# NEW YORK
# Civil Practice Law and Rules

## 1997 REDBOOK BENDER PAMPHLET EDITION

**CPLR**
with Judicial Conference Notes and Statutory Cross
References

## CPLR TIMETABLE

## SELECTED PRACTICE PROVISIONS

## SPECIAL FEATURE
An Analysis of Practice Under New York's
Commencement by Filing Law

## COURT DIRECTORY

*As Amended by the 1996 Regular Legislative Session
through September 24, 1996*
REVISED INDEX

## MATTHEW ◆ BENDER

## Questions About This Publication?

For assistance with replacement pages, shipments, billing or other customer service matters, please call our

Customer Services Department at ............................ 1–800–833–9844

Outside the United States and Canada
please call ...................................................................... (518) 487–3000
or fax .............................................................................. (518) 462–3788
To place an order, call ................................................. 1–800–223–1940
or contact your Matthew Bender representative.

FOR EDITORIAL ASSISTANCE or reprint permission, please call
   Anthony Vlahos, J.D., at ............................. 1-800-9257 Ext. 2441
      or
   Nancy Schwell, J.D., at .............................. 1-800-9257 Ext. 2348

MATTHEW BENDER & CO., INC.
EDITORIAL OFFICES
TWO PARK AVENUE, NEW YORK, NY 10016-5675 (212) 448-2000
201 MISSION STREET, SAN FRANCISCO, CA 94105–1831 (415) 908-3200

## NOTE

# TABLE OF CONTENTS

Table of 1996 CPLR Amendments .................................................. **T–1**
CPLR Timetable ............................................................................. **T–3**
New York Court System ............................................................... **T–66**

## CIVIL PRACTICE LAW AND RULES

| ART | Chapter 8 of the Consolidated Laws | PAGE |
|---|---|---|
| 1. | Short title; applicability and definitions. (§§ 101–107.) .............. | 1–1 |
| 2. | Limitations of time. (§§ 201–218.) ..................................... | 2–1 |
| 3. | Jurisdiction and service, appearance and choice of court. (§§ 301–318, 320–322, 325–328.) ........................................ | 3–1 |
| 4. | Special proceedings. (§§ 401–411.) ..................................... | 4–1 |
| 5. | Venue. (§§ 501–513.) ...................................................... | 5–1 |
| 6. | Joinder of claims, consolidation and severance. (§§ 601–604.) ... | 6–1 |
| 9. | Class actions. (§§ 901–909.) ............................................. | 9–1 |
| 10. | Parties generally. (§§ 1001–1026.) ..................................... | 10–1 |
| 11. | Poor persons. (§§ 1101–1103.) .......................................... | 11–1 |
| 12. | Infants, incompetents and conservatees. (§§ 1201–1211.) ............ | 12–1 |
| 13. | Actions by the state. (§§ 1301–1303.) .................................. | 13–1 |
| 13-A. | Proceeds of crime—forfeiture. (§§ 1310–1352.) ..................... | 13A–1 |
| 13-B. | Civil remedies; enterprise corruption. (§§ 1353–1355.) .............. | 13B–1 |
| 14. | Contribution. (§§ 1401–1404.) ........................................... | 14–1 |
| 14-A. | Damage actions: effect of contributory negligence and assumption of risk. (§§ 1411–1413.) .................................................. | 14A–1 |
| 15. | Actions against persons jointly liable. (§§ 1501–1502.) .............. | 15–1 |
| 16. | Limited liability of persons jointly liable. (§§ 1600–1603.) ......... | 16–1 |
| 20. | Mistakes, defects, irregularities and extensions of time. (§§ 2001–2005.) .............................................................. | 20–1 |
| 21. | Papers. (§§ 2101–2106.) .................................................. | 21–1 |
| 22. | Stay, motions, orders and mandates. (§§ 2201, 2211–2223.) ....... | 22–1 |
| 23. | Subpoenas, oaths and affirmations. (§§ 2301–2310.) ................ | 23–1 |
| 24. | Publication. (§§ 2401–2402.) ............................................ | 24–1 |
| 25. | Undertakings. (§§ 2501–2513.) .......................................... | 25–1 |
| 26. | Property paid into court. (§§ 2601–2609.) ............................. | 26–1 |
| 27. | Disposition of property in litigation. (§§ 2701–2703.) ............... | 27–1 |
| 30. | Remedies and pleading. (§§ 3001–3005, 3011–3026, 3031–3037, 3041–3045.) ................................................................ | 30–1 |
| 31. | Disclosure. (§§ 3101–3118, 3120–3126, 3130–3133, 3140.) ........... | 31–1 |
| 32. | Accelerated judgment. (§§ 3201, 3211–3222.) ........................ | 32–1 |
| 34. | Calendar practice; trial preferences. (§§ 3401–3407.) ............... | 34–1 |
| 40. | Trial generally. (§§ 4001, 4011–4019.) ................................. | 40–1 |
| 41. | Trial by a jury. (§§ 4101–4113.) ........................................ | 41–1 |
| 42. | Trial by the court. (§§ 4201, 4211–4213.) ............................. | 42–1 |
| 43. | Trial by a referee. (§§ 4301, 4311–4321.) ............................. | 43–1 |

44.     Trial motions. (§§ 4401–4406.) .................................... 44–1
45.     Evidence. (§§ 4501–4546 ................................. 45–1
50.     Judgments generally. (§§ 5001–5004, 5011–5021.) ................. 50–1
50-A.   Periodic payment of judgments in medical and dental malpractice
        actions. (§§ 5031–5039) ........................................ 50A–1
50-B.   Periodic payment of judgments in personal injury, injury to
        property and wrongful death actions. (§§ 5041–5049.) ............ 50B–1
51.     Enforcement of judgments and orders generally.
        (§§ 5101–5107.) ................................................ 51–1
52.     Enforcement of money judgments. (§§ 5201–5211, 5221–5242,
        5250–5252.) .................................................... 52–1
53.     Recognition of foreign country money judgments.
        (§§ 5301–5309.) ................................................ 53–1
54.     Enforcement of judgments entitled to full faith and credit.
        (§§ 5401–5408.) ................................................ 54–1
55.     Appeals generally. (§§ 5501, 5511–5532.) ....................... 55–1
56.     Appeals to the court of appeals. (§§ 5601–5602, 5611–5615.) .... 56–1
57.     Appeals to the appellate division. (§§ 5701–5704, 5711–5713.) .... 57–1
60.     Provisional remedies generally. (§ 6001.) ...................... 60–1
61.     Arrest. (Repealed.) ............................................ 61–1
62.     Attachment. (§§ 6201–6204, 6210–6226.) ......................... 62–1
63.     Injunction. (§§ 6301, 6311–6315, 6330.) ........................ 63–1
64.     Receivership. (§§ 6401–6405.) .................................. 64–1
65.     Notice of pendency. (§§ 6501, 6511–6515.) ...................... 65–1
70.     Habeas corpus. (§§ 7001–7012.) ................................. 70–1
71.     Recovery of chattel. (§§ 7101–7112.) ........................... 71–1
72.     Recovery of penalty or forfeiture. (§§ 7201–7205.) ............. 72–1
75.     Arbitration. (§§ 7501–7514.) ................................... 75–1
75-A.   Health care arbitration. (§§ 7550–7565.) ....................... 75A–1
76.     Proceeding to enforce agreement for determination of issue.
        (§ 7601.) ...................................................... 76–1
77.     Proceeding relating to express trust. (§§ 7701–7706.) .......... 77–1
78.     Proceeding against body or officer. (§§ 7801–7806.) ............ 78–1
80.     Fees. (§§ 8001–8022.) .......................................... 80–1
81.     Costs generally. (§§ 8101–8110.) ............................... 81–1
82.     Amount of costs. (§§ 8201–8204.) ............................... 82–1
83.     Disbursements and additional allowances. (§§ 8301–8303-a.) ..... 83–1
84.     Taxation of costs. (§§ 8401–8404.) ............................. 84–1
85.     Security for costs. (§§ 8501–8503.) ............................ 85–1
86.     Counsel fees and expenses in certain actions against the state.
        (§§ 8600–8605.) ................................................ 86–1
87.     Punitive damage awards; public share. (Repealed.) .............. 87–1
90.     Failure or adjournment of term of court. (§§ 9001–9003.) ........ 90–1
94.     Admission to practice. (§§ 9401–9407.) ......................... 94–1
97.     Records of clerks of the courts. (§§ 9701–9703.) ............... 97–1
98.     Actions against villages. (§§ 9801–9804.) ...................... 98–1
100.    Repeal; saving clauses; effective date. (§§ 10001–10005.) ........... 100–1

# APPENDIX
# SELECTED PRACTICE PROVISIONS

| TITLES INCLUDED | PAGE |
|---|---|
| Constitution of the State of New York | CONST–1 |
| Business Corporation Law (BCL) | BCL–1 |
| Court of Claims Act (CCA) | CCA–1 |
| Criminal Procedure Law (CPL) | CPL–1 |
| Debtor and Creditor Law (DCL) | DCL–1 |
| Domestic Relations Law (DRL) | DRL–1 |
| Education Law | ED–1 |
| Estates, Powers and Trusts Law (EPTL) | EPTL–1 |
| General Associations Law | GAL–1 |
| General Construction Law | GCL–1 |
| General Municipal Law | GML–1 |
| General Obligations Law | GOL–1 |
| Insurance Law | INS–1 |
| Judiciary Law | JUD–1 |
| Lien Law | LIEN–1 |
| New York City Civil Court Act | NYCCCA–1 |
| Professional Disciplinary Rules | PDR–1 |
| Public Health Law | PHL–1 |
| Public Officers Law | POL–1 |
| Real Property Law | RPL–1 |
| Surrogate's Court Procedure Act (SCPA) | SCPA–1 |
| Uniform Commercial Code (UCC) | UCC–1 |
| Vehicle and Traffic Law | VTL–1 |
| SPECIAL FEATURE: An Analysis of Practice Under New York's Commencement by Filing Law | CH.216–1 |
| Court Directory | CD–1 |

# TABLE OF 1996 CPLR AMENDMENTS

| CPLR Section or Rule | Amendment | Effective Date |
|---|---|---|
| 203(c)(1) | Amended to delete the words "with the court." | 9/1/97 |
| 214(6) | Amended to add the words "regardless of whether the underlying theory is based in contract or tort." | 9/4/96 |
| 214–d | New section, "Limitations on certain actions against licensed engineers and architects," added. | 10/1/96 |
| 304 | Amended to expand the definition of "filing" and add a new last sentence requiring date stamping of the original and a copy of the filed papers. | 9/1/97 |
| 305(a) | Amended to delete final sentence and replace with new final sentence to make reference to CPLR § 1003. | 4/2/96 |
| 306–a | Amended to delete the words, "with the clerk of the court" from the first sentence. | 9/1/97 |
| 311 | Amended to number opening paragraph as subdivision (a) and add new subdivision (b) governing situations where service under subdivision (a) is impracticable. | 1/1/97 |
| 312-a(a) | Amended to delete the phrase ", an authorized employee or the plaintiff, the plaintiff's attorney or an employee of the attorney" and replace it with "or any other person." | 7/30/96 |
| 601 | Amended to number the existing paragraph as (a) and add a new subdivision (b) dealing with joinder of claims in consumer credit transactions. | 1/1/97 |
| 1003 | Amended to allow the addition of parties at any stage by leave of court or stipulation of all parties, or once without leave within 20 days after service of original summons or within 20 days after service of a pleading responding to it. | 4/2/96 |
| 1401 | Amended to add references to G.O.L. § 18-201, Workers' Comp. L. §§ 11 and 29, and any other state or federal workers' compensation law. | 9/10/96 |
| 1601(1) | Amended to add reference to a "grave injury" pursuant to Workers' Comp. L. § 11. | 9/10/96 |
| 1602(4), (12) | Amended subdivision (4) to add reference to a "grave injury" pursuant to Workers' Comp. L. § 11; added new subdivision (12). | 9/10/96 |
| 1603 | Amended to add reference to § 1601(1). | 9/10/96 |
| 2101(a) | Amended to add the words, "orders of protection, temporary orders of protection." | 6/11/96 |
| 2219(a) | Amended to allow, upon request of any party, the reduction to writing or other recording of an order or ruling made by a judge. | 1/1/97 |
| 3015(e) | Amended to add reference to Putnam county. | 8/8/96 |
| 3116(a) | Amended to require a witness to return a signed deposition within 60 days and to prohibit changes to the transcript by a witness more than 60 days after submission to the witness for examination. | 1/1/97 |

| CPLR Section or Rule | Amendment | Effective Date |
|---|---|---|
| 3117(a)(2) | Amended to allow the deposition of a party to become admissible upon application of an adversely interested party. | 1/1/97 |
| 3211(e) | Amended to add a clause which deems an objection of improper service waived, if the objecting party does not move for judgment within 60 days after serving the pleading that raised the objection. | 1/1/97 |
| 3211(h) | New subdivision (h), "Standards for motions to dismiss certain cases involving licensed architects, engineers or landscape architects," added. | 10/1/96 |
| 3212(a) | Amended to allow court to set a date after which no motion for summary judgment may be made; in the absence of such a date, the motion must be made no later than 120 days after filing the note of issue. | 1/1/97 |
| 3212(i) | New subdivision (i), "Standards for summary judgment in certain cases involving licensed architects, engineers or landscape architects," added. | 10/1/96 |
| 3214(b) | Amended to provide that if a motion under R 3211, 3212 or § 3213 is based solely on the defense of improper service, disclosure shall not be stayed unless the court orders otherwise. | 1/1/97 |
| 4109 | Amended to equalize the number of peremptory challenges for plaintiffs and defendants and to allow the court to allocate a side's combined total of peremptory challenges among those parties in such manner as may be appropriate. | 10/24/96 |
| 4539 | Amended to number the existing section as subdivision (a) and add a new subdivision (b) dealing with reproduction by a process which stores an image. | 11/1/96 |
| 5513 | Amended subdivision (a) to add the phrase "by a party" and amended subdivision (b) to add the phrase "seeking permission to appeal." | 1/1/97 |
| 6312 | Amended to add new subdivision (c), "Issues of fact" and to replace the word "paper" with the word "evidence" in subdivision (a). | 1/1/97 |
| 8003(b) | Amended to eliminate the distinction between types of actions for purposes of determining a referee's compensation, to increase the statutory maximum compensation for referees to $500 and to allow the court to authorize payment of additional compensation where the referee sells property for $50,000 or more. | 6/26/96 |
| 8011(b) | Amended subparagraph (1) to add a reference to Article 18 of the Uniform Justice Court Act. | 1/1/97 |
| 8020(a) | Amended to add an addition fee of $25 to be paid to the clerk for placing a cause on a calendar for trial or inquest after a request for judicial intervention. | 7/23/96 |

| CPLR Section or Rule | Amendment | Effective Date |
|---|---|---|
| 8022 | Amended the heading by replacing the word "appeal" with the words "appeals and proceedings before appellate courts" and amended subdivision (b) to entitle the clerks of appellate divisions to a fee upon the filing of a notice of petition or order to show cause commencing a special proceeding. | 7/23/96 |

# CPLR TIMETABLE

**Introductory Note:** This timetable is arranged in chronological order, following the usual sequence of litigation.

The column on the left lists the act—such as filing or service of papers or giving of notice—that is required of counsel, sheriff or court. The second column indicates the time period available to handle the matter. The third column cites the applicable rule or statute. The fourth column comments on the time period or on the attorney's further tasks or options, or provides further references.

Generally, the Civil Practice Law and Rules are cited, but other relevant provisions are indicated, including the New York Codes, Rules and Regulations regarding appellate proceedings and proceedings in the Supreme and County Courts. In the section on Appeals, after the first reference to 22 NYCRR, only the rule number is provided. The timetable does not include statutes or rules specific to Family Court proceedings, real property actions and proceedings, criminal matters, or Surrogate's Court proceedings.

This timetable is intended as a handy reference guide only and is not a substitute for thorough research. Counsel should refer directly to each statute and rule cited for further details and should see the applicable text in *Weinstein, Korn & Miller, New York Civil Practice—Civil Practice Law & Rules* for discussion thereof.

Timetable

## CONTENTS

LIMITATION—INTERPOSITION OF
CLAIM . . . . . . . . . . . . . . . . . . . . . . 7
PROVISIONAL REMEDIES . . . . . . . . . . . . 13
    Injunction . . . . . . . . . . . . . . . . . . . . 14
    Attachment . . . . . . . . . . . . . . . . . . . . 14
    Receivership . . . . . . . . . . . . . . . . . . . . 16
    Notice of pendency . . . . . . . . . . . . . . . . 17
    Seizure of chattel . . . . . . . . . . . . . . . . . 18
UNDERTAKINGS . . . . . . . . . . . . . . . . . 19
SPECIAL PROCEEDINGS . . . . . . . . . . . . . 21
    Habeas corpus . . . . . . . . . . . . . . . . . 24
    Article 78 proceeding . . . . . . . . . . . . . . 24
    Arbitration . . . . . . . . . . . . . . . . . . . . 25
SERVICE OF SUMMONS AND
COMPLAINT . . . . . . . . . . . . . . . . . . . . 27
SECURITY FOR COSTS . . . . . . . . . . . . . 31
PLEADINGS . . . . . . . . . . . . . . . . . . . . 32
DEFENSE OF ACTION . . . . . . . . . . . . . . 32
    Answer or appearance . . . . . . . . . . . . . . 33
PRE-TRIAL MOTION OR DEMANDS . . . . . . 34
BILL OF PARTICULARS . . . . . . . . . . . . . 37
DISCLOSURE . . . . . . . . . . . . . . . . . . . 38
ACCELERATED JUDGMENT . . . . . . . . . . . 44
    Default judgment . . . . . . . . . . . . . . . . . 44
    Voluntary discontinuance . . . . . . . . . . . . . 46
    Judgment by confession . . . . . . . . . . . . . . 46
    Tender . . . . . . . . . . . . . . . . . . . . . . . 46
    Offer to liquidate damages conditionally . . . . 46
    Offer to compromise . . . . . . . . . . . . . . . 46
CALENDAR PRACTICE . . . . . . . . . . . . . . 47
    Placing case on calendar—filing note of issue
    and certificate of readiness . . . . . . . . . . . 47
    Filing of demand for trial by jury . . . . . . . . 48
TRIAL . . . . . . . . . . . . . . . . . . . . . . . 49
SUBMISSION OF ORDERS, JUDGMENTS AND
DECREES—SUPREME AND COUNTY
COURTS . . . . . . . . . . . . . . . . . . . . . . 50
POST-TRIAL MOTIONS . . . . . . . . . . . . . . 51
TAXATION OF COSTS . . . . . . . . . . . . . . 52
ENFORCEMENT OF JUDGMENTS . . . . . . . 52
    Foreign judgments . . . . . . . . . . . . . . . . 55
APPEALS . . . . . . . . . . . . . . . . . . . . . . 55
    In general . . . . . . . . . . . . . . . . . . . . . 55

Timetable

Court of Appeals . . . . . . . . . . . . . . . . . .    56
Appellate Divisions . . . . . . . . . . . . . . . . .    59
Appeals under NYS Human Rights Law . . . .    65
Appellate Terms—References . . . . . . . . . . .    65

## LIMITATION—INTERPOSITION OF CLAIM

| Act To Be Performed | Time Period Available | Statute or Rule | Comments |
|---|---|---|---|
| Action on a bond | Within 20 years of accrual | CPLR 211(a) | |
| Action to enforce money judgment | Within 20 years of docketing | CPLR 211(b) | Presumption of payment and satisfaction; not strictly speaking a statute of limitations. |
| Action for recovery of real property by State or grantee of State | Within 20 years of accrual | CPLR 211(c), (d) | |
| Action for support, alimony or maintenance | Within 20 years of accrual | CPLR 211(e) | |
| Action for recovery of real property | Within 10 years of seizing or possession of property by plaintiff or plaintiff's predecessor in interest | CPLR 212(a) | |
| Action to annul letters patent or grant of real property | Within 10 years after determination of voidness | CPLR 212(b) | |
| Action to redeem from a mortgage | Within 10 years of breach of condition of mortgage or date of recording of deed | CPLR 212(c) | |
| Action for which there is no prescribed limitation | Six years | CPLR 213(1) | |

| Act To Be Performed | Time Period Available | Statute or Rule | Comments |
|---|---|---|---|
| Action on contractual obligation or liability | Six years | CPLR 213(2) | Exceptions: See CPLR 213-a; UCC Art. 2 sales; see § 2-725 (normally four years), *infra*; actions based on breach of home sale warranty (see General Business Law Article 36-B), generally within one year after the warranty period, or within four years of the warranty date, whichever is later. |
| Action on a sealed instrument | Six years | CPLR 213(3) | |
| Action on a bond or note secured by mortgage on real property | Six years | CPLR 213(4) | |
| Action by State for spoliation or misappropriation of public property | Six years | CPLR 213(5) | Computed for discovery of facts by State. |
| Action based on mistake | Six years | CPLR 213(6) | |
| Shareholder's derivative action | Six years | CPLR 213(7) | |
| Action based on fraud | Six years | CPLR 213(8) | Computed from discovery by plaintiff or time plaintiff should have discovered fraud with due diligence. |

| Act To Be Performed | Time Period Available | Statute or Rule | Comments |
|---|---|---|---|
| Forfeiture action to recover proceeds of crime or instrumentality of crime | Within five years of commission of crime | CPLR 1311(1) | |
| Action for breach of contract for sale | Four years after cause of action has accrued | UCC 2-725 | By original agreement, the parties may reduce the period to not less than one year but may not extend it. See also CPLR 203(f). |
| Action on residential rent overcharge | Four years | CPLR 213-a | |
| Action against enforcement officer for nonpayment of money collected on an execution | Three years | CPLR 214(1) | |
| Action for statutory liability, penalty or forfeiture | Three years | CPLR 214(2) | *Exceptions:* See CPLR 213 (six years) and 215 (one year). |
| Replevin action | Three years | CPLR 214(3) | |
| Property damage action | Three years | CPLR 214(4) | Exception: See CPLR 214-c |
| Personal injury action | Three years | CPLR 214(5) | *Exceptions:* See CPLR 214-b ("Agent Orange," two years), 214-c, and 215 (assault, battery, false imprisonment, one year). |

Timetable

| Act To Be Performed | Time Period Available | Statute or Rule | Comments |
|---|---|---|---|
| Malpractice other than medical, dental or podiatric malpractice | Three years | CPLR 214(6) | |
| Annulment on ground of fraud | Three years | CPLR 214(7) | Computed from discovery by spouse whose consent was induced by fraud. |
| Action to recover for exposure to latent toxic substances | Three years | CPLR 214-c | Computed from date of discovery or date discovery should have occurred, with reasonable diligence. See CPLR 214-c(4) re applicable period when discovery of cause of injury is alleged to have occurred less than five years after discovery of injury; see also uncodified revival provisions in sections 4 and 5 of L. 1986, C. 682. See CPLR 214-c(6) re dates of acts or omissions to which the statute applies. |

| Act To Be Performed | Time Period Available | Statute or Rule | Comments |
|---|---|---|---|
| Medical, dental or podiatric malpractice | Two and one-half years | CPLR 214-a | Computed from act or omission or from last treatment if continuous treatment. *Exception:* Foreign object in body, one year from discovery or discovery of facts which would reasonably lead to discovery, whichever is earlier. |
| Action to recover for "Agent Orange" (phenoxy herbicides) injury | Two years; no later than 6/16/92 | CPLR 214-b | Computed from date of discovery or date discovery should have occurred, with reasonable diligence. Restricted to member of armed forces in Indo-China 1/1/62-5/7/75. |
| Action against licensed engineers and architects | Ten years | CPLR 214-d | Notice must be given 90 days before commencement of any action based upon professional performance, conduct or omission occuring more than ten years prior to the date of the claim. |
| Action for damages by a victim of a criminal offense | Seven years after date of the crime | CPLR 213-b | |

Timetable

| Act To Be Performed | Time Period Available | Statute or Rule | Comments |
|---|---|---|---|
| Wrongful death action | Two years, or at least one year from termination of criminal action *vs.* same defendant with respect to same event or occurrence. | EPTL 5-4.1 | Written claim within one year. |
| Contract action against village | 18 months | CPLR 9802 | |
| Tort action against municipality | Notice of claim; within 90 days | GML § 50-e | |
| | Actions must be commenced within one year and 90 days of accrual | GML § 50-i | *Exception:* Wrongful death, two years to commence action. |
| Action for intentional tort | One year | CPLR 215(3) | |
| Action against sheriff, coroner, constable for official act or omission | One year | CPLR 215(1) | |
| Action on arbitration award | One year | CPLR 215(5) | |
| Action to enforce penalty or forfeiture given to private prosecutor | One year | CPLR 215(4) | |
| Action against officer for escape of civil prisoner | One year | CPLR 215(2) | |
| Action to recover or enforce penalty for interest overcharge | One year | CPLR 215(6) | |

| Act To Be Performed | Time Period Available | Statute or Rule | Comments |
|---|---|---|---|
| Action by tenant against landlord for retaliation | One year | CPLR 215(7) | See RPL § 223-b(3). |
| Proceeding to set aside judicial sale | Within one year after sale | CPLR 2003 | Does not apply to judicial sales made pursuant to UCC Art. 9. |
| Article 78 proceeding; actions complaining about conduct that would constitute a union's breach of its duty of fair representation | Four months, but may be shorter | CPLR 217 | Consult relevant statute authorizing proceeding.<br><br>*Exception:* With leave of court, if petitioner was under statutorily defined disability, two years. |
| **PROVISIONAL REMEDIES** | | | |
| Election of remedy | May be required by court on motion for provisional remedy | CPLR 6001 | Applies to seizure of chattel as well as attachment, injunction, receivership and notice of pendency. |
| Interposition of claim in complaint when order for provisional remedy is granted | Summons and complaint must be filed, and index number secured. See CPLR 203(c), added in 1992. Summons and complaint to be served within 120 days thereafter. See CPLR 306–b. | CPLR 203(b)(3) | Provisional remedy here *excludes* attachment but *includes* seizure of chattel. |

Timetable

| Act To Be Performed | Time Period Available | Statute or Rule | Comments |
|---|---|---|---|
| **Injunction** | | | |
| Application for preliminary injunction or temporary restraining order | No time constraints | CPLR 6301, 6313 | T.R.O. may be granted pending hearing for preliminary injunction, where immediate and irreparable injury would otherwise result. |
| Service of notice of motion for preliminary injunction | With summons or at any time thereafter and prior to judgment | CPLR 6311(1) | |
| Posting of undertaking by plaintiff seeking preliminary injunction | Required prior to granting of preliminary injunction | CPLR 6312(b) | *Exceptions:* Does not apply to State, municipal corporation or certain public officers. See CPLR 2512, 4110-a, 2505. |
| **Attachment** | | | |
| Posting of undertaking | On motion for order of attachment | CPLR 6212(b) | |
| Granting of order of attachment without notice | Before or after service of summons and at any time prior to judgment | CPLR 6211(a) | On grounds for attachment, see CPLR 6201. |
| Granting of temporary restraining order prohibiting transfer of assets by garnishee | Permitted upon motion on notice for order of attachment | CPLR 6210 | |

| Act To Be Performed | Time Period Available | Statute or Rule | Comments |
|---|---|---|---|
| Plaintiff's filing of order of attachment and supporting papers, summons and complaint | Within 10 days after granting of order | CPLR 6212(c) | |
| Action is commenced by filing summons and complaint and securing an index number pursuant to CPLR 203(c). See also CPLR 306–a and 306–b, effective July 1, 1992. | Within 60 days after order of attachment is granted. Application may be made for extension of time, prior to expiration of time | CPLR 6213 | Required to make order of attachment valid. If defendant dies prior to service within the 60-day period, summons must be served upon executor or administrator within 60 days after letters are issued. CPLR 6213. |
| Levy by sheriff pursuant to order of attachment | At any time prior to final judgment | CPLR 6211(a) | Levy upon personal property made by service of order of attachment, normally valid for 90 days. CPLR 6214(e). See also CPLR 6214(d). *Compare* CPLR 6215 (levy by seizure), 6216 (levy upon real property). As to attachment or levy upon a security or share, see UCC § 8–317. |

| Act To Be Performed | Time Period Available | Statute or Rule | Comments |
|---|---|---|---|
| Sheriff's filing of inventory of property seized | Within 15 days after service of order of attachment or "forthwith" after such order has been vacated or annulled | CPLR 6218(b) | |
| Garnishee's service upon sheriff of statement regarding debts to defendant | Within 10 days after service of order of attachment or sooner if court directs | CPLR 6219 | |
| Plaintiff's motion for order confirming order of attachment | Within five days after levy | CPLR 6211(b) | |
| Defendant's demand for papers | At any time after levy | CPLR 6212(d) | |
| Plaintiff's service of papers upon defendant | Not more than one day after service of demand for same | CPLR 6212(d) | |
| Motion to vacate or modify order of attachment | Prior to application of property or debt to the satisfaction of judgment | CPLR 6223 | By defendant, garnishee or any person having an interest in the property or debt. |
| **Receivership** | | | |
| Appointment of temporary receiver | Before or after service of summons and at any time prior to judgment | CPLR 6401(a) | Motion made by person not already a party constitutes an appearance in the action. See also CPLR 5228. |

| Act To Be Performed | Time Period Available | Statute or Rule | Comments |
|---|---|---|---|
| Duration of temporary receivership | Does not continue after final judgment unless otherwise directed by court | CPLR 6401(c) | |
| Removal of receiver | At any time by court upon motion of any party or on its own initiative | CPLR 6405 | |
| **Notice of Pendency** | | | |
| Filing of notice of pendency | Before or after service of summons and at any time prior to judgment | CPLR 6511(a) | Unless complaint has already been filed in county where property is situated, complaint shall be filed with the notice of pendency. |
| Effectiveness of notice of pendency filed before an action is commenced | Only if: Summons is served on defendant within 30 days after filing of notice of penalty *or* | CPLR 6512 | |
| | First publication of summons is made pursuant to order and is completed subsequently within 30 days after filing of notice of pendency *or* | | |

| Act To Be Performed | Time Period Available | Statute or Rule | Comments |
|---|---|---|---|
| | If defendant dies before service of summons within 30-day period, summons must be served on executor or administrator within 60 days after letters are issued | | |
| Duration of notice of pendency | Three years from date of filing | CPLR 6513 | Extension may be granted before expiration. |
| Cancellation by stipulation or by plaintiff | At any time prior to entry of judgment | CPLR 6514(d), (e) | See CPLR 6514(a), (b) (mandatory cancellation, discretionary cancellation by court). |
| **Seizure of Chattel** | | | |
| Plaintiff's motion for order confirming *ex parte* order of seizure | Within five days after seizure | CPLR 7102(d)(4) | |
| Sheriff's retention of custody of chattel | For 10 days after seizure pursuant to order granted on notice and until served with an order of confirmation where seizure is pursuant to *ex parte* order | CPLR 7102(f) | |

| Act To Be Performed | Time Period Available | Statute or Rule | Comments |
|---|---|---|---|
| Sheriff's delivery of chattel to plaintiff | After 10-day period if sheriff not served with notice of exception to plaintiff's surety, notice of motion for an impounding or returning order, or the necessary papers to reclaim the chattel | CPLR 7102(f) | As to reclaiming chattel, see CPLR 7103. |
| Sheriff's filing of return | Within 20 days after delivery of chattel | CPLR 7107 | |
| Notice of motion to punish sheriff for not filing return before hearing on contempt | At least 10 days' notice to sheriff | CPLR 7107 | |
| **UNDERTAKINGS** | | | |
| Exception to surety | Within 10 days after receipt of a copy of the undertaking | CPLR 2506 | May only be taken where a certificate of qualification (Ins. L. § 1111) is not filed with the undertaking. |

| Act To Be Performed | Time Period Available | Statute or Rule | Comments |
| --- | --- | --- | --- |
| Surety's motion to justify | Within 10 days after service of notice of exception | CPLR 2507(a) | If motion to justify is not timely made, the undertaking is without effect except that surety remains liable until new undertaking is allowed. See CPLR 2507(b). Motion can also be made by person in whose behalf the undertaking was given. |
| Surety's motion on notice to be discharged from liability for act or omission of fiduciary | Subsequent to court order or the time when new undertaking satisfactory to court is filed | CPLR 2510 | Court may restrain fiduciary from acting pending order discharging surety. |
| Account of fiduciary following surety's motion for discharge | Within such time as court orders but not exceeding 20 days | CPLR 2510(a) | |

| Act To Be Performed | Time Period Available | Statute or Rule | Comments |
| --- | --- | --- | --- |
| **SPECIAL PROCEEDINGS** | | | |
| Service of notice of petition, petition and affidavits | At least eight days before return date | CPLR 403(b) | Court may grant order to show cause to be served in lieu of notice of petition at a time and in a manner specified therein. CPLR 403(d). |
| Filing of notice of petition and petition and securing an index number pursuant to CPLR 203(c), effective July 1, 1992, followed by service of notice of petition or order to show cause and petition as required by CPLR 306–b, effective July 1, 1992. | | | |
| Service of answer and any supporting affidavits | At least two days before return date; but if notice of petition served at least 12 days before return date so demands, answer must be served at least seven days before return date | CPLR 403(b) | Add five days if service is by mail. CPLR 2103(b)(2) |

| Act To Be Performed | Time Period Available | Statute or Rule | Comments |
|---|---|---|---|
| Service of reply and any supporting affidavits | At or before hearing date; but if answer was served at least seven days before return date in compliance with demand in notice of petition served at least 12 days before return date, reply must be served at least one day before hearing date | CPLR 403(b) | |
| Respondent's raising objection in point of law | In answer or by motion to dismiss petition, upon notice within the time allowed for answer | CPLR 404(a) | |
| Respondent's time to serve and file answer if motion to dismiss petition is denied | Unless otherwise specified by order, within five days after service of order with notice of entry | CPLR 404(a) | |
| Re-notice, by petitioner, for hearing | Two days' notice | CPLR 404(a) | Petitioner may object in point of law to new matter, in reply or by motion to strike on hearing day. CPLR 404(b). |
| Re-notice, by respondent, for a hearing | Upon service of the answer upon seven days' notice | CPLR 404(a) | |
| Motion to correct defects | Within time allowed for responsive pleading | CPLR 405(b) | By serving notice of motion or order to show cause. |

| Act To Be Performed | Time Period Available | Statute or Rule | Comments |
| --- | --- | --- | --- |
| Service of responsive pleading after service of amended pleading | Within five days | CPLR 405(b) | Where party cannot serve responsive pleading until papers are corrected, and court so orders. |
| Service of responsive pleading if motion to correct is denied | Within two days after service of order denying motion with notice of entry, unless order specifies otherwise | CPLR 405(b) | Where time to serve responsive pleading has been extended. |
| Re-notice for hearing after motion to correct | Two days' notice | CPLR 405(b) | |
| Petitioner's motion to correct | In reply or by motion on hearing or re-hearing date | CPLR 405(c) | |
| Notice of motion in special proceeding, made before return date | Shall be noticed to be heard at return date of petition | CPLR 406 | |
| Severance of claim or party | At any time, by court | CPLR 407 | |
| Service of notice to admit | Not later than three days before return date of petition | CPLR 408 | Does not apply to Surrogate's Court proceedings or to proceedings relating to express trusts (CPLR Art. 77); see CPLR Art. 31. |

Timetable

| Act To Be Performed | Time Period Available | Statute or Rule | Comments |
| --- | --- | --- | --- |
| Service of statement denying or setting forth reasons for failing to admit or deny | Not later than one day before return date of petition, unless otherwise ordered by court on *ex parte* motion | CPLR 408 | Does not apply to Surrogate's Court proceedings or to proceedings relating to express trusts (CPLR Art. 77); see CPLR Art. 31. |
| Furnishing of papers | At hearing | CPLR 409(a) | |
| **Habeas Corpus** | | | |
| Filing of return to writ of habeas corpus | At time specified in writ or, if returnable forthwith, within 24 hours after service | CPLR 7008(a) | |
| Service of written notice of habeas corpus hearing, where detention is by virtue of a mandate | By personal service, eight days before hearing, or as court directs | CPLR 7009(a) | |
| **Article 78 Proceeding** | | | |
| Service of notice of petition and answer | At least 20 days before time when petition is noticed to be heard | CPLR 7804(c) | Unless court grants order to show cause in lieu of notice of petition. |
| Service of reply and any supporting affidavits | At least one day before return date | CPLR 7804(c) | |
| Service and filing of respondent's answer following denial of motion to dismiss petition | Within five days after service of order with notice of entry | CPLR 7804(f) | See CPLR 7804(f) re objections in point of law. |

| Act To Be Performed | Time Period Available | Statute or Rule | Comments |
|---|---|---|---|
| Re-notice, by petitioner, for hearing | Two days' notice | CPLR 7804(f) | Petitioner may object in point of law to new matter, in reply or on day of hearing. |
| Re-notice, by respondent, for a hearing | Upon service of the answer upon seven days' notice | CPLR 7804(f) | |
| **Arbitration** | | | |
| Arbitration of damages in medical, dental or podiatric malpractice actions | Upon a concession of liability by defendant, defendant may demand that plaintiff elect whether to consent to arbitration of damages. Demand may be made at any time before service of bill of particulars but no later than 60 days after filing of notice of medical, podiatric or dental malpractice | CPLR 3045 | Within 20 days after receipt of demand, plaintiff shall elect whether to arbitrate damages; if defendant serves a concession of liability within 20 days of such election, issue of damages shall be subject to arbitration under CPLR Article 75-A. |

| Act To Be Performed | Time Period Available | Statute or Rule | Comments |
|---|---|---|---|
| Application to stay arbitration | Within 20 days after service of demand for arbitration or notice of intention to arbitrate | CPLR 7503(c) | As to compulsory arbitration in civil actions for sum of money, see 22 NYCRR § 28.2. As to grievance arbitration involving public employers and recognized or certified employee organizations, see 4 NYCRR § 207.4 and Civ. Serv. L. Art. 14. |
| Notice of arbitration hearing | At least eight days' notice | CPLR 7506(b) | |
| Making of award by confession | At any time within 3 months after statement verified | CPLR 7508(b) | |
| Written application for modification of award by arbitrator | Within 20 days after delivery of award to applicant | CPLR 7509 | |
| Service of written objection to modification of arbitrator's award | Within 10 days of receipt of notice of application for modification | CPLR 7509 | |
| Disposition, by arbitrators, of application | Within 30 days | CPLR 7509 | |
| Application for confirmation of award | Within one year after delivery of award to applicant | CPLR 7510 | Unless award is vacated or modified; see CPLR 7510, 7511. |

| Act To Be Performed | Time Period Available | Statute or Rule | Comments |
|---|---|---|---|
| Application to vacate or modify arbitration award | Within 90 days after delivery of award | CPLR 7511(a) | |
| **SERVICE OF SUMMONS AND COMPLAINT** | | | |
| Filing of proof of service by delivery to person of suitable age and discretion and mailing to last known residence or to actual place of business (as provided in CPLR 308(2)), within 20 days of each other | Within 20 days of delivery or mailing, whichever occurs later | CPLR 308(2) | Service is complete 10 days after such filing, except in matrimonial actions where such service is made pursuant to order in accordance with DRL § 232(a). |
| Filing of proof of service by "nail and mail" within 20 days of each other (mailing requirement may be satisfied by either mailing to last known residence or actual place of business as provided in CPLR 308(4)) | Within 20 days of affixing or mailing, whichever occurs later | CPLR 308(4) | Service is complete 10 days after such filing, except in matrimonial actions where such service is made pursuant to order in accordance with DRL § 232(a). |
| Notice by mailing copy of summons prior to entry of default judgment in nonpayment action | At least 20 days prior to entry | CPLR 3215(f)(3) | |

| Act To Be Performed | Time Period Available | Statute or Rule | Comments |
| --- | --- | --- | --- |
| Service of summons by publication | At least once in each of four successive weeks | CPLR 316(a) | *Exception:* In matrimonial action, at least once in each of 3 successive weeks. Consult CPLR 316(a).<br><br>Pleading, order and papers to be filed on or before first day of publication. See CPLR 316(a). In matrimonial actions, copy of summons to be mailed on or before first day of publication. See CPLR 316(b). |
| Time of publication | First publication required within 30 days after order | CPLR 316(c) | Service is complete on 28th day after first publication, except in matrimonial action, complete on 21st day. Service is complete earlier if defendant appears during period of publication of summons against him. See also CPLR 2402. |

| Act To Be Performed | Time Period Available | Statute or Rule | Comments |
|---|---|---|---|
| Service of complaint where summons served without complaint | (1) Defendant may serve written demand for complaint within 20 days after service if served personally or within 30 days if service of summons was other than personal.<br><br>(2) If defendant does not make demand for complaint, complaint is to be served within 20 days after defendant's notice of appearance.<br><br>(3) Complaint shall be served 20 days after defendant makes demand for same. | CPLR 3012(b) | Service of demand extends time for defendant to appear to within 20 days after service of complaint. |

| Act To Be Performed | Time Period Available | Statute or Rule | Comments |
|---|---|---|---|
| Service when summons is delivered to sheriff (outside NYC) or county clerk (in NYC) | For actions in the supreme court or the county courts, CPLR 203(c), 306–a, and 306–b, all effective July 1, 1992, obviate the need to deliver the summons to a sheriff or clerk for service; actions in those courts are commenced for statute of limitations and other purposes by filing the summons and complaint with the clerk and securing an index number, with service generally within 120 days thereafter. See CPLR 203(c), 306–a and 306–b. The time limitations in CPLR 203(b)(5) continue to apply to actions in the lower courts.<br><br>Service must be made personally on defendant within 60 days after period of limitation would have expired but for this provision<br><br>*or* | CPLR 203(b)(5) | Required to timely interpose claim in complaint. |

| Act To Be Performed | Time Period Available | Statute or Rule | Comments |
|---|---|---|---|
| | First publication must be made within 60 days after period of limitation would have expired but for this provision, and publication is completed subsequently *or* | | |
| | If defendant dies within 60-day period, and before service, service must be made upon executor or administrator within 60 days after letters are issued | | |
| Addition of parties to action | At any stage of the action by leave of court or by stipulation of all parties who have appeared. Without leave of court, once as of right, within 20 days after service of the original summons or before the time to respond to the summons has expired, or within 20 days after service of a pleading responding to it | CPLR 1003 | |

Timetable

| Act To Be Performed | Time Period Available | Statute or Rule | Comments |
|---|---|---|---|
| Amendment of complaint to assert claim against third-party defendant | Within 20 days after service of the answer to the third-party complaint on plaintiff's attorney | CPLR 1009 | |
| Extension of time where paper is served by mail | Five days | CPLR 2103(b)(2) | |
| **SECURITY FOR COSTS** | | | |
| Plaintiff's giving security for costs by undertaking | Within 30 days from date of court order | CPLR 8502 | If not timely given, court may dismiss complaint upon motion and may award costs to defendant. See CPLR 8503. |
| **PLEADINGS** | | | |
| Service of amended pleading if motion to correct is granted | Within 10 days after service of notice of entry of order | CPLR 3024(c) | |
| Amendment of pleadings without leave of court | Within 20 days after service, or at any time before period for responding to it expires, or within 20 days after service of responsive pleading | CPLR 3025(a) | |
| Amendments and supplemental pleadings by leave | At any time by leave of court or by stipulation of all parties | CPLR 3025(b) | |

| Act To Be Performed | Time Period Available | Statute or Rule | Comments |
| --- | --- | --- | --- |
| Service of answer or reply to amended or supplemental pleadings | Within 20 days after service | CPLR 3025(d) | |
| **DEFENSE OF ACTION** | | | |
| Defense of action by person served other than by personal delivery or personal delivery to agent | Within one year after obtaining knowledge of entry of judgment but not more than five years after entry | CPLR 317 | Court must make finding defendant did not receive summons in time to defend and finding that he had a meritorious defense. |
| **Answer or Appearance** | | | |
| Defendant's appearance by answer, notice of appearance or motion having effect of extending time to answer | Within 20 days after service if service of summons was made on defendant personally | CPLR 320(a), 3012(a) | If summons served without complaint, time to appear is extended until 20 days after service of complaint pursuant to defendant's demand. See CPLR 3012(b). |
| | Within 30 days after service complete, if service of summons was other than personal | CPLR 320(a), 3012(c) | Includes service on attorney as agent, delivery to person of suitable age and discretion and mailing, service pursuant to court order. See CPLR 303, 308(2)–(5), 313, 314, 315. |

| Act To Be Performed | Time Period Available | Statute or Rule | Comments |
|---|---|---|---|
| | | | If summons served without complaint, time to appear is extended until 20 days after service of complaint pursuant to defendant's demand. See CPLR 3012(b). |
| Service of copy of written authority by attorney for nonresident defendant or service of notice of filing same | Within 20 days after appearing or making a motion | CPLR 322(b) | |
| Service of answer or reply, generally | Within 20 days after service of pleading to which it responds | CPLR 3012(a) | |

**PRE-TRIAL MOTIONS OR DEMANDS**

| Act To Be Performed | Time Period Available | Statute or Rule | Comments |
|---|---|---|---|
| Service of defendant's demand for change of place of trial on ground of improper venue | With answer or before answer served | CPLR 511(a) | |
| Defendant's motion to change place of trial | Within 15 days after service of demand, unless within five days plaintiff serves written consent | CPLR 511(b) | |

| Act To Be Performed | Time Period Available | Statute or Rule | Comments |
|---|---|---|---|
| Motion for change of place of trial on other ground | Within a "reasonable time after commencement of the action" | CPLR 511(a) | |
| Motion for order to determine whether action will be maintained as class action | Within 60 days after time to serve a responsive pleading has expired for all named defendants | CPLR 902 | |
| Service of notice of motion and supporting affidavits | At least eight days before return date | CPLR 2214(b) | Add five days for service by mail. CPLR 2103. |
| Service of answering affidavits | At least two days before return date; but at least seven days before return date if notice of motion served at least 12 days before return date so demands | CPLR 2214(b) | Add five days for service by mail. CPLR 2103. |
| Service of reply affidavits | At least two days before return date if answering affidavit was served at least seven days before return date where notice of motion was served at least 12 days before return date and so demanded | CPLR 2214(b) | Add five days for service by mail. CPLR 2103. |
| Service of notice of cross-motion | At least three days before return date | CPLR 2215 | |

| Act To Be Performed | Time Period Available | Statute or Rule | Comments |
|---|---|---|---|
| Furnishing papers to court and adverse party | At hearing | CPLR 2214(c) | |
| Service of a subpoena *duces tecum* upon a hospital or upon a department or bureau of a municipal corporation or of the state | At least three days before the return date | CPLR 2306(a) | |
| Motion for subpoena *duces tecum* upon library; municipal or state department, bureau or officer | At least one day's notice | CPLR 2307 | |
| Time for taking procedural steps where parties will be substituted | Extended until 15 days after substitution | CPLR 1022 | Includes time for making motion for new trial, taking appeal, or making motion for permission to appeal. If action is dismissed under CPLR 1021, period is similarly extended until 15 days after dismissal. |
| Service of notice of motion to correct pleadings | Within 20 days after service of challenged pleading | CPLR 3024(c) | If motion is denied, responsive pleading must be served within 10 days after service of notice of entry of the order. |

| Act To Be Performed | Time Period Available | Statute or Rule | Comments |
|---|---|---|---|
| Service of notice of motion for order directing settlement of statement terms and determination of controversy under New York Simplified Procedure for Court Determination of Disputes | Eight days' notice or as court deems appropriate | CPLR 3034(2) | If motion is granted, amended pleading must be served within 10 days after service of notice of entry of the order. |
| Order determining a motion relating to a provisional remedy | Within 20 days after submission of motion | CPLR 2219 | |
| Order determining any other motion | Within 60 days after submission of motion | CPLR 2219 | |
| **BILL OF PARTICULARS** | | | |
| Service of bill of particulars | Within 20 days after demand | CPLR 3042(a) | |
| Motion to vacate or modify demand for bill of particulars | Within 10 days after receipt of notice | CPLR 3042(a) | |

Timetable

| Act To Be Performed | Time Period Available | Statute or Rule | Comments |
|---|---|---|---|
| Motion for order of preclusion or order directing service of further bill of particulars | Within 10 days after receipt of bill claimed to be insufficient | CPLR 3042(d) | Unless special circumstances exist. |
| Amendment of bill of particulars as of course, in an action in which a note of issue is required to be filed | Once, before trial, prior to filing note of issue | CPLR 3042(g) | |
| Service of supplemental bill of particulars without leave | Not less than 30 days prior to trial | CPLR 3043(b) | In personal injury actions. |
| **DISCLOSURE** | | | |
| Objection to disclosure, inspection, or examination | Within 20 days of service of a notice under rule 3120 or section 3121 | CPLR 3122 | Party to whom notice is directed must state the reasons for the objection with "reasonable particularity." |
| Service of subpoena *duces tecum* upon hospital; municipal or state department or bureau or officer | At least three days before time fixed for production of records unless court otherwise orders | CPLR 2306(a) | Where subpoena requires production of patient records, transcript certified by head of hospital, department, bureau (or by assistant), or officer. |

| Act To Be Performed | Time Period Available | Statute or Rule | Comments |
|---|---|---|---|
| Service of subpoena *duces tecum* upon library; municipal or state department or bureau or officer | At least 24 hours before time fixed for production of records unless court otherwise orders | CPLR 2307 | Where subpoena requires production of books, papers or other things. |
| Service of subpoena on non-party witness, or employee or officer of a party | At least 20 days before examination | CPLR 3106(b) | |
| Notification that a different deponent will be produced | At least 10 days prior to scheduled deposition | CPLR 3106(d) | |
| Review of proceedings where witness fails to comply with subpoena and has been committed to jail | Within 90 days | CPLR 2308(c) | Periodic review after not more than 90 days. |
| Service of notice of taking oral deposition | On 20 days' notice, unless court directs otherwise | CPLR 3107 | A party to be examined may serve notice of at least 10 days for examination of another party, his agent or employee, at same time and place. |
| Service of written cross-questions | Within 15 days after service of written questions and notice | CPLR 3109(a) | |
| Service of written redirect questions | Within seven days after service of written cross-questions | CPLR 3109(a) | |

| Act To Be Performed | Time Period Available | Statute or Rule | Comments |
| --- | --- | --- | --- |
| Service of written recross-questions | Within five days after being served with written redirect questions | CPLR 3109(a) | Otherwise, errors and irregularities are waived. |
| Service of written objection to errors in notice for taking deposition | At least three days before time for taking deposition | CPLR 3112 | Otherwise, objections are waived. |
| Service of written objection to form of written questions | Within time allowed for serving succeeding questions or within three days after service | CPLR 3115(e) | |
| Compliance with demand for address of party | Within 10 days of service of demand | CPLR 3118 | |
| Exchange of medical information in personal injury and wrongful death actions | | | See Uniform Rules for NYS Trial Courts § 202.17 (Supreme and County Courts). |
| Service of written request for admission as to matters of fact, papers, documents and photographs | At any time after service of answer or after expiration of 20 days from service of summons, whichever is sooner, but not later than 20 days before trial | CPLR 3123(a) | Deemed admitted unless within 20 days after service or as court allows, adverse party serves sworn statement of denial or explanation. See CPLR 3123(a). |

| Act To Be Performed | Time Period Available | Statute or Rule | Comments |
|---|---|---|---|
| Service of written interrogatories | After commencement of the action but not before the defendant's time to serve a responsive pleading has expired, except by leave of court | CPLR 3132 | |
| Motion to strike out interrogatory | Within 10 days after service of interrogatories | CPLR 3133(a) | Answer to interrogatory is thereby deferred until court rules on objections, CPLR 3133(b). |
| Service of answers or objections to interrogatories | Within 20 days after service of interrogatories | CPLR 3133 | a party who objects to answering an interrogatory need not move for an order to strike, but may instead set forth the objection in the response |
| Motion for review of order of referee supervising disclosure | Within five days after order is made | CPLR 3104(d) | |
| Exchange and filing of statements of net worth in actions and proceedings involving alimony, maintenance, support and equitable distribution | Within 20 days after receipt of written demand or if not demanded, it shall be filed by each party within 10 days after joinder of issue | DRL § 236(B), Fam. Ct. Act § 464, Uniform Rules for NYS Trial Courts § 202.16 (Supreme and County Courts) | |

| Act To Be Performed | Time Period Available | Statute or Rule | Comments |
| --- | --- | --- | --- |
| Exchange and filing of proposed disposition in actions and proceedings involving alimony, maintenance, support and equitable distribution | | | See § 202.16(d)(3) of the Uniform Rules for NYS Trial Courts, which provides that the statement of proposed disposition be filed with the note of issue (§ 202.21) and that the other party shall file such statement within 20 days "of such service." |

| Act To Be Performed | Time Period Available | Statute or Rule | Comments |
| --- | --- | --- | --- |
| Amendment or supplementation of responses | Whenever the responding party subsequently learns that a response was incorrect or incomplete when given, or when the responding party learns that a response "though correct and complete when made, no longer is correct and complete." | CPLR 3101(h) | The duty to amend or supplement a previous response arises only when the failure to act would be materially misleading |

**Editor's note: L. 1996, ch. 117, amended CPLR 3116(a). Beginning January 1, 1997, the following time restrictions apply:]**

| | | | |
| --- | --- | --- | --- |
| Signature and return of deposition; changes made to deposition | ithin 60 days after receipt of the deposition by the witness for examination | CPLR 3116(a) | If the witness fails to return the deposition, it may be used as fully as though signed. No changes may be made to the deposition more than 60 days after transmission to the witness for examination |

**ACCELERATED JUDGMENT**

| | | | |
| --- | --- | --- | --- |
| Motion to dismiss for improper service where objecting party raises the objection in the answer | Within 60 days after service of the answer | CPLR 3211(e) | Failure to move for dismissal will result in waiver of the objection. The court may extend the time on the ground of "undue hardship" |

Timetable

| Act To Be Performed | Time Period Available | Statute or Rule | Comments |
|---|---|---|---|
| Extension of time to serve pleading where notice of motion to dismiss cause of action (CPLR 3211[a]) or to dismiss defense (CPLR 3211[b]) is made before service of pleading responsive to cause of action or defense | Until 10 days after service of notice of entry of order | CPLR 3211(f) | |
| Motion for summary judgment | Any time after issue has been joined but no later than 120 days after filing the note of issue | CPLR 3212(a) | However, the court may set a date by with any such motion shall be made, which must be no earlier than 30 days after filing the note of issue. The court may extend either date upon a showing of good cause |
| Notice of motion for summary judgment in lieu of complaint | Minimum of 20 days after service of summons if personal service or 30 days if other than personal service | CPLR 3213, 320(a) | If hearing date is later than minimum time, plaintiff may require defendant to serve copy of answering papers within extended period of time, not exceeding 10 days prior to hearing date. CPLR 3213. |

| Act To Be Performed | Time Period Available | Statute or Rule | Comments |
| --- | --- | --- | --- |
| **Default Judgment** | | | |
| Plaintiff's application for default judgment (claim for sum certain) | Within one year after default | CPLR 3215(a) | If plaintiff fails to comply, court shall dismiss complaint. See CPLR 3215(c). See also CPLR 1203. |
| Defendant's application for judgment for costs | Within one year after default | CPLR 3215(a) | |
| Notice of default motion to be provided to defendant who has appeared | At least five days | CPLR 3215(f)(1) | If application is made to court, unless otherwise provided in specific action. |
| Notice of default motion to be provided to defendant who has not appeared | If more than one year has elapsed since default, at least five days' notice | CPLR 3215(f)(1) | Unless court orders otherwise. |
| Notice, to be given to defendant, of reference or assessment by jury | At least five days | CPLR 3215(f)(2) | If defendant who has not appeared serves demand for notice, before motion for judgment is heard. |
| Additional notice required to take a default judgment against a natural person based upon nonpayment of a contractual obligation | At least 20 days before entry of judgment | CPLR 3215(f)(3) | Does not apply to small claims part of any court or to any summary proceeding to recover possession of real property or to actions affecting title to real property. |

Timetable

| Act To Be Performed | Time Period Available | Statute or Rule | Comments |
|---|---|---|---|
| Motion to dismiss for want of prosecution | At least one year must have elapsed since joinder of issue | CPLR 3216(b) | See CPLR 3216 for other requirements, including written demand for service and filing of note of issue within 90 days after receipt. |
| **Voluntary Discontinuance** | | | |
| Service of notice of discontinuance | At any time before a responsive pleading is served or within 20 days after service of pleading asserting the claim, whichever is earlier | CPLR 3217(a)(1) | See CPLR 3217 for other methods of discontinuance. See also Uniform Rules for NYS Trial Courts § 202.28 (Supreme and County Courts), re filing stipulation to discontinue action within 20 days of discontinuance. |
| **Judgment by Confession** | | | |
| Filing of defendant's affidavit by confession | Within three years after execution | CPLR 3218(b) | May not be entered after defendant's death. |
| **Tender** | | | |
| Deposit of payment with court clerk and service upon claimant of written tender of payment | Not later than 10 days before trial | CPLR 3219 | In contract action, by party against whom a separate judgment may be taken. Claimant may withdraw amount within 10 days. |
| Offer To Liquidate Damages Conditionally | Not later than 10 days before trial | CPLR 3220 | |

| Act To Be Performed | Time Period Available | Statute or Rule | Comments |
|---|---|---|---|
| Offer To Compromise | Not later than 10 days before trial | CPLR 3221 | *Exception:* Matrimonial action. |
| **CALENDAR PRACTICE** | | | |
| Placing case on calendar—filing note of issue and certificate of readiness | At any time after issue is joined, or at least 40 days after completion of service of summons | CPLR 3402(a) | File within 10 days after service of note of issue. See also Uniform Rules for NYS Trial Courts § 202.21 (Supreme and County Courts). |
| Service of note of issue upon new party | Within five days | CPLR 3402(b) | |
| Filing statement with clerk on bringing in new party | Within five days | CPLR 3402(b) | |
| Service of notice of motion for preference | With note of issue, by party serving note of issue, *or* 10 days after such service by any other party (*or* thereafter during pendency of action by party who reaches age 70 *or* who is terminally ill) | CPLR 3403(b) | |
| Abandonment of case in Supreme Court or County Court marked "Off" or struck from calendar or unanswered on calendar roll | If not restored within one year | CPLR 3404 | Case shall be dismissed without necessity for order. |

Timetable

| Act To Be Performed | Time Period Available | Statute or Rule | Comments |
|---|---|---|---|
| Notice of dental, medical or podiatric malpractice actions. | Within 60 days after issue is joined | CPLR 3406, Uniform Rules for NYS Trial Courts § 202.56 (Supreme and County Courts) | |
| Filing of demand for trial by jury | Within 15 days after service of note of issue | CPLR 4102(a) | File with proof of service upon each party. If trial by jury has been demanded of only some of the issues, any other party within 10 days after service of demand may serve and file demand for trial by jury of any other issues triable by jury. CPLR 4102(b). See also Uniform Rules for Trial Courts § 202.21(c) (Supreme and County Courts). |
| Motion for trial by referee or advisory jury | Within 20 days after note of issue is filed | CPLR 4015 | *Exceptions:* Where issue to be tried arises on a motion or pursuant to a judgment. |

| Act To Be Performed | Time Period Available | Statute or Rule | Comments |
| --- | --- | --- | --- |
| Motion to strike case from calendar | Within 20 days after service of note of issue and certificate of readiness (does not apply to tax assessment review proceedings) | Uniform Rules for NYS Trial Courts § 202.21 (Supreme and County Courts) | After the 20-day period, no motion shall be allowed except for good cause shown. |
| **TRIAL** | | | |
| Decision of court | Within 60 days after final submission of cause or matter or within 60 days after motion for new trial or to confirm or reject (CPLR 4403), whichever is later | CPLR 4213(c) | |
| First hearing by referee | Within 20 days after date of order of reference | CPLR 4313 | |
| Filing of referee's decision | Within 30 days after final submission of cause or matter | CPLR 4319 | If not timely filed, court may grant new trial. |
| Filing of referee's report, findings of fact and conclusions of law | Within 30 days after final submission of cause or matter | CPLR 4320(b) | Transcript to be filed with report, unless otherwise stipulated. |

| Act To Be Performed | Time Period Available | Statute or Rule | Comments |
|---|---|---|---|
| Motion to confirm or reject judicial hearing officer's or referee's report | Plaintiff shall move on notice within 15 days after notice of filing was given. If plaintiff fails to make motion, defendant shall make motion within 30 days after notice of filing | Uniform Rules for NYS Trial Courts § 202.44 (Supreme and County Courts) | |

## SUBMISSION OF ORDERS, JUDGMENTS AND DECREES—SUPREME AND COUNTY COURTS

| Act To Be Performed | Time Period Available | Statute or Rule | Comments |
|---|---|---|---|
| Submission of proposed order or judgment for signature (with proof of service) where order is directed to be settled or submitted for signature | Within 60 days after signing and filing of decision directing that order be settled or submitted | Uniform Rules for NYS Trial Courts § 202.48 | |
| Service of copy of proposed order of judgment with notice of settlement where settlement is directed by court | If by personal service, not less than 5 days before date of settlement<br><br>If by mail, not less than 10 days before date of settlement | Uniform Rules for NYS Trial Courts § 202.48 | |

| Act To Be Performed | Time Period Available | Statute or Rule | Comments |
|---|---|---|---|
| Service of proposed counter-order or judgment | If by personal service, not less than 2 days before date of settlement<br><br>If by mail, not less than 7 days, before date of settlement | Uniform Rules for NYS Trial Court § 202.48 | |
| **POST-TRIAL MOTIONS** | | | |
| Motion for new trial or to confirm or reject verdict of advisory jury or report of referee to report | Within 15 days after verdict or filing of referee's report and prior to further trial | CPLR 4403 | |
| Post-trial motion for judgment and new trial | Within 15 days after decision, verdict or discharge of jury | CPLR 4405 | |
| Motion to relieve party from judgment or order, on ground of excusable default | Within one year after service of copy of judgment or order with written notice of entry, upon moving party, or if entered by moving party, within one year after such entry | CPLR 5015(a)(1) | See also CPLR 2005, 3012(d) concerning delay or default resulting from law office failure. |
| Petition for remission or mitigation of forfeiture of proceeds of crime | Within one year of entry of judgment of forfeiture | CPLR 1311(7) | |

| Act To Be Performed | Time Period Available | Statute or Rule | Comments |
|---|---|---|---|
| **TAXATION OF COSTS** | | | |
| Taxation on notice | Five days' notice | CPLR 8402 | |
| Notice of retaxation | Five days' notice | CPLR 8403 | Service within five days after service of bill of costs without notice. |
| **ENFORCEMENT OF JUDGMENTS** | | | |
| Mailing of copy of satisfaction-piece to judgment debtor | Within 10 days after date of filing | CPLR 5020(a) | |
| Execution of satisfaction-piece by attorney for judgment creditor | Within 10 years after entry of judgment | CPLR 5020(b) | |
| Civil penalty for failure of judgment creditor to execute and file satisfaction-piece | On failure to comply with CPLR 5020(a) or (d) within 20 days after receiving full satisfaction | CPLR 5020(c) | If the City of New York is the judgment creditor, written demand is first required. |
| Entry upon return of execution arising out of small claims action | Within 90 days after receipt of judgment by sheriff | CPLR 5021(b) | |
| Leave to issue execution to levy upon real property after death of party against whom order awarding possession was obtained | Upon 20 days' notice to occupants of real property and to heirs or devisees | CPLR 5102 | |

| Act To Be Performed | Time Period Available | Statute or Rule | Comments |
|---|---|---|---|
| Expiration of judgment lien existing against real property at time of judgment debtor's death | Two years thereafter or 10 years after filing of judgment-roll, whichever is later | CPLR 5208 | |
| Service of restraining notice | If "notice to judgment debtor or obligor" (CPLR 5222[e]) has not been given to judgment debtor or obligor within one year before service of restraining notice, copy of restraining notice and notice to judgment debtor or obligor shall be mailed by first class or personally delivered to each judgment debtor obligor within four days of service of restraining notice | CPLR 5222(d) | |
| Return of answers to information subpoena | Within seven days after receipt | CPLR 5224(a)(3) | |
| Deposition or examination of books and papers | Not less than 10 days' notice, unless court orders shorter notice | CPLR 5224(c) | |
| Subsequent examination | Within one year, requires leave of court | CPLR 5224(f) | |

| Act To Be Performed | Time Period Available | Statute or Rule | Comments |
|---|---|---|---|
| Return of execution to court clerk or to support collection unit | Within 60 days after issuance unless served in accordance with CPLR 5231 or 5232(a) | CPLR 5230(c), 5231, 5232(a) | May be extended in writing by judgment creditor's attorney or by the support collection unit, for not more than 60 additional days. |
| Service of income execution upon debtor | Within 20 days after delivery to sheriff | CPLR 5231(d) | |
| Levy upon default or failure to serve debtor | After 20 days | CPLR 5231(e) | |
| Accounting by sheriff of monies collected | At least once every ninety days from the time a levy is made | CPLR 5231(k) | |
| Voidness of levy | At expiration of 90 days after service of execution, or as provided by court | CPLR 5232(a) | *Exceptions:* As to debts paid to sheriff or support collection unit or as to which proceeding under CPLR 5225 or 5227 has been brought. |
| Service by sheriff or support collection unit of copy of execution, and notice to judgment debtor or obligor | Within four days after service of execution upon garnishee | CPLR 5232(c) | |
| Priority of other judgment creditors | For 60 days after order is filed, unless otherwise specified or unless extended by order within the 60 days | See CPLR 5234(c) | If order is filed before property or debt is levied upon. |

| Act To Be Performed | Time Period Available | Statute or Rule | Comments |
|---|---|---|---|
| Levy upon real property | 10 years after filing of judgment-roll | CPLR 5235 | |
| Sale of real property levied upon | Between 56th and 63rd day after first publication of copy of notice of sale | CPLR 5236(a) | As to notice of sale, see CPLR 5236(c). |
| Sheriff's delivery to purchaser, of proofs re sale, and deed | Within 10 days after sale | CPLR 5236(f) | |
| **Foreign judgments** | | | |
| Filing of foreign judgment | Within 90 days of date of authentication | CPLR 5402(a) | |
| Mailing of notice of filing | Within 30 days after filing of judgment | CPLR 5403 | Proceeds shall not be distributed earlier than 30 days after filing of proof of service. |
| **APPEALS** | | | |
| **In general** | | | |
| Taking of appeal as of right, or moving for permission to appeal | Within 30 days after service of copy of judgment or order and notice of entry | CPLR 5513(a), (b) | If attorney dies within 30-day period, extended to 60 days from date of death. CPLR 5514(b). |

| Act To Be Performed | Time Period Available | Statute or Rule | Comments |
|---|---|---|---|
| Taking of cross-appeal | Same as above, *or* within 10 days after service of notice of appeal or motion for permission to appeal, whichever is longer | CPLR 5513(c) | |
| **Court of Appeals** | | | |
| Filing and service of appellant's jurisdictional statement | Within 10 days from time appeal is taken | 22 NYCRR § 500.2(a), (d) | Statement may include request that appeal be considered for expedited resolution. See § 500.4(d). |
| | | | If party will assert that a statute is unconstitutional, written notice to attorney general must be given at time of filing jurisdictional statement. See § 500.2(d). |
| Sua sponte examination of merits— | | | |
| —Appellant's service and submission to Court of written comments and arguments | Within 20 days of clerk's inquiry | § 500.4(f) | If either party objects to summary considerations, written comments and arguments justifying that position should accompany the submission. § 500.4(f). |

| Act To Be Performed | Time Period Available | Statute or Rule | Comments |
|---|---|---|---|
| —Respondent's service and filing of submission | 15 days after receipt of appellant's submission | § 500.4(f) | If either party objects to summary consideration, written comments and arguments justifying that position should accompany the submission. § 500.4(f). |
| Filing and service of appellant's record materials and brief | Within 60 days from taking the appeal unless another due date has been set by the court | §§ 500.5(d), (f), 500.9(a) | Appeal will be dismissed for failure of appellant to proceed or file papers if Court had no notice of pending appeal and 80 days pass from date of taking appeal without compliance with filing provisions. § 500.9(a). If Court had notice of appeal and appellant does not comply, dismissal after 20-day notice by clerk, subject to extension. See § 500.9(b). |

Timetable

| Act To Be Performed | Time Period Available | Statute or Rule | Comments |
|---|---|---|---|
| | | | Liberal extension of time, with reasonable grounds, permit-file papers if Court had no notice of pending appeal and 80 days pass from date of taking appeal without compliance with filing provisions. § 500.9(d). If Court had notice of appeal and appellant does not comply, dismissal after 20-day notice by clerk, subject to extension. See § 500.9(b). |
| Filing and service of respondent's brief and appendix | Within 45 days of service of appellant's papers unless another due date has been set by the court | § 500.7(a) | Liberal extension of time permitted. § 500.9(d). If noncompliance, preclusion after 20-day notice by clerk, subject to extension. See § 500.9(c). |
| Filing and service of reply brief | Within 10 days of receipt of respondent's brief | § 500.5(f) | Liberal extension of time permitted. § 500.9(d). Where cross-appeals are filed, cross-appellant may serve reply brief to main appellant's responsive brief. § 500.5(f). |

| Act To Be Performed | Time Period Available | Statute or Rule | Comments |
| --- | --- | --- | --- |
| Motions to Court of Appeals | On eight days' notice (13 if service by mail) | § 500.11(a) | |
| Service of notice of motion for reargument | Within 30 days after appeal or motion decided, unless otherwise permitted by Court | § 500.11(g)(3) | |
| Withdrawal of appeal or motion | At any time prior to argument or submission | § 500.16 | By stipulation signed by all parties (and in criminal appeals, by defendant personally). § 500.16. |
| Other provisions relating to appeals | | See §§ 500.10, 500.11(d), (e) | |
| **Appellate Divisions** | | | |
| Filing of record (appendix system) | 1st Dep't: Within 30 days after settlement of transcript or statement in lieu of transcript | § 600.5(a)(1) | See CPLR 5525, 5526, 5528(a)(5). |
| | 2d Dep't: Appellant shall subpoena from the clerk of the court from which the appeal is taken all papers constituting the record on appeal and cause them to be filed with the clerk of this court prior to the filing of the appendix | § 670.9(b) | See CPLR 5525, 5528(f)(5), 5532. |

| Act To Be Performed | Time Period Available | Statute or Rule | Comments |
|---|---|---|---|
| Filing of original record, stipulated and settled | 3d Dep't: See §§ 800.4(b), 800.7(b) and consult court clerk | | |
| | 4th Dep't: Within 60 days of filing and serving notice of appeal | § 1000.5(c)(1) | |
| | 4th Dep't: Within 60 days of filing and serving notice of appeal or order of transfer | § 1000.5(b)(2) | Within five days of its return by respondent. § 1000.5(c)(4). |
| Filing of agreed statement in lieu of record | 1st Dep't: Within 30 days after approval | § 600.5(b)(2) | See CPLR 5527. |
| | 2d Dep't: See § 670.10 and CPLR 5531 | § 670.9(c) | |
| | 3d Dep't: Same as above | § 800.4(d) | |
| | 4th Dep't: See § 1000.5(d) and CPLR 5527 | | |
| Filing of optional full record | 1st Dep't: Within 30 days after settlement of transcript of proceedings | § 600.5(c) | See CPLR 5526, 5528(a)(5). |
| | 2d Dep't: See § 670.10 and CPLR 5528(a)(5) | § 670.9(a) | |

| Act To Be Performed | Time Period Available | Statute or Rule | Comments |
| --- | --- | --- | --- |
| Filing of records in case where record does not involve settlement or approval | *1st Dep't:* Within 30 days after taking of notice of appeal | § 600.5(d) | |
| | *2d Dep't:* Together with the brief | § 670.9(b)(3) | Where transcript or statement not involved. |
| Placing appeal on calendar | | | |
| *1st Dep't:* By filing note of issue with proof of service | Within 20 days after filing record on appeal, statement in lieu of record or papers in transferred Art. 78 proceeding at least 57 days before first day of term. | § 600.11(a)(1), (b); see § 600.4 | *Exception:* Submission of controversy is placed on calendar at time of filing agreed statement of facts.<br><br>Papers and briefs must be filed within nine months of date of notice of appeal (in Art. 78 proceeding, from date of order of transfer to App. Div.). See § 600.11(a)(3). |
| *2d Dep't:* Same as above | See § 670.9 | § 670.8(a) | Similarly, see § 800.12. |
| *3d Dep't:* Not specified | Not specified by Rule or CPLR | | |
| *4th Dep't:* See § 1000.8 | Not specified by Rule or CPLR | | |

| Act To Be Performed | Time Period Available | Statute or Rule | Comments |
| --- | --- | --- | --- |
| Appellant's filing of main brief | *2d Dep't:* See § 670.9 | § 670.8(a) | File with record. |
| | *3d Dep't:* Generally, within 60 days after service of notice of appeal | § 800.9(a) | |
| Filing of answering (respondent's) brief | *1st Dep't:* At least 27 days before first day of term | § 600.11(c) | |
| | *2d Dep't:* Within 30 days after service of appellant's brief | § 670.8(b) | |
| | *3d Dep't:* Within 30 days from service of appellant's brief, *or* must apply to court within 10 days for extension | § 800.9(b) | |
| | *4th Dep't:* Within 30 days of service of appellant's brief | §§ 1000.5(b)(3), (c)(3) | |
| Filing of reply brief | *1st Dep't:* Within nine days after service of answering brief | § 600.11(c) | |
| | *2d Dep't:* Within 10 days after service of respondent's brief | § 670.8(b) | |
| | *3d Dep't:* Within 10 days after service of respondent's brief | § 800.9(c) | |
| | *4th Dep't:* Within nine days of service of respondent's brief | §§ 1000.5(b)(4), (c)(5) | |

| Act To Be Performed | Time Period Available | Statute or Rule | Comments |
|---|---|---|---|
| **Cross appeals** | | | |
| Filing and service of record and brief | *4th Dep't:* On appeal, unless otherwise ordered by court | § 1000.5(b)(5) | |
| Filing by respondent/cross appellant | *1st Dep't:* Within 30 days after perfection of appellant's appeal | § 600.11(d) | |
| | *2d Dep't:* 30 days after service of appellant's main brief | § 670.8(c)(2) | Filing and service of adverse party's answering brief. |
| | *3d Dep't:* Within 30 days after service of first brief | § 800.9(e) | Filing and service of answering brief and appendix. |
| | *4th Dep't:* Within 30 days after service of main brief | § 1000.5(b)(5) | Filing and service of answering brief (or brief and appendix). |
| Filing of reply brief by first appellant | *2d Dep't:* Within 30 days after service of answering brief | § 670.8(c)(2) | |
| | *3d Dep't:* Within 10 days after service of answering brief | § 800.9(e) | |
| | *4th Dep't:* Within nine days of service of answering brief | § 1000.5(b)(5) | |
| Filing of reply brief to cross-appeal | *1st Dep't:* Within nine days after reply to the answering brief filed | § 600.11(d) | |

| Act To Be Performed | Time Period Available | Statute or Rule | Comments |
|---|---|---|---|
| | 2d Dep't: Within 10 days after service of reply to answering brief | § 670.8(c)(2) | |
| | 3d Dep't: Within 10 days after service of appellant's reply brief | § 800.9(e) | |
| | 4th Dep't: Within four days of service of reply to answering brief | § 1000.5(b)(5) | |
| Written notification to clerk of time desired for argument | 1st Dep't: On or before the court's scheduled date in that particular term | § 600.11(f)(1) | |
| Request for change of date of argument | 3d Dep't: At least 14 days prior to commencement of term | § 800.11 | |
| Notice of intention to apply for permission to argue certain appeals | 2d Dep't: At least seven days prior to calendar date | § 670.19(c) | Notice must be given to court and opposing party. |
| Filing of stipulation of adjournment | 1st Dep't: Not later than 26 days before first day of term for which appeal has been noticed | § 600.11(g) | |
| Motion for reargument | 1st Dep't: Within 30 days after appeal has been decided | § 600.14(a) | |

| Act To Be Performed | Time Period Available | Statute or Rule | Comments |
| --- | --- | --- | --- |
| Other provisions relating to appeals | | CPLR 5530(a), 5519(c), 5525(c)(1), (d), 5527 | *2d Dep't:* See §§ 670.9(b), 670.10(c), 670.12-670.14, 670.18.<br><br>*3d Dep't:* See §§ 800.5(b), 800.8(c), 800.13, 800.18-800.22.<br><br>*4th Dep't:* See §§ 1000.2–1000.5, 1000.7.<br><br>See §§ 600.7(c) (1st Dep't), 670.17 (2nd Dep't), 800.20 (3rd Dep't), 1000.5(j) (4th Dep't). |
| **Appeals Under NYS Human Rights Law** | | | |

Timetable

# NEW YORK COURT SYSTEM

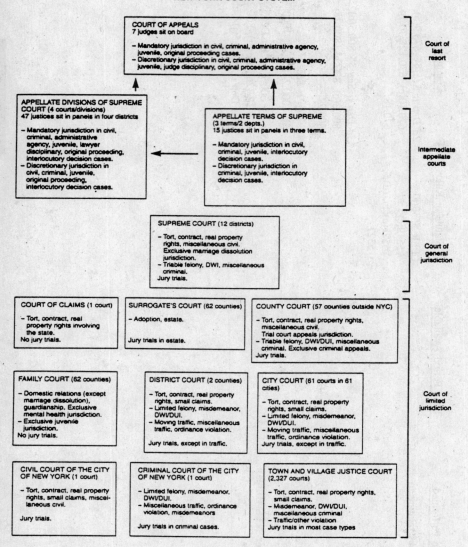

**COURT OF APPEALS**
7 judges sit on board

– Mandatory jurisdiction in civil, criminal, administrative agency, juvenile, original proceeding cases.
– Discretionary jurisdiction in civil, criminal, administrative agency, juvenile, judge disciplinary, original proceeding cases.

> Court of last resort

**APPELLATE DIVISIONS OF SUPREME COURT (4 courts/divisions)**
47 justices sit in panels in four districts

– Mandatory jurisdiction in civil, criminal, administrative agency, juvenile, lawyer disciplinary, original proceeding, interlocutory decision cases.
– Discretionary jurisdiction in civil, criminal, juvenile, original proceeding, interlocutory decision cases.

**APPELLATE TERMS OF SUPREME COURT**
(3 terms/2 depts.)
15 justices sit in panels in three terms.

– Mandatory jurisdiction in civil, criminal, juvenile, interlocutory decision cases.
– Discretionary jurisdiction in criminal, juvenile, interlocutory decision cases.

> Intermediate appellate courts

**SUPREME COURT (12 districts)**

– Tort, contract, real property rights, miscellaneous civil. Exclusive marriage dissolution jurisdiction.
– Triable felony, DWI, miscellaneous criminal.
Jury trials.

> Court of general jurisdiction

**COURT OF CLAIMS (1 court)**

– Tort, contract, real property rights involving the state.
No jury trials.

**SURROGATE'S COURT (62 counties)**

– Adoption, estate.

Jury trials in estate.

**COUNTY COURT (57 counties outside NYC)**

– Tort, contract, real property rights, miscellaneous civil. Trial court appeals jurisdiction.
– Triable felony, DWI/DUI, miscellaneous criminal. Exclusive criminal appeals.
Jury trials.

**FAMILY COURT (62 counties)**

– Domestic relations (except marriage dissolution), guardianship. Exclusive mental health jurisdiction.
– Exclusive juvenile jurisdiction.
No jury trials.

**DISTRICT COURT (2 counties)**

– Tort, contract, real property rights, small claims.
– Limited felony, misdemeanor, DWI/DUI.
– Moving traffic, miscellaneous traffic, ordinance violation.

Jury trials, except in traffic.

**CITY COURT (61 courts in 61 cities)**

– Tort, contract, real property rights, small claims.
– Limited felony, misdemeanor, DWI/DUI.
– Moving traffic, miscellaneous traffic, ordinance violation.
Jury trials, except in traffic.

> Court of limited jurisdiction

**CIVIL COURT OF THE CITY OF NEW YORK (1 court)**

– Tort, contract, real property rights, small claims, miscellaneous civil.

Jury trials.

**CRIMINAL COURT OF THE CITY OF NEW YORK (1 court)**

– Limited felony, misdemeanor, DWI/DUI.
– Miscellaneous traffic, ordinance violation, misdemeanors

Jury trials in criminal cases.

**TOWN AND VILLAGE JUSTICE COURT (2,327 courts)**

– Tort, contract, real property rights, small claims.
– Misdemeanor, DWI/DUI, miscellaneous criminal
– Traffic/other violation
Jury trials in most case types

Source: Court Statistics Project of the National Center for State Courts. State Court Caseload Statistics, 1987 Report. Williamsburg, VA National Center for State Courts (a joint effort of the Conference of State Court Administrators and the National Center for State Courts.) 1989.

# CIVIL PRACTICE LAW AND RULES

**As amended by the 1996 Regular Legislative Session through
September 24, 1996**

An Act in relation to civil practice and prescribing rules of civil procedure governing generally the civil procedure in the courts of the state of New York and before the judges thereof, constituting chapter eight of the consolidated laws.

# ARTICLE 1

## SHORT TITLE; APPLICABILITY AND DEFINITIONS

### SUMMARY OF ARTICLE

§ 101.    Short title; application.
§ 102.    Amendment, rescission or adoption of rules.
§ 103.    Form of civil judicial proceedings.
    (a)  One form of action.
    (b)  Action or special proceeding.
    (c)  Improper form.
§ 104.    Construction.
§ 105.    Definitions.
    (a)  Applicability.
    (b)  Action and special proceeding.
    (c)  Attorney.
    (d)  Civil judicial proceeding.
    (e)  Clerk.
    (f)  Consumer credit transaction.
    (g)  Court and judge.
    (h)  Domestic and foreign corporation.
    (i)  Garnishee.
    (j)  Infant, infancy.
    (k)  Judgment.
    (l)  Judgment creditor.
    (m)  Judgment debtor.
    (n)  Judicial hearing officer.
    (o)  Law.
    (p)  Matrimonial action.
    (q)  Money judgment.
    (r)  Place where action triable.
    (s)  Real property.
    (t)  Type size requirement.
    (u)  Verified pleading.
§ 106.    Civil and criminal prosecutions not merged.
§ 107.    Appendix of official forms.

CPLR

## § 101. Short title; application.

This chapter shall be known as the civil practice law and rules, and may be cited as "CPLR." The civil practice law and rules shall govern the procedure in civil judicial proceedings in all courts of the state and before all judges, except where the procedure is regulated by inconsistent statute. The civil practice law and rules shall succeed the civil practice act and rules of civil practice and shall be deemed substituted therefor throughout the statutes and rules of the state. Reference to a provision in the civil practice law and rules may, except when such provision is being enacted or amended, be made without indicating whether it is a rule or section.

### 1964 AMENDMENTS

L. 1964, ch. 252, eff. Sept. 1, 1964, added the last sentence.

## § 102. Amendment, rescission or adoption of rules.

The civil practice rules are herein designated "rule." Any rule in this chapter may be amended, or rescinded, or additional civil practice rules may be adopted, not inconsistent with the constitution, by act of the legislature. No rule so amended, rescinded or adopted shall abridge or enlarge the substantive rights of any party.

### CROSS REFERENCES

**Judiciary Law § 229,** referred to in this section, was repealed by L. 1978, ch. 156, eff. May 19, 1978. **Judiciary Law § 215,** which replaced former § 229, does not refer to the power of the judicial conference to change the rules of the CPLR.

### 1986 AMENDMENTS

L. 1986, ch. 334, eff. July 17, 1986, deleted the reference to **Judiciary Law** § 229(3).

## § 103. Form of civil judicial proceedings.

(a) One form of action. There is only one form of civil action. The distinctions between actions at law and suits in equity, and the forms of those actions and suits, have been abolished.

(b) Action or special proceeding. All civil judicial proceedings shall be prosecuted in the form of an action, except where prosecution in the form of a special proceeding is authorized. Except where otherwise prescribed by law, procedure in special proceedings shall be the same as in actions, and the provisions of the civil practice law and rules applicable to actions shall be applicable to special proceedings.

(c) Improper form. If a court has obtained jurisdiction over the parties, a civil judicial proceeding shall not be dismissed solely because it is not brought in the proper form, but the court shall make whatever order is required for its proper prosecution.

## § 104. Construction.

The civil practice law and rules shall be liberally construed to secure the just, speedy and inexpensive determination of every civil judicial proceeding.

## § 105. Definitions.

(a) Applicability. Unless the context requires otherwise, the definitions in this section apply to the civil practice law and rules.

(b) Action and special proceeding. The word "action" includes a special proceeding; the words "plaintiff" and "defendant" include the petitioner and the respondent, respectively, in a special proceeding; and the words "summons" and "complaint" include the notice of petition and the petition, respectively, in a special proceeding.

(c) Attorney. The word "attorney" includes a party prosecuting or defending an action in person.

(d) Civil judicial proceeding. A "civil judicial proceeding" is a prosecution, other than a criminal action, of an independent application to a court for relief.

(e) Clerk. The word "clerk," as used in any provision respecting an action or any proceedings therein, means the clerk of the court in which the action is triable.

(f) Consumer credit transaction. The term "consumer credit transaction" means a transaction wherein credit is extended to an individual and the money, property, or service which is the subject of the transaction is primarily for personal, family or household purposes.

(g) Court and judge. The word "court," as used in any provision concerning a motion, order or special proceeding, includes a judge thereof authorized to act out of court with respect to such motion, order or special proceeding.

(h) Domestic and foreign corporation. A "domestic corporation" is a corporation created by or under the laws of the state, or a corporation located in the state and created by or under the laws of the United States, or a corporation created by or pursuant to the laws in force in the colony of New York before April nineteenth, seventeen hundred seventy-five. Every other corporation is a "foreign corporation."

(i) Garnishee. A "garnishee" is a person who owes a debt to a judgment debtor, or a person other than the judgment debtor who has property in his possession or custody in which a judgment debtor has an interest.

(j) Infant, infancy. The word "infant," as used in this chapter, means a person who has not attained the age of eighteen years. The word "infancy" means the state of being an infant.

(k) Judgment. The word "judgment" means a final or interlocutory judgment.

CPLR

(l) Judgment creditor. A "judgment creditor" is a person in whose favor a money judgment is entered or a person who becomes entitled to enforce it.

(m) Judgment debtor. A "judgment debtor" is a person, other than a defendant not summoned in the action, against whom a money judgment is entered.

(n) Judicial hearing officer. A "judicial hearing officer" means a person so designated pursuant to provisions of article twenty-two of the judiciary law.

(o) Law. The word "law" means any statute or any civil practice rule.

(p) Matrimonial action. The term "matrimonial action" includes actions for a separation, for an annulment or dissolution of a marriage, for a divorce, for a declaration of the nullity of a void marriage, for a declaration of the validity or nullity of a foreign judgment of divorce and for a declaration of the validity or nullity of a marriage.

(q) Money judgment. A "money judgment" is a judgment, or any part thereof, for a sum of money or directing the payment of a sum of money.

(r) Place where action triable. The place where an action is "triable" means the place where the action is pending; or, if no action has been commenced, any proper place of trial or any proper place to commence the action; or, after entry of judgment, the place where the judgment was entered.

(s) Real property. "Real property" includes chattels real.

(t) Type size requirement. Whenever a requirement relating to size of type is stated in point size, the type size requirement shall be deemed met if the x-height of the type is a minimum of forty-five percent of the specified point size. each point shall be measured as .351 millimeter. The x-height size shall be measured as it appears on the page. The x-height is the height of the lower case letters, exclusive of ascenders or dissenters

(u) Verified pleading. A "verified pleading" may be utilized as an affidavit whenever the latter is required.

### 1994 AMENDMENTS

L. 1994, ch. 100, eff. May 16, 1994, amended CPLR 105 by relettering former subdivision (t) as subdivision (u) and adding a new subdivision (t) pertaining to type size requirements.

### 1983 AMENDMENTS

L. 1983, ch. 840, eff. April 1, 1983, relettered subdivisions (n) through (s) to be (o) through (t) and added a new subdivision (n).

### 1974 AMENDMENTS

L. 1974, ch. 924, eff. Sept. 1, 1974, added a new Subd. (j) defining the words "infant" and "infancy," and relettered accordingly.

### 1973 AMENDMENTS

L. 1973, ch. 238, eff. Sept. 1, 1973, added a new Subd. (f) defining "consumer credit transaction," and relettered accordingly.

## § 106. Civil and criminal prosecutions not merged.

Where the violation of a right admits of both a civil and criminal prosecution, the one is not merged in the other.

## § 107. Appendix of official forms.

The state administrator shall have the power to adopt, amend and rescind an appendix of forms. Forms adopted pursuant to this section shall be sufficient under the civil practice law and rules and shall illustrate the simplicity and brevity of statement which the civil practice law and rules contemplate.

### CROSS REFERENCES

L. 1978, ch. 156, eff. May 19, 1978, replaced the "state administrator" with a "chief administrator of the courts." See **Judiciary Law Article 7-A.**

### 1974 AMENDMENTS

L. 1974, ch, 615, eff. May 30, 1974, transferred the power to adopt, amend and rescind an appendix of official forms from the judicial conference to the state administrator.

### 1967 AMENDMENTS

L. 1967, ch. 646, effective Sept. 1, 1967, added Section 107, authorizing the Judicial Conference to promulgate an appendix of official CPLR forms.

CPLR

# ARTICLE 2

# LIMITATIONS OF TIME

---

## SUMMARY OF ARTICLE

§ 201.     Application of article.

§ 202.     Cause of action accruing without the state.

§ 203.     Methods of computing periods of limitation generally.
     (a)   Accrual of cause of action and interposition of claim.
     (b)   Claim in complaint where action commenced by service.
     (c)   Claim in complaint where action commenced by filing.
     (d)   Defense or counterclaim.
     (e)   Effect upon defense or counterclaim of termination of action because of death or by dismissal or voluntary discontinuance.
     (f)   Claim in amended pleading.
     (g)   Time computed from actual or imputed discovery of facts.

§ 204.     Stay of commencement of action; demand for arbitration.
     (a)   Stay.
     (b)   Arbitration.

§ 205.     Termination of action.
     (a)   New action by plaintiff.
     (b)   Defense or counterclaim.
     (c)   Application.

§ 206.     Computing periods of limitation in particular actions.
     (a)   Where demand necessary.
     (b)   Based on misconduct of agent.
     (c)   Based on breach of covenant of seizin or against incumbrances.
     (d)   Based on account.

§ 207.     Defendant's absence from state or residence under false name.

§ 208.     Infancy, insanity.

§ 209.     War.
     (a)   Cause of action accruing in foreign country.
     (b)   Right of alien.
     (c)   Non-enemy in enemy country or enemy-occupied territory.

§ 210.     Death of claimant or person liable; cause of action accruing after death and before grant of letters.
     (a)   Death of claimant.
     (b)   Death of person liable.
     (c)   Cause of action accruing after death and before grant of letters.

§ 211.     Actions to be commenced within twenty years.
     (a)   On a bond.
     (b)   On a money judgment.
     (c)   By state for real property.

      (d)  By grantee of state for real property.

      (e)  For support, alimony or maintenance.

§ 212.     Actions to be commenced within ten years.

      (a)  Possession necessary to recover real property.

      (b)  Annulment of letters patent.

      (c)  To redeem from a mortgage.

§ 213.     Actions to be commenced within six years: where not otherwise provided for; on contract; on sealed instrument; on bond or note, and mortgage upon real property; by state based on misappropriation of public property; based on mistake; by corporation against director, officer or stockholder; based on fraud.

§ 213-a.   Actions to be commenced within four years; residential rent overcharge.

§ 213-b.   Action by a victim of a criminal offense.

§ 214.     Actions to be commenced within three years: for non-payment of money collected on execution; for penalty created by statute; to recover chattel; for injury to property; for personal injury; for malpractice other than medical, dental or podiatric malpractice; to annul a marriage on the ground of fraud.

§ 214-a.   Action for medical, dental or podiatric malpractice to be commenced within two years and six months; exceptions.

§ 214-b.   Action to recover damages for personal injury caused by contact with or exposure to phenoxy herbicides.

§ 214-c.   Certain actions to be commenced within three years of discovery.

§ 214-d.   Limitations on certain actions against licensed engineers and architects.

§ 215.     Actions to be commenced within one year: against sheriff, coroner or constable; for escape of prisoner; for assault, battery, false imprisonment, malicious prosecution, libel or slander; for violation of right of privacy; for penalty given to informer; on arbitration award.

§ 216.     Abbreviation of period to one year after notice.

      (a)  Action to recover money.

      (b)  Action to recover property.

§ 217.     Proceeding against body or officer; actions complaining about conduct that would constitute a union's breach of its duty of fair representation; four months.

§ 218.     Transitional provisions.

      (a)  Actions barred at effective date.

      (b)  Cause of action accrued and not barred at effective date.

---

## § 201. Application of article.

An action, including one brought in the name or for the benefit of the state, must be commenced within the time specified in this article unless a different time is prescribed by law or a shorter time is prescribed by written agreement. No court shall extend the time limited by law for the commencement of an action.

## § 202. Cause of action accruing without the state.

An action based upon a cause of action accruing without the state cannot be commenced after the expiration of the time limited by the laws of either the state or the place without the state where the cause of action accrued, except that where the cause of action accrued in favor of a resident of the state the time limited by the laws of the state shall apply.

## § 203. Method of computing periods of limitation generally.

(a) Accrual of cause of action and interposition of claim. The time within which an action must be commenced, except as otherwise expressly prescribed, shall be computed from the time the cause of action accrued to the time the claim is interposed.

(b) Claim in complaint where action commenced by service. In an action which is commenced by service, a claim asserted in the complaint is interposed against the defendant or a co-defendant united in interest with such defendant when:

1. the summons is served upon the defendant; or

2. first publication of the summons against the defendant is made pursuant to an order, and publication is subsequently completed; or

3. an order for a provisional remedy other than attachment is granted, if, within thirty days thereafter, the summons is served upon the defendant or first publication of the summons against the defendant is made pursuant to an order and publication is subsequently completed, or, where the defendant dies within thirty days after the order is granted and before the summons is served upon the defendant or publication is completed, if the summons is served upon the defendant's executor or administrator within sixty days after letters are issued; for this purpose seizure of a chattel in an action to recover a chattel is a provisional remedy; or

4. an order of attachment is granted, if the summons is served in accordance with the provisions of section 6213; or

5. the summons is delivered to the sheriff of that county outside the city of New York or is filed with the clerk of that county within the city of New York in which the defendant resides, is employed or is doing business, or if none of the foregoing is known to the plaintiff after reasonable inquiry, then of the county in which the defendant is known to have last resided, been employed or been engaged in business, or in which the cause of action arose; or if the defendant is a corporation, of a county in which it may be served or in which the cause of action arose; provided that:

(i) the summons is served upon the defendant within sixty days after the period of limitation would have expired but for this provision; or

(ii) first publication of the summons against the defendant is made pursuant to an order within sixty days after the period of limitation would have expired but for this provision and publication is subsequently completed; or

(iii) the summons is served upon the defendant's executor or administrator within sixty days after letters are issued, where the defendant dies within sixty days after the period of limitation would have expired but for this provision and before the summons is served upon the defendant or publication is completed.

6. in an action to be commenced in a court not of record, the summons is delivered for service upon the defendant to any officer authorized to serve it in a county, city or town in which the defendant resides, is employed or is doing business, or if none of the foregoing be known to the plaintiff after reasonable inquiry, then in a county, city or town in which defendant is known to have last resided, been employed or been engaged in business, or, where the defendant is a corporation, in a county, city or town in which it may be served, if the summons is served upon the defendant within sixty days after the period of limitation would have expired but for this provision; or, where the defendant dies within sixty days after the period of limitation would have·expired but for this provision and before the summons is served upon the defendant, if the summons is served upon his executor or administrator within sixty days after letters are issued.

(c) Claim in complaint where action commenced by filing. In an action which is commenced by filing, a claim asserted in the complaint is interposed against the defendant or a co-defendant united in interest with such defendant when:

1. the summons and complaint or summons with notice is filed with the clerk of the court; or [Effective until 8/31/97]

1.[Effective 9/1/97] the summons and complaint or summons with notice is filed; or

2. a court signs an order after finding that circumstances prevent the immediate filing of the summons and complaint or summons with notice with the clerk of the court. The court shall specify in the order the time and date, no later than five days after the signing of the order, by which such filing is to occur.

(d) Defense or counterclaim. A defense or counterclaim is interposed when a pleading containing it is served. A defense or counterclaim is not barred if it was not barred at the time the claims asserted in the complaint were interposed, except that if the defense or counterclaim arose from the transactions, occurrences, or series of transactions or occurrences, upon which a claim asserted in the complaint depends, it is not barred to the extent of the demand in the complaint notwithstanding that it was barred at the time the claims asserted in the complaint were interposed.

(e) Effect upon defense or counterclaim of termination of action because of death or by dismissal or voluntary discontinuance. Where a defendant has served an answer containing a defense or counterclaim and the action is terminated because of the plaintiff's death or by dismissal or voluntary discontinuance, the time which elapsed between the commencement and termination of the action is not a part of the time within which an action must be commenced to recover upon the claim in the defense or counterclaim or the time within which the defense or counterclaim may be interposed in another action brought by the plaintiff or his successor in interest.

(f) Claim in amended pleading. A claim asserted in an amended pleading is deemed to have been interposed at the time the claims in the original pleading were interposed, unless the original pleading does not give notice of the transactions, occurrences, or series of transactions or occurrences, to be proved pursuant to the amended pleading.

(g) Time computed from actual or imputed discovery of facts. Except as provided in article two of the uniform commercial code or in section two hundred fourteen–a of this chapter, where the time within which an action must be commenced is computed from the time when facts were discovered or from the time when facts could with reasonable diligence have been discovered, or from either of such times, the action must be commenced within two years after such actual or imputed discovery or within the period otherwise provided, computed from the time the cause of action accrued, whichever is longer.

CPLR

### CROSS REFERENCES

Reference to U.C.C. Article 2 in subd. (f), *supra*, refers to U.C.C. § 2-725, which appears in Appendix, *infra*.

### 1996 AMENDMENTS

L. 1996, ch. 606, eff. Sept. 1, 1997, and applicable to all actions or special proceedings commenced on or after such date, amended subparagraph (c)(1) by deleting the words "with the court.'

### 1992 AMENDMENTS

L. 1992, ch. 216, eff. July 1, 1992, amended CPLR 203 by adding to the catch line of subdivision (b) the words ". . . where action commenced by service. In an action which is commenced by service, . . ."; by deleting the language added by L. 1992, ch. 55, pertaining to the requirement that an index number be obtained pursuant to CPLR 306-a; by deleting the phrase "the summons is filed, an index number obtained, and" at the beginning of subparagraphs (i), (ii), and (iii); by adding as an entirely new provision the present subdivision (c); by renumbering former subdivisions (c), (d), (e), and (f) as subdivisions (d), (e), (f), and (g) respectively; and by replacing the pronoun "him" with "the defendant" throughout the section.

L. 1992, ch. 55, eff. for all actions pending on July 1, 1992, amended CPLR 203(b)(5) by adding the language pertaining to the requirement that an index number be obtained pursuant to CPLR 306-a, and the phrase "the summons is filed, an index number obtained, and" at the beginning of subparagraphs (i), (ii), and (iii). These amendments, however, were superseded by L. 1992, ch. 216, discussed *supra*.

## 1979 AMENDMENTS

L. 1979, ch. 404, eff. Jan. 1, 1980, amended CPLR 203 subdivision (b) paragraph 5 by repealing the former provision and enacting the statute in its present form.

## 1977 AMENDMENTS

L. 1977, ch. 494, eff. Sept. 1, 1977, amended paragraph (5) of subd. (b).

## 1976 AMENDMENTS

L. 1976, ch. 722, eff. Sept. 1, 1976, amended paragraph (5) of subd. (b). 203(b).

## 1975 AMENDMENTS

L. 1975, ch. 109, eff. July 1, 1975, amended Subd. (f) by adding the phrase "or in section two hundred fourteen-a of this chapter" after the words "the uniform commercial code", thereby excluding medical malpractice actions based on discovery of foreign objects in the body of the patient from the two year computation of CPLR 203(f). The amendment applies to acts of malpractice occurring on or after July 1, 1975.

## 1970 AMENDMENTS

L. 1970, ch. 397, eff. Sept. 1, 1970, amended subdivision (b)(3) by excluding attachment from the operation of this provision, thereby conforming the section to the provisions of CPLR 6213; added a new subdivision (b)(4); and renumbered accordingly.

## 1966 AMENDMENTS

L. 1966, ch. 138, eff. Sept. 1, 1966, amended Subd. (f) by inserting after the title the words "Except as provided in article 2 of the uniform commercial code." See U.C.C. § 2-725 in Appendix, *infra*.

## 1965 AMENDMENTS

L. 1965, ch. 112, eff. Sept. 1, 1965, amended Subd. (b)(4) [now (b)(5)].

L. 1965, ch. 113, eff. Sept. 1, 1965, amended Subd. (b)(5) [now (b)(6)].

L. 1965, ch. 196, eff. Sept. 1, 1965, amended Subd. (d).

L. 1965, ch. 56, eff. Sept. 1, 1965, amended Subd. (f). Amendment recommended by the Judicial Conference Feb. 1, 1965, Report to the Legislature: "Two problems are presented by the present provision: (1) to what actions does the alternative formula apply; and (2) how is the time the cause of action accrued' ascertained?

"As to the first problem, § 203(f) confines its application to those cases where the time within which an action must be commenced is computed either from actual or imputed discovery. This would seem clearly to include those actions referred to in § 213(6) (by way of § 206(c)), and in § 213(7), as they are presently constituted, since both of these provisions expressly refer to actual or imputed discovery. But what of those provisions which refer solely to discovery,' (e.g., §§ 206(a)(1), 206(b), 213(5), 214(7)) and which may be construed to mean only actual discovery? Must the case be one where the statute of limitations turns on actual *or* imputed discovery before the alternative formula of § 203(f) is to apply?

"The Conference perceives no reason in logic or policy why the principle of § 203(f) should be confined to cases where running of the statute is suspended pending actual *or* imputed discovery, but should not apply to cases where running of the statute is suspended until actual discovery. In the ordinary case, the time of actual discovery will be later than that of imputed discovery, and it would be anomalous, to say the least, to put pressure upon a plaintiff to whom discovery is imputed to bring his action expeditiously, while at the same time permitting a plaintiff with actual knowledge to wait out the full statutory period. The Conference therefore proposes to make the alternative formula of § 203(f) generally applicable to all actions where the time of discovery is a factor in computing the statute of limitations.

". . . this proposed change may affect the courts' interpretation of § 214(7) (action to annul a marriage for fraud) as well as of Domestic Relations Law §§ 171 and 200 (actions for divorce or separation based on adultery). . . ."

## § 204.  Stay of commencement of action; demand for arbitration.

(a) Stay. Where the commencement of an action has been stayed by a court or by statutory prohibition, the duration of the stay is not a part of the time within which the action must be commenced.

(b) Arbitration. Where it shall have been determined that a party is not obligated to submit a claim to arbitration, the time which elapsed between the demand for arbitration and the final determination that there is no obligation to arbitrate is not a part of the time within which an action upon such claim must be commenced. The time within which the action must be commenced shall not be extended by this provision beyond one year after such final determination.

## § 205.  Termination of action.

(a) New action by plaintiff. If an action is timely commenced and is terminated in any other manner than by a voluntary discontinuance, a failure to obtain personal jurisdiction over the defendant, a dismissal of the complaint for neglect to prosecute the action, or a final judgment upon the merits, the plaintiff, or, if the plaintiff dies, and the cause of action survives, his or her executor or administrator, may commence a new action upon the same transaction or occurrence or series of transactions or occurrences within six months after the termination provided that the new action would have been timely commenced at the time of commencement of the prior action and that service upon defendant is effected within such six-month period.

(b) Defense or counterclaim. Where the defendant has served an answer and the action is terminated in any manner, and a new action upon the same transaction or occurrence or series of transactions or occurrences is commenced by the plaintiff or his successor in interest, the assertion of any cause of action or defense by the defendant in the new action shall be timely if it was timely asserted in the prior action.

(c) Application. This section also applies to a proceeding brought under the workers' compensation law.

### 1992 AMENDMENTS

L. 1992, ch. 216, eff. July 1, 1992, amended section 205 by adding to subdivision (a) the words "a failure to obtain personal jurisdiction over the defendant," and the words "and that service upon defendant is effected within such six-month period"; and by making the language gender neutral.

### 1978 AMENDMENTS

L. 1978, ch. 51, eff. April 11, 1978, amended subdivisions (a) and (b) by eliminating language providing that a new action commenced under the section be limited to a suit upon the same "cause of action" and substituting the provision that the new action be based upon the same "transaction or occurrence," provided that the cause would have been timely when the original action was brought.

### 1965 AMENDMENTS

L. 1965, ch. 233, eff. Sept. 1, 1965, amended section by dividing it into three subdivisions.

## § 206. Computing periods of limitation in particular actions.

(a) Where demand necessary. Except as provided in article 3 of the uniform commercial code, where a demand is necessary to entitle a person to commence an action, the time within which the action must be commenced shall be computed from the time when the right to make the demand is complete, except that

1. where a right grows out of the receipt or detention of money or property by a trustee, agent, attorney or other person acting in a fiduciary capacity, the time within which the action must be commenced shall be computed from the time when the person having the right to make the demand discovered the facts upon which the right depends; and

2. where there was a deposit of money to be repaid only upon a special demand, or a delivery of personal property not to be returned specifically or in kind at a fixed time or upon a fixed contingency, the time within which the action must be commenced shall be computed from the demand for repayment or return.

(b) Based on misconduct of agent. Where a judgment is entered against a principal in an action based upon an injury resulting from the act or omission of his deputy or agent, the time within which an action by the principal against the deputy or agent to recover damages by reason of such judgment must be commenced shall be computed, from the time when the action against the principal was finally determined. Where an injury results from the representation by a person that he is an agent with authority to execute a contract in behalf of a principal, the time within which an action to recover damages for breach of warranty of authority must be commenced by the person injured against the purported agent shall be computed from the time the person injured discovered the facts constituting lack of authority.

(c) Based on breach of covenant of seizin or against incumbrances. In an action based upon breach of a covenant of seizin or against incumbrances, the time within which the action must be commenced shall be computed from an eviction.

(d) Based on account. In an action based upon a mutual, open and current account, where there have been reciprocal demands between the parties, the time within which the action must be commenced shall be computed from the time of the last transaction in the account on either side.

### CROSS REFERENCES

Reference to **U.C.C. Article 3** in subd. (a), *supra*, refers to **U.C.C. § 3-122(3)**, which appears in Appendix, *infra*.

### 1966 AMENDMENTS

L. 1966, ch. 138, eff. Sept. 1, 1966, amended Subd. (a) by inserting after the title the words "Except as provided in article 3 of the uniform commercial code, where."

Amendment recommended by the Judicial Conference Feb. 1, 1966, Report to the Legislature: "CPLR 206(a) provides a cause of action on a demand instrument accrues when the right to make the demand is complete'. U.C.C. § 3-122(3), however, provides that such a cause of action accrues upon demand' and provides further that notice of dishonor is a demand'. The bar should be apprised of the existence of this plain inconsistency so as to avoid possible pitfalls."

### 1965 AMENDMENTS

L. 1965, ch. 248, eff. Sept. 1, 1965, repealed Subd. (c), and relettered Subds. (d) and (e) to (c) and (d), respectively. Former Subd. (c) transferred to and made part of new § 213(9), now § 213(8).

## § 207.  Defendant's absence from state or residence under false name.

If, when a cause of action accrues against a person, he is without the state, the time within which the action must be commenced shall be computed from the time he comes into or returns to the state. If, after a cause of action has accrued against a person, that person departs from the state and remains continuously absent therefrom for four months or more, or that person resides within the state under a false name which is unknown to the person entitled to commence the action, the time of his absence or residence within the state under such a false name is not a part of the time within which the action must be commenced. If an action is commenced against a person described above, the time within which service must be made on such person in accordance with subdivisions (a) and (b) of section three hundred six–b of this chapter shall be computed in accordance with this section. This section does not apply:

1. while there is in force a designation, voluntary or involuntary, made pursuant to law, of a person to whom a summons may be delivered within the state with the same effect as if served personally within the state; or

2. while a foreign corporation has one or more officers or other persons in the state on whom a summons against such corporation may be served; or

3. while jurisdiction over the person of the defendant can be obtained without personal delivery of the summons to the defendant within the state.

### CROSS REFERENCES

Examples of designation referred to in subd. (1), *supra*, may be found in **Vehicle and Traffic Law §§ 253-254** and **Business Corporations Law §§ 304, 306 and 307**. See Appendix, *infra*.

### 1992 AMENDMENTS

L. 1992, ch. 216, eff. July 1, 1992, amended CPLR 207 by adding the next to last sentence to subdivision (a), beginning with the words "If an action is commenced . . .."; and by making the language gender neutral.

## § 208.  Infancy, insanity.

If a person entitled to commence an action is under a disability because of infancy or insanity at the time the cause of action accrues, and the time otherwise limited for commencing the action is three years or more and expires no later than three years after the disability ceases, or the person under the disability dies, the time within which the action must be commenced shall be extended to three years after the disability ceases or the person under the disability dies, whichever event first occurs; if the time otherwise limited is less than three years, the time shall be extended by the period of disability. The time within which the action must be commenced shall not be extended by this provision beyond ten years after the cause of action accrues, except, in any action other than for medical, dental or podiatric malpractice, where the person was under a disability due to infancy. This section shall not apply to an action to recover a penalty or forfeiture, or against a sheriff or other officer for an escape.

### CROSS REFERENCES

As to claims against the State, see **N.Y. Const. Art. 3 § 19** in Appendix, *infra*.

Also see **Court of Claims Act § 10 (5)** in Appendix, *infra*.

### 1986 AMENDMENTS

L. 1986, ch. 485, eff. July 21, 1986, and applicable to acts, omissions or failures occurring on or after such date, amended the eleventh line of CPLR 208 by inserting the words "or podiatric" after the word "dental."

### 1985 AMENDMENTS

L. 1985, ch. 760, eff. July 1, 1985 and applicable to any acts, omissions or failures occurring on or after that date, amended the second sentence of CPLR 208 by inserting the words "or dental" between "medical" and "malpractice."

### 1975 AMENDMENTS

L. 1975, ch. 109, eff. July 1, 1975, amended the second sentence of CPLR 208 by adding the phrase ", in any action other than for medical malpractice," after the word "except," thereby limiting to a maximum of ten years the extended period for commencing an infant's action where the cause of action is for medical malpractice. The amendment applies to acts of malpractice occurring on or after July 1, 1975.

CPLR

### 1974 AMENDMENTS

L. 1974, ch. 924, eff. Sept. 1, 1974, amended the first sentence of CPLR 208 by adding the words "under a disability because of infancy or insanity" and by deleting after the phrase "at the time the cause of action accrues" the words "under the age of twenty-one years or insane." The second sentence of the section was amended by inserting the last five words "a disability due to infancy" and deleting the words "the age of twenty-one years." A person is under the disability of infancy if he is under the age of eighteen years. See CPLR 105(j) enacted simultaneously with the amendment to CPLR 208.

### 1973 AMENDMENTS

L. 1973, ch. 687, eff. Sept. 9, 1973, amended CPLR 208 by deleting from the first sentence "or imprisoned on a criminal charge or conviction for a term less than for life"; and by adding "or" before "insane" in the first sentence.

## § 209.　War.

(a) Cause of action accruing in foreign country. Where a cause of action, whether originally accrued in favor of a resident or non-resident of the state, accrued in a foreign country with which the United States or any of its allies were then or subsequently at war, or territory then or subsequently occupied by the government of such foreign country, the time which elapsed between the commencement of the war, or of such occupation, and the termination of hostilities with such country, or of such occupation, is not a part of the time within which the action must be commenced. This section shall neither apply to nor in any manner affect an action brought pursuant to section six hundred twenty-five of the banking law against a banking organization or against the superintendent of banks.

(b) Right of alien. Where a person is unable to commence an action in the courts of the state because any party is an alien subject or citizen of a foreign country at war with the United States or any of its allies, whether the cause of action accrued during or prior to the war, the time which elapsed between the commencement of the war and the termination of hostilities with such country is not a part of the time within which the action must be commenced.

(c) Non-enemy in enemy country or enemy-occupied territory. Where a person entitled to commence an action, other than a person entitled to the benefits of subdivision (b), is a resident of, or a sojourner in, a foreign country with which the United States or any of its allies are at war, or territory occupied by the government of such foreign country, the period of such residence or sojourn during which the war continues or the territory is so occupied is not a part of the time within which the action must be commenced.

## § 210.　Death of claimant or person liable; cause of action accruing after death and before grant of letters.

(a) Death of claimant. Where a person entitled to commence an action dies before the expiration of the time within which the action must be commenced and the cause of action survives, an action may be commenced by his representative within one year after his death.

(b) Death of person liable. The period of eighteen months after the death, within or without the state, of a person against whom a cause of action exists is not a part of the time within which the action must be commenced against his executor or administrator.

(c) Cause of action accruing after death and before grant of letters. In an action by an executor or administrator to recover personal property wrongfully taken after the death and before the issuance of letters, or to recover damages for taking, detaining or injuring personal property within that period, the time within which the action must be commenced shall be computed from the time the letters are issued or from three years after the death, whichever event first occurs. Any distributee, next of kin, legatee or creditor who was under a disability prescribed in section 208 at the time the cause of action accrued, may, within two years after the disability ceases, commence an action to recover such damages or the value of such property as he would have received upon a final distribution of the estate if an action had been timely commenced by the executor or administrator.

## § 211. Actions to be commenced within twenty years.

(a) On a bond. An action to recover principal or interest upon a written instrument evidencing an indebtedness of the state of New York or of any person, association or public or private corporation, originally sold by the issuer after publication of an advertisement for bids for the issue in a newspaper of general circulation and secured only by a pledge of the faith and credit of the issuer, regardless of whether a sinking fund is or may be established for its redemption, must be commenced within twenty years after the cause of action accrues. This subdivision does not apply to actions upon written instruments evidencing an indebtedness of any corporation, association or person under the jurisdiction of the public service commission, the commissioner of transportation, the interstate commerce commission, the federal communications commission, the civil aeronautics board, the federal power commission, or any other regulatory commission or board of a state or of the federal government. This subdivision applies to all causes of action, including those barred on April eighteenth, nineteen hundred fifty, by the provisions of the civil practice act then effective.

(b) On a money judgment. A money judgment is presumed to be paid and satisfied after the expiration of twenty years from the time when the party recovering it was first entitled to enforce it. This presumption is conclusive, except as against a person who within the twenty years acknowledges an indebtedness, or makes a payment, of all or part of the amount recovered by the judgment, or his heir or personal representative, or a person whom he otherwise represents. Such an acknowledgment must be in writing and signed by the person to be charged. Property acquired by an enforcement order or by levy upon an execution is a payment, unless the person to be charged shows that it did not include property claimed by him. If such an acknowledgment or payment is made, the judgment is conclusively presumed to be paid and satisfied as against any person after the expiration of twenty years after the last acknowledgment or payment made by him. The presumption created by this subdivision may be availed of under an allegation that the action was not commenced within the time limited.

(c) By state for real property. The state will not sue a person for or with respect to real property, or the rents or profits thereof, by reason of the right or title of the state to the same, unless the cause of action accrued, or the state, or those from whom it claims, have received the rents and profits of the real property or of some part thereof, within twenty years before the commencement of the action.

(d) By grantee of state for real property. An action shall not be commenced for or with respect to real property by a person claiming by virtue of letters patent or a grant from the state, unless it might have been maintained by the state, as prescribed in this section, if the patent or grant had not been issued or made.

(e) For support, alimony or maintenance. An action or proceeding to enforce any temporary order, permanent order or judgment of any court of competent jurisdiction which awards support, alimony or maintenance, regardless of whether or not arrears have been reduced to a money judgment, must be commenced within twenty years from the date of a default in payment. This section shall only apply to orders which have been entered subsequent to the date upon which this section shall become effective.

### 1987 AMENDMENTS

L. 1987, ch. 815, eff. Aug. 7, 1987, and applicable to any action or proceeding commenced on or after such date, added a new subdivision (e), making a twenty-year limitation period applicable to actions or proceedings to enforce orders or judgments awarding support, alimony or maintenance. Note that as to orders, the section applies only to those entered subsequent to Aug. 7, 1987.

### 1970 AMENDMENTS

L. 1970, ch. 267, § 7, eff. March 1, 1971, amended Subd. (a) to provide that the subdivision shall not apply to actions upon a written instrument evidencing an indebtedness of any corporation, association or person under the jurisdiction of the Commissioner of Transportation.

### 1965 AMENDMENTS

L. 1965, ch. 214, eff. Sept. 1, 1965, added new Subd. (d).

## § 212.  Actions to be commenced within ten years.

(a) Possession necessary to recover real property. An action to recover real property or its possession cannot be commenced unless the plaintiff, or his predecessor in interest, was seized or possessed of the premises within ten years before the commencement of the action.

(b) Annulment of letters patent. Where letters patent or a grant of real property, issued or made by the state, are declared void on the ground of fraudulent suggestion or concealment, forfeiture, mistake or ignorance of a material fact, wrongful detaining or defective title, an action to recover the premises may be commenced by the state or by a subsequent patentee or grantee, or his successor in interest, within ten years after the determination is made.

(c) To redeem from a mortgage. An action to redeem real property from a mortgage with or without an account of rents and profits may be commenced by the mortgagor or his successors in interest, against the mortgagee in possession, or against the purchaser of the mortgaged premises at a foreclosure sale in an action in which the mortgagor or his successors in interest were not excluded from their interest in the mortgaged premises, or against a successor in interest of either, unless the mortgagee, purchaser or successor was continually possessed of the premises for ten years after the breach or non-fulfillment of a condition or covenant of the mortgage, or the date of recording of the deed of the premises to the purchaser.

### 1964 AMENDMENTS

L. 1964, ch. 388, eff. Sept. 1, 1964, made mechanical correction.

§ 213. **Actions to be commenced within six years: where not otherwise provided for; on contract; on sealed instrument; on bond or note, and mortgage upon real property; by state based on misappropriation of public property; based on mistake; by corporation against director, officer or stockholder; based on fraud.**

The following actions must be commenced within six years:

1. an action for which no limitation is specifically prescribed by law;

2. an action upon a contractual obligation or liability, express or implied, except as provided in section two hundred thirteen-a of this article or article 2 of the uniform commercial code or article 36-B of the general business law;

3. an action upon a sealed instrument;

4. an action upon a bond or note, the payment of which is secured by a mortgage upon real property, or upon a bond or note and mortgage so secured, or upon a mortgage of real property, or any interest therein;

5. an action by the state based upon the spoliation or other misappropriation of public property; the time within which the action must be commenced shall be computed from discovery by the state of the facts relied upon;

6. an action based upon mistake;

7. an action by or on behalf of a corporation against a present or former director, officer or stockholder for an accounting, or to procure a judgment on the ground of fraud, or to enforce a liability, penalty or forfeiture, or to recover damages for waste or for an injury to property or for an accounting in conjunction therewith;

8. an action based upon fraud; the time within which the action must be commenced shall be computed from the time the plaintiff or the person under whom he claims discovered the fraud, or could with reasonable diligence have discovered it.

### CROSS REFERENCES

Reference to **U.C.C. Article 2** in subd. (2), *supra*, refers to **U.C.C. § 2-725,** which appears in Appendix, *infra*.

As to promises and waivers affecting the time limit for commencement of a mortgage foreclosure action, and the effect of part payment upon such time limit, see **General Obligations Law §§ 17-105 and 17-107.**

**General Business Law** article 36-B, referred to in subdivision 2, was added by the legislature in 1988, and concerns warranties on sales of new homes.

### 1988 AMENDMENTS

L. 1988, ch. 709, eff. March 1, 1989, applicable to all new homes for which contracts of sale are entered into on or after the effective date.

### 1983 AMENDMENTS

L. 1983, ch. 403, eff. April 1, 1984 and applicable to actions and proceedings commencing on and after that date, amended CPLR 213(2) by inserting a reference to CPLR 213-a.

### 1975 AMENDMENTS

L. 1975, ch. 43, eff. Sept. 1, 1975, upon the recommendation of the Judicial Conference, amended section heading by deleting "to establish a will;" and by repealing Subd. (7), as well as renumbering former Subds. (8) and (9) to Subds. (7) and (8).

The 1975 Judicial Conference Report stated:

"Section 213 is a statute of limitations governing actions to be commenced in six years. Subdivision 7 lists an action to establish a will, and contains discovery and imputed discovery provisions where the will has been lost, concealed or destroyed.

"Article 8 (sections 200–204) of the Decedent Estate Law, which provided for an action to establish a will or construe a device was repealed by L. 1966, ch. 952, eff. Sept. 1, 1967, when the new Estates, Powers and Trust Law became effective.

"Thus, the retention of a six year statute of limitations on an action to establish a will in the Supreme Court, when the statutory basis for the action no longer exists, is an anomaly and misleading to lawyers, and the provision should be repealed, as proposed.

"Although there is no statute of limitations on a proceeding to probate a will in Surrogate's Court (see *In re of Canfield*, 165 Misc. 66 (Surr. Ct. Kings Co. 1937)), the proposed repeal would not necessitate the enactment of such a statute. The purpose of such a provision would be to quiet titles (see Uniform Probate Code, Section 3—108) and this purpose is accomplished by EPTL 3—3.8. That provision validates title of a bona fide purchaser of real property from the distributees unless a will containing a different disposition of the property has been admitted to probate within two years after the testator's death. In addition, SCPA 2113 sets forth the procedure for probate of heirship, in order to determine who the distributees are and to create a record of their interests."

### 1966 AMENDMENTS

L. 1966, ch. 138, eff. Sept. 1, 1966, inserted the words "except as provided in article 2 of the uniform commercial code" before the semicolon in Subd. (2).

Amendment recommended by the Judicial Conference Feb. 1, 1966, Report to the Legislature: "The purpose of this amendment is to put the bar on notice of the provision in U.C.C. § 2-725(1) that the period of limitations on an action for breach of a contract of sale of goods is four years. Where the cause of action is based on breach of warranty of goods sold this four-year period conflicts with CPLR 213(2) (providing a six-year period for contract actions), possibly conflicts with CPLR 213(9) (providing a six-year period for fraud actions), and possibly conflicts with CPLR 214(4) and (5) (providing a three-year period for actions for damages for property and personal injury)."

### 1965 AMENDMENTS

L. 1965, ch. 248, eff. Sept. 1, 1965, amended Subd. (6) by deleting the words "fraud or," and by adding a new Subd. (9), now Subd. (8), and by changing the catch-line accordingly.

Amendment recommended by the Judicial Conference Feb. 1, 1965, Report to the Legislature: "The apparent breadth of the language of § 206(c) might mislead practitioners to conclude that its discovery rules apply to any action in which fraud or an element of fraud is involved. The intention of the revisers, however, was to confine § 206(c) to actions for actual fraud within the meaning of § 213(6). Moreover, in the area of constructive fraud it has long been the rule that the statute of limitations begins to run upon commission of the fraud rather than upon its discovery. See *Buttles v. Smith,* 281 N.Y. 226, 236, 22 N.E.2d 350, 353 (1939). If § 206(c) were interpreted to alter this rule, vast and revolutionary changes would be wrought in the law of creditors' rights and fraudulent conveyances, changes which the revisers most certainly would have alluded to had they been intended.

"The Conference therefore believes that the substance of the provisions of § 206(c) should be placed in § 213 in a new subdivision, subdivision (9), [now subdivision (8),] thereby making it clear that the discovery provision applies only to actions for actual fraud.

"The proposed amendment to § 213(6) is designed to separate the provisions relating to fraud from those relating to mistake, as to which no change is proposed."

## § 213-a. Actions to be commenced within four years: residential rent overcharge.

An action on a residential rent overcharge shall be commenced within four years of such overcharge.

### 1983 AMENDMENTS

L. 1983, ch. 403, eff. April 1, 1984, added section 213-a. The section is applicable to actions and proceedings commencing on and after April 1, 1984.

### § 213-b. Action by a victim of a criminal offense.

Notwithstanding any other limitation set forth in this article or in article five of the estates, powers and trusts law, an action by a crime victim, or the representative of a crime victim, as defined in subdivision six of section six hundred twenty-one of the executive law, may be commenced to recover damages from a defendant convicted of a crime which is the subject of such action, for any injury or loss resulting therefrom within seven years of the date of the crime.

#### 1992 AMENDMENTS

L. 1992, ch. 618, eff. July 24, 1992 and applying only to actions commenced on or after the effective date, added CPLR 213-b, providing that a crime victim may commence a civil action for damages against the criminal defendant within seven years of the date of the crime.

### § 214. Actions to be commenced within three years: for non-payment of money collected on execution; for penalty created by statute; to recover chattel; for injury to property; for personal injury; for malpractice other than medical, dental or podiatric malpractice; to annul a marriage on the ground of fraud.

The following actions must be commenced within three years:

1. an action against a sheriff, constable or other officer for the non-payment of money collected upon an execution;

2. an action to recover upon a liability, penalty or forfeiture created or imposed by statute except as provided in sections 213 and 215;

3. an action to recover a chattel or damages for the taking or detaining of a chattel;

4. an action to recover damages for an injury to property except as provided in section 214–c;

5. an action to recover damages for a personal injury except as provided in sections 214–b, 214–c and 215;

6. an action to recover damages for malpractice, other than medical, dental or podiatric malpractice, regardless of whether the underlying theory is based in contract or tort; and

7. an action to annul a marriage on the ground of fraud; the time within which the action must be commenced shall be computed from the time the plaintiff discovered the facts constituting the fraud, but if the plaintiff is a person other than the spouse whose consent was obtained by fraud, the time within which the action must be commenced shall be computed from the time, if earlier, that that spouse discovered the facts constituting the fraud.

CPLR

### 1996 AMENDMENTS

L. 1996, ch. 623, eff. Sept. 4, 1996, amended subdivision (6) by adding the words "regardless of whether the underlying theory is based in contract or tort.'

### 1994 AMENDMENTS

L. 1994, ch. 88, eff. May 10, 1994, again extended the period for commencing actions set forth in L. 1981, ch. 266, until June 16, 1996. The 1994 legislation also slightly enlarged the period of inclusion of the provision, so that it effectively begins on December 22, 1961, rather than January 1, 1962.

### 1986 AMENDMENTS

L. 1986, ch. 485, eff. July 21, 1986, and applicable to acts, omissions or failures occurring on or after such date, amended CPLR 214 to exclude actions for podiatric malpractice from those actions which must be commenced within three years; L. 1986, ch. 682, eff. July 30, 1986, and applicable to actions commenced or claims filed on or after such date, amended CPLR 214(4) and (5) by adding references to new section 214–c.

### 1985 AMENDMENTS

L. 1985, ch. 760, eff. July 1, 1985, and applicable to any acts, omissions or failures occurring on or after that date, amended CPLR 214(6) to exclude actions for dental malpractice.

### 1981 AMENDMENTS

L. 1981, ch. 266, eff. June 16, 1981, amended CPLR 214(5) to exclude personal injury actions covered by CPLR 214-b from those actions which must be commenced within three years.

### 1975 AMENDMENTS

L. 1975, ch. 109, eff. July 1, 1975, amended the section to exclude medical malpractice actions from its coverage; such actions are now treated under § 214–a, *infra*. The amendment applies to acts of malpractice occurring on or after July 1, 1975. The three-year statute of limitations contained in CPLR 214 is still applicable to causes of action for medical malpractice based upon acts occurring before July 1, 1975.

## § 214–a.  Action for medical, dental or podiatric malpractice to be commenced within two years and six months; exceptions.

An action for medical, dental or podiatric malpractice must be commenced within two years and six months of the act, omission or failure complained of or last treatment where there is continuous treatment for the same illness, injury or condition which gave rise to the said act, omission or failure; provided, however, that where the action is based upon the discovery of a foreign object in the body of the patient, the action may be commenced within one year of the date of such discovery or of the date of discovery of facts which would reasonably lead to such discovery, whichever is earlier. For the purpose of this section the term "continuous treatment" shall not include examinations undertaken at the request of the patient for the sole purpose of ascertaining the state of the patient's condition. For the purpose of this section the term "foreign object" shall not include a chemical compound, fixation device or prosthetic aid or device.

### 1986 AMENDMENTS

L. 1986, ch. 485, eff. July 21, 1986, and applicable to acts, omissions or failures occurring on or after such date, amended CPLR 214–a to apply to actions for podiatric malpractice.

### 1985 AMENDMENTS

L. 1985, ch. 760, eff. July 1, 1985, and applicable to any acts, omissions or failures occurring on or after that date, amended CPLR 214-a to apply to actions for dental malpractice.

### 1975 AMENDMENTS

L. 1975, ch. 109, eff. July 1, 1975, added Section 214-a. The amendment applies to acts of malpractice occurring on or after July 1, 1975. The three-year statute of limitations contained in CPLR 214 is still applicable to causes of action for medical malpractice based upon acts occurring before July 1, 1975.

## § 214-b.    Action to recover damages for personal injury caused by contact with or exposure to phenoxy herbicides.

Notwithstanding any provision of law to the contrary, an action to recover damages for personal injury caused by contact with or exposure to phenoxy herbicides while serving as a member of the armed forces of the United States in Indo-China from January first, nineteen hundred sixty-two through May seventh, nineteen hundred seventy-five, may be commenced within two years from the date of discovery of such injury, or within two years from the date when through the exercise of reasonable diligence the cause of such injury should have been discovered, whichever is later.

### 1994 AMENDMENTS

L. 1994, ch. 88, eff. May 10, 1994, again extended the period for commencing actions set forth in L. 1981, ch. 266, until June 16, 1996. The 1994 legislation also slightly enlarged the period of inclusion of the provision, so that it effectively begins on Dec. 22, 1961, rather than Jan. 1, 1962.

### 1992 AMENDMENTS

L. 1992, ch. 251, eff. June 30, 1992, amended L. 1981, ch. 266, § 4, by extending the time limitations for the actions described therein to June 16, 1994.

### 1990 AMENDMENTS

L. 1990, ch. 227, eff. June 15, 1990, amended L. 1981, ch. 266, § 4 to read as follows:

§ 4. Every cause of action for an injury or death caused by contact with or exposure to phenoxy herbicides while serving as a member of the armed forces of the United States in Indo-China from January 1, 1962 through May 7, 1975, which is or would be barred prior to June 16, 1985, because the applicable period of limitation has expired is hereby revived or extended as the case may be, and an action thereon may be commenced and prosecuted provided such action is commenced not later than June 16, 1992.

### 1988 AMENDMENTS

L. 1988, ch. 170, eff. June 27, 1988, amended L. 1981, ch. 266, § 4, to read as follows:

§ 4. Every cause of action for an injury or death caused by contact with or exposure to phenoxy herbicides while serving as a member of the armed forces of the United States in Indo-China from January first, nineteen hundred sixty-two through May seventh, nineteen hundred seventy-five, which is or would be barred prior to June sixteenth, nineteen hundred eighty-five, because the applicable period of limitation has expired is hereby revived or extended as the case may be, and an action thereon may be commenced and prosecuted provided such action is commenced not later than June sixteenth, nineteen hundred ninety.

### 1987 AMENDMENTS

L. 1987, ch. 194, eff. June 29, 1987, amended L. 1981, ch. 266, § 4, to read as follows:

§ 4. Every cause of action for an injury or death caused by contact with or exposure to phenoxy herbicides while serving as a member of the armed forces of the United States in Indo-China from January first, nineteen hundred sixty-two through May seventh, nineteen hundred seventy-five, which is or would be barred prior to June sixteenth, nineteen hundred eighty-five, because the applicable period of limitation has expired is hereby revived or extended as the case may be, and an action thereon may be commenced and prosecuted provided such action is commenced not later than June sixteenth, nineteen hundred eighty-eight.

### 1985 AMENDMENTS

L. 1985, ch. 498, eff. July 24, 1985, amended L. 1981, ch. 266, § 4, to read as follows:

§ 4. Every cause of action for an injury or death caused by contact with or exposure to phenoxy herbicides while serving as a member of the armed forces of the United States in Indo-China from January first, nineteen hundred sixty-two through May seventh, nineteen hundred seventy-five, which is or would be barred prior to June sixteenth, nineteen hundred eighty-five, because the applicable period of limitation has expired is hereby revived or extended as the case may be, and an action thereon may be commenced and prosecuted provided such action is commenced not later than June sixteenth, nineteen hundred eighty-seven.

### 1983 AMENDMENTS

L. 1983, ch. 358, eff. June 26, 1983, amended L. 1981, ch. 266, § 4 to read as follows:

§ 4. Every cause of action for an injury or death caused by contact with or exposure to phenoxy herbicides while serving as a member of the armed forces of the United States in Indo-China from January first, nineteen hundred sixty-two through May seventh, nineteen hundred seventy-five, which is or would be barred prior to June sixteenth, nineteen hundred eighty-five, because the applicable period of limitation has expired is hereby revived or extended as the case may be, and an action thereon may be commenced and prosecuted provided such action is commenced not later than June sixteenth, nineteen hundred eighty-five.

**1982 AMENDMENTS**

L. 1982, ch. 153, eff. June 1, 1982, amended CPLR 214-b by deleting the words "March twenty-ninth, nineteen hundred seventy-three" and adding the words "May seventh, nineteen hundred seventy-five." In addition, L. 1981, ch. 266, § 4, was also amended to reflect the same extension of time limitations for personal injury or death caused by contact with or exposure to phenoxy herbicides.

**1981 AMENDMENTS**

L. 1981, ch. 266, eff. June 16, 1981, added section 214-b. L. 1981, ch. 266, § 4 provides as follows:

§ 4. Every cause of action for an injury or death caused by contact with or exposure to phenoxy herbicides while serving as a member of the armed forces of the United States in Indo-China from January first, nineteen hundred sixty-two through March twenty-ninth, nineteen hundred seventy-three, which is barred as of the effective date of this act because the applicable period of limitation has expired is hereby revived, and an action thereon may be commenced and prosecuted provided such action is commenced within one year of the effective date of this act.

## § 214-c. Certain actions to be commenced within three years of discovery.

1. In this section: "exposure" means direct or indirect exposure by absorption, contact, ingestion, inhalation, implantation or injection.

2. Notwithstanding the provisions of section 214, the three year period within which an action to recover damages for personal injury or injury to property caused by the latent effects of exposure to any substance or combination of substances, in any form, upon or within the body or upon or within property must be commenced shall be computed from the date of discovery of the injury by the plaintiff or from the date when through the exercise of reasonable diligence such injury should have been discovered by the plaintiff, whichever is earlier.

3. For the purposes of sections fifty-e and fifty-i of the general municipal law, section thirty-eight hundred thirteen of the education law and the provisions of any general, special or local law or charter requiring as a condition precedent to commencement of an action or special proceeding that a notice of claim be filed or presented within a specified period of time after the claim or action accrued, a claim or action for personal injury or injury to property caused by the latent effects of exposure to any substance or combination of substances, in any form, upon or within the body or upon or within property shall be deemed to have accrued on the date of discovery of the injury by the plaintiff or on the date when through the exercise of reasonable diligence the injury should have been discovered, whichever is earlier.

4. Notwithstanding the provisions of subdivisions two and three of this section, where the discovery of the cause of the injury is alleged to have occurred less than five years after discovery of the injury or when with reasonable diligence such injury should have been discovered, whichever is earlier, an action may

be commenced or a claim filed within one year of such discovery of the cause of the injury; provided, however, if any such action is commenced or claim filed after the period in which it would otherwise have been authorized pursuant to subdivision two or three of this section the plaintiff or claimant shall be required to allege and prove that technical, scientific or medical knowledge and information sufficient to ascertain the cause of his injury had not been discovered, identified or determined prior to the expiration of the period within which the action or claim would have been authorized and that he has otherwise satisfied the requirements of subdivisions two and three of this section.

5. This section shall not be applicable to any action for medical or dental malpractice.

6. This section shall be applicable to acts, omissions or failures occurring prior to, on or after July first, nineteen hundred eighty-six, except that this section shall not be applicable to any act, omission or failure:

(a) which occurred prior to July first, nineteen hundred eighty-six, and

(b) which caused or contributed to an injury that either was discovered or through the exercise of reasonable diligence should have been discovered prior to such date, and

(c) an action for which was or would have been barred because the applicable period of limitation had expired prior to such date.

### 1992 AMENDMENTS

L. 1992, ch. 551, eff. July 24, 1992, amended Subdivision (1) by broadening the definition of "exposure" to include exposure by implantation.

### 1986 AMENDMENTS

L. 1986, ch. 682, eff. July 30, 1986, and applicable to actions commenced or claims filed on or after such date, added new section 214-c, providing for a three-year discovery statute of limitations for cases involving exposure to latent toxic substances. See uncodified revival provisions contained in sections 4 and 5 of ch. 682, applicable to enumerated substances.

## § 214-d. Limitations on certain actions against licensed engineers and architects.

1. Any person asserting a claim for personal injury, wrongful death or property damage, or a cross or third-party claim for contribution or indemnification arising out of an action for personal injury, wrongful death or property damage, against a licensed architect, engineer, or landscape architect or against a partnership, professional corporation or limited liability company lawfully practicing architecture, engineering or landscape architecture which is based upon the professional performance, conduct or omission by such licensed architect, engineer, or landscape architect or such firm occurring more than ten years prior to the date of such claim, shall give written notice of such claim to each such architect, engineer, or landscape architect or such firm at least ninety days before the

commencement of any action or proceeding against such licensed architect, engineer, or landscape architect or such firm including any cross or third-party action or claim. The notice of claim shall identify the performance, conduct or omissions complained of, on information and belief, and shall include a request for general and special damages. Service of such written notice of claim may be made by any of the methods permitted for personal service of a summons upon a natural person, partnership or professional corporation. A notice of claim served in accordance with this section shall be filed, together with proof of service thereof, in any court of this state in which an action, proceeding or cross or third-party claim arising out of such conduct may be commenced or interposed, within thirty days of the service of the notice of claim. Upon the filing of any such notice of claim, a county clerk shall collect an index number fee in accordance with section eight thousand eighteen of this chapter and an index number shall be assigned.

2. In such pleadings as are subsequently filed in any court, each party shall represent that it has fully complied with the provisions of this section.

3. Service of a notice as provided in this section shall toll the applicable statute of limitations to and including a period of one hundred twenty days following such service.

4. From and after the date of service of the notice provided for in subdivision one of this section, the claimant shall have the right to serve a demand for discovery and production of documents and things for inspection, testing, copying or photographing in accordance with rule three thousand one hundred twenty of this chapter. Such demand shall be governed by the procedures of article thirty-one of this chapter. In addition, the claimant shall have the right to the examination before trial of such licensed architect, engineer, or landscape architect or such firm or to serve written interrogatories upon such licensed architect, engineer, or landscape architect or such firm after service of and compliance with a demand for production and inspection in accordance with this section. The court may, at any time at its own initiative or on motion of such licensed architect, engineer, or landscape architect or such firm deny, limit, condition or restrict such examination before trial or written interrogatories upon a showing that such claimant has failed to establish reasonable necessity for the information sought or failed to establish that the information sought by such examination or interrogatories cannot reasonably be determined from the documents or things provided in response to a demand for production and inspection served in accordance with this section. Such examination before trial or interrogatories shall otherwise be governed by article thirty-one of this chapter.

5. After the expiration of ninety days from service of the notice provided in subdivision one of this section, the claimant may commence or interpose an action, proceeding or cross or third-party claim against such licensed architect, engineer, or landscape architect or such firm. The action shall proceed in every

CPLR

respect as if the action were one brought on account of conduct occurring less than ten years prior to the claim described in said action, unless the defendant architect, engineer, or landscape architect or such firm shall have made a motion under rule three thousand two hundred eleven or three thousand two hundred twelve of this chapter, in which event the action shall be stayed pending determination of the motion. Such motion shall be granted upon a showing that such claimant has failed to comply with the notice of claim requirements of this section or for the reasons set forth in subdivision (h) of rule three thousand two hundred eleven or subdivision (i) of rule three thousand two hundred twelve of this chapter; provided, however, such motion shall not be granted if the moving party is in default of any disclosure obligation as set forth in subdivision four of this section.

6. No claim for personal injury, or wrongful death or property damage, or a cross or third-party claim for contribution or indemnification arising out of an action for personal injury, wrongful death or property damage may be asserted against a licensed architect, engineer, or landscape architect or such firm arising out of conduct by such licensed architect, engineer, or landscape architect or such firm occurring more than ten years prior to the accrual of such claim shall be commenced or interposed against any such licensed architect, engineer, or landscape architect or such firm unless it shall appear by and as an allegation in the complaint or necessary moving papers that the claimant has complied with the requirements of this section. Upon the commencement of such a proceeding or action or interposition of such cross or third-party claim, a county clerk shall not be entitled to collect an index number fee and such action, proceeding or cross or third-party claim shall retain the previously assigned index number. Such action, proceeding or cross or third-party claim shall otherwise be governed by the provisions of this chapter.

7. The provisions of this section shall apply only to a licensed architect, engineer, or landscape architect or such firm practicing architecture, engineering or landscape architecture in the state of New York at the time the conduct complained of occurred and shall not apply to any person or entity, including but not limited to corporations, which was not licensed as an architect, engineer, or landscape architect or such firm in this state or to a firm not lawfully practicing architecture, engineering or landscape architecture at the time the conduct complained of occurred.

8. The provisions of this section shall not be construed to in any way alter or extend any applicable statutes of limitations except as expressly provided herein.

**Added** by L. 1996, ch. 682, eff. Oct. 1, 1996.

### § 215. Actions to be commenced within one year: against sheriff, coroner or constable; for escape of prisoner; for assault, battery, false imprisonment, malicious prosecution, libel or slander; for violation of right of privacy; for penalty given to informer; on arbitration award.

The following actions shall be commenced within one year:

1. an action against a sheriff, coroner or constable, upon a liability incurred by him by doing an act in his official capacity or by omission of an official duty, except the non-payment of money collected upon an execution;

2. an action against an officer for the escape of a prisoner arrested or imprisoned by virtue of a civil mandate;

3. an action to recover damages for assault, battery, false imprisonment, malicious prosecution, libel, slander, false words causing special damages, or a violation of the right of privacy under section fifty-one of the civil rights law;

4. an action to enforce a penalty or forfeiture created by statute and given wholly or partly to any person who will prosecute; if the action is not commenced within the year by a private person, it may be commenced on behalf of the state, within three years after the commission of the offense, by the attorney-general or the district attorney of the county where the offense was committed; and

5. an action upon an arbitration award.

6. an action to recover any overcharge of interest or to enforce a penalty for such overcharge.

7. an action by a tenant pursuant to subdivision three of section two hundred twenty-three-b of the real property law.

8. Whenever it is shown that a criminal action against the same defendant has been commenced with respect to the event or occurrence from which a claim governed by this section arises, the plaintiff shall have at least one year from the termination of the criminal action as defined in section 1.20 of the criminal procedure law in which to commence the civil action, notwithstanding that the time in which to commence such action has already expired or has less than a year remaining.

CPLR

#### CROSS REFERENCES

**Real Prop. Law § 223-b** referred to above deals with prohibitions against retaliation by a landlord against a tenant.

Termination of criminal action is defined in **Criminal Procedure Law § 1.20(16).**

#### 1983 AMENDMENTS

L. 1983, ch. 95, eff. May 17, 1983, and applying to all pending civil and criminal actions, added subdivision (8).

**1979 AMENDMENTS**

L. 1979, ch. 693, eff. Sept. 1, 1979, amended CPLR 215 by adding subdivision (7).

**1969 AMENDMENTS**

L. 1969, ch. 1141, eff. July 1, 1969, repealed Subd. (7), dealing with the enforcement of the New York State Truth-in-Lending Act, also repealed in 1969.

**1968 AMENDMENTS**

L. 1968, ch. 1072, eff. July 1, 1969, added Subds. (6) and (7).

## § 216.   Abbreviation of period to one year after notice.

(a) Action to recover money. 1. No action for the recovery of any sum of money due and payable under or on account of a contract, or for any part thereof, shall be commenced by any person who has made claim to the sum, after the expiration of one year from the giving of notice, as hereinafter provided, to the claimant that an action commenced by another person is pending to recover the sum, or any part thereof, exceeding fifty dollars in amount. This limitation shall not be construed to enlarge the time within which the cause of action of the claimant would otherwise be barred.

2. If any person shall make claim for the recovery of any sum of money due and payable under or on account of a contract, and an action has theretofore been, or shall thereafter be, commenced by another person to recover the sum, or any part thereof, exceeding fifty dollars in amount, the defendant in such action may, within twenty days from the date of service upon him of the complaint or from the date of receipt by him of the claim, whichever occurs later, make a motion before the court in which the action is pending for an order permitting the defendant to give notice to the claimant that the action is pending. The court in which the action is pending shall grant the order where it appears that a person not a party to the action has made claim against the defendant for the sum of money, or any part thereof, exceeding fifty dollars in amount; that the action was brought without collusion between the defendant and the plaintiff; and that the claimant cannot, with due diligence, be served with process in such a manner as to obtain jurisdiction over his person. The order shall provide, among such other terms and conditions as justice may require, that notice shall be given to the claimant by sending by registered mail a copy of the summons and complaint in the action and the order and a notice addressed to the claimant at his last known address. In the event that registration of mail directed to any country or part thereof shall be discontinued or suspended, notice to a claimant whose last known address is within such country or part thereof shall be given by ordinary mail, under such terms and conditions as the court may direct. Proof that the notice has been mailed shall be filed within ten days from the date of the order; otherwise the order becomes inoperative. Upon such filing, notice shall be deemed to have been given on the tenth day after the date of such order.

3. Upon proof by affidavit or otherwise, to the satisfaction of the court, that the conditions of this subdivision have been satisfied and that there is no collusion between the claimant and the defendant, the court shall make an order staying further prosecution of the action for a period not to exceed one year from the date when the notice shall have been given to the claimant. At the time of the granting of such order or at any time thereafter, the court, upon the motion of any party, shall, as a condition of the granting of the order or its continuation, impose upon the defendant such terms as justice may require as to the furnishing of an undertaking in an amount to be fixed by the court. The stay shall be vacated and the undertaking, if any has been given, may be discharged or modified, as justice may require, upon proof to the court by any party to the action that the claimant has intervened or has instituted another action in any court of this state to recover the said sum of money, or any part thereof, exceeding fifty dollars.

4. A motion for any relief as prescribed in this subdivision shall be made on notice to all other parties to the action.

5. Whenever claims are made by two or more persons, each claiming to be, to the exclusion of the other, the duly authorized deputy, officer or agent to demand, receive, collect, sue for or recover the same sum of money due and payable under or on account of a contract, or any part thereof, exceeding fifty dollars in amount, for and on behalf of the same person, each person making such a claim shall be deemed an adverse claimant. Notwithstanding that an action has been commenced in the name of or on behalf of the person for whom he claims to be the duly authorized deputy, officer or agent, any such adverse claimant may be notified of the pendency of an action as provided in this subdivision and may intervene in the action and be designated as claiming to be or as the alleged deputy, officer or agent.

6. Whenever an action has been commenced for the recovery of any sum of money exceeding fifty dollars due and payable under or on account of a contract and the records of the defendant show that a person other than the plaintiff has the right, exclusive of other deputies, officers or agents of the plaintiff, to demand, sue for and recover the same sum of money, or any part thereof, exceeding fifty dollars in amount, either in his own name, on his own behalf, or as the authorized deputy, officer or agent for the plaintiff, and the defendant has received no notice of transfer, revocation, or other change in right or authority acceptable to it, the person so appearing on the records shall be deemed to have made an adverse claim to the sum of money and may be treated as an adverse claimant.

(b) Action to recover property. When an action has been commenced to recover specific personal property, including certificates of stocks, bonds, notes or other securities or obligations, exceeding fifty dollars in value, held by the defendant within the state, or to enforce a vested or contingent interest or lien upon such property, and a person not a party to the action asserts a claim to

CPLR

the whole or any part of the same property or to a right, interest or lien upon it which is adverse to the plaintiff's claim, and the court in which the action is pending has no jurisdiction over the adverse claimant to direct the issuance of process or if the same be issued it would be without effect notwithstanding that the action seeks to have declared, enforced, regulated, defined or limited, rights, interests or liens upon specific personal property within the state, the defendant in the action may within twenty days from the date of service upon him of the complaint or within twenty days of the date of the receipt by him of the adverse claim, whichever shall occur later, make a motion before the court for leave to give notice to the adverse claimant of the pending action in the same manner as provided in subdivision (a). Upon the granting of such an order, the provisions of subdivision (a) shall apply insofar as they are compatible with the subject matter of the action.

### § 217.  Proceeding against body or officer; actions complaining about conduct that would constitute a union's breach of its duty of fair representation; four months.

1. Unless a shorter time is provided in the law authorizing the proceeding, a proceeding against a body or officer must be commenced within four months after the determination to be reviewed becomes final and binding upon the petitioner or the person whom he represents in law or in fact, or after the respondent's refusal, upon the demand of the petitioner or the person whom he represents, to perform its duty; or with leave of the court where the petitioner or the person whom he represents, at the time such determination became final and binding upon him or at the time of such refusal, was under a disability specified in section 208, within two years after such time.

2. (a) Any action or proceeding against an employee organization subject to article fourteen of the civil service law or article twenty of the labor law which complains that such employee organization has breached its duty of fair representation regarding someone to whom such employee organization has a duty shall be commenced within four months of the date the employee or former employee knew or should have known that the breach has occurred, or within four months of the date the employee or former employee suffers actual harm, whichever is later.

(b) Any action or proceeding by an employee or former employee against an employer subject to article fourteen of the civil service law or article twenty of the labor law, an essential element of which is that an employee organization breached its duty of fair representation to the person making the complaint, shall be commenced within four months of the date the employee or former employee knew or should have known that the breach has occurred, or within four months of the date the employee or former employee suffers actual harm, whichever is later.

**1990 AMENDMENTS**

L. 1990, ch. 467, eff. July 11, 1990, adding the words "actions complaining about conduct that would constitute a union's breach of its duty of fair representation;" to the heading; dividing the section into subdivisions; and adding subdivision 2.

## § 218. Transitional provisions.

(a) Actions barred at effective date. Nothing in this article shall authorize any action to be commenced which is barred when this article becomes effective, except insofar as the right to commence the action may be revived by an acknowledgment or payment.

(b) Cause of action accrued and not barred at effective date. Where a cause of action accrued before, and is not barred when this article becomes effective, the time within which an action must be commenced shall be the time which would have been applicable apart from the provisions of this article, or the time which would have been applicable if the provisions of this article had been in effect when the cause of action accrued, whichever is longer.

CPLR

# ARTICLE 3

## JURISDICTION AND SERVICE, APPEARANCE AND CHOICE OF COURT

### SUMMARY OF ARTICLE

§ 301.　　Jurisdiction over persons, property or status.

§ 302.　　Personal jurisdiction by acts of non-domiciliaries.

　　(a)　Acts which are the basis of jurisdiction.

　　(b)　Personal jurisdiction over non-resident defendant in matrimonial actions or family court proceedings.

　　(c)　Effect of appearance.

§ 303.　　Designation of attorney as agent for service.

§ 304.　　Method of commencing action or special proceeding.

R 305.　　Summons; supplemental summons; amendment.

　　(a)　Summons; supplemental summons.

　　(b)　Summons and notice.

　　(c)　Amendment.

R 306.　　Proof of service.

　　(a)　Generally.

　　(b)　Personal service.

　　(c)　Other service.

　　(d)　Form.

　　(e)　Admission of service.

§ 306–a.　Index number in an action commenced in supreme or county court.

§ 306–b.　Filing proof of service in an action commenced in supreme or county court.

§ 307.　　Personal service upon the state.

§ 308.　　Personal service upon a natural person.

§ 309.　　Personal service upon an infant, incompetent or conservatee.

　　(a)　Upon an infant.

　　(b)　Upon a person judicially declared to be incompetent.

　　(c)　Upon a conservatee.

§ 310.　　Personal service upon a partnership.

§ 311.　　Personal service upon a corporation or governmental subdivision.

§ 312.　　Personal service upon a court, board or commission.

§ 312-a.　Personal service by mail.

　　(a)　Service.

　　(b)　Completion of service and time to answer.

　　(c)　Affirmation.

　　(d)　Form.

　　(e)　Subsequent service.

　　(f)　Disbursements.

CPLR

§ 313.      Service without the state giving personal jurisdiction.
§ 314.      Service without the state not giving personal jurisdiction in certain actions.
§ 315.      Service by publication authorized.
R 316.      Service by publication.
    (a)  Contents of order; form of publication; filing.
    (b)  Mailing to accompany publication in matrimonial actions.
    (c)  Time of publication; when service complete.
§ 317.      Defense by person to whom summons not personally delivered.
R 318.      Designation of agent for service.
§ 319.      [Not used.]
R 320.      Defendant's appearance.
    (a)  Requirement of appearance.
    (b)  When appearance confers personal jurisdiction, generally.
    (c)  When appearance confers personal jurisdiction, in certain actions; limited appearance.
    (d)  Appearance after first publication.
§ 321.      Attorneys.
    (a)  Appearance in person or by attorney.
    (b)  Change or withdrawal of attorney.
    (c)  Death, removal or disability of attorney.
R 322.      Authority for appearance of attorney in real property action.
    (a)  Authority of plaintiff's attorney.
    (b)  Authority of non-resident defendant's attorney.
    (c)  Agencies or wholly-owned corporations of the United States.
§§ 323–324.  [Not used.]
§ 325.      Grounds for removal.
    (a)  By supreme court for mistake in choice of the court.
    (b)  From court of limited jurisdiction.
    (c)  On consent to court of limited jurisdiction.
    (d)  Without consent to court of limited jurisdiction.
    (e)  From supreme court to surrogate's court where decedent's estate affected.
    (f)  To supreme court where county judge incapacitated.
    (g)  From one local court to another.
R 326.      Procedure on removal.
    (a)  Stay of proceedings.
    (b)  Order and subsequent proceedings.
    (c)  Fees and disbursements.
R 327.      Inconvenient forum.
R 328.      Assistance to tribunals and litigants outside the state.
    (a)  Pursuant to court order.
    (b)  Without court order.
    (c)  Effect.

## § 301. Jurisdiction over persons, property or status.

A court may exercise such jurisdiction over persons, property, or status as might have been exercised heretofore.

**CROSS REFERENCES**

As to subject matter jurisdiction of the courts, generally, see **Constitutional** and **Judiciary Law** provisions in the Appendix, *infra*.

## § 302. Personal jurisdiction by acts of non-domiciliaries.

(a) Acts which are the basis of jurisdiction. As to a cause of action arising from any of the acts enumerated in this section, a court may exercise personal jurisdiction over any non-domiciliary, or his executor or administrator, who in person or through an agent:

1. transacts any business within the state or contracts anywhere to supply goods or services in the state; or

2. commits a tortious act within the state, except as to a cause of action for defamation of character arising from the act; or

3. commits a tortious act without the state causing injury to person or property within the state, except as to a cause of action for defamation of character arising from the act, if he

(i) regularly does or solicits business, or engages in any other persistent course of conduct, or derives substantial revenue from goods used or consumed or services rendered, in the state, or

(ii) expects or should reasonably expect the act to have consequences in the state and derives substantial revenue from interstate or international commerce; or

4. owns, uses or possesses any real property situated within the state.

(b) Personal jurisdiction over non-resident defendant in matrimonial actions or family court proceedings. A court in any matrimonial action or family court proceeding involving a demand for support, alimony, maintenance, distributive awards or special relief in matrimonial actions may exercise personal jurisdiction over the respondent or defendant notwithstanding the fact that he or she no longer is a resident or domiciliary of this state, or over his or her executor or administrator, if the party seeking support is a resident of or domiciled in this state at the time such demand is made, provided that this state was the matrimonial domicile of the parties before their separation, or the defendant abandoned the plaintiff in this state, or the claim for support, alimony, maintenance, distributive awards or special relief in matrimonial actions accrued under the laws of this state or under an agreement executed in this state. The family court may exercise personal jurisdiction over a non-resident respondent to the extent provided in sections one hundred fifty-four and one thousand thirty-six of the family court act.

CPLR

(c) Effect of appearance. Where personal jurisdiction is based solely upon this section, an appearance does not confer such jurisdiction with respect to causes of action not arising from an act enumerated in this section.

### 1995 AMENDMENTS

L. 1995, ch. 441, eff. Oct. 31, 1995, amended CPLR 302(b) by deleting the reference to Article 10 of the Family Court Act and by adding the references to sections 154 and 1036 of the Family Court Act.

### 1991 AMENDMENTS

L. 1991, ch. 69, eff. April 22, 1991, amended CPLR 302(b) by adding the last sentence.

### 1982 AMENDMENTS

L. 1982, ch. 505, eff. Sept. 1, 1982, amended CPLR 302(b) by deleting the words "obligation to pay" and inserting the words "claim for."

### 1980 AMENDMENTS

L. 1980, ch. 281, eff. July 19, 1980, amended CPLR 302(b) by adding references to ". . . maintenance, distributive awards or special relief in matrimonial actions. . . ."

### 1979 AMENDMENTS

L. 1979, ch. 252, eff. Sept. 1, 1979, amended CPLR 302 subd. (a) par. 1, by expanding the "transaction of business" contact to include the situation where one "contracts anywhere to supply goods or services in the state"; and amended subd. (b) by making the catch line clearer and by correcting a printer's error in the body of the provision.

### 1974 AMENDMENTS

L. 1974, ch. 859, eff. June 7, 1974, added a new subdivision (b) entitled "Personal jurisdiction over non-resident defendant" and relettered former subdivision (b) as subdivision (c).

### 1966 AMENDMENTS

L. 1966, ch. 590, eff. Sept. 1, 1966, amended Subd. (a).

Amendment recommended by the Judicial Conference Feb. 1, 1966, Report to the Legislature: "The interpretation of CPLR 302(a)(2) by the Court of Appeals in [*Feathers v. McLucas,* 15 N.Y.2d 443, 261 N.Y.S.2d 8, 209 N.E.2d 68 (1965)] has disclosed a serious gap in this provision. . . . It is now settled that CPLR 302(a)(2) reaches a non-resident who commits a tortious act or omission within the state but does not reach a non-resident who causes a tortious injury within the state through an act or omission committed outside the state (unless he can be held to have transacted business within the state within the meaning of CPLR 302(a)(1)). . . . In view of this serious gap in the coverage afforded by CPLR 302(a)(2) the Judicial Conference believes that an amendment is required which will be broad enough to protect New York residents yet not so broad as to burden unfairly non-residents whose connection with the state is remote and who could not reasonably be expected to foresee that their acts outside of New York could have harmful consequences in New York. The line of distinction is subtle and its statutory delineation requires the utmost care. . . .

"It is suggested, therefore, that as a matter of policy, jurisdiction should not be exercised over a person who causes tortious injuries in the state by an act or omission outside the state unless he had other contacts with the state or unless he was engaged in extensive business activities on an interstate or international level and does an act which he should reasonably foresee might have potential consequences within New York State.

"Accordingly, the proposed amendment set forth above cures the gap in CPLR 302(a)(2) reflected in the *Feathers* case by renumbering present paragraph (3) to be paragraph (4) and by adding a new paragraph (3) thereto . . .

"The jurisdiction of the court under proposed CPLR 302(a)(3) over the non-domiciliary who commits a tortious act outside of the state causing injury within the state is limited to a cause of action arising out of such tortious act. However, there is no necessary connection between the àct' committed without the state and the additional àcts' of contact mentioned in subparagraph (i) or the deriving of substantial revenue from interstate or international commerce mentioned in subparagraph (ii). Neither is there a necessary connection between the àct' from which the cause of action arose and the àct' of foreseeing mentioned in subparagraph (ii) except that the same act which gives rise to the cause of action also causes the consequences within the state which the non-domiciliary expects or should reasonably expect. It should also be noted that the statutory requirement of foreseeability relates to forum consequences generally and not to the specific event which produced injury within the state. For example, using again the facts of the *Feathers* case as illustration, the requirement of reasonable expectation of potential forum consequences would be satisfied if the foreign corporation which manufactured the defective gas tank knew that it was intended for use in New York.

"Finally, in the event that non-resident plaintiffs seek to avail themselves of the expanded long-arm' jurisdiction over non-resident defendants, the doctrine of forum non conveniens' is available in appropriate cases."

## § 303. Designation of attorney as agent for service.

The commencement of an action in the state by a person not subject to personal jurisdiction is a designation by him of his attorney appearing in the action or of the clerk of the court if no attorney appears, as agent, during the pendency of the action, for service of a summons pursuant to section 308, in any separate action in which such a person is a defendant and another party to the action is a plaintiff if such separate action would have been permitted as a counterclaim had the action been brought in the supreme court.

### 1972 AMENDMENTS

L. 1972, ch. 487, eff. Sept. 1, 1972, amended CPLR 303 by adding "pursuant to section 308" after "service of a summons."

## § 304. Method of commencing action or special proceeding.

An action is commenced by filing a summons and complaint or summons with notice with the clerk of the court in the county in which the action is brought. A special proceeding is commenced by filing a notice of petition or order to show cause and a petition with the clerk of the court in the county in which the special proceeding is brought. Where a court finds that circumstances prevent immediate filing with the clerk of the court, the signing of an order requiring the subsequent filing at a specific time and date not later than five days thereafter shall commence the action. For purposes of this section, and for purposes of section two hundred three of this chapter, filing shall mean the delivery of the summons with notice or summons and complaint to the clerk together with any fee required as specified in rule twenty-one hundred two of this chapter for filing [*Effective until 8/31/97*].

[*Effective 9/1/97*] An action is commenced by filing a summons and complaint or summons with notice. A special proceeding is commenced by filing a notice of petition or order to show cause and a petition. Where a court finds that circumstances prevent immediate filing, the signing of an order requiring the subsequent filing at a specific time and date not later than five days thereafter shall commence the action. For purposes of this section, and for purposes of sections two hundred three and three hundred six-a of this chapter, filing shall mean the delivery of the summons with notice, summons and complaint, notice of petition or order to show cause to the clerk of the court in the county in which the action or special proceeding is brought or any other person designated by the clerk of the court for that purpose together with any fee required as specified in rule twenty-one hundred two of this chapter for filing. At such time of filing, the original and a copy of such papers shall be date stamped by a court clerk who shall file the original and maintain a record of the date of the filing and who shall immediately return the copy to the party who brought the filing.

### 1996 AMENDMENTS

L. 1996, ch. 606, eff. Sept. 1, 1997, and applicable to all actions or special proceedings commenced on or after such date. amended the section by deleting the words "with the clerk of court" from the first two sentences, adding a reference to section 306-a, expanding the definition of "filing" and adding a new last sentence.

### 1994 AMENDMENTS

L. 1994, ch. 563, eff. July 26, 1994, amended CPLR 304 by inserting the words "and a petition."

## R 305. Summons; supplemental summons; amendment.

(a) Summons; supplemental summons. A summons shall specify the basis of the venue designated and if based upon the residence of the plaintiff it shall specify the plaintiff's address, and also shall bear the index number assigned and the date of filing with the clerk of the court. A third-party summons shall also specify the date of filing of the third-party summons with the clerk of the court. The summons in an action arising out of a consumer credit transaction shall prominently display at the top of the summons the words "consumer credit transaction" and, where a purchaser, borrower or debtor is a defendant, shall specify the county of residence of a defendant, if one resides within the state, and the county where the consumer credit transaction took place, if it is within the state. Where, upon order of the court or by stipulation of all parties or as of right pursuant to section 1003, a new party is joined in the action and the joinder is not made upon the new party's motion, a supplemental summons specifying the pleading which the new party must answer shall be filed with the clerk of the court and served upon such party.

(b) Summons and notice. If the complaint is not served with the summons, the summons shall contain or have attached thereto a notice stating the nature of the action and the relief sought, and, except in an action for medical malpractice, the sum of money for which judgment may be taken in case of default.

(c) Amendment. At any time, in its discretion and upon such terms as it deems just, the court may allow any summons or proof of service of a summons to be amended, if a substantial right of a party against whom the summons issued is not prejudiced.

### CROSS REFERENCES

As to the summons in a matrimonial action, see **Domestic Relations Law §§ 211 and 232(a)**, in Appendix, *infra*.

### 1996 AMENDMENTS

L. 1996, ch. 39, eff. April 2, 1996, amended subdivision (a) by deleting the final sentence and replacing with a new final sentence, which makes reference to § 1003, Nonjoinder and misjoinder of parties.

### 1992 AMENDMENTS

L. 1992, ch. 216, eff. July 1, 1992, amended subdivision (a) by adding to the first sentence the words ". . . and also shall bear the index number assigned and the date of filing with the clerk of the court. A third-party summons shall also specify the date of filing of the third-party summons with the clerk of the court"; by adding to the final sentence the words "filed with the clerk of the court and"; and by making the language gender neutral.

### 1978 AMENDMENTS

L. 1978, ch. 528, eff. Jan. 1, 1979, amended subd. (b) so as to require service of notice of the nature of the action whenever the summons is served without a complaint, and, with the exception of medical malpractice suits, to uniformly require inclusion in such notice of the sum for which a default judgment may be taken.

Amendment recommended by the Judicial Conference in its report to the 1978 Legislature, wherein it stated:

"The permissive language now contained in CPLR 305(b) (the summons may contain . . . .') constitutes a serious trap for the unwary practitioner who is not familiar with the provisions of CPLR 3215(e) governing proof of default. Under that provision, absent proof of service of the summons and complaint, a 305(b) notice is needed to preserve plaintiff's right to obtain a default judgment (*McDermott v. Hoening*, 32 A.D. 2d 838 (2nd Dept. 1969); *see* 1 Weinstein, Korn & Miller, New York Civil Practice - CPLR , ¶ 305.12 (Matthew Bender)). It is not clear whether and how a plaintiff who has served an unaccompanied summons without notice may, on his own initiative, serve the complaint on the defendant who neither appeared nor made a demand for the complaint . . .

"Under the proposed amendment the uncertainty now surrounding default practice under CPLR 305(b) and 3215(c), (e) would be avoided by the mandatory notice provision. That provision would be in harmony with modern notions of notice pleading. It would assure the defendant at least basic information concerning the nature of the plaintiff's claim and the relief sought. In order to accomplish that aim the content of the mandatory notice would be clarified. The language of the rule which now requires a statement of the object of the action and the relief sought' would be amended to provide instead for a brief recital of the nature of the action and the relief sought.' The present verbiage could be misread as a redundancy denoting merely a requirement to specify the type of relief sought in terms of damages or other remedy. Such misreading led to the downfall of the plaintiff's action in a negligence case where the court voided a summons served without complaint on the ground that it failed to disclose the object of the action, even though it set forth the damages demanded (*Arden v. Loew's Hotels Inc.*, 40 A.D. 2d 894 (3rd Dept. 1972).

"A different kind of technical defect that may render an unaccompanied summons jurisdictionally void for default purposes is typified by *A.J. Eckert Co. v. George A. Fuller Co., Inc.* 51 A.D. 2d 844 (3rd Dept. 1976). In that case an application to the court for judgment by default was denied when the summons stated the object of the action (claim for the balance due under a contract and damages for breach thereof ') but failed to set forth the sum for which judgment would be taken in case of default as required by CPLR 3215(b). To avoid mishaps of that sort the present requirement that in an action for a sum certain or for a sum which by computation can be made certain, the notice must state the sum of money for which judgment will be taken' would be expanded to include any kind of action seeking monetary relief, whether liquidated or unliquidated. The sole exception would be an action to recover damages for medical malpractice where CPLR 3017(c) bars the pleader from stating the amount of damages sought. To require a statement of the sum to which the pleader deems himself entitled in the summons would flout the purpose of that statute.

"The proposed amplification of language with respect to the statement of money damages, liquidated or unliquidated, reiterates more compactly the present practice. The language in rule 305(b) proposed to be deleted, which refers to actions for a sum certain, was derived from rule 46 of the former rules of civil practice, which provided for a short form of complaint for enumerated categories of contract actions (*see* 1 Weinstein, Korn & Miller, New York Civil Practice ¶ 305.12 (Matthew Bender). L. 1965 ch. 749 amended Rule 305(b) to permit service of a notice, contained in the summons or attached to it, stating the object of the action and the relief sought, as well as the original notice where the suit was for a sum certain. Thus, under the present law, a notice may be served in any action. If the action is one involving liquidated damages, the sum certain or able to be made certain by computation must be stated in the 305(b) notice, in order to allow entry of a default judgment by the clerk (CPLR 3215(a)). If the damages are unliquidated, the sum must be stated in the 305(b) notice, under the rubric of relief sought' in order to satisfy the requirement of CPLR 3215(b) that the judgment by default not exceed in amount or differ in type from that demanded in the complaint or stated in the notice served pursuant to subdivision (b) of rule 305.' The same applies in an equitable proceeding, such as for specific performance or an injunction, where alternative or incidental money damages are demanded. In short, the proposed language serves as a reminder that a statement of the monetary relief sought in a summons served without complaint is always needed in order to protect plaintiff's rights on default.

"Matrimonial actions would be governed by analogous amendments to Domestic Relations Law, sections 211 and 232 . . . .

"Finally, the question may be asked whether a deviation from the notice standards prescribed by rule 305(b), as proposed to be amended, would constitute a jurisdictional defect or a mere irregularity. The complete absence of any notice would certainly constitute a jurisdictional defect when the summons is not accompanied by the complaint (*see McDermott v. Hoenig*, 32 A.D. 2d 838, 302 N.Y.S.2d 280 (2d Dept 1969)). In accordance with present practice, the court would have to determine whether a defective notice is correctable or, under the circumstances of a particular case, renders the summons jurisdictionally void for purposes of a default proceeding."

### 1973 AMENDMENTS

L. 1973, ch. 238, eff. Sept. 1, 1973, amended CPLR 305(a) by adding a new second sentence setting forth the requirements for a summons in an action arising out of a consumer credit transaction.

### 1965 AMENDMENTS

L. 1965, ch. 749, eff. Sept. 1, 1965, amended subd. (b). See comments at 1978 amendment notes.

**CPLR**

## R 306. Proof of service.

(a) Generally. Proof of service shall specify the papers served, the person who was served and the date, time, address, or, in the event there is no address, place and manner of service, and set forth facts showing that the service was made by an authorized person and in an authorized manner.

(b) Personal service. Whenever service is made pursuant to this article by delivery of the summons to an individual, proof of service shall also include, in addition to any other requirement, a description of the person to whom it was so delivered including, but not limited to, sex, color of skin, hair color, approximate age, approximate weight and height, and other identifying features.

(c) Other service. Where service is made pursuant to subdivision four of section three hundred eight of this chapter, proof of service shall also specify the dates, addresses and the times of attempted service pursuant to subdivisions one, two or three of such section.

(d) Form. Proof of service shall be in the form of a certificate if the service is made by a sheriff or other authorized public officer, in the form of an affidavit if made by any other person, or in the form of a signed acknowledgment of receipt of a summons and complaint, or summons and notice or notice of petition as provided for in section 312-a of this article.

(e) Admission of service. A writing admitting service by the person to be served is adequate proof of service.

### CROSS REFERENCES

See **General Business Law § 89-c** as to records required to be kept by process servers.

## § 306–a.   Index number in an action commenced in supreme or county court.

(a) Upon filing the summons and complaint or summons with notice with the clerk of the court in an action commenced in supreme or county court, an index number shall be assigned and the fee required by subdivision (a) of section eight thousand eighteen of this chapter shall be pais. Upon the filing of a summons and complaint against a person not already a party, as permitted under section one thousand seven or rule one thousand eleven of this chapter, the fee required by subdivision (a) of section eight thousand eighteen of this chapter shall be paid, but a separate index number shall not be assigned [*Effective until 8/31/97*]

(a) [*Effective 9/1/97*] Upon filing the summons and complaint or summons with notice in an action commenced in supreme or county court, an index number shall be assigned and the fee required by subdivision (a) of section eight thousand eighteen of this chapter shall be paid. Upon the filing of a summons and complaint against a person not already a party, as permitted under section one thousand seven or rule one thousand eleven of this chapter, the fee required by subdivision (a) of section eight thousand eighteen of this chapter shall be paid, but a separate index number shall not be assigned.

(b) If a person other than the plaintiff or third-party plaintiff who served the summons or third-party summons obtains the index number and pays the fee therefor, the clerk shall issue an order directing the plaintiff or the third-party plaintiff to pay such person the amount of the fee paid. If such fee is not paid within thirty days of service of the order with notice of entry, the person who paid the fee, in addition to any other remedies available at law, may apply to the clerk for an order dismissing the action without prejudice.

**1992 AMENDMENTS**

L. 1992, ch. 216, eff. July 1, 1992, repealed prior versions of CPLR 306–a. CPLR 306–a(a) now provides that a party who files in the supreme or county courts a summons and complaint, or summons with notice, must secure an index number at the time of filing. CPLR 306–a(b) provides that if someone other than the plaintiff purchases the index number, that person is entitled to an order from the clerk of the court, requiring reimbursement by the plaintiff (or the third-party plaintiff) within 30 days of service of the order with notice of entry. If the plaintiff fails to comply, the paying individual may apply to the clerk for an order dismissing the action, but without prejudice.

L. 1992, ch. 55, eff. for all actions that were "pending" on July 1, 1992, amended subdivision (a) by deleting the reference to third-party actions. More important, it provided that unless a summons was filed with the clerk and an index number purchased before process was served, service would be ineffective. It also deleted former subdivision (b) and replaced it with the current subdivision (b) dealing with third-party actions, and revised subdivision (c). These amendments, however, were superseded by L. 1992, ch. 216, discussed *supra*.

## § 306–b. Filing proof of service in an action commenced in supreme or county court.

(a) Proof of service of the summons and complaint, summons with notice, or of the third-party summons and complaint shall be filed with the clerk of the court within one hundred twenty days after the date of filing of the summons and complaint, summons with notice or third-party summons and complaint, provided that in an action or proceeding where the applicable statute of limitations is four months or less, such proof of service must be filed not later than fifteen days after the date on which the applicable statute of limitations expires. If proof of service is not filed and there has been no appearance by the defendant within the time provided in this section for filing proof of service, the action or third-party action shall be deemed dismissed as to the non-appearing party with respect to whom no proof of service has been filed, without prejudice and without costs.

(b) If an action dismissed for failure to file proof of service pursuant to this section or for failure to effect proper service was timely commenced, the plaintiff may commence a new action, despite the expiration of the statute of limitations after the commencement of the original action, upon the same transaction or occurrence or series of transactions or occurrences within one hundred twenty days of such dismissal provided that service upon the defendant is effected within such one hundred twenty day period. Where the claim asserted is in a proceeding against a body or officer which must be commenced within four months or less, the plaintiff must commence the new action and serve the defendant with * fifteen days of such dismissal.

* [**Editor's note:** So in original. Probably should read "within."]

**1992 AMENDMENTS**

L. 1992, ch. 216, eff. July 1, 1992, added CPLR 306–b.

CPLR

## § 307.  Personal service upon the state.

1. Personal service upon the state shall be made by delivering the summons to an assistant attorney-general at an office of the attorney-general or to the attorney-general within the state.

2. Personal service on a state officer sued solely in an official capacity or state agency, which shall be required to obtain personal jurisdiction over such an officer or agency, shall be made by (1) delivering the summons to such officer or to the chief executive officer of such agency or to a person designated by such chief executive officer to receive service, or (2) by mailing the summons by certified mail, return receipt requested, to such officer or to the chief executive officer of such agency, and by personal service upon the state in the manner provided by subdivision one of this section. Service by certified mail shall not be complete until the summons is received in a principal office of the agency and until personal service upon the state in the manner provided by subdivision one of this section is completed. For purposes of this subdivision, the term "principal office of the agency" shall mean the location at which the office of the chief executive officer of the agency is generally located. Service by certified mail shall not be effective unless the front of the envelope bears the legend "URGENT LEGAL MAIL" in capital letters. The chief executive officer of every such agency shall designate at least one person, in addition to himself or herself, to accept personal service on behalf of the agency. For purposes of this subdivision the term state agency shall be deemed to refer to any agency, board, bureau, commission, division, tribunal or other entity which constitutes the state for purposes of service under subdivision one of this section.

### 1993 AMENDMENTS

L. 1993, ch. 420, eff. Oct. 19, 1993, amended subdivision (2) by replacing the clause that began "In the event any provision of law . . ." with the clause "Personal service on a state officer sued solely in an official capacity or state agency, which shall be required to obtain personal jurisdiction over such an officer or agency."

### 1992 AMENDMENTS

L. 1992, ch. 44, eff. Jan. 1, 1993, amended subdivision (2) to add a provision authorizing personal service upon specified state agency officers by certified mail, return receipt requested, in an envelope bearing the legend "URGENT LEGAL MAIL."

### 1985 AMENDMENTS

L. 1985, ch. 290, eff. Nov. 1, 1985, added subdivision (2).

## § 308.  Personal service upon a natural person.

Personal service upon a natural person shall be made by any of the following methods:

1. by delivering the summons within the state to the person to be served; or

2. by delivering the summons within the state to a person of suitable age and discretion at the actual place of business, dwelling place or usual place of abode of the person to be served and by either mailing the summons to the person to be served at his or her last known residence or by mailing the summons by first class mail to the person to be served at his or her actual place of business in an envelope bearing the legend "personal and confidential" and not indicating on the outside thereof, by return address or otherwise, that the communication is from an attorney or concerns an action against the person to be served, such delivery and mailing to be effected within twenty days of each other; proof of such service shall be filed with the clerk of the court designated in the summons within twenty days of either such delivery or mailing, whichever is effected later; service shall be complete ten days after such filing; proof of service shall identify such person of suitable age and discretion and state the date, time and place of service, except in matrimonial actions where service hereunder may be made pursuant to an order made in accordance with the provisions of subdivision a of section two hundred thirty-two of the domestic relations law; or

3. by delivering the summons within the state to the agent for service of the person to be served as designated under rule 318, except in matrimonial actions where service hereunder may be made pursuant to an order made in accordance with the provisions of subdivision a of section two hundred thirty-two of the domestic relations law;

4. where service under paragraphs one and two cannot be made with due diligence, by affixing the summons to the door of either the actual place of business, dwelling place or usual place of abode within the state of the person to be served and by either mailing the summons to such person at his or her last known residence or by mailing the summons by first class mail to the person to be served at his or her actual place of business in an envelope bearing the legend "personal and confidential" and not indicating on the outside thereof, by return address or otherwise, that the communication is from an attorney or concerns an action against the person to be served, such affixing and mailing to be effected within twenty days of each other; proof of such service shall be filed with the clerk of the court designated in the summons within twenty days of either such affixing or mailing, whichever is effected later; service shall be complete ten days after such filing, except in matrimonial actions where service hereunder may be made pursuant to an order made in accordance with the provisions of subdivision a of section two hundred thirty-two of the domestic relations law;

5. in such manner as the court, upon motion without notice, directs, if service is impracticable under paragraphs one, two and four of this section.

6. For purposes of this section, "actual place of business" shall include any location that the defendant, through regular solicitation or advertisement, has held out as its place of business.

CPLR

## CROSS REFERENCES

**D.R.L.** § **232,** referred to in subds. (2), (3) and (4), *supra,* appears in Appendix, *infra.*

See also **Vehicle and Traffic Law** § **253** regarding service on non-residents and § **254** regarding service on residents who depart from the state and on residents' executors and administrators who are non-residents or who depart from the state, in Appendix, *infra.*

## 1994 AMENDMENTS

L. 1994, ch. 131, eff. Jan. 1, 1995, added CPLR 308(6) pertaining to "actual place of business."

## 1988 AMENDMENTS

L. 1988, ch. 125, eff. Jan. 1, 1989, amended subdivision 2 to require delivery and mailing to be accomplished within 20 days of each other, and subdivision 4 to require affixing and mailing to be accomplished within 20 days of each other; to require proof of service—under both subdivisions—to be filed within 20 days of whichever service is accomplished later; to make statute gender neutral.

## 1987 AMENDMENTS

L. 1987, ch. 115, eff. July 15, 1987, amended paragraphs two and four by providing alternative means of satisfying mailing requirement of substituted service and "nailing and mailing" procedures.

## 1986 AMENDMENTS

L. 1986, ch. 77, eff. Jan. 1, 1987, repealed the undesignated paragraph following paragraph (5) of CPLR 308 relating to the additional notice required to take a default judgment in an action against a natural person based upon nonpayment of a contractual obligation. New paragraph (3) of CPLR 3215(f) now governs.

## 1977 AMENDMENTS

L. 1977, ch. 344, eff. Jan. 1, 1978, amended CPLR 308 by adding a new undesignated paragraph which provides that in an action against a natural person for nonpayment of a contractual obligation additional notice must be given at least 20 days prior to the entry of a default judgment and which describes the procedures for service of such notice.

## 1974 AMENDMENTS

L. 1974, ch. 765, eff. July 7, 1974, amended paragraphs two, three and four of CPLR 308 by deleting the words "except in matrimonial actions" at the beginning of each paragraph and by adding the clause "except in matrimonial actions where service hereunder may be made pursuant to an order made in accordance with the provisions of subdivision a of section two hundred thirty-two of the domestic relations law."

## 1971 AMENDMENTS

L. 1971, ch. 176, eff. Sept. 1, 1971, amended CPLR 308.

This amendment was recommended by the Judicial Conference February 1, 1971 Report to the Legislature, wherein it was stated:

"Paragraph 4 would be amended to provide that in order to avail himself of substituted service by ñailing and mailing,' a party must make diligent attempts at prior service under paragraphs 1 *and* 2, rather than under paragraphs 1, 2 *or* 3, as at present . . .

"In addition, minor verbal improvements would be made in paragraph 4 . . .

"A similar change is proposed in paragraph 5, to allow the use of a special mode of service according to court order where diligent attempts have failed under paragraphs 1, 2 *and* 4, rather than under paragraphs 1, 2, 3 *or* 4, as at present.

"Paragraphs 1 and 2 would be amended to add the disjunctive word òr' at the end of each, to clarify that paragraphs 1, 2 or 3 offer alternatives for effecting service and that each of the specified modes can be used as a first preference.

"Paragraph 2 would also be made stylistically consistent with paragraph 4 by changing the word àddress' therein to ̀residence.' "

### 1970 AMENDMENTS

L. 1970, ch. 852, eff. Sept. 1, 1970, repealed former CPLR 308 and inserted a new section 308.

### 1968 AMENDMENTS

L. 1968, ch. 276, eff. Sept. 1, 1968, amended Subd. (3) [now (4)] to require that proof of substituted service be filed within twenty days after such service.

## § 309. Personal service upon an infant, incompetent or conservatee.

(a) Upon an infant. Personal service upon an infant shall be made by personally serving the summons within the state upon a parent or any guardian or any person having legal custody or, if the infant is married, upon an adult spouse with whom the infant resides, or, if none are within the state, upon any other person with whom he resides, or by whom he is employed. If the infant is of the age of fourteen years or over, the summons shall also be personally served upon him within the state.

(b) Upon a person judicially declared to be incompetent. Personal service upon a person judicially declared to be incompetent to manage his affairs and for whom a committee has been appointed shall be made by personally serving the summons within the state upon the committee and upon the incompetent, but the court may dispense with service upon the incompetent.

(c) Upon a conservatee. Personal service on a person for whom a conservator has been appointed shall be made by personally serving the summons within the state upon the conservator and upon the conservatee, but the court may dispense with service upon the conservatee.

### CROSS REFERENCES

If defendant is a patient of any hospital, school or alcoholism facility as defined **Mental Hygiene Law §** 1.05; see **14 N.Y.C.R.R. §** 22.2 regarding service of process.

### 1981 AMENDMENTS

L. 1981, ch. 115, eff. May 18, 1981, added a new subdivision (c).

1968 AMENDMENTS

L. 1968, ch. 844, eff. Sept. 1, 1968, amended Subd. (a) by expanding the category
of persons upon whom service of a summons must be made in place of an infant.

## § 310.   Personal service upon a partnership.

(a) Personal service upon persons conducting a business as a partnership may
be made by personally serving the summons upon any one of them.

(b) Personal service upon said partnership may also be made within the state
by delivering the summons to the managing or general agent of the partnership
or the person in charge of the office of the partnership within the state at such
office and by either mailing the summons to the partner thereof intended to be
served by first class mail to his last known residence or to the place of business
of the partnership. Proof of such service shall be filed within twenty days with
the clerk of the court designated in the summons; service shall be complete ten
days after such filing; proof of service shall identify the person to whom the
summons was so delivered and state the date, time of day and place of service.

(c) Where service under subdivisions (a) and (b) of this section cannot be
made with due diligence, it may be made by affixing a copy of the summons
to the door of the actual place of business of the partnership within the state
and by either mailing the summons by first class mail to the partner intended
to be so served to such person to his last known residence or to said person
at the office of said partnership within the state. Proof of such service shall be
filed within twenty days thereafter with the clerk of the court designated in the
summons; service shall be complete ten days after filing.

(d) Personal service on such partnership may also be made by delivering the
summons to any other agent or employee of the partnership authorized by
appointment to receive service; or to any other person designated by the
partnership to receive process in writing, filed in the office of the clerk of the
county wherein such partnership is located.

(e) If service is impracticable under subdivisions (a), (b) and (c) of this section,
it may be made in such manner as the court, upon motion without notice directs.

### CROSS REFERENCES

See also **General Associations Law** §§ 12, 13 as to service upon unincorporated
associations in Appendix, *infra*.

See **Partnership Law** § 120-g regarding service on a foreign limited partnership.

1991 AMENDMENTS

L. 1991, ch. 338, eff. July 15, 1991, relettered as subdivision (a) the first
undesignated paragraph and deleted the phrase "within the state" following the word
"summons," and added new subdivisions (b), (c), (d) and (e).

## § 311.*    Personal service upon a corporation or governmental subdivision.

(a) Personal service upon a corporation or governmental subdivision shall be made by delivering the summons as follows:

1. upon any domestic or foreign corporation, to an officer, director, managing or general agent, or cashier or assistant cashier or to any other agent authorized by appointment or by law to receive service;

2. upon the city of New York, to the corporation counsel or to any person designated to receive process in a writing filed in the office of the clerk of New York county;

3. upon any other city, to the mayor, comptroller, treasurer, counsel or clerk; or, if the city lacks such officers, to an officer performing a corresponding function under another name;

4. upon a county, to the chair or clerk of the board of supervisors, clerk, attorney or treasurer;

5. upon a town, to the supervisor or the clerk;

6. upon a village, to the mayor, clerk, or any trustee;

7. upon a school district, to a school officer, as defined in the education law; and

8. upon a park, sewage or other district, to the clerk, any trustee or any member of the board.

(b) If service upon a domestic or foreign corporation in time to secure and file the proof of service called for by subdivision (a) of section three hundred six-b of this article is impracticable under paragraph one of subdivision (a) of this section or any other law, service upon the corporation may be made in such manner, and proof of service may take such form, as the court, upon motion without notice, directs.

> \* **[Editor's note:** This version of § 311 is effective as of January 1, 1997. Through December 31, 1996, former § 311 remains in effect. It reads as follows:
>
> Personal service upon a corporation or governmental subdivision shall be made by delivering the summons as follows:
>
> 1. upon any domestic or foreign corporation, to an officer, director, managing or general agent, or cashier or assistant cashier or to any other agent authorized by appointment or by law to receive service;
>
> 2. upon the city of New York, to the corporation counsel or to any person designated by him to receive process in a writing filed in the office of the clerk of New York county;
>
> 3. upon any other city, to the mayor, comptroller, treasurer, counsel or clerk; or, if the city lacks such officers, to an officer performing a corresponding function under another name;
>
> 4. upon a county, to the chairman or clerk of the board of supervisors, clerk, attorney or treasurer;

5. upon a town, to the supervisor or the clerk;

6. upon a village, to the mayor, clerk, or any trustee;

7. upon a school district, to a school officer, as defined in the education law; and

8. upon a park, sewage or other district, to the clerk, any trustee or any member of the board.]

### CROSS REFERENCES

See **B.C.L.** §§ **304, 306 and 307,** in Appendix, *infra* , as to service upon secretary of state or other designated agent of corporation.

See **General Municipal Law** §§ **50-e, 50-h and 50-i** , in Appendix, *infra,* as to notice of claim against public corporation or officer.

See **Education Law** § **2, paragraph 13,** in Appendix, *infra* , for definition of "school officer," referred to in paragraph 7, *supra.*

See **Insurance Law** §§ **59 and 59a** for service on the Superintendent of Insurance as attorney for authorized and unauthorized insurers.

### 1996 AMENDMENTS

L. 1996, ch. 337, eff. Jan. 1, 1997, amended the section by numbering the opening paragraph as subdivision (a); adding new subdivision (b) governing situations where service under subdivision (a) is impracticable; and making the section gender neutral.

### 1977 AMENDMENTS

L. 1977, ch. 17, eff. March 22, 1977, amended paragraph 8 by striking the reference to a "school" district. A 1976 amendment enacted paragraph 7 to govern service upon a school district.

### 1976 AMENDMENTS

L. 1976, ch. 745, eff. Sept. 1, 1976, added paragraph (7) to CPLR 311 and renumbered accordingly.

Amendment recommended by the Judicial Conference in its Report to the 1976 Legislature, in which it stated:

"The purpose of the proposed amendment is to broaden the category of persons designated by law as persons to whom a summons, and thus a notice of claim, in a Supreme Court action against a school district may be delivered to include those identified in section 2 of the Education Law. By so doing, notice to school officers to whom parents are most likely to give notice will constitute effective notice, thereby avoiding results like that Mr. Justice Bernard S. Meyer felt compelled to reach in *Bayer* v. *Board of Education,* 58 Misc. 2d 259 (Sup. Ct. Nassau Co. 1968). In that case a letter stating a claim was timely served upon the superintendent of schools but the action was dismissed because the superintendent was not one of those identified by statute as a person upon whom service could be made. The recommended change adopts one of the solutions suggested by Mr. Justice Meyer in his decision."

## § 312.   Personal service upon a court, board or commission.

Personal service upon a court consisting of three or more judges may be made by delivering the summons to any one of them. Personal service upon a board or commission having a chairman or other presiding officer, secretary or clerk, by whatever official title he is called, may be made by delivering the summons to him. Personal service upon a board or commission of a town or village may also be made by delivering the summons to the clerk of the town or village. Personal service upon any other board or commission shall be made by delivering the summons to any one of the members.

### 1987 AMENDMENTS

> L. 1987, ch. 109, eff. June 8, 1987, added the provision that personal service upon a board of commission of a town or village may also be made by delivering the summons to the clerk of the town or village.

### § 312-a.  Personal service by mail.

(a) Service. As an alternative to the methods of personal service authorized by section 307, 308, 310, 311 or 312 of this article, a summons and complaint, or summons and notice, or notice of petition and petition may be served by the plaintiff or any other person by mailing to the person or entity to be served, by first class mail, postage prepaid, a copy of the summons and complaint, or summons and notice or notice of petition and petition, together with two copies of a statement of service by mail and acknowledgment of receipt in the form set forth in subdivision (d) of this section, with a return envelope, postage prepaid, addressed to the sender.

(b) Completion of service and time to answer. 1. The defendant, an authorized employee of the defendant, defendant's attorney or an employee of the attorney must complete the acknowledgement of receipt and mail or deliver one copy of it within thirty (30) days from the date of receipt. Service is complete on the date the signed acknowledgment of receipt is mailed or delivered to the sender. The signed acknowledgment of receipt shall constitute proof of service.

2. Where a complaint or petition is served with the summons or notice of petition, the defendant shall serve an answer within twenty (20) days after the date the signed acknowledgement of receipt is mailed or delivered to the sender.

(c) Affirmation. The acknowledgement of receipt of service shall be subscribed and affirmed as true under penalties of perjury and shall have the same force and effect as an affidavit.

(d) Form. The statement of service by mail and the acknowledgement of receipt of such service shall be in substantially the following form:

Statement of Service by Mail and
Acknowledgment of Receipt by Mail of
Summons and Complaint or Summons and Notice
or Notice of Petition and Petition

A. Statement of service
by mail

To: (Insert the name and address of the person or entity to be served.) The enclosed summons and complaint, or summons and notice, or notice of petition and petition (strike out inapplicable terms) are served pursuant to section 312-a of the Civil Practice Law and Rules.

To avoid being charged with the expense of service upon you, you must sign, date and complete the acknowledgment part of this form and mail or deliver one copy of the completed form to the sender within thirty (30) days from the date you receive it. You should keep a copy for your records or your attorney. If you wish to consult an attorney, you should do so as soon as possible before the thirty (30) days expire.

If you do not complete and return the form to the sender within thirty (30) days, you (or the party on whose behalf you are being served) will be required to pay expenses incurred in serving the summons and complaint, or summons and notice, or notice of petition and petition in any other manner permitted by law, and the cost of such service as permitted by law will be entered as a judgment against you.

If you have received a complaint or petition with this statement, the return of this statement and acknowledgment does not relieve you of the necessity to answer the complaint or petition. The time to answer expires twenty (20) days after the day you mail or deliver this form to the sender. If you wish to consult with an attorney, you should do so as soon as possible before the twenty (20) days expire.

If you are served on behalf of a corporation, unincorporated association, partnership or other entity, you must indicate under your signature your relationship to the entity. If you are served on behalf of another person and you are authorized to receive process, you must indicate under your signature your authority.

It is a crime to forge a signature or to make a false entry on this statement or on the acknowledgment.

## B. ACKNOWLEDGMENT OF RECEIPT OF SUMMONS AND COMPLAINT
## OR SUMMONS AND NOTICE OR NOTICE OF PETITION AND PETITION

I received a summons and complaint, or summons and notice, or notice of petition and petition (strike out inapplicable terms) in the above-captioned matter at (insert address). PLEASE CHECK ONE OF THE FOLLOWING:

IF 2 IS CHECKED, COMPLETE AS INDICATED:

    1.   ☐   I am not in military service.

    2.   ☐   I am in military service, and my rank, serial number and branch of service are as follows:

Rank . . . . . . . .

Serial number . . . . . . . .

Branch of Service . . . . . . . .

### TO BE COMPLETED REGARDLESS OF MILITARY STATUS:

Date: . . . . . . . .
    (Date this Acknowledgment is executed)
I affirm the above as true under penalty of perjury.

. . . . . . . . . . . . . .
Signature

. . . . . . . . . . . . . .
Print name

. . . . . . . . . . . . .
Name of Defendant for which acting

Position with Defendant for which acting (i.e., officer, attorney, etc.)

### PLEASE COMPLETE ALL BLANKS INCLUDING DATES

(e) Subsequent service. Where a duly executed acknowledgment is not returned, upon the subsequent service of process in another manner permitted by law, the summons or notice of petition or paper served with the summons or notice of petition shall indicate that an attempt previously was made to effect service pursuant to this section.

CPLR

(f) Disbursements. Where the signed acknowledgment of receipt is not returned within thirty (30) days after receipt of the documents mailed pursuant to subdivision (a) of this section, the reasonable expense of serving process by an alternative method shall be taxed by the court on notice pursuant to section 8402 of this chapter as a disbursement to the party serving process, and the court shall direct immediate judgment in that amount.

### 1996 AMENDMENTS

L. 1996, ch. 368, eff. July 30, 1996, amended subdivision (a) by deleting the phrase ", an authorized employee of the plaintiff, the plaintiff's attorney or an employee of the attorney" and replacing it with the words "or any other person."

### 1993 AMENDMENTS

L. 1993, ch. 459, eff. Jan. 1, 1994, amended CPLR 312-a by adding the words "an authorized employee of the plaintiff" to subdivision (a); by adding the words "an authorized employee of the defendant" and the number "30" to subdivision (b); by changing "a copy" in subdivision (b) to "one copy"; by adding the number "20 to subdivision (b)(2); by adding the letter "A." before the words "STATEMENT OF SERVICE BY MAIL" in subdivision (d); by adding the words "strike out inapplicable terms" to subdivision (d); by adding the sentence beginning "You should keep a copy ..." to subdivision (d); by replacing "may" with "will" immediately preceding "be required to pay expenses incurred in serving the summons ..." in subdivision (d); by replacing "may" with "will" immediately preceding "be entered as a judgment against you" in subdivision (d); by deleting lines for the insertion of the signature, printed name, and address immediately following the sentence beginning "It is a crime to ..." in subdivision (d); by adding the letter "B." before "ACKNOWLEDGMENT OF RECEIPT ..." in subdivision (d); by adding the words "strike out inapplicable terms" to the sentence beginning "I received a summons ..." in subdivision (d); by adding the words "TO BE COMPLETED REGARDLESS OF MILITARY STATUS:" in subdivision (d); by replacing the words "Relationship to entity/Authority to Receive Service of Process" in subdivision (d) with the words "Name Of Defendant For Which Acting/Position With Defendant For Which Acting (i.e. Officer, Attorney, etc.)"; by adding the words "Please Complete All Blanks Including Dates" in subdivision (d); by adding to subdivision (f) the words "on notice pursuant to section 8402 of this chapter"; and replacing in subdivision (f) the words "if that party is awarded costs in the action or proceeding" with "and the court shall direct immediate judgment in that amount."

### 1992 AMENDMENTS

L. 1992, ch. 216, eff. July 1, 1992, amended subdivision (b)(1) by deleting from the beginning of the second sentence the words "An action is commenced and service" and replacing them with the word "Service."

### 1991 AMENDMENTS

L. 1991, ch. 249, eff. July 1, 1991, deleted the Jan. 1, 1992 repeal date.

### 1989 AMENDMENTS

L. 1989, ch. 274, eff. Jan. 1, 1990 until Jan.1, 1992, added a trial period for effectuating personal service by mail.

**CROSS REFERENCES**

Conforming amendments were also enacted to several court acts; *see* **Civil Practice Annual of New York (Matthew Bender):** the Uniform District Court Act, the New York City Civil Court Act, the Uniform City Court Act and the Uniform Justice Court Act, *see also* proof of service amendment to CPLR 306, *supra.* Enacting language mandated that the "chief administrator of the courts shall monitor and survey the cost of personal service following the effective date of this act and shall report findings with respect thereto, including appropriate recommendations to the legislature and the governor, on or before April 1, 1991."

## § 313.   Service without the state giving personal jurisdiction.

A person domiciled in the state or subject to the jurisdiction of the courts of the state under section 301 or 302, or his executor or administrator, may be served with the summons without the state, in the same manner as service is made within the state, by any person authorized to make service within the state who is a resident of the state or by any person authorized to make service by the laws of the state, territory, possession or country in which service is made or by any duly qualified attorney, solicitor, barrister, or equivalent in such jurisdiction.

## § 314.   Service without the state not giving personal jurisdiction in certain actions.

Service may be made without the state by any person authorized by section 313 in the same manner as service is made within the state:

1. in a matrimonial action; or

2. where a judgment is demanded that the person to be served be excluded from a vested or contingent interest in or lien upon specific real or personal property within the state; or that such an interest or lien in favor of either party be enforced, regulated, defined or limited; or otherwise affecting the title to such property, including an action of interpleader or defensive interpleader; or

3. where a levy upon property of the person to be served has been made within the state pursuant to an order of attachment or a chattel of such person has been seized in an action to recover a chattel.

## § 315.   Service by publication authorized.

The court, upon motion without notice, shall order service of a summons by publication in an action described in section 314 if service cannot be made by another prescribed method with due diligence.

## R 316.   Service by publication.

(a) Contents of order; form of publication; filing. An order for service of a summons by publication shall direct that the summons be published together with the notice to the defendant, a brief statement of the nature of the action

**CPLR**

and the relief sought, and, except in an action for medical malpractice, the sum of money for which judgment may be taken in case of default and, if the action is brought to recover a judgment affecting the title to, or the possession, use or enjoyment of, real property, a brief description of the property, in two newspapers, at least one in the English language, designated in the order as most likely to give notice to the person to be served, for a specified time, at least once in each of four successive weeks, except that in a matrimonial action publication in one newspaper in the English language, designated in the order as most likely to give notice to the person to be served, at least once in each of three successive weeks shall be sufficient. The summons, complaint, or summons and notice in an action for divorce or separation, order and papers on which the order was based shall be filed on or before the first day of publication.

(b) Mailing to accompany publication in matrimonial actions. An order for service of a summons by publication in a matrimonial action shall also direct that on or before the first day of publication a copy of the summons be mailed to the person to be served unless a place where such person probably would receive mail cannot with due diligence be ascertained and the court dispenses with such mailing. A notice of publication shall be enclosed.

(c) Time of publication; when service complete. The first publication of the summons shall be made within thirty days after the order is granted. Service by publication is complete on the twenty-eighth day after the day of first publication, except that in a matrimonial action it is complete on the twenty-first day after the day of first publication.

### 1979 AMENDMENTS

L. 1979, ch. 191, eff. Jan. 1, 1980, amended CPLR 316 subd. (c) by changing the time within which first publication of the summons must be made from 20 to 30 days from the granting of the order.

The Judicial Conference Report on the CPLR to the 1979 Legislature noted that the twenty day period is unduly short and that: ". . . There is some judicial authority to the effect that the present 20 day period is jurisdictional so that if plaintiff makes the first publication on the twenty-first day no jurisdiction will be acquired (*Caton v. Caton*, 72 Misc. 2d 544 (Sup. Ct. Monroe Co. 1972))."

### 1978 AMENDMENTS

L. 1978, ch. 528, eff. Jan. 1, 1979, amended subd. (a) to conform the notice provisions therein to analogous provisions in CPLR 305(b), as amended. See 1978 amendment note under CPLR 305, *supra,* for detailed Judicial Conference commentary on the amendment.

### 1972 AMENDMENTS

Proposal No. 1 made by the Judicial Conference Report to the 1972 Legislature amended Subd. (c), eff. Sept. 1, 1972, by adding to the second sentence thereof the clause, "except that in a matrimonial action it is complete on the twenty-first day after the day of first publication."

### 1970 AMENDMENTS

Proposal No. 1 made by Judicial Conference Jan. 2, 1970 Report to the 1970 Legislature, eff. Sept. 1, 1970: Subd. (a) amended by adding to the first sentence thereof, the clause, "except that in a matrimonial action publication in one newspaper in the English language, designated in the order as most likely to give notice to the person to be served, at least once in each of three successive weeks shall be sufficient."

### 1969 AMENDMENTS

L. 1969, ch. 274, eff. Sept. 1, 1969, amended Subd. (a) by adding that ". . . summons and notice in an action for divorce or separation" shall be filed on or before the first day of publication.

## § 317. Defense by person to whom summons not personally delivered.

A person served with a summons other than by personal delivery to him or to his agent for service designated under rule 318, within or without the state, who does not appear may be allowed to defend the action within one year after he obtains knowledge of entry of the judgment, but in no event more than five years after such entry, upon a finding of the court that he did not personally receive notice of the summons in time to defend and has a meritorious defense. If the defense is successful, the court may direct and enforce restitution in the same manner and subject to the same conditions as where a judgment is reversed or modified on appeal. This section does not apply to an action for divorce, annulment or partition.

### 1964 AMENDMENTS

L. 1964, ch. 388, eff. Sept. 1, 1964, substituted "section" in place of "rule" in last sentence.

## R 318. Designation of agent for service.

A person may be designated by a natural person, corporation or partnership as an agent for service in a writing, executed and acknowledged in the same manner as a deed, with the consent of the agent endorsed thereon. The writing shall be filed in the office of the clerk of the county in which the principal to be served resides or has its principal office. The designation shall remain in effect for three years from such filing unless it has been revoked by the filing of a revocation, or by the death, judicial declaration of incompetency or legal termination of the agent or principal.

### 1987 AMENDMENTS

L. 1987, ch. 788, eff. Nov. 5, 1987, and applicable only to designations filed on and after such date, amended CPLR 318 to provide that a writing designating an agent for service be "executed and acknowledged in the same manner as a deed."

§ 319.  [Not used].

## R 320.  Defendant's appearance.

(a) Requirement of appearance. The defendant appears by serving an answer or a notice of appearance, or by making a motion which has the effect of extending the time to answer. An appearance shall be made within twenty days after service of the summons, except that if the summons was served on the defendant by delivering it to an official of the state authorized to receive service in his behalf or if it was served pursuant to section 303, subdivision two, three, four or five of section 308, or sections 313, 314 or 315, the appearance shall be made within thirty days after service is complete. If the complaint is not served with the summons, the time to appear may be extended as provided in subdivision (b) of section 3012.

(b) When appearance confers personal jurisdiction, generally. Subject to the provisions of subdivision (c), an appearance of the defendant is equivalent to personal service of the summons upon him, unless an objection to jurisdiction under paragraph eight of subdivision (a) of rule 3211 is asserted by motion or in the answer as provided in rule 3211.

(c) When appearance confers personal jurisdiction, in certain actions; limited appearance. When the court's jurisdiction is not based upon personal service on the defendant, an appearance is not equivalent to personal service upon the defendant:

1. in a case specified in subdivision (3) of section 314, if jurisdiction is based solely upon a levy on defendant's property within the state pursuant to an order of attachment; or

2. in any other case specified in section 314 if an objection to jurisdiction under paragraphs eight or nine of subdivision (a) of rule 3211, or both, is asserted by motion or in the answer as provided in rule 3211, unless the defendant proceeds with the defense after asserting the objection to jurisdiction and the objection is not ultimately sustained.

(d) Appearance after first publication. Where the defendant appears during the period of publication of a summons against him, the service by publication shall be deemed completed by the appearance.

### 1978 AMENDMENTS

L. 1978, ch. 528, eff. Jan. 1, 1979, amended subdivision (a) of CPLR 320 by adding the final sentence making cross-reference to CPLR 3012(b), which, as amended, grants an extension of time to appear to a defendant who makes a timely demand for the complaint. See 1978 amendment note under CPLR 3012, *infra,* for detailed Judicial Conference commentary on the amendment.

### 1970 AMENDMENTS

L. 1970, ch. 852, eff. Sept. 1, 1970, amended Subd. (a) by adding reference to CPLR 308(5).

## 1969 AMENDMENTS

Amendment No. 1 made by Judicial Conference Feb. 1, 1969, Report to the 1969 Legislature, effective Sept. 1, 1969: Subd. (c) amended.

The Judicial Conference Report stated, in part:

". . . subdivision (c) of Rule 320 of the CPLR [is] amended by incorporating therein a provision for a limited appearance in attachment-based cases. The amendment would provide that in cases where jurisdiction is based solely on a levy on defendant's property within the state pursuant to an order of attachment, defendant's appearance is not equivalent to personal service on the defendant. In any other case where the defendant is subject to the court's in rem jurisdiction under CPLR 314, the existing provisions of Rule 320 (c) which prohibit a limited appearance, would remain unchanged. . . .

". . . it should be noted that the proposed amendment of Rule 320 (c) operates automatically. No notice of a limited appearance would be required. The automatic operation of the amendment parallels CPLR 302 (b) [now 302(c)] which, notwithstanding defendant's appearance, automatically restricts a plaintiff to the prosecution of claims covered by the long-arm statute. . . .

"The Committee is fully aware that problems of res judicata (collateral estoppel) are bound to arise as a result of the proposed amendment. It will be the traditional task of the courts to work out these problems on a case by case basis, keeping in mind the general purpose and intent of the proposed amendment."

## 1965 AMENDMENTS

Amendment No. 2 made by Judicial Conference Feb. 1, 1965, Report to the Legislature, effective Sept. 1, 1965, added the words "as provided in rule 3211" at end of Subd. (b) for the reason: "The present language of subdivision (b) appears to contravene the traditional policy of favoring the disposition of jurisdictional defenses before defenses going to the merits. The consequences may be highly undesirable. The court may be required to determine issues going to the merits, possibly in favor of the plaintiff, even in a case where later jurisdictional objection by the defendant would necessitate dismissal.

"If such later jurisdictional objection were sustained after a ruling on a defense on the merits adverse to the defendant, a serious problem of *res judicata* would be involved in a second action with the same parties based on the same cause. It is far from clear whether or not a re-litigation of the same defense on the merits would be permitted on the ground that the determination thereof in the first action is void because rendered by a court not having jurisdiction.

"A solution to this dilemma is recommended by way of an amendment to 3211(e) [*infra* ] to which the proposed amendment of 320(b) makes reference and is ancillary."

Amendment No. 3 made by Judicial Conference Feb. 1, 1965, Report to the Legislature, effective Sept. 1, 1965, deleted the words "at the time of appearance" appearing before "by motion or in the answer" and added the words "as provided in rule 3211" after words "by motion or in the answer" in Subd. (c).

See further discussion in 1965 Amendments to Rule 3211, *infra.*

## 1964 AMENDMENTS

Amendment No. 1 made by Judicial Conference Feb. 1, 1964, Report to the Legislature, effective Sept. 1, 1964: Words "at the time of appearance" appearing before "by motion or in the answer" in Subd. (b) deleted for the reason "The requirement that an objection to jurisdiction of the person of the defendant must be asserted àt the time of appearance' in order to be effective is inconsistent with rule

CPLR

3211(e) and may prove a trap for the unwary. In order to avoid such an unintended result the proposed change should be made."

## § 321.  Attorneys.

(a) Appearance in person or by attorney. A party, other than one specified in section 1201 of this chapter, may prosecute or defend a civil action in person or by attorney, except that a corporation or voluntary association shall appear by attorney, except as otherwise provided in sections 1809 and 1809–A of the New York city civil court act, sections 1809 and 1809–A of the uniform district court act and sections 1809 and 1809–A of the uniform city court act, and except as otherwise provided in section 501 and section 1809 of the uniform justice court act. If a party appears by attorney such party may not act in person in the action except by consent of the court.

(b) Change or withdrawal of attorney. 1. Unless the party is a person specified in section 1201, an attorney of record may be changed by filing with the clerk a consent to the change signed by the retiring attorney and signed and acknowledged by the party. Notice of such change of attorney shall be given to the attorneys for all parties in the action or, if a party appears without an attorney, to the party.

2. An attorney of record may withdraw or be changed by order of the court in which the action is pending, upon motion on such notice to the client of the withdrawing attorney, to the attorneys of all other parties in the action or, if a party appears without an attorney, to the party, and to any other person, as the court may direct.

(c) Death, removal or disability of attorney. If an attorney dies, becomes physically or mentally incapacitated, or is removed, suspended or otherwise becomes disabled at any time before judgment, no further proceeding shall be taken in the action against the party for whom he appeared, without leave of the court, until thirty days after notice to appoint another attorney has been served upon that party either personally or in such manner as the court directs.

### CROSS REFERENCES

**New York City Civil Court Act § 1809,** referred to in Subd. (a) governing procedures relating to corporations, insurers and assignees in small claims matters, *supra,* appears in the Appendix, *infra;* § 1809 of **U.D.C.A., U.C.C.A. and U.J.C.A.** is identical to **N.Y.C. Civ. Ct. Act § 1809.** U.J.C.A. § 501, "Appearance by Corporations," was enacted by L. 1987, ch. 653, eff. Jan. 1, 1988.

See **SCPA §§ 401 and 402** as to appearance in Surrogate's Court.

See also the "Commercial Claims" provisions of **N.Y.C. Civ. Ct. Act Art. 18-A** (L. 1987, ch. 653, eff. Jan. 1, 1991), **U.D.C.A. Art. 18-A** (L. 1987, ch. 653, eff. Jan. 1, 1989), and **U.C.C.A. Art. 18-A** (L. 1987, ch. 653, eff. Jan. 1, 1989), governing actions for money not in excess of $1,500, where the claimant is a corporation, partnership or association.

### 1991 AMENDMENTS

L. 1991, ch. 236, eff. July 1, 1991, amended subdivision (a) by adding references to sections 1809 and 1809-A of the N.Y.C. Civ. Ct. Act, the U.D.C.A. and the U.C.C.A.

### 1987 AMENDMENTS

L. 1987, ch. 653, eff. Jan. 1, 1988, amended subdivision (a) to add references to sections 501 and 1809 of the uniform justice court act.

### 1980 AMENDMENTS

L. 1980, ch. 119, eff. Jan. 1, 1981, amended CPLR 321(b) by adding new paragraph 2 clarifying the procedure for change or withdrawal of an attorney in a pending action and altering the language of paragraph 1 to reflect the change.

In its report to the 1980 Legislature, the Judicial Conference noted that new paragraph 2 ". . . sets forth that the procedure for the change shall be a mere motion, thus clarifying that a special proceeding need not be brought for this purpose. And rather than attempt to set forth whom to notify, the amendment leaves it to the court to determine. It does this by requiring the motion to be òn such notice to such persons as the court may direct,' i.e., it contemplates the procedure of an order to show cause. This will enable the court to determine, on a case by case basis, who shall be notified, and how. There may be many parties, and the action may have been quiescent for a time. Leaving it to the court to determine whom to notify, and by what method, permits the factors applicable to the individual case to be weighed."

### 1976 AMENDMENTS

L. 1976, ch. 200, eff. Sept. 1, 1976, amended Subd. (a) of CPLR 321 by eliminating a provision governing appearance of closely held corporations by an officer or shareholder in defense of small claims actions; the act transferred that provision, without change in substance, to § 1809 of the various court acts, with an appropriate cross-reference in CPLR 321 (a).

### 1975 AMENDMENTS

L. 1975, ch. 176, eff. Sept. 1, 1975, amended Subd. (a) by adding a provision permitting defense of small claims actions by shareholders or officers of certain closely held corporations.

### 1964 AMENDMENTS

L. 1964, ch. 511, eff. Sept. 1, 1964, added to subdivision (b): "Notice of such change of attorney shall be given to the attorney for all parties in the action or if a party appears without an attorney to the party."

## R 322.   Authority for appearance of attorney in real property action.

(a) Authority of plaintiff's attorney. Where the defendant in an action affecting real property has not been served with evidence of the authority of the plaintiff's attorney to begin the action, he may move at any time before answering for an order directing the production of such evidence. Any writing by the plaintiff or his agent requesting the attorney to begin the action or ratifying his conduct of the action on behalf of the plaintiff is prima facie evidence of the attorney's authority.

CPLR

(b) Authority of non-resident defendant's attorney. The attorney for a non-resident defendant in an action affecting real property shall file with the clerk written authority for his appearance, executed and acknowledged in the form required to entitle a deed to be recorded, and shall serve either a copy of such authority or notice of such filing on the plaintiff's attorney within twenty days after appearing or making a motion.

(c) Agencies or wholly-owned corporations of the United States. This rule does not apply to an attorney representing an official, agency or instrumentality of, or corporation wholly owned by, the United States.

## §§ 323-324. [Not used].

## § 325. Grounds for removal.

(a) By supreme court for mistake in choice of the court. Where a mistake was made in the choice of the court in which an action is commenced, the supreme court, upon motion, may remove the action to the proper court, upon such terms as may be just.

(b) From court of limited jurisdiction. Where it appears that the court in which an action is pending does not have jurisdiction to grant the relief to which the parties are entitled, a court having such jurisdiction may remove the action to itself upon motion. A waiver of jury trial in the first court is inoperative after the removal.

(c) On consent to court of limited jurisdiction. Where it appears that the amount of damages sustained are less than demanded, and a lower court would have had jurisdiction of the action but for the amount of damages demanded, the court in which an action is pending may remove it to the lower court upon reduction of the amount of damages demanded to a sum within the jurisdictional limits of the lower court and upon consent of all parties to the action other than a defendant who has interposed no counterclaim and over whom the lower court would have had jurisdiction if the action had originally been commenced there. A waiver of jury trial in the first court is inoperative after the removal.

(d) Without consent to court of limited jurisdiction. The appellate division, if it determines that the calendar conditions in a lower court so permit, may by rule provide that a court in which an action is pending may, in its discretion, remove such action without consent to such lower court where it appears that the amount of damages sustained may be less than demanded, and the lower court would have had jurisdiction but for the amount of damages demanded. If the action is so removed, then the verdict or judgment shall be subject to the limitation of monetary jurisdiction of the court in which the action was originally commenced and shall be lawful to the extent of the amount demanded within such limitation. A waiver of jury trial in the first court is inoperative after the removal.

(e) From supreme court to surrogate's court where decedent's estate affected. Where an action pending in the supreme court affects the administration of a decedent's estate which is within the jurisdiction of the surrogate's court, the supreme court, upon motion, may remove the action to such surrogate's court upon the prior order of the surrogate's court. The right of jury trial shall be preserved in the subsequent proceedings.

(f) To supreme court where county judge incapacitated. Where a county judge is incapable of acting in an action pending in the county court, the supreme court may remove the action to itself. An objection to jurisdiction that might have been taken in the county court may be taken in the supreme court after the removal.

(g) From one local court to another. Where it is unlikely that an action or proceeding pending in a district court, town court, village court or city court will be disposed of within a reasonable period of time because of (i) death, disability or other incapacity or disqualification of all the judges of such court, or (ii) inability of such court to form a jury in such action or proceeding, a judge of the county court of the county in which such lower court is located, may, upon motion of any party to such action or proceeding, order that it be transferred for disposition by the lower court to any other district court, town court, village court or city court in the same or an adjoining county, provided that such other court has jurisdiction of the subject matter of the action or proceeding and jurisdiction over the classes of persons named as parties.

### CROSS REFERENCES

See Appendix, *infra,* for **Constitutional and Judiciary Law** provisions as to subject matter jurisdiction, generally; note particularly **Section 19** of **Article VI** of the **New York State Constitution** as to transfer of actions and proceedings.

### 1988 AMENDMENTS

L. 1988, ch. 397, eff. July 1, 1988, added new subdivision (g) permitting removal from one local (*i.e.*, district, town, village, or city) court to another in the same or an adjoining county, when (i) all judges in the transferring court are unavailable, or (ii) a jury cannot be impaneled in the transferring county.

### 1968 AMENDMENTS

L. 1968, ch. 502, eff. Sept. 1, 1968, added present Subd. (d) and relettered former Subds. (d) and (e) to be Subd. (e) and (f) respectively.

### 1966 AMENDMENTS

L. 1966, ch. 961, amended Subd. (e) by deleting "of the county of Bronx, Kings, Nassau, New York, Queens, Richmond or Westchester" following the phrase "jurisdiction of the surrogate's court" found in the first sentence, effective Sept. 1, 1967, thereby making the provision applicable to all surrogate's courts.

## R 326. Procedure on removal.

(a) Stay of proceedings. An order to stay proceedings for the purpose of moving for removal may be made by the court in which the action is pending or the court to which removal is sought.

(b) Order and subsequent proceedings. Where an order of removal is made by a court other than the court in which the action is pending, a certified copy of the order shall be filed with the clerk of the court in which the action is pending. Upon such filing or upon entry of an order of removal by him, the clerk of the court in which an action is pending shall forthwith deliver to the clerk of the court to which it has been ordered removed all papers and records in the action and certified copies of all minutes and entries which shall be filed, entered or recorded, as the case requires, in the office of the latter clerk. Subsequent proceedings shall be had in the court to which it has been ordered removed as if the action had been originally commenced there and no process, provisional remedy or other proceeding taken in the court from which the action was removed shall be invalid as the result of the removal.

(c) Fees and disbursements. If at the time the order of removal is entered any filing, trial, or jury demand fees have been paid, such fees shall be credited against the fees which, for the same purpose, shall be required in the court to which the action has been ordered removed. A party entitled to tax disbursements after the removal may include fees paid by him prior to the time the order of removal is entered.

### 1964 AMENDMENTS

Amendment No. 2 made by the Judicial Conference Feb. 1, 1964, Report to the Legislature, effective Sept. 1, 1964, rephrased the first sentence of Subd. (c).

## R 327. Inconvenient forum.

(a) When the court finds that in the interest of substantial justice the action should be heard in another forum, the court, on the motion of any party, may stay or dismiss the action in whole or in part on any conditions that may be just. The domicile or residence in this state of any party to the action shall not preclude the court from staying or dismissing the action.

(b) Notwithstanding the provisions of subdivision (a) of this rule, the court shall not stay or dismiss any action on the ground of inconvenient forum, where the action arises out of or relates to a contract, agreement or undertaking to which section 5-1402 of the general obligations law applies, and the parties to the contract have agreed that the law of this state shall govern their rights or duties in whole or in part.

### CROSS REFERENCES

General Obligations Law § 5-1402, dealing with the enforceability of choice of forum clauses, appears in the Appendix, *infra*.

**CPLR**

### 1984 AMENDMENTS

Subdivision (b) was added by L. 1984, ch. 421, eff. July 19, 1984. Subdivision (b) is applicable to contracts entered into after July 19, 1984 and to contracts entered into on or before July 19, 1984 in connection with any action or proceeding commenced on or after that date.

### 1972 AMENDMENTS

Rule 327 was added to the CPLR by Proposal No. 2 of the Judicial Conference Report to the 1972 Legislature, effective Sept. 1, 1972.

## R 328. Assistance to tribunals and litigants outside the state.

(a) Pursuant to court order. Upon application by any interested person or in response to letters rogatory issued by a tribunal outside the state, the supreme court or a county court of the state may order service upon any person who is domiciled or can be found within the state of any document issued in connection with a proceeding in a tribunal outside the state. The order shall direct the manner of service.

(b) Without court order. Service in connection with a proceeding in a tribunal outside the state may be made within the state without an order of court.

(c) Effect. Service under this rules does not, of itself, require the recognition or enforcement of an order, judgment or decree rendered outside the state.

### CROSS REFERENCES

See also **28 U.S.C.** § **1696** as to service by order of federal district court of documents issued in connection with proceedings in a foreign country or an international tribunal.

### 1973 AMENDMENTS

Rule 328 was added to the CPLR by proposal No. 1 of the Judicial Conference Report to the 1973 Legislature, effective Sept. 1, 1973.

The 1973 Judicial Conference Report stated:

"This proposal would adopt section 2.04 of the Uniform Interstate and International Procedure Act as CPLR Rule 328 to provide that the Supreme Court or County Courts could order service of documents originating outside New York State on persons domiciled or found within the state. It would be made clear that this would not prevent such service without court order, and that service made pursuant to the provision would not, without more, entitle out-of-state judgments based on such service to recognition. That the same assistance can be rendered pursuant to 28 U.S.C.A. § 1696 would not render the proposal superfluous, for it would reduce present expense and delay when a foreign request for assistance is addressed to a New York State court.

"Although the cases which have denied such assistance (*In re Letters Rogatory Out of First Civil Court of City of Mexico*, 261 Fed. 652 (S.D.N.Y. 1919); *Matter of Romero*, 56 Misc. 319 (Sup. Ct. N.Y. Co. 1907)) have probably lost whatever authority they once possessed, it is appropriate to dispel any doubt in this regard in view of the increasing importance of interstate and international cooperation in such matters due to the increase of litigation with cosmopolitan aspects."

# ARTICLE 4

# SPECIAL PROCEEDINGS

---

### SUMMARY OF ARTICLE

§ 401.　　Parties.
§ 402.　　Pleadings.
§ 403.　　Notice of petition; service; order to show cause.
　　　(a)　Notice of petition.
　　　(b)　Time for service of notice of petition and answer.
　　　(c)　Manner of service.
　　　(d)　Order to show cause.
§ 404.　　Objections in point of law.
　　　(a)　By respondent.
　　　(b)　By petitioner.
§ 405.　　Correction of defects in papers.
　　　(a)　Motion to correct.
　　　(b)　Time limits; pleading after disposition.
　　　(c)　Petitioner's motion.
R 406.　　Motions.
§ 407.　　Severance.
§ 408.　　Disclosure.
R 409.　　Hearing.
　　　(a)　Furnishing of papers; filing.
　　　(b)　Summary determination.
§ 410.　　Trial.
R 411.　　Judgment.

---

## § 401.　Parties.

The party commencing a special proceeding shall be styled the petitioner and any adverse party the respondent. After a proceeding is commenced, no party shall be joined or interpleaded and no third-party practice or intervention shall be allowed, except by leave of court.

## § 402.　Pleadings.

There shall be a petition, which shall comply with the requirements for a complaint in an action, and an answer where there is an adverse party. There shall be a reply to a counterclaim denominated as such and there may be a reply to new matter in the answer in any case. The court may permit such other pleadings as are authorized in an action upon such terms as it may specify. Where there is no adverse party the petition shall state the result of any prior application for similar relief and shall specify the new facts, if any, that were not previously shown.

### 1965 AMENDMENTS

L. 1965, ch. 773, eff. Sept. 1, 1965, added the words "and shall specify the new facts, if any, that were not previously shown" at the end of the section.

## § 403. Notice of petition; service; order to show cause.

(a) Notice of petition. A notice of petition shall specify the time and place of the hearing on the petition and the supporting affidavits, if any, accompanying the petition.

(b) Time for service of notice of petition and answer. A notice of petition, together with the petition and affidavits specified in the notice, shall be served on any adverse party at least eight days before the time at which the petition is noticed to be heard. An answer and supporting affidavits, if any, shall be served at least two days before such time. A reply, together with supporting affidavits, if any, shall be served at or before such time. An answer shall be served at least seven days before such time if a notice of petition served at least twelve days before such time so demands; whereupon any reply shall be served at least one day before such time.

(c) Manner of service. A notice of petition shall be served in the same manner as a summons in an action.

(d) Order to show cause. The court may grant an order to show cause to be served, in lieu of a notice of petition at a time and in a manner specified therein.

### 1988 AMENDMENT

L. 1988, ch. 761, eff. Feb. 24, 1989, amended subdivision (b) to increase the time for serving an answer and supporting affidavits from one day to two days, and to increase the time periods contained in the last sentence for service of an answer from five to seven days if a notice of petition served at least twelve days before (formerly ten days) so demands.

## § 404. Objections in point of law.

(a) By respondent. The respondent may raise an objection in point of law by setting it forth in his answer or by a motion to dismiss the petition, made upon notice within the time allowed for answer. If the motion is denied, the court may permit the respondent to answer, upon such terms as may be just; and unless the order specifies otherwise, such answer shall be served and filed within five days after service of the order with notice of entry; and the petitioner may re-notice the matter for hearing upon two days' notice , or the respondent may re-notice the matter for hearing upon service of the answer upon seven days' notice.

(b) By petitioner. The petitioner may raise an objection in point of law to new matter contained in the answer by setting it forth in his reply or by moving to strike such matter on the day the petition is noticed or re-noticed to be heard.

### 1993 AMENDMENTS

L. 1993, ch. 202, eff. July 6, 1993, amended subdivision (a) by allowing respondents to "re-notice the matter for hearing upon service of the answer upon two days' notice."

## § 405. Correction of defects in papers.

(a) Motion to correct. Either party may move to cure a defect or omission in the record, or to strike scandalous or prejudicial matter unnecessarily inserted in a pleading, or for a more definite statement of a pleading which is so vague or ambiguous that he cannot reasonably be required to frame a response.

(b) Time limits; pleading after disposition. A party shall make a motion under this section by serving a notice of motion or order to show cause within the time allowed for his responsive pleading. Unless the court so orders on motion made without notice on the ground that the party is unable to plead until the papers are corrected, the motion shall not extend the time for such responsive pleading. If the motion is granted, the party who made the motion shall serve and file his responsive pleading within five days after service of the amended pleading. If the motion is denied and the time to serve a responsive pleading has been extended, the party shall serve and file his responsive pleading within two days after service of the order denying the motion with notice of entry, unless the order specifies otherwise. A party may re-notice the matter for hearing upon two days' notice.

(c) Petitioner's motion. The petitioner may raise the objections specified in subdivision (a) in his reply or by motion on the day on which the petition has been noticed or re-noticed to be heard.

## R 406. Motions.

Motions in a special proceeding, made before the time at which the petition is noticed to be heard, shall be noticed to be heard at that time.

## § 407. Severance.

The court may at any time order a severance of a particular claim, counter-claim or cross-claim, or as to a particular party, and order that, as to such claim or party, the special proceeding continue as an action or as a separate special proceeding.

## § 408.   Disclosure.

Leave of court shall be required for disclosure except for a notice under section 3123. A notice under section 3123 may be served at any time not later than three days before the petition is noticed to be heard and the statement denying or setting forth the reasons for failing to admit or deny shall be served not later than one day before the petition is noticed to be heard, unless the court orders otherwise on motion made without notice. This section shall not be applicable to proceedings in a surrogate's court, nor to proceedings relating to express trusts pursuant to article 77, both of which shall be governed by article 31.

### 1976 AMENDMENTS

L. 1976, ch. 193, eff. Sept. 1, 1976, amended CPLR 408 to provide that the section shall not apply to proceedings relating to express trusts pursuant to Article 77, and that disclosure in such proceedings shall be governed by the general disclosure provisions of article 31.

CPLR 7701 was amended by the same chapter to provide for examination of trustees in special proceedings relating to express trusts.

Amendment of CPLR 408 and CPLR 7701 was recommended by the Judicial Conference Report to the 1976 Legislature, wherein it stated:

"This bill would conform the practice under the CPLR relating to *inter vivos* trust proceedings to that in Surrogate's Court, thus rectifying a previous legislative oversight.

"At present, by virtue of the general provisions of CPLR 408, a court order is required for disclosure in *inter vivos* trust proceedings, whereas in testamentary trust proceedings, under SCPA 2211, no such order is necessary. SCPA 2211 also provides that in testamentary trust accountings the fiduciary may be examined under oath by any party to the proceeding, either before or after filing objections. There is no comparable provision in Article 77 of the CPLR with respect to *inter vivos* trusts.

"There is no good reason why the procedure in *inter vivos* trust accountings should be different in this respect from testamentary trust accountings. The general provision in CPLR 408, which requires a court order for disclosure in all special proceedings, was originated by the revisers in order to preserve the summary nature of special proceedings. They felt that to allow disclosure on notice before the hearing would almost certainly extend the eight day notice of petition period. However, this general rule should bend to certain exceptions where examination, because of its inherent importance, should be obtainable more conveniently. Such an exception should apply when a fiduciary is making an accounting, so that interested parties may be afforded full protection. This is already the rule in testamentary trust proceedings in Surrogate's Court."

### 1964 AMENDMENTS

L. 1964, ch. 477, eff. April 10, 1964, added the sentence: "This section shall not be applicable to proceedings in a surrogate's court, which shall be governed by article 31 of this act."

# R 409.   Hearing.

(a) Furnishing of papers; filing. Upon the hearing, each party shall furnish to the court all papers served by him. The petitioner shall furnish all other papers not already in the possession of the court necessary to the consideration of the questions involved. Where such papers are in the possession of an adverse party, they shall be produced by such party at the hearing on notice served with the petition. The court may require the submission of additional proof. All papers furnished to the court shall be filed unless the court orders otherwise.

(b) Summary determination. The court shall make a summary determination upon the pleadings, papers and admissions to the extent that no triable issues of fact are raised. The court may make any orders permitted on a motion for summary judgment.

## § 410. Trial.

If triable issues of fact are raised they shall be tried forthwith and the court shall make a final determination thereon. If issues are triable of right by jury, the court shall give the parties an opportunity to demand a jury trial of such issues. Failure to make such demand within the time limited by the court, or, if no such time is limited, before trial begins, shall be deemed a waiver of the right to trial by jury.

## R 411. Judgment.

The court shall direct that a judgment be entered determining the rights of the parties to the special proceeding.

CPLR

# ARTICLE 5

# VENUE

## SUMMARY OF ARTICLE

§ 501.    Contractual provisions fixing venue.
§ 502.    Conflicting venue provisions.
§ 503.    Venue based on residence.
    (a)  Generally.
    (b)  Executor, administrator, trustee, committee, conservator, general or testamentary guardian, or receiver.
    (c)  Corporation.
    (d)  Unincorporated association, partnership, or individually-owned business.
    (e)  Assignee.
    (f)  Consumer credit transaction.
§ 504.    Actions against counties, cities, towns, villages, school districts and district corporations.
§ 505.    Actions involving public authorities.
    (a)  Generally.
    (b)  Against New York city transit authority.
§ 506.    Where special proceeding commenced.
    (a)  Generally.
    (b)  Proceeding against body or officer.
§ 507.    Real property actions.
§ 508.    Actions to recover a chattel.
§ 509.    Venue in county designated.
§ 510.    Grounds for change of place of trial.
R 511.    Change of place of trial.
    (a)  Time for motion or demand.
    (b)  Demand for change of place of trial upon ground of improper venue, where motion made.
    (c)  Stay of proceedings.
    (d)  Order, subsequent proceedings and appeal.
R 512.    Change of place of trial of action or issue triable without a jury.
§ 513.    Misplacement of venue in consumer credit transactions.

## § 501. Contractual provisions fixing venue.

Subject to the provisions of subdivision two of section 510, written agreement fixing place of trial, made before an action is commenced, shall be enforced upon a motion for change of place of trial.

## § 502. Conflicting venue provisions.

Where, because of joinder of claims or parties, there is a conflict of provisions under this article, the court, upon motion, shall order as the place of trial one proper under this article as to at least one of the parties or claims.

## § 503. Venue based on residence.

(a) Generally. Except where otherwise prescribed by law, the place of trial shall be in the county in which one of the parties resided when it was commenced; or, if none of the parties then resided in the state, in any county designated by the plaintiff. A party resident in more than one county shall be deemed a resident of each such county.

(b) Executor, administrator, trustee, committee, conservator, general or testamentary guardian, or receiver. An executor, administrator, trustee, committee, conservator, general or testamentary guardian, or receiver shall be deemed a resident of the county of his appointment as well as the county in which he actually resides.

(c) Corporation. A domestic corporation, or a foreign corporation authorized to transact business in the state, shall be deemed a resident of the county in which its principal office is located; except that such a corporation, if a railroad or other common carrier, shall also be deemed a resident of the county where the cause of the action arose.

(d) Unincorporated association, partnership, or individually-owned business. A president or treasurer of an unincorporated association, suing or being sued on behalf of the association, shall be deemed a resident of any county in which the association has its principal office, as well as the county in which he actually resides. A partnership or an individually-owned business shall be deemed a resident of any county in which it has its principal office, as well as the county in which the partner or individual owner suing or being sued actually resides.

(e) Assignee. In an action for a sum of money only, brought by an assignee other than an assignee for the benefit of creditors or a holder in due course of a negotiable instrument, the assignee's residence shall be deemed the same as that of the original assignor at the time of the original assignment.

(f) Consumer credit transaction. In an action arising out of a consumer credit transaction where a purchaser, borrower or debtor is a defendant, the place of trial shall be the residence of a defendant, if one resides within the state or the county where such transaction took place, if it is within the state, or, in other cases, as set forth in subdivision (a).

CPLR

### 1981 AMENDMENTS

L. 1981, ch. 115, eff. May 15, 1981, amended CPLR 503(b) by adding the conservator of a conservatee to those persons whose county of appointment is a basis of venue in addition to the county of their residence.

### 1973 AMENDMENTS

L. 1973, ch. 238, eff. Sept. 1, 1973, added a new Subd. (f).

### 1965 AMENDMENTS

L. 1965, ch. 114, eff. Sept. 1, 1965, amended Subd. (e) by inserting the word "original" before the word "assignor" and before the word "assignment" in the last clause.

Amendment recommended by the Judicial Conference Feb. 1, 1965, Report to the Legislature: "This amendment is designed to make it clear that venue rules may not be evaded by the stratagem of consecutive assignments."

## § 504.  Actions against counties, cities, towns, villages, school districts and district corporations.

Notwithstanding the provisions of any charter heretofore granted by the state, and subject to the provisions of subdivision (b) of section 506, the place of trial of all actions against counties, cities, towns, villages, school districts and district corporations or any of their officers, boards or departments shall be, for:

1. a county, in such county;

2. a city, except the city of New York, town, village, school district or district corporation, in the county in which such city, town, village, school district or district corporation is situated, or if such school district or district corporation is situated in more than one county, in either county; and

3. the city of New York, in the county within the city in which the cause of action arose, or if it arose outside of the city, in the county of New York.

### 1966 AMENDMENTS

L. 1966, ch. 444, eff. Sept. 1, 1966, added reference to school districts and district corporations.

## § 505.  Actions involving public authorities.

(a) Generally. The place of trial of an action by or against a public authority constituted under the laws of the state shall be in the county in which the authority has its principal office or where it has facilities involved in the action.

(b) Against New York city transit authority. The place of trial of an action against the New York city transit authority shall be in the county within the city of New York in which the cause of action arose, or, if it arose outside of the city, in the county of New York.

## § 506. Where special proceeding commenced.

(a) Generally. Unless otherwise prescribed in subdivision (b) or in the law authorizing the proceeding, a special proceeding may be commenced in any county within the judicial district where the proceeding is triable.

(b) Proceeding against body or officer. A proceeding against a body or officer shall be commenced in any county within the judicial district where the respondent made the determination complained of or refused to perform the duty specifically enjoined upon him by law, or where the proceedings were brought or taken in the course of which the matter sought to be restrained originated, or where the material events otherwise took place, or where the principal office of the respondent is located, except that

1. a proceeding against a justice of the supreme court or a judge of a county court or the court of general sessions shall be commenced in the appellate division in the judicial department where the action, in the course of which the matter sought to be enforced or restrained originated, is triable, unless a term of the appellate division in that department is not in session, in which case the proceeding may be commenced in the appellate division in an adjoining judicial department; and

2. a proceeding against the regents of the university of the state of New York, the commissioner of education, the commissioner of taxation and finance, the tax appeals tribunal except as provided in section two thousand sixteen of the tax law, the public service commission, the commissioner or the department of transportation relating to articles three, four, five, six, seven, eight, nine or ten of the transportation law or to the railroad law, the water resources board, the comptroller or the department of agriculture and markets, shall be commenced in the supreme court, Albany county.

3. notwithstanding the provisions of paragraph two of this subdivision, a proceeding against the commissioner of education pursuant to section forty-four hundred four of the education law may be commenced in the supreme court in the county of residence of the petitioner.

4. a proceeding against the New York city tax appeals tribunal established by section one hundred sixty-eight of the New York city charter shall be commenced in the appellate division of the supreme court, first department.

### CROSS REFERENCES

Education Law § 4404, referred to in subdivision (b), paragraph 3, *supra*, governs the procedure for appealing the decision of a school board's committee on the handicapped regarding the educational placement and plan for a handicapped child.

### 1992 AMENDMENTS

L. 1992, ch. 47, eff. April 7, 1992, amended Subd. (b)(2) to include the reference to section two thousand sixteen of the tax law, and L. 1992, ch. 808, eff. Oct. 1, 1992, added Subd. (b)(4), providing that a proceeding against the New York City

Tax Appeals Tribunal must be commenced in the Appellate Division, First Department.

### 1988 AMENDMENTS

L. 1988, ch. 41, eff. April 9, 1988, and applicable to all special proceedings commenced on or after April 9, 1988 pursuant to Education Law § 4404.

### 1986 AMENDMENTS

L. 1986, ch. 282, eff. Sept. 1, 1987, amended Subd. (b)(2) to include proceedings against the commissioner of taxation and finance and the tax appeals tribunal. Such amendments are applicable to all proceedings commenced in the division of tax appeals on or after such date and shall apply to all proceedings commenced prior to such date which have not been the subject of a final and irrevocable administrative action as of such effective date, to the extent ch. 282 can be made applicable. Any proceeding for which a hearing has been commenced prior to the effective date shall be subject to automatic review by the tax appeals tribunal which shall render the decision in such proceeding unless there is a prior settlement.

### 1970 AMENDMENTS

L. 1970, ch. 267, § 8, eff. March 1, 1971, amended Subd. (b)(2) to include a proceeding against the Commissioner of Transportation or the Department of Transportation relating to Articles Three through Ten of the Transportation Law or to the Railroad Law.

## § 507.   Real property actions.

The place of trial of an action in which the judgment demanded would affect the title to, or the possession, use or enjoyment of, real property shall be in the county in which any part of the subject of the action is situated.

## § 508.   Actions to recover a chattel.

The place of trial of an action to recover a chattel may be in the county in which any part of the subject of the action is situated at the time of the commencement of the action.

## § 509.   Venue in county designated.

Notwithstanding any provision of this article, the place of trial of an action shall be in the county designated by the plaintiff, unless the place of trial is changed to another county by order upon motion, or by consent as provided in subdivision (b) of rule 511.

### 1965 AMENDMENTS

L. 1965, ch. 773, eff. Sept. 1, 1965, added the words "or by consent as provided in subdivision (b) of rule 511" to the end of the section.

## § 510.   Grounds for change of place of trial.

The court, upon motion, may change the place of trial of an action where:

**CPLR**

1. the county designated for that purpose is not a proper county; or

2. there is reason to believe that an impartial trial cannot be had in the proper county; or

3. the convenience of material witnesses and the ends of justice will be promoted by the change.

## R 511.   Change of place of trial.

(a) Time for motion or demand. A demand under subdivision (b) for change of place of trial on the ground that the county designated for that purpose is not a proper county shall be served with the answer or before the answer is served. A motion for change of place of trial on any other ground shall be made within a reasonable time after commencement of the action.

(b) Demand for change of place of trial upon ground of improper venue, where motion made. The defendant shall serve a written demand that the action be tried in a county he specifies as proper. Thereafter the defendant may move to change the place of trial within fifteen days after service of the demand, unless within five days after such service plaintiff serves a written consent to change the place of trial to that specified by the defendant. Defendant may notice such motion to be heard as if the action were pending in the county he specified, unless plaintiff within five days after service of the demand serves an affidavit showing either that the county specified by the defendant is not proper or that the county designated by him is proper.

(c) Stay of proceedings. No order to stay proceedings for the purpose of changing the place of trial shall be granted unless it appears from the papers that the change is sought with due diligence.

(d) Order, subsequent proceedings and appeal. Upon filing of consent by the plaintiff or entry of an order changing the place of trial by the clerk of the county from which it is changed, the clerk shall forthwith deliver to the clerk of the county to which it is changed all papers filed in the action and certified copies of all minutes and entries, which shall be filed, entered or recorded, as the case requires, in the office of the latter clerk. Subsequent proceedings shall be had in the county to which the change is made as if it had been designated originally as the place of trial, except as otherwise directed by the court. An appeal from an order changing the place of trial shall be taken in the department in which the motion for the order was heard and determined.

### 1965 AMENDMENTS

Amendment No. 4 made by Judicial Conference Feb. 1, 1965, Report to the Legislature, effective Sept. 1, 1965, added the following sentence to the end of paragraph (d): "An appeal from an order changing the place of trial shall be taken in the department in which the motion for the order was heard and determined."

L. 1965, ch. 773, eff. Sept. 1, 1965, added the words "upon ground of improper venue" before the words "where motion is made" in the catch line to Subd. (b).

Amendment recommended by the Judicial Conference Feb. 1, 1965, Report to the Legislature: "Since the demand procedure for change of place of trial is to be used by defendant only where the ground for change is that the county designated is improper, the suggested change in the catch-line of the applicable subdivision, by so specifying, should assist practitioners and help to prevent possible misuse of the demand procedure and its special provisions. Under the demand procedure, if the plaintiff does not consent to defendant's demand to change venue, the defendant may move for such relief in the county specified as proper in the demand unless plaintiff supports his choice by proper affidavit. In contrast, a motion to change venue on other grounds (impartial trial or convenience of material witnesses) must be made in the county designated by the plaintiff or in one of the alternative counties permitted by § 2212(a). The proposed amendment will alert the bar to the limited application of the demand procedure for change of venue."

### 1964 AMENDMENTS

L. 1964, ch. 388, eff. Sept. 1, 1964, made mechanical corrections in subd. (b).

## R 512. Change of place of trial of action or issue triable without a jury.

The place of trial of an action or any issue triable without a jury may be, in the discretion of the court, in any county within the judicial district in which the action is triable. After the trial, the decision and all other papers relating to the trial shall be filed and the judgment entered in the county where the action is pending.

## § 513. Misplacement of venue in consumer credit transactions.

(a) In an action arising out of a consumer credit transaction, the clerk shall not accept a summons for filing when it appears upon its face that the proper venue is a county other than the county where such summons is offered for filing.

(b) The clerk shall indicate upon the summons the date of the rejection and shall enter such date in a register maintained by him together with the name of the counties in which the summons may properly be filed.

(c) Notwithstanding subdivisions one and three of section three hundred eight, where a summons has been rejected for filing by virtue of this section, service is complete ten days after such summons is filed in the proper county with proof of service upon the defendant of the summons, together with proof of service upon the defendant by registered or certified mail of a notice setting forth the following:

1. the proper county,

2. the date of filing of the summons,

3. the date within which the answer or notice of appearance is to be filed, and

4. the address at which it is to be filed.

CPLR

### 1973 AMENDMENTS

L. 1973, ch. 238, eff. Sept. 1, 1973, added new CPLR 513, concerning misplacement of venue in consumer credit transactions.

# ARTICLE 6

# JOINDER OF CLAIMS, CONSOLIDATION AND SEVERANCE

## SUMMARY OF ARTICLE

§ 601.      Joinder of claims.
§ 602.      Consolidation.
       (a)   Generally.
       (b)   Cases pending in different courts.
§ 603.      Severance and separate trials.
§ 604.      Change by supreme court of place of trial of action pending in another
           court.

**CPLR**

## § 601.*   Joinder of claims.

(a) The plaintiff in a complaint or the defendant in an answer setting forth a counterclaim or cross-claim may join as many claims as he may have against an adverse party. There may be like joinder of claims when there are multiple parties.

(b) Two or more plaintiffs may join no more than five claims in any one action or proceeding against the same defendant arising out of separate consumer credit transactions, provided that the plaintiffs are represented by the same attorney.

*[Editor's note: This version of § 601 is effective as of January 1, 1997. Through December 31, 1996, former § 601 remains in effect. It reads as follows:

**§ 601. Joinder of claims.**

The plaintiff in a complaint or the defendant in an answer setting forth a counterclaim or cross-claim may join as many claims as he may have against an adverse party. There may be like joinder of claims when there are multiple parties.]

### 1996 AMENDMENTS

L. 1996, ch. 602, eff. Jan. 1, 1997, amended the section by numbering the existing paragraph as (a) and adding a new subdivision (b).

## § 602.   Consolidation.

(a) Generally. When actions involving a common question of law or fact are pending before a court, the court, upon motion, may order a joint trial of any or all the matters in issue, may order the actions consolidated, and may make such other orders concerning proceedings therein as may tend to avoid unnecessary costs or delay.

(b) Cases pending in different courts. Where an action is pending in the supreme court it may, upon motion, remove to itself an action pending in another court and consolidate it or have it tried together with that in the supreme court. Where an action is pending in the county court, it may, upon motion, remove to itself an action pending in a city, municipal, district or justice court in the county and consolidate it or have it tried together with that in the county court.

## § 603.   Severance and separate trials.

In furtherance of convenience or to avoid prejudice the court may order a severance of claims, or may order a separate trial of any claim, or of any separate issue. The court may order the trial of any claim or issue prior to the trial of the others.

## § 604.   Change by supreme court of place of trial of action pending in another court.

Upon motion of any party, the supreme court may order that an issue of fact in an action pending in another court, except an action relating to real property pending in a county court, be tried in the supreme court in another county upon such terms as may be just. After the trial, the clerk of the county in which it has taken place shall certify the minutes thereof, which shall be filed with the clerk of the court in which the action is pending. Subsequent proceedings shall be the same as if the issue had been tried in the court in which the action is pending.

# ARTICLE 9

# CLASS ACTIONS

---

## SUMMARY OF ARTICLE

§ 901.      Prerequisites to a class action.
§ 902.      Order allowing class action.
§ 903.      Description of class.
§ 904.      Notice of class action.
§ 905.      Judgment.
§ 906.      Actions conducted partially as class actions.
R 907.      Orders in conduct of class actions.
R 908.      Dismissal, discontinuance or compromise.
R 909.      Attorneys' fees.

**CPLR**

---

## § 901. Prerequisites to a class action.

a. One or more members of a class may sue or be sued as representative parties on behalf of all if:

1. the class is so numerous that joinder of all members, whether otherwise required or permitted, is impracticable;

2. there are questions of law or fact common to the class which predominate over any questions affecting only individual members;

3. the claims or defenses of the representative parties are typical of the claims or defenses of the class;

4. the representative parties will fairly and adequately protect the interest of the class; and

5. a class action is superior to other available methods for the fair and efficient adjudication of the controversy.

b. Unless a statute creating or imposing a penalty, or a minimum measure or recovery specifically authorizes the recovery thereof in a class action, an action to recover a penalty, or minimum measure of recovery created or imposed by statute may not be maintained as a class action.

### 1975 AMENDMENTS

L. 1975, ch. 207, eff. Sept. 1, 1975, upon the recommendation of the Judicial Conference, added new Article 9 (CPLR 901–909), to govern class actions in lieu of former CPLR 1005.

The 1975 Judicial Conference Report stated, in part:

"The basic changes in New York class action procedure are designed to achieve two major goals:

"1. to set up a flexible, functional scheme whereby class actions could qualify without the present undesirable and socially detrimental restrictions; and

"2. to prescribe basic guidelines for judicial management of class actions.

"The present provision has remained in force without substantial change since the addition of its predecessor to the Field Code (L. 1849, ch. 438). . . . Under the present law, unless the subject matter of the controversy is a limited fund or specific property, or the relief sought is common to the class in the sense that satisfaction of the individual claims before the court also automatically satisfies the claims of all other class members (see 18 N.Y. Jud. Council Rep. 217, 230 (1952)), a class action can qualify only if a bond of privity' exists between the multiple parties forming the class. (*Society Milion Athena, Inc. v. National Bank of Greece*, 281 N.Y. 282 (1939)). In the main, class actions in New York are confined to the closely associated relationships growing out of trusts, partnerships, or joint ventures, and ownership of corporate stock. (*Hall v. Coburn Corp. of Amer.*, 26 N.Y. 2d 396, 402 (1970)). . . .

"The basic feature of the proposed bill is the abandonment of the sterile notion of privity which for over 120 years has blocked the effective implementation of the class action device, producing results under which class actions were not permitted where they should have been and were allowed where they should not have been.' *see* 2 Weinstein, Korn & Miller, New York Civil Practice - CPLR ¶ 1005.02 (Matthew Bender). For a critical discussion of illustrative cases see 18 Jud. Council Rep. 217 (1952); *see* 2 Weinstein, Korn & Miller, New York Civil Practice - CPLR ¶ 1005.11(Matthew Bender); Homburger, State Class Actions and the Federal Rule (17 Judicial Conference Report (1972), reprinted from 71 Colum. L. Rev. 609, 612–21 (1971)). In place of the amorphous privity concept, the bill would substitute functional criteria which would take into account the practicalities of life and pressing contemporary needs of our society while at the same time assuring adequate judicial control of the remedy. . . .

". . . the proposed bill adopts the general scheme of the Federal Rule, but is simpler in its basic structure and more consistent in its functional orientation. For a detailed explanation of the modifications of the Federal Rule, *see* Homburger, State Class Actions and the Federal Rule (17 Judicial Conference Report (1972) reprinted from 71 Colum. L. Rev. 609 (1971)). . . .

"Section 901 contains a unitary scheme of prerequisites for all class actions, as opposed to the overlapping and more complex classification scheme of the Federal Rule. The reach of proposed section 901 is co-extensive with Federal Rule 23(a) and (b) (1), (2) and (3). Like the Federal Rule the proposed section states the prerequisites to the class actions in pragmatic and functional terms avoiding any reference to the abstract nature of the substantive rights involved."

## § 902.    Order allowing class action.

Within sixty days after the time to serve a responsive pleading has expired for all persons named as defendants in an action brought as a class action, the plaintiff shall move for an order to determine whether it is to be so maintained. An order under this section may be conditional, and may be altered or amended before the decision on the merits on the court's own motion or on motion of the parties. The action may be maintained as a class action only if the court finds that the prerequisites under section 901 have been satisfied. Among the matters which the court shall consider in determining whether the action may proceed as a class action are:

1. the interest of members of the class in individually controlling the prosecution or defense of separate actions;

2. the impracticability or inefficiency of prosecuting or defending separate actions;

3. the extent and nature of any litigation concerning the controversy already commenced by or against members of the class;

4. the desirability or undesirability of concentrating the litigation of the claim in the particular forum;

5. the difficulties likely to be encountered in the management of a class action.

### 1975 AMENDMENTS

L. 1975, ch. 207, eff. Sept. 1, 1975, upon the recommendation of the Judicial Conference, added new Article 9 (CPLR 901–909), to govern class actions in lieu of former CPLR 1005. See comments to CPLR 901.

The 1975 Judicial Conference Report, covering proposed CPLR 902, modified by the legislature, and further amended by L. 1975, ch. 474, eff. Sept. 1, 1975, stated:

"Proposed section 902 would adopt the federal policy of determining, at least tentatively, the propriety of maintaining a class action in the initial stages of the proceedings. A wide range of discretion would enable the court to vary the order at any time before reaching a decision on the merits. The section lists factors which the court should consider in determining the propriety of maintaining a class action. In contrast to the Federal Rule, these factors would be significant in any class action and the proposed section would expressly include impracticability or inefficiency of prosecuting or defending separate actions among the relevant factors. The list is non-exhaustive. For example, the apparent merits of the claims asserted may have a bearing on the court's determination."

## § 903. Description of class.

The order permitting a class action shall describe the class. When appropriate the court may limit the class to those members who do not request exclusion from the class within a specified time after notice.

### 1975 AMENDMENTS

L. 1975, ch. 207, eff. Sept. 1, 1975, upon the recommendation of the Judicial Conference, added new Article 9 (CPLR 901–909), to govern class actions in lieu of former CPLR 1005. See comments to CPLR 901.

The 1975 Judicial Conference Report stated:

"In addition to requiring the description of the class by the order permitting the action, the bill would give to the court discretionary power to direct notice to each member that he may request exclusion from the class within a specified time after notification. Presumably the court would exercise its discretion in favor of granting a right to opt-out when representation of the entire class is not needed for a just disposition of the controversy, when the class members have a significant practical interest in individually controlling the litigation, and when individual notice is feasible without imposing a prohibitive economic or administrative burden on the parties."

CPLR

## § 904. Notice of class action.

(a) In class actions brought primarily for injunctive or declaratory relief, notice of the pendency of the action need not be given to the class unless the court finds that notice is necessary to protect the interests of the represented parties and that the cost of notice will not prevent the action from going forward.

(b) In all other class actions, reasonable notice of the commencement of a class action shall be given to the class in such manner as the court directs.

(c) The content of the notice shall be subject to court approval. In determining the method by which notice is to be given, the court shall consider

I. the cost of giving notice by each method considered

II. the resources of the parties and

III. the stake of each represented member of the class, and the likelihood that significant numbers of represented members would desire to exclude themselves from the class or to appear individually, which may be determined, in the court's discretion, by sending notice to a random sample of the class.

(d) I. Preliminary determination of expenses of notification. Unless the court orders otherwise, the plaintiff shall bear the expense of notification. The court may, if justice requires, require that the defendant bear the expense of notification, or may require each of them to bear a part of the expense in proportion to the likelihood that each will prevail upon the merits. The court may hold a preliminary hearing to determine how the costs of notice should be apportioned.

II. Final determination. Upon termination of the action by order or judgment, the court may, but shall not be required to, allow to the prevailing party the expenses of notification as taxable disbursements under article eighty-three of the civil practice law and rules.

### 1975 AMENDMENTS

L. 1975, ch. 207, eff. Sept. 1, 1975, upon the recommendation of the Judicial Conference, added new Article 9 (CPLR 901–909), to govern class actions in lieu of former CPLR 1005. See comments to CPLR 901.

The 1975 Judicial Conference Report, covering proposed CPLR 904, substantially expanded by the legislature, stated, in part:

". . . The flexible scheme, proposed in the bill, requires notice in such manner as the court directs, subject however to the court's power to dispense with notice in appropriate cases. The court should grant dispensation sparingly, as, for example, in cases where notice would be burdensome and costly, the interests of the individual member of the class in controlling the litigation minimal, and effective representation of the class interests attainable without notification.

"The bill would round out the notice provisions by allocating the financial and mechanical burden of notification to the plaintiff unless the court orders otherwise, a provision not contained in the federal counterpart. A reallocation of that burden may be appropriate, depending on the relative strength of two competing policies, as viewed in the light of the circumstances of a particular case: protection of the opponent of the class from harassment on the one hand, and the accessibility of the courts to claimants seeking a determination of the merits of the controversy on the other. A flexible rule giving the court a wide range of discretion is needed. Factors bearing on the exercise of the court's discretion include the meritoriousness of the claims asserted on behalf of the class, the financial status of the representative of the class and their opponent, the interest of the latter in obtaining a binding adjudication, and the availability of inexpensive notification facilities to the opponent of the class. . . .

"Finally, the bill contains express provision, also not contained in the Federal Rule, requiring court approval of the content of the notice in order to forestall the transmittal of improper or misleading information to the class membership."

## § 905. Judgment.

The judgment in an action maintained as a class action, whether or not favorable to the class, shall include and describe those whom the court finds to be members of the class.

### 1975 AMENDMENTS

L. 1975, ch. 207, eff. Sept. 1, 1975, upon the recommendation of the Judicial Conference, added new Article 9 (CPLR 901–909), to govern class actions in lieu of former CPLR 1005. See comments to CPLR 901.

The 1975 Judicial Conference Report stated:

"As under the Federal Rule, the judgment under the proposed section would embrace the entire class whether or not it is favorable to the class. The binding effect on a nonappearing member of the class could of course be determined only in a subsequent action to which such member is a party."

## § 906. Actions conducted partially as class actions.

When appropriate,

1. an action may be brought or maintained as a class action with respect to particular issues, or

2. a class may be divided into subclasses and each subclass treated as a class.

The provisions of this article shall then be construed and applied accordingly.

### 1975 AMENDMENTS

L. 1975, ch. 207, eff. Sept. 1, 1975, upon the recommendation of the Judicial Conference, added new Article 9 (CPLR 901–909), to govern class actions in lieu of former CPLR 1005. See comments to CPLR 901.

The 1975 Judicial Conference Report stated:

"Following the lead of the Federal Rule, the proposed section expressly authorizes class treatment with respect to particular issues and the formation of subclasses."

## R 907. Orders in conduct of class actions.

In the conduct of class actions the court may make appropriate orders:

1. determining the course of proceedings or prescribing measures to prevent undue repetition or complication in the presentation of evidence or argument;

CPLR

2. requiring, for the protection of the members of the class, or otherwise for the fair conduct of the action, that notice be given in such manner as the court may direct to some or all of the members of any step in the action, or of the proposed extent of the judgment, or of the opportunity of members to signify whether they consider the representation fair and adequate, or to appear and present claims or defenses, or otherwise to come into the action;

3. imposing conditions on the representative parties or on intervenors;

4. requiring that the pleadings be amended to eliminate therefrom allegations as to representation of absent persons, and that the action proceed accordingly;

5. directing that a money judgment favorable to the class be paid either in one sum, whether forthwith or within such period as the court may fix, or in such installments as the court may specify;

6. dealing with similar procedural matters.

The orders may be altered or amended as may be desirable from time to time.

### 1975 AMENDMENTS

L. 1975, ch. 207, eff. Sept. 1, 1975, upon the recommendation of the Judicial Conference, added new Article 9 (CPLR 901–909), to govern class actions in lieu of former CPLR 1005. See comments to CPLR 901.

The 1975 Judicial Conference Report stated:

"The proposed rule like the Federal Rule would provide important guidelines that assist the court in the management of the action. Deviating from the Federal Rule, proposed rule 907 authorizes the court in the exercise of its discretion to determine whether represented parties may enter an appearance without first seeking permission to intervene, and to tailor the effect of an appearance to the exigencies of the particular case. There is also a special provision, not found in the federal rule, which would allow the court to set terms for payment of a judgment to a victorious class in accordance with the financial capacity of the defendant so as to avoid harsh economic and social consequences such as loss of employment. The desirability of this change is self-evident."

## R 908. Dismissal, discontinuance or compromise.

A class action shall not be dismissed, discontinued, or compromised without the approval of the court. Notice of the proposed dismissal, discontinuance, or compromise shall be given to all members of the class in such manner as the court directs.

### 1975 AMENDMENTS

L. 1975, ch. 207, eff. Sept. 1, 1975, upon the recommendation of the Judicial Conference, added new Article 9 (CPLR 901–909), to govern class actions in lieu of former CPLR 1005. See comments to CPLR 901.

The Judicial Conference Report stated:

"The proposed provision is stricter than the present law. In addition to court approval, it requires in all cases notice to the members of the class in such manner as the court directs."

## R 909.   Attorneys' fees.

If a judgment in an action maintained as a class action is rendered in favor of the class, the court in its discretion may award attorneys' fees to the representatives of the class based on the reasonable value of legal services rendered and if justice requires, allow recovery of the amount awarded from the opponent of the class.

### 1975 AMENDMENTS

L. 1975, ch. 207, eff. Sept. 1, 1975, upon the recommendation of the Judicial Conference, added new Article 9 (CPLR 901–909), to govern class actions in lieu of former CPLR 1005. See comments to CPLR 901.

CPLR 909 was not among the eight proposals of the Judicial Conference for class actions. It was added by the legislature to new Article 9.

CPLR

# ARTICLE 10

# PARTIES GENERALLY

## SUMMARY OF ARTICLE

§ 1001.    Necessary joinder of parties.
    (a)  Parties who should be joined.
    (b)  When joinder excused.
§ 1002.    Permissive joinder of parties.
    (a)  Plaintiffs.
    (b)  Defendants.
    (c)  Separate relief; separate trials.
§ 1003.    Nonjoinder and misjoinder of parties.
§ 1004.    When joinder unnecessary.
§ 1005.    [Repealed.]
§ 1006.    Interpleader.
    (a)  Stakeholder; claimant; action of interpleader.
    (b)  Defensive interpleader.
    (c)  Effect of pendency of another action against stakeholder.
    (d)  Abolition of former grounds for objection.
    (e)  Issue of independent liability.
    (f)  Discharge of stakeholder.
    (g)  Deposit of money as basis for jurisdiction.
§ 1007.    When third-party practice allowed.
§ 1008.    Answer of third-party defendant; defenses.
R 1009.    Claim by plaintiff against third-party defendant.
R 1010.    Dismissal or separate trial of third-party complaint.
R 1011.    Successive third-party proceedings; counterclaims.
§ 1012.    Intervention as of right; notice to attorney-general where constitutionality in issue.
    (a)  Intervention as of right.
    (b)  Notice to attorney-general where constitutionality in issue.
    (c)  Notice to comptroller of the state of New York where public retirement benefits are in issue.
§ 1013.    Intervention by permission.
§ 1014.    Proposed intervention pleading.
§ 1015.    Substitution upon death.
    (a)  Generally.
    (b)  Devolution of rights or liabilities on other parties.
§ 1016.    Substitution of committee or conservator.
§ 1017.    Substitution in case of receivership or dissolution of a corporation.
§ 1018.    Substitution upon transfer of interest.
§ 1019.    Substitution of public officers.

CPLR

§ 1020.     Substitution of indemnitors for executing or attaching officer.

§ 1021.     Substitution procedure; dismissal for failure to substitute; presentation of appeal.

§ 1022.     Substitution: extension of time for taking procedural steps.

§ 1023.     Public body or officer described by official title.

§ 1024.     Unknown parties.

§ 1025.     Partnerships and unincorporated associations.

§ 1026.     Review of determinations by administrative officers of the unified court system.

---

## § 1001.   Necessary joinder of parties.

(a) Parties who should be joined. Persons who ought to be parties if complete relief is to be accorded between the persons who are parties to the action or who might be inequitably affected by a judgment in the action shall be made plaintiffs or defendants. When a person who should join as a plaintiff refuses to do so, he may be made a defendant.

(b) When joinder excused. When a person who should be joined under subdivision (a) has not been made a party and is subject to the jurisdiction of the court, the court shall order him summoned. If jurisdiction over him can be obtained only by his consent or appearance, the court, when justice requires, may allow the action to proceed without his being made a party. In determining whether to allow the action to proceed, the court shall consider:

1. whether the plaintiff has another effective remedy in case the action is dismissed on account of the nonjoinder;

2. the prejudice which may accrue from the nonjoinder to the defendant or to the person not joined;

3. whether and by whom prejudice might have been avoided or may in the future be avoided;

4. the feasibility of a protective provision by order of the court or in the judgment; and

5. whether an effective judgment may be rendered in the absence of the person who is not joined.

## § 1002.   Permissive joinder of parties.

(a) Plaintiffs. Persons who assert any right to relief jointly, severally, or in the alternative arising out of the same transaction, occurrence, or series of transactions or occurrences, may join in one action as plaintiffs if any common question of law or fact would arise.

(b) Defendants. Persons against whom there is asserted any right to relief jointly, severally, or in the alternative, arising out of the same transaction, occurrence, or series of transactions or occurrences, may be joined in one action as defendants if any common question of law or fact would arise.

(c) Separate relief; separate trials. It shall not be necessary that each plaintiff be interested in obtaining, or each defendant be interested in defending against, all the relief demanded or as to every claim included in an action; but the court may make such orders as will prevent a party from being embarrassed, delayed, or put to expense by the inclusion of a party against whom he asserts no claim and, who asserts no claim against him, and may order separate trials or make other orders to prevent prejudice.

## § 1003. Nonjoinder and misjoinder of parties.

Nonjoinder of a party who should be joined under section 1001 is a ground for dismissal of an action without prejudice unless the court allows the action to proceed without that party under the provisions of that section. Misjoinder of parties is not a ground for dismissal of an action. Parties may be added at any stage of the action by leave of court or by stipulation of all parties who have appeared, or once without leave of court within twenty days after service of the original summons or at anytime before the period for responding to that summons expires or within twenty days after service of a pleading responding to it. Parties may be dropped by the court, on motion of any party or on its own initiative, at any stage of the action and upon such terms as may be just. The court may order any claim against a party severed and proceeded with separately.

### 1996 AMENDMENTS

L. 1996, ch. 39, eff. April 2, 1996, amended the section to add a new third sentence, beginning with the words, "Parties may be added," and ending with "pleading responding to it" and made the section gender neutral.

### 1964 AMENDMENTS

L. 1964, ch. 388, eff. Sept. 1, 1964, amended first sentence at the end thereof to change "rule" to "section."

## § 1004. When joinder unnecessary.

Except where otherwise prescribed by order of the court, an executor, administrator, guardian of the property of an infant, committee of the property of a judicially declared incompetent, conservator of the property of a conservatee, trustee of an express trust, insured person who has executed to his insurer either a loan or subrogation receipt, trust agreement or other similar agreement, or person with whom or in whose name a contract has been made for the benefit of another, may sue or be sued without joining with him the person for or against whose interest the action is brought.

CPLR

**1981 AMENDMENTS**

L. 1981, ch. 115, eff. May 18, 1981, amended CPLR 1004 by adding the conservator of a conservatee's property as one who may sue or be sued without joining with him the person for or against whom the action is brought.

## § 1005. [Repealed].

## § 1006. Interpleader.

(a) Stakeholder; claimant; action of interpleader. A stakeholder is a person who is or may be exposed to multiple liability as the result of adverse claims. A claimant is a person who has made or may be expected to make such a claim. A stakeholder may commence an action of interpleader against two or more claimants.

(b) Defensive interpleader. A defendant stakeholder may bring in a claimant who is not a party by filing a summons and interpleader complaint. Service of process upon such a claimant shall be by serving upon such claimant a summons and interpleader complaint and all prior pleadings served in the action.

(c) Effect of pendency of another action against stakeholder. If a stakeholder seeks to bring in a claimant pursuant to subdivision (b) and there is pending in a court of the state an action between the claimant and the stakeholder based upon the same claim, the appropriate court, on motion, upon such terms as may be just, may dismiss the interpleader complaint and order consolidation or joint trial of the actions, or may make the claimant a party and stay the pending action until final disposition of the action in which interpleader is so granted, and may make such further order as may be just.

(d) Abolition of former grounds for objection. It is not ground for objection to interpleader that the claims of the several claimants or the titles on which their claims depend do not have a common origin or are not identical but are adverse to and independent of one another, or that the stakeholder avers that he is not liable in whole or in part to any or all of the claimants.

(e) Issue of independent liability. Where the issue of an independent liability of the stakeholder to a claimant is raised by the pleadings or upon motion, the court may dismiss the claim of the appropriate claimant, order severance or separate trials, or require the issue to be tried in the action.

(f) Discharge of stakeholder. After the time for all parties to plead has expired, the stakeholder may move for an order discharging him from liability in whole or in part to any party. The stakeholder shall submit proof by affidavit or otherwise of the allegations in his pleading. The court may grant the motion and require payment into court, delivery to a person designated by the court or retention to the credit of the action, of the subject matter of the action to be disposed of in accordance with further order or the judgment. An order under subdivision (g) shall not discharge the stakeholder from liability to any claimant until an order granted under this subdivision is complied with. The court shall impose such terms relating to payment of expenses, costs and disbursements as may be just and which may be charged against the subject matter of the action. If the court shall determine that a party is entitled to interest, in the absence of an agreement by the stakeholder as to the rate of interest, he shall be liable to such party for interest to the date of discharge at a rate no greater than the lowest discount rate of the Federal Reserve Bank of New York for discounts for, and advances to, member banks in effect from time to time during the period for which, as found by the court, interest should be paid.

(g) Deposit of money as basis for jurisdiction. Where a stakeholder is otherwise entitled to proceed under this section for the determination of a right to, interest in or lien upon a sum of money, whether or not liquidated in amount, payable in the state pursuant to a contract or claimed as damages for unlawful retention of specific real or personal property in the state, he may move, either before or after an action has been commenced against him, for an order permitting him to pay the sum of money or part of it into court or to a designated person or to retain it to the credit of the action. Upon compliance with a court order permitting such deposit or retention, the sum of money shall be deemed specific property within the state within the meaning of paragraph two of section 314.

**1994 AMENDMENTS**

L. 1994, ch. 563, eff. July 26, 1994, amended CPLR 1006(b) by adding the words "filing a summons and interpleader complaint. Service of process upon such a claimant shall be made by."

## § 1007.  When third-party practice allowed.

After the service of his answer, a defendant may proceed against a person not a party who is or may be liable to that defendant for all or part of the plaintiff's claim against that defendant, by filing pursuant to section three hundred four of this chapter a third-party summons and complaint with the clerk of the court in the county in which the main action is pending, for which a separate index number shall not be issued but a separate index number fee shall be collected. The third-party summons and complaint and all prior pleadings served in the action shall be served upon such person within one hundred twenty days of the filing. A defendant serving a third-party complaint shall be styled a third-party plaintiff and the person so served shall be styled a third-party defendant. The defendant shall also serve a copy of such third-party complaint upon the plaintiff's attorney simultaneously upon issuance for service of the third-party complaint on the third-party defendant.

**1992 AMENDMENTS**

L. 1992, ch. 216, eff. July 1, 1992, amended CPLR 1007 by deleting from the first sentence the words "serving upon such person a summons and third-party complaint and all prior pleadings served in the action" and by replacing them with the clause that begins with the words "filing pursuant to"; by adding the second sentence; and by making the language gender neutral.

CPLR

**1984 AMENDMENTS**

L. 1984, ch. 329, eff. Jan. 1, 1985, amended CPLR 1007 by specifying that the third-party complaint shall be served upon plaintiff's attorney simultaneously with service on the third-party defendant.

## § 1008.   Answer of third-party defendant; defenses.

The third-party defendant shall answer the claim asserted against him by serving copies of his answer upon the third-party plaintiff. The third-party defendant may assert against the plaintiff in his answer any defenses which the third-party plaintiff has to the plaintiff's claim. The third-party defendant shall have the rights of a party adverse to the other parties in the action, including the right to counter-claim, cross-claim and appeal.

## R 1009.   Claim by plaintiff against third-party defendant.

Within twenty days after service of the answer to the third-party complaint upon plaintiff's attorney, the plaintiff may amend his complaint without leave of court to assert against the third-party defendant any claim plaintiff has against the third-party defendant.

**1984 AMENDMENTS**

L. 1984, ch. 329, eff. Jan. 1, 1985, amended CPLR 1009.

**1972 AMENDMENTS**

Proposal No. 3 of the Judicial Conference Report to the 1972 Legislature amended CPLR 1009, effective Sept. 1, 1972, ". . . to allow plaintiff to assert any claim he has against the third-party defendant. [Previously, the rule restricted] the plaintiff to any claim he might have asserted if the third-party defendant had been joined originally as a defendant."

## R 1010.   Dismissal or separate trial of third-party complaint.

The court may dismiss a third-party complaint without prejudice, order a separate trial of the third-party claim or of any separate issue thereof, or make such other order as may be just. In exercising its discretion, the court shall consider whether the controversy between the third-party plaintiff and the third-party defendant will unduly delay the determination of the main action or prejudice the substantial rights of any party.

## R 1011.   Successive third-party proceedings; counterclaims.

A third-party defendant may proceed pursuant to section 1007 against any person who is or may be liable to him for all or part of the third-party claim. When a counterclaim is asserted against a plaintiff, he may proceed pursuant to section 1007 as if he were a defendant.

## § 1012.　Intervention as of right; notice to attorney-general where constitutionality in issue.

(a) Intervention as of right. Upon timely motion, any person shall be permitted to intervene in any action

1. when a statute of the state confers an absolute right to intervene; or

2. when the representation of the person's interest by the parties is or may be inadequate and the person is or may be bound by the judgment; or

3. when the action involves the disposition or distribution of, or the title or a claim for damages for injury to, property and the person may be affected adversely by the judgment.

(b) Notice to attorney-general where constitutionality in issue. When the constitutionality of a statute of the state is involved in an action to which the state is not a party, the court shall notify the attorney-general, who shall be permitted to intervene in support of its constitutionality.

(c) Notice to comptroller of the state of New York where public retirement benefits are in issue. Where public retirement benefits, paid, payable, claimed, or sought to be paid by a state retirement system or any other retirement system established for public employees within this state or any subdivision thereof, or the interpretation of any provisions of law or rules governing any such retirement system or the operation thereof, are involved in an action to which the comptroller of the state of New York is not a party, the court shall notify said comptroller, who shall be permitted, in his discretion, to intervene in such action or to file a brief amicus curiae.

### 1972 AMENDMENTS

L. 1972, ch. 360, eff. Sept. 1, 1972, added Subd. (c).

## § 1013.　Intervention by permission.

Upon timely motion, any person may be permitted to intervene in any action when a statute of the state confers a right to intervene in the discretion of the court, or when the person's claim or defense and the main action have a common question of law or fact. In exercising its discretion, the court shall consider whether the intervention will unduly delay the determination of the action or prejudice the substantial rights of any party.

## § 1014.　Proposed intervention pleading.

A motion to intervene shall be accompanied by a proposed pleading setting forth the claim or defense for which intervention is sought.

CPLR

## § 1015.　Substitution upon death.

(a) Generally. If a party dies and the claim for or against him is not thereby extinguished the court shall order substitution of the proper parties.

(b) Devolution of rights or liabilities on other parties. Upon the death of one or more of the plaintiffs or defendants in an action in which the right sought to be enforced survives only to the surviving plaintiffs or against the surviving defendants, the action does not abate. The death shall be noted on the record and the action shall proceed.

## § 1016.　Substitution of committee or conservator.

If a party is adjudicated incompetent or a conservator has been appointed, the court shall order substitution of his committee or conservator.

### 1981 AMENDMENTS

L. 1981, ch. 115, eff. May 18, 1981, amended CPLR 1016 by rewording the title and text to designate an incompetent's committee and a conservatee's conservator as the persons to be substituted in their respective places.

## § 1017.　Substitution in case of receivership or dissolution of a corporation.

If a receiver is appointed for a party, or a corporate party is dissolved, the court shall order substitution of the proper parties.

## § 1018.　Substitution upon transfer of interest.

Upon any transfer of interest, the action may be continued by or against the original parties unless the court directs the person to whom the interest is transferred to be substituted or joined in the action.

## § 1019.　Substitution of public officers.

If a person made a party in his capacity as public officer dies or otherwise ceases to hold office, the action may be continued by or against his successor if it is shown to the court that there is need for so continuing it. Before a substitution is made his successor and, unless the court otherwise orders, the party shall be given reasonable notice of the motion and accorded an opportunity to object. When, in accordance with section 1023, an officer is described by his official title and his name is not added, no substitution is necessary.

## § 1020.　Substitution of indemnitors for executing or attaching officer.

Where an action is brought against an officer to recover a chattel levied upon by virtue of an execution or order of attachment, or to recover damages for the detention or sale of such a chattel, and an undertaking indemnifying the officer against such acts has been given, the court may order that the indemnitor be substituted for the officer.

## § 1021.  Substitution procedure; dismissal for failure to substitute; presentation of appeal.

A motion for substitution may be made by the successors or representatives of a party or by any party. If a person who should be substituted does not appear voluntarily he may be made a party defendant. If the event requiring substitution occurs before final judgment and substitution is not made within a reasonable time, the action may be dismissed as to the party for whom substitution should have been made, however, such dismissal shall not be on the merits unless the court shall so indicate. If the event requiring substitution occurs after final judgment, substitution may be made in either the court from or to which an appeal could be or is taken, or the court of original instance, and if substitution is not made within four months after the event requiring substitution, the court to which the appeal is or could be taken may dismiss the appeal, impose conditions or prevent it from being taken. Whether or not it occurs before or after final judgment, if the event requiring substitution is the death of a party, and timely substitution has not been made, the court, before proceeding further, shall, on such notice as it may in its discretion direct, order the persons interested in the decedent's estate to show cause why the action or appeal should not be dismissed.

### 1975 AMENDMENTS

L. 1975, ch. 25, eff. March 25, 1975, amended the third sentence of the section by adding thereto: "however, such dismissal shall not be on the merits unless the court shall so indicate."

### 1970 AMENDMENTS

L. 1970, ch. 93, eff. Sept. 1, 1970, amended the section by adding thereto, "Whether or not it occurs before or after final judgment, if the event requiring substitution is the death of a party, and timely substitution has not been made, the court, before proceeding further, shall, on such notice as it may in its discretion direct, order the persons interested in the decedent's estate to show cause why the action or appeal should not be dismissed."

The amendment was recommended by the Judicial Conference Jan. 2, 1970, Report to the Legislature, wherein it was stated, in part:

"At present, CPLR 1021 allows the court to dismiss an action or appeal for unreasonable failure to substitute parties. Where the event requiring substitution is the death of a party, this provision conflicts with CPLR 5016 (d), which provides that no verdict or decision shall be rendered against a deceased party.

"Under this amendment, the court will be able to dispose of the matter in one proceeding, rather than denying the motion to dismiss without prejudice to renewal after appointment of a representative. . . ." (See § 5016(d).)

CPLR

## § 1022. Substitution: extension of time for taking procedural steps.

Unless the court orders otherwise, if the time for making a motion for a new trial or for taking an appeal or for making a motion for permission to appeal or for taking any other procedural step in the action has not expired before the occurrence of an event permitting substitution of a party, the period is extended as to all parties until fifteen days after substitution is made, or, in case of dismissal of the action under section 1021, is extended as to all parties until fifteen days after such dismissal.

## § 1023. Public body or officer described by official title.

When a public officer, body, board, commission or other public agency may sue or be sued in its official capacity, it may be designated by its official title, subject to the power of the court to require names to be added.

## § 1024. Unknown parties.

A party who is ignorant, in whole or in part, of the name or identity of a person who may properly be made a party, may proceed against such person as an unknown party by designating so much of his name and identity as is known. If the name or remainder of the name becomes known all subsequent proceedings shall be taken under the true name and all prior proceedings shall be deemed amended accordingly.

## § 1025. Partnerships and unincorporated associations.

Two or more persons conducting a business as a partnership may sue or be sued in the partnership name, and actions may be brought by or against the president or treasurer of an unincorporated association on behalf of the association in accordance with the provisions of the general associations law.

## § 1026. Review of determinations by administrative officers of the unified court system.

In any action or proceeding brought to review a determination of the chief judge of the court of appeals, of the court of appeals or of the administrative board of the courts, made pursuant to the provisions of article seven-A of the judiciary law or section twenty-eight of article six of the constitution, the only proper party to be named therein shall be the chief administrator of the courts, in his representative capacity. No action or proceeding so instituted shall name the chief judge, the court of appeals or any member thereof, or the administrative board or any member thereof as a party.

### CROSS REFERENCES

Article 7-A of the Judiciary Law, enacted by L. 1978, ch. 156, eff. May 19, 1978, provides for administration of the unified court system. N.Y. Const. Art. 6, § 28 appears in the Appendix, *infra*.

### 1978 AMENDMENTS

L. 1978, ch. 156, eff. May 19, 1978, added § 1026.

CPLR

# ARTICLE 11

# POOR PERSONS

---

## SUMMARY OF ARTICLE

§ 1101.    Motion for permission to proceed as a poor person; affidavit; certificate; notice; waiver of fee; when motion not required.
    (a)   Motion; affidavit.
    (b)   Certificate.
    (c)   Notice.
    (d)   Waiver of fee in certain cases.
    (e)   When motion not required.
§ 1102.    Privileges of poor person.
    (a)   Attorney.
    (b)   Stenographic transcript.
    (c)   Appeals.
    (d)   Costs and fees.
§ 1103.    Distribution of recovery in favor of poor person.

CPLR

---

## § 1101.   Motion for permission to proceed as a poor person; affidavit; certificate; notice; waiver of fee; when motion not required.

(a) Motion; affidavit. Upon motion of any person, the court in which an action is triable, or to which an appeal has been or will be taken, may grant permission to proceed as a poor person. Where a motion for leave to appeal as a poor person is brought to the court in which an appeal has been or will be taken, such court shall hear such motion on the merits and shall not remand such motion to the trial court for consideration. The moving party shall file an affidavit setting forth the amount and sources of his or her income and listing his or her property with its value; that he or she is unable to pay the costs, fees and expenses necessary to prosecute or defend the action or to maintain or respond to the appeal; the nature of the action; sufficient facts so that the merit of the contentions can be ascertained; and whether any other person is beneficially interested in any recovery sought and, if so, whether every such person is unable to pay such costs, fees and expenses. An executor, administrator or other representative may move for permission on behalf of a deceased, infant or incompetent poor person.

(b) Certificate. The court may require the moving party to file with the affidavit a certificate of an attorney stating that the attorney has examined the action and believes there is merit to the moving party's contentions.

(c) Notice. Except as provided in subdivisions (d) and (e) of this section, if an action has already been commenced, notice of the motion shall be served on all parties, and notice shall also be given to the county attorney in the county in which the action is triable or the corporation counsel if the action is triable in the city of New York.

(d) Waiver of fee in certain cases. A plaintiff may seek to commence his or her action without payment of the fee required by filing the form affidavit, attesting that such plaintiff is unable to pay the costs, fees and expenses necessary to prosecute or defend the action, which shall be available in the clerk's office along with the summons and complaint or summons with notice or third-party summons and complaint. The case will be given an index number, or, in courts other than the supreme or county courts, any necessary filing number and the application will be submitted to a judge of the court. If the court approves the application, the plaintiff will by written order be given notice that all fees and costs relating to the filing and service shall be waived. If the court denies the application the plaintiff will by written order be given notice that the case will be dismissed if the fee is not paid within one hundred twenty days of the date of the order.

(e) When motion not required. Where a party is represented in a civil action by a legal aid society or a legal services or other nonprofit organization, which has as its primary purpose the furnishing of legal services to indigent persons, or by private counsel working on behalf of or under the auspices of such society or organization, all fees and costs relating to the filing and service shall be waived without the necessity of a motion and the case shall be given an index number, or, in a court other than the supreme or county court, an appropriate filing number, provided that a determination has been made by such society, organization or attorney that such party is unable to pay the costs, fees and expenses necessary to prosecute or defend the action, and that an attorney's certification that such determination has been made is filed with the clerk of the court along with the summons and complaint or summons with notice or third-party summons and complaint or otherwise provided to the clerk of the court.

### 1994 AMENDMENTS

L. 1994, ch. 563, eff. July 26, 1994, amended CPLR 1101(c) by replacing the word "If" with the words "Except as provided in subdivisions (d) and (e) of this section, if."

### 1992 AMENDMENTS

L. 1992, ch. 216, eff. July 1, 1992, amended CPLR 1101 by inserting into the catchline the words "waiver of fee; when motion not required"; by adding new subdivisions (d) and (e); and by making the language gender neutral.

### 1987 AMENDMENTS

L. 1987, ch. 312, eff. Oct. 18, 1987, amended Subd. (a) to add the requirement that an appellate court to which a motion for leave to appeal as a poor person has been or will be taken, shall hear such motion on the merits.

### 1981 AMENDMENTS

L. 1981, ch. 478, eff. July 7, 1981, amended CPLR 1101(c) to substitute the corporation counsel for the commissioner of finance as one upon whom a motion for permission to proceed as a poor person must be served in an action triable in New York City.

### 1978 AMENDMENTS

L. 1978, ch. 655, eff. July 24, 1978, amended Subd. (c) by substituting "commissioner of finance" for "finance administrator."

### 1969 AMENDMENTS

L. 1969, ch. 407, eff. May 9, 1969, amended Subd. (c) by substituting "finance administrator" for "director of finance."

### 1966 AMENDMENTS

L. 1966, ch. 455, eff. Sept. 1, 1966, amended Subd. (c) by adding after the word "parties" the words "and notice shall also be given to the county attorney in the county in which the action is triable or the director of finance if the action is triable in the city of New York."

## § 1102. Privileges of poor person.

(a) Attorney. The court in its order permitting a person to proceed as a poor person may assign an attorney.

(b) Stenographic transcript. Where a party has been permitted by order to appeal as a poor person, the court clerk, within two days after the filing of said order with him, shall so notify the court stenographer, who, within twenty days of such notification shall make and certify two typewritten transcripts of the stenographic minutes of said trial or hearing, and shall deliver one of said transcripts to the poor person or his attorney, and file the other with the court clerk together with an affidavit of the fact and date of such delivery and filing. The expense of such transcripts shall be a county charge or, in the counties within the city of New York, a city charge, as the case may be, payable to the stenographer out of the court fund upon the certificate of the judge presiding at the trial or hearing. A poor person may be furnished with a stenographic transcript without fee by order of the court in proceedings other than appeal, the fee therefor to be paid by the county or, in the counties within the city of New York by the city, as the case may be, in the same manner as is paid for transcripts on appeal. Notwithstanding this or any other provision of law, fees paid for stenographic transcripts with respect to those proceedings specified in paragraph (a) of subdivision one of section thirty-five of the judiciary law shall be paid by the state in the manner prescribed by subdivision four of section thirty-five of the judiciary law.

(c) Appeals. On an appeal or motion for permission to appeal a poor person may submit typewritten briefs and appendices, furnishing one legible copy for each appellate justice.

(d) Costs and fees. A poor person shall not be liable for the payment of any costs or fees unless a recovery by judgment or by settlement is had in his favor in which event the court may direct him to pay out of the recovery all or part of the costs and fees, a reasonable sum for the services and expenses of his attorney and any sum expended by the county or city under subdivision (b).

### 1969 AMENDMENTS

L. 1969, ch. 681, eff. Sept. 1, 1969, amended Subd. (b) by adding thereto the last sentence.

### 1966 AMENDMENTS

L. 1966, ch. 455, eff. Sept. 1, 1966, enacted a new Subd. (b).

### 1965 AMENDMENTS

L. 1965, ch. 773, eff. Sept. 1, 1965, amended subdivisions (c) and (d).

### 1964 AMENDMENTS

L. 1964, ch. 576, eff. April 16, 1964, amended Subd. (b).

## § 1103. Distribution of recovery in favor of poor person.

Any recovery by judgment or by settlement had in favor of a poor person, shall be paid to the clerk of the court in which the order permitting the person to proceed as a poor person was entered, to await distribution pursuant to court order.

# ARTICLE 12

# INFANTS, INCOMPETENTS AND CONSERVATEES

## SUMMARY OF ARTICLE

§ 1201.   Representation of infant, incompetent person or conservatee.

R 1202.   Appointment of guardian ad litem.
    (a)  By whom motion made.
    (b)  Notice of motion.
    (c)  Consent.

§ 1203.   Default judgment.

§ 1204.   Compensation of guardian ad litem.

§ 1205.   Liability for costs of infant, judicially declared incompetent, or conservatee, or representative.

§ 1206.   Disposition of proceeds of claim of infant, judicially declared incompetent or conservatee.

§ 1207.   Settlement of action or claim by infant, judicially declared incompetent or conservatee, by whom motion made; special proceeding; notice; order of settlement.

R 1208.   Settlement procedure; papers; representation.
    (a)  Affidavit of infant's or incompetent's representative.
    (b)  Affidavit of attorney.
    (c)  Medical or hospital report.
    (d)  Appearance before court.
    (e)  Representation.
    (f)  Preparation of papers by attorney for adverse party.

§ 1209.   Arbitration of controversy involving infant, judicially declared incompetent or conservatee.

R 1210.   Guardian of infant.
    (a)  Petition for appointment; by whom presented; contents.
    (b)  Hearing.
    (c)  Undertaking.
    (d)  Direction as to management of estate.
    (e)  Filing of certified copy of order of appointment.

R 1211.   Allowance for infant's support.
    (a)  Petition to supreme court, county court or surrogate's court; contents.
    (b)  Notice.

## § 1201.   Representation of infant, incompetent person or conservatee.

Unless the court appoints a guardian ad litem, an infant shall appear by the guardian of his property or, if there is no such guardian, by a parent having legal custody, or, if there is no such parent, by another person or agency having legal custody, or, if the infant is married, by an adult spouse residing with the infant, a person judicially declared to be incompetent shall appear by the committee of his property, and a conservatee shall appear by the conservator of his property. A person shall appear by his guardian ad litem if he is an infant and has no guardian of his property, parent, or other person or agency having legal custody, or adult spouse with whom he resides, or if he is an infant, person judicially declared to be incompetent or a conservatee as defined in section 77.01 of the Mental Hygiene Law and the court so directs because of a conflict of interest or for other cause, or if he is an adult incapable of adequately prosecuting or defending his rights.

### CROSS REFERENCES

See **Mental Hygiene Law § 77.01** as to definition of a conservatee. See **§ 78.15** as to duties and powers of the committee of an incompetent. **§ 78.15(e)** provides for maintenance of proceedings by the committee.

See **SCPA Article 17** as to appointment and powers of guardians and custodians of infants' property.

See **SCPA § 402** as to appearance for infant, incompetent or person under disability in Surrogate's Court.

### Editor's Note

Articles 77 and 78 of the Mental Hygiene Law were replaced by Article 81, eff. April 1, 1993. CPLR § 1201 remains operative for certain parties. *See* L.1992, ch. 698, eff. April 1, 1993, as amended by L. 1993, ch. 32, eff. April 1, 1993.

### 1981 AMENDMENTS

L. 1981, ch. 115, eff. May 18, 1981, amended CPLR 1201 by adding a conservatee as one who shall be represented by another in an action brought by or against him.

### 1974 AMENDMENTS

L. 1974, ch. 606, eff. May 30, 1974, amended CPLR 1201 by providing for the appearance of an infant by an agency having legal custody.

### 1968 AMENDMENTS

L. 1968, ch. 844, eff. Sept. 1, 1968, amended CPLR 1201 to read as above by specifying persons who must represent an infant or incompetent in an action or proceeding.

## R 1202.   Appointment of guardian ad litem.

(a) By whom motion made. The court in which an action is triable may appoint a guardian ad litem at any stage in the action upon its own initiative or upon the motion of:

1. an infant party if he is more than fourteen years of age; or

2. a relative, friend, a guardian or committee of the property or conservator; or

3. any other party to the action if a motion has not been made under paragraph one or two within ten days after completion of service.

(b) Notice of motion. Notice of a motion for appointment of a guardian ad litem for a person shall be served upon the guardian of his property, upon his committee or upon his conservator, or, if he has no such guardian, committee, or conservator, upon the person with whom he resides. Notice shall also be served upon the person who would be represented if he is more than fourteen years of age and has not been judicially declared to be incompetent.

(c) Consent. No order appointing a guardian ad litem shall be effective until a written consent of the proposed guardian has been submitted to the court together with an affidavit stating facts showing his ability to answer for any damage sustained by his negligence or misconduct.

**CROSS REFERENCES**

See SCPA §§ 403 and 404 as to appointment of guardian ad litem in Surrogate's Court.

**1981 AMENDMENTS**

L. 1981, ch. 115, eff. May 18, 1981, amended CPLR 1202(a) and (b) by adding a conservatee's conservator as one who may move to appoint a guardian ad litem and as one who must be served with notice of such a motion.

## § 1203. Default judgment.

No judgment by default may be entered against an infant or a person judicially declared to be incompetent unless his representative appeared in the action or twenty days have expired since appointment of a guardian ad litem for him. No default judgment may be entered against an adult incapable of adequately protecting his rights for whom a guardian ad litem has been appointed unless twenty days have expired since the appointment.

## § 1204. Compensation of guardian ad litem.

A court may allow a guardian ad litem a reasonable compensation for his services to be paid in whole or part by any other party or from any recovery had on behalf of the person whom such guardian represents or from such person's other property. No order allowing compensation shall be made except on an affidavit of the guardian or his attorney showing the services rendered.

**CROSS REFERENCES**

See SCPA § 405 as to compensation of guardian ad litem in Surrogate's Court, and SCPA § 2307 as to commissioners of fiduciaries generally.

CPLR

## § 1205. Liability for costs of infant, judicially declared incompetent, or conservatee, or representative.

An infant, a person judicially declared to be incompetent, a conservatee, a person for whom a guardian ad litem has been appointed, or a representative of any such person, shall not be liable for costs unless the court otherwise orders.

### 1981 AMENDMENTS

L. 1981, ch. 115, eff. May 18, 1981, amended CPLR 1205 by adding conservatees as persons who shall not be liable for costs in an action, unless otherwise ordered by the court.

## § 1206. Disposition of proceeds of claim of infant, judicially declared incompetent or conservatee.

Except as provided in EPTL 7-4.9, any property to which an infant, a person judicially declared to be incompetent or a conservatee is entitled, after deducting any expenses allowed by the court, shall be distributed to the guardian of his property, the committee of his property or conservator to be held for the use and benefit of such infant, incompetent or conservatee except that:

(a) in the case of an infant who is married to and resides with an adult spouse, the court may order that the property be distributed to such adult spouse for the use and benefit of the infant; or (b) if the value of the property does not exceed ten thousand dollars the court may order the property distributed to a person with whom such infant, incompetent or conservatee resides or who has some interest in his welfare to be held for the use and benefit of such infant, incompetent or conservatee; or (c) the court may order that money constituting any part of the property be deposited in one or more specified insured banks or trust companies or savings banks or insured state or federal credit unions or be invested in one or more specified accounts in insured savings and loan associations, or it may order that a structured settlement agreement be executed, which shall include any settlement whose terms contain provisions for the payment of funds on an installment basis, provided that with respect to future installment payments, the court may order that each party liable for such payments shall fund such payments, in an amount necessary to assure the future payments, in the form of an annuity contract executed by a qualified insurer and approved by the superintendent of insurance pursuant to articles fifty-A and fifty-B of this chapter. The court may elect that the money be deposited in a high interest yield account such as an insured "savings certificate" or an insured "money market" account. The court may further elect to invest the money in one or more insured or guaranteed United States treasury or municipal bills, notes or bonds. This money is subject to withdrawal only upon order of the court, except that no court order shall be required to pay over to the infant who has attained the age of eighteen years all moneys so held unless the depository is in receipt of an order from a court of competent jurisdiction directing it to withhold such payment beyond the infant's eighteenth birthday. Notwithstanding the preceding sentence, the ability of an infant who has attained the age of eighteen years to accelerate the receipt of future installment payments pursuant to a structured settlement agreement shall be governed by the terms of such agreement. The reference to the age of twenty-one years in any order made pursuant to this subdivision or its predecessor, prior to September first, nineteen hundred seventy-four, directing payment to the infant without further court order when he reaches the age of twenty-one years, shall be deemed to designate the age of eighteen years; or

(d) the court may order that the property be held for the use and benefit of such infant, incompetent or conservatee as provided by subdivision (d) of section 1210.

### CROSS REFERENCES

EPTL § 7-4.9 provides that a will or other instrument may authorize distribution to a minor by means of distribution to a custodian.

See also SCPA § 2220 as to payment of share of infant or incompetent in settlement of fiduciary's accounts.

### 1995 AMENDMENTS

L. 1995, ch. 205, eff. July 26, 1995, amended CPLR 1206(b) by increasing the value of the property which a court may order distributed from five to ten thousand dollars.

L. 1995, ch. 464, eff. Aug. 2, 1995, amended CPLR 1206(c) to authorize the court to order deposits with savings banks and insured state or federal credit unions.

### 1988 AMENDMENTS

L. 1988, ch. 635, eff. Oct. 1, 1988, amended subd. (c) to provide for structured settlement agreements.

### 1986 AMENDMENTS

L. 1986, ch. 125, eff. Sept. 1, 1986, amended Subd. (b) of CPLR 1206 by changing the value of the property which a court may order distributed to five thousand dollars.

### 1982 AMENDMENTS

L. 1982, ch. 177, eff. Sept. 6, 1982, amended CPLR 1206(c) to permit the court to elect to deposit the proceeds of the claim of an infant, incompetent or conservatee in a high interest yield account or in U.S. treasury or municipal bills, notes or bonds.

### 1981 AMENDMENTS

L. 1981, ch. 73, eff. Sept. 1, 1981, amended CPLR 1206(b) to increase from one to three thousand dollars the limit on the value of property a court may order distributed on behalf of an infant, incompetent or conservatee. It shall apply to the estates of decedents dying on or after the effective date.

L. 1981, ch. 115, eff. May 18, 1981, amended CPLR 1206 and subdivisions (b) and (d) to add a conservatee as one whose property may be disposed of in accordance with its provisions and add the conservator as one to whom such property may be distributed.

### 1975 AMENDMENTS

L. 1975, ch. 228, eff. Sept. 1, 1975, amended subdivision (c) of CPLR 1206 by deleting a clause which had provided that the court *may direct* that a payout be made to the infant on demand upon reaching the age of eighteen years, without *further* court order, and substituting a provision that the payout may be made on demand, on reaching eighteen years, absent *any* court order, and that an order permitting payment would only be required to countermand an existing order to withhold payment beyond the infant's eighteenth birthday.

The amendment further provided that an order made prior to September 1, 1974 directing payment without further court order when the infant reaches twenty-one years of age shall be deemed to designate the age as eighteen years.

### 1974 AMENDMENTS

L. 1974, ch. 924, eff. Sept. 1, 1974, amended Subd. (c) providing for the removal of funds from a depository by an infant upon demand "when he reaches the age of eighteen years." Previously the provision applied to an infant "when he reaches the age of twenty-one years."

### 1973 AMENDMENTS

L. 1973, ch. 455, eff. June 5, 1973, amended the introductory paragraph of CPLR 1206 by adding thereto "Except as provided in EPTL 7-4.8."

### 1968 AMENDMENTS

L. 1968, ch. 844, eff. Sept. 1, 1968, amended CPLR 1206 by the addition of Subd. (a) and by the addition to Subd. (c) of the final clause in the first sentence, beginning with the word "unless."

## § 1207. Settlement of action or claim by infant, judicially declared incompetent or conservatee, by whom motion made; special proceeding; notice; order of settlement.

Upon motion of a guardian of the property or guardian ad litem of an infant or, if there is no such guardian, then of a parent having legal custody of an infant, or if there is no such parent, by another person having legal custody, or if the infant is married, by an adult spouse residing with the infant, or of the committee of the property of a person judicially declared to be incompetent, or of the conservator of the property of a conservatee, the court may order settlement of any action commenced by or on behalf of the infant, incompetent or conservatee. If no action has been commenced, a special proceeding may be commenced upon petition of such a representative for settlement of any claim by the infant, incompetent or conservatee in any court where an action for the amount of the proposed settlement could have been commenced. Unless otherwise provided by rule of the chief administrator of the courts, if no motion term is being held and there is no justice of the supreme court available in a county where the action or an action on the claim is triable, such a motion may be made, or special proceeding may be commenced, in a county court and the county judge shall act with the same power as a justice of the supreme court even though the amount of the settlement may exceed the jurisdictional limits of the county court. Notice of the motion or petition shall be given as directed by the court. An order on such a motion shall have the effect of a judgment. Such order, or the judgment in a special proceeding, shall be entered without costs and shall approve the fee for the infant's, incompetent's or conservatee's attorney, if any.

### 1986 AMENDMENTS

L. 1986, ch. 355, eff. July 17, 1986, amended CPLR 1207 by adding "Unless otherwise provided for by rule of the chief administrator of the courts" after the sentence ending "could have been commenced."

### 1981 AMENDMENTS

L. 1981, ch. 115, eff. May 18, 1981, amended CPLR 1207 to add conservatees as persons whose actions and claims are to be settled according to this section's provisions.

### 1971 AMENDMENTS

L. 1971, ch. 571, eff. Sept. 1, 1971, amended CPLR 1207 by deleting "resident" from the third sentence, and by adding "available" after the phrase "there is no justice of the supreme court."

### 1969 AMENDMENTS

L. 1969, ch. 209, eff. Sept. 1, 1969, included within the category of those who may settle an infant's claim, all those representatives mentioned in CPLR 1201.

## R 1208.    Settlement procedure; papers; representation.

(a) Affidavit of infant's or incompetent's representative. An affidavit of the infant's or incompetent's representative shall be included in the supporting papers and shall state:

1. his name, residence and relationship to the infant or incompetent;

2. the name, age and residence of the infant or incompetent;

3. the circumstances giving rise to the action or claim;

4. the nature and extent of the damages sustained by the infant or incompetent, and if the action or claim is for damages for personal injuries to the infant or incompetent, the name of each physician who attended or treated the infant or incompetent or who was consulted, the medical expenses, the period of disability, the amount of wages lost, and the present physical condition of the infant or incompetent;

5. the terms and proposed distribution of the settlement and his approval of both;

6. the facts surrounding any other motion or petition for settlement of the same claim, of an action to recover on the same claim or of the same action;

7. whether reimbursement for medical or other expenses has been received from any source; and

8. whether the infant's or incompetent's representative or any member of the infant's or incompetent's family has made a claim for damages alleged to have been suffered as a result of the same occurrence giving rise to the infant's or incompetent's claim and, if so, the amount paid or to be paid in settlement of such claim or if such claim has not been settled the reasons therefor.

(b) Affidavit of attorney. If the infant or incompetent or his representative is represented by an attorney, an affidavit of the attorney shall be included in the supporting papers and shall state:

1. his reasons for recommending the settlement;

2. that directly or indirectly he has neither become concerned in the settlement at the instance of a party or person opposing, or with interests adverse to, the infant or incompetent nor received nor will receive any compensation from such party, and whether or not he has represented or now represents any other person asserting a claim arising from the same occurrence; and

3. the services rendered by him.

(c) Medical or hospital report. If the action or claim is for damages for personal injuries to the infant or incompetent, one or more medical or hospital reports, which need not be verified, shall be included in the supporting papers.

(d) Appearance before court. On the hearing, the moving party or petitioner, the infant or incompetent, and his attorney shall attend before the court unless attendance is excused for good cause.

(e) Representation. No attorney having or representing any interest conflicting with that of an infant or incompetent may represent the infant or incompetent.

(f) Preparation of papers by attorney for adverse party. If the infant or incompetent is not represented by an attorney the papers may be prepared by the attorney for an adverse party or person and shall state the fact.

### CROSS REFERENCES

See **Judiciary Law § 474** as to special requirements for attorney's contingent fee arrangements on infants' claims.

### 1968 AMENDMENTS

L. 1968, ch. 844, eff. Sept. 1, 1968, amended the caption and text of CPLR 1208 by having it read as above in Subds. (a), (b), (c) and (d) and by repealing Subd. (g).

### 1967 AMENDMENTS

L. 1967, ch. 578, eff. July 1, 1967, added Subd. (g), (repealed in 1968).

### 1964 AMENDMENTS

L. 1964, ch. 195, eff. Sept. 1, 1964, deleted words "of each" and "each" in first sentence of Subd. (c), dealing with affidavit of physician. First sentence formerly read: "If the action or claim is for damages for personal injuries to the infant or incompetent, affidavits of each of one or more physicians shall be included in the supporting papers and each shall state: . . ."

## § 1209. Arbitration of controversy involving infant, judicially declared incompetent or conservatee.

A controversy involving an infant, person judicially declared to be incompetent or conservatee, shall not be submitted to arbitration except pursuant to a court order made upon application of the representative of such infant, incompetent or conservatee.

### 1981 AMENDMENTS

L. 1981, ch. 115, eff. May 18, 1981, amended CPLR 1209 to add a controversy involving a conservatee to those governed by this section.

## R 1210. Guardian of infant.

(a) Petition for appointment; by whom presented; contents. An infant, if of the age of fourteen years or more, or a relative or friend of an infant, may present a petition to the court for appointment of a guardian. The petition shall state the age and residence of the infant, the name and residence of any living parent and of the person proposed as guardian, the relationship, if any, which such person bears to the infant, and the nature, status and value of the infant's estate.

(b) Hearing. The court shall ascertain the age of the infant, the amount of his personal property, the gross amount or value of the rents and profits of his real estate during his minority, and the sufficiency of the security offered by the proposed guardian. If the infant is of the age of fourteen years or more, the court shall examine him as to his voluntary nomination of or preference for a suitable guardian; if he is under the age of fourteen, the court shall select and appoint a suitable guardian.

(c) Undertaking. The court shall make an order requiring or dispensing wholly or partly with an undertaking, in an amount and according to the conditions set forth in section seventeen hundred eight of the surrogate's court procedure act.

(d) Direction as to management of estate. The court in its discretion may direct that the principal of the estate or any part of it be invested in bonds of the state of New York or of the United States, or invested in bonds or other obligations of any county, city, town, village or school district of the state of New York, or deposited with any bank, trust company, insured savings and loan association or insured savings bank or insured state or federal credit union which has been designated as a depository for such fund; or invested in a bond and mortgage on unincumbered and improved property within the state, having a value, to be shown to the satisfaction of the court, of at least double the amount of principal invested, for the benefit of the infant, and may direct that only the interest or income be received by the guardian.

(e) Filing of certified copy of order of appointment. Upon the appointment of a guardian of the person or property, or both, of an infant the guardian shall file a certified copy of the order of his appointment with the clerk of the surrogate's court of the county in which he has been appointed.

CPLR

## CROSS REFERENCES

**SCPA § 1708,** referred to in Subd. (c), *supra,* appears in Appendix, *infra.*

See also **SCPA § 801,** in Appendix, *infra,* as to amount, conditions, sureties and obligees of the undertaking.

## 1995 AMENDMENTS

L. 1995, ch. 464, eff. Aug. 2, 1995, amended CPLR 1210(d) by adding the words "or insured state or federal credit union."

## 1983 AMENDMENTS

L. 1983, ch. 37, eff. Sept. 1, 1983, amended Subd. (d) by allowing for investment in county, city, town, village and school district bonds by guardians or infants.

## 1975 AMENDMENTS

L. 1975, ch. 490, eff. Sept. 1, 1975, amended Subd. (d) by adding insured savings and loan associations and insured savings banks as depositories for funds deposited by guardians of infants.

## 1969 AMENDMENTS

Amendment made by Judicial Conference Feb. 1, 1969, Report to the 1969 Legislature, eff. Sept 1, 1969, eliminated the word "general" from the term "general guardian" in the catch line and in subdivisions (a) and (e) of Rule 1210 to effect consistency of terminology with the new Surrogate's Court Procedure Act (Art. 17).

## 1966 AMENDMENTS

L. 1966, ch. 961, added a new Subd. (e), eff. Sept. 1, 1967.

# R 1211.   Allowance for infant's support.

(a) Petition to supreme court, county court or surrogate's court; contents. A petition to the supreme court, county court or the surrogate's court for the application of an infant's property or a portion thereof to the infant's support, maintenance or education shall set forth in detail:

1. the amount and nature of the infant's property, where it is situated and how invested, his income from such property or any other source and any claim against the infant;

2. whether or not the infant's parents are living and, if either of them is living, all circumstances relative to their ability to support the infant, and if neither of them is living, the names of other persons legally obligated to support the infant and the circumstances relative to their ability to support the infant; and

3. the terms of any previous order made by any court within or without the state for similar relief and the disposition made of any property pursuant thereto.

(b) Notice. Such notice as the court shall direct shall be given to:

1. the guardian of the property of the infant, if the petition is presented by a person other than such guardian;

2. the infant's father if he is living or, if not, then to the infant's mother or, if neither parent is living, then to the person with whom the infant resides; and

3. the infant if he is of the age of fourteen years or more.

### 1972 AMENDMENTS

L. 1972, ch. 276, eff. Sept. 1, 1972, added "county court" to Subd. (a).

# ARTICLE 13

# ACTIONS BY THE STATE

————

## SUMMARY OF ARTICLE

§ 1301.    Actions in behalf of the people to be brought in the name of the state.
§ 1302.    Action brought on relation of a person.
§ 1303.    Procedure in action brought by the state.

————

CPLR

## § 1301.   Actions in behalf of the people to be brought in the name of the state.

An action brought in behalf of the people, except an action to recover a penalty or forfeiture expressly given by law to a particular officer, shall be brought in the name of the state.

## § 1302.   Action brought on relation of a person.

Where an action is brought by the attorney-general on the relation or information of a person having an interest in the question, the complaint shall allege, and the title of the action shall show, that the action is so brought. As a condition of bringing an action for the benefit of a person having an interest in the question, the attorney-general shall require the relator to give an undertaking to indemnify the state against costs and expenses.

## § 1303.   Procedure in action brought by the state.

Except as otherwise specially prescribed by statute or rule the proceedings in an action brought by the state shall be the same as in an action by a private person.

# ARTICLE 13-A

# PROCEEDS OF A CRIME—FORFEITURE

---

## SUMMARY OF ARTICLE

§ 1310.   Definitions.
§ 1311.   Forfeiture actions.
§ 1311-a. Subpoena duces tecum.
§ 1312.   Provisional remedies; generally.
§ 1313.   Debt or property subject to attachment; proper garnishee.
§ 1314.   Attaching creditor's rights in personal property.
§ 1315.   Discharge of garnishee's obligation.
§ 1316.   Order of attachment on notice; temporary restraining order; contents.
§ 1317.   Order of attachment without notice.
   (1)   When granted; contents.
   (2)   Confirmation of order.
§ 1318.   Motion papers; filing; demand; damages.
   (1)   Affidavit; other papers.
   (2)   Filing.
   (3)   Demand for papers.
   (4)   Damages.
§ 1319.   Service of summons.
§ 1320.   Levy upon personal property by service of order.
   (1)   Method of levy.
   (2)   Effect of levy; prohibition of transfer.
   (3)   Seizure by claiming agent; notice of satisfaction.
   (4)   Proceeding to compel payment or delivery.
   (5)   Failure to proceed.
§ 1321.   Levy upon personal property by seizure.
§ 1322.   Levy upon real property.
§ 1323.   Additional undertaking to carrier garnishee.
§ 1324.   Claiming agent's duties after levy.
   (1)   Retention of property.
   (2)   Inventory.
§ 1325.   Garnishee's statement.
§ 1326.   Disclosure.
§ 1327.   Proceedings to determine adverse claims.
§ 1328.   Discharge of attachment.
§ 1329.   Vacating or modifying attachment.
   (1)   Motion to vacate or modify.
   (2)   Burden of proof.
§ 1330.   Annulment of attachment.
§ 1331.   Return of property; directions to clerk and claiming agent.

CPLR

§ 1332.     Disposition of attachment property after execution issued; priority of orders of attachment.

§ 1333.     Grounds for preliminary injunction and temporary restraining order.

§ 1334.     Motion papers.

§ 1335.     Temporary restraining order.
     (1)   Generally.
     (2)   Service.

§ 1336.     Vacating or modifying preliminary injunction or temporary restraining order.

§ 1337.     Ascertaining damages sustained by reason of preliminary injunction or temporary restraining order.

§ 1338.     Appointment and powers of temporary receiver.
     (1)   Appointment of temporary receiver; joinder of moving party.
     (2)   Powers of temporary receiver.
     (3)   Duration of temporary receivership.

§ 1339.     Oath.

§ 1340.     Undertaking.

§ 1341.     Accounts.

§ 1342.     Removal.

§ 1343.     Notice of pendency; constructive notice.

§ 1344.     Filing, content and indexing of notice of pendency.
     (1)   Filing.
     (2)   Content, designation of index.
     (3)   Indexing.

§ 1345.     Service of summons.

§ 1346.     Duration of notice of pendency.

§ 1347.     Motion for cancellation of notice of pendency.
     (1)   Mandatory cancellation.
     (2)   Discretionary cancellation.
     (3)   Costs and expenses.
     (4)   Cancellation by stipulation.
     (5)   Cancellation by a claiming authority.

§ 1348.     Undertaking for cancellation of notice of pendency.

§ 1349.     Disposal of property.

§ 1350.     Rules of procedure; in general.

§ 1351.     Application of article.

§ 1352.     Preservation of other rights and remedies.

---

## § 1310. Definitions.

In this article:

1. "Property" means and includes: real property, personal property, money, negotiable instruments, securities, or any thing of value or any interest in a thing of value.

2. "Proceeds of a crime" means any property obtained through the commission of a felony crime defined in subdivisions five and six hereof, and includes any appreciation in value of such property.

3. "Substituted proceeds of a crime" means any property obtained by the sale or exchange of proceeds of a crime, and any gain realized by such sale or exchange.

4. "Instrumentality of a crime" means any property, other than real property and any buildings, fixtures, appurtenances, and improvements thereon, whose use contributes directly and materially to the commission of a crime defined in subdivisions five and six hereof.

4–a. "Real property instrumentality of a crime" means an interest in real property the use of which contributes directly and materially to the commission of a specified felony offense.

4–b. "Specified felony offense" means:

(a) a conviction of a person for a violation of section 220.18, 220.21, 220.41, or 220.43 of the penal law, or where the accusatory instrument charges one or more of such offenses, conviction upon a plea of guilty to any of the felonies for which such plea is otherwise authorized by law or a conviction of a person for conspiracy to commit a violation of section 220.18, 220.21, 220.41, or 220.43 of the penal law, where the controlled substances which are the object of the conspiracy are located in the real property which is the subject of the forfeiture action; or

(b) on three or more occasions, engaging in conduct constituting a violation of any of the felonies defined in section 220.09, 220.16, 220.18, 220.21, 220.31, 220.34, 220.39, 220.41, 220.43 or 221.55 of the penal law, which violations do not constitute a single criminal offense as defined in subdivision one of section 40.10 of the criminal procedure law, or a single criminal transaction, as defined in paragraph (a) of subdivision two of section 40.10 of the criminal procedure law, and at least one of which resulted in a conviction of such offense, or where the accusatory instrument charges one or more of such felonies, conviction upon a plea of guilty to a felony for which such plea is otherwise authorized by law; or

(c) a conviction of a person for a violation of section 220.09, 220.16, 220.34 or 220.39 of the penal law, or a conviction of a criminal defendant for a violation of section 221.30 of the penal law, or where the accusatory instrument charges any such felony, conviction upon a plea of guilty to a felony for which the plea is otherwise authorized by law, together with evidence which: (i) provides substantial indicia that the defendant used the real property to engage in a continual, ongoing course of conduct involving the unlawful mixing, compounding, manufacturing, warehousing, or packaging of controlled substances or where the conviction is for a violation of section 221.30 of the penal law, marijuana, as part of an illegal trade or business for gain; and (ii) establishes, where the conviction is for possession of a controlled substance or where the conviction is for a violation of section 221.30 of the penal law, marijuana, that such possession was with the intent to sell it.

5. "Post-conviction forfeiture crime" means any felony defined in the penal law or any other chapter of the consolidated laws of the state.

6. "Pre-conviction forfeiture crime" means only a felony defined in article two hundred twenty or section 221.30 or 221.55 of the penal law.

7. "Court" means a superior court.

8. "Defendant" means a person against whom a forfeiture action is commenced and includes a "criminal defendant" and a "non-criminal defendant."

9. "Criminal defendant" means a person who has criminal liability for a crime defined in subdivisions five and six hereof. For purposes of this article, a person has criminal liability when (a) he has been convicted of a post-conviction forfeiture crime, or (b) the claiming authority proves by clear and convincing evidence that such person has committed an act in violation of article two hundred twenty or section 221.30 or 221.55 of the penal law.

10. "Non-criminal defendant" means a person, other than a criminal defendant, who possesses an interest in the proceeds of a crime, the substituted proceeds of a crime or in an instrumentality of a crime.

11. "Claiming authority" means the district attorney having jurisdiction over the offense or the attorney general for purpose of those crimes for which the attorney general has criminal jurisdiction in a case where the underlying criminal charge has been, is being or is about to be brought by the attorney general, or the appropriate corporation counsel or county attorney, provided that the corporation counsel or county attorney may act as a claiming authority only with the consent of the district attorney or the attorney general, as appropriate.

12. "Claiming agent" means and shall include all persons described in subdivision thirty-four of section 1.20 of the criminal procedure law, and sheriffs, undersheriffs and deputy sheriffs of counties within the city of New York.

13. "Fair consideration" means fair consideration is given for property, or obligation, (a) when in exchange for such property, or obligation, as a fair equivalent therefor, and in good faith, property is conveyed or an antecedent debt is satisfied, or (b) when such property, or obligation is received in good faith to secure a present advance or antecedent debt in amount not disproportionately small as compared with the value of the property, or obligation obtained.

14. "District attorney" means and shall include all persons described in subdivision thirty-two of section 1.20 of the criminal procedure law and the special assistant district attorney in charge of the office of prosecution, special narcotics courts of the city of New York.

### CROSS REFERENCES

Article 220 of the **Penal Law**, referred to in paragraph (6), deals with controlled substances offenses; **Penal Law §§ 221.30 and 221.55 cover the criminal possession and sale of marihuana in the first degree. Criminal Procedure Law** § 1.20(34), referred to in paragraph 12, lists persons included within the term "police officer."

### 1990 AMENDMENTS

L. 1990, ch. 655, eff. Nov. 1, 1990, amended CPLR 1310 by adding subdivisions (4–a), defining "real property instrumentality of a crime," and (4–b), defining "specified felony offense," and by amending subdivision (11) by replacing the words "the defendant in the forfeiture action is a person against whom a" with "the underlying."

### 1986 AMENDMENTS

L. 1986, ch. 8, eff. Nov. 1, 1986, added new subdivision (14) defining "district attorney"; L. 1986, ch. 174, eff. Nov. 1, 1986, amended subdivision (12) to include sheriffs, undersheriffs and deputy sheriffs of counties in the city of New York, within the definition of "claiming agent."

### 1984 AMENDMENTS

L. 1984, ch. 669, eff. Aug. 1, 1984, repealed former Article 13-A and added a new Article 13-A, comprising CPLR 1310 through CPLR 1352. New Article 13-A is applicable to crimes committed on and after Aug. 1, 1984.

## § 1311.  Forfeiture actions.

1. A civil action may be commenced by the appropriate claiming authority against a criminal defendant to recover the property which constitutes the proceeds of a crime, the substituted proceeds of a crime, an instrumentality of a crime or the real property instrumentality of a crime or to recover a money judgment in an amount equivalent in value to the property which constitutes the proceeds of a crime, the substituted proceeds of a crime, an instrumentality of a crime, or the real property instrumentality of a crime. A civil action may be commenced against a non-criminal defendant to recover the property which constitutes the proceeds of a crime, the substituted proceeds of a crime, an instrumentality of a crime or the real property instrumentality of a crime, provided, however, that a judgment of forfeiture predicated upon clause (A) of subparagraph (iv) of paragraph (b) of subdivision three hereof shall be limited to the amount of the proceeds of the crime. Any action under this article must be commenced within five years of the commission of the crime and shall be civil, remedial, and in personam in nature and shall not be deemed to be a penalty or criminal forfeiture for any purpose. Except as otherwise specially provided by statute, the proceedings under this article shall be governed by this chapter. An action under this article is not a criminal proceeding and may not be deemed to be a previous prosecution under article forty of the criminal procedure law.

(a) Actions relating to post-conviction forfeiture crimes. An action relating to a post-conviction forfeiture crime must be grounded upon a conviction of a felony defined in subdivision five of section one thousand three hundred ten of this article, or upon criminal activity arising from a common scheme or plan of which such a conviction is a part, or upon a count of an indictment or information alleging a felony which was dismissed at the time of a plea of guilty to a felony in satisfaction of such count. A court may not grant forfeiture until such conviction has occurred. However, an action may be commenced, and a court may grant a provisional remedy provided under this article, prior to such conviction having occurred. An action under this paragraph must be dismissed at any time after sixty days of the commencement of the action unless the conviction upon which the action is grounded has occurred, or an indictment or information upon which the asserted conviction is to be based is pending in a superior court. An action under this paragraph shall be stayed during the pendency of a criminal action which is related to it; provided, however, that such stay shall not prevent the granting or continuance of any provisional remedy provided under this article or any other provisions of law.

(b) Actions relating to pre-conviction forfeiture crimes. An action relating to a pre-conviction forfeiture crime need not be grounded upon conviction of a pre-conviction forfeiture crime, provided, however, that if the action is not grounded upon such a conviction, it shall be necessary in the action for the claiming authority to prove the commission of a pre-conviction forfeiture crime by clear and convincing evidence. An action under this paragraph shall be stayed during the pendency of a criminal action which is related to it; provided, that upon motion of a defendant in the forfeiture action or the claiming authority, a court may, in the interest of justice and for good cause, and with the consent of all parties, order that the forfeiture action proceed despite the pending criminal action; and provided that such stay shall not prevent the granting or continuance of any provisional remedy provided under this article or any other provision of law.

2. All defendants in a forfeiture action brought pursuant to this article shall have the right to trial by jury on any issue of fact.

3. In a forfeiture action pursuant to this article the following burdens of proof shall apply:

(a) In a forfeiture action commenced by a claiming authority against a criminal defendant, except for those facts referred to in paragraph (b) of subdivision nine of section one thousand three hundred ten and paragraph (b) of subdivision one of this section which must be proven by clear and convincing evidence, the burden shall be upon the claiming authority to prove by a preponderance of the evidence the facts necessary to establish a claim for forfeiture.

(b) In a forfeiture action commenced by a claiming authority against a non-criminal defendant:

(i) in an action relating to a pre-conviction forfeiture crime, the burden shall be upon the claiming authority to prove by clear and convincing evidence the commission of the crime by a person, provided, however, that it shall not be necessary to prove the identity of such person.

(ii) if the action relates to the proceeds of a crime, except as provided in subparagraph (i) hereof, the burden shall be upon the claiming authority to prove by a preponderance of the evidence the facts necessary to establish a claim for forfeiture and that the non-criminal defendant either (A) knew or should have known that the proceeds were obtained through the commission of a crime, or (B) fraudulently obtained his or her interest in the proceeds to avoid forfeiture.

(iii) if the action relates to the substituted proceeds of a crime, except as provided in subparagraph (i) hereof, the burden shall be upon the claiming authority to prove by a preponderance of the evidence the facts necessary to establish a claim for forfeiture and that the non-criminal defendant either (A) knew that the property sold or exchanged to obtain an interest in the substituted proceeds was obtained through the commission of a crime, or (B) fraudulently obtained his or her interest in the substituted proceeds to avoid forfeiture.

(iv) if the action relates to an instrumentality of a crime, except as provided for in subparagraph (i) hereof, the burden shall be upon the claiming authority to prove by a preponderance of the evidence the facts necessary to establish a claim for forfeiture and that the non-criminal defendant either (A) knew that the instrumentality was or would be used in the commission of a crime or (B) knowingly obtained his or her interest in the instrumentality to avoid forfeiture.

(v) if the action relates to a real property instrumentality of a crime, the burden shall be upon the claiming authority to prove those facts referred to in subdivision four-b of section thirteen hundred ten of this article by clear and convincing evidence. The claiming authority shall also prove by a clear and convincing evidence that the non-criminal defendant knew that such property was or would be used for the commission of specified felony offenses, and either (a) knowingly and unlawfully benefited from such conduct or (b) voluntarily agreed to the use of such property for the commission of such offenses by consent freely given. For purposes of this subparagraph, a non-criminal defendant knowingly and unlawfully benefits from the commission of a specified felony offense when he derives in exchange for permitting the use or occupancy of such real property by a person or persons committing such specified offense a substantial benefit that would otherwise not accrue as a result of the lawful use or occupancy of such real property. "Benefit" means benefit as defined in subdivision seventeen of section 10.00 of the penal law.

(c) In a forfeiture action commenced by a claiming authority against a non-criminal defendant the following rebuttable presumptions shall apply:

(i) a non-criminal defendant who did not pay fair consideration for the proceeds of a crime, the substituted proceeds of a crime or the instrumentality of a crime, shall be presumed to know that such property was the proceeds of a crime, the substituted proceeds of a crime, or an instrumentality of a crime.

CPLR

(ii) a non-criminal defendant who obtains an interest in the proceeds of a crime, substituted proceeds of a crime or an instrumentality of a crime with knowledge of an order of provisional remedy relating to said property issued pursuant to this article, shall be presumed to know that such property was the proceeds of a crime, substituted proceeds of a crime, or an instrumentality of a crime.

(iii) in an action relating to a post-conviction forfeiture crime, a non-criminal defendant who the claiming authority proves by clear and convincing evidence has criminal liability under section 20.00 of the penal law for the crime of conviction or for criminal activity arising from a common scheme or plan of which such crime is a part and who possesses an interest in the proceeds, the substituted proceeds, or an instrumentality of such criminal activity is presumed to know that such property was the proceeds of a crime, the substituted proceeds of a crime, or an instrumentality of a crime.

(iv) a non-criminal defendant who participated in or was aware of a scheme to conceal or disguise the manner in which said non-criminal obtained his or her interest in the proceeds of a crime, substituted proceeds of a crime, or an instrumentality of a crime is presumed to know that such property was the proceeds of a crime, the substituted proceeds of a crime, or an instrumentality of a crime.

(d) In a forfeiture action commenced by a claiming authority against a defendant, the following rebuttable presumption shall apply: all currency or negotiable instruments payable to the bearer shall be presumed to be the proceeds of a pre-conviction forfeiture crime when such currency or negotiable instruments are (i) found in close proximity to a controlled substance unlawfully possessed by the defendant in an amount sufficient to constitute a violation of section 220.18 or 220.21 of the penal law, or (ii) found in close proximity to any quantity of a controlled substance or marihuana unlawfully possessed by such defendant in a room, other than a public place, under circumstances evincing an intent to unlawfully mix, compound, distribute, package or otherwise prepare for sale such controlled substance or marihuana.

(e) The presumption set forth pursuant to paragraph (d) of this subdivision shall be rebutted by credible and reliable evidence which tends to show that such currency or negotiable instrument payable to the bearer is not the proceeds of a preconviction forfeiture crime. In an action tried before a jury, the jury shall be so instructed. Any sworn testimony of a defendant offered to rebut the presumption and any other evidence which is obtained as a result of such testimony, shall be inadmissible in any subsequent proceeding relating to the forfeiture action, or in any other civil or criminal action, except in a prosecution for a violation of article two hundred ten of the penal law. In an action tried before a jury, at the commencement of the trial, or at such other time as the court reasonably directs, the claiming authority shall provide notice to the court and to the defendant of its intent to request that the court charge such presumption.

3–a. Conviction of a person in a criminal action upon an accusatory instrument which includes one or more of the felonies specified in subdivision four-b of section thirteen hundred ten of this article, of any felony other than such felonies, shall not preclude a defendant, in any subsequent proceeding under this article where that conviction is at issue, from adducing evidence that the conduct underlying the conviction would not establish the elements of any of the felonies specified in such subdivision other than the one to which the criminal defendant pled guilty. If the defendant does adduce such evidence, the burden shall be upon the claiming authority to prove, by clear and convincing evidence, that the conduct underlying the criminal conviction would establish the elements of the felony specified in such subdivision. Nothing contained in this subdivision shall affect the validity of a settlement of any forfeiture action negotiated between the claiming authority and a criminal defendant contemporaneously with the taking of a plea of guilty in a criminal action to any felony defined in article two hundred twenty or section 221.30 or 221.55 of the penal law, or to a felony conspiracy to commit the same.

4. The court in which a forfeiture action is pending may dismiss said action in the interests of justice upon its own motion or upon an application as provided for herein.

(a) At any time during the pendency of a forfeiture action, the claiming authority who instituted the action, or a defendant may (i) apply for an order dismissing the complaint and terminating the forfeiture action in the interest of justice, or (ii) may apply for an order limiting the forfeiture to an amount equivalent in value to the value of property constituting the proceeds or substituted proceeds of a crime in the interest of justice.

(b) Such application for the relief provided in paragraph (a) hereof must be made in writing and upon notice to all parties. The court may, in its discretion, direct that notice be given to any other person having an interest in the property.

(c) An application for the relief provided for in paragraph (a) hereof must be brought exclusively in the superior court in which the forfeiture action is pending.

(d) The court may grant the relief provided in paragraph (a) hereof if it finds that such relief is warranted by the existence of some compelling factor, consideration or circumstance demonstrating that forfeiture of the property of* any part thereof, would not serve the ends of justice. Among the factors, considerations and circumstances the court may consider, among others, are:

(i) the seriousness and circumstances of the crime to which the property is connected relative to the impact of forfeiture of property upon the person who committed the crime; or

(ii) the adverse impact of a forfeiture of property upon innocent persons; or

(iii) the appropriateness of a judgment of forfeiture in an action relating to pre-conviction forfeiture crime where the criminal proceeding based on the crime to which the property is allegedly connected results in an acquittal of the criminal defendant or a dismissal of the accusatory instrument on the merits; or

(iv) in the case of an action relating to an instrumentality, whether the value of the instrumentality substantially exceeds the value of the property constituting the proceeds or substituted proceeds of a crime.

(e) The court must issue a written decision stating the basis for an order issued pursuant to this subdivision.

4–a. (a) The court in which a forfeiture action relating to real property is pending may, upon its own motion or upon the motion of the claiming authority which instituted the action, the defendant, or any other person who has a lawful property interest in such property, enter an order:

(i) appointing an administrator pursuant to section seven hundred seventy-eight of the real property actions and proceedings law when the owner of a dwelling is a defendant in such action, and when persons who are not defendants in such action lawfully occupy one or more units within such dwelling, in order to maintain and preserve the property on behalf of such persons or any other person or entity who has a lawful property interest in such property, or in order to remedy any other condition which is dangerous to life, health or safety; or

(ii) otherwise limiting, modifying or dismissing the forfeiture action in order to preserve or protect the lawful property interest of any non-criminal defendant or any other person who is not a criminal defendant, or the lawful property interest of a defendant which is not subject to forfeiture; or

(iii) where such action involves interest in a residential leasehold or a statutory tenancy, directing that upon entry of a judgment of forfeiture, the lease or statutory tenancy will be modified as a matter of law to terminate only the interest of the defendant or defendants, and to continue the occupancy or tenancy of any other person or persons who lawfully reside in such demised premises, with such rights as such parties would otherwise have had if the defendant's interest had not been forfeited pursuant to this article.

(b) For purposes of this subdivision the term "owner" has the same meaning as prescribed for that term in section seven hundred eighty-one of the real property actions and proceedings law and the term "dwelling" shall mean any building or structure or portion thereof which is principally occupied in whole or part as the home, residence or sleeping place of one or more human beings.

5. An action for forfeiture shall be commenced by service pursuant to this chapter of a summons with notice or summons and verified complaint. No person shall forfeit any right, title, or interest in any property who is not a defendant in the action. The claiming authority shall also file a copy of such papers with the state division of criminal justice services; provided, however, failure to file such papers shall not be grounds for any relief by a defendant in this section.

6. On the motion of any party to the forfeiture action, and for good cause shown, a court may seal any papers, including those pertaining to any provisional

remedy, which relate to the forfeiture action until such time as the property which is the subject of the forfeiture action has been levied upon. A motion to seal such papers may be made ex parte and in camera.

7. Remission. In addition to any other relief provided under this chapter, at any time within one year after the entry of a judgment of forfeiture, any person, claiming an interest in the property subject to forfeiture who did not receive actual notice of the forfeiture action may petition the judge before whom the forfeiture action was held for a remission or mitigation of the forfeiture and restoration of the property or the proceeds of any sale resulting from the forfeiture, or such part thereof, as may be claimed by him. The court may restore said property upon such terms and conditions as it deems reasonable and just if (i) the petitioner establishes that he or she was without actual knowledge of the forfeiture action or any related proceeding for a provisional remedy and did not know or should not have known that the forfeited property was connected to a crime or fraudulently conveyed and (ii) the court determines that restoration of the property would serve the ends of justice.

8. The total amount that may be recovered by the claiming authority against all criminal defendants in a forfeiture action or actions involving the same crime shall not exceed the value of the proceeds of the crime or substituted proceeds of the crime, whichever amount is greater, and, in addition, the value of any forfeited instrumentality used in the crime. Any such recovery against criminal defendants for the value of the proceeds of the crime or substituted proceeds of the crime shall be reduced by an amount which equals the value of the same proceeds of the same crime or the same substituted proceeds of the same crime recovered against all non-criminal defendants. Any such recovery for the value of an instrumentality of a crime shall be reduced by an amount which equals the value of the same instrumentality recovered against any non-criminal defendant.

The total amount that may be recovered against all non-criminal defendants in a forfeiture action or actions involving the same crime shall not exceed the value of the proceeds of the crime or the substituted proceeds of the crime, whichever amount is greater, and, in addition, the value of any forfeited instrumentality used in the crime. Any such recovery against non-criminal defendants for the value of the proceeds of the crime or substituted proceeds of the crime shall be reduced by an amount which equals the value of the proceeds of the crime or substituted proceeds of the crime recovered against all criminal defendants. A judgment against a non-criminal defendant pursuant to clause A of subparagraph (iv) of paragraph (b) of subdivision three of this section shall be limited to the amount of the proceeds of the crime. Any recovery for the value of an instrumentality of the crime shall be reduced by an amount equal to the value of the same instrumentality recovered against any criminal defendant.

9. Any defendant in a forfeiture action who knowingly and intentionally conceals, destroys, dissipates, alters, removes from the jurisdiction, or otherwise

disposes of, property specified in a provisional remedy ordered by the court or in a judgment of forfeiture in knowing contempt of said order or judgment shall be subject to criminal liability and sanctions under sections 80.05 and 215.80 of the penal law.

10. The proper venue for trial of an action for forfeiture is:

(a) In the case of an action for post-conviction forfeiture commenced after conviction, the county where the conviction occurred.

(b) In all other cases, the county where a criminal prosecution could be commenced under article twenty of the criminal procedure law, or, in the case of an action commenced by the office of prosecution, special narcotics courts of the city of New York, under section one hundred seventy-seven-b of the judiciary law.

11. (a) Any stipulation or settlement agreement between the parties to a forfeiture action shall be filed with the clerk of the court in which the forfeiture action is pending. No stipulation or settlement agreement shall be accepted for filing unless it is accompanied by an affidavit from the claiming authority that written notice of the stipulation or settlement agreement, including the terms of such, has been given to the state crime victims board, the state division of criminal justice services, and in the case of a forfeiture based on a felony defined in article two hundred twenty or section 221.30 or 221.55 of the penal law, to the state division of substance abuse services.

(b) No judgment or order of forfeiture shall be accepted for filing unless it is accompanied by an affidavit from the claiming authority that written notice of judgment or order, including the terms of such, has been given to the state crime victims board, the state division of criminal justice services, and in the case of a forfeiture based on a felony defined in article two hundred twenty or section 221.30 or 221.55 of the penal law, to the state division of substance abuse services.

(c) Any claiming authority or claiming agent which receives any property pursuant to chapter thirteen of the food and drug laws (21 U.S.C. § 801 *et seq.*) of the United States and/or chapter four of the customs duties laws (19 U.S.C. § 1301 *et seq.*) of the United States and/or chapter 96 of the crimes and criminal procedure laws (18 U.S.C. § 1961 *et seq.*) of the United States shall provide an affidavit to the commissioner of the division of criminal justice services stating the estimated present value of the property received.

12. Property acquired in good faith by an attorney as payment for the reasonable and bona fide fees of legal services or reimbursement of reasonable and bona fide expenses related to the representation of a defendant in connection with a civil or criminal forfeiture proceeding or a related criminal matter, shall be exempt from a judgment of forfeiture. For purposes of this subdivision and subdivision four of section one thousand three hundred twelve of this article, "bona fide" means that the attorney who acquired such property had no

reasonable basis to believe that the fee transaction was a fraudulent or sham transaction designed to shield property from forfeiture, hide its existence from governmental investigative agencies, or was conducted for any purpose other than for legitimate legal representation.

* [**Editor's note:** So in original. Probably should read "or."]

## CROSS REFERENCES

Article 40 of the **Criminal Procedure Law**, referred to in paragraph (1), provides for an exemption from prosecution by reason of previous prosecution; **Penal Law** § 20.00, referred to in paragraph (3)(c)(iii), sets forth the basis for criminal liability for conduct of another; **Penal Law** § 215.80, referred to in paragraph (9), makes it a class A misdemeanor for a defendant in an Article 13-A forfeiture action to unlawfully dispose of assets subject to forfeiture; **Penal Law** § 80.05, also referred to in paragraph (9), sets forth the fine for a violation of **Penal Law** § 215.80; Article 20 of the **Criminal Procedure Law**, referred to in paragraph 10(b), sets forth the principles governing the geographical jurisdiction of offenses; **Judiciary Law** § 177-b, also referred to in paragraph 10(b), establishes special narcotics parts within the Supreme Courts of cities with a population of one million or more.

## 1990 AMENDMENTS

L. 1990, ch. 655, eff. Nov. 1, 1990, amended CPLR 1311(a) by including the real property instrumentality of a crime among the property that may be recovered in a civil forfeiture action against a criminal defendant; adding paragraphs (b)(v), (d) and (e) to subdivision (3); adding subdivision (3–a); adding subdivision (4–a); amending subdivision (5) to mandate that the claiming authority file a copy of a summons with notice or summons and verified complaint with the state division of criminal justice services; and adding subdivisions (11) and (12).

## 1985 AMENDMENTS

L. 1985, ch. 379, eff. Nov. 1, 1985, amended paragraph 10(b) to provide that in the case of an action commenced by the office of prosecution, venue for trial of a forfeiture action is in the special narcotics courts of New York City.

## 1984 AMENDMENTS

L. 1984, ch. 669, eff. Aug. 1, 1984, repealed former Article 13-A and added a new Article 13-A, comprising CPLR 1310 through CPLR 1352. New Article 13-A is applicable to crimes committed on and after the effective date.

## § 1311–a.  Subpoena duces tecum.

1. At any time before an action pursuant to this article is commenced, the claiming authority may, pursuant to the provisions of subdivision two of this section, apply without notice for the issuance of a subpoena duces tecum.

2. An application for a subpoena duces tecum pursuant to this section:

(a) shall be made in the judicial district in which the claiming authority may commence an action pursuant to this article, and shall be made in writing to a justice of the supreme court, or a judge of the county court; and

(b) shall be supported by an affidavit, and such other written documentation as may be submitted which: (i) sets forth the identity of the claiming authority and certifies that the applicant is authorized to make the application on the claiming authority's behalf; (ii) demonstrates reasonable grounds to believe that the execution of the subpoena would be reasonably likely to lead to information about the nature and location of any debt or property against which a forfeiture judgment may be enforced; (iii) states whether any other such subpoena or provisional remedy has been previously sought or obtained with respect to the subject matter of the subpoena or the matter to which it relates; (iv) contains a factual statement which sets forth the basis for the issuance of the subpoena, including a particular description of the nature of the information sought to be obtained; (v) states whether the issuance of the subpoena is sought without notice to any interested party; and (vi) where the application seeks the issuance of the subpoena without notice to any interested party, contains a statement setting forth the factual basis for the claiming authority's belief that providing notice of the application for the issuance of the subpoena may result in any property being destroyed, removed from the jurisdiction of the court, or otherwise being unavailable for forfeiture or to satisfy a money judgment that may be entered in the forfeiture action, and may interfere with law enforcement investigations or judicial proceedings.

3. An application made pursuant to this section may be granted, in the court's discretion, upon a determination that the application meets the requirements set forth in subdivision two of this section; provided, however, that no such subpoena may be issued or directed to an attorney with regard to privileged records or documents or attorney work-product relating to a client. When a subpoena has been issued pursuant to this section, the claiming authority shall have the right to possession of the subpoenaed material. The possession shall be for a period of time, and on such reasonable terms and conditions, as the court may direct. The reasonableness of such possession, time, terms and conditions shall be determined with consideration for, among other things, (a) the good cause shown by the party issuing the subpoena or in whose behalf the subpoena is issued, (b) the rights and legitimate needs of the person subpoenaed and (c) the feasibility and appropriateness of making copies of the subpoenaed material. Where the application seeks a subpoena to compel the production of an original record or document, the court in its discretion may order the production of a certified transcript or certified copy thereof.

4. Upon a determination pursuant to subdivision three of this section that the subpoena should be granted, the court shall issue the subpoena, seal all papers relating thereto, and direct that the recipient shall not, except as otherwise ordered by the court, disclose the fact of issuance or the subject of the subpoena to any person or entity; provided, however, that the court may require that notice be given to any interested party prior to the issuance of the subpoena, or at any time thereafter, when: (a) an order granting a provisional remedy pursuant to this article with respect to the subject matter of the subpoena or the matter to which it relates has been served upon the defendant whose books and records are the subject matter of the subpoena, whether such books and records are in

the possession of the defendant or a third party; or (b) the court determines that providing notice of the application (i) will not result in any property being destroyed, removed from the jurisdiction of the court, or otherwise being unavailable for forfeiture or to satisfy a money judgment that may be entered in the forfeiture action and (ii) will not interfere with law enforcement investigations or judicial proceedings. For purposes of this section, "interested party" means any person whom the court determines might have an interest in the property subject to the forfeiture action brought pursuant to this article.

5. Notwithstanding the provisions of subdivision four of this section, where a subpoena duces tecum has been issued pursuant to this section without notice to any interested party, the claiming authority shall serve written notice of the fact and date of the issuance of the subpoena duces tecum, and of the fact that information was obtained thereby, upon any interested party not later than ninety days after the date of compliance with such subpoena, or upon commencement of a forfeiture action, whichever occurs first; provided, however, where the action has not been commenced and upon a showing of good cause, service of the notice required herein may be postponed by order of the court for a reasonable period of time. The court, upon the filing of a motion by any interested party served with such notice, may, in its discretion, make available to such party or the party's counsel for inspection such portions of the information obtained pursuant to the subpoena as the court directs.

6. Nothing contained in this section shall be construed to diminish or impair any right of subpoena or discovery that may otherwise be provided for by law to the claiming authority or to a defendant in a forfeiture action.

CPLR

### 1990 AMENDMENTS
L. 1990. ch. 655, eff. Nov. 1, 1990.

## § 1312.  Provisional remedies; generally.

1. The provisional remedies of attachment, injunction, receivership and notice of pendency provided for herein, shall be available in all actions to recover property or for a money judgment under this article.

2. On a motion for a provisional remedy, the claiming authority shall state whether any other provisional remedy has previously been sought in the same action against the same defendant. The court may require the claiming authority to elect between those remedies to which it would otherwise be entitled.

3. A court may grant an application for a provisional remedy when it determines that: (a) there is a substantial probability that the claiming authority will prevail on the issue of forfeiture and that failure to enter the order may result in the property being destroyed, removed from the jurisdiction of the court, or otherwise be unavailable for forfeiture; (b) the need to preserve the availability of the property through the entry of the requested order outweighs the hardship on any party against whom the order may operate; and (c) in an action relating

to real property, that entry of the requested order will not substantially diminish, impair, or terminate the lawful property interest in such real property of any person or persons other than the defendant or defendants.

4. Upon motion of any party against whom a provisional remedy granted pursuant to this article is in effect, the court may issue an order modifying or vacating such provisional remedy if necessary to permit the moving party to obtain funds for the payment of reasonable living expenses, other costs or expenses related to the maintenance, operation, or preservation of property which is the subject of any such provisional remedy or reasonable and bona fide attorneys' fees and expenses for the representation of the defendant in the forfeiture proceeding or in a related criminal matter relating thereto, payment for which is not otherwise available from assets of the defendant which are not subject to such provisional remedy. Any such motion shall be supported by an affidavit establishing the unavailability of other assets of the moving party which are not the subject of such provisional remedy for payment of such expenses or fees.

### 1990 AMENDMENTS

L. 1990, ch. 655, eff. Nov. 1, 1990, amended CPLR 1312 by adding part (c) of subdivision (3), setting forth the basis for granting an application for a provisional remedy in an action relating to real property, and by adding subdivision (4).

### 1984 AMENDMENTS

L. 1984, ch. 669, eff. Aug. 1, 1984, repealed former Article 13-A and added a new Article 13-A, comprising CPLR 1310 through CPLR 1352. New Article 13-A is applicable to crimes committed on and after Aug. 1, 1984.

## § 1313. Debt or property subject to attachment; proper garnishee.

Any debt or property against which a forfeiture judgment may be enforced as provided under this article is subject to attachment. The proper garnishee of any such property or debt is the person designated as a proper garnishee for purposes of enforcing money judgments in section five thousand two hundred one of this chapter. For the purpose of applying the provisions to attachment, references to a "judgment debtor" in section five thousand two hundred one and in subdivision (i) of section one hundred five of this chapter shall be construed to mean "defendant."

### 1984 AMENDMENTS

L. 1984, ch. 669, eff. Aug. 1, 1984, repealed former Article 13-A and added a new Article 13-A, comprising CPLR 1310 through CPLR 1352. New Article 13-A is applicable to crimes committed on and after Aug. 1, 1984.

## § 1314. Attaching creditor's rights in personal property.

Where the claiming authority has delivered an order of attachment to a claiming agent, the claiming authority's rights in a debt owed to a defendant or in an interest of a defendant in personal property against which debt or property a judgment may be enforced, are superior to the extent of the amount of the attachment to the rights of any transferee of the debt or property, except:

1. A transferee who acquired the debt or property before it was levied upon for fair consideration and without knowledge of the order of attachment; or

2. A transferee who acquired the debt or property for fair consideration after it was levied upon without knowledge of the levy while it was not in the possession of the claiming agent.

### 1984 AMENDMENTS

L. 1984, ch. 669, eff. Aug. 1, 1984, repealed former Article 13-A and added a new Article 13-A, comprising CPLR 1310 through CPLR 1352. New Article 13-A is applicable to crimes committed on and after Aug. 1, 1984.

## § 1315.  Discharge of garnishee's obligation.

A person who, pursuant to an order of attachment, pays or delivers to the claiming agent money or other personal property in which a defendant has or will have an interest, or so pays a debt he or she owes the defendant, is discharged from his or her obligation to the defendant to the extent of the payment or delivery.

### 1984 AMENDMENTS

L. 1984, ch. 669, eff. Aug. 1, 1984, repealed former Article 13-A and added a new Article 13-A, comprising CPLR 1310 through CPLR 1352. New Article 13-A is applicable to crimes committed on and after Aug. 1, 1984.

## § 1316.  Order of attachment on notice; temporary restraining order; contents.

Upon a motion on notice for an order of attachment, the court may, without notice to the defendant, grant a temporary restraining order prohibiting the transfer of assets by a garnishee as provided in subdivision two of section one thousand three hundred twenty of this article. The contents of the order of attachment granted pursuant to this section shall be as provided in subdivision one of section one thousand three hundred seventeen of this article.

### 1984 AMENDMENTS

L. 1984, ch. 669, eff. Aug. 1, 1984, repealed former Article 13-A and added a new Article 13-A, comprising CPLR 1310 through CPLR 1352. New Article 13-A is applicable to crimes committed on and after Aug. 1, 1984.

## § 1317.  Order of attachment without notice.

1. When granted; contents. An order of attachment may be granted without notice, before or after service of summons and at any time prior to judgment. It shall specify the amount to be secured by the order of attachment including

CPLR

any interest, costs and any claiming agent's fees and expenses, be endorsed with the name and address of the claiming authority and shall be directed to a claiming agent in any county or in the city of New York where any property in which the defendant has an interest is located or where a garnishee may be served. The order shall direct the claiming agent to levy within his or her jurisdiction, at any time before final judgment, upon such property in which the defendant has an interest and upon such debts owing to the defendant as will satisfy the amount specified in the order of attachment.

2. Confirmation of order. An order of attachment granted without notice shall provide that within a period not to exceed five days after levy, the claiming authority shall move, on such notice as the court shall direct to the defendant, the garnishee, if any, and the claiming agent, for an order confirming the order of attachment. If the claiming authority fails to make such motion within the required period, the order of attachment and levy thereunder shall have no further effect and shall be vacated upon motion. Upon the motion to confirm, the provisions of subdivision two of section one thousand three hundred twenty-nine of this article shall apply. An order of attachment granted without notice may provide that the claiming agent refrain from taking any property levied upon into his actual custody, pending further order of the court.

### 1984 AMENDMENTS

L. 1984, ch. 669, eff. Aug. 1, 1984, repealed former Article 13-A and added a new Article 13-A, comprising CPLR 1310 through CPLR 1352. New Article 13-A is applicable to crimes committed on and after Aug. 1, 1984.

## § 1318.   Motion papers; filing; demand; damages.

1. Affidavit; other papers. On a motion for an order of attachment, or for an order to confirm an order of attachment, the claiming authority shall show, by affidavit and such other written evidence as may be submitted, that there is a cause of action and showing grounds for relief as required by section one thousand three hundred twelve of this article.

2. Filing. Within ten days after the granting of an order of attachment, the claiming authority shall file it and the affidavit and other papers upon which it was based and the summons and complaint or proposed complaint in the action. A court for good cause shown may extend the time for such filing upon application of the claiming authority. Unless the time for filing has been extended, the order shall be invalid if not so filed, except that a person upon whom it is served shall not be liable for acting upon it as if it were valid without knowledge of the invalidity.

3. Demand for papers. At any time after property has been levied upon, the defendant may serve upon the claiming authority a written demand that the papers upon which the order of attachment was granted and the levy made be served upon him or her. As soon as practicable after service of the demand, the claiming authority shall cause the papers demanded to be served by mailing

the same to the address specified in the demand. A demand under this subdivision shall not of itself constitute an appearance in the action.

4. Damages. The claiming authority shall be liable to the defendant for all costs and damages, including reasonable attorney's fees, which may be sustained by reason of the attachment if the defendant recovers judgment, or if it is finally decided that the claiming authority was not entitled to an attachment of the defendant's property. In order to establish the claiming authority's liability, the defendant must prove by a preponderance of the evidence that in obtaining the order of attachment the claiming authority acted without reasonable cause, and not in good faith.

### 1984 AMENDMENTS

L. 1984, ch. 669, eff. Aug. 1, 1984, repealed former Article 13-A and added a new Article 13-A, comprising CPLR 1310 through CPLR 1352. New Article 13-A is applicable to crimes committed on and after the effective date.

## § 1319.  Service of summons.

An order of attachment granted before service is made on the defendant against whom the attachment is granted is valid only if, within sixty days after the order is granted, a summons is served upon the defendant or first publication of the summons against the defendant is made pursuant to an order and publication is subsequently completed, except that a person upon whom the order of attachment is served shall not be liable for acting upon it as if it were valid without knowledge of the invalidity. If the defendant dies within sixty days after the order is granted and before the summons is served upon him or her or publication is completed, the order is valid only if the summons is served upon his or her executor or administrator within sixty days after letters are issued. Upon such terms as may be just and upon good cause shown the court may extend the time, not exceeding sixty days, within which the summons must be served or publication commenced pursuant to this section, provided that the application for extension is made before the expiration of the time fixed.

### 1992 AMENDMENTS

L. 1992, ch. 216, eff. July 1, 1992, amended the first sentence of CPLR 1319 by deleting the words "an action is commenced" after the words "attachment granted before" and inserting in their place "service is made on the defendant against whom the attachment is granted."

### 1984 AMENDMENTS

L. 1984, ch. 669, eff. Aug. 1, 1984, repealed former Article 13-A and added a new Article 13-A, comprising CPLR 1310 through CPLR 1352. New Article 13-A is applicable to crimes committed on and after Aug. 1, 1984.

## § 1320.  Levy upon personal property by service of order.

1. Method of levy. The claiming agent shall levy upon any interest of the defendant in personal property, or upon any debt owed to the defendant, by

serving a copy of the order of attachment upon the garnishee, or upon the defendant if property to be levied upon is in the defendant's possession or custody, in the same manner as a summons except that such service shall not be made by delivery of a copy to a person authorized to receive service of summons solely be* a designation filed pursuant to a provision of law other than rule three hundred eighteen of this chapter.

2. Effect of levy; prohibition of transfer. A levy by service of an order of attachment upon a person other than the defendant is effective only if, at the time of service, such person owes a debt to the defendant or such person is in the possession or custody of property in which such person knows or has reason to believe the defendant has an interest, or if the claiming authority has stated in a notice which shall be served with the order that a specified debt is owed by the person served to the defendant or that the defendant has an interest in specified property in the possession or custody of the person served. All property in which the defendant is known or believed to have an interest then in and thereafter coming into the possession or custody of such a person, including any specified in the notice, and all debts of such person, including any specified in the notice, then due and thereafter coming due to the defendant, shall be subject to the levy. Unless the court orders otherwise, the person served with the order shall forthwith transfer or deliver all such property, and pay all such debts upon maturity, up to the amount specified in order of attachment, to the claiming agent and execute any document necessary to effect the payment, transfer or delivery. After such payment, transfer or delivery, property coming into the possession or custody of the garnishee, or debt incurred by him or her, shall not be subject to the levy. Until such payment, transfer or delivery is made, or until the expiration of ninety days after the service of the order of attachment upon him or her, or of such further time as is provided by any subsequent order of the court served upon him or her, whichever event first occurs, the garnishee is prohibited to make or suffer any sale, assignment or transfer of, or any interference with any such property, or pay over or otherwise dispose of any such debt, to any person other than the claiming agent except upon direction of the claiming agent or pursuant to an order of the court. A garnishee, however, may collect or redeem an instrument received by him or her for such purpose and he or she may sell or transfer in good faith property held as collateral or otherwise pursuant to pledge thereof or at the direction of any person other than the defendant authorized to direct sale or transfer, provided that the proceeds in which the defendant has an interest be retained subject to the levy. A claiming authority who has specified personal property or debt to be levied upon in a notice served with an order of attachment shall be liable to the owner of the property or the person to whom the debt is owed, if other than the defendant, for any damages sustained by reason of the levy. In order to establish the claiming authority's liability, the owner of the property of** the person to whom the debt is owed must prove by a preponderance of the evidence that, in causing the levy to occur, the claiming authority acted without reasonable cause and not in good faith.

3. Seizure by claiming agent; notice of satisfaction. Where property or debts have been levied upon by service of an order of attachment, the claiming agent shall take into his or her actual custody all such property capable of delivery and shall collect and receive all such debts. When the claiming agent has taken into his or her actual custody property or debts having value sufficient to satisfy the amount specified in the order of attachment, the claiming agent shall notify the defendant and each person upon whom the order of attachment was served that the order of attachment has been fully executed.

4. Proceeding to compel payment or delivery. Where property or debts have been levied upon by service of an order of attachment, the claiming authority may commence a special proceeding against the garnishee served with the order to compel the payment, delivery or transfer to the claiming agent of such property or debts, or to secure a judgment against the garnishee. Notice of petition shall also be served upon the parties to the action and the claiming agent. A garnishee may assert any defense or counterclaim which he or she may have asserted against the defendant. The court may permit any adverse claimant to intervene in the proceeding and may determine his or her rights in accordance with section one thousand three hundred twenty-seven of this article.

5. Failure to proceed. At the expiration of ninety days after a levy is made by service of the order of attachment, or of such further time as the court, upon motion of the claiming authority on notice to the parties to the action, has provided, the levy shall be void except as to property or debts which the claiming agent has taken into his or her actual custody, collected or received or as to which a proceeding under subdivision four hereof has been commenced.

\* [**Editor's note:** So in original. Probably should read "by."]
\*\* [**Editor's note:** So in original. Probably should be "or."]

### 1984 AMENDMENTS

L. 1984, ch. 669, eff. Aug. 1, 1984, repealed former Article 13-A and added a new Article 13-A, comprising CPLR 1310 through CPLR 1352. New Article 13-A is applicable to crimes committed on and after Aug. 1, 1984.

## § 1321.  Levy upon personal property by seizure.

If the claiming authority shall so direct the collecting agent, as an alternative to the method prescribed by section one thousand three hundred twenty of this article, shall levy upon property capable of delivery by taking the property into his actual custody. In cases in which the collecting agent is a sheriff, the sheriff may require that the claiming authority furnish indemnity that is either satisfactory to the sheriff or is fixed by the court. The collecting agent shall within four days serve a copy of the order of attachment in the manner prescribed by subdivision one of section one thousand three hundred twenty of this article upon the person from whose possession or custody the property was taken.

### 1984 AMENDMENTS

L. 1984, ch. 669, eff. Aug. 1, 1984, repealed former Article 13-A and added a new Article 13-A, comprising CPLR 1310 through CPLR 1352. New Article 13-A is applicable to crimes committed on and after Aug. 1, 1984.

## § 1322. Levy upon real property.

The claiming agent shall levy upon any interest of the defendant in real property by filing with the clerk of the county in which the property is located a notice of attachment endorsed with the name and address of the claiming authority and stating the names of the parties to the action, the amount specified in the order of attachment and a description of the property levied upon. The clerk shall record and index the notice in the same books, in the same manner and with the same effect, as a notice of the pendency of an action.

### 1984 AMENDMENTS

L. 1984, ch. 669, eff. Aug. 1, 1984, repealed former Article 13-A and added a new Article 13-A, comprising CPLR 1310 through CPLR 1352. New Article 13-A is applicable to crimes committed on and after Aug. 1, 1984.

## § 1323. Additional undertaking to carrier garnishee.

A garnishee who is a common carrier may transport or deliver property actually loaded on a conveyance, notwithstanding the service upon him or her of an order of attachment, if it was loaded without reason to believe that an order of attachment affecting the property had been granted, unless the claiming authority gives an undertaking in an amount fixed by the court, that the claiming authority shall pay any such carrier all expenses and damages which may be incurred for unloading the property and for detention of the conveyance necessary for that purpose.

### 1984 AMENDMENTS

L. 1984, ch. 669, eff. Aug. 1, 1984, repealed former Article 13-A and added a new Article 13-A, comprising CPLR 1310 through CPLR 1352. New Article 13-A is applicable to crimes committed on and after Aug. 1, 1984.

## § 1324. Claiming agent's duties after levy.

1. Retention of property. The claiming agent shall hold and safely keep all property or debts paid, delivered, transferred or assigned to him or her or taken into his or her custody to answer any judgment that may be obtained against the defendant in the action, unless otherwise directed by the court or the claiming authority, subject to the payment of the claiming agent's fees and expenses, if any. Any money shall be held for the benefit of the parties to the action in an interest-bearing trust account at a national or state bank or trust company. If the urgency of the case requires, the court may direct sale or other disposition of property, specifying the manner and terms thereof, with notice to the parties to the action and the garnishee who has possession of such property.

2. Inventory. Within fifteen days after service of an order of attachment or forthwith after such order has been vacated or annulled, the claiming agent shall file an inventory of property seized, a description of real property levied upon, the names and addresses of all persons served with the order of attachment, and an estimate of the value of all property levied upon.

### 1984 AMENDMENTS

L. 1984, ch. 669, eff. Aug. 1, 1984, repealed former Article 13-A and added a new Article 13-A, comprising CPLR 1310 through CPLR 1352. New Article 13-A is applicable to crimes committed on and after Aug. 1, 1984.

## § 1325.   Garnishee's statement.

Within ten days after service upon a garnishee of an order of attachment, or within such shorter time as the court may direct, the garnishee shall serve upon the claiming agent a statement specifying all debts of the garnishee to the defendant, when the debts are due, all property in the possession or custody of the garnishee in which the defendant has an interest, and the amounts and value of the debts and property specified. If the garnishee has money belonging to, or is indebted to, the defendant in at least the amount of the attachment, he or she may limit his or her statement to that fact.

### 1984 AMENDMENTS

L. 1984, ch. 669, eff. Aug. 1, 1984, repealed former Article 13-A and added a new Article 13-A, comprising CPLR 1310 through CPLR 1352. New Article 13-A is applicable to crimes committed on and after Aug. 1, 1984.

## § 1326.   Disclosure.

Upon motion of any interested person, at any time after the granting of an order of attachment and prior to final judgment in the action, upon such notice as the court may direct, the court may order disclosure by any person of information regarding any property in which the defendant has or may have interest, or any debts owed or which may be owed to the defendant.

### 1984 AMENDMENTS

L. 1984, ch. 669, eff. Aug. 1, 1984, repealed former Article 13-A and added a new Article 13-A, comprising CPLR 1310 through CPLR 1352. New Article 13-A is applicable to crimes committed on and after Aug. 1, 1984.

## § 1327.   Proceedings to determine adverse claims.

Prior to the application of property or debt to the satisfaction of a judgment, any person, other than a party to the action, who has an interest in the property subject to forfeiture may commence a special proceeding against the claiming authority to determine the rights of adverse claimants to the property or debt, and in such proceeding shall serve a notice of petition upon the claiming agent and upon each party in the same manner as a notice of motion. The proceeding may be commenced in the county where the property was levied upon, or in the county where the order of attachment is filed. The court may vacate or discharge the attachment, void the levy, direct the disposition of the property or debt, direct that undertakings be provided or released, or direct that damages be awarded. Where there appear to be disputed questions of fact, the court shall order a separate trial, indicating the person who shall have possession of the property pending a decision and the undertaking, if any, which such person shall give. If the court determines that the adverse claim was fraudulent or made without any reasonable basis whatsoever, it may require the claimant to pay the claiming authority the reasonable expenses incurred in the proceeding, including reasonable attorney's fees, and any other damages suffered by reason of the claim. The commencement of the proceeding shall not of itself subject the adverse claimant to personal jurisdiction with respect to any matter other than the claim asserted in the proceeding.

### 1994 AMENDMENTS

L. 1994, ch. 563, eff. July 26, 1994, amended CPLR 1327 by replacing the words "by serving" with the words "and in such proceeding shall serve."

### 1984 AMENDMENTS

L. 1984, ch. 669, eff. Aug. 1, 1984, repealed former Article 13-A and added a new Article 13-A, comprising CPLR 1310 through CPLR 1352. New Article 13-A is applicable to crimes committed on and after Aug. 1, 1984.

## § 1328.  Discharge of attachment.

1. A defendant whose property or debt has been levied upon may move, upon notice to the claiming authority and the claiming agent, for any* order discharging the attachment as to all or part of the property or debt upon payment of the claiming agent's fees and expenses, if any. On such a motion, the defendant shall give an undertaking, in an amount equal to the value of the property or debt sought to be discharged, that the defendant will pay to the claiming authority the amount of any judgment which may be recovered in the action against him or her, not exceeding the amount of the undertaking. Making a motion or giving an undertaking under this section shall not of itself constitute an appearance in the action.

2. When a motion to discharge is made in the case of property levied upon pursuant to a claimed violation of the tax law, the amount of the undertaking required shall be an amount equal to the lesser of:

(a) The amount specified in subdivision one of this section; or

(b) The aggregate amount of all unpaid tax and civil penalties for such violation.

* [**Editor's note**: So in original. Probably should be "an."]

**1985 AMENDMENTS**

L. 1985, ch. 65, eff. April 17, 1985, added subdivision (2).

**1984 AMENDMENTS**

L. 1984, ch. 669, eff. Aug. 1, 1984, repealed former Article 13-A and added a
new Article 13-A, comprising CPLR 1310 through CPLR 1352. New Article 13-A
is applicable to crimes committed on and after Aug. 1, 1984.

## § 1329.   Vacating or modifying attachment.

1. Motion to vacate or modify. Prior to the application of property or debt
to the satisfaction of a judgment, the defendant, the garnishee or any person
having an interest in the property or debt may move, on notice to each party
and the claiming agent, for an order vacating or modifying the order of attachment. Upon the motion, the court may give the claiming authority a reasonable
opportunity to correct any defect. If, after the defendant has appeared in the
action, the court determines that the attachment is unnecessary to the security
of the claiming authority, it shall vacate the order of attachment. Such a motion
shall not of itself constitute an appearance in the action.

2. Burden of proof. Upon a motion to vacate or modify an order of attachment
the claiming authority shall have the burden of establishing the grounds for the
attachment, the need for continuing the levy and the probability that he or she
will succeed on the merits.

**1984 AMENDMENTS**

L. 1984, ch. 669, eff. Aug. 1, 1984, repealed former Article 13-A and added a
new Article 13-A, comprising CPLR 1310 through CPLR 1352. New Article 13-A
is applicable to crimes committed on and after the effective date.

## § 1330.   Annulment of attachment.

An order of attachment is annulled when the action in which it was granted
abates or is discontinued or a judgment entered therein in favor of the claiming
authority is fully satisfied, or a judgment is entered therein in favor of the
defendant. In the last specified case a stay of proceedings suspends the effect
of the annulment, and a reversal or vacating of the judgment revives the order
of attachment.

**1984 AMENDMENTS**

L. 1984, ch. 669, eff. Aug. 1, 1984, repealed former Article 13-A and added a
new article 13-A, comprising CPLR 1310 through CPLR 1352. New Article 13-A
is applicable to crimes committed on and after the effective date.

## § 1331.   Return of property; directions to clerk and claiming agent.

Upon motion of any interested person, on notice to the claiming agent and
each party, the court may direct the clerk of any county to cancel a notice of
attachment and may direct the claiming agent to dispose of, account for, assign,

CPLR

return or release any property or debt, or the proceeds thereof, or any undertaking, or to file additional inventories or returns, subject to the payment of the claiming agent's fees, and expenses, if any. The court shall direct that notice of the motion be given to the claiming authority and plaintiffs in other orders of attachment, if any, and to the judgment creditors of executions, if any, affecting any property or debt, or the proceeds thereof, sought to be returned or released.

### 1984 AMENDMENTS

L. 1984, ch. 669, eff. Aug. 1, 1984, repealed former Article 13-A and added a new Article 13-A, comprising CPLR 1310 through CPLR 1352. New Article 13-A is applicable to crimes committed on and after the effective date.

## § 1332. Disposition of attachment property after execution issued; priority of orders of attachment.

Where an execution is issued upon a judgment entered against the defendant, the claiming agent's duty with respect to custody and disposition of property or debt levied upon pursuant to an order of attachment is the same as if he or she had levied upon it pursuant to the execution. The priority among two or more orders of attachment against the same defendant shall be in the order in which they were delivered to the officer who levied upon the property or debt. The priority between an order of attachment and an execution, or a payment, delivery or receivership order, is set forth in section five thousand two hundred thirty-four of this chapter.

### 1984 AMENDMENTS

L. 1984, ch. 669, eff. Aug. 1, 1984, repealed former Article 13-A and added a new Article 13-A, comprising CPLR 1310 through CPLR 1352. New Article 13-A is applicable to crimes committed on and after the effective date.

## § 1333. Grounds for preliminary injunction and temporary restraining order.

A preliminary injunction may be granted in any action under this article, whether for money damages or otherwise, where it appears that the defendant threatens or is about to do, or is doing or procuring or suffering to be done, an act in violation of the claiming authority's rights respecting the subject of the action, and thereby tending to render a resulting judgment ineffectual. A temporary restraining order may be granted pending a hearing for a preliminary injunction where it appears that immediate and irreparable injury, loss or damage will result unless the defendant is restrained before the hearing can be had. A preliminary injunction may be granted only upon notice to the defendant. Notice of the motion may be served with the summons or at any time thereafter and prior to judgment.

**1984 AMENDMENTS**

L. 1984, ch. 669, eff. Aug. 1, 1984, repealed former Article 13-A and added a new Article 13-A, comprising CPLR 1310 through CPLR 1352. New Article 13-A is applicable to crimes committed on and after the effective date.

## § 1334.  Motion papers.

Affidavit; other papers. On a motion for a preliminary injunction the claiming authority shall show, by affidavit and such other written evidence as may be submitted, that there is a cause of action and showing grounds for relief as required by section one thousand three hundred twelve of this article.

**1984 AMENDMENTS**

L. 1984, ch. 669, eff. Aug. 1, 1984, repealed former Article 13-A and added a new Article 13-A, comprising CPLR 1310 through CPLR 1352. New Article 13-A is applicable to crimes committed on and after the effective date.

## § 1335.  Temporary restraining order.

1. Generally. If, on a motion for a preliminary injunction, the claiming authority shall show that immediate and irreparable injury, loss or damages may result unless the defendant is restrained before a hearing can be had, a temporary restraining order may be granted without notice. Upon granting a temporary restraining order, the court shall set the hearing for the preliminary injunction at the earliest possible time.

2. Service. Unless the court orders otherwise, a temporary restraining order together with the papers upon which it was based, and a notice of hearing for the preliminary injunction, shall be personally served in the same manner as a summons.

**1984 AMENDMENTS**

L. 1984, ch. 669, eff. Aug. 1, 1984, repealed former Article 13-A and added a new Article 13-A, comprising CPLR 1310 through CPLR 1352. New Article 13-A is applicable to crimes committed on and after Aug. 1, 1984.

## § 1336.  Vacating or modifying preliminary injunction or temporary restraining order.

A defendant enjoined by a preliminary injunction may move at any time, on notice to the claiming authority, to vacate or modify it. On motion, without notice, made by a defendant enjoined by a temporary restraining order, the judge who granted it, or in his or her absence or disability, another judge, may vacate or modify the order. An order granted without notice and vacating or modifying a temporary restraining order shall be effective when, together with the papers upon which it is based, it is filed with the clerk and served upon the claiming authority. As a condition to granting an order vacating or modifying a preliminary injunction or a temporary restraining order, a court may require the

CPLR

defendant to give an undertaking, in an amount to be fixed by the court, that the defendant shall pay to the claiming authority any loss sustained by reason of the vacating or modifying order.

**1984 AMENDMENTS**

L. 1984, ch. 669, eff. Aug. 1, 1984, repealed former Article 13-A and added a new Article 13-A, comprising CPLR 1310 through CPLR 1352. New Article 13-A is applicable to crimes committed on and after Aug. 1, 1984.

## § 1337. Ascertaining damages sustained by reason of preliminary injunction or temporary restraining order.

The damages sustained by reason of a preliminary injunction or temporary restraining order may be ascertained upon motion on such notice to all interested persons as the court shall direct. Where the defendant enjoined was an officer of a corporation or joint-stock association or a representative of another person, the damages sustained by such corporation, association or person represented, to the amount of such excess, may also be ascertained. The amount of damages so ascertained is conclusive upon all persons who were served with notice of the motion and such amount may be recovered by the person entitled thereto in a separate action. In order to establish the claiming authority's liability for damages, the person seeking such damages must prove by a preponderance of the evidence that, in causing the temporary restraining order or preliminary injunction to be granted, the claiming authority acted without reasonable cause and not in good faith.

**1984 AMENDMENTS**

L. 1984, ch. 669, eff. Aug. 1, 1984, repealed former Article 13-A and added a new Article 13-A, comprising CPLR 1310 through CPLR 1352. New Article 13-A is applicable to crimes committed on and after Aug. 1, 1984.

## § 1338. Appointment and powers of temporary receiver.

1. Appointment of temporary receiver; joinder of moving party. Upon motion of the claiming authority on* any other person having an apparent interest in property which is the subject of an action pursuant to this article, a temporary receiver of the property may be appointed, before or after service of summons and at any time prior to judgment, or during the pendency of an appeal, where there is danger that the property will be removed from the state, or lost, materially injured or destroyed. A motion made by a person not already a party to the action constitutes an appearance in the action and the person shall be joined as a party.

2. Powers of temporary receiver. The court appointing a receiver may authorize him or her to take and hold real and personal property, and sue for, collect and sell debts or claims, upon such conditions and for such purposes as the court shall direct. A receiver shall have no power to employ counsel unless

expressly so authorized by order of the court. Upon motion of the receiver or a party, powers granted to a temporary receiver may be extended or limited or the receivership may be extended to another action involving the property.

3. Duration of temporary receivership. A temporary receivership shall not continue after final judgment unless otherwise directed by the court.

\* [**Editor's note:** So in original. Probably should be "or."]

### 1984 AMENDMENTS

L. 1984, ch. 669, eff. Aug. 1, 1984, repealed former Article 13-A and added a new Article 13-A, comprising CPLR 1310 through CPLR 1352. New Article 13-A is applicable to crimes committed on and after Aug. 1, 1984.

## § 1339. Oath.

A temporary receiver, before entering upon his or her duties, shall be sworn faithfully and fairly to discharge the trust committed to him or her. The oath may be administered by any person authorized to take acknowledgments of deeds by the real property law. The oath may be waived upon consent of all parties.

### CROSS REFERENCES

See **Real Prop. L.** § 298 *et seq.,* in Appendix, *infra,* for provisions authorizing the taking of acknowledgments of deeds.

### 1984 AMENDMENTS

L. 1984, ch. 669, eff. Aug. 1, 1984, repealed former Article 13-A and added a new Article 13-A, comprising CPLR 1310 through CPLR 1352. New Article 13-A is applicable to crimes committed on and after Aug. 1, 1984.

## § 1340. Undertaking.

A temporary receiver shall give an undertaking in an amount to be fixed by the court making the appointment, that he or she will faithfully discharge his or her duties.

### 1984 AMENDMENTS

L. 1984, ch. 669, eff. Aug. 1, 1984, repealed former Article 13-A and added a new Article 13-A, comprising CPLR 1310 through CPLR 1352. New Article 13-A is applicable to crimes committed on and after Aug. 1, 1984.

## § 1341. Accounts.

A temporary receiver shall keep written accounts itemizing receipts and expenditures, and describing the property and naming the depository of receivership funds, which shall be open to inspection by any person having an apparent interest in the property. [Upon motion of the receiver or of any person having an apparent interest in the property,]\* the court may require the keeping of particular records or direct or limit inspection or require presentation of a temporary receiver's accounts. Notice of a motion for the presentation of a temporary receiver's accounts shall be served upon the sureties on his or her undertaking as well as upon each party.

\* [**Editor's note:** Bracketed material has apparently been omitted due to an oversight.]

### 1984 AMENDMENTS

L. 1984, ch. 669, eff. Aug. 1, 1984, repealed former Article 13-A and added a new Article 13-A, comprising CPLR 1310 through CPLR 1352. New Article 13-A is applicable to crimes committed on and after Aug. 1, 1984.

## § 1342. Removal.

Upon motion of any party or upon its own initiative, the court which appointed a receiver may remove him or her at any time.

### 1984 AMENDMENTS

L. 1984, ch. 669, eff. Aug. 1, 1984, repealed former Article 13-A and added a new Article 13-A, comprising CPLR 1310 through CPLR 1352. New Article 13-A is applicable to crimes committed on and after Aug. 1, 1984.

## § 1343. Notice of pendency; constructive notice.

A notice of pendency may be filed in any action brought pursuant to this article in which the judgment demanded would affect the title to, or the possession, use or enjoyment of, real property. The pendency of such an action is constructive notice, from the time of filing of the notice only, to a purchaser from, or incumbrancer against, any defendant named in a notice of pendency indexed in a block index against a block in which property affected is situated or any defendant against whose name a notice of pendency is indexed. A person whose conveyance or incumbrance is recorded after the filing of the notice is bound by all proceedings taken in the action after such filing to the same extent as if he or she were a party.

### 1984 AMENDMENTS

L. 1984, ch. 669, eff. Aug. 1, 1984, repealed former Article 13-A and added a new Article 13-A, comprising CPLR 1310 through CPLR 1352. New Article 13-A is applicable to crimes committed on and after Aug. 1, 1984.

## § 1344. Filing, content and indexing of notice of pendency.

1. Filing. In a case specified in section one thousand three hundred forty-three of this article the notice of pendency shall be filed in the office of the clerk of any county where property affected is situated, before or after service of a summons and at any time prior to judgment. Unless it has already been filed in that county, the complaint shall be filed with the notice of pendency.

2. Content, designation of index. A notice of pendency shall state the names of the parties to the action, that the action is for forfeiture pursuant to this article and a description of the property affected. A notice of pendency filed with a

clerk who maintains a block index shall contain a designation of the number of each block on the land map of a county which is affected by the notice. A notice of pendency filed with a clerk who does not maintain a block index shall contain a designation of the names of each defendant against whom the notice is directed to be indexed.

3. Indexing. Each county clerk with whom a notice of pendency is filed shall immediately record and index it against the blocks or names designated. A county clerk who does not maintain a block index shall index a notice of pendency of an action for partition against the names of each claiming authority and each defendant not designated as wholly fictitious.

### 1984 AMENDMENTS

L. 1984, ch. 669, eff. Aug. 1, 1984, repealed former Article 13-A and added a new Article 13-A, comprising CPLR 1310 through CPLR 1352. New Article 13-A is applicable to crimes committed on and after Aug. 1, 1984.

## § 1345.  Service of summons.

A notice of pendency filed before an action is commenced is effective only if, within thirty days after filing, a summons is served upon the defendant or first publication of the summons against the defendant is made pursuant to an order and publication is subsequently completed. If the defendant dies within thirty days after filing and before the summons served upon him or her or publication is completed, the notice is effective only if the summons is served upon his or her executor or administrator within sixty days after letters are issued.

### 1984 AMENDMENTS

L. 1984, ch. 669, eff. Aug. 1, 1984, repealed former Article 13-A and added a new Article 13-A, comprising CPLR 1310 through CPLR 1352. New Article 13-A is applicable to crimes committed on and after Aug. 1, 1984.

## § 1346.  Duration of notice of pendency.

A notice of pendency shall be effective for a period of three years from the date of filing. Before expiration of a period or extended period, the court, upon motion of the claiming authority and upon such notice as it may require, for good cause shown, may grant an extension for a like additional period. An extension order shall be filed, recorded and indexed before expiration of the prior period.

### 1984 AMENDMENTS

L. 1984, ch. 669, eff. Aug. 1, 1984, repealed former Article 13-A and added a new Article 13-A, comprising CPLR 1310 through CPLR 1352. New Article 13-A is applicable to crimes committed on and after Aug. 1, 1984.

## § 1347. Motion for cancellation of notice of pendency.

1. Mandatory cancellation. The court, upon motion of any person aggrieved and upon such notice as it may require, shall direct any county clerk to cancel a notice of pendency, if service of a summons has not been completed within the time limited by section one thousand three hundred forty-five of this article; or if the action has been settled, discontinued or abated; or if the time to appeal from a final judgment against the claiming authority has expired.

2. Discretionary cancellation. The court, upon a motion of any person aggrieved and upon such notice as it may require, may direct any county clerk to cancel a notice of pendency, if the claiming authority has not commenced or prosecuted the action in good faith.

3. Costs and expenses. The court, in an order canceling a notice of pendency under this section, may direct the claiming authority to pay any costs and expenses occasioned by the filing and cancellation, in addition to any costs of the action. In order to establish the claiming authority's liability for such costs and expenses, the person seeking such costs and expenses must prove by a preponderance of the evidence that, in causing the notice to pendency to be filed, the claiming authority acted without reasonable cause and not in good faith.

4. Cancellation by stipulation. At any time prior to entry of judgment, a notice of pendency shall be cancelled by the county clerk without an order, on the filing with him or her of:

(a) An affidavit by the claiming authority showing which defendants have been served with process, which defendants are in default in appearing or answering, and which defendants have appeared or answered and by whom; and

(b) A stipulation consenting to the cancellation, signed by the claiming authority and by the attorneys for all the defendants who have appeared or answered including those who have waived all notices, and executed and acknowledged, in the form required to entitle a deed to be recorded, by the defendants who have been served with process and have not appeared but whose time to do so has not expired, and by any defendants who have appeared in person.

5. Cancellation by a claiming authority. At any time prior to the entry of a judgment a notice of pendency of action shall be cancelled by the county clerk without an order on the filing with him or her of an affidavit by the claiming authority showing that there have been no appearances and that the time to appear has expired for all parties.

### 1984 AMENDMENTS

L. 1984, ch. 669, eff. Aug. 1, 1984, repealed former Article 13-A and added a new Article 13-A, comprising CPLR 1310 through CPLR 1352. New Article 13-A is applicable to crimes committed on and after Aug. 1, 1984.

## § 1348.   Undertaking for cancellation of notice of pendency.

The court, upon motion of any person aggrieved and upon such notice of pendency as it may require, may direct any county clerk to cancel a notice of pendency, upon such terms as are just, whether or not the judgment demanded would affect specific real property, if the moving party shall give an undertaking in an amount to be fixed by the court, and if the court finds that adequate relief can be secured to the claiming authority by the giving of such an undertaking.

### 1984 AMENDMENTS

L. 1984, ch. 669, eff. Aug. 1, 1984, repealed former Article 13-A and added a new Article 13-A, comprising CPLR 1310 through CPLR 1352. New Article 13-A is applicable to crimes committed on and after Aug. 1, 1984.

## § 1349.   Disposal of property.

1. Any judgment or order of forfeiture issued pursuant to this article shall include provisions for the disposal of the property found to have been forfeited.

2. If any other provision of law expressly governs the manner of disposition of property subject to the judgment or order of forfeiture, that provision of law shall be controlling. Upon application by a claiming agent for reimbursement of moneys directly expended by a claiming agent in the underlying criminal investigation for the purchase of contraband which were converted into a non-monetary form or which have not been otherwise recovered, the court shall direct such reimbursement from money forfeited pursuant to this article. Upon application of the claiming agent, the court may direct that any vehicles, vessels or aircraft forfeited pursuant to this article be retained by the claiming agent for law enforcement purposes, unless the court determines that such property is subject to a perfected lien, in which case the court may not direct that the property be retained unless all such liens on the property to be retained have been satisfied or pursuant to the court's order will be satisfied. In the absence of an application by the claiming agent, the claiming authority may apply to the court to retain such property for law enforcement purposes. Upon such application, the court may direct that such property be retained by the claiming authority for law enforcement purposes, unless the court determines that such property is subject to a perfected lien. If not so retained, the judgment or order shall direct the claiming authority to sell the property in accordance with article fifty-one of this chapter, and that the proceeds of such sale and any other moneys realized as a consequence of any forfeiture pursuant to this article shall be apportioned and paid in the following descending order of priority:

(a) Amounts ordered to be paid by the court in satisfaction of any lien or claim against property forfeited. A fine imposed pursuant to the penal law shall not be deemed to constitute a lien or claim for purposes of this section;

(b) Amounts ordered to be paid by the defendant in any other action or proceeding as restitution, reparations or damages to a victim of the crime, which crime constitutes the basis upon which forfeiture was effected under this article, to the extent such amounts remain unpaid;

(c) Amounts ordered to be paid by the defendant in any other action or proceeding as restitution, reparations or damages to a victim of any crime committed by the defendant even though such crime did not constitute the basis for forfeiture under this article, to the extent that such amounts remain unpaid;

(d) Amounts actually expended by a claiming authority or claiming agent, which amounts are substantiated by vouchers or other evidence, for the:

(i) Maintenance and operation of real property attached pursuant to this article. Expenditures authorized by this subparagraph are limited to mortgage, tax and other financial obligations imposed by law and those other payments necessary to provide essential services and repairs to real property whose occupants are innocent of the criminal conduct which led to the attachment or forfeiture; and

(ii) proper storage, cleanup and disposal of hazardous substances or other materials, the disposal of which is governed by the environmental conservation law, when such storage, cleanup or disposal is required by circumstances attendant to either the commission of the crime or the forfeiture action, or any order entered pursuant thereto;

(e) In addition to amounts, if any, distributed pursuant to paragraph (d) of this subdivision, fifteen percent of all moneys realized through forfeiture to the claiming authority in satisfaction of actual costs and expenses incurred in the investigation, preparation and litigation of the forfeiture action, including that proportion of the salaries of the attorneys, clerical and investigative personnel devoted thereto, plus all costs and disbursements taxable under the provisions of this chapter;

(f) In addition to amounts, if any, distributed pursuant to paragraph (d) of this subdivision, five percent of all moneys realized through forfeiture to the claiming agent in satisfaction of actual costs incurred for protecting, maintaining and forfeiting the property including that proportion of the salaries of attorneys, clerical and investigative personnel devoted thereto;

(g) Forty percent of all moneys realized through forfeiture which are remaining after distributions pursuant to paragraphs (a) through (f) of this subdivision, to the substance abuse service fund established pursuant to section ninety-seven-w of the state finance law;

(h) All moneys remaining after distributions pursuant to paragraphs (a) through (g) of this subdivision shall be distributed as follows:

(i) seventy-five percent of such moneys shall be deposited to a law enforcement purposes subaccount of the general fund of the state where the claiming agent is an agency of the state or the political subdivision or public authority of which the claiming agent is a part, to be used for law enforcement use in the investigation of penal law offenses;

(ii) the remaining twenty-five percent of such moneys shall be deposited to a prosecution services subaccount of the general fund of the state where the claiming authority is the attorney general or the political subdivision of which the claiming authority is a part, to be used for the prosecution of penal law offenses.

Where multiple claiming agents participated in the forfeiture action, funds available pursuant to subparagraph (i) of this paragraph shall be disbursed to the appropriate law enforcement purposes subaccounts in accordance with the terms of a written agreement reflecting the participation of each claiming agent entered into by the participating claiming agents.

3. All moneys distributed to the claiming agent and the claiming authority pursuant to paragraph (h) of subdivision two of this section shall be used to enhance law enforcement efforts and not in supplantation of ordinary budgetary costs including salaries of personnel, and expenses of the claiming authority or claiming agent during the fiscal year in which this section takes effect.

4. The claiming authority shall report the disposal of property and collection of assets pursuant to this section to the state crime victims board, the state division of criminal justice services and the state division of substance abuse services.

CPLR

### 1990 AMENDMENTS

L. 1990, ch. 655, eff. Nov. 1, 1990, repealed former § 1349 and added new § 1349.

## § 1350.  Rules of procedure; in general.

The civil practice law and rules shall govern the procedure in proceedings and actions commenced under this article, except where the procedure is regulated by any inconsistent provisions herein.

### 1984 AMENDMENTS

L. 1984, ch. 669, eff. Aug. 1, 1984, repealed former Article 13-A and added a new Article 13-A, comprising CPLR 1310 through CPLR 1352. New Article 13-A is applicable to crimes committed on and after the effective date.

## § 1351.  Application of article.

If any provision of this article or the application thereof to any person or circumstances shall be adjudged by any court of competent jurisdiction to be invalid or unconstitutional, such judgment shall not affect, impair or invalidate the remainder thereof, but shall be confined (i) in its operation of the provision, or (ii) in its application to the person or circumstance directly involved in the controversy in which such judgment shall have been rendered.

### 1984 AMENDMENTS

L. 1984, ch. 669, eff. Aug. 1, 1984, repealed former Article 13-A and added a new Article 13-A, comprising CPLR 1310 through CPLR 1352. New Article 13-A is applicable to crimes committed on and after the effective date.

## § 1352. Preservation of other rights and remedies.

The remedies provided for in this article are not intended to substitute for or limit or supersede the lawful authority of any public officer or agency or other person to enforce any other right or remedy provided for by law.

### 1984 AMENDMENTS

L. 1984, ch. 669, eff. Aug. 1, 1984, repealed former Article 13-A and added a new Article 13-A, comprising CPLR 1310 through CPLR 1352. New Article 13-A is applicable to crimes committed on and after the effective date.

# ARTICLE 13-B

# CIVIL REMEDIES; ENTERPRISE CORRUPTION

### SUMMARY OF ARTICLE

§ 1353.    Civil remedies.
§ 1354.    Joinder of a party.
§ 1355.    Civil actions notice.

## § 1353.  Civil remedies.

1. Upon or after conviction of a person of any subdivision of section 460.20 of the penal law, the court may, after making due provision for the rights of innocent persons, enjoin future activity by the person so convicted or an enterprise he controls or in whose control he participates upon a showing that injunctive action is necessary to prevent further violation of that section. In such case the court may:

(a) order the defendant to divest himself of any interest in a specified enterprise;

(b) impose reasonable restrictions upon the future activities or investments of the defendant, including prohibiting the defendant from engaging in the same type of endeavor as the enterprise in which he was engaged in violation of section 460.20 of the penal law;

(c) order the dissolution of any enterprise he controls or the reorganization of any enterprise he controls or of which he participates in the control;

(d) order the suspension or revocation of a license, permit or prior approval granted by any agency of the state or any political subdivision thereof to the defendant or to any enterprise controlled by him or in whose control he participates, provided however, that when the court orders such license, permit or approval revoked or suspended for a period of more than two years, the court shall set a period of time within two years of the date of such revocation or suspension after which the defendant or enterprise may petition the court to permit the defendant or enterprise to request restoration or renewal of such license, permit or approval, by the agency or board empowered to grant it, after notice to and hearing of the party who brought the action in which the revocation or suspension was ordered;

CPLR

(e) order the revocation of the certificate of incorporation of a corporation organized under the laws of the state in which the defendant has a controlling interest or the revocation of authorization for a foreign corporation in which the defendant has a controlling interest to conduct business within the state upon a finding that the board of directors or a high managerial agent acting on behalf of the corporation, in conducting the affairs of the corporation, has authorized or engaged in activity made unlawful by section 460.20 of the penal law and that such action is necessary for the prevention of future criminal activity made unlawful by section 460.20 of the penal law.

2. The attorney general, the deputy attorney general in charge of the statewide organized crime task force, or any district attorney may institute civil proceedings in the supreme court under this section. Any action brought under this article shall constitute a special proceeding. In any action brought under this article, the supreme court shall proceed as soon as practicable to the hearing and determination thereof. Pending final determination, the supreme court may, at any time, enter such injunctions, prohibitions, or restraining orders or take such actions, including the acceptance of satisfactory performance bonds, ordering of disclosure under article thirty-one of this chapter, or other action as the court may deem proper.

### 1986 AMENDMENTS

L. 1986, ch. 516, eff. Nov. 1, 1986, permits commencement of a civil or criminal action against a person based upon his participation in a pattern of criminal activity beginning before such date only if his participation in the pattern also specifically includes one criminal act which was a felony and which was committed on or after such date; also added new Article 13-B, comprising CPLR 1353 through 1355.

## § 1354.   Joinder of a party.

A person or enterprise not convicted of the crime of enterprise corruption may be made a party to a civil action under this article, whenever joinder of such person or enterprise is necessary pursuant to section 1001 of this chapter.

### 1986 AMENDMENTS

L. 1986, ch. 516, eff. Nov. 1, 1986, permits commencement of a civil or criminal action against a person based upon his participation in a pattern of criminal activity beginning before such date only if his participation in the pattern also specifically includes one criminal act which was a felony and which was committed on or after such date; also added new Article 13-B, comprising CPLR 1353 through 1355.

## § 1355.   Civil actions notice.

Within fifteen days of commencing a civil proceeding pursuant to this article, the prosecutor bringing such action must notify those district attorneys who were affected district attorneys within the meaning of section 460.60 of the penal law in the prior criminal proceeding.

## 1986 AMENDMENTS

L. 1986, ch. 516, eff. Nov. 1, 1986, permits commencement of a civil or criminal action against a person based upon his participation in a pattern of criminal activity beginning before such date only if his participation in the pattern also specifically includes one criminal act which was a felony and which was committed on or after such date; also added new Article 13-B, comprising CPLR 1353 through 1355.

# ARTICLE 14

# CONTRIBUTION

## SUMMARY OF ARTICLE

§ 1401.  Claim for contribution.
§ 1402.  Amount of contribution.
§ 1403.  How contribution claimed.
§ 1404.  Rights of persons entitled to damages not affected; rights of indemnity or subrogation preserved.

## § 1401.  Claim for contribution.

Except as provided in sections 15-108 and 18-201 of the general obligations law, sections eleven and twenty-nine of the workers' compensation law, or the workers' compensation law of any other state or the federal government, two or more persons who are subject to liability for damages for the same personal injury, injury to property or wrongful death, may claim contribution among them whether or not an action has been brought or a judgment has been rendered against the person from whom contribution is sought.

### CROSS REFERENCES

**G.O.L. § 15-108** appears in Appendix, *infra*.

See **Insurance Law § 167, paragraph (3)**, in Appendix, *infra*, as to the inapplicability to contribution claims of the inter-spousal automobile liability coverage exception.

### 1996 AMENDMENTS

L. 1996, ch. 635, eff. Sept. 10, 1996, amended the section to add references to G.O.L. § 18–201, Workers' Compensation Law §§ 11 and 29, and any other state or federal workers' compensation law.

### 1974 AMENDMENTS

L. 1974, ch. 742, eff. Sept. 1, 1974, upon the recommendation of the Judicial Conference, repealed former Article 14, entitled "Actions Between Joint Tort-Feasors", and enacted a new Article 14, comprising sections 1401-1404, entitled "Contribution".

The 1974 Judicial Conference Report stated:

"The proposals submitted herewith are directed towards two principal goals:

"First, they would codify and clarify the fundamental rule embodied in [*Dole v. Dow Chem. Co.*, 30 N.Y.2d 143 (1972),] and its progeny (1) that there is no longer the requirement of a joint money judgment against tortfeasors if contribution is to be allowed among them; and (2) that the courts are no longer restricted to either apportioning liability for contribution on a *pro rata* basis, if the statutory prerequisites for contribution have been met, or shifting responsibility entirely from one tortfeasor to another under the primary-secondary tortfeasor doctrine of indemnification. Instead, under proposed new article 14, which the Committee recommends, the courts may apportion the shares of the contributing tortfeasors on the basis of their comparative degrees of culpability.

"Second, a proposed amendment of section 15-108 of the General Obligations Law would remove the disincentive to settle which presently exists under *Dole* for a tortfeasor because he remains subject to contribution to other tortfeasors against whom a judgment in favor of the injured party may be rendered. Under the proposed statutory scheme, the settling tortfeasor would no longer be subject to a claim for contribution by other persons who are liable to the injured party; neither could he assert a claim for contribution against them. Rather, under the proposed amendment, the claim of the injured party against other tortfeasors would be reduced by the amount of the settlement or by the amount of the equitable share of the damages attributable to the released tortfeasor, which ever is the greater.

"[Section 1401] is made applicable to persons subject to liability for the same harm. This provision is broader than that ascribed to a rule encompassing only joint tortfeasors' as that phrase has sometimes been construed. . . . [It applies] also, where otherwise appropriate, to concurrent tortfeasors,' . . . successive and independent tortfeasors,' . . . and to alternative tortfeasors. . . .

"The section is not limited to unintentional tortfeasors. . . . The existence of a procedure in new Article 14 for apportioning liability on the basis of relative degrees of culpability permits the use of the Article where one of the tortfeasors is guilty of intentional misconduct or reckless misconduct while another is not, without fear that the intentional wrongdoer will be rewarded' by the presence of a non-intentional wrongdoer. . . .

"While it is expected that in the usual situation in which this Article will be applied, each of the wrongdoers will be charged with the commission of a tort, the Article is not so limited. It is the fact of liability to the same person for the same harm rather than the legal theory upon which tort liability is based which controls.

"For instance, this Article applies in those factual situations in which one or more of the wrongdoers is charged with a breach of warranty. . . . Any conceptual problem arising from an attempt to measure comparative fault, when warranty liability is ostensibly not based upon fault, has been solved by the formulation of the applicable standard of comparison set forth in section 1402.

"When liability to the injured person is predicated upon the violation of a statute, difficult questions concerning the appropriateness of applying the proposed Article arise when the violation of the statute gives rise to strict or absolute liability and does not merely constitute negligence per se. . . . It seems clear that in those strict or absolute liability cases in which every person subject to a claim for contribution has violated the statute, the proposed Article should apply, for its application will foster the goal of loss distribution among wrongdoers without interfering with any legislative policy of deterrence which might have been a motivating factor in the passage of the act.

"However, where only one of the wrongdoers is charged with violating a statute imposing absolute liability, and such wrongdoer attempts to assert a claim for contribution against one who is liable only for common law negligence, resolution of the issue is more difficult. It is suggested that courts should apply this Article in such cases unless it is clear that the legislative policy which led to the passage of the statute would be frustrated by the granting of contribution in favor of the person who violated the statute. . . .

"[The] requirement of common liability is considered essential in a contribution statute. . . . However, there may be situations in which one party may not be liable to the injured person but should nonetheless be responsible for contribution. For instance, where, at the time he is sued for contribution, the alleged wrongdoer is not subject to suit directly by the injured party because the statute of limitations has run on that claim, it may nonetheless be proper to subject him to a claim for contribution under this Article if all other requirements of this Article are met. . . .

"The proposed statutory language is broad enough to permit contribution in such cases because the person against whom contribution is sought was 'subject to liability' even though he could not be held liable to the injured person directly at the time he was sued for contribution if he chose to assert the defense of the statute of limitations. Similarly, the proposed statute is not intended to change existing law where contribution is presently permitted despite the fact that the one against whom it is sought had a personal defense against the injured party other than the statute of limitations (e.g., in *Dole* the claim against Dole's employer was barred by the Workmen's Compensation Law, yet the employer was required to contribute his share to the recovery obtained against Dow Chemical Co.). . . ."

## § 1402. Amount of contribution.

The amount of contribution to which a person is entitled shall be the excess paid by him over and above his equitable share of the judgment recovered by the injured party; but no person shall be required to contribute an amount greater than his equitable share. The equitable shares shall be determined in accordance with the relative culpability of each person liable for contribution.

### 1974 AMENDMENTS

Article added by L. 1974, ch. 742, eff. Sept. 1, 1974.

The 1974 Judicial Conference Report stated, in part:

"The phrase 'relative culpability' is used here in lieu of 'relative degrees of negligence' or 'fault' because this Article permits contribution even when one or more of the wrongdoers is not charged with negligence, or is charged only with a breach of warranty, frequently referred to as a 'no-fault' theory of liability. . . . The phrase is designed to make clear that the setting of 'relative responsibility' which *Dole* sought, and which section 1402 permits, can be accomplished even where some of the tortfeasors are not negligent or at fault. . . .

"It is to be expected that when this section is applied, the 'relative degrees of culpability' will be expressed in terms of percentages as is currently done under *Dole* and its progeny. . . .

"While the claim for contribution may be asserted prior to payment of any amount to the injured person, thus assuring expeditious resolution of the issue of whether a right to contribution exists, the proposed section precludes enforcement of those rights until the person seeking to enforce his right of contribution has paid to the injured person more than his equitable share of the damages.

"This rule has been taken, with appropriate modifications, from the former contribution statute (CPLR § 1401) and is consistent with the rule that where a third-party claim for indemnity against loss has been asserted, and a conditional or provisional judgment has been entered, the judgment cannot be enforced until the original defendant has satisfied all or part of the original plaintiff's judgment. . . .

"Taken, with appropriate modifications, from former section 1401, this section provides, in part, that no person is obligated to pay more to a fellow wrongdoer for contribution than the equitable share of the entire damages which has been assessed against him.

"The effect of this rule is to place upon the wrongdoer who pays the judgment the risk that other wrongdoers responsible for contribution are solvent. To illustrate: If P sues A, B and C, and receives a judgment for $12,000 against each, the equitable share of each A, B and C being assessed as 1/3, if A pays the $12,000 to P, and C is insolvent, A can recover only $4,000 from B, not $6,000, and thus A will bear the entire financial loss resulting from the insolvency of C."

## § 1403.   How contribution claimed.

A cause of action for contribution may be asserted in a separate action or by cross-claim, counterclaim or third-party claim in a pending action.

### 1974 AMENDMENTS

Article added by L. 1974, ch. 742, eff. Sept. 1, 1974.

The 1974 Judicial Conference Report stated, in part:

"A separate action may be necessary where the person against whom contribution is sought is not subject to jurisdiction in the court in which the primary action has been brought. It may also be necessary in those cases in which the existence of a wrongdoer who is subject to liability for contribution is not discovered until after the primary action has been completed or is discovered so late that to introduce the claim for contribution into the primary action would unfairly delay the determination of the injured person's claim.

"However, the assertion of a claim for contribution in a separate action should be discouraged, for it adds to the burden of already crowded courts, creates the possibility of inconsistent verdicts in the two actions and makes more difficult the assessment of equitable shares in multi-party situations in which one of three or more wrongdoers is not joined in the initial action. Therefore, it is hoped that separate actions for contribution will not be instituted if it is possible to resolve the issue in the primary action brought by the injured person."

## § 1404.   Right of persons entitled to damages not affected; rights of indemnity or subrogation preserved.

(a) Nothing contained in this article shall impair the rights of any person entitled to damages under existing law.

(b) Nothing contained in this article shall impair any right of indemnity or subrogation under existing law.

### 1974 AMENDMENTS

Article added by L. 1974, ch. 742, eff. Sept. 1, 1974.

The 1974 Judicial Conference Report stated, in part:

"The function of subdivision (a) of this section is to assure that this Article is interpreted consistently with the views of the Court of Appeals . . . to the end that the traditional doctrine of joint and several liability among multiple wrongdoers . . .

is not changed by the operation of this Article. This section should not be construed, however, as limiting the effect of General Obligations Law § 15-108.

"In keeping with the premise that *Dole* was intended essentially to modify the law of contribution, leaving much of the traditional common law of indemnity unchanged, . . . subdivision (b) of section 1404 states that in those factual situations in which the Court of Appeals would continue to apply the common law rules of indemnity . . . nothing contained in this Article should be construed to preclude them from so doing.

"In addition, it is to be expected that whenever the existing common law rules of indemnity are applied to shift the entire financial responsibility from one tortfeasor to another, there is to be no subsequent claim for contribution under this Article.

"To the extent that one party possesses rights in accordance with the laws of subrogation and the existence of those rights would not be inconsistent with the purpose and intent of this Article, those rights should continue to be enforceable."

CPLR

# ARTICLE 14-A

## DAMAGE ACTIONS: EFFECT OF CONTRIBUTORY NEGLIGENCE AND ASSUMPTION OF RISK

---

### SUMMARY OF ARTICLE

§ 1411.      Damages recoverable when contributory negligence or assumption of risk is established.

§ 1412.      Burden of pleading; burden of proof.

§ 1413.      Applicability.

---

**CPLR**

### § 1411.   Damages recoverable when contributory negligence or assumption of risk is established.

In any action to recover damages for personal injury, injury to property, or wrongful death, the culpable conduct attributable to the claimant or to the decedent, including contributory negligence or assumption of risk, shall not bar recovery, but the amount of damages otherwise recoverable shall be diminished in the proportion which the culpable conduct attributable to the claimant or decedent bears to the culpable conduct which caused the damages.

#### 1975 AMENDMENTS

L. 1975, ch. 69, eff. Sept. 1, 1975, upon the recommendation of the Judicial Conference, added new Article 14-A (CPLR 1411–1413), providing new rules as to the effect of contributory negligence and assumption of risk in damage actions, aimed at completing the application of the principle of comparative negligence to contribution among joint tortfeasors, commenced by *Dole v. Dow Chemical Co.*, 30 N.Y.2d 143 (1972), by extending that principle to the case-in-chief.

The 1975 Judicial Conference Report stated, in part:

"(a) Because contributory fault is a defense in actions based upon a theory of strict products liability (*Codling v. Paglia*, 32 N.Y.2d 330 (1973)) and those based upon a theory of breach of warranty, [*Velez v. Craine & Clark Lumber Corp.*, 33 N.Y.2d 117 (1973)] and because àssumption of risk' has been held to be a defense in an action based upon strict products liability (*Bolm v. Triumph Corp.*, 33 N.Y.2d 151, 157 (1973); *accord*, Restatement (Second) of Torts § 402 A, comment N (1965)), this article is applicable not only to negligence actions, but to all actions brought to recover damages for personal injury, injury to property or wrongful death whatever the legal theory upon which the suit is based.

"(b) The phrase c̀ulpable conduct' is used instead of ǹegligent conduct' because this article will apply to cases where the conduct of one or more of the parties will be found to be not negligent, but will nonetheless be a factor in determining the amount of damages. For example, in *Velez* v. *Craine & Clark Lumber Corp.* (33 N.Y.2d 117 (1973)), defendant was found to have breached a warranty but was not chargeable with negligence. Under existing law, the contributory negligence of the plaintiff would be a complete bar to recovery. This article permits the apportionment of damages in cases such as *Velez* in which the plaintiff's negligence may be the only *negligence*, but the defendant's conduct is nonetheless culpable' and therefore to be considered in determining damages.

\* \* \*

"The phrase is consistent with that used in section 1402 of the CPLR which provides that contribution šhall be determined in accordance with the relative culpability of each person . . .' and is used in this article for the same reason that led to its adoption in article fourteen of the CPLR. . . .

"(c) This article equates the defenses of contributory negligence and assumption of risk by providing that neither shall continue to serve as a complete defense in actions to which this article applies. This is consistent with the result reached in the vast majority of states that have adopted some form of comparative negligence (*e.g.*, Oregon Laws 1971, ch. 688 ssl; *McConville* v. *State Farm Mutual Automobile Ins. Co.*, 15 Wisc. 2d 374, 113 N.W.2d 14 (1962); *Lyons* v. *Redding Construction Co.*, 83 Wash. 2d 86, 515 P.2d 821 (1973). *But see Dendy* v. *City of Pascagola*, 193 So. 2d 559 (Miss. 1967)). The statute is also consistent with the position taken by the New York courts, which have found that there is a borderline where the concept of contributory negligence merges almost imperceptibly into that of acceptance of a risk. . . . Very often the difference is chiefly one of terminology.' *McFarlane* v. *City of Niagara Falls*, 247 N.Y. 340, 349, 160 N.E. 391 (1928) (Cardozo).

\* \* \*

". . . Just as there has been a general softening of the rigidities of the doctrine of contributory negligence' with à tendency to treat it almost always as a question of fact' (*Rossman* v. *La Grega*, 28 N.Y.2d 300, 306 (1971)), as well as a growing recognition that the great issue is not liability but the damages recoverable for injuries' (*Andre* v. *Pomeroy*, —N.Y.2d — (1974) (Breitel, dissenting)), it is expected that the courts will treat assumption of risk as a form of culpable conduct under this article.

"In appropriate cases, of course, the finder of fact may determine that the plaintiff's conduct in assuming the risk is the sole culpable conduct, and diminish damages accordingly.

"(d) Àssumption of risk' and contributory negligence' are not the only doctrines that might be included within the phrase culpable conduct.' The Court of Appeals has recently determined that ùse of [a] . . . product for other than its normally intended purpose or other than in the manner normally intended' is a form of contributory fault' which bars recovery in an action based upon a theory of strict products liability (*Codling* v. *Paglia*, 32 N.Y.2d 330, 343, 298 N.E.2d 622 (1973)); that defense constitutes a form of culpable conduct.' So too, the patent danger' rule, made applicable in negligence actions in *Campo* v. *Schofield* (301 N.Y. 458, (1950)), and recently applied to strict products liability cases should be considered within the framework of this article as a factor to be weighed by the trier of fact in determining whether to diminish damages. *Bolm* v. *Triumph Corp.*, 33 N.Y.2d 151, 159 (1973) (the issue . . . presents a question of fact . . .'

"Neither the specific examples of culpable conduct mentioned in the statute nor those used in this comment are necessarily exhaustive of the range of culpable conduct' which may properly be considered. Judicial development of the concept of culpable conduct' consistent with the goals of this article is not precluded.

"(e) In determining the total culpable conduct which caused the damages,' the culpable conduct of the defendant as well as that of the claimant must be considered. The defendant's culpable conduct may include, but is not necessarily limited to, negligence, breach of warranty, a violation of statute giving rise to civil liability, conduct giving rise to liability upon a theory of strict liability, and intentional misconduct.

"(f) In applying this article, not only the culpable conduct of the claimant or decedent is to be considered, but also any culpable conduct which is legally attributable to him though actually committed or performed by another. However, this article is not intended to create vicarious liability or to expand the doctrine of imputed contributory negligence, and should be interpreted in harmony with recent decisional law which severely restricts, if it does not entirely eliminate, the doctrine of imputed of vicarious contributory negligence. *Kalechman* v. *Drew Auto Rental, Inc.*, 33 N.Y.2d 397 (1973).

"(g) This article requires that the culpable conduct attributable to the decedent or claimant be compared with the total culpable conduct which caused the damages. Several specific policy decisions have been incorporated thereby.

(1) *Joint and Several Liability*. It is not intended that this article change the present rule of joint and several liability among tortfeasors (*Barrett* v. *The Third Avenue Ry. Co.*, 45 N.Y. 628 (1871); *Gleich* v. *Volpe*, 32 N.Y.2d 517, 523–524 (1973)), nor is it intended to preclude judicial reconsideration of the rule.

(2) *Causal Culpability*. Only culpable conduct which was a substantial factor in causing the harm for which recovery is sought is to be considered in determining the amount by which damages are to be diminished. . . .

(3) *Culpability of Non-party*. It is possible that a person whose culpable conduct contributed to the damages may not be a party to the action instituted by the claimant, as where one of several tortfeasors has settled with the claimant, or is unknown, or is not subject to the jurisdiction of the court in which the claimant has filed suit.

In the usual case the requirement that claimant's conduct be compared with the total culpable conduct of all persons, whether or not parties to the action, should not add to the complexity of the trial nor should it impose unfair burdens upon any party to the action. It is included primarily to reflect the compatibility of this article with article fourteen of the CPLR, and section 15–108 of the General Obligations Law. . . .

"If the claimant sues tortfeasor A and not tortfeasor B, the culpable conduct attributable to claimant should be considered in light of the total culpable conduct—that of the claimant, of A, and of B. As under present law (*Barrett* v. *The Third Avenue Ry. Co.*, 45 N.Y.628 (1871 )), A will be liable for the full amount of claimant's damages less the percentage found attributable to the claimant. There is, therefore, no incentive for A to demonstrate that B was also culpable. *Cf,* James, *Connecticut's Comparative Negligence Statute:* An Analysis of Some Problems, 6 *Conn. L. Rev.* 207, 219-221 (1974).

"Where B has settled with claimant, however, A will not only wish to demonstrate that claimant was chargeable with culpable conduct, but will also wish to have the finder of fact determine the percentage of culpability attributable to B, since it is possible that judgment will be entered against A only after the damages suffered by claimant have been twice reduced—once to reflect claimant's culpable conduct, and once to reflect B's culpability. *See N.Y. Gen. Obl. Law* section 15-108 . . .; CPLR rule 4533(b).

**CPLR**

"(h) . . .Because the New York courts have consistently recognized that where contributory negligence is not claimed as a bar to recovery, the doctrine of last clear chance is not to be applied (*e.g., Polk* v. *New York Central R.R. Co.,* 10 A.D. 2d 703 (1st Dept. 1960); *Jasinski* v. *New York Central R.R. Co.,* 21 A.D. 2d 456 (4th Dept. 1964), it was thought unnecessary to include an express provision in this article abolishing the doctrine. See *Cushman* v. *Perkins,* 245 A.2d 846 (Maine 1968).

"The continued separate existence of the doctrine of last clear chance cannot be justified; the factors which the doctrine took into consideration can more appropriately be considered in determining the čulpable conduct' and the issue of causation of damages under this article. . . .

"(i) . . . This article permits a finding that while each of the parties is culpable, each is entitled to recover some portion of his damages. For instance, if plaintiff sues for $5,000 and defendant asserts in a counterclaim that he is entitled to $10,000 in damages, the finder of fact could determine that each was negligent, and that the culpability of each party was fifty percent, thus entitling plaintiff to $2500 and defendant to $5,000.

"It is the intent of this proposed legislation that no casualty insurance company, or other insurer, shall apply as a set-off to payment pursuant to a policy of insurance any amount by which a recovery against its insured was diminished by reason of a counterclaim or cross-claim asserted by the insured pursuant to this article. . . .

"Section 3019(d) of the CPLR provides that a separate judgment may not be had for a cause of action contained in a counterclaim or cross-claim unless the court so orders. It appears, therefore, that the normal procedure when such claim is asserted is to try both the claim and counterclaim together, and to enter only a single judgment for the difference between the amounts awarded in each claim. *See* 3 Weinstein, Korn & Miller, New York Civil Practice - CPLR ¶ 3019.02 (Matthew Bender).

"Because there are legitimate policy reasons for preferring that routine use of multiple judgments be avoided (*see e.g., Illinois McGraw Elec. Co.* v. *John J. Walters, Inc.,* 7 N.Y.2d 874 (1959); *Pease & Elliman, Inc.* v. *926 Park Avenue Corp.,* 23 App. Div. 2d 361 (1st Dept. 1965); *Dalminter, Inc.* v. *Dalmine, S.P.A.,* 28 App. Be N.Y Div. 2d 852 (1st Dept.), *aff'd,* 23 N.Y.2d 653 (1968)), entry of two judgments has not been made mandatory in all cases.

"Confident that the legislative intent will be fulfilled and that existing legislation and procedural rules are adequate to accomplish that result, it was deemed unnecessary to provide a specific prohibition against set-off. (*See, e.g.,* Rhode Island Stat. Ann. Section 9–20–4.1 (1971))."

## § 1412. Burden of pleading; burden of proof.

Culpable conduct claimed in diminution of damages, in accordance with section fourteen hundred eleven, shall be an affirmative defense to be pleaded and proved by the party asserting the defense.

### 1975 AMENDMENTS

L. 1975, ch. 69, eff. Sept. 1, 1975, upon the recommendation of the Judicial Conference, added new Article 14-A (CPLR 1411–1413), as to the effect of contributory negligence and assumption of risk in damage actions. See comments to CPLR 1411.

The 1975 Judicial Conference Report stated, in part:

"(a) The New York Court of Appeals has noted: Àlthough New York has clung to a rule that a living plaintiff must establish his own freedom from negligence, it is the majority rule in this country that in all negligence actions, including those maintained by living persons for injury or property damage, the defendant claiming contributory negligence of the plaintiff has the burden of showing it. . . . And it is likewise the general rule where contributory negligence is an affirmative defense the injured person "is presumed to have used due . . . care.' " *Rossman v. LaGrega*, 28 N.Y.2d 300, 304 (1971). This section brings New York law on the issue into conformity with the majority rule and represents the culmination of the gradual but persistent erosion of the rule that freedom from contributory negligence must be pleaded and proven by the plaintiff. . . . *Wartels v. County Asphalt, Inc.*, 29 N.Y.2d 381 (1972) (Unusual facts reduced plaintiff's burden of proof close to the vanishing point'); *Codling v. Paglia*, 32 N.Y.2d 330, 343 (1973) (contributory fault of the plaintiff is a *defense* to an action for strict products liability') (emphasis added).

"(b) Because they are both manifestations of the same or similar considerations... . . . burden of pleading and burden of proof are usually parallel.' James, Civil Procedure p. 265 (1965). This is generally true in New York (*see* 3 Weinstein, Korn & Miller, New York Civil Practice - CPLR ¶ 3018.14 (Matthew Bender)), and there is no reason to make an exception where one seeks to diminish damages otherwise recoverable by asserting, pursuant to this article, that the claimant's culpable conduct contributed to his harm. This article may be viewed as having created a partial defense, the effect of which is to mitigate damages, and such defenses traditionally must be pleaded affirmatively. *See* 3 Weinstein, Korn & Miller, New York Civil Practice - CPLR ¶ 3018.17 (Matthew Bender); *Cf. Rehill v. Rehill*, 306 N.Y. 126 (1953)."

## § 1413.  Applicability.

This article shall apply to all causes of action accruing on or after September first, nineteen hundred seventy-five.

### 1975 AMENDMENTS

L. 1975, ch. 69, eff. Sept. 1, 1975, upon the recommendation of the Judicial Conference, added new Article 14-A (CPLR 1411–1413), as to the effect of contributory negligence and assumption of risk in damage actions. See comments to CPLR 1411.

The 1975 Judicial Conference Report stated, in part:

"(a) A clear majority of states which have passed legislation establishing some form of comparative negligence have specifically provided that the statute should be applied prospectively only, to causes of action that arise after the effective date of the statute (e.g. Texas Law. 1973, ch. 28, ss. 4), while the remaining few provide either that the statute shall be applied to actions filed after the effective date of the statute (Rhode Isl. Stat. Ann. ss9–20–4), or to trials commenced after the effective date of the statute (Minnesota Laws 1969, ch. 624 ss.2). Where the statute has been silent, the courts have uniformly applied the statute only prospectively. *E.g., Joseph v. Lowery*, 495 P.2d 273 (Oregon 1972).

"While at least one court has upheld the validity of a statutory provision calling for retroactive application of a comparative negligence statute (*Peterson v. City of Minneapolis*, 173 N.W.2d 353 (1969)), the result in New York of litigation challenging such a provision is not free from doubt. . . .

"In order to avoid the uncertainty and confusion which might result from the retroactive application of the statute, and to protect the legitimate expectations of potential litigants and others who placed reliance upon present law, this statute is made applicable only to causes of action which accrue after its effective date.

CPLR

"(b) The word àccrue' used in this article should be given the meaning attached to it for purposes of determining the period within which an action must be commenced. CPLR 203(a). It is not unlikely that the rules for the determination of the date of accrual of some causes of action may be subject to changing judicial interpretations (*see e.g., Flanagan* v. *Mt. Eden General Hospital*, 24 N.Y.2d 427 (1969); *compare Mendel* v. *Pittsburgh Plate Glass Co.*, 25 N.Y.2d 340 (1969) with *Rivera* v. *Berkeley Superwash, Inc.*, 44 App. Div. 2d 316 (2d Dept. 1974)), and it is intended that this article be interpreted to reflect any such developments.

"(c) Under present law it is possible that one claimant will pursue two causes of action for the same or similar injury and that each cause of action will have a different accrual date. *Compare Mendel* v. *Pittsburgh Plate Glass Co.*, 25 N.Y.2d 340 (1969), *Schmidt* v. *Merchants Dispatch Transp. Co.*, 270 N.Y. 287 (1936). *Cf. Caffaro* v. *Trayna*, 35 N.Y.2d 245 (1973). In such transitional cases, when appropriate, the court should apply this article to all related causes of action tried together with a claim to which this article does apply."

# ARTICLE 15

# ACTIONS AGAINST PERSONS JOINTLY LIABLE

## SUMMARY OF ARTICLE

§ 1501.    Actions against persons jointly liable; service of summons; judgment.
§ 1502.    Provisional remedies and defenses in subsequent action against co-obligor.

## § 1501.    Actions against persons jointly liable; service of summons; judgment.

Where less than all of the named defendants in an action based upon a joint obligation, contract or liability are served with the summons, the plaintiff may proceed against the defendants served, unless the court otherwise directs, and if the judgment is for the plaintiff it may be taken against all the defendants.

### CROSS REFERENCES

See **General Obligations Law § 15-102** in Appendix, *infra,* as to effect of judgment upon non-party co-obligor.

## § 1502.    Provisional remedies and defenses in subsequent action against co-obligor.

A subsequent action against a co-obligor who was not summoned in the original action must be maintained in order to procure a judgment enforceable against his individually held property for the sum remaining unpaid upon the original judgment, and such action shall be regarded as based upon the same obligation, contract or liability as the original judgment for the purpose of obtaining any provisional remedy. The complaint in the subsequent action shall be verified. The defendant in the subsequent action may raise any defenses or counterclaims that he might have raised in the original action if the summons had been served on him when it was first served on a co-obligor, and may raise objections to the original judgment, and defenses or counterclaims that have arisen since it was entered.

CPLR

# ARTICLE 16

# LIMITED LIABILITY OF PERSONS JOINTLY LIABLE

## SUMMARY OF ARTICLE

§ 1600.    Definitions.
§ 1601.    Limited liability of persons jointly liable.
§ 1602.    Application.
§ 1603.    Burdens of proof.

## § 1600. Definitions.

As used in this article the term "non-economic loss" includes but is not limited to pain and suffering, mental anguish, loss of consortium or other damages for non-economic loss.

### 1986 AMENDMENTS

L. 1986, ch. 682, eff. July 30, 1986, and applicable to actions commenced or claims filed on or after such date, except for actions commenced pursuant to § 4 or claims filed pursuant to § 5 of L. 1986, ch. 682 (revival provisions for certain toxic tort actions), added new Article 16 (CPLR 1600–1603).

## § 1601. Limited liability of persons jointly liable.

1. Notwithstanding any other provision of law, when a verdict or decision in an action or claim for personal injury is determined in favor of a claimant in an action involving two or more tortfeasors jointly liable or in a claim against the state and the liability of a defendant is found to be fifty percent or less of the total liability assigned to all persons liable, the liability of such defendant to the claimant for non-economic loss shall not exceed that defendant's equitable share determined in accordance with the relative culpability of each person causing or contributing to the total liability for non-economic loss; provided, however that the culpable conduct of any person not a party to the action shall not be considered in determining any equitable share herein if the claimant proves that with due diligence he or she was unable to obtain jurisdiction over such person in said action (or in a claim against the state, in a court of this state); and further provided that the culpable conduct of any person shall not be considered in determining any equitable share herein to the extent that action

against such person is barred because the claimant has not sustained a "grave injury"as defined in section eleven of the workers' compensation law.

2. Nothing in this section shall be construed to affect or impair any right of a tortfeasor under section 15-108 of the general obligations law.

### 1996 AMENDMENTS

L. 1996, ch. 635, eff. Sept. 10, 1996, amended subdivision (1) by adding at the end the clause "and further provided . . . section eleven of the workers' compensation law.'

### 1986 AMENDMENTS

L. 1986, ch. 682, eff. July 30, 1986, and applicable to actions commenced or claims filed on or after such date, except for actions commenced pursuant to § 4 or claims filed pursuant to § 5 of L. 1986, ch. 682 (revival provisions for certain toxic tort actions), added new Article 16 (CPLR 1600–1603).

## § 1602.  Application.

The limitations set forth in this article shall:

1. apply to any claim for contribution or indemnification, but shall not include:

(a) a claim for indemnification if, prior to the accident or occurrence on which the claim is based, the claimant and the tortfeasor had entered into a written contract in which the tortfeasor had expressly agreed to indemnify the claimant for the type of loss suffered; or

(b) a claim for indemnification by a public employee, including indemnification pursuant to section fifty-k of the general municipal law or section seventeen or eighteen of the public officers law.

2. not be construed to impair, alter, limit, modify, enlarge, abrogate or restrict (i) the limitations set forth in section twenty-a of the court of claims act; (ii) any immunity or right of indemnification available to or conferred upon any defendant for any negligent or wrongful act or omission; (iii) any right on the part of any defendant to plead and prove an affirmative defense as to culpable conduct attributable to a claimant or decedent which is claimed by such defendant in the diminution of damages in any action; and (iv) any liability arising by reason of a non-delegable duty or by reason of the doctrine of respondeat superior.

3. not apply to administrative proceedings.

4. not apply to claims under the workers' compensation law or to a claim against a defendant where claimant has sustained a 'grave injury' as defined in section eleven of the workers' compensation law to the extent of the equitable share of any person against whom the claimant is barred from asserting a cause of action because of the applicability of the workers' compensation law provided, however, that nothing in this subdivision shall be construed to create, impair, alter, limit, modify, enlarge, abrogate, or restrict any theory of liability upon which any person may be held liable.

5. not apply to actions requiring proof of intent.

6. not apply to any person held liable by reason of his use, operation, or ownership of a motor vehicle or motorcycle, as those terms are defined respectively in sections three hundred eleven and one hundred twenty-five of the vehicle and traffic law.

7. not apply to any person held liable for causing claimant's injury by having acted with reckless disregard for the safety of others.

8. not apply to any person held liable by reason of the applicability of article ten of the labor law.

9. not apply to any person held liable for causing claimant's injury by having unlawfully released into the environment a substance hazardous to public health, safety or the environment, a substance acutely hazardous to public health, safety or the environment or a hazardous waste, as defined in articles thirty-seven and twenty-seven of the environmental conservation law and in violation of article seventy-one of such law; provided, however, that nothing herein shall require that the violation of said article by such person has resulted in a criminal conviction or administrative adjudication of liability.

10. not apply to any person held liable in a product liability action where the manufacturer of the product is not a party to the action and the claimant establishes by a preponderance of the evidence that jurisdiction over the manufacturer could not with due diligence be obtained and that if the manufacturer were a party to the action, liability for claimant's injury would have been imposed upon said manufacturer by reason of the doctrine of strict liability, to the extent of the equitable share of such manufacturer.

11. not apply to any parties found to have acted knowingly or intentionally, and in concert, to cause the acts or failures upon which liability is based; provided, however, that nothing in this subdivision shall be construed to create, impair, alter, limit, modify, enlarge, abrogate, or restrict any theory of liability upon which said parties may be held liable to the claimant.

12. In conjunction with the other provisions of this article not be construed to create or enlarge actions for contribution or indemnity barred because of the applicability of the workers' compensation law of this state, any other state or the federal government, or section 18-201 of the general obligations law.

### 1996 AMENDMENTS

L. 1996, ch. 635, eff. Sept. 10, 1996, amended subdivision (4) by deleting the words "such defendant has impleaded a third party"; adding the phrase "claimant has sustained a "grave injury" . . . equitable share of any person"; deleting the words", to the extent of the equitable share of said third party"; and adding at the end of the subdivision the clause, "provided, however, that nothing . . . any person may be held liable"; added subdivision (12).

**1986 AMENDMENTS**

L. 1986, ch. 682, eff. July 30, 1986, and applicable to actions commenced or claims filed on or after such date, except for actions commenced pursuant to § 4 or claims filed pursuant to § 5 of L. 1986, ch. 682 (revival provisions for certain toxic tort actions), added new Article 16 (CPLR 1600–1603).

## § 1603. Burdens of proof.

In any action or claim for damages for personal injury a party asserting that the limitations on liability set forth in this article do not apply shall allege and prove by a preponderance of the evidence that one or more of the exemptions set forth in subdivision one of section sixteen hundred one or section sixteen hundred two applies. A party asserting limited liability pursuant to this article shall have the burden of proving by a preponderance of the evidence its equitable share of the total liability.

**1996 AMENDMENTS**

L. 1996, ch. 635, eff. Sept. 10, 1996, amended the section to add a reference to § 1601(1).

**1986 AMENDMENTS**

L. 1986, ch. 682, eff. July 30, 1986, and applicable to actions commenced or claims filed on or after such date except for actions commenced pursuant to § 4 or claims filed pursuant to § 5 of L. 1986, ch. 682 (revival provisions for certain toxic tort actions), added new Article 16 (CPLR 1600–1603).

# ARTICLE 20

## MISTAKES, DEFECTS, IRREGULARITIES AND EXTENSIONS OF TIME

### SUMMARY OF ARTICLE

§ 2001.    Mistakes, omissions, defects and irregularities.
§ 2002.    Error in ruling of court.
§ 2003.    Irregularity in judicial sale.
§ 2004.    Extensions of time generally.
§ 2005.    Excusable delay or default.

CPLR

### § 2001.   Mistakes, omissions, defects and irregularities.

At any stage of an action, the court may permit a mistake, omission, defect or irregularity to be corrected, upon such terms as may be just, or, if a substantial right of a party is not prejudiced, the mistake, omission, defect or irregularity shall be disregarded.

### § 2002.   Error in ruling of court.

An error in a ruling of the court shall be disregarded if a substantial right of a party is not prejudiced.

### § 2003.   Irregularity in judicial sale.

At any time within one year after a sale made pursuant to a judgment or order, but not thereafter, the court, upon such terms as may be just, may set the sale aside for a failure to comply with the requirements of the civil practice law and rules as to the notice, time or manner of such sale, if a substantial right of a party was prejudiced by the defect. This section does not apply to judicial sales made pursuant to article 9 of the uniform commercial code.

#### 1966 AMENDMENTS

L. 1966, ch. 138, eff. Sept. 1, 1966, added the sentence "This section does not apply to judicial sales made pursuant to article 9 of the uniform commercial code."

Amendment recommended by the Judicial Conference Feb. 1, 1966, Report to the Legislature: "CPLR 2003 permits a court, within one year of a judicial sale, to set aside the sale on grounds of any of the irregularities specified. U.C.C. § 9-501(1), however, permits a secured creditor, after default, either to sell the collateral himself or to reduce his claim to a judgment and sale. U.C.C. § 9-504(4) provides that the purchaser at such sale takes good title despite the failure of the creditor to comply with all relevant provisions of the U.C.C. or the requirements òf any judicial proceedings.' Thus there is a possible conflict between the U.C.C.'s policy respecting sales under secured transactions and the CPLR's policy as to judicial sales generally. The change is proposed in order to place attorneys on notice of the U.C.C. provision."

## § 2004.  Extensions of time generally.

Except where otherwise expressly prescribed by law, the court may extend the time fixed by any statute, rule or order for doing any act, upon such terms as may be just and upon good cause shown, whether the application for extension is made before or after the expiration of the time fixed.

## § 2005.  Excusable delay or default.

Upon an application satisfying the requirements of subdivision (d) of section 3012 or subdivision (a) of rule 5015, the court shall not, as a matter of law, be precluded from exercising its discretion in the interests of justice to excuse delay or default resulting from law office failure.

### 1983 AMENDMENTS

L. 1983, ch. 318, added CPLR 2005 in relation to excusable default and extension of time. ch. 318, § 3 provides:

§ 3. This act shall take effect immediately and shall be deemed and construed as remedial in nature and application and shall apply in every action and proceeding heretofore commenced and which either: still is pending before a court; or the time for taking of an appeal from any order or judgment in such action has not yet expired, and in all actions and proceedings hereafter commenced.

# ARTICLE 21

# PAPERS

## SUMMARY OF ARTICLE

R 2101.     Form of papers.
       (a)    Quality, size and legibility.
       (b)    Language.
       (c)    Caption.
       (d)    Indorsement by attorney.
       (e)    Copies.
       (f)    Defects in form; waiver.
R 2102.     Filing of papers.
R 2103.     Service of papers.
       (a)    Who can serve.
       (b)    Upon an attorney.
       (c)    Upon a party.
       (d)    Filing.
       (e)    Parties to be served.
       (f)    Definitions.
R 2104.     Stipulations.
§ 2105.     Certification by attorney.
R 2106.     Affirmation of truth of statement by attorney, physician, osteopath or
           dentist.

## R 2101. Form of papers.

(a) Quality, size and legibility. Each paper served or filed shall be durable, white and, except for summonses, subpoenas, notices of appearance, notes of issue, orders of protection, temporary orders of protection and exhibits, shall be eleven by eight and one-half inches in size. The writing shall be legible and in black ink. Beneath each signature shall be printed the name signed. The letters in the summons shall be in clear type of no less than twelve-point in size. Each other printed or typed paper served or filed, except an exhibit, shall be in clear type of no less than ten-point in size.

(b) Language. Each paper served or filed shall be in the English language which, where practicable, shall be of ordinary usage. Where an affidavit or exhibit annexed to a paper served or filed is in a foreign language, it shall be accompanied by an English translation and an affidavit by the translator stating his qualifications and that the translation is accurate.

(c) Caption. Each paper served or filed shall begin with a caption setting forth the name of the court, the venue, the title of the action, the nature of the paper and the index number of the action if one has been assigned. In a summons, a complaint or a judgment the title shall include the names of all parties, but in all other papers it shall be sufficient to state the name of the first named party on each side with an appropriate indication of any omissions.

(d) Indorsement by attorney. Each paper served or filed shall be indorsed with the name, address and telephone number of the attorney for the party serving or filing the paper, or if the party does not appear by attorney, with the name, address and telephone number of the party.

(e) Copies. Except where otherwise specifically prescribed, copies, rather than originals, of all papers, including orders, affidavits and exhibits may be served or filed. Where it is required that the original be served or filed and the original is lost or withheld, the court may authorize a copy to be served or filed.

(f) Defects in form; waiver. A defect in the form of a paper, if a substantial right of a party is not prejudiced, shall be disregarded by the court, and leave to correct shall be freely given. The party on whom a paper is served shall be deemed to have waived objection to any defect in form unless, within two days after the receipt thereof, he returns the paper to the party serving it with a statement of particular objections.

### 1996 AMENDMENTS

L. 1996, ch. 131, eff. June 11, 1996, amended subdivision (a) by adding the words "orders of protection, temporary orders of protection.'

### 1994 AMENDMENTS

L. 1994, ch. 100, eff. Jan. 1, 1995, amended subdivision (a) by adding the final two sentences; by deleting the provision excepting summonses, subpoenas, notices of appearance, notes of issue and exhibits from the general requirement that all papers served or filed must be on eleven-by-eight-and-one-half-inch paper; and by deleting an obsolete provision extending the time during which non-conforming size forms could be used.

### 1974 AMENDMENTS

CPLR 2101(a) was amended by proposal No. 1 of the Judicial Conference Report to the 1974 Legislature, eff. Sept. 1, 1974, to provide that courts or other public agencies shall have until Sept. 1, 1976 to utilize their present stock of forms larger than eleven by eight and one-half inches.

### 1973 AMENDMENTS

CPLR 2101(a) was amended by proposal No. 2 of the Judicial Conference Report to the 1973 Legislature, eff. Sept. 1, 1973, to provide that in all actions and proceedings commenced on or after Sept. 1, 1974, all papers served or filed, except for summonses, subpoenas, notices of appearance, notes of issue and exhibits, shall be eleven by eight and one half inches in size.

**1965 AMENDMENTS**

L. 1965, ch. 773, eff. Sept. 1, 1965, amended Subd. (d).

**1964 AMENDMENTS**

L. 1964, ch. 388, eff. Sept. 1, 1964, amended Subd. (e).

## R 2102. Filing of papers.

Except where otherwise prescribed by law or order of court, papers required to be filed shall be filed with the clerk of the court in which the action is triable. In a proceeding not brought in a court, papers required to be filed shall be filed with the clerk of the county in which the proceeding is brought.

## R 2103. Service of papers.

(a) Who can serve. Except where otherwise prescribed by law or order of court, papers may be served by any person not a party of the age of eighteen years or over.

(b) Upon an attorney. Except where otherwise prescribed by law or order of court, papers to be served upon a party in a pending action shall be served upon the party's attorney. Where the same attorney appears for two or more parties, only one copy need be served upon the attorney. Such service upon an attorney shall be made:

1. by delivering the paper to the attorney personally; or

2. by mailing the paper to the attorney at the address designated by that attorney for that purpose or, if none is designated, at that attorney's last known address; service by mail shall be complete upon mailing; where a period of time prescribed by law is measured from the service of a paper and service is by mail, five days shall be added to the prescribed period; or

3. if the attorney's office is open, by leaving the paper with a person in charge, or if no person is in charge, by leaving it in a conspicuous place; or if the attorney's office is not open, by depositing the paper, enclosed in a sealed wrapper directed to the attorney, in the attorney's office letter drop or box; or

4. by leaving it at the attorney's residence within the state with a person of suitable age and discretion. Service upon an attorney shall not be made at the attorney's residence unless service at the attorney's office cannot be made; or

5. by transmitting the paper to the attorney by electronic means, provided that a telephone number or other station or other limitation, if any, is designated by the attorney for that purpose. Service by electronic means shall be complete upon the receipt by the sender of a signal from the equipment of the attorney served indicating that the transmission was received, and the mailing of a copy of the paper to that attorney. The designation of a telephone number or other station for service by electronic means in the address block subscribed on paper served or filed in the course of an action or proceeding shall constitute consent

CPLR

to service by electronic means in accordance with this subdivision. An attorney may change or rescind a number or address designated for service of documents by serving a notice on the other parties; or

6. by dispatching the paper to the attorney by overnight delivery service at the address designated by the attorney for that purpose or, if none is designated, at the attorney's last known address. Service by overnight delivery service shall be complete upon deposit of the paper enclosed in a properly addressed wrapper into the custody of the overnight delivery service for overnight delivery, prior to the latest time designated by the overnight delivery service for overnight delivery. Where a period of time prescribed by law is measured from the service of a paper and service is by overnight delivery, one business day shall be added to the prescribed period. "Overnight delivery service" means any delivery service which regularly accepts items for overnight delivery to any address in the state.

(c) Upon a party. If a party has not appeared by an attorney or the party's attorney cannot be served, service shall be upon the party by a method specified in paragraph one, two, four, five or six of subdivision (b) of this rule.

(d) Filing. If a paper cannot be served by any of the methods specified in subdivisions (b) and (c), service may be made by filing the paper as if it were a paper required to be filed.

(e) Parties to be served. Each paper served on any party shall be served on every other party who has appeared, except as otherwise may be provided by court order or as provided in section 3012 or in subdivision (f) of section 3215. Upon demand by a party, the plaintiff shall supply that party with a list of those who have appeared and the names and addresses of their attorneys.

(f) Definitions. For the purposes of this rule:

1. "Mailing" means the deposit of a paper enclosed in a first class postpaid wrapper, addressed to the address designated by a person for that purpose or, if none is designated, at that person's last known address, in a post office or official depository under the exclusive care and custody of the United States Postal Service within the state;

2. "Electronic means" means any method of transmission of information between two machines designed for the purpose of sending and receiving such transmissions, and which results in the fixation of the information transmitted in a tangible medium of expression.

### 1990 AMENDMENTS

L. 1990, ch. 244, eff. June 15, 1990, renumbering paragraph 5 of CPLR 2103(b) to be paragraph 6; adding a new paragraph 5, designating service by electronic means as an additional method of service on a party's attorney; and amending CPLR 2103(c) to include reference to paragraph 6.

### 1989 AMENDMENTS

L. 1989, ch. 478, eff. Jan. 1, 1990, amended CPLR 2103(b)(5) to provide for the use of overnight mail, and it re-enacted subdivision 2 without the change made by Chapter 461.

### 1982 AMENDMENTS

L. 1982, ch. 20, eff. Jan. 1, 1983, amended CPLR 2103(b)(2) to increase from three to five the number of days for service of a paper by mail.

### 1971 AMENDMENTS

Amendment No. 1 made by the Judicial Conference February 1, 1971 Report to the 1971 Legislature, eff. Sept. 1, 1971, amended CPLR 2103(e), by providing, *inter alia*, that each paper served on any party shall be served on every other party who has appeared.

## R 2104.  Stipulations.

An agreement between parties or their attorneys relating to any matter in an action, other than one made between counsel in open court, is not binding upon a party unless it is in a writing subscribed by him or his attorney or reduced to the form of an order and entered.

## § 2105.  Certification by attorney.

Where a certified copy of a paper is required by law, an attorney admitted to practice in the courts of the state may certify that it has been compared by him with the original and found to be a true and complete copy. Such a certificate, when subscribed by such attorney, has the same effect as if made by a clerk.

### 1970 AMENDMENTS

L. 1970, ch. 307, eff. Sept. 1, 1970, amended the section to allow any attorney duly admitted to practice in the state of New York to certify papers under this section.

### 1964 AMENDMENTS

L. 1964, ch. 349, eff. Sept. 1, 1964. Amendment was recommended by the Judicial Conference Feb. 1, 1964, Report to the Legislature: "In its present form § 2105 could possibly be interpreted to apply not only to members of the New York bar but also to out-of-state attorneys and even to a party not admitted to practice who appears *pro se* (see § 105(c)). Such a result seems unintended and the proposed change is designed to preclude it."

## R 2106.  Affirmation of truth of statement by attorney, physician, osteopath or dentist.

The statement of an attorney admitted to practice in the courts of the state, or of a physician, osteopath or dentist, authorized by law to practice in the state, who is not a party to an action, when subscribed and affirmed by him to be true under the penalties of perjury, may be served or filed in the action in lieu of and with the same force and effect as an affidavit.

### 1973 AMENDMENTS

CPLR 2106 was amended by proposal No. 3 of the Judicial Conference Report to the 1973 Legislature, effective Sept. 1, 1973, to provide that non-party physicians, osteopaths and dentists licensed to practice in the state may file in an action a statement affirmed by them in lieu of an affidavit.

# ARTICLE 22

# STAY, MOTIONS, ORDERS AND MANDATES

---

## SUMMARY OF ARTICLE

§ 2201.    Stay.

§§ 2202–2210.    [Not used.]

§ 2211.    Application for order; when motion made.

§ 2212.    Where motion made, in supreme court action.
    (a)  Motions on notice.
    (b)  Ex parte motions.
    (c)  Motions before a county court or judge.
    (d)  Rules of the chief administrator of the courts.

§ 2213.    Where motion made, in county court action.
    (a)  Ex parte motions.
    (b)  Motions that may be made before the supreme court or a justice thereof.
    (c)*

\* [Editor's note: No official heading.]

R 2214.    Motion papers; service; time.
    (a)  Notice of motion.
    (b)  Time for service of notice and affidavits.
    (c)  Furnishing papers to the court.
    (d)  Order to show cause.

R 2215.    Relief demanded by other than moving party.

R 2216.    [Repealed.]

R 2217.    Prior motion; ex parte motion; transfer of motion.
    (a)  Prior motion.
    (b)  Affidavit on ex parte motion.
    (c)  Transfer of motion.
    (d)  Rules of the chief administrator of the courts.

§ 2218.    Trial of issue raised on motion.

R 2219.    Time and form of order.
    (a)  Time and form of order determining motion, generally.
    (b)  Signature on appellate court order.

R 2220.    Entry and filing of order; service.
    (a)  Entry and filing.
    (b)  Service.

R 2221.    Motion affecting prior order.

R 2222.    Docketing order as judgment.

R 2223.    Duties of officer receiving mandate.

CPLR

---

### § 2201.　Stay.

Except where otherwise prescribed by law, the court in which an action is pending may grant a stay of proceedings in a proper case, upon such terms as may be just.

### §§ 2202-2210.　[Not used.]

### § 2211.　Application for order; when motion made.

A motion is an application for an order. A motion on notice is made when a notice of the motion or an order to show cause is served.

### § 2212.　Where motion made, in supreme court action.

(a) Motions on notice. A motion on notice in an action in the supreme court shall be noticed to be heard in the judicial district where the action is triable or in a county adjoining the county where the action is triable. Unless statute, civil practice rule or local court rule provides otherwise, the motion shall be noticed to be heard before a motion term or, upon order to show cause granted by a justice, before that justice out of court.

(b) Ex parte motions. A motion in an action in the supreme court that may be made without notice may be made at a motion term or to a justice out of court in any county in the state.

(c) Motions before a county court or judge. The chief administrator of the courts may by rule provide for the hearing of motions on notice or ex parte motions in an action or proceeding in the supreme court by a term of the county court or a county judge in the county in which venue is laid during periods in which no supreme court trial or special term is in session in the county.

(d) Rules of the chief administrator of the courts. The chief administrator may by rule exclude motions within a department, district or county from the operation of subdivisions (a), (b) and (c) of this section, provided, however, that the practice in counties within the city of New York shall be uniform.

#### 1986 AMENDMENTS

L. 1986, ch. 355, eff. July 17, 1986, amended Subd. (c) of CPLR 2212 by replacing references to the departments of the appellate division with "chief administrator of the courts"; Subd. (d) of CPLR 2212 was amended by replacing the reference to appellate division rules with "rules of the chief administrator of the courts" and by making other changes, including the addition of a reference to subdivision (c).

#### 1965 AMENDMENTS

L. 1965, ch. 149, eff. Sept. 1, 1965, amended Subd. (c), to make it clear that a county judge may hear a Supreme Court motion if there is no Supreme Court trial or special term in session in the county.

## § 2213.  Where motion made, in county court action.

(a) Ex parte motions. A motion in an action in a county court that may be made without notice may be made before a motion term of the county court or before the county judge out of court in any county in the state.

(b) Motions that may be made before the supreme court or a justice thereof. When no motion term is being held and there is no county judge available within the county, any motion in an action in a county court, whether or not on notice, may be made or noticed to be heard before a motion term of the supreme court or, upon order to show cause granted by a justice of the supreme court, before such justice out of court, in the judicial district where the action is triable or in a county adjoining the county where the action is triable, except a motion under article forty-four or a motion for an order that would dispose of the action, in whole or in part, in any manner other than by settlement under section 1207.

(c) The chief administrator of the courts may by rule exclude motions from the operation of this section within a department, district or county.

### 1986 AMENDMENTS

L. 1986, ch. 355, eff. July 17, 1986, amended CPLR 2213 by adding the word "available" in the second sentence of subdivision (b); by designating last sentence of section as subdivision (c) and by making other changes to subdivision (c), including replacing "appellate division" with "chief administrator of the courts."

## R 2214.  Motion papers; service; time.

(a) Notice of motion. A notice of motion shall specify the time and place of the hearing on the motion, the supporting papers upon which the motion is based, the relief demanded and the grounds therefor. Relief in the alternative or of several different types may be demanded.

(b) Time for service of notice and affidavits. A notice of motion and supporting affidavits shall be served at least eight days before the time at which the motion is noticed to be heard. Answering affidavits shall be served at least two days before such time. Answering affidavits shall be served at least seven days before such time if a notice of motion served at least twelve days before such time so demands; whereupon any reply affidavits shall be served at least one day before such time.

(c) Furnishing papers to the court. Each party shall furnish to the court all papers served by him. The moving party shall furnish at the hearing all other papers not already in the possession of the court necessary to the consideration of the questions involved. Where such papers are in the possession of an adverse party, they shall be produced by him at the hearing on notice served with the motion papers. Only papers served in accordance with the provisions of this rule shall be read in support of, or in opposition to, the motion unless the court for good cause shall otherwise direct.

(d) Order to show cause. The court in a proper case may grant an order to show cause, to be served in lieu of a notice of motion, at a time and in a manner specified therein. An order to show cause against a state body or officers must be served in addition to service upon the defendant or respondent state body or officers upon the attorney general by delivery to an assistant attorney general at an office of the attorney general in the county in which venue of the action is designated or if there is no office of the attorney general in such county, at the office of the attorney general nearest such county.

### 1984 AMENDMENTS

L. 1984, ch. 177, eff. Aug. 6, 1984, amended CPLR 2214(b) by increasing the time for service of a notice of motion demanding answering affidavits and for service of the answering affidavits.

### 1972 AMENDMENTS

L. 1972, ch. 455, eff. May 24, 1972 and ch. 752, eff. May 30, 1972, amended CPLR 2214(d) by adding new last sentence providing that an order to show cause served on a state body or officers must also be served on the attorney general.

## R 2215.  Relief demanded by other than moving party.

At least three days prior to the time at which the motion is noticed to be heard, a party may serve upon the moving party a notice of cross-motion demanding relief, with or without supporting papers. Relief in the alternative or of several different types may be demanded; relief need not be responsive to that demanded by the moving party.

### 1980 AMENDMENTS

L. 1980, ch. 132, eff. Jan. 1, 1981, amended CPLR 2215 by adding the requirement that a party who has been moved against and who wishes to make his or her own application for relief by way of a cross-motion specifically serve on the movant a notice of cross-motion.

In making its recommendation to the 1980 Legislature, the Judicial Conference Report on the CPLR noted that this was an attempt to prevent a non-moving party's application for affirmative relief from being buried in the other party's papers, an event which takes the moving party by surprise and adds unnecessary chores for the motion judge. The Report stated, "The main idea is to have the covering paper clue the reader in to the whole mission of the accompanying papers, and to avoid the situation in which a demand for cross-relief comes up as almost a hidden incident of affidavits opposing the main motion. The inclusion of a general relief clause, with which a notice of motion ordinarily ends in New York practice, will still cover other items of relief reasonably supportable on the papers, and a general relief clause may also be used in the notice of cross-motion. The proposal is intended to clarify the obligations of a cross-movant. It is not intended to place any restriction on the court's powers to grant affirmative relief."

**R 2216.  [Repealed.]**

**R 2217.  Prior motion; ex parte motion; transfer of motion.**

(a) Prior motion. Any motion may be referred to a judge who decided a prior motion in the action.

(b) Affidavit on ex parte motion. An ex parte motion shall be accompanied by an affidavit stating the result of any prior motion for similar relief and specifying the new facts, if any, that were not previously shown.

(c) Transfer of motion. If a motion is made to a judge who is or will be for any reason unable to hear it, it may be transferred by order of such judge or by written stipulation of the parties to any other judge to whom it might originally have been made.

(d) Rules of the chief administrator of the courts. The chief administrator may by rule exclude motions within a department, district or county from the operation of subdivisions (a) and (c) of this rule.

### 1986 AMENDMENTS

L. 1986, ch. 355, eff. July 17, 1986, amended CPLR 2217 by adding new Subd. (d), "Rules of the chief administrator of the courts."

**§ 2218.  Trial of issue raised on motion.**

The court may order that an issue of fact raised on a motion shall be separately tried by the court or a referee. If the issue is triable of right by jury, the court shall give the parties an opportunity to demand a jury trial of such issue. Failure to make such demand within the time limited by the court, or, if no such time is limited, before trial begins, shall be deemed a waiver of the right to trial by jury. An order under this rule shall specify the issue to be tried.

**R 2219.  Time and form of order.**

(a)* Time and form of order determining motion, generally. An order determining a motion relating to a provisional remedy shall be made within twenty days, and an order determining any other motion shall be made within sixty days, after the motion is submitted for decision. The order shall be in writing and shall be the same in form whether made by a court or a judge out of court. An order determining a motion made upon supporting papers shall be signed with the judge's signature or initials by the judge who made it, state the court of which he or she is a judge and the place and date of the signature, recite the papers used on the motion, and give the determination or direction in such detail as the judge deems proper. Except in a town or village court or where otherwise provided by law, upon the request of any party, an order or ruling made by a judge, whether upon written or oral application or sua sponte, shall be reduced to writing or otherwise recorded.

CPLR

* [**Editor's note:** This version of R 2219(a) is effective as of January 1, 1997. Through December 31, 1996, former R 2219(a) remains in effect. It reads as follows:

(a) Time and form of order determining motion, generally. An order determining a motion relating to a provisional remedy shall be made within twenty days, and an order determining any other motion shall be made within sixty days, after the motion is submitted for decision. The order shall be in writing and shall be the same in form whether made by a court or a judge out of court. An order determining a motion made upon supporting papers shall be signed with the judge's signature or initials by the judge who made it, state the court of which he is a judge and the place and date of the signature, recite the papers used on the motion, and give the determination or direction in such detail as the judge deems proper.]

(b) Signature on appellate court order. An order of an appellate court shall be signed by a judge thereof except that, upon written authorization by the presiding judge, it may be signed by the clerk of the court or, in his absence or disability, by a deputy clerk.

### 1996 AMENDMENTS

L. 1996, ch. 38, eff. January 1, 1996, amended subdivision (a) by adding a new final sentence and making the subdivision gender neutral.

## R 2220. Entry and filing of order; service.

(a) Entry and filing. An order determining a motion shall be entered and filed in the office of the clerk of the court where the action is triable, and all papers used on the motion and any opinion or memorandum in writing shall be filed with that clerk unless the order dispenses with such filing. When a statute or civil practice rule requires such filing and entry in a county other than that in which the order was made, the party prevailing on the motion shall file the order and the papers used on the motion with the proper clerk after receiving them. If a party fails to file any papers required to be filed under this subdivision, the order may be vacated as irregular, with costs.

(b) Service. Service of an order shall be made by serving a copy of the order.

### 1964 AMENDMENTS

Amendment No. 3 made by the Judicial Conference Feb. 1, 1964, Report to the Legislature, eff. Sept. 1, 1964, deleted the word "certified" formerly appearing before "copy of the order" in subd. (b).

## R 2221. Motion affecting prior order.

(a) A motion for leave to renew or to reargue a prior motion, for leave to appeal from, or to stay, vacate or modify, an order shall be made, on notice, to the judge who signed the order, unless he is for any reason unable to hear it, except that:

1. if the order was made upon a default such motion may be made, on notice, to any judge of the court; and

2. if the order was made without notice such motion may be made, without notice, to the judge who signed it, or, on notice, to any other judge of the court.

(b) Rules of the chief administrator of the courts. The chief administrator may by rule exclude motions within a department, district or county from the operation of subdivision (a) of this rule.

A motion made to other than a proper judge under this rule shall be transferred to the proper judge.

### 1986 AMENDMENTS

L. 1986, ch. 355, eff. July 17, 1986, amended CPLR 2221 by dividing the material following the heading into Subd. (a) and by adding new Subd. (b), "Rules of the chief administrator of the courts."

## R 2222. Docketing order as judgment.

At the request of any party the clerk shall docket as a judgment an order directing the payment of money, including motion costs, or affecting the title to, or the possession, use or enjoyment of, real property, provided, however, that where the clerk maintains a section and block index, an order affecting the title to, or the possession, use or enjoyment of, real property may be entered in such index in lieu thereof.

### 1970 AMENDMENTS

L. 1970, ch. 661, eff. May 8, 1970, amended the section by adding thereto the following: "provided, however, that where the clerk maintains a section and block index, an order affecting the title to, or the possession, use or enjoyment of, real property may be entered in such index in lieu thereof."

## R 2223. Duties of officer receiving mandate.

An officer to whom a mandate is delivered to be executed shall:

1. execute the mandate according to its command;

2. give without compensation to the person delivering the mandate, if requested, a written receipt describing the mandate and specifying the day and hour of receiving it;

3. deliver without compensation to the person served, if requested, a copy of the mandate; and

4. return the mandate together with his return thereon, by delivering or mailing it to the clerk's office.

CPLR

# ARTICLE 23

# SUBPOENAS, OATHS AND AFFIRMATIONS

## SUMMARY OF ARTICLE

§ 2301.   Scope of subpoena.
§ 2302.   Authority to issue.
   (a)   Without court order.
   (b)   Issuance by court.
§ 2303.   Service of subpoena; payment of fees in advance.
§ 2304.   Motion to quash, fix conditions or modify.
§ 2305.   Attendance required pursuant to subpoena; possession of books, records, documents or papers.
   (a)   When person required to attend.
   (b)   Subpoena duces tecum; attendance by substitute.
   (c)   Inspection, examination and audit of records.
§ 2306.   Hospital records; medical records of department or bureau of a municipal corporation or of the state.
   (a)   Transcript or reproduction.
   (b)   Delivery to clerk.
§ 2307.   Books, papers and other things of a library, department or bureau of a municipal corporation or of the state.
§ 2308.   Disobedience of subpoena.
   (a)   Judicial.
   (b)   Non-judicial.
   (c)   Review of proceedings.
§ 2309.   Oaths and affirmations.
   (a)   Persons authorized to administer.
   (b)   Form.
   (c)   Oaths and affirmations taken without the state.
   (d)   Form of certificate of oath or affirmation administered by officer of the armed forces of the United States.
§ 2310.   Exclusions from article.

## § 2301. Scope of subpoena.

A subpoena requires the attendance of a person to give testimony. A subpoena duces tecum requires production of books, papers and other things.

CPLR

1964 AMENDMENTS

L. 1964, ch. 388, eff. Sept. 1, 1964, deleted the word "form" from the caption.

## § 2302.  Authority to issue.

(a) Without court order. Subpoenas may be issued without a court order by the clerk of the court, a judge where there is no clerk, the attorney general, an attorney of record for a party to an action, an administrative proceeding or an arbitration, an arbitrator, a referee, or any member of a board, commission or committee authorized by law to hear, try or determine a matter or to do any other act, in an official capacity, in relation to which proof may be taken or the attendance of a person as a witness may be required, provided, however, that a subpoena to compel production of a patient's clinical record maintained pursuant to the provisions of section 33.13 of the mental hygiene law shall be accompanied by a court order.

(b) Issuance by court. A subpoena to compel production of an original record or document where a certified transcript or copy is admissible in evidence, or to compel attendance of any person confined in a penitentiary or jail, shall be issued by the court. Unless the court orders otherwise, a motion for such subpoena shall be made on at least one day's notice to the person having custody of the record, document or person confined. A subpoena to produce a prisoner so confined shall be issued by a judge to whom a petition for habeas corpus could be made under subdivision (b) of section 7002 of the civil practice law and rules or a judge of the court of claims, if the matter is pending before the court of claims or a judge of the surrogate's court if the matter is pending before the surrogates* court, or a judge of the family court, if the matter is pending before the family court.

\* [Editor's note: So in original. Probably should read "surrogate's."]

### CROSS REFERENCES

See Judiciary Law § 2-b in Appendix, *infra*, as to power of court to issue subpoenas.

1989 AMENDMENTS

L. 1989, ch. 183, eff. Aug. 23, 1989.

1982 AMENDMENTS

L. 1982, ch. 139, eff. June 1, 1982, amended CPLR 2302(b) by adding the words "or a judge of the surrogate's court if the matter is pending before the surrogates court, or a judge of the family court, if the matter is pending before the family court."

1980 AMENDMENTS

L. 1980, ch. 77, eff. Feb. 13, 1980, amended CPLR 2302(b) by adding the words "or a judge of the court of claims, if the matter is pending before the court of claims."

**1964 AMENDMENTS**

L. 1964, ch. 519, eff. April 10, 1964, inserted in Subd. (a) the words "the attorney general", clarifying his authority to issue subpoenas.

## § 2303.   Service of subpoena; payment of fees in advance.

A subpoena shall be served in the same manner as a summons, except that where service of a subpoena is made pursuant to subdivision two or four of section three hundred eight of this chapter, the filing of proof of service shall not be required and service shall be deemed complete upon the later of the delivering or mailing of the subpoena, if made pursuant to subdivision two of section three hundred eight of this chapter, or upon the later of the affixing or mailing of the subpoena, if made pursuant to subdivision four of section three hundred eight of this chapter. Any person subpoenaed shall be paid or tendered in advance authorized traveling expenses and one day's witness fee.

**1982 AMENDMENTS**

L. 1982, ch. 618, eff. July 22, 1982, amended CPLR 2303 by adding the exception for service of a subpoena pursuant to CPLR 308.

## § 2304.   Motion to quash, fix conditions or modify.

A motion to quash, fix conditions or modify a subpoena shall be made promptly in the court in which the subpoena is returnable. If the subpoena is not returnable in a court, a request to withdraw or modify the subpoena shall first be made to the person who issued it and a motion to quash, fix conditions or modify may thereafter be made in the supreme court. Reasonable conditions may be imposed upon the granting or denial of a motion to quash or modify.

**1964 AMENDMENTS**

L. 1964, ch. 388, eff. Sept. 1, 1964 inserted "a" before "request" in the second sentence.

## § 2305.   Attendance required pursuant to subpoena; possession of books, records, documents or papers.

(a) When person required to attend. A subpoena may provide that the person subpoenaed shall appear on the date stated and any recessed or adjourned date of the trial hearing or examination. If he is given reasonable notice of such recess or adjournment, no further process shall be required to compel his attendance on the adjourned date. At the end of each day's attendance, the person subpoenaed may demand his fee for the next day on which he is to attend. If the fee is not then paid, he shall be deemed discharged.

(b) Subpoena duces tecum; attendance by substitute. Any person may comply with a subpoena duces tecum by having the requisite books, documents or things produced by a person able to identify them and testify respecting their origin, purpose and custody.

(c) Inspection, examination and audit of records. Whenever by statute any department or agency of government, or officer thereof, is authorized to issue a subpoena requiring the production of books, records, documents or papers, the issuing party shall have the right to the possession of such material for a period of time, and on terms and conditions, as may reasonably be required for the inspection, examination or audit of the material. The reasonableness of such possession, time, terms, and conditions shall be determined with consideration for, among other things, (i) the good cause shown by the issuing party, (ii) the rights and needs of the person subpoenaed, and (iii) the feasibility and appropriateness of making copies of the material. The cost of reproduction and transportation incident thereto shall be borne by the person or party issuing the subpoena unless the court determines otherwise in the interest of justice.

### 1977 AMENDMENTS

L. 1977, ch. 451, eff. July 19, 1977, amended CPLR 2305 by adding a new subd. (c) which controls possession of materials subpoenaed by a governmental authority.

### § 2306. Hospital records; medical records of department or bureau of a municipal corporation or of the state.

(a) Transcript or reproduction. Where a subpoena duces tecum is served upon a hospital, or upon a department or bureau of a municipal corporation or of the state, or an officer thereof, requiring the production of records relating to the condition or treatment of a patient, a transcript or a full sized legible reproduction certified as correct by the superintendent or head of the hospital, department or bureau or his assistant, or the officer, may be produced unless otherwise ordered by a court. Such a subpoena shall be served at least three days before the time fixed for the production of the records unless otherwise ordered by a court.

(b) Delivery to clerk. Where a court has designated a clerk to receive records described in subdivision (a), delivery may be made to him at or before the time fixed for their production. The clerk shall give a receipt for the records and notify the person subpoenaed when they are no longer required. The records shall be delivered in a sealed envelope indicating the title of the action, the date fixed for production and the name and address of the attorney appearing on the subpoena. They shall be available for inspection pursuant to the rules or order of the court.

### CROSS REFERENCES

Regarding public access to government records, see **Public Officers Law, Article 6** (Freedom of Information Law) in Appendix, *infra.*

### 1986 AMENDMENTS

L. 1986, ch. 4, eff. Jan. 1, 1987, amended CPLR 2306(a) by allowing full size legible reproductions of hospital records in response to a subpoena duces tecum and changing the time for service of a subpoena duces tecum from twenty-four hours to three days before the time fixed for the production of the records.

### § 2307. Books, papers and other things of a library, department or bureau of a municipal corporation or of the state.

Issuance by court. A subpoena duces tecum to be served upon a library, or a department or bureau of a municipal corporation or of the state, or an officer thereof, requiring the production of any books, papers or other things, shall be issued by a justice of the supreme court in the district in which the book, paper or other thing is located or by a judge of the court in which an action for which it is required is triable. Unless the court orders otherwise, a motion for such subpoena shall be made on at least one day's notice to the library, department, bureau or officer having custody of the book, document or other thing and the adverse party. Such subpoena must be served upon such library, or such department or bureau of such municipal corporation or of the state or an officer having custody of the book, document or other thing and the adverse party at least twenty-four hours before the time fixed for the production of such records unless in the case of an emergency the court shall by order dispense with such notice otherwise required. Compliance with a subpoena duces tecum may be made by producing a full-sized legible reproduction of the item or items required to be produced certified as complete and accurate by the person in charge of such library, department or bureau, or a designee of such person, and no personal appearance to certify such item or items shall be required of such person or designee, unless the court shall order otherwise pursuant to subdivision (d) of rule 2214 of this chapter. Where a stipulation would serve the same purpose as production of the book, document or other thing and the subpoena is required because the parties will not stipulate, the judge may impose terms on any party, including the cost of production of the book or document, and require such cost to be paid as an additional fee to the library, department or officer.

#### CROSS REFERENCES

Regarding public access to government records, see **Public Officers Law, Article 6** (Freedom of Information Law) in Appendix, *infra*.

#### 1991 AMENDMENTS

L. 1991, ch. 389, eff. Jan. 1, 1992, removed the designation for Subd. (a), amended the first paragraph to provide that compliance with a subpoena duces tecum could be made by producing a full-sized legible reproduction of the item or items required to be produced, and deleted Subd. (b).

#### 1976 AMENDMENTS

L. 1976, ch. 419, eff. Sept. 1, 1976, amended Subd. (a) to provide that the subpoena must be served upon the custodian and upon the adverse party at least 24 hours before the time fixed for production, unless emergency circumstances exist, in which case the court may dispense with such notice requirements.

### § 2308. Disobedience of subpoena.

(a) Judicial. Failure to comply with a subpoena issued by a judge, clerk or officer of the court shall be punishable as a contempt of court. If the witness is a party the court may also strike his pleadings. A subpoenaed person shall also be liable to the person on whose behalf the subpoena was issued for a penalty not exceeding fifty dollars and damages sustained by reason of the failure to comply. A court may issue a warrant directing a sheriff to bring the witness into court. If a person so subpoenaed attends or is brought into court, but refuses without reasonable cause to be examined, or to answer a legal and pertinent question, or to produce a book, paper or other thing which he was directed to produce by the subpoena, or to subscribe his deposition after it has been correctly reduced to writing, the court may forthwith issue a warrant directed to the sheriff of the county where the person is, committing him to jail, there to remain until he submits to do the act which he was so required to do or is discharged according to law. Such a warrant of commitment shall specify particularly the cause of the commitment and, if the witness is committed for refusing to answer a question, the question shall be inserted in the warrant.

(b) Non-judicial. Unless otherwise provided, if a person fails to comply with a subpoena which is not returnable in a court, the issuer or the person on whose behalf the subpoena was issued may move in the supreme court to compel compliance. If the court finds that the subpoena was authorized, it shall order compliance and may impose costs not exceeding fifty dollars. A subpoenaed person shall also be liable to the person on whose behalf the subpoena was issued for a penalty not exceeding fifty dollars and damages sustained by reason of the failure to comply. A court may issue a warrant directing a sheriff to bring the witness before the person or body requiring his appearance. If a person so subpoenaed attends or is brought before such person or body, but refuses without reasonable cause to be examined, or to answer a legal and pertinent question, or to produce a book, paper or other thing which he was directed to produce by the subpoena, or to subscribe his deposition after it has been correctly reduced to writing, the court, upon proof by affidavit, may issue a warrant directed to the sheriff of the county where the person is, committing him to jail, there to remain until he submits to do the act which he was so required to do or is discharged according to law. Such a warrant of commitment shall specify particularly the cause of the commitment and, if the witness is committed for refusing to answer a question, the question shall be inserted in the warrant.

(c) Review of proceedings. Within ninety days after the offender shall have been committed to jail he shall, if not then discharged by law, be brought, by the sheriff, or other officer, as a matter of course personally before the court issuing the warrant of commitment and a review of the proceedings shall then be held to determine whether the offender shall be discharged from commitment. At periodic intervals of not more than ninety days following such review, the offender, if not then discharged by law from such commitment, shall be brought, by the sheriff, or other officer, personally before the court issuing the warrant of commitment and further reviews of the proceedings shall then be held to determine whether he shall be discharged from commitment. The clerk of the court before which such review of the proceedings shall be held, or the judge or justice of such court in case there be no clerk, shall give reasonable notice in writing of the date, time and place of each such review to each party or his attorney who shall have appeared of record in the proceeding resulting in the issuance of the warrant of commitment, at their last known address.

### CROSS REFERENCES

See selected provisions governing procedures to punish for contempt under **Judiciary Law, Article 19,** Appendix, *infra*.

### 1977 AMENDMENTS

L. 1977, ch. 25, eff. Sept. 1, 1977, amended the first sentence of subd. (b) by providing that the "person on whose behalf the subpoena was issued" may move in the supreme court to compel compliance with the subpoena. Previously only the "issuer" of the subpoena could so move.

### 1965 AMENDMENTS

L. 1965, ch. 231, eff. May 17, 1965, added a new subdivision (c).

## § 2309. Oaths and affirmations.

(a) Persons authorized to administer. Unless otherwise provided, an oath or affirmation may be administered by any person authorized to take acknowledgments of deeds by the real property law. Any person authorized by the laws of this state to receive evidence may administer an oath or affirmation for that purpose. An oath to a juror or jurors may be administered by a clerk of court and his deputies. This section shall not apply to an oath of office.

(b) Form. An oath or affirmation shall be administered in a form calculated to awaken the conscience and impress the mind of the person taking it in accordance with his religious or ethical beliefs.

(c) Oaths and affirmations taken without the state. An oath or affirmation taken without the state shall be treated as if taken within the state if it is accompanied by such certificate or certificates as would be required to entitle a deed acknowledged without the state to be recorded within the state if such deed had been acknowledged before the officer who administered the oath or affirmation.

(d) Form of certificate of oath or affirmation administered by officer of the armed forces of the United States. The certificate of an oath or affirmation administered within or without the state or the United States, by an officer of the armed forces of the United States authorized by the real property law to take acknowledgment of deeds, shall state:

1. the rank and serial number of the officer before whom the oath or affirmation is taken and the command to which he is attached;

2. that the person taking the oath or affirmation was, at the time of taking it, a person enlisted or commissioned in or serving in or with the armed forces of the United States or the dependent of such a person, or a person attached to or accompanying the armed forces of the United States; and

CPLR

3. the serial number of the person who takes, or whose dependent takes the oath or affirmation, if such person is enlisted or commissioned in the armed forces of the United States. The place where such oath or affidavit is taken need not be disclosed.

### CROSS REFERENCES

**Real Prop. L.** provisions authorizing the taking of acknowledgments of deeds, referred to in Subd. (a), *supra*, may be found in **Real Prop. L. § 298,** *et seq.*, in Appendix, *infra*.

### 1964 AMENDMENTS

L. 1964, ch. 287, eff. Sept. 1, 1964, added next to last sentence to Subd. (a) and deleted words "or an oath administered to jurors" in last sentence. The last sentence formerly read: "This section shall not apply to an oath of office or an oath administered to jurors."

## § 2310. Exclusions from article.

The provisions of this article shall not apply to subpoenas issued in proceedings before the New York state labor relations board.

# ARTICLE 24

# PUBLICATION

---

## SUMMARY OF ARTICLE

§ 2401.    Order when publication cannot be made.
§ 2402.    Computation of time for publication of notice.

---

## § 2401. Order when publication cannot be made.

1. Where because of circumstances beyond the control of a party required to publish, publication required by any statute, rule or court order cannot be made or completed in the specified place or newspaper in the required manner, the court may by order require such other publication as will not unduly prejudice any other party.

2. Notwithstanding the provisions of paragraph 1, if publication required by any statute, rule or court order has been commenced and cannot be completed because of the suspension or termination of publication by a newspaper, publication may be completed in any other newspaper which complies with the statute, rule, or order without further court order.

### 1971 AMENDMENTS

L. 1971, ch. 927, eff. June 25, 1971, amended CPLR 2401 by adding a new paragraph 2.

## § 2402. Computation of time for publication of notice.

The period of publication of a legal notice shall be computed by excluding the first day of publication and including the day on which the act or event of which notice is given is to take place or which completes the full period of publication.

CPLR

# ARTICLE 25

# UNDERTAKINGS

———

## SUMMARY OF ARTICLE

§ 2501.   Undertaking; definition.
§ 2502.   Surety; form of affidavit; two or more undertakings; condition; acknowledgment.
    (a)   Surety; form of affidavit.
    (b)   Two or more undertakings.
    (c)   Condition.
    (d)   Acknowledgment.
§ 2503.   Undertaking of more than one thousand dollars; real property; lien.
    (a)   Creation of lien.
    (b)   Affidavit of surety.
    (c)   Filing of affidavit; recording.
    (d)   Release of lien.
§ 2504.   Waiver of undertaking; removal and change of parties.
    (a)   Waiver of undertaking.
    (b)   Removal and change of parties.
§ 2505.   Filing of undertaking; service upon adverse party; time when effective.
§ 2506.   Exception to surety; allowance where no exception taken.
    (a)   Exception to surety.
    (b)   Allowance where no exception taken.
§ 2507.   Justification of surety.
    (a)   Motion to justify.
    (b)   Failure to justify.
§ 2508.   Motion for new or additional undertaking.
§ 2509.   Control of assets by agreement with surety.
§ 2510.   Discharge of surety on the undertaking of a fiduciary.
    (a)   Motion; new undertaking; accounting.
    (b)   Settlement of account.
§ 2511.   Liability of surety.
§ 2512.   Undertaking by the state, municipal corporation or public officer.
§ 2513.   Action on undertaking to a public officer, board or municipal corporation.

CPLR

———

## § 2501. Undertaking; definition.

Undertaking includes

1. Any obligation, whether or not the principal is a party thereto, which contains a covenant by a surety to pay the required amount, as specified therein, if any required condition, as specified therein or as provided in subdivision (c) section 2502, is not fulfilled; and

2. any deposit, made subject to the required condition, of the required amount in legal tender of the United States or in face value of unregistered bonds of the United States or of the state.

## § 2502. Surety; form of affidavit; two or more undertakings; condition; acknowledgment.

(a) Surety; form of affidavit. Unless the court orders otherwise, surety shall be:

1. an insurance company authorized to execute the undertaking within the state, or

2. a natural person, except an attorney, who shall execute with the undertaking his affidavit setting forth his full name and address and that he is domiciled within the state and worth at least the amount specified in the undertaking exclusive of liabilities and of property exempt from application to the satisfaction of a judgment.

(b) Two or more undertakings. Where two or more undertakings are authorized or required to be given, they may be contained in the same instrument.

(c) Condition. Where no condition is specified in an undertaking in an action or proceeding, the condition shall be that the principal shall faithfully and fairly discharge the duties and fulfill the obligations imposed by law, or court order. Where the condition specifies that the undertaking is to be void upon payment of an amount or performance of an act, the undertaking shall be construed in accordance with the provisions of section 7-301 of the general obligations law.

(d) Acknowledgment. The undertaking shall be acknowledged in the form required to entitle a deed to be recorded.

### CROSS REFERENCES

G.O.L. § 7-301, referred to in Subd. (c), *supra*, appears in Appendix, *infra*.

### 1970 AMENDMENTS

L. 1970, ch. 848, eff. Sept. 1, 1970, amended Subd. (c). The amendment was recommended by the Judicial Conference Jan. 2, 1970, Report to the Legislature wherein it was stated: "This bill would amend CPLR 2502(c) and 2511 to eliminate the last sentence of each provision, which are substantive provisions governing the extent of the surety's liability in judicial and non-judicial proceedings. These sentences would be combined and placed in the General Obligations Law, as new section 7-301, which would make it clear that the scope of the new provision extends to all undertakings in a penal sum. There would be cross-references to this new section in the CPLR provision, which henceforth would apply only to undertakings given in an action or judicial proceeding."

## § 2503. Undertaking of more than one thousand dollars; real property; lien.

(a) Creation of lien. Unless the court orders otherwise, an undertaking in an amount of more than one thousand dollars, which is not a deposit of legal tender of the United States or in face value of unregistered bonds of the United States or of the state, upon which natural persons are surety shall be secured by real property located in the state which shall be worth the amount specified in the undertaking exclusive of all encumbrances. Such undertaking shall create a lien on the real property when recorded in the individual surety bond liens docket in the office of the clerk or register of the county where the real property is located.

(b) Affidavit of surety. The affidavit of the surety shall contain, in addition to the information required by subdivision (a) of section 2502:

1. a statement that the surety or sureties is or are the sole owner or owners of the real property offered as security;

2. a description of the property, sufficiently identified to establish the lien of the undertaking;

3. a statement of the total amount of the liens, unpaid taxes, and other encumbrances against each property offered; and

4. a statement of the assessed value of each property offered, its market value, and the value of the equity over and above all encumbrances, liens and unpaid taxes.

(c) Filing of affidavit; recording. A duplicate original of the affidavit required by this rule shall be filed in the office of the clerk or register of the county where the real property is located. The following information shall be entered on the individual surety bond liens docket in the office of the clerk or register of the county where the real property is located;

1. the names of the sureties listed in alphabetical order;

2. the amount of the undertaking;

3. a description of the real property or properties offered as security thereunder, sufficiently identified to clearly establish the lien of the undertaking;

4. the date of such recording;

5. the title of the action, proceeding or estate; and

6. the court in which the papers are filed.

CPLR

(d) Release of lien. The clerk or register of the county where the property is located shall make an entry, which shall constitute a release of the lien for all purposes and as to all persons, upon

1. the filing of a consent acknowledged by the person for whose benefit the undertaking was given in the form required to entitle a deed to be recorded; or

2. the order of the court, discharging the surety, made upon motion with such notice to other persons as the court may direct.

## § 2504. Waiver of undertaking; removal and change of parties.

(a) Waiver of undertaking. Unless the court orders otherwise, an undertaking may be waived by the written consent of all parties.

(b) Removal and change of parties. The liability on an undertaking shall remain in effect in favor of the party for whose benefit it was given, notwithstanding a removal of the action or a change of parties.

## § 2505. Filing of undertaking; service upon adverse party; time when effective.

An undertaking together with any affidavit required by this article shall be filed with the clerk of the court in which the action is triable, or, upon an appeal, in the office where the judgment or order of the court of original instance is entered, and a copy shall be served upon the adverse party. The undertaking is effective when so served and filed.

### 1965 AMENDMENTS

L. 1965, ch. 773, eff. Sept. 1, 1965, deleted the word "pending" in the phrase "the court in which the action is pending" in the first sentence of the section and substituted therefor the word "triable."

Amendment recommended by the Judicial Conference Feb. 1, 1965, Report to the Legislature: "Since undertakings are frequently given before service of summons or after judgment, the proposed change is necessary in order to preclude uncertainty as to the proper place for filing undertakings in such situations, where no action is pending."

## § 2506. Exception to surety; allowance where no exception taken.

(a) Exception to surety. If a certificate of qualification issued pursuant to subsections (b), (c) and (d) of section one thousand one hundred eleven of the insurance law is not filed with the undertaking, a party may except to the sufficiency of a surety by written notice of exception served upon the adverse party within ten days after receipt of a copy of the undertaking. Where the undertaking has been served upon a party by the sheriff, the notice of exception shall be served on the sheriff and on the adverse party. Exceptions deemed by the court to have been taken unnecessarily, or for vexation or delay, may, upon notice, be set aside, with costs.

(b) Allowance where no exception taken. Where no exception to sureties is taken within ten days or where exceptions taken are set aside the undertaking is allowed.

### 1984 AMENDMENTS

L. 1984, ch. 805, eff. Sept. 1, 1984, amended CPLR 2506(a) to conform the references to the recodified Insurance Law.

### 1976 AMENDMENTS

L. 1976, ch. 314, eff. Sept. 1, 1976, amended Subd. (a) to provide that exception to sufficiency of a surety may only be taken where a certificate of qualification is not filed with the undertaking.

## § 2507.  Justification of surety.

(a) Motion to justify. Within ten days after service of notice of exception, the surety excepted to or the person upon whose behalf the undertaking was given shall move to justify, upon notice to the adverse party and to the sheriff if he was served with the undertaking. The surety shall be present upon the hearing of such motion to be examined under oath. If the court find the surety sufficient, it shall make an appropriate indorsement on the undertaking. A certificate of qualification issued pursuant to subsections (b), (c) and (d) of section one thousand one hundred eleven of the insurance law shall be accepted in lieu of a justification.

(b) Failure to justify. If a motion to justify is not made within ten days after the notice of exception is served, the undertaking shall then be without effect, except as provided in this subdivision. Unless otherwise provided by order of court, a surety on an undertaking excepted to and not justified shall remain liable until a new undertaking is given and allowed, but the original undertaking shall be otherwise without effect.

### 1984 AMENDMENTS

L. 1984, ch. 805, eff. Sept. 1, 1984, amended CPLR 2507(a) to conform the references to the recodified Insurance Law.

## § 2508.  Motion for new or additional undertaking.

Upon motion of any interested person, upon notice to the parties and surety, and to the sheriff, where he was required to be served with the undertaking, the court may order a new or additional undertaking, a justification or rejustification of sureties, or new or additional sureties. Unless otherwise provided by order of court, a surety, on the original undertaking shall remain liable until such order is complied with, but the original undertaking shall be otherwise without effect.

## § 2509.  Control of assets by agreement with surety.

Any person of whom an undertaking is required may agree with his surety for the deposit of any assets for which his surety may be held responsible with a bank, or safe deposit or trust company, authorized to do business in the state, if such deposit is otherwise proper and in such manner as to prevent withdrawal without the written consent of the surety or an order of court, made on notice to the surety. The agreement shall not affect the liability of the principal or surety as established by the terms of the undertaking.

## § 2510.　Discharge of surety on the undertaking of a fiduciary.

(a) Motion; new undertaking; accounting. Surety on the undertaking of any fiduciary may move with notice to the person upon whose behalf the undertaking was given, to be discharged from liability for any act or omission of such fiduciary subsequent to the order of the court or the time when a new undertaking satisfactory to the court is filed. The court may restrain such fiduciary from acting pending the order discharging such surety from liability. Upon the hearing, the court shall order the fiduciary to give a new undertaking and to account, within such time as the court orders but not exceeding twenty days, for all his acts. If a new undertaking is filed the fiduciary shall account for his acts up to and including the date of such filing. Where the fiduciary does not comply with the order to account, the surety may make and file such account with the same effect as though filed by the fiduciary, and may utilize any disclosure device in obtaining information necessary for such an accounting. The court shall make such provisions with respect to commissions, allowances, disbursement and costs as it deems just.

(b) Settlement of account. When such account has been filed, the court, upon sufficient notice, shall order all persons interested in the proceedings to attend a settlement of the account at a time and place specified, and such settlement shall be made and the rights and liabilities of all parties to the proceeding shall be determined and enforced. After settlement of the account, the court shall make an order relieving the surety from any act or omission of the fiduciary subsequent to the date of such order or the time when a new undertaking satisfactory to the court was filed, whichever is earlier. Upon written demand by the fiduciary, the surety shall return any compensation paid for the unexpired portion of such suretyship.

## § 2511.　Liability of surety.

Where two or more persons are surety on an undertaking in an action or proceeding, they shall be jointly and severally liable. The amount recoverable from a surety shall be determined in accordance with the provisions of section 7-301 of the General Obligations Law.

### CROSS REFERENCES

See **G.O.L.** § 7-301 in Appendix, *infra*.

**1970 AMENDMENTS**

L. 1970, ch. 848, eff. Sept. 1, 1970. See Judicial Conference comments under CPLR 2502, 1970 amendments.

## § 2512. Undertaking by the state, municipal corporation or public officer.

1. Any provision of law authorizing or requiring an undertaking to be given by a party shall be construed as excluding the state, a domestic municipal corporation or a public officer in behalf of the state or of such a corporation. Such parties shall, however, be liable for damages as provided in such provision of law in an amount not exceeding an amount which shall be fixed by the court whenever it would require an undertaking of a private party.

2. Where an appeal is taken by any such party, only the court to which the appeal is taken may fix the amount which shall limit the liability for damages pursuant to this section.

**1976 AMENDMENTS**

L. 1976, ch. 264, eff. Sept. 1, 1976, amended CPLR 2512 to provide that not only municipalities, as previously provided, but also the state, or a public officer, shall be liable for damages in an amount fixed by the court while being exempt from giving undertakings. The amendment also added paragraph (2), providing that where such parties appeal, only the court to which an appeal is taken may fix the maximum liability.

## § 2513. Action on undertaking to a public officer, board or municipal corporation.

A person for whose benefit an undertaking has been given to a public officer, board or municipal corporation of the state may move, on notice to persons interested in the disposition of the proceeds, for leave to bring an action in his own name for breach of a condition.

# ARTICLE 26

# PROPERTY PAID INTO COURT

## SUMMARY OF ARTICLE

§ 2601.　　Payment of money or securities into court.
　　　(a)　Discharge of party paying money into court.
　　　(b)　Delivery of money and securities to county treasurer; commissioner of finance of city of New York.
　　　(c)　Title to funds paid into court.
　　　(d)　Subsequent control of money or securities paid into court.
§ 2602.　　Payment into court of property other than money or securities; deposit with warehouse or safe deposit company.
§ 2603.　　Cost of administration of property paid into court.
§ 2604.　　Calculation of gross sum in lieu of income.
R 2605.　　Duties of depositories.
R 2606.　　Obtaining order for payment out of court.
R 2607.　　Payment of property paid into court.
§ 2608.　　Liability of custodian.
R 2609.　　Deposit by referee appointed to sell property.

## § 2601.　Payment of money or securities into court.

(a) Discharge of party paying money into court. A party paying money into court pursuant to the direction of the court is discharged thereby from all further liability to the extent of the money so paid in.

(b) Delivery of money and securities to county treasurer; commissioner of finance of city of New York. All moneys and securities paid into court shall be delivered either by the party making the payment into court or when an officer other than the county treasurer first receives them, by that officer, to the county treasurer of the county where the action is triable or to such other county treasurer as the court specially directs. Where money or securities are received by an officer other than the county treasurer, he shall deliver them to the county treasurer within two days after he receives them. The commissioner of finance of the city of New York shall be considered the treasurer of each of the counties included within that city.

(c) Title to funds paid into court. Title for the benefit of interested parties is vested in the county treasurer to whom any security is transferred pursuant to this article. Any security purchased by the county treasurer as an investment of money paid into court shall be purchased in the name of his office. He may bring an action upon or in relation to a security in his official or representative character.

(d) Subsequent control of money or securities paid into court. A court may direct that money or securities in the custody of a county treasurer pursuant to this section be transferred or invested as it deems proper.

### 1978 AMENDMENTS

L. 1978, ch. 655, eff. July 24, 1978 amended Subd. (b) by substituting "commissioner of finance" wherever "finance administrator" appears.

### 1969 AMENDMENTS

L. 1969, ch. 407, eff. May 9, 1969, amended Subd. (b) by substituting "finance administrator" wherever "director of finance" appears.

### 1964 AMENDMENTS

L. 1964, ch. 576, eff. April 16, 1964, in Subd. (b) substituted "director of finance" for "treasurer" of the city of New York, in the caption, and in the last sentence.

## § 2602.  Payment into court of property other than money or securities; deposit with warehouse or safe deposit company.

Property paid into court, other than money or securities, shall not be delivered to the county treasurer. The court may direct that such property be deposited in a warehouse or safe deposit company upon the filing of a bond for the cost of such storage by the party paying the property into court or the party who requested such disposition, as the court may provide. It may make such other or subsequent disposition as it deems proper.

## § 2603.  Cost of administration of property paid into court.

A party entitled to the income of any property paid into court shall be charged with the expense of administering such property and of receiving and paying over the income thereof.

## § 2604.  Calculation of gross sum in lieu of income.

A gross sum payable to a party in lieu of the income of a sum of money paid into court for his benefit shall be calculated according to article four of the real property actions and proceedings law.

### CROSS REFERENCES

R.P.A.P.L. Article 4, referred to in CPLR 2604, *supra*, relates to the valuation of interests in real property, covering interest rates as well as mortality and other tables.

**1966 AMENDMENTS**

L. 1966, ch. 233, eff. April 25, 1966, deleted the entire section after the words "shall be calculated according to" and substituted therefor the words "article four of the real property actions and proceedings law."

## R 2605.   Duties of depositories.

When property paid into court is deposited with any depository, the entry of such deposit in the books of the depository shall contain a short reference to the title of the cause or matter in relation to which the deposit is made and shall specify the time from which any interest or accumulation on the deposit, if any, is to commence. On or before the first day of February in each year, such depository shall transmit to the appellate division of the supreme court in the department in which the depository is situated a statement describing the property in its custody, including interest or accumulation, if any, to the credit of each cause or matter on the last preceding first day of January.

## R 2606.   Obtaining order for payment out of court.

Unless otherwise directed by the judgment or order under which the property was paid into court, an order for the payment of property out of court shall be made only:

1. on motion with notice to all parties who have appeared or filed a notice of claim to such property; or

2. by special proceeding. In either case the petition shall be accompanied by a copy of the judgment, order or other paper under which the property was paid into court, together with a certificate of the county treasurer or other depository of the property, showing the present condition and amount thereof, and stating separately, in the case of money, the amount of principal and interest.

**1974 AMENDMENTS**

L. 1974, ch. 878, eff. Sept. 1, 1974, amended paragraph 2 of CPLR 2606, which previously read "2. by special proceeding; the petition shall be accompanied by . . .," to read "2. by special proceeding. In either case the petition shall be accompanied. . . ."

## R 2607.   Payment of property paid into court.

No property paid into court, or income from such property, shall be paid out except upon order of the court directing payment to a specified person, except that if the property so paid into court, or the income from such property, inclusive of interest, does not exceed fifty dollars, a county treasurer may pay the same, without a court order, to the person entitled thereto or his authorized attorney. When the whole or remaining balance of all payments of money into court in an action, or the whole or remaining balance of a distributive share thereof, or any security or other property, is directed to be paid out of court, the order must direct the payment of all accrued income belonging to the party to whom such money or distributive share or remaining balance thereof, or security or other property is paid. A certified copy of the order directing payment shall be delivered to the county treasurer or other custodian of the property. The custodian, in the case of money, shall draw a draft payable to the order of the party entitled thereto specifying the title of the cause or matter on account of which the draft is made and the date of the order authorizing the draft. A certified copy of the order, accompanied by a draft in the case of money, shall be delivered to the depository of the property before it shall pay out any property. If an order directs that periodic payments be made, the filing of one copy of the order shall be sufficient to authorize the payment of subsequent drafts in pursuance thereof. Any other provision of law to the contrary notwithstanding, if an order directing payment by the county treasurer is made by the court, the copy of the order to be delivered to the county treasurer and the depository as herein provided shall be certified by the clerk of the court to be a true copy of the original of such order on file in his office.

### 1971 AMENDMENTS

L. 1971, ch. 154, eff. April 21, 1971, amended CPLR 2607 by adding new last sentence.

## § 2608. Liability of custodian.

No liability shall attach to a custodian of property paid into court because of a payment made by him in good faith in accordance with the direction of an order of the court or as provided in rule 2607.

### 1964 AMENDMENTS

L. 1964, ch. 388, eff. Sept. 1, 1964, changed reference to "rule 2606" to "rule 2607."

## R 2609. Deposit by referee appointed to sell property.

Money received by a referee appointed to sell property shall be deposited forthwith by the referee, in his name as referee, in a bank or trust company authorized to transact business in this state, or with the chief fiscal officer or county treasurer of the county in which the action or proceeding is pending, as the court shall designate. Such moneys when paid to the chief fiscal officer of the county or county treasurer shall not be withdrawn except as directed by the judgment or order under which the deposit is made, or by an order under rule 2606.

### 1976 AMENDMENTS

L. 1976, ch. 86, eff. March 30, 1976, amended CPLR 2609 by adding county treasurer as an additional proper designee for deposit of money received by a referee appointed to sell property, and by including deposits with the county treasurer under the provision prohibiting withdrawal absent direction by the court.

**1974 AMENDMENTS**

L. 1974, ch. 90, eff. Sept. 1, 1974, amended the Rule.

CPLR

# ARTICLE 27

# DISPOSITION OF PROPERTY IN LITIGATION

## SUMMARY OF ARTICLE

§ 2701.    When court may order disposition of property.
§ 2702.    Sale of property.
§ 2703.    Enforcement of order directing disposition of property.

## § 2701.    When court may order disposition of property.

The court, upon motion or on its own initiative, with such notice as it deems proper, may order personal property capable of delivery which is the subject of the action, paid into court, or delivered to such person as it may direct, with such security as the court shall direct, and subject to its further direction if:

1. a party has such property in his possession, custody or control as trustee for another party or where it belongs or is due to another party; or

2. a party has such property in his possession, custody or control and it belongs or is due to another party, where special circumstances make it desirable that payment or delivery to such other party should be withheld; or

3. the ownership of such property will depend on the outcome of a pending action and no party is willing to accept possession or custody of it during the pendency of the action.

### 1964 AMENDMENTS

L. 1964, ch. 422, eff. Sept. 1, 1964. Amendment was recommended by the Judicial Conference Feb. 1, 1964, Report to the Legislature: "Subdivision 1, as presently worded, permits an order for payment of property into court only where the party to whom it belongs would not have the benefit, use or control of it —i.e., if the party is unable to accept delivery because of special circumstances such as residence in a country where confiscation of the property would be effected. Subdivision 2 covers only those cases where an action is pending and no party is willing to accept possession or custody during pendency of the action. Thus, no provision now exists covering the disposition of property belonging to a party who is able to accept delivery or payment. The proposed changes are designed to provide for this presently omitted situation while also preserving the existing provisions. This would be in accord with analogous provisions of the C.P.A., and no change from the C.P.A. was apparently intended."

CPLR

## § 2702.   Sale of property.

On motion of any party, the court may order the sale, in such manner and on such terms as it deems proper, of any personal property capable of delivery which is the subject of the action if it shall appear likely that its value will be substantially decreased during the pendency of the action. Any party to the action may purchase such property at a judicially-directed sale held pursuant to this section without prejudice to his claim.

### 1965 AMENDMENTS

L. 1965, ch. 773, eff. Sept. 1, 1965, deleted the word "rule" in the last sentence and substituted therefor the word "section."

## § 2703.   Enforcement of order directing disposition of property.

Where the court has directed disposition of personal property capable of delivery and the direction is disobeyed, the court by order, in addition to punishing the disobedience as a contempt, may require the sheriff to take and dispose of the property in accordance with its direction.

### 1964 AMENDMENTS

L. 1964, ch. 262, eff. Sept. 1, 1964, deleted the last sentence of this section and reenacted the same as CPLR § 5107. It read: "The court may require the sheriff to convey real property in conformity with its directions." The change was recommended by the Judicial Conference; see amendment notes to CPLR 5107.

# ARTICLE 30

# REMEDIES AND PLEADING

---

## SUMMARY OF ARTICLE

§ 3001.    Declaratory judgment.
§ 3002.    Actions and relief not barred for inconsistency.
     (a)   Action against several persons.
     (b)   Action against agent and undisclosed principal.
     (c)   Action for conversion and on contract.
     (d)   Action on contract and to reform.
     (e)   Claim for damages and rescission.
     (f)   Vendee's lien not to depend upon form of action.
§ 3003.    Action for periodic payments due under pension or retirement contract no bar to action for future installments.
§ 3004.    Where restoration of benefits before judgment unnecessary.
§ 3005.    Relief against mistake of law.
§§ 3006–3010.   [Not used.]
§ 3011.    Kinds of pleadings.
§ 3012.    Service of pleadings and demand for complaint.
     (a)   Service of pleadings.
     (b)   Service of complaint where summons served without complaint.
     (c)   Additional time to serve answer where summons and complaint not personally delivered to person to be served within the state.
     (d)   Extension of time to appear or plead.
§ 3012-a.   Certificate of merit in medical, dental and podiatric malpractice actions.
§ 3013.    Particularity of statements generally.
R 3014.    Statements.
R 3015.    Particularity as to specific matters.
     (a)   Conditions precedent.
     (b)   Corporate status.
     (c)   Judgment, decision or determination.
     (d)   Signatures.
     (e)   License to do business.
R 3016.    Particularity in specific actions.
     (a)   Libel or slander.
     (b)   Fraud or mistake.
     (c)   Separation or divorce.
     (d)   Judgment.
     (e)   Law of foreign country.
     (f)   Sale and delivery of goods or performing of labor or services.
     (g)   Personal injury.

CPLR

     (h)  Gross negligence or intentional infliction of harm by certain directors, officers or trustees of certain corporations, associations, organizations or trusts.

§ 3017.    Demand for relief.
     (a)  Generally.
     (b)  Declaratory judgment.
     (c)  Medical or dental malpractice action or action against a municipal corporation.

§ 3018.    Responsive pleadings.
     (a)  Denials.
     (b)  Affirmative defenses.

§ 3019.    Counterclaims and cross-claims.
     (a)  Subject of counterclaims.
     (b)  Subject of cross-claims.
     (c)  Counterclaim against trustee or nominal plaintiff.
     (d)  Cause of action in counterclaim or cross-claim deemed in complaint.

§ 3020.    Verification.
     (a)  Generally.
     (b)  When answer must be verified.
     (c)  Defense not involving the merits.
     (d)  By whom verification made.

R 3021.    Form of affidavit of verification.
R 3022.    Remedy for defective verification.
R 3023.    Construction of verified pleading.
R 3024.    Motion to correct pleadings.
     (a)  Vague or ambiguous pleadings.
     (b)  Scandalous or prejudicial matter.
     (c)  Time limits; pleading after disposition.

R 3025.    Amended and supplemental pleadings.
     (a)  Amendments without leave.
     (b)  Amendments and supplemental pleadings by leave.
     (c)  Amendment to conform to the evidence.
     (d)  Responses to amended or supplemental pleadings.

§ 3026.    Construction.

§§ 3027–3030.    [Not used.]

§ 3031.    Simplified procedure for court determination of disputes—action without pleadings.

R 3032.    Contents of statement.
§ 3033.    Contracts to submit; enforcement of submission.
R 3034.    Motion procedure to settle statement terms.
§ 3035.    Simplified procedure authorized.
     (a)  Implementation and pre-trial.
     (b)  Technical rules of evidence dispensed.
     (c)  Practice.

R 3036.    Court determination.
§ 3037.    Appeal.

§§ 3038–3040.    [Not used.]

§ 3041.      Bill of particulars in any case.
R 3042.      Procedure for bill of particulars.
     (a)   Demand.
     (b)   Amendment.
     (c)   Failure to respond or to comply with a demand.
     (d)   Penalties for refusal to comply.
     (e)   Service of improper or unduly burdensome demands.
R 3043.      Bill of particulars in personal injury actions.
     (a)   Specified particulars.
     (b)   Supplemental bill of particulars without leave.
     (c)   Discretion of court.
§ 3044.      Verification of bill of particulars.
§ 3045.      Arbitration of damages in medical, dental or podiatric malpractice
            actions.

CPLR

## § 3001. Declaratory judgment.

The supreme court may render a declaratory judgment having the effect of a final judgment as to the rights and other legal relations of the parties to a justiciable controversy whether or not further relief is or could be claimed. If the court declines to render such a judgment it shall state its grounds.

## § 3002. Actions and relief not barred for inconsistency.

(a) Action against several persons. Where causes of action exist against several persons, the commencement or maintenance of an action against one, or the recovery against one of a judgment which is unsatisfied, shall not be deemed an election of remedies which bars an action against the others.

(b) Action against agent and undisclosed principal. Where causes of action exist against an agent and his undisclosed principal, the commencement or maintenance, after disclosure of the principal, of an action against either, or the recovery of a judgment against either which is unsatisfied, shall not be deemed an election of remedies which bars an action against the other.

(c) Action for conversion and on contract. Where causes of action exist against several persons for the conversion of property and upon express or implied contract, the commencement or maintenance of an action against one, or the recovery against one of a judgment which is unsatisfied, either for the conversion or upon the contract, shall not be deemed an election of remedies which bars an action against the others either for the conversion or upon the contract.

(d) Action on contract and to reform. A judgment denying recovery in an action upon an agreement in writing shall not be deemed to bar an action to reform such agreement and to enforce it as reformed.

(e) Claim for damages and rescission. A claim for damages sustained as a result of fraud or misrepresentation in the inducement of a contract or other transaction, shall not be deemed inconsistent with a claim for rescission or based upon rescission. In an action for rescission or based upon rescission the aggrieved party shall be allowed to obtain complete relief in one action, including rescission, restitution of the benefits, if any, conferred by him as a result of the transaction, and damages to which he is entitled because of such fraud or misrepresentation; but such complete relief shall not include duplication of items of recovery.

(f) Vendee's lien not to depend upon form of action. When relief is sought, in an action or by way of defense or counterclaim, by a vendee under an agreement for the sale or exchange of real property, because of the rescission, failure, invalidity or disaffirmance of such agreement, a vendee's lien upon the property shall not be denied merely because the claim is for rescission, or is based upon the rescission, failure, invalidity or disaffirmance of such agreement.

### § 3003. Action for periodic payments due under pension or retirement contract no bar to action for future installments.

The commencement or maintenance of an action for the recovery of payments which have become due under the terms of a written agreement providing for the payment of a pension or retirement compensation or deferred compensation for a period of years or for life, whether or not such agreement is part of an employment contract, shall not be deemed to bar subsequent actions to recover payments thereafter becoming due under the terms of such agreement.

### § 3004. Where restoration of benefits before judgment unnecessary.

A party who has received benefits by reason of a transaction that is void or voidable because of fraud, misrepresentation, mistake, duress, infancy or incompetency, and who, in an action or by way of defense or counterclaim, seeks rescission, restitution, a declaration or judgment that such transaction is void, or other relief, whether formerly denominated legal or equitable, dependent upon a determination that such transaction was void or voidable, shall not be denied relief because of a failure to tender before judgment restoration of such benefits; but the court may make a tender of restoration a condition of its judgment, and may otherwise in its judgment so adjust the equities between the parties that unjust enrichment is avoided.

### § 3005. Relief against mistake of the law.

When relief against a mistake is sought in an action or by way of defense or counterclaim, relief shall not be denied merely because the mistake is one of law rather than one of fact.

**§§ 3006-10. [Not used.]**

**§ 3011. Kinds of pleadings.**

There shall be a complaint and an answer. An answer may include a counterclaim against a plaintiff and a cross-claim against a defendant. A defendant's pleading against another claimant is an interpleader complaint, or against any other person not already a party is a third-party complaint. There shall be a reply to a counterclaim denominated as such, an answer to an interpleader complaint, or third-party complaint and an answer to a cross-claim that contains a demand for an answer. If no demand is made, the cross-claim shall be deemed denied or avoided. There shall be no other pleading unless the court orders otherwise.

### 1977 AMENDMENTS

L. 1977, ch. 26, eff. Sept. 1, 1977, amended CPLR 3011 to provide that an answer to a cross-claim is required only where the cross-claim demands an answer. If no demand is made, the cross-claim is deemed denied or avoided.

The Judicial Conference, in recommending the amendment in its 1977 Report to the Legislature, stated in part:

". . . . In cases arising out of the same incident, where there are multiple plaintiffs each suing numerous defendants, as for example under the theory of *Dole* v. *Dow Chemical Company,* 30 N.Y. 2d 143 (1972), the preparation and service of mandatory answers to cross-claims becomes extremely burdensome.

"This bill would mitigate the problem by providing for an answer to a cross-claim only when it contains a demand for an answer . . . . The result will be to require answers to cross-claims when they serve a purpose but not otherwise, thereby serving the convenience of the courts and the parties and eliminating much unnecessary paperwork."

**§ 3012. Service of pleadings and demand for complaint.**

(a) Service of pleadings. The complaint may be served with the summons. A subsequent pleading asserting new or additional claims for relief shall be served upon a party who has not appeared in the manner provided for service of a summons. In any other case, a pleading shall be served in the manner provided for service of papers generally. Service of an answer or reply shall be made within twenty days after service of the pleading to which it responds.

(b) Service of complaint where summons served without complaint. If the complaint is not served with the summons, the defendant may serve a written demand for the complaint within the time provided in subdivision (a) of rule 320 for an appearance. Service of the complaint shall be made within twenty days after service of the demand. Service of the demand shall extend the time to appear until twenty days after service of the complaint. If no demand is made, the complaint shall be served within twenty days after service of the notice of appearance. The court upon motion may dismiss the action if service of the complaint is not made as provided in this subdivision. A demand or motion under this subdivision does not of itself constitute an appearance in the action.

(c) Additional time to serve answer where summons and complaint not personally delivered to person to be served within the state. If the complaint is served with the summons and the service is made on the defendant by delivering the summons and complaint to an official of the state authorized to receive service in his behalf or if service of the summons and complaint is made pursuant to section 303, paragraphs two, three, four or five of section 308 or sections 313, 314 or 315, service of an answer shall be made within thirty days after service is complete.

(d) Extension of time to appear or plead. Upon the application of a party, the court may extend the time to appear or plead, or compel the acceptance of a pleading untimely served, upon such terms as may be just and upon a showing of reasonable excuse for delay or default.

### 1983 AMENDMENTS

L. 1983, ch. 318, eff. June 21, 1983, amended CPLR 3012 by adding a new subd. (d) to provide for an extension of time to appear or plead. ch. 318, § 3 provides:

§ 3. This act shall take effect immediately and shall be deemed and construed as remedial in nature and application and shall apply in every action and proceeding heretofore commenced and which either: still is pending before a court; or the time for taking of an appeal from any order or judgment in such action has not yet expired, and in all actions and proceedings hereafter commenced.

### 1978 AMENDMENTS

L. 1978, ch. 534, eff. Jan. 1, 1979, amended Subd. (b).

### 1970 AMENDMENTS

L. 1970, ch. 852, eff. Sept. 1, 1970, amended Subd. (c).

### 1964 AMENDMENTS

L. 1964, ch. 388, eff. Sept. 1, 1964, amended Subd. (c).

## § 3012-a.  Certificate of merit in medical, dental and podiatric malpractice actions.

(a) In any action for medical, dental or podiatric malpractice, the complaint shall be accompanied by a certificate, executed by the attorney for the plaintiff, declaring that:

(1) the attorney has reviewed the facts of the case and has consulted with at least one physician in medical malpractice actions, at least one dentist in dental malpractice actions or at least one podiatrist in podiatric malpractice actions who is licensed to practice in this state or any other state and who the attorney reasonably believes is knowledgeable in the relevant issues involved in the particular action, and that the attorney has concluded on the basis of such review and consultation that there is a reasonable basis for the commencement of such action; or

(2) the attorney was unable to obtain the consultation required by paragraph one of this subdivision because a limitation of time, established by article two

of this chapter, would bar the action and that the certificate required by paragraph one of this subdivision could not reasonably be obtained before such time expired. If a certificate is executed pursuant to this subdivision, the certificate required by this section shall be filed within ninety days after service of the complaint; or

(3) the attorney was unable to obtain the consultation required by paragraph one of this subdivision because the attorney had made three separate good faith attempts with three separate physicians, dentists or podiatrists, in accordance with the provisions of paragraph one of this subdivision to obtain such consultation and none of those contacted would agree to such a consultation.

(b) Where a certificate is required pursuant to this section, a single certificate shall be filed for each action, even if more than one defendant has been named in the complaint or is subsequently named.

(c) Where the attorney intends to rely solely on the doctrine of "res ipsa loquitur", this section shall be inapplicable. In such cases, the complaint shall be accompanied by a certificate, executed by the attorney, declaring that the attorney is solely relying on such doctrine and, for that reason, is not filing a certificate required by this section.

(d) If a request by the plaintiff for the records of the plaintiff's medical or dental treatment by the defendants has been made and such records have not been produced, the plaintiff shall not be required to serve the certificate required by this section until ninety days after such records have been produced.

(e) For purposes of this section, and subject to the provisions of section thirty-one hundred one of this chapter, an attorney who submits a certificate as required by paragraph one or two of subdivision (a) of this section and the physician, dentist or podiatrist with whom the attorney consulted shall not be required to disclose the identity of the physician, dentist or podiatrist consulted and the contents of such consultation; provided, however, that when the attorney makes a claim under paragraph three of subdivision (a) of this section that he was unable to obtain the required consultation with the physician, dentist or podiatrist, the court may, upon the request of a defendant made prior to compliance by the plaintiff with the provisions of section thirty-one hundred of this chapter, require the attorney to divulge to the court the names of physicians, dentists or podiatrists refusing such consultation.

(f) The provisions of this section shall not be applicable to a plaintiff who is not represented by an attorney.

(g) The plaintiff may, in lieu of serving the certificate required by this section, provide the defendant or defendants with the information required by paragraph one of subdivision (d) of section thirty-one hundred one of this chapter within the period of time prescribed by this section.

CPLR

### 1987 AMENDMENTS

L. 1987, ch. 507, eff. July 30, 1987, and applicable to any acts, omissions or failures occurring on or after such date, amended section to apply to podiatric malpractice actions.

### 1986 AMENDMENTS

L. 1986, ch. 266, eff. July 8, 1986 and applicable to actions commenced on or after such date, added new section 3012-a, relating to certificates of merit in medical and dental malpractice actions.

## § 3013.  Particularity of statements generally.

Statements in a pleading shall be sufficiently particular to give the court and parties notice of the transactions, occurrences, or series of transactions or occurrences, intended to be proved and the material elements of each cause of action or defense.

## R 3014.  Statements.

Every pleading shall consist of plain and concise statements in consecutively numbered paragraphs. Each paragraph shall contain, as far as practicable, a single allegation. Reference to and incorporation of allegations may subsequently be by number. Prior statements in a pleading shall be deemed repeated or adopted subsequently in the same pleading whenever express repetition or adoption is unnecessary for a clear presentation of the subsequent matters. Separate causes of action or defenses shall be separately stated and numbered and may be stated regardless of consistency. Causes of action or defenses may be stated alternatively or hypothetically. A copy of any writing which is attached to a pleading is a part thereof for all purposes.

## R 3015.  Particularity as to specific matters.

(a) Conditions precedent. The performance or occurrence of a condition precedent in a contract need not be pleaded. A denial of performance or occurrence shall be made specifically and with particularity. In case of such denial, the party relying upon the performance or occurrence shall be required to prove on the trial only such performance or occurrence as shall have been so specified.

(b) Corporate status. Where any party is a corporation, the complaint shall so state and, where known, it shall specify the state, country or government by or under whose laws the party was created.

(c) Judgment, decision or determination. A judgment, decision or other determination of a court, judicial or quasi-judicial tribunal, or of a board or officer, may be pleaded without stating matter showing jurisdiction to render it.

(d) Signatures. Unless specifically denied in the pleadings each signature on a negotiable instrument is admitted.

(e) License to do business. Where the plaintiff's cause of action against a consumer arises from the plaintiff's conduct of a business which is required by state or local law to be licensed by the department of consumer affairs of the city of New York, the Suffolk county department of consumer affairs, the Westchester county department of consumer affairs/weight-measures, the county of Rockland, the county of Putnam or the Nassau county department of consumer affairs, the complaint shall allege, as part of the cause of action, that plaintiff is duly licensed and shall contain the name and number, if any, of such license and the governmental agency which issued such license; provided, however, that where the plaintiff does not have a license at the commencement of the action the plaintiff may, subject to the provisions of rule thirty hundred twenty-five of this article, amend the complaint with the name and number of an after-acquired license and the name of the governmental agency which issued such license or move for leave to amend the complaint in accordance with such provisions. The failure of the plaintiff to comply with this subdivision will permit the defendant to move for dismissal pursuant to paragraph seven of subdivision (a) of rule thirty-two hundred eleven of this chapter.

CPLR

### 1996 AMENDMENTS

L. 1996, ch. 465, eff. August 8, 1996, amended subdivision (e) to add a reference to Putnam county.

### 1990 AMENDMENTS

L. 1990, ch. 654, eff. July 18, 1990, amended CPLR 3015(e) to apply to a plaintiff licensed by the Westchester county department of consumer affairs/weight-measures.

### 1986 AMENDMENTS

L. 1986, ch. 26, eff. April 3, 1986, amended CPLR 3015(e) to apply to a plaintiff licensed by the Rockland County Department of Consumer Affairs.

### 1985 AMENDMENTS

L. 1985, ch. 26, eff. April 2, 1985, amended CPLR 3015(e) to apply to a plaintiff licensed by the Suffolk County Department of Consumer Affairs.

### 1984 AMENDMENTS

L. 1984, ch. 243, eff. July 19, 1984, amended CPLR 3015(e) to apply to a plaintiff licensed by the Nassau County Department of Consumer Affairs.

### 1983 AMENDMENTS

L. 1983, ch. 817, eff. July 30, 1983, and applicable to all actions commenced on and after that date, added CPLR 3015(e).

### 1972 AMENDMENTS

Former Subd. (d) was deleted and former Subd. (e) was relettered Subd. (d) by Proposal No. 4 of the Judicial Conference Report to the 1972 Legislature, eff. Sept. 1, 1972.

The 1972 Judicial Conference Report stated in part:

"Subdivision (d) of Rule 3015, which requires that special damages be itemized in the pleading, would be deleted. The itemization of special damages is a proper function of the bill of particulars which has been retained substantially unchanged from prior law.

"Rule 3015 (d) was originally proposed when the Advisory Committee on Practice and Procedure decided to abolish the bill of particulars (1 Adv. Comm. Rpt. 65-66 (1957)). It was retained by oversight when the Legislature restored the bill of particulars (5th Rpt. Leg. Doc. (1961) No. 15, pp. 422, 437–440. . . .).

"The proposed repeal of Rule 3015 (d) would implement the intent of both the Advisory Committee and the Legislature. Deletion is not intended to change case law requiring the pleading of special damages forming an element of a cause of action, as required by CPLR 3013. Case law requires the pleading of special damages independent of Rule 3015 (d) (see *Keefe* v. *Lee*, 197 N.Y. 68 (1909))."

### 1964 AMENDMENTS

Amendment No. 4 made by the Judicial Conference Feb. 1, 1964, Report to the Legislature, eff. Sept. 1, 1964, added the new subdivision (e), now Subd. (d). The Judicial Conference stated: "The first sentence of § 3018(a) permits a party to raise by a general denial the question of the authenticity of a signature on a negotiable instrument. Sections 3-307 and 8-105 (2)(a) of the Uniform Commercial Code, however, provide that every signature on a negotiable instrument is admitted unless specifically denied in the proper pleading. In the view of the Judicial Conference the proposed change is not only necessary for the sake of conformity with the Code but is also desirable in itself as a matter of sound pleading procedure."

## R 3016.  Particularity in specific actions.

(a) Libel or slander. In an action for libel or slander, the particular words complained of shall be set forth in the complaint, but their application to the plaintiff may be stated generally.

(b) Fraud or mistake. Where a cause of action or defense is based upon misrepresentation, fraud, mistake, wilful default, breach of trust or undue influence, the circumstances constituting the wrong shall be stated in detail.

(c) Separation or divorce. In an action for separation or divorce, the nature and circumstances of a party's alleged misconduct, if any, and the time and place of each act complained of, if any, shall be specified in the complaint or counterclaim as the case may be.

(d) Judgment. In an action on a judgment, the complaint shall state the extent to which any judgment recovered by the plaintiff against the defendant, or against a person jointly liable with the defendant, on the same cause of action has been satisfied.

(e) Law of foreign country. Where a cause of action or defense is based upon the law of a foreign country or its political subdivision, the substance of the foreign law relied upon shall be stated.

(f) Sale and delivery of goods or performing of labor or services. In an action involving the sale and delivery of goods, or the performing of labor or services, or the furnishing of materials, the plaintiff may set forth and number in his verified complaint the items of his claim and the reasonable value or agreed price of each. Thereupon the defendant by his verified answer shall indicate specifically those items he disputes and whether in respect of delivery or performance, reasonable value or agreed price.

(g) Personal injury. In an action designated in subsection (a) of section five thousand one hundred four of the insurance law, for personal injuries arising out of negligence in the use or operation of a motor vehicle in this state, the complaint shall state that the plaintiff has sustained a serious injury, as defined in subsection (d) of section five thousand one hundred two of the insurance law, or economic loss greater than basic economic loss, as defined in subsection (a) of section five thousand one hundred two of the insurance law.

(h) Gross negligence or intentional infliction of harm by certain directors, officers or trustees of certain corporations, associations, organizations or trusts. In an action or proceeding based upon the conduct of a director, officer or trustee described in section seven hundred twenty-a of the not-for-profit corporation law, or subdivision six of section 20.09 of the arts and cultural affairs law, the complaint shall be verified and shall state whether or not said complaint is based upon gross negligence or intentional infliction of harm.

## CROSS REFERENCES

**Insurance Law §§ 5102 and 5104,** referred to in Subd. (g), *supra*, contain essential provisions of the "no fault" automobile insurance act; §§ 5102–5104, § 5108 are included in the Appendix, *infra.*

### 1991 AMENDMENTS

L. 1991, ch. 656, eff. July 26, 1991, amended CPLR 3016(h) to replace a reference to Gen. Mun. L. § 305 with a reference to Arts and Cultural Affairs L. § 20.09.

### 1990 AMENDMENTS

L. 1990, ch. 904, eff. July 30, 1990, amended CPLR 3016(h) to include actions or proceedings based upon the conduct of a director, officer or trustee as described in subdivision six of section three hundred five of the General Municipal Law.

### 1986 AMENDMENTS

L. 1986, ch. 220, eff. June 28, 1986 and applicable only to those causes of action arising on or after that date, added new Subd. (h) to CPLR 3016, requiring a verified complaint in actions based upon § 720(a) of the Not-For-Profit Corporation Law, stating whether the complaint is based upon gross negligence or intentional infliction of harm.

### 1984 AMENDMENTS

L. 1984, ch. 805, eff. Sept. 1, 1984, amended CPLR 3016(g) to conform the references to the recodified Insurance Law.

### 1976 AMENDMENTS

L. 1976, ch. 87, eff. April 29, 1976, amended Subd. (c).

**1974 AMENDMENTS**

L. 1974, ch. 575, eff. Sept. 1, 1974, added Subd. (g).

## § 3017. Demand for relief.

(a) Generally. Except as otherwise provided in subdivision (c) of this section, every complaint, counterclaim, cross-claim, interpleader complaint, and third-party complaint shall contain a demand for the relief to which the pleader deems himself entitled. Relief in the alternative or of several different types may be demanded. Except as provided in section 3215, the court may grant any type of relief within its jurisdiction appropriate to the proof whether or not demanded, imposing such terms as may be just.

(b) Declaratory judgment. In an action for a declaratory judgment, the demand for relief in the complaint shall specify the rights and other legal relations on which a declaration is requested and state whether further or consequential relief is or could be claimed and the nature and extent of any such relief which is claimed.

(c) Medical or dental malpractice action or action against a municipal corporation. In an action for medical or dental malpractice or in an action against a municipal corporation, as defined in section 2 of the General Municipal Law, the complaint, counterclaim, cross-claim, interpleader complaint, and third-party complaint shall contain a prayer for general relief but shall not state the amount of damages to which the pleader deems himself entitled. If the action is brought in the supreme court, the pleading shall also state whether or not the amount of damages sought exceeds the jurisdictional limits of all lower courts which would otherwise have jurisdiction, provided, however, that a party against whom an action for medical or dental malpractice is brought or the municipal corporation, may at any time request a supplemental demand setting forth the total damages to which the pleader deems himself entitled. A supplemental demand shall be provided by the party bringing the action within fifteen days of the request. In the event the supplemental demand is not served within fifteen days, the court, on motion, may order that it be served. A supplemental demand served pursuant to this subdivision shall be treated in all respects as a demand made pursuant to subdivision (a) of this section.

**1989 AMENDMENTS**

L. 1989, ch. 442, eff. Aug. 15, 1989 added dental malpractice.

**1980 AMENDMENTS**

L. 1980, ch. 686, eff. June 26, 1981, amended CPLR 3017(c) to include actions against a municipal corporation.

**1976 AMENDMENTS**

L. 1976, ch. 955, eff. Aug. 26, 1976, added Subd. (c), banning ad damnum clauses in medical malpractice pleadings, and amended Subd. (a) accordingly.

## § 3018. Responsive pleadings.

(a) Denials. A party shall deny those statements known or believed by him to be untrue. He shall specify those statements as to the truth of which he lacks knowledge or information sufficient to form a belief and this shall have the effect of a denial. All other statements of a pleading are deemed admitted, except that where no responsive pleading is permitted they are deemed denied or avoided.

(b) Affirmative defenses. A party shall plead all matters which if not pleaded would be likely to take the adverse party by surprise or would raise issues of fact not appearing on the face of a prior pleading such as arbitration and award, collateral estoppel, culpable conduct claimed in diminution of damages as set forth in article fourteen A, discharge in bankruptcy, facts showing illegality either by statute or common law, fraud, infancy or other disability of the party defending, payment, release, res judicata, statute of frauds, or statute of limitation. The application of this subdivision shall not be confined to the instances enumerated.

### 1980 AMENDMENTS

L. 1980, ch. 111, eff. May 7, 1980, as amended by ch. 504, eff. June 24, 1980, amended CPLR 3018(b) by expanding the enumeration of affirmative defenses that must be pleaded under this section to specifically include pleadings relating to contributory negligence.

## § 3019. Counterclaims and cross-claims.

(a) Subject of counterclaims. A counterclaim may be any cause of action in favor of one or more defendants or a person whom a defendant represents against one or more plaintiffs, a person whom a plaintiff represents or a plaintiff and other persons alleged to be liable.

(b) Subject of cross-claims. A cross-claim may be any cause of action in favor of one or more defendants or a person whom a defendant represents against one or more defendants, a person whom a defendant represents or a defendant and other persons alleged to be liable. A cross-claim may include a claim that the party against whom it is asserted is or may be liable to the cross-claimant for all or part of a claim asserted in the action against the cross-claimant.

(c) Counterclaim against trustee or nominal plaintiff. In an action brought by a trustee or in the name of a plaintiff who has no actual interest in the contract upon which it is founded, a claim against the plaintiff shall not be allowed as a counterclaim, but a claim existing against the person beneficially interested shall be allowed as a counterclaim to the extent of the plaintiff's claim, if it might have been so allowed in an action brought by the person beneficially interested.

(d) Cause of action in counterclaim or cross-claim deemed in complaint. A cause of action contained in a counterclaim or a cross-claim shall be treated, as far as practicable, as if it were contained in a complaint, except that separate process, trial or judgment may not be had unless the court so orders. Where a person not a party is alleged to be liable a summons and answer containing the counterclaim or cross-claim shall be filed, whereupon he or she shall become a defendant. Service upon such a defendant shall be by serving a summons and answer containing the counterclaim or cross-claim. Such defendant shall serve a reply or answer as if he or she were originally a party.

### 1994 AMENDMENTS

L. 1994, ch. 563, eff. July 26, 1994, amended CPLR 3019(d) by replacing the words "he shall be served with a summons and a copy of the answer containing the counterclaim or cross-claim," with the words "a summons and answer containing the counterclaim or cross-claim shall be filed"; by adding the words "or she"; and by adding the words "Service upon such a defendant shall be by serving a summons and answer containing the counterclaim or cross claim. Such defendant."

### 1966 AMENDMENTS

L. 1966, ch. 182, eff. Sept. 1, 1966, repealed Subd. (c) and Subd. (d), and redesignated Subd. (e) and Subd. (f) as Subd. (c) and Subd. (d) respectively.

Amendment was recommended by the Judicial Conference Feb. 1, 1966, Report to the Legislature: "U.C.C. § 9-318(1) is inconsistent with CPLR 3019(c). The U.C.C. provision makes the rights of an assignee of a contract of sale subject to (a) all the terms of the contract and any defenses or claims arising therefrom, and (b) any other defense or claim of the debtor against the assignor which accrues before the account debtor receives notification of the assignment. On the other hand, CPLR 3019(c) provides that a defendant can assert against the assignee a claim èxisting' against the assignor àt the time of the assignment' and belonging to the defendant before notification of the assignment. In this respect CPLR 3019(c) has also for four years been in conflict with § 13-105 of the General Obligations Law (formerly § 41 of the Personal Property Law). Èxisting' means màtured' at the time of assignment. See *James Talcott, Inc. v. Winco Sales Corp.*, 28 Misc. 2d 612 (App. Term 1st Dept. 1960). The U.C.C. permits an account debtor to assert a claim arising out of the same transaction regardless of when it accrued, and any *other* claim if it accrued prior to notification of the assignment.

"CPLR 3019(d), relating to counterclaims against an assignee of a negotiable instrument who is not a holder in due course, is amply covered by U.C.C. § 3-306, dealing with the same matter.

"The U.C.C. establishes the substantive rules of claims and defenses against assignees of secured contracts or negotiable instruments (Sections 9-318(1) and 3-306). The substantive law regulating claims and defenses of an obligor against an assignee in transactions other than those covered by the Uniform Commercial Code is contained in General Obligations Law § 13-105. Accordingly, CPLR 3019(c) and (d) should be eliminated."

## § 3020. Verification.

(a) Generally. A verification is a statement under oath that the pleading is true to the knowledge of the deponent, except as to matters alleged on information and belief, and that as to those matters he believes it to be true. Unless otherwise specified by law, where a pleading is verified, each subsequent pleading shall also be verified, except the answer of an infant and except as to matter in the pleading concerning which the party would be privileged from testifying as a witness. Where the complaint is not verified, a counterclaim, cross-claim or third-party claim in the answer may be separately verified in the same manner and with the same effect as if it were a separate pleading.

(b) When answer must be verified. An answer shall be verified:

1. when the complaint charges the defendant with having confessed or suffered a judgment, executed a conveyance, assignment or other instrument, or transferred or delivered money or personal property with intent to hinder, delay or defraud his creditors, or with being a party or privy to such a transaction by another person with like intent towards the creditors of that person, or with any fraud whatever affecting a right or the property of another; or

2. in an action against a corporation to recover damages for the non-payment of a promissory note or other evidence of debt for the absolute payment of money upon demand or at a particular time.

(c) Defense not involving the merits. A defense which does not involve the merits of the action shall be verified.

(d) By whom verification made. The verification of a pleading shall be made by the affidavit of the party, or, if two or more parties united in interest are pleading together, by at least one of them who is acquainted with the facts, except:

1. if the party is a domestic corporation, the verification shall be made by an officer thereof and shall be deemed a verification by the party;

2. if the party is the state, a governmental subdivision, board, commission, or agency, or a public officer in behalf of any of them, the verification may be made by any person acquainted with the facts; and

3. if the party is a foreign corporation, or is not in the county where the attorney has his office, or if there are two or more parties united in interest and pleading together and none of them acquainted with the facts is within that county, or if the action or defense is founded upon a written instrument for the payment of money only which is in the possession of an agent or the attorney, or if all the material allegations of the pleading are within the personal knowledge of an agent or the attorney, the verification may be made by such agent or attorney.

### 1973 AMENDMENTS

L. 1973, ch. 88, eff. Sept. 1, 1973, amended CPLR 3020(d)(2).

### 1964 AMENDMENTS

L. 1964, ch. 388, eff. Sept. 1, 1964, made mechanical corrections.

## R 3021. Form of affidavit of verification.

The affidavit of verification must be to the effect that the pleading is true to the knowledge of the deponent, except as to the matters therein stated to be alleged on information and belief, and that as to those matters he believes it to be true. If it is made by a person other than the party, he must set forth in the affidavit the grounds of his belief as to all matters not stated upon his knowledge and the reason why it is not made by the party.

## R 3022. Remedy for defective verification.

A defectively verified pleading shall be treated as an unverified pleading. Where a pleading is served without a sufficient verification in a case where the adverse party is entitled to a verified pleading, he may treat it as a nullity, provided he gives notice with due diligence to the attorney of the adverse party that he elects so to do.

## R 3023. Construction of verified pleading.

The allegations or denials in a verified pleading must, in form, be stated to be made by the party pleading. Unless they are stated to be made upon the information and belief of the party, they must be regarded for all purposes, including a criminal prosecution, as having been made upon the knowledge of the person verifying the pleading. An allegation that the party has not sufficient knowledge or information to form a belief with respect to a matter, must, for the same purposes, be regarded as an allegation that the person verifying the pleading has not such knowledge or information.

## R 3024. Motion to correct pleadings.

(a) Vague or ambiguous pleadings. If a pleading is so vague or ambiguous that a party cannot reasonably be required to frame a response he may move for a more definite statement.

(b) Scandalous or prejudicial matter. A party may move to strike any scandalous or prejudicial matter unnecessarily inserted in a pleading.

(c) Time limits; pleading after disposition. A notice of motion under this rule shall be served within twenty days after service of the challenged pleading. If the motion is denied, the responsive pleading shall be served within ten days after service of notice of entry of the order and, if it is granted, an amended pleading complying with the order shall be served within that time.

## R 3025. Amended and supplemental pleadings.

(a) Amendments without leave. A party may amend his pleading once without leave of court within twenty days after its service, or at any time before the period for responding to it expires, or within twenty days after service of a pleading responding to it.

(b) *Amendments and supplemental pleadings by leave.* A party may amend his pleading, or supplement it by setting forth additional or subsequent transactions or occurrences, at any time by leave of court or by stipulation of all parties. Leave shall be freely given upon such terms as may be just including the granting of costs and continuances.

(c) *Amendment to conform to the evidence.* The court may permit pleadings to be amended before or after judgment to conform them to the evidence, upon such terms as may be just including the granting of costs and continuances.

(d) *Responses to amended or supplemental pleadings.* Except where otherwise prescribed by law or order of the court, there shall be an answer or reply to an amended or supplemental pleading if an answer or reply is required to the pleading being amended or supplemented. Service of such an answer or reply shall be made within twenty days after service of the amended or supplemental pleading to which it responds.

## § 3026. Construction.

Pleadings shall be liberally construed. Defects shall be ignored if a substantial right of a party is not prejudiced.

### 1964 AMENDMENTS

L. 1964, ch. 388, eff. Sept. 1, 1964, made mechanical corrections.

## §§ 3027-30. [Not used.]

## § 3031. Simplified procedure for court determination of disputes—action without pleadings.

An action may be commenced without the service of a summons, or may be continued after the service of a summons, without pleadings, by the filing of a statement, signed and acknowledged by all the parties or signed by their attorneys, specifying plainly and concisely the claims and defenses between the parties and the relief requested. Signing constitutes a certificate that the issues are genuine, and such filing, together with a note of issue, to be filed at the same time, shall constitute the joinder of issues in the action. The procedure in any action commenced under this section shall constitute "the New York Simplified Procedure for Court Determination of Disputes" and it shall be sufficient so to identify the procedure in any contract or other document referring to it. A submission of a controversy under this procedure shall constitute a waiver by the parties of the right to trial by jury.

## R 3032. Contents of statement.

The statement required when an action is commenced without summons, or continued after the service of a summons without pleadings, shall set forth plainly and concisely the claims and defenses in dispute between the parties and the relief sought, including the amount of money demanded, if any. With the permission of the court, amended or supplemental statements may be served and filed at any time.

**1964 AMENDMENTS**

L. 1964, ch. 388, eff. Sept. 1, 1964, made mechanical corrections.

## § 3033.  Contracts to submit; enforcement of submission.

1. Any written contract, otherwise valid under the substantive law, to submit any existing or future controversy to the court pursuant to section 3031 is valid and enforceable and shall be construed as an implied consent of the parties to the jurisdiction of the supreme court of this state to enforce it pursuant to the procedures of rule 3036, and to enter judgment thereon, and shall constitute a waiver by the parties of the right to trial by jury.

2. If the parties to a dispute arising under a contract to submit a controversy to the court under section 3031 are unable to agree on a statement of claims and defenses and relief sought pursuant to that section, the court on motion shall settle the terms of the statement. In deciding the motion the court shall consider and determine any questions as to the existence of the contract or its validity or the failure of any party to perform it. If a substantial issue of fact be raised as to the making of the contract or submission or the failure to comply therewith, the court or judge shall proceed to trial of such issue without a jury, unless either party should demand a jury trial.

## R 3034.  Motion procedure to settle statement terms.

1. A party aggrieved by the failure of another to perform under a contract to submit a controversy, upon filing a statement, signed and acknowledged by the party, specifying the claim and the relief requested, may move for an order directing settlement of the terms of the statement, if necessary, and the determination of the controversy pursuant to the New York Simplified Procedure for Court Determination of Disputes.

2. Eight days notice of the motion, or such other notice as the court shall deem appropriate, shall be served upon the party alleged to be in default, in such a manner as the court shall direct.

3. If there is no substantial question as to the making of the contract or submission, or the failure to comply therewith, the court shall proceed with the determination of the controversy pursuant to the simplified procedure and these rules. If the court shall find that a substantial issue of fact has been raised as to the making of the contract or submission, or the failure to comply therewith, and the motion shall not have been denied as a matter of law, the court shall proceed expeditiously with the trial thereof without a jury, unless either party upon argument of the motion shall have demanded in writing a trial by jury of the issue of the making of the contract or submission, in which event the

court shall proceed as promptly as may be practicable with such trial before a jury.

### § 3035.　Simplified procedure authorized.

(a) Implementation and pre-trial. The procedure in any action under the New York simplified procedure for court determination of disputes authorized by sections 3031 and 3033 shall be as provided in rule 3036 adopted to implement the provisions hereof, which is designed to promote the speedy hearing of such actions and to provide for such actions a procedure that is as simple and informal as circumstances will permit. A pre-trial conference may be held relative to the disposition of questions of law which might be conclusive in the action and avoid a trial.

(b) Technical rules of evidence dispensed. The technical rules of evidence shall be dispensed with to the extent specified in such rule 3036.

(c) Practice. The practice under this procedure relating to motions to stay or to transfer pending actions, and relating to venue, assessment of costs, entry of judgment, judgment by default, and the continuance of the action in case of death or incompetency of parties shall be as prescribed in the rules adopted pursuant hereto.

### R 3036.　Court determination.

1. Except upon a trial under paragraph three of rule 3034 of the issue of the making of the contract or submission, the rules as to the admissibility of evidence, except as provided by statutes relating to privileged communications, and as to procedure shall be dispensed with unless the court shall otherwise direct, and shall not apply to or exclude, limit, or restrict the taking of any testimony and the adducing of any proof.

2. In any action brought pursuant to the simplified procedure for court determination of disputes in which the court shall be of the opinion that evidence by an impartial expert would be of material aid to the just determination of the action, it may direct that such evidence be obtained. The fee and expenses of such expert shall be paid by the parties as, in its discretion, the court may direct.

3. Any action or proceeding, other than one brought in accordance with the simplified procedure, which presents an issue referable to the court for determination under the simplified procedure may be stayed by the court in which such action or proceeding is pending, or by the supreme court.

4. If the court directs a party to the contract or submission to serve a statement within a given time, and the party fails to do so, or if a party fails to appear upon proper notice, judgment by default may be awarded.

5. At a pre-trial conference, or at any other time on motion of any party or on its own motion, on notice to the parties, and upon such terms and conditions

CPLR

as in its discretion may seem proper, the court may (a) order or allow any party to serve an additional or amended statement of facts; (b) direct pre-trial disclosure of evidence and discovery and inspection of books, records and documents; (c) permit the taking of depositions for use at the hearing; (d) limit or restrict the number of experts to be heard as witnesses; (e) clarify and define the issues to be tried; (f) stay or transfer and consolidate with the action any other civil action or proceeding pending in any court between parties the action; (g) grant summary judgment in favor of any party as in rule 3212 provided.

6. After a statement complying with the requirements of rule 3032 or settled in accordance with rule 3034 has been filed, any party may serve and file a note of issue. Trial of the action shall commence on the date specified in such note of issue or as soon thereafter as may be practicable. Completion of preliminary procedures required by local court rules prior to the placing of a case upon the calendar for trial shall not be required in actions under the New York Simplified Procedure for Court Determination of Disputes.

7. The judgment roll shall consist of the submission or contract; the statement of claims and defenses; each paper submitted to the court upon a motion and each order of the court thereon: a copy of the judgment and of each paper necessarily affecting the judgment.

8. Those provisions of the civil practice law and rules pertaining to venue, entry and enforcement of judgment and the continuance of a civil action in case of the death or incompetency of parties shall apply to actions under the simplified procedure.

9. Costs and disbursements may be awarded by the court in its discretion. If awarded, the amount thereof must be included in the judgment.

### 1964 AMENDMENTS

L. 1964, ch. 388, eff. Sept. 1, 1964, changed "subdivision 3" in the first sentence of paragraph (1) to read "paragraph three."

## § 3037. Appeal.

An appeal may be taken only from a judgment, or an order determining the making of the contract or submission or the failure to comply therewith. There shall be no appeal from an intermediate order of the court or of a judge in an action under the simplified procedure provisions, except with the permission of the trial or appellate court, but such order or orders may be reviewed on the appeal from a judgment entered under these provisions. A decision of the trial judge on the facts shall be final if there is any substantial evidence to support it.

**§§ 3038-40. [Not used.]**

**§ 3041. Bill of particulars in any case.**

Any party may require any other party to give a bill of particulars of such party's claim, or a copy of the items of the account alleged in a pleading. As used elsewhere in this article, the term "bill of particulars" shall include "copy of the items of an account."

### 1994 AMENDMENTS

L. 1994, ch. 562, eff. for actions commenced on or after Jan. 1, 1995, amended CPLR 3041 by replacing "his" with "such party's," and by adding the final sentence.

### CROSS REFERENCES

Restrictions on the use of written interrogatories in conjunction with a demand for a bill of particulars are dealt with in CPLR § 3130, *infra*.

## R 3042. Procedure for bill of particulars.

(a) Demand. A demand for a bill of particulars shall be made by serving a written demand stating the items concerning which particulars are desired. Within thirty days of service of a demand for a bill of particulars, the party on whom the demand is made shall serve a bill of particulars complying with each item of the demand, except any item to which the party objects, in which event the reasons for the objection shall be stated with reasonable particularity. The assertion of an objection to one or more of the items in the demand shall not relieve the party on whom the demand is made from the obligation to respond in full within thirty days of service of the demand to the items of the demand to which no objection has been made.

(b) Amendment. In any action or proceeding in a court in which a note of issue is required to be filed, a party may amend the bill of particulars once as of course prior to the filing of a note of issue.

(c) Failure to respond or to comply with a demand. If a party fails to respond to a demand in a timely fashion or fails to comply fully with a demand, the party seeking the bill of particulars may move to compel compliance, or, if such failure is willful, for the imposition of penalties pursuant to subdivision (d) of this rule.

(d) Penalties for refusal to comply. If a party served with a demand for a bill of particulars willfully fails to provide particulars which the court finds ought to have been provided pursuant to this rule, the court may make such final or conditional order with regard to the failure or refusal as is just, including such relief as is set forth in section thirty-one hundred twenty-six of this chapter.

(e) Service of improper or unduly burdensome demands. If the court concludes that the demand for particulars, or a part thereof, is improper or unduly burdensome, in addition to vacating or modifying the demand, the court may make such order with regard to the improper or unduly burdensome demand as is just.

CPLR

### 1994 AMENDMENT

L. 1994, ch. 562, eff. for actions commenced on or after Jan. 1, 1995, amended CPLR 3042 by replacing all of subdivision (a); by deleting subdivisions (b), (c), (d), (e) and (f); by relettering subdivision (g) as subdivision (b); and by completely replacing subdivisions (c), (d) and (e).

### 1984 AMENDMENTS

L. 1984, ch. 294, eff. Sept. 1, 1984, amended CPLR 3042(a) by increasing the time within which a bill of particulars must be served to twenty days after the demand for the bill.

### 1978 AMENDMENTS

L. 1978, ch. 296, eff. June 19, 1978, added a new subdivision (g), which allowed amendment of a bill of particulars once as a matter of course, and relettered former subdivision (g) as subdivision (h). Subdivision (g) was subsequently amended by L. 1978, ch. 297, eff. June 19, 1978, which added the opening clause pertaining to proceedings in which a note of issue is required to be filed.

### 1974 AMENDMENTS

CPLR 3042(a) was amended by proposal No. 3 of the Judicial Conference Report to the 1974 Legislature, eff. Sept. 1, 1974, by substituting the term "five days," which appeared in the second sentence, with the term "ten days."

## R 3043.   Bill of particulars in personal injury actions.

(a) Specified particulars. In actions to recover for personal injuries the following particulars may be required:

(1) The date and approximate time of day of the occurrence;

(2) Its approximate location;

(3) General statement of the acts or omissions constituting the negligence claimed;

(4) Where notice of a condition is a prerequisite, whether actual or constructive notice is claimed;

(5) If actual notice is claimed, a statement of when and to whom it was given;

(6) Statement of the injuries and description of those claimed to be permanent, and in an action designated in subsection (a) of section five thousand one hundred four of the insurance law, for personal injuries arising out of negligence in the use or operation of a motor vehicle in this state, in what respect plaintiff has sustained a serious injury, as defined in subsection (d) of section five thousand one hundred two of the insurance law, or economic loss greater than basic economic loss, as defined in subsection (a) of section five thousand one hundred two of the insurance law;

(7) Length of time confined to bed and to house;

(8) Length of time incapacitated from employment; and

(9) Total amounts claimed as special damages for physicians' services and medical supplies; loss of earnings, with name and address of the employer; hospital expenses; nurses' services.

(b) Supplemental bill of particulars without leave. A party may serve a supplemental bill of particulars with respect to claims of continuing special damages and disabilities without leave of court at any time, but not less than thirty days prior to trial. Provided however that no new cause of action may be alleged or new injury claimed and that the other party shall upon seven days notice, be entitled to newly exercise any and all rights of discovery but only with respect to such continuing special damages and disabilities.

(c) Discretion of court. Nothing contained in the foregoing shall be deemed to limit the court in denying in a proper case, any one or more of the foregoing particulars, or in a proper case, in granting other, further or different particulars.

### CROSS REFERENCES

**Insurance Law §§ 5102 and 5104,** referred to in paragraph (6) of Subd. (a), *supra,* contain essential provisions of the "no fault" automobile insurance act; §§ 5102–5104, and § 5109 are included in the Appendix, *infra.*

### 1984 AMENDMENTS

L. 1984, ch. 805, eff. Sept. 1, 1984, amended CPLR 3043(a)(6) to conform the references to the recodified Insurance Law.

### 1979 AMENDMENTS

L. 1979, ch. 590, eff. Sept. 1, 1979, amended CPLR 3043 by adding a new subdivision (b), and by relettering the former subdivision (b) subdivision (c).

### 1974 AMENDMENTS

L. 1974, ch. 575, eff. Sept. 1, 1974, amended CPLR 3043(a)(6) by adding the provisions relating to an action brought pursuant to Insurance Law § 673(1) for personal injuries arising out of negligence in the use or operation of a motor vehicle in the state.

## § 3044.   Verification of bill of particulars.

If a pleading is verified, a subsequent bill of particulars shall also be verified. A bill of particulars of any pleading with respect to a cause of action for negligence shall be verified whether such pleading be verified or not.

### 1994 AMENDMENTS

L. 1994, ch. 562, eff. for actions commenced on or after Jan. 1, 1995, amended CPLR 3044 by deleting the words "or a copy of the items of account of that pleading."

### 1964 AMENDMENTS

L. 1964, ch. 291, eff. Sept. 1, 1964, substituted the first sentence for former first sentence which read: "A bill of particulars of a verified pleading or a copy of the items of an account alleged therein, shall be verified."

CPLR

## § 3045. Arbitration of damages in medical, dental or podiatric malpractice actions.

(a) At any time after service of a bill of particulars but no later than sixty days after filing of the notice of dental, medical or podiatric malpractice action pursuant to rule thirty-four hundred six of this chapter, any defendant in such an action may demand that the plaintiff elect whether to consent to the arbitration of damages upon a concession of liability in accordance with the provisions of this section.

(b) Within twenty days after receipt of such a demand, the plaintiff shall elect whether to arbitrate damages in such an action pursuant to such a concession of liability by the defendant or defendants in the action. If the defendant or defendants serve a concession of liability upon the plaintiff within twenty days after receipt of such an election, the issue of damages, including the proximate cause thereof, shall be subject to arbitration in accordance with the provisions of article seventy-five-A of this chapter. A concession of the liability, made pursuant to this section, shall not be binding on the defendant for any other purpose.

### 1987 AMENDMENTS

L. 1987, ch. 507, eff. July 30, 1987, and applicable to any acts, omissions or failures occurring on or after such date, amended section to apply to podiatric malpractice actions.

### 1986 AMENDMENTS

L. 1986, ch. 266, eff. July 8, 1986 and applicable to actions in which notice pursuant to CPLR 3406 has been filed, added new section 3045 providing for arbitration of damages in medical and dental malpractice actions. CPLR 3045 applies to actions in which the notice pursuant to CPLR 3406 is filed on or after July 8, 1986.

# ARTICLE 31

# DISCLOSURE

## SUMMARY OF ARTICLE

§ 3101.    Scope of disclosure.
    (a)  Generally.
    (b)  Privileged matter.
    (c)  Attorney's work product.
    (d)  Trial preparation.
    (e)  Party's statement.
    (f)  Contents of insurance agreement.
    (g)  Accident reports.
    (h)  Amendment or supplementation of responses.
    (i)  [Audio-visual materials.]
§ 3102.    Method of obtaining disclosure.
    (a)  Disclosure devices.
    (b)  Stipulation or notice normal method.
    (c)  Before action commenced; real property actions.
    (d)  After trial commenced.
    (e)  Action pending in another jurisdiction.
    (f)  Action to which state is party.
§ 3103.    Protective orders.
    (a)  Prevention of abuse.
    (b)  Suspension of disclosure pending application for a protective order.
    (c)  Suppression of information improperly obtained.
§ 3104.    Supervision of disclosure.
    (a)  Motion for, and extent of, supervision of disclosure.
    (b)  Selection of referee.
    (c)  Powers of referee; motions referred to person supervising disclosure.
    (d)  Review of order of referee.
    (e)  Payment of expenses of referee.
R 3105.    Notice to party in default.
R 3106.    Priority of depositions; witnesses; prisoners; designation of deponent.
    (a)  Normal priority.
    (b)  Witnesses.
    (c)  Prisoners.
    (d)  Designation of deponent.
R 3107.    Notice of taking oral questions.
R 3108.    Written questions; when permitted.
R 3109.    Notice of taking deposition on written questions.
    (a)  Notice of taking; service of questions and cross-questions.
    (b)  Officer asking written questions.

CPLR

R 3110.  Where the deposition is to be taken within the state.
R 3111.  Production of things at the examination.
R 3112.  Errors in notice for taking depositions.
R 3113.  Conduct of the examination.
    (a)  Persons before whom depositions may be taken.
    (b)  Oath of witness; recording of testimony; objections; continuous examination; written questions read by examining officer.
    (c)  Examination and cross-examination.
R 3114.  Examination of witness who does not understand the English language.
R 3115.  Objections to qualification of person taking deposition; competency; questions and answers.
    (a)  Objection when deposition offered in evidence.
    (b)  Errors which might be obviated if made known promptly.
    (c)  Disqualification of person taking deposition.
    (d)  Competency of witnesses or admissibility of testimony.
    (e)  Form of written questions.
R 3116.  Signing deposition; physical preparation; copies.
    (a)  Signing.
    (b)  Certification and filing by officer.
    (c)  Exhibits.
    (d)  Expenses of taking.
    (e)  Errors of officer or person transcribing.
R 3117.  Use of depositions.
    (a)  Impeachment of witnesses; parties; unavailable witnesses.
    (b)  Use of part of deposition.
    (c)  Substitution of parties; prior actions.
    (d)  Effect of using deposition.
R 3118.  Demand for address of party or of person who possessed an assigned cause of action or defense.
§ 3119.  [Not used.]
R 3120.  Discovery and production of documents and things for inspection, testing, copying or photographing.
    (a)  As against party.
    (b)  As against non-party.
§ 3121.  Physical or mental examination.
    (a)  Notice of examination.
    (b)  Copy of report.
R 3122.  Objection to disclosure, inspection or examination; compliance.
§ 3123.  Admissions as to matters of fact, papers, documents and photographs.
    (a)  Notice to admit; admission unless denied or denial excused.
    (b)  Effect of admission.
    (c)  Penalty for unreasonable denial.
R 3124.  Failure to disclose; motion to compel disclosure.
R 3125.  Place where motion to compel disclosure made.
§ 3126.  Penalties for refusal to comply with order or to disclose.
§§ 3127–3129.  [Not used.]
§ 3130.  Use of interrogatories.
§ 3131.  Scope of interrogatories.

R 3132.    Service of interrogatories.
R 3133.    Service of answers or objections to interrogatories.
    (a)  Service of an answer or objection.
    (b)  Form of answers & objections to interrogatories.
    (c)  Amended answers.
R 3134.    [Repealed].
§ 3140.    Disclosure of appraisals in proceedings for condemnation, appropriation or review of tax assessments.

---

## § 3101.   Scope of disclosure.

(a) Generally. There shall be full disclosure of all matter material and necessary in the prosecution or defense of an action, regardless of the burden of proof, by:

(1) a party, or the officer, director, member, agent or employee of a party;

(2) a person who possessed a cause of action or defense asserted in the action;

(3) a person about to depart from the state, or without the state, or residing at a greater distance from the place of trial than one hundred miles, or so sick or infirm as to afford reasonable grounds of belief that he or she will not be able to attend the trial, or a person authorized to practice medicine, dentistry or podiatry who has provided medical, dental or podiatric care or diagnosis to the party demanding disclosure, or who has been retained by such party as an expert witness; and

(4) any other person, upon notice stating the circumstances or reasons such disclosure is sought or required.

(b) Privileged matter. Upon objection by a person entitled to assert the privilege, privileged matter shall not be obtainable.

(c) Attorney's work product. The work product of an attorney shall not be obtainable.

(d) Trial preparation.

1. Experts. (i) Upon request, each party shall identify each person whom the party expects to call as an expert witness at trial and shall disclose in reasonable detail the subject matter on which each expert is expected to testify, the substance of the facts and opinions on which each expert is expected to testify, the qualifications of each expert witness and a summary of the grounds for each expert's opinion. However, where a party for good cause shown retains an expert an insufficient period of time before the commencement of trial to give appropriate notice thereof, the party shall not thereupon be precluded from introducing the expert's testimony at the trial solely on grounds of noncompliance with this

paragraph. In that instance, upon motion of any party, made before or at trial, or on its own initiative, the court may make whatever order may be just. In an action for medical, dental or podiatric malpractice, a party, in responding to a request, may omit the names of medical, dental or podiatric experts but shall be required to disclose all other information concerning such experts otherwise required by this paragraph.

(ii) In an action for medical, dental or podiatric malpractice, any party may, by written offer made to and served upon all other parties and filed with the court, offer to disclose the name of, and to make available for examination upon oral deposition, any person the party making the offer expects to call as an expert witness at trial. Within twenty days of service of the offer, a party shall accept or reject the offer by serving a written reply upon all parties and filing a copy thereof with the court. Failure to serve a reply within twenty days of service of the offer shall be deemed a rejection of the offer. If all parties accept the offer, each party shall be required to produce his or her expert witness for examination upon oral deposition upon receipt of a notice to take oral deposition in accordance with rule thirty-one hundred seven of this chapter. If any party, having made or accepted the offer, fails to make that party's expert available for oral deposition, that party shall be precluded from offering expert testimony at the trial of the action.

(iii) Further disclosure concerning the expected testimony of any expert may be obtained only by court order upon a showing of special circumstances and subject to restrictions as to scope and provisions concerning fees and expenses as the court may deem appropriate. However, a party, without court order, may take the testimony of a person authorized to practice medicine, dentistry or podiatry who is the party's treating or retained expert, as described in paragraph three of subdivision (a) of this section, in which event any other party shall be entitled to the full disclosure authorized by this article with respect to that expert without court order.

2. Materials. Subject to the provisions of paragraph one of this subdivision, materials otherwise discoverable under subdivision (a) of this section and prepared in anticipation of litigation or for trial by or for another party, or by or for that other party's representative (including an attorney, consultant, surety, indemnitor, insurer or agent), may be obtained only upon a showing that the party seeking discovery has substantial need of the materials in the preparation of the case and is unable without undue hardship to obtain the substantial equivalent of the materials by other means. In ordering discovery of the materials when the required showing has been made, the court shall protect against disclosure of the mental impressions, conclusions, opinions or legal theories of an attorney or other representative of a party concerning the litigation.

(e) Party's statement. A party may obtain a copy of his own statement.

(f) Contents of insurance agreement. A party may obtain discovery of the existence and contents of any insurance agreement under which any person carrying on an insurance business may be liable to satisfy part or all of a judgment which may be entered in the action or to indemnify or reimburse for payments made to satisfy the judgment. Information concerning the insurance agreement is not by reason of disclosure admissible in evidence at trial. For purpose of this subdivision, an application for insurance shall not be treated as part of an insurance agreement.

(g) Accident reports. Except as is otherwise provided by law, in addition to any other matter which may be subject to disclosure, there shall be full disclosure of any written report of an accident prepared in the regular course of business operations or practices of any person, firm, corporation, association or other public or private entity, unless prepared by a police or peace officer for a criminal investigation or prosecution and disclosure would interfere with a criminal investigation or prosecution.

(h) Amendment or supplementation of responses. A party shall amend or supplement a response previously given to a request for disclosure promptly upon the party's thereafter obtaining information that the response was incorrect or incomplete when made, or that the response, though correct and complete when made, no longer is correct and complete, and the circumstances are such that a failure to amend or supplement the response would be materially misleading. Where a party obtains such information an insufficient period of time before the commencement of trial appropriately to amend or supplement the response, the party shall not thereupon be precluded from introducing evidence at the trial solely on the grounds of noncompliance with this subdivision. In that instance, upon motion of any party, made before or at trial, or on its own initiative, the court may make whatever order may be just. Further amendment or supplementation may be obtained by court order.

(i) In addition to any other matter which may be subject to disclosure, there shall be full disclosure of any films, photographs, video tapes or audio tapes, including transcripts or memoranda thereof, involving a person referred to in paragraph one of subdivision (a) of this section. There shall be disclosure of all portions of such material, including out-takes, rather than only those portions a party intends to use. The provisions of this subdivision shall not apply to materials compiled for law enforcement purposes which are exempt from disclosure under section eighty-seven of the public officers law.

### CROSS REFERENCES

See **D.R.L. § 236 Part B(4)** in Appendix, *infra*, as to compulsory financial disclosure in matrimonial actions.

As to public access to government records, see **Public Officers Law, Article 6** (Freedom of information law) in Appendix, *infra*.

See **Judiciary Law § 148-a** in Appendix, *infra* regarding medical malpractice panels.

### 1993 AMENDMENTS

L. 1993, ch. 98, eff. Jan. 1, 1994, amended CPLR 3101(a) by making the section applicable to dentistry and podiatry and by making the section gender neutral; amended CPLR 3101(b) by replacing the word "party" with the words "person entitled to assert the privilege"; and added a new subdivision (h) addressing amendment or supplementation of a response previously given to a disclosure request.

L. 1993, ch. 574, eff. Sept. 1, 1993, added a new subdivision (i) to provide for comprehensive disclosure of all audio-visual materials involving any person designated in CPLR 3101(a)(1).

### 1991 AMENDMENTS

L. 1991, ch. 165, eff. Oct. 1, 1991, amended CPLR 3101(d)(1)(ii) by deleting the provision allowing a party to condition an offer to disclose an expert witness's name and make him available for deposition on all parties' waiving a hearing of the matter before the malpractice panel, and the provision specifying that if this offer was conditioned upon a waiver of the malpractice panel's hearing of the matter, the panel shall not be utilized. The October 1, 1991 effective date applies only to actions where, as of this date, the medical malpractice panel has not signed and forwarded to all parties a formal written recommendation concerning the question of liability.

### 1988 AMENDMENTS

L. 1988, ch. 184, eff. July 1, 1988, renumbered subparagraph (ii) as (iii), and added new subparagraph (ii) permitting consensual deposition of expert witnesses, in lieu of malpractice panel in medical, dental and podiatric actions.

### 1986 AMENDMENTS

L. 1986, ch. 485, eff. July 21, 1986, and applicable to acts, omissions or failures occurring on or after such date, amended CPLR 3101(d)(i) to provide that in actions for podiatric malpractice, a party responding to a request for pretrial disclosure of expert testimony may omit the names of podiatric experts; CPLR 3101(d)(ii) was amended to provide that in podiatric malpractice actions a party may, without court order, take the testimony of a person authorized to practice podiatry who is the party's treating or retained expert.

### 1985 AMENDMENTS

L. 1985, ch. 294, eff. July 1, 1985, and applicable to any actions commenced on or after that date, deleted former subdivision (d) and added a new subdivision (d).

### 1984 AMENDMENTS

L. 1984, ch. 294, eff. Sept. 1, 1984, amended CPLR 3101(a)(4) to provide for disclosure by any other person, upon notice stating the circumstances or reasons disclosure is sought.

### 1980 AMENDMENTS

L. 1980, ch. 283, eff. Sept. 1, 1980, added new subdivision (g).

### 1979 AMENDMENTS

L. 1979, ch. 268, eff. Jan. 1, 1980, amended CPLR 3101 subd. (a) par. 3 by providing for disclosure by "a person authorized to practice medicine who has provided medical care or diagnosis to the party demanding disclosure, or who has been retained by him as an expert witness."

The Judicial Conference Report to the 1979 Legislature noted that this amendment ". . . would liberalize the special circumstances' rule only with respect to the physicians specified. Thus, unavailability or special circumstances would still have to be shown to obtain the deposition of any physician who provided medical care or diagnosis to the adverse party or who has been retained as an expert witness by the adverse party. There is a strong judicial trend toward liberalizing the special circumstances' provision of CPLR 3101(a). In Villano v. Conde Nast Publications, Inc., 361 N.Y.S.2d 351, 46 A.D.2d 118 (1st Dept. 1973) the defendant moved to examine the plaintiff's treating physicians in an action for invasion of privacy, claiming special circumstances.' The Appellate Division reversed Special Term's denial of the motion, stating that a mere showing by the lawyer that he needs such witnesses' pre-trial depositions to prepare fully for the trial should suffice as a special circumstance.' There remains a need for statutory provision clearly permitting a party to take the deposition, without the necessity of showing special circumstances, of a person authorized to practice medicine who has provided medical care or diagnosis to that party, or who has been retained by him as an expert witness. This measure would supply just such a provision and thereby provide an additional and valuable tool for the trial lawyer. It would ease the burden on litigants, lawyers, courts and physicians, especially where shortages of physicians exist. Coupled with CPLR 3117(a)(4), it would reduce the expense of litigation occasioned by physicians personally testifying at trial."

### 1975 AMENDMENTS

L. 1975, ch. 668, eff. Aug. 6, 1975, amended CPLR 3101 by adding a new Subd. (f), providing for disclosure of the contents of insurance agreements.

## § 3102. Method of obtaining disclosure.

(a) Disclosure devices. Information is obtainable by one or more of the following disclosure devices: depositions upon oral questions or without the state upon written questions, interrogatories, demands for addresses, discovery and inspection of documents or property, physical and mental examinations of persons, and requests for admission.

(b) Stipulation or notice normal method. Unless otherwise provided by the civil practice law and rules, or by the court, disclosure shall be obtained by stipulation or on notice without leave of the court.

(c) Before action commenced. Before an action is commenced, disclosure to aid in bringing an action, to preserve information or to aid in arbitration, may be obtained, but only by court order. The court may appoint a referee to take testimony.

(d) After trial commenced. Except as provided in section 5223, during and after trial, disclosure may be obtained only by order of the trial court on notice.

(e) Action pending in another jurisdiction. When under any mandate, writ or commission issued out of any court of record in any other state, territory, district or foreign jurisdiction, or whenever upon notice or agreement, it is required to take the testimony of a witness in the state, he may be compelled to appear and testify in the same manner and by the same process as may be employed for the purpose of taking testimony in actions pending in the state. The supreme court or a county court shall make any appropriate order in aid of taking such a deposition.

(f) Action to which state is party. In an action in which the state is properly a party, whether as plaintiff, defendant or otherwise, disclosure by the state shall be available as if the state were a private person.

### CROSS REFERENCES

As to public access to government records, see **Public Officers Law, Article 6** (Freedom of information law) in Appendix, *infra*.

### 1993 AMENDMENTS

L. 1993, ch. 98, eff. Jan. 1, 1994, amended CPLR 3102(c) to eliminate the requirement that a copy of any deposition that was obtained before an action was commenced, and that was intended for use in an action involving title to realty, be recorded, and amended CPLR 3102(f) by deleting the disclosure exception for interrogatories and requests for admissions.

### 1984 AMENDMENTS

L. 1984, ch. 294, eff. Sept. 1, 1984, amended CPLR 3102(f) by eliminating the provision that disclosure by the state may be obtained only by order of the court in which the action is pending.

### 1967 AMENDMENTS

L. 1967, ch. 638, eff. July 1, 1967, amended caption and text of Subd. (f) to permit adverse party to obtain disclosure against state in any action to which state is properly a party, upon court order, excepting interrogatories and requests for admissions. Formerly, Subd. (f) specified that "In an action in the court of claims, disclosure may be obtained only by order of that court."

### 1964 AMENDMENTS

L. 1964, ch. 388, eff. Sept. 1, 1964, made mechanical corrections.

## § 3103. Protective orders.

(a) Prevention of abuse. The court may at any time on its own initiative, or on motion of any party or of any person from whom discovery is sought, make a protective order denying, limiting, conditioning or regulating the use of any disclosure device. Such order shall be designed to prevent unreasonable annoyance, expense, embarrassment, disadvantage, or other prejudice to any person or the courts.

(b) Suspension of disclosure pending application for protective order. Service of a notice of motion for a protective order shall suspend disclosure of the particular matter in dispute.

(c) Suppression of information improperly obtained. If any disclosure under this article has been improperly or irregularly obtained so that a substantial right of a party is prejudiced, the court, on motion, may make an appropriate order, including an order that the information be suppressed.

**1993 AMENDMENTS**

L. 1993, ch. 98, eff. Jan. 1, 1994, amended CPLR 3103(a) by replacing the word "witness" with the words "of any person from whom discovery is sought."

## § 3104. Supervision of disclosure.

(a) Motion for, and extent of, supervision of disclosure. Upon the motion of any party or witness on notice to all parties or on its own initiative without notice, the court in which an action is pending may by one of its judges or a referee supervise all or part of any disclosure procedure.

(b) Selection of referee. A judicial hearing officer may be designated as a referee under this section, or the court may permit all of the parties in an action to stipulate that a named attorney may act as referee. In such latter event the stipulation shall provide for payment of his fees which shall, unless otherwise agreed, be taxed as disbursements.

(c) Powers of referee; motions referred to person supervising disclosure. A referee under this section shall have all the powers of the court under this article except the power to relieve himself of his duties, to appoint a successor, or to adjudge any person guilty of contempt. All motions or applications made under this article shall be returnable before the judge or referee, designated under this section and after disposition, if requested by any party, his order shall be filed in the office of the clerk.

(d) Review of order of referee. Any party or witness may apply for review of an order made under this section by a referee. The application shall be by motion made in the court in which the action is pending within five days after the order is made. Service of a notice of motion for review shall suspend disclosure of the particular matter in dispute. If the question raised by the motion may affect the rights of a witness, notice shall be served on him personally or by mail at his last known address. It shall set forth succinctly the order complained of, the reason it is objectionable and the relief demanded.

(e) Payment of expenses of referee. Except where a judicial hearing officer has been designated a referee hereunder, the court may make an appropriate order for the payment of the reasonable expenses of the referee.

**1983 AMENDMENTS**

L. 1983, ch. 840, eff. April 1, 1983, amended CPLR 3104(b) and (e).

**1963 AMENDMENTS**

L. 1963, ch. 307, eff. Sept. 1, 1963, amended CPLR 3104(d) by adding: "Service of a notice of motion for review shall suspend disclosure of the particular matter in dispute."

## R 3105. Notice to party in default.

When a party is in default for failure to appear, he shall not be entitled to notice or service of any copy required under this article.

## R 3106. Priority of depositions; witnesses; prisoners; designation of deponent.

(a) Normal priority. After an action is commenced, any party may take the testimony of any person by deposition upon oral or written questions. Leave of the court, granted on motion, shall be obtained if notice of the taking of the deposition of a party is served by the plaintiff before that party's time for serving a responsive pleading has expired.

(b) Witnesses. Where the person to be examined is not a party or a person who at the time of taking the deposition is an officer, director, member or employee of a party, he shall be served with a subpoena. Unless the court orders otherwise, on motion with or without notice, such subpoena shall be served at least twenty days before the examination. Where a motion for a protective order against such an examination is made, the witness shall be notified by the moving party that the examination is stayed.

(c) Prisoners. The deposition of a person confined under legal process may be taken only by leave of the court.

(d) Designation of deponent. A party desiring to take the deposition of a particular officer, director, member or employee of a person shall include in the notice or subpoena served upon such person the identity, description or title of such individual. Such person shall produce the individual so designated unless they shall have, no later than ten days prior to the scheduled deposition, notified the requesting party that another individual would instead be produced and the identity, description or title of such individual is specified. If timely notification has been so given, such other individual shall instead be produced.

### 1985 AMENDMENTS

L. 1985, ch. 327, eff. July 11, 1985, amended CPLR 3106(d) to change the first sentence to read "notice or subpoena."

### 1984 AMENDMENTS

L. 1984, ch. 294, eff. Sept. 1, 1984, amended subdivisions (a) and (b) and added subdivision (d).

## R 3107. Notice of taking oral questions.

A party desiring to take the deposition of any person upon oral examination shall give to each party twenty days' notice, unless the court orders otherwise. The notice shall be in writing, stating the time and place for taking the deposition, the name and address of each person to be examined, if known, and, if any name is not known, a general description sufficient to identify him or the particular class or group to which he belongs. The notice need not enumerate the matters upon which the person is to be examined. A party to be examined pursuant to notice served by another party may serve notice of at least ten days for the examination of any other party, his agent or employee, such examination to be noticed for and to follow at the same time and place.

### CROSS REFERENCES

Restrictions on the taking of a deposition under this section, together with the service of written interrogatories, are dealt with in **CPLR 3130**, *infra.*

### 1984 AMENDMENTS

L. 1984, ch. 294, eff. Sept. 1, 1984, amended CPLR 3107 by increasing the notice of oral deposition to 20 days and increasing the notice for examination of any other party at the same time and place to 10 days.

### 1964 AMENDMENTS

L. 1964, ch. 388, eff. Sept. 1, 1964, made mechanical corrections.

## R 3108. Written questions; when permitted.

A deposition may be taken on written questions when the examining party and the deponent so stipulate or when the testimony is to be taken without the state. A commission or letters rogatory may be issued where necessary or convenient for the taking of a deposition outside of the state.

## R 3109. Notice of taking deposition on written questions.

(a) Notice of taking; service of questions and cross-questions. A party desiring to take the deposition of any person upon written questions shall serve such questions upon each party together with a notice stating the name and address of the person to be examined, if known, and, if the name is not known, a general description sufficient to identify him or the particular class or group to which he belongs, and the name or descriptive title and address of the officer before whom the deposition is to be taken. Within fifteen days thereafter a party so served may serve written cross-questions upon each party. Within seven days thereafter the original party may serve written redirect questions upon each party. Within five days after being served with written redirect questions, a party may serve written recross-questions upon each party.

(b) Officer asking written questions. A copy of the notice and copies of all written questions served shall be delivered by the party taking the deposition to the officer designated in the notice. The officer shall proceed promptly to take the testimony of the witness in response to the written questions and to prepare the deposition.

### 1984 AMENDMENTS

L. 1984, ch. 294, eff. Sept. 1, 1984, amended CPLR 3107(a) by increasing the time for service of cross-questions, redirect questions and recross-questions.

## R 3110. Where the deposition is to be taken within the state.

A deposition within the state on notice shall be taken:

1. when the person to be examined is a party or an officer, director, member or employee of a party, within the county in which he resides or has an office

for the regular transaction of business in person or where the action is pending; or

2. when any other person to be examined is a resident, within the county in which he resides, is regularly employed or has an office for the regular transaction of business in person, or if he is not a resident, within the county in which he is served, is regularly employed or has an office for the regular transaction of business in person; or

3. when the party to be examined is a public corporation or any officer, agent or employee thereof, within the county in which the action is pending; the place of such examination shall be the office of any of the attorneys for such a public corporation or any officer, agent or authorized employee thereof unless the parties stipulate otherwise.

For the purpose of this rule New York city shall be considered one county.

### 1994 AMENDMENTS

L. 1994, ch. 603, eff. Oct. 1, 1994, amended CPLR 3110(3) by deleting the words "in the court in which the action is pending" and replacing them with the words "the office of any of the attorneys for such a public corporation or any officer, agent or authorized employee thereof."

## R 3111.  Production of things at the examination.

The notice or subpoena may require the production of books, papers and other things in the possession, custody or control of the person to be examined to be marked as exhibits, and used on the examination. The reasonable production expenses of a non-party witness shall be defrayed by the party seeking discovery.

### 1994 AMENDMENTS

L. 1994, ch. 100, eff. May 16, 1994, amended by adding the final sentence providing for the payment of expenses to a non-party who is required to produce items to be used at an examination.

## R 3112.  Errors in notice for taking depositions.

All errors and irregularities in the notice for taking a deposition are waived unless at least three days before the time for taking the deposition written objection is served upon the party giving the notice.

## R 3113.  Conduct of the examination.

(a) Persons before whom depositions may be taken. Depositions may be taken before any of the following persons except an attorney, or employee of an attorney, for a party or prospective party and except a person who would be disqualified to act as a juror because of interest in the event of consanguinity or affinity to a party:

1. within the state, a person authorized by the laws of the state to administer oaths;

2. without the state but within the United States or within a territory or possession subject to the jurisdiction of the United States, a person authorized to take acknowledgments of deeds outside of the state by the real property law of the state or to administer oaths by the laws of the United States or of the place where the deposition is taken; and

3. in a foreign country, any diplomatic or consular agent or representative of the United States, appointed or accredited to, and residing within, the country, or a person appointed by commission or under letters rogatory, or an officer of the armed forces authorized to take the acknowledgment of deeds.

Officers may be designated in notices or commissions either by name or descriptive title and letters rogatory may be addressed "To the Appropriate Authority in (here name the state or country)."

(b) Oath of witness; recording of testimony; objections; continuous examination; written questions read by examining officer. The officer before whom the deposition is to be taken shall put the witness on oath and shall personally, or by someone acting under his direction, record the testimony. The testimony shall be recorded by stenographic or other means, subject to such rules as may be adopted by the appellate division in the department where the action is pending. All objections made at the time of the examination to the qualifications of the officer taking the deposition or the person recording it, or to the manner of taking it, or to the testimony presented, or to the conduct of any person, and any other objection to the proceedings, shall be noted by the officer upon the deposition and the deposition shall proceed subject to the right of a person to apply for a protective order. The deposition shall be taken continuously and without unreasonable adjournment, unless the court otherwise orders or the witness and parties present otherwise agree. In lieu of participating in an oral examination, any party served with notice of taking a deposition may transmit written questions to the officer, who shall propound them to the witness and record the answers.

(c) Examination and cross-examination. Examination and cross-examination of deponents shall proceed as permitted in the trial of actions in open court. When the deposition of a party is taken at the instance of an adverse party, the deponent may be cross-examined by his own attorney. Cross-examination need not be limited to the subject matter of the examination in chief.

CROSS REFERENCES

Real Property Law provisions authorizing the taking of acknowledgments of deeds, referred to in paragraph (2) of Subd. (a), *supra*, may be found in **Real Prop. L. § 298**, *et seq.*, in Appendix, *infra*.

The following rules apply to the use of electronic recording of depositions in civil cases:

New York and Bronx Counties, 22 N.Y.C.R.R. § 660.25;

Second Department, 22 N.Y.C.R.R. § 685, 685.1–685.12;

CPLR

Third Department, 22 N.Y.C.R.R. § 830.1–830.12;
Fourth Department, 22 N.Y.C.R.R. § 1030.1–1030.11.

### 1993 AMENDMENTS

L. 1993, ch. 98, eff. Jan. 1, 1994, amended CPLR 3113(a)(2) by replacing the word "dominion" with the word "jurisdiction".

### 1977 AMENDMENTS

CPLR 3113(b) was amended by proposal No. 1 of the Judicial Conference, in its Report to the 1977 Legislature, eff. Sept. 1, 1977, to provide that recording of testimony at the examination may be by stenographic or other means. As explained by the 1977 Judicial Conference: "This measure would expressly permit testimony to be perpetuated on videotape."

## R 3114.  Examination of witness who does not understand the English language.

If the witness to be examined does not understand the English language, the examining party must, at his own expense, provide a translation of all questions and answers. Where the court settles questions, it may settle them in the foreign language and in English. It may use the services of one or more experts whose compensation shall be paid by the party seeking the examination and may be taxed as a disbursement.

## R 3115.  Objections to qualification of person taking deposition; competency; questions and answers.

(a) Objection when deposition offered in evidence. Subject to the other provisions of this rule, objection may be made at the trial or hearing to receiving in evidence any deposition or part thereof for any reason which would require the exclusion of the evidence if the witness were then present and testifying.

(b) Errors which might be obviated if made known promptly. Errors and irregularities occurring at the oral examination in the manner of taking the deposition, in the form of the questions or answers, in the oath or affirmation, or in the conduct of persons, and errors of any kind which might be obviated or removed if objection were promptly presented, are waived unless reasonable objection thereto is made at the taking of the deposition.

(c) Disqualification of person taking deposition. Objection to the taking of a deposition because of disqualification of the person by whom it is to be taken is waived unless made before the taking of the deposition begins or as soon thereafter as the disqualification becomes known or could be discovered with reasonable diligence.

(d) Competency of witnesses or admissibility of testimony. Objections to the competency of a witness or to the admissibility of testimony are not waived by failure to make them before or during the taking of the deposition, unless the ground of the objection is one which might have been obviated or removed if objection had been made at that time.

(e) Form of written questions. Objections to the form of written questions are waived unless served in writing upon the party propounding the questions within the time allowed for serving succeeding questions or within three days after service.

### R 3116. Signing deposition; physical preparation; copies.

(a)* Signing. The deposition shall be submitted to the witness for examination and shall be read to or by him or her, and any changes in form or substance which the witness desires to make shall be entered at the end of the deposition with a statement of the reasons given by the witness for making them. The deposition shall then be signed by the witness before any officer authorized to administer an oath. If the witness fails to sign and return the deposition within sixty days, it may be used as fully as though signed. No changes to the transcript may be made by the witness more than sixty days after submission to the witness for examination.

> *[**Editor's note:** This version of R 3116(a) is effective as of January 1, 1997. Through December 31, 1996, former R 3116(a) remains in effect. It reads as follows:
>
> (a) Signing. The deposition shall be submitted to the witness for examination and shall be read to or by him or her, and any changes in form or substance which the witness desires to make shall be entered at the end of the deposition with a statement of the reasons given by the witness for making them. The deposition shall then be signed by the witness before any officer authorized to administer an oath. If the witness fails to sign the deposition, it may be used as fully as though signed.]

(b) Certification and filing by officer. The officer before whom the deposition was taken shall certify on the deposition that the witness was duly sworn by him and that the deposition is a true record of the testimony given by the witness. He shall list all appearances by the parties and attorneys. If the deposition was taken on written questions, he shall attach to it the copy of the notice and written questions received by him. He shall then securely seal the deposition in an envelope endorsed with the title of the action and the index number of the action, if one has been assigned, and marked "Deposition of (here insert name of witness)" and shall promptly file it with, or send it by registered or certified mail to the clerk of the court where the case is to be tried. The deposition shall always be open to the inspection of the parties, each of whom is entitled to make copies thereof. If a copy of the deposition is furnished to each party or if the parties stipulate to waive filing, the officer need not file the original but may deliver it to the party taking the deposition.

(c) Exhibits. Documentary evidence exhibited before the officer or exhibits marked for identification during the examination of the witness shall be annexed to and returned with the deposition. However, if requested by the party producing documentary evidence or an exhibit, the officer shall mark it for identification as an exhibit in the case, give each party an opportunity to copy or inspect it, and return it to the party offering it, and it may then be used in the same manner as if annexed to and returned with the deposition.

CPLR

(d) Expenses of taking. Unless the court orders otherwise, the party taking the deposition shall bear the expense thereof.

(e) Errors of officer or person transcribing. Errors and irregularities of the officer or the person transcribing the deposition are waived unless a motion to suppress the deposition or some part thereof is made with reasonable promptness after such defect is, or with due diligence might have been, ascertained.

### 1996 AMENDMENTS

L. 1996, ch. 117, eff. Jan. 1, 1997, amended subdivision (a) to add to the third sentence the phrases "and return" and "within sixty days"; and to add a new final sentence.

### 1993 AMENDMENTS

L. 1993, ch. 98, eff. Jan. 1, 1994, amended CPLR 3116(a) to simplify and reform the procedure relating to the signing of depositions.

### 1978 AMENDMENTS

L. 1978, ch. 292, eff. Sept. 1, 1978, amended subdivision (a), setting forth separate requirements as to signing of the deposition when the witness is an adverse party.

The Governor's memorandum of approval stated in part:

"This bill is designed to expedite preparation for trial and to minimize the effect of dilatory practices of an adverse party witness who refuses to sign and return a deposition.

"Specifically, the bill would provide that if a deposition is forwarded to a witness who is an adverse party and that witness is given 30 days written notice to return the deposition signed, if the witness fails to so return the deposition, the deposition may then be used as fully as though signed."

### 1966 AMENDMENTS

Amendment No. 1, eff. Sept. 1, 1966, made by the Judicial Conference Feb. 1, 1966, Report to the Legislature, amended Subd. (a).

## R 3117. Use of depositions.

(a) Impeachment of witnesses; parties; unavailable witnesses. At the trial or upon the hearing of a motion or an interlocutory proceeding, any part or all of a deposition, so far as admissible under the rules of evidence, may be used in accordance with any of the following provisions:

1. any deposition may be used by any party for the purpose of contradicting or impeaching the testimony of the deponent as a witness;

2.* the deposition testimony of a party or of any person who was a party when the testimony was given or of any person who at the time the testimony was given was an officer, director, member, employee or managing or authorized agent of a party, may be used for any purpose by any party who was adversely interested when the deposition testimony was given or who is adversely interested when the deposition testimony is offered in evidence;

* [**Editor's note:** This version of R 3117(a)(2) is effective as of January 1, 1997. Through December 31, 1996, former R 3117(a)(2) remains in effect. It reads as follows:

2. the deposition of a party or of any one who at the time of taking the deposition was an officer, director, member, or managing or authorized agent of a party, or the deposition of an employee of a party produced at the taking of the deposition by that party, may be used for any purpose by any adversely interested party;]

3. the deposition of any person may be used by any party for any purpose against any other party who was present or represented at the taking of the deposition or who had the notice required under these rules, provided the court finds:

(i) that the witness is dead; or

(ii) that the witness is at a greater distance than one hundred miles from the place of trial or is out of the state, unless it appears that the absence of the witness was procured by the party offering the deposition; or

(iii) that the witness is unable to attend or testify because of age, sickness, infirmity, or imprisonment; or

(iv) that the party offering the deposition has been unable to procure the attendance of the witness by diligent efforts; or

(v) upon motion or notice, that such exceptional circumstances exist as to make its use desirable, in the interest of justice and with due regard to the importance of presenting the testimony of witnesses orally in open court;

4. the deposition of a person authorized to practice medicine may be used by any party without the necessity of showing unavailability or special circumstances, subject to the right of any party to move pursuant to section 3103 to prevent abuse.

(b) Use of part of deposition. If only part of a deposition is read at the trial by a party, any other party may read any other part of the deposition which ought in fairness to be considered in connection with the part read.

(c) Substitution of parties; prior actions. Substitution of parties does not affect the right to use depositions previously taken. When an action has been brought in any court of any state or of the United States and another action involving the same subject matter is afterward brought between the same parties or their representatives or successors in interest all depositions taken in the former action may be used in the latter as if taken therein.

(d) Effect of using deposition. A party shall not be deemed to make a person his own witness for any purpose by taking his deposition. The introduction in evidence of the deposition or any part thereof for any purpose other than that of contradicting or impeaching the deponent makes the deponent the witness of the party introducing the deposition, but this shall not apply to the use of a deposition as described in paragraph two of subdivision (a). At the trial, any party may rebut any relevant evidence contained in a deposition, whether introduced by him or by any other party.

CPLR

## 1996 AMENDMENTS

L. 1996, ch. 117, eff. Jan. 1, 1997, amended subparagraph (a)(2) by adding the word "testimony" following "the deposition" at the beginning of the subparagraph; by adding the phrase "or of any person who at the time the testimony was given" following the phrase "of a party"; by replacing the phrase "or any one" to "of any person"; by replacing the phrase "of taking the deposition" with "the testimony was given"; by adding "employee" to the list of persons giving testimony and deleting "or the deposition of an employee of a party produced at the taking of the deposition by that party"; and by deleting the phrase "adversely interested" and adding the phrase "who is adversely interested when the deposition testimony is offered in evidence" at the end of the subparagraph.

## 1993 AMENDMENTS

L. 1993, ch. 86, eff. June 1, 1993, amended CPLR 3117(a)(2) by adding the words "at the taking of the deposition."

## 1979 AMENDMENTS

L. 1979, ch. 268, eff. Jan. 1, 1980, amended CPLR 3117 subd. (a) par. 4 by eliminating the words "medical witness" and substituting the phrase "person authorized to practice medicine."

## 1977 AMENDMENTS

CPLR 3117(a) was amended by proposal No. 2 of the Judicial Conference in its Report to the 1977 Legislature, eff. Sept. 1, 1977, by the addition of paragraph (4), permitting use of a deposition of a medical witness by any party without a showing of unavailability or special circumstances.

The 1977 Judicial Conference noted in part:

"The term medical witness' as used in the proposed amendment is intended to apply to a medical witness other than one who is a party to the action, as the context of the subdivision clearly indicates. The rules governing the use of depositions of parties are contained in paragraph 2 of subdivision (a) of this section and would, of course, govern the deposition of a party who also happened to be a medical person."

## R 3118.   Demand for address of party or of person who possessed an assigned cause of action or defense.

A party may serve on any party a written notice demanding a verified statement setting forth the post office address and residence of the party, of any specified officer or member of the party and of any person who possessed a cause of action or defense asserted in the action which has been assigned. The demand shall be complied with within ten days of its service.

## R 3119.   [Not used].

## R 3120.   Discovery and production of documents and things for inspection, testing, copying or photographing.

(a) As against party:

1. After commencement of an action, any party may serve on any other party notice:

(i) to produce and permit the party seeking discovery, or someone acting on his or her behalf, to inspect, copy, test or photograph any designated documents or any things which are in the possession, custody or control of the party served; or

(ii) to permit entry upon designated land or other property in the possession, custody or control of the party served for the purpose of inspecting, measuring, surveying, sampling, testing, photographing or recording by motion pictures or otherwise the property or any specifically designated object or operation thereon.

2. The notice shall specify the time, which shall be not less than twenty days after service of the notice, and the place and manner of making the inspection, copy, test, or photograph, or of the entry upon the land or other property and, in the case of an inspection, copying, testing or photographing, shall set forth the items to be inspected, copied, tested or photographed by individual item or by category, and shall describe each item and category with reasonable particularity.

(b) As against non-party. A person not a party may be directed by order to do whatever a party may be directed to do under subdivision (a). The motion for such order shall be on notice to all adverse parties; the non-party shall be served with the notice of motion in the same manner as a summons. The order shall contain, in addition to such specifications as the notice is required to contain under paragraph two of subdivision (a), provision for the defraying of the expenses of the non-party.

CPLR

### CROSS REFERENCES

As to public access to government records, see **Public Officers Law, Article 6** (Freedom of information law) in Appendix, *infra*.

### 1993 AMENDMENTS

L. 1993, ch. 98, eff. Jan. 1, 1994, amended CPLR 3120(a)(1) by eliminating the requirement that the notice to produce documents specifically identify the documents being requested, and amended 3120(a)(2) to provide that a notice to produce may identify the items sought either individually or by category.

### 1984 AMENDMENTS

L. 1984, ch. 294, eff. Sept. 1, 1984, amended CPLR 3120(a)(2) by providing that the time to be specified on the notice of inspection shall be not less than 20 days after service of the notice.

### 1966 AMENDMENTS

Amendment No. 2, eff. Sept. 1, 1966, made by the Judicial Conference Feb. 1, 1966, Report to the Legislature. " The proposed amendment would make it clear that full discovery of documents and things is available against a non-party witness, by court order. This would appear to be in accord with the intent of the revisers. The burden on the non-party witness is minimized by the requirement that the order provide for the defraying of his expenses. As a protection to the non-party the notice of motion would be required to be served in the same manner as a summons."

## § 3121.  Physical or mental examination.

(a) Notice of examination. After commencement of an action in which the mental or physical condition or the blood relationship of a party, or of an agent, employee or person in the custody or under the legal control of a party, is in controversy, any party may serve notice on another party to submit to a physical, mental or blood examination by a designated physician, or to produce for such examination his agent, employee or the person in his custody or under his legal control. The notice may require duly executed and acknowledged written authorizations permitting all parties to obtain, and make copies of, the records of specified hospitals relating to such mental or physical condition or blood relationship; where a party obtains a copy of a hospital record as a result of the authorization of another party, he shall deliver a duplicate of the copy to such party. A copy of the notice shall be served on the person to be examined. It shall specify the time, which shall be not less than twenty days after service of the notice, and the conditions and scope of the examination.

(b) Copy of report. A copy of a detailed written report of the examining physician setting out his findings and conclusions shall be delivered by the party seeking the examination to any party requesting to exchange therefor a copy of each report in his control of an examination made with respect to the mental or physical condition in controversy.

### 1984 AMENDMENTS

L. 1984, ch. 294, eff. Sept. 1, 1984, amended CPLR 3121(a) by providing that the time to be specified on the notice of physical or mental examination shall be not less than 20 days after service of the notice.

## R 3122.  Objection to disclosure, inspection or examination; compliance.

(a) Within twenty days of service of a notice under rule 3120 or section 3121, the party to whom the notice is directed, if that party objects to the disclosure, inspection or examination, shall serve a response which shall state with reasonable particularity the reasons for each objection. If objection is made to part of an item or category, the part shall be specified. The party seeking disclosure under rule 3120 or section 3121 may move for an order under rule 3124 with respect to any objection to, or other failure to respond to or permit inspection as requested by, the notice or any part thereof.

(b) Whenever a person is required pursuant to such a notice or order to produce documents for inspection, and where such person withholds one or more documents that appear to be within the category of the documents required by the notice or order to be produced, such person shall give notice to the party seeking the production and inspection of the documents that one or more such documents are being withheld. This notice shall indicate the legal ground for withholding each such document, and shall provide the following information as to each such document, unless the party withholding the document states that divulgence of such information would cause disclosure of the allegedly privileged information: (1) the type of document; (2) the general subject matter of the document; (3) the date of the document; and (4) such other information as is sufficient to identify the document for a subpoena duces tecum.

### 1993 AMENDMENTS

L. 1993, ch. 98, eff. Jan. 1, 1994, amended CPLR 3122(a) to modify the procedure to be followed by a party who objects to a disclosure request. The time limit within which a party who is served with a disclosure request under CPLR 3120 or CPLR 3121 must raise an objection was increased from 10 to 20 days. Also, the method for raising an objection was fundamentally altered: instead of moving for a protective order, the objecting party need only serve upon the party seeking disclosure a response stating the reasons for each objection with "reasonable particularity." Additionally, 3122(b) was added to set forth the method by which a party who declines to produce some or all of the documents described in a disclosure request must notify the party seeking the disclosure of the basis upon which material has been withheld.

### 1979 AMENDMENTS

L. 1979, ch. 80, eff. Sept. 1, 1979, amended CPLR 3122 by changing the time within which a party may serve a notice of motion for a protective order from 5 to 10 days from the date of service of notice under CPLR 3120 or 3121.

The Judicial Conference Report on the CPLR to the 1979 Legislature noted that the five day time period was unrealistic and burdensome, and that: ". . . The frequently expressed objection of the bar to the unworkable shortness of the time period of CPLR 3122, and the growing number of judicial decisions granting relaxation thereof, is compelling reason for immediate extension of that time period, as proposed in this bill."

## § 3123. Admissions as to matters of fact, papers, documents and photographs.

(a) Notice to admit; admission unless denied or denial excused. At any time after service of the answer or after the expiration of twenty days from service of the summons, whichever is sooner, and not later than twenty days before the trial, a party may serve upon any other party a written request for admission by the latter of the genuineness of any papers or documents, or the correctness or fairness of representation of any photographs, described in and served with the request, or of the truth of any matters of fact set forth in the request, as to which the party requesting the admission reasonably believes there can be no substantial dispute at the trial and which are within the knowledge of such other party or can be ascertained by him upon reasonable inquiry. Copies of the papers, documents or photographs shall be served with the request unless copies have already been furnished. Each of the matters of which an admission is requested shall be deemed admitted unless within twenty days after service thereof or within such further time as the court may allow, the party to whom the request is directed serves upon the party requesting the admission a sworn statement either denying specifically the matters of which an admission is requested or setting forth in detail the reasons why he cannot truthfully either admit or deny those matters. If the matters of which an admission is requested cannot be fairly admitted without some material qualification or explanation, or if the matters constitute a trade secret or such party would be privileged or disqualified from testifying as a witness concerning them, such party may, in lieu of a denial or statement, serve a sworn statement setting forth in detail his claim and, if the claim is that the matters cannot be fairly admitted without some material qualification or explanation, admitting the matters with such qualification or explanation.

(b) Effect of admission. Any admission made, or deemed to be made, by a party pursuant to a request made under this rule is for the purpose of the pending action only and does not constitute an admission by him for any other purpose nor may it be used against him in any other proceeding; and the court, at any time, may allow a party to amend or withdraw any admission on such terms as may be just. Any admission shall be subject to all pertinent objections to admissibility which may be interposed at the trial.

(c) Penalty for unreasonable denial. If a party, after being served with a request under subdivision (a) does not admit and if the party requesting the admission thereafter proves the genuineness of any such paper or document, or the correctness or fairness of representation of any such photograph, or the truth of any such matter of fact, he may move at or immediately following the trial for an order requiring the other party to pay him the reasonable expenses incurred in making such proof, including reasonable attorney's fees. Unless the court finds that there were good reasons for the denial or the refusal otherwise to admit or that the admissions sought were of no substantial importance, the order shall be made irrespective of the result of the action. Upon a trial by jury, the motion for such an order shall be determined by the court outside the presence of the jury.

## R 3124. Failure to disclose; motion to compel disclosure.

If a person fails to respond to or comply with any request, notice, interrogatory, demand, question or order under this article, except a notice to admit under section 3123, the party seeking disclosure may move to compel compliance or a response.

### 1993 AMENDMENTS

L. 1993, ch. 98, eff. Jan. 1, 1994, added this section, replacing former CPLR 3124.

## R 3125. Place where motion to compel disclosure made.

Unless otherwise provided by rule of the chief administrator of the courts, the county in which a deposition is being taken or an examination or inspection is being sought may be treated by the moving party as the county in which the action is pending for purposes of section 3124.

**1986 AMENDMENTS**

L. 1986, ch. 355, eff. July 17, 1986, amended CPLR 3125 by adding the phrase "Unless otherwise provided by rule of the chief administrator of the courts" to the beginning of the paragraph.

## § 3126. Penalties for refusal to comply with order or to disclose.

If any party, or a person who at the time a deposition is taken or an examination or inspection is made, is an officer, director, member, employee or agent of a party or otherwise under a party's control, refuses to obey an order for disclosure or wilfully fails to disclose information which the court finds ought to have been disclosed, pursuant to this article, the court may make such orders with regard to the failure or refusal as are just, among them:

1. an order that issues to which the information is relevant shall be deemed resolved for purposes of the action in accordance with the claims of the party obtaining the order; or

2. an order prohibiting the disobedient party from supporting or opposing designated claims or defenses, from producing in evidence designated things or items of testimony, or from introducing any evidence of the physical, mental or blood condition sought to be determined, or from using certain witnesses; or

3. an order striking out pleadings or parts thereof, or staying further proceedings until the order is obeyed, or dismissing the action or any part thereof, or rendering a judgment by default against the disobedient party.

**1993 AMENDMENTS**

L. 1993, ch. 98, eff. Jan. 1, 1994, replaced the words "notice duly served" with the words "this article" in the opening paragraph of the section.

**1978 AMENDMENTS**

L. 1978, ch. 42, eff. April 4, 1978, amended the opening paragraph by adding the words "pursuant to notice duly served," thus eliminating any ambiguity as to the applicability of the section to those instances where disclosure is sought upon notice, without court order.

## §§ 3127-3129. [Not used].

## § 3130. Use of interrogatories.

1. Except as otherwise provided herein, after commencement of an action, any party may serve upon any other party written interrogatories. Except in a matrimonial action, a party may not serve written interrogatories on another party and also demand a bill of particulars of the same party pursuant to section 3041. In the case of an action to recover damages for personal injury, injury to property or wrongful death predicated solely on a cause or causes of action for negligence, a party shall not be permitted to serve interrogatories on and conduct a deposition of the same party pursuant to rule 3107 without leave of court.

2. After the commencement of a matrimonial action or proceeding, upon motion brought by either party, upon such notice to the other party and to the non-party from whom financial disclosure is sought, and given in such manner as the court shall direct, the court may order a non-party to respond under oath to written interrogatories limited to furnishing financial information concerning a party, and further provided such information is both reasonable and necessary in the prosecution or the defense of such matrimonial action or proceeding.

### 1986 AMENDMENTS

L. 1986, ch. 257, eff. Sept. 1, 1986, amended subdivision (1) to except matrimonial actions from prohibition against service of written interrogatories and demand for bill of particulars upon same party, and L. 1986, ch. 467, eff. Aug. 20, 1986 (which amended CPLR 3130(1) without incorporating changes made by L. 1986, ch. 257), to provide that in actions to recover damages for personal injury, injury to property or wrongful death predicated solely on a cause of action for negligence, parties cannot serve interrogatories on or conduct depositions of the same party pursuant to CPLR 3107 without leave of court.

### 1983 AMENDMENTS

L. 1983, ch. 275, eff. July 10, 1983, amended CPLR 3130 by designating the opening paragraph subd. (1) and adding a new subd. (2).

### 1979 AMENDMENTS

L. 1979, ch. 197, eff. Sept. 1, 1979, amended CPLR 3130 ". . . to remove the prohibition on the use of interrogatories in actions to recover damages for an injury to property or personal injury resulting from negligence, or in wrongful death actions. . . . [I]n addition, the bill adds a requirement that in an action to recover damages for injury to property or personal injury resulting from negligence or in a wrongful death action, a party may not demand both interrogatories and an oral deposition without leave of the court." For additional information, see Governor's Memorandum filed with Assembly Bill 555/B.

## § 3131.　Scope of interrogatories.

Interrogatories may relate to any matters embraced in the disclosure requirement of section 3101 and the answers may be used to the same extent as the depositions of a party. Interrogatories may require copies of such papers, documents or photographs as are relevant to the answers required, unless opportunity for this examination and copying be afforded.

### 1975 AMENDMENTS

L. 1975, ch. 859, eff. Sept. 8, 1975, amended the second sentence by adding the word, "papers," prior to the phrase "documents or photographs".

## R 3132.　Service of interrogatories.

After commencement of an action, any party may serve written interrogatories upon any other party. Interrogatories may not be served upon a defendant before that defendant's time for serving a responsive pleading has expired, except by leave of court granted with or without notice. A copy of the interrogatories and of any order made under this rule shall be served on each party.

### 1993 AMENDMENTS

L. 1993, ch. 98, eff. Jan. 1, 1994, amended CPLR 3132 by modifying the time limits for serving interrogatories in certain cases. Leave of court is required when a plaintiff seeks to serve interrogatories upon a defendant whose time to answer has not expired.

### R 3133. Service of answers or objections to interrogatories.

(a) Service of an answer or objection. Within twenty days after service of interrogatories, the party upon whom they are served shall serve upon each of the parties a copy of the answer to each interrogatory, except one to which the party objects, in which event the reasons for the objection shall be stated with reasonable particularity.

(b) Form of answers and objections to interrogatories. Interrogatories shall be answered in writing under oath by the party served, if an individual, or, if the party served is a corporation, a partnership or a sole proprietorship, by an officer, director, member, agent or employee having the information. Each question shall be answered separately and fully, and each answer shall be preceded by the question to which it responds.

(c) Amended answers. Except with respect to amendment or supplementation of responses pursuant to subdivision (h) of section 3101, answers to interrogatories may be amended or supplemented only by order of the court upon motion.

### 1993 AMENDMENTS

L. 1993, ch. 98, eff. Jan. 1, 1994, amended CPLR 3133 to extend the time for responding to interrogatories from 10 to 20 days. A party who objects to answering an interrogatory need not move for an order to strike, but may instead simply set forth the objection to the interrogatory in the response.

### R 3134. [Repealed.]

### § 3140. Disclosure of appraisals in proceedings for condemnation, appropriation or review of tax assessments.

Notwithstanding the provisions of subdivisions (c) and (d) of section 3101, the chief administrator of the courts shall adopt rules governing the exchange of appraisal reports intended for use at the trial in proceedings for condemnation, appropriation or review of tax assessments.

### 1993 AMENDMENTS

L. 1993, ch. 98, eff. Jan. 1, 1994, amended CPLR 3140 to correct a typographical error and to replace the words "appellate division in each judicial department" with the words "chief administrator of the courts."

CPLR

## 1967 AMENDMENTS

L. 1967, ch. 640, eff. Sept. 1, 1967, added Section 3140 requiring appellate divisions to adopt rules governing the exchange of appraisal reports.

# ARTICLE 32

# ACCELERATED JUDGMENT

---

## SUMMARY OF ARTICLE

§ 3201.     Confession of judgment before default on certain installment contracts invalid.

§§ 3202–3210.   [Not used.]

R 3211.     Motion to dismiss.
  (a)  Motion to dismiss cause of action.
  (b)  Motion to dismiss defense.
  (c)  Evidence permitted; immediate trial; motion treated as one for summary judgment.
  (d)  Facts unavailable to opposing party.
  (e)  Number, time and waiver of objections; motion to plead over.
  (f)  Extension of time to plead.
  (g)  Standards for motions to dismiss in certain cases involving public petition and participation.
  (h)  Standards for motion to dismiss in certain cases involving licensed architects, engineers or landscape architects.

R 3212.     Motion for summary judgment.
  (a)  Time; kind of action.
  (b)  Supporting proof; grounds; relief to either party.
  (c)  Immediate trial.
  (d)  [Repealed.]
  (e)  Partial summary judgment; severance.
  (f)  Facts unavailable to opposing party.
  (g)  Limitation of issues of fact for trial.
  (h)  Standards for summary judgment in certain cases involving public petition and participation.
  (i)  Standards for summary judgment in certain cases involving licensed architects, engineers or landscape architects.

§ 3213.     Motion for summary judgment in lieu of complaint.

R 3214.     Motions heard by judge supervising disclosure; stay of disclosure.
  (a)  Judge supervising disclosure.
  (b)  Stay of disclosure.

§ 3215.     Default judgment.
  (a)  Default and entry.
  (b)  Procedure before court.
  (c)  Default not entered within one year.
  (d)  Multiple defendants.
  (e)  Place of application to court.
  (f)  Proof.

(g)  Notice.

(h)  Judgment for excess where counterclaim interposed.

(i)  Default judgment for failure to comply with stipulation of settlement.

R 3216.  Want of prosecution.

R 3217.  Voluntary discontinuance.

(a)  Without an order.

(b)  By order of court.

(c)  Effect of discontinuance.

§ 3218.  Judgment by confession.

(a)  Affidavit of defendant.

(b)  Entry of judgment.

(c)  Execution where the judgment is not all due.

(d)  Confession by joint debtors.

R 3219.  Tender.

R 3220.  Offer to liquidate damages conditionally.

R 3221.  Offer to compromise.

R 3222.  Action on submitted facts.

(a)  Commencement.

(b)  Subsequent proceedings.

---

## § 3201. Confession of judgment before default on certain installment contracts invalid.

Notwithstanding the provisions of section thirty-two hundred eighteen, no judgment by confession shall be entered on any affidavit which was executed prior to the time a default in the payment of an installment occurs in connection with the purchase of fifteen hundred dollars or less of any commodities for any use other than a commercial or business use upon any plan of deferred payments whereby the price or cost is payable in two or more installments. Any judgment entered in violation of this section is void and unenforceable.

## §§ 3202-3210.  [Not used.]

## R 3211.  Motion to dismiss.

(a) Motion to dismiss cause of action. A party may move for judgment dismissing one or more causes of action asserted against him on the ground that:

1. a defense is founded upon documentary evidence; or

2. the court has not jurisdiction of the subject matter of the cause of action; or

3. the party asserting the cause of action has not legal capacity to sue; or

4. there is another action pending between the same parties for the same cause of action in a court of any state or the United States; the court need not dismiss upon this ground but may make such order as justice requires; or

5. the cause of action may not be maintained because of arbitration and award, collateral estoppel, discharge in bankruptcy, infancy or other disability of the moving party, payment, release, res judicata, statute of limitations, or statute of frauds; or

6. with respect to a counterclaim, it may not properly be interposed in the action; or

7. the pleading fails to state a cause of action; or

8. the court has not jurisdiction of the person of the defendant; or

9. the court has not jurisdiction in an action where service was made under section 314 or 315; or

10. the court should not proceed in the absence of a person who should be a party.

11. the party is immune from liability pursuant to section seven hundred twenty-a of the not-for-profit corporation law. Presumptive evidence of the status of the corporation, association, organization or trust under section 501(c)(3) of the internal revenue code may consist of production of a letter from the United States internal revenue service reciting such determination on a preliminary or final basis or production of an official publication of the internal revenue service listing the corporation, association, organization or trust as an organization described in such section, and presumptive evidence of uncompensated status of the defendant may consist of an affidavit of the chief financial officer of the corporation, association, organization or trust. On a motion by a defendant based upon this paragraph the court shall determine whether such defendant is entitled to the benefit of section seven hundred twenty-a of the not-for-profit corporation law or subdivision six of section 20.09 of the arts and cultural affairs law and, if it so finds, whether there is a reasonable probability that the specific conduct of such defendant alleged constitutes gross negligence or was intended to cause the resulting harm. If the court finds that the defendant is entitled to the benefits of that section and does not find reasonable probability of gross negligence or intentional harm, it shall dismiss the cause of action as to such defendant.

(b) Motion to dismiss defense. A party may move for judgment dismissing one or more defenses, on the ground that a defense is not stated or has no merit.

(c) Evidence permitted; immediate trial; motion treated as one for summary judgment. Upon the hearing of a motion made under subdivision (a) or (b), either party may submit any evidence that could properly be considered on a motion for summary judgment. Whether or not issue has been joined, the court, after adequate notice to the parties, may treat the motion as a motion for summary judgment. The court may, when appropriate for the expeditious disposition of the controversy, order immediate trial of the issues raised on the motion.

CPLR

(d) Facts unavailable to opposing party. Should it appear from affidavits submitted in opposition to a motion made under subdivision (a) or (b) that facts essential to justify opposition may exist but cannot then be stated, the court may deny the motion, allowing the moving party to assert the objection in his responsive pleading, if any, or may order a continuance to permit further affidavits to be obtained or disclosure to be had and may make such other order as may be just.

(e)* Number, time and waiver of objections; motion to plead over. At any time before service of the responsive pleading is required, a party may move on one or more of the grounds set forth in subdivision (a), and no more than one such motion shall be permitted. Any objection or defense based upon a ground set forth in paragraphs one, three, four, five and six of subdivision (a) is waived unless raised either by such motion or in the responsive pleading. A motion based upon a ground specified in paragraphs two, seven or ten of subdivision (a) may be made at any subsequent time or in a later pleading, if one is permitted; an objection that the summons and complaint, summons with notice, or notice of petition and petition was not properly served, is waived if, having raised such an objection in a pleading, the objecting party does not move for judgment on that ground within sixty days after serving the pleading, unless the court extends the time upon the ground of undue hardship. The foregoing sentence shall not apply in any proceeding under subdivision one or two of section seven hundred eleven of the real property actions and proceedings law. The papers in opposition to a motion based on improper service shall contain a copy of the proof of service, whether or not previously filed. An objection based upon a ground specified in paragraphs eight or nine of subdivision (a) is waived if a party moves on any of the grounds set forth in subdivision (a) without raising such objection or if, having made no objection under subdivision (a), he does not raise such objection in the responsive pleading. Where a motion is made on the ground set forth in paragraph seven of subdivision (a), or on the ground that a defense is not stated, if the opposing party desires leave to plead again in the event the motion is granted, he shall so state in his opposing papers and may set forth evidence that could properly be considered on a motion for summary judgment in support of a new pleading; leave to plead again shall not be granted unless the court is satisfied that the opposing party has good ground to support his cause of action or defense; the court may require the party seeking leave to plead again to submit evidence to justify the granting of such leave.

*[Editor's note: This version of R 3211(e) is effective as of January 1, 1997. Through December 31, 1996, former R 3211(e) remains in effect. It reads as follows:

(e) Number, time and waiver of objections; motion to plead over. At any time before service of the responsive pleading is required, a party may move on one or more of the grounds set forth in subdivision (a), and no more than one such motion shall be permitted. Any objection or defense based upon a ground set forth in paragraphs one, three, four, five and six of subdivision (a) is waived unless raised either by such motion or in the responsive pleading. A motion based upon a ground specified in paragraphs two, seven or ten of subdivision (a) may be made at any subsequent time or in a later pleading, if one is permitted. An objection based upon a ground specified in paragraphs eight or nine of subdivision (a) is waived if a party moves on any of the grounds set forth in subdivision (a) without raising such objection or if, having made no objection under subdivision (a), he does not raise such objection in the responsive pleading. Where a motion is made on the ground set forth in paragraph seven of subdivision (a), or on the ground that a defense is not stated, if the opposing party desires leave to plead again in the event the motion is granted, he shall so state in his opposing papers and may set forth evidence that could properly be considered on a motion for summary judgment in support of a new pleading; leave to plead again shall not be granted unless the court is satisfied that the opposing party has good ground to support his cause of action or defense; the court may require the party seeking leave to plead again to submit evidence to justify the granting of such leave.]

(f) Extension of time to plead. Service of a notice of motion under subdivision (a) or (b) before service of a pleading responsive to the cause of action or defense sought to be dismissed extends the time to serve the pleading until ten days after service of notice of entry of the order.

(g) Standards for motions to dismiss in certain cases involving public petition and participation. A motion to dismiss based on paragraph seven of subdivision (a) of this section, in which the moving party has demonstrated that the action, claim, cross claim or counterclaim subject to the motion is an action involving public petition and participation as defined in paragraph (a) of subdivision one of section seventy-six-a of the civil rights law, shall be granted unless the party responding to the motion demonstrates that the cause of action has a substantial basis in law or is supported by a substantial argument for an extension, modification or reversal of existing law. The court shall grant preference in the hearing of such motion.

(h) Standards for motions to dismiss in certain cases involving licensed architects, engineers or landscape architects. A motion to dismiss based on paragraph seven of subdivision (a) of this rule, in which the moving party has demonstrated that the action, claim, cross claim or counterclaim subject to the motion is an action in which a notice of claim must be served on a licensed architect, engineer ot landscpae architect pursuant to the provisions of subdivision one of section two hundred fourteen of this chapter, shall be granted unless the party responding to the motion demonstratesthat a substantial basis in law exists to believe that the performance, conduct or omission complained of such licensed architect, engineer or landscape architect or such firm as set forth in the noptice of claim was negligent and that such performance, conduct or omission was a proximate 'cause of personal injury, wrongful death or property damage complained of by the claimant or is supported by a substantial argument for an extension, modification or reversal of existing law. The court shall grant a preference in the hearing of such motion.

**CROSS REFERENCES**

As to subject matter jurisdiction of the courts, generally, see **Constitutional** and **Judiciary Law** provisions in the Appendix, *infra*.

CPLR

## 1996 AMENDMENTS

L. 1996, ch. 501, eff. Jan. 1, 1997, amended subdivision (e) to add a clause which deems an objection of improper service waived, if the objecting party does not move for judgment within 60 days after serving the pleading that raised the objection. This does not apply in any proceeding under RPAPL § 711(1) or (2); L. 1996, ch. 682, eff. Oct. 1, 1996, added new subdivision (h)..

## 1992 AMENDMENTS

L. 1992, ch. 767, eff. Jan. 1, 1993, added subdivision (g), providing the standards for motions to dismiss in certain cases involving public petition and participation.

## 1991 AMENDMENTS

L. 1991, ch. 656, eff. July 26, 1991, amended CPLR 3211(a)(11) to replace a reference to Gen. Mun. L. § 305 with a reference to Arts and Cultural Affairs L. § 20.09.

## 1990 AMENDMENTS

L. 1990, ch. 904, eff. July 30, 1990, amended paragraph (11) of subdivision (a) of CPLR 3211 to include the reference to subdivision six of section three hundred five of the general municipal law.

## 1986 AMENDMENTS

L. 1986, ch. 220, eff. June 28, 1986 and applicable only to those causes of action arising on or after that date, added new paragraph (11) to CPLR 3211(a), providing for a motion to dismiss when a party is immune from liability under § 720(a) of the Not-For-Profit Corporation Law.

## 1973 AMENDMENTS

CPLR 3211(c) was amended by proposal No. 4 of the Judicial Conference Report to the 1973 Legislature, eff. Sept. 1, 1973, to provide that the court may treat a motion to dismiss as one for summary judgment whether or not issue has been joined, but only upon adequate notice to the parties.

## 1965 AMENDMENTS

Amendment No. 5 made by Judicial Conference Feb. 1, 1965, Report to the Legislature, eff. Sept. 1, 1965, added the words "or has no merit" at the end of Subd. (b) for the reason: "As the provision is presently worded, a defense raised in the answer which has no merit but which is not invalid on its face may not be the subject of a motion to dismiss, should the provision be interpreted literally. The spirit of the CPLR, and specifically of 3211, is to the contrary, and therefore, the rule should expressly permit the early testing of the merit of a defense."

Amendment No. 6 made by Judicial Conference Feb. 1, 1965, Report to the Legislature, eff. Sept. 1, 1965, inserted the words "paragraphs one, three, four, five and six of" after the phrase "Any objection or defense based upon a ground set forth in" and deleted the words "except that a" after the words "responsive pleading" and inserted the word "A" therein to start a new sentence beginning "A motion based upon a ground specified . . ." and in that same sentence deleted the words "by motion" and immediately following that sentence inserted a new sentence to read "An objection based upon a ground specified in paragraphs eight or nine of subdivision (a) is waived if a party moves on any of the grounds set forth in subdivision (a) without raising such objection or if, having made no objection under subdivision (a), he does not raise such objection in the responsive pleading" and deleted the words "in subdivision (b)" substituting therefor the words "on the ground that a defense is not stated" and after the words "opposing papers and" deleted the words "in them" and substituted therefor the word "may" all in the third sentence and at the end of the third sentence added the final clause "the court may require the party seeking leave to plead again to submit evidence to justify the granting of such leave" all in Subd. (e) for the reason: "This amendment is designed to enable the court to determine any issue of jurisdiction over the person or of jurisdiction *in rem* or *quasi in rem* before it is required to determine any issue reaching the merits of the case [see amendments to CPLR 320(b) and (c) *supra* ].

"The present text of R 3211 (e) creates problems for the lawyer who has prepared his pleading with misplaced confidence in its adequacy. If he fails to comply with the present requirement that evidence supporting leave to plead again be set forth in his papers opposing a motion to dismiss, he may find himself not only with a dismissed pleading, but also unable to make a belated request for leave to plead again, and, if he is asserting an affirmative claim, faced with the alternatives of appeal from the order of dismissal or the commencement of a new action. The problem may be acute where the statute of limitations is about to expire.

"On the other hand, the cautious pleader, though satisfied with the adequacy of his pleading, may feel obliged, in order to avoid the foregoing problems, not only to seek leave in his opposing papers to plead again, but also to submit his supporting evidence in those papers, thus indicating to the court a perhaps unwarranted defeatist attitude. If, having done so, he nevertheless succeeds in overcoming the motion to dismiss, he finds not only that his labors were unnecessary but also that he has prematurely laid bare much of his case and much of the evidence upon which he ultimately intends to rely to prove his case.

"This portion of the rule has been subject to much criticism from bench and bar which the Conference feels justified, while at the same time believing that the former practice of granting leave to plead again without any evidentiary showing should not be restored . . . the proposed amendment steers a desirable middle course by dispensing with the present requirement that supporting evidence must be set forth in the papers opposing the motion to dismiss. The proposed amendment would leave to the court's discretion the timing and method for the submission of evidence supporting a request for leave to plead again, while retaining the present requirement that the request for leave to plead again must be stated in the papers opposing the motion to dismiss.

"The proposed change with respect to a motion to dismiss a defense is necessitated by the [change in rule 3211 (b)]."

L. 1965, ch. 773, eff. Sept. 1, 1965, deleted the word "or" in the final phrase of Subd. (d) "or may make such other order as may be just" and substituted therefor the word "and."

Amendment recommended by the Judicial Conference Feb. 1, 1965, Report to the Legislature: "The amendment is proposed to prevent possible misconstruction which would preclude the granting of unspecified just relief as well as the specific relief set forth in this subdivision relating to motions to dismiss."

## 1964 AMENDMENTS

Amendment No. 6 made by the Judicial Conference Feb. 1, 1964, Report to the Legislature, eff. Sept. 1, 1964, added the words "and award" after the word "arbitration" in paragraph 5 of Subd. (a).

CPLR

## R 3212.   Motion for summary judgment.

(a)* Time; kind of action. Any party may move for summary judgment in any action, after issue has been joined; provided however, that the court may set a date after which no such motion may be made, such date being no earlier than thirty days after the filing of the note of issue. If no such date is set by the court, such motion shall be made no later than one hundred twenty days after the filing of the note of issue, except with leave of court on good cause shown.

> * [**Editor's note:** This version of R 3212(a) is effective as of January 1, 1997. Through December 31, 1996, former R 3212(a) remains in effect. It reads as follows:
>
> (a) Time; kind of action. Any party may move for summary judgment in any action, after issue has been joined.]

(b) Supporting proof; grounds; relief to either party. A motion for summary judgment shall be supported by affidavit, by a copy of the pleadings and by other available proof, such as depositions and written admissions. The affidavit shall be by a person having knowledge of the facts; it shall recite all the material facts; and it shall show that there is no defense to the cause of action or that the cause of action or defense has no merit. The motion shall be granted if, upon all the papers and proof submitted, the cause of action or defense shall be established sufficiently to warrant the court as a matter of law in directing judgment in favor of any party. Except as provided in subdivision (c) of this rule the motion shall be denied if any party shall show facts sufficient to require a trial of any issue of fact. If it shall appear that any party other than the moving party is entitled to a summary judgment, the court may grant such judgment without the necessity of a cross-motion.

(c) Immediate trial. If it appears that the only triable issues of fact arising on a motion for summary judgment relate to the amount or extent of damages, or if the motion is based on any of the grounds enumerated in subdivision (a) or (b) of rule 3211, the court may, when appropriate for the expeditious disposition of the controversy, order an immediate trial of such issues of fact raised by the motion, before a referee, before the court, or before the court and a jury, whichever may be proper.

(d) [Repealed.]

(e) Partial summary judgment; severance. In a matrimonial action summary judgment may not be granted in favor of the non-moving party. In any other action summary judgment may be granted as to one or more causes of action, or part thereof, in favor of any one or more parties, to the extent warranted, on such terms as may be just. The court may also direct:

1. that the cause of action as to which summary judgment is granted shall be severed from any remaining cause of action; or

2. that the entry of the summary judgment shall be held in abeyance pending the determination of any remaining cause of action.

(f) Facts unavailable to opposing party. Should it appear from affidavits submitted in opposition to the motion that facts essential to justify opposition may exist but cannot then be stated, the court may deny the motion or may order a continuance to permit affidavits to be obtained or disclosure to be had and may make such other order as may be just.

(g) Limitation of issues of fact for trial. If a motion for summary judgment is denied or is granted in part, the court, by examining the papers before it and, in the discretion of the court, by interrogating counsel, shall, if practicable, ascertain what facts are not in dispute or are incontrovertible. It shall thereupon make an order specifying such facts and they shall be deemed established for all purposes in the action. The court may make any order as may aid in the disposition of the action.

(h) Standards for summary judgment in certain cases involving public petition and participation. A motion for summary judgment, in which the moving party has demonstrated that the action, claim, cross claim or counterclaim subject to the motion is an action involving public petition and participation, as defined in paragraph (a) of subdivision one of section seventy-six-a of the civil rights law, shall be granted unless the party responding to the motion demonstrates that the action, claim, cross claim or counterclaim has a substantial basis in fact and law or is supported by a substantial argument for an extension, modification or reversal of existing law. The court shall grant preference in the hearing of such motion.

(i) Standards for summary judgment in certain cases involving licensed architects, engineers or landscape architects. A motion for summary judgment, in which the moving party has demonstrated that the action, claim, cross claim or counterclaim subject to the motion is an action in which a notice of claim must be served on a licensed architect, engineer or landscape architect pursuant to the provisions of subdivision one of section two hundred fourteen of this chapter, shall be granted unless the party responding to the motion demonstrates that a substantial basis in fact and in law exists to believe that the performance, conduct or omission complained of such licensed architect, engineer or landscape architect or such firm as set forth in the notice of claim was negligent and that such performance, conduct or omission was a proximate cause of personal injury, wrongful death or property damage complained of by the claimant or is supported by a substantial argument for an extension, modification or reversal of existing law. The court shall grant a preference in the hearing of such motion.

CPLR

### 1996 AMENDMENTS

L. 1996, ch. 492, eff. Jan. 1, 1997, amended subdivision (a) by adding the words beginning, "provided, however . . ." and continuing to the end of the subdivision; L. 1996, Ch. 682, eff. Oct. 1, 1996, added new subdivision (i).

### 1992 AMENDMENTS

L. 1992, ch. 767, eff. Jan. 1, 1993, added subdivision (h), providing the standards for summary judgment in certain cases involving public petition and participation.

## 1984 AMENDMENTS

L. 1984, ch. 827, eff. Aug. 5, 1984, amended CPLR 3212(e) by providing that partial summary judgment may not be granted in matrimonial actions. L. 1984, ch. 828, eff. Aug. 5, 1984, provides that the application of ch. 827 shall be determined in accordance with the provisions of CPLR 10003.

## 1978 AMENDMENTS

L. 1978, ch. 532, eff. Jan. 1, 1979, repealed former subdivision (d) of CPLR 3212, and deleted references thereto in subdivisions (a) and (e). Former subdivision (d) had provided that summary judgment in matrimonial actions was only available to defendants upon documentary evidence or official records establishing a defense, and was not available to plaintiffs at all. The effect of the amendment is to permit the entry of summary judgment for the plaintiff or the defendant in a matrimonial action as in any other action.

## 1973 AMENDMENTS

. CPLR 3212(c) was repealed and a new subdivision (c) was enacted by proposal No. 5 of the Judicial Conference Report to the 1973 Legislature, effective Sept. 1, 1973.

. The 1973 Judicial Conference Report stated:

"This proposal would amend subdivision (c) of Rule 3212, which now provides that on a motion for summary judgment the court may order an immediate trial of any issue of fact as to the amount or extent of damages, in order to permit the court to order immediate trial also of any issue of fact which presently can be raised upon a motion to dismiss (see CPLR 3211 (a) (b) (c)).

"The specific defenses enumerated under Rule 3211(a) are of the kind that commonly form the bases for summary judgment, especially when the defense is founded upon documentary evidence (Rule 3211(a) (1)). Furthermore, a motion to dismiss based on failure to state a cause of action (Rule 3211(a) (7)) often raises the same issues as a motion for summary judgment, and when matters outside the pleading are submitted (Rule 3211(c)) the motion is almost indistinguishable from one for summary judgment.

"Despite these substantial similarities, there exists a formal asymmetry in that on a motion to dismiss the court may order immediate trial of the issues raised on the motion (Rule 3211(c)), while on a motion for summary judgment any triable issue other than as to damages requires denial of the motion (Rule 3212(b)).

"Thus, in the light of the foregoing and because Rule 3211(c) permits motions to dismiss to be converted into motions for summary judgment, the proposed amendment clarifying and conforming practice under the two rules should be effected (*see* 4 Weinstein, Korn & Miller, New York Civil Practice - CPLR ¶ 3212.03 (Matthew Bender); see also Ass'n of the Bar of the City of New York, Report of the Committee on State Legislation 190-191 (1961)).

"The proposed amendment would allow the court under the conditions stated to consider other issues of fact, in addition to the sole present category of disputed damages, the resolution of which would be dispositive."

L. 1973, ch. 651, eff. Sept. 1, 1973, amended CPLR 3212(b) by deleting from the penultimate sentence "other than an issue as to the amount or extent of the damages"; and by adding to the penultimate sentence "Except as provided in subdivision (c) of this rule."

CPLR

#### 1965 AMENDMENTS

L. 1965, ch. 773, eff. Sept. 1, 1965, deleted the words "or" and "is" in the last phrase of Subd. (f) "or may make such other order as is just" and substituted therefor the words "and" and "may be" respectively.

Amendment recommended by the Judicial Conference Feb. 1, 1965, Report to the Legislature: "The change is proposed in order to make 3212(f) consistent with the language of 3211(d). . . ." See amendment and notes to 3211(d), *supra.*

## § 3213.   Motion for summary judgment in lieu of complaint.

When an action is based upon an instrument for the payment of money only or upon any judgment, the plaintiff may serve with the summons a notice of motion for summary judgment and the supporting papers in lieu of a complaint. The summons served with such motion papers shall require the defendant to submit answering papers on the motion within the time provided in the notice of motion. The minimum time such motion shall be noticed to be heard shall be as provided by subdivision (a) of rule 320 for making an appearance, depending upon the method of service. If the plaintiff sets the hearing date of the motion later than the minimum time therefor, he may require the defendant to serve a copy of his answering papers upon him within such extended period of time, not exceeding ten days, prior to such hearing date. No default judgment may be entered pursuant to subdivision (a) of section 3215 prior to the hearing date of the motion. If the motion is denied, the moving and answering papers shall be deemed the complaint and answer, respectively, unless the court orders otherwise.

#### 1969 AMENDMENTS

L. 1969, ch. 210, eff. Sept. 1, 1969, amended the section to reflect intention that summary procedure may be used where action is based on "any judgment."

#### 1967 AMENDMENTS

L. 1967, ch. 377, eff. Sept. 1, 1967, amended section to read as above by adding next to last sentence and by revising wording of section to achieve a greater degree of clarity.

#### 1965 AMENDMENTS

L. 1965, ch. 350, eff. Sept. 1, 1965, deleted the words "returnable at least twenty days after service" at the end of the first sentence, and added the second, third and fourth sentences.

## R 3214.   Motions heard by judge supervising disclosure; stay of disclosure.

(a) Judge supervising disclosure. Unless the chief administrator of the courts has, by rule, provided otherwise, if a case has been assigned to a judge to supervise disclosure pursuant to section 3104, all motions preliminary to trial shall be referred to such judge whenever practicable.

(b)* Stay of disclosure. Service of a notice of motion under rule 3211, 3212, or section 3213 stays disclosure until determination of the motion unless the court orders otherwise. If the motion is based solely on the defense that the summons and complaint, summons with notice, or notice of petition and petition was not properly served, disclosure shall not be stayed unless the court orders otherwise.

* [**Editor's note:** This version of R 3214(b) is effective as of January 1, 1997. Through December 31, 1996, former R 3214(b) remains in effect. It reads as follows:

(b) Stay of disclosure. Service of a notice of motion under rule 3211, 3212, or section 3213 stays disclosure until determination of the motion unless the court orders otherwise.]

### 1996 AMENDMENTS

L. 1996, ch. 501, eff. Jan. 1, 1997, amended subdivision (b) to add a new last sentence.

### 1986 AMENDMENTS

L. 1986, ch. 355, eff. July 17, 1986, amended subdivision (a) by adding the phrase "Unless the chief administrator of the courts has, by rule, provided otherwise," to the beginning of the subdivision, and substituting "such judge" for "him."

## § 3215.　Default judgment.

(a) Default and entry. When a defendant has failed to appear, plead or proceed to trial of an action reached and called for trial, or when the court orders a dismissal for any other neglect to proceed, the plaintiff may seek a default judgment against him. If the plaintiff's claim is for a sum certain or for a sum which can by computation be made certain, application may be made to the clerk within one year after the default. The clerk, upon submission of the requisite proof, shall enter judgment for the amount demanded in the complaint or stated in the notice served pursuant to subdivision (b) of rule 305, plus costs and interest. Upon entering a judgment against less than all defendants, the clerk shall also enter an order severing the action as to them. When a plaintiff has failed to proceed to trial of an action reached and called for trial, or when the court orders a dismissal for any other neglect to proceed, the defendant may make application to the clerk within one year after the default and the clerk, upon submission of the requisite proof, shall enter judgment for costs. Where the case is not one in which the clerk can enter judgment, the plaintiff shall apply to the court for judgment.

(b) Procedure before court. The court, with or without a jury, may make an assessment or take an account or proof, or may direct a reference. When a reference is directed, the court may direct that the report be returned to it for further action or, except where otherwise prescribed by law, that judgment be entered by the clerk in accordance with the report without any further application. Except in a matrimonial action, no finding of fact in writing shall be necessary to the entry of a judgment on default. The judgment shall not exceed in amount or differ in type from that demanded in the complaint or stated in the notice served pursuant to subdivision (b) of rule 305.

(c) Default not entered within one year. If the plaintiff fails to take proceedings for the entry of judgment within one year after the default, the court shall not enter judgment but shall dismiss the complaint as abandoned, without costs, upon its own initiative or on motion, unless sufficient cause is shown why the complaint should not be dismissed. A motion by the defendant under this subdivision does not constitute an appearance in the action.

(d) Multiple defendants. Whenever a defendant has answered and one or more other defendants have failed to appear, plead, or proceed to trial of an action reached and called for trial, notwithstanding the provisions of subdivision (c) of this section, upon application to the court within one year after the default of any such defendant, the court may enter an ex parte order directing that proceedings for the entry of a judgment or the making of an assessment, the taking of an account or proof, or the direction of a reference be conducted at the time of or following the trial or other disposition of the action against the defendant who has answered. Such order shall be served on the defaulting defendant in such manner as shall be directed by the court.

(e) Place of application to court. An application to the court under this section may be made, except where otherwise prescribed by rules of the chief administrator of the courts, by motion at any trial term in which the action is triable or at any special term in which a motion in the action could be made. Any reference shall be had in the county in which the action is triable, unless the court orders otherwise.

(f) Proof. On any application for judgment by default, the applicant shall file proof of service of the summons and the complaint, or a summons and notice served pursuant to subdivision (b) of rule 305 or subdivision (a) of rule 316, and proof by affidavit made by the party of the facts constituting the claim, the default and the amount due. Where a verified complaint has been served it may be used as the affidavit of the facts constituting the claim and the amount due; in such case, an affidavit as to the default shall be made by the party or his attorney. When jurisdiction is based on an attachment of property, the affidavit must state that an order of attachment granted in the action has been levied on the property of the defendant, describe the property and state its value. Proof of mailing the notice required by subdivision (f), where applicable, shall also be filed.

(g) Notice.

1. Except as otherwise provided with respect to specific actions, whenever application is made to the court or to the clerk, any defendant who has appeared is entitled to at least five days' notice of the time and place of the application, and if more than one year has elapsed since the default any defendant who has not appeared is entitled to the same notice unless the court orders otherwise.

CPLR

The court may dispense with the requirement of notice when a defendant who has appeared has failed to proceed to trial of an action reached and called for trial.

2. Where an application for judgment must be made to the court, the defendant who has failed to appear may serve on the plaintiff at any time before the motion for judgment is heard a written demand for notice of any reference or assessment by a jury which may be granted on the motion. Such a demand does not constitute an appearance in the action. Thereupon at least five days' notice of the time and place of the reference or assessment by a jury shall be given to the defendant by service on the person whose name is subscribed to the demand, in the manner prescribed for service of papers generally.

3. (i) When a default judgment based upon nonappearance is sought against a natural person in an action based upon nonpayment of a contractual obligation an affidavit shall be submitted that additional notice has been given by or on behalf of the plaintiff at least twenty days before the entry of such judgment by mailing a copy of the summons by first-class mail to the defendant at his place of residence in an envelope bearing the legend "personal and confidential" and not indicating on the outside of the envelope that the communication is from an attorney or concerns an alleged debt. In the event such mailing is returned as undeliverable by the post office before the entry of a default judgment, or if the place of residence of the defendant is unknown, a copy of the summons shall then be mailed in the same manner to the defendant at the defendant's place of employment if known; if neither the place of residence nor the place of employment of the defendant is known, then the mailing shall be to the defendant at his last known residence.

(ii) The additional notice may be mailed simultaneously with or after service of the summons on the defendant. An affidavit of mailing pursuant to this paragraph shall be executed by the person mailing the notice and shall be filed with the judgment. Where there has been compliance with the requirements of this paragraph, failure of the defendant to receive the additional notice shall not preclude the entry of default judgment.

(iii) This requirement shall not apply to cases in the small claims part of any court or to any summary proceeding to recover possession of real property or to actions affecting title to real property.

4. (i) When a default judgment based upon non-appearance is sought against a domestic or authorized foreign corporation which has been served pursuant to paragraph (b) of section three hundred six of the business corporation law, an affidavit shall be submitted that an additional service of the summons by first class mail has been made upon the defendant corporation at its last known address at least twenty days before the entry of judgment.

(ii) The additional service of the summons by mail may be made simultaneously with or after the service of the summons on the defendant corporation pursuant to paragraph (b) of section three hundred six of the business corporation law, and shall be accompanied by a notice to the corporation that service is being made or has been made pursuant to that provision. An affidavit of mailing pursuant to this paragraph shall be executed by the person mailing the summons and shall be filed with the judgment. Where there has been compliance with the requirements of this paragraph, failure of the defendant corporation to receive the additional service of summons and notice provided for by this paragraph shall not preclude the entry of default judgment.

(iii) This requirement shall not apply to cases in the small claims part or commercial claims part of any court, or to any summary proceeding to recover possession of real property, or to actions affecting title to real property.

(h) Judgment for excess where counterclaim interposed. In an action upon a contract where the complaint demands judgment for a sum of money only, if the answer does not deny the plaintiff's claim but sets up a counterclaim demanding an amount less than the plaintiff's claim, the plaintiff upon filing with the clerk an admission of the counterclaim may take judgment for the excess as upon a default.

(i) Default judgment for failure to comply with stipulation of settlement.

1. Where, after commencement of an action, a stipulation of settlement is made, providing, in the event of failure to comply with the stipulation, for entry without further notice of a judgment in a specified amount with interest, if any, from a date certain, the clerk shall enter judgment on the stipulation and an affidavit as to the failure to comply with the terms thereof, together with a complaint or a concise statement of the facts on which the claim was based.

2. Where, after commencement of an action, a stipulation of settlement is made, providing, in the event of failure to comply with the stipulation, for entry without further notice of a judgment dismissing the action, the clerk shall enter judgment on the stipulation and an affidavit as to the failure to comply with the terms thereof, together with the pleadings or a concise statement of the facts on which the claim and the defense were based.

**CROSS REFERENCES**

As to default in matrimonial actions, see **Domestic Relations Law,** §§ 211 and 232(a), in Appendix, *infra.*

**1994 AMENDMENTS**

L. 1994, ch. 100, eff. May 11, 1994, amended the first sentence of CPLR 3215(g)(1) by replacing "if" with "whenever"; replacing "must be" with "is"; by replacing "if judgment is entered by" with "to"; and by replacing "motion" with "application." The second sentence of CPLR 3215(g)(1) was also amended by deleting the word "also" following the words "The court may."

**1992 AMENDMENTS**

L. 1992, ch. 255, eff. Jan. 1, 1993, added new Subd. (d) and relettered former Subds. (d)–(h) as (e)–(i), respectively.

CPLR

## 1990 AMENDMENTS

L. 1990, ch. 584, eff. Aug. 17, 1990, amended CPLR 3215(f)(1) by deleting the opening sentence and adding the words "or if judgment is entered by the clerk;" L. 1990, ch. 419, eff. Jan. 1, 1991, added subdivision (f)(4).

## 1986 AMENDMENTS

L. 1986, ch. 77, eff. Jan. 1, 1987, added new paragraph (3) to CPLR 3215(f) governing additional notice requirements in actions based upon nonpayment of contractual obligations, superseding repealed provisions of CPLR 308, and amended subdivision (e) to reflect this change.

L. 1986, ch. 355, eff. July 17, 1986, amended Subd. (d) of CPLR 3215 by replacing "local court rules" with "rules of the chief administrator of the courts."

## 1977 AMENDMENTS

L. 1977, ch. 344, eff. Jan. 1, 1978, amended CPLR 3215(e) by adding a provision requiring the filing of proof of mailing of the summons to defendant prior to entry of a default judgment in those actions where such additional notice is required by CPLR 308.

## 1968 AMENDMENTS

L. 1968, ch. 720, eff. Sept. 1, 1968, added second sentence to Subd. (f)(1) and added the phrase "who has failed to appear" to the first sentence of Subd. (f)(2).

## 1967 AMENDMENTS

L. 1967, ch. 31, eff. Sept. 1, 1967, added paragraph (2) to Subd. (h).

## 1966 AMENDMENTS

L. 1966, ch. 487, eff. Sept. 1, 1966, added a new Subd. (h).

## 1965 AMENDMENTS

L. 1965, ch. 148, eff. Sept. 1, 1965, amended Subd. (e), by adding the words "or subdivision (a) of rule 316" after the words "pursuant to subdivision (b) of rule 305" in the first sentence.

## 1964 AMENDMENTS

L. 1964, ch. 290, eff. Sept. 1, 1964, amended Subd. (e) to make it clear that a verified complaint may be used in place of an affidavit of facts.

# R 3216.　Want of prosecution.

(a) Where a party unreasonably neglects to proceed generally in an action or otherwise delays in the prosecution thereof against any party who may be liable to a separate judgment, or unreasonably fails to serve and file a note of issue, the court, on its own initiative or upon motion, may dismiss the party's pleading on terms. Unless the order specifies otherwise, the dismissal is not on the merits.

(b) No dismissal shall be directed under any portion of subdivision (a) of this rule and no court initiative shall be taken or motion made thereunder unless the following conditions precedent have been complied with:

(1) Issue must have been joined in the action;

(2) One year must have elapsed since the joinder of issue;

(3) The court or party seeking such relief, as the case may be, shall have served a written demand by registered or certified mail requiring the party against whom such relief is sought to resume prosecution of the action and to serve and file a note of issue within ninety days after receipt of such demand, and further stating that the default by the party upon whom such notice is served in complying with such demand within said day period will serve as a basis for a motion by the party serving said demand for dismissal as against him for unreasonably neglecting to proceed.

(c) In the event that the party upon whom is served the demand specified in subdivision (b)(3) of this rule serves and files a note of issue within such ninety day period, the same shall be deemed sufficient compliance with such demand and diligent prosecution of the action; and in such event, no such court initiative shall be taken and no such motion shall be made, and if taken or made, the court initiative or motion to dismiss shall be denied.

(d) After an action has been placed on the calendar by the service and filing of a note of issue, with or without any such demand, provided, however, if such demand has been served, within the said ninety day period, the action may not be dismissed by reason of any neglect, failure or delay in prosecution of the action prior to the said service and filing of such note of issue.

(e) In the event that the party upon whom is served the demand specified in subdivision (b)(3) of this rule fails to serve and file a note of issue within such ninety day period, the court may take such initiative or grant such motion unless the said party shows justifiable excuse for the delay and a good and meritorious cause of action.

(f) The provisions of this rule shall not apply to proceedings within rule thirty-four hundred four.

### 1978 AMENDMENTS

L. 1978, ch. 4, eff. Sept. 1, 1978, amended subdivisions (b), (c), (d), and (e) by changing the forty-five day period to a ninety day period.

### 1967 AMENDMENTS

L. 1967, ch. 770, eff. Sept. 1, 1967, repealed former 3216 and added the present rule.

## R 3217.  Voluntary discontinuance.

(a) Without an order. Any party asserting a claim may discontinue it without an order.

1. by serving upon all parties to the action a notice of discontinuance at any time before a responsive pleading is served or within twenty days after service

of the pleading asserting the claim, whichever is earlier, and filing the notice with proof of service with the clerk of the court; or

2. by filing with the clerk of the court before the case has been submitted to the court or jury a stipulation in writing signed by the attorneys of record for all parties, provided that no party is an infant, incompetent person for whom a committee has been appointed or conservatee and no person not a party has an interest in the subject matter of the action.

3. by filing with the clerk of the court before the case has been submitted to the court or jury a certificate or notice of discontinuance stating that any parcel of land which is the subject matter of the action is to be excluded pursuant to paragraph (e) of subdivision two of section eleven hundred twenty-two of the real property tax law.

(b) By order of court. Except as provided in subdivision (a), an action shall not be discontinued by a party asserting a claim except upon order of the court and upon terms and conditions, as the court deems proper. After the cause has been submitted to the court or jury to determine the facts the court may not order an action discontinued except upon the stipulation of all parties appearing in the action.

(c) Effect of discontinuance. Unless otherwise stated in the notice, stipulation or order of discontinuance, the discontinuance is without prejudice, except that a discontinuance by means of notice operates as an adjudication on the merits if the party has once before discontinued by any method an action based on or including the same cause of action in a court of any state or the United States.

### CROSS REFERENCES

Provisions requiring leave of court to discontinue an action are contained in **CPLR 908,** as to class actions; **B.C.L. § 626(d),** as to shareholders' derivative actions; **Environmental Conservation Law § 71-0505,** as to suits involving title to state lands in forest preserve counties; **Condemnation Law §§ 18 and 56,** as to condemnation proceedings.

### 1989 AMENDMENTS

L. 1989, ch. 736, eff. July 24, 1989 added paragraph 3 of subdivision (a).

### 1981 AMENDMENTS

L. 1981, ch. 115, eff. May 18, 1981, amended CPLR 3217(a)(2) by adding a conservatee as a party whose presence in an action will prevent voluntary discontinuance of that action by stipulation without a court order.

## § 3218. Judgment by confession.

(a) Affidavit of defendant. Except as provided in section thirty-two hundred one, a judgment by confession may be entered, without an action, either for money due or to become due, or to secure the plaintiff against a contingent liability in behalf of the defendant, or both, upon an affidavit executed by the defendant;

1. stating the sum for which judgment may be entered, authorizing the entry of judgment, and stating the county where the defendant resides or, if he is a non-resident, the county in which entry is authorized;

2. if the judgment to be confessed is for money due or to become due, stating concisely the facts out of which the debt arose and showing that the sum confessed is justly due or to become due; and

3. if the judgment to be confessed is for the purpose of securing the plaintiff against a contingent liability, stating concisely the facts constituting the liability and showing that the sum confessed does not exceed the amount of the liability.

(b) Entry of judgment. At any time within three years after the affidavit is executed, it may be filed with the clerk of the county where the defendant stated in his affidavit that he resided when it was executed or, if the defendant was then a non-resident, with the clerk of the county designated in the affidavit. Thereupon the clerk shall enter a judgment in the supreme court for the sum confessed. He shall tax costs to the amount of fifteen dollars, besides disbursements taxable in an action. The judgment may be docketed and enforced in the same manner and with the same effect as a judgment in an action in the supreme court. No judgment by confession may be entered after the defendant's death.

(c) Execution where the judgment is not all due. Where the debt for which the judgment is entered is not all due, execution may be issued only for the sum which has become due. The execution shall be in the form prescribed for an execution upon a judgment for the full amount recovered, except that it shall direct the sheriff to collect only the sum due, stating the amount with interest and the costs of the judgment. Notwithstanding the issuance and collection of such an execution, the judgment shall remain in force as security for the sum or sums to become due after the execution is issued. When further sums become due, further executions may be issued in the same manner.

(d) Confession by joint debtors. One or more joint debtors may confess a judgment for a joint debt due or to become due. Where all the joint debtors do not unite in the confession, the judgment shall be entered and enforced against only those who confessed it and it is not a bar to an action against the other joint debtors upon the same demand.

## R 3219. Tender.

At any time not later than ten days before trial, any party against whom a cause of action based upon contract, express or implied, is asserted, and against whom a separate judgment may be taken, may, without court order, deposit with the clerk of the court for safekeeping, an amount deemed by him to be sufficient to satisfy the claim asserted against him, and serve upon the claimant a written tender of payment to satisfy such claim. A copy of the written tender shall be filed with the clerk when the money is so deposited. The clerk shall place money so received in the safe or vault of the court to be provided for the safekeeping thereof, there to be kept by him until withdrawal by claimant or return to the depositor or payment thereof to the county treasurer or commissioner of finance of the city of New York, as hereinafter provided. Within ten days after such deposit the claimant may withdraw the amount deposited upon filing a duly acknowledged statement that the withdrawal is in satisfaction of the claim. The clerk shall thereupon enter judgment dismissing the pleading setting forth the claim, without costs.

Where there is no withdrawal within such ten-day period, the amount deposited shall, upon request, be repaid to the party who deposited it. If the tender is not accepted and the claimant fails to obtain a more favorable judgment, he shall not recover interest or costs from the time of the offer, but shall pay costs for defending against the claim from that time. A tender shall not be made known to the jury.

Money received by the clerk of the court for safekeeping as hereinabove provided and later withdrawn by claimant or repaid to the depositor pursuant to the provisions hereof shall not be deemed paid into court. If the deposit is neither withdrawn by claimant nor returned to the depositor upon his request at the expiration of the ten-day period, the amount of such deposit shall be deemed paid into court as of the day following the expiration of the ten-day period and the clerk shall pay the amount of the deposit to the county treasurer or commissioner of finance of the city of New York, in accordance with section twenty-six hundred one of the civil practice law and rules. Withdrawal of such amount thereafter shall be in accordance with the provisions of rule twenty-six hundred seven. Fees for services rendered therein by a county treasurer or the commissioner of finance of the city of New York are set forth in section eight thousand ten.

### 1978 AMENDMENTS

L. 1978, ch. 655, eff. July 24, 1978, amended CPLR 3219 by substituting "commissioner of finance" wherever "finance administrator" appears.

### 1969 AMENDMENTS

L. 1969, ch. 407, eff. May 9, 1969, substituted "finance administrator" wherever "director of finance" appears.

### 1966 AMENDMENTS

L. 1966, ch. 581, eff. June 14, 1966, amended the first and second paragraphs of CPLR 3219 and added the third paragraph.

### 1965 AMENDMENTS

L. 1965, ch. 773, eff. Sept. 1, 1965, amended the first paragraph of CPLR 3219.

### 1964 AMENDMENTS

L. 1964, ch. 388, eff. Sept. 1, 1964, substituted the words "acknowledged statement" for the words "authenticated statement" in the fourth sentence of the first paragraph.

### R 3220.    Offer to liquidate damages conditionally.

At any time not later than ten days before trial, any party against whom a cause of action based upon contract, express or implied, is asserted may serve upon the claimant a written offer to allow judgment to be taken against him for a sum therein specified, with costs then accrued, if the party against whom the claim is asserted fails in his defense. If within ten days thereafter the claimant serves a written notice that he accepts the offer, and damages are awarded to him on the trial, they shall be assessed in the sum specified in the offer. If the offer is not so accepted and the claimant fails to obtain a more favorable judgment he shall pay the expenses necessarily incurred by the party against whom the claim is asserted, for trying the issue of damages from the time of the offer. The expenses shall be ascertained by the judge or referee before whom the case is tried. An offer under this rule shall not be made known to the jury.

### R 3221.    Offer to compromise.

Except in a matrimonial action, at any time not later than ten days before trial, any party against whom a claim is asserted, and against whom a separate judgment may be taken, may serve upon the claimant a written offer to allow judgment to be taken against him for a sum or property or to the effect therein specified, with costs then accrued. If within ten days thereafter the claimant serves a written notice that he accepts the offer, either party may file the summons, complaint and offer, with proof of acceptance, and thereupon the clerk shall enter judgment accordingly. If the offer is not accepted and the claimant fails to obtain a more favorable judgment, he shall not recover costs from the time of the offer, but shall pay costs from that time. An offer of judgment shall not be made known to the jury.

### R 3222.    Action on submitted facts.

(a) Commencement. An action, except a matrimonial action, may be commenced by filing with the clerk a submission of the controversy, acknowledged by all parties in the form required to entitle a deed to be recorded. The submission shall consist of a case, containing a statement of the facts upon which the controversy depends, and a statement that the controversy is real and that the submission is made in good faith for the purpose of determining the rights of the parties. If made to the supreme court, the submission shall specify the particular county clerk with whom the papers are to be filed.

(b) Subsequent proceedings. Subsequent proceedings shall be had according to the civil practice law and rules except that:

1. an order of attachment or a preliminary injunction shall not be granted;

2. the controversy shall be determined on the case alone;

3. if the submission is made to the supreme court, it shall be heard and determined either by the court, or by the appellate division, or, with his consent, by a specified judge or referee, as the parties may stipulate;

4. on such a submission the court, judge or referee may find facts by inference from the facts stipulated; and

5. if the statement of facts in the case is not sufficient to enable the court to enter judgment the submission shall be dismissed or the court shall allow the filing of an additional statement.

### 1986 AMENDMENTS

L. 1986, ch. 355, eff. July 17, 1986, amended Subd. (b)(3) of CPLR 3222 to provide that submissions made to the Supreme Court can be heard and determined by that court in addition to the Appellate Division; reference to Special Term was deleted.

### 1984 AMENDMENTS

L. 1984, ch. 313, eff. July 3, 1984, amended CPLR 3222(b)(1) by deleting the reference to an order of arrest.

# ARTICLE 34

# CALENDAR PRACTICE; TRIAL PREFERENCES

## SUMMARY OF ARTICLE

R 3401.   Rules for the hearing of causes.
R 3402.   Note of issue.
    (a)  Placing case on calendar.
    (b)  New parties.
R 3403.   Trial preferences.
    (a)  Preferred cases.
    (b)  Obtaining preference.
R 3404.   Dismissal of abandoned cases.
R 3405.   Arbitration of certain claims.
R 3406.   Mandatory filing and pre-calendar conference in dental, podiatric and
        medical malpractice actions.
    (a)  Mandatory filing.
    (b)  Pre-calendar conference.
R 3407.   Preliminary conference in personal injury actions involving certain
        terminally ill parties.
    (a)  Request for conference.
    (b)  Preliminary conference.

## R 3401.   Rules for the hearing of causes.

The chief administrator of the courts shall adopt rules regulating the hearing of causes, which may include the filing of notes of issue, the preparation and publication of calendars and the calendar practice for the courts of the unified court system. Insofar as practicable, such rules within the city of New York shall be uniform.

### 1986 AMENDMENTS

L. 1986, ch. 355, eff. July 17, 1986, amended CPLR 3401, by changing the title to "Rules for the hearing of causes," and making other changes to reflect transfer of rule-making power from appellate divisions to the chief administrator of the courts.

## R 3402.   Note of issue.

(a) Placing case on calendar. At any time after issue is first joined, or at least forty days after service of a summons has been completed irrespective of joinder of issue, any party may place a case upon the calendar by filing, within ten days after service, with proof of such service two copies of a note of issue with the clerk and such other data as may be required by the applicable rules of the court in which the note is filed. The clerk shall enter the case upon the calendar as of the date of the filing of the note of issue.

(b) New parties. A party who brings in a new party shall within five days thereafter serve him with the note of issue and file a statement with the clerk advising him of the bringing in of such new party and of any change in the title of the action, with proof of service of the note of issue upon the new party, and of such statement upon all parties who have appeared in the action. The case shall retain its place upon the calendar unless the court otherwise directs.

### 1968 AMENDMENTS

L. 1968, ch. 19, eff. Sept. 1, 1968, increased from "five" to "ten" days the time specified in Subd. (a) within which a party may place a case upon the calendar after service of a note of issue.

## R 3403. Trial preferences.

(a) Preferred cases. Civil cases shall be tried in the order in which notes of issue have been filed, but the following shall be entitled to a preference:

1. an action brought by or against the state, or a political subdivision of the state, or an officer or board of officers of the state or a political subdivision of the state, in his or its official capacity, on the application of the state, the political subdivision, or the officer or board of officers;

2. an action where a preference is provided for by statute; and

3. an action in which the interests of justice will be served by an early trial;

4. in any action upon the application of a party who has reached the age of seventy years.

5. an action to recover damages for medical, dental or podiatric malpractice.

6. an action to recover damages for personal injuries where the plaintiff is terminally ill and alleges that such terminal illness is a result of the conduct, culpability or negligence of the defendant.

(b) Obtaining preference. Unless the court otherwise orders, notice of a motion for preference shall be served with the note of issue by the party serving the note of issue, or ten days after such service by any other party; or thereafter during the pendency of the action upon the application of a party who reaches the age of seventy years, or who is terminally ill.

### CROSS REFERENCES

**State Finance Law § 123-c** provides that a citizen-taxpayer action shall have preference over all other causes in all courts.

### 1990 AMENDMENTS

L. 1990, ch. 670, eff. July 22, 1990, amended CPLR 3403 by adding a new paragraph (a)(6), granting trial preference to an action to recover damages for personal injuries where the plaintiff is terminally ill and alleges that the terminal illness is a result of the defendant's conduct, culpability or negligence, and by adding the words "or who is terminally ill" to the end of subdivision (b).

### 1986 AMENDMENTS

L. 1986, ch. 485, eff. July 21, 1986, and applicable to acts, omissions or failures occurring on or after such date, amended CPLR 3403(a)(5) to apply to podiatric malpractice actions.

### 1985 AMENDMENTS

L. 1985, ch. 760, eff. July 1, 1985, and applicable to any acts, omissions or failures occurring on or after that date, amended CPLR 3403(a)(5) to provide a trial preference for dental malpractice cases.

### 1979 AMENDMENTS

L. 1979, ch. 61, eff. April 9, 1979, amended CPLR 3403 subds. (a)(4) and (b) by changing the age requirement for trial preference from seventy five years to seventy years.

### 1975 AMENDMENTS

L. 1975, ch. 109, eff. July 1, 1975, amended Subd. (a) by adding new paragraph 5, providing a trial preference for medical malpractice cases. The amendment applies to acts of malpractice occurring on or after July 1, 1975.

### 1970 AMENDMENTS

L. 1970, ch. 907, eff. Sept. 1, 1970, added new subparagraph 4 to Subd. (a).

L. 1970, ch. 907, eff. Sept. 1, 1970, amended Subd. (b) by adding new language beginning with "or thereafter" to the end of the subdivision.

## R 3404.   Dismissal of abandoned cases.

A case in the supreme court or a county court marked "off" or struck from the calendar or unanswered on a clerk's calendar call, and not restored within one year thereafter, shall be deemed abandoned and shall be dismissed without costs for neglect to prosecute. The clerk shall make an appropriate entry without the necessity of an order.

## R 3405.   Arbitration of certain claims.

The chief judge of the court of appeals may promulgate rules for the arbitration of claims for the recovery of a sum of money not exceeding six thousand dollars, exclusive of interest, pending in any court or courts except the civil court of the city of New York, and not exceeding ten thousand dollars, exclusive of interest, pending in the civil court of the city of New York. Such rules must permit a jury trial de novo upon demand by any party following the determination of the arbitrators and may require the demander to pay the cost of arbitration;

CPLR

and shall also provide for all procedures necessary to initiate, conduct and determine the arbitration. A judgment may be entered upon the arbitration award. The rules shall further provide for the recruitment and qualifications of the arbitrators and for their compensation; except that such rules may authorize use of judicial hearing officers as arbitrators. All expenses for compensation, reimbursement and administration under this rule shall be a state charge to be paid out of funds appropriated to the administrative office for the courts for that purpose.

### 1992 AMENDMENTS

L. 1992, ch. 55, eff. April 10, 1992, amended this rule by providing that the rules promulgated by the chief judge of the Court of Appeals for the arbitration of certain claims may authorize use of judicial hearing officers as arbitrators.

### 1990 AMENDMENTS

L. 1990, ch. 30, eff. May 22, 1990, amended R. 3405, exempting the civil court for the city of New York from the $6,000 limitation and establishing an alternative $10,000 limitation for those courts.

### 1978 AMENDMENTS

L. 1978, ch. 156, eff. May 19, 1978, added § 3405.

## R 3406.  Mandatory filing and pre-calendar conference in dental, podiatric and medical malpractice actions.

(a) Mandatory filing. Not more than sixty days after issue is joined, the plaintiff in an action to recover damages for dental, medical or podiatric malpractice shall file with the clerk of the court in which the action is commenced a notice of dental, medical or podiatric malpractice action, on a form to be specified by the chief administrator of the courts. Together with such notice, the plaintiff shall file: (i) proof of service of such notice upon all other parties to the action; (ii) proof that, if demanded, authorizations to obtain medical, dental, podiatric and hospital records have been served upon the defendants in the action; and (iii) such other papers as may be required to be filed by rule of the chief administrator of the courts. The time for filing a notice of dental, medical or podiatric malpractice action may be extended by the court only upon a motion made pursuant to section two thousand four of this chapter.

(b) Pre-calendar conference. The chief administrator of the courts, in accordance with such standards and administrative policies as may be promulgated pursuant to section twenty-eight of article six of the constitution, shall adopt special calendar control rules for actions to recover damages for dental, podiatric or medical malpractice. Such rules shall require a pre-calendar conference in such an action, the purpose of which shall include, but not be limited to, encouraging settlement, simplifying or limiting issues and establishing a timetable for disclosure, establishing a timetable for offers and depositions pursuant to subparagraph (ii) of paragraph one of subdivision (d) of section thirty-one hundred one of this chapter, future conferences, and trial. The timetable for disclosure shall provide for the completion of disclosure not later than twelve months after the notice of dental, podiatric or medical malpractice is filed and shall require that all parties be ready for the trial of the case not later than eighteen months after such notice is filed. The initial pre-calendar conference shall be held after issue is joined in a case but before a note of issue is filed. To the extent feasible, the justice convening the pre-calendar conference shall hear and decide all subsequent pre-trial motions in the case and shall be assigned the trial of the case. The chief administrator of the courts also shall provide for the imposition of costs or other sanctions, including imposition of reasonable attorney's fees, dismissal of an action, claim, cross-claim, counterclaim or defense, or rendering a judgment by default for failure of a party or a party's attorney to comply with these special calendar control rules or any order of a court made thereunder. The chief administrator of the courts, in the exercise of discretion, may provide for exemption from the requirement of a pre-calendar conference in any judicial district or a county where there exists no demonstrated need for such conferences.

**CPLR**

### CROSS REFERENCES

See **22 N.Y.C.R.R. § 202.56 of the Uniform Rules** for the Supreme Court and County Court as to the form of the notice of medical, dental or podiatric malpractice action, and as to other special rules relevant to such actions.

### 1991 AMENDMENTS

L. 1991, ch. 165, eff. Oct. 1, 1991, amended CPLR 3406(b) by deleting the requirement that the initial pre-calendar conference be held before a medical malpractice panel hearing is scheduled. The October 1, 1991 effective date applies only to actions where, as of this date, the medical malpractice panel members have not signed and forwarded to all parties a formal written recommendation concerning the question of liability.

### 1988 AMENDMENTS

L. 1988, ch.184, eff. July 1, 1988, amended subdivision (b) and its heading to add podiatric cases to the scope of the rule; and to add scheduling of reciprocal expert depositions to the scope of the pre-trial conference.

### 1986 AMENDMENTS

L. 1986, ch. 485, eff. July 21, 1986, and applicable to acts, omissions or failures occurring on or after such date, amended CPLR 3406(a) to apply to podiatric malpractice actions.

### 1985 AMENDMENTS

L. 1985, ch. 294, eff. July 1, 1985, and applicable to any action for dental or medical malpractice commenced on or after such date, added Rule 3406.

**R 3407. Preliminary conference in personal injury actions involving certain terminally ill parties.**

(a) Request for conference. At any time, a party to an action who is terminally ill, and who asserts in a pleading in such action that such terminal illness is the result of the culpable conduct of another party to such action, may request an expedited preliminary conference in such action. Such request shall be filed in writing with the clerk of the court, and shall be accompanied by a physician's affidavit stating that the party is terminally ill, the nature of the terminal illness, and the duration of life expectancy of such party, if known. The court shall hold a preliminary conference in such action within twenty days after the filing of such a request.

(b) 1. Preliminary conference. At such preliminary conference, the court shall issue an order establishing a schedule for the completion of all discovery proceedings, to be completed within ninety days after the date of the preliminary conference, unless it can be demonstrated for good cause that a longer period is necessary.

2. At such preliminary conference, the court shall issue an order that a note of issue and certificate of readiness be filed in such action within a period of time specified in the order, that the action receive a preference in trial, and that the trial be commenced within one year from the date of such order. In its discretion, and upon application of any party, the court may advance or adjourn such trial date based on the circumstances of the case.

3. Notwithstanding the provisions of subdivision (b) of rule 3214 of this chapter, the service or pendency of a motion under rule 3211, 3212 or section 3213 of this chapter shall not stay disclosure in an action where a preliminary conference order has been entered pursuant to this rule.

**1992 AMENDMENTS**

L. 1992, ch. 582, eff. Sept. 1, 1992, added Rule 3407, which governs filings by terminally ill plaintiffs.

# ARTICLE 40

# TRIAL GENERALLY

---

## SUMMARY OF ARTICLE

§ 4001.　Powers of referees.
§§ 4002–4009.　[Not used.]
§ 4010.　[Repealed.]
R 4011.　Sequence of trial.
R 4012.　Marked pleadings furnished.
R 4013.　Trial elsewhere than at courthouse.
R 4014.　Duration of trial.
R 4015.　Time for motion for referee or advisory jury.
R 4016.　Opening and closing statements.
§ 4017.　Objections.
R 4018.　Increased damages.
R 4019.　Recording in camera interviews of infants.

CPLR

---

## § 4001.　Powers of referees.

A court may appoint a referee to determine an issue, perform an act, or inquire and report in any case where this power was heretofore exercised and as may be hereafter authorized by law.

## §§ 4002–4009.　[Not used.]

## § 4010.　[Repealed.]

## R 4011.　Sequence of trial.

The court may determine the sequence in which the issues shall be tried and otherwise regulate the conduct of the trial in order to achieve a speedy and unprejudiced disposition of the matters at issue in a setting of proper decorum.

## R 4012.　Marked pleadings furnished.

The party who has filed the note of issue shall furnish the judge who is to preside at the trial with copies of each pleading, where they have not been superseded by the pre-trial order, plainly marked to indicate which statements are admitted and which controverted by the responsive pleading.

## R 4013. Trial elsewhere than at courthouse.

Upon stipulation of the parties, the judge who is to preside at the trial of an issue may direct trial in whole or in part at a specified place other than the courthouse.

## R 4014. Duration of trial.

Notwithstanding the expiration of the term at which it was commenced, a trial shall continue until it is completed.

## R 4015. Time for motion for referee or advisory jury.

A motion for trial by a referee or an advisory jury shall be made within twenty days after note of issue is filed, except where the issue to be tried arises on a motion or pursuant to a judgment.

## R 4016. Opening and closing statements.

Before any evidence is offered, an attorney for each plaintiff having a separate right, and an attorney for each defendant having a separate right, may make an opening statement. At the close of all the evidence on the issues tried, an attorney for each such party may make a closing statement in inverse order to opening statements.

## § 4017. Objections.

Formal exceptions to rulings of the court are unnecessary. At the time a ruling or order of the court is requested or made a party shall make known the action which he requests the court to take or, if he has not already indicated it, his objection to the action of the court. Failure to so make known objections, as prescribed in this section or in section 4110-b, may restrict review upon appeal in accordance with paragraphs three and four of subdivision (a) of section 5501.

### 1973 AMENDMENTS

L. 1973, ch. 233, eff. Sept. 1, 1973, amended CPLR 4017 by deleting the third sentence, and by inserting in the last sentence, "as prescribed in this section or in section 4110-b." See CPLR 4110-b, *infra*.

## R 4018. Increased damages.

Where increased damages are granted by statute, the decision, report or verdict shall specify the sum awarded as single damages, and judgment shall be entered for the increased amount.

## R 4019. Recording in camera interviews of infants.

(a) A court shall not conduct an in camera interview of an infant in any action or proceeding to fix temporary or permanent custody or to modify judgments and orders of custody concerning marital separation, divorce, annulment of marriage and dissolution of marriage unless a stenographic record of such interview is made.

(b) If an appeal is taken to the appellate division from a judgment or order of the court on any such action or proceeding, the stenographic record of any such interview shall be made a part of the record and forwarded under seal to the appellate division.

### 1985 AMENDMENTS

L. 1985, ch. 785, eff. Aug. 1, 1985, and applicable to actions and proceedings conducted on or after that date, added CPLR 4019.

CPLR

# ARTICLE 41

# TRIAL BY A JURY

## SUMMARY OF ARTICLE

§ 4101.　Issues triable by a jury revealed before trial.
§ 4102.　Demand and waiver of trial by jury; specification of issues.
    (a)　Demand.
    (b)　Specification of issues.
    (c)　Waiver.
    (d)　Local rules.
    (e)　Relief by court.
§ 4103.　Issues triable by a jury revealed at trial; demand and waiver of trial by jury.
§ 4104.　Number of jurors.
§ 4105.　Persons who constitute the jury.
§ 4106.　Alternate jurors.
R 4107.　Judge present at examination of jurors.
§ 4108.　Challenges generally.
§ 4109.　Peremptory challenges.
§ 4110.　Challenges for cause.
    (a)　Challenge to the favor.
    (b)　Disqualification of juror for relationship.
§ 4110-a.　Competency of inhabitants as justices or jurors; undertakings not required of village.
§ 4110-b.　Instructions to jury; objection.
§ 4110-c.　Trial jury; viewing of premises.
R 4111.　General and special verdicts and written interrogatories.
    (a)　General and special verdict defined.
    (b)　Special verdict.
    (c)　General verdict accompanied by answers to interrogatories.
    (d)　Itemized verdict in medical, dental or podiatric malpractice actions.
    (e)　Itemized verdict in certain actions against a public employer for personal injury and wrongful death.
    (f)　Itemized verdict in certain actions.
R 4112.　Entry of verdict.
§ 4113.　Disagreement by jury.
    (a)　Unanimous verdict not required.
    (b)　Procedure where jurors disagree.

CPLR

## § 4101. Issues triable by a jury revealed before trial.

In the following actions, the issues of fact shall be tried by a jury unless a jury trial is waived or a reference is directed under section 4317, except that equitable defenses and equitable counterclaims shall be tried by the court:

1. an action in which a party demands and sets forth facts which would permit a judgment for a sum of money only;

2. an action of ejectment; for dower; for waste; for abatement of and damages for a nuisance; to recover a chattel; or for determination of a claim to real property under article fifteen of the real property actions and proceedings law; and

3. any other action in which a party is entitled by the constitution or by express provision of law to a trial by jury.

## § 4102. Demand and waiver of trial by jury; specification of issues.

(a) Demand. Any party may demand a trial by jury of any issue of fact triable of right by a jury, by serving upon all other parties and filing a note of issue containing a demand for trial by jury. Any party served with a note of issue not containing such a demand may demand a trial by jury by serving upon each party a demand for a trial by jury and filing such demand in the office where the note of issue was filed within fifteen days after service of the note of issue. A demand shall not be accepted for filing unless a note of issue is filed in the action. If no party shall demand a trial by jury as provided herein, the right to trial by jury shall be deemed waived by all parties. A party may not withdraw a demand for trial by jury without the consent of the other parties, regardless of whether another party previously filed a note of issue without a demand for trial by jury.

(b) Specification of issues. In his demand a party may specify the issues which he wishes tried by jury; otherwise he shall be deemed to have demanded trial by jury of all issues so triable. If he has demanded trial by jury of only some of the issues, any other party within ten days after service of the demand may serve and file a demand for trial by jury of any other issues in the action so triable.

(c) Waiver. A party who has demanded the trial of an issue of fact by a jury under this section waives his right by failing to appear at the trial, by filing a written waiver with the clerk or by oral waiver in open court. A waiver does not withdraw a demand for trial by jury without the consent of the other parties. A party shall not be deemed to have waived the right to trial by jury of the issues of fact arising upon a claim, by joining it with another claim with respect to which there is no right to trial by jury and which is based upon a separate transaction; or of the issues of fact arising upon a counterclaim, cross-claim or third party claim, by asserting it in an action in which there is no right to trial by jury.

(d) Local rules. The chief administrator of the courts may by rule provide that a party shall be deemed to have demanded trial by jury by filing a note of issue not containing an express waiver of trial by jury.

(e) Relief by court. The court may relieve a party from the effect of failing to comply with this section if no undue prejudice to the rights of another party would result.

#### 1990 AMENDMENTS

L. 1990, ch. 582, eff. Jan. 1, 1991, amended CPLR 4102(a) to provide that one party cannot withdraw a demand for a jury trial unless the other parties consent, even if another party previously filed a note of issue without a demand for a jury trial.

#### 1986 AMENDMENTS

L. 1986, ch. 355, eff. July 17, 1986, amended CPLR 4102(d) to reflect the transfer of rule-making power from the appellate divisions to the chief administrator of the courts.

#### 1968 AMENDMENTS

L. 1968, ch. 19, eff. Sept. 1, 1968, increased from "ten" to "fifteen" days the time specified in Subd. (a) within which a party must file a demand for a trial by jury after receipt of a note of issue not containing such demand.

## § 4103. Issues triable by a jury revealed at trial; demand and waiver of trial by jury.

When it appears in the course of a trial by the court that the relief required, although not originally demanded by a party, entitles the adverse party to a trial by jury of certain issues of fact, the court shall give the adverse party an opportunity to demand a jury trial of such issues. Failure to make such demand within the time limited by the court shall be deemed a waiver of the right to trial by jury. Upon such demand, the court shall order a jury trial of any issues of fact which are required to be tried by jury.

## § 4104. Number of jurors.

A jury shall be composed of six persons.

#### 1972 AMENDMENTS

L. 1972, ch. 185, § 1, eff. May 28, 1972, repealed former Section 4104 and inserted a new Section 4104 in its place.

## § 4105. Persons who constitute the jury.

The first six persons who appear as their names are drawn and called, and are approved as indifferent between the parties, and not discharged or excused, must be sworn and constitute the jury to try the issue.

### 1972 AMENDMENTS

L. 1972, ch. 185, § 2, eff. May 28, 1972, amended CPLR 4105 by deleting the phrase "The first twelve, or, if a jury of six is demanded" that formerly appeared at the beginning of the Section.

## § 4106. Alternate jurors.

Unless the court, in its discretion, orders otherwise, one or two additional jurors, to be known as "alternate jurors," may be drawn upon the request of a party. Such jurors shall be drawn at the same time, from the same source, in the same manner, and have the same qualifications as the regular jurors, and be subject to the same examinations and challenges. They shall be seated with, take the oath with, and be treated in the same manner as the regular jurors, except that after final submission of the case, the court shall discharge the alternate jurors. If, before the final submission of the case, a regular juror dies, or becomes ill, or for any other reason is unable to perform his duty, the court may order him to be discharged and draw the name of an alternate, who shall replace the discharged juror in the jury box, and be treated as if he had been selected as one of the regular jurors.

### 1972 AMENDMENTS

L. 1972, ch. 336, eff. Sept. 1, 1972, amended CPLR 4106 by deleting the first sentence of the Section, which read, "The court, in its discretion, may direct the calling of one or two additional jurors, to be known as àlternate jurors'," and substituting the present first sentence.

## R 4107. Judge present at examination of jurors.

On application of any party, a judge shall be present at the examination of the jurors.

### 1964 AMENDMENTS

Amendment No. 7 made by the Judicial Conference Feb. 1, 1964, Report to the Legislature, effective Sept. 1, 1964, substituted the word "a" in place of "the" before the word "judge" for the reason: "This change is suggested in order to prevent an interpretation that the judge to be present at the voir dire must be the judge' assigned to try the case —an interpretation which could cause serious problems if such judge were then sitting at another trial. If this change is made, the specification of the particular judge to be present at voir dire will be left to implementing local court rules.

"The Judicial Conference is aware of the objections to Rule 4107 voiced by some judges who feel that a judge's presence at voir dire should be discretionary. On the other hand, there are situations on voir dire where the presence of a judge is essential in order to prevent serious harm. The Judicial Conference believes that the results of experience under the rule should be awaited before considering the advisability of its repeal. Its present proposal is designed to alleviate at least to some extent the problems which are involved in the courts in metropolitan centers when a judge's presence is required at the examination of jurors."

## § 4108. Challenges generally.

An objection to the qualifications of a juror must be made by a challenge unless the parties stipulate to excuse him. A challenge of a juror, or a challenge to the panel or array of jurors, shall be tried and determined by the court.

## § 4109. Peremptory challenges.

The plaintiff or plaintiffs shall have a combined total of three peremptory challenges plus one peremptory challenge for every two alternate jurors. The defendant or defendants (other than any third-party defendant or defendants) shall have a combined total of three peremptory challenges, plus one peremptory challenge for every two alternate jurors. The court, in its discretion before the examination of jurors begins, may grant an equal number of additional challenges to both sides as may be appropriate. In any case where a side has two or more parties, the court, in its discretion, may allocate that side's combined total of peremptory challenges among those parties in such manner as may be appropriate.

### 1996 AMENDMENTS

L. 1996, ch. 655, eff. Oct. 24, 1996, and applicable only to actions and proceedings in which the examination of jurors begins on or after such effective date, amended the section to equalize the number of peremptory challenges for plaintiffs and defendants and added a new last sentence.

### 1972 AMENDMENTS

L. 1972, ch. 185, § 3, eff. May 28, 1972, amended CPLR 4109 by substituting "three" for "six" in the first sentence of the Section.

## § 4110. Challenges for cause.

(a) Challenge to the favor. The fact that a juror is in the employ of a party to the action; or if a party to the action is a corporation, that he is a shareholder or a stockholder therein; or, in an action for damages for injuries to person or property, that he is a shareholder, stockholder, director, officer or employee, or in any manner interested, in any insurance company issuing policies for protection against liability for damages for injury to persons or property; shall constitute a ground for a challenge to the favor as to such juror. The fact that a juror is a resident of, or liable to pay taxes in, a city, village, town or county which is a party to the action shall not constitute a ground for challenge to the favor as to such juror.

(b) Disqualification of juror for relationship. Persons shall be disqualified from sitting as jurors if related within the sixth degree by consanguinity or affinity to a party. The party related to the juror must raise the objection before the case is opened; any other party must raise the objection no later than six months after the verdict.

CPLR

## § 4110-a. Competency of inhabitants as justices or jurors; undertakings not required of village.

In an action brought by or against a village it shall not be an objection against the person acting as justice or juror in such action that he is a resident of the village or subject to taxation therein. It shall not be necessary for the village to give a bond, undertaking or security to appeal or to obtain a provisional remedy, or to take or prevent any other proceeding; or to do or perform any act or thing notwithstanding any provision of any other law to the contrary, but the village shall be liable to the same extent as if it had given the bond, undertaking or security otherwise required by or in pursuance of law.

**1972 AMENDMENTS**

L. 1972, ch. 890, eff. Sept. 1, 1973, added new CPLR 4110-a.

## § 4110-b. Instructions to jury; objection.

At the close of the evidence or at such earlier time during the trial as the court reasonably directs, any party may file written requests that the court instruct the jury on the law as set forth in the requests. The court, out of the hearing of the jury, shall inform counsel of its proposed action upon the requests prior to their arguments to the jury, but the court shall instruct the jury after the arguments are completed. No party may assign as error the giving or the failure to give an instruction unless he objects thereto before the jury retires to consider its verdict stating the matter to which he objects and the grounds of his objection. Opportunity shall be given to make the objection out of the hearing of the jury.

**1973 AMENDMENTS**

L. 1973, ch. 233, eff. Sept. 1, 1973, added new CPLR 4110-b.

## § 4110-c. Trial jury; viewing of premises.

1. When during the course of a trial the court is of the opinion that a viewing or observation by the jury of the premises or place where alleged injuries to person or property were sustained in an accident or occurrence claimed to have been the cause thereof or of any other premises or place involved in the case will be helpful to the jury in determining any material factual issue, it may in its discretion, at any time before the commencement of the summations, order that the jury be conducted to such premises or place for such purpose in accordance with the provisions of this section.

2. In such case, the jury must be kept together throughout under the supervision of an appropriate public servant or servants appointed by the court, and the court itself must be present throughout. The parties to the action and counsel for them may as a matter of right be present throughout, but such right may be waived.

3. The purpose of such an inspection is solely to permit visual observation by the jury of the premises or place in question and neither the court, the parties, counsel nor the jurors may engage in discussion or argumentation concerning the significance or implications of anything under observation or concerning any issue in the case.

### 1982 AMENDMENTS

L. 1982, ch. 116, eff. Sept. 1, 1982, added new CPLR 4110-c.

## R 4111. General and special verdicts and written interrogatories.

(a) General and special verdict defined. The court may direct the jury to find either a general verdict or a special verdict. A general verdict is one in which the jury finds in favor of one or more parties. A special verdict is one in which the jury finds the facts only, leaving the court to determine which party is entitled to judgment thereon.

(b) Special verdict. When the court requires a jury to return a special verdict, the court shall submit to the jury written questions susceptible of brief answer or written forms of the several findings which might properly be made or it shall use any other appropriate method of submitting the issues and requiring written findings thereon. The court shall give sufficient instruction to enable the jury to make its findings upon each issue. If the court omits any issue of fact raised by the pleadings or evidence, each party waives his right to a trial by jury of the issue so omitted unless before the jury retires he demands its submission to the jury. As to an issue omitted without demand, the court may make an express finding or shall be deemed to have made a finding in accordance with the judgment.

(c) General verdict accompanied by answers to interrogatories. When the court requires the jury to return a general verdict, it may also require written answers to written interrogatories submitted to the jury upon one or more issues of fact. The court shall give sufficient instruction to enable the jury to render a general verdict and to answer the interrogatories. When the answers are consistent with each other but one or more is inconsistent with the general verdict, the court shall direct the entry of judgment in accordance with the answers, notwithstanding the general verdict, or it shall require the jury to further consider its answers and verdict or it shall order a new trial. When the answers are inconsistent with each other and one or more is inconsistent with the general verdict, the court shall require the jury to further consider its answers and verdict or it shall order a new trial.

(d) Itemized verdict in medical, dental or podiatric malpractice actions. In a medical, dental or podiatric malpractice action the court shall instruct the jury that if the jury finds a verdict awarding damages it shall in its verdict specify the applicable elements of special and general damages upon which the award is based and the amount assigned to each element, including but not limited to medical expenses, dental expenses, podiatric expenses, loss of earnings, impairment of earning ability, and pain and suffering. In a medical, dental or podiatric malpractice action, each element shall be further itemized into amounts intended to compensate for damages which have been incurred prior to the verdict and amounts intended to compensate for damages to be incurred in the future. In itemizing amounts intended to compensate for future damages, the jury shall set forth the period of years over which such amounts are intended to provide compensation. In actions in which Article Fifty-A or Fifty-B of this chapter applies, in computing said damages, the jury shall be instructed to award the full amount of future damages, as calculated, without reduction to present value.

(e) Itemized verdict in certain actions against a public employer for personal injury and wrongful death. In an action against a public employer or a public employee who is subject to indemnification by a public employer with respect to such action or both, as such terms are defined in subdivision (b) of section forty-five hundred forty-five, for personal injury or wrongful death arising out of an injury sustained by a public employee while acting within the scope of his public employment or duties, the court shall instruct the jury that if the jury finds a verdict awarding damages it shall in its verdict specify the applicable elements of special and general damages upon which the award is based and the amount assigned to each element, including but not limited to medical expenses, loss of earnings, impairment of earning ability, and pain and suffering.

(f) Itemized verdict in certain actions. In an action brought to recover damages for personal injury, injury to property or wrongful death, which is not subject to subdivisions (d) and (e) of this rule, the court shall instruct the jury that if the jury finds a verdict awarding damages, it shall in its verdict specify the applicable elements of special and general damages upon which the award is based and the amount assigned to each element including, but not limited to, medical expenses, dental expenses, loss of earnings, impairment of earning ability, and pain and suffering. Each element shall be further itemized into amounts intended to compensate for damages that have been incurred prior to the verdict and amounts intended to compensate for damages to be incurred in the future. In itemizing amounts intended to compensate for future damages, the jury shall set forth the period of years over which such amounts are intended to provide compensation. In actions in which Article Fifty-A or Fifty-B of this chapter applies, in computing said damages, the jury shall be instructed to award the full amount of future damages, as calculated, without reduction to present value.

### 1994 AMENDMENTS

L. 1994, ch. 100, eff. May 16, 1994, amended CPLR 4111(d) and (f) by inserting the words "In actions in which Article Fifty-A or Fifty-B of this chapter applies."

## 1988 AMENDMENTS

L. 1988, ch. 184, eff. July 1, 1988, amended L. 1986, ch. 682, § 12, L. 1985, ch. 294, § 25, and L. 1984, ch. 701, § 5, to make subsections (d), (e), and (f) applicable to all actions in which trial has not begun as of August 1, 1988.

## 1986 AMENDMENTS

L. 1986, ch. 485, eff. July 21, 1986 and applicable to acts, omissions or failures occurring on or after such date, amended CPLR 4111(d) to apply to podiatric malpractice actions; L. 1986, ch. 682, eff. July 30, 1986, and applicable to actions commenced or claims filed on or after such date, amended CPLR 4111 by adding new Subd. (f) requiring an itemized verdict in certain actions to recover damages for personal injury, injury to property or wrongful death.

## 1985 AMENDMENTS

L. 1985, ch. 294, eff. July 1, 1985, and applicable to any action for dental or medical malpractice commenced on or after that date, and L. 1985, ch. 760, eff. July 1, 1985, and applicable to any acts, omissions or failures occurring on or after that date, amended subdivision (d) to apply to dental malpractice actions and to provide for further itemization as to past and future damages in medical or dental malpractice actions.

## 1984 AMENDMENTS

L. 1984, ch. 701, eff. Oct. 1, 1984, and applicable to all actions commenced on or after that date, added subdivision (e).

## 1976 AMENDMENTS

L. 1976, ch. 955, eff. Aug. 26, 1976, added subd. (d), providing for itemized verdicts in medical malpractice actions.

# R 4112.  Entry of verdict.

When the jury renders a verdict, the clerk shall make an entry in his minutes specifying the time and place of the trial, the names of the jurors and witnesses, the general verdict and any answers to written interrogatories, or the questions and answers or other written findings constituting the special verdict and the direction, if any, which the court gives with respect to subsequent proceedings.

# § 4113.  Disagreement by jury.

(a) Unanimous verdict not required. A verdict may be rendered by not less than five-sixths of the jurors constituting a jury.

(b) Procedure where jurors disagree. Where five-sixths of the jurors constituting a jury cannot agree after being kept together for as long as is deemed reasonable by the court, the court shall discharge the jury and direct a new trial before another jury.

# ARTICLE 42

# TRIAL BY THE COURT

## SUMMARY OF ARTICLE

§ 4201.   Powers of referees to report.
R 4211.   Issues to be decided by the court.
R 4212.    Advisory jury; referee to report.
§ 4213.   Decision of the court.
    (a)  Requests for findings.
    (b)  Form of decision.
    (c)  Time for decision.

## § 4201.  Powers of referees to report.

A referee to inquire and report shall have the power to issue subpoenas, to administer oaths and to direct the parties to engage in and permit such disclosure proceedings as will expedite the disposition of the issues.

## R 4211.  Issues to be decided by the court.

The court shall decide any issue not required to be tried by a jury unless it is referred to a referee to determine pursuant to section 4317.

### 1968 AMENDMENTS

Proposal No. 1, eff. Sept. 1, 1968, made by the Judicial Conference Feb. 1, 1968, Report to the Legislature, inserted cross-reference to "section" in place of reference to "rule" as mechanical correction.

## R 4212.  Advisory jury; referee to report.

Upon the motion of any party as provided in rule 4015 or on its own initiative, the court may submit any issue of fact required to be decided by the court to an advisory jury or upon a showing of some exceptional condition requiring it or in matters of account, to a referee to report. An order under this rule shall specify the issues to be submitted. The procedures to be followed in the use of an advisory jury shall be the same as those for a jury selected under article forty-one. Where no issues remain to be tried, the court shall render decision directing judgment in the action.

## § 4213. Decision of the court.

(a) Requests for findings. Before the case is finally submitted, the court shall afford the parties an opportunity to submit requests for findings of fact. Each request shall be numbered and so phrased that the court may conveniently pass upon it.

(b) Form of decision. The decision of the court may be oral or in writing and shall state the facts it deems essential. In a medical, dental or podiatric malpractice action or in an action against a public employer or a public employee who is subject to indemnification by a public employer with respect to such action or both, as such terms are defined in subdivision (b) of section forty-five hundred forty-five, for personal injury or wrongful death arising out of an injury sustained by a public employee while acting within the scope of his public employment or duties, and in any other action brought to recover damages for personal injury, injury to property, or wrongful death, a decision awarding damages shall specify the applicable elements of special and general damages upon which the award is based and the amount assigned to each element, including but not limited to medical expenses, dental expenses, podiatric expenses, loss of earnings, impairment of earning ability, and pain and suffering. In a medical, dental or podiatric malpractice action, and in any other action brought to recover damages for personal injury, injury to property, or wrongful death, each element shall be further itemized into amounts intended to compensate for damages which have been incurred prior to the decision and amounts intended to compensate for damages to be incurred in the future. In itemizing amounts intended to compensate for future damages, the court shall set forth the period of years over which such amounts are intended to provide compensation. In computing said damages, the court shall award the full amount of future damages, as calculated, without reduction to present value.

(c) Time for decision. The decision of the court shall be rendered within sixty days after the cause or matter is finally submitted or within sixty days after a motion under rule 4403, whichever is later, unless the parties agree to extend the time.

### 1986 AMENDMENTS

L. 1986, ch. 485, eff. July 21, 1986, and applicable to acts, omissions or failures occurring on or after such date, amended CPLR 4213(b) to apply to podiatric malpractice actions, and L. 1986, ch. 682, eff. July 30, 1986, and applicable to actions commenced or claims filed on or after such date, which amended CPLR 4213(b) without incorporating changes made by L. 1986, ch. 485, to apply to actions involving personal injury, injury to property or wrongful death.

### 1985 AMENDMENTS

L. 1985, ch. 294, eff. July 1, 1985, and applicable to any action for dental or medical malpractice commenced on or after that date, and L. 1985, ch. 760, eff. July 1, 1985, and applicable to any acts, omissions or failures occurring on or after that date, amended subdivision (b) to provide that a decision awarding damages in a medical or dental malpractice action include dental expenses in its specification of damages and further itemize as to past and future damages.

### 1984 AMENDMENTS

L. 1984, ch. 701, eff. Oct. 1, 1984, and applicable to all actions commenced on or after that date, amended subdivision (b) to provide that a decision awarding damages in an action against a public employer for personal injury or wrongful death itemize special and general damages constituting the award.

### 1976 AMENDMENTS

L. 1976, ch. 955, eff. Aug. 26, 1976, amended Subd. (b) to provide that a decision awarding damages in a medical malpractice action itemize special and general damages constituting the award.

CPLR

# ARTICLE 43

# TRIAL BY A REFEREE

---

## SUMMARY OF ARTICLE

§ 4301.   Powers of referee to determine.
§§ 4302-4310.   [Not used.]
R 4311.   Order of reference.
R 4312.   Number of referees; qualifications.
R 4313.   Notice.
R 4314.   Successor referee.
R 4315.   Referee to be sworn.
R 4316.   Procedure where more than one referee.
§ 4317.   When reference to determine may be used.
   (a)  Upon consent of the parties.
   (b)  Without consent of the parties.
§ 4318.   Conduct of trial.
§ 4319.   Decision.
§ 4320.   Reference to report.
   (a)  Conduct of trial.
   (b)  Report; transcript.
R 4321.   Fees and expenses.

---

## § 4301.   Powers of referee to determine.

A referee to determine an issue or to perform an act shall have all the powers of a court in performing a like function; but he shall have no power to relieve himself of his duties, to appoint a successor or to adjudge any person except a witness before him guilty of contempt. For the purposes of this article the term referee shall be deemed to include judicial hearing officer.

### 1983 AMENDMENTS

L. 1983, ch. 840, eff. April 1, 1983, amended CPLR 4301.

### 1964 AMENDMENTS

L. 1964, ch. 388, eff. Sept. 1, 1964, changed the word "referees" in the caption to read "referee."

**§§ 4302-4310.   [Not used.]**

## R 4311.   Order of reference.

An order of reference shall direct the referee to determine the entire action or specific issues, to report issues, to perform particular acts, or to receive and report evidence only. It may specify or limit the powers of the referee and the time for the filing of his report and may fix a time and place for the hearing.

## R 4312.   Number of referees; qualifications.

1. A court may designate either one or three referees; provided, however, a judicial hearing officer may be designated a referee, in which case there shall be only one referee. Except by consent of the parties, no person shall be designated a referee unless he is an attorney admitted to practice in the state and in good standing. Where a referee may be designated by the parties, they may designate any number of referees.

2. Except in matrimonial actions or where the reference is to a judicial hearing officer, a person to whom all the parties object may not be designated as a referee. In matrimonial actions, only a judicial hearing officer or a special referee appointed by the chief administrator of the courts may be designated to determine an issue. In a matrimonial action the court shall not order a reference to a referee nominated by a party.

3. No person shall serve as referee who holds the position of court clerk, or clerk, secretary or stenographer to a judge; or who is the partner or clerk of an attorney for any party to the action or occupies the same office with such attorney except as provided in paragraph five of this rule.

4. A judge shall not serve as a referee in an action brought in a court of which he is a judge except by the written consent of the parties, and, in that case, he cannot receive any compensation as referee.

5. In uncontested matrimonial actions, a court clerk, law secretary, or any other non-judicial employee of the court, who is an attorney in good standing admitted to practice in the state, may be appointed by an administrative judge to serve without fee as a referee for the purpose of hearing and reporting to the court.

### 1983 AMENDMENTS

L. 1983, ch. 840, eff. April 1, 1983, amended CPLR 4312(1) and (2).

### 1980 AMENDMENTS

L. 1980, ch. 187, eff. June 2, 1980, made permanent the changes in CPLR 4312 enacted by the 1976 Legislature and extended by the 1978 Legislature relating to the appointment of referees in uncontested matrimonial actions. See comments at 1976 amendment notes.

## 1976 AMENDMENTS

L. 1976, ch. 699, eff. Sept. 1, 1976, and to remain in force and effect until August 31, 1978 [extended to August 30, 1980 by L. 1978, ch. 94, eff. April 25, 1978.] added a new paragraph (5) and a cross-reference thereto in paragraph (3).

Amendment recommended by the Judicial Conference in its report to the 1976 Legislature, wherein it stated, in part:

"The statistics of the Tenth Judicial District (Nassau and Suffolk Counties) strikingly indicate the large numbers of uncontested matrimonial processed by the courts. In that District the court disposed of 4,732 uncontested matrimonial actions in 1974 as contrasted with 2,291 in 1971; the statistical estimate is that the present workload of these cases consumes the full time of three judges. The time that a judge spends in these cases can be more effectively utilized and may be conserved by the appointment of a referee to hear and report, with the determination by the court.

"The power of appointment is vested in the administrative judge to facilitate speedy implementation as the need arises, since he is acquainted with local calendar conditions and availability of personnel for immediate assignment without disruption of other functions.

"This amendment is supplementary to, and in no way diminishes or affects the existing power of the Appellate Division, pursuant to CPLR 4312(2) and 4317 to designate special referees, who also may be court personnel such as law assistants, to hear and determine matrimonial actions without fee. It would, however, facilitate references to hear and report in uncontested matrimonial actions by permitting a more flexible use of qualified court personnel by an administrative judge."

CPLR

## R 4313.　Notice.

Except where the reference is to a judicial hearing officer or a special referee, upon the entry of an order of reference, the clerk shall send a copy of the order to the referee. Unless the order of reference otherwise provides, the referee shall forthwith notify the parties of a time and place for the first hearing to be held within twenty days after the date of the order or shall forthwith notify the court that he declines to serve.

### 1983 AMENDMENTS

L. 1983, ch. 840, eff. April 1, 1983, amended CPLR 4313.

## R 4314.　Successor referee.

Upon being notified that a referee declines or fails to serve, or in case of death, resignation or removal of a referee, or if a new trial is granted after a reference, on motion of any party or on its own initiative, the court may designate a successor referee, unless a stipulation upon which the order of reference is based expressly provides otherwise.

## R 4315.　Referee to be sworn.

A referee, other than a judicial hearing officer or a special referee, before entering upon his duties, shall be sworn faithfully and fairly to do such acts and make such determination and report as the order requires. The oath may be administered by any person authorized to take acknowledgments of deeds by the real property law. The oath may be waived upon consent of all parties.

**1983 AMENDMENTS**

L. 1983, ch. 840, eff. April 1, 1983, amended CPLR 4315.

### R 4316. Procedure where more than one referee.

Where the reference is to more than one referee all must meet together and hear all the allegations and proofs of the parties; but a majority may appoint a time and place for the trial, decide any question which arises upon the trial, sign a report or settle a case. Any of them may administer an oath to a witness; and a majority of those present at a time and place appointed for the trial may adjourn the trial to a future day.

### § 4317. When reference to determine may be used.

(a) Upon consent of the parties. The parties may stipulate that any issue shall be determined by a referee. Upon the filing of the stipulation with the clerk, the clerk shall forthwith enter an order referring the issue for trial to the referee named therein. Where the stipulation does not name a referee, the court shall designate a referee. Leave of court and designation by it of the referee is required for references in matrimonial actions; actions against a corporation to obtain a dissolution, to appoint a receiver of its property, or to distribute its property, unless such action is brought by the attorney-general; or actions where a defendant is an infant.

(b) Without consent of the parties. On motion of any party or on its own initiative, the court may order a reference to determine a cause of action or an issue where the trial will require the examination of a long account, including actions to foreclose mechanic's liens; or to determine an issue of damages separately triable and not requiring a trial by jury; or where otherwise authorized by law.

### § 4318. Conduct of trial.

Unless otherwise specified in the order of reference, the referee shall conduct the trial in the same manner as a court trying an issue without a jury. The provisions of article forty-four applicable to trial by the court shall apply to a reference pursuant to this article.

**1964 AMENDMENTS**

L. 1964, ch. 388, eff. Sept. 1, 1964, substituted the word "article" for the word "rule" at the end of the last sentence.

## § 4319. Decision.

The decision of a referee shall comply with the requirements for a decision by the court and shall stand as the decision of a court. Unless otherwise specified in the order of reference, the referee shall file his decision within thirty days after the cause or matter is finally submitted. If it is not filed within the required time, upon the motion of a party before it is filed, the court may grant a new trial and, in that event, the referee shall not be entitled to any fees.

## § 4320. Reference to report.

(a) Conduct of trial. A referee to report shall conduct the trial in the same manner as a court trying an issue without a jury.

(b) Report; transcript. The referee shall file his report, setting forth findings of fact and conclusions of law, within thirty days after the cause or matter is finally submitted. Unless otherwise stipulated, a transcript of the testimony together with the exhibits or copies thereof shall be filed with the report.

## R 4321. Fees and expenses.

1. An order or a stipulation for a reference shall determine the basis and method of computing the referee's fees and provide for their payment. The court may make an appropriate order for the payment of the reasonable expenses of the referee. Unless the court otherwise orders or the stipulation otherwise provides, such fees and expenses of the referee shall be taxed as costs.

2. This section shall not apply where the reference is to a judicial hearing officer.

### 1983 AMENDMENTS

L. 1983, ch. 840, eff. April 1, 1983, amended CPLR 4321 by numbering the opening paragraph (1) and adding a new subdivision (2).

CPLR

# ARTICLE 44

## TRIAL MOTIONS

### SUMMARY OF ARTICLE

R 4401.　Motion for judgment during trial.
§ 4401–a.　Motion for judgment.
R 4402.　Motion for continuance or new trial during trial.
R 4403.　Motion for new trial or to confirm or reject or grant other relief after reference to report or verdict of advisory jury.
R 4404.　Post-trial motion for judgment and new trial.
　　(a)　Motion after trial where jury required.
　　(b)　Motion after trial where jury not required.
R 4405.　Time and judge before whom post-trial motion made.
R 4406.　Single post-trial motion.

CPLR

### R 4401.　Motion for judgment during trial.

Any party may move for judgment with respect to a cause of action or issue upon the ground that the moving party is entitled to judgment as a matter of law, after the close of the evidence presented by an opposing party with respect to such cause of action or issue, or at any time on the basis of admissions. Grounds for the motion shall be specified. The motion does not waive the right to trial by jury or to present further evidence even where it is made by all parties.

### § 4401-a.　Motion for judgment.

A motion for judgment at the end of the plaintiff's case must be granted as to any cause of action for medical malpractice based solely on lack of informed consent if the plaintiff has failed to adduce expert medical testimony in support of the alleged qualitative insufficiency of the consent.

#### CROSS REFERENCES

See **Public Health Law** § 2805-d in Appendix, *infra*, as to limitation of medical malpractice action based upon lack of informed consent.

#### 1975 AMENDMENTS

L. 1975, ch. 109, eff. July 1, 1975, added Section 4401–a. The new section applies to acts of malpractice occurring on or after July 1, 1975.

## R 4402.   Motion for continuance or new trial during trial.

At any time during the trial, the court, on motion of any party, may order a continuance or a new trial in the interest of justice on such terms as may be just.

## R 4403.   Motion for new trial or to confirm or reject or grant other relief after reference to report or verdict of advisory jury.

Upon the motion of any party or on his own initiative, the judge required to decide the issue may confirm or reject, in whole or in part, the verdict of an advisory jury or the report of a referee to report; may make new findings with or without taking additional testimony; and may order a new trial or hearing. The motion shall be made within fifteen days after the verdict or the filing of the report and prior to further trial in the action. Where no issues remain to be tried the court shall render decision directing judgment in the action.

## R 4404.   Post-trial motion for judgment and new trial.

(a) Motion after trial where jury required. After a trial of a cause of action or issue triable of right by a jury, upon the motion of any party or on its own initiative, the court may set aside a verdict or any judgment entered thereon and direct that judgment be entered in favor of a party entitled to judgment as a matter of law or it may order a new trial of a cause of action or separable issue where the verdict is contrary to the weight of the evidence, in the interest of justice or where the jury cannot agree after being kept together for as long as is deemed reasonable by the court.

(b) Motion after trial where jury not required. After a trial not triable of right by a jury, upon the motion of any party or on its own initiative, the court may set aside its decision or any judgment entered thereon. It may make new findings of fact or conclusions of law, with or without taking additional testimony, render a new decision and direct entry of judgment, or it may order a new trial of a cause of action or separable issue.

## R 4405.   Time and judge before whom post-trial motion made.

A motion under this article shall be made before the judge who presided at the trial within fifteen days after decision, verdict or discharge of the jury. The court shall have no power to grant relief after argument or submission of an appeal from the final judgment.

### 1965 AMENDMENTS

L. 1965, ch. 673, eff. July 2, 1965, deleted the word "rule" and substituted therefor the word "article" in the first sentence.

**R 4406.    Single post-trial motion.**

In addition to motions made orally immediately after decision, verdict or discharge of the jury, there shall be only one motion under this article with respect to any decision by a court, or to a verdict on issues triable of right by a jury; and each party shall raise by the motion or by demand under rule 2215 every ground for post-trial relief then available to him.

# ARTICLE 45

# EVIDENCE

## SUMMARY OF ARTICLE

§ 4501.   Self-incrimination.
§ 4502.   Spouse.
    (a) Incompetency where issue adultery.
    (b) Confidential communication privileged.
§ 4503.   Attorney.
    (a) Confidential communication privileged; nonjudicial proceedings.
    (b) Wills.
§ 4504.   Physician, dentist, podiatrist, chiropractor and nurse.
    (a) Confidential information privileged.
    (b) Identification by dentist; crime committed against patient under sixteen.
    (c) Mental or physical condition of deceased patient.
    (d) Proof of negligence; unauthorized practice of medicine.
§ 4505.   Confidential communication to clergy privileged.
§ 4506.   Eavesdropping evidence; admissibility; motion to suppress in certain cases.
§ 4507.   Psychologist.
§ 4508.   Social worker.
    (a) Confidential information privileged.
    (b) Limitations on waiver.
§ 4509.   Library records.
§ 4510.   Rape crisis counselor.
    (a) Definitions.
    (b) Confidential information priveledged.
    (c) Who may waive the priveledge.
    (d) Limitation in waiver.
R 4511.   Judicial notice of law.
    (a) When judicial notice shall be taken without request.
    (b) When judicial notice may be taken without request; when it shall be taken on request.
    (c) Determination by court; review as matter of law.
    (d) Evidence to be received on matter to be judicially noticed.
§ 4512.   Competency of interested witness or spouse.
§ 4513.   Competency of person convicted of crime.
R 4514.   Impeachment of witness by prior inconsistent statement.
R 4515.   Form of expert opinion.
R 4516.   Proof of age of child.
R 4517.   Prior testimony by unavailable witness.

R 4518.     Business records.
        (a)  Generally.
        (b)  Hospital bills.
        (c)  Other records.
        (d)*
        (e)*
        (f)*
    * [Editor's note: No official heading.]
§ 4519.     Personal transaction or communication between witness and decedent
                or mentally ill person.
R 4520.     Certificate or affidavit of public officer.
R 4521.     Lack of record.
R 4522.     Ancient filed maps, surveys and records affecting real property.
R 4523.     Search by title insurance or abstract company.
R 4524.     Conveyance of real property without the state.
R 4525.     Copies of statements under article nine of the uniform commercial code.
R 4526.     Marriage certificate.
§ 4527.     Death or other status of missing person.
        (a)  Presumed death.
        (b)  Death, internment, capture and other status.
R 4528.     Weather conditions.
R 4529.     Inspection certificate issued by United States department of agriculture.
§ 4530.     Certificate of population.
        (a)  Prima facie evidence.
        (b)  Conclusive evidence.
R 4531.     Affidavit of service or posting notice by person unavailable at trial.
R 4532.     Self-authentication of newspapers and periodicals of general circulation.
R 4532-a.   X-rays, magnetic resonance images, computed axial tomographs, posi-
                tron emission tomographs, electromyograms, sonograms and fetal
                heart rate monitor strips in personal injury actions.
R 4533.     Market reports.
R 4533-a.   Prima facie proof of damages.
R 4533-b.   Proof of payment by joint tortfeasor.
R 4534.     Standard of measurement used by surveyor.
R 4535.     [Repealed.]
R 4536.     Proof of writing by comparison of handwriting.
R 4537.     Proof of writing subscribed by witness.
R 4538.     Acknowledged, proved or certified writing; conveyance of real property
                without the state.
R 4539.     Reproductions of original.
R 4540.     Authentication of official record of court or government office in the
                United States.
        (a)  Copies permitted.
        (b)  Certificate of officer of the state.
        (c)  Certificate of officer of another jurisdiction.
        (d)  Printed tariff or classification subject to public service commission,
                commissioner of transportation or interstate commerce commission.
R 4541.     Proof of proceedings before justice of the peace.

  (a) Of the state.
  (b) Of another state.
R 4542. Proof of foreign records and documents.
  (a) Foreign record.
  (b) Final certification.
  (c) Lack of record.
§ 4543. Proof of facts or writing by methods other than those authorized in this article.
§ 4544. Contracts in small print.
§ 4545. Admissibility of collateral source of payment.
  (a) Action for medical, dental or podiatric malpractice.
  (b) Certain actions against a public employer for personal injury and wrongful death.
  (c) Actions for personal injury, injury to property or wrongful death.
§ 4546. Loss of earnings and impairment of earning ability in actions for medical, dental or podiatric malpractice.

CPLR

---

## § 4501. Self-incrimination.

A competent witness shall not be excused from answering a relevant question, on the ground only that the answer may tend to establish that he owes a debt or is otherwise subject to a civil suit. This section does not require a witness to give an answer which will tend to accuse himself of a crime or to expose him to a penalty or forfeiture, nor does it vary any other rule respecting the examination of a witness.

## § 4502. Spouse.

(a) Incompetency where issue adultery. A husband or wife is not competent to testify against the other in an action founded upon adultery, except to prove the marriage, disprove the adultery, or disprove a defense after evidence has been introduced tending to prove such defense.

(b) Confidential communication privileged. A husband or wife shall not be required, or, without consent of the other if living, allowed, to disclose a confidential communication made by one to the other during marriage.

## § 4503. Attorney.

(a) Confidential communication privileged; nonjudicial proceedings. Unless the client waives the privilege, an attorney or his employee, or any person who obtains without the knowledge of the client evidence of a confidential communication made between the attorney or his employee and the client in the course of professional employment, shall not disclose, or be allowed to disclose such communication, nor shall the client be compelled to disclose such communication, in any action, disciplinary trial or hearing, or administrative action, proceeding or hearing conducted by or on behalf of any state, municipal or local governmental agency or by the legislature or any committee or body thereof. Evidence of any such communication obtained by any such person, and evidence resulting therefrom, shall not be disclosed by any state, municipal or local governmental agency or by the legislature or any committee or body thereof. The relationship of an attorney and client shall exist between a professional service corporation organized under article fifteen of the business corporation law to practice as an attorney and counselor-at-law and the clients to whom it renders legal services.

(b) Wills. In any action involving the probate, validity or construction of a will, an attorney or his employee shall be required to disclose information as to the preparation, execution or revocation of any will or other relevant instrument, but he shall not be allowed to disclose any communication privileged under subdivision (a) which would tend to disgrace the memory of the decedent.

### 1977 AMENDMENTS

L. 1977, ch. 418, eff. July 12, 1977, amended CPLR 4503(a) by adding the last sentence.

## § 4504. Physician, dentist, podiatrist, chiropractor and nurse.

(a) Confidential information privileged. Unless the patient waives the privilege, a person authorized to practice medicine, registered professional nursing, licensed practical nursing, dentistry, podiatry or chiropractic shall not be allowed to disclose any information which he acquired in attending a patient in a professional capacity, and which was necessary to enable him to act in that capacity. The relationship of a physician and patient shall exist between a medical corporation, as defined in article forty-four of the public health law, a professional service corporation organized under article fifteen of the business corporation law to practice medicine, a university faculty practice corporation organized under section fourteen hundred twelve of the not-for-profit corporation law to practice medicine or dentistry, and the patients to whom they respectively render professional medical services.

A patient who, for the purpose of obtaining insurance benefits, authorizes the disclosure of any such privileged communication to any person shall not be deemed to have waived the privilege created by this subdivision. For purposes of this subdivision:

1. "person" shall mean any individual, insurer or agent thereof, peer review committee, public or private corporation, political subdivision, government agency, department or bureau of the state, municipality, industry, co-partnership, association, firm, trust, estate or any other legal entity whatsoever; and

2. "insurance benefits" shall include payments under a self-insured plan.

(b) Identification by dentist; crime committed against patient under sixteen. A dentist shall be required to disclose information necessary for identification of a patient. A physician, dentist, podiatrist, chiropractor or nurse shall be required to disclose information indicating that a patient who is under the age of sixteen years has been the victim of a crime.

(c) Mental or physical condition of deceased patient. A physician or nurse shall be required to disclose any information as to the mental or physical condition of a deceased patient privileged under subdivision (a), except information which would tend to disgrace the memory of the decedent, either in the absence of an objection by a party to the litigation or when the privilege has been waived:

1. by the personal representative, or the surviving spouse, or the next of kin of the decedent; or

2. in any litigation where the interests of the personal representative are deemed by the trial judge to be adverse to those of the estate of the decedent, by any party in interest; or

3. if the validity of the will of the decedent is in question, by the executor named in the will, or the surviving spouse or any heir-at-law or any of the next of kin or any other party in interest.

(d) Proof of negligence; unauthorized practice of medicine. In any action for damages for personal injuries or death against a person not authorized to practice medicine under article 131 of the education law for any act or acts constituting the practice of medicine, when such act or acts were a competent producing proximate or contributing cause of such injuries or death, the fact that such person practiced medicine without being so authorized shall be deemed prima facie evidence of negligence.

**CPLR**

### CROSS REFERENCES

See **Penal Law § 265.25,** which requires that certain wounds be reported to police authorities by the attending physician or hospital representative.

### 1993 AMENDMENTS

L. 1993, ch. 555, eff. July 28, 1993, amended CPLR 4504(a) to include not-for-profit university faculty practice corporations licensed to practice medicine or dentistry.

### 1991 AMENDMENTS

L. 1991, ch. 457, eff. July 19, 1991, amended CPLR 4504 by adding the references to "podiatrist" and "podiatry."

### 1990 AMENDMENTS

L. 1990, ch. 800, eff. July 25, 1990, amended CPLR 4504 by adding the references to "chiropractor" and "chiropractic."

### 1984 AMENDMENTS

L. 1984, ch. 913, eff. Oct. 5, 1984, amended CPLR 4504(a) to provide that the authorization of disclosure of any privileged communication for the purpose of obtaining insurance benefits shall not be deemed a waiver of the privilege created by the subdivision.

### 1971 AMENDMENTS

L. 1971, ch. 1139, eff. July 6, 1971, amended CPLR 4504(a) by creating a physician-patient relationship between a medical corporation, as defined in Public Health Law article 44, a professional service corporation organized under Business Corporation Law article 15, and the patients to whom they respectively render professional medical services.

L. 1971, ch. 987, eff. Sept. 1, 1971, amended CPLR 4504 by adding a new subdivision (d).

### 1966 AMENDMENTS

L. 1966, ch. 252, eff. Sept. 1, 1966, amended Subd. (a) by adding the words "registered professional nursing, licensed practical nursing" after the phrase "a person authorized to practice medicine" and deleted the words "or a registered professional or licensed practical nurse" after the words "or dentistry."

## § 4505.   Confidential communication to clergy privileged.

Unless the person confessing or confiding waives the privilege, a clergyman, or other minister of any religion or duly accredited Christian Science practitioner, shall not be allowed to disclose a confession or confidence made to him in his professional character as spiritual advisor.

### 1965 AMENDMENTS

L. 1965, ch. 520, eff. June 28, 1965, added the words "or confiding," "or duly accredited Christian Science practitioner," and "or confidence" to the section.

## § 4506.   Eavesdropping evidence; admissibility; motion to suppress in certain cases.

1. The contents of any overheard or recorded communication, conversation or discussion, or evidence derived therefrom, which has been obtained by conduct constituting the crime of eavesdropping, as defined by section 250.05 of the penal law, may not be received in evidence in any trial, hearing or proceeding before any court or grand jury, or before any legislative committee, department, officer, agency, regulatory body, or other authority of the state, or a political subdivision thereof; provided, however, that such communication, conversation, discussion or evidence, shall be admissible in any civil or criminal trial, hearing or proceeding against a person who has, or is alleged to have, committed such crime of eavesdropping.

2. As used in this section, the term "aggrieved person" means:

(a) A person who was a sender or receiver of a telephonic or telegraphic communication which was intentionally overheard or recorded by a person other than the sender or receiver thereof, without the consent of the sender or receiver, by means of any instrument, device or equipment; or

(b) A party to a conversation or discussion which was intentionally overheard or recorded, without the consent of at least one party thereto, by a person not present threat, by means of any instrument, device or equipment; or

(c) A person against whom the overhearing or recording described in paragraphs (a) and (b) was directed.

3. An aggrieved person who is a party in any civil trial, hearing or proceeding before any court, or before any department, officer, agency, regulatory body, or other authority of the state, or a political subdivision thereof, may move to suppress the contents of any overheard or recorded communication, conversation or discussion or evidence derived therefrom, on the ground that:

(a) The communication, conversation or discussion was unlawfully overheard or recorded; or

(b) The eavesdropping warrant under which it was overheard or recorded is insufficient on its face; or

(c) The eavesdropping was not done in conformity with the eavesdropping warrant.

4. The motion prescribed in subdivision three of this section must be made before the judge or justice who issued the eavesdropping warrant. If no eavesdropping warrant was issued, such motion must be made before a justice of the supreme court of the judicial district in which the trial, hearing or proceeding is pending. The aggrieved person must allege in his motion papers that an overheard or recorded communication, conversation or discussion, or evidence derived therefrom, is subject to suppression under subdivision three of this section, and that such communication, conversation or discussion, or evidence, may be used against him in the civil trial, hearing or proceeding in which he is a party. The motion must be made prior to the commencement of such trial, hearing or proceeding, unless there was no opportunity to make such motion or the aggrieved person was not aware of the grounds of the motion. If the motion is granted, the contents of the overheard or recorded communication, conversation or discussion or evidence derived therefrom, may not be received in evidence in any trial, hearing or proceeding.

**1969 AMENDMENTS**

L. 1969, ch. 1147, eff. June 25, 1969, repealed section 4506 and added new section 4506.

## § 4507.  Psychologist.

The confidential relations and communications between a psychologist registered under the provisions of article one hundred fifty-three of the education law and his client are placed on the same basis as those provided by law between attorney and client, and nothing in such article shall be construed to require any such privileged communications to be disclosed.

CPLR

A client who, for the purpose of obtaining insurance benefits, authorizes the disclosure of any such privileged communication to any person shall not be deemed to have waived the privilege created by this section. For purposes of this section:

1. "person" shall mean any individual, insurer or agent thereof, peer review committee, public or private corporation, political subdivision, government agency, department or bureau of the state, municipality, industry, co-partnership, association, firm, trust, estate or any other legal entity whatsoever; and

2. "insurance benefits" shall include payments under a self-insured plan.

### 1984 AMENDMENTS

L. 1984, ch. 913, eff. Oct. 5, 1984, amended CPLR 4507 to provide that the authorization of disclosure of any privileged communication for the purpose of obtaining insurance benefits shall not be deemed a waiver of the privilege created by the section.

### 1968 AMENDMENTS

L. 1968, ch. 274, eff. May 14, 1968, added CPLR 4507 and CPLR 4508.

## § 4508. Social worker.

(a) Confidential information privileged. A person duly registered as a certified social worker under the provisions of article one hundred fifty-four of the education law shall not be required to disclose a communication made by his client to him, or his advice given thereon, in the course of his professional employment, nor shall any clerk, stenographer or other person working for the same employer as the certified social worker or for the certified social worker be allowed to disclose any such communication or advice given thereon; except

1. that a certified social worker may disclose such information as the client may authorize;

2. that a certified social worker shall not be required to treat as confidential a communication by a client which reveals the contemplation of a crime or harmful act;

3. where the client is a child under the age of sixteen and the information acquired by the certified social worker indicates that the client has been the victim or subject of a crime, the certified social worker may be required to testify fully in relation thereto upon any examination, trial or other proceeding in which the commission of such crime is a subject of inquiry;

4. where the client waives the privilege by bringing charges against the certified social worker and such charges involve confidential communications between the client and certified social worker.

(b) Limitations on waiver. A client who, for the purpose of obtaining insurance benefits, authorizes the disclosure of any such privileged communication to any person shall not be deemed to have waived the privilege created by this section. For purposes of this subdivision:

1. "person" shall mean any individual, insurer or agent thereof, peer review committee, public or private corporation, political subdivision, government agency, department, or bureau of the state, municipality, industry, co-partnership, association, firm, trust, estate or any other legal entity whatsoever; and

2. "insurance benefits" shall include payments under a self-insured plan.

### 1985 AMENDMENTS

L. 1985, ch. 96, eff. July 20, 1985, deleted the cross reference to Education Law § 7707 and added subdivision (b).

### 1968 AMENDMENTS

L. 1968, ch. 274, eff. May 14, 1968, added CPLR 4508.

## § 4509. Library records.

Library records, which contain names or other personally identifying details regarding the users of public, free association, school, college and university libraries and library systems of this state, including but not limited to records related to the circulation of library materials, computer database searches, interlibrary loan transactions, reference queries, requests for photocopies of library materials, title reserve requests, or the use of audio-visual materials, films or records, shall be confidential and shall not be disclosed except that such records may be disclosed to the extent necessary for the proper operation of such library and shall be disclosed upon request or consent of the user or pursuant to subpoena, court order or where otherwise required by statute.

### 1988 AMENDMENTS

L. 1988, ch. 112, eff. June 13, 1988, amended § 4509 to eliminate the restriction to "circulation" records, broadening the category of records deemed confidential.

### 1982 AMENDMENTS

L. 1982, ch. 14, eff. March 10, 1982, added new CPLR 4509.

## § 4510. Rape crisis counselor.

(a) Definitions. When used in this section, the following terms shall have the following meanings:

1. "Rape crisis program" means any office, institution or center which has been approved pursuant to subdivision fifteen of section two hundred six of the public health law, offering counseling and assistance to clients concerning sexual offenses, sexual abuses or incest.

2. "Rape crisis counselor" means any person who has been certified by an approved rape crisis program as having satisfied the training standards specified in subdivision fifteen of section two hundred six of the public health law, and

who, regardless of compensation, is acting under the direction and supervision of an approved rape crisis program.

3. "Client" means any person who is seeking or receiving the services of a rape crisis counselor for the purpose of securing counseling or assistance concerning any sexual offenses, sexual abuse, incest or attempts to commit sexual offenses, sexual abuse, or incest, as defined in the penal law.

(b) Confidential information privileged. A rape crisis counselor shall not be required to disclose a communication made by his or her client to him or her, or advice given thereon, in the course of his or her services nor shall any clerk, stenographer or other person working for the same program as the rape crisis counselor or for the rape crisis counselor be allowed to disclose any such communication or advice given thereon nor shall any records made in the course of the services given to the client or recording of any communications made by or to a client be required to be disclosed, nor shall the client be compelled to disclose such communication or records, except:

1. that a rape crisis counselor may disclose such otherwise confidential communication to the extent authorized by the client;

2. that a rape crisis counselor shall not be required to treat as confidential a communication by a client which reveals the intent to commit a crime or harmful act;

3. in a case in which the client waives the privilege by instituting charges against the rape crisis counselor or the rape crisis program and such action or proceeding involves confidential communications between the client and the rape crisis counselor.

(c) Who may waive the privilege. The privilege may only be waived by the client, the personal representative of a deceased client, or, in the case of a client who has been adjudicated incompetent or for whom a conservator has been appointed, the committee or conservator.

(d) Limitation on waiver. A client who, for the purposes of obtaining compensation under article twenty-two of the executive law or insurance benefits, authorizes the disclosure of any privileged communication to an employee of the crime victims board or an insurance representative shall not be deemed to have waived the privilege created by this section.

### 1993 AMENDMENTS

L. 1993, ch. 432, eff. Jan. 22, 1994, added new CPLR 4510.

## R 4511.   Judicial notice of law.

(a) When judicial notice shall be taken without request. Every court shall take judicial notice without request of the common law, constitutions and public statutes of the United States and of every state, territory and jurisdiction of the United States and of the official compilation of codes, rules and regulations of the state except those that relate solely to the organization or internal management of an agency of the state and of all local laws and county acts.

(b) When judicial notice may be taken without request; when it shall be taken on request. Every court may take judicial notice without request of private acts and resolutions of the congress of the United States and of the legislature of the state; ordinances and regulations of officers, agencies or governmental subdivisions of the state or of the United States; and the laws of foreign countries or their political subdivisions. Judicial notice shall be taken of matters specified in this subdivision if a party requests it, furnishes the court sufficient information to enable it to comply with the request, and has given each adverse party notice of his intention to request it. Notice shall be given in the pleadings or prior to the presentation of any evidence at the trial, but a court may require or permit other notice.

(c) Determination by court; review as matter of law. Whether a matter is judicially noticed or proof is taken, every matter specified in this section shall be determined by the judge or referee, and included in his findings or charged to the jury. Such findings or charge shall be subject to review on appeal as a finding or charge on a matter of law.

(d) Evidence to be received on matter to be judicially noticed. In considering whether a matter of law should be judicially noticed and in determining the matter of law to be judicially noticed, the court may consider any testimony, document, information or argument on the subject, whether offered by a party or discovered through its own research. Whether or not judicial notice is taken, a printed copy of a statute or other written law or a proclamation, edict, decree or ordinance by an executive contained in a book or publication, purporting to have been published by a government or commonly admitted as evidence of the existing law in the judicial tribunals of the jurisdiction where it is in force, is prima facie evidence of such law and the unwritten or common law of a jurisdiction may be proved by witnesses or printed reports of cases of the courts of the jurisdiction.

### § 4512. Competency of interested witness or spouse.

Except as otherwise expressly prescribed, a person shall not be excluded or excused from being a witness, by reason of his interest in the event or because he is a party or the spouse of a party.

### § 4513. Competency of person convicted of crime.

A person who has been convicted of a crime is a competent witness; but the conviction may be proved, for the purpose of affecting the weight of his testimony, either by cross-examination, upon which he shall be required to answer any relevant question, or by the record. The party cross-examining is not concluded by such person's answer.

CPLR

## R 4514. Impeachment of witness by prior inconsistent statement.

In addition to impeachment in the manner permitted by common law, any party may introduce proof that any witness has made a prior statement inconsistent with his testimony if the statement was made in a writing subscribed by him or was made under oath.

CROSS REFERENCES

See **Criminal Procedure Law § 60.35,** as to impeachment of own witness in criminal cases by proof of prior contradictory statement.

## R 4515. Form of expert opinion.

Unless the court orders otherwise, questions calling for the opinion of an expert witness need not be hypothetical in form, and the witness may state his opinion and reasons without first specifying the data upon which it is based. Upon cross-examination, he may be required to specify the data and other criteria supporting the opinion.

## R 4516. Proof of age of child.

Whenever it becomes necessary to determine the age of a child, he may be produced and exhibited to enable the court or jury to determine his age by a personal inspection.

## R 4517. Prior testimony by unavailable witness.

In a civil action, if a witness' testimony is not available because of privilege, death, physical or mental illness, absence beyond the jurisdiction of the court to compel appearance by its process or absence because the proponent of his statement does not know and with diligence has been unable to ascertain his whereabouts, or because he is incompetent to testify by virtue of section 4519, his testimony, taken or introduced in evidence at a former trial, together with all exhibits and documents introduced in connection with it, may be introduced in evidence by any party upon any trial of the same subject-matter in the same or another action between the same parties or their representatives, subject to any objection to admissibility other than hearsay. Such testimony may not be used if the witness' unavailability was procured by, or through the culpable neglect or wrongdoing of, the proponent of his statement. The original stenographic notes of testimony taken by a stenographer who has since died or become incompetent may be read in evidence by any person whose competency to read them accurately is established to the satisfaction of the court.

1964 AMENDMENTS

Amendment No. 8, eff. Sept. 1, 1964, made by the Judicial Conference Feb. 1, 1964, Report to the Legislature, added the words "or because he is incompetent to testify by virtue of section 4519," following the phrase "unable to ascertain his whereabouts," in the first sentence.

## R 4518. Business records.

(a) Generally. Any writing or record, whether in the form of an entry in a book or otherwise, made as a memorandum or record of any act, transaction, occurrence or event, shall be admissible in evidence in proof of that act, transaction, occurrence or event, if the judge finds that it was made in the regular course of any business and that it was the regular course of such business to make it, at the time of the act, transaction, occurrence or event, or within a reasonable time thereafter. All other circumstances of the making of the memorandum or record, including lack of personal knowledge by the maker, may be proved to affect its weight, but they shall not affect its admissibility. The term business includes a business, profession, occupation and calling of every kind.

(b) Hospital bills. A hospital bill is admissible in evidence under this rule and is prima facie evidence of the facts contained, provided it bears a certification by the head of the hospital or by a responsible employee in the controller's or accounting office that the bill is correct, that each of the items was necessarily supplied and that the amount charged is reasonable. This subdivision shall not apply to any proceeding in a surrogate's court nor in any action instituted by or on behalf of a hospital to recover payment for accommodations or supplies furnished or for services rendered by or in such hospital, except that in a proceeding pursuant to section one hundred eighty-nine of the lien law to determine the validity and extent of the lien of a hospital, such certified hospital bills are prima facie evidence of the fact of services and of the reasonableness of any charges which do not exceed the comparable charges made by the hospital in the care of workmen's compensation patients.

(c) Other records. All records, writings and other things referred to in sections 2306 and 2307 are admissible in evidence under this rule and are prima facie evidence of the facts contained, provided they bear a certification or authentication by the head of the hospital, laboratory, department or bureau of a municipal corporation or of the state, or by an employee delegated for that purpose or by a qualified physician. Where a hospital record is in the custody of a warehouse, or "warehouseman" as that term is defined by paragraph (h) of subdivision one of section 7-102 of the uniform commercial code, pursuant to a plan approved in writing by the state commissioner of health, admissibility under this subdivision may be established by a certification made by the manager of the warehouse that sets forth (i) the authority by which the record is held, including but not limited to a court order, order of the commissioner, or order or resolution of the governing body or official of the hospital, and (ii) that the record has been in the exclusive custody of such warehouse or warehousemen since its receipt from the hospital or, if another has had access to it, the name and address of such person and the date on which and the circumstances under which such access was had. Any warehouseman providing a certification as required by this subdivision shall have no liability for acts or omissions relating thereto, except for intentional misconduct, and the warehouseman is authorized to assess and collect a reasonable charge for providing the certification described by this subdivision.

(d) Any records or reports relating to the administration and analysis of a blood genetic marker or DNA test administered pursuant to sections four hundred eighteen and five hundred thirty-two of the family court act are admissible in evidence under this rule and are prima facie evidence of the facts contained provided they bear a certification or authentication by the head of the hospital, laboratory, department or bureau of a municipal corporation or of the state or by an employee delegated for that purpose, or by a qualified physician. If such record or report relating to the administration and analysis of a blood genetic marker or DNA test or tests administered pursuant to sections four hundred eighteen and five hundred thirty-two of the family court act indicates at least a ninety-five percent probability of paternity, the admission of such record or report shall create a rebuttable presumption of paternity, and shall, if unrebutted, establish the paternity of and liability for the support of a child pursuant to articles four and five of the family court act.

(e) Notwithstanding any other provision of law, a record or report relating to the administration and analysis of a blood genetic marker or DNA test certified in accordance with subdivision (d) of this rule and administered pursuant to sections four hundred eighteen and five hundred thirty-two of the family court act is admissible in evidence under this rule without the need for foundation testimony or further proof of authenticity or accuracy unless objections to the record or report are made in writing no later than twenty days before a hearing at which the record or report may be introduced into evidence or thirty days after receipt of the test results, whichever is earlier.

(f) Notwithstanding any other provision of law, records or reports of support payments and disbursements maintained pursuant to title six-a of article three of the social services law by the department of social services or the fiscal agent under contract to the department for the provision of centralized collection and disbursement functions are admissible in evidence under this rule, provided that they bear a certification by an official of a social services district attesting to the accuracy of the content of the record or report of support payments and that in attesting to the accuracy of the record or report such official has received confirmation from the department of social services or the fiscal agent under contract to the department for the provision of centralized collection and disbursement functions pursuant to section one hundred eleven-h of the social services law that the record or report of support payments reflects the processing of all support payments in the possession of the department or the fiscal agent as of a specified date, and that the document is a record or report of support payments maintained pursuant to title six-a of article three of the social services law. If so certified, such record or report shall be admitted into evidence under this rule without the need for additional foundation testimony. Such records shall be the basis for a permissive inference of the facts contained therein unless the trier of fact finds good cause not to draw such inference.

## 1995 AMENDMENTS

L. 1995, ch. 81, § 236, eff. July 1, 1995, added a new subdivision (f) pertaining to social service support records.

## 1994 AMENDMENTS

L. 1994, ch. 170, eff. June 15, 1994, amended CPLR 4518 by deleting from subdivision (c) the reference to blood genetic marker tests (*cf.* 1984 amendment note, *infra*) and by adding new subdivisions (d) and (e) to specifically regulate those tests and the resulting reports.

## 1992 AMENDMENTS

L. 1992, ch. 381, eff. July 17, 1992, amended Subdivision (c) by adding the language following the sentence ending with the words "qualified physician."

## 1984 AMENDMENTS

L. 1984, ch. 792, eff. Aug. 5, 1984, and applicable to any action or proceeding pending on or commenced after Aug. 5, 1984, amended CPLR 4518(c) by substituting blood genetic marker test for blood grouping or human leucocyte antigen test.

## 1983 AMENDMENTS

L. 1983, ch. 311, eff. June 21, 1983, amended CPLR 4518(c) by providing for certification of blood test results by a laboratory or a qualified physician.

## 1982 AMENDMENTS

L. 1982, ch. 695, eff. July 22, 1982, amended CPLR 4518(c) to include reports of blood tests and HLA tests among those business records which are admissible into evidence.

## 1970 AMENDMENTS

Amendment No. 2 made by Judicial Conference Jan. 2, 1970, Report to the 1970 Legislature, effective Sept. 1, 1970, amended by adding thereto new Subd. (c).

## § 4519.  Personal transaction or communication between witness and decedent or mentally ill person.

Upon the trial of an action or the hearing upon the merits of a special proceeding, a party or a person interested in the event, or a person from, through or under whom such a party or interested person derives his interest or title by assignment or otherwise, shall not be examined as a witness in his own behalf or interest, or in behalf of the party succeeding to his title or interest against the executor, administrator or survivor of a deceased person or the committee of a mentally ill person, or a person deriving his title or interest from, through or under a deceased person or mentally ill person, by assignment or otherwise, concerning a personal transaction or communication between the witness and the deceased person or mentally ill person, except where the executor, administrator, survivor, committee or person so deriving title or interest is examined

CPLR

in his own behalf, or the testimony of a mentally ill person or deceased person is given in evidence, concerning the same transaction or communication. A person shall not be deemed interested for the purposes of this section by reason of being a stockholder or officer of any banking corporation which is a party to the action or proceeding, or interested in the event thereof. No party or person interested in the event, who is otherwise competent to testify, shall be disqualified from testifying by the possible imposition of costs against him or the award of costs to him. A party or person interested in the event or a person from, through or under whom such a party or interested person derives his interest or title by assignment or otherwise, shall not be qualified for the purposes of this section, to testify in his own behalf or interest, or in behalf of the party succeeding to his title or interest, to personal transactions or communications with the donee of a power of appointment in an action or proceeding for the probate of a will, which exercises or attempts to exercise a power of appointment granted by the will of a donor of such power, or in an action or proceeding involving the construction of the will of the donee after its admission to probate.

Nothing contained in this section, however, shall render a person incompetent to testify as to the facts of an accident or the results therefrom where the proceeding, hearing, defense or cause of action involves a claim of negligence or contributory negligence in an action wherein one or more parties is the representative of a deceased or incompetent person based upon, or by reason of, the operation or ownership of a motor vehicle being operated upon the highways of the state, or the operation or ownership of aircraft being operated in the air space over the state, or the operation or ownership of a vessel on any of the lakes, rivers, streams, canals or other waters of this state, but this provision shall not be construed as permitting testimony as to conversations with the deceased.

### 1978 AMENDMENTS

L. 1978, ch. 550, eff. July 24, 1978, amended CPLR 4519 by eliminating use of the term "lunatic" throughout, and replacing it with the term "mentally ill person."

## R 4520. Certificate or affidavit of public officer.

Where a public officer is required or authorized, by special provision of law, to make a certificate or an affidavit to a fact ascertained, or an act performed, by him in the course of his official duty, and to file or deposit it in a public office of the state, the certificate or affidavit so filed or deposited is prima facie evidence of the facts stated.

## R 4521. Lack of record.

A statement signed by an officer or a deputy of an officer having legal custody of specified official records of the United States or of any state, territory or jurisdiction of the United States, or of any court thereof, or kept in any public office thereof, that he has made diligent search of the records and has found no record or entry of a specified nature, is prima facie evidence that the records contain no such record or entry, provided that the statement is accompanied by a certificate that legal custody of the specified official records belongs to such person, which certificate shall be made by a person described in rule 4540.

**1964 AMENDMENTS**

L. 1964, ch. 388, eff. Sept. 1, 1964, substituted the word "rule" in place of the word "section" before "4540" in the last line.

### R 4522.  Ancient filed maps, surveys and records affecting real property.

All maps, surveys and official records affecting real property, which have been on file in the state in the office of the register of any county, any county clerk, any court of record or any department of the city of New York for more than ten years, are prima facie evidence of their contents.

### R 4523.  Search by title insurance or abstract company.

A search affecting real property, when made and certified to by a title insurance, abstract or searching company, organized under the laws of this state, may be used in place of, and with the same legal effect as, an official search.

### R 4524.  Conveyance of real property without the state.

A record of a conveyance of real property situated within another state, territory or jurisdiction of the United States, recorded therein pursuant to its laws, is prima facie evidence of conveyance and of due execution.

### R 4525.  Copies of statements under article nine of the uniform commercial code.

A copy of a statement which is noted or certified by a filing officer pursuant to section 9-407(1) of the uniform commercial code and which states that the copy is a true copy is prima facie evidence of the facts stated in the notation or certification and that the copy is a true copy of a statement filed in the office of the filing officer.

**1965 AMENDMENTS**

L. 1965, ch. 729, eff. July 21, 1965, repealed former Rule 4525 and enacted a new Rule 4525.

### R 4526.  Marriage certificate.

An original certificate of a marriage made by the person by whom it was solemnized within the state, or the original entry thereof made pursuant to law in the office of the clerk of a city or a town within the state, is prima facie evidence of the marriage.

CPLR

## § 4527.  Death or other status of missing person.

(a) Presumed death. A written finding of presumed death, made by any person authorized to make such findings by the federal missing persons act is prima facie evidence of the death, and the date, circumstances and place of disappearance. In the case of a merchant seaman, a written finding of presumed death, made by the maritime war emergency board or by the war shipping administration or the successors or assigns of such board or administration in connection with war risk insurance is prima facie evidence of the death, and the date, circumstances and place of disappearance.

(b) Death, internment, capture and other status. An official written report or record that a person is missing, missing in action, interned in a neutral country, or beleaguered, besieged or captured by an enemy, or is dead, or is alive, made by an officer or employee of the United States authorized by law of the United States to make it is prima facie evidence of such fact.

### CROSS REFERENCES

The **Federal Missing Persons Act,** referred to in Subd. (a), *supra,* appears in 5 USCA § 5561, *et seq.*

## R 4528.  Weather conditions.

Any record of the observations of the weather, taken under the direction of the United States weather bureau, is prima facie evidence of the facts stated.

## R 4529.  Inspection certificate issued by United States department of agriculture.

An inspection certificate issued by the authorized agents of the United States department of agriculture on file with the United States secretary of agriculture is prima facie evidence of the facts stated.

## § 4530.  Certificate of population.

(a) Prima facie evidence. A certificate of the officer in charge of the census of the United States, attested by the United States secretary of commerce, giving the result of the census is, except as hereinafter provided, prima facie evidence of such result.

(b) Conclusive evidence. Where the population of the state or a subdivision, or a portion of a subdivision of the state is required to be determined according to the federal or state census or enumeration last preceding a particular time, a certificate of the officer in charge of the census of the United States, attested by the United States secretary of commerce, as to such population as shown by such federal census, or a certificate of the secretary of state as to such population as shown by such state enumeration, is conclusive evidence of such population.

## R 4531. Affidavit of service or posting notice by person unavailable at trial.

An affidavit by a person who served, posted or affixed a notice, showing such service, posting or affixing is prima facie evidence of the service, posting or affixing if the affiant is dead, mentally ill or cannot be compelled with due diligence to attend at the trial.

### 1978 AMENDMENTS

L. 1978, ch. 550, eff. July 24, 1978, amended CPLR 4531 by eliminating use of the term "insane" and replacing it with the term "mentally ill."

## R 4532. Self-authentication of newspapers and periodicals of general circulation.

Extrinsic evidence of authenticity as a condition precedent to admissibility is not required with respect to printed materials purporting to be newspapers or periodicals of general circulation; provided however, nothing herein shall be deemed to preclude or limit the right of a party to challenge the authenticity of such printed material, by extrinsic evidence or otherwise, prior to admission by the court or to raise the issue of authenticity as an issue of fact.

### 1986 AMENDMENTS

L. 1986, ch. 89, eff. May 23, 1986, amended CPLR 4532 by allowing for the self-authentication of newspapers and periodicals of general circulation and removing the need for extrinsic evidence of authenticity as a condition precedent to admissibility.

## R 4532-a. X-rays, magnetic resonance images, computed axial tomographs, positron emission tomographs, electromyograms, sonograms and fetal heart rate monitor strips in personal injury actions.

In an action in which a claim for personal injuries is asserted, an X-ray, magnetic resonance image, computed axial tomograph, positron emission tomograph, electromyogram, sonogram or fetal heart rate monitor strips of any party thereto is admissible in evidence provided:

(1) that there is photographically inscribed on such X-ray, magnetic resonance image, computed axial tomograph, positron emission tomograph, electromyogram, sonogram or fetal heart rate monitor strips the name of the injured party, the date when taken, the identifying number thereof, and the name and address of the physician under whose supervision the same was taken;

(2) that at least ten days before the date of trial of the action, the attorney for the party intending to offer such X-ray, magnetic resonance image, computed axial tomograph, positron emission tomograph, electromyogram, sonogram or fetal heart rate monitor strips, serve upon the attorney or attorneys for the party or parties against whom said x-ray, magnetic resonance image, computed axial

CPLR

tomograph, positron emission tomograph, electromyogram, sonogram or fetal heart rate monitor strips is to be offered, a notice of his intention to offer such X-ray, magnetic resonance image, computed axial tomograph, positron emission tomograph, electromyogram, sonogram or fetal heart rate monitor strips in evidence during the trial and that the same is available for inspection at his office, provided that such X-ray, magnetic resonance image, computed axial tomograph, positron emission tomograph, electromyogram, sonogram or fetal heart rate monitor strips has or have not been previously so examined; and

(3) that the notice aforesaid is accompanied by an affidavit of such physician identifying the X-ray, magnetic resonance image, computed axial tomograph, positron emission tomograph, electromyogram, sonogram or fetal heart rate monitor strips and attesting to the information inscribed thereon, and further attesting that, if called as a witness in the action, he would so testify.

Nothing contained in this section, however, shall prohibit the admissibility of an X-ray, magnetic resonance image, computed axial tomograph, positron emission tomograph, electromyogram, sonogram or fetal heart rate monitor strips in evidence in a personal injury action where otherwise admissible.

### 1993 AMENDMENTS

L. 1993, ch. 482, eff. July 26, 1993, amended CPLR 4532-a to provide that certain designated medical test results — X-ray, magnetic resonance image, computed axial tomograph, positron emission tomograph, electromyogram, sonogram and fetal heart rate monitor strip — can be admissible evidence.

### 1979 AMENDMENTS

L. 1979, ch. 124, eff. Sept. 1, 1979, amended CPLR 4532-a subds. (1) and (3) by eliminating the word radiologist and substituting therefor the word physician.

### 1972 AMENDMENTS

Proposal No. 5 of the Judicial Conference Report to the 1972 Legislature, effective Sept. 1, 1972, amended Subd. (1) by deleting the words "and age" which appeared between "the name" and "of the injured party."

### 1970 AMENDMENTS

L. 1970, ch. 772, eff. Sept. 1, 1970, added new Rule 4532-a.

## R 4533. Market reports.

A report of a regularly organized stock or commodity market published in a newspaper or periodical of general circulation or in an official publication or trade journal is admissible in evidence to prove the market price or value of any article regularly sold or dealt in on such market. The circumstances of the preparation of such a report may be shown to affect its weight, but they shall not affect its admissibility.

## 1964 AMENDMENTS

L. 1964, ch. 388, eff. Sept. 1, 1964, substituted "Market" for "Stock market" reports in caption. In the first sentence after the word "circulation" the words "or in an official publication or trade journal" were inserted.

# R 4533-a.   Prima facie proof of damages.

An itemized bill or invoice, receipted or marked paid, for services or repairs of an amount not in excess of two thousand dollars is admissible in evidence and is prima facie evidence of the reasonable value and necessity of such services or repairs itemized therein in any civil action provided it bears a certification by the person, firm or corporation, or an authorized agent or employee thereof, rendering such services or making such repairs and charging for the same, and contains a verified statement that no part of the payment received therefor will be refunded to the debtor, and that the amounts itemized therein are the usual and customary rates charged for such services or repairs by the affiant or his employer; and provided further that a true copy of such itemized bill or invoice together with a notice of intention to introduce such bill or invoice into evidence pursuant to this rule is served upon each party at least ten days before the trial. No more than one bill or invoice from the same person, firm or corporation to the same debtor shall be admissible in evidence under this rule in the same action.

CPLR

## 1988 AMENDMENTS

L. 1988, ch. 249, eff. July 8, 1988, amended 4533-a to increase from fifteen hundred to two thousand dollars the maximum amount of a bill or invoice admissible as prima facie proof of damages.

## 1981 AMENDMENTS

L. 1981, ch. 355, eff. June 29, 1981, amended CPLR 4533-a by increasing the amount of an itemized bill admissible as prima facie evidence of the value of services or repairs from one thousand to fifteen hundred dollars.

## 1975 AMENDMENTS

L. 1975, ch. 103, eff. Sept. 1, 1975, substituted the phrase "one thousand" for "five hundred" before the word "dollars" in the first sentence.

## 1970 AMENDMENTS

Amendment No. 3 made by the Judicial Conference Jan. 2, 1970, Report to the 1970 Legislature, effective Sept. 1, 1970 amended CPLR 4533-a.

The Judicial Conference Report stated, in part: "Enacted in 1966 to facilitate proof of repairs in petty automobile accident cases, CPLR 4533-a has been the target of much criticism as well as praise, some of it aimed at the philosophy of the rule, much of it at its draftsmanship. The rule, as originally conceived, permitted a plaintiff to prove damage to his automobile, in amount less than three hundred dollars, simply by putting his repair bill into evidence. Where the bill exceeded three hundred dollars, the case was regarded as serious enough for the plaintiff to incur the expense of calling the garage mechanic as a witness.

"In 1968, the Judicial Conference, on the advice of the Committee, amended the rule, greatly expanding it. This expansion was undoubtedly sound so far as its basic thrust was concerned. The 1968 amendment provided that bills for any professional or other specialized services or repairs' could be offered. However, the scope of the Rule was limited to actions involving tortious damages to a person or property.' Most significantly, under the 1968 amendment, a bill in *any* amount could be admitted, although it could not authorize an award' of more than three hundred dollars. The possibility of putting large doctors' bills before the jury without calling the doctors as witnesses has disturbed many attorneys. Numerous suggestions for repeal, modification, clarification, expansion and limitation of CPLR 4533-a, many of them contradictory of one another, were received by the Judicial Conference and the Advisory Committee.

"The Judicial Conference, upon the advice of the Committee, commissioned Professor Joseph M. McLaughlin, of the Fordham University Law School, to study the various suggestions received in respect to this Rule and to formulate recommended amendments. . . . The Committee carefully considered Professor McLaughlin's findings and recommendations and, after extensive discussion, arrived at the following conclusions:

"1. The fundamental concept that bills should be admitted as proof of reasonable value of the services performed is sound, at least in small cases. A plaintiff, even in a personal injury action, should not be compelled to spend a few hundred dollars to obtain the testimony of a doctor that the doctor's bill for, say, seventy-five dollars is reasonable and necessary. This, indeed, is the primary philosophy underlying the Rule. It is eminently sound.

"2. The bill, however, should not be evidence of anything but reasonable value and necessity of the services or repairs. If there is an issue as to whether the services were for injuries proximately caused by the defendant, other proof will be required.

"3. The Rule should apply to bills in an amount of less than $500. However, while the procedure would thus be available for bills in a larger amount than at present, the practice of allowing submission of bills in *any* amount could be discontinued. There is merit in the contention voiced by members of the bar that a jury which sees a bill in excess of the amount it may award will nevertheless be unduly influenced thereby in fixing the amount of the verdict.

"4. If the concept of self-proving (in the sense of prima facie proof) bills has validity, which the Committee believes it does in small cases, it should not be confined to tort cases. Accordingly, it is recommended that the new Rule be extended to all civil actions.

"5. The mere service of a bill upon the defendant does not tell him that the plaintiff intends to offer the bill without calling as a witness the person who sent the bill. This is the key point to the procedure authorized by the Rule. Accordingly, it is recommended that the rule include a notice provision to that effect.

"6. To prevent abuse, it is suggested that the Rule contain a limitation that no more than one bill from the same source to the same debtor may be admitted under these provisions.

"In addition to the amendments necessary to implement these conclusions, some simplification of the language of the present rule seems desirable."

### 1968 AMENDMENTS

Proposal No. 2, effective Sept. 1, 1968, made by the Judicial Conference Feb. 1, 1968, Report to the Legislature, rescinded former rule 4533-a and promulgated a new rule 4533-a.

CPLR

## 1966 AMENDMENTS

L. 1966, ch. 263, eff. Sept. 1, 1966, added new rule 4533-a.

## R 4533-b. Proof of payment by joint tortfeasor.

In an action for personal injury, injury to property or for wrongful death, any proof as to payment by or settlement with another joint tortfeasor, or one claimed to be a joint tortfeasor, offered by a defendant in mitigation of damages, shall be taken out of the hearing of the jury. The court shall deduct the proper amount, as determined pursuant to section 15-108 of the general obligations law, from the award made by the jury.

### CROSS REFERENCES

See **G.O.L.§ 15-108** in Appendix, *infra*.

### 1974 AMENDMENTS

L. 1974, ch. 742, eff. Sept. 1, 1974, upon the recommendation of the Judicial Conference, amended Rule 4533-b by adding to the first sentence the phrases "or for wrongful death," "or settlement with another" and "or one claimed to be a joint tortfeasor." The second sentence which read "the court shall deduct the amount of such payment . . ." was amended to read "the court shall deduct the proper amount, as determined pursuant to section 15-108 of the general obligations law. . . ."

The 1974 Judicial Conference Report stated:

"(a) In addition to adding 'wrongful death' actions to those included within the scope of this rule, this rule has been amended in order to conform it to the newly revised General Obligations Law § 15-108. In accordance with that section, it is possible that damages may be mitigated by an amount in excess of the payment made by a joint tortfeasor, and this Rule provides that the court shall deduct the 'proper amount' in accordance with General Obligations Law § 15-108.

"(b) While the Rule refers to 'joint tortfeasor' it is intended that the phrase be construed to also include all those who may claim contribution in accordance with Article 14 of the CPLR whether or not they are 'joint tortfeasors', in the technical sense in which that phrase is sometimes used."

### 1971 AMENDMENTS

L. 1971, ch. 244, eff. Sept. 1, 1971, added new Rule 4533-b.

The Judicial Conference 1971 report to the 1971 Legislature, Feb. 1, 1971, in recommending the adoption of CPLR 4533-b stated:

"The purpose of the proposed amendment is to modify the rule of *Livant* v. *Livant*, 18 A.D. 2d 383 (First Dept., 1963), under which payments made by one of several joint tortfeasors may be alleged and proved in mitigation in the presence of the jury. Henceforth the proof of such payment would be kept from the jury and at the conclusion of the trial, in the event of a verdict in favor of plaintiff, the trial court would deduct the amount of such settlement from the award.

"The principal reason for changing the rule of *Livant* as proposed is the concern that under the present practice the jury will tend to return a nominal verdict where a prior payment is revealed, and if there are multiple defendants, to think that the tortfeasor who settled before was the only wrongdoer merely because he settled. The proposed amendment would continue to allow mitigation of damages in such circumstances but without the very real possibility that the plaintiff will not be made whole. The proposed amendment would encourage settlements by the holdout defendant, who, under the present rule, may prefer to hazard a nominal award by the jury. The proposed amendment represents the rule in a number of jurisdictions (cf. *Livant* (*supra*) at 386), most notably in Illinois (*DeLude* v. *Rimek,* 351 Ill. App. 466; *Jackson* v. *Hursey*, 1 Ill. App. 2d 598; *Ryan* v. *Monson*, 33 Ill. App. 2d 406).

"In New York, the prejudicial effect in a consolidated action of admitting evidence of a settlement by a party who remains in the lawsuit has been recognized (*Bove* v. *Medeo*, 19 A.D. 2d 646 (Second Dept., 1963) and *Burger* v. *L.I.R.R.*, 24 A.D. 2d 509 (Second Dept., 1965)). Yet the rule of *Livant,* with its contrary thrust, continues in authority. In the interest of justice and consistency, that rule should be abrogated as proposed."

### R 4534.　Standard of measurement used by surveyor.

An official certificate of any state, county, city, village, or town sealer elected or appointed pursuant to the laws of the state, or the statement under oath of a surveyor, that the chain or measure used by him conformed to the state standard at the time a survey was made is prima facie evidence of conformity, and an official certificate made by any sealer that the implement used in measuring such chain or other measure was the one provided the sealer pursuant to the provisions of the laws of the state is prima facie evidence of that fact.

### R 4535.　[Repealed.]

### R 4536.　Proof of writing by comparison of handwriting.

Comparison of a disputed writing with any writing proved to the satisfaction of the court to be the handwriting of the person claimed to have made the disputed writing shall be permitted.

### R 4537.　Proof of writing subscribed by witness.

Unless a writing requires a subscribing witness for its validity, it may be proved as if there was no subscribing witness.

### R 4538.　Acknowledged, proved or certified writing; conveyance of real property without the state.

Certification of the acknowledgment or proof of a writing, except a will, in the manner prescribed by law for taking and certifying the acknowledgment or proof of a conveyance of real property within the state is prima facie evidence that it was executed by the person who purported to do so. A conveyance of real property, situated within another state, territory or jurisdiction of the United States, which has been duly authenticated, according to the laws of that state, territory or jurisdiction, so as to be read in evidence in the courts thereof, is admissible in evidence in the state.

## R 4539.   Reproductions of original.

(a) If any business, institution, or member of a profession or calling, in the regular course of business or activity has made, kept or recorded any writing, entry, print or representation and in the regular course of business has recorded, copied, or reproduced it by any process, including reproduction, which accurately reproduces or forms a durable medium for reproducing the original, such reproduction, when satisfactorily identified, is as admissible in evidence as the original, whether the original is in existence or not, and an enlargement or facsimile of such reproduction is admissible in evidence if the original reproduction is in existence and available for inspection under direction of the court. The introduction of a reproduction does not preclude admission of the original.

(b) A reproduction created by any process which stores an image of any writing, entry, print or representation and which does not permit additions, deletions, or changes without leaving a record of such additions, deletions, or changes, when authenticated by competent testimony or affidavit which shall include the manner or method by which tampering or degradation of the reproduction is prevented, shall be as admissible in evidence as the original.

### 1996 AMENDMENTS

L. 1996, ch. 27, eff. Nov. 1, 1996, numbered the existing paragraph as subdivision (a) and added the phrase "including reproduction" and added a new subdivision (b) dealing with reproduction by a process which stores an image.

## R 4540.   Authentication of official record of court or government office in the United States.

(a) Copies permitted. An official publication, or a copy attested as correct by an officer or a deputy of an officer having legal custody of an official record of the United States or of any state, territory or jurisdiction of the United States, or of any of its courts, legislature, offices, public bodies or boards is prima facie evidence of such record.

(b) Certificate of officer of the state. Where the copy is attested by an officer of the state, it shall be accompanied by a certificate signed by, or with a facsimile of the signature of, the clerk of a court having legal custody of the record, and, except where the copy is used in the same court or before one of its officers, with the seal of the court affixed; or signed by, or with a facsimile of the signature of, the officer having legal custody of the original, or his deputy or clerk, with his official seal affixed; or signed by, or with a facsimile of the signature of, the presiding officer, secretary or clerk of the public body or board and, except where it is certified by the clerk or secretary of either house of the legislature, with the seal of the body or board affixed. If the certificate is made by a county clerk, the county seal shall be affixed.

(c) Certificate of officer of another jurisdiction. Where the copy is attested by an officer of another jurisdiction, it shall be accompanied by a certificate

CPLR

that such officer has legal custody of the record, and that his signature is believed to be genuine, which certificate shall be made by a judge of a court of record of the district or political subdivision in which the record is kept, with the seal of the court affixed; or by any public officer having a seal of office and having official duties in that district or political subdivision with respect to the subject matter of the record, with the seal of his office affixed.

(d) Printed tariff or classification subject to public service commission, commissioner of transportation or interstate commerce commission. A printed copy of a tariff or classification which shows a public service commission or commissioner of transportation number of this state and an effective date, or a printed copy of a tariff or classification which shows an interstate commerce commission number and an effective date, is admissible in evidence, without certification, and is prima facie evidence of the filed original tariff or classification.

**1970 AMENDMENTS**

L. 1970, ch. 267, § 9, eff. March 1, 1971, amended Subd. (d) to include the Commissioner of Transportation.

## R 4541. Proof of proceedings before justice of the peace.

(a) Of the state. A transcript from the docket-book of a justice of the peace of the state, subscribed by him, and authenticated by a certificate signed by the clerk of the county in which the justice resides, with the county seal affixed, to the effect that the person subscribing the transcript is a justice of the peace of that county, is prima facie evidence of any matter stated in the transcript which is required by law to be entered by the justice in his docket-book.

(b) Of another state. A transcript from the docket-book of a justice of the peace of another state, of his minutes of the proceedings in a cause, of a judgment rendered by him, of an execution issued thereon or of the return of an execution, when subscribed by him, and authenticated as prescribed in this subdivision is prima facie evidence of his jurisdiction in the cause and of the matters shown by the transcript. The transcript shall be authenticated by a certificate of the justice to the effect that it is in all respects correct and that he had jurisdiction of the cause; and also by a certificate of the clerk or prothonotary of the county in which the justice resides, with his official seal affixed, to the effect that the person subscribing the certificate attached to the transcript is a justice of the peace of that county.

## R 4542. Proof of foreign records and documents.

(a) Foreign record. A foreign official record, or an entry therein, when admissible for any purpose, may be evidenced by an official publication thereof; or a copy thereof, attested by a person authorized to make the attestation, and accompanied by a final certification as to the genuineness of the signature and official position

1. of the attesting person, or

2. of any foreign official whose certificate of genuineness of signature and official position

(i) relates to the attestation, or

(ii) is in a chain of certificates of genuineness of signature and official position relating to the attestation.

(b) Final certification. A final certification may be made by a secretary of an embassy or legation, consul general, consul, vice consul, or consular agent of the United States, or a diplomatic or consular official of the foreign country assigned or accredited to the United States. If reasonable opportunity has been given to all parties to investigate the authenticity and accuracy of the documents, the court may, for good cause shown, admit an attested copy without final certification, or permit the foreign official record to be evidenced by an attested summary with or without a final certification.

(c) Lack of record. A written statement that after diligent search no record or entry of a specified tenor was found to exist in the foreign records designated by the statement, authenticated in compliance with the requirements set forth in subdivisions (a) and (b) for a copy of a foreign record is admissible as evidence that the records contain no such record or entry.

### 1972 AMENDMENTS

Proposal No. 6 of the Judicial Conference Report to the 1972 Legislature, effective Sept. 1, 1972, amended Subd. (b) by adding the words "agent of the United States, or a diplomatic or consular" between the words "or consular" and "official of the foreign country."

### 1969 AMENDMENTS

Amendment by Judicial Conference Feb. 1, 1969, Report to the 1969 Legislature, effective Sept. 1, 1969, repealed rule 4542 and added new rule 4542. "[T]he new rule 4542 . . . is substantially similar to the parallel provision of the Uniform Interstate and International Procedure Act. . . ."

## § 4543. Proof of facts or writing by methods other than those authorized in this article.

Nothing in this article prevents the proof of a fact or a writing by any method authorized by any applicable statute or by the rules of evidence at common law.

## § 4544. Contracts in small print.

The portion of any printed contract or agreement involving a consumer transaction or a lease for space to be occupied for residential purposes where the print is not clear and legible or is less than eight points in depth or five and one-half points in depth for upper case type may not be received in evidence in any trial, hearing or proceeding on behalf of the party who printed or prepared such contract or agreement, or who caused said agreement or contract to be printed or prepared. As used in the immediately preceding sentence, the term "consumer transaction" means a transaction wherein the money, property or service which is the subject of the transaction is primarily for personal, family or household purposes. No provision of any contract or agreement waiving the provisions of this section shall be effective. The provisions of this section shall not apply to agreements or contracts entered into prior to the effective date of this section.

### 1979 AMENDMENTS

L. 1979, ch. 474, eff. Sept. 1, 1979, amended CPLR 4544 to clarify the admissibility of contracts printed in small type. The statute had previously stated that such contracts were inadmissible if they were unclear and if the print was too small. The Legislature deleted the word "and" adding the word "or."

### 1975 AMENDMENTS

L. 1975, ch. 370, eff. July 1, 1976, added new CPLR 4544.

## § 4545.  Admissibility of collateral source of payment.

(a) Action for medical, dental or podiatric malpractice. In any action for medical, dental or podiatric malpractice where the plaintiff seeks to recover for the cost of medical care, dental care, podiatric care, custodial care or rehabilitation services, loss of earnings or other economic loss, evidence shall be admissible for consideration by the court to establish that any such past or future cost or expense was or will, with reasonable certainty, be replaced or indemnified, in whole or in part, from any collateral source such as insurance (except for life insurance), social security (except those benefits provided under title XVIII of the social security act), workers' compensation or employee benefit programs (except such collateral sources entitled by law to liens against any recovery of the plaintiff). If the court finds that any such cost or expense was or will, with reasonable certainty, be replaced or indemnified from any collateral source, it shall reduce the amount of the award by such finding, minus an amount equal to the premiums paid by the plaintiff for such benefits for the two-year period immediately preceding the accrual of such action and minus an amount equal to the projected future cost to the plaintiff of maintaining such benefits. In order to find that any future cost or expense will, with reasonable certainty, be replaced or indemnified by the collateral source, the court must find that the plaintiff is legally entitled to the continued receipt of such collateral source, pursuant to a contract or otherwise enforceable agreement, subject only to the continued payment of a premium and such other financial obligations as may be required by such agreement.

(b) Certain actions against a public employer for personal injury and wrongful death. 1. In any action against a public employer or a public employee who is subject to indemnification by a public employer with respect to such action or both for personal injury or wrongful death arising out of an injury sustained by a public employee while acting within the scope of his public employment or duties, where the plaintiff seeks to recover for the cost of medical care, custodial care or rehabilitation services, loss of earnings or other economic loss, evidence shall be admissible for consideration by the court to establish that any such cost or expense was replaced or indemnified, in whole or in part, from a collateral source provided or paid for, in whole or in part, by the public employer, including but not limited to paid sick leave, medical benefits, death benefits, dependent benefits, a disability retirement allowance and social security (except those benefits provided under title XVIII of the social security act) but shall not include those collateral sources entitled by law to liens against any recovery of the plaintiff. If the court finds that any such cost or expense was replaced or indemnified from any such collateral source, it shall reduce the amount of the award by such finding, minus an amount equal to the contributions of the injured public employee for such benefit.

2. As used in this subdivision, the term "public employer" means the state of New York, a county, city, town, village or any other political subdivision of the state, any public authority operating a rapid transit, commuter railroad, omnibus, marine, airport or aviation facility, a school district or any governmental entity operating a public school, college or university and any municipal housing authority. The term "public employee" means any person holding a position by election, appointment or employment in the service of a public employer, while acting within the scope of his public employment or duties, whether or not compensated, or a volunteer expressly authorized to participate in a volunteer program sponsored by a public employer but does not include an independent contractor. The term public employee includes a former employee, his estate or judicially appointed personal representative.

3. For the purposes of this subdivision a certified report of the actuary of the appropriate public employee retirement system shall be admissible evidence of the present value of any death benefit, dependent benefit or disability retirement allowance.

4. The provisions of this subdivision shall not be construed to affect, alter or amend any provisions of the workers' compensation law or to apply to any claims under such law.

(c) Actions for personal injury, injury to property or wrongful death. In any action brought to recover damages for personal injury, injury to property or wrongful death, where the plaintiff seeks to recover for the cost of medical care, dental care, custodial care or rehabilitation services, loss of earnings or other economic loss, evidence shall be admissible for consideration by the court to establish that any such past or future cost or expense was or will, with reasonable certainty, be replaced or indemnified, in whole or in part, from any collateral source such as insurance (except for life insurance), social security (except those benefits provided under title XVIII of the social security act), workers' compensation or employee benefit programs (except such collateral sources

CPLR

entitled by law to liens against any recovery of the plaintiff). If the court finds that any such cost or expense was or will, with reasonable certainty, be replaced or indemnified from any collateral source, it shall reduce the amount of the award by such finding, minus an amount equal to the premiums paid by the plaintiff for such benefits for the two-year period immediately preceding the accrual of such action and minus an amount equal to the projected future cost to the plaintiff of maintaining such benefits. In order to find that any future cost or expense will, with reasonable certainty, be replaced or indemnified by the collateral source, the court must find that the plaintiff is legally entitled to the continued receipt of such collateral source, pursuant to a contract or otherwise enforceable agreement, subject only to the continued payment of a premium and such other financial obligations as may be required by such agreement.

### 1986 AMENDMENTS

L. 1986, ch. 220, eff. June 28, 1986, and applicable to actions or proceedings commenced on or after such date, added subdivision (c) providing that specified damages recovered in actions for personal injury, injury to property or wrongful death, may be reduced by recovery from collateral sources. L. 1986, ch. 485, eff. July 21, 1986, and applicable to acts, omissions or failures occurring on or after such date, amended subdivision (a) to apply to podiatric malpractice actions.

### 1985 AMENDMENTS

L. 1985, ch. 294, eff. July 1, 1985, and applicable to any action for dental or medical malpractice commenced on or after such date, amended subdivision (a) to apply to dental malpractice actions and to provide for the admissibility of collateral sources to payment for future costs.

### 1984 AMENDMENTS

L. 1984, ch. 701, eff. Oct. 1, 1984, and applicable to actions commenced on or after that date, added CPLR 4545.

## § 4546. Loss of earnings and impairment of earning ability in actions for medical, dental or podiatric malpractice.

1. In any action for medical, dental or podiatric malpractice where the plaintiff seeks to recover damages for loss of earnings or impairment of earning ability, evidence shall be admissible for consideration by the court, outside of the presence of the jury, to establish the federal, state and local personal income taxes which the plaintiff would have been obligated by law to pay.

2. In any such action, the court shall instruct the jury not to deduct federal, state and local personal income taxes in determining the award, if any, for loss of earnings and impairment of earning ability. The court shall further instruct the jury that any reduction for such taxes from any award shall, if warranted, be made by the court.

3. In any such action, the court shall, if warranted by the evidence, reduce any award for loss of earnings or impairment of earning ability by the amount

of federal, state and local personal income taxes which the court finds, with reasonable certainty, that the plaintiff would have been obligated by law to pay.

### 1987 AMENDMENTS

L. 1987, ch. 507, eff. July 30, 1987, and applicable to any acts, omissions or failures occurring on or after such date, amended section to apply to podiatric malpractice actions.

### 1986 AMENDMENTS

L. 1986, ch. 266, eff. July 8, 1986, and applicable to actions commenced on or after such date, added new CPLR 4546.

CPLR

# ARTICLE 50

# JUDGMENTS GENERALLY

---

## SUMMARY OF ARTICLE

§ 5001.    Interest to verdict, report or decision.
    (a)  Actions in which recoverable.
    (b)  Date from which computed.
    (c)  Specifying date; computing interest.
§ 5002.    Interest from verdict, report or decision to judgment.
§ 5003.    Interest upon judgment.
§ 5003–a.  Prompt payment following settlement.
§ 5004.    Rate of interest.
§§ 5005–5010.  [Not used.]
§ 5011.    Definition and content of judgment.
R 5012.    Judgment upon part of cause of action; upon several causes.
R 5013.    Effect of judgment dismissing claim.
§ 5014.    Action upon judgment.
R 5015.    Relief from judgment or order.
    (a)  On motion.
    (b)  On stipulation.
    (c)  On application of an administrative judge.
    (d)  Restitution.
R 5016.    Entry of judgment.
    (a)  What constitutes entry.
    (b)  Judgment upon verdict.
    (c)  Judgment upon decision.
    (d)  After death of party.
    (e)  Final judgment after interlocutory judgment.
R 5017.    Judgment-roll.
    (a)  Preparation and filing.
    (b)  Content.
§ 5018.    Docketing of judgment.
    (a)  Docketing by clerk; docketing elsewhere by transcript.
    (b)  Docketing of judgment of court of United States.
    (c)  Form of docketing.
§ 5019.    Validity and correction of judgment or order; amendment of docket.
    (a)  Validity and correction of judgment or order.
    (b)  Subsequent judgment or order affecting judgment or lien.
    (c)  Change in judgment creditor.
    (d)  Certificate of county clerk.
§ 5020.    Satisfaction-piece.
    (a)  Generally.

**CPLR**

    (b) Attorney of record.
§ 5020-a. Payment of judgment in certain cases.
§ 5021. Entry of satisfaction.
    (a) Entry upon satisfaction-piece, court order, deposit into court, discharge of compounding joint debtor.
    (b) Entry upon return of execution.
    (c) Entry upon certificate.

----

## § 5001. Interest to verdict, report or decision.

(a) Actions in which recoverable. Interest shall be recovered upon a sum awarded because of a breach of performance of a contract, or because of an act or omission depriving or otherwise interfering with title to, or possession or enjoyment of, property, except that in an action of an equitable nature, interest and the rate and date from which it shall be computed shall be in the court's discretion.

(b) Date from which computed. Interest shall be computed from the earliest ascertainable date the cause of action existed, except that interest upon damages incurred thereafter shall be computed from the date incurred. Where such damages were incurred at various times, interest shall be computed upon each item from the date it was incurred or upon all of the damages from a single reasonable intermediate date.

(c) Specifying date; computing interest. The date from which interest is to be computed shall be specified in the verdict, report or decision. If a jury is discharged without specifying the date, the court upon motion shall fix the date, except that where the date is certain and not in dispute, the date may be fixed by the clerk of the court upon affidavit. The amount of interest shall be computed by the clerk of the court, to the date the verdict was rendered or the report or decision was made, and included in the total sum awarded.

### 1992 AMENDMENTS

L. 1992, ch. 55, eff. April 10, 1992, amended Subd. (a) by expanding the list of actions in which interest is recoverable to include actions based on the imposition of a civil penalty, and amended Subd. (b) to provide the basis for determining the date from which interest is computed in that type of action.

## § 5002. Interest from verdict, report or decision to judgment.

Interest shall be recovered upon the total sum awarded, including interest to verdict, report or decision, in any action, from the date the verdict was rendered or the report or decision was made to the date of entry of final judgment. The amount of interest shall be computed by the clerk of the court and included in the judgment.

## § 5003.　Interest upon judgment.

Every money judgment shall bear interest from the date of its entry. Every order directing the payment of money which has been docketed as a judgment shall bear interest from the date of such docketing.

## § 5003–a.　Prompt payment following settlement.

(a) When an action to recover damages has been settled, any settling defendant, except those defendants to whom subdivisions (b) and (c) of this section apply, shall pay all sums due to any settling plaintiff within twenty-one days of tender, by the settling plaintiff to the settling defendant, of a duly executed release and a stipulation discontinuing action executed on behalf of the settling plaintiff.

(b) When an action to recover damages has been settled and the settling defendant is a municipality or any subdivision thereof, or any public corporation that is not indemnified by the state, it shall pay all sums due to any settling plaintiff within ninety days of tender, by the settling plaintiff to it, of duly executed release and a stipulation discontinuing action executed on behalf of the settling plaintiff. The provisions of this paragraph shall not inure to the benefit of any insurance carrier for a municipality or any subdivision thereof, or any public corporation that is not indemnified by the state. Any such insurance carrier shall pay all sums due to any settling plaintiff in accordance with the provisions of subdivision (a) of this section.

(c) When an action to recover damages has been settled and the settling defendant is the state, an officer or employee of the state entitled to indemnification pursuant to section seventeen of the public officers law, or a public benefit corporation indemnified by the state, payment of all sums due to any settling plaintiff shall be made within ninety days of the comptroller's determination that all papers required to effectuate the settlement have been received by him. The provisions of this paragraph shall not inure to the benefit of any insurance carrier for the state, an officer or employee of the state entitled to indemnification pursuant to section seventeen of the public officers law, or a public benefit corporation indemnified by the state. Any such insurance carrier shall pay all sums due to any settling plaintiff in accordance with the provisions of subdivision (a) of this section.

(d) In an action which requires judicial approval of settlement, other than an action to which subdivision (c) of this section applies, the plaintiff shall also tender a copy of the order approving such settlement with the duly executed release and stipulation discontinuing action executed on behalf of the plaintiff.

(e) In the event that a settling defendant fails to promptly pay all sums as required by subdivisions (a), (b), and (c) of this section, any unpaid plaintiff may enter judgment, without further notice, against such settling defendant who has not paid. The judgment shall be for the amount set forth in the release,

CPLR

together with costs and lawful disbursements, and interest on the amount set forth in the release from the date that the release and stipulation discontinuing action were tendered.

(f) Nothing in this section shall apply to settlements subject to article seventy-four of the insurance law or to future installment payments to be paid pursuant to a structured settlement agreement.

(g) The term "tender", as used herein, shall mean either to personally deliver or to mail, by registered or certified mail, return receipt requested.

### 1992 AMENDMENTS

L. 1992, ch. 269, eff. June 30, 1992, added this section. L. 1992, ch. 270, eff. June 30, 1992, amended Subd. (f) by adding the words "or to future installment payments to be paid pursuant to a structured settlement agreement."

## § 5004.   Rate of interest.

Interest shall be at the rate of nine per centum per annum, except where otherwise provided by statute.

### CROSS REFERENCES

See **General Municipal Law** § 3–a as to rate of interest on judgments and accrued claims against municipal corporations.

### 1981 AMENDMENTS

L. 1981, ch. 258, eff. June 25, 1981, amended CPLR 5004 by increasing the rate of interest on judgments from six to nine percent. In actions in which interest is to be computed from a date prior to the effective date hereof, it shall be computed at six percent until such date and at nine percent thereafter.

### 1972 AMENDMENTS

L. 1972, ch. 358, eff. Sept. 1, 1972, amended CPLR 5004.

## §§ 5005-5010.   [Not used.]

## § 5011.   Definition and content of judgment.

A judgment is the determination of the rights of the parties in an action or special proceeding and may be either interlocutory or final. A judgment shall refer to, and state the result of, the verdict or decision, or recite the default upon which it is based. A judgment may direct that property be paid into court when the party would not have the benefit or use or control of such property or where special circumstances make it desirable that payment or delivery to the party entitled to it should be withheld.

## R 5012.   Judgment upon part of cause of action; upon several causes.

The court, having ordered a severance, may direct judgment upon a part of a cause of action or upon one or more causes of action as to one or more parties.

## R 5013. Effect of judgment dismissing claim.

A judgment dismissing a cause of action before the close of the proponent's evidence is not a dismissal on the merits unless it specifies otherwise, but a judgment dismissing a cause of action after the close of the proponent's evidence is a dismissal on the merits unless it specifies otherwise.

## § 5014. Action upon judgment.

Except as permitted by section 15-102 of the general obligations law, an action upon a money judgment entered in a court of the state may only be maintained between the original parties to the judgment where:

1. ten years have elapsed since the first docketing of the judgment; or

2. the judgment was entered against the defendant by default for want of appearance and the summons was served other than by personal delivery to him or to his agent for service designated under rule 318, either within or without the state; or

3. the court in which the action is sought to be brought so orders on motion with such notice to such other persons as the court may direct.

An action may be commenced under subdivision one of this section during the year prior to the expiration of ten years since the first docketing of the judgment. The judgment in such action shall be designated a renewal judgment and shall be so docketed by the clerk. The lien of a renewal judgment shall take effect upon the expiration of ten years from the first docketing of the original judgment.

### CROSS REFERENCES

See G.O.L. § 15-102 in Appendix, *infra.*

### 1986 AMENDMENTS

L. 1986, ch. 123, eff. Sept. 1, 1986, added a new closing paragraph providing for renewal judgments.

### 1965 AMENDMENTS

L. 1965, ch. 115, eff. April 26, 1965, amended the first paragraph by substituting reference to section "15-102 of the general obligations" law for reference to "two hundred thirty-two of the debtor and creditor" law.

### 1964 AMENDMENTS

L. 1964, ch. 485, eff. Sept. 1, 1964, amended paragraph 2.

## R 5015. Relief from judgment or order.

(a) On motion. The court which rendered a judgment or order may relieve a party from it upon such terms as may be just, on motion of any interested person with such notice as the court may direct, upon the ground of:

**CPLR**

1. excusable default, if such motion is made within one year after service of a copy of the judgment or order with written notice of its entry upon the moving party, or, if the moving party has entered the judgment or order, within one year after such entry; or

2. newly-discovered evidence which, if introduced at the trial, would probably have produced a different result and which could not have been discovered in time to move for a new trial under section 4404; or

3. fraud, misrepresentation, or other misconduct of an adverse party; or

4. lack of jurisdiction to render the judgment or order; or

5. reversal, modification or vacatur of a prior judgment or order upon which it is based.

(b) On stipulation. The clerk of the court may vacate a default judgment entered pursuant to section 3215 upon the filing with him of a stipulation of consent to such vacatur by the parties personally or by their attorneys.

(c) On application of an administrative judge. An administrative judge, upon a showing that default judgments were obtained by fraud, misrepresentation, illegality, unconscionability, lack of due service, violations of law, or other illegalities or where such default judgments were obtained in cases in which those defendants would be uniformly entitled to interpose a defense predicated upon but not limited to the foregoing defenses, and where such default judgments have been obtained in a number deemed sufficient by him to justify such action as set forth herein, and upon appropriate notice to counsel for the respective parties, or to the parties themselves, may bring a proceeding to relieve a party or parties from them upon such terms as may be just. The disposition of any proceeding so instituted shall be determined by a judge other than the administrative judge.

(d) Restitution. Where a judgment or order is set aside or vacated, the court may direct and enforce restitution in like manner and subject to the same conditions as where a judgment is reversed or modified on appeal.

### 1978 AMENDMENTS

L. 1978, ch. 156, eff. May 19, 1978, added new subdivision (c) and relettered former subdivision (c) as subdivision (d). The new CPLR 5015(c) replaces former § 217-a of the Judiciary Law, repealed by L. 1978, ch. 156.

### 1972 AMENDMENTS

Proposal No. 7 of the Judicial Conference Report to the 1972 Legislature, effective Sept. 1, 1972, amended Rule 5015 by inserting a new Subd. (b), by relettering former Subd. (b) as Subd. (c), and by inserting the words "or vacated" in Subd. (c). Subd. (c) was relettered subd. (d) in 1978.

## R 5016. Entry of judgment.

(a) What constitutes entry. A judgment is entered when, after it has been signed by the clerk, it is filed by him.

(b) Judgment upon verdict. Judgment upon the general verdict of a jury after a trial by jury as of right shall be entered by the clerk unless the court otherwise directs; if there is a special verdict, the court shall direct entry of an appropriate judgment.

(c) Judgment upon decision. Judgment upon the decision of a court or a referee to determine shall be entered by the clerk as directed therein. When relief other than for money or costs only is granted, the court or referee shall, on motion, determine the form of the judgment.

(d) After death of party. No verdict or decision shall be rendered against a deceased party, but if a party dies before entry of judgment and after a verdict, decision or accepted offer to compromise pursuant to rule 3221, judgment shall be entered in the names of the original parties unless the verdict, decision or offer is set aside. This provision shall not bar dismissal of an action or appeal pursuant to section 1021.

(e) Final judgment after interlocutory judgment. Where an interlocutory judgment has been directed, a party may move for final judgment when he becomes entitled thereto.

**1970 AMENDMENTS**

L. 1970, ch. 93, eff. Sept. 1, 1970, amended Subd. (d) by adding new last sentence thereto.

The amendment was recommended by the Judicial Conference Jan. 2, 1970 Report to the Legislature, wherein it was stated in part:

"At present, CPLR 1021 allows the court to dismiss an action or appeal for unreasonable failure to substitute parties. Where the event requiring substitution is the death of a party, this provision conflicts with CPLR 5016(d), which provides that no verdict or decision shall be rendered against a deceased party.

"Under this amendment, the court will be able to dispose of the matter in one proceeding, rather than denying the motion to dismiss without prejudice to renewal after appointment of a representative." (See CPLR 1021.)

## R 5017. Judgment-roll.

(a) Preparation and filing. A judgment-roll shall be prepared by the attorney for the party at whose instance the judgment is entered or by the clerk. It shall be filed by the clerk when he enters judgment, and shall state the date and time of its filing.

(b) Content. The judgment-roll shall contain the summons, pleadings, admissions, each judgment and each order involving the merits or necessarily affecting the final judgment. If the judgment was taken by default, it shall also contain the proof required by subdivision (f) of section 3215 and the result of any assessment, account or reference under subdivision (b) of section 3215. If a trial was had, it shall also contain the verdict or decision, any tender or offer made pursuant to rules 3219, 3220 or 3221, and any transcript of proceedings then on file. If any appeal was taken, it shall also contain the determination and

CPLR

opinion of each appellate court and the papers on which each appeal was heard. In an action to recover a chattel, it shall also contain the sheriff's return. In an action on submitted facts under rule 3222, the judgment-roll shall consist of the case, submission, affidavit, each judgment and each order necessarily affecting the final judgment. The judgment-roll of a judgment by confession under section 3218 shall consist of the affidavit and a copy of the judgment.

## 1994 AMENDMENTS

L. 1994, ch. 89, eff. May 10, 1994, amended CPLR 5017(b) to change the reference to CPLR 3215(f).

## § 5018. Docketing of judgment.

(a) Docketing by clerk; docketing elsewhere by transcript. Immediately after filing the judgment-roll the clerk shall docket a money judgment, and at the request of any party specifying the particular adverse party or parties against whom docketing shall be made, the clerks shall so docket a judgment affecting the title to real property, provided however, that where the clerk maintains a section and block index, a judgment affecting the title to, or the possession, use or enjoyment of, real property may be entered in such index in lieu thereof. If the judgment is upon a joint liability of two or more persons the words "not summoned" shall be written next to the name of each defendant who was not summoned. Upon the filing of a transcript of the docket of a judgment of a court other than the supreme, county or a family court, the clerk of the county in which the judgment was entered shall docket the judgment. Upon the filing of a transcript of the docket of a judgment which has been docketed in the office of the clerk of the county in which it was entered, the clerk of any other county in the state shall docket the judgment. Whenever a county clerk dockets a judgment by transcript under this subdivision, he shall notify the clerk who issued it, who, upon receiving such notification, shall make an entry on the docket of the judgment in his office indicating where the transcript has been filed. A judgment docketed by transcript under this subdivision shall have the same effect as a docketed judgment entered in the supreme court within the county where it is docketed.

(b) Docketing of judgment of court of United States. A transcript of the judgment of a court of the United States rendered or filed within the state may be filed in the office of the clerk of any county and upon such filing the clerk shall docket the judgment in the same manner and with the same effect as a judgment entered in the supreme court within the county.

(c) Form of docketing. A judgment is docketed by making an entry in the proper docket book as follows:

1. under the surname of the judgment debtor first named in the judgment, the entry shall consist of:

(i) the name and last known address of each judgment debtor and his trade or profession if stated in the judgment;

(ii) the name and last known address of the judgment creditor;

(iii) the sum recovered or directed to be paid in figures;

(iv) the date and time the judgment-roll was filed;

(v) the date and time of docketing;

(vi) the court and county in which judgment was entered; and

(vii) the name and office address of the attorney for the judgment creditor;

2. under the surname of every other judgment debtor, if any, the entry shall consist of his name and last known address and an appropriate cross-reference to the first entry.

If no address is known for the judgment debtor or judgment creditor, an affidavit executed by the party at whose instance the judgment is docketed or his attorney shall be filed stating that the affiant has no knowledge of an address.

(d) A county clerk may adopt a new docketing system utilizing electro-mechanical, electronic or any other method he deems suitable for maintaining the dockets.

**CPLR**

### 1991 AMENDMENTS

L. 1991, ch. 648, eff. July 26, 1991, added subdivision (d).

### 1970 AMENDMENTS

L. 1970, ch. 661, eff. May 8, 1970, amended Subd. (a) by inserting in the first sentence, "provided, however, that where the clerk maintains a section and block index, a judgment affecting the title to, or the possession, use or enjoyment of, real property may be entered in such index in lieu thereof."

### 1966 AMENDMENTS

L. 1966, ch. 707, eff. Sept. 1, 1966, amended Subd. (a). Amendment recommended by the Judicial Conference Feb. 1, 1966, Report to the Legislature: "CPLR 2222 provides for permissive docketing as a judgment of an order affecting title, possession, use or enjoyment of real property while CPLR 5018(a) mandates the docketing of a judgment affecting title to real property.

"In these circumstances the Judicial Conference believes that CPLR 5018(a) should be amended to conform to the request procedure for real property docketing provided in CPLR 2222. Mandatory docketing of all judgments affecting title to real property seems an unnecessary burden since in most cases such a judgment will be recorded and docketing will be pointless. It would appear sufficient to provide only for permissive docketing in the unusual case where it is requested by a party to the action who believes it essential to protect his rights. In such a case it seems reasonable to require that the party requesting docketing specify the particular adverse party or parties against whom the judgment is to be docketed."

### 1965 AMENDMENTS

L. 1965, ch. 773, eff. Sept. 1, 1965, amended subd. (c).

**1964 AMENDMENTS**

L. 1964, ch. 292, eff. Sept. 1, 1964, amended the first sentence of Subd. (a).

## § 5019. Validity and correction of judgment or order; amendment of docket.

(a) Validity and correction of judgment or order. A judgment or order shall not be stayed, impaired or affected by any mistake, defect or irregularity in the papers or procedures in the action not affecting a substantial right of a party. A trial or an appellate court may require the mistake, defect or irregularity to be cured.

(b) Subsequent judgment or order affecting judgment or lien. When a docketed judgment or the lien thereof is affected in any way by a subsequent order or judgment or retaxation of costs, the clerk of the court in which the judgment was entered shall make an appropriate entry on the docket of the judgment. In the case of a judgment of a court other than the supreme, county or a family court which has been docketed by the clerk of the county in which it was entered, such county clerk shall make an appropriate entry on his docket upon the filing of a certified copy of the order or judgment effecting the change or a certificate of the change issued by the clerk of the court in which the judgment was entered. Unless the order or judgment effecting the change otherwise provides, the duration of the judgment lien on real property shall be measured from the filing of the judgment-roll.

(c) Change in judgment creditor. A person other than the party recovering a judgment who becomes entitled to enforce it, shall file in the office of the clerk of the court in which the judgment was entered or, in the case of a judgment of a court other than the supreme, county or a family court which has been docketed by the clerk of the county in which it was entered, in the office of such county clerk, a copy of the instrument on which his authority is based, acknowledged in the form required to entitle a deed to be recorded, or, if his authority is based on a court order, a certified copy of the order. Upon such filing the clerk shall make an appropriate entry on his docket of the judgment.

(d) Certificate of county clerk. Upon the filing of a certificate of change of the docket of any judgment docketed with the clerk of the county in which it was entered, issued by such county clerk, the clerk of any court or county where the judgment has been docketed shall make an appropriate entry on his docket of the judgment.

## § 5020. Satisfaction-piece.

(a) Generally. When a person entitled to enforce a judgment receives satisfaction or partial satisfaction of the judgment, he shall execute and file with the proper clerk pursuant to subdivision (a) of section 5021, a satisfaction-piece or partial satisfaction-piece acknowledged in the form required to entitle a deed to be recorded, which shall set forth the book and page where the judgment is docketed. A copy of the satisfaction-piece or partial satisfaction-piece filed with the clerk shall be mailed to the judgment debtor by the person entitled to enforce the judgment within ten days after the date of filing.

(b) Attorney of record. Within ten years after the entry of a judgment the attorney of record or the attorney named on the docket for the judgment creditor may execute a satisfaction-piece or a partial satisfaction-piece, but if his authority was revoked before it was executed, the judgment may nevertheless be enforced against a person who had actual notice of the revocation before a payment on the judgment was made or a purchase of property bound by it was effected.

(c) When the judgment is fully satisfied, if the person required to execute and file with the proper clerk pursuant to subdivisions (a) and (d) hereof fails or refuses to do so within twenty days after receiving full satisfaction, then the judgment creditor shall be subject to a penalty of one hundred dollars recoverable by the judgment debtor pursuant to Section 7202 of the civil practice law and rules or article eighteen of either the New York City civil court act, uniform district court act or uniform city court act; provided, however, that such penalty shall not be recoverable when a city with a population greater than one million persons is the judgment creditor, unless such judgment creditor shall fail to execute and file a satisfaction–piece with the proper clerk pursuant to subdivisions (a) and (d) hereof within twenty days after having been served by the judgment debtor with a written demand therefor by certified mail, return receipt requested.

(d) Where a transcript of the docket of a judgment has been docketed in any other county of the state pursuant to subdivision (a) of section 5018, the person required to execute and file with the proper clerk pursuant to subdivision (a) hereof shall, upon receiving full satisfaction, file a certificate of the clerk of the county in which the judgment was entered, in accordance with subdivision (c) of section 5021, with the clerks of all other counties in which such judgment has been docketed.

### 1979 AMENDMENTS

L. 1979, ch. 148, eff. June 28, 1979, amended CPLR 5020 subd. (a) by eliminating the requirement that the judgment debtor bear the cost of the filing and mailing of the satisfaction piece.

### 1977 AMENDMENTS

L. 1977, ch. 41, eff. Sept. 1, 1977, amended subd. (b) by extending from five to ten years the period after the entry of judgment within which an attorney may execute a satisfaction piece or a partial satisfaction piece.

### 1975 AMENDMENTS

L. 1975, ch. 575, eff. Aug. 1, 1975, amended Subd. (c) by adding a new proviso, barring a recovery of the statutory penalty when a city, having a population of greater than one million, is the judgment creditor, unless such city fails to execute and file a satisfaction-piece pursuant to Subds. (a) and (d), within 20 days after having been served by the judgment debtor with a written demand for a satisfaction-piece.

### 1974 AMENDMENTS

L. 1974, ch. 601, eff. July 1, 1974, amended CPLR 5020 by adding a new subdivision (d) and amending subds. (a) and (c).

### 1969 AMENDMENTS

L. 1969, ch. 213, eff. Sept. 1, 1969, amended Subd. (b) by extending to five years the time within which an attorney may execute a satisfaction-piece.

L. 1969, ch. 1051, eff. Sept. 1, 1969, amended Subd. (b) by extending to five years the time within which an attorney may execute a satisfaction-piece and added new Subd. (c).

## § 5020-a.  Payment of judgment in certain cases.

When a judgment debtor has shown to the satisfaction of the clerk of the court from which an execution has been issued that a sum of money which satisfies the judgment had been sent to the last known address of the judgment creditor by registered or certified mail, return receipt requested, but was returned as unclaimed or undeliverable by the post office, the judgment debtor may deposit with the clerk of such court a certified check in an amount equal to the sum of money which satisfies the judgment. Upon receipt of such check any additional charges relating to an execution shall cease to accrue against the judgment debtor and the clerk shall forthwith notify each sheriff to whom an execution was issued that such execution is hereby rescinded. Such notice shall not be effective upon the sheriff until its receipt by him from the clerk. Provided, however, no entry of the satisfaction on the docket of the judgment made * be made by the clerk except pursuant to the provisions of section 5021.

\* [**Editor's note:** So in original. Probably should read "may."]

### 1981 AMENDMENTS

L. 1981, ch. 274, eff. Sept. 1, 1981, enacted a new section 5020-a.

## § 5021.  Entry of satisfaction.

(a) Entry upon satisfaction-piece, court order, deposit into court, discharge of compounding joint debtor. The clerk of the court in which the judgment was entered or, in the case of a judgment of a court other than the supreme, county or a family court which has been docketed by the clerk of the county in which it was entered, such county clerk, shall make an entry of the satisfaction or partial satisfaction on the docket of the judgment upon:

1. the filing of a satisfaction-piece or partial satisfaction-piece; or

2. the order of the court, made upon motion with such notice to other persons as the court may require, when the judgment has been wholly or partially satisfied but the judgment debtor cannot furnish the clerk with a satisfaction-piece or partial satisfaction-piece; or

3. the deposit with the clerk of a sum of money which satisfies or partially satisfies the judgment pursuant to an order of the court, made upon motion with such notice to other persons as the court may require, permitting such deposit; such an order shall not be made unless the court is satisfied that there are no outstanding executions on which sheriff's fees have not been paid; or

4. the filing of an instrument specified in article eight of the debtor and creditor law, executed by a creditor releasing or discharging a compounding joint debtor; in such case, the entry on the docket of the judgment shall state that the judgment is satisfied as to the compounding debtor only.

(b) Entry upon return of execution. A sheriff shall return an execution to the clerk of the court from which the execution issued if such execution is wholly or partially satisfied, and the clerk shall make an appropriate entry on his docket of the judgment. The sheriff shall also deliver to the person making payment, upon request, a certified copy of the execution and of the return of satisfaction or partial satisfaction. Upon the filing of such copy with the clerk of the county where the execution was satisfied, such clerk shall enter satisfaction or partial satisfaction on his docket of the judgment. Provided however that, in addition, a return of execution arising out of an action brought pursuant to article eighteen of the New York city civil court act, article eighteen of the uniform city court act, article eighteen of the uniform district court act or article eighteen of the uniform justice court act shall be made and entered whether wholly or partially satisfied, or unsatisfied, within ninety days after receipt of the judgment by the sheriff and the clerk shall make an appropriate entry on his docket of the judgment.

(c) Entry upon certificate. Upon the filing of a certificate of the clerk of the county in which the judgment was entered, stating that the judgment has been wholly or partially satisfied, the clerk of any court or county where a judgment has been docketed shall make an appropriate entry on his docket of the judgment.

CPLR

### CROSS REFERENCES

**Article 8 of the Debtor and Creditor Law**, referred to in paragraph (4) of Subd. (a), *supra*, was repealed by L. 1963, ch. 664, eff. Sept. 27, 1964; relevant provisions of the former article are now contained in **General Obligations Law § 15-101**, *et seq.*

**Article 18 of N.Y.C. Civ. Ct. Act, U.C.C.A., U.D.C.A., and U.J.C.A.**, referred to in Subd. (b), *supra*, are the small claims articles of the respective acts; provision for return of *unsatisfied* executions in small claims actions was necessitated by enactment in 1975 of § 1811 (now § 1812) of the respective court acts, wherein a showing of prior unsatisfied judgments is a precondition to the use of special enforcement procedures; see **N.Y.C. Civ. Ct. Act § 1812** in Appendix, *infra*.

### 1976 AMENDMENTS

L. 1976, ch. 156, eff. Sept. 1, 1976, amended Subd. (b) to provide for the return of an unsatisfied execution in actions brought under the small claims provisions of the Uniform Justice Court Act.

### 1975 AMENDMENTS

L. 1975, ch. 486, eff. Sept. 1, 1975, amended Subd. (b) by adding a new fourth sentence, requiring the making and entry of a return of execution arising out of small claims actions brought under Articles 18 of the N.Y.C. Civ. Ct. Act, U.C.C.A., or U.D.C.A., whether wholly or partially satisfied, or unsatisfied, within 90 days after sheriff's receipt of judgment, with an appropriate entry on judgment docket by the court clerk.

### 1970 AMENDMENTS

L. 1970, ch. 660, eff. May 8, 1970, amended Subd. (b) by deleting the requirements that the sheriff endorse his return on the execution and that the clerk maintain a record of all returns of executions; and by adding at the end of the first sentence the phrase "and the clerk shall make an appropriate entry on his docket of the judgment." The subdivision as amended requires the clerk of the issuing court to enter on his docket of the judgment whether the execution was returned wholly or partially satisfied.

### 1965 AMENDMENTS

L. 1965, ch. 773, eff. Sept. 1, 1965, amended Subd. (b).

# ARTICLE 50-A

# PERIODIC PAYMENT OF JUDGMENTS IN MEDICAL AND DENTAL MALPRACTICE ACTIONS

## SUMMARY OF ARTICLE

§ 5031.    Basis for determining judgment to be entered.
§ 5032.    Form of security.
§ 5033.    Posting and maintaining security.
§ 5034.    Failure to make payment.
§ 5035.    Effect of death of judgment creditor.
§ 5036.    Adjustment of payments.
§ 5037.    Settlements.
§ 5038.    Assignment of periodic installments.
§ 5039.    Duties of superintendent of insurance.

## § 5031. Basis for determining judgment to be entered.

In order to determine what judgment is to be entered on a verdict in an action to recover damages for dental, medical or podiatric malpractice under this article, the court shall proceed as follows:

(a) The court shall apply to the findings of past and future damages any applicable rules of law, including set-offs, credits, comparative negligence pursuant to section fourteen hundred eleven of this chapter, additurs, and remittiturs, in calculating the respective amounts of past and future damages claimants are entitled to recover and defendants are obligated to pay.

(b) The court shall enter judgment in lump sum for past damages, for future damages not in excess of two hundred fifty thousand dollars, and for any damages, fees or costs payable in lump sum or otherwise under subdivisions (c) and (d) of this section. For the purposes of this section, any lump sum payment of a portion of future damages shall be deemed to include the elements of future damages in the same proportion as such elements comprise of the total award for future damages as determined by the trier of fact.

(c) Payment of litigation expenses and that portion of the attorney's fees related to past damages shall be payable in a lump sum. Payment of that portion of the attorney's fees related to future damages for which, pursuant to this article, the claimant is entitled to a lump sum payment shall also be payable in a lump sum. Payment of that portion of the attorney's fees related to the future periodically paid damages shall also be payable in a lump sum, based on the present value of the annuity contract purchased to provide payment of such future periodically paid damages pursuant to subdivision (e) of this section.

(d) Upon election of a subrogee or a lien holder, including an employer or insurer who provides workers' compensation, filed within the time permitted by rule of court, any part of future damages allocable to reimbursement of payments previously made by the subrogee or the lien holder shall be paid in lump sum to the subrogee or the lien holder in such amount as is calculable and determinable under the law in effect at the time of such payment.

(e) With respect to awards of future damages in excess of two hundred fifty thousand dollars in an action to recover damages for dental, medical or podiatric malpractice, the court shall enter judgment as follows:

After making any adjustments prescribed by subdivisions (b), (c) and (d) of this section, the court shall enter a judgment for the amount of the present value of an annuity contract that will provide for the payment of the remaining amounts of future damages in periodic installments. The present value of such contract shall be determined in accordance with generally accepted actuarial practices by applying the discount rate in effect at the time of the award to the full amount of the remaining future damages, as calculated pursuant to this subdivision. The period of time over which such periodic payments shall be made and the period of time used to calculate the present value of the annuity contract shall be the period of years determined by the trier of fact in arriving at the itemized verdict; provided, however, that the period of time over which such periodic payments shall be made and the period of time used to calculate the present value for damages attributable to pain and suffering shall be ten years or the period of time determined by the trier of fact, whichever is less. The court, as part of its judgment, shall direct that the defendants and their insurance carriers shall be required to offer and to guarantee the purchase and payment of such an annuity contract. Such annuity contract shall provide for the payment of the annual payments of such remaining future damages over the period of time determined pursuant to this subdivision. The annual payment for the first year shall be calculated by dividing the remaining amount of future damages by the number of years over which such payments shall be made and the payment due in each succeeding year shall be computed by adding four percent to the previous year's payment. Where payment of a portion of the future damages terminates in accordance with the provisions of this article, the four percent added payment shall be based only upon that portion of the damages that remains subject to continued payment. Unless otherwise agreed, the annual sum so arrived at shall be paid in equal monthly installments and in advance.

(f) With the consent of the claimant and any party liable, in whole or in part, for the judgment, the court shall enter judgment for the amount found for future damages attributable to said party as such are determinable without regard to the provisions of this article.

**1986 AMENDMENTS**

L. 1986, ch. 485, eff. July 21, 1986, and applicable to acts, omissions or failures occurring on or after such date, amended CPLR 5031 to apply to podiatric malpractice actions.

**1985 AMENDMENTS**

L. 1985, ch. 294, eff. July 1, 1985, added Article 50-A, comprising CPLR 5031–5039. Article 50-A is applicable to any action for dental or medical malpractice commenced on or after July 1, 1985.

## § 5032. Form of security.

Security authorized or required for payment of a judgment for periodic installments entered in accordance with this article must be in the form of an annuity contract, executed by a qualified insurer and approved by the superintendent of insurance pursuant to section five thousand thirty-nine of this article, and approved by the court.

**1985 AMENDMENTS**

L. 1985, ch. 294, eff. July 1, 1985, added Article 50-A, comprising CPLR 5031–5039. Article 50-A is applicable to any action for dental or medical malpractice commenced on or after July 1, 1985.

## § 5033. Posting and maintaining security.

(a) If the court enters a judgment for periodic installments, each party liable for all or a portion of such judgment shall separately or jointly with one or more others post security in an amount necessary to secure payment for the amount of the judgment for future periodic installments within thirty days after the date the judgment is entered. A liability insurer having a contractual obligation and any other person adjudged to have an obligation to pay all or part of a judgment for periodic installments on behalf of a judgment debtor is obligated to post security to the extent of its contractual or adjudged obligation if the judgment debtor has not done so.

(b) A judgment creditor or successor in interest and any party having rights may move that the court find that security has not been posted and maintained with regard to a judgment obligation owing to the moving party. Upon so finding, the court shall order that security complying with this article be posted within thirty days. If security is not posted within that time and subdivision (c) of this section does not apply, the court shall enter a judgment for the lump sum as such sum is determinable under the law without regard to this article.

(c) If a judgment debtor who is the only person liable for a portion of a judgment for periodic installments fails to post and maintain security, the right to lump sum payment described in subdivision (b) of this section applies only against that judgment debtor and the portion of the judgment so owed.

(d) If more than one party is liable for all or a portion of a judgment requiring security under this article and the required security is posted by one or more

CPLR

but fewer than all of the parties liable, the security requirements are satisfied and those posting security may proceed under subdivision (b) of this section to enforce rights for security or lump sum payment to satisfy or protect rights of reimbursement from a party not posting security.

1985 AMENDMENTS

L. 1985, ch. 294, eff. July 1, 1985, added Article 50-A, comprising CPLR 5031–5039. Article 50-A is applicable to any action for dental or medical malpractice commenced on or after July 1, 1985.

### § 5034. Failure to make payment.

If at any time following entry of judgment, a judgment debtor fails for any reason to make a payment in a timely fashion according to the terms of this article, the judgment creditor may petition the court which rendered the original judgment for an order requiring payment by the judgment debtor of the outstanding payments in a lump sum. In calculating the amount of the lump sum judgment, the court shall total the remaining periodic payments due and owing to the judgment creditor, as calculated pursuant to subdivision (b) of section five thousand thirty-one of this article, and shall not convert these amounts to their present value. The court may also require the payment of interest on the outstanding judgment.

1985 AMENDMENTS

L. 1985, ch. 294, eff. July 1, 1985, added Article 50-A, comprising CPLR 5031–5039. Article 50-A is applicable to any action for dental or medical malpractice commenced on or after July 1, 1985.

### § 5035. Effect of death of judgment creditor.

(a) Unless otherwise agreed between the parties at the time security is posted pursuant to section five thousand thirty-three of this article, in all cases covered by this article in which future damages are payable in periodic installments, the liability for payment of any installments for medical, dental or other costs of health care or noneconomic loss not yet due at the death of the judgment creditor terminates upon the death of the judgment creditor.

(b) The portion of any periodic payment allocable to loss of future earnings shall not be reduced or terminated by reason of the death of the judgment creditor, but shall be paid to persons to whom the judgment creditor owed a duty of support immediately prior to his death to the extent that such duty of support exists under applicable law at the time of the death of the judgment creditor. Such payments to such persons shall continue for the remainder of the period as originally found by the jury or until such duty of support ceases to exist, whichever occurs first. In such cases, the court which rendered the original judgment may, upon petition of any party in interest, modify the judgment to award and apportion the future payments of such unpaid future damages in accordance with this subdivision which apportioned amounts shall be payable in the future as provided for in this article. In the event that the judgment creditor does not owe a duty of support to any person at the time of the death of the judgment creditor or such duty ceases to exist, the remaining payments shall be considered part of the estate of the judgment creditor. In such cases, the court which rendered the original judgment may, upon petition of any party in interest, convert those portions of such periodic payments allocable to the loss of future earnings to a lump sum by calculating the present value of such payments in order to assist in the settlement of the estate of the judgment creditor.

### 1985 AMENDMENTS

L. 1985, ch. 294, eff. July 1, 1985, added Article 50-A, comprising CPLR 5031–5039. Article 50-A is applicable to any action for dental or medical malpractice commenced on or after July 1, 1985.

## § 5036. Adjustment of payments.

(a) If, at the time after entry of judgment, a judgment creditor or successor in interest can establish that the continued payment of the judgment in periodic installments will impose a hardship, the court may, in its discretion, order that the remaining payments or a portion thereof shall be made to the judgment creditor in a lump sum. The court shall, before entering such an order, find that: (i) unanticipated and substantial medical, dental or other needs have arisen that warrant the payment of the remaining payments, or a portion thereof, in a lump sum; (ii) ordering such a lump sum payment would not impose an unreasonable financial burden on the judgment debtor or debtors; (iii) ordering such a lump sum payment will accommodate the future medical and other needs of the judgment creditor; and (iv) ordering such a lump sum payment would further the interests of justice.

(b) If a lump sum payment is ordered by the court, such payment shall be made by the medical malpractice insurance association created pursuant to article fifty-five of the insurance law and shall not be the obligation of the insurer providing the initial annuity contract. Such insurer shall thereafter make all future payments due under its annuity contract to the association, except that, if the lump sum payment ordered by the court is a portion of the remaining periodic payments, such insurer shall appropriately apportion future payments due under its annuity contract between the association and the judgment creditor or successor in interest. Such lump sum payment to be paid to the judgment creditor or successor in interest by the association shall be calculated on the basis of the present value of the annuity contract, which shall be based on its cost at such time, for remaining periodic payments, or portions thereof, that are converted into a lump sum payment. In no event shall such lump sum payment be greater than the present value of the annuity contract for the remaining periodic payments.

CPLR

### CROSS REFERENCES

**Insurance Law Article 55**, referred to in subdivision (b), governs the operations and management of the Medical Malpractice Insurance Association.

### 1988 AMENDMENTS

L. 1988, ch. 184, eff. July 1, 1988, repealed subdivision (b) and replaced it with a new (b) requiring lump-sum payments to be made by the medical malpractice insurance association (See Insurance Law § 55).

### 1985 AMENDMENTS

L. 1985, ch. 294, eff. July 1, 1985, added Article 50-A, comprising CPLR 5031–5039. Article 50-A is applicable to any action for dental or medical malpractice commenced on or after July 1, 1985.

## § 5037. Settlements.

Nothing in this article shall be construed to limit the right of a plaintiff, defendant and any insurer to settle dental, medical or podiatric malpractice claims as they consider appropriate and in their complete discretion.

### 1986 AMENDMENTS

L. 1986, ch. 485, eff. July 21, 1986, and applicable to acts, omissions or failures occurring on or after such date, amended CPLR 5037 to apply to podiatric malpractice actions.

### 1985 AMENDMENTS

L. 1985, ch. 294, eff. July 1, 1985, added Article 50-A, comprising CPLR 5031–5039. Article 50-A is applicable to any action for dental or medical malpractice commenced on or after July 1, 1985.

## § 5038. Assignment of periodic installments.

An assignment of or an agreement to assign any right to periodic installments for future damages contained in a judgment entered under this article is enforceable only as to amounts: (a) to secure payment of alimony, maintenance, or child support; (b) for the cost of products, services, or accommodations provided or to be provided by the assignee for medical, dental or other health care; or (c) for attorney's fees and other expenses of litigation incurred in securing the judgment.

### 1985 AMENDMENTS

L. 1985, ch. 294, eff. July 1, 1985, added Article 50-A, comprising CPLR 5031–5039. Article 50-A is applicable to any action for dental or medical malpractice commenced on or after July 1, 1985.

## § 5039. Duties of superintendent of insurance.

The superintendent of insurance shall establish rules and procedures for determining which insurers, self-insurers, plans or arrangements are financially qualified to provide the security required under this article and to be designated as qualified insurers.

### 1985 AMENDMENTS

L. 1985, ch. 294, eff. July 1, 1985, added Article 50-A, comprising CPLR 5031–5039. Article 50-A is applicable to any action for dental or medical malpractice commenced on or after July 1, 1985.

# ARTICLE 50–B

# PERIODIC PAYMENT OF JUDGMENTS IN PERSONAL INJURY, INJURY TO PROPERTY AND WRONGFUL DEATH ACTIONS

---

## SUMMARY OF ARTICLE

§ 5041.  Basis for determining judgment to be entered.
§ 5042.  Form of security.
§ 5043.  Posting and maintaining security.
§ 5044.  Failure to make payment.
§ 5045.  Effect of death of judgment creditor.
§ 5046.  Adjustment of payments.
§ 5047.  Settlements.
§ 5048.  Assignment of periodic installments.
§ 5049.  Duties of superintendent of insurance.

**CPLR**

---

## § 5041.  Basis for determining judgment to be entered.

In order to determine what judgment is to be entered on a verdict in an action to recover damages for personal injury, injury to property or wrongful death under this article, and not subject to article fifty-A of this chapter, the court shall proceed as follows:

(a) The court shall apply to the findings of past and future damages any applicable rules of law, including set-offs, credits, comparative negligence pursuant to section fourteen hundred eleven of this chapter, additurs, and remittiturs, in calculating the respective amounts of past and future damages claimants are entitled to recover and defendants are obligated to pay.

(b) The court shall enter judgment in lump sum for past damages, for future damages not in excess of two hundred fifty thousand dollars, and for any damages, fees or costs payable in lump sum or otherwise under subdivisions (c) and (d) of this section. For the purposes of this section, any lump sum payment of a portion of future damages shall be deemed to include the elements of future damages in the same proportion as such elements comprise of the total award for future damages as determined by the trier of fact.

(c) Payment of litigation expenses and that portion of the attorney's fees related to past damages shall be payable in a lump sum. Payment of that portion of the attorney's fees related to future damages for which, pursuant to this article, the claimant is entitled to a lump sum payment shall also be payable in a lump sum. Payment of that portion of the attorney's fees related to the future periodically paid damages shall also be payable in a lump sum, based on the present value of the annuity contract purchased to provide payment of such future periodically paid damages pursuant to subdivision (e) of this section.

(d) Upon election of a subrogee or a lien holder, including an employer or insurer who provides workers' compensation, filed within the time permitted by rule of court, any part of future damages allocable to reimbursement of payments previously made by the subrogee or the lien holder shall be paid in lump sum to the subrogee or the lien holder in such amount as is calculable and determinable under the law in effect at the time of such payment.

(e) With respect to awards of future damages in excess of two hundred fifty thousand dollars in an action to recover damages for personal injury, injury to property or wrongful death, the court shall enter judgment as follows:

After making any adjustment prescribed by subdivision (b), (c) and (d) of this section, the court shall enter a judgment for the amount of the present value of an annuity contract that will provide for the payment of the remaining amounts of future damages in periodic installments. The present value of such contract shall be determined in accordance with generally accepted actuarial practices by applying the discount rate in effect at the time of the award to the full amount of the remaining future damages, as calculated pursuant to this subdivision. The period of time over which such periodic payments shall be made and the period of time used to calculate the present value of the annuity contract shall be the period of years determined by the trier of fact in arriving at the itemized verdict; provided, however, that the period of time over which such periodic payments shall be made and the period of time used to calculate the present value for damages attributable to pain and suffering shall be ten years or the period of time determined by the trier of fact, whichever is less. The court, as part of its judgment, shall direct that the defendants and their insurance carriers shall be required to offer and to guarantee the purchase and payment of such an annuity contract. Such annuity contract shall provide for the payment of the annual payments of such remaining future damages over the period of time determined pursuant to this subdivision. The annual payment for the first year shall be calculated by dividing the remaining amount of future damages by the number of years over which such payments shall be made and the payment due in each succeeding year shall be computed by adding four percent to the previous year's payment. Where payment of a portion of the future damages terminates in accordance with the provisions of this article, the four percent added payment shall be based only upon that portion of the damages that remains subject to continued payment. Unless otherwise agreed, the annual sum so arrived at shall be paid in equal monthly installments and in advance.

(f) With the consent of the claimant and any party liable, in whole or in part, for the judgment, the court shall enter judgment for the amount found for future damages attributable to said party as such are determinable without regard to the provisions of this article.

**1986 AMENDMENTS**

L. 1986, ch. 682, eff. July 30, 1986, and applicable to actions commenced or claims filed on or after such date, added new Article 50–B, comprising CPLR 5041 through 5049.

## § 5042. Form of security.

Security authorized or required for payment of a judgment for periodic installments entered in accordance with this article must be in the form of an annuity contract, executed by a qualified insurer and approved by the superintendent of insurance pursuant to section five thousand forty-nine of this article, and approved by the court.

**1986 AMENDMENTS**

L. 1986, ch. 682, eff. July 30, 1986, and applicable to actions commenced or claims filed on or after such date, added new Article 50–B, comprising CPLR 5041 through 5049.

## § 5043. Posting and maintaining security.

(a) If the court enters a judgment for periodic installments, each party liable for all or a portion of such judgment shall separately or jointly with one or more others post security in an amount necessary to secure payment for the amount of the judgment for future periodic installments within thirty days after the date the judgment is entered. A liability insurer having a contractual obligation and any other person adjudged to have an obligation to pay all or part of a judgment for periodic installments on behalf of a judgment debtor is obligated to post security to the extent of its contractual or adjudged obligation if the judgment debtor has not done so.

(b) A judgment creditor or successor in interest and any party having rights may move that the court find that security has not been posted and maintained with regard to a judgment obligation owing to the moving party. Upon so finding, the court shall order that security complying with this article be posted within thirty days. If security is not posted within that time and subdivision (c) of this section does not apply, the court shall enter a judgment for the lump sum as such sum is determinable under the law without regard to this article.

(c) If a judgment debtor who is the only person liable for a portion of a judgment for periodic installments fails to post and maintain security, the right to lump sum payment described in subdivision (b) of this section applies only against that judgment debtor and the portion of judgment so owed.

(d) If more than one party is liable for all or a portion of a judgment requiring security under this article and the required security is posted by one or more but fewer than all of the parties liable, the security requirements are satisfied and those posting security may proceed under subdivision (b) of this section to enforce rights for security or lump sum payment to satisfy or protect rights of reimbursement from a party not posting security.

### 1986 AMENDMENTS

L. 1986, ch. 682, eff. July 30, 1986, and applicable to actions commenced or claims filed on or after such date, added new Article 50–B, comprising CPLR 5041 through 5049.

## § 5044. Failure to make payment.

If at any time following entry of judgment, a judgment debtor fails for any reason to make a payment in a timely fashion according to the terms of this article, the judgment creditor may petition the court which rendered the original judgment for an order requiring payment by the judgment debtor of the outstanding payments in a lump sum. In calculating the amount of the lump sum judgment, the court shall total the remaining periodic payments due and owing to the judgment creditor, as calculated pursuant to subdivision (b) of section five thousand forty-one of this article, and shall not convert these amounts to their present value. The court may also require the payment of interest on the outstanding judgment.

### 1986 AMENDMENTS

L. 1986, ch. 682, eff. July 30, 1986, and applicable to actions commenced or claims filed on or after such date, added new Article 50–B, comprising CPLR 5041 through 5049.

## § 5045. Effect of death of judgment creditor.

(a) Unless otherwise agreed between the parties at the time security is posted pursuant to section five thousand forty-three of this article, in all cases covered by this article in which future damages are payable in periodic installments, the liability for payment of any installments for medical, dental or other costs of health care or non-economic loss not yet due at the death of the judgment creditor terminates upon the death of the judgment creditor.

(b) The portion of any periodic payment allocable to loss of future earnings shall not be reduced or terminated by reason of the death of the judgment creditor, but shall be paid to persons to whom the judgment creditor owed a duty of support immediately prior to his death to the extent that such duty of support exists under applicable law at the time of the death of the judgment creditor. Such payments to such persons shall continue for the remainder of the period as originally found by the jury or until such duty of support ceases to exist, whichever occurs first. In such cases, the court which rendered the original judgment may, upon petition of any party in interest, modify the judgment to award and apportion the future payments of such unpaid future damages in accordance with this subdivision which apportioned amounts shall be payable in the future as provided for in this article. In the event that the judgment credit does not owe a duty of support to any person at the time of the death of the judgment creditor or such duty ceases to exist, the remaining payments shall be considered part of the estate of the judgment creditor. In such cases, the court which rendered the original judgment may, upon petition of any party in interest, convert those portions of such periodic payments allocable to the loss of future earnings to a lump sum by calculating the present value of such payments in order to assist in the settlement of the estate of the judgment creditor.

### 1986 AMENDMENTS

L. 1986, ch. 682, eff. July 30, 1986, and applicable to actions commenced or claims filed on or after such date, added new Article 50–B, comprising CPLR 5041 through 5049.

## § 5046. Adjustment of payments.

(a) If, at any time after entry of judgment, a judgment creditor or successor in interest can establish that the continued payment of the judgment in periodic installments will impose a hardship, the court may, in its discretion, order that the remaining payments or a portion thereof shall be made to the judgment creditor in a lump sum. The court shall, before entering such an order, find that: (i) unanticipated and substantial medical, dental or other health needs have arisen that warrant the payment of the remaining payments, or a portion thereof, in a lump sum; (ii) ordering such a lump sum payment would not impose an unreasonable financial burden on the judgment debtor or debtors; (iii) ordering such a lump sum payment will accommodate the future medical, dental and other health needs of the judgment creditor; and (iv) ordering such a lump sum payment would further the interests of justice.

(b) If a lump sum payment is ordered by the court, such lump sum shall be calculated on the basis of the present value of remaining periodic payments, or portions thereof, that are converted into a lump sum payment. Unless specifically waived by all parties, the annuity contract executed pursuant to section five thousand forty-two of this article shall contain a provision authorizing such a lump sum payment if such payment is approved pursuant to this section. The remaining future periodic payments, if any, shall be reduced accordingly. For the purposes of this section, present value shall be calculated based on the interest rate and mortality assumptions at the time such a lump sum payment is made as determined by the insurer who has provided the annuity contract, in accordance with regulations issued by the superintendent of insurance.

### 1986 AMENDMENTS

L. 1986, ch. 682, eff. July 30, 1986, and applicable to actions commenced or claims filed on or after such date, added new Article 50–B, comprising CPLR 5041 through 5049.

## § 5047. Settlements.

Nothing in this article shall be construed to limit the right of a plaintiff, defendant or defendants and any insurer to settle property damage, personal injury or wrongful death claims as they consider appropriate and in their complete discretion.

### 1986 AMENDMENTS

L. 1986, ch. 682, eff. July 30, 1986, and applicable to actions commenced or claims filed on or after such date, added new Article 50–B, comprising CPLR 5041 through 5049.

## § 5048. Assignment of periodic installments.

An assignment of or an agreement to assign any right to periodic installments for future damages contained in a judgment entered under this article is enforceable only as to amounts: (a) to secure payment of alimony, maintenance, or child support; (b) for the cost of products, services, or accommodations provided or to be provided by the assignee for medical, dental or other health care; or (c) for attorney's fees and other expenses of litigation incurred in securing the judgment.

### 1986 AMENDMENTS

L. 1986, ch. 682, eff. July 30, 1986, and applicable to actions commenced or claims filed on or after such date, added new Article 50–B, comprising CPLR 5041 through 5049.

## § 5049. Duties of superintendent of insurance.

The superintendent of insurance shall establish rules and procedures for determining which insurers, self-insurers, plans or arrangements are financially qualified to provide the security required under this article and to be designated as qualified insurers.

### 1986 AMENDMENTS

L. 1986, ch. 682, eff. July 30, 1986, and applicable to actions commenced or claims filed on or after such date, added new Article 50–B, comprising CPLR 5041 through 5049.

# ARTICLE 51

## ENFORCEMENT OF JUDGMENTS AND ORDERS GENERALLY

### SUMMARY OF ARTICLE

§ 5101.    Enforcement of money judgment or order.
§ 5102.    Enforcement of judgment or order awarding possession of real property or a chattel.
§ 5103.    Enforcement of judgment or order directing sale of real property.
    (a)  Entry in county where real property situated.
    (b)  Place and mode of sale; security.
§ 5104.    Enforcement of judgment or order by contempt.
§ 5105.    Alternative enforcement of judgment or order.
§ 5106.    Appointment of receiver.
§ 5107.    Conveyance by sheriff.

### § 5101.  Enforcement of money judgment or order.

A money judgment and an order directing the payment of money, including motion costs, may be enforced as prescribed in article fifty-two. An order of support, alimony or maintenance of any court of competent jurisdiction where arrears/past-due support have not been reduced to judgment, including motion costs, may be enforced as prescribed in article fifty-two upon the default of a debtor as such term is defined in paragraph seven of subdivision (a) of section fifty-two hundred forty-one of this article, except that for the purposes of this section only, a default shall not be founded upon retroactive child support obligations as defined in paragraph (a) of subdivision one of section four hundred forty of the family court act and subdivision one of section two hundred forty, and paragraph b of subdivision nine of section two hundred thirty-six of the domestic relations law. The establishment of a default shall be subject to the procedures established for the determination of a mistake of fact for income executions pursuant to subdivision (e) of section fifty-two hundred forty-one of this article.

#### 1993 AMENDMENTS

L. 1993, ch. 59, eff. July 1, 1993, to address the enforceability of support, alimony or maintenance orders upon the debtor's default.

## § 5102. Enforcement of judgment or order awarding possession of real property or a chattel.

A judgment or order, or a part thereof, awarding possession of real property or a chattel may be enforced by an execution, which shall particularly describe the property and designate the party to whom the judgment or order awards its possession. The execution shall comply with the provisions of section 5230, except that it shall direct the sheriff to deliver possession of the property to the party designated. In an action to recover a chattel, where the judgment awards possession of the chattel and in the alternative its value, the execution shall also direct the sheriff, if the chattel cannot be found within his county, to levy upon real and personal property as upon an execution to enforce a money judgment. After the death of a party against whom a judgment or order awarding possession of real property has been obtained, an order granting leave to issue such execution may be granted upon twenty days' notice, to be served in the same manner as a summons, to the occupants of the real property and to the heirs or devisees of the deceased party.

## § 5103. Enforcement of judgment or order directing sale of real property.

(a) Entry in county where real property situated. Where real property directed by a judgment or order to be sold is not situated in the county in which the judgment or order is entered, the judgment or order shall also be entered by the clerk of the county in which the property is situated upon filing with him a certified copy of the judgment or order. A purchaser of the property is not required to pay the purchase money or accept a deed until the judgment or order is so entered.

(b) Place and mode of sale; security. Where a judgment or order directs that real property shall be sold, it shall be sold in such manner as the judgment or order may direct in the county where it is situated by the sheriff of that county or by a referee appointed by the court for the purpose. If the property is situated in more than one county, it may be sold in a county in which any part is situated unless the judgment or order directs otherwise. If a referee is appointed to sell the property, the court may require him to give an undertaking in an amount fixed by it for the proper application of the proceeds of the sale. The conveyance shall specify in the granting clause the party whose right, title or interest is directed to be sold by the judgment or order and is being conveyed.

## § 5104. Enforcement of judgment or order by contempt.

Any interlocutory or final judgment or order, or any part thereof, not enforceable under either article fifty-two or section 5102 may be enforced by serving a certified copy of the judgment or order upon the party or other person required thereby or by law to obey it and, if he refuses or wilfully neglects to obey it, by punishing him for a contempt of the court.

## § 5105.  Alternative enforcement of judgment or order.

An interlocutory or final judgment or order, or any part thereof, may be enforced either by the method prescribed in article fifty-two or that prescribed in section 5104, or both, where such judgment or part:

1. requires the payment of money into court or to an officer of, or receiver appointed by, the court, except where the money is due upon an express or implied contract or as damages for non-performance of a contract; or

2. requires a trustee or person acting in a fiduciary relationship to pay a sum of money for a willful default or dereliction of his duty.

## § 5106.  Appointment of receiver.

A court, by or after judgment, may appoint a receiver of property which is the subject of an action, to carry the judgment into effect or to dispose of the property according to its directions. Unless the court otherwise orders, such a receivership shall be subject to the provisions of article sixty-four.

## § 5107.  Conveyance by sheriff.

The court may require the sheriff to convey real property in conformity with its directions.

**1964 AMENDMENTS**

L. 1964, ch. 262, eff. Sept. 1, 1964, deleted the last sentence of CPLR 2703 and reenacted the same as CPLR 5107.

**CPLR**

# ARTICLE 52

# ENFORCEMENT OF MONEY JUDGMENTS

## SUMMARY OF ARTICLE

§ 5201.  Debt or property subject to enforcement; proper garnishee.
   (a)  Debt against which a money judgment may be enforced.
   (b)  Property against which a money judgment may be enforced.
   (c)  Proper garnishee for particular property or debt.
§ 5202.  Judgment creditor's rights in personal property.
   (a)  Execution creditor's rights.
   (b)  Other judgment creditor's rights.
§ 5203.  Priorities and liens upon real property.
   (a)  Priority and lien on docketing judgment.
   (b)  Extension of lien.
§ 5204.  Release of lien or levy upon appeal.
§ 5205.  Personal property exempt from application to the satisfaction of money judgments.
   (a)  Exemption for personal property.
   (b)  Exemption of cause of action and damages for taking or injuring exempt personal property.
   (c)  Trust exemption.
   (d)  Income exemptions.
   (e)  Exemptions to members of armed forces.
   (f)  Exemption for unpaid milk proceeds.
   (g)  Security deposit exemption.
   (h)  [Exemption for personal property necessary for debtor's health and welfare.]
   (i)  Exemption for life insurance policies.
§ 5206.  Real property exempt from application to the satisfaction of money judgments.
   (a)  Exemption of homestead.
   (b)  Homestead exemption after owner's death.
   (c)  Suspension of occupation as affecting homestead.
   (d)  Exemption of homestead exceeding ten thousand dollars in value.
   (e)  Sale of homestead exceeding ten thousand dollars in value.
   (f)  Exemption of burying ground.
§ 5207.  Enforcement involving the state.
§ 5208.  Enforcement after death of judgment debtor; leave of court; extension of lien.
§ 5209.  Discharge of garnishee's obligation.
§ 5210.  Power of court to punish for contempt.
§ 5211.  Privilege on examination; immunity.

CPLR

§§ 5212–5220.   [Not used.]

§ 5221.   Where enforcement proceeding commenced.
    (a)   Court and county in which proceeding commenced.
    (b)   Notices, subpoenas and motions.

§ 5222.   Restraining notice.
    (a)   Issuance; on whom served; form; service.
    (b)   Effect of restraint; prohibition of transfer; duration.
    (c)   Subsequent notice.
    (d)   Notice to judgment debtor or obligor.
    (e)   Content of notice.
    (f)   [Definitions.]
    (g)   Restraining notice in the form of magnetic tape.

§ 5223.   Disclosure.

R 5224.   Subpoena; procedure.
    (a)   Kinds and service of subpoena.
    (b)   Fees.
    (c)   Time and place of examination.
    (d)   Conduct of examination.
    (e)   Signing deposition; physical preparation.
    (f)   Subsequent examination.

§ 5225.   Payment or delivery of property of judgment debtor.
    (a)   Property in the possession of judgment debtor.
    (b)   Property not in the possession of judgment debtor.
    (c)   Documents to effect payment or delivery.

§ 5226.   Installment payment order.

§ 5227.   Payment of debts owed to judgment debtor.

§ 5228.   Receivers.
    (a)   Appointment of receiver.
    (b)   Extension of receivership.

§ 5229.   Enforcement before judgment entered.

§ 5230.   Executions.
    (a)   Form.
    (b)   Issuance.
    (c)   Return.
    (d)   Records of sheriff or support collection unit.
    (e)   [Definitions.]

§ 5231.   Income execution.
    (a)   Form.
    (b)   Issuance.
    (c)   Definition of earnings and disposable earnings.
    (d)   Service upon debtor.
    (e)   Levy upon default or failure to serve debtor.
    (f)   Withholding of installments.
    (g)   Statement on income execution.
    (h)   Levy upon money payable by municipal corporation or the state.
    (i)   Modification.
    (j)   Priority; delivery to another sheriff.
    (k)   Accounting by sheriff.

**§ 5232.**　　Levy upon personal property.
　　(a)　Levy by service of execution.
　　(b)　Levy by seizure.
　　(c)　Notice to judgment debtor or obligor.
　　(d)　[Definitions.]
**§ 5233.**　　Sale of personal property.
　　(a)　Public auction.
　　(b)　Public notice.
　　(c)　Order for immediate sale or disposition.
　　(d)　Unsaleable material.
**§ 5234.**　　Distribution of proceeds of personal property; priorities.
　　(a)　Distribution of proceeds of personal property.
　　(b)　Priority among execution creditors.
　　(c)　Priority of other judgment creditors.
**§ 5235.**　　Levy upon real property.
**§ 5236.**　　Sale of real property.
　　(a)　Time of sale; public auction.
　　(b)　Sale of mortgaged property.
　　(c)　Notice of sale.
　　(d)　Notice of postponement of sale.
　　(e)　Effect of notice as against judgment creditors.
　　(f)　Conveyance; proof of notice.
　　(g)　Disposition of proceeds of sale.
**§ 5237.**　　Failure of title to property sold.
**§ 5238.**　　Directions to the sheriff.
**§ 5239.**　　Proceeding to determine adverse claims.
**§ 5240.**　　Modification or protective order; supervision of enforcement.
**§ 5241.**　　Income execution for support enforcement
　　(a)　Definitions.
　　(b)　Issuance.
　　(c)　Execution for support enforcement; form.
　　(d)　Notice to debtor.
　　(e)　Determination of mistake of fact.
　　(f)　Levy.
　　(g)　Deduction from income.
　　(h)　Priority.
　　(i)　Levy upon money payable by the state.
**§ 5242.**　　Income deduction order for support enforcement.
**§§ 5243–5249.**　　[Not used.]
**§ 5250.**　　Arrest of judgment debtor.
**§ 5251.**　　Disobedience of subpoena, restraining notice or order; false swearing; destroying notice of sale.
**§ 5252.**　　Discrimination against employees and prospective employees based upon wage assignment or income execution.

CPLR

## § 5201. Debt or property subject to enforcement; proper garnishee.

(a) Debt against which a money judgment may be enforced. A money judgment may be enforced against any debt, which is past due or which is yet to become due, certainly or upon demand of the judgment debtor, whether it was incurred within or without the state, to or from a resident or non-resident, unless it is exempt from application to the satisfaction of the judgment. A debt may consist of a cause of action which could be assigned or transferred accruing within or without the state.

(b) Property against which a money judgment may be enforced. A money judgment may be enforced against any property which could be assigned or transferred, whether it consists of a present or future right or interest and whether or not it is vested, unless it is exempt from application to the satisfaction of the judgment. A money judgment entered upon a joint liability of two or more persons may be enforced against individual property of those persons summoned and joint property of such persons with any other persons against whom the judgment is entered.

(c) Proper garnishee for particular property or debt.

1. Where property consists of a right or share in the stock of an association or corporation, or interests or profits therein, for which a certificate of stock or other negotiable instrument is not outstanding, the corporation, or the president or treasurer of the association on behalf of the association, shall be the garnishee.

2. Where property consists of a right or interest to or in a decedent's estate or any other property or fund held or controlled by a fiduciary, the executor or trustee under the will, administrator or other fiduciary shall be the garnishee.

3. Where property consists of an interest in a partnership, any partner other than the judgment debtor, on behalf of the partnership, shall be the garnishee.

4. Where property or a debt is evidenced by a negotiable instrument for the payment of money, a negotiable document of title or a certificate of stock of an association or corporation, the instrument, document or certificate shall be treated as property capable of delivery and the person holding it shall be the garnishee; except that in the case of a security which is transferable in the manner set forth in section 8-320 of the uniform commercial code, the firm or corporation which carries on its books an account in the name of the judgment debtor in which is reflected such security, shall be the garnishee; provided, however, that if such security has been pledged, the pledgee shall be the garnishee.

### CROSS REFERENCES

U.C.C. § 8-320, referred to in paragraph (4) of Subd. (c), *supra*, deals with transfer or pledge within a central depository system.

**1964 AMENDMENTS**

L. 1964, ch. 298, eff. Sept. 1, 1964, amended paragraph 4 of Subd. (c) to add the provision following the semi-colon in respect to a security transferable in the manner set forth in the Uniform Commercial Code § 8-320.

## § 5202. Judgment creditor's rights in personal property.

(a) Execution creditor's rights. Where a judgment creditor has delivered an execution to a sheriff, the judgment creditor's rights in a debt owed to the judgment debtor or in an interest of the judgment debtor in personal property, against which debt or property the judgment may be enforced, are superior to the extent of the amount of the execution to the rights of any transferee of the debt or property, except:

1. a transferee who acquired the debt or property for fair consideration before it was levied upon; or

2. a transferee who acquired a debt or personal property not capable of delivery for fair consideration after it was levied upon without knowledge of the levy.

(b) Other judgment creditor's rights. Where a judgment creditor has secured an order for delivery of, payment of, or appointment of a receiver of, a debt owed to the judgment debtor or an interest of the judgment debtor in personal property, the judgment creditor's rights in the debt or property are superior to the rights of any transferee of the debt or property, except a transferee who acquired the debt or property for fair consideration and without notice of such order.

**CROSS REFERENCES**

As to definition of fair consideration, see **Debtor and Creditor Law § 272**, in Appendix, *infra*.

## § 5203. Priorities and liens upon real property.

(a) Priority and lien on docketing judgment. No transfer of an interest of the judgment debtor in real property, against which property a money judgment may be enforced, is effective against the judgment creditor either from the time of the docketing of the judgment with the clerk of the county in which the property is located until ten years after filing of the judgment-roll, or from the time of the filing with such clerk of a notice of levy pursuant to an execution until the execution is returned, except:

1. a transfer or the payment of the proceeds of a judicial sale, which shall include an execution sale, in satisfaction either of a judgment previously so docketed or of a judgment where a notice of levy pursuant to an execution thereon was previously so filed; or

2. a transfer in satisfaction of a mortgage given to secure the payment of the purchase price of the judgment debtor's interest in the property; or

CPLR

3. a transfer to a purchaser for value at a judicial sale, which shall include an execution sale; or

4. when the judgment was entered after the death of the judgment debtor; or

5. when the judgment debtor is the state, an officer, department, board or commission of the state, or a municipal corporation; or

6. when the judgment debtor is the personal representative of a decedent and the judgment was awarded in an action against him in his representative capacity.

(b) Extension of lien. Upon motion of the judgment creditor, upon notice to the judgment debtor, served personally or by registered or certified mail, return receipt requested, to the last known address of the judgment debtor, the court may order that the lien of a money judgment upon real property be effective after the expiration of ten years from the filing of the judgment-roll, for a period no longer than the time during which the judgment creditor was stayed from enforcing the judgment, or the time necessary to complete advertisement and sale of real property in accordance with section 5236, pursuant to an execution delivered to a sheriff prior to the expiration of ten years from the filing of the judgment roll. The order shall be effective from the time it is filed with the clerk of the county in which the property is located and an appropriate entry is made upon the docket of the judgment.

### 1972 AMENDMENTS

L. 1972, ch. 968, eff. Sept. 1, 1972, added new subparagraph (a)(6).

### 1965 AMENDMENTS

L. 1965, ch. 974, eff. Sept. 1, 1965, inserted the words "which shall include an execution sale" in Subd. (a), paragraphs 1 and 3.

### 1964 AMENDMENTS

L. 1964, ch. 388, eff. Sept. 1, 1964, corrected the cross-reference in Subd. (b) to "5235" to read "5236".

## § 5204. Release of lien or levy upon appeal.

Upon motion of the judgment debtor, upon notice to the judgment creditor, the sheriff and the sureties upon the undertaking, the court may order, upon such terms as justice requires, that the lien of a money judgment, or that a levy made pursuant to an execution issued upon a money judgment, be released as to all or specified real or personal property upon the ground that the judgment debtor has given an undertaking upon appeal sufficient to secure the judgment creditor.

### 1970 AMENDMENTS

L. 1970, ch. 600, eff. July 1, 1970, amended the section by requiring that the sheriff receive notice of a motion to release a lien of a money judgment or a levy made pursuant to an execution issued upon a money judgment.

### § 5205. Personal property exempt from application to the satisfaction of money judgments.

(a) Exemption for personal property. The following personal property when owned by any person is exempt from application to the satisfaction of a money judgment except where the judgment is for the purchase price of the exempt property or was recovered by a domestic, laboring person or mechanic for work performed by that person in such capacity:

1. all stoves kept for use in the judgment debtor's dwelling house and necessary fuel therefor for sixty days; one sewing machine with its appurtenances;

2. the family bible, family pictures, and school books used by the judgment debtor or in the family; and other books, not exceeding fifty dollars in value, kept and used as part of the family or judgment debtor's library;

3. a seat or pew occupied by the judgment debtor or the family in a place of public worship;

4. domestic animals with the necessary food for those animals for sixty days, provided that the total value of such animals and food does not exceed four hundred fifty dollars; all necessary food actually provided for the use of the judgment debtor or his family for sixty days;

5. all wearing apparel, household furniture, one mechanical, gas or electric refrigerator, one radio receiver, one television set, crockery, tableware and cooking utensils necessary for the judgment debtor and the family;

6. a wedding ring; a watch not exceeding thirty-five dollars in value; and

7. necessary working tools and implements, including those of a mechanic, farm machinery, team, professional instruments, furniture and library, not exceeding six hundred dollars in value, together with the necessary food for the team for sixty days, provided, however, that the articles specified in this paragraph are necessary to the carrying on of the judgment debtor's profession or calling.

(b) Exemption of cause of action and damages for taking or injuring exempt personal property. A cause of action, to recover damages for taking or injuring personal property exempt from application to the satisfaction of a money judgment, is exempt from application to the satisfaction of a money judgment. A money judgment and its proceeds arising out of such a cause of action is exempt, for one year after the collection thereof, from application to the satisfaction of a money judgment.

(c) Trust exemption. 1. Except as provided in paragraphs four and five of this subdivision, all property while held in trust for a judgment debtor, where the trust has been created by, or the fund so held in trust has proceeded from, a person other than the judgment debtor, is exempt from application to the satisfaction of a money judgment.

CPLR

2. For purposes of this subdivision, all trusts, custodial accounts, annuities, insurance contracts, monies, assets or interests established as part of, and all payments from, either any trust or plan, which is qualified as an individual retirement account under section four hundred eight of the United States Internal Revenue Code of 1986, as amended, or a Keogh (HR-10), retirement or other plan established by a corporation, which is qualified under section 401 of the United States Internal Revenue Code of 1986, as amended, or created as a result of rollovers from such plans pursuant to sections 402 (a) (5), 403 (a) (4) or 408 (d) (3) of the Internal Revenue Code of 1986, as amended, shall be considered a trust which has been created by or which has proceeded from a person other than the judgment debtor, even though such judgment debtor is (i) in the case of an individual retirement account plan, an individual who is the settlor of and depositor to such account plan, or (ii) a self-employed individual, or (iii) a partner of the entity sponsoring the Keogh (HR-10) plan, or (iv) a shareholder of the corporation sponsoring the retirement or other plan.

3. All trusts, custodial accounts, annuities, insurance contracts, monies, assets, or interests described in paragraph two of this subdivision shall be conclusively presumed to be spendthrift trusts under this section and the common law of the state of New York for all purposes, including, but not limited to, all cases arising under or related to a case arising under sections one hundred one to thirteen hundred thirty of title eleven of the United States Bankruptcy Code, as amended.

4. This subdivision shall not impair any rights an individual has under a qualified domestic relations order as that term is defined in section 414(p) of the United States Internal Revenue Code of 1986, as amended.

5. Additions to an asset described in paragraph two of this subdivision shall not be exempt from application to the satisfaction of a money judgment if (i) made after the date that is ninety days before the interposition of the claim on which such judgment was entered, or (ii) deemed to be fraudulent conveyances under article ten of the debtor and creditor law.

(d) Income exemptions. The following personal property is exempt from application to the satisfaction of a money judgment, except such part as a court determines to be unnecessary for the reasonable requirements of the judgment debtor and his dependents:

1. ninety per cent of the income or other payments from a trust the principal of which is exempt under subdivision (c); provided, however, that with respect to any income or payments made from trusts, custodial accounts, annuities, insurance contracts, monies, assets or interest established as part of an individual retirement account plan or as part of a Keogh (HR-10), retirement or other plan described in paragraph two of subdivision (c) of this section, the exception in this subdivision for such part as a court determines to be unnecessary for the reasonable requirements of the judgment debtor and his dependents shall not apply, and the ninety percent exclusion of this paragraph shall become a one hundred percent exclusion;

2. ninety per cent of the earnings of the judgment debtor for his personal services rendered within sixty days before, and at any time after, an income execution is delivered to the sheriff or a motion is made to secure the application of the judgment debtor's earnings to the satisfaction of the judgment; and

3. payments pursuant to an award in a matrimonial action, for the support of a wife, where the wife is the judgment debtor, or for the support of a child, where the child is the judgment debtor; where the award was made by a court of the state, determination of the extent to which it is unnecessary shall be made by that court.

(e) Exemptions to members of armed forces. The pay and bounty of a non-commissioned officer, musician or private in the armed forces of the United States or the state of New York; a land warrant, pension or other reward granted by the United States, or by a state, for services in the armed forces; a sword, horse, medal, emblem or device of any kind presented as a testimonial for services rendered in the armed forces of the United States or a state; and the uniform, arms and equipments which were used by a person in the service, are exempt from application to the satisfaction of a money judgment; provided, however, that the provisions of this subdivision shall not apply to the satisfaction of any order or money judgment for the support of a person's child, spouse, or former spouse.

(f) Exemption for unpaid milk proceeds. Ninety per cent of any money or debt due or to become due to the judgment debtor for the sale of milk produced on a farm operated by him and delivered for his account to a milk dealer licensed pursuant to article twenty-one of the agriculture and markets law is exempt from application to the satisfaction of a money judgment.

(g) Security deposit exemption. Money deposited as security for the rental of real property to be used as the residence of the judgment debtor or the judgment debtor's family; and money deposited as security with a gas, electric, water, steam, telegraph or telephone corporation, or a municipality rendering equivalent utility services, for services to judgment debtor's residence or the residence of judgment debtor's family, are exempt from application to the satisfaction of a money judgment.

(h) The following personal property is exempt from application to the satisfaction of money judgment, except such part as a court determines to be unnecessary for the reasonable requirements of the judgment debtor and his dependents:

1. any and all medical and dental accessions to the human body and all personal property or equipment that is necessary or proper to maintain or assist in sustaining or maintaining one or more major life activities or is utilized to provide mobility for a person with a permanent disability; and

2. any guide dog, service dog or hearing dog, as those terms are defined in section one hundred eight of the agriculture and markets law, or any animal

CPLR

trained to aid or assist a person with a permanent disability and actually being so used by such person, together with any and all food or feed for any such dog or other animal.

(i) Exemption for life insurance policies. The right of a judgment debtor to accelerate payment of part or all of the death benefit or special surrender value under a life insurance policy, as authorized by paragraph one of subsection (a) of section one thousand one hundred thirteen of the insurance law, or enter into a viatical settlement pursuant to the provisions of article seventy-eight of the insurance law, is exempt from application to the satisfaction of a money judgment.

### CROSS REFERENCES

See **Debtor and Creditor Law, Article 10-A,** in Appendix, *infra,* regarding exemptions for debtors in federal bankruptcy proceedings.

### 1995 AMENDMENTS

L. 1995, ch. 93, section 1, eff. Sept. 1, 1995, amended CPLR 5205(c)(2) by deleting the words "the corpus of" from the first sentence [following the word "either"], by replacing the word "qualifying" with the words "or plan, which is qualified," by adding the words "in the case of an individual retirement account plan, an individual who is the settlor of and depositor to such account plan," and by renumbering the remaining categories.

L. 1995, ch. 93, § 2, eff. Sept. 1, 1995, amended CPLR 5205(d)(1) by adding to subparagraph (1) the words "an individual retirement account plan or as part of."

### 1994 AMENDMENTS

L. 1994, ch. 127, eff. Sept. 1, 1994, amended CPLR 5205(c)(2), to add to the trust exemption provisions the corpus of a federally qualified Individual Retirement Account trust.

### 1993 AMENDMENTS

L. 1993, ch. 638, eff. Aug. 4, 1993, added subdivision (i) to exempt from application to the satisfaction of a money judgment the right of a judgment debtor to accelerate payment of part or all of the death benefit or special surrender value provided in a life insurance policy, or to enter into a viatical settlement as the owner of a life insurance policy covering catastrophic or life-threatening illness and providing that the insured may agree to accept compensation in return for assigning the right to receive a death benefit.

### 1989 AMENDMENTS

L. 1989, ch. 84, eff. May 11, 1989; ch. 84 superseded by L. 1989, ch. 280, eff. July 7, 1989.

### 1987 AMENDMENTS

L. 1987, ch. 108, eff. June 8, 1987, amended subd. (c) by designating language following words "Trust exemption," as par. 1, adding references therein to pars. 3 and 4, and adding pars. 2, 3 and 4.

**1986 AMENDMENTS**

L. 1986, ch. 404, eff. July 21, 1986, amended CPLR 5205(h)(2) to exempt "service dogs" (dogs that assist persons with disabilities) from property applicable to the satisfaction of a money judgment.

**1980 AMENDMENTS**

L. 1980, ch. 116, eff. May 13, 1980, amended CPLR 5205 by adding new subdivision (h).

**1979 AMENDMENTS**

L. 1979, ch. 148, eff. June 28, 1979, amended subd. (d) par. 1 by making a technical correction.

**1978 AMENDMENTS**

L. 1978, ch. 17, eff. March 14, 1978, added subdivision (g).

**1977 AMENDMENTS**

L. 1977, ch. 516, eff. July 1, 1977, amended subd. (e) to provide that exemptions to members of the armed forces shall not apply to the satisfaction of any order or money judgment for support of a child, spouse or former spouse.

**1976 AMENDMENTS**

L. 1976, ch. 129, eff. Sept. 1, 1976, amended Subd. (a), deleted former Subd. (b), and relettered the remaining subdivisions accordingly, in order to eliminate an improper sex distinction in the designation of items constituting exempt personal property.

L. 1976, ch. 697, eff. Aug. 23, 1976, amended paragraph 5 of Subd. (a) by adding one television set to the list of personal property exempt from application to the satisfaction of a money judgment.

**1965 AMENDMENTS**

L. 1965, ch. 623, eff. June 28, 1965, amended subsection (f), by raising the exemption from 60% to 90%.

## § 5206. Real property exempt from application to the satisfaction of money judgments.

(a) Exemption of homestead. Property of one of the following types, not exceeding ten thousand dollars in value above liens and encumbrances, owned and occupied as a principal residence, is exempt from application to the satisfaction of a money judgment, unless the judgment was recovered wholly for the purchase price thereof:

1. a lot of land with a dwelling thereon,

2. shares of stock in a cooperative apartment corporation, or

3. units of a condominium apartment.

4. a mobile home

But no exempt homestead shall be exempt from taxation or from sale for non-payment of taxes or assessments.

(b) Homestead exemption after owner's death. The homestead exemption continues after the death of the person in whose favor the property was exempted for the benefit of the surviving spouse and surviving children until the majority of the youngest surviving child and until the death of the surviving spouse.

(c) Suspension of occupation as affecting homestead. The homestead exemption ceases if the property ceases to be occupied as a residence by a person for whose benefit it may so continue, except where the suspension of occupation is for a period not exceeding one year, and occurs in consequence of injury to, or destruction of, the dwelling house upon the premises.

(d) Exemption of homestead exceeding ten thousand dollars in value. The exemption of a homestead is not void because the value of the property exceeds ten thousand dollars but the lien of a judgment attaches to the surplus.

(e) Sale of homestead exceeding ten thousand dollars in value. A judgment creditor may commence a special proceeding in the county in which the homestead is located against the judgment debtor for the sale, by a sheriff or receiver, of a homestead exceeding ten thousand dollars in value. The court may direct that the notice of petition be served upon any other person. The court, if it directs such a sale, shall so marshall the proceeds of the sale that the right and interest of each person in the proceeds shall correspond as nearly as may be to his right and interest in the property sold. Money, not exceeding ten thousand dollars, paid to a judgment debtor, as representing his interest in the proceeds, is exempt for one year after the payment, unless, before the expiration of the year, he acquires an exempt homestead, in which case, the exemption ceases with respect to so much of the money as was not expended for the purchase of that property; and the exemption of the property so acquired extends to every debt against which the property sold was exempt. Where the exemption of property sold as prescribed in this subdivision has been continued after the judgment debtor's death, or where he dies after the sale and before payment to him of his proportion of the proceeds of the sale, the court may direct that portion of the proceeds which represents his interest be invested for the benefit of the person or persons entitled to the benefit of the exemption, or be otherwise disposed of as justice requires.

(f) Exemption of burying ground. Land, set apart as a family or private burying ground, is exempt from application to the satisfaction of a money judgment, upon the following conditions only:

1. a portion of it must have been actually used for that purpose;

2. it must not exceed in extent one-fourth of an acre; and

3. it must not contain any building or structure, except one or more vaults or other places of deposit for the dead, or mortuary monuments.

CROSS REFERENCES

See **Debtor and Creditor Law, Article 10-A,** in Appendix, *infra,* regarding exemptions for debtors in federal bankruptcy proceedings.

## 1980 AMENDMENTS

L. 1980, ch. 717, eff. June 26, 1980, amended CPLR 5206(a) by adding mobile homes to the list of properties qualifying for the homestead exemption.

## 1977 AMENDMENTS

L. 1977, ch. 181, § 1, eff. Aug. 22, 1977, amended subd. (a) by making the homestead exemption applicable to shares in a cooperative apartment corporation and units of a condominium, and by increasing the value of the exemption from "two thousand dollars" to "ten thousand dollars . . . above liens and encumbrances;" deleted former subd. (b), which had required that property intended to be held as an exempt homestead be designated as such, and which had provided for the recording of such designation; relettered the remaining subdivisions accordingly, and deleted references therein to designation of exempt property; amended subds. (d) and (e) by increasing the value of the exemption from two thousand to ten thousand dollars; eliminated requirements from subd. (f) that land intended for use as burying ground must be so designated in order to attain exempt status, and that such designation be recorded as provided; and deleted former subd. (h) which had provided for cancellation of exemption of real property.

L. 1977, ch. 181, section 2 provided that the act shall not affect the application of property to the satisfaction of a money judgment for a debt contracted before the effective date. The section, as it appeared prior to the 1977 amendment is set forth below:

"§ 5206.    **Real property exempt from application to the satisfaction of money judgments.**

"(a) Exemption of homestead. A lot of land, with one or more buildings thereon, not exceeding two thousand dollars in value, owned and occupied as a principal residence by any person, and designated for that purpose, is exempt from application to the satisfaction of a money judgment, unless the judgment was recovered wholly for a debt contracted before the designation of the property, or for the purchase price thereof. But no property designated as an exempt homestead shall be exempt from taxation or from sale for non-payment of taxes or assessments.

"(b) Designation of exempt homestead. In order to be exempted as a homestead, a conveyance thereof, stating in substance that it is designed to be held as a homestead, exempt from application to the satisfaction of a money judgment, must be recorded, as prescribed by law; or a notice containing a full description of the property and stating that it is designed to be so held shall be subscribed by the owner, acknowledged or proved, and certified, in like manner as a deed to be recorded in the county where the property is situated, and must be recorded in the office of the recording officer of that county, in a book kept for that purpose, and styled the "homestead exemption book." In those counties where the clerk of the county is not the recording officer, designations heretofore recorded in the office of the clerk of the county shall be transferred to the office of the recording officer of that county.

"(c) Homestead exemption after owner's death. The homestead exemption continues after the death of the person in whose favor the property was exempted for the benefit of the youngest surviving child and until the death of the surviving spouse.

"(d) Suspension of occupation as affecting homestead. The homestead exemption ceases if the property ceases to be occupied as a residence by a person for whose benefit it may so continue, except where the suspension of occupation is for a period not exceeding one year, and occurs in consequence of injury to, or destruction of, the dwelling house upon the premises.

"(e) Exemption of homestead exceeding two thousand dollars in value. The exemption of a homestead is not void because the value of the property designated as exempt exceeds two thousand dollars but the lien of a judgment attaches to the surplus.

"(f) Sale of homestead exceeding two thousand dollars in value. A judgment creditor may commence a special proceeding in the county in which the homestead is located against the judgment debtor for the sale, by a sheriff or receiver, of a homestead exceeding two thousand dollars in value. The court may direct that the notice of petition be served upon any other person. The court, if it directs such a sale, shall so marshall the proceeds of the sale that the right and interest of each person in the proceeds shall correspond as nearly as may be to his right and interest in the property sold. Money, not exceeding two thousand dollars, paid to a judgment debtor, as representing his interest in the proceeds, is exempt for one year after the payment, unless, before the expiration of the year, he causes real property to be designated as an exempt homestead, in which case, the exemption ceases with respect to so much of the money as was not expended for the purchase of that property; and the exemption of the property so designated extends to every debt against which the property sold was exempt. Where the exemption of property sold as prescribed in this subdivision has been continued after the judgment debtor's death, or where he dies after the sale and before payment to him of his proportion of the proceeds of the sale, the court may direct that portion of the proceeds which represents his interest be invested for the benefit of the person or persons entitled to the benefit of the exemption, or be otherwise disposed of as justice requires.

"(g) Exemption of burying ground. Land, set apart as a family or private burying ground and heretofore designated as prescribed by law in order to exempt the same, or hereafter designated as prescribed in this subdivision for that purpose, is exempt from application to the satisfaction of a money judgment, upon the following conditions only:

"1. a portion of it must have been actually used for that purpose;

"2. it must not exceed in extent one-fourth of an acre; and

"3. it must not contain at the time of its designation, or at any time afterwards, any building or structure, except one or more vaults or other places of deposit for the dead, or mortuary monuments.

"In order to designate land to be exempted as prescribed in this subdivision, a notice containing a full description of the land to be exempted and stating that it has been set apart for a family or private burying ground must be subscribed by the owner; acknowledged or proved, and certified, in like manner as a deed to be recorded in the county where the land is situated; and recorded in the office of the clerk or register of that county, in the proper book for recording deeds, at least three days before the sale of the land by virtue of a procedure to secure its application to the satisfaction of a judgment.

"(h) Cancellation of exemption of real property. The owner of real property exempt as prescribed in this section may subscribe a notice, at any time, and personally acknowledge the execution thereof before an officer authorized by law to take the acknowledgment of a deed, to the effect that he cancels all exemptions from application of the property, or a particular part thereof, fully described in the notice, to the satisfaction of a money judgment. The cancellation takes effect when such a notice is recorded as prescribed in this section for recording a notice to effect the exemption so canceled. Nothing herein contained shall be so construed as to prevent a husband and wife from jointly conveying or mortgaging property so exempt."

CPLR

### 1976 AMENDMENTS

L. 1976, ch. 129, eff. Sept. 1, 1976, amended Subd. (a) by deleting a provision which made the section applicable to the principal residence of a "woman or householder" and providing that the exemption apply instead to "any person."

### 1969 AMENDMENTS

L. 1969, ch. 961, eff. Jan. 1, 1970, amended subds. (a), (d) and (e).

## § 5207.   Enforcement involving the state.

None of the procedures for the enforcement of money judgments are applicable to a judgment against the state. All procedures for the enforcement of money judgments against other judgment debtors are applicable to the state, its officers, agencies and subdivisions, as a garnishee, except where otherwise prescribed by law, and except that an order in such a procedure shall only provide for the payment of moneys not claimed by the state, and no judgment shall be entered against the state, or any officer, department, board or commission thereof, in such a procedure. This section shall not be deemed to grant any court jurisdiction to hear and determine claims or actions against the state not otherwise given by law to such court.

## § 5208.   Enforcement after death of judgment debtor; leave of court; extension of lien.

Except where otherwise prescribed by law, after the death of a judgment debtor, an execution upon a money judgment shall not be levied upon any debt owed to him or any property in which he has an interest, nor shall any other enforcement procedure be undertaken with respect to such debt or property, except upon leave of the surrogate's court which granted letters testamentary or letters of administration upon the estate. If such letters have not been granted within eighteen months after the death, leave to issue such an execution or undertake such enforcement procedure may thereafter be granted, upon motion of the judgment creditor upon such notice as the court may require, by any court from which the execution could issue or in which the enforcement procedure could be commenced. A judgment lien existing against real property at the time of a judgment debtor's death shall expire two years thereafter or ten years after filing of the judgment-roll, whichever is later.

### CROSS REFERENCES

As to obtaining leave from the Surrogate's Court to issue execution against decedent's estate, see **Surrogate's Court Procedures Act § 1812,** in Appendix, *infra.*

Also see **Surrogate's Court Procedures Act § 1811** regarding expenses preferred to debts and claims, and **Estates Powers and Trusts Law § 11-4.6** regarding leave to issue execution against personal representative of decedent.

## § 5209.  Discharge of garnishee's obligation.

A person who, pursuant to an execution or order, pays or delivers, to the judgment creditor or a sheriff or receiver, money or other personal property in which a judgment debtor has or will have an interest, or so pays a debt he owes the judgment debtor, is discharged from his obligation to the judgment debtor to the extent of the payment or delivery.

## § 5210.  Power of court to punish for contempt.

Every court in which a special proceeding to enforce a money judgment may be commenced, shall have power to punish a contempt of court committed with respect to an enforcement procedure.

### CROSS REFERENCES

See selected provisions governing procedures to punish for contempt under **Judiciary Law, Article 19**, in Appendix, *infra.*

## § 5211.  Privilege on examination; immunity.

The court may confer immunity upon any witness in accordance with the provisions of section 50.20 of the criminal procedure law for testimony or evidence in an enforcement procedure relating to disposition of property in which the judgment debtor has an interest, or relating to his or another person's claim to be entitled, as against the judgment creditor or a receiver, to hold property derived from or through the judgment debtor, or to be discharged from the payment of a debt which was due to the judgment debtor; provided, however, that no immunity shall be conferred except upon twenty-four hours' prior written notice to the appropriate district attorney having an official interest therein.

### CROSS REFERENCES

**CPL §§ 50.10 and 50.20,** providing for compulsion of evidence by offer of immunity, appear in the Appendix, *infra.*

### 1971 AMENDMENTS

L. 1971, ch. 1097, eff. Sept. 1, 1971, amended CPLR 5211 by deleting the reference to the Code of Criminal Procedure and substituting reference to the Criminal Procedure Law § 50.20.

### 1967 AMENDMENTS

L. 1967, ch. 680, eff. Sept. 1, 1967, inserted reference to Code of Criminal Procedure in place of reference to Penal Law.

## §§ 5212-5220.  [Not used.]

## § 5221.  Where enforcement proceeding commenced.

(a) Court and county in which proceeding commenced.

1. If the judgment sought to be enforced was entered in the city court of any city outside the city of New York, and the respondent resides or is regularly employed or has a place for the regular transaction of business in person within the county in which the court is or was located, a special proceeding authorized by this article shall be commenced in that court or in the county court of that county.

2. If the judgment sought to be enforced was entered in a district court, or by a justice of the peace whose office has been or is by law to be abolished and whose jurisdiction has been or is by law to be superseded by a district court, and the respondent resides or is regularly employed or has a place for the regular transaction of business in person within the county in which such district court is established, a special proceeding authorized by this article shall be commenced in such district court.

3. If the judgment sought to be enforced was entered in the municipal court of the city of New York, the city court of the city of New York or the civil court of the city of New York, and the respondent resides or is regularly employed or has a place for the regular transaction of business in person within that city, a special proceeding authorized by this article shall be commenced in the civil court of the city of New York.

4. In any other case, if the judgment sought to be enforced was entered in any court of this state, a special proceeding authorized by this article shall be commenced, either in the supreme court or a county court, in a county in which the respondent resides or is regularly employed or has a place for the regular transaction of business in person or, if there is no such county, in any county in which he may be served or the county in which the judgment was entered.

5. If no court in which a special proceeding authorized by this article could be commenced is in session, the special proceeding may be commenced in the supreme court or a county court in any county within the judicial district in which the proceeding could otherwise be commenced or in any county adjoining the county in which the proceeding could otherwise be commenced.

(b) Notices, subpoenas and motions. A notice or subpoena authorized by this article may be issued from, and a motion authorized by this article may be made before, any court in which a special proceeding authorized by this article could be commenced if the person served with the notice, subpoena or notice of motion were respondent.

### 1989 AMENDMENTS

L. 1989, ch. 124, eff. June 2, 1989, amended paragraph 1 of subdivision (a) to eliminate the list of cities and substitute the phrase "any city outside the city of New York."

### 1983 AMENDMENTS

L. 1983, ch. 341, eff. Sept. 1, 1983, amended CPLR 5221(a)(1) by adding Binghamton and Jamestown to the list of city courts to which the statute applies.

CPLR

## 1980 AMENDMENTS

L. 1980, ch. 289, eff. Sept. 1, 1980, amended CPLR 5221(a)(1) by adding a reference to the courts of the city of White Plains.

## 1979 AMENDMENTS

L. 1979, ch. 92, eff. Sept. 1, 1979, amended par. 1 of subd. (a) of CPLR 5221 by adding the cities of Lockport, Niagara Falls and North Tonawanda to the list of cities to which the statute applies.

## 1976 AMENDMENTS

L. 1976, ch. 164, eff. May 18, 1976, amended CPLR 5221(a)(1) by adding thereto the City Court of New Rochelle.

## 1971 AMENDMENTS

L. 1971, ch. 1069, eff. Sept. 1, 1971, amended CPLR 5221(a)(1) by adding thereto the City Court of Long Beach.

## 1970 AMENDMENTS

L. 1970, ch. 554, eff. Sept. 1, 1970, amended Subd. (a)(1) by adding thereto the City Court of Rome.

## 1965 AMENDMENTS

L. 1965, ch. 518, eff. Sept. 1, 1965, renumbered paragraphs 2, 3 and 4 of Subd. (a), to 3, 4 and 5 respectively, and added a new paragraph 2 which begins "If the judgment sought to be enforced was entered in a district court . . ."

## § 5222.  Restraining notice.

(a) Issuance; on whom served; form; service. A restraining notice may be issued by the clerk of the court or the attorney for the judgment creditor as officer of the court, or by the support collection unit designated by the appropriate social services district. It may be served upon any person, except the employer of a judgment debtor or obligor where the property sought to be restrained consists of wages or salary due or to become due to the judgment debtor or obligor. It shall be served personally in the same manner as a summons or by registered or certified mail, return receipt requested or if issued by the support collection unit, by regular mail. It shall specify all of the parties to the action, the date that the judgment or order was entered, the court in which it was entered, the amount of the judgment or order and the amount then due thereon, the names of all parties in whose favor and against whom the judgment or order was entered, it shall set forth subdivision (b) and shall state that disobedience is punishable as a contempt of court, and it shall contain an original signature or copy of the original signature of the clerk of the court or attorney or the name of the support collection unit which issued it. Service of a restraining notice upon a department or agency of the state or upon an institution under its direction shall be made by serving a copy upon the head of the department, or the person designated by him or her and upon the state department of audit and control at its office in Albany; a restraining notice served upon a state board, commission, body or agency which is not within any department of the state shall be made by serving the restraining notice upon the state department of audit and control at its office in Albany. Service at the office of a department of the state in Albany may be made by the sheriff of any county by registered or certified mail, return receipt requested, or if issued by the support collection unit, by regular mail.

(b) Effect of restraint; prohibition of transfer; duration. A judgment debtor or obligor served with a restraining notice is forbidden to make or suffer any sale, assignment, transfer or interference with any property in which he or she has an interest, except upon direction of the sheriff or pursuant to an order of the court, until the judgment or order is satisfied or vacated. A restraining notice served upon a person other than the judgment debtor or obligor is effective only if, at the time of service, he or she owes a debt to the judgment debtor or obligor or he or she is in the possession or custody of property in which he or she knows or has reason to believe the judgment debtor or obligor has an interest, or if the judgment creditor or support collection unit has stated in the notice that a specified debt is owed by the person served to the judgment debtor or obligor or that the judgment debtor or obligor has an interest in specified property in the possession or custody of the person served. All property in which the judgment debtor or obligor is known or believed to have an interest then in and thereafter coming into the possession or custody of such a person, including any specified in the notice, and all debts of such a person, including any specified in the notice, then due and thereafter coming due to the judgment debtor or obligor, shall be subject to the notice. Such a person is forbidden to make or suffer any sale, assignment or transfer of, or any interference with, any such property, or pay over or otherwise dispose of any such debt, to any person other than the sheriff or the support collection unit, except upon direction of the sheriff or pursuant to an order of the court, until the expiration of one year after the notice is served upon him or her, or until the judgment or order is satisfied or vacated, whichever event first occurs. A judgment creditor or support collection unit which has specified personal property or debt in a restraining notice shall be liable to the owner of the property or the person to whom the debt is owed, if other than the judgment debtor or obligor, for any damages sustained by reason of the restraint. If a garnishee served with a restraining notice withholds the payment of money belonging or owed to the judgment debtor or obligor in an amount equal to twice the amount due on the judgment or order, the restraining notice is not effective as to other property or money.

(c) Subsequent notice. Leave of court is required to serve more than one restraining notice upon the same person with respect to the same judgment or order.

(d) Notice to judgment debtor or obligor. If a notice in the form prescribed in subdivision (e) has not been given to the judgment debtor or obligor within

CPLR

a year before service of a restraining notice, a copy of the restraining notice together with the notice to judgment debtor or obligor shall be mailed by first class mail or personally delivered to each judgment debtor or obligor who is a natural person within four days of the service of the restraining notice. Such notice shall be mailed to the defendant at his or her residence address; or in the event such mailing is returned as undeliverable by the post office, or if the residence address of the defendant is unknown, then to the defendant in care of the place of employment of the defendant if known, in an envelope bearing the legend "personal and confidential" and not indicating on the outside thereof, by the return address or otherwise, that the communication is from an attorney or concerns a judgment or order; or if neither the residence address nor the place of employment of the defendant is known then to the defendant at any other known address.

(e) Content of notice. The notice required by subdivision (d) shall be in substantially the following form and may be included in the restraining notice:

## NOTICE TO JUDGMENT DEBTOR OR OBLIGOR

Money or property belonging to you may have been taken or held in order to satisfy a judgment or order which has been entered against you. Read this carefully.

## YOU MAY BE ABLE TO GET YOUR MONEY BACK

State and federal laws prevent certain money or property from being taken to satisfy judgments or orders. Such money or property is said to be "exempt". The following is a partial list of money which may be exempt:

1. Supplemental security income, (SSI);
2. Social security;
3. Public assistance (welfare);
4. Alimony or child support;
5. Unemployment benefits;
6. Disability benefits;
7. Workers' compensation benefits;
8. Public or private pensions; and
9. Veterans benefits.

If you think that any of your money that has been taken or held is exempt, you must act promptly because the money may be applied to the judgment or order. If you claim that any of your money that has been taken or held is exempt, you may contact the person sending this notice.

Also, YOU MAY CONSULT AN ATTORNEY, INCLUDING LEGAL AID IF YOU QUALIFY. The law (New York civil practice law and rules, article four and sections fifty-two hundred thirty-nine and fifty-two hundred forty) provides a procedure for determination of a claim to an exemption.

(f) For the purposes of this section "order" shall mean an order issued by a court of competent jurisdiction directing the payment of support, alimony or maintenance upon which a "default" as defined in paragraph seven of subdivision (a) of section fifty-two hundred forty-one of this article has been established subject to the procedures established for the determination of a "mistake of fact" for income executions pursuant to subdivision (e) of section fifty-two hundred forty-one of this article except that for the purposes of this section only a default shall not be founded upon retroactive child support obligations as defined in paragraph (a) of subdivision one of section four hundred forty of the family court act and subdivision one of section two hundred forty and paragraph b of subdivision nine of section two hundred thirty-six of the domestic relations law.

(g) Restraining notice in the form of magnetic tape. Where such person consents thereto in writing, a restraining notice in the form of magnetic tape may be served upon a person other than the judgment debtor or obligor. A restraining notice in such form shall contain all of the information required to be specified in a restraining notice under subdivision (a), except for the original signature or copy of the original signature of the clerk or attorney who issued the restraining notice. The provisions of this subdivision notwithstanding, the notice required by subdivisions (d) and (e) shall be given to the judgment debtor or obligor in the written form set forth therein.

CPLR

### 1994 AMENDMENTS

L. 1994, ch. 35, eff. April 4, 1994, added a new subdivision (g) pertaining to restraining notices in the form of magnetic tape.

### 1993 AMENDMENTS

L. 1993, ch. 59, eff. July 1, 1993, amended subdivision (a) by adding the words "or by the support collection unit designated by the appropriate social services district"; by adding the words "support collection unit" throughout the section; by adding the words "or obligor" following the words "judgment debtor" throughout the section; by adding the words "or if issued by the support collection unit, by regular mail" to the third sentence and the final sentence of subdivision (a); to add the words "or order" following the word "judgment" throughout the section; to add the words "or the name of the support collection unit which" to the fifth sentence of subdivision (a); to add the words "or her" following the words "to him" throughout the section; and to add a new subdivision (f).

### 1991 AMENDMENTS

L. 1991, ch. 314, eff. July 15, 1991, amended subdivision (a) by requiring that a restraining notice contain the original signature or copy of the original signature of the clerk of the court or attorney who issued it.

### 1982 AMENDMENTS

L. 1982, ch. 882, eff. Sept. 1, 1982, amended CPLR 5222 by adding two new subdivisions (d) and (e).

### 1969 AMENDMENTS

L. 1969, ch. 1137, eff. May 26, 1969, amended Subd. (a) by adding to the second sentence thereof, "except the employer of a judgment debtor where the property sought to be restrained consists of wages or salary due or to become due to the judgment debtor."

### 1968 AMENDMENTS

L. 1968, ch. 743, eff. Sept. 1, 1968, inserted last two sentences in Subd. (a) pertaining to service of a restraining notice upon the state of New York.

## § 5223. Disclosure.

At any time before a judgment is satisfied or vacated, the judgment creditor may compel disclosure of all matter relevant to the satisfaction of the judgment, by serving upon any person a subpoena, which shall specify all of the parties to the action, the date of the judgment, the court in which it was entered, the amount of the judgment and the amount then due thereon, and shall state that false swearing or failure to comply with the subpoena is punishable as a contempt of court.

## R 5224. Subpoena; procedure.

(a) Kinds and service of subpoena. Any or all of the following kinds of subpoenas may be served:

1. a subpoena requiring attendance for the taking of a deposition upon oral or written questions at a time and place named therein; or

2. a subpoena duces tecum requiring the production of books and papers for examination at a time and place named therein; or

3. an information subpoena, accompanied by a copy and original of written questions and a prepaid, addressed return envelope. Service of an information subpoena may be made by registered or certified mail, return receipt requested. Answers shall be made in writing under oath by the person upon whom served, if an individual, or by an officer, director, agent or employee having the information, if a corporation, partnership or sole proprietorship. Each question shall be answered separately and fully and each answer shall refer to the question to which it responds. Answers shall be returned together with the original of the questions within seven days after receipt.

(b) Fees. A judgment debtor served with a subpoena under this section and any other person served with an information subpoena shall not be entitled to any fee. Any other person served with a subpoena requiring attendance or the production of books and papers shall be paid or tendered in advance authorized traveling expenses and one day's witness fee.

(c) Time and place of examination. A deposition on oral or written questions or an examination of books and papers may proceed upon not less than ten days' notice to the person subpoenaed, unless the court orders shorter notice, before any person authorized by subdivision (a) of rule 3113. An examination shall be held during business hours and, if taken within the state, at a place specified in rule 3110. Upon consent of the witness, an examination may be held at any other place within the state and before any officer authorized to administer an oath.

(d) Conduct of examination. The officer before whom the deposition is to be taken shall put the witness on oath. If requested by the person conducting the examination, the officer shall personally, or by some one acting under his direction, record and transcribe the testimony and shall list all appearances by the parties and attorneys. Examination and cross-examination of the witness shall proceed as permitted in the trial of actions in open court. Cross-examination need not be limited to the subject matter of the examination in chief. All objections made at the time of the examination to the qualifications of the officer taking the deposition, or of a person recording it, or to the manner of taking it, or to the testimony presented, or to the conduct of any person, and any other objection to the proceedings, shall be noted by the officer upon the deposition and the deposition shall proceed subject to the right of a person to apply for a protective order. The deposition shall be taken continuously and without unreasonable adjournment, unless the court orders or the witness agrees otherwise. If the witness does not understand the English language, the judgment creditor shall, at his own expense, provide a translation of all questions and answers. Unless the court orders otherwise, a person other than the judgment debtor served with a subpoena duces tecum requiring the production of books of account may produce in place of the original books of account a sworn transcript of such accounts as are relevant.

(e) Signing deposition; physical preparation. At the request of the person conducting the examination, a deposition on written questions or a deposition on oral questions which has been transcribed shall be submitted to the witness and shall be read to or by him, and any changes in form or substance which the witness desires to make shall be entered upon the deposition with a statement of the reasons given by the witness for making them; and the deposition shall then be signed by the witness before any officer authorized to administer an oath. If the witness fails to sign the deposition, the officer before whom the deposition was taken shall sign it and state on the record the fact of the witness's failure or refusal to sign together with any reason given. The deposition may then be used as fully as though signed. Where testimony is transcribed, the officer before whom the deposition was taken shall certify on the deposition that the witness was duly sworn by him and that the deposition is a true record of the testimony given by the witness.

(f) Subsequent examination. Leave of court is required to compel a judgment debtor to appear for the taking of his deposition or to compel the production by him of books and papers within one year after the conclusion of a previous examination of him with respect to the same judgment.

CPLR

## 1994 AMENDMENTS

L. 1994, ch. 302, eff. July 20, 1994, amended CPLR 5224(b) by adding the words "and any other person served with an information subpoena" and by deleting the final sentence relating to fees.

## § 5225.  Payment or delivery of property of judgment debtor.

(a) Property in the possession of judgment debtor. Upon motion of the judgment creditor, upon notice to the judgment debtor, where it is shown that the judgment debtor is in possession or custody of money or other personal property in which he has an interest, the court shall order that the judgment debtor pay the money, or so much of it as is sufficient to satisfy the judgment, to the judgment creditor and, if the amount to be so paid is insufficient to satisfy the judgment, to deliver any other personal property, or so much of it as is of sufficient value to satisfy the judgment, to a designated sheriff. Notice of the motion shall be served on the judgment debtor in the same manner as a summons or by registered or certified mail, return receipt requested.

(b) Property not in the possession of judgment debtor. Upon a special proceeding commenced by the judgment creditor, against a person in possession or custody of money or other personal property in which the judgment debtor has an interest, or against a person who is a transferee of money or other personal property from the judgment debtor, where it is shown that the judgment debtor is entitled to the possession of such property or that the judgment creditor's rights to the property are superior to those of the transferee, the court shall require such person to pay the money, or so much of it as is sufficient to satisfy the judgment to the judgment creditor and, if the amount to be so paid is insufficient to satisfy the judgment, to deliver any other personal property, or so much of it as is of sufficient value to satisfy the judgment, to a designated sheriff. Costs of the proceedings shall not be awarded against a person who did not dispute the judgment debtor's interest or right to possession. Notice of the proceeding shall also be served upon the judgment debtor in the same manner as a summons or by registered or certified mail, return receipt requested. The court may permit the judgment debtor to intervene in the proceeding. The court may permit any adverse claimant to intervene in the proceeding and may determine his rights in accordance with section 5239.

(c) Documents to effect payment or delivery. The court may order any person to execute and deliver any document necessary to effect payment or delivery.

## 1964 AMENDMENTS

L. 1964, ch. 388, eff. Sept. 1, 1964, corrected the cross-reference to "5238" in Subd. (b) to read "5239."

## § 5226.  Installment payment order.

Upon motion of the judgment creditor, upon notice to the judgment debtor, where it is shown that the judgment debtor is receiving or will receive money from any source, or is attempting to impede the judgment creditor by rendering services without adequate compensation, the court shall order that the judgment debtor make specified installment payments to the judgment creditor. Notice of the motion shall be served on the judgment debtor in the same manner as a summons or by registered or certified mail, return receipt requested. In fixing the amount of the payments, the court shall take into consideration the reasonable requirements of the judgment debtor and his dependents, any payments required to be made by him or deducted from the money he would otherwise receive in satisfaction of other judgments and wage assignments, the amount due on the judgment, and the amount being or to be received, or, if the judgment debtor is attempting to impede the judgment creditor by rendering services without adequate compensation, the reasonable value of the services rendered.

### § 5227.   Payment of debts owed to judgment debtor.

Upon a special proceeding commenced by the judgment creditor, against any person who it is shown is or will become indebted to the judgment debtor, the court may require such person to pay to the judgment creditor the debt upon maturity, or so much of it as is sufficient to satisfy the judgment, and to execute and deliver any document necessary to effect payment; or it may direct that a judgment be entered against such person in favor of the judgment creditor. Costs of the proceeding shall not be awarded against a person who did not dispute the indebtedness. Notice of the proceeding shall also be served upon the judgment debtor in the same manner as a summons or by registered or certified mail, return receipt requested. The court may permit the judgment debtor to intervene in the proceeding. The court may permit any adverse claimant to intervene in the proceeding and may determine his rights in accordance with section 5239.

### § 5228.   Receivers.

(a) Appointment of receiver. Upon motion of a judgment creditor, upon such notice as the court may require, the court may appoint a receiver who may be authorized to administer, collect, improve, lease, repair or sell any real or personal property in which the judgment debtor has an interest or to do any other acts designed to satisfy the judgment. As far as practicable, the court shall require that notice be given to the judgment debtor and to any other judgment creditors of the judgment debtor. The order of appointment shall specify the property to be received, the duties of the receiver and the manner in which they are to be performed. A receiver shall have no power to employ counsel unless expressly so authorized by order of the court. A receiver shall be entitled to necessary expenses and to such commissions, not exceeding five percent of the sums received and disbursed by him, as the court which appointed him allows, but if a judgment creditor is appointed receiver, he shall not be entitled to compensation. If a receiver has been appointed, a court making an order directing payment, or delivery, of property shall direct that payment, or delivery, be made to the receiver rather than to a sheriff. Sections 6402, 6403, 6404 and 6405 are applicable to receivers appointed under this subdivision.

(b) Extension of receivership. Where a receiver has been appointed, the court, upon motion of a judgment creditor, upon such notice as it may require, shall extend the receivership to his judgment.

## § 5229.  Enforcement before judgment entered.

In any court, before a judgment is entered, upon motion of the party in whose favor a verdict or decision has been rendered, the trial judge may order examination of the adverse party and order him restrained with the same effect as if a restraining notice had been served upon him after judgment.

### 1964 AMENDMENTS

L. 1964, ch. 279, eff. Sept. 1, 1964, added the words "In any court" at the beginning of the sentence.

## § 5230.  Executions.

(a) Form. An execution shall specify the date that the judgment or order was entered, the court in which it was entered, the amount of the judgment or order and the amount due thereon and it shall specify the names of the parties in whose favor and against whom the judgment or order was entered. An execution shall direct that only the property in which a named judgment debtor or obligor who is not deceased has an interest, or the debts owed to the named judgment debtor or obligor, be levied upon or sold thereunder and shall specify the last known address of that judgment debtor or obligor. Where the judgment or order was entered in a court other than the supreme, county or a family court, the execution shall also specify the date on which a transcript of the judgment or order was filed with the clerk of the county in which the judgment was entered. Where jurisdiction in the action was based upon a levy upon property or debt pursuant to an order of attachment, the execution shall also state that fact, describe all property and debts levied upon, and direct that only such property and debts be sold thereunder. Where the judgment or order was recovered for all or part of a mortgage debt, the execution shall also describe the mortgaged property, specify the book and page where the mortgage is recorded, and direct that no part of the mortgaged property be levied upon or sold thereunder.

(b) Issuance. At any time before a judgment or order is satisfied or vacated, an execution may be issued from the supreme court, county court or a family court, in the county in which the judgment was first docketed, by the clerk of the court or the attorney for the judgment creditor as officer of the court, to the sheriffs of one or more counties of the state, directing each of them to satisfy the judgment or order out of the real and personal property of the judgment debtor or obligor and the debts due to him or her. Where the judgment or order is for support and is payable to the support collection unit designated by the appropriate social services district, such unit shall be authorized to issue the execution and to satisfy the judgment or order out of the real and personal property of the judgment debtor or obligor and the debts due to him or her.

(c) Return. An execution shall be returned to the clerk of the court from which it was issued or to the support collection unit within sixty days after issuance unless the execution has been served in accordance with section 5231 or subdivision (a) of section 5232. The time may be extended in writing for a period of not more than sixty additional days by the attorney for the judgment creditor or by the support collection unit. Further like extensions may be given by the attorney for the judgment creditor or by the support collection unit unless another execution against the same judgment debtor or obligor has been delivered to the same enforcement officer and has not been returned.

(d) Records of sheriff or support collection unit. Each sheriff or support collection unit shall keep a record of executions delivered showing the names of the parties and the judgment debtor or obligor; the dates of issue and return; the date and time of delivery, which shall be endorsed upon the execution; the amount due at the time the execution was delivered; and the amount of the judgment or order and of the sheriff's fees unpaid, if any, at the time of the return.

(e) For the purposes of this section "order" shall mean an order issued by a court of competent jurisdiction directing the payment of support, alimony or maintenance upon which a "default" as defined in paragraph seven of subdivision (a) of section fifty-two hundred forty-one of this article has been established subject to the procedures established for the determination of a "mistake of fact" for income executions pursuant to subdivision (e) of section fifty-two hundred forty-one of this article, except that for the purposes of this section only, a default shall not be founded upon retroactive child support obligations as defined in paragraph (a) of subdivision one of section four hundred forty of the family court act and subdivision one of section two hundred forty, and paragraph b of subdivision nine of section two hundred thirty-six of the domestic relations law.

1993 AMENDMENTS

L. 1993, ch. 59, eff. July 1, 1993, added a new final sentence to subdivision (b); added a new subdivision (e); added the word "orders" following the word "judgments" throughout the section; added the word "obligor" following the word "judgment debtor" throughout the section; and added references to "support collection unit" throughout the section.

## § 5231. Income execution.

(a) Form. An income execution shall specify, in addition to the requirements of subdivision (a) of section 5230, the name and address of the person from whom the judgment debtor is receiving or will receive money; the amount of money, the frequency of its payment and the amount of the installments to be collected therefrom; and shall contain a notice to the judgment debtor that he shall commence payment of the installments specified to the sheriff forthwith and that, upon his default, the execution will be served upon the person from whom he is receiving or will receive money.

(b) Issuance. Where a judgment debtor is receiving or will receive money from any source, an income execution for installments therefrom of not more than ten percent thereof may be issued and delivered to the sheriff of the county in which the judgment debtor resides or, where the judgment debtor is a non-resident, the county in which he is employed; provided, however, that (i) no amount shall be withheld from the judgment debtor's earnings pursuant to an income execution for any week unless the disposable earnings of the judgment debtor for that week exceed thirty times the federal minimum hourly wage prescribed in the Fair Labor Standards Act of 1938 as in effect at the time the earnings are payable; (ii) the amount withheld from the judgment debtor's earnings pursuant to an income execution for any week shall not exceed twenty-five percent of the disposable earnings of the judgment debtor for that week, or, the amount by which the disposable earnings of the judgment debtor for that week exceed thirty times the federal minimum hourly wage prescribed by the Fair Labor Standards Act of 1938 as in effect at the time the earnings are payable, whichever is less; (iii) if the earnings of the judgment debtor are also subject to deductions for alimony, support or maintenance for family members or former spouses pursuant to section five thousand two hundred forty-one or section five thousand two hundred forty-two of this article, the amount withheld from the judgment debtor's earnings pursuant to this section shall not exceed the amount by which twenty-five percent of the disposable earnings of the judgment debtor for that week exceeds the amount deducted from the judgment debtor's earnings in accordance with section five thousand two hundred forty-one or section five thousand two hundred forty-two of this article. Nothing in this section shall be construed to modify, abrogate, impair, or affect any exemption from the satisfaction of a money judgment otherwise granted by law.

(c) Definition of earnings and disposable earnings. (i) As used herein earnings means compensation paid or payable for personal services, whether denominated as wages, salary, commission, bonus, or otherwise, and includes periodic payments pursuant to a pension or retirement program.

(ii) As used herein disposable earnings means that part of the earnings of any individual remaining after the deduction from those earnings of any amounts required by law to be withheld.

(d) Service upon debtor. Within twenty days after an income execution is delivered to the sheriff, the sheriff shall serve a copy of it upon the judgment debtor, in the same manner as a summons or, in lieu thereof, by certified mail return receipt requested provided an additional copy is sent by regular mail to the debtor. If service is by mail as herein provided, the person effecting service shall retain the receipt together with a post office certificate of mailing as proof of such service.

(e) Levy upon default or failure to serve debtor. If a judgment debtor fails to pay installments pursuant to an income execution served upon him for a period of twenty days, or if the sheriff is unable to serve an income execution upon the judgment debtor within twenty days after the execution is delivered to the sheriff, the sheriff shall levy upon the money that the judgment debtor is receiving or will receive by serving a copy of the income execution, indorsed to indicate the extent to which paid installments have satisfied the judgment, upon the person from whom the judgment debtor is receiving or will receive money personally within the county in the same manner as a summons or by certified mail return receipt requested, except that such service shall not be made by delivery to a person authorized to receive service of summons solely by a designation filed pursuant to a provision of law other than rule 318.

(f) Withholding of installments. A person served with an income execution shall withhold from money then or thereafter due to the judgment debtor installments as provided therein and pay them over to the sheriff. If such person shall fail to so pay the sheriff, the judgment creditor may commence a proceeding against him for accrued installments. If the money due to the judgment debtor consists of salary or wages and his employment is terminated by resignation or dismissal at any time after service of the execution, the levy shall thereafter be ineffective, and the execution shall be returned, unless the debtor is reinstated or re-employed within ninety days after such termination.

(g) Statement on income execution. Any income execution delivered to the sheriff on or after the effective date of this act shall contain the following statement:

THIS INCOME EXECUTION DIRECTS THE WITHHOLDING OF UP TO TEN PERCENT OF THE JUDGMENT DEBTOR'S GROSS INCOME. IN CERTAIN CASES, HOWEVER, STATE OR FEDERAL LAW DOES NOT PERMIT THE WITHHOLDING OF THAT MUCH OF THE JUDGMENT DEBTOR'S GROSS INCOME. THE JUDGMENT DEBTOR IS REFERRED TO NEW YORK CIVIL PRACTICE LAW AND RULES § 5231 AND 15 UNITED STATES CODE § 1671 ET SEQ.

I. LIMITATIONS ON THE AMOUNT THAT CAN BE WITHHELD.

A. AN INCOME EXECUTION FOR INSTALLMENTS FROM A JUDGMENT DEBTOR'S GROSS INCOME CANNOT EXCEED TEN PERCENT (10%) OF THE JUDGMENT DEBTOR'S GROSS INCOME.

B. IF A JUDGMENT DEBTOR'S WEEKLY DISPOSABLE EARNINGS ARE LESS THAN THIRTY (30) TIMES THE CURRENT FEDERAL MINIMUM WAGE (    , PER HOUR), OR (    ), NO DEDUCTION CAN BE MADE FROM THE JUDGMENT DEBTOR'S EARNINGS UNDER THIS INCOME EXECUTION.

CPLR

C. A JUDGMENT DEBTOR'S WEEKLY DISPOSABLE EARNINGS CANNOT BE REDUCED BELOW THE AMOUNT ARRIVED AT BY MULTIPLYING THIRTY (30) TIMES THE CURRENT FEDERAL MINIMUM WAGE (   , PER HOUR), OR (   ), UNDER THIS INCOME EXECUTION.

D. IF DEDUCTIONS ARE BEING MADE FROM A JUDGMENT DEBTOR'S EARNINGS UNDER ANY ORDERS FOR ALIMONY, SUPPORT OR MAINTENANCE FOR FAMILY MEMBERS OR FORMER SPOUSES, AND THOSE DEDUCTIONS EQUAL OR EXCEED TWENTY-FIVE PERCENT (25%) OF THE JUDGMENT DEBTOR'S DISPOSABLE EARNINGS, NO DEDUCTION CAN BE MADE UNDER THIS INCOME EXECUTION.

E. IF DEDUCTIONS ARE BEING MADE FROM A JUDGMENT DEBTOR'S EARNINGS UNDER ANY ORDERS FOR ALIMONY, SUPPORT OR MAINTENANCE FOR FAMILY MEMBERS OR FORMER SPOUSES, AND THOSE DEDUCTIONS ARE LESS THAN TWENTY-FIVE PERCENT (25%) OF THE JUDGMENT DEBTOR'S DISPOSABLE EARNINGS, DEDUCTIONS MAY BE MADE FROM THE JUDGMENT DEBTOR'S EARNINGS UNDER THIS INCOME EXECUTION. HOWEVER, THE AMOUNT ARRIVED AT BY ADDING THE DEDUCTIONS FROM EARNINGS MADE UNDER THE EXECUTION TO THE DEDUCTIONS MADE FROM EARNINGS UNDER ANY ORDERS FOR ALIMONY, SUPPORT OR MAINTENANCE FOR FAMILY MEMBERS OR FORMER SPOUSES CANNOT EXCEED TWENTY-FIVE PERCENT (25%) OF THE JUDGMENT DEBTOR'S DISPOSABLE EARNINGS.

NOTE: NOTHING IN THIS NOTICE LIMITS THE PROPORTION OR AMOUNT WHICH MAY BE DEDUCTED UNDER ANY ORDER FOR ALIMONY, SUPPORT OR MAINTENANCE FOR FAMILY MEMBERS OR FORMER SPOUSES.

II. EXPLANATION OF LIMITATIONS.

DEFINITIONS:

DISPOSABLE EARNINGS

DISPOSABLE EARNINGS ARE THAT PART OF AN INDIVIDUAL'S EARNINGS LEFT AFTER DEDUCTING THOSE AMOUNTS THAT ARE REQUIRED BY LAW TO BE WITHHELD (FOR EXAMPLE, TAXES, SOCIAL SECURITY, AND UNEMPLOYMENT INSURANCE, BUT NOT DEDUCTIONS FOR UNION DUES, INSURANCE PLANS, ETC.).

GROSS INCOME

GROSS INCOME IS SALARY, WAGES OR OTHER INCOME, INCLUDING ANY AND ALL OVERTIME EARNINGS, COMMISSIONS, AND INCOME FROM TRUSTS, BEFORE ANY DEDUCTIONS ARE MADE FROM SUCH INCOME.

ILLUSTRATIONS REGARDING EARNINGS:

| IF DISPOSABLE EARNINGS IS: | AMOUNT TO PAY OR DEDUCT FROM EARNINGS UNDER THIS INCOME EXECUTION IS: |
|---|---|
| (A) 30 TIMES FEDERAL MINIMUM WAGE (     ) OR LESS | NO PAYMENT OR DEDUCTION ALLOWED |
| (B) MORE THAN 30 TIMES FEDERAL MINIMUM WAGE (     ) AND LESS THAN 40 TIMES FEDERAL MINIMUM WAGE (     ) | THE LESSER OF: THE EXCESS OVER 30 TIMES THE FEDERAL MINIMUM WAGE (     ) IN DISPOSABLE EARNINGS, OR 10% OF GROSS EARNINGS |
| (C) 40 TIMES THE FEDERAL MINIMUM WAGE (     ) OR MORE | THE LESSER OF: 25% OF DISPOSABLE EARNINGS OR 10% OF GROSS EARNINGS. |

III.     NOTICE: YOU MAY BE ABLE TO CHALLENGE THIS INCOME EXECUTION THROUGH THE PROCEDURES PROVIDED IN CPLR § 5231(g)* AND CPLR § 5240

IF YOU THINK THAT THE AMOUNT OF YOUR INCOME BEING DEDUCTED UNDER THIS INCOME EXECUTION EXCEEDS THE AMOUNT PERMITTED BY STATE OR FEDERAL LAW, YOU SHOULD ACT PROMPTLY BECAUSE THE MONEY WILL BE APPLIED TO THE JUDGMENT. IF YOU CLAIM THAT THE AMOUNT OF YOUR INCOME BEING DEDUCTED UNDER THIS INCOME EXECUTION EXCEEDS THE AMOUNT PERMITTED BY STATE OR FEDERAL LAW, YOU SHOULD CONTACT YOUR EMPLOYER OR OTHER PERSON PAYING YOUR INCOME. FURTHER, YOU MAY CONSULT AN ATTORNEY, INCLUDING LEGAL AID IF YOU QUALIFY. NEW YORK STATE LAW PROVIDES TWO PROCEDURES THROUGH WHICH AN INCOME EXECUTION CAN BE CHALLENGED:

CPLR § 5231(i) MODIFICATION. AT ANY TIME, THE JUDGMENT DEBTOR MAY MAKE A MOTION TO A COURT FOR AN ORDER MODIFYING AN INCOME EXECUTION.

CPLR § 5240 MODIFICATION OR PROTECTIVE ORDER: SUPERVISION OF ENFORCEMENT. AT ANY TIME, THE JUDGMENT DEBTOR MAY MAKE A MOTION TO A COURT FOR AN ORDER DENYING, LIMITING, CONDITIONING, REGULATING, EXTENDING OR MODIFYING THE USE OF ANY POST-JUDGMENT ENFORCEMENT PROCEDURE, INCLUDING THE USE OF INCOME EXECUTIONS.

(h) Levy upon money payable by municipal corporation or the state. The levy of an income execution served upon a municipal or public benefit corporation, or board of education, shall be effective fifteen days after such service. Such an execution shall specify the title or position of the judgment debtor and the bureau, office, department or subdivision in which he is employed and the municipal or public benefit corporation, or board of education, shall be entitled to a fee of two dollars upon being served. A levy upon money payable directly by a department of the state, or by an institution under its jurisdiction, shall be made by serving the income execution upon the head of the department, or upon a person designated by him, at the office of the department in Albany; a levy upon money payable directly upon the state comptroller's warrant, or directly by a state board, commission, body or agency which is not within any department of the state, shall be made by serving the income execution upon the state department of audit and control at its office in Albany. Service at the office of a department of the state in Albany may be made by the sheriff of any county by registered or certified mail, return receipt requested.

(i) Modification. At any time, the judgment creditor or the judgment debtor may move, upon such notice as the court may direct, for an order modifying an income execution.

(j) Priority; delivery to another sheriff. Two or more income executions issued against the same judgment debtor, specifying the same person from whom the money is received and delivered to the same or different enforcement officers shall be satisfied out of that money in the order in which the executions are delivered to an officer authorized to levy in the county, town or city in which the debtor resides or, where the judgment debtor is a non-resident, the county, town or city in which he is employed. If an income execution delivered to a sheriff is returned unsatisfied in whole or in part because the sheriff to whom it was delivered is unable to find within the county the person from whom the judgment debtor is receiving or will receive money, the execution may be delivered to the sheriff of any county in which such person may be found. The priority of an income execution delivered to a sheriff within twenty days after its return by each previous sheriff shall be determined by the time of delivery to the first sheriff.

(k) Accounting by sheriff. It shall be the duty of the sheriff to whom such income execution shall be delivered, from time to time and at least once every ninety days from the time a levy shall be made thereunder, to account for and pay over to the person entitled thereto all monies collected thereon, less his lawful fees and expenses for collecting the same.

\* [Editor's note: So in original. Probably should read "5231(i)."]

**CROSS REFERENCES**

Personal Property Law § 48-a deals with the manner of collection of income executions, the percentage of earnings deductible and restrictions against multiple deductions.

## 1990 AMENDMENTS

L. 1990, ch. 178, eff. May 24, 1990, amended CPLR 5231 subdivision (b) by deleting "earnings from any person" and adding "money from any source;" adding to subparagraphs (i), (ii) and (iii) the words "from the judgment debtor's earnings;" and adding a new final sentence: "Nothing in this section shall be construed to modify, abrogate, impair or affect any exemption from the satisfaction of a money judgment otherwise granted by law." The same enactment amended subdivision (g) by changing the first sentence from "state and federal law`to "state or federal law;" replacing the references in I(D) and I(E) to "gross income" with "earnings," and adding to phrases "from the judgment debtor's earnings" and "from earnings;" changing the phrase in I(E) from "the income execution" to "this income execution;" modifying the Illustrations portion of the prescribed form by adding the phrase "regarding earnings" after "Illustrations;" adding "from earnings" after "Amount to Pay or Deduct;" replacing "Gross Income" with "Gross Earnings;" modifying Part III, the Notice portion of the prescribed form by changing the reference from CPLR 5231(g) to CPLR 5231(i); changing "earnings" to "income;" and changing "state and federal law" to "state or federal law."

L. 1990, ch. 183, eff. May 24, 1990, amended CPLR 5231 subdivision (d) by providing that one additional copy of the income execution by sent to the debtor by regular mail, and by repealing that part of the subdivision that provided that a copy of the income execution be sent by regular mail to the debtor in care of his last known employer.

## 1987 AMENDMENTS

L. 1987, ch. 829, eff. Aug. 7, 1987, added new subdivisions (c) and (g), amended subdivision (b), amended and relettered subdivision (f) and relettered the remaining subdivisions accordingly.

## 1986 AMENDMENTS

L. 1986, ch. 241, eff. July 31, 1986, amended former Subd.(i) [relettered Subd. (k) in 1987] by reducing the amount of time for an accounting of monies collected by a sheriff from at least once every six months to ninety days.

## 1975 AMENDMENTS

L. 1975, ch. 88, eff. May 13, 1975, amended subds. (c) and (d).

## 1970 AMENDMENTS

L. 1970, ch. 298, eff. Sept. 1, 1970, amended Subd. (b) by increasing the amount which a judgment debtor receives for which an income execution may be issued from more than thirty dollars to more than eighty-five dollars per week.

# § 5232. Levy upon personal property.

(a) Levy by service of execution. The sheriff or support collection unit designated by the appropriate social services district shall levy upon any interest of the judgment debtor or obligor in personal property not capable of delivery, or upon any debt owed to the judgment debtor or obligor, by serving a copy of the execution upon the garnishee, in the same manner as a summons, except that such service shall not be made by delivery to a person authorized to receive service of summons solely by a designation filed pursuant to a provision of law other than rule 318. In the event the garnishee is the state of New York, such levy shall be made in the same manner as an income execution pursuant to section 5231 of this article. A levy by service of the execution is effective only if, at the time of service, the person served owes a debt to the judgment debtor or obligor or he or she is in the possession or custody of property not capable of delivery in which he or she knows or has reason to believe the judgment debtor or obligor has an interest, or if the judgment creditor or support collection unit has stated in a notice which shall be served with the execution that a specified debt is owed by the person served to the judgment debtor or obligor or that the judgment debtor or obligor has an interest in specified property not capable of delivery in the possession or custody of the person served. All property not capable of delivery in which the judgment debtor or obligor is known or believed to have an interest then in or thereafter coming into the possession or custody of such a person, including any specified in the notice, and all debts of such a person, including any specified in the notice, then due or thereafter coming due to the judgment debtor or obligor, shall be subject to the levy. The person served with the execution shall forthwith transfer all such property, and pay all such debts upon maturity, to the sheriff or to the support collection unit and execute any document necessary to effect the transfer or payment. After such transfer or payment, property coming into the possession or custody of the garnishee, or debt incurred by him, or her shall not be subject to the levy. Until such transfer or payment is made, or until the expiration of ninety days after the service of the execution upon him or her, or of such further time as is provided by any order of the court served upon him or her, whichever event first occurs, the garnishee is forbidden to make or suffer any sale, assignment or transfer of, or any interference with, any such property, or pay over or otherwise dispose of any such debt, to any person other than the sheriff or the support collection unit, except upon direction of the sheriff or the support collection unit or pursuant to an order of the court. At the expiration of ninety days after a levy is made by service of the execution, or of such further time as the court, upon motion of the judgment creditor or support collection unit has provided, the levy shall be void except as to property or debts which have been transferred or paid to the sheriff or to the support collection unit or as to which a proceeding under sections 5225 or 5227 has been brought. A judgment creditor who, or support collection unit which, has specified personal property or debt to be levied upon in a notice served with an execution shall be liable to the owner of the property or the person to whom the debt is owed, if other than the judgment debtor or obligor, for any damages sustained by reason of the levy.

(b) Levy by seizure. The sheriff or support collection unit of the appropriate social services district shall levy upon any interest of the judgment debtor in personal property capable of delivery by taking the property into custody without interfering with the lawful possession of pledgees and lessees. The sheriff or support collection unit shall forthwith serve a copy of the execution in the manner prescribed by subdivision (a) upon the person from whose possession or custody the property was taken.

(c) Notice to judgment debtor or obligor. Where an execution does not state that a notice in the form presented by subdivision (e) of section fifty-two hundred twenty-two of this chapter has been duly served upon the judgment debtor or obligor within a year, the sheriff or support collection unit shall, not later than four days after service of the execution upon any garnishee, mail by first class mail, or personally deliver, to each judgment debtor or obligor who is a natural person, a copy of the execution together with such notice. The sheriff or support collection unit shall specify on the notice to judgment debtor or obligor the name and address of the judgment creditor or the judgment creditor's attorney or the support collection unit. The notice shall be mailed to the judgment debtor or obligor at his or her residence address; and in the event such mailing is returned as undeliverable by the post office, or if the residence address of the judgment debtor or obligor is unknown, then to the judgment debtor or obligor in care of the place of employment of the judgment debtor or obligor if known, in an envelope bearing the legend "personal and confidential" and not indicating on the outside thereof, by the return address or otherwise, that the communication is from a sheriff or support collection unit or concerns a debt; or if neither the residence nor the place of employment of the judgment debtor or obligor is known, then to the judgment debtor or obligor at any other known address.

(d) For the purposes of this section "obligor" shall mean an individual other than a judgment debtor obligated to pay support, alimony or maintenance pursuant to an order of a court of competent jurisdiction who has been found to be in "default" of such order as such term is defined in paragraph seven of subdivision (a) of section fifty-two hundred forty-one of this article and the establishment of such default has been subject to the procedures established for the determination of a "mistake of fact" for income executions pursuant to subdivision (e) of section fifty-two hundred forty-one of this article, except that for the purposes of this section only, a default shall not be founded upon retroactive child support obligations as defined in paragraph (c) of subdivision one of section four hundred forty and subdivision one of section two hundred forty, and paragraph b of subdivision nine of section two hundred thirty-six of the domestic relations law.

### 1993 AMENDMENTS

L. 1993, ch. 59, eff. July 1, 1993, added references to "support collection unit" throughout the section; added the words "or her" after the word "him" throughout the section; added the words "or obligor" following the words "judgment debtor" throughout the section; substituted the words "this article" in place of the words "civil practice law and rules" in subdivision (a); and added a new subdivision (d).

### 1982 AMENDMENTS

L. 1982, ch. 882, eff. Sept. 1, 1982, amended CPLR 5232 by adding a new subdivision (c).

CPLR

## 1968 AMENDMENTS

L. 1968, ch. 743, eff. Sept. 1, 1968, inserted second sentence in Subd. (a) pertaining to a levy when the state of New York is the garnishee.

## § 5233. Sale of personal property.

(a) Public auction. The interest of the judgment debtor in personal property obtained by a sheriff pursuant to execution or order, other than legal tender of the United States, shall be sold by the sheriff at public auction at such time and place and as a unit or in such lots, or combination thereof, as in his judgment will bring the highest price, but no sale may be made to that sheriff or to his deputy or undersheriff. The property shall be present and within the view of those attending the sale unless otherwise ordered by the court.

(b) Public notice. A printed notice of the time and place of the sale shall be posted at least six days before the sale in three public places in the town or city in which the sale is to be held, provided however, in the city of New York, in lieu of posting such notice may be advertised in the auction columns of any morning newspaper published daily and Sunday in such city an edition of which appears on the newsstands the previous night and has a circulation of not less than three hundred thousand. An omission to so post or advertise notice, or the defacing or removal of a posted notice, does not affect the title of a purchaser without notice of the omission or offense.

(c) Order for immediate sale or disposition. The court may direct immediate sale or other disposition of property with or without notice if the urgency of the case requires.

(d) Unsaleable material. If property seized by the sheriff is considered by him to be material which, by law, may not be sold, he shall apply to the court for a determination whether the property can legally be sold. Reasonable notice of such application shall also be given to the owner of such property. If the court decides the property may not be legally sold, it shall order appropriate disposition of the property which may include its destruction.

## 1979 AMENDMENTS

L. 1979, ch. 457, eff. July 5, 1979, amended CPLR 5233 by adding a new subdivision (d).

## 1976 AMENDMENTS

L. 1976, ch. 795, eff. July 24, 1976, amended Subd. (b) to provide that in New York City the notice may be published in a qualifying newspaper in lieu of posting.

## § 5234. Distribution of proceeds of personal property; priorities.

(a) Distribution of proceeds of personal property. After deduction for and payment of fees, expenses and any taxes levied upon sale, delivery, transfer or payment, the proceeds of personal property or debt acquired by a receiver or a sheriff or other officer authorized to enforce the judgment shall be distributed to the judgment creditor and any excess shall be paid over to the judgment debtor. No distribution of proceeds shall be made until fifteen days after service of the execution except upon order of the court.

(b) Priority among execution creditors. Where two or more executions or orders of attachment are issued against the same judgment debtor or obligor and delivered to the same enforcement officer or issued by the support collection unit designated by the appropriate social services district, they shall be satisfied out of the proceeds of personal property or debt levied upon by the officer or by the support collection unit in the order in which they were delivered, such executions for child support shall have priority over any other assignment, levy or process. Where two or more executions or orders of attachment are issued against the same judgment debtor or obligor and delivered to different enforcement officers, and personal property or debt is levied upon within the jurisdiction of all of the officers, the proceeds shall be first applied in satisfaction of the execution or order of attachment delivered to the officer who levied, and thereafter shall be applied in satisfaction of the executions or orders of attachment delivered to those of the other officers who, before the proceeds are distributed, make a demand upon the officer who levied, in the order of such demands, except that such executions for child support shall have priority over any other assignment, levy or process. Where there is more than one past-due child support order, the proceeds shall be applied to the orders in proportion to the amount each order's claim bears to the combined total. Nothing herein shall be deemed to defeat or impair the rights of any secured party as such term is defined in paragraph (m) of subsection one of section 9–105 of the uniform commercial code. An execution or order of attachment returned by an officer before a levy or delivered to him after the proceeds of the levy have been distributed shall not be satisfied out of those proceeds.

(c) Priority of other judgment creditors. Where personal property or debt has been ordered delivered, transferred or paid, or a receiver thereof has been appointed by order, or a receivership has been extended thereto by order, and the order is filed before the property or debt is levied upon, the rights of the judgment creditor who secured the order are superior to those of the judgment creditor entitled to the proceeds of the levy. Where two or more such orders affecting the same interest in personal property or debt are filed, the proceeds of the property or debt shall be applied in the order of filing. Where delivery, transfer, or payment to the judgment creditor, a receiver, or a sheriff or other officer is not completed within sixty days after an order is filed, the judgment creditor who secured the order is divested of priority, unless otherwise specified in the order or in an extension order filed within the sixty days.

### 1993 AMENDMENTS

L. 1993, ch. 59, eff. July 1, 1993, added the words "or obligor" following the words "judgment debtor"; added the words "or issued by the support collection unit designated by the appropriate social services district" after the words "same enforcement officer"; added the words "or by the support collection unit" following the words "by the officer"; added the words "such executions for child support shall have priority over any other assignment, levy or process" following the words "in which they were delivered"; added the words "except that such executions for child support shall have priority over any other assignment, levy or process" following the words "in the order of such demands"; and added the two sentences immediately preceding the last sentence in subdivision (b).

### 1982 AMENDMENTS

L. 1982, ch. 882, eff. Sept. 1, 1982, amended CPLR 5234 by adding a new sentence at the end of subdivision (a).

## § 5235. Levy upon real property.

After the expiration of ten years after the filing of the judgment-roll, the sheriff shall levy upon any interest of the judgment debtor in real property, pursuant to an execution other than one issued upon a judgment for any part of a mortgage debt upon the property, by filing with the clerk of the county in which the property is located a notice of levy describing the judgment, the execution and the property. The clerk shall record and index the notice against the name of the judgment debtor, or against the property, in the same books, and in the same manner as a notice of the pendency of an action.

## § 5236. Sale of real property.

(a) Time of sale; public auction. Between the fifty-sixth and the sixty-third day after the first publication of a copy of the notice of sale, unless the time is extended by order or the sale postponed by the sheriff, the interest of the judgment debtor in real property which has been levied upon under an execution delivered to the sheriff or which was subject to the lien of the judgment at the time of such delivery shall be sold by the sheriff pursuant to the execution at public auction at such time and place within the county where the real property is situated and as a unit or in such parcels, or combination thereof, as in his judgment will bring the highest price, but no sale may be made to that sheriff or to his deputy or undersheriff. If the property is situated in more than one county, it may be sold in a county in which any part is situated, unless the court orders otherwise.

(b) Sale of mortgaged property. Real property mortgaged shall not be sold pursuant to an execution issued upon a judgment recovered for all or part of the mortgage debt.

(c) Notice of sale. A printed notice of the time and place of the sale containing a description of the property to be sold shall be posted at least fifty-six days before the sale in three public places in the town or city in which the property is located, and, if the sale is to be held in another town or city, in three public places therein. Service by the sheriff of a copy of said notice on the judgment debtor shall be made as provided in section 308. A list containing the name and address of the judgment debtor and of every judgment creditor whose judgment was a lien on the real property to be sold and of every person who had of record any interest in or lien on such property forty-five days prior to the day fixed for the sale shall be furnished the sheriff by the judgment creditor, and each person on the list shall be served by the sheriff with a copy of the notice by personal delivery or by registered or certified mail, return receipt requested, at least thirty days prior to the day fixed for the sale. A copy of the notice shall be published at least once in each of four periods of fourteen successive days, the first of which periods may be measured from any day between the fifty-sixth and sixty-third days, preceding the time fixed for the sale in a newspaper published in the county in which the property is located or, if there is none, in a newspaper published in an adjoining county. An omission to give any notice required by this or the following subdivision, or the defacing or removal of a notice posted pursuant to either, does not affect the title of a purchaser without notice of the omission or offense.

(d) Notice of postponement of sale. Any person may, in a writing served on the sheriff either by personal delivery or by registered or certified mail, return receipt requested, request that the sheriff notify him in the event that a scheduled sale is postponed. Such writing shall contain the person's name and mailing address. If the sale is for any reason postponed, notice of the postponed date need be given only to:

1. those whose requests, made as above provided, have been received by the sheriff at least five days prior to the postponed date,

2. those who appeared at the time and place previously appointed for the sale, and

3. the judgment debtor at his last known address.

The notice may be served either by personal delivery or by registered or certified mail, return receipt requested. Unless the court shall otherwise direct, it need not be posted or published.

(e) Effect of notice as against judgment creditors. A judgment creditor duly notified pursuant to subdivisions (c) or (d) who fails to deliver an execution to the sheriff prior to the sale shall have no further lien on the property and, except as against the judgment debtor, no further interest in the proceeds of the sale.

(f) Conveyance; proof of notice. Within ten days after the sale, the sheriff shall execute and deliver to the purchaser proofs of publication, service and posting of the notice of sale, and a deed which shall convey the right, title and interest sold. Such proofs may be filed and recorded in the office of the clerk of the county where the property is located.

(g) Disposition of proceeds of sale. After deduction for and payment of fees, expenses and any taxes levied on the sale, transfer or delivery, the sheriff making

CPLR

a sale of real property pursuant to an execution shall, unless the court otherwise directs,

1. distribute the proceeds to the judgment creditors who have delivered executions against the judgment debtor to the sheriff before the sale, which executions have not been returned, in the order in which their judgments have priority, and

2. pay over any excess to the judgment debtor.

### 1975 AMENDMENTS

L. 1975, ch. 570, eff. Sept. 1, 1975, amended Subd. (c) by rewording it so as to resolve the conflict between the section and CPLR 308, as amended in 1970.

### 1969 AMENDMENTS

L. 1969, ch. 1089, eff. Jan. 1, 1970, amended subds. (c) and (d).

### 1968 AMENDMENTS

L. 1968, ch. 498, eff. Sept. 1, 1968, amended the second sentence of Subd. (c) to expand the class of those persons who are to be given notice of the sale of realty pursuant to an execution to include anyone whose interest was of record thirty days prior to the sale.

### 1967 AMENDMENTS

L. 1967, ch. 57, eff. Sept. 1, 1967, amended Subd. (c) to require that notice of sale be given to owner of fee title if owner, at time of execution, is other than the judgment debtor.

### 1965 AMENDMENTS

L. 1965, ch. 974, eff. Sept. 1, 1965, amended subds. (a) and (c), added new subds. (d) and (e), and relettered subds. (d) and (e) to be subds. (f) and (g), respectively. In relation to the amendment of subd. (c) the Judicial Conference noted:

"The net effect of the time changes proposed would be that only creditors with liens at least 30 days old prior to the sale, instead of 20 days old, would be notified. The levying judgment creditor could complete his list of the judgment creditors and mortgagees on or after the 30th day before the sale instead of the 20th day. . . . The sheriff would have a possible 15 days in which to effect service on the listed judgment creditors and mortgagees instead of 10 days. . . . The notified judgment creditors would have 15 days prior to the sale in which to issue and deliver their own executions to the sheriff. . . .

"The sheriffs have expressed some apprehension that the present provision as it relates to the time of sale might be construed as permitting the sale only on the 63rd day following the first publication. The purpose of the present provision, however, is to permit the sale to take place on any day between the 56th and the 63rd day after first publication. The proposed amendment, requested by the sheriffs, is designed to clarify this point."

### 1964 AMENDMENTS

L. 1964, ch. 347, eff. Sept. 1, 1964, amended the third sentence of Subd. (c) to change the time periods for publication.

### § 5237.   Failure of title to property sold.

The purchaser of property sold by a sheriff pursuant to execution or order may recover the purchase money from the judgment creditors who received the proceeds if the property is recovered from such purchaser in consequence of an irregularity in the sale or a vacatur, reversal or setting aside of the judgment upon which the execution or order was based. If a judgment for the purchase money is so recovered against a judgment creditor in consequence of an irregularity in the sale, such judgment creditor may enforce his judgment as if no levy or sale had been made, and, for that purpose, he may move without notice for an order restoring any lien or priority or amending any docket entry affected by the sale.

### § 5238.   Directions to the sheriff.

Upon motion of any party, on notice to the sheriff and all other parties, the court may direct the sheriff to dispose of, account for, assign, return or release all or any part of any property or debt, or the proceeds thereof, or to file additional returns, subject to the payment of the sheriff's fees and expenses. As far as practicable, the court shall direct that notice of the motion be given to any other judgment creditors, at the addresses shown on the judgment docket and to any persons who have secured orders of attachment affecting any property or debt, or the proceeds thereof, sought to be returned or released.

### § 5239.   Proceeding to determine adverse claims.

Prior to the application of property or debt by a sheriff or receiver to the satisfaction of a judgment, any interested person may commence a special proceeding against the judgment creditor or other person with whom a dispute exists to determine rights in the property or debt. Service of process in such a proceeding shall be made by service of a notice of petition upon the respondent, the sheriff or receiver, and such other person as the court directs, in the same manner as a notice of motion. The proceeding may be commenced in the county where the property was levied upon, or in a court or county specified in subdivision (a) of section 5221. The court may vacate the execution or order, void the levy, direct the disposition of the property or debt, or direct that damages be awarded. Where there appear to be disputed questions of fact, the court shall order a separate trial, indicating the person who shall have possession of the property pending a decision and the undertaking, if any, which such person shall give. If the court determines that any claim asserted was fraudulent, it may require the claimant to pay to any party adversely affected thereby the reasonable expenses incurred by such party in the proceeding, including reasonable attorneys' fees, and any other damages suffered by reason of the claim. The court may permit any interested person to intervene in the proceeding.

CPLR

L. 1994, ch. 563, eff. July 26, 1994, amended CPLR 5239 by deleting the words "by serving" in the first sentence and inserting in their place the words "Service of process in such a proceeding shall be made by service of."

L. 1965, ch. 974, eff. Sept. 1, 1965, amended the section.

## § 5240. Modification or protective order; supervision of enforcement.

The court may at any time, on its own initiative or the motion of any interested person, and upon such notice as it may require, make an order denying, limiting, conditioning, regulating, extending or modifying the use of any enforcement procedure. Section 3104 is applicable to procedures under this article.

## § 5241. Income execution for support enforcement.

(a) Definitions. As used in this section and in section fifty-two hundred forty-two of this chapter, the following terms shall have the following meanings:

1. "Order of support" means any temporary or final order, judgment, agreement or stipulation incorporated by reference in such judgment or decree in a matrimonial action or family court proceeding, or any foreign support order, judgment or decree, registered pursuant to section thirty-seven-a of the domestic relations law which directs the payment of alimony, maintenance, support or child support.

2. "Debtor" means any person directed to make payments by an order of support.

3. "Creditor" means any person entitled to enforce an order of support, including a support collection unit.

4. "Employer" means any employer, future employer, former employer, union or employees' organization.

5. "Income payor" includes:

(i) the auditor, comptroller, trustee or disbursing officer of any pension fund, benefit program, policy of insurance or annuity;

(ii) the state of New York or any political subdivision thereof, or the United States; and

(iii) any person, corporation, trustee, unincorporated business or association, partnership, financial institution, bank, savings and loan association, credit union, stock purchase plan, stock option plan, profit sharing plan, stock broker, commodities broker, bond broker, real estate broker, insurance company, entity or institution.

6. "Income" includes any earned, unearned, taxable or non-taxable income, workers' compensation, disability benefits, unemployment insurance benefits

and federal social security benefits as defined in 42 U.S.C. section 662(f)(2), but excluding public assistance benefits paid pursuant to the social services law and federal supplemental security income.

7. "Default" means the failure of a debtor to remit to a creditor three payments on the date due in the full amount directed by the order of support, or the accumulation of arrears equal to or greater than the amount directed to be paid for one month, whichever first occurs.

8. "Mistake of fact" means any error in the amount of current support or arrears or in the identity of the debtor or that the order of support does not exist or has been vacated.

9. "Support collection unit" means any support collection unit established by a social services district pursuant to the provisions of section one hundred eleven-h of the social services law, or a local public agency where such agency is responsible for the performance of all the functions of the support collection unit pursuant to an agreement under the provisions of section one hundred eleven-h of the social services law.

10. "Date of withholding" means the date on which the income would otherwise have been paid or made available to the debtor were it not withheld by the employer or income payor.

11. "Health insurance benefits" means any medical, dental, optical and prescription drugs and health care services or other health care benefits which may be provided for dependents through an employer or organization, including such employers or organizations which are self-insured.

(b) Issuance. (1) When a debtor is in default, an execution for support enforcement may be issued by the support collection unit, or by the sheriff, the clerk of court or the attorney for the creditor as an officer of the court. Where a debtor is receiving or will receive income, an execution for deductions therefrom in amounts not to exceed the limits set forth in subdivision (g) of this section may be served upon an employer or income payor after notice to the debtor. The amount of the deductions to be withheld shall be sufficient to ensure compliance with the direction in the order of support, and shall include an additional amount to be applied to the reduction of arrears. The creditor may amend the execution before or after service upon the employer or income payor to reflect additional arrears or payments made by the debtor after notice pursuant to subdivision (d) of this section, or to conform the execution to the facts found upon a determination made pursuant to subdivision (e) of this section.

(2) Where the order of support orders the debtor to provide health insurance benefits for specified dependents, an execution for medical support enforcement may, except as provided for herein, be issued by the support collection unit, or by the sheriff, the clerk of court or the attorney for the creditor as an officer of the court. Such execution for medical support enforcement may require the debtor's employer or organization to purchase on behalf of the debtor and the

CPLR

debtor's dependents such available health insurance benefits as are ordered by the order of support. Such execution shall, consistent with the order of support, direct the employer or organization to provide to the issuer of the execution any identification cards and benefit claim forms and to withhold from the debtor's income the employee's share of the cost of such health insurance benefits. An execution for medical support enforcement shall not require a debtor's employer or organization to purchase or otherwise acquire health insurance or health insurance benefits that would not otherwise be available to the debtor by reason of his employment or membership. Nothing herein shall be deemed to obligate or otherwise hold any employer or organization responsible for an option exercised by the debtor in selecting medical insurance coverage by an employee or member.

(3) Any inconsistent provisions of this title or other law notwithstanding, in anycase in which a parent is required by a court order to provide health coverage for a child and the parent is eligible for health insurance benefits as defined in this section through an employer or organization, including those which are self-insured, doing business in the state, such employer or organization must, in addition to implementing the provisions of a duly executed and served medical support execution, as such term is defined in this section:

(i) permit such parent immediately to enroll under such health insurance benefit coverage any such dependent who is otherwise eligible for such coverage without regard to any seasonal enrollment restrictions;

(ii) if such a parent is enrolled but fails to make application to obtain coverage of such dependent child, immediately enroll such dependent child under such health benefit coverage upon application by such child's other parent or by the department or social services district furnishing medical assistance to such child, and

(iii) not disenroll, or eliminate coverage of, such a child unless the employer or organization has provided satisfactory written evidence that:

(A) such court order is no longer in effect, or

(B) the child is or will be enrolled in comparable health coverage through another insurer which will take effect not later than the effective date of such disenrollment, or

(C) such employer or organization has eliminated health insurance coverage for all similarly situated employees.

(c) Execution for support enforcement; form. (1) The execution shall contain the caption of the order of support, and specify the date that the order of support was entered, the court in which it was entered, the amount of the periodic payments directed, the amount of arrears, the nature of the default and the names of the debtor and creditor. In addition, the execution shall include:

(i) the name and address of the employer or income payor from whom the debtor is receiving or will receive income;

(ii) the amount of the deductions to be made therefrom on account of current support, and the amount to be applied to the reduction of arrears;

(iii) a notice that deductions will apply to current and subsequent income;

(iv) a notice that the execution will be served upon any current or subsequent employer or income payor unless a mistake of fact is shown within fifteen days, a notice of the manner in which a mistake of fact may be asserted, and a notice that, if the debtor claims a mistake of fact, a determination will be made within forty-five days after notice to the debtor as provided in subdivision (d) of this section, and that the debtor will receive written notice whether the execution will be served and of the time that deductions will begin;

(v) a notice that the employer or income payor must commence deductions no later than the first pay period that occurs after fourteen days following the service of the execution and that payment must be remitted within ten days of the date that the debtor is paid;

(vi) a notice that the execution is binding until further notice;

(vii) a notice of the substance of the provisions of section fifty-two hundred fifty-two of this chapter and that a violation thereof is punishable as a contempt of court by fine or imprisonment or both;

(viii) a notice of the limitations upon deductions from wages set forth in subdivision (g) of this section;

(ix) a notice that an employer must notify the issuer promptly when the debtor terminates employment and provide the debtor's last address and the name and address of the new employer, if known.

(2) In addition, if the execution includes provisions to enforce medical support, the execution shall include:

(i) a notice that the debtor has been ordered by the court to enroll the dependents in any available health insurance benefits and to maintain such coverage for such dependents as long as such benefits remain available;

(ii) a notice inquiring of the employer or organization as to whether such health insurance benefits are presently in effect for the eligible dependents named in the execution, the date such benefits were or become available, and directing that the response to such inquiry immediately be forwarded to the issuer of such execution;

(iii) a statement directing the employer or organization to purchase on behalf of the debtor any available health insurance benefits to be made available to the debtor's dependents as directed by the execution, including the enrollment of such eligible dependents in such benefit plans and the provision to the issuer of the execution of any identification cards and benefit claim forms;

(iv) a statement directing the employer or organization to deduct from the debtor's income such amount which is the debtor's share of the premium, if any, for such health insurance benefits who are otherwise eligible for such coverage without regard to any seasonal enrollment restrictions;

(v) a notice that the debtor's employer must notify the issuer promptly at any time the debtor terminates or changes such health insurance benefits;

(vi) a statement that the debtor's employer or organization shall not be required to purchase or otherwise acquire health insurance or health insurance benefits that would not otherwise be available to the debtor by reason of his employment or membership; and

(vii) a statement that failure to enroll the eligible dependents in such health insurance plan or benefits or failure to deduct from the debtor's income the debtor's share of the premium for such plan or benefits shall make such organization jointly and severally liable for all medical expenses incurred on the behalf of the debtor's dependents named in the execution while such dependents are not so enrolled to the extent of the insurance benefits that should have been provided under the execution.

(d) Notice to debtor. The creditor shall serve a copy of the execution upon the debtor by regular mail to the debtor at his last known residence or such other place where he is likely to receive notice, or in the same manner as a summons may be served.

(e) Determination of mistake of fact. Where the execution has been issued by the support collection unit, the debtor may assert a mistake of fact and shall have an opportunity to make a submission in support of the objection within fifteen days from service of a copy thereof. Thereafter, the agency shall determine the merits of the objection, and shall notify the debtor of its determination within forty-five days after notice to the debtor as provided in subdivision (d) of this section. If the objection is disallowed, the debtor shall be notified that the income execution will be served on the employer or income payor, and of the time that deductions will begin. Where the income execution has been issued by an attorney as officer of the court, or by the sheriff, or by the clerk of the court, the debtor may assert a mistake of fact within fifteen days from service of a copy thereof by application to the supreme court or to the family court having jurisdiction in accordance with section four hundred sixty-one of the family court act. If application is made to the family court, such application shall be by petition on notice to the creditor and it shall be heard and determined in accordance with the provisions of section four hundred thirty-nine of the family court act, and a determination thereof shall be made, and the debtor notified thereof within forty-five days of the application. If application is made to the supreme court such application shall be by petition on notice to the creditor and, it shall be heard and determined in accordance with the provisions of article four of the civil practice law and rules, and a determination thereof shall be made, and the debtor notified thereof within forty-five days of the application.

(f) Levy. If a debtor fails to show mistake of fact within fifteen days, or after a determination pursuant to subdivision (e) of this section has been made, or if the creditor is unable to serve the execution upon the debtor, the creditor may levy upon the income that the debtor is receiving or will receive by serving the execution upon the employer or income payor personally in the same manner as a summons or by regular mail, except that such service shall not be made by delivery to a person authorized to receive service of summons solely by a designation filed pursuant to a provision of law other than rule 318.

(g) Deduction from income. (1) An employer or income payor served with an income execution shall commence deductions from income due or thereafter due to the debtor no later than the first pay period that occurs fourteen days after service of the execution, and shall remit payments to the creditor within ten days of the date that the debtor is paid. Each payment remitted by an employer or income payor shall include, in addition to the identity and social security number of the debtor, the date and amount of each withholding of the debtor's income included in the payment. An employer or income payor shall be liable to the creditor for failure to deduct the amounts specified, provided however that deduction of the amounts specified by the employer or income payor shall not relieve the debtor of the underlying obligation of support. If such person shall fail to so pay the creditor, the creditor may commence a proceeding against him or her for accrued deductions, together with interest and reasonable attorney's fees. If the money due to the debtor consists of salary or wages and his or her employment is terminated by resignation or dismissal at any time after service of the execution, the levy shall thereafter be ineffective, and the execution shall be returned, unless the debtor is reinstated or re-employed within ninety days after such termination. An employer must notify the issuer promptly when the debtor terminates employment and provide the debtor's last address and the name and address of the new employer, if known. Where the income is compensation paid or payable to the debtor for personal services, the amount of the deductions to be withheld shall not exceed the following:

(i) Where a debtor is currently supporting a spouse or dependent child other than the creditor, the amount of the deductions to be withheld shall not exceed fifty percent of the earnings of the debtor remaining after the deduction therefrom of any amounts required by law to be withheld ("disposable earnings"), except that if any part of such deduction is to be applied to the reduction of arrears which shall have accrued more than twelve weeks prior to the beginning of the week for which such earnings are payable, the amount of such deduction shall not exceed fifty-five percent of disposable earnings.

(ii) Where a debtor is not currently supporting a spouse or dependent child other than the creditor, the amount of the deductions to be withheld shall not exceed sixty percent of the earnings of the debtor remaining after the deduction therefrom of any amounts required by law to be withheld ("disposable earnings"), except that if any part of such deduction is to be applied to the reduction of arrears which shall have accrued more than twelve weeks prior to the beginning of the week for which such earnings are payable, the amount of such deduction shall not exceed sixty-five percent of disposable earnings.

(2) If an employer, income payor or organization is served with an execution for medical support enforcement, such employer or income payor shall purchase on behalf of the debtor any available health insurance benefits to be made available to the debtor's dependents as ordered by the execution, including the immediate enrollment of such eligible dependents in such benefit plans and the provision to the issuer of the execution of any identification cards and benefit claim forms, and shall commence deductions from income due or thereafter due to the debtor of such amount which is the debtor's share of the premium, if any, for such health insurance benefits who are otherwise eligible for such coverage without regard to any seasonal enrollment restrictions and shall provide a confirmation of such enrollment to the issuer of such execution. If such employer or organization shall fail to so enroll such eligible dependents or to deduct from the debtor's income the debtor's share of the premium, such employer or organization shall be jointly and severally liable for all medical expenses incurred on the behalf of the debtor's dependents named in the execution while such dependents are not so enrolled to the extent of the insurance benefits that should have been provided under such execution. Except as otherwise provided by law, nothing herein shall be deemed to obligate an employer or organization to maintain or continue an employee's or member's health insurance benefits.

(h) Priority. A levy pursuant to this section or an income deduction order pursuant to section 5242 of this chapter shall take priority over any other assignment, levy or process. If an employer or income payor is served with more than one execution to this section, or with an execution pursuant to this section and also an order pursuant to section 5242 of this chapter, and if the combined total amount of the deductions to be withheld exceeds the limits set forth in subdivision (g) of this section, the employer or income payor shall withhold the maximum amount permitted thereby and pay to each creditor that proportion thereof which such creditor's claim bears to the combined total. Any additional deduction authorized by subdivision (g) of this section to be applied to the reduction of arrears shall be applied to such arrears in proportion to the amount of arrears due to each creditor.

(i) Levy upon money payable by the state. A levy upon money payable directly by a department of the state, or by an institution under its jurisdiction, shall be made by serving the income execution upon the head of the department, or upon a person designated by him, at the office of the department in Albany; a levy upon money payable directly upon the state comptroller's warrant, or directly by a state board, commission, body or agency which is not within any department of the state, shall be made by serving the execution upon the state department of audit and control at its office in Albany. Service at the office of a department or any agency or institution of the state in Albany may be made by registered or certified mail, return receipt requested.

### 1994 AMENDMENTS

L. 1994, ch. 170, eff. June 9, 1994, amended CPLR 5241(b)(2) by deleting the final sentence pertaining to executions for medical support enforcement, and by adding a new subparagraph (3); amended CPLR 5241(c)(2)(iv) by deleting the words "no later than the first enrollment period allowable under the applicable provider's terms of enrollment subsequent to the service of the execution," and inserting in their place the words "who are otherwise eligible for such coverage without regard to any seasonal enrollment restrictions"; amended CPLR 5241(g)(1)(ii) by deleting the final sentence, which read "The provisions of this paragraph shall not apply to executions for medical support enforcement as described in paragraph two of subdivision (b) of this section"; amended CPLR 5241(g)(2) by adding the word "immediate" and by deleting the words "no later than the first enrollment subsequent to the service of the execution" and inserting in their place the words "who are otherwise eligible for such coverage without regard to any seasonal enrollment restrictions."

### 1993 AMENDMENTS

L. 1993, ch. 59, eff. July 1, 1993, amended subdivision (a) by adding a new paragraph (11), defining "health insurance benefits," and amended subdivisions (b), (c) and (g).

### 1990 AMENDMENTS

L. 1990, ch. 818, eff. Sept. 30, 1990, amended CPLR 5241 by adding a new paragraph (a)(10), and by adding a provision to subdivision (g) mandating that each payment remitted by an employer or income payor include the identity and social security number of the debtor, as well as the date and amount of each withholding of the debtor's income included in the payment.

### 1988 AMENDMENTS

L. 1988, ch. 327, eff. July 25, 1988, and applying to all judgments, orders or agreements or stipulations incorporated by reference in a judgment, relating to actions for divorce, separation or annulment of a marriage or of support, entered or issued both before and after such date. The amendment added "agreements or stipulations incorporated by reference in a judgment" to the definition of "order of support".

### 1987 AMENDMENTS

L. 1987, ch. 815, eff. Aug. 7, 1987, and applicable to any action or proceeding commenced on or after such date, amended Subd. (e) to add the provision that determinations of mistake of fact applications on income executions issued by the sheriff or the clerk of the court, shall be made by the court; and deleting the provision that such determinations be made by the issuer; to add reference to Family Court Act § 461; to provide that applications to the Family Court be brought by petition on notice to the creditor; to add the last sentence specifying the procedure for application to the supreme court on a mistake of fact.

### 1985 AMENDMENTS

L. 1985, ch. 809, eff. Nov. 1, 1985, added CPLR 5241.

## § 5242.   Income deduction order for support enforcement.

(a) Upon application of a creditor, for good cause shown, and upon such terms as justice may require, the court may correct any defect, irregularity, error or omission in an income execution for support enforcement issued pursuant to section 5241 of this article.

(b) Upon application of a creditor, for good cause shown, the court may enter an income deduction order for support enforcement. In determining good cause, the court may take into consideration evidence of the degree of such debtor's past financial responsibility, credit references, credit history, and any other matter the court considers relevant in determining the likelihood of payment in accordance with the order of support. Proof of default establishes a prima facie case against the debtor, which can be overcome only by proof of the debtor's inability to make the payments. Unless the prima facie case is overcome, the court shall enter an income deduction order for support enforcement pursuant to this section.

(c)(1) When the court enters an order of support on behalf of persons other than those in receipt of public assistance or in receipt of services pursuant to section one hundred eleven-g of the social services law, or registers pursuant to section thirty-seven-a of the domestic relations law an order of support which has been issued by a foreign jurisdiction and which is not to be enforced pursuant to title six-A of article three of the social services law, where the court determines that the respondent earns wages that could be subject to an income deduction order, the court shall issue an income deduction order to obtain payment of the order at the same time it issues or registers the order. The court shall enter the income deduction order unless the court finds and sets forth in writing (i) the reasons that there is good cause not to require immediate income withholding; or (ii) that an agreement providing for an alternative arrangement has been reached between the parties. Such agreement may include a written agreement or an oral stipulation, made on the record, that results in a written order. For purposes of this subdivision, good cause shall mean substantial harm to the debtor. The absence of an arrearage or the mere issuance of an income deduction order shall not constitute good cause. When the court determines that there is good cause not to issue an income deduction order immediately or when the parties agree to an alternative arrangement as provided in this paragraph, the court shall state expressly in the order of support the basis for its decision. In entering the income deduction order, the court shall specify an amount to be withheld by the debtor's employer, which shall be sufficient to ensure compliance with the order of support and also shall include an additional amount to be applied to the reduction of arrears, if any, and shall specify the names, addresses, and social security numbers of the parties to the support proceeding and the mailing address of the unit within the state department of social services designated to receive such deductions. The court shall transmit copies of such order to the parties and to such unit.

(2) An employer served with an income deduction order entered pursuant to this subdivision shall commence deductions from the income due or thereafter due to the debtor no later than the first pay period that occurs fourteen days

after service of the income deduction order, and shall remit payments to the state department of social services pursuant to subdivision fourteen of section one hundred eleven-b of the social services law within ten days of the date that the debtor is paid. Each payment remitted by the employer shall be made payable to the creditor named in the order, and shall include the names, addresses, and social security numbers of the debtor and the creditor, and the date and the amount of each withholding of the debtor's income included in the payment. An employer shall be liable to the creditor for failure to deduct the amounts specified in the income deduction order, provided however that deduction by the employer of the amounts specified shall not relieve the debtor of the underlying obligation of support. If an employer shall fail to so pay the creditor, the creditor may commence a proceeding against the employer for accrued deductions, together with interest and reasonable attorney's fees. If the debtor's employment is terminated by resignation or dismissal at any time after service of the income deduction order, the order shall cease to have force and effect unless the debtor is reinstated or re-employed by the same employer. An employer must notify the creditor promptly when the debtor terminates employment and must provide the debtor's last address and the name and address of the debtor's new employer, if known. Where the income is compensation paid or payable to the debtor for personal services, the amount withheld by the employer shall not exceed the following:

(i) Where the debtor currently is supporting a spouse or dependent child other than the creditor's dependent child, the amount withheld shall not exceed fifty percent of the earnings of the debtor remaining after the deduction therefrom of any amounts required by law to be withheld ("disposable earnings"), except that if any part of the deduction is to be applied to the reduction of arrears which shall have accrued more than twelve weeks prior to the beginning of the week for which such earnings are payable, the amount withheld shall not exceed fifty-five percent of disposable earnings.

(ii) Where the debtor currently is not supporting a spouse or dependent child other than the creditor's dependent child, the amount withheld shall not exceed sixty percent of the earnings of the debtor remaining after the deduction therefrom of any amounts required by law to be withheld ("disposable earnings"), except that if any part of the deduction is to be applied to the reduction of arrears which shall have accrued more than twelve weeks prior to the beginning of the week for which such earnings are payable, the amount withheld shall not exceed sixty-five percent of disposable earnings.

(d) An order pursuant to this section shall take priority over any other assignment, levy or process. If an employer or income payor is served with more than one income deduction order pertaining to a single employee pursuant to this section, or with an order issued pursuant to this section and also an execution pursuant to section 5241 of this chapter, and if the combined total amount of the income to be withheld exceeds the limits set forth in subdivision (c) of this

CPLR

section, the employer or income payor shall withhold the maximum amount permitted thereby and pay to each creditor that proportion thereof which such creditor's claim bears to the combined total.

(e) An employer or income payor shall be liable to the creditor for failure to deduct the amounts specified, provided however that deduction of the amounts specified by the employer or income payor shall not relieve the debtor of the underlying obligation of support.

(f) A creditor shall not be required to issue process under section 5241 of this article prior to obtaining relief pursuant to this section.

(g) Where the court issues an income deduction order for support enforcement payable to the support collection unit, as defined in paragraph nine of subdivision (a) of section 5241 of this article, each payment remitted by an employer or income payor shall include, in addition to the identity and social security number of the debtor, the date and amount of each withholding of the debtor's income included in the payment.

### 1994 AMENDMENTS

L. 1994, ch. 170, eff. June 15, 1994, amended CPLR 5242 by adding a new subdivision (c) authorizing the court to issue an income deduction order in certain cases, based upon a determination that the respondent earns wages in New York and that enforcement may not otherwise be available; by renumbering former subdivisions (c) through (f) to become subdivisions (d) through (g); and by adding to subdivision (d) all of the language after the initial sentence, providing that if multiple support enforcement orders are served, whether pursuant to CPLR 5241, CPLR 5242 or both, the employer shall deduct the maximum amount authorized and distribute the deduction to each creditor in proportion to the amount of that creditor's claim.

### 1990 AMENDMENTS

L. 1990, ch. 818, eff. Sept. 30, 1990, amended CPLR 5242 by adding subdivision (f).

### 1987 AMENDMENTS

L. 1987, ch. 815, eff. Aug. 7, 1987, and applicable to any action or proceeding commenced on or after such date, added new subd. (e), which provides that a creditor is not required to issue process under CPLR 5241 before obtaining relief under CPLR 5242.

### 1985 AMENDMENTS

L. 1985, ch. 809, eff. Nov. 1, 1985, added CPLR 5242.

## §§ 5243-5249.   [Not used.]

## § 5250.   Arrest of judgment debtor.

Upon motion of the judgment creditor without notice, where it is shown that the judgment debtor is about to depart from the state, or keeps himself concealed therein, and that there is reason to believe that he has in his possession or custody property in which he has an interest, the court may issue a warrant directed to the sheriff of any county in which the judgment debtor may be located. The warrant shall command the sheriff to arrest the judgment debtor forthwith and bring him before the court. The sheriff shall serve a copy of the warrant and the papers upon which it was based upon the judgment debtor at the time he makes the arrest. When the judgment debtor is brought before the court, the court may order that he give an undertaking, in a sum to be fixed by the court, that he will attend before the court for examination and that he will obey the terms of any restraining notice contained in the order.

### CROSS REFERENCES

See selected provisions governing procedures to punish for contempt under **Judiciary Law, Article 19,** in Appendix, *infra.*

## § 5251. Disobedience of subpoena, restraining notice or order; false swearing; destroying notice of sale.

Refusal or willful neglect of any person to obey a subpoena or restraining notice issued, or order granted, pursuant to this title; false swearing upon an examination or in answering written questions; and willful defacing or removal of a posted notice of sale before the time fixed for the sale, shall each be punishable as a contempt of court.

### CROSS REFERENCES

See selected provisions governing procedures to punish for contempt under **Judiciary Law, Article 19,** in Appendix, *infra.*

### 1965 AMENDMENTS

L. 1965, ch. 773, eff. Sept. 1, 1965, amended the section.

## § 5252. Discrimination against employees and prospective employees based upon wage assignment or income execution.

1. No employer shall discharge, lay off or discipline an employee or refuse to hire a prospective employee because one or more wage assignments or income executions have been served upon such employer or a former employer against the employee's or prospective employee's wages or because of the pendency of any action or judgment against such employee or prospective employee for nonpayment of any alleged contractual obligation.

2. An employee or prospective employee may institute a civil action for damages for wages lost as a result of a violation of this section within ninety days after such violation. Damages recoverable shall not exceed lost wages for six weeks and in such action the court also may order the reinstatement of such discharged employee or the hiring of such prospective employee. Except as provided for in subdivision (g) of section fifty-two hundred forty-one, not more than ten per centum of the damages recovered in such action shall be subject

CPLR

to any claims, attachments or executions by any creditors, judgment creditors or assignees of such employee or prospective employee. A violation of this section may also be punished as a contempt of court pursuant to the provisions of section seven hundred fifty-three of the judiciary law.

### 1985 AMENDMENTS

L. 1985, ch. 809 eff. Nov. 1, 1985, amended CPLR 5252 to apply to prospective employees, to cross refer to CPLR 5241(g) governing the maximum amount deductible for support enforcement, and to make violation of the section punishable as a contempt of court.

### 1977 AMENDMENTS

L. 1977, ch. 344, eff. Jan. 1, 1978, amended CPLR 5252 by adding the provision to subd. (1) prohibiting discharge of an employee because of pendency of action or judgment against such employee for nonpayment of a contractual obligation.

### 1974 AMENDMENTS

L. 1974, ch. 981, eff. Sept. 1, 1974, amended subd. (1) of section 5252 by inserting the reference to "one or more wage assignments" and by prohibiting an employer from discharging or laying off an employee because income "executions" have been served upon the employer against the employee's wages. Previously the section referred to "an income execution" in the singular. In addition the word "employees'" was amended to read "employee's."

Prior to the enactment of chapter 981 of the L. of 1974, ch. 753 of the L. of 1974, eff. Sept. 1, 1974, provided for a more limited amendment of CPLR 5252 by inserting a reference to a "wage assignment" and by changing the word "employees' " to read "employee's." The provisions of chapter 753 of the Laws of 1974 pertaining to CPLR 5252 have been superseded by the provisions of chapter 981 of the Laws of 1974.

### 1969 AMENDMENTS

L. 1969, ch. 1138, eff. May 26, 1969, amended paragraph (1) by deleting "provided, however, that this provision shall not apply if more than one income execution against such employee is served upon the employer within any period of twelve consecutive months after January first, nineteen hundred sixty-seven."

### 1966 AMENDMENTS

L. 1966, ch. 613, eff. Jan. 1, 1967, added new section 5252.

# ARTICLE 53

# RECOGNITION OF FOREIGN COUNTRY
# MONEY JUDGMENTS

---

## SUMMARY OF ARTICLE

§ 5301.  Definitions.
    (a)  Foreign state.
    (b)  Foreign country judgment.
§ 5302.  Applicability.
§ 5303.  Recognition and enforcement.
§ 5304.  Grounds for non-recognition.
    (a)  No recognition.
    (b)  Other grounds for non-recognition.
§ 5305.  Personal jurisdiction.
    (a)  Bases of jurisdiction.
    (b)  Other bases of jurisdiction.
§ 5306.  Stay in case of appeal.
§ 5307.  Recognition in other situations.
§ 5308.  Uniformity of interpretation.
§ 5309.  Citation.

---

## § 5301.  Definitions.

As used in this article the following definitions shall be applicable.

(a) Foreign state. "Foreign state" in this article means any governmental unit other than the United States, or any state, district, commonwealth, territory, insular possession thereof, or the Panama Canal Zone or the Trust Territory of the Pacific Islands.

(b) Foreign country judgment. "Foreign country judgment" in this article means any judgment of a foreign state granting or denying recovery of a sum of money, other than a judgment for taxes, a fine or other penalty, or a judgment for support in matrimonial or family matters.

### 1979 AMENDMENTS

L. 1979, ch. 119. eff. Jan. 1, 1980, amended CPLR 5301 subd. (a) by eliminating the Ryukyu Islands from the list of exceptions to the term "foreign state". The exception was once appropriate, when the Ryukyu Islands were under the treaty control of the United States. However, they were returned to Japan in 1972.

## 1970 AMENDMENTS

L. 1970, ch. 981, eff. Sept. 1, 1970, added new Article 53 (CPLR 5301-5309) concerning the recognition of foreign country money judgments.

The new Article 53 was recommended by the Judicial Conference Jan. 2, 1970 Report to the Legislature wherein it was stated:

"This bill would insert into the CPLR a new Article 53 entitled Recognition of Foreign Country Money Judgments'. This would in effect, incorporate in New York law the Ùniform Foreign Money-Judgments Recognition Act' which has already been adopted by seven states, among them California and Illinois. . . .

*"The basic purpose of this proposal is to procure for New York judgments in foreign countries much better reciprocal treatment at the hands of foreign courts than they now receive.* The lack of recognition of New York judgments in foreign countries stems frequently from the fact that many foreign countries of civil law background do not accept *decisional* law as proof that New York treats foreign judgments liberally, but they rather require *statutory* proof of this fact. It is the opinion of experts in the field of international litigation that this codifying legislation would answer the reciprocity requirements of many foreign countries and would therefore result in obtaining better treatment for New York citizens engaged in litigation abroad.

"The Uniform Act codifies, rather than reforms, existing decisional law in New York and other states respecting the recognition of foreign country judgments. Indeed, New York's standards of recognition are even more liberal than those prescribed by the Uniform Act. The liberal tendency of New York courts in respect to the recognition of foreign country judgments is reflected in a long line of cases. Two such examples are *Coudenhove-Kalergi v. Dieterle* (36 N.Y.S.2d 313; Sup. Ct. 1942) wherein the New York court recognized an award of an arbitration tribunal in Germany over the objection that this was not a final judgment of a court of record and *Regierungspraesident Land Nordrheim Westfolen v. Rosenthal* (17 A.D.2d 145, 232 N.Y.S.2d 963; 1962) wherein the New York court enforced a revocation award of a German administrative tribunal. Neither of these decisions would be authorized by the provisions of Article 53 but neither would be overruled by this Article since they represent an aspect of decisional law more liberal than Article 53 and the New York courts would be free to exceed Article 53 in liberality if they should so choose under a saving clause contained in the draft statute.

"Article 53 as proposed would be applicable only to judgments of foreign countries and not to judgments of United States courts or sister-state courts. Only money judgments would be recognizable under the proposed article and only those which are final, conclusive and enforceable where rendered. Qualifying foreign country judgments would be enforceable by the procedures presently provided in the CPLR for the enforcement of judgments (action on the judgment or motion for summary judgment in lieu of complaint).

"A foreign country judgment under this bill, *would be refused* recognition in New York if the judgment was rendered under a system which does not provide impartial tribunals or procedures compatible with the requirements of due process, or if the foreign court did not have personal jurisdiction over the defendants. In addition, the New York court, in its discretion, *could refuse* recognition in a wide variety of instances specified in the bill and conforming to present case law.

"Provision is also made for a stay of the New York proceedings if an appeal is pending in the foreign country."

## § 5302. Applicability.

This article applies to any foreign country judgment which is final, conclusive and enforceable where rendered even though an appeal therefrom is pending or it is subject to appeal.

## § 5303. Recognition and enforcement.

Except as provided in section 5304, a foreign country judgment meeting the requirements of section 5302 is conclusive between the parties to the extent that it grants or denies recovery of a sum of money. Such a foreign judgment is enforceable by an action on the judgment, a motion for summary judgment in lieu of complaint, or in a pending action by counterclaim, cross-claim or affirmative defense.

## § 5304. Grounds for non-recognition.

(a) No recognition. A foreign country judgment is not conclusive if:

1. the judgment was rendered under a system which does not provide impartial tribunals or procedures compatible with the requirements of due process of law;

2. the foreign court did not have personal jurisdiction over the defendant.

(b) Other grounds for non-recognition. A foreign country judgment need not be recognized if:

1. the foreign court did not have jurisdiction over the subject matter;

2. the defendant in the proceedings in the foreign court did not receive notice of the proceedings in sufficient time to enable him to defend;

3. the judgment was obtained by fraud;

4. the cause of action on which the judgment is based is repugnant to the public policy of this state;

5. the judgment conflicts with another final and conclusive judgment;

6. the proceeding in the foreign court was contrary to an agreement between the parties under which the dispute in question was to be settled otherwise than by proceedings in that court; or

7. in the case of jurisdiction based only on personal service, the foreign court was a seriously inconvenient forum for the trial of the action.

## § 5305. Personal jurisdiction.

(a) Bases of jurisdiction. The foreign country judgment shall not be refused recognition for lack of personal jurisdiction if:

1. the defendant was served personally in the foreign state;

CPLR

2. the defendant voluntarily appeared in the proceedings, other than for the purpose of protecting property seized or threatened with seizure in the proceedings or of contesting the jurisdiction of the court over him;

3. the defendant prior to the commencement of the proceedings had agreed to submit to the jurisdiction of the foreign court with respect to the subject matter involved;

4. the defendant was domiciled in the foreign state when the proceedings were instituted, or, being a body corporate had its principal place of business, was incorporated, or had otherwise acquired corporate status, in the foreign state;

5. the defendant had a business office in the foreign state and the proceedings in the foreign court involved a cause of action arising out of business done by the defendant through that office in the foreign state; or

6. the defendant operated a motor vehicle or airplane in the foreign state and the proceedings involved a cause of action arising out of such operation.

(b) Other bases of jurisdiction. The courts of this state may recognize other bases of jurisdiction.

### § 5306. Stay in case of appeal.

If the defendant satisfies the court either that an appeal is pending or that he is entitled and intends to appeal from the foreign country judgment, the court may stay the proceedings until the appeal has been determined or until the expiration of a period of time sufficient to enable the defendant to prosecute the appeal.

### § 5307. Recognition in other situations.

This article does not prevent the recognition of a foreign country judgment in situations not covered by this article.

### § 5308. Uniformity of interpretation.

This article shall be so construed as to effectuate its general purpose to make uniform the law of those states which enact these provisions.

### § 5309. Citation.

This article may be cited as the "Uniform Foreign Country Money-Judgments Recognition Act."

# ARTICLE 54

# ENFORCEMENT OF JUDGMENTS
# ENTITLED TO FULL FAITH AND CREDIT

## SUMMARY OF ARTICLE

§ 5401.   Definition.
§ 5402.   Filing and status of foreign judgments.
    (a)  Filing.
    (b)  Status of foreign judgments.
§ 5403.   Notice of filing.
§ 5404.   Stay.
    (a)  Based upon security in foreign jurisdiction.
    (b)  Based upon other grounds.
§ 5405.   Fees.
§ 5406.   Optional procedure.
§ 5407.   Uniformity of interpretation.
§ 5408.   Citation.

**CPLR**

## § 5401.  Definition.

In this article "foreign judgment" means any judgment, decree, or order of a court of the United States or of any other court which is entitled to full faith and credit in this state, except one obtained by default in appearance, or by confession of judgment.

### 1970 AMENDMENTS

L. 1970, ch. 982, eff. Sept. 1, 1970, added new Article 54 (CPLR 5401-5408) concerning the enforcement of judgments entitled to full faith and credit.

The new Article 54 was recommended by the Judicial Conference Jan. 2, 1970, Report to the Legislature wherein it was stated in part: "This proposal would insert into the CPLR a new Article 54, captioned Ènforcement of Judgments Entitled to Full Faith and Credit'. It would thereby incorporate into the law of New York the major features of the 1964 Uniform Enforcement of Foreign Judgments Act, recommended for adoption in New York in a study prepared for the Judicial Conference by Professor Barbara Kulzer of the State University of New York at Buffalo (now of Rutgers University School of Law), published in the *Thirteenth Annual Report of the Judicial Conference* (1968). The terms Ỳoreign judgment' and Àmerican judgment' as used in this discussion to describe the scope of this bill are identical in meaning; they include judgments of courts of states of the United States and courts in the Federal jurisdiction; they *do not* include judgments of courts of foreign countries. . . .

"Article 54 would provide a registration procedure for the enforcement of American judgments. This procedure is similar to that used in the Federal District Courts for the registration of federal judgments for money or property (28 U.S.C. § 1963) and is based upon the 1964 Uniform Enforcement of Foreign Judgments Act. *However, it is more conservative in its approach than the Uniform Act. The Uniform Act would apply to default and consent judgments. Article 54 would expressly exclude default and consent judgments from its scope.*

"The purpose of this bill is to cure a procedural defect in our law in respect to the modes of enforcement of American judgments which has been criticized by legal writers for upwards of 40 years and which has led to the enactment of 28 U.S.C. § 1963 for federal courts, and to the drafting of the 1948 Uniform Enforcement of Foreign Judgments Act as well as the revised 1964 Uniform Enforcement of Foreign Judgments Act for state courts. Proposed Article 54 is designed to provide for American judgments, *aside from default and consent judgments*, which are sought to be enforced in New York, the simpler, speedier and less expensive method of enforcement which is now available in the Federal system for the enforcement of judgments of United States district courts. It is comparable to registration systems now in successful operation in Canada and Australia. The Uniform Act has been adopted by seven sister states.

"Proposed Article 54 would establish a procedure whereby a copy of any foreign judgment entitled to full faith and credit and not rendered by default or by consent, if properly authenticated, could be filed within 90 days of authentication in the office of any county clerk. The clerk, under the proposed Article, would treat the foreign judgment in the same manner as a judgment of the Supreme Court of this state. A judgment so filed would have the same effect and be subject to the same procedures, defenses and proceedings for reopening, vacating, or staying as a judgment of the Supreme Court of this state and could be enforced or satisfied in like manner. The Article would permit the court to stay enforcement for good cause shown.

"The right of a judgment creditor to proceed by an action on the judgment or a motion for summary judgment in lieu of complaint instead of proceeding under this Article remains unimpaired.

"The success of the Federal courts in working with a registration enforcement procedure very similar to that here proposed indicates the practicality and desirability of this proposal. It should be necessary as a matter of equity only to ensure that a defendant has his full day in court. If he has his full day in court in one state, it should be unnecessary, in a federal system such as ours, especially in view of our full faith and credit concepts, that he be given another full day in court in every state where the winning plaintiff attempts to enforce his judgment. Indeed, the present procedures are most inequitable to the plaintiff who has fairly won his case against a defendant whose properties happen to be located in other states. This proposal is more extensively discussed in the CPLR Report of the Judicial Conference to the 1969 Legislature.

. . . .

"The bill . . . contains a provision for notice of registration to the judgment debtor. More specifically, the notice provision would require that within 30 days after the filing of the judgment and the affidavit, the judgment creditor shall mail notice of filing of the foreign judgment to the judgment debtor at his last known address and, while execution may issue immediately, the proceeds of the execution shall not be distributed to the judgment creditor earlier than 30 days after filing of proof of service. . . . [The] notice by mail . . . is timed so that normally it will not interfere with the judgment creditor's collection efforts; yet it will alert the judgment debtor to the filing of the judgment and enable him to raise objections before distribution of the proceeds of an execution. Notice will also enable the judgment debtor to ensure the discharge of a registered judgment if he satisfies the judgment without being aware of the registration."

## § 5402.    Filing and status of foreign judgments.

(a) Filing. A copy of any foreign judgment authenticated in accordance with an act of congress or the statutes of this state may be filed within ninety days of the date of authentication in the office of any county clerk of the state. The judgment creditor shall file with the judgment an affidavit stating that the judgment was not obtained by default in appearance or by confession of judgment, that it is unsatisfied in whole or in part, the amount remaining unpaid, and that its enforcement has not been stayed, and setting forth the name and last known address of the judgment debtor.

(b) Status of foreign judgments. The clerk shall treat the foreign judgment in the same manner as a judgment of the supreme court of this state. A judgment so filed has the same effect and is subject to the same procedures, defenses and proceedings for reopening, vacating, or staying as a judgment of the supreme court of this state and may be enforced or satisfied in like manner.

## § 5403.    Notice of filing.

Within thirty days after filing of the judgment and the affidavit, the judgment creditor shall mail notice of filing of the foreign judgment to the judgment debtor at his last known address. The proceeds of an execution shall not be distributed to the judgment creditor earlier than thirty days after filing of proof of service.

## § 5404.    Stay.

(a) Based upon security in foreign jurisdiction. If the judgment debtor shows the supreme court that an appeal from the foreign judgment is pending or will be taken, or that a stay of execution has been granted, the court shall stay enforcement of the foreign judgment until the appeal is concluded, the time for appeal expires, or the stay of execution expires or is vacated, upon proof that the judgment debtor has furnished the security for the satisfaction of the judgment required by the state in which it was rendered.

(b) Based upon other grounds. If the judgment debtor shows the supreme court any ground upon which enforcement of a judgment of the supreme court of this state would be stayed, the court shall stay enforcement of the foreign judgment for an appropriate period, upon requiring the same security for satisfaction of the judgment which is required in this state.

CPLR

## § 5405.   Fees.

When a foreign judgment is filed pursuant to this article, an index number shall be assigned in accordance with the provisions of subdivision (a) of section 8018 and the fee shall be as prescribed therein.

## § 5406.   Optional procedure.

The right of a judgment creditor to proceed by an action on the judgment or a motion for summary judgment in lieu of complaint, instead of proceeding under this article, remains unimpaired.

## § 5407.   Uniformity of interpretation.

This article shall be so construed as to effectuate its general purpose to make uniform the law of those states which enact these provisions.

## § 5408.   Citation.

This article may be cited as the "Uniform Enforcement of Foreign Judgments Act."

# ARTICLE 55

# APPEALS GENERALLY

---

## SUMMARY OF ARTICLE

§ 5501.    Scope of review.
    (a)   Generally, from final judgment.
    (b)   Court of appeals.
    (c)   Appellate division.
    (d)   Appellate term.

§§ 5502–5510.   [Not used.]

§ 5511.    Permissible appellant and respondent.

§ 5512.    Appealable paper; entry of order made out of court.
    (a)   Appealable paper.
    (b)   Entry of order made out of court.

§ 5513.    Time to take appeal, cross-appeal or move for permission to appeal.
    (a)   Time to take appeal as of right.
    (b)   Time to move for permission to appeal.
    (c)   Additional time where adverse party takes appeal or moves for permission to appeal.

§ 5514.    Extension of time to take appeal or to move for permission to appeal.
    (a)   Alternate method of appeal.
    (b)   Disability of attorney.
    (c)   Other extensions of time; substitutions or omissions.

§ 5515.    Taking an appeal; notice of appeal.

R 5516.    Motion for permission to appeal.

§ 5517.    Subsequent orders.
    (a)   Appeal not affected by certain subsequent orders.
    (b)   Review of subsequent orders.

§ 5518.    Preliminary injunction or temporary restraining order by appellate division.

§ 5519.    Stay of enforcement.
    (a)   Stay without court order.
    (b)   Stay in action defended by insurer.
    (c)   Stay and limitation of stay by court order.
    (d)   Undertaking.
    (e)   Continuation of stay.
    (f)   Proceedings after stay.
    (g)   Appeals in medical, dental or podiatric malpractice judgments.

§ 5520.    Omissions; appeal by improper method.
    (a)   Omissions.
    (b)   Appeal by permission instead of as of right.
    (c)   Defects in form.

R 5521.    Preferences.
R 5522.    Disposition of appeal.
§ 5523.    Restitution.
R 5524.    Entry of order; remittitur and further proceedings.
   (a) Entry of order in appellate court.
   (b) Remittitur and further proceedings.
R 5525.    Preparation and settlement of transcript; statement in lieu of transcript.
   (a) Preparation of transcript.
   (b) Omission of part of transcript.
   (c) Settlement of transcript.
   (d) Statement in lieu of stenographic transcript.
   (e) Special rules prescribing time limitations in settlement of transcript or statement in lieu thereof authorized.
R 5526.    Content and form of record on appeal.
R 5527.    Statement in lieu of record on appeal.
R 5528.    Content of briefs and appendices.
   (a) Appellant's brief and appendix.
   (b) Respondent's brief and appendix.
   (c) Appellant's reply brief and appendix.
   (d) Joint appendix.
   (e) Sanction.
R 5529.    Form of briefs and appendices.
   (a) Form of reproduction; size; paper; binding.
   (b) Numbering.
   (c) Page headings.
   (d) Quotations.
   (e) Citations of decisions.
   (f) Questions and answers.
R 5530.    Filing record and briefs; service of briefs.
   (a) Generally.
   (b) Upon cross-appeal.
   (c) Special rules prescribing times for filing and serving authorized.
R 5531.    Description of action.
R 5532.    Stipulation in lieu of certification.

---

## § 5501.  Scope of review.

(a) Generally, from final judgment. An appeal from a final judgment brings up for review:

1. any non-final judgment or order which necessarily affects the final judgment, including any which was adverse to the respondent on the appeal from the final judgment and which, if reversed, would entitle the respondent to prevail in whole or in part on that appeal, provided that such non-final judgment or order has not previously been reviewed by the court to which the appeal is taken;

2. any order denying a new trial or hearing which has not previously been reviewed by the court to which the appeal is taken;

3. any ruling to which the appellant objected or had no opportunity to object or which was a refusal or failure to act as requested by the appellant, and any charge to the jury, or failure or refusal to charge as requested by the appellant, to which he objected;

4. any remark made by the judge to which the appellant objected; and

5. a verdict after a trial by jury as of right, when the final judgment was entered in a different amount pursuant to the respondent's stipulation on a motion to set aside the verdict as excessive or inadequate; the appellate court may increase such judgment to a sum not exceeding the verdict or reduce it to a sum not less than the verdict.

(b) Court of appeals. The court of appeals shall review questions of law only, except that it shall also review questions of fact where the appellate division, on reversing or modifying a final or interlocutory judgment, has expressly or impliedly found new facts and a final judgment pursuant thereto is entered. On an appeal pursuant to subdivision (d) of section fifty-six hundred one, or subparagraph (ii) of paragraph one of subdivision (a) of section fifty-six hundred two, or subparagraph (ii) of paragraph two of subdivision (b) of section fifty-six hundred two, only the non-final determination of the appellate division shall be reviewed.

(c) Appellate division. The appellate division shall review questions of law and questions of fact on an appeal from a judgment or order of a court of original instance and on an appeal from an order of the supreme court, a county court or an appellate term determining an appeal. In reviewing a money judgment in an action in which an itemized verdict is required by rule forty-one hundred eleven of this chapter in which it is contended that the award is excessive or inadequate and that a new trial should have been granted unless a stipulation is entered to a different award, the appellate division shall determine that an award is excessive or inadequate if it deviates materially from what would be reasonable compensation.

(d) Appellate term. The appellate term shall review questions of law and questions of fact.

CPLR

### CROSS REFERENCES

See **N.Y. Const., Art. VI, §§ 3** (Court of appeals), **5** (Appellate courts generally), **8** (Appellate term) and **11** (Appellate jurisdiction of county courts), in Appendix, *infra.*

### 1988 AMENDMENTS

L. 1988, ch. 184, eff. July 1, 1988, amending L. 1986, ch. 682, to make subdivision (c) applicable to all actions in which trial has not begun as of August 1, 1988.

**1986 AMENDMENTS**

L. 1986, ch. 682, eff. July 30, 1986 and applicable to actions commenced or claims filed on or after such date, amended CPLR 5501(c) by adding provisions relating to review of money judgments in actions in which an itemized verdict is required and it is contended that the award is excessive or inadequate.

## §§ 5502-5510. [Not used.]

## § 5511. Permissible appellant and respondent.

An aggrieved party or a person substituted for him may appeal from any appealable judgment or order except one entered upon the default of the aggrieved party. He shall be designated as the appellant and the adverse party as the respondent.

## § 5512. Appealable paper; entry of order made out of court.

(a) Appealable paper. An initial appeal shall be taken from the judgment or order of the court of original instance and an appeal seeking review of an appellate determination shall be taken from the order entered in the office of the clerk of the court whose order is sought to be reviewed. If a timely appeal is taken from a judgment or order other than that specified in the last sentence and no prejudice results therefrom and the proper paper is furnished to the court to which the appeal is taken, the appeal shall be deemed taken from the proper judgment or order.

(b) Entry of order made out of court. Entry of an order made out of court and filing of the papers on which the order was granted may be compelled by order of the court from or to which an appeal from the order might be taken.

## § 5513.* Time to take appeal, cross-appeal or move for permission to appeal.

(a) Time to take appeal as of right. An appeal as of right must be taken within thirty days after service by a party upon the appellant of a copy of the judgment or order appealed from and written notice of its entry, except that when the appellant has served a copy of the judgment or order and written notice of its entry, the appeal must be taken within thirty days thereof.

(b) Time to move for permission to appeal. The time within which a motion for permission to appeal must be made shall be computed from the date of service by a party upon the party seeking permission of a copy of the judgment or order to be appealed from and written notice of its entry, or, where permission has already been denied by order of the court whose determination is sought to be reviewed, of a copy of such order and written notice of its entry, except that when such party seeking permission to appeal has served a copy of such judgment or order and written notice of its entry, the time shall be computed from the date of such service. A motion for permission to appeal must be made within thirty days.

(c) Additional time where adverse party takes appeal or moves for permission to appeal. A party upon whom the adverse party has served a notice of appeal or motion papers on a motion for permission to appeal may take an appeal or make a motion for permission to appeal within ten days after such service or within the time limited by subdivision (a) or (b) of this section, whichever is longer, if such appeal or motion is otherwise available to such party.

* [**Editor's note:** This version of § 5513 is effective as of January 1, 1997. Through December 31, 1996, former § 5513 remains in effect. It reads as follows:

(a) Time to take appeal as of right. An appeal as of right must be taken within thirty days after service upon the appellant of a copy of the judgment or order appealed from and written notice of its entry, except that when the appellant has served a copy of the judgment or order and written notice of its entry, his appeal must be taken within thirty days thereof.

(b) Time to move for permission to appeal. The time within which a motion for permission to appeal must be made shall be computed from the date of service upon the party seeking permission of a copy of the judgment or order to be appealed from and written notice of its entry, or, where permission has already been denied by order of the court whose determination is sought to be reviewed, of a copy of such order and written notice of its entry, except that when such party has served a copy of such judgment or order and written notice of its entry, the time shall be computed from the date of such service. A motion for permission to appeal must be made within thirty days.

(c) Additional time where adverse party takes appeal or moves for permission to appeal. A party upon whom the adverse party has served a notice of appeal or motion papers on a motion for permission to appeal may take an appeal or make a motion for permission to appeal within ten days after such service or within the time limited by subdivision (a) or (b) of this section, whichever is longer, if such appeal or motion is otherwise available to him.]

### 1996 AMENDMENTS

L. 1996, ch. 214, eff. Jan. 1, 1997, amended subdivisions (a) and (b) by adding the phrase "by a party"; further amended subdivision (b) by adding the phrase "seeking permission to appeal"; and made the section gender neutral.

### 1977 AMENDMENTS

L. 1977, ch. 30, eff. Sept. 1, 1977, repealed former subdivision (b) governing the time to take a cross-appeal and relettered former subdivision (c), governing time to move for permission to appeal, to be subdivision (b). The matter repealed in former subdivision (b) is now covered in new subdivision (c) enacted by L. 1977, ch. 30, eff. Sept. 1, 1977.

The effect of the amendment is to specifically provide that the ten-day minimal period for cross-appeal be applicable in those instances where either the appeal or the cross-appeal, or both, are made by motion for permission to appeal, and that such ten-day period not be limited to instances where the appeal or cross-appeal is taken as of right.

CPLR

### 1970 AMENDMENTS

L. 1970, ch. 108, eff. Sept. 1, 1970, amended Subd. (a) to provide that when an appellant has served a copy of the judgment or order and written notice of its entry, his appeal must be taken within thirty days thereof; amended Subd. (c) [now (b)] to provide that when a party seeking permission to appeal has served a copy of the judgment or order and written notice of its entry, the time to appeal shall be computed from the date of such service.

## § 5514.   Extension of time to take appeal or to move for permission to appeal.

(a) Alternate method of appeal. If an appeal is taken or a motion for permission to appeal is made and such appeal is dismissed or motion is denied and, except for time limitations in section 5513, some other method of taking an appeal or of seeking permission to appeal is available, the time limited for such other method shall be computed from the dismissal or denial unless the court to which the appeal is sought to be taken orders otherwise.

(b) Disability of attorney. If the attorney for an aggrieved party dies, is removed or suspended, or becomes physically or mentally incapacitated or otherwise disabled before the expiration of the time limited for taking an appeal or moving for permission to appeal without having done so, such appeal may be taken or such motion for permission to appeal may be served within sixty days from the date of death, removal or suspension, or commencement of such incapacity or disability.

(c) Other extensions of time; substitutions or omissions. No extension of time shall be granted for taking an appeal or for moving for permission to appeal except as provided in this section, section 1022, or section 5520.

## § 5515.   Taking an appeal; notice of appeal.

1. An appeal shall be taken by serving on the adverse party a notice of appeal and filing it in the office where the judgment or order of the court of original instance is entered except that where an order granting permission to appeal is made, the appeal is taken when such order is entered. A notice shall designate the party taking the appeal, the judgment or order or specific part of the judgment or order appealed from and the court to which the appeal is taken.

2. Whenever an appeal is taken to the court of appeals, a copy of the notice of appeal shall be sent forthwith to the clerk of the court of appeals by the clerk of the office where the notice of appeal is required to be filed pursuant to this section.

3. Where leave to appeal to the court of appeals is granted by permission of the appellate division, a copy of the order granting such permission to appeal shall be sent forthwith to the clerk of the court of appeals by the clerk of the appellate division.

### 1975 AMENDMENTS

L. 1975, ch. 491, eff. Aug. 28, 1975, amended the first paragraph by designating it Subd. (1), and adding new Subds. (2) and (3), requiring the clerk of the court of original instance, or the Appellate Division Clerk, to forward to the Court of Appeals Clerk a copy of the notice of appeal, or the order granting permission to appeal.

## R 5516. Motion for permission to appeal.

A motion for permission to appeal shall be noticed to be heard at a motion day at least eight days and not more than fifteen days after notice of the motion is served, unless there is no motion day during that period, in which case at the first motion day thereafter.

### 1978 AMENDMENTS

L. 1978, ch. 209, eff. June 2, 1978, amended CPLR 5516 by adoption of proposals made by the Judicial Conference in its Report to the 1978 Legislature, in which it stated:

"CPLR 5516, which governs motions for permission to appeal, and which now provides that such motion shall be noticed to be heard àt the next motion day more than seven days' after the notice is served, would be amended to provide instead that such motions shall be noticed to be heard àt least eight days and not more than fifteen days' after the notice is served. The proposed amendment would clarify the rule so as to assure avoidance of potential problems.

"The phrase more than seven days' means the same as àt least eight days' and therefore a motion under CPLR 5516 served by mail must be made on 11 days' notice, pursuant to CPLR 2103(b)(2) which provides, *inter alia*, that where a period of time prescribed by law is measured from the service of a paper and service is by mail, three days shall be added to the prescribed period.'

"The wording of CPLR 5516, however, could easily be misread by the practitioner to result in the addition of 3 days to 7 days in the instance of service by mail. This would result in a jurisdictionally defective motion (*see* 7 Weinstein, Korn & Miller, New York Civil Practice - CPLR ¶ 5516.01 (Matthew Bender)).

"The difficulty is complicated by the fact that CPLR 5516 requires a motion for permission to appeal to be noticed to be heard àt the next motion day.' This phrase could be literally construed to mean that there is only one day on which such motion can be made returnable, rather than on any of the days specified in the rules of the appellate courts.

"The proposed change would allow the clerk to move the return date further ahead if necessary to prevent a jurisdictional defect, thus conforming the language to the intent of the draftsmen (*see* 7 Weinstein, Korn & Miller, New York Civil Practice - CPLR ¶ 5516.01(Matthew Bender))."

### 1968 AMENDMENTS

Proposal No. 3, eff. Sept. 1, 1968, made by the Judicial Conference Feb. 1, 1968, Report to the Legislature, inserted word "seven" in place of word "four."

## § 5517. Subsequent orders.

(a) Appeal not affected by certain subsequent orders. An appeal shall not be affected by:

1. the granting of a motion for reargument or the granting of an order upon reargument making the same or substantially the same determination as is made in the order appealed from; or

2. the granting of a motion for resettlement of the order appealed from; or

3. the denial of a motion, based on new or additional facts, for the same or substantially the same relief applied for in the motion on which the order appealed from was made.

(b) Review of subsequent orders. A court reviewing an order may also review any subsequent order made upon a motion specified in subdivision (a), if the subsequent order is appealable as of right.

## § 5518. Preliminary injunction or temporary restraining order by appellate division.

The appellate division may grant, modify or limit a preliminary injunction or temporary restraining order pending an appeal or determination of a motion for permission to appeal in any case specified in section 6301.

## § 5519. Stay of enforcement.

(a) Stay without court order. Service upon the adverse party of a notice of appeal or an affidavit of intention to move for permission to appeal stays all proceedings to enforce the judgment or order appealed from pending the appeal or determination on the motion for permission to appeal where:

1. the appellant or moving party is the state or any political subdivision of the state or any officer or agency of the state or of any political subdivision of the state; provided that where a court, after considering an issue specified in question four of section seventy-eight hundred three of this chapter, issues a judgment or order directing reinstatement of a license held by a corporation with no more than five stockholders and which employs no more than ten employees, a partnership with no more than five partners and which employs no more than ten employees, a proprietorship or a natural person, the stay provided for by this paragraph shall be for a period of fifteen days; or

2. the judgment or order directs the payment of a sum of money, and an undertaking in that sum is given that if the judgment or order appealed from, or any part of it, is affirmed, or the appeal is dismissed, the appellant or moving party shall pay the amount directed to be paid by the judgment or order, or the part of it as to which the judgment or order is affirmed; or

3. the judgment or order directs the payment of a sum of money, to be paid in fixed installments, and an undertaking in a sum fixed by the court of original instance is given that the appellant or moving party shall pay each installment which becomes due pending the appeal and that if the judgment or order appealed from, or any part of it, is affirmed, or the appeal is dismissed, the appellant

or moving party shall pay any installments or part of installments then due or the part of them as to which the judgment or order is affirmed; or

4. the judgment or order directs the assignment or delivery of personal property, and the property is placed in the custody of an officer designated by the court of original instance to abide the direction of the court to which the appeal is taken, or an undertaking in a sum fixed by the court of original instance is given that the appellant or moving party will obey the direction of the court to which the appeal is taken; or

5. the judgment or order directs the execution of any instrument, and the instrument is executed and deposited in the office where the original judgment or order is entered to abide the direction of the court to which the appeal is taken; or

6. the appellant or moving party is in possession or control of real property which the judgment or order directs be conveyed or delivered, and an undertaking in a sum fixed by the court of original instance is given that the appellant or moving party will not commit or suffer to be committed any waste and that if the judgment or order appealed from, or any part of it, is affirmed, or the appeal is dismissed, the appellant or moving party shall pay the value of the use and occupancy of such property, or the part of it as to which the judgment or order is affirmed, from the taking of the appeal until the delivery of possession of the property; if the judgment or order directs the sale of mortgaged property and the payment of any deficiency, the undertaking shall also provide that the appellant or moving party shall pay any such deficiency; or

7. the judgment or order directs the performance of two or more of the acts specified in subparagraphs two through six and the appellant or moving party complies with each applicable subparagraph.

(b) Stay in action defended by insurer. If an appeal is taken from a judgment or order entered against an insured in an action which is defended by an insurance corporation, or other insurer, on behalf of the insured under a policy of insurance the limit of liability of which is less than the amount of said judgment or order, all proceedings to enforce the judgment or order to the extent of the policy coverage shall be stayed pending the appeal, and no action shall be commenced or maintained against the insurer for payment under the policy pending the appeal, where the insurer:

1. files with the clerk of the court in which the judgment or order was entered a sworn statement of one of its officers, describing the nature of the policy and the amount of coverage together with a written undertaking that if the judgment or order appealed from, or any part of it, is affirmed, or the appeal is dismissed, the insurer shall pay the amount directed to be paid by the judgment or order, or the part of it as to which the judgment or order is affirmed, to the extent of the limit of liability in the policy, plus interest and costs;

2. serves a copy of such sworn statement and undertaking upon the judgment creditor or his attorney; and

**CPLR**

3. delivers or mails to the insured at the latest address of the insured appearing upon the records of the insurer, written notice that the enforcement of such judgment or order, to the extent that the amount it directs to be paid exceeds the limit of liability in the policy, is not stayed in respect to the insured. A stay of enforcement of the balance of the amount of the judgment or order may be imposed by giving an undertaking, as provided in paragraph two of subdivision (a), in an amount equal to that balance.

(c) Stay and limitation of stay by court order. The court from or to which an appeal is taken or the court of original instance may stay all proceedings to enforce the judgment or order appealed from pending an appeal or determination on a motion for permission to appeal in a case not provided for in subdivision (a) or subdivision (b), or may grant a limited stay or may vacate, limit or modify any stay imposed by subdivision (a), subdivision (b) or this subdivision, except that only the court to which an appeal is taken may vacate, limit or modify a stay imposed by paragraph one of subdivision (a).

(d) Undertaking. On an appeal from an order affirming a judgment or order, the undertaking shall secure both the order and the judgment or order which is affirmed.

(e) Continuation of stay. If the judgment or order appealed from is affirmed or modified, the stay shall continue for five days after service upon the appellant of the order of affirmance or modification with notice of its entry in the court to which the appeal was taken. If an appeal is taken or a motion is made for permission to appeal from such an order, before the expiration of the five days, the stay shall continue until five days after service of notice of the entry of the order determining such appeal or motion. When a motion for permission to appeal is involved, the stay, or any other stay granted pending determination of the motion for permission to appeal, shall:

(i) if the motion is granted, continue until five days after the appeal is determined; or

(ii) if the motion is denied, continue until five days after the movant is served with the order of denial with notice of its entry.

(f) Proceedings after stay. A stay of enforcement shall not prevent the court of original instance from proceeding in any matter not affected by the judgment or order appealed from or from directing the sale of perishable property.

(g) Appeals in medical, dental or podiatric malpractice judgments. In an action for medical, dental or podiatric malpractice, if an appeal is taken from a judgment in excess of one million dollars and an undertaking in the amount of one million dollars or the limit of insurance coverage available to the appellant for the occurrence, whichever is greater, is given together with a joint undertaking by the appellant and any insurer of the appellant's professional liability that, during the period of such stay, the appellant will make no fraudulent conveyance without fair consideration as described in section two hundred seventy-three-a of the debtor and creditor law, the court to which such an appeal is taken shall stay all proceedings to enforce the judgment pending such appeal if it finds that there is a reasonable probability that the judgment may be reversed or determined excessive. In making a determination under this subdivision, the court shall not consider the availability of a stay pursuant to subdivision (a) or (b) of this section. Liability under such joint undertaking shall be limited to fraudulent conveyances made by the appellant subsequent to the execution of such undertaking and during the period of such stay, but nothing herein shall limit the liability of the appellant for fraudulent conveyances pursuant to article ten of the debtor and creditor law or any other law. An insurer that pays money to a beneficiary of such a joint undertaking shall thereupon be subrogated, to the extent of the amount to be paid, to the rights and interests of such beneficiary, as a judgment creditor, against the appellant on whose behalf the joint undertaking was executed.

### 1988 AMENDMENTS

L. 1988, ch. 184, eff. July 1, 1988, added new subdivision (g) governing stays in large-verdict (*i.e.*, one million dollars and above) medical, dental, and podiatric malpractice actions. L. 1988, ch. 493, eff. Sept. 1, 1988, amended 5519(a) paragraph 1 to set at 15 days an automatic stay pending appeal by the state or a political subdivision or agency of the state, of an adverse decision in specified Article 78 proceedings.

### 1979 AMENDMENTS

L. 1979, ch. 239, eff. Jan. 1, 1980, amended CPLR 5519 subd. (e) by making certain stylistic changes and by clarifying the meaning of the statute with respect to procedures for continuation of a stay of proceedings where an appeal as of right is timely taken, or a timely motion is made for permission to take an appeal from an affirmance or modification of an order determining a prior appeal.

The Judicial Conference report on the CPLR to the 1979 Legislature stated that the statute, ". . . has been troublesome for lack of precision and because reference to motions for permission to appeal was not included . . .

"CPLR 5519(e) now provides for continuance of the stay after the determination of the first appeal, for five days from service upon the appellant of the notice of entry, in the court to which the first appeal was taken, of the order determining that appeal. Where an appeal is taken from such an order, the stay continues until determination of the appeal. *DFI Communications Inc. v. Greenberg*, 394 N.Y.S.2d 586, 41 N.Y.2d 1017, 363 N.E. 2d 312 (1977) held that a motion to continue the stay is unnecessary since the filing of the notice of appeal automatically continues the stay. CPLR 5519(e) would be clarified to reflect the decision by providing for such automatic continuation if the second appeal is taken within the designated 5-day period after the determination of the first appeal, except that the 5-day period would now be measured from service on appellant of the order of affirmation or modification as well as the notice of entry. It would also be provided that the stay continue until 5 days after determination of the appeal.

"CPLR 5519(e) would be further clarified by providing a similar mechanism to govern the continuation of a stay where a motion for permission to appeal is made. Absence of such specific provision has generated unnecessary applications in such cases for continuation of the stay until determination of the appeal (*Created*

*Gemstones, Inc. v. Union Carbide Corporation*, 408 N.Y.S.2d 507, 45 N.Y.2d 772, 380 N.E.2d 333 (1978)). Thus, where a motion for permission to appeal is made within the designated 5-day period, any stay would continue until the motion is granted or denied. If the motion is granted, whether or not the designated 5-day period has elapsed, the stay would continue until 5 days after the determination of the appeal. If the motion is denied, the stay would continue for 5 days after the movant is served with the order of denial with notice of its entry.

"The last sentence of CPLR 5519(e), which relates to the duration of any stay granted pending a motion for permission to appeal, would be stricken as unnecessary because of the proposed amendments."

### 1975 AMENDMENTS

L. 1975, ch. 70, eff. Sept. 1, 1975, upon the recommendation of the Judicial Conference, amended Subd. (e).

### 1965 AMENDMENTS

L. 1965, ch. 744, eff. Sept. 1, 1965, deleted the words "and the judgment or order directs either the payment of a sum of money, the assignment or delivery of personal property, or the conveyance of real property" in paragraph 1 of subdivision (a).

## § 5520. Omissions; appeal by improper method.

(a) Omissions. If an appellant either serves or files a timely notice of appeal or notice of motion for permission to appeal, but neglects through mistake or excusable neglect to do another required act within the time limited, the court from or to which the appeal is taken or the court of original instance may grant an extension of time for curing the omission.

(b) Appeal by permission instead of as of right. An appeal taken by permission shall not be dismissed upon the ground that the appeal would lie as of right and was not taken within the time limited for an appeal as of right, provided the motion for permission was made within the time limited for taking the appeal.

(c) Defects in form. Where a notice of appeal is premature or contains an inaccurate description of the judgment or order appealed from, the appellate court, in its discretion, when the interests of justice so demand, may treat such a notice as valid.

### 1979 AMENDMENTS

L. 1979, ch. 120, eff. Jan. 1, 1980, amended CPLR 5520 subd. (a) by ". . . supplying a missing reference therein to a notice of motion for permission to appeal . . .", the Judicial Conference Report on the CPLR to the 1979 Legislature stated. The report continued:

"CPLR 5520(a) provides that the court of original instance or the court from or to which an appeal is taken may grant an extension of time to cure an omission by mistake or excusable neglect on the part of an appellant who has either served or filed a timely notice of appeal, but has omitted some other act necessary to perfect the appeal.

"No good reason exists for the failure to extend the benefit of this provision to a notice of motion for leave to appeal . . . This obviously unintended deficiency would be corrected by this bill, which specifically includes a notice of motion for permission to appeal within the scope of the provision."

### 1966 AMENDMENTS

L. 1966, ch. 594, eff. Sept. 1, 1966, added new Subd. (c).

## R 5521. Preferences.

(a) Preferences in the hearing of an appeal may be granted in the discretion of the court to which the appeal is taken.

(b) Consistent with the provisions of section one thousand one hundred twelve of the family court act, appeals from orders, judgments or decrees in proceedings brought pursuant to articles three, seven and ten and part one of article six of the family court act, and pursuant to sections three hundred fifty-eight-a, three hundred eighty-four-b and three hundred ninety-two of the social services law, shall be given preference and may be brought on for argument on such terms and conditions as the court may direct, upon application of any party or counsel for a minor who is the subject of the proceedings.

### 1991 AMENDMENTS

L. 1991, ch. 582, eff. Jan. 1, 1992, relettered the previously undesignated first paragraph as subdivision (a) and added new subdivision (b).

## R 5522. Disposition of appeal.

(a) A court to which an appeal is taken may reverse, affirm, or modify, wholly or in part, any judgment or order before it, as to any party. The court shall render a final determination or, where necessary or proper, remit to another court for further proceedings. A court reversing or modifying a judgment or order without opinion shall briefly state the grounds of its decision.

(b) In an appeal from a money judgment in an action in which an itemized verdict is required by rule forty-one hundred eleven of this chapter in which it is contended that the award is excessive or inadequate, the appellate division shall set forth in its decision the reasons therefor, including the factors it considered in complying with subdivision (c) of section fifty-five hundred one of this chapter.

### 1988 AMENDMENTS

L. 1988, ch. 184, eff. July 1, 1988, amended L. 1986, ch. 682, to make subdivision (b) applicable to all actions in which trial has not begun as of August 1, 1988.

### 1986 AMENDMENTS

L. 1986, ch. 682, eff. July 30, 1986, and applicable to actions commenced or claims filed on or after such date, amended CPLR 5522 by restructuring the rule and adding new paragraph (b), requiring the Appellate Division, in appeals from money judgments in actions where an itemized verdict is required by CPLR 4111, to set forth in its decision the reasons it found such award to be excessive or inadequate.

CPLR

### 1977 AMENDMENTS

CPLR 5522 was amended by proposal No. 3 of the Judicial Conference in its Report to the 1977 Legislature, effective September 1, 1977, by eliminating the requirement that a court affirming a judgment or order without opinion briefly state the grounds of its decision. The 1977 amendment reverts to the text as it read before the amendment effected by ch. 407 of the Laws of 1975.

### 1975 AMENDMENTS

L. 1975, ch. 407, eff. Sept. 1, 1975, amended CPLR 5522.

## § 5523. Restitution.

A court reversing or modifying a final judgment or order or affirming such a reversal or modification may order restitution of property or rights lost by the judgment or order, except that where the title of a purchaser in good faith and for value would be affected, the court may order the value or the purchase price restored or deposited in court.

## R 5524. Entry of order; remittitur and further proceedings.

(a) Entry of order in appellate court. An order of a court to which an appeal is taken shall be entered in the office of the clerk of that court.

(b) Remittitur and further proceedings. A copy of the order of the court to which an appeal is taken determining the appeal, together with the record on appeal, shall be remitted to the clerk of the court of original instance except that where further proceedings are ordered in another court, they shall be remitted to the clerk of such court. The entry of such copy shall be authority for any further proceedings. Any judgment directed by the order shall be entered by the clerk of the court to which remission is made.

## R 5525. Preparation and settlement of transcript; statement in lieu of transcript.

(a) Preparation of transcript. Where a stenographic record of the proceedings is made, the appellant, within the time for taking the appeal, shall serve upon the stenographic reporter a request for a transcript of the proceedings and, unless the appellant is the state or any political subdivision of the state or an officer or agency of the state or of any political subdivision of the state, shall deposit a sum sufficient to pay the fee. As soon as possible after receiving such notice the reporter shall serve upon the appellant the ribbon copy and a carbon copy of the typewritten transcript, or two copies of the transcript if it is reproduced by any other means. The appellate division in each department may by rule applicable in the department to all appeals taken from judgments or orders entered in the department, provide that only a ribbon copy of the typewritten transcript be prepared and provide for the use of such copy by the parties and the court.

(b) Omission of part of transcript. The parties may stipulate that only a portion of the record be transcribed. No transcript is necessary where a party appeals from a judgment entered upon a referee's report, or a decision of the court upon a trial without a jury, and he relies only upon exceptions to rulings on questions of law made after the case is finally submitted.

(c) Settlement of transcript.

1. Within fifteen days after receiving the transcript from the court reporter or from any other source, the appellant shall make any proposed amendments and serve them and a copy of the transcript upon the respondent. Within fifteen days after such service the respondent shall make any proposed amendments or objections to the proposed amendments of the appellant and serve them upon the appellant. At any time thereafter and on at least four days' notice to the adverse party, the transcript and the proposed amendments and objections thereto shall be submitted for settlement to the judge or referee before whom the proceedings were had if the parties cannot agree on the amendments to the transcript. The original of the transcript shall be corrected by the appellant in accordance with the agreement of the parties or the direction of the court and its correctness shall be certified to thereon by the parties or the judge or referee before whom the proceedings were had. When he serves his brief upon the respondent the appellant shall also serve a conformed copy of the transcript or deposit it in the office of the clerk of the court of original instance who shall make it available to respondent.

2. If the appellant has timely proposed amendments and served them with a copy of the transcript on respondent, and no amendments or objections are proposed by the respondent within the time limited by paragraph 1, the transcript, certified as correct by the court reporter, together with appellant's proposed amendments, shall be deemed correct without the necessity of a stipulation by the parties certifying to its correctness or the settlement of the transcript by the judge or referee. The appellant shall affix to such transcript an affirmation, certifying to his compliance with the time limitation, the service of the notice provided by paragraph 3 and the respondent's failure to propose amendments or objections within the time prescribed.

3. Appellant shall serve on respondent together with a copy of the transcript and the proposed amendments, a notice of settlement containing a specific reference to subdivision (c) of this rule, and stating that if respondent fails to propose amendments or objections within the time limited by paragraph 1, the provisions of paragraph 2 shall apply.

(d) Statement in lieu of stenographic transcript. Where no stenographic record of the proceedings is made, the appellant, within ten days after taking his appeal, shall prepare and serve upon the respondent a statement of the proceedings from the best available sources, including his recollection, for use instead of a transcript. The respondent may serve upon the appellant objections or proposed amendments to the statement within ten days after such service. The statement,

CPLR

with objections or proposed amendments, shall be submitted for settlement to the judge or referee before whom the proceedings were had.

(e) Special rules prescribing time limitations in settlement of transcript or statement in lieu thereof authorized. The appellate division in each department may by rule applicable in the department prescribe other limitations of time different from those prescribed in subdivisions (c) and (d) for serving transcripts, or statements in lieu of transcripts, and proposed amendments or objections, and for submission thereof for settlement.

### 1975 AMENDMENTS

CPLR 5525(c) was amended by Proposal No. 1 of the Judicial Conference Report to the 1975 Legislature, effective September 1, 1975, by designating the text of the first paragraph of Subd. (c) as Paragraph "1."; by changing the ten day time limits in the first and second sentences to fifteen day time limits; by inserting in the first sentence, following the phrase "after receiving the transcript," the clause "from the court reporter or from any other source"; and by adding thereto two new paragraphs, numbered Paragraphs "2." and "3."

## R 5526.    Content and form of record on appeal.

The record on appeal from a final judgment shall consist of the notice of appeal, the judgment-roll, the corrected transcript of the proceedings or a statement pursuant to subdivision (d) of rule 5525 if a trial or hearing was held, any relevant exhibits, or copies of them, in the court of original instance, any other reviewable order, and any opinions in the case. The record on appeal from an interlocutory judgment or any order shall consist of the notice of appeal, the judgment or order appealed from, the transcript, if any, the papers and other exhibits upon which the judgment or order was founded and any opinions in the case. All printed or reproduced papers comprising the record on appeal shall be eleven inches by eight and one-half inches. The subject matter of each page of the record shall be stated at the top thereof, except that in the case of papers other than testimony, the subject matter of the paper may be stated at the top of the first page of each paper, together with the page numbers of the first and last pages thereof. In the case of testimony, the name of the witness, by whom he was called and whether the testimony is direct, cross, redirect or recross examination shall be stated at the top of each page.

### 1976 AMENDMENTS

Proposal No. 1, effective September 1, 1976, made by the Judicial Conference 1976 Report to the Legislature, amended CPLR 5526 by adding the last two sentences specifying the form of page headings.

### 1968 AMENDMENTS

Proposal No. 4, effective Sept. 1, 1968, made by the Judicial Conference Feb. 1, 1968 Report to the Legislature, amended caption and text of rule 5526 to read as above. (See 1975 Amendments.)

**R 5527. Statement in lieu of record on appeal.**

When the questions presented by an appeal can be determined without an examination of all the pleadings and proceedings, the parties may prepare and sign a statement showing how the questions arose and were decided in the court from which the appeal is taken and setting forth only so much of the facts averred and proved or sought to be proved as are necessary to a decision of the questions. The statement may also include portions of the transcript of the proceedings and other relevant matter. It shall include a copy of the judgment or order appealed from, the notice of appeal and a statement of the issues to be determined. Within twenty days after the appellant has taken his appeal, the statement shall be presented to the court from which the appeal is taken for approval as the record on appeal. The court may make corrections or additions necessary to present fully the questions raised by the appeal. The approved statement shall be printed as a joint appendix.

**R 5528. Content of briefs and appendices.**

(a) Appellant's brief and appendix. The brief of the appellant shall contain in the following order:

1. a table of contents, which shall include the contents of the appendix, if it is not bound separately, with references to the initial page of each paper printed and of the direct, cross, and redirect examination of each witness;

2. a concise statement, not exceeding two pages, of the questions involved without names, dates, amounts or particulars, with each question numbered, set forth separately and followed immediately by the answer, if any, of the court from which the appeal is taken;

3. a concise statement of the nature of the case and of the facts which should be known to determine the questions involved, with supporting references to pages in the appendix;

4. the argument for the appellant which shall be divided into points by appropriate headings distinctively printed; and

5. an appendix, which may be bound separately, containing only such parts of the record on appeal as are necessary to consider the questions involved, including those parts the appellant reasonably assumes will be relied upon by the respondent; provided, however, that the appellate division in each department may by rule applicable in the department authorize an appellant at his election to proceed upon a record on appeal printed or reproduced in like manner as an appendix, and in the event of such election an appendix shall not be required.

(b) Respondent's brief and appendix. The brief of the respondent shall conform to the requirements of subdivision (a), except that a counterstatement of the questions involved or a counterstatement of the nature and facts of the case shall be included only if the respondent disagrees with the statement of

CPLR

the appellant and the appendix shall contain only such additional parts of the record as are necessary to consider the questions involved.

(c) Appellant's reply brief and appendix. Any reply brief of the appellant shall conform to the requirements of subdivision (a) without repetition.

(d) Joint appendix. A joint appendix bound separately may be used. It shall be filed with the appellant's brief.

(e) Sanction. For any failure to comply with subdivision (a), (b) or (c) the court to which the appeal is taken may withhold or impose costs.

## R 5529. Form of briefs and appendices.

(a) Form of reproduction; size; paper; binding.

1. Briefs and appendices may be either printed or reproduced by offset printing, mimeographing or any other method of reproduction approved by the state administrator. Paper shall be of a quality approved by the state administrator.

2. Printed briefs and appendices shall be on white paper eleven inches along the bound edge by eight and one-half inches. The printed portion of each page, exclusive of marginal references, shall be seven and one-sixth inches by four and one-sixth inches. Printing shall be in a clear type of no less than eleven-point size but footnotes may be printed in type of no less than nine-point size.

3. Briefs and appendices reproduced by offset printing, mimeographing or any method of reproduction other than printing shall be on white paper eleven inches along the bound edge by eight and one-half inches. The bound margin shall be at least one inch, and typed matter shall not exceed seven by nine and one–half inches, with double spacing between each line of text. The reproduction shall be a facsimile of the material neatly prepared on the typewriter in clear type of no less than elite in size.

(b) Numbering. Pages of briefs shall be numbered consecutively. Pages of appendices shall be separately numbered consecutively, each number preceded by the letter A.

(c) Page headings. The subject matter of each page of the appendix shall be stated at the top thereof, except that in the case of papers other than testimony, the subject matter of the paper may be stated at the top of the first page of each paper, together with the page numbers of the first and last pages thereof. In the case of testimony, the name of the witness, by whom he was called and whether the testimony is direct, cross, redirect, or recross examination shall be stated at the top of each page.

(d) Quotations. Asterisks or other appropriate means shall be used to indicate omissions in quoted excerpts. Reference shall be made to the source of the excerpts quoted. Where an excerpt in the appendix is testimony of a witness quoted from the record the beginning of each page of the transcript shall be indicated by parenthetical insertion of the transcript page number.

(e) Citations of decisions. New York decisions shall be cited from the official reports, if any. All other decisions shall be cited from the official reports, if any, and also from the National Reporter System if they are there reported. Decisions not reported officially or in the National Reporter System shall be cited from the most available source.

(f) Questions and answers. The answer to a question in the appendix shall not begin a new paragraph.

### 1976 AMENDMENTS

Proposal No. 1, effective September 1, 1976, made by the Judicial Conference 1976 Report to the Legislature, amended Subd. (c) to permit subject matter of the paper to be stated at the top of the first page only, instead of requiring such statement at the top of every page.

### 1975 AMENDMENTS

Proposal No. 2 of the 1975 Judicial Conference, effective September 1, 1975, amended CPLR 5529(a)(3).

### 1968 AMENDMENTS

Proposal No. 5, effective Sept. 1, 1968, made by the Judicial Conference Feb. 1, 1968 Report to the Legislature amended paragraphs (2) and (3) of subdivision (a).

## R 5530. Filing record and briefs; service of briefs.

(a) Generally. Within twenty days after settlement of the transcript or after settlement of the statement in lieu of stenographic transcript or after approval of the statement in lieu of record, the appellant shall file with the clerk of the court to which the appeal is taken the record on appeal or statement in lieu of record, and the required number of copies of his brief, and shall also serve upon the adverse party three copies of his brief. The respondent shall file and serve a like number of copies of his brief within fifteen days after service of the appellant's brief. The appellant may file and serve a like number of copies of a reply brief within ten days after service of the respondent's brief.

(b) Upon cross-appeal. Unless the court to which the appeals are taken otherwise orders, where both parties take an appeal from the same judgment or order, the plaintiff, or appellant in the court from which the appeal is taken, shall file and serve his brief first. The answering brief shall be filed and served within fifteen days after service of the first brief and shall include the points and arguments on the cross-appeal. A reply brief shall be filed and served within fifteen days after service of the answering brief, and shall include answering points and arguments on the cross-appeal. A reply brief to the cross-appeal may thereafter be served and filed within ten days after the service of the reply to the first brief.

(c) Special rules prescribing times for filing and serving authorized. The appellate division in each department may by rule applicable in the department prescribe other limitations of time different from those prescribed in subdivisions (a) and (b) for filing and serving records on appeal, or statements in lieu of records, and briefs in appeals taken therein.

### R 5531.  Description of action.

The appellant shall file together with the record on appeal, in both criminal and civil actions, a statement containing the following information listed and numbered in the following order:

1. the index number of the case in the court below,

2. the full names of the original parties and any change in the parties,

3. the court and county in which the action was commenced,

4. the date the action was commenced and the dates on which each pleading was served,

5. a brief description of the nature and object of the action,

6. a statement as to whether the appeal is from a judgment or an order or both, the dates of entry of each judgment or order appealed from, and the name of the judge or justice who directed the entry of the judgment or made the order being appealed, and

7. a statement as to the method of appeal being used:

(a) whether the appeal is on full record, printed or reproduced, or

(b) on the original record, in which event, state whether the appendix method is being used, or leave to prosecute the appeal on the original record was granted by the court or by statute.

The statement shall be prefixed to the papers constituting the record on appeal. A copy of this statement shall be filed with the clerk at the time the record on appeal is filed.

**1974 AMENDMENTS**

L. 1974, ch. 433, eff. Sept. 1, 1974, amended paragraphs 6 and 7.

**1966 AMENDMENTS**

Amendment No. 3, effective Sept. 1, 1966, made by the Judicial Conference Feb. 1, 1966, Report to the Legislature. The reason stated was that the requirement of "CPLR 5531 that the statement referred to therein be filed with the appellant's brief if a brief is filed has caused some confusion among the bar because of the change from Rule 234 of the Rules of Civil Practice, under which the statement was required to be prefixed to the papers on appeal. The former practice, which resulted in earlier filing of the statement than at present and its inclusion in the record on appeal, is preferable for administrative purposes. For these reasons it seems desirable to revert to the former practice.

"Since the statement required by CPLR 5531 is also used for statistical purposes by the Judicial Conference, the proposed change would require that an additional copy be filed. This will facilitate transmission of the information contained in the statement by the clerk of the appellate court to the Judicial Conference."

### 1964 AMENDMENTS

Amendment No. 10 made by the Judicial Conference Feb. 1, 1964, Report to the Legislature, pursuant to Judiciary Law § 229, effective Sept. 1, 1964, revised the requirements of the statement to be filed with the record on appeal.

## R 5532. Stipulation in lieu of certification.

The parties or their attorneys may stipulate as to the correctness of the entire record on appeal or any portion thereof in lieu of certification.

### 1964 AMENDMENTS

Amendment No. 9 made by the Judicial Conference Feb. 1, 1964, Report to the Legislature, effective Sept. 1, 1964, added this new Rule 5532.

CPLR

# ARTICLE 56

# APPEALS TO THE COURT OF APPEALS

## SUMMARY OF ARTICLE

§ 5601.    Appeals to the court of appeals as of right.
    (a)  Dissent.
    (b)  Constitutional grounds.
    (c)  From order granting new trial or hearing, upon stipulation for judgment absolute.
    (d)  Based upon nonfinal determination of appellate division.
§ 5602.    Appeals to the court of appeals by permission.
    (a)  Permission of appellate division or court of appeals.
    (b)  Permission of appellate division.
§§ 5603–5610.   [Not used.]
§ 5611.    When appellate division order deemed final.
§ 5612.    Presumptions as to determinations of questions of fact.
    (a)  Appeal from reversal or modification.
    (b)  Appeal on certified questions of law.
§ 5613.    Disposition upon reversal or modification.
§ 5614.    Disposition upon certified questions.
§ 5615.    Disposition upon appeal from order granting new trial or hearing.

## § 5601.  Appeals to the court of appeals as of right.

(a) Dissent. An appeal may be taken to the court of appeals as of right in an action originating in the supreme court, a county court, a surrogate's court, the family court, the court of claims or an administrative agency, from an order of the appellate division which finally determines the action, where there is a dissent by at least two justices on a question of law in favor of the party taking such appeal.

(b) Constitutional grounds. An appeal may be taken to the court of appeals as of right:

1. from an order of the appellate division which finally determines an action where there is directly involved the construction of the constitution of the state or of the United States; and

2. from a judgment of a court of record of original instance which finally determines an action where the only question involved on the appeal is the

validity of a statutory provision of the state or of the United States under the constitution of the state or of the United States.

(c) From order granting new trial or hearing, upon stipulation for judgment absolute. An appeal may be taken to the court of appeals as of right in an action originating in the supreme court, a county court, a surrogate's court, the family court, the court of claims or an administrative agency, from an order of the appellate division granting or affirming the granting of a new trial or hearing where the appellant stipulates that, upon affirmance, judgment absolute shall be entered against him.

(d) Based upon nonfinal determination of appellate division. An appeal may be taken to the court of appeals as of right from a final judgment entered in a court of original instance, from a final determination of an administrative agency or from a final arbitration award, or from an order of the appellate division which finally determines an appeal from such a judgment or determination, where the appellate division has made an order on a prior appeal in the action which necessarily affects the judgment, determination or award and which satisfies the requirements or subdivision (a) or of paragraph one of subdivision (b) except that of finality.

## CROSS REFERENCES

See N.Y. Const., Art. VI, §§ 3 (Court of appeals), 5 (Appellate courts generally), 8 (Appellate term) and 11 (Appellate jurisdiction of county courts), in Appendix, *infra*.

## 1986 AMENDMENTS

L. 1986, ch. 316, eff. Jan. 1, 1987, and applicable to every notice of appeal filed or motion for leave to appeal to the court of appeals made on or after such date, amended Subd. (d) of CPLR 5601 by providing for appeal as of right to the Court of Appeals from a final arbitration award.

## 1985 AMENDMENTS

L. 1985, ch. 300, eff. Jan. 1, 1986, and applicable to every notice of appeal taken or motion for leave to appeal to the Court of Appeals made on or after that date, amended CPLR 5601(a) to limit appeals as of right to the Court of Appeals to cases where there is a dissent by at least two justices of the Appellate Division on a question of law in favor of the party taking the appeal.

## 1973 AMENDMENTS

L. 1973, ch. 95, § 1, eff. immediately and retroactive to and deemed to be in full force and effect from and after March 1, 1973, amended L. 1969, ch. 999 by eliminating the time limit on the effectiveness of ch. 999. This makes the 1969 amendment of CPLR 5601(a) (L. 1969, ch. 999, as amended by L. 1971, ch. 44) permanent. See "1971" and "1969 Amendments," *infra*.

L. 1973, ch. 95, § 2, amended CPLR 5601 (a) by deleting "stated" before "question of law," and by making grammatical changes.

## 1971 AMENDMENTS

L. 1971, ch. 44, eff. March 1, 1971 until March 1, 1973, amended L. 1969, ch. 999, § 2, entitled "An Act to Amend the Civil Practice Law and Rules, in Relation to Appeals as of Right to the Court of Appeals" (CPLR 5601(a)), by extending the effective date of ch. 999 until March 1, 1973.

### 1969 AMENDMENTS

L. 1969, ch. 999, eff. Sept. 2, 1969 until March 1, 1971, amended Subd. (a) by deleting "of such judgment or order"; by dividing the material following "an order of the appellate division which finally determines the action," into subparagraphs (i), (ii) and (iii); by adding to new subparagraph (i), "on a stated question of law in favor of the party taking such appeal"; and by adding to new subparagraph (iii), "thereof in a substantial respect, which is within the power of the court of appeals to review on such appeal, and the party taking the appeal is aggrieved by the modification."

### 1967 AMENDMENTS

L. 1967, ch. 342, eff. Sept. 1, 1967, added reference to family court in Subd. (a) and Subd. (c).

## § 5602.  Appeals to the court of appeals by permission.

(a) Permission of appellate division or court of appeals. An appeal may be taken to the court of appeals by permission of the appellate division granted before application to the court of appeals, or by permission of the court of appeals upon refusal by the appellate division or upon direct application. Permission by an appellate division for leave to appeal shall be pursuant to rules authorized by that appellate division. Permission by the court of appeals for leave to appeal shall be pursuant to rules authorized by the court which shall provide that leave to appeal be granted upon the approval of two judges of the court of appeals. Such appeal may be taken:

1. in an action originating in the supreme court, a county court, a surrogate's court, the family court, the court of claims, an administrative agency or an arbitration,

(i) from an order of the appellate division which finally determines the action and which is not appealable as of right, or

(ii) from a final judgment of such court, final determination of such agency or final arbitration award where the appellate division has made an order on a prior appeal in the action which necessarily affects the final judgment, determination or award and the final judgment, determination or award is not appealable as of right pursuant to subdivision (d) of section 5601 of this article; and

2. in a proceeding instituted by or against one or more public officers or a board, commission or other body of public officers or a court or tribunal, from an order of the appellate division which does not finally determine such proceeding, except that the appellate division shall not grant permission to appeal from an order granting or affirming the granting of a new trial or hearing.

(b) Permission of appellate division. An appeal may be taken to the court of appeals by permission of the appellate division:

1. from an order of the appellate division which does not finally determine an action, except an order described in paragraph two of subdivision (a) or subparagraph (iii) of paragraph two of subdivision (b) of this section or in subdivision (c) of section 5601;

2. in an action originating in a court other than the supreme court, a county court, a surrogate's court, the family court, the court of claims or an administrative agency,

(i) from an order of the appellate division which finally determines the action, and which is not appealable as of right pursuant to paragraph one of subdivision (b) of section 5601, or

(ii) from a final judgment of such court or a final determination of such agency where the appellate division has made an order on a prior appeal in the action which necessarily affects the final judgment or determination and the final judgment or determination is not appealable as of right pursuant to subdivision (d) of section 5601, or

(iii) from an order of the appellate division granting or affirming the granting of a new trial or hearing where the appellant stipulates that, upon affirmance, judgment absolute shall be entered against him.

### 1986 AMENDMENTS

L. 1986, ch. 316, eff. Jan. 1, 1987, and applicable to every notice of appeal filed or motion for leave to appeal to the court of appeals made on or after such date, amended Subd. (1)(a) of CPLR 5602 by providing for appeal by permission in an action originating in an arbitration from a final arbitration award.

### 1985 AMENDMENTS

L. 1985, ch. 300, eff. Jan. 1, 1986, and applicable to every notice of appeal taken or motion for leave to appeal to the court of appeals made on or after that date, amended CPLR 5602(a) to provide that permission for leave to appeal to the Court of Appeals shall be pursuant to rules authorized by the Appellate Division and the Court of Appeals.

### 1967 AMENDMENTS

L. 1967, ch. 342, eff. Sept. 1, 1967, added reference to family court in Subd. (a)(1) and Subd. (b)(2).

## §§ 5603-5610. [Not used.]

## § 5611. When appellate division order deemed final.

If the appellate division disposes of all the issues in the action its order shall be considered a final one, and a subsequent appeal may be taken only from that order and not from any judgment or order entered pursuant to it. If the aggrieved party is granted leave to replead or to perform some other act which would defeat the finality of the order, it shall not take effect as a final order until the expiration of the time limited for such act without his having performed it.

## § 5612. Presumptions as to determinations of questions of fact.

(a) Appeal from reversal or modification. On an appeal from an order of the appellate division reversing, modifying or setting aside a determination and rendering a final or interlocutory determination, except when it reinstates a verdict, the court of appeals shall presume that questions of fact as to which no findings are made in the order or opinion of the appellate division were not considered by it, where such findings are required to be made by paragraph two of subdivision (b)* of rule 5712.

(b) Appeal on certified questions of law. On an appeal on certified questions of law, the court of appeals shall presume that questions of fact as to which no findings are made in the order granting permission to appeal or in the order appealed from or in the opinion of the appellate division were determined in favor of the party who is respondent in the court of appeals.

\* [**Editor's note:** So in original. Reference probably should be to subdivision (c) of rule 5712.]

## § 5613. Disposition upon reversal or modification.

The court of appeals, upon reversing or modifying a determination of the appellate division, when it appears or must be presumed that questions of fact were not considered by the appellate division, shall remit the case to that court for determination of questions of fact raised in the appellate division.

## § 5614. Disposition upon certified questions.

The order of the court of appeals determining an appeal upon certified questions shall certify its answers to the questions certified and direct entry of the appropriate judgment or order.

## § 5615. Disposition upon appeal from order granting new trial or hearing.

When an appeal to the appellate division presented questions of fact and a further appeal is taken pursuant to subdivision (c) of section 5601, or subparagraph (iii) of paragraph two of subdivision (b) of section 5602, the court of appeals shall affirm the order appealed from and shall render judgment or order absolute against the appellant unless the order or opinion of the appellate division recites either that the questions of fact have not been considered or that the court has considered the questions of fact and has determined that it would not grant a new trial or hearing upon those questions.

CPLR

# ARTICLE 57

# APPEALS TO THE APPELLATE DIVISION

---

## SUMMARY OF ARTICLE

§ 5701.  Appeals to appellate division from supreme and county courts.
    (a)  Appeals as of right.
    (b)  Orders not appealable as of right.
    (c)  Appeals by permission.
§ 5702.  Appeals to appellate division from other courts of original instance.
§ 5703.  Appeals to appellate division from appellate courts.
    (a)  From appellate terms.
    (b)  From other appellate courts.
§ 5704.  Review of ex parte orders.
    (a)  By appellate division.
    (b)  By appellate term.
§§ 5705–5710.  [Not used.]
§ 5711.  Where appeal heard.
§ 5712.  Content of order determining appeal.
    (a)  Dissents.
    (b)  Order of affirmance.
    (c)  Order of reversal or modification.
§ 5713.  Content of order granting permission to appeal to court of appeals.

---

## § 5701.  Appeals to appellate division from supreme and county courts.

(a) Appeals as of right. An appeal may be taken to the appellate division as of right in an action, originating in the supreme court or a county court:

1. from any final or interlocutory judgment except one entered subsequent to an order of the appellate division which disposes of all the issues in the action; or

2. from an order not specified in subdivision (b), where the motion it decided was made upon notice and it:

(i) grants, refuses, continues or modifies a provisional remedy; or

(ii) settles, grants or refuses an application to resettle a transcript or statement on appeal; or

(iii) grants or refuses a new trial; except where specific questions of fact arising upon the issues in an action triable by the court have been tried by a jury, pursuant to an order for that purpose, and the order grants or refuses a new trial upon the merits; or

(iv) involves some part of the merits; or

(v) affects a substantial right; or

(vi) in effect determines the action and prevents a judgment from which an appeal might be taken; or

(vii) determines a statutory provision of the state to be unconstitutional, and the determination appears from the reasons given for the decision or is necessarily implied in the decision; or

3. from an order, where the motion it decided was made upon notice, refusing to vacate or modify a prior order, if the prior order would have been appealable as of right under paragraph two had it decided a motion made upon notice.

(b) Orders not appealable as of right. An order is not appealable to the appellate division as of right where it:

1. is made in a proceeding against a body or officer pursuant to article 78; or

2. requires or refuses to require a more definite statement in a pleading; or

3. orders or refuses to order that scandalous or prejudicial matter be stricken from a pleading.

(c) Appeals by permission. An appeal may be taken to the appellate division from any order which is not appealable as of right in an action originating in the supreme court or a county court by permission of the judge who made the order granted before application to a justice of the appellate division; or by permission of a justice of the appellate division in the department to which the appeal could be taken, upon refusal by the judge who made the order or upon direct application.

### CROSS REFERENCES

See N.Y. Const., Art. VI, §§ 3 (Court of appeals), 5 (Appellate courts generally), 8 (Appellate term) and 11 (Appellate jurisdiction of county courts), in Appendix, *infra*.

## § 5702.  Appeals to appellate division from other courts of original instance.

An appeal may be taken to the appellate division from any judgment or order of a court of original instance other than the supreme court or a county court in accordance with the statute governing practice in such court.

## § 5703. Appeals to appellate division from appellate courts.

(a) From appellate terms. An appeal may be taken to the appellate division, from an order of the appellate term which determines an appeal from a judgment or order of a lower court, by permission of the appellate term or, in case of refusal, of the appellate division. When permission to appeal is sought from an order granting or affirming the granting of a new trial or hearing, the appellant shall stipulate that, upon affirmance, judgment absolute may be entered against him.

(b) From other appellate courts. An appeal may be taken to the appellate division as of right from an order of a county court or a special term of the supreme court which determines an appeal from a judgment of a lower court.

## § 5704. Review of ex parte orders.

(a) By appellate division. The appellate division or a justice thereof may vacate or modify any order granted without notice to the adverse party by any court or a judge thereof from which an appeal would lie to such appellate division; and the appellate division may grant any order or provisional remedy applied for without notice to the adverse party and refused by any court or a judge thereof from which an appeal would lie to such appellate division.

(b) By appellate term. The appellate term in the first or second judicial department or a justice thereof may vacate or modify any order granted without notice to the adverse party by any court or a judge thereof from which an appeal would lie to such appellate term; and such appellate term may grant any order or provisional remedy applied for without notice to the adverse party and refused by any court or a judge thereof from which an appeal would lie to such appellate term.

CPLR

### 1972 AMENDMENTS

L. 1972, ch. 435, eff. Sept. 1, 1972 amended CPLR 5704(a).

The 1972 Judicial Conference Report stated:

"At present, section 5704 (a) specifies, substantially, that the Appellate Division or a Justice thereof may vacate or modify an ex parte order of the Supreme Court ( or a Justice thereof) only; and that the Appellate Division may grant an ex-parte order or provisional remedy refused by the Supreme Court (or a Justice thereof) only. The proposed amendment would remove the foregoing arbitrary limitation to the Supreme Court by providing that the specified power to the review extends to similar orders or decisions of any court, or a Judge thereof, from which an appeal would lie to the Appellate Division.

### 1966 AMENDMENTS

L. 1966, ch. 577, eff. Sept. 1, 1966, amended Subd. (b) by deleting references to the Civil Court of the City of New York and the Justices thereof, and substituting therefore references to "any court or a judge thereof from which an appeal would lie to such appellate term."

§§ 5705–5710.　[Not used.]

## § 5711.　Where appeal heard.

Except as provided in subdivision (d) of rule 511, an appeal to the appellate division shall be brought in the department embracing the county in which the judgment or order appealed from is entered and there heard and determined unless, in furtherance of justice, the appeal is sent to another department.

### 1965 AMENDMENTS

L. 1965, ch. 338, eff. Sept. 1, 1965, added the words "Except as provided in subdivision (d) of rule 511" at the beginning of the section.

## § 5712.　Content of order determining appeal.

(a) Dissents. Every order of the appellate division determining an appeal shall state whether one or more justices dissent from the determination.

(b) Order of affirmance. Whenever the appellate division, although affirming a final or interlocutory judgment or order, reverses or modifies any findings of fact, or makes new findings of fact, its order shall comply with the requirement of subdivision (c).

(c) Order of reversal or modification. Whenever the appellate division reverses or modifies or sets aside a determination and thereupon makes a determination, except when it reinstates a verdict, its order shall state whether its determination is upon the law, or upon the facts, or upon the law and the facts:

1. if the determination is stated to be upon the law alone, the order shall also state whether or not the findings of fact below have been affirmed; and

2. if the determination is stated to be upon the facts, or upon the law and the facts, the order shall also specify the findings of fact which are reversed or modified, and set forth any new findings of fact made by the appellate division with such particularity as was employed for the statement of the findings of fact in the court of original instance; except that the order need not specify the findings of fact which are reversed or modified nor set forth any new findings of fact if the appeal is either from a determination by the court without any statement of the findings of fact or from a judgment entered upon a general verdict without answers to interrogatories.

### 1964 AMENDMENTS

L. 1964, ch. 388, eff. Sept. 1, 1964, corrected "court or original instance" in Subd. (c)(2) to read "court of original instance."

## § 5713.　Content of order granting permission to appeal to court of appeals.

When the appellate division grants permission to appeal to the court of appeals, its order granting such permission shall state that questions of law have arisen which in its opinion ought to be reviewed. When the appeal is from a non-final order, the order granting such permission shall also state that the findings of fact have been affirmed, or reversed or modified and new findings of fact made, or have not been considered, shall specify the findings of fact which have been reversed or modified and set forth new findings of fact with at least the same particularity as was employed for the findings of fact below and shall certify the questions of law decisive of the correctness of its determination or of any separable portion of it.

# ARTICLE 60

# PROVISIONAL REMEDIES GENERALLY

---

## SUMMARY OF ARTICLE

§ 6001.     Kinds of provisional remedies; when remedy available to defendant.

---

## § 6001.  Kinds of provisional remedies; when remedy available to defendant.

The provisional remedies are attachment, injunction, receivership and notice of pendency. On a motion for a provisional remedy, the plaintiff shall state whether any other provisional remedy has been secured or sought in the same action against the same defendant, and the court may require the plaintiff to elect between those remedies to which he would otherwise be entitled; for this purpose, seizure of a chattel in an action to recover a chattel is a provisional remedy. A cause of action contained in a counterclaim or a cross-claim, and a judgment demanded thereon, shall entitle the defendant to the same provisional remedies to which he would be entitled if he were the plaintiff, the party against whom the judgment is demanded were the defendant and the cause of action were contained in a complaint.

### 1984 AMENDMENTS

L. 1984, ch. 313, eff. July 3, 1984, amended CPLR 6001 by deleting the reference to the provisional remedy of arrest.

CPLR

# ARTICLE 61

# ARREST

[**Editor's note:** *L. 1979, ch. 409, eff. June 29, 1979, repealed Article 61 of CPLR.*]

# ARTICLE 62

# ATTACHMENT

## SUMMARY OF ARTICLE

§ 6201.   Grounds for attachment.
§ 6202.   Debt or property subject to attachment; proper garnishee.
§ 6203.   Attaching creditor's rights in personal property.
§ 6204.   Discharge of garnishee's obligation.
§ 6210.   Order of attachment on notice; temporary restraining order; contents.
§ 6211.   Order of attachment without notice.
   (a)   When granted; contents.
   (b)   Confirmation of order.
R 6212.   Motion papers; undertaking; filing; demand; damages.
   (a)   Affidavit; other papers.
   (b)   Undertaking.
   (c)   Filing.
   (d)   Demand for papers.
   (e)   Damages.
§ 6213.   Service of summons.
§ 6214.   Levy upon personal property by service of order.
   (a)   Method of levy.
   (b)   Effect of levy; prohibition of transfer.
   (c)   Seizure by sheriff; notice of satisfaction.
   (d)   Proceeding to compel payment or delivery.
   (e)   Failure to proceed.
§ 6215.   Levy upon personal property by seizure.
§ 6216.   Levy upon real property.
§ 6217.   Additional undertaking to carrier garnishee.
§ 6218.   Sheriff's duties after levy.
   (a)   Retention of property.
   (b)   Inventory.
§ 6219.   Garnishee's statement.
§ 6220.   Disclosure.
§ 6221.   Proceeding to determine adverse claims.
§ 6222.   Discharge of attachment.
§ 6223.   Vacating or modifying attachment.
   (a)   Motion to vacate or modify.
   (b)   Burden of proof.
§ 6224.   Annulment of attachment.
§ 6225.   Return of property; directions to clerk and sheriff.
§ 6226.   Disposition of attached property after execution issued; priority of orders of attachment.

## § 6201. Grounds for attachment.

An order of attachment may be granted in any action, except a matrimonial action, where the plaintiff has demanded and would be entitled, in whole or in part, or in the alternative, to a money judgment against one or more defendants, when:

1. the defendant is a nondomiciliary residing without the state, or is a foreign corporation not qualified to do business in the state; or

2. the defendant resides or is domiciled in the state and cannot be personally served despite diligent efforts to do so; or

3. the defendant, with intent to defraud his creditors or frustrate the enforcement of a judgment that might be rendered in plaintiff's favor, has assigned, disposed of, encumbered or secreted property, or removed it from the state or is about to do any of these acts; or

4. the action is brought by the victim or the representative of the victim of a crime, as defined in subdivision six of section six hundred twenty-one of the executive law, against the person or the legal representative or assignee of the person convicted of committing such crime and seeks to recover damages sustained as a result of such crime pursuant to section six hundred thirty-two-a of the executive law; or

5. the cause of action is based on a judgment, decree or order of a court of the United States or of any other court which is entitled to full faith and credit in this state, or on a judgment which qualifies for recognition under the provisions of article 53.

### 1992 AMENDMENTS

L. 1992, ch. 618, eff. July 24, 1992 and applying only to actions commenced on or after the effective date, renumbered prior Subdivision (4) as (5) and added a new Subdivision (4), expanding the list of situations in which an order of attachment may be granted to include a civil action for damages brought by a crime victim or his or her representative against the person convicted of committing the crime or that person's representative or assignee.

### 1977 AMENDMENTS

L. 1977, ch. 860, eff. Sept. 1, 1977, amended CPLR 6201 by adoption of proposals made by the Judicial Conference in its Report to the 1977 Legislature, in which it stated:

"The proposed amendment of subparagraph 1 of this section would subject foreign corporations to attachment only where such corporations are not qualified to do business in the state. There is never a need for a jurisdictional attachment when a foreign corporation has obtained a certificate of authority to do business in New York.

"Present subparagraph 3 is eliminated as archaic and unnecessary. While at one time such a provision was needed to secure jurisdiction in certain cases, the provision has been outmoded by the availability of new jurisdictional tools (CPLR 308(5)). Moreover, the provision largely overlaps with present subparagraphs 1 and 2. The Weinstein, Korn and Miller Treatise (§ 6201.11) [7A Weinstein, Korn & Miller, New York Civil Practice - CPLR ¶ 6201] properly points out that it is difficult to imagine an instance in which attachment could be granted under subparagraph 3 against a defendant trying to avoid service that would not fall within subparagraphs 1 and 2.' If the defendant is a resident or domiciliary, or a corporation qualified to do business in the state, the plaintiff should be able to effect personal service without resorting to attachment. If the defendant is a nondomiciliary residing without the state or a foreign corporation not qualified to do business in the state, attachment is available under subparagraph 1 as proposed to be amended.

"Paragraphs 5, 6 and 8 are repealed because each of the provisions grounds attachment solely on the nature of the action (fraud in inducing contract (paragraph 5)); (peculation (paragraph 6)); conversion, fraud or deceit (paragraph 8)). The present statute, in authorizing attachment in these cases, apparently indulges in the unproved presumption that defendants charged with the stated wrongs are more likely to indulge in conduct frustrating the enforcement of a future judgment in plaintiff's favor than defendants in other cases. The provisions are of dubious constitutional validity. There is no reason why a defendant charged, for example, with conversion is more likely to tamper with his property than one sued for assault, wrongful death or negligence. In the absence of compelling reasons, drastic interference with the free use and enjoyment of defendant's property should not be authorized on the basis of limited judicial cognition, long before defendant has his full day in court and his liability has been established.

"Paragraph 7 would be renumbered paragraph 4, but would otherwise remain as it presently reads, because attachment should be available to secure judgments entitled to full faith and credit or qualifying for registration under Article 53. These are situations sui generis where the defendant had his day in court, or at least an opportunity for a day in court, although the court was foreign rather than domestic."

### CROSS REFERENCES

**Domestic Relations Law** § 233 deals with the sequestration of defendant's property for the purpose of securing quasi in rem jurisdiction in matrimonial actions.

### 1970 AMENDMENTS

L. 1970, ch. 980, eff. Sept. 1, 1970, amended the section by adding a new Subd. (7) , renumbered as Subd. (4) by L. 1977, ch. 860, eff. Sept. 1, 1977, and by renumbering former Subd. (7) as Subd. (8).

## § 6202.  Debt or property subject to attachment; proper garnishee.

Any debt or property against which a money judgment may be enforced as provided in section 5201 is subject to attachment. The proper garnishee of any such property or debt is the person designated in section 5201; for the purpose of applying the provisions to attachment, references to a "judgment debtor" in section 5201 and in subdivision ( i ) of section 105 shall be construed to mean "defendant."

### 1977 AMENDMENTS

L. 1977, ch. 860, eff. Sept. 1, 1977, amended CPLR 6202 by correcting the former cross-reference to subd. (h) of section 105 to refer to subd. (i) of section 105, as relettered by L. 1973, ch. 238.

CPLR

## § 6203. Attaching creditor's rights in personal property.

Where a plaintiff has delivered an order of attachment to a sheriff, the plaintiff's rights in a debt owed to the defendant or in an interest of the defendant in personal property against which debt or property a judgment may be enforced, are superior to the extent of the amount of the attachment to the rights of any transferee of the debt or property, except:

1. a transferee who acquired the debt or property before it was levied upon for fair consideration or without knowledge of the order of attachment; or

2. a transferee who acquired the debt or property for fair consideration after it was levied upon without knowledge of the levy while it was not in the possession of the sheriff.

## § 6204. Discharge of garnishee's obligation.

A person who, pursuant to an order of attachment, pays or delivers to the sheriff money or other personal property in which a defendant has or will have an interest, or so pays a debt he owes the defendant, is discharged from his obligation to the defendant to the extent of the payment or delivery.

## § 6210. Order of attachment on notice; temporary restraining order; contents.

Upon a motion on notice for an order of attachment, the court may, without notice to the defendant, grant a temporary restraining order prohibiting the transfer of assets by a garnishee as provided in subdivision (b) of section 6214. The contents of the order of attachment granted pursuant to this section shall be as provided in subdivision (a) of section 6211.

### 1977 AMENDMENTS

L. 1977, ch. 860, eff. Sept. 1, 1977, added section 6210, as proposed by the Judicial Conference in its Report to the 1977 Legislature, in which it stated:

"Proposed new CPLR 6210 would effect two basic changes. It would expressly provide in statutory form that the plaintiff may apply for an order of attachment on notice. It would further provide that the court may prohibit the transfer of assets by a garnishee or the defendant, as provided in CPLR 6214 (b), through a temporary restraining order, issued ex parte.

"At present the only explicit provision governing the granting of an order of attachment to the plaintiff sets forth an ex parte procedure (CPLR 6211). Thus, proposed CPLR 6210 would codify plaintiff's option of proceeding on notice which was always available in practice, although not spelled out in a separate provision in the CPLR. However, the plaintiff's option was rarely used because the motion-on-notice method offered no protection to plaintiff in restraining the transfer of assets by the garnishee before the hearing.

"Spelling out the proposed procedure, with the restraining order component, would codify a practice employed by some courts as a result of constitutional concerns about the ex parte procedure. The utility of obtaining an order of attachment on notice is enhanced by permitting the use of an ex parte temporary restraining order pending the hearing on the motion. This both encourages pre-attachment hearings (protecting defendants) and permits use of a temporary restraining order (protecting plaintiffs).

"Ordinarily the most practicable method of moving on notice for an order of attachment, while simultaneously seeking a temporary restraining order without notice, would be to proceed by order to show cause on a single set of motion papers. However, nothing would preclude a plaintiff from proceeding on separate motion papers, by ordinary motion on notice, for an order of attachment and for a temporary restraining order. The temporary restraining order is designed to protect the plaintiff during the period which will elapse from the time the plaintiff moves for an order of attachment to the time the sheriff is able to levy upon each garnishee under the order, after it has been granted.

"By making reference to CPLR 6211(a), this provision also makes it clear that the contents of an order of attachment obtained on notice are the same as the contents of an order of attachment obtained ex parte."

## § 6211.  Order of attachment without notice.

(a) When granted; contents. An order of attachment may be granted without notice, before or after service of summons and at any time prior to judgment. It shall specify the amount to be secured by the order of attachment including any interest, costs and sheriff's fees and expenses, be indorsed with the name and address of the plaintiff's attorney and shall be directed to the sheriff of any county or of the city of New York where any property in which the defendant has an interest is located or where a garnishee may be served. The order shall direct the sheriff to levy within his jurisdiction, at any time before final judgment, upon such property in which the defendant has an interest and upon such debts owing to the defendant as will satisfy the amount specified in the order of attachment.

(b) Confirmation of order. Except where an order of attachment is granted on the ground specified in subdivision one of section 6201, an order of attachment granted without notice shall provide that within a period not to exceed five days after levy, the plaintiff shall move, on such notice as the court shall direct to the defendant, the garnishee, if any, and the sheriff, for an order confirming the order of attachment. Where an order of attachment without notice is granted on the ground specified in subdivision one of section 6201, the court shall direct that the statement required by section 6219 be served within five days, that a copy thereof be served upon the plaintiff, and the plaintiff shall move within ten days after levy for an order confirming the order of attachment. If the plaintiff upon motion shall show that the statement has not been served and that the plaintiff will be unable to satisfy the requirement of subdivision (b) of section 6223 until the statement has been served, the court may grant one extension of the time to move for confirmation for a period not to exceed ten days. If plaintiff fails to make such motion within the required period, the order of attachment and any levy thereunder shall have no further effect and shall be vacated upon motion. Upon the motion to confirm, the provisions of subdivision (b) of section 6223 shall apply. An order of attachment granted without notice may provide that the sheriff refrain from taking any property levied upon into his actual custody, pending further order of the court.

### 1985 AMENDMENTS

L. 1985, ch. 566, eff. Sept. 1, 1985, amended CPLR 6211(b) in relation to confirmation of an order of attachment without notice granted on the ground specified in CPLR 6201(1) (defendant is a nondomiciliary or a corporation not qualified to do business within the state).

### 1977 AMENDMENTS

L. 1977, ch. 860, eff. Sept. 1, 1977, amended CPLR 6211 by adoption of proposals made by the Judicial Conference in its Report to the 1977 Legislature, in which it stated in part:

"The present section, now headed òrder of attachment,' would be amended to make it clear that it applies to an order granted ex parte. The section would be divided into two subdivisions, (a) and (b), the text of subdivision (b) being new.

"Subdivision (a) would be clarified to indicate that the amount specified in the order of attachment is the amount to be secured by that order, including any interest, costs and sheriff's fees and expenses.

"New subdivision (b) would provide that where the ex parte motion for attachment is used, the defendant is protected by the requirement that within a period not to exceed five days after the levy, the plaintiff shall move, on such notice as the court shall direct to the defendant, the garnishee, if any, and the sheriff, for an order confirming the order of attachment. If plaintiff fails to make such motion, the order of attachment and any levy thereunder shall have no further effect. Thus, where an ex parte motion for attachment is used, the defendant is protected by the requirement that the levy be swiftly followed by a motion by the plaintiff to confirm the attachment. This procedure largely codifies the minimum guidelines for attachment contained in the directive of October 28, 1974 of Honorable Edward Thompson, Administrative Judge of the Civil Court of the City of New York, and a similar rule promulgated by the Appellate Division, Fourth Judicial Department (22 N.Y.C.R.R. § 1039.13).

"Under the procedure established by the proposed amendment, a garnishee would no longer be bound by the levy or the attachment if the motion to confirm was not made within five days of the levy, or within a shorter period set by the court. Although a motion of vacatur is not required to void an attachment and levy under this provision, it is permitted. A defendant, for example, may desire to make a motion to secure an order formally vacating the attachment in order to lay a procedural foundation for recovering damages suffered on account of an improper attachment."

## R 6212. Motion papers; undertaking; filing; demand; damages.

(a) Affidavit; other papers. On a motion for an order of attachment or for an order to confirm an order of attachment, the plaintiff shall show, by affidavit and such other written evidence as may be submitted, that there is a cause of action, that it is probable that the plaintiff will succeed on the merits, that one or more grounds for attachment provided in section 6201 exist, and that the amount demanded from the defendant exceeds all counterclaims known to the plaintiff.

(b) Undertaking. On a motion for an order of attachment, the plaintiff shall give an undertaking, in a total amount fixed by the court, but not less than five hundred dollars, a specified part thereof conditioned that the plaintiff shall pay to the defendant all costs and damages, including reasonable attorney's fees, which may be sustained by reason of the attachment if the defendant recovers judgment or if it is finally decided that the plaintiff was not entitled to an attachment of the defendant's property, and the balance conditioned that the plaintiff shall pay to the sheriff all of his allowable fees. The attorney for the plaintiff shall not be liable to the sheriff for such fees. The surety on the undertaking shall not be discharged except upon notice to the sheriff.

(c) Filing. Within ten days after the granting of an order of attachment, the plaintiff shall file it and the affidavit and other papers upon which it was based and the summons and complaint in the action. Unless the time for filing has been extended, the order shall be invalid if not so filed, except that a person upon whom it is served shall not be liable for acting upon it as if it were valid without knowledge of the invalidity.

(d) Demand for papers. At any time after property has been levied upon, the defendant may serve upon the plaintiff a written demand that the papers upon which the order of attachment was granted and the levy made be served upon him. Not more than one day after service of the demand, the plaintiff shall cause the papers demanded to be served at the address specified in the demand. A demand under this subdivision shall not of itself constitute an appearance in the action.

(e) Damages. The plaintiff shall be liable to the defendant for all costs and damages, including reasonable attorney's fees, which may be sustained by reason of the attachment if the defendant recovers judgment, or if it is finally decided that the plaintiff was not entitled to an attachment of the defendant's property. Plaintiff's liability shall not be limited by the amount of the undertaking.

### 1977-1978 AMENDMENTS

L. 1977, ch. 15, eff. Sept. 1, 1977, amended subd. (b) by adding the final sentence thereof, requiring notice to the sheriff of discharge of the surety. Section 2 of L. 1977, ch. 15 provided that the act shall take effect on Sept. 1, 1977 and shall expire one year from that date. L. 1978, ch. 530, eff. July 24, 1978, repealed the expiration date of September 1, 1978, thus ending the provisional status of the notice requirement. L. 1977, ch. 860, eff. Sept. 1, 1977, amended CPLR 6212 by adoption of proposals made by the Judicial Conference in its Report to the 1977 Legislature, in which it stated:

"Subdivision (a) would be amended to contain a new requirement that the plaintiff's affidavit, on the motion for an order of attachment or for a confirming order, show that it is probable that the plaintiff will succeed on the merits and that one or more grounds for attachment exist. This would conform the statutory requirement to dicta in the United States Supreme Court cases cited previously . . . An erroneous cross-reference would also be corrected.

"Subdivision (b) would be amended to increase the $250 minimum amount of an undertaking to $500 to reflect inflation since 1963 when the CPLR became effective and to make it clear that reasonable attorney's fees are recoverable costs under the undertaking.

"Subdivision (e) is new."

## § 6213. Service of summons.

An order of attachment granted before service is made on the defendant against whom the attachment is granted is valid only if, within sixty days after the order is granted, a summons is served upon the defendant or first publication of the summons against the defendant is made pursuant to an order and publication is subsequently completed, except that a person upon whom the order of attachment is served shall not be liable for acting upon it as if it were valid without knowledge of the invalidity. If the defendant dies within sixty days after the order is granted and before the summons is served upon him or publication is completed, the order is valid only if the summons is served upon his executor or administrator within sixty days after letters are issued. Upon such terms as may be just and upon good cause shown the court may extend the time, not exceeding sixty days, within which the summons must be served or publication commenced pursuant to this section, provided that the application for extension is made before the expiration of the time fixed.

### 1992 AMENDMENTS

L. 1992, ch. 216, eff. July 1, 1992, amended the first sentence of CPLR 6213 by deleting the words "an action is commenced" after the words "attachment granted before" and inserting in their place "service is made on the defendant against whom the attachment is granted."

### 1969 AMENDMENTS

L. 1969, ch. 208, eff. Sept. 1, 1969; thirty day limitation for service of summons increased to sixty days and last sentence added permitting the court to extend the time, not exceeding sixty days, within which the summons must be served or publication commenced.

## § 6214. Levy upon personal property by service of order.

(a) Method of levy. The sheriff shall levy upon any interest of the defendant in personal property, or upon any debt owed to the defendant, by serving a copy of the order of attachment upon the garnishee, or upon the defendant if property to be levied upon is in the defendant's possession or custody, in the same manner as a summons except that such service shall not be made by delivery of a copy to a person authorized to receive service of summons solely by a designation filed pursuant to a provision of law other than rule 318.

(b) Effect of levy; prohibition of transfer. A levy by service of an order of attachment upon a person other than the defendant is effective only if, at the time of service, such person owes a debt to the defendant or such person is in the possession or custody of property in which such person knows or has reason to believe the defendant has an interest, or if the plaintiff has stated in a notice which shall be served with the order that a specified debt is owed by the person served to the defendant or that the defendant has an interest in specified property in the possession or custody of the person served. All property in which the defendant is known or believed to have an interest then in and thereafter coming into the possession or custody of such a person, including any specified in the notice, and all debts of such a person, including any specified in the notice, then due and thereafter coming due to the defendant, shall be subject to the levy. Unless the court orders otherwise, the person served with the order shall forthwith transfer or deliver all such property, and pay all such debts upon maturity, up to the amount specified in the order of attachment, to the sheriff and execute any document necessary to effect the payment, transfer or delivery. After such payment, transfer or delivery, property coming into the possession or custody of the garnishee, or debt incurred by him, shall not be subject to the levy. Until such payment, transfer or delivery is made, or until the expiration of ninety days after the service of the order of attachment upon him, or of such further time as is provided by any subsequent order of the court served upon him, whichever event first occurs, the garnishee is forbidden to make or suffer any sale, assignment or transfer of, or any interference with any such property, or pay over or otherwise dispose of any such debt, to any person other than the sheriff, except upon direction of the sheriff or pursuant to an order of the court. A garnishee, however, may collect or redeem an instrument received by him for such purpose and he may sell or transfer in good faith property held as collateral or otherwise pursuant to pledge thereof or at the direction of any person other than the defendant authorized to direct sale or transfer, provided that the proceeds in which the defendant has an interest be retained subject to the levy. A plaintiff who has specified personal property or debt to be levied upon in a notice served with an order of attachment shall be liable to the owner of the property or the person to whom the debt is owed, if other than the defendant, for any damages sustained by reason of the levy.

(c) Seizure by sheriff; notice of satisfaction. Where property or debts have been levied upon by service of an order of attachment, the sheriff shall take into his actual custody all such property capable of delivery and shall collect and receive all such debts. When the sheriff has taken into his actual custody property or debts having value sufficient to satisfy the amount specified in the order of attachment, the sheriff shall notify the defendant and each person upon whom the order of attachment was served that the order of attachment has been fully executed.

(d) Proceeding to compel payment or delivery. Where property or debts have been levied upon by service of an order of attachment, the plaintiff may commence a special proceeding against the garnishee served with the order to compel the payment, delivery or transfer to the sheriff of such property or debts, or to secure a judgment against the garnishee. Notice of petition shall also be served upon the parties to the action and the sheriff. A garnishee may interpose any defense or counterclaim which he might have interposed against the defendant if sued by him. The court may permit any adverse claimant to intervene in the proceeding and may determine his rights in accordance with section 6221.

(e) Failure to proceed. At the expiration of ninety days after a levy is made by service of the order of attachment, or of such further time as the court, upon motion of the plaintiff on notice to the parties to the action, has provided, the levy shall be void except as to property or debts which the sheriff has taken into his actual custody, collected or received or as to which a proceeding under subdivision (d) has been commenced.

### 1977 AMENDMENTS

L. 1977, ch. 860, eff. Sept. 1, 1977, amended CPLR 6214 by adoption of proposals made by the Judicial Conference in its Report to the 1977 Legislature, in which it stated:

"The amendments to the several subdivisions of this section, relating to levy by the sheriff upon personal property pursuant to an order of attachment, are designed to clarify the language and to require that parties and other interested persons receive appropriate notice of proceedings authorized under the statute. The addition of the phrase ùnless the court orders otherwise' in § 6214(b) in respect to the transfer of assets to the sheriff is required to conform to new § 6211(b) which permits the court in its discretion in an ex parte order of attachment to provide that the sheriff refrain from taking the property levied upon into his actual custody."

### 1965 AMENDMENTS

L. 1965, ch. 773, eff. Sept. 1, 1965, deleted the word "manual" in the phrase "capable of manual delivery" in Subd. (c).

## § 6215.   Levy upon personal property by seizure.

If the plaintiff shall so direct and shall furnish the sheriff indemnity satisfactory to him or fixed by the court, the sheriff, as an alternative to the method prescribed by section 6214, shall levy upon property capable of delivery by taking the property into his actual custody. The sheriff shall forthwith serve a copy of the order of attachment in the manner prescribed by subdivision (a) of section 6214 upon the person from whose possession or custody the property was taken.

### 1963 AMENDMENTS

L. 1963 , ch. 532, deleted the word "rule" from the cross-reference to "section 6214" in the first sentence of CPLR 6215.

## § 6216.   Levy upon real property.

The sheriff shall levy upon any interest of the defendant in real property by filing with the clerk of the county in which the property is located a notice of attachment indorsed with the name and address of the plaintiff's attorney and stating the names of the parties to the action, the amount specified in the order of attachment and a description of the property levied upon. The clerk shall record and index the notice in the same books, in the same manner and with the same effect, as a notice of the pendency of an action.

### 1977 AMENDMENTS

L. 1977, ch. 860, eff. Sept. 1, 1977, amended CPLR 6216 by adoption of proposals made by the Judicial Conference in its Report to the 1977 Legislature, in which it stated:

"The phrase the amount of plaintiff's claim' would be superseded by the phrase the amount specified in the order of attachment,' which is more precise. It applies to all items to be secured by the order of attachment, including interest, costs and the sheriff's fees and expenses."

## § 6217.  Additional undertaking to carrier garnishee.

A garnishee who is a common carrier may transport or deliver property actually loaded on a conveyance, notwithstanding the service upon him of an order of attachment, if it was loaded without reason to believe that an order of attachment affecting the property had been granted, unless the plaintiff gives an undertaking in an amount fixed by the court, that the plaintiff shall pay any such carrier all expenses and damages which may be incurred for unloading the property and for detention of the conveyance necessary for that purpose.

## § 6218.  Sheriff's duties after levy.

(a) Retention of property. The sheriff shall hold and safely keep all property or debts paid, delivered, transferred or assigned to him or taken into his custody to answer any judgment that may be obtained against the defendant in the action, unless otherwise directed by the court or the plaintiff, subject to the payment of the sheriff's fees and expenses. Any money shall be held for the benefit of the parties to the action in an interest-bearing trust account at a national or state bank or trust company. If the urgency of the case requires, the court may direct sale or other disposition of property, specifying the manner and terms thereof, with notice to the parties to the action and the garnishee who had possession of such property.

(b) Inventory. Within fifteen days after service of an order of attachment or forthwith after such order has been vacated or annulled, the sheriff shall file an inventory of property seized, a description of real property levied upon, the names and addresses of all persons served with the order of attachment, and an estimate of the value of all property levied upon.

### 1977 AMENDMENTS

L. 1977, ch. 860, eff. Sept. 1, 1977, amended CPLR 6218 by adoption of proposals made by the Judicial Conference in its Report to the 1977 Legislature, in which it stated:

"This provision would be amended to assure that any attached monies shall be held for the benefit of the parties to the action in an interest-bearing trust account at a national or state bank or trust company . . .

"The provision would also be amended to require notice to parties and garnishees when the court directs the sale or other disposition of attached property."

### 1964 AMENDMENTS

L. 1964, ch. 342, eff. Sept. 1, 1964, amended Subd. (b), to change period for filing of inventory from 10 to 15 days.

## § 6219. Garnishee's statement.

Within ten days after service upon a garnishee of an order of attachment, or within such shorter time as the court may direct, the garnishee shall serve upon the sheriff a statement specifying all debts of the garnishee to the defendant, when the debts are due, all property in the possession or custody of the garnishee in which the defendant has an interest, and the amounts and value of the debts and property specified. If the garnishee has money belonging to, or is indebted to, the defendant in at least the amount of the attachment, he may limit his statement to that fact.

## § 6220. Disclosure.

Upon motion of any interested person, at any time after the granting of an order of attachment and prior to final judgment in the action, upon such notice as the court may direct, the court may order disclosure by any person of information regarding any property in which the defendant has an interest, or any debts owing to the defendant.

## § 6221. Proceedings to determine adverse claims.

Prior to the application of property or debt to the satisfaction of a judgment, any interested person may commence a special proceeding against the plaintiff to determine the rights of adverse claimants to the property or debt. Service of process in such a proceeding shall be made by serving a notice of petition upon the sheriff and upon each party in the same manner as a notice of motion. The proceeding may be commenced in the county where the property was levied upon, or in the county where the order of attachment is filed. The court may vacate or discharge the attachment, void the levy, direct the disposition of the property or debt, direct that undertakings be provided or released, or direct that damages be awarded. Where there appear to be disputed questions of fact, the court shall order a separate trial, indicating the person who shall have possession of the property pending a decision and the undertaking, if any, which such person shall give. If the court determines that the adverse claim was fraudulent, it may require the claimant to pay the plaintiff the reasonable expenses incurred in the proceeding, including reasonable attorney's fees, and any other damages suffered by reason of the claim. The commencement of the proceeding shall not of itself subject the adverse claimant to personal jurisdiction with respect to any matter other than the claim asserted in the proceeding.

### 1994 AMENDMENTS

L. 1994, ch. 563, eff. July 26, 1994, amended CPLR 6221 by adding to the phrase "Service of process in such a proceeding shall be made."

### 1977 AMENDMENTS

L. 1977, ch. 860, eff. Sept. 1, 1977, amended CPLR 6221 by adoption of proposals made by the Judicial Conference in its Report to the 1977 Legislature, in which it stated:

"This section, governing proceedings to determine adverse claims, would be clarified by providing that the commencement of the proceeding shall not of itself subject the adverse claimant to personal jurisdiction with respect to any matter other than the claim asserted in the proceeding."

## § 6222.　Discharge of attachment.

A defendant whose property or debt has been levied upon may move, upon notice to the plaintiff and the sheriff, for an order discharging the attachment as to all or a part of the property or debt upon payment of the sheriff's fees and expenses. On such a motion, the defendant shall give an undertaking, in an amount equal to the value of the property or debt sought to be discharged, that the defendant will pay to the plaintiff the amount of any judgment which may be recovered in the action against him, not exceeding the amount of the undertaking. Making a motion or giving an undertaking under this section shall not of itself constitute an appearance in the action.

## § 6223.　Vacating or modifying attachment.

(a) Motion to vacate or modify. Prior to the application of property or debt to the satisfaction of a judgment, the defendant, the garnishee or any person having an interest in the property or debt may move, on notice to each party and the sheriff, for an order vacating or modifying the order of attachment. Upon the motion, the court may give the plaintiff a reasonable opportunity to correct any defect. If, after the defendant has appeared in the action, the court determines that the attachment is unnecessary to the security of the plaintiff, it shall vacate the order of attachment. Such a motion shall not of itself constitute an appearance in the action.

(b) Burden of proof. Upon a motion to vacate or modify an order of attachment the plaintiff shall have the burden of establishing the grounds for the attachment, the need for continuing the levy and the probability that he will succeed on the merits.

### 1977 AMENDMENTS

L. 1977, ch. 860, eff. Sept. 1, 1977, amended CPLR 6223 by adoption of proposals made by the Judicial Conference in its Report to the 1977 Legislature, in which it stated:

"At present this section, which is headed Vacating or modifying attachment,' has no subdivisions. It would be divided into two subdivisions under the amendment. Subdivision (a) would be entitled Motion to vacate or modify.'

"At present, §6223 provides that on this motion the court shall give the plaintiff a reasonable opportunity to correct any defect. The proposed amendment would give the court discretion to provide the plaintiff with a reasonable opportunity to correct any defect, since the court may feel that correction may or may not be wise under the circumstances.

"A new subdivision (b), entitled burden of proof,' would be added to provide that upon a motion to vacate or modify an order of attachment the plaintiff shall have the burden of establishing the grounds for the attachment, the need for continuing the levy and the probability that he will succeed on the merits.

"The recent line of cases of the Supreme Court of the United States on provisional remedies, referred to previously [*Carey v. Sugar*, 425 U.S. 73, 96 S. Ct. 1208, 47 L. Ed. 2d 587 (1976); *North Georgia Finishing, Inc. v. Di-Chem Inc.*, 419 U.S. 601, 95 S. Ct. 719, 42 L. Ed. 2d 751 (1975); *Mitchell v. W. T. Grant Company*, 416 U.S. 600, 94 S. Ct. 1895, 40 L. Ed. 2d 406 (1974); *Fuentes v. Shevin*, 407 U. S. 67, 92 S. Ct. 1983, 32 L. Ed. 2d 556 (1972); *Sniadach v. Family Finance Corp. of Bay View*, 395 US 337, 89 SCt 1820, 23 L. Ed. 2d 349 (1969)], indicates the desirability of the proposed amendment.

"When the court has granted an order of attachment without a prior hearing the court must determine at a post-taking hearing brought on by the plaintiff on motion whether to confirm the order. The standards of confirming or granting an order are the same. Where the court grants an order of attachment before a hearing, or where the defendant has defaulted, the court must apply these standards on the basis of the papers and proof presented by the plaintiff. In other instances there will usually be opposing papers and proof presented by the defendant. The burden of proof will be upon the plaintiff in all cases.

"The Supreme Court in *North Georgia Finishing, Inc. v. Di-Chem*, 419 U.S. 601 (1975), required àn early hearing at which the creditor would be required to demonstrate at least probable cause' for the taking. The concurring opinion of Justice Powell which represents the minimal position of the Court states: Due process further requires that the State afford an opportunity for a prompt post-garnishment judicial hearing in which the garnishor has the burden of showing probable cause to continue the garnishment for a sufficient period of time to allow proof and satisfaction of the alleged debt.' 419 U.S. at 611.

"The court must in addition find that the plaintiff has presented a prima facie case and with reasonable probability will be entitled to final judgment. This provision resembles a provision found in the revised claim and delivery procedures in California. California Code of Civil Procedure § 510(e) Supp. 1973. As in *Long Island Trust Co. v. Porta Aluminum Corp.* 44 A.D. 2d 118 (2nd Dept. 1974), if the court cannot find probable cause to believe that plaintiff will succeed, the court should refuse to grant or confirm an order of attachment. By a cross-reference contained in proposed new CPLR 6211 (b), this provision on the burden of proof is made applicable to the motion to confirm.

"Any determination made by the court on a motion to confirm, modify, or vacate an order of attachment, in respect to the probability that the plaintiff will ultimately prevail on the merits, is, of course, inadmissible on the merits of the action in the case-in-chief."

## § 6224.  Annulment of attachment.

An order of attachment is annulled when the action in which it was granted abates or is discontinued, or a judgment entered therein in favor of the plaintiff is fully satisfied, or a judgment is entered therein in favor of the defendant. In the last specified case a stay of proceedings suspends the effect of the annulment, and a reversal or vacating of the judgment revives the order of attachment.

### § 6225. Return of property; directions to clerk and sheriff.

Upon motion of any interested person, on notice to the sheriff and each party, the court may direct the clerk of any county to cancel a notice of attachment and may direct the sheriff to dispose of, account for, assign, return or release any property or debt, or the proceeds thereof, or any undertakings, or to file additional inventories or returns, subject to the payment of the sheriff's fees and expenses. The court shall direct that notice of the motion be given to the plaintiffs in other orders of attachment, if any, and to the judgment creditors of executions, if any, affecting any property or debt, or the proceeds thereof, sought to be returned or released.

### § 6226. Disposition of attached property after execution issued; priority of orders of attachment.

Where an execution is issued upon a judgment entered against the defendant, the sheriff's duty with respect to custody and disposition of property or debt levied upon pursuant to an order of attachment is the same as if he had levied upon it pursuant to the execution. The priority among two or more orders of attachment against the same defendant shall be in the order in which they were delivered to the officer who levied upon the property or debt. The priority between an order of attachment and an execution, or a payment, delivery or receivership order, is set forth in section 5234.

CPLR

# ARTICLE 63

# INJUNCTION

---

## SUMMARY OF ARTICLE

§ 6301.　　Grounds for preliminary injunction and temporary restraining order.

§ 6311.　　Preliminary injunction.

R 6312.　　Motion papers; undertaking; issues of fact.

　　(a)　Affidavit; other papers.

　　(b)　Undertaking.

　　(c)　Issues of fact.

§ 6313.　　Temporary restraining order.

　　(a)　Generally.

　　(b)　Service.

　　(c)　Undertaking.

§ 6314.　　Vacating or modifying preliminary injunction or temporary restraining order.

§ 6315.　　Ascertaining damages sustained by reason of preliminary injunction or temporary restraining order.

§ 6330.　　Obscene prints and articles; jurisdiction.

---

## § 6301.　Grounds for preliminary injunction and temporary restraining order.

A preliminary injunction may be granted in any action where it appears that the defendant threatens or is about to do, or is doing or procuring or suffering to be done, an act in violation of the plaintiff's rights respecting the subject of the action, and tending to render the judgment ineffectual, or in any action where the plaintiff has demanded and would be entitled to a judgment restraining the defendant from the commission or continuance of an act, which, if committed or continued during the pendency of the action, would produce injury to the plaintiff. A temporary restraining order may be granted pending a hearing for a preliminary injunction where it appears that immediate and irreparable injury, loss or damage will result unless the defendant is restrained before the hearing can be had.

CPLR

## § 6311.  Preliminary injunction.

1. A preliminary injunction may be granted only upon notice to the defendant. Notice of the motion may be served with the summons or at any time thereafter and prior to judgment. A preliminary injunction to restrain a public officer, board or municipal corporation of the state from performing a statutory duty may be granted only by the supreme court at a term in the department in which the officer or board is located or in which the duty is required to be performed.

2. Notice of motion for a preliminary injunction to restrain state officers or boards of state officers under the provisions of this section must be upon notice served upon the defendant or respondent, state officers or board of state officers and must be served upon the attorney general by delivery of such notice to an assistant attorney general at an office of the attorney general in the county in which venue of the action is designated or if there is no office of the attorney general in such county, at the office of the attorney general nearest such county.

### 1972 AMENDMENTS

L. 1972, ch. 455, eff. May 24, 1972 and ch. 752, eff. May 30, 1972, amended CPLR 6311 by adding subparagraph 2 and numbering the prior matter as subparagraph 1.

## R 6312.*  Motion papers; undertaking; issues of fact.

(a) Affidavit; other evidence. On a motion for a preliminary injunction the plaintiff shall show, by affidavit and such other evidence as may be submitted, that there is a cause of action, and either that the defendant threatens or is about to do, or is doing or procuring or suffering to be done, an act in violation of the plaintiff's rights respecting the subject of the action and tending to render the judgment ineffectual; or that the plaintiff has demanded and would be entitled to a judgment restraining the defendant from the commission or continuance of an act, which, if committed or continued during the pendency of the action, would produce injury to the plaintiff.

(b) Undertaking. Except as provided in section 2512, prior to the granting of a preliminary injunction, the plaintiff shall give an undertaking in an amount to be fixed by the court, that the plaintiff, if it is finally determined that he or she was not entitled to an injunction, will pay to the defendant all damages and costs which may be sustained by reason of the injunction, including:

1. if the injunction is to stay proceedings in another action, on any ground other than that a report, verdict or decision was obtained by actual fraud, all damages and costs which may be, or which have been, awarded in the other action to the defendant as well as all damages and costs which may be awarded him or her in the action in which the injunction was granted; or,

2. if the injunction is to stay proceedings in an action to recover real property, or for dower, on any ground other than that a verdict, report or decision was obtained by actual fraud, all damages and costs which may be, or which have

been, awarded to the defendant in the action in which the injunction was granted, including the reasonable rents and profits of, and any wastes committed upon, the real property which is sought to be recovered or which is the subject of the action for dower, after the granting of the injunction; or,

3. if the injunction is to stay proceedings upon a judgment for a sum of money on any ground other than that the judgment was obtained by actual fraud, the full amount of the judgment as well as all damages and costs which may be awarded to the defendant in the action in which the injunction was granted.

(c) Issues of fact. Provided that the elements required for the issuance of a preliminary injunction are demonstrated in the plaintiff's papers, the presentation by the defendant of evidence sufficient to raise an issue of fact as to any of such elements shall not in itself be grounds for denial of the motion. In such event the court shall make a determination by hearing or otherwise whether each of the elements required for issuance of a preliminary injunction exists.

* [**Editor's note:** This version of R 6312 is effective as of January 1, 1997. Through December 31, 1996, former R 6312 remains in effect. It reads as follows:

### R 6312. Motion papers; undertaking.

(a) Affidavit; other papers. On a motion for a preliminary injunction the plaintiff shall show, by affidavit and such other evidence as may be submitted, that there is a cause of action, and either that the defendant threatens or is about to do, or is doing or procuring or suffering to be done, an act in violation of the plaintiff's rights respecting the subject of the action and tending to render the judgment ineffectual; or that the plaintiff has demanded and would be entitled to a judgment restraining the defendant from the commission or continuance of an act, which, if committed or continued during the pendency of the action, would produce injury to the plaintiff.

(b) Undertaking. Except as provided in section 2512, prior to the granting of a preliminary injunction, the plaintiff shall give an undertaking in an amount to be fixed by the court, that the plaintiff, if it is finally determined that he was not entitled to an injunction, will pay to the defendant all damages and costs which may be sustained by reason of the injunction, including,

1. if the injunction is to stay proceedings in another action, on any ground other than that a report, verdict or decision was obtained by actual fraud, all damages and costs which may be, or which have been, awarded in the other action to the defendant as well as all damages and costs which may be awarded him in the action in which the injunction was granted; or,

2. if the injunction is to stay proceedings in an action to recover real property, or for dower, on any ground other than that a verdict, report or decision was obtained by actual fraud, all damages and costs which may be, or which have been, awarded to the defendant in the action in which the injunction was granted, including the reasonable rents and profits of, and any wastes committed upon, the real property which is sought to be recovered or which is the subject of the action for dower, after the granting of the injunction; or,

3. if the injunction is to stay proceedings upon a judgment for a sum of money on any ground other than that the judgment was obtained by actual fraud, the full amount of the judgment as well as all damages and costs which may be awarded to the defendant in the action in which the injunction was granted.]

CPLR

**1996 AMENDMENTS**

L. 1996, ch. 24, eff. Jan. 1, 1997, amended the heading by adding the words, "issues of fact"; amended subdivision (a) by replacing the word "paper" with "evidence"; amended subdivision (b) by deleting the comma at the end and replacing with a colon; added a new subdivision (c) entitled "Issues of fact"; and made the section gender neutral.

## § 6313. Temporary restraining order.

(a) Generally. If, on a motion for a preliminary injunction, the plaintiff shall show that immediate and irreparable injury, loss or damages will result unless the defendant is restrained before a hearing can be had, a temporary restraining order may be granted without notice. Upon granting a temporary restraining order, the court shall set the hearing for the preliminary injunction at the earliest possible time. No temporary restraining order may be granted in an action arising out of a labor dispute as defined in section eight hundred seven of the labor law, nor against a public officer, board or municipal corporation of the state to restrain the performance of statutory duties.

(b) Service. Unless the court orders otherwise, a temporary restraining order together with the papers upon which it was based, and a notice of hearing for the preliminary injunction, shall be personally served in the same manner as a summons.

(c) Undertaking. Prior to the granting of a temporary restraining order the court may, in its discretion, require the plaintiff to give an undertaking in an amount to be fixed by the court, containing terms similar to those set forth in subdivision (b) of rule 6312, and subject to the exception set forth therein.

**CROSS REFERENCES**

See **Article 7-A of the State Finance Law §§ 123-123j,** authorizing temporary restraining orders against public servants, notwithstanding the provisions of CPLR 6313, in citizen taxpayer suits for improper disbursement of state funds or property.

**1982 AMENDMENTS**

L. 1982, ch. 235, eff. June 15, 1982, amended CPLR 6313(a) by deleting the last sentence which had made this section inapplicable to the attorney-general in a proceeding under Article 23-A of the **General Business Law.**

**1964 AMENDMENTS**

L. 1964, ch. 263, eff. Sept. 1, 1964, added new Subd. (c).

## § 6314. Vacating or modifying preliminary injunction or temporary restraining order.

A defendant enjoined by a preliminary injunction may move at any time, on notice to the plaintiff, to vacate or modify it. On motion, without notice, made by a defendant enjoined by a temporary restraining order, the judge who granted it, or in his absence or disability, another judge, may vacate or modify the order.

An order granted without notice and vacating or modifying a temporary restraining order shall be effective when, together with the papers upon which it is based, it is filed with the clerk and served upon the plaintiff. As a condition to granting an order vacating or modifying a preliminary injunction or a temporary restraining order, a court may require the defendant, except where the defendant is a public body or officer, to give an undertaking, in an amount to be fixed by the court, that the defendant shall pay to the plaintiff any loss sustained by reason of the vacating or modifying order.

### § 6315.   Ascertaining damages sustained by reason of preliminary injunction or temporary restraining order.

The damages sustained by reason of a preliminary injunction or temporary restraining order may be ascertained upon motion on such notice to all interested persons as the court shall direct. Where the defendant enjoined was an officer of a corporation or joint-stock association or a representative of another person, and the amount of the undertaking exceeds the damages sustained by the defendant by reason of the preliminary injunction or temporary restraining order, the damages sustained by such corporation, association or person represented, to the amount of such excess, may also be ascertained. The amount of damages so ascertained is conclusive upon all persons who were served with notice of the motion and such amount may be recovered by the person entitled thereto in a separate action.

### § 6330.   Obscene prints and articles; jurisdiction.

The supreme court has jurisdiction to enjoin the sale or distribution of obscene prints and articles, as hereinafter specified:

1. The district attorney of any county, the chief executive officer of any city, town or village or the corporation counsel, or if there be none, the chief legal officer of any city, town, or village, in which a person, firm or corporation publishes, sells or distributes or displays or is about to sell or distribute or display or has in his possession with intent to sell or display or distribute or is about to acquire possession with intent to sell, display or distribute any book, magazine, pamphlet, comic book, story paper, writing, paper, picture, motion picture, drawing, photograph, figure, image or any written or printed matter of an indecent character, which is obscene, lewd, lascivious, filthy, indecent or disgusting, or which contains an article or instrument of indecent or immoral use or purports to be for indecent or immoral use or purpose; or in any other respect defined in section 235.00 of the penal law, may maintain an action for an injunction against such person, firm or corporation in the supreme court to prevent the sale or further sale or the distribution or further distribution or the acquisition, publication or possession within the state of any book, magazine, pamphlet, comic book, story paper, writing, paper, picture, motion picture, drawing, photograph, figure or image or any written or printed matter of an indecent character, herein described or described in section 235.00 of the penal law.

2. The person, firm or corporation sought to be enjoined shall be entitled to a trial of the issues within one day after joinder of issue and a decision shall be rendered by the court within two days of the conclusion of the trial.

3. In the event that a final order or judgment of injunction be entered in favor of such officer of the city, town or village and against the person, firm or corporation sought to be enjoined, such final order of* judgment shall contain a provision directing the person, firm or corporation to surrender to such peace officer, acting pursuant to his special duties, or police officer, as the court may direct or to the sheriff of the county in which the action was brought any of the matter described in paragraph one hereof and such officer or sheriff shall be directed to seize and destroy the same.

4. In any action brought as herein provided such officer of the city, town or village shall not be required to file any undertaking before the issuance of an injunction order provided for in paragraph two hereof, shall not be liable for costs and shall not be liable for damages sustained by reason of the injunction order in cases where judgment is rendered in favor of the person, firm or corporation sought to be enjoined.

5. Every person, firm or corporation who sells, distributes, or acquires possession with intent to sell or distribute any of the matter described in paragraph one hereof, after the service upon him of a summons and complaint in an action brought by such officer of any county, city, town or village pursuant to this section is chargeable with knowledge of the contents thereof.

6. The court, in its adjudication, may (1) grant the relief sought (2) deny the relief sought or (3) enjoin the sale, further sale, display, distribution, further distribution, acquisition, publication, or possession of the material, to persons under the age of seventeen, upon a finding that the material is of the kind described in paragraph a or b of subdivision one of section 235.21 of the penal law.

\* [**Editor's note:** So in original. Probably should read "or."]

### 1980 AMENDMENTS

L. 1980, ch. 843, eff. Sept. 1, 1980, amended subdivision three of CPLR 6330 by inserting a reference to police officers, as well as qualifying the term peace officer by adding the words ". . . acting pursuant to his special duties."

### 1972 AMENDMENTS

L. 1972, ch. 826, eff. Aug. 31, 1972, amended CPLR 6330(1) by including "displays" of indecent matter, adding "motion picture," making a technical amendment, and by adding a new paragraph (6).

### 1971 AMENDMENTS

L. 1971, ch. 545, § 8, eff. Sept. 1, 1971, added new CPLR 6330. It is derived from former section 22-a of the Code of Criminal Procedure.

# ARTICLE 64

# RECEIVERSHIP

## SUMMARY OF ARTICLE

§ 6401.     Appointment and powers of temporary receiver.
        (a)   Appointment of temporary receiver; joinder of moving party.
        (b)   Powers of temporary receiver.
        (c)   Duration of temporary receivership.
§ 6402.     Oath.
§ 6403.     Undertaking.
§ 6404.     Accounts.
§ 6405.     Removal.

## § 6401. Appointment and powers of temporary receiver.

(a) Appointment of temporary receiver; joinder of moving party. Upon motion of a person having an apparent interest in property which is the subject of an action in the supreme or a county court, a temporary receiver of the property may be appointed, before or after service of summons and at any time prior to judgment, or during the pendency of an appeal, where there is danger that the property will be removed from the state, or lost, materially injured or destroyed. A motion made by a person not already a party to the action constitutes an appearance in the action and the person shall be joined as a party.

(b) Powers of temporary receiver. The court appointing a receiver may authorize him to take and hold real and personal property, and sue for, collect and sell debts or claims, upon such conditions and for such purposes as the court shall direct. A receiver shall have no power to employ counsel unless expressly so authorized by order of the court. Upon motion of the receiver or a party, powers granted to a temporary receiver may be extended or limited or the receivership may be extended to another action involving the property.

(c) Duration of temporary receivership. A temporary receivership shall not continue after final judgment unless otherwise directed by the court.

## § 6402. Oath.

A temporary receiver, before entering upon his duties, shall be sworn faithfully and fairly to discharge the trust committed to him. The oath may be administered by any person authorized to take acknowledgments of deeds by the real property law. The oath may be waived upon consent of all parties.

**CROSS REFERENCES**

See **Real Prop. L. § 298,** *et seq.,* in Appendix, *infra,* for provisions authorizing the taking of acknowledgments of deeds.

## § 6403.　Undertaking.

A temporary receiver shall give an undertaking in an amount to be fixed by the court making the appointment, that he will faithfully discharge his duties.

## § 6404.　Accounts.

A temporary receiver shall keep written accounts itemizing receipts and expenditures, and describing the property and naming the depository of receivership funds, which shall be open to inspection by any person having an apparent interest in the property. Upon motion of the receiver or of any person having an apparent interest in the property, the court may require the keeping of particular records or direct or limit inspection or require presentation of a temporary receiver's accounts. Notice of a motion for the presentation of a temporary receiver's accounts shall be served upon the sureties on his undertaking as well as upon each party.

## § 6405.　Removal.

Upon motion of any party or upon its own initiative, the court which appointed a receiver may remove him at any time.

# ARTICLE 65

# NOTICE OF PENDENCY

## SUMMARY OF ARTICLE

§ 6501.     Notice of pendency; constructive notice.

§§ 6502–6510.     [Not used.]

R 6511.     Filing, content and indexing of notice of pendency.
      (a)   Filing.
      (b)   Content; designation of index.
      (c)   Indexing.
      (d)   Electronic indexing.

§ 6512.     Service of summons.

§ 6513.     Duration of notice of pendency.

§ 6514.     Motion for cancellation of notice of pendency.
      (a)   Mandatory cancellation.
      (b)   Discretionary cancellation.
      (c)   Costs and expenses.
      (d)   Cancellation by stipulation.
      (e)   Cancellation by plaintiff.

§ 6515.     Undertaking for cancellation of notice of pendency; security by plaintiff.

## § 6501.   Notice of pendency; constructive notice.

A notice of pendency may be filed in any action in a court of the state or of the United States in which the judgment demanded would affect the title to, or the possession, use or enjoyment of, real property, except in a summary proceeding brought to recover the possession of real property. The pendency of such an action is constructive notice, from the time of filing of the notice only, to a purchaser from, or incumbrancer against, any defendant named in a notice of pendency indexed in a block index against a block in which property affected is situated or any defendant against whose name a notice of pendency is indexed. A person whose conveyance or incumbrance is recorded after the filing of the notice is bound by all proceedings taken in the action after such filing to the same extent as a party.

### 1993 AMENDMENT

L. 1993, ch. 657, eff. Jan. 1, 1994, amended to specifically exclude summary proceedings brought to recover possession of real property.

**§§ 6502-6510.  [Not used.]**

## R 6511.  Filing, content and indexing of notice of pendency.

(a) Filing. In a case specified in section 6501, the notice of pendency shall be filed in the office of the clerk of any county where property affected is situated, before or after service of summons and at any time prior to judgment. Unless it has already been filed in that county, the complaint shall be filed with the notice of pendency.

(b) Content; designation of index. A notice of pendency shall state the names of the parties to the action, the object of the action and a description of the property affected. A notice of pendency filed with a clerk who maintains a block index shall contain a designation of the number of each block on the land map of the county which is affected by the notice. Except in an action for partition a notice of pendency filed with a clerk who does not maintain a block index shall contain a designation of the names of each defendant against whom the notice is directed to be indexed.

(c) Indexing. Each county clerk with whom a notice of pendency is filed shall immediately record it and index it against the blocks or names designated. A county clerk who does not maintain a block index shall index a notice of pendency of an action for partition against the names of each plaintiff and each defendant not designated as wholly fictitious.

(d) Electronic indexing. A county clerk may adopt a new indexing system utilizing electro-mechanical, electronic or any other method he deems suitable for maintaining the indexes.

### 1991 AMENDMENTS

L. 1991, ch. 648, eff. July 26, 1991, added subdivision (d).

## § 6512.  Service of summons.

A notice of pendency is effective only if, within thirty days after filing, a summons is served upon the defendant or first publication of the summons against the defendant is made pursuant to an order and publication is subsequently completed. If the defendant dies within thirty days after filing and before the summons is served upon him or publication is completed, the notice is effective only if the summons is served upon his executor or administrator within sixty days after letters are issued.

### 1994 AMENDMENTS

L. 1994, ch. 563, eff. July 26, 1994, amended CPLR 6512 by deleting the words "filed before an action is commenced" after the words "notice of pendency."

### § 6513.  Duration of notice of pendency.

A notice of pendency shall be effective for a period of three years from the date of filing. Before expiration of a period or extended period, the court, upon motion of the plaintiff and upon such notice as it may require, for good cause shown, may grant an extension for a like additional period. An extension order shall be filed, recorded and indexed before expiration of the prior period.

### § 6514.  Motion for cancellation of notice of pendency.

(a) Mandatory cancellation. The court, upon motion of any person aggrieved and upon such notice as it may require, shall direct any county clerk to cancel a notice of pendency, if service of a summons has not been completed within the time limited by section 6512; or if the action has been settled, discontinued or abated; or if the time to appeal from a final judgment against the plaintiff has expired; or if enforcement of a final judgment against the plaintiff has not been stayed pursuant to section 5519.

(b) Discretionary cancellation. The court, upon motion of any person aggrieved and upon such notice as it may require, may direct any county clerk to cancel a notice of pendency, if the plaintiff has not commenced or prosecuted the action in good faith.

(c) Costs and expenses. The court, in an order canceling a notice of pendency under this section, may direct the plaintiff to pay any costs and expenses occasioned by the filing and cancellation, in addition to any costs of the action.

(d) Cancellation by stipulation. At any time prior to entry of judgment, a notice of pendency shall be canceled by the county clerk without an order, on the filing with him of

1. an affidavit by the attorney for the plaintiff showing which defendants have been served with process, which defendants are in default in appearing or answering, and which defendants have appeared or answered and by whom, and

2. a stipulation consenting to the cancellation, signed by the attorney for the plaintiff and by the attorneys for all the defendants who have appeared or answered including those who have waived all notices, and executed and acknowledged, in the form required to entitle a deed to be recorded, by the defendants who have been served with process and have not appeared but whose time to do so has not expired, and by any defendants who have appeared in person.

(e) Cancellation by plaintiff. At any time prior to the entry of judgment a notice of pendency of action shall be canceled by the county clerk without an order, on the filing with him of an affidavit by the attorney for the plaintiff showing that there have been no appearances and that the time to appear has expired for all parties.

CPLR

**1971 AMENDMENTS**

L. 1971, ch. 668, eff. June 22, 1971, added new CPLR 6514(e) providing for cancellation of notice of pendency of action by plaintiff.

**1967 AMENDMENTS**

L. 1967, ch. 440, eff. Sept. 1, 1967, added Subd. (d) permitting cancellation of notice of pendency by stipulation.

## § 6515.  Undertaking for cancellation of notice of pendency; security by plaintiff.

In any action other than one to foreclose a mortgage or for partition or dower, the court, upon motion of any person aggrieved and upon such notice as it may require, may direct any county clerk to cancel a notice of pendency, upon such terms as are just, whether or not the judgment demanded would affect specific real property, if the moving party shall give an undertaking in an amount to be fixed by the court, and if:

1. the court finds that adequate relief can be secured to the plaintiff by the giving of such an undertaking; or

2. in such action, the plaintiff fails to give an undertaking, in an amount to be fixed by the court, that the plaintiff will indemnify the moving party for the damages that he may incur if the notice is not canceled.

**1973 AMENDMENTS**

L. 1973, ch. 1029, eff. Sept. 1, 1973 amended paragraph (2) of CPLR 6515 by eliminating the restriction of paragraph 2 to actions for specific performance only.

# ARTICLE 70

# HABEAS CORPUS

---

## SUMMARY OF ARTICLE

§ 7001.   Application of article; special proceeding.
§ 7002.   Petition.
   (a)   By whom made.
   (b)   To whom made.
   (c)   Content.
§ 7003.   When the writ shall be issued.
   (a)   Generally.
   (b)   Successive petitions for writ.
   (c)   Penalty for violation.
§ 7004.   Content of writ.
   (a)   For whom issued.
   (b)   To whom directed.
   (c)   Before whom returnable.
   (d)   When returnable.
   (e)   Expenses; undertaking.
§ 7005.   Service of the writ.
§ 7006.   Obedience to the writ.
   (a)   Generally; defects in form.
   (b)   Compelling obedience.
   (c)   Precept to bring up person detained.
§ 7007.   Warrant preceding or accompanying writ.
§ 7008.   Return.
   (a)   When filed and served.
   (b)   Content.
§ 7009.   Hearing.
   (a)   Notice before hearing.
   (b)   Reply to return.
   (c)   Hearing to be summary.
   (d)   Sickness or infirmity of person detained.
   (e)   Custody during proceeding.
§ 7010.   Determination of proceeding.
   (a)   Discharge.
   (b)   Bail.
   (c)   Remand.
§ 7011.   Appeal.
§ 7012.   Redetention after discharge.

## § 7001.  Application of article; special proceeding.

Except as otherwise prescribed by statute, the provisions of this article are applicable to common law or statutory writs of habeas corpus and common law writs of certiorari to inquire into detention. A proceeding under this article is a special proceeding.

## § 7002.  Petition.

(a) By whom made. A person illegally imprisoned or otherwise restrained in his liberty within the state, or one acting on his behalf or a party in a child abuse proceeding subsequent to an order of the family court, may petition without notice for a writ of habeas corpus to inquire into the cause of such detention and for deliverance. A judge authorized to issue writs of habeas corpus having evidence, in a judicial proceeding before him, that any person is so detained shall, on his own initiative, issue a writ of habeas corpus for the relief of that person.

(b) To whom made. Except as provided in paragraph five of this subdivision, a petition for the writ shall be made to:

1. the supreme court in the judicial district in which the person is detained; or

2. the appellate division in the department in which the person is detained; or

3. any justice of the supreme court; or

4. a county judge being or residing within the county in which the person is detained; where there is no judge within the county capable of issuing the writ, or if all within the county capable of doing so have refused, the petition may be made to a county judge being or residing within an adjoining county.

5. in a city having a population of one million or more inhabitants, a person held as a trial inmate in a city detention institution shall petition for a writ to the supreme court in the county in which the charge for which the inmate is being detained is pending. Such inmate may also petition for a writ to the appellate division in the department in which he is detained or to any justice of the supreme court provided that the writ shall be made returnable before a justice of the supreme court held in the county in which the charge for which the inmate is being detained is pending.

(c) Content. The petition shall be verified and shall state, or shall be accompanied by an affidavit which shall state,

1. that the person in whose behalf the petition is made is detained, naming the person by whom he is detained and the place of detention if they are known, or describing them if they are not known; where the detention is by virtue of a mandate, a copy of it shall be annexed to the petition, or sufficient reason why a copy could not be obtained shall be stated;

2. the cause or pretense of the detention, according to the best knowledge and belief of the petitioner;

3. that a court or judge of the United States does not have exclusive jurisdiction to order him released;

4. if the writ is sought because of an illegal detention, the nature of the illegality;

5. whether any appeal has been taken from any order by virtue of which the person is detained, and, if so, the result;

6. the date, and the court or judge to whom made, of every previous application for the writ, the disposition of each such application and of any appeal taken, and the new facts, if any, presented in the petition that were not presented in any previous application; and

7. if the petition is made to a county judge outside the county in which the person is detained, the facts which authorize such judge to act.

### 1986 AMENDMENTS

L. 1986, ch. 355, eff. July 17, 1986, amended CPLR 7002(b)(1) and (5) by deleting references to special term.

### 1971 AMENDMENTS

L. 1971, ch. 803, eff. July 1, 1971 amended CPLR 7002 (b) the addition of new paragraph 5.

### 1969 AMENDMENTS

L. 1969, ch. 264, eff. June 1, 1969, amended Subd. (a) by adding that ". . . party in a child abuse proceeding subsequent to an order of the family court" may petition for a writ of habeas corpus.

## § 7003. When the writ shall be issued.

(a) Generally. The court to whom the petition is made shall issue the writ without delay on any day, or, where the petitioner does not demand production of the person detained or it is clear that there is no disputable issue of fact, order the respondent to show cause why the person detained should not be released. If it appears from the petition or the documents annexed thereto that the person is not illegally detained or that a court or judge of the United States has exclusive jurisdiction to order him released, the petition shall be denied.

(b) Successive petitions for writ. A court is not required to issue a writ of habeas corpus if the legality of the detention has been determined by a court of the state on a prior proceeding for a writ of habeas corpus and the petition presents no ground not theretofore presented and determined and the court is satisfied that the ends of justice will not be served by granting it.

(c) Penalty for violation. For a violation of this section in refusing to issue the writ, a judge, or, if the petition was made to a court, each member of the court who assents to the violation, forfeits to the person detained one thousand dollars to be recovered by an action in his name or in the name of the petitioner to his use.

## § 7004. Content of writ.

(a) For whom issued. The writ shall be issued on behalf of the state, and where issued upon the petition of a private person, it shall show that it was issued upon his relation.

(b) To whom directed. The writ shall be directed to, and the respondent shall be, the person having custody of the person detained.

(c) Before whom returnable. A writ to secure the discharge of a person from a state institution shall be made returnable before a justice of the supreme court or a county judge being or residing within the county in which the person is detained; if there is no such judge it shall be made returnable before the nearest accessible supreme court justice or county judge. In all other cases, the writ shall be made returnable in the county where it was issued, except that where the petition was made to the supreme court or to a supreme court justice outside the county in which the person is detained, such court or justice may make the writ returnable before any judge authorized to issue it in the county of detention.

(d) When returnable. The writ may be made returnable forthwith or on any day or time certain, as the case requires.

(e) Expenses; undertaking. A court issuing a writ directed to any person other than a public officer may require the petitioner to pay the charges of bringing up the person detained and to deliver an undertaking to the person having him in custody in an amount fixed by the court, to pay the charges for taking back the person detained if he should be remanded. Service of the writ shall not be complete until such charge is paid or tendered and such undertaking is delivered.

### 1964 AMENDMENTS

L. 1964, ch. 388, eff. Sept. 1, 1964, made a mechanical correction.

## § 7005. Service of the writ.

A writ of habeas corpus may be served on any day. Service shall be made by delivering the writ and a copy of the petition to the person to whom it is directed. If he cannot with due diligence be found, the writ may be served by leaving it and a copy of the petition with any person who has custody of the person detained at the time. Where the person to whom the writ is directed conceals himself or refuses admittance, the writ may be served by affixing it and a copy of the petition in a conspicuous place on the outside either of his dwelling or of the place where the person is detained and mailing a copy of the writ and the petition to him at such dwelling or place, unless the court which issues the writ determines, for good cause shown, that such mailing shall be dispensed with, or directs service in some other manner which it finds reasonably calculated to give notice to such person of the proceeding. If the person detained is in the custody of a person other than the one to whom the writ is directed, a copy of the writ may be served upon the person having such custody with the same effect as if the writ had been directed to him.

### 1970 AMENDMENTS

L. 1970, ch. 395, eff. Sept. 1, 1970, amended the section by adding new material to the penultimate sentence, after the word "detained."

The amendment was recommended by the Judicial Conference Jan. 2, 1970 Report to the Legislature which stated, in part:

"This bill would amend CPLR 7005, which prescribes methods of service of the writ of habeas corpus, to provide a more desirable method for service where the person to whom the writ is directed conceals himself or refuses admittance. Presently, under such circumstances, the statute prescribes service by affixing the writ and a copy of the petition in a conspicuous place on the outside either of his dwelling place or of the place where the person is detained. No adequate reason appears for the existence of a difference between the method of substituted service of the writ of habeas corpus, which requires only the ñailing' of the writ, and the method of substituted service of process, which requires ñailing and mailing'.

"Although there is need for haste in some habeas corpus matters, emotions frequently run high in such situations, and the evidence of concealment or refusal is often circumstantial. Where the need for haste is paramount, the proposed bill would allow the court, upon good cause shown, to dispense with mailing or to direct service in some other manner which it finds reasonably calculated to give notice. The latter clause of the proposed amendment would introduce desirable flexibility into service of the writ, allowing even greater haste when warranted, than is presently possible. For example, the court could direct that service be made orally by use of the telephone or of an electric bullhorn, if the circumstances of the case were sufficiently urgent to warrant doing so."

## § 7006. Obedience to the writ.

(a) Generally; defects in form. A person upon whom the writ or a copy thereof is served, whether it is directed to him or not, shall make a return to it and, if required by it, produce the body of the person detained at the time and place specified, unless the person detained is too sick or infirm to make the required trip. A writ of habeas corpus shall not be disobeyed for defect of form so long as the identity of the person detained may be derived from its contents.

(b) Compelling obedience. If the person upon whom the writ or a copy thereof is served refuses or neglects fully to obey it, without showing sufficient cause, the court before whom the writ is returnable, upon proof of its service, shall forthwith issue a warrant of attachment against him directed to the sheriff in any county in which such person may be found requiring him to be brought before the court issuing the warrant; he may be ordered committed in close custody to the county jail until he complies with the order of the court. Where such person is a sheriff, the warrant shall be directed to a person specifically designated to execute it. Such person shall have power to call to his aid the same assistance as the sheriff in executing the warrant; a sheriff shall be committed to a jail in a county other than his own.

(c) Precept to bring up person detained. A court issuing a warrant of attachment as prescribed in subdivision (b) may at the same time, or thereafter, issue a precept to the person to whom the warrant is directed ordering him immediately to bring before the court the person detained.

## § 7007. Warrant preceding or accompanying writ.

A court authorized to issue a writ of habeas corpus, upon satisfactory proof that a person is wrongfully detained and will be removed from the state or suffer irreparable injury before he can be relieved by habeas corpus, shall issue a warrant of attachment directed to an appropriate officer requiring him immediately to bring the person detained before the court. A writ of habeas corpus directed to the person having custody of the person detained shall also be issued. Where it appears that the detention constitutes a criminal offense, the warrant may order the apprehension of the person responsible for the detention, who shall then be brought before the court issuing the warrant and examined as in a criminal case.

## § 7008. Return.

(a) When filed and served. The return shall consist of an affidavit to be served in the same manner as an answer in a special proceeding and filed at the time and place specified in the writ, or, where the writ is returnable forthwith, within twenty-four hours after its service.

(b) Content. The affidavit shall fully and explicitly state whether the person detained is or has been in the custody of the person to whom the writ is directed, the authority and cause of the detention, whether custody has been transferred to another, and the facts of and authority for any such transfer. A copy of any mandate by virtue of which the person is detained shall be annexed to the affidavit, and the original mandate shall be produced at the hearing; where the mandate has been delivered to the person to whom the person detained was transferred, or a copy of it cannot be obtained, the reason for failure to produce it and the substance of the mandate shall be stated in the affidavit.

## § 7009. Hearing.

(a) Notice before hearing. Where the detention is by virtue of a mandate, the court shall not adjudicate the issues in the proceeding until written notice of the time and place of the hearing has been served either personally eight days prior to the hearing, or in any other manner or time as the court may order,

1. where the mandate was issued in a civil cause, upon the person interested in continuing the detention or upon his attorney; or,

2. where a person is detained by order of the family court, or by order of any court while a proceeding affecting him is pending in the said family court, upon the judge who made the order. In all such proceedings the court shall be represented by the corporation counsel of the city of New York, or outside the city of New York, by the county attorney; or,

3. in any other case, upon the district attorney of the county in which the person was detained when the writ was served and upon the district attorney of the county from which he was committed.

(b) Reply to return. The petitioner or the person detained may deny under oath, orally or in writing, any material allegation of the answering affidavits or allege any fact showing that the person detained is entitled to be discharged.

(c) Hearing to be summary. The court shall proceed in a summary manner to hear the evidence produced in support of and against the detention and to dispose of the proceeding as justice requires.

(d) Sickness or infirmity of person detained. Where it is proved to the satisfaction of the court that the person detained is too sick or infirm to be brought to the appointed place, the hearing may be held without his presence, may be adjourned, or may be held at the place where the prisoner is detained.

(e) Custody during proceeding. Pending final disposition, the court may place the person detained in custody or parole him or admit him to bail as justice requires.

## § 7010. Determination of proceeding.

(a) Discharge. If the person is illegally detained a final judgment shall be directed discharging him forthwith. No person detained shall be discharged for a defect in the form of the commitment, or because the person detaining him is not entitled to do so if another person is so entitled. A final judgment to discharge a person may be enforced by the court issuing the order by attachment in the manner prescribed in subdivision (b) of section 7006.

(b) Bail. If the person detained has been admitted to bail but the amount fixed is so excessive as to constitute an abuse of discretion, and he is not ordered discharged, the court shall direct a final judgment reducing bail to a proper amount. If the person detained has been denied bail, and he is not ordered discharged, the court shall direct a final judgment admitting him to bail forthwith, if he is entitled to be admitted to bail as a matter of right, or if it appears that the denial of bail constituted an abuse of discretion. Such judgment must fix the amount of bail, specify the time and place at which the person detained is required to appear, and order his release upon bail being given in accordance with the criminal procedure law.

(c) Remand. If the person detained is not ordered discharged and not admitted to bail, a final judgment shall be directed dismissing the proceeding, and, if he was actually produced in court, remanding him to the detention from which he

CPLR

was taken, unless the person then detaining him was not entitled to do so, in which case he shall be remanded to proper detention.

### CROSS REFERENCES

Criminal Procedure Law bail provisions referred to in Subd. (b), *supra*, appear in **Crim. Pro. L. §§ 500-550.10.**

### 1971 AMENDMENTS

L. 1971, ch. 1097, eff. Sept. 1, 1971, amended CPLR 7010(b) by deleting the reference to the Code of Criminal Procedure and substituting reference to the Criminal Procedure Law.

## § 7011. Appeal.

An appeal may be taken from a judgment refusing to grant a writ of habeas corpus or refusing an order to show cause issued under subdivision (a) of section 7003, or from a judgment made upon the return of such writ or order to show cause. A person to whom notice is given pursuant to subdivision (a) of section 7009 is a party for purposes of appeal. The attorney-general may appeal in the name of the state in any case where a district attorney might do so. Where an appeal from a judgment admitting a person to bail is taken by the state, his release shall not be stayed thereby.

## § 7012. Redetention after discharge.

A person discharged upon the return of a writ of habeas corpus shall not be detained for the same cause, except by virtue of a subsequent lawful mandate.

# ARTICLE 71

# RECOVERY OF CHATTEL

---

## SUMMARY OF ARTICLE

§ 7101.   When action may be brought.
§ 7102.   Seizure of chattel on behalf of plaintiff.
    (a)  Seizure of chattel.
    (b)  Service.
    (c)  Affidavit.
    (d)  Order of seizure.
    (e)  Undertaking.
    (f)  Disposition of chattel by sheriff.
§ 7103.   Reclaiming, impounding or returning chattel.
    (a)  Reclaiming chattel.
    (b)  Impounding chattel.
    (c)  Returning chattel.
    (d)  Additional parties.
§ 7104.   Seizing, reclaiming or returning less than all chattels.
§ 7105.   Sale of perishable property.
§ 7106.   Payment of sheriff's fees and expenses; liability of sheriff.
    (a)  Payment of sheriff's fees and expenses.
    (b)  Liability of sheriff.
§ 7107.   Sheriff's return.
§ 7108.   Judgment; execution in certain cases; enforcement by contempt.
    (a)  Generally.
    (b)  Where value of chattel should not be awarded; execution.
    (c)  Failure of jury to fix sum.
§ 7109.   Unique chattel.
    (a)  Injunction, temporary restraining order.
    (b)  Judgment enforceable by contempt.
§ 7110.   Sheriff's powers.
§ 7111.   Action on undertaking.
§ 7112.   Testimony by deposition to ascertain location of chattel.

---

## § 7101.   When action may be brought.

An action under this article may be brought to try the right to possession of a chattel.

## § 7102. Seizure of chattel on behalf of plaintiff.

(a) Seizure of chattel. When the plaintiff delivers to a sheriff an order of seizure, the papers on which the order was granted, the undertaking and a summons and complaint bearing the index number and the date of filing with the clerk of the court, in the action to recover the chattel, he shall seize the chattel in accordance with the provisions of the order and without delay.

(b) Service. The sheriff shall serve upon the person from whose possession the chattel is seized a copy of the order of seizure, the papers on which the order was granted, and the undertaking delivered to him by the plaintiff. Unless the order of seizure provides otherwise, the papers delivered to him by the plaintiff, shall be personally served by the sheriff on each defendant not in default in the same manner as a summons or as provided in section 314; if a defendant has appeared he shall be served in the manner provided for service of papers generally.

(c) Affidavit. The application for an order of seizure shall be supported by an affidavit which shall clearly identify the chattel to be seized and shall state:

1. that the plaintiff is entitled to possession by virtue of facts set forth;

2. that the chattel is wrongfully held by the defendant named;

3. whether an action to recover the chattel has been commenced, the defendants served, whether they are in default, and, if they have appeared, where papers may be served upon them;

4. the value of each chattel or class of chattels claimed, or the aggregate value of all chattels claimed;

5. if the plaintiff seeks the inclusion in the order of seizure of a provision authorizing the sheriff to break open, enter and search for the chattel, the place where the chattel is located and facts sufficient to establish probable cause to believe that the chattel is located at the place;

6. that no defense to the claim is known to the plaintiff; and

7. if the plaintiff seeks an order of seizure without notice, facts sufficient to establish that unless such order is granted without notice, it is probable the chattel will become unavailable for seizure by reason of being transferred, concealed, disposed of, or removed from the state, or will become substantially impaired in value.

(d) Order of seizure. 1. Upon presentation of the affidavit and undertaking and upon finding that it is probable the plaintiff will succeed on the merits and the facts are as stated in the affidavit, the court may grant an order directing the sheriff of any county where the chattel is found to seize the chattel described in the affidavit and including, if the court so directs, a provision that, if the chattel is not delivered to the sheriff, he may break open, enter and search for the chattel in the place specified in the affidavit. The plaintiff shall have the burden of establishing the grounds for the order.

2. Upon a motion for an order of seizure, the court, without notice to the defendant, may grant a temporary restraining order that the chattel shall not be removed from the state if it is a vehicle, aircraft or vessel or, otherwise, from its location, transferred, sold, pledged, assigned or otherwise disposed of or permitted to become subject to a security interest or lien until further order of the court. Unless the court otherwise directs, the restraining order does not prohibit a disposition of the chattel to the plaintiff. Disobedience of the order may be punished as contempt of court.

3. An order as provided in paragraph one of this subdivision may be granted without notice only if, in addition to the other prerequisites for the granting of the order, the court finds that unless such order is granted without notice it is probable the chattel will become unavailable for seizure by reason of being transferred, concealed, disposed of, or removed from the state, or will become substantially impaired in value.

4. An order of seizure granted without notice shall provide that the plaintiff shall move for an order confirming the order of seizure on such notice to the defendant and sheriff and within such period, not to exceed five days after seizure, as the court shall direct. Unless the motion is made within such period, the order of seizure shall have no further effect and shall be vacated on motion and any chattel seized thereunder shall be returned forthwith to the defendant. Upon the motion to confirm, the plaintiff shall have the burden of establishing the grounds for confirmation.

(e) Undertaking. The undertaking shall be executed by sufficient surety, acceptable to the court. The condition of the undertaking shall be that the surety is bound in a specified amount, not less than twice the value of the chattel stated in the plaintiff's affidavit, for the return of the chattel to any person to whom possession is awarded by the judgment, and for payment of any sum awarded by the judgment against the person giving the undertaking. A person claiming only a lien on or security interest in the chattel may except to the plaintiff's surety.

(f) Disposition of chattel by sheriff. Unless the court orders otherwise, the sheriff shall retain custody of a chattel for a period of ten days after seizure where seizure is pursuant to an order granted on notice, and until served with an order of confirmation where seizure is pursuant to an order granted without notice. At the expiration of such period, the sheriff shall deliver the chattel to the plaintiff if there has not been served upon him a notice of exception to plaintiff's surety, a notice of motion for an impounding or returning order, or the necessary papers to reclaim the chattel. Upon failure of the surety on plaintiff's undertaking to justify, the sheriff shall deliver possession of the chattel to the person from whom it was seized.

### 1994 AMENDMENTS

L. 1994, ch. 563, eff. July 26, 1994, amended CPLR 7102(a) by deleting the word "and" following "order was granted"; deleting the clause "if an action to recover a

**CPLR**

chattel has not been commenced" following "the undertaking and"; and by adding the phrase "in the action to recover the chattel."

## 1992 AMENDMENTS

L. 1992, ch. 216, eff. July 1, 1992, amended subdivision (a) by adding the words "bearing the index number and the date of filing with the clerk of the court."

## 1978 AMENDMENTS

L. 1978, ch. 81, eff. Jan. 1, 1979, amended CPLR 7102. The amendments were recommended by the Judicial Conference in its Report to the 1978 Legislature, wherein it stated:

"The purpose of this proposal to amend CPLR Article 71 is twofold: (1) to assure that New York's statutory replevin procedure is constitutional and (2) to replace the vague reference to due process in the present statute with specific statements of the requirements of due process, thus affording clear guidance to the bench and bar.

"In 1970, a three-judge federal court held that the provision of Article 71 permitting the prejudgment seizure of chattels by the plaintiff in a replevin action without an order of a judge or of a court of competent jurisdiction . . .' violated the Fourth Amendment of the United States Constitution as applied to the states by the Fourteenth Amendment and the procedural due process requirements of the Fourteenth Amendment (*LaPrease v. Raymours Furniture Company*, (D.C.N.Y.) 315 F.Supp. 716, 725 (N.D.N.Y. 1970)).

"Article 71 was amended in 1971 (L. 1971, ch. 1051) to comply with the requirements of constitutional due process suggested by the *LaPrease* decision. However, as amended, Article 71 simply authorizes the courts to grant the order of seizure and to direct the sheriff to break into the place where the chattel is located when it is constitutional to do so (see CPLR 7102(d) (1)).

"In 1972, when the United States Supreme Court decided *Fuentes v. Shevin*, 92 S.Ct. 1983, 407 U.S. 67, 32 L.Ed. 556 (1972), it appeared that constitutional due process required notice and a hearing aimed at establishing the probable validity of the underlying claim before the chattel may be seized, except in unusual circumstances (see *Fuentes*, 407 U.S. at 93, 97). In *Fuentes* the Court held unconstitutional the Florida and Pennsylvania replevin statutes that allowed seizure of goods by a sheriff without notice, hearing, and judicial order.

"Shortly after *Fuentes* was decided, the judges and clerks of the Civil Court of the City of New York were directed to deny all applications for the prejudgment seizure of chattels unless the defendant had been given notice and an opportunity to be heard (Edward Thompson, J.S.C., Administrative Judge, Notice to Clerks of Special Term (July 11, 1972)).

"However, in 1974, the United States Supreme Court held constitutional the Louisiana replevin statute allowing ex parte pre-judgment seizure of property (*Mitchell v. W. T. Grant Company*, 94 S.Ct. 1895, 416 U.S. 600, 40 L.Ed.2d 406 (1974)). Furthermore, in *Mitchell* and in a 1975 opinion, *North Georgia Finishing Co., Inc. v. Di-Chem, Inc.*, 95 S.Ct. 719, 419 U.S. 601, 42 L.Ed.2d 751 (1975), the Court clarified due process requirements and established a balancing test to determine the constitutionality of a replevin procedure.

"Due process requires notice and . . . opportunity for a hearing or other safeguard against mistaken repossession . . . .' (*North Georgia Finishing Co., Inc. v. Di-Chem, Inc.*, 95 S.Ct. 719, 419 U.S. at 606, 42 L.Ed.2d 751 (1975), holding unconstitutional the impounding, in a commercial litigation, of respondent's bank account pursuant to a Georgia garnishment statute because of the absence of a prompt hearing at which the creditor would be required to demonstrate at least probable cause' to justify the garnishment). The replevin procedure must accommodate the conflicting interests of the plaintiff and defendant and minimize the risk of mistaken repossession (*Mitchell v. W. T. Grant Co.,* 94 S.Ct. 1895, 416 U.S. at 607, 618, 40 L.Ed.2d 406 (1974)). Plaintiffs are concerned that property they they [sic] are entitled to possess will deteriorate in the hands of the defendant or will become unavailable. Defendants are interested in enjoying the use and possession of property they are entitled to and in being compensated for all damages if the order of seizure is mistakenly granted.

"The ex parte procedure in *Mitchell* constitutionally accommodated the interests of both parties and minimized the risk of mistaken repossession. The main features of that procedure are: 1) the plaintiff must establish the probability of success; 2) the plaintiff must present the factual basis of his claim instead of conclusory allegations; 3) there is judicial supervision throughout; 4) the defendant is entitled to an early post-seizure hearing in which the plaintiff must prove his claim; 5) the plaintiff must put up a bond to guarantee the defendant against damages and expenses resulting from mistaken repossession.

"Whether the Fourth Amendment applies to replevin procedures was not decided by the United States Supreme Court in *Fuentes, Mitchell,* or *North Georgia Finishing Co., Inc.* However, lower federal courts have held that the Fourth Amendment applies to orders of seizure authorizing the sheriff to forcibly enter and search the place where the chattel is located (*LaPrease,* 315 F.Supp. at 721-22; *Hamrick v. Ashland Finance Co. of W. Va.,* (D.C.W.Va) 423 F.Supp. 1033, 1036-37 (S.D.W.Va. 1976)).

"Using the guidance provided by the United States Supreme Court in *Mitchell* and *North Georgia Finishing Co., Inc.* on the procedural due process problem and by lower federal courts on the Fourth Amendment problem, it is now possible to amend Article 71 to assure that it is constitutional and to rectify the failure of the 1971 amendment to Art. 71 to establish clear and easily usable standards to guide attorneys and the courts in taking action under the statute.' Edward Thompson, J.S.C., Administrative Judge, *Notice to Judges and Clerks, No. 176* (March 17, 1972 (quoting Governor Rockefeller's statement on signing the measure amending Article 71 in 1971)).

"This proposal to amend Article 71 establishes procedures for granting the order of seizure on notice (revised section 7102(d)(1)) and the order of seizure without notice (new section 7102(d)(3)). A temporary restraining order is available in both proceedings (see revised section 7102(d)(2)). If a seizure is made pursuant to an order of seizure without notice, new section 7102(d)(4) provides for an early hearing to minimize the risk and harm of mistaken repossession, and a new provision of section 7108(a) makes the plaintiff liable to the defendant for all damages if the order of seizure without notice is not confirmed under new section 7102(d)(4).

"Because of Fourth Amendment concerns, the revised section governing the order of seizure requires probable cause to believe that the chattel is located as specified before the court may authorize the sheriff to break in and search (see revised section 7102(d)(1)). In addition, if the order of seizure is without notice, the court must find exigent circumstances under new section 7102(d)(3).

"The Committee has considered the replevin provisions in light of *Shaffer v. Heitner,* (U.S.Del.), 97 S.Ct. 2569, 45 U.S.L.W. 4849 (U.S. Supreme Court, June 24, 1977) which held that when the property serving as the basis for the exercise of jurisdiction by a state court in a quasi-in-rem action is completely unrelated to the plaintiff's cause of action, the presence of the property alone is not sufficient to support the state's jurisdiction under due process. The Committee has concluded that no revision of the replevin article is necessary in light of *Shaffer* because in replevin the property to be seized is the very subject matter of the underlying claim.

"The Advisory Committee wishes to highlight a major change made by the bill that could otherwise be overlooked. The substitution of may' for shall' in section 7102(d)(1) and (2) makes replevin a discretionary remedy. This is justified because, although not formally a provisional remedy, replevin is functionally a provisional remedy since it involves a prejudgment seizure of property. All the provisional remedies save lis pendens are discretionary and in view of the drastic nature of the remedy and the infinite variety of possible fact patterns, replevin should also be discretionary.

*Subdivision (a)*. "The amendment to section 7102(a) provides that the documents to be delivered by the plaintiff to the sheriff shall include, among other things, the papers on which the order was granted. This amendment is not intended to change the meaning of section 7102(a). Rather, the amendment simply makes it clear that the court examines the papers, and grants the order before the order, and the papers on which the order was granted are given to the sheriff and that the sheriff then acts pursuant to court order."

*Subdivision (b)*. "The amendment to section 7102(b) provides that the documents that the sheriff shall serve upon the person from whose possession the chattel is seized include, in addition to a copy of the order of seizure, copies of the papers on which the order was granted, and the undertaking delivered to the sheriff by the plaintiff. The purpose of this amendment is to conform section 7102(b) to section 7102 (a) as amended."

*Subdivision (c)*. "The purpose of the proposed amendments to section 7102(c) is to coordinate the affidavit requirements with the factual issues that the court must focus on in deciding whether to issue an order of seizure under revised section 7102(d)(1) or new section 7102(d)(3).

"The general reference in section 7102(c)(5) to due process has been deleted and replaced by a specific statement of the due process standard. Under revised paragraph (5) of section 7102(c), if the plaintiff seeks the inclusion in the order of seizure of a provision authorizing the sheriff to break open, enter and search for the chattel, the affidavit shall state where the chattel is located and facts sufficient to establish probable cause to believe that such chattel is located there.

"The statement in revised paragraph (5) is necessary to enable the court to determine under revised section 7102(d)(1) whether the order of seizure should authorize the sheriff to break in and search for the chattel. The plaintiff's factual statement must show that the information and the informant are reliable and credible (*see Aguilar v. State of Texas*, 84 S.Ct. 1509, 378 U.S. 108, 12 L.Ed.2d 723 (1964)).

"Under new paragraph (6), the plaintiff must state that he knows of no defense to his claim. The statement focuses attention on the possibility that defenses to the claim exist that would defeat plaintiff's right to possession of the chattel. If an order of seizure without notice is granted and, at the hearing on the plaintiff's motion for an order of confirmation under new paragraph (4) of section 7102(d), the defendant establishes that he has a defense to the claim and that the plaintiff knew about the defense at the time of plaintiff's motion for an order of seizure without notice, the court, in ruling on the motion for an order of confirmation and in assessing damages, may consider the fact that the plaintiff stated in his affidavit that he knew of no defense.

"New paragraph (6) of section 7102(c) also is in aid of section 601 of the General Business Law which prohibits a principal creditor (as defined in section 600 of the General Business Law) or his agent from claiming or attempting or threatening to enforce a right with knowledge or reason to know that the right does not exist. N.Y. General Business Law § 601.

"Under new paragraph (7) of section 7102(c), if the plaintiff seeks an order of seizure without notice, he shall state facts sufficient to establish that unless such order is granted without notice it is probable the chattel will become unavailable for seizure by reason of being transferred, concealed, disposed of, or removed from the state, or will become substantially impaired in value.

"The statement in new paragraph (7) of section 7102(c) is necessary to enable the court to decide under new paragraph (3) of section 7102(d) whether to grant an order of seizure without notice."

*Subdivision (d).* "Section 7102(d) has been divided into four paragraphs: (1), (2), (3), and (4). As amended, section 7102(d) spells out the due process requirements for an order of seizure and for authorizing the sheriff to break in and search, permits the court to grant a temporary restraining order, and establishes the procedure for the new requirement that an order of seizure without notice must be confirmed.

"Revised paragraph (1) of section 7102(d) is the core provision governing orders of seizure. It governs the order of seizure on notice and, in conjunction with new paragraphs (3) and (4) of section 7102(d), the order of seizure without notice.

"Paragraph (1), as revised, permits the court to grant an order of seizure upon presentation of the affidavit and undertaking and upon finding that it is probable that the plaintiff will succeed on the merits and the facts are as stated in the affidavit. This proposed provision states that the court may' grant an order of seizure, rather than shall' grant an order of seizure as at present, to make it clear that the court has discretion to prevent unfair and mistaken deprivations of property . . .' (*Fuentes,* 407 U.S. at 97), and to conform the replevin procedure, which is functionally a provisional remedy, to other provisional remedies which are discretionary. The court must find it probable' that the plaintiff will succeed on the merits because due process requires that the plaintiff establish the probability that his case will succeed' (*Mitchell,* 94 S.Ct. 1895, 416 U.S. at 609, 40 L.Ed.2d 406. Accord, *Fuentes,* 407 U.S. at 97; *Long Is. Trust Co. v. Porta Aluminum,* 354 N.Y.S.2d 134, 44 A.D.2d 118, 124 (2nd Dept. 1974)).

"Revised paragraph (1) of section 7102(d) also provides that if the facts are as stated in the affidavit, the court may include in the order of seizure a provision that, if the chattel is not delivered to the sheriff, the sheriff may break open, enter and search for the chattel in the place specified in the affidavit. Thus, if the court finds probable cause to believe that the chattel is located at the place specified in the affidavit, the court may authorize the sheriff to break into and search that place if the chattel is not delivered to the sheriff. Under the Fourth Amendment, the location of the chattel must be specified and there must be probable cause to believe that the chattel is located at that place (*LaPrease v. Raymours Furniture Company,* (D.C.N.Y.) 315 F.Supp. 716, 721 (N.D.N.Y. 1970); *Hamrick v. Ashland Finance Co. of W. Va.,* (D.C.W.Va.) 423 F.Supp. 1033, 1036-37 (S.D.W.Va. 1976)). The court is given discretion to permit the sheriff to break in and search because the Fourth Amendment requires that breaking and entering be allowed only in the court's sound discretion. (*Hamrick,* (D.C.W.Va.) 432 F.Supp. at 1036).

"Finally, revised paragraph (1) of section 7102(d) provides that the plaintiff shall have the burden of establishing the grounds for the order. The purpose of this provision is to clarify that the plaintiff has the burden to establish all the grounds for the granting of the order of seizure.

"Revised paragraph (2) of section 7102(d) provides that the court, without notice to the defendant, may grant a temporary restraining order upon any motion for an order of seizure, not, as at present, only when the order of seizure does not include a provision authorizing the sheriff to break in and search. As with the granting of an order of seizure and the inclusion of the breaking and search provision, the authority to grant a temporary restraining order is discretionary, not, as at present, mandatory.

"The temporary restraining order in new paragraph (2) of section 7102(d) provides the plaintiff with the immediate protection of having the status quo preserved without significantly interfering with the defendant's use and possession of the chattel. The temporary restraining order is available even if the court decides that the order of seizure without notice is inappropriate.

"By providing for the granting of a temporary restraining order upon a motion for an order of seizure, revised paragraph (2) of section 7102(d) encourages plaintiffs to proceed on notice. When a plaintiff weighs the need to proceed without notice against the cost of proceeding without notice (*e.g.,* the greater proof requirements under new paragraph (3) of section 7102(d) and the greater potential damages liability under revised section 7108(a)), the fact that a temporary restraining order is available to protect his interest in the property if he moves for an order of seizure on notice may lead him to proceed on notice.

"New paragraph (3) of section 7102(d) has been added to govern the order of seizure without notice. Under new paragraph (3), an order as provided in section 7102(d)(1) may be granted without notice only if, in addition to the other prerequisites for the granting of the order, the court finds that unless such order is granted without notice it is probable that the chattel will become unavailable for seizure by reason of being transferred, concealed, disposed of, or removed from the state, or will become substantially impaired in value.

"After the decisions in *LaPrease and Fuentes,* which raised doubts about the constitutionality of the ex parte order of seizure, the Civil Court of the City of New York, since 1972, has granted orders of seizure only on notice to the defendant and has protected plaintiffs in special situations by granting ṡtays' enjoining defendants from disposing of or destroying the chattels in dispute (see Edward Thompson, J.S.C., Administrative Judge, *Notice to Clerks of Special Term* (July 11, 1972) and *Directive to Judges, Clerks and Special Term II Clerks No. 219* (December 5, 1972)).

"It is now clear that an ex parte replevin procedure is constitutional if it accommodates the interests of the plaintiff and the defendant and minimizes the risk and harm of mistaken repossession (see *Mitchell,* 94 S.Ct. 1895, 416 U.S. 600, 40 L.Ed. 2d 406). Under new paragraph (3) of section 7102(d), the court has discretion to grant an order of seizure without notice if the court finds it probable that the plaintiff will succeed on the merits and that the facts are as stated in the affidavit and the court finds that, unless such order of seizure is granted without notice, it is probable that the chattel will become unavailable for seizure by reason of being transferred, concealed, disposed of, or removed from the state or will become substantially impaired in value.

"The harm to the defendant that would flow from mistaken repossession is minimized by the early post-seizure hearing provided for in new paragraph (4) of section 7102(d).

"New paragraph (3) of section 7102(d) also takes into account the concern that a number of judges have expressed about the constitutionality of including in an ex parte order of seizure permission for the sheriff to break in and search (see, *e.g., LaPrease,* (D.C.N.Y.) 315 F.Supp. at 721-22; Edward Thompson J.S.C., Administrative Judge, *Notice to Judges and Clerks, No. 176* (March 17, 1972)). Because the danger of mistaken repossession is greater when the order is granted ex parte and because the interference with the defendant's expectation of privacy is greater when the sheriff is permitted to break in and search, new paragraph (3) requires not only probable cause to believe that the chattel is located as specified in the affidavit (as is required by revised section 7102(d)(1)), but also that the court be satisfied that, unless the order is granted without notice, the chattel will become unavailable for seizure by reason of being transferred, concealed, disposed of, or removed from the state, or will become substantially impaired in value. This exigency requirement comports with Judge Thompson's *Notice to Judges and Clerks, No. 176* (March 17, 1972).

"New paragraph (4) of section 7102(d) provides that an order of seizure granted without notice shall provide that the plaintiff shall move for an order confirming the order of seizure on such notice to the defendant and sheriff and within such period, not to exceed five days after seizure, as the court shall direct. Unless the motion is made within such period, the order of seizure shall have no further effect and shall be vacated on motion and any chattel seized thereunder shall be returned forthwith to the defendant. Upon the motion to confirm, the plaintiff shall have the burden of establishing the grounds for confirmation.

"Thus, where the order of seizure without notice is used, the defendant is protected by the requirement that the seizure be swiftly followed by a hearing and order of confirmation or else the order of seizure will be void and the chattel will be returned to the defendant. At the hearing on the motion for the order of confirmation, the court has discretion to confirm the order of seizure if the plaintiff establishes all the grounds for the granting of the order of seizure without notice under section 7102(d)(3). Where the order of seizure is granted without notice, due process requires an early noticed hearing with the plaintiff having the burden of establishing the probability of success in establishing his claim.

"Although a motion to vacate is not required to void the seizure, it is permitted. A defendant may, for example, wish to secure an order vacating the seizure in order to lay a procedural foundation for recovering damages on account of improper seizure."

*Subdivision (f).* "This amendment provides that, where seizure is pursuant to an order granted on notice, unless the court orders otherwise, the sheriff shall retain custody of the chattel for a period of ten days after seizure, and, where seizure is pursuant to an order granted without notice, unless the court orders otherwise, the sheriff shall retain custody of the chattel for a period of ten days after seizure and until served with an order of confirmation.

"The purpose of this revision is to coordinate section 7102(f) with new paragraph (4) of section 7102(d), which governs the confirmation of the order of seizure without notice.

"The word èither' that appears in the second sentence of section 7102(f) has been deleted for grammatical reasons."

**1971 AMENDMENTS**

L. 1971, ch. 1051, eff. July 2, 1971, amended CPLR 7102.

## § 7103. Reclaiming, impounding or returning chattel.

(a) Reclaiming chattel. A chattel may be reclaimed by any person claiming the right to its possession, except a defendant claiming only a lien thereon or security interest therein, by service upon the sheriff, and upon all parties to the action, of a notice that the reclaiming party requires a return of all or part of the chattels replevied; an undertaking executed as required by subdivision (e) of section 7102 and an affidavit stating that the reclaiming party is entitled to possession by virtue of facts set forth. The sheriff shall retain custody of the

CPLR

chattel for ten days after such papers have been served upon him. At the expiration of such period he shall deliver the chattel to the person serving the notice if there has not been served upon him a notice of exception to sureties or a notice of motion for an impounding order. Upon failure by the surety to justify, the sheriff shall deliver possession of the chattel to the plaintiff. If more than one person serves a reclaiming notice on the sheriff, the sheriff shall move, on notice to all parties, to have the court determine to whom the chattel shall be delivered.

(b) Impounding chattel. A chattel which is in the custody of the sheriff may be impounded pending judgment or further order of the court, upon motion of any person claiming the right to its possession, upon notice to the sheriff and to all parties to the action. The motion shall be granted if the chattel is of such a nature, or the circumstances are such, that the moving party, if found to be entitled to possession, would not be adequately compensated for its loss by the payment of its pecuniary value. An undertaking shall accompany the motion, in an amount not less than two hundred and fifty dollars, that the moving party will indemnify the sheriff for all expenses incurred by him in transporting, handling and safekeeping the chattel pending determination of the motion, and, if the motion is granted, pending judgment or further order of the court. All expenses resulting from impounding shall be taxed as disbursements in the action as the court may direct.

(c) Returning chattel. 1. If a chattel which is in the custody of the sheriff is personal property which if owned by a defendant would be exempt from application to the satisfaction of a money judgment, if the value of the possession of the chattel to the defendant is greater than the value of its possession to the plaintiff, if the interest of the plaintiff would not thereby be prejudiced and if the interests of justice so require, upon motion of the defendant, upon notice to the sheriff and to all parties to the action, and on such terms and on such security and conditions as to the court may seem proper, the court may order its return to the defendant.

2. If the court orders the return of the chattel to the defendant, it shall grant a restraining order that the chattel shall not be removed from the state if it is a vehicle, aircraft or vessel or, otherwise, from its location, transferred, sold, pledged, assigned or otherwise disposed of or permitted to become subject to a security interest or lien until further order of the court. Unless the court otherwise directs, the restraining order does not prohibit a disposition of the chattel to the plaintiff. Disobedience of the order may be punished as a contempt of court.

(d) Additional parties. A motion under this section, or service upon plaintiff of a notice of reclamation or exception to surety by a person not a party to the action, makes such a person a party to the action. Plaintiff shall serve a copy of the complaint upon such person within twenty days after he becomes a party.

**CPLR**

### 1971 AMENDMENTS

L. 1971, ch. 1051, eff. July 2, 1971, amended subd. (a), added new subd. (c) and relettered former subd. (c) to be subd. (d).

## § 7104. Seizing, reclaiming or returning less than all chattels.

Where the seizure of two or more chattels is required by the order of seizure, the sheriff shall seize those chattels which can be found. Less than all of the seized chattels may be impounded, reclaimed, or returned. The value of the chattels seized, as stated in the affidavit of the plaintiff, or as determined by the court upon application of the defendant, shall be the value for the purposes of subsequent undertakings in the action. Unless the court orders otherwise, the sheriff may, at any time before entry of judgment, seize those chattels not yet seized; the proceedings for reclaiming, impounding or returning a chattel subsequently seized are the same as on a former seizure.

### 1978 AMENDMENTS

L. 1978, ch. 81, eff. Jan. 1, 1979, amended CPLR 7104 by adoption of proposals made by the Judicial Conference in its Report to the 1978 Legislature, in which it stated:

"Section 7104 has been amended to provide that the value of the chattels seized for the purposes of subsequent undertakings in the action shall be as stated in the affidavit or as determined by the court upon application of the defendant.

"The purpose of this amendment is to make it clear that in determining the value of the chattel, the court may take into consideration the value that the defendant asserts is the value of the chattel as well as the value that the plaintiff has alleged in his affidavit. This amendment is intended to obviate the danger that the plaintiff may have overvalued or undervalued the chattel because of mistake or for other reasons. For example, the plaintiff may have undervalued the chattel in order to be able to put up a smaller bond under section 7102(e); the plaintiff may have overvalued the chattel in order to show that it is urgent that an order of seizure be granted."

See notes under the 1978 amendment to CPLR 7102 for the extensive commentary by the Judicial Conference recommending the 1978 amendment of Article 71.

### 1971 AMENDMENTS

L. 1971, ch. 1051, eff. July 2, 1971, amended CPLR 7104.

## § 7105. Sale of perishable property.

Upon motion with such notice as the court may require, the court may order the sheriff to sell perishable property which has been seized. The court shall prescribe the time and place of the sale, and the manner and time in which notice thereof shall be given. Unless the court orders otherwise, the sheriff, after deducting his fees and necessary expenses, shall pay the proceeds into court to be held pending determination of the action.

### § 7106.   Payment of sheriff's fees and expenses; liability of sheriff.

(a) Payment of sheriff's fees and expenses. The sheriff shall not deliver a chattel to the person entitled to possession unless such person shall, upon request, pay to the sheriff his lawful fees and the expenses necessarily incurred in taking and keeping the chattel. Such fees and expenses shall be taxed as costs in the action or may be taxed immediately upon motion and the sheriff may be required to refund any amount not found to be necessarily incurred.

(b) Liability of sheriff. A sheriff is liable for damages caused by his delivery of a chattel in violation of this article only to the extent that such damages can not be collected from the party to whom the chattel was delivered, or his surety. When a chattel is delivered by the sheriff to any party, as prescribed in this article, the sheriff ceases to be responsible for the sufficiency of the sureties of any party; until then, he is responsible for the sufficiency of the sureties of any party.

### § 7107.   Sheriff's return.

The sheriff shall file with the clerk a return within twenty days after he has delivered a chattel; it shall include all papers delivered to or served on him and a statement of all action taken by him. Where the sheriff has not filed a return before the hearing of a motion made by any party to punish him for contempt for such failure, he may be punished for contempt. At least ten days' notice of such motion shall be given to the sheriff.

### § 7108.   Judgment; execution in certain cases; enforcement by contempt.

(a) Generally. Damages for wrongful taking or detention or for injury to or depreciation of a chattel may be awarded to a party. If an order of seizure granted without notice is not confirmed as required pursuant to paragraph four of subdivision (d) of section 7102, the plaintiff, unless the court orders otherwise upon good cause shown, shall be liable to the defendant for all costs and damages, including reasonable attorney's fees, which may be sustained by reason of the granting of the order of seizure without notice, and the plaintiff's liability shall not be limited to the amount of the undertaking. Except as provided in subdivision (b), judgment shall award possession of each chattel to the prevailing party or, if the action is discontinued or dismissed, to the person from whom it was seized; and where the person awarded possession is not in possession when judgment is entered, it shall in the alternative, award the value of each chattel at the time of trial or the sum for which it was sold under section 7105, decreased by the value of the interest of an unsuccessful party.

(b) Where value of chattel should not be awarded; execution. A verdict, report or decision in favor of the defendant where the chattel is in possession of the plaintiff at the time it is rendered shall not fix the value of the chattel where:

1. the plaintiff is the owner of the chattel but it was rightfully distrained doing damage, and the value of the chattel is greater than the damages sustained by the defendant; or

2. the plaintiff is the owner of the chattel, but the defendant has a special property therein, the value of which is less than the value of the chattel.

The verdict, report or decision shall state why the value of the chattel is not fixed, and the final judgment shall award to the defendant the amount of damages or value of his special property and, if such sum is not collected, possession of the chattel. An execution shall direct the sheriff to deliver possession of the chattel to the defendant unless the party in possession pays the sum awarded to the defendant with interest and sheriff's fees and in case the chattel cannot be found within his county, then to satisfy that sum from the property of the party against whom the judgment is entered. If the chattel is in possession of the defendant, it may remain in his possession until the amount awarded is paid.

(c) Failure of jury to fix sum. If the jury shall fail to fix any sum required to be fixed by this section, such sum shall be fixed by a jury empanelled for the purpose upon motion made before the judge who presided at the trial within fifteen days after verdict.

### 1978 AMENDMENTS

L. 1978, ch. 81, eff. Jan. 1, 1979, amended CPLR 7108 by adoption of proposals made by the Judicial Conference in its Report to the 1978 Legislature, in which it stated:

"A new sentence has been added to section 7108(a) to provide that if an order of seizure granted without notice is not confirmed as required pursuant to section 7102(d)(4), the plaintiff, unless the court orders otherwise upon good cause shown, shall be liable to the defendant for all costs and damages, including reasonable attorney's fees, which may be sustained by reason of the granting of the order of seizure without notice, and the plaintiff's liability shall not be limited to the amount of the undertaking.

"This provision protects defendants and, by not limiting damages to the amount of the undertaking, provides an incentive to plaintiffs to move on notice for an order of seizure."

See notes under the 1978 amendment to CPLR 7102 for the extensive commentary by the Judicial Conference recommending the 1978 amendment of Article 71.

## § 7109.  Unique chattel.

(a) Injunction, temporary restraining order. Where the chattel is unique, the court may grant a preliminary injunction or temporary restraining order that the chattel shall not be removed from the state, transferred, sold, pledged, assigned or otherwise disposed of until the further order of the court.

(b) Judgment enforceable by contempt. Where the chattel is unique, the court, in addition to granting a judgment under section 7108, may direct that a party in possession deliver the chattel to the party entitled to possession. Disobedience of a judgment or order so directing may be punished as a contempt of court.

If a party accepts the value of the chattel awarded to him by the judgment, he shall have no claim to the chattel.

## § 7110. Sheriff's powers.

If the order of seizure so provides, the sheriff in accordance with the order of seizure, may break open, enter and search for the chattel in the place where the chattel may be and take the chattel into his possession.

### 1971 AMENDMENTS

L. 1971, ch. 1051, eff. July 2, 1971, amended CPLR 7110 by deleting all the language after the word "powers" in the catchline; by deleting and adding language to reflect the charges made in Article 71 by the repeal of the use of a requisition and the substitution of an order of seizure in its stead.

## § 7111. Action on undertaking.

An action on an undertaking cannot be maintained after final judgment until the return, wholly or partly unsatisfied, of an execution on the judgment for delivery of possession of the chattel or for payment of a sum of money in lieu of the chattel.

## § 7112. Testimony by deposition to ascertain location of chattel.

A party to an action to recover a chattel may move, upon such notice as the court may direct, upon a showing that he lacks knowledge of the location of the chattel or a part thereof, for an order to examine any person for the purpose of obtaining information with reference to such location. The order may be granted before or after service of summons and complaint, or anytime before or after final judgment, and may also restrain the adverse party from acting in violation of whatever rights the moving party may have in the chattel, upon the execution of a reasonable undertaking, with sufficient sureties, to reimburse the adverse party for all damages wrongfully caused by such restraint.

### 1978 AMENDMENTS

L. 1978, ch. 81, eff. Jan. 1, 1979, amended CPLR 7112 by adoption of proposals made by the Judicial Conference in its Report to the 1978 Legislature, in which it stated:

"A new phrase has been added to provide that a motion to examine any person for the purpose of obtaining information with reference to the location of a chattel shall be upon such notice as the court may direct.' "

See notes under the 1978 amendment to CPLR 7102 for the extensive commentary by the Judicial Conference recommending the 1978 amendment of Article 71.

### 1968 AMENDMENTS

L. 1968, ch. 355, eff. Sept. 1, 1968, added CPLR 7112.

# ARTICLE 72

# RECOVERY OF PENALTY OR FORFEITURE

## SUMMARY OF ARTICLE

§ 7201.　Action by state.
   (a)　Statutory penalty or forfeiture.
   (b)　Forfeiture on conviction for treason.
   (c)　Forfeiture of recognizance.
§ 7202.　Action by person aggrieved.
§ 7203.　Action by common informer.
   (a)　When maintainable.
   (b)　Service.
   (c)　Action not barred by collusive recovery.
§ 7204.　Recovery of part of penalty or forfeiture.
§ 7205.　Defense of good faith reliance on judicial decision.

## § 7201.　Action by state.

(a) Statutory penalty or forfeiture. Where property has been forfeited or a penalty incurred to the state or to an officer, for its use, pursuant to statute, the attorney-general, or the district attorney of the county in which the action is triable, if such an action has not already been brought by the attorney-general, shall commence an action to recover the property or penalty. A recovery in such an action bars the recovery in any other action brought for the same cause.

(b) Forfeiture on conviction for treason. Where personal property is forfeited to the state upon a conviction of outlawry for treason, the attorney-general shall commence an action to recover the property or its value.

(c) Forfeiture of recognizance. Where the condition of a recognizance is broken, the recognizance is wholly forfeited by an order of the court directing its prosecution. Where a recognizance to the state is forfeited, it is not necessary to allege or prove any damages.

## § 7202.　Action by person aggrieved.

Where a penalty or forfeiture is given by a statute to a person aggrieved by the act or omission of another, the person aggrieved may commence an action to recover it.

## § 7203.   Action by common informer.

(a) When maintainable. Where a penalty or forfeiture is given by a statute to any person, an action to recover it may be maintained by any person in his own name; but the action cannot be compromised or settled without the leave of the court.

(b) Service. The summons can be served only by an officer authorized by law to collect upon an execution issued out of the same court. The summons cannot be countermanded by the plaintiff before service. Immediately after it has been served, the officer shall file it with his certificate of service with the judge who issued it or with the clerk of the court.

(c) Action not barred by collusive recovery. The plaintiff may recover, notwithstanding the recovery of a judgment, for or against the defendant, in an action brought by another person, if the former judgment was recovered collusively and fraudulently.

## § 7204.   Recovery of part of penalty or forfeiture.

Where a statute gives a pecuniary penalty or forfeiture not exceeding a specified sum, the whole sum or a part proportionate to the offense may be awarded.

## § 7205.   Defense of good faith reliance on judicial decision.

No action for a penalty or forfeiture may be brought for an act done in good faith and pursuant to a construction given to a statute by a decision of an appellate court and adjudged lawful thereby, where such act was done prior to a reversal or the overruling of such decision.

# ARTICLE 75

# ARBITRATION

## SUMMARY OF ARTICLE

§ 7501.   Effect of arbitration agreement.
§ 7502.   Applications to the court; venue; statutes of limitation; provisional remedies.
    (a)  Applications to the court; venue.
    (b)  Limitation of time.
    (c)  Provisional remedies.
§ 7503.   Application to compel or stay arbitration; stay of action; notice of intention to arbitrate.
    (a)  Application to compel arbitration; stay of action.
    (b)  Application to stay arbitration.
    (c)  Notice of intention to arbitrate.
§ 7504.   Court appointment of arbitrator.
§ 7505.   Powers of arbitrator.
§ 7506.   Hearing.
    (a)  Oath of arbitrator.
    (b)  Time and place.
    (c)  Evidence.
    (d)  Representation by attorney.
    (e)  Determination by majority.
    (f)  Waiver.
§ 7507.   Award; form; time; delivery.
§ 7508.   Award by confession.
    (a)  When available.
    (b)  Time of award.
    (c)  Person or agency making award.
§ 7509.   Modification of award by arbitrator.
§ 7510.   Confirmation of award.
§ 7511.   Vacating or modifying award.
    (a)  When application made.
    (b)  Grounds for vacating.
    (c)  Grounds for modifying.
    (d)  Rehearing.
    (e)  Confirmation.
§ 7512.   Death or incompetency of a party.
§ 7513.   Fees and expenses.
§ 7514.   Judgment on an award.
    (a)  Entry.
    (b)  Judgment-roll.

CPLR

---

## § 7501. Effect of arbitration agreement.

A written agreement to submit any controversy thereafter arising or any existing controversy to arbitration is enforceable without regard to the justiciable character of the controversy and confers jurisdiction on the courts of the state to enforce it and to enter judgment on an award. In determining any matter arising under this article, the court shall not consider whether the claim with respect to which arbitration is sought is tenable, or otherwise pass upon the merits of the dispute.

## § 7502. Applications to the court; venue; statutes of limitation; provisional remedies.

(a) Applications to the court; venue. A special proceeding shall be used to bring before a court the first application arising out of an arbitrable controversy which is not made by motion in a pending action. The proceeding shall be brought in the court and county specified in the agreement; or, if none be specified, in a court in the county in which one of the parties resides or is doing business, or, if there is no such county, in a court in any county; or in a court in the county in which the arbitration was held. All subsequent applications shall be made by motion in the pending action or the special proceeding.

(b) Limitation of time. If, at the time that a demand for arbitration was made or a notice of intention to arbitrate was served, the claim sought to be arbitrated would have been barred by limitation of time had it been asserted in a court of the state, a party may assert the limitation as a bar to the arbitration on an application to the court as provided in section 7503 or subdivision (b) of section 7511. The failure to assert such bar by such application shall not preclude its assertion before the arbitrators, who may, in their sole discretion, apply or not apply the bar. Except as provided in subdivision (b) of section 7511, such exercise of discretion by the arbitrators shall not be subject to review by a court on an application to confirm, vacate or modify the award.

(c) Provisional remedies. The supreme court in the county in which an arbitration is pending, or, if not yet commenced, in a county specified in subdivision (a), may entertain an application for an order of attachment or for a preliminary injunction in connection with an arbitrable controversy, but only upon the ground that the award to which the applicant may be entitled may be rendered ineffectual without such provisional relief. The provisions of articles 62 and 63 of this chapter shall apply to the application, including those relating to undertakings and to the time for commencement of an action (arbitration shall be deemed an action for this purpose) if the application is made before commencement, except that the sole ground for the granting of the remedy shall be as stated above. The form of the application shall be as provided in subdivision (a).

**1985 AMENDMENTS**

L. 1985, ch. 253, eff. Jan. 1, 1986, added subdivision (c) to CPLR 7502.

## § 7503. Application to compel or stay arbitration; stay of action; notice of intention to arbitrate.

(a) Application to compel arbitration; stay of action. A party aggrieved by the failure of another to arbitrate may apply for an order compelling arbitration. Where there is no substantial question whether a valid agreement was made or complied with, and the claim sought to be arbitrated is not barred by limitation under subdivision (b) of section 7502, the court shall direct the parties to arbitrate. Where any such question is raised, it shall be tried forthwith in said court. If an issue claimed to be arbitrable is involved in an action pending in a court having jurisdiction to hear a motion to compel arbitration, the application shall be made by motion in that action. If the application is granted, the order shall operate to stay a pending or subsequent action, or so much of it as is referable to arbitration.

(b) Application to stay arbitration. Subject to the provisions of subdivision (c), a party who has not participated in the arbitration and who has not made or been served with an application to compel arbitration, may apply to stay arbitration on the ground that a valid agreement was not made or has not been complied with or that the claim sought to be arbitrated is barred by limitation under subdivision (b) of section 7502.

(c) Notice of intention to arbitrate. A party may serve upon another party a demand for arbitration or a notice of intention to arbitrate, specifying the agreement pursuant to which arbitration is sought and the name and address of the party serving the notice, or of an officer or agent thereof if such party is an association or corporation, and stating that unless the party served applies to stay the arbitration within twenty days after such service he shall thereafter be precluded from objecting that a valid agreement was not made or has not been complied with and from asserting in court the bar of a limitation of time. Such notice or demand shall be served in the same manner as a summons or by registered or certified mail, return receipt requested. An application to stay arbitration must be made by the party served within twenty days after service upon him of the notice or demand, or he shall be so precluded. Notice of such application shall be served in the same manner as a summons or by registered or certified mail, return receipt requested. Service of the application may be made upon the adverse party, or upon his attorney if the attorney's name appears on the demand for arbitration or the notice of intention to arbitrate. Service of the application by mail shall be timely if such application is posted within the prescribed period. Any provision in an arbitration agreement or arbitration rules

CPLR

which waives the right to apply for a stay of arbitration is hereby declared null and void.

### 1973 AMENDMENTS

L. 1973, ch. 1028, eff. Sept. 1, 1973, amended CPLR 7503(c) by changing the ten day period for applying to stay arbitration to twenty days; by providing that service of the application to stay arbitration may be made upon the adverse party's attorney if his name appears on the notice of intention to arbitrate or on the demand; by providing that service of the application by mail shall be timely if made within the prescribed period; by adding to the first, second and third sentence references to demands for arbitration to conform to CPLR 7502(b); and by adding a requirement that any provision in an arbitration agreement which waives the right to apply for a stay be deemed void.

### 1964 AMENDMENTS

L. 1964, ch. 388, eff. Sept. 1, 1964, deleted comma formerly appearing between "be" and "arbitrated" in Subd. (b).

## § 7504. Court appointment of arbitrator.

If the arbitration agreement does not provide for a method of appointment of an arbitrator, or if the agreed method fails or for any reason is not followed, or if an arbitrator fails to act and his successor has not been appointed, the court, on application of a party, shall appoint an arbitrator.

## § 7505. Powers of arbitrator.

An arbitrator and any attorney of record in the arbitration proceeding has the power to issue subpoenas. An arbitrator has the power to administer oaths.

## § 7506. Hearing.

(a) Oath of arbitrator. Before hearing any testimony, an arbitrator shall be sworn to hear and decide the controversy faithfully and fairly by an officer authorized to administer an oath.

(b) Time and place. The arbitrator shall appoint a time and place for the hearing and notify the parties in writing personally or by registered or certified mail not less than eight days before the hearing. The arbitrator may adjourn or postpone the hearing. The court, upon application of any party, may direct the arbitrator to proceed promptly with the hearing and determination of the controversy.

(c) Evidence. The parties are entitled to be heard, to present evidence and to cross-examine witnesses. Notwithstanding the failure of a party duly notified to appear, the arbitrator may hear and determine the controversy upon the evidence produced.

(d) Representation by attorney. A party has the right to be represented by an attorney and may claim such right at any time as to any part of the arbitration or hearings which have not taken place. This right may not be waived. If a party is represented by an attorney, papers to be served on the party shall be served upon his attorney.

(e) Determination by majority. The hearing shall be conducted by all the arbitrators, but a majority may determine any question and render an award.

(f) Waiver. Except as provided in subdivision (d), a requirement of this section may be waived by written consent of the parties and it is waived if the parties continue with the arbitration without objection.

## § 7507. Award; form; time; delivery.

Except as provided in section 7508, the award shall be in writing, signed and affirmed by the arbitrator making it within the time fixed by the agreement, or, if the time is not fixed, within such time as the court orders. The parties may in writing extend the time either before or after its expiration. A party waives the objection that an award was not made within the time required unless he notifies the arbitrator in writing of his objection prior to the delivery of the award to him. The arbitrator shall deliver a copy of the award to each party in the manner provided in the agreement, or, if no provision is so made, personally or by registered or certified mail, return receipt requested.

### 1981 AMENDMENTS

L. 1981, ch. 952, eff. July 31, 1981, amended CPLR 7507 by requiring that an arbitrator now affirm a written arbitration award instead of acknowledging it.

## § 7508. Award by confession.

(a) When available. An award by confession may be made for money due or to become due at any time before an award is otherwise made. The award shall be based upon a statement, verified by each party, containing an authorization to make the award, the sum of the award or the method of ascertaining it, and the facts constituting the liability.

(b) Time of award. The award may be made at any time within three months after the statement is verified.

(c) Person or agency making award. The award may be made by an arbitrator or by the agency or person named by the parties to designate the arbitrator.

## § 7509. Modification of award by arbitrator.

On written application of a party to the arbitrators within twenty days after delivery of the award to the applicant, the arbitrators may modify the award upon the grounds stated in subdivision (c) of section 7511. Written notice of the application shall be given to other parties to the arbitration. Written objection to modification must be served on the arbitrators and other parties to the arbitration within ten days of receipt of the notice. The arbitrators shall dispose

CPLR

of any application made under this section in writing, signed and acknowledged by them, within thirty days after either written objection to modification has been served on them or the time for serving said objection has expired, whichever is earlier. The parties may in writing extend the time for such disposition either before or after its expiration.

## § 7510. Confirmation of award.

The court shall confirm an award upon application of a party made within one year after its delivery to him, unless the award is vacated or modified upon a ground specified in section 7511.

## § 7511. Vacating or modifying award.

(a) When application made. An application to vacate or modify an award may be made by a party within ninety days after its delivery to him.

(b) Grounds for vacating.

1. The award shall be vacated on the application of a party who either participated in the arbitration or was served with a notice of intention to arbitrate if the court finds the rights of that party were prejudiced by:

(i) corruption, fraud or misconduct in procuring the award; or

(ii) partiality of an arbitrator appointed as a neutral; except where the award was by confession; or

(iii) an arbitrator, or agency or person making the award exceeded his power or so imperfectly executed it that a final and definite award upon the subject matter submitted was not made; or

(iv) failure to follow the procedure of this article, unless the party applying to vacate the award continued with the arbitration with notice of the defect and without objection.

2. The award shall be vacated on the application of a party who neither participated in the arbitration nor was served with a notice of intention to arbitrate if the court finds that:

(i) the rights of that party were prejudiced by one of the grounds specified in paragraph one; or

(ii) a valid agreement to arbitrate was not made; or

(iii) the agreement to arbitrate had not been complied with; or

(iv) the arbitrated claim was barred by limitation under subdivision (b) of section 7502.

(c) Ground for modifying. The court shall modify the award if:

1. there was a miscalculation of figures or a mistake in the description of any person, thing or property referred to in the award; or

2. the arbitrators have awarded upon a matter not submitted to them and the award may be corrected without affecting the merits of the decision upon the issues submitted; or

3. the award is imperfect in a matter of form, not affecting the merits of the controversy.

(d) Rehearing. Upon vacating an award, the court may order a rehearing and determination of all or any of the issues either before the same arbitrator or before a new arbitrator appointed in accordance with this article. Time in any provision limiting the time for a hearing or award shall be measured from the date of such order or rehearing, whichever is appropriate, or a time may be specified by the court.

(e) Confirmation. Upon the granting of a motion to modify, the court shall confirm the award as modified; upon the denial of a motion to vacate or modify, it shall confirm the award.

### CROSS REFERENCES

See **Insurance Law** § 675 as to arbitration of "no-fault" claims against insurers. Special provisions for review of arbitrators' awards are contained therein.

## § 7512. Death or incompetency of a party.

Where a party dies after making a written agreement to submit a controversy to arbitration, the proceedings may be begun or continued upon the application of, or upon notice to, his executor or administrator or, where it relates to real property, his distributee or devisee who has succeeded to his interest in the real property. Where a committee of the property or of the person of a party to such an agreement is appointed, the proceedings may be continued upon the application of, or notice to, the committee. Upon the death or incompetency of a party, the court may extend the time within which an application to confirm, vacate or modify the award or to stay arbitration must be made. Where a party has died since an award was delivered, the proceedings thereupon are the same as where a party dies after a verdict.

## § 7513. Fees and expenses.

Unless otherwise provided in the agreement to arbitrate, the arbitrators' expenses and fees, together with other expenses, not including attorney's fees, incurred in the conduct of the arbitration, shall be paid as provided in the award. The court, on application, may reduce or disallow any fee or expense it finds excessive or allocate it as justice requires.

## § 7514. Judgment on an award.

(a) Entry. A judgment shall be entered upon the confirmation of an award.

(b) Judgment-roll. The judgment-roll consists of the original or a copy of the agreement and each written extension of time within which to make an award;

CPLR

the statement required by section 7508 where the award was by confession; the award; each paper submitted to the court and each order of the court upon an application under sections 7510 and 7511; and a copy of the judgment.

### 1964 AMENDMENTS

L. 1964, ch. 388, eff. Sept. 1, 1964, changed reference in Subd. (b) to section "seventy-five hundred eight" to the figures "7508."

# ARTICLE 75-A

# HEALTH CARE ARBITRATION

## SUMMARY OF ARTICLE

§ 7550. Definitions.
§ 7551. Applicability.
§ 7552. Health care arbitration proceedings.
§ 7553. Costs of the proceeding.
§ 7554. Selection of arbitrators.
§ 7555. Screening for bias; communication with arbitrator candidates.
§ 7556. Demand for arbitration; minors; consolidation of proceedings.
§ 7557. Reparation offers; denials of liability.
§ 7558. Depositions and discovery; rules of the arbitration administrator; adjournments.
§ 7559. Hearing; evidence; record; neutral experts.
§ 7560. Subpoenas.
§ 7561. Use of depositions; enforcement of discovery procedures.
§ 7562. Witnesses' fees and mileage; arbitrators' fees and expenses.
§ 7563. Briefs; awards; decision.
§ 7564. Form of decision; costs upon frivolous claims and counterclaims.
§ 7565. Modification and judicial review of decision.

CPLR

## § 7550. Definitions.

As used in this article:

(a) "Arbitration administrator" means an entity designated by the superintendent of insurance to administer the arbitration of disputes pursuant to this article.

(b) "Hospital" has the same meaning as is set forth in subdivision ten of section twenty-eight hundred one of the public health law.

(c) "Health maintenance organization" has the same meaning as is set forth in subdivision one of section forty-four hundred one of the public health law and shall include health maintenance organizations authorized pursuant to article forty-three of the insurance law.

(d) "Health care provider" includes any person or entity employed or otherwise involved in the provision of health care or treatment.

**1986 AMENDMENTS**

L. 1986, ch. 266, eff. July 8, 1986, added new Article 75-a, comprising CPLR 7550 through 7565.

## § 7551. Applicability.

The provisions of this article shall apply to all claims for damages because of injury or death resulting from health care or treatment rendered or failed to be rendered to enrollees and other covered family members of health maintenance organizations and all other claims, cross-claims, counter-claims, and claims for contribution and indemnity arising from claims subject to agreements to arbitrate made pursuant to section forty-four hundred six-a of the public health law and to arbitrations authorized pursuant to section thirty hundred forty-five of this chapter.

**1986 AMENDMENTS**

L. 1986, ch. 266, eff. July 8, 1986, added new Article 75-a, comprising CPLR 7550 through 7565.

## § 7552. Health care arbitration proceedings.

(a) Proceedings pursuant to this article shall be commenced and conducted in accordance with article seventy-five of this chapter, except as otherwise provided by this article, and in accordance with rules promulgated by the arbitration administrator and approved by the superintendent of insurance.

(b) The standards of duty, practice, or care to be applied to a physician, dentist, hospital, health maintenance organization or other health care provider in the arbitration shall be the same standards as would be applied in a comparable medical or dental malpractice action.

(c) Damages shall be determined in accordance with provisions of law applicable to medical and dental malpractice actions. Attorney contingency fee agreements shall be valid and subject to provisions of law applicable to medical and dental malpractice actions.

**1986 AMENDMENTS**

L. 1986, ch. 266, eff. July 8, 1986, added new Article 75-a, comprising CPLR 7550 through 7565.

## § 7553. Costs of the proceeding.

The administrative expense of arbitrations shall be paid from the arbitration fund established pursuant to section five thousand six hundred three of the insurance law.

**1986 AMENDMENTS**

L. 1986, ch. 266, eff. July 8, 1986, added new Article 75-a, comprising CPLR 7550 through 7565.

## § 7554. Selection of arbitrators.

(a) An arbitration under this article shall be heard by a panel of three arbitrators. The chairperson of the panel shall be an attorney who shall be appointed to serve in such capacity on a full-time basis for a fixed term. The chairperson shall have jurisdiction over prehearing procedures. Qualifications for the selection of such chairpersons shall be established by the arbitration administrator, subject to the approval of the superintendent of insurance.

(b) Except as otherwise provided in subdivision (e) of this section, the remaining two arbitrators, hereinafter referred to as associate arbitrators, shall be selected from a pool of candidates established pursuant to the rules and procedures promulgated by the arbitration administrator and approved by the superintendent of insurance. Attorneys whose practice substantially involves representation in personal injury matters, physicians, dentists, hospital and health maintenance organization personnel and other health care providers shall not be eligible to serve as associate arbitrators. The rules and procedures pertaining to selection of associate arbitrators under this article shall provide that the arbitration administrator send simultaneously to each party an identical list of associate arbitrator candidates, together with a brief biographical statement on each candidate. A party may strike from the list any names which is unacceptable and shall number the remaining names in order of preference. When the lists are returned to the arbitration administrator they shall be compared and the first two mutually agreeable associate arbitrator candidates shall be invited to serve.

(c) When two mutually agreed upon associate arbitrators have not been selected from the first list, a second list of such candidates shall be sent in the manner provided for in subdivision (b) of this section.

(d) If a complete panel is not selected by mutual agreement of the parties pursuant to subdivisions (b) and (c) of this section, then, under applicable rules and procedures of the arbitration administrator, which are approved by the superintendent of insurance, the arbitration administrator shall appoint the remaining associate arbitrators. Any appointment of an associate arbitrator by the arbitration administrator shall be subject to challenge by any party for cause. To be sufficient, a challenge must allege facts which establish that community, professional or other pressures are likely to influence the objectivity of the appointed associate arbitrator. A decision on a request to strike an arbitrator for cause shall be made by the arbitration administrator.

(e) The parties shall not be restricted to the associate arbitrator candidates submitted for consideration. If all parties mutually agree upon one or more associate arbitrators, such arbitrators shall be invited to serve.

**1986 AMENDMENTS**

L. 1986, ch. 266, eff. July 8, 1986, added new Article 75-a, comprising CPLR 7550 through 7565.

CPLR

## § 7555.   Screening for bias; communication with arbitrator candidates.

(a) Prior to inclusion on a list of proposed associate arbitrators, the arbitration administrator shall make an appropriate initial screening for bias and shall require associate arbitrator candidates for a particular case to complete a current personal disclosure statement under oath. In addition to other relevant information, the statement shall disclose any personal acquaintance with any of the parties or their counsel and the nature of such acquaintance. If the statement reveals facts which suggest the possibility of partiality, the arbitration administrator shall communicate those facts to the parties.

(b) No party shall communicate with an associate arbitrator candidate, directly or indirectly, except through the arbitration administrator, at any time after the filing of the demand for arbitration. Any candidate who is aware of such communication shall immediately notify the arbitration administrator.

### 1986 AMENDMENTS

L. 1986, ch. 266, eff. July 8, 1986, added new Article 75-a, comprising CPLR 7550 through 7565.

## § 7556.   Demand for arbitration; minors; consolidation of proceedings.

(a) Any person subject to an arbitration agreement may seek to compel arbitration, pursuant to section seventy-five hundred three or section thirty-hundred forty-five of this chapter.

(b) Notwithstanding the provisions of section twelve hundred nine of this chapter, a minor child and a person judicially determined to be incompetent shall be bound to arbitrate disputes, controversies, or issues upon the execution of an arbitration election on the person's behalf by a parent, legal guardian, committee, conservator or other person legally authorized to enroll such minor or incompetent person in a health maintenance organization, in accordance with the provisions of section forty-five hundred six-a of the public health law.

(c) Separate arbitration proceedings brought pursuant to this article, which involve common question of law and fact, shall be consolidated into a single arbitration proceeding.

(d) Except for arbitrations commenced pursuant to section thirty hundred forty-five of this chapter, any case involving a person who is not bound to participate in the arbitration proceeding pursuant to subdivision (e) of section forty-four hundred six-a of the public health law shall not be subject to the arbitration proceeding, unless such person and all parties who are subject to the arbitration consent to the arbitration of the claim. Absent such consent, any party may seek to stay such arbitrations, pursuant to section seventy-five hundred three of this chapter, notwithstanding any time limits that may otherwise apply to such a stay, and require the matter to proceed as a civil action. In the event that such an arbitration is stayed, the arbitration administrator shall forthwith transfer the case to the clerk of the court in the venue designated by the plaintiff, where the case shall be expeditiously reviewed and assigned in accordance with rules promulgated by the chief administrator of the courts. If the demand for arbitration was made or a notice of intention to arbitrate was served within the limitations of time specified by article two of this chapter, and the arbitration was subsequently stayed and transferred to a court, the action shall be deemed to have been timely commenced, in accordance with the provisions of subdivision (a) of section two hundred five of this chapter.

**1986 AMENDMENTS**

L. 1986, ch. 266, eff. July 8, 1986, added new Article 75-a, comprising CPLR 7550 through 7565.

### § 7557. Reparation offers; denials of liability.

All communications incidental to settlement made orally or in writing by any party shall not be disclosed to the arbitration panel, unless all parties consent to such disclosure.

**1986 AMENDMENTS**

L. 1986, ch. 266, eff. July 8, 1986, added new Article 75-a, comprising CPLR 7550 through 7565.

### § 7558. Depositions and discovery; rules of the arbitration administrator; adjournments.

(a) After the appointment of the panel of arbitrators and notwithstanding inconsistent provisions of sections four hundred eight and three thousand one hundred two of this chapter, the parties to the arbitration may take depositions and obtain discovery regarding the subject matter of the arbitration and, to that end, use and exercise the same rights, remedies, and obligations in the arbitration as if the subject matter of the arbitration were pending in a civil action.

(b) The arbitration administrator shall promulgate rules, subject to the approval of the superintendent of insurance, to ensure the expeditious completion of discovery and the prompt commencement and conclusion of the hearing, consistent with applicable provisions of rule thirty-four hundred six of this chapter.

(c) An adjournment at the request of counsel for any of the parties may be granted only by the chairperson of the panel for good cause shown. A proceeding under this article shall be treated in the same manner as an action or proceeding in supreme court for the purpose of any claim by counsel of actual engagement.

**1986 AMENDMENTS**

L. 1986, ch. 266, eff. July 8, 1986, added new Article 75-a, comprising CPLR 7550 through 7565.

## § 7559. Hearing; evidence; record; neutral experts.

(a) An arbitration hearing shall be informal and the rules of evidence shall be those applicable to arbitrations conducted pursuant to article seventy-five of this chapter.

(b) Testimony at the hearing shall be taken under oath and a record of the proceedings shall be made by a recording device. Any party may obtain a copy of the recording of the proceeding, which shall be provided without charge. A party, at that party's expense, may also utilize the services of a stenographic reporter. The cost of any transcription ordered by the panel of arbitrators for its own use shall be deemed part of the cost of the proceedings.

(c) The panel on its own motion may call a neutral expert witness who shall be subject to cross-examination by the parties. The cost of the expert will be deemed a cost of the proceeding.

### 1986 AMENDMENTS

L. 1986, ch. 266, eff. July 8, 1986, added new Article 75-a, comprising CPLR 7550 through 7565.

## § 7560. Subpoenas.

The chairperson of the panel and any attorney of record in the proceeding has the power to issue subpoenas, in accordance with section seventy-five hundred five of this chapter.

### 1986 AMENDMENTS

L. 1986, ch. 266, eff. July 8, 1986, added new Article 75-a, comprising CPLR 7550 through 7565.

## § 7561. Use of depositions; enforcement of discovery procedures.

(a) On application of a party to the arbitration, the chairperson may permit the deposition of a witness to be used as evidence, in accordance with the provisions of rule three thousand one hundred seventeen of this chapter.

(b) Depositions shall be taken in the manner prescribed by law for the taking of depositions in civil actions.

(c) The chairperson may enforce the failure of parties to comply with applicable discovery obligations in the same manner as a court, pursuant to section three thousand one hundred twenty-six of this chapter, including through the imposition of costs, payable to the arbitration fund, provided, however, that the chairperson shall not have the power to find a party in contempt.

### 1986 AMENDMENTS

L. 1986, ch. 266, eff. July 8, 1986, added new Article 75-a, comprising CPLR 7550 through 7565.

### § 7562. Witnesses' fees and mileage; arbitrator's fees and expenses.

(a) Except for the parties to the arbitration and their agents, officers, and employees, all witnesses appearing pursuant to subpoena are entitled to receive fees and mileage in the same amount and under the same circumstances as prescribed by law for witnesses in civil actions. The fee and mileage of a witness subpoenaed upon the application of a party to the arbitration shall be paid by that party. The fee and mileage of a witness subpoenaed solely at the request of an arbitrator shall be deemed to be a cost of the proceeding.

(b) Each arbitrator's salary or fees and expenses, together with any other costs of the proceeding shall be paid from the arbitration administration fund established pursuant to section five thousand six hundred three of the insurance law. The range of such salary or fees and expenses and the manner of their payment shall be established by regulation of the superintendent of insurance.

#### 1986 AMENDMENTS

L. 1986, ch. 266, eff. July 8, 1986, added new Article 75-a, comprising CPLR 7550 through 7565.

### § 7563. Briefs; award; decision.

(a) The panel may order that written briefs be submitted within thirty days after the close of hearings. In written briefs each party may summarize the evidence and testimony and may propose a comprehensive award of compensatory elements.

(b) The panel of arbitrators shall render its decision by majority vote and the decision shall be rendered within thirty days after the close of the hearing or the receipt of briefs, if briefs are requested.

#### 1986 AMENDMENTS

L. 1986, ch. 266, eff. July 8, 1986, added new Article 75-a, comprising CPLR 7550 through 7565.

### § 7564. Form of decision; costs upon frivolous claims and counterclaims.

(a) The decision in the arbitration proceeding shall be in the form required by sections seven thousand five hundred seven and four thousand two hundred thirteen of this chapter and shall be filed with the arbitration administrator.

(b) The panel of arbitrators shall be empowered to award costs and reasonable attorney's fees to a successful party in an arbitration, if the panel finds that the action, claim, counterclaim, defense or cross claim of an unsuccessful party is frivolous, in accordance with the provisions and subject to the limitations of section eight thousand three hundred three-a of this chapter. The arbitration fee paid by the claimant shall be recoverable by the claimant in the event an award is made to the claimant.

CPLR

**1986 AMENDMENTS**

L. 1986, ch. 266, eff. July 8, 1986, added new Article 75-a, comprising CPLR 7550 through 7565.

## § 7565. Modification and judicial review of decision.

A decision of a panel of arbitrators shall be binding on all parties, unless modified or vacated pursuant to section seven thousand five hundred nine or seven thousand five hundred eleven of this chapter.

**1986 AMENDMENTS**

L. 1986, ch. 266, eff. July 8, 1986, added new Article 75-A, comprising CPLR 7550 through 7565.

## ARTICLE 76

# PROCEEDING TO ENFORCE AGREEMENT FOR DETERMINATION OF ISSUE

---

### SUMMARY OF ARTICLE

§ 7601.    Special proceeding to enforce agreement that issue or controversy be determined by a person named or to be selected.

---

§ 7601.    **Special proceeding to enforce agreement that issue or controversy be determined by a person named or to be selected.**

A special proceeding may be commenced to specifically enforce an agreement, other than one contained in the standard fire insurance policy of the state, that a question of valuation, appraisal or other issue or controversy be determined by a person named or to be selected. The court may enforce such an agreement as if it were an arbitration agreement, in which case the proceedings shall be conducted as if brought under article seventy-five. Where there is a defense which would require dismissal of an action for breach of the agreement, the proceeding shall be dismissed.

CPLR

# ARTICLE 77

# PROCEEDING RELATING TO EXPRESS TRUST

---

### SUMMARY OF ARTICLE

§ 7701.    Special proceeding relating to express trust.
§ 7702.    Verified account accompanying petition.
§ 7703.    Joinder and representation of persons interested in trust property.
§ 7704.    Reference.
§ 7705.    Recording or filing instrument settling account.
§ 7706.    Order on filing instrument settling account.

---

### § 7701.   Special proceeding relating to express trust.

A special proceeding may be brought to determine a matter relating to any express trust except a voting trust, a mortgage, a trust for the benefit of creditors, a trust to carry out any plan of reorganization of real property acquired on foreclosure or otherwise of a mortgage or mortgages against which participation certificates have been issued and guaranteed by a corporation and for which the superintendent of insurance or the superintendent of banks has been or may hereafter be appointed rehabilitator or liquidator or conservator, a trust to carry out any plan of reorganization pursuant to sections one hundred nineteen through one hundred twenty-three of the real property law or pursuant to section seventy-seven B of the national bankruptcy act, and trusts for cemetery purposes, as provided for by sections 8-1.5 and 8-1.6 of the estates, powers and trusts law.

Any party to the proceeding shall have the right to examine the trustees, under oath, either before or after filing an answer or objections, as to any matter relating to their administration of the trust, in accordance with the provisions of article thirty-one.

#### 1976 AMENDMENTS

L. 1976, ch. 193, eff. Sept. 1, 1976, amended the section by updating the cross-references contained therein, without changing substance, and by adding the final paragraph providing for examination of trustees.

CPLR 408, which requires leave of court for disclosure in special proceedings, was also amended by Chapter 193, so as to exclude Article 77 proceedings from the provisions of § 408, and to provide that disclosure in such proceedings be governed by the general provisions of Article 31.

CPLR

Amendment of CPLR 408 and CPLR 7701 was recommended by the Judicial Conference Report to the 1976 Legislature, wherein it stated:

"This bill would conform the practice under the CPLR relating to *inter vivos* trust proceedings to that in Surrogate's Court, thus rectifying a previous legislative oversight.

"At present, by virtue of the general provisions of CPLR 408, a court order is required for disclosure in *inter vivos* trust proceedings, whereas in testamentary trust proceedings, under SCPA 2211, no such order is necessary. SCPA 2211 also provides that in testamentary trust accountings the fiduciary may be examined under oath by any party to the proceeding, either before or after filing objections. There is no comparable provision in Article 77 of the CPLR with respect to *inter vivos* trusts.

"There is no good reason why the procedure in *inter vivos* trust accountings should be different in this respect from testamentary trust accountings."

### 1964 AMENDMENTS

L. 1964, ch. 322, eff. Sept. 1, 1964, amended the section to clarify its meaning and scope.

## § 7702. Verified account accompanying petition.

A petition by a trustee praying that his intermediate or final account be judicially settled shall be accompanied by an account verified in the form required by section twenty-two hundred nine of the surrogate's court procedure act.

### CROSS REFERENCES

See SCPA § 2209 in Appendix, *infra.*

### 1970 AMENDMENTS

L. 1970, ch. 348, eff. Sept. 1, 1970, amended the section to provide that a trustee seeking to have his account judicially settled shall submit, with his petition, an account verified in the form required by section 2209 of the Surrogate's Court Procedure Act.

## § 7703. Joinder and representation of persons interested in trust property.

The provisions as to joinder and representation of persons interested in estates as provided in the surrogate's court procedure act shall govern joinder and representation of persons interested in express trusts. For these purposes, the term "will" used in the surrogate's court procedure act shall be construed to mean the instrument creating the trust.

### CROSS REFERENCES

See SCPA § 315 ("Joinder and representation of persons interested in estates.") in appendix, *infra.*

### 1981 AMENDMENTS

L. 1981, ch. 178, eff. June 2, 1981, which applies to estates of deceased persons and trusts in existence after such date, repealed CPLR 7703 ("Representation in case of remainder to class") and substituted a new section 7703.

## § 7704.  Reference.

No referee shall be appointed to examine and audit a trustee's account, or to hear and report on or to determine any questions arising upon the settlement of such account, where:

1. a question of law exclusively is involved; or

2. no objections have been filed to the transactions set forth in the account by any of the persons interested in the trust or by any representative authorized under section 1201 to appear for an infant or incompetent interested in the trust or by a guardian ad litem of a person not in being interested in the trust.

### 1964 AMENDMENTS

L. 1964, ch. 388, eff. Sept. 1, 1964, inserted "a" before "question" in Subd. (1).

## § 7705.  Recording or filing instrument settling account.

There may be recorded or filed in the office of the clerk or register of the county where any trustee under an express trust not created by will, if an individual, resides, or, if a corporation, has its principal office, any instrument settling an account, in whole or in part, executed by one or more such trustees and by one or more of the persons interested in the subject-matter of the trust, none of whom is under the disability of infancy or incompetency. Every such instrument to be recorded or filed shall be acknowledged; and if recorded the record thereof, or a certified copy of the record or instrument shall be prima facie evidence of the contents of such instrument and its due execution.

### 1981 AMENDMENTS

L. 1981, ch. 199, eff. June 9, 1981, amended CPLR 7705.

## § 7706.  Order on filing instrument settling account.

Where an instrument described in section seven thousand seven hundred five of this article has been executed by all of the persons who would be necessary parties in a proceeding under section seven thousand seven hundred one of this article, none of whom is under the disability of infancy or incompetency, one or more of the trustees may present to the court a petition showing the names and post office addresses of all persons interested in the trust, whether or not the trust has been fully executed, that the petitioner has fully accounted and made full disclosure in writing of his administration of the trust to all persons interested, and praying that his intermediate or final account be judicially settled. There shall be filed with the petition the instrument described in section seven thousand seven hundred five of this article. The court may thereupon make an order settling the petitioner's account and discharging the petitioner and sureties on his bond, if any, from any further liability to all persons interested therein.

CPLR

**1981 AMENDMENTS**

L. 1981, ch. 199, eff. June 9, 1981, added a new section 7706 to the CPLR.

# ARTICLE 78

# PROCEEDING AGAINST BODY OR OFFICER

## SUMMARY OF ARTICLE

§ 7801.  Nature of proceeding.
§ 7802.  Parties.
    (a)  Definition of "body or officer."
    (b)  Persons whose terms of office have expired; successors.
    (c)  Prohibition in favor of another.
    (d)  Other interested persons.
§ 7803.  Questions raised.
§ 7804.  Procedure.
    (a)  Special proceeding.
    (b)  Where proceeding brought.
    (c)  Time for service of notice of petition and answer.
    (d)  Pleadings.
    (e)  Answering affidavits; record to be filed; default.
    (f)  Objections in point of law.
    (g)  Hearing and determination; transfer to appellate division.
    (h)  Trial.
    (i)  Appearance by judicial officer.
§ 7805.  Stay.
§ 7806.  Judgment.

CPLR

## § 7801.  Nature of proceeding.

Relief previously obtained by writs of certiorari to review, mandamus or prohibition shall be obtained in a proceeding under this article. Wherever in any statute reference is made to a writ or order of certiorari, mandamus or prohibition, such reference shall, so far as applicable, be deemed to refer to the proceeding authorized by this article. Except where otherwise provided by law, a proceeding under this article shall not be used to challenge a determination:

1. which is not final or can be adequately reviewed by appeal to a court or to some other body or officer or where the body or officer making the determination is expressly authorized by statute to rehear the matter upon the petitioner's application unless the determination to be reviewed was made upon a rehearing, or a rehearing has been denied, or the time within which the petitioner can procure a rehearing has elapsed; or

2. which was made in a civil action or criminal matter unless it is an order summarily punishing a contempt committed in the presence of the court.

## § 7802. Parties.

(a) Definition of "body or officer." The expression "body or officer" includes every court, tribunal, board, corporation, officer, or other person, or aggregation of persons, whose action may be affected by a proceeding under this article.

(b) Persons whose terms of office have expired; successors. Whenever necessary to accomplish substantial justice, a proceeding under this article may be maintained against an officer exercising judicial or quasi-judicial functions, or member of a body whose term of office has expired. Any party may join the successor of such officer or member of a body or other person having custody of the record of proceedings under review.

(c) Prohibition in favor of another. Where the proceeding is brought to restrain a body or officer from proceeding without or in excess of jurisdiction in favor of another, the latter shall be joined as a party.

(d) Other interested persons. The court may direct that notice of the proceeding be given to any person. It may allow other interested persons to intervene.

### 1981 AMENDMENTS

L. 1981, ch. 502, eff. July 15, 1981, amended CPLR 7802(b) by deleting the requirement of serving a notice of a proceeding under Article 78 upon the attorney-general when it is brought against an officer exercising judicial or quasi-judicial functions or a member of a body whose term of office has expired. That service requirement is now found at CPLR 7804(c).

## § 7803. Questions raised.

The only questions that may be raised in a proceeding under this article are:

1. whether the body or officer failed to perform a duty enjoined upon it by law; or

2. whether the body or officer proceeded, is proceeding or is about to proceed without or in excess of jurisdiction; or

3. whether a determination was made in violation of lawful procedure, was affected by an error of law or was arbitrary and capricious or an abuse of discretion, including abuse of discretion as to the measure or mode of penalty or discipline imposed; or

4. whether a determination made as a result of a hearing held, and at which evidence was taken, pursuant to direction by law is, on the entire record, supported by substantial evidence.

## § 7804. Procedure.

(a) Special proceeding. A proceeding under this article is a special proceeding.

(b) Where proceeding brought. A proceeding under this article shall be brought in the supreme court in the county specified in subdivision (b) of section 506 except as that subdivision otherwise provides.

(c) Time for service of notice of petition and answer. Unless the court grants an order to show cause to be served in lieu of a notice of petition at a time and in a manner specified therein, a notice of petition, together with the petition and affidavits specified in the notice, shall be served on any adverse party at least twenty days before the time at which the petition is noticed to be heard. An answer and supporting affidavits, if any, shall be served at least five days before such time. A reply, together with supporting affidavits, if any, shall be served at least one day before such time. In the case of a proceeding pursuant to this article against a state body or officers, or against members of a state body or officers whose terms have expired as authorized by subdivision (b) of section 7802 of this chapter, commenced either by order to show cause or notice of petition, in addition to the service thereof provided in this section, the order to show cause or notice of petition must be served upon the attorney general by delivery of such order or notice to an assistant attorney general at an office of the attorney general in the county in which venue of the proceeding is designated, or if there is no office of the attorney general within such county, at the office of the attorney general nearest such county. In the case of a proceeding pursuant to this article against members of bodies of governmental subdivisions whose terms have expired as authorized by subdivision (b) of section 7802 of this chapter, the order to show cause or notice of petition must be served upon such governmental subdivision in accordance with section 311 of this chapter.

(d) Pleadings. There shall be a verified petition, which may be accompanied by affidavits or other written proof. Where there is an adverse party there shall be a verified answer, which must state pertinent and material facts showing the grounds of the respondent's action complained of. There shall be a reply to a counterclaim denominated as such and there shall be a reply to new matter in the answer or where the accuracy of proceedings annexed to the answer is disputed. The court may permit such other pleadings as are authorized in an action upon such terms as it may specify.

(e) Answering affidavits; record to be filed; default. The body or officer shall file with the answer a certified transcript of the record of the proceedings under consideration, unless such a transcript has already been filed with the clerk of the court. The respondent shall also serve and submit with the answer affidavits or other written proof showing such evidentiary facts as shall entitle him to a trial of any issue of fact. The court may order the body or officer to supply any defect or omission in the answer, transcript or an answering affidavit.

Statements made in the answer, transcript or an answering affidavit are not conclusive upon the petitioner. Should the body or officer fail either to file and serve an answer or to move to dismiss, the court may either issue a judgment in favor of the petitioner or order that an answer be submitted.

(f) Objections in point of law. The respondent may raise an objection in point of law by setting it forth in his answer or by a motion to dismiss the petition, made upon notice within the time allowed for answer. If the motion is denied, the court shall permit the respondent to answer, upon such terms as may be just; and unless the order specifies otherwise, such answer shall be served and filed within five days after service of the order with notice of entry; and the petitioner may re-notice the matter for hearing upon two days' notice, or the respondent may re-notice the matter for hearing upon service of the answer upon seven days' notice. The petitioner may raise an objection in point of law to new matter contained in the answer by setting it forth in his reply or by moving to strike such matter on the day the petition is noticed or re-noticed to be heard.

(g) Hearing and determination; transfer to appellate division. Where the substantial evidence issue specified in question four of section 7803 is not raised, the court in which the proceeding is commenced shall itself dispose of the issues in the proceeding. Where such an issue is raised, the court shall first dispose of such other objections as could terminate the proceeding, including but not limited to lack of jurisdiction, statute of limitations and res judicata, without reaching the substantial evidence issue. If the determination of the other objections does not terminate the proceeding, the court shall make an order directing that it be transferred for disposition to a term of the appellate division held within the judicial department embracing the county in which the proceeding was commenced. When the proceeding comes before it, whether by appeal or transfer, the appellate division shall dispose of all issues in the proceeding, or, if the papers are insufficient, it may remit the proceeding.

(h) Trial. If a triable issue of fact is raised in a proceeding under this article, it shall be tried forthwith. Where the proceeding was transferred to the appellate division, the issue of fact shall be tried by a referee or by a justice of the supreme court and the verdict, report or decision rendered after the trial shall be returned to, and the order thereon made by, the appellate division.

(i) Appearance by judicial officer. Notwithstanding any other provision of law, where a proceeding is brought under this article against a justice, judge, referee or judicial hearing officer appointed by a court and (1) it is brought by a party to a pending action or proceeding, and (2) it is based upon an act or acts performed by the respondent in that pending action or proceeding either granting or denying relief sought by a party thereto, and (3) the respondent is not a named party to the pending action or proceeding, in addition to service on the respondent, the petitioner shall serve a copy of the petition together with copies of all moving papers upon all other parties to the pending action or proceeding. All such parties shall be designated as respondents. Unless ordered by the court upon application of a party the respondent justice, judge, referee or judicial hearing officer need not appear in the proceeding in which case the allegations of the petition shall not be deemed admitted or denied by him. Upon election of the justice, judge, referee, or judicial hearing officer not to appear, any ruling, order or judgment of the court in such proceeding shall bind said respondent. If such respondent does appear he shall respond to the petition and shall be entitled to be represented by the attorney general. If such respondent does not elect to appear all other parties shall be given notice thereof.

### 1993 AMENDMENTS

L. 1993, ch. 202, eff. July 6, 1993, amended subdivision (f) by allowing respondents to "re-notice the matter for hearing upon service of the answer upon seven days' notice."

### 1990 AMENDMENTS

L. 1990, ch. 575, eff. Jan. 1, 1991, amended CPLR 7804(g) to require the court, when the substantial evidence issue specified in CPLR 7803(4) is raised, to first dispose of those objections that could terminate the proceeding, such as lack of jurisdiction, statute of limitations and res judicata, before reaching the substantial evidence issue; and deleting the words "the court may, however, itself pass on objections in point of law."

### 1987 AMENDMENTS

L. 1987, ch. 384, eff. July 23, 1987, amended CPLR 7804(i), making provisions applicable to proceedings brought by a party to a pending action or proceeding, and eliminating the requirement that the proceeding be brought by a party to a "pending criminal action" or proceeding "involving the custody of a child."

### 1986 AMENDMENTS

L. 1986, ch. 355, eff. July 17, 1986, amended CPLR 7804 (b) and (h) by deleting references to special term and trial term.

### 1983 AMENDMENTS

L. 1983, ch. 840, eff. April 1, 1983, amended CPLR 7804(i).

### 1981 AMENDMENTS

L. 1981, ch. 502, eff. July 15, 1981, amended subdivision (c) of CPLR 7804 by expanding the kinds of Article 78 proceedings wherein service of initiatory papers must be made upon the attorney-general to include proceedings against members of a state body or officers whose terms have expired as authorized by CPLR 7802(b) and by requiring that in any proceeding pursuant to Article 78 which is brought against a member of a governmental subdivision whose term has expired as authorized by CPLR 7802(b), the order to show cause or notice of petition must be served upon such governmental subdivision in accordance with CPLR 311.

L. 1981, ch. 580, eff. Aug. 14, 1981, amended CPLR 7804 by adding a new subdivision (i).

### 1972 AMENDMENTS

L. 1972, ch. 455, eff. May 24, 1972, and ch. 752, eff. May 30, 1972, amended CPLR 7804(c) by providing that in an Article 78 proceeding against a state body

CPLR

of officers, the order to show cause or notice of petition must be served on the attorney general.

## 1965 AMENDMENTS

L. 1965, ch. 814, eff. Sept. 1, 1965, amended subds. (d) and (e).

Amendments recommended by the Judicial Conference Feb. 1, 1965, Report to the Legislature: "Article 78 proceedings under the C.P.A. were summary in nature. The recommended change restores language inadvertently omitted in the CPLR, and permits the disposition of these proceedings on the return day expeditiously as an application for summary judgment, in accordance with practice under the C.P.A. See the 1937 *Report of the Judicial Council* (page 129 et seq.)"

## § 7805.　Stay.

On the motion of any party or on its own initiative, the court may stay further proceedings, or the enforcement of any determination under review, upon terms including notice, security and payment of costs, except that the enforcement of an order or judgment granted by the appellate division in a proceeding under this article may be stayed only by order of the appellate division or the court of appeals. Unless otherwise ordered, security given on a stay is effective in favor of a person subsequently joined as a party under section 7802.

## § 7806.　Judgment.

The judgment may grant the petitioner the relief to which he is entitled, or may dismiss the proceeding either on the merits or with leave to renew. If the proceeding was brought to review a determination, the judgment may annul or confirm the determination in whole or in part, or modify it, and may direct or prohibit specified action by the respondent. Any restitution or damages granted to the petitioner must be incidental to the primary relief sought by the petitioner, and must be such as he might otherwise recover on the same set of facts in a separate action or proceeding suable in the supreme court against the same body or officer in its or his official capacity.

# ARTICLE 80

# FEES

---

## SUMMARY OF ARTICLE

§ 8001. **Persons subpoenaed; examination before trial; transcripts of records.**
    (a) **Persons subpoenaed.**
    (b) **Persons subpoenaed upon an examination before trial.**
    (c) **Transcripts of records.**
§ 8002. **Stenographers.**
§ 8003. **Referees.**
    (a) **Generally.**
    (b) **Upon sale of real property.**
§ 8004. **Commissions of receivers.**
    (a) **Generally.**
    (b) **Allowance where funds depleted.**
§ 8005. **Commissions of trustees; advance payment of fees of an attorney-trustee.**
§ 8006. **Premiums on undertakings by fiduciaries.**
§ 8007. **Printers.**
§ 8008. **Fees and expenses of officer to be paid before transmission of paper.**
§ 8009. **Oaths; acknowledgments; certification or exemplification.**
§ 8010. **County treasurers.**
§ 8011. **Fixed fees of sheriffs.**
    (a) **Order of attachment.**
    (b) **Property execution.**
    (c) **Income execution; service upon judgment debtor.**
    (d) **Income execution; levy upon default or failure to serve judgment debtor.**
    (e) **Recovery of chattel.**
    (f) **Summary proceeding.**
    (g) **Sales.**
    (h) **Summons, subpoenas and other mandates.**
    (i) **Undertakings; returns; copies.**
    (j) **Prisoners.**
    (k) **Jurors; view; constables' services.**
§ 8011–a. **[Repealed.]**
§ 8011–b. **[Repealed.]**
§ 8012. **Mileage fees, poundage fees, additional compensation, and limitation on compensation of sheriffs.**
    (a) **Mileage fees.**
    (b) **Poundage fees.**
    (c) **Additional compensation.**
    (d) **Mileage fees in the city of New York.**

§ 8013.    Expenses of sheriffs.
 (a)  Publication of notice of sale.
 (b)  Appraisal of attached property.
 (c)  Other expenses.
 (d)  Payment in advance.
§ 8014.    Collection of sheriff's fees on execution.
§ 8015.    County clerk where sheriff is a party or otherwise disqualified.
§ 8016.    Clerks of courts of record generally.
 (a)  Fees of clerks in actions.
 (b)  Certifying judgment-roll on appeal.
§ 8017.    Exemption of the state and counties, and agencies and officers thereof, from fees of clerks.
§ 8018.    Index number fees of county clerks.
 (a)  Amount of fee.
 (b)  Exemptions from index number fee.
 (c)  Endorsement of index number on papers.
 (d)  Additional services without fee where index number assigned.
§ 8019.    County clerks generally.
 (a)  Application.
 (b)  Legible copies.
 (c)  Notice to county clerk.
 (d)  Exemptions for state or city of New York.
 (e)  Size of page and type.
 (f)  Copies of records.
§ 8020.    County clerks as clerks of court.
 (a)  Placing cause on calendar.
 (b)  Calendar fee for transferred cause, joint trial, retrial, or separate trial.
 (c)  Filing demand for jury trial.
 (d)  [Repealed.]
 (e)  Jury fee for transferred cause, joint trial, retrial, or separate trial.
 (f)  Certification, exemplification, and copies of papers.
 (g)  Searches.
 (h)  Production of court records.
§ 8021.    County clerks other than as clerks of court.
 (a)  Services in connection with papers or instruments relating to real property and not filed under the uniform commercial code.
 (b)  Filing, other than in connection with papers or instruments relating to real property or filed under the uniform commercial code.
 (c)  Certification, issuing certificates, other papers and copies of papers, records, and related services, other than in connection with papers or instruments relating to real property or filed under the uniform commercial code.
 (d)  Searches of records not filed under the uniform commercial code.
 (e)  Production of records.
 (f)  Services rendered pursuant to part four of article nine of the uniform commercial code.
 (g)  Services rendered in relation to federal tax liens filed pursuant to the lien law.

### § 8022.   Fee on civil appeals and proceedings before appellate courts.

---

### § 8001.   Persons subpoenaed; examination before trial; transcripts of records.

(a) Persons subpoenaed. Any person whose attendance is compelled by a subpoena, whether or not actual testimony is taken, shall receive for each day's attendance fifteen dollars for attendance fees and twenty-three cents as travel expenses for each mile to the place of attendance from the place where he or she was served, and return. There shall be no mileage fee for travel wholly within a city.

(b) Persons subpoenaed upon an examination before trial. If a witness who is not a party, or agent or employee of a party, is subpoenaed to give testimony, or produce books, papers and other things at an examination before trial, he shall receive an additional three dollars for each day's attendance.

(c) Transcripts of records. Wherever the preparation of a transcript of records is required in order to comply with a subpoena, the person subpoenaed shall receive an additional fee of ten cents per folio upon demand.

#### 1988 AMENDMENTS

L. 1988, ch. 23, eff. Jan. 1, 1989, amended subdivision (a) to increase subpoenaed-witness fees from two to fifteen dollars for attendance, and from eight to twenty-three cents per mile for travel expenses; and to make statute gender neutral.

### § 8002.   Stenographers.

Unless otherwise agreed or provided by law, a stenographer is entitled, for a copy fully written out from his stenographic notes of testimony or other proceedings taken in a court, and furnished upon request to a party or his attorney, to the fee set forth in the rules promulgated by the chief administrator of the courts.

#### 1984 AMENDMENTS

L. 1984, ch. 846, eff. Aug. 5, 1984, amended CPLR 8002 by providing that the fee shall be that set forth in the rules promulgated by the chief administrator. The new fee is applicable only to transcripts ordered on or after the date of the formal promulgation of the rules and regulations by the chief administrator of the courts. The former fee was 30 cents per folio.

#### 1973 AMENDMENTS

L. 1973, ch. 458, eff. Sept. 1, 1973, amended CPLR 8002 by increasing the fee to thirty cents for each folio.

CPLR

**1965 AMENDMENTS**

L. 1965, ch. 980, eff. Sept. 1, 1965, increased the fee to twenty cents per folio.

## § 8003. Referees.

(a) Generally. A referee is entitled, for each day spent in the business of the reference, to fifty dollars unless a different compensation is fixed by the court or by the consent in writing of all parties not in default for failure to appear or plead.

(b) Upon sale of real property. A referee appointed to sell real property pursuant to a judgment is entitled to the same fees and disbursements as those allowed to a sheriff. Where a referee is required to take security upon a sale, or to distribute, apply, or ascertain and report upon the distribution or application of any of the proceeds of the sale, he or she is also entitled to one-half of the commissions upon the amount secured, distributed or applied as are allowed by law to an executor or administrator for receiving and paying out money. Commissions in excess of fifty dollars shall not be allowed upon a sum bid by a party, and applied upon that party's judgment, without being paid to the referee. A referee's compensation, including commissions, upon a sale pursuant to a judgment in any action cannot exceed five hundred dollars, unless the property sold for fifty thousand dollars or more, in which event the referee may receive such additional compensation as to the court may seem proper.

(c) This section shall not apply to judicial hearing officers who have been designated referees.

**1996 AMENDMENTS**

L. 1996, ch. 225, eff. June 26, 1996, amended the final sentence of subdivision (b) to change the phrase "an action to foreclose a mortgage" to "any action"; to delete the phrase "two hundred dollars, or pursuant to any other judgment," prior to the phrase "five hundred dollars"; to increase the sum of ten thousand dollars to fifty thousand dollars; and to make the section gender neutral.

**1983 AMENDMENTS**

L. 1983, ch. 840, eff. April 1, 1983, added CPLR 8003(c).

**1976 AMENDMENTS**

L. 1976, ch. 700, eff. Aug. 23, 1976, amended CPLR 8003 by increasing fees for referees.

## § 8004. Commissions of receivers.

(a) Generally. A receiver, except where otherwise prescribed by statute, is entitled to such commissions, not exceeding five percent upon the sums received and disbursed by him, as the court by which he is appointed allows, but if in any case the commissions, so computed, do not amount to one hundred dollars, the court, may allow the receiver such a sum, not exceeding one hundred dollars, as shall be commensurate with the services he rendered.

(b) Allowance where funds depleted. If, at the termination of a receivership, there are no funds in the hands of the receiver, the court, upon application of the receiver, may fix the compensation of the receiver and the fees of his attorney, in accordance with the respective services rendered, and may direct the party who moved for the appointment of the receiver to pay such sums, in addition to the necessary expenditures incurred by the receiver. This subdivision shall not apply to a receiver or his attorney appointed pursuant to article twenty-three-a of the general business law.

CROSS REFERENCES

**Article 23-A of the General Business Law,** referred to in Subd. (b), *supra,* deals with fraudulent practices with respect to stocks, bonds and other securities.

## § 8005. Commissions of trustees; advance payment of fees of an attorney-trustee.

A trustee of an express trust shall be entitled to commissions and the allowance of his expenses and compensation and, if he be an attorney admitted to practice in this state, to the allowance of a sum on account of his compensation for legal services theretofore rendered to the trust, in the same manner and amount as that provided by sections twenty-one hundred eleven, twenty-three hundred eight and twenty-three hundred eleven of the surrogate's court procedure act for testamentary trustees, if the trust was established on or before August thirty-first, nineteen hundred fifty-six, or as that provided by sections twenty-one hundred eleven, twenty-three hundred nine and twenty-three hundred eleven of the surrogate's court procedure act for testamentary trustees, if the trust was established after August thirty-first, nineteen hundred fifty-six or as that provided for by sections twenty-one hundred eleven and twenty-three hundred eleven for testamentary trustees and twenty-three hundred twelve of the surrogate's court procedure act except that the statements required thereunder to be furnished annually in order to retain certain annual commissions need be furnished during the settlor's lifetime only to beneficiaries currently receiving income. The court shall make such determinations and allowances as the named sections require or authorize the surrogate to make, and the term "will" used in those sections shall be construed to mean the instrument creating the trust and the phrase "the court from which his letters were issued" shall be construed to mean the court having jurisdiction of the trust.

1984 AMENDMENTS

L. 1984, ch. 936, éff. Aug. 6, 1984, amended CPLR 8005 by adding references to SCPA §§ 2211, 2311 and 2312. L. 1984, ch. 936, § 12, reads as follows:

§ 12. This act shall take effect immediately, and shall apply to any trust whether in existence on or after the effective date of this act provided, however, nothing contained in this act shall be deemed to change, alter, reduce, eliminate or otherwise affect the right of any trustee to any receiving or paying commission or annual commission which such trustee has earned or is entitled to claim or be paid immediately prior to the effective date of this act and further provided however that an individual trustee shall continue to receive commissions in the manner provided for an individual trustee under sections twenty-three hundred eight and twenty-three hundred nine of the surrogate's court procedure act, as the case may be, in effect immediately before the effective date of this act until the end of the then current trust year, and thereafter, at the rates then in effect under such sections.

### 1980 AMENDMENTS

L. 1980, ch. 185, eff. June 2, 1980, amended CPLR 8005 to provide for the advance payment of fees to an attorney who is also a trustee of an express trust.

### 1972 AMENDMENTS

L. 1972, ch. 172, eff. April 25, 1972, amended CPLR 8005 be deleting references to Surrogate's Court Act §§ 285-a, 285-b, and 285-d and substituting references to Surrogate's Court Procedure Act §§ 2308, 2309, and 2311.

### 1965 AMENDMENTS

L. 1965, ch. 542, eff. June 1, 1965, amended section.

Amendment recommended jointly by the Temporary State Commission on the Law of Estates and the Judicial Conference. The phrase "on the settlement of the account" was eliminated to make it clear that the trustees are entitled to commissions not only on the settlement of the account but also annually in the same manner and amount as under the Surrogate's Court Act. Reference to § 285-d was inserted to enable inter vivos trustees to make an ex parte application for advance payment of commissions in the same manner as testamentary trustees under the Surrogate's Court Act. Reference to annual statements was inserted to make it clear that an inter vivos trustee must make the same broad disclosures to beneficiaries as testamentary trustees except that while the settlor of the trust is alive the statements need only be furnished to the beneficiaries currently receiving income. See Report No. 7.11B [Leg. Doc. (1964) No. 19, p. 691] and 1964 Supplement to same.

## § 8006.   Premiums on undertakings by fiduciaries.

A receiver, assignee, guardian, trustee, committee, conservator or person appointed under section one hundred eleven of the real property law or under section twenty of the personal property law, required by law to give an undertaking as such, may include as a part of his necessary expenses such reasonable sum, not exceeding one percent per annum upon the amount of such undertaking paid his surety thereon, as the court appointing him shall allow.

### CROSS REFERENCES

Real Prop. L. § 111 and Pers. Prop. L. § 20 were repealed by EPTL § 14-1.1 (L. 1966, ch. 952, eff. Sept. 1, 1967) and their provisions were reenacted, with minor revisions, as **EPTL §7-2.3.**

### 1981 AMENDMENTS

L. 1981, ch. 115, eff. May 18, 1981, amended CPLR 8006 by adding a reference to a conservator.

## § 8007. Printers.

Except where otherwise prescribed by law, the proprietor of a newspaper is entitled for publishing a summons, notice, order or other advertisement, required to be published by law or by the order of any court, or of the clerk of a court, to twenty-nine cents per line of a column width not less than ten pica ems, provided that in computing such charge per line the line shall average at least five words for each insertion in newspapers having a circulation of less than two thousand five hundred; twenty-nine and one-half cents per line for newspapers having two thousand five hundred or more circulation and less than five thousand; thirty and one-half cents per line for newspapers having five thousand or more circulation and less than seven thousand five hundred; thirty-one and one-half cents per line for newspapers having seven thousand five hundred or more circulation and less than ten thousand; thirty-two and one-half cents per line for newspapers having ten thousand or more circulation and less than fifteen thousand; and three and one-half cents per line, in addition to the thirty-two and one-half cents for the initial fifteen thousand circulation, for each additional five thousand circulation up to thirty-five thousand circulation and one and one-half cents per line for each additional five thousand possessed by a newspaper. To all of the above rates nine cents per line shall be added to the initial insertion charge of each separate advertisement. To all of the above rates for the initial insertion eight cents per line shall also be added for tabular matter or intricate composition. In reckoning line charges allowance shall be made for date lines, paragraph endings, titles, signatures and similar short lines as full lines where the same are set to conform to the usual rules of composition. Display advertising shall be charged agate measurement (fourteen lines to each inch), ten to thirteen pica ems wide, depending on the makeup of the newspaper publishing such copy. This rate shall not apply to any newspaper printed, principally circulated or having its principal office in the counties of New York or Bronx within the first judicial district or in the county of Kings within the second judicial district or in the county of Nassau within the tenth judicial district or in the county of Queens within the eleventh judicial district or in the county of Westchester within the ninth judicial district or in any city having a population of over one hundred seventy-five thousand inhabitants within the eighth judicial district, where the rate for such publication may be equal to but shall not exceed the regularly established classified advertising rate of such newspapers. Every newspaper making claim for compensation under the provisions of this section must be established at least one year and entered in the post office as second class matter.

### 1991 AMENDMENTS

L. 1991, ch. 449, eff. Sept. 1, 1991.

### 1990 AMENDMENTS

L. 1990, ch. 776, eff. Sept. 1, 1990.

CPLR

### 1988 AMENDMENTS

L. 1988, ch. 354, eff. Aug. 28, 1988, amended 8007 to exempt Westchester County from the fee structure for display advertising of legal notices.

### 1984 AMENDMENTS

L. 1984, ch. 679, eff. Sept. 1, 1984.

### 1980 AMENDMENTS

L. 1980, ch. 500, eff. Sept. 1, 1980.

### 1979 AMENDMENTS

L. 1979, ch. 719, eff. Sept. 1, 1979.

### 1974 AMENDMENTS

L. 1974, ch. 691, sec. 2, eff. Jan. 1, 1975.

### 1971 AMENDMENTS

L. 1971, ch. 1198, eff. Jan. 1, 1972.

### 1966 AMENDMENTS

L. 1966, ch. 885 and ch. 458, eff. Jan. 1, 1967.

## § 8008. Fees and expenses of officer to be paid before transmission of paper.

Each provision of law requiring a judge, clerk or other officer to transmit a paper to another officer, for the benefit of a party, is to be construed as requiring the transmission only at the request of the person so to be benefited, and upon payment by him of the fees allowed by law for the paper transmitted, or any copy or certificate connected therewith, and the expenses specified in section sixty-eight of the public officers law.

### CROSS REFERENCES

See **Public Officers Law § 68** in Appendix, *infra.*

## § 8009. Oaths; acknowledgments; certification or exemplification.

Any authorized officer is entitled, for the services specified to the following fees:

1. for administering an oath or affirmation, and certifying it when required, except where another fee is specially prescribed by statute, two dollars;

2. for taking and certifying the acknowledgment or proof of the execution of a written instrument, two dollars for one person and two dollars for each additional person, and two dollars for swearing each witness thereto; and

3. for certifying or exemplifying a typewritten or printed copy of any document, paper, book or record in his custody, twenty-five cents for each folio with a minimum of one dollar.

**1991 AMENDMENTS**

L. 1991, ch. 143, eff. July 23, 1991.

**1972 AMENDMENTS**

L. 1972, ch. 734 and ch. 735, eff. July 1, 1972.

## § 8010. County treasurers.

The treasurer of a county or the commissioner of finance of the city of New York is entitled for the services specified to the following fees:

1. two per cent upon a sum of money paid out of court by him;

2. one-half of one per cent upon a sum of money invested by him;

3. two per cent of the par value of investments transferred or assigned out of court by him, when the investments have been made by him;

4. two per cent of the par value of securities deposited into court and received by him, to be paid at the time of the deposit by the parties making it; and

5. one dollar for each certificate issued by him certifying as to the amount of deposit to the credit of court funds.

**1978 AMENDMENTS**

L. 1978, ch. 655, eff. July 24, 1978, amended CPLR 8010.

**1970 AMENDMENTS**

L. 1970, ch. 547, eff. July 1, 1970, amended subparagraph (5).

**1969 AMENDMENTS**

L. 1969, ch. 407, eff. May 9, 1969.

**1964 AMENDMENTS**

L. 1964, ch. 576, eff. April 16, 1964.

## § 8011. Fixed fees of sheriffs.

For the services specified, a sheriff is entitled to the following fees and, where indicated, these shall be paid in advance.

(a) Order of attachment.

1. For receiving an order of attachment, entering it in the appropriate books, and return when required, ten dollars, in advance.

2. For levying upon real or personal property, twenty-six dollars and fifty cents, in advance.

3. For each additional levy upon real or personal property by virtue of an order of attachment, twenty-six dollars and fifty cents, in advance.

4. For serving a copy of an order of attachment on a defendant, and for serving a copy on each additional defendant, ten dollars, in advance.

CPLR

5. For serving a summons with or without a complaint, ten dollars, in advance.

6. For making and filing a description of real property, or an inventory of personal property, levied upon by virtue of an order of attachment, or an estimate of the value thereof, ten dollars.

7. Mileage for services covered in paragraphs two, three and four of this subdivision, in advance, provided, however, that where the services covered in such paragraphs are performed at the same time and place, there shall be only one mileage fee.

(b) Property execution.

1.* For receiving an execution against property, entering it in the appropriate books, and return when required, ten dollars, in advance, except that in an execution which arises out of an action brought pursuant to article eighteen of the uniform district court act, article eighteen of the uniform city court act, article eighteen of the New York city civil court act or article eighteen of the uniform justice court act, the fees provided in this subdivision shall not be collected in advance.

*[**Editor's note:** This version of § 8011(b)(1) is effective as of January 1, 1997. Through December 31, 1996, former § 8011(b)(1) remains in effect. It reads as follows:

1. For receiving an execution against property, entering it in the appropriate books, and return when required, ten dollars, in advance, except that in an execution which arises out of an action brought pursuant to article eighteen of the uniform district court act, article eighteen of the uniform city court act or article eighteen of the New York City civil court act, the fees provided in this subdivision shall not be collected in advance.]

2. For levying upon property by virtue of an execution, ten dollars.

3. For making an inventory of property levied upon by virtue of an execution, ten dollars.

4. Mileage for services covered in paragraphs two and three of this subdivision, in advance, provided however, that where the services covered in such paragraphs are performed at the same time, there shall be only one mileage fee.

(c) Income execution; service upon judgment debtor.

1. For receiving an income execution, entering it in appropriate books, and return when required, ten dollars, in advance.

2. For serving the income execution upon the judgment debtor, ten dollars, in advance.

3. Mileage for service covered in paragraph two of this subdivision, unless such execution is served by mail.

(d) Income execution; levy upon default or failure to serve judgment debtor.

1. For serving an income execution, entering it in the appropriate books, and return when required, ten dollars, in advance.

2. For levying upon the money that the judgment debtor is receiving or will receive, ten dollars, in advance.

3. Mileage for services covered in paragraph two of this subdivision unless such levy is made by mail.

(e) Recovery of chattel.

1. For receiving an order to recover chattel, entering it in the appropriate books, and return when required, ten dollars, in advance.

2. For executing the order of seizure against the defendant's chattel or chattels, fifty dollars, in advance.

3. For executing the order of seizure against the chattel or chattels of an additional defendant or any other person in whose possession said chattel or chattels may be found, twenty-six dollars and fifty cents, in advance.

4. For serving an additional copy of the required papers, ten dollars, in advance.

5. For serving the summons with or without a complaint, ten dollars, in advance.

6. Mileage for services covered in paragraphs two, three, four and five of this subdivision, in advance, provided however, that where the services covered in such paragraphs are performed at the same time and place, there shall be only one mileage fee.

(f) Summary proceeding.

1. Notice of petition and petition.

(i) For receiving a notice of petition and petition, obtaining an index number when required, entering it in the appropriate books, and return, ten dollars, in advance.

(ii) For serving the notice of petition on a tenant or other person in possession, ten dollars, in advance.

(iii) For serving the notice of petition on each additional tenant, undertenant, subtenant, person or persons in possession, or person or persons not in possession to be served, ten dollars, in advance.

(iv) For making an affidavit or military or nonmilitary service, ten dollars for each affidavit, in advance.

(v) Mileage for services covered in subparagraph (ii) of this paragraph, and where person or persons named in the petition are to be served at an address or addresses other than the premises described in the petition, additional mileage shall be paid, in advance, except where two or more notices of petition are to be served at the same time, within the same site or location, there shall be only one mileage fee.

2. Warrant of eviction or any mandate requiring delivery of possession of real property and removal of person or persons in possession.

CPLR

(i) For requisitioning, receiving, entering in the appropriate books, and for the return of a warrant of eviction or any other mandate, ten dollars, in advance.

(ii) For service of notice of eviction on a person or persons to be served, ten dollars for each person to be served, in advance.

(iii) Mileage of services covered in subparagraph (ii) of this paragraph, in advance, except where two or more notices of eviction are to be served at the same time, within the same site or location, there shall be only one mileage fee.

(iv) For executing a warrant of eviction or any mandate requiring him or her to put a person in possession of real property and removing person or persons in possession, fifty dollars, in advance.

(v) Mileage for services covered in subparagraph (iv) of this paragraph, in advance.

(g) Sales.

1. For posting of notice, including advertising real or personal property for sale by virtue of an execution, order of attachment, or other mandate, or in pursuance of a direction contained in a judgment, or for a notice of postponement of a sale, ten dollars.

2. For drawing and executing a conveyance upon a sale of real property, twenty dollars, to be paid by the grantee, in advance.

3. For attending a sale of real or personal property, ten dollars.

4. For conducting a sale of real or personal property, ten dollars.

5. Mileage for services covered in paragraphs three and four of this subdivision provided, however, that where the services covered in such paragraphs are performed at the same time and place, there shall be only one mileage fee.

(h) Summons, subpoenas and other mandates.

1. For serving a summons, with or without a complaint or notice, for serving a subpoena, or for serving civil process, ten dollars, in advance.

2. For serving or executing an order of arrest, or any other mandate for the service or execution of which no other fee is specifically prescribed by law, thirty dollars, in advance.

3. Mileage for services covered in paragraphs one and two of this subdivision, in advance.

4. For receiving a precept issued by commissioners appointed to inquire concerning the incompetency of a person, the fee allowed the clerk by subdivision (a) of section eight thousand twenty of this article for placing a cause on the calendar, and for notifying a county clerk or commissioner or jurors pursuant to such a precept, the fee, if any, allowed the clerk by subdivision (c) of section eight thousand twenty of this article for filing a demand for jury trial.

(i) Undertakings; returns; copies.

1. For taking any undertaking which the sheriff is authorized to take one dollar and fifty cents, and the notary's fees to any affidavit or acknowledgments.

2. For making a copy of a description or any inventory of property levied upon by virtue of an order of attachment, or of a summons or complaint, or other mandate, or an affidavit or any other paper served by him or her, ten dollars, in advance.

3. For a certified copy of an execution, and of the return or satisfaction thereupon, or for a certified copy of any undertaking which he is authorized to take, ten dollars.

(j) Prisoners.

1. For each person committed to or discharged from prison, ten dollars, in advance, to be paid by the person at whose instance he or she is imprisoned.

2. For attending before an officer for the purpose of surrendering a prisoner, or receiving into custody a prisoner surrendered, in exoneration of his or her bail, ten dollars, for all his or her services upon such a surrender or receipt.

(k) Jurors; view; constables' services.

1. For notifying jurors to attend upon a writ of inquiry, two dollars and fifty cents for each juror notified, including the making and return of the inquisition, when required; and for attending a jury when required in such a case, twenty-eight dollars.

2. For attending a view, ten dollars for each day.

3. For any services which may be rendered by a constable, other than those specifically provided for in this section, section eight thousand twelve or eight thousand thirteen of this article, to the same fees as are allowed by law to a constable for those services.

### 1996 AMENDMENTS

L. 1996, ch. 190, eff. January 1, 1997, amended subparagraph (b)(1) by adding a reference to Article 18 of the Uniform Justice Court Act.

### 1992 AMENDMENTS

L. 1992, ch. 55, eff. April 10, 1992, added this section, replacing former CPLR 8011, 8011-a and 8011-b.

CPLR

§ 8011-a.   [Repealed.]

§ 8011-b.   [Repealed.]

### § 8012.   Mileage fees, poundage fees, additional compensation, and limitation on compensation of sheriffs.

(a) Mileage fees. A sheriff is entitled to twenty-three cents for each mile necessarily travelled in performing the following services, payable in advance:

1. in serving or executing a mandate upon or against one person, or upon or against two or more persons in the course of one journey, computed from the nearest office of the sheriff in the county to the place of service or execution, and return;

2. in serving or executing two or more mandates in one action upon or against one person at one time, computed from the nearest office of the sheriff in the county to the place of service or execution, and return; and

3. in attending a view, computed from the nearest office of the sheriff in the county to the place of attendance, and return.

(b) Poundage fees.

1. A sheriff is entitled, for collecting money by virtue of an execution, an order of attachment, or an attachment for the payment of money in an action, or a warrant for the collection of money issued by the comptroller or by a county treasurer or by any agency of the state or a political subdivision thereof, or for collecting a fine by virtue of a commitment for civil contempt, to poundage of, in the counties within the city of New York, five per cent of the sum collected and in all other counties, five percent upon the first two hundred fifty thousand dollars collected, and three percent upon the residue of the sum collected.

2. Where a settlement is made after a levy by virtue of an execution, the sheriff is entitled to poundage upon the value of property levied upon, not exceeding the sum at which the settlement is made. Where an execution is vacated or set aside, the sheriff is entitled to poundage upon the value of the property levied upon, not exceeding the amount specified in the execution and the court may order the party liable therefor to pay the same to the sheriff.

3. Where a settlement is made, either before or after judgment, after a levy by virtue of an order of attachment, the sheriff is entitled to poundage upon the value of the property levied upon, not exceeding the sum at which the settlement is made. Where an order of attachment is vacated or set aside, the sheriff is entitled to poundage upon the value of the property levied upon, not exceeding the amount specified in the order of attachment, and the court may order the party at whose instance the order of attachment was granted to pay the same to the sheriff. Where an order of attachment is otherwise discharged by order of the court, the sheriff is entitled to the same poundage, to be paid by the party at whose instance the order of attachment is discharged, and the

sheriff is entitled to retain the property levied upon until the poundage is paid. The maximum amount upon which poundage shall be computed, if such a settlement is made or the order of attachment is vacated or set aside, is one million dollars.

(c) Additional compensation. A sheriff is entitled in any case, including an instance in which a mandate has been stayed, vacated or set aside, or a settlement has been made after a levy, to such additional compensation for his trouble and expenses in taking possession of and preserving property under any mandate or in removing a person in possession of real property and the said person's property, as the court allows, and the court may make an order requiring the party liable therefor to pay the same to the sheriff.

(d) Mileage fees in the city of New York. For mileage travelled wholly within the city of New York the sheriff of the city of New York shall be entitled to fifteen dollars payable in advance, as provided in section eight thousand eleven-a of this chapter.

**CPLR**

### 1987 AMENDMENTS

L. 1987, ch. 218, eff. Sept. 1, 1987, amended subd. (d) to increase the mileage fees of the sheriff in the city of New York, from ten dollars to fifteen dollars.

### 1985 AMENDMENTS

L. 1985, ch. 565, eff. July 26, 1985, amended CPLR 8012(a) to increase the sheriff's mileage fee to twenty-three cents per mile.

### 1976 AMENDMENTS

L. 1976, ch. 695, eff. July 24, 1976, amended CPLR 8012(d) by increasing the sheriff's mileage fee in the city of New York and adding a reference to the general provisions governing sheriff's fees in New York city in the newly enacted CPLR 8011-a.

### 1972 AMENDMENTS

L. 1972, ch. 734 and ch. 735, eff. July 1, 1972, amended CPLR 8012(b)(1).

L. 1972, ch. 734, eff. July 1, 1972, repealed CPLR 8012(d), relettered subdivision (e) as (d), and amended new subdivision (d).

### 1970 AMENDMENTS

L. 1970, ch. 859, § 4, eff. July 1, 1970, amended CPLR 8012(b)(1).

### 1969 AMENDMENTS

L. 1969, ch. 441, eff. July 1, 1969, added new subdivision (e), now (d).

## § 8013. Expenses of sheriffs.

(a) Publication of notice of sale. A sheriff, where real property is to be sold by virtue of an execution or in pursuance of a direction contained in a judgment, is entitled to reimbursement for printer's fees, paid by him for the publication of a notice of the sale. Where the notice is published more than four times, or the sale is postponed, the expense of continuing the publication, or of publishing the notice of postponement, shall be paid by the person requesting it. Where two or more executions against the property of one judgment debtor are in the hands of the sheriff at the time when the proceeds are distributed, the sheriff is entitled to reimbursement for printer's fees upon only the execution issued upon the judgment first docketed in the county.

(b) Appraisal of attached property. A sheriff, where an estimate of the value of property levied upon by virtue of an order of attachment is made, shall be entitled to reimbursement for such compensation to appraisers actually employed thereupon as the court which granted the order of attachment may allow.

(c) Other expenses. A sheriff is entitled to reimbursement of all expenses necessarily incurred in the execution of any mandate and in the protection, presentation, transportation or sale of property.

(d) Payment in advance. A sheriff, whenever he deems it necessary, may require payment to him in advance to cover any or all expenses for which he is entitled to reimbursement; advance payments made in connection with a mandate or direction affecting property shall be repaid by the sheriff out of the proceeds of the sale of the property, if any.

### § 8014. Collection of sheriff's fees on execution.

The fees of a sheriff, upon an execution against property, which are not required by statute to be paid by a particular person and which are not included in the bill of costs of the party in whose favor the execution is issued, shall be collected by virtue of the execution in the same manner as the sum therein directed to be collected.

### § 8015. County clerk where sheriff is a party or otherwise disqualified.

A county clerk is entitled for the services specified to the following fees:

1. for performing any duty of a sheriff in an action in which the sheriff, for any cause, is disqualified, the same compensation to which a sheriff is entitled for the same services; and

2. for confining a sheriff in a house by virtue of a mandate, and maintaining him while there, two dollars for each day, to be paid by the sheriff, before he is entitled to be discharged.

### § 8016. Clerks of courts of record generally.

(a) Fees of clerks in actions. Except where a greater fee is allowed by another statute for the same service, each clerk of a court of record, except the clerk of the civil court of the city of New York, except a county clerk, except clerks of the family courts, and except the clerks of the district courts, is entitled for the services specified to the following fees, payable in advance:

1. upon the trial of an action, or the hearing, upon the merits, of a special proceeding, from the party bringing it on, one dollar;

2. for entering final judgment, including the filing of the judgment-roll and a copy of the judgment to insert therein, fifty cents, and fifteen cents in addition for each folio, exceeding five, contained in the judgment;

3. for entering any order or an interlocutory judgment, fifty cents, and fifteen cents in addition for each folio, exceeding five;

4. for a certified or other copy of an order, record or other paper in an action brought or transferred to the court of which he is clerk and entered or filed in his office, ten cents for each folio;

5. for a certified transcript of the docket of a judgment, fifty cents; and

6. for filing a transcript or docketing or redocketing a judgment thereupon, fifty cents, and fifty cents in addition for each defendant, exceeding two.

(b) Certifying judgment-roll on appeal. Where, on an appeal from a judgment or order, a party shall present to the clerk of a court of record, except the clerk of the civil court of the city of New York, except a county clerk, except clerks of the family courts, and except the clerks of the district courts, a printed copy of the judgment-roll or order appealed from, it shall be the duty of the clerk to compare and certify the same, for which service he shall be entitled to be paid at the rate of fifty cents per page or portion thereof, unless a greater fee is allowed by another statute.

**1969 AMENDMENTS**

L. 1969, ch. 219, eff. Sept. 1, 1969, amended Subd. (a) and Subd. (b) by excepting clerks of the district courts from the provisions respecting fees of clerks in civil actions. Fees payable to clerks of the district courts provided for in Uniform District Court Act § 1911.

**1965 AMENDMENTS**

L. 1965, ch. 437, eff. Sept. 1, 1965, added words "and except clerks of the family courts" to Subds. (a) and (b).

## § 8017. Exemption of the state and counties, and agencies and officers thereof, from fees of clerks.

(a) Notwithstanding any other provision of this article or any other general, special or local law relating to fees of clerks, no clerk shall charge or collect a fee from the state, or an agency or officer thereof, for any service rendered in an action in which any of them is involved, nor shall any clerk charge or collect a fee for filing, recording or indexing any paper, document, map or proceeding filed, recorded or indexed for the county, or an agency or officer thereof acting in an official capacity, nor for furnishing a transcript, certification or copy of any paper, document, map or proceeding to be used for official purposes.

CPLR

(b) Notwithstanding any other provision of law the exemption of subdivision (a) of this section shall not apply to the fees of clerks where the action is on behalf of the New York State Higher Education Services Corporation to recover money due as a result of default of a student loan.

### 1988 AMENDMENTS

L. 1988, ch. 192, eff. July 31, 1988, relocated the previously-misplaced "(a)" after the section heading.

### 1984 AMENDMENTS

L. 1984, ch. 858, eff. Aug. 5, 1984, added CPLR 8017(b).

### 1965 AMENDMENTS

L. 1965, ch. 147, eff. Sept. 1, 1965, repealed former § 8017 entitled "Exemption of actions by the state or state agencies from fees of clerks." Former 8017-a, entitled "Exemption of counties from fees of county clerks" was revised and enacted as a new § 8017.

## § 8018.  Index number fees of county clerks.

(a) Amount of fee. A county clerk is entitled, for the assignment of an index number to an action pending in a court of which he is clerk, to a fee of one-hundred sixty-five dollars, payable in advance.

The filing of a transcript of judgment in the county clerk's office is not to be deemed an action pending in the supreme or county court of the county in which it is filed, nor does it constitute the commencement of an action in such courts.

In addition, a county clerk is entitled, for the assignment of an index number to an action pending in a court of which he or she is clerk, to the following fee: an additional five dollars, to be paid monthly by the county clerk to the commissioner of education, after deducting twenty-five cents, for deposit into the New York state local government records management improvement fund.

(b) Exemptions from index number fee. No fee shall be charged for the assignment of an index number:

1. upon the filing of an order of the appellate term of the supreme court or of an order or certificate of commitment under the mental hygiene law; or

2. upon the transfer of papers from the clerk of any other court, pursuant to an order for change of venue; or

3. to a criminal case or to any action at the request of a public agency, officer or poor person entitled by law to exemption from payment of fees to a county clerk; or

4. to any case in a county court on appeal from a judgment or order of the district court or a town, village or city court.

(c) Endorsement of index number on papers. No paper in an action in the supreme or a county court, other than an order submitted for signature to a judge out of court, shall be submitted for any purpose to the supreme or county court or to a clerk thereof unless there is endorsed on such paper the index number of the action assigned by the clerk of the county.

(d) Additional services without fee where index number assigned. A county clerk who has assigned an index number shall charge no further fee in the action to which the index number is assigned:

1. for the filing, entering, indexing, or docketing, and in the counties within the city of New York, for recording, as required by statute, of any and all papers in the action, or preliminary thereto or supplementary to judgment;

2. for furnishing an extract of minutes for filing with the clerk of the court, for affixing a certificate to a filed paper, for taxing costs, for sealing writs, for issuing commissions, for certifying a copy of the clerk's minutes to accompany papers transmitted upon entry of an order for change of venue, or for entering a judgment in the action;

3. for docketing of a satisfaction, a partial satisfaction, an assignment, a reversal, a modification, an amendment, a cancellation or a continuance of a previous entry or docket of a previously filed paper in the action;

4. for certifying a copy of an order of an appellate term of the supreme court for transmittal to the civil court of the city of New York or a city, municipal or district court, or for certifying a copy of an order for use in a division of the clerk's office or for transmittal to a city or county treasurer;

5. for docketing of a return of execution, satisfied, unsatisfied or partially satisfied;

6. for filing a notice or order continuing or canceling a notice of pendency of action or a notice of attachment against real property; and

7. for discharging a judgment of record by deposit with the clerk.

### 1990 AMENDMENTS

L. 1990, ch. 190, eff. May 25, 1990, amended CPLR 8018(a) to increase the fee for an index number from one hundred dollars to one hundred sixty-five dollars.

### 1989 AMENDMENTS

Unnumbered paragraph three of subdivision (a), relating to additional fees, was added by L. 1989, ch. 78, eff. Aug. 1, 1989, but to be deemed repealed on Dec. 31, 1995; paragraph 4 of subdivision (b) was added by L. 1989, ch. 488, eff. July 16, 1989.

### 1988 AMENDMENTS

L. 1988, ch. 192, eff. July 31, 1988, repealed subdivision (e), and included its provisions in the amended subdivision (d) as paragraphs (5), (6) and (7).

CPLR

### 1987 AMENDMENTS

L. 1987, ch. 825, eff. Nov. 5, 1987, amended subd. (a) to increase the fee to a county clerk for the assignment of an index number from thirty-five dollars to one-hundred dollars.

### 1983 AMENDMENTS

L. 1983, ch. 15, eff. April 1, 1983, amended CPLR 8018(a).

### 1981 AMENDMENTS

L. 1981, ch. 997, eff. July 31, 1981, amended CPLR 8018(a).

### 1980 AMENDMENTS

L. 1980, ch. 39, eff. April 1, 1980, amended CPLR 8018(a).

### 1977 AMENDMENTS

L. 1977, ch. 33, section 1, eff. April 1, 1977, amended subd. (a).

L. 1977, ch. 688, eff. Sept. 1, 1977, amended subd. (e)(2).

### 1972 AMENDMENTS

L. 1972, ch. 734, eff. July 1, 1972, amended subdivisions (a)(1) and (e)(3) by increasing fees.

L. 1972, ch. 709, eff. Sept. 1, 1972, renumbered subdivision (a)(2) as (a)(3) and added new subdivision (a)(2).

### 1971 AMENDMENTS

L. 1971, ch. 404, eff. July 1, 1971 amended CPLR 8018(a)(1) and (e)(3).

### 1970 AMENDMENTS

L. 1970, ch. 105, eff. March 24, 1970, amended Subd. (a)(1).

### 1966 AMENDMENTS

L. 1966, ch. 752, eff. Sept. 1, 1966, amended Subd. (e).

### 1964 AMENDMENTS

L. 1964, ch. 286, eff. Sept. 1, 1964, added new unnumbered paragraph at end of Subd. (a).

## § 8019. County clerks generally.

(a) Application. The fees of a county clerk specified in this article shall supersede the fees allowed by any other statute for the same services, except in so far as the administrative code of the city of New York sets forth different fees for the city register of the city of New York and the county clerk of Richmond, and except that such fees do not include the block fees as set out in the Nassau county administrative code, which are to be charged in addition to the fees specified in this article. This subdivision does not apply to the fees specified in subdivision (f) of section 8021.

(b) Legible copies. Whenever a paper or document, presented to a county clerk for filing or recording, is not legible or otherwise suitable for copying or recording by the photocopying process, the county clerk may require a legible or suitable copy thereof along with such paper or document, and the same fees shall be payable for the copy as are payable for the paper or document.

(c) Notice to county clerk. A county clerk need not make an entry which is required by a court order unless proper notice is given to the clerk by a party to the action or a person legally interested therein.

(d) Exemptions for state or city of New York. A clerk of a county within the city of New York shall not charge or receive any fee from the city of New York or the state of New York or from any agency or officer of either acting in official capacity.

(e) Size of page and type. For purposes of this article, the size of each page accepted by a county clerk for recording and indexing shall not exceed nine inches by fourteen inches, except that in the counties of Cattaraugus, Columbia, Delaware, Herkimer, Monroe and Otsego, the size of the page shall not exceed eight and a half inches by fourteen inches, and every printed portion thereof shall be plainly printed in not smaller than eight point type. The county clerk acting as recording officer may in special circumstances accept a page exceeding the size or with smaller print than that prescribed herein, on such terms and at such fee, subject to review by the supreme court, as he may deem appropriate, but the fee for such recording and indexing shall not be less than double the fees otherwise chargeable by law therefor.

(f) Copies of records. The following fees, up to a maximum of thirty dollars per record shall be payable to a county clerk or register for copies of the records of the office except records filed under the uniform commercial code:

1. to prepare a copy of any paper or record on file in his office, except as otherwise provided, fifty cents per page with a minimum fee of one dollar;

2. to certify a prepared copy of any record or paper on file, fifty cents per page with a minimum fee of four dollars;

3. to prepare and certify a copy of any record or paper on file, one dollar per page with a minimum fee of four dollars; and

4. to prepare and certify a copy of a certificate of honorable discharge, except as provided for in the military law, two dollars.

### 1988 AMENDMENTS

L. 1988, ch. 192, eff. July 31, 1988, added new subdivision (f) setting fees for copying and certification of county clerk or county register records.

### 1965 AMENDMENTS

L. 1965, ch. 773, eff. Sept. 1, 1965, made mechanical changes.

### 1964 AMENDMENTS

L. 1964, ch. 476, eff. Sept. 27, 1964, added to Subd. (a): "This subdivision does not apply to the fees specified in subdivision (f) of section eight thousand twenty-one of this chapter." This amendment is part of law amending the Uniform Commercial Code and relates thereto. See CPLR 8021.

## § 8020.  County clerks as clerks of court.

Whenever a county clerk renders a service in his capacity as clerk of the supreme or a county court, in an action pending in such court, he is entitled to the fees specified in this section, payable in advance.

(a) Placing cause on calendar. For placing a cause on a calendar for trial or inquest, one hundred dollars in the supreme court and county court; except that where rules of the chief administrator of the courts require that a request for judicial intervention be made in an action pending in supreme court or county court, the county clerk shall be entitled to a fee of seventy-five dollars, payable before a judge may be assigned pursuant to such request, and thereafter, for placing such a cause on a calendar for trial or inquest, the county clerk shall be entitled to an additional fee of twenty-five dollars, and no other fee may be charged thereafter pursuant to this subdivision.

(b) Calendar fee for transferred cause, joint trial, retrial, or separate trial. Where a cause which has been placed upon a calendar is transferred before trial to a court for which a larger calendar fee is prescribed, the difference in calendar fee shall be paid at the time the cause is placed upon the calendar of the latter court, except that no additional fee shall be required when the action is transferred for the purpose of consolidation or trial jointly with another action. No separate calendar fee shall be imposed for a retrial of a cause or for the trial of a separate issue in a cause.

(c) Filing demand for jury trial. For filing a demand for a jury trial in the following counties, where the right to a jury trial is duly demanded:

1. in the counties within the city of New York, fifty dollars in the supreme court;

2. in all other counties, fifty dollars in the supreme court and county court.

(d) [**Editor's note:** *Repealed;* see discussion under "1972 Amendments" below.]

(e) Jury fee for transferred cause, joint trial, retrial or separate trial. Where a cause in which a jury has been demanded is transferred before trial to a court for which a larger jury fee is prescribed, the difference in the jury fee shall be paid at the time the cause is placed upon the calendar of the latter court, except that no additional fee shall be required when the action is transferred for the purpose of consolidation or trial jointly with another action in which a jury fee has previously been paid. No separate jury fee shall be imposed for a retrial of a cause or for the trial of a separate issue in a cause.

(f) Certification, exemplification, and copies of papers.

1. For issuing any certificate, in counties within the city of New York, eight dollars, and in all other counties, four dollars, except as otherwise expressly provided in this article.

2. For a certificate of exemplification, exclusive of certification, in counties within the city of New York, twenty-five dollars, and in all other counties, ten dollars.

(g) Searches. For certifying to a search of any court records for a consecutive two-year period or fraction thereof, for each name so searched, five dollars.

(h) Production of court records. For each day or part thereof in attendance in any action pursuant to a subpoena duces tecum, twenty dollars, and in addition thereto, mileage fees of twelve cents per mile each way and the necessary expenses of the messenger, except that if the subpoena duces tecum be served within the city of New York and the place of attendance is within the city of New York, then actual transportation costs shall be charged instead of the mileage fees.

### 1996 AMENDMENTS

L. 1996, ch. 309, eff. July 23, 1996, amended subdivision (a) by adding an additional fee to be paid to the clerk for placing a cause on a calendar for trial or inquest after a request for judicial intervention.

### 1992 AMENDMENTS

L. 1992, ch. 55, eff. April 15, 1992, amended CPLR 8020(f) to set forth the amounts payable to a county clerk acting in the capacity of court clerk for issuing any certificate or a certificate of exemplification in a county within New York City.

### 1990 AMENDMENTS

L. 1990, ch. 190, eff. May 25, 1990, amended CPLR 8020(a) to increase the fee for placing a case on the calendar for trial or inquest from seventy dollars to one hundred dollars, and to increase the fee for assigning a judge pursuant to a request for judicial intervention from fifty dollars to seventy-five dollars.

### 1988 AMENDMENTS

L. 1988, ch. 192, eff. July 31, 1988, deleted paragraphs 2, 3, and 4 from subdivision (f), and renumbered paragraph 5 as paragraph 2.

### 1987 AMENDMENTS

L. 1987, ch. 825, eff. Nov. 5, 1987, amended Subd. (a), clarifying language by deleting subsections (1) and (2) which had distinguished between the Supreme Court in counties within the city of New York, and the Supreme Court and County Court in all other counties, and adding the exception for the payment of the fee of fifty dollars where the rules of the chief administrator of the courts require that a request for judicial intervention be made in a pending action.

### 1983 AMENDMENTS

L. 1983, ch. 15, eff. April 1, 1983, amended CPLR 8020(a) and (c).

L. 1983, ch. 784, eff. Aug. 29, 1983, amended CPLR 8020(f), (g) and (h).

CPLR

### 1980 AMENDMENTS

L. 1980, ch. 39, eff. April 1, 1980, amended CPLR 8020(a) and (c).

### 1977 AMENDMENTS

L. 1977, ch. 33, sections 2 and 3, eff. April 1, 1977, amended subdivisions (a) and (c).

### 1972 AMENDMENTS

L. 1972, ch. 185, § 4, eff. May 28, 1972, repealed Subdivisions (c) and (d) and inserted a new Subdivision (c). Subdivision (d) was not replaced nor were subsequent subdivisions relettered.

L. 1972, ch. 709, eff. Sept. 1, 1972, added new Subd. (a)(3).

L. 1972, ch. 734, eff. July 1, 1972, amended CPLR 8020 (a)(1), (c)(1), (f), (g) and (h) by increasing the fees payable.

### 1971 AMENDMENTS

L. 1971, ch. 404, eff. July 1, 1971, and ch. 829, eff. Sept. 1, 1971, amended Subds. (a), (c), (f) and (g).

### 1970 AMENDMENTS

L. 1970, ch. 440, eff. May 1, 1970, amended paragraph (a).

L. 1970, ch. 104, eff. March 24, 1970, amended Subd. (h).

### 1969 AMENDMENTS

L. 1969, ch. 801, eff. Sept. 1, 1969, amended subd. (a)(2).

### 1968 AMENDMENTS

L. 1968, ch. 14, eff. Sept. 1, 1968, added paragraph 4-a to Subd. (a), since repealed.

## § 8021. County clerks other than as clerks of court.

Whenever a county clerk renders a service other than in his capacity as clerk of the supreme or a county court, or other than in an action pending in a court of which he is clerk, he is entitled to the fees specified in this section, payable in advance.

(a) Services in connection with papers or instruments relating to real property and not filed under the uniform commercial code.

1. For filing any paper, document or other instrument of any nature or description which is required or permitted by law to be filed in his office, five dollars, except as otherwise expressly provided in this article and in article twelve of the real property law.

2. For filing and indexing any map, ten dollars.

3. For affixing and indexing a notice of foreclosure of a mortgage, as prescribed in section fourteen hundred four of the real property actions and proceedings law, ten dollars.

4. a. For recording, entering, indexing and endorsing a certificate on any instrument, five dollars and, in addition thereto, three dollars for each page or

portion of a page and fifty cents for each additional town, city, block or other indices in which such instrument is to be indexed as directed by the endorsement thereon. On the assignment of a mortgage which assigns more than one mortgage or on a release of lease which releases more than one lease, then there shall be an additional fee of three dollars for every mortgage assigned or lease released in excess of one.

b. For recording, entering, indexing and endorsing a certificate on any instrument, an additional fee of five dollars to be paid monthly by county clerks to the commissioner of education, after deducting twenty-five cents, for deposit into the New York state local government records management improvement fund.

5. For re-indexing a recorded instrument, two dollars for each town, city, block or other indices so re-indexed upon presentation of the instrument with such additional endorsement thereon or, if the original instrument is not obtainable, by request in writing sworn to by an interested party, setting forth the facts.

6. For copying and mailing any map, such fees as may be fixed by the county clerk subject to review by the supreme court.

7. For entering a cross reference of the record of any instrument on the margin of the record of any other instrument referred to therein by liber and page, fifty cents for each cross reference.

8. For examining the record of each assignment of mortgage or other instrument recited in a certificate of discharge of mortgage, fifty cents.

9. For searching for any filed or recorded instrument, upon a written request specifying the kind of instrument, the location by town, city or block if a real property instrument, and the names and period to be searched, such fee as may be fixed by the county clerk subject to review by the supreme court.

10. For filing or recording a notice of pendency of action or a notice of attachment against real property, or an amended notice of pendency of action or an amended notice of action against real property, in counties within the city of New York, thirty-five dollars, and in all other counties, fifteen dollars, but no fee shall be charged for filing or recording a notice or order continuing or canceling same.

11. For filing federal tax liens payment shall be made in the manner provided by section two hundred forty-three of the lien law.

(b) Filing, other than in connection with papers or instruments relating to real property or filed under the uniform commercial code.

1. For filing any paper, document or other instrument of any nature or description which is required or permitted by law to be filed in his office, five dollars, except as otherwise expressly provided in this article, and except that no fee shall be charged for filing a commission of appointment to public office or an oath of office of a public officer or employee, other than a notary public or commissioner of deeds.

CPLR

2. For filing any certificate, instrument or document in relation to a corporation, or any certificate pursuant to section forty-nine-a of the personal property law, or any certificate, instrument or document in relation to a joint stock association, limited partnership, continued use of firm name or registration of hotel name, in counties within the city of New York, one hundred dollars, and in all other counties, twenty-five dollars. For filing any certificate pursuant to section one hundred thirty of the general business law, in counties within the city of New York, one hundred dollars, and in all other counties, twenty-five dollars. No fee shall be charged for filing proof of publication or a cancellation, discontinuance or dissolution certificate.

3. For filing an assignment of or order for the payment of salary or wages, in counties within the city of New York, ten dollars, and in all other counties, five dollars. No fee shall be charged for filing of a satisfaction, assignment, cancellation or vacation thereof.

4. For filing a notice of mechanics lien, or a notice of lending, in counties within the city of New York, thirty dollars, and in all other counties, fifteen dollars. No fee shall be charged for filing a notice or order continuing, amending or canceling same, but when a mechanics lien is discharged by deposit with a clerk of the court, there shall be a fee of three dollars in all counties other than those within the city of New York.

5. For filing, examining and entering an absolute bill of sale of chattels, or any instrument affecting chattels, or a copy of the foregoing, or an assignment of any such instrument, or a satisfaction of a chattel mortgage or conditional bill of sale, in all counties except those within the city of New York, one dollar and fifty cents. For filing, examining and entering a notice of lien on merchandise, one dollar and fifty cents. Every instrument affecting chattels must be endorsed on the outside thereof with the character of the instrument, the names of all the parties thereto and the location of the property affected thereby, which must be distinguished from the address of the parties by the words "property located at," or similar words.

6. For filing a notice of hospital lien, five dollars. No fee shall be charged for filing a satisfaction, partial satisfaction, modification, assignment, cancellation, discharge of amendment thereof.

7. For filing a transcript of judgment, in counties within the city of New York, twenty-five dollars, and in all other counties, ten dollars. No fee shall be charged for filing a certificate or order of satisfaction, partial satisfaction, modification, assignment, reversal, cancellation or amendment, of judgment or lien.

8. For filing and indexing a certificate of appointment or official character of a notary public, or for filing and indexing a certificate of appointment as commissioner of deeds, ten dollars.

9. For filing an assignment of money due on a contract, or an order on owner, twenty-five dollars. No fee shall be charged for filing a notice or order continuing, amending or canceling same.

10. For filing a building loan contract, in counties within the city of New York, fifty dollars, and in all other counties, twenty-five dollars.

11. (a) For recording any instrument required by statute to be recorded, in counties within the city of New York, ten dollars, and in all other counties, five dollars, and, in addition thereto, three dollars for each page or portion of a page recorded, except that the charge for instruments of surrender and orders of commitment required to be filed and recorded pursuant to section three hundred eighty-four of the social services law shall be ten dollars per instrument or order in counties within the city of New York, and in all other counties, five dollars per instrument or order.

(b) For recording any instrument required by statute to be recorded, an additional fee of five dollars to be paid monthly by county clerks to the commissioner of education, after deducting twenty-five cents, for deposit into the New York state local government records management improvement fund.

(c) Certification, issuing certificates, other papers and copies of papers, records, and related services, other than in connection with papers or instruments relating to real property or filed under the uniform commercial code.

1. For issuing any certificate, except as otherwise expressly provided for in this article, in counties within the city of New York, ten dollars, and in all other counties, five dollars.

2. For an execution of a judgment, five dollars.

3. For issuing a transcript of the docket of a judgment or other lien, in counties within the city of New York, fifteen dollars, and in all other counties, five dollars.

4. For issuing a certificate of appointment of a notary public, five dollars.

5. For issuing a certificate authenticating an official act by a notary public, commissioner of deeds or other public officer, three dollars, except that no fee shall be charged for a certificate on a paper required by the United States veterans' administration.

6. For issuing an official receipt for any instrument affecting personal property, two dollars.

7. For a certificate of exemplification, exclusive of certification, ten dollars.

8. For preparing and certifying a copy of a marriage record, five dollars.

9. No fee shall be charged to any county officer, employee or institution required to file or record any instrument in connection with the official duties thereof, or to any public official in connection with the filing of his undertaking.

(d) Searches of records not filed under the uniform commercial code. For certifying to a search of any records, other than those in an action or relating to real property, for a consecutive two-year period or fraction thereof, for each name so searched, five dollars; except that in the counties within the city of New York, when the records so searched are the census records of the state

CPLR

of New York, the charge shall be one dollar for a consecutive two-year period or fraction thereof.

(e) Production of records. The production in any action of any filed or recorded paper, document, map or other instrument which is part of the public records and papers of a county clerk's office, except the papers in an action which have been filed with the county clerk in his capacity as clerk of the court, is hereby prohibited in the interest of the safety and preservation thereof, unless the county clerk consents to such production, or the judge presiding in the court in which such production is sought so orders. Instead of the original, a certified copy of such filed or recorded paper, document, map or other instrument shall be produced in evidence as provided in section 4540 without an order. In the event that the original is to be produced on order of such judge, there shall be a fee for each day or part thereof in attendance pursuant to a subpoena duces tecum of twenty dollars and, in addition thereto, mileage fees of twelve cents per mile each way and the necessary expenses of the messenger, except that if the subpoena duces tecum be served within the city of New York and the place of attendance is within the city of New York, then actual transportation cost shall be charged instead of the mileage fees. In the event that a certified photo copy of the records subpoenaed is produced, there shall be the same fee as if the original was produced on the order of a judge.

(f) Services rendered pursuant to part four of article nine of the uniform commercial code.

1. For filing, indexing and furnishing filing data for a financing statement or a continuation statement on a form conforming to standards prescribed by the secretary of state, three dollars, or if the statement otherwise conforms to the requirements of part four of such article, four dollars and fifty cents, plus, in either case,

(a) if the statement covers collateral which is crops or goods which are or are to become fixtures, fifty cents and, in addition;

(b) if the real estate is in the city of New York or the county of Nassau, any block fees allowed by the administrative code of the city of New York or the Nassau county administrative code;

(c) for each additional person, firm or organization, beyond the first, named as a debtor in the statement, seventy-five cents.

2. For filing and indexing an assignment or statement of assignment on a form conforming to standards prescribed by the secretary of state, of a security interest included in or accompanying a termination statement, three dollars, or if the assignment or statement of assignment otherwise conforms to the requirements of part four of such article, four dollars and fifty cents, plus, in either case, for each additional person, firm or organization, beyond the first, named as a debtor in the assignment or statement, seventy-five cents.

3. For filing and indexing a termination statement, including sending or delivering the financing statement and any continuation statement, statement of assignment or statement of release pertaining thereto, or an acknowledgment of the filing of the termination statement, one dollar and fifty cents and, otherwise, shall be three dollars, plus, in each case an additional fee of seventy-five cents for each name more than one against which the termination statement is required to be indexed.

4. For filing, indexing and furnishing filing data for a financing statement indicating an assignment of a security interest in the collateral on a form conforming to standards prescribed by the secretary of state, three dollars, or if the financing statement otherwise conforms to the requirements of part four of such article, four dollars and fifty cents, and seventy-five cents for each additional person, firm or organization, beyond the first, named as a debtor in the statement.

5. For filing, indexing and furnishing filing data about a statement of assignment on a form conforming to standards prescribed by the secretary of state, separate from a financing statement, three dollars, or if the statement of assignment otherwise conforms to the requirements of part four of such article, four dollars and fifty cents plus, in either case, for each additional person, firm or organization, beyond the first, named as a debtor in the statement, seventy-five cents.

6. For filing and noting a statement of release of collateral on a form conforming to standards prescribed by the secretary of state, three dollars, or if the statement of release otherwise conforms to the requirements of part four of such article, four dollars and fifty cents plus, in either case, for each additional person, firm or organization, beyond the first, named as a debtor in the statement, seventy-five cents.

7. For noting the file number and date and hour of the filing of the original upon a copy thereof furnished by the person filing any financing statement, termination statement, statement of assignment, or statement of release, and delivering or sending the copy to such person, when the filed statement contains more than one page or the statements and copy are not on forms conforming to standards prescribed by the secretary of state, an amount equal to the product of one dollar and fifty cents multiplied by the number of pages the filed statement contains.

8. For issuing a certificate showing whether there is on file a presently effective financing statement naming a particular debtor and any statement of assignment thereof or statement of release of collateral pertaining thereto, and if there is, giving the date and hour of filing of each such statement and the names and addresses of each secured party therein, four dollars and fifty cents if the request for the certificate is on a form conforming to standards prescribed by the secretary of state or, otherwise, seven dollars and fifty cents.

9. For furnishing a copy of any filed financing statement, continuation statement, termination statement, statement of assignment or statement of release, one dollar and fifty cents per page; provided, however, that the county clerk may furnish duplicate copies of microfilm records of all financing statements, continuation statements, termination statements, statements of assignment and statements of release filed during any month to any person requesting the same at a fee, to be determined by the county clerk, of less than one dollar and fifty cents per page.

(g) Services rendered in relation to federal tax liens filed pursuant to the lien law.

1. For filing and indexing a notice of lien for taxes payable to the United States of America and certificates and notices affecting such liens, four dollars and fifty cents.

2. For issuing a certificate showing whether there is on file on the date and hour stated therein, any notice of federal tax lien or certificate or notice affecting such lien, filed on or after July third, nineteen hundred sixty-six, and if there is, giving the date and hour of filing each such notice or certificate, four dollars and fifty cents.

### CROSS REFERENCES

Reference in Subd. (a)(1), *supra*, to provisions of Article 12 of the Real Property Law refers to **Real Prop. L. § 432,** which sets forth fees to be charged for registering title to real property.

**Lien Law § 243,** referred to in Subd. (a)(13), *supra*, providing for fees payable for filing Internal Revenue tax lien, appears in Appendix, *infra*.

**Pers. Prop. L. § 49-a,** referred to in Subd. (b)(2), *supra*, provides for statement to be filed by lenders upon assignment.

**Gen. Bus. L. § 130,** referred to in Subd. (b)(2), *supra*, provides for the filing of certificates by persons conducting business under an assumed name or as partners.

**S.S.L. § 384,** referred to in Subd. (b)(11), *supra*, pertains to guardianship of destitute or dependent children.

**U.C.C. Article 9, Part 4,** referred to in Subd. (f)(1), *supra*, deals with filing to perfect a security interest.

### 1992 AMENDMENTS

L. 1992, ch. 55, eff. April 15, 1992, amended CPLR 8021(a)(10); (b)(2), (3), (4), (7), (10), and (11)(a); and (c)(1) and (3), by setting forth the amount payable to a clerk of a county within New York City, who is not acting as a court clerk, for performing the services described in these subsections.

### 1989 AMENDMENTS

L. 1989, ch. 78, eff. July 30, 1989, amended paragraph 4 of subdivision (a) and paragraph 11 of subdivision (b) regarding additional fees; however, these provisions will be deemed repealed on Dec. 31, 1995.

### 1988 AMENDMENTS

L. 1988, ch. 192, eff. July 31, 1988, deleted paragraphs 6 and 7 from subdivision (a), renumbered paragraphs 8 through 13 as 6 through 11, and amended renumbered paragraph 10 to include recording a notice or amended notice of pendency; amended paragraph 10 of subdivision (b) to eliminate restriction to the counties within New York City; deleted paragraphs 6, 8 and 9 from subdivision (c), renumbered paragraph 7 as 6 and 10 through 12 as 7 through 9.

### 1983 AMENDMENTS

L. 1983, ch. 783, eff. Aug. 29, 1983, amended CPLR 8021(a)–(g).

### 1982 AMENDMENTS

L. 1982, ch. 692, eff. Aug. 21, 1982, amended subds. (f) and (g).

### 1977 AMENDMENTS

L. 1977, ch. 688, eff. Sept. 1, 1977, amended subds. (a)(4), (b)(7), (b)(8), (c)(3) and (c)(4).

### 1972 AMENDMENTS

L. 1972, chs. 324, 734 and 735, eff. July 1, 1975, amended Subd. (a)(4).

L. 1972, chs. 734 and 735, eff. July 1, 1975, also amended Subd. (b), (c), (d) and (e) by increasing fees.

### 1971 AMENDMENTS

L. 1971, ch. 404, eff. July 1, 1971, amended CPLR 8021(a), (b), (c), (d) and (e).

### 1969 AMENDMENTS

L. 1969, ch. 680, eff. May 21, 1969, amended Subd. (f)(4).

### 1968 AMENDMENTS

L. 1968, ch. 133, eff. July 1, 1968, amended Subd. (a) by adding paragraph (13).

L. 1968, ch. 721, eff. Sept. 1, 1968, amended Subd. (b)(11).

### 1967 AMENDMENTS

L. 1967, ch. 338, eff. April 18, 1967, added Subd. (g).

L. 1967, ch. 680, eff. Sept. 1, 1967, amended subd. (b)(2).

L. 1967, ch. 689, eff. April 27, 1967, amended Subd. (f).

### 1965 AMENDMENTS

L. 1965, ch. 128, eff. Sept. 1, 1965, amended Subd. (b).

L. 1965, ch. 773, eff. Sept. 1, 1965, amended subd. (a)(3).

### 1964 AMENDMENTS

L. 1964, ch. 476, eff. Sept. 27, 1964, amending the Uniform Commercial Code, made related amendments to CPLR 8021.

## § 8022. Fee on civil appeals and proceedings before appellate courts.

(a) A county clerk, upon filing a notice of appeal, is entitled to a fee of fifty dollars, payable in advance.

CPLR

(b) The clerks of the appellate divisions of the supreme court and the clerk of the court of appeals are entitled, upon the filing of a record on a civil appeal or a statement in lieu of record on a civil appeal, as required by rule 5530 of this chapter, to a fee of two hundred fifty dollars, payable in advance. The clerks of the appellate divisions also shall be entitled to such fee upon the filing of a notice of petition or order to show cause commencing a special proceeding in their respective courts.

### 1996 AMENDMENTS

L. 1996 ch. 390, eff. July 23, 1996, amended the heading by replacing the word "appeal" with the words, "appeals and proceedings before appellate courts"; amended paragraph (b) by adding the last sentence.

### 1990 AMENDMENTS

L. 1990 ch. 190, eff. May 25, 1990, amended CPLR 8022 by adding a new subdivision (a) authorizing a county clerk to receive a fee of fifty dollars before filing a notice of appeal; and by renumbering the former provision to become subdivision (b), and increasing the fee on appeal to the Appellate Division and Court of Appeals from two hundred dollars to two hundred fifty dollars.

### 1987 AMENDMENTS

L. 1987, ch. 825, eff. Nov. 5, 1987, added section 8022.

# ARTICLE 81

# COSTS GENERALLY

### SUMMARY OF ARTICLE

§ 8101.    Costs in an action.
§ 8102.    Limitation of costs where action brought in higher court.
§ 8103.    Costs where parties prevail upon separate issues.
§ 8104.    Costs in consolidated, severed or removed action.
§ 8105.    Costs where more than one plaintiff or defendant.
§ 8106.    Costs upon motion.
§ 8107.    Costs upon appeal.
§ 8108.    Specification of denial or award of costs.
§ 8109.    Defendant's costs against the state.
     (a)   Action brought for benefit of municipal corporation.
     (b)   Payment of defendant's costs against the state.
§ 8110.    Costs against a fiduciary.

## § 8101.   Costs in an action.

The party in whose favor a judgment is entered is entitled to costs in the action, unless otherwise provided by statute or unless the court determines that to so allow costs would not be equitable, under all of the circumstances.

## § 8102.   Limitation of costs where action brought in higher court.

A plaintiff is not entitled to costs:

1. in an action brought in the supreme court in a county within the city of New York which could have been brought, except for the amount claimed, in the civil court of the city of New York, unless he shall recover six thousand dollars or more; or,

2. in an action brought in the supreme court in a county not within the city of New York which could have been brought, except for the amount claimed, in any court of limited monetary jurisdiction in the county, unless he shall recover five hundred dollars or more; or,

3. in an action brought in the county court which could have been brought, except for the amount claimed, in any court of lesser monetary jurisdiction in the county, unless he shall recover two hundred fifty dollars or more.

## § 8103. Costs where parties prevail upon separate issues.

Upon the recovery of a judgment in favor of the plaintiff, the court may award costs in the action to a defendant without denying costs to the plaintiff, if it determines that a cause of action upon which the defendant prevailed is not substantially the same as any cause of action upon which the plaintiff recovered the judgment.

## § 8104. Costs in consolidated, severed or removed action.

Where two or more actions are consolidated, costs shall be awarded in the consolidated action as if it had been instituted as a single action, unless the order of consolidation otherwise provides. Where an action is severed into two or more actions, costs shall be awarded in each such action as if it had been instituted as a separate action, unless the order of severance otherwise provides. Where an action is removed, except pursuant to subdivision (d) of section three hundred twenty-five of this chapter, costs in the action shall be awarded as if it had been instituted in the court to which it is removed, unless the order of removal otherwise provides and as limited by section eighty-one hundred two of this chapter. Where an action is removed pursuant to subdivision (d) of section three hundred twenty-five of this chapter, costs in the action shall be awarded as if it had remained in the court from which it was removed, as limited by section eighty-one hundred two of this chapter.

### 1990 AMENDMENTS

L. 1990, ch. 64, eff. Jan. 1, 1991, amended § 8104 by providing that costs in an action removed pursuant to § 325(d) shall be awarded as if the action had remained in the court from which it was removed, as limited by § 8102.

## § 8105. Costs where more than one plaintiff or defendant.

Where a judgment is entered in favor of two or more parties, they shall be entitled, in all, to the same costs in the action as a single party, unless the court otherwise orders.

## § 8106. Costs upon motion.

Costs upon a motion may be awarded to any party, in the discretion of the court, and absolutely or to abide the event of the action.

## § 8107. Costs upon appeal.

The party in whose favor an appeal is decided in whole or in part is entitled to costs upon the appeal, whether or not he is entitled to costs in the action, unless otherwise provided by statute, rule or order of the appellate court. Where a new trial is directed upon appeal, costs upon the appeal may be awarded absolutely or to abide the event.

### § 8108.   Specification of denial or award of costs.

A denial of costs in an action to a party in whose favor the judgment is entered, an award of costs in an action to a party against whom the judgment is entered, an award of separate costs in an action to one or more parties, or an apportionment of costs among several parties, shall be made in the direction of the court for judgment, or in the report or decision upon which judgment is entered, or, upon motion of the party to be benefited thereby, by an order of the judge or referee who presided at the trial. The decision on a motion shall specify the amount of costs awarded upon the motion, if any, and each party to whom they are awarded. The decision on appeal shall specify the disposition made in regard to costs.

### § 8109.   Defendant's costs against the state.

(a) Action brought for benefit of municipal corporation. Costs awarded to the defendant in an action brought by the state for the benefit of a municipal corporation shall be awarded against the municipal corporation and not against the state.

(b) Payment of defendant's costs against the state. Where costs are awarded to the defendant and against the state in an action brought by a public officer, and the proceedings have not been stayed, the comptroller shall draw his warrant upon the treasurer for the payment of the costs out of any money in the treasury appropriated for that purpose, upon the production to him of an exemplified copy of the judgment or order awarding the costs, a copy of a taxed bill of costs and a certificate of the attorney-general to the effect that the action was brought pursuant to law. The fees of the clerk for the exemplified copy shall be certified thereupon by him and included in the warrant.

### § 8110.   Costs against a fiduciary.

Where costs are awarded against a fiduciary, they shall be chargeable only upon the estate, fund or person he represents, unless the court directs them to be paid personally for mismanagement or bad faith in the prosecution or defense of the action.

CPLR

# ARTICLE 82

# AMOUNT OF COSTS

### SUMMARY OF ARTICLE

§ 8201.     Amount of costs in an action.

§ 8202.     Amount of costs on motion.

§ 8203.     Amount of costs on appeal to appellate division and appellate term.

§ 8204.     Amount of costs on appeal to court of appeals.

### § 8201.   Amount of costs in an action.

Costs awarded in an action shall be in the amount of:

1. two hundred dollars for all proceedings before a note of issue is filed; plus

2. two hundred dollars for all proceedings after a note of issue is filed and before trial; plus

3. three hundred dollars for each trial, inquest or assessment of damages.

#### 1988 AMENDMENTS

L. 1988, ch. 101, eff. Jan. 1, 1989, applicable to all bills of costs entered on or after effective date, regardless of when claim accrued or action was commenced, amended 8201 to increase costs awarded in proceedings before note of issue is filed from fifty dollars (or twenty-five dollars outside New York City) to two hundred dollars in all counties; to increase costs awarded after note of issue is filed but before trial from one hundred dollars (or fifty dollars outside New York City) to two hundred dollars in all counties; and to increase costs awarded for each trial, inquest or assessment of damages from one hundred fifty dollars (or seventy-five dollars outside New York City) to three hundred dollars in all counties.

#### 1972 AMENDMENTS

L. 1972, ch. 734 and ch. 735, eff. July 1, 1972, amended CPLR 8021 by increasing the costs in an action in New York City.

### § 8202.   Amount of costs on motion.

Costs awarded on a motion shall be in an amount fixed by the court, not exceeding one hundred dollars.

CPLR

### 1988 AMENDMENTS

L. 1988, ch. 101, eff. Jan. 1, 1989, applicable to all bills of costs entered on or after effective date, regardless of when claim accrued or action was commenced, amended to increase costs awarded on a motion from forty dollars (or twenty dollars outside New York City) to one hundred dollars for all counties.

### 1972 AMENDMENTS

L. 1972, ch. 734 and ch. 735, eff. July 1, 1972, amended CPLR 8202 by increasing the costs on a motion in New York City.

## § 8203. Amount of costs on appeal to appellate division and appellate term.

(a) Unless the court awards a lesser amount, costs awarded on an appeal to the appellate division shall be in the amount of two hundred fifty dollars.

(b) Costs on an appeal from a county court to an appellate term may be awarded by the appellate term in its discretion, and if awarded shall be as follows:

1. to the appellant upon reversal, not more than thirty dollars;

2. to the respondent upon affirmance, not more than twenty-five dollars;

3. to either party on modification, not more than twenty-five dollars.

On appeal from any other court to an appellate term costs shall be governed by the provisions of the applicable court act.

### 1988 AMENDMENTS

L. 1988, ch. 101, eff. Jan. 1, 1989, applicable to all bills of costs entered on or after effective date, regardless of when claim accrued or action was commenced, amended subdivision (a) to eliminate the differential between pre-argument and argument costs, setting costs at two hundred fifty dollars.

### 1972 AMENDMENTS

L. 1972, ch. 391, eff. Sept. 1, 1972, amended CPLR 8203 by adding to the title, "appellate term," by lettering the prior material as subdivision (a), and by adding new subdivision (b).

L. 1972, ch. 734 eff. July 1, 1972, amended CPLR 8203. Effect of amendment canceled by L. 1972, ch. 735, eff. July 1, 1972.

## § 8204. Amount of costs on appeal to court of appeals.

Unless the court awards a lesser amount, costs awarded on an appeal to the court of appeals shall be in the amount of five hundred dollars.

### 1988 AMENDMENTS

L. 1988, ch. 101, eff. Jan. 1, 1989, applicable to all bills of costs entered on or after effective date, regardless of when claim accrued or action was commenced, amended 8204 to eliminate the pre-argument/argument costs differential, and to set costs at five hundred dollars.

## 1972 AMENDMENTS

L. 1972, ch. 734, eff. July 1, 1972, amended CPLR 8204. Effect of amendment cancelled by L. 1972, ch. 735, eff. July 1, 1972.

# ARTICLE 83

# DISBURSEMENTS AND ADDITIONAL ALLOWANCES

---

## SUMMARY OF ARTICLE

§ 8301. Taxable disbursements.
    (a) Disbursements in action or on appeal.
    (b) Disbursements on motion.
    (c) Disbursements to party not awarded costs.
    (d) Reasonable fees taxable.
§ 8302. Additional allowance to plaintiff as of right in real property actions.
    (a) Actions in which allowance made.
    (b) Amount of allowance.
    (c) Additional allowance where action settled.
    (d) Additional allowance in foreclosure action.
§ 8303. Additional allowance in the discretion of the court.
    (a) Discretionary allowance in action.
    (b) Discretionary allowance on enforcement motion.
§ 8303-a. Costs upon frivolous claims and counterclaims in actions to recover damages for personal injury, injury to property or wrongful death.
[§ 8303-a. Costs upon frivolous claims and counterclaims in podiatric, dental and medical malpractice actions.]

---

## § 8301. Taxable disbursements.

(a) Disbursements in action or on appeal. A party to whom costs are awarded in an action or on appeal is entitled to tax his necessary disbursements for:

1. the legal fees of witnesses and of referees and other officers;

2. the reasonable compensation of commissioners taking depositions;

3. the legal fees for publication, where publication is directed pursuant to law;

4. the legal fees paid for a certified copy of a paper necessarily obtained for use on the trial;

5. the expense of securing copies of opinions and charges of judges;

6. the reasonable expenses of printing the papers for a hearing, when required;

7. the prospective charges for entering and docketing the judgment;

8. the sheriff's fees for receiving and returning one execution;

9. the reasonable expense of taking, and making two transcripts of testimony on an examination before trial, not exceeding two hundred fifty dollars in any one action;

10. the expenses of searches made by title insurance, abstract or searching companies, or by any public officer authorized to make official searches and certify to the same, or by the attorney for the party to whom costs are awarded, taxable at rates not exceeding the cost of similar official searches;

11. the reasonable expenses actually incurred in securing an undertaking to stay enforcement of a judgment subsequently reversed; and

12. such other reasonable and necessary expenses as are taxable according to the course and practice of the court, by express provision of law or by order of the court.

(b) Disbursements on motion. Upon motion of any party made after the determination of a motion, or upon its own initiative, the court may allow any party thereto to tax as disbursements his reasonable and necessary expenses of the motion.

(c) Disbursements to party not awarded costs. The court may allow taxation of disbursements by a party not awarded costs in an action or on appeal; and shall allow taxation of disbursements by a party not awarded costs in an action for a sum of money only where he recovers the sum of fifty dollars or more.

(d) Reasonable fees taxable. Where an expense for a service performed, other than a search, is a taxable disbursement, the court may allow its taxation in an amount equal to the reasonable sum actually and necessarily expended therefor, if it is the usual charge made by private persons for the service, although it is in excess of the fee allowed a public officer.

## § 8302. Additional allowance to plaintiff as of right in real property actions.

(a) Actions in which allowance made. A plaintiff, if a judgment is entered in his favor and he recovers costs, is entitled to an additional allowance, in an action:

1. to foreclose a mortgage upon real property; or

2. for the partition of real property; or

3. to compel the determination of a claim to real property.

(b) Amount of allowance. An additional allowance under this rule shall be computed upon the amount found to be due upon the mortgage, or the value of the property which is partitioned or the claim to which is determined, at the rate of:

1. ten per cent of a sum not exceeding two hundred dollars; plus

2. five per cent of any additional sum not exceeding eight hundred dollars; plus

3. two per cent of any additional sum not exceeding two thousand dollars; plus

4. one per cent of any additional sum not exceeding five thousand dollars.

(c) Additional allowance where action settled. Where an action specified in subdivision (a) is settled before judgment, the plaintiff is entitled to an additional allowance upon the amount paid upon the settlement, computed at one-half of the rates set forth in subdivision (b).

(d) Additional allowance in foreclosure action. In an action to foreclose a mortgage upon real property, a plaintiff entitled to an additional allowance pursuant to subdivision (a) or (c) shall also be entitled to the sum of fifty dollars. Where a part of the mortgage debt is not due, if the judgment directs the sale of the whole property, the additional allowance specified in subdivision (a) shall be computed as provided in subdivision (b) upon the whole sum unpaid upon the mortgage. If the judgment directs the sale of a part only, it shall be computed upon the sum actually due, and if the court thereafter grants an order directing the sale of the remainder or a part thereof, it shall be computed upon the amount then due. The aggregate of additional allowances so computed shall not exceed the sum which would have been allowed if the entire sum secured by the mortgage had been due when the judgment was entered.

## § 8303.   Additional allowance in the discretion of the court.

(a) Discretionary allowance in action. Whether or not costs have been awarded, the court before which the trial was had, or in which judgment was entered, on motion, may award:

1. to any party to an action to foreclose a mortgage upon real property, a sum not exceeding two and one half per cent of the sum due or claimed to be due upon such mortgage, and not exceeding the sum of three hundred dollars; or

2. to any party to a difficult or extraordinary case, where a defense has been interposed, a sum not exceeding five per cent of the sum recovered or claimed, or of the value of the subject matter involved, and not exceeding the sum of three thousand dollars; or

3. to any party to an action for the partition of real property, a sum not exceeding five per cent of the value of the subject matter involved and not exceeding the sum of three thousand dollars; or

4. to the fiduciary or to any party to an action which involves the construction of a will or an inter vivos trust instrument, such sums as it deems reasonable for counsel fees and other expenses necessarily incurred with respect to such

CPLR

construction in the action; and the court may direct that the whole or any part of such allowance shall be paid to the attorney rendering the services in the action, and may provide that the determination of the amount of any allowance in connection therewith be reserved for a supplemental order to be entered after the time to appeal has expired, or if an appeal be taken, then after final determination of the appeal; and a court on appeal may make a like award and direction on appeal; or

5. to the attorney for the petitioner in a proceeding to dispose of an infant's property, such sum as to the court may seem just and proper; or

6. to the plaintiffs in an action or proceeding brought by the attorney-general under articles twenty-two, twenty-two-a, twenty-three-a or thirty-three or section five hundred twenty-a of the general business law, or under subdivision twelve of section sixty-three of the executive law, or under article twenty-three of the arts and cultural affairs law, or in an action or proceeding brought by the attorney-general under applicable statutes to dissolve a corporation or for usurpation of public office, or unlawful exercise of franchise or of corporate right, a sum not exceeding two thousand dollars against each defendant.

(b) Discretionary allowance on enforcement motion. The court, on a motion relating to the enforcement of a judgment, may award to the judgment creditor a sum not exceeding five per cent of the judgment or fifty dollars, whichever is more.

### 1988 AMENDMENTS

L. 1988, ch. 500, eff. Aug. 1, 1988, amended paragraph 6 of subdivision (a) to permit discretionary award of costs to plaintiff in an action brought under General Business Law § 520-a (requirements for credit card transaction forms); L. 1988, ch. 547, eff. Nov. 1, 1988, amended paragraph 6 of subdivision (a) to delete reference to former General Business Law Article 26-A (regulation of theatrical syndication financing) and to add reference to Arts and Cultural Affairs Law Article 23, paralleling the legislature's relocation of this section by L. 1983, ch. 876, § 1.

### 1982 AMENDMENTS

L. 1982, ch. 846, eff. Sept. 1, 1982, amended CPLR 8303(a)(6) by adding a reference to General Business Law § 33.

### 1971 AMENDMENTS

L. 1971, ch. 430, eff. Sept. 1, 1971, amended CPLR 8303(a) (6) by adding a reference to General Business Law Article 22-a.

### 1966 AMENDMENTS

L. 1966, ch. 224, eff. Sept. 1, 1966, amended Subd. (a).

The amendments were recommended by the Judicial Conference Feb. 1, 1966, Report to the Legislature: "Both CPLR 8301 and CPLR 8302 are applicable only to a party to whom costs are awarded. The silence of CPLR 8303(a) on this point has occasioned some confusion. The provision should be clarified to reflect the revisers' intention that a party may be eligible for an additional allowance even though he is not the party who taxes costs (See 1960 N.Y.Leg.Doc.No. 20, p. 331)." The change to § 8303(a)(1) is one of form merely.

"§ 1513 of the Civil Practice Act, the counterpart of CPLR 8303(a)(1), provided explicitly that it applied only to mortgages on real property. Since no change in substance was intended by the revisers, CPLR 8303(a)(1) should be clarified accordingly in order to prevent any misconstruction. The proposed clarification would also remove an inconsistency with CPLR 8302(a)(1), which expressly applies to mortgages on real property only."

### 1965 AMENDMENTS

L. 1965, ch. 577, eff. June 28, 1965, amended paragraph 6 of Subd. (a).

[Editor's note: Two versions of CPLR 8303-a follow. The first version reflects amendments made by L. 1986, ch. 220, eff. June 28, 1986; the second version represents that published and amended by L. 1986, ch. 485, eff. July 21, 1986. Because of material discrepancies, both versions are being printed in their entireties.]

## § 8303-a.  Costs upon frivolous claims and counterclaims in actions to recover damages for personal injury, injury to property or wrongful death.

(a) If in an action to recover damages for personal injury, injury to property or wrongful death, an action or claim is commenced or continued by a plaintiff or a counterclaim, defense or cross claim is commenced or continued by a defendant that is found, at any time during the proceedings or upon judgment, to be frivolous by the court, the court shall award to the successful party costs and reasonable attorney's fees not exceeding ten thousand dollars.

(b) The costs and fees awarded under subdivision (a) of this section shall be assessed either against the party bringing the action, claim, cross claim, defense or counterclaim or against the attorney for such party, or against both, as may be determined by the court, based upon the circumstances of the case. Such costs and fees shall be in addition to any other judgment awarded to the successful party.

(c) In order to find the action, claim, counterclaim, defense or cross claim to be frivolous under subdivision (a) of this section, the court must find one or more of the following:

(i) the action, claim, counterclaim, defense or cross claim was commenced, used or continued in bad faith, solely to delay or prolong the resolution of the litigation or to harass or maliciously injure another;

(ii) the action, claim, counterclaim, defense or cross claim was commenced or continued in bad faith without any reasonable basis in law or fact and could not be supported by a good faith argument for an extension, modification or reversal of existing law. If the action, claim, counterclaim, defense or cross claim was promptly discontinued when the party or the attorney learned or should have learned that the action, claim, counterclaim, defense or cross claim lacked such a reasonable basis, the court may find that the party or the attorney did not act in bad faith.

CPLR

**1986 AMENDMENTS**

L. 1986, ch. 220, eff. June 28, 1986, and applicable to actions or proceedings commenced on or after such date, amended paragraph (a) by providing for costs upon frivolous claims and counterclaims in actions for personal injury, injury to property or wrongful death, and deleting references to dental and medical malpractice actions.

**1985 AMENDMENTS**

L. 1985, ch. 294, eff. July 1, 1985, and applicable to any action for dental or medical malpractice commenced on or after such date, added CPLR 8303-a.

## § 8303-a.   Costs upon frivolous claims and counterclaims in podiatric, dental and medical malpractice actions.

(a) If in a dental, medical or podiatric malpractice action, an action or claim is commenced or continued by a plaintiff or a counterclaim, defense or cross claim is commenced or continued by a defendant that is found, at any time during the proceedings or upon judgment, to be frivolous by the court, the court shall award to the successful party costs and reasonable attorney's fees not exceeding ten thousand dollars.

(b) The costs and fees awarded under subdivision (a) of this section shall be assessed either against the party bringing the action, claim, cross claim, defense or counterclaim or against the attorney for such party, or against both, as may be determined by the court, based upon the circumstances of the case. Such costs and fees shall be in addition to any other judgment awarded to the successful party.

(c) In order to find the action, claim, counterclaim, defense or cross claim to be frivolous under subdivision (a) of this section, the court must find one or more of the following:

(i) the action, claim, counterclaim, defense or cross claim was commenced, used or continued in bad faith, solely to delay or prolong the resolution of the litigation or to harass or maliciously injure another;

(ii) the action, claim, counterclaim, defense or cross claim was commenced or continued in bad faith without any reasonable basis in law or fact and could not be supported by a good faith argument for an extension, modification or reversal of existing law. If the action, claim, counterclaim, defense or cross claim was promptly discontinued when the party or the attorney learned or should have learned that the action, claim, counterclaim, defense or cross claim lacked such a reasonable basis, the court may find that the party or the attorney did not act in bad faith.

**1986 AMENDMENTS**

L. 1986, ch. 485, eff. July 21, 1986, amended CPLR 8303-a to apply to podiatric malpractice actions. Such amendment is applicable to acts, omissions or failures occurring on or after such date.

# ARTICLE 84

# TAXATION OF COSTS

---

## SUMMARY OF ARTICLE

§ 8401.    Computation by clerk.
§ 8402.    Taxation with notice.
§ 8403.    Taxation without notice.
§ 8404.    Judicial review of taxation or retaxation.

---

## § 8401.   Computation by clerk.

Costs, disbursements and additional allowances shall be taxed by the clerk upon the application of the party entitled thereto. A valuation of property necessary for fixing an additional allowance shall be ascertained by the court, unless it has been fixed by the decision of the court, verdict of the jury, or report of the referee or commissioners, upon which the judgment is entered. The clerk, whether or not objection is made, shall examine the bills presented to him for taxation; shall satisfy himself that all the items allowed by him are correct and allowable; and shall strike out all items of disbursements, other than the prospective charges expressly allowed by law, not supported by affidavit showing that they have been necessarily incurred and are reasonable in amount. The clerk shall insert in the judgment the total of the amount taxed as costs, disbursements and additional allowances.

## § 8402.   Taxation with notice.

Costs may be taxed upon at least five days' notice to each adverse party interested in reducing the amount thereof except one against whom judgment was entered on default in appearance. A copy of the bill of costs, specifying the items in detail, and a copy of any supporting affidavits shall be served with the notice.

## § 8403.   Taxation without notice.

Costs may also be taxed without notice. A party who has taxed costs without notice shall immediately serve a copy of the bill of costs upon each party who is entitled to notice under section 8402. Within five days after such service, any such party may serve notice of retaxation of costs upon five days' notice to the party who has taxed the costs, specifying the item as to which retaxation is sought.

## § 8404.  Judicial review of taxation or retaxation.

Upon motion of any interested party, on notice, the court may allow or disallow any item objected to before the clerk; or it may order a retaxation before the clerk and it may specify the grounds or the proof upon which an item may be allowed or disallowed.

# ARTICLE 85

# SECURITY FOR COSTS

## SUMMARY OF ARTICLE

§ 8501.   Security for costs.
    (a)   As of right.
    (b)   In court's discretion.
§ 8502.   Stay and dismissal on failure to give security.
§ 8503.   Undertaking.

## § 8501.   Security for costs.

(a) As of right. Except where the plaintiff has been granted permission to proceed as a poor person or is the petitioner in a habeas corpus proceeding, upon motion by the defendant without notice, the court or a judge thereof shall order security for costs to be given by the plaintiffs where none of them is a domestic corporation, a foreign corporation licensed to do business in the state or a resident of the state when the motion is made.

(b) In court's discretion. Upon motion by the defendant with notice, or upon its own initiative, the court may order the plaintiff to give security for costs in an action by or against an assignee or trustee for the benefit of creditors, a trustee, a receiver or debtor in possession in bankruptcy, an official trustee or a committee of a person imprisoned in this state, an executor or administrator, the committee of a person judicially declared to be incompetent, the conservator of a conservatee, a guardian ad litem, or a receiver.

### 1981 AMENDMENTS

L. 1981, ch. 115, eff. May 18, 1981, amended CPLR 8501(b) by adding actions by or against a conservator of a conservatee to those actions in which a court may, in its discretion, require the plaintiff to give security for costs.

## § 8502.   Stay and dismissal on failure to give security.

Until security for costs is given pursuant to the order of the court, all proceedings other than to review or vacate such order shall be stayed. If the plaintiff shall not have given security for costs at the expiration of thirty days from the date of the order, the court may dismiss the complaint upon motion by the defendant, and award costs in his favor.

CPLR

## § 8503.  Undertaking.

Security for costs shall be given by an undertaking in an amount of five hundred dollars in counties within the city of New York, and two hundred fifty dollars in all other counties, or such greater amount as shall be fixed by the court that the plaintiff shall pay all legal costs awarded to the defendant.

### 1972 AMENDMENTS

L. 1972, ch. 734 and ch. 735, eff. July 1, 1972, increased the amount of the undertaking for security for costs in New York City to five hundred dollars.

# ARTICLE 86

# COUNSEL FEES AND EXPENSES IN CERTAIN ACTIONS AGAINST THE STATE

## SUMMARY OF ARTICLE

§ 8600.    Intent and short title.
§ 8601.    Fees and other expenses in certain actions against the state.
    (a) When awarded
    (b) Application for fees
§ 8602.    Definitions.
    (a) Actions to which Article 86 applies.
    (b) Amount of fees and expenses.
    (c) Final judgment or settlement.
    (d) Individuals entitled to fees and expenses.
    (e) "Position of the state" defined.
    (f) "Prevailing party" defined.
    (g) "State" defined.
§ 8603.    Interest.
§ 8604.    Annual report.
§ 8605.    Applicability.
    (a) Effect of Article 86 on actions not against the state.
    (b) Fees incurred in administrative proceedings.
    (c) Recovery of fees or expenses under other statutes, laws and rules or common law.

CPLR

## § 8600. Intent and short title.

It is the intent of this article, which may hereafter be known and cited as the "New York State Equal Access to Justice Act," to create a mechanism authorizing the recovery of counsel fees and other reasonable expenses in certain actions against the state of New York, similar to the provisions of federal law contained in 28 U.S.C. § 2412(d) and the significant body of case law that has evolved thereunder.

### 1990 AMENDMENTS

L. 1990, ch. 73, eff. April 1, 1990 to March 31, 1992, amended CPLR 8600 to replace the erroneous reference to 5 U.S.C. § 504 with the correct reference, 28 U.S.C. § 2412(d).

## § 8601. Fees and other expenses in certain actions against the state.

(a) When awarded. In addition to costs, disbursements and additional allowances awarded pursuant to sections eight thousand two hundred one through eight thousand two hundred four and eight thousand three hundred one through eight thousand three hundred three of this chapter, and except as otherwise specifically provided by statute, a court shall award to a prevailing party, other than the state, fees and other expenses incurred by such party in any civil action brought against the state, unless the court finds that the position of the state was substantially justified or that special circumstances make an award unjust. Whether the position of the state was substantially justified shall be determined solely on the basis of the record before the agency or official whose act, acts, or failure to act gave rise to the civil action. Fees shall be determined pursuant to prevailing market rates for the kind and quality of the services furnished, except that fees and expenses may not be awarded to a party for any portion of the litigation in which the party has unreasonably protracted the proceedings.

(b) Application for fees. A party seeking an award of fees and other expenses shall, within thirty days of final judgment in the action, submit to the court an application which sets forth (1) the facts supporting the claim that the party is a prevailing party and is eligible to receive an award under this section, (2) the amount sought, and (3) an itemized statement from every attorney or expert witness for whom fees or expenses are sought stating the actual time expended and the rate at which such fees and other expenses are claimed.

### 1990 AMENDMENTS

L. 1990, ch. 73, eff. April 1, 1990 to March 31, 1992, amended CPLR 8601 to provide discussion of fees and other expenses in certain actions against the state; and amended to replace the original references to "plaintiff or petitioner" with "party;" the original references to "defendant" with "state;" and the reference to "action" in the final sentence of subdivision (a) with "act, acts."

## § 8602. Definitions. ·

For the purpose of this article:

(a) "Action" means any civil action or proceeding brought to seek judicial review of an action of the state as defined in subdivision (g) of this section, including an appellate proceeding, but does not include an action brought in the court of claims.

(b) "Fees and other expenses" means the reasonable expenses of expert witnesses, the reasonable cost of any study, analysis, consultation with experts, and like expenses, and reasonable attorney fees, including fees for work performed by law students or paralegals under the supervision of an attorney incurred in connection with an administrative proceeding and judicial action.

(c) "Final judgment" means a judgment that is final and not appealable, and settlement.

(d) "Party" means (i) an individual whose net worth, not including the value of a homestead used and occupied as a principal residence, did not exceed fifty thousand dollars at the time the civil action was filed; (ii) any owner of an unincorporated business or any partnership, corporation, association, real estate developer or organization which had no more than one hundred employees at the time the civil action was filed, (iii) any organization described in section 501(c)(3) of the Internal Revenue Code of 1954 (26 U.S.C. 501(c)(3)) exempt from taxation under section 501(a) of such Code regardless of the number of employees.

(e) "Position of the state" means the act, acts or failure to act from which judicial review is sought.

(f) "Prevailing party" means a plaintiff or petitioner in the civil action against the state who prevails in whole or in substantial part where such party and the state prevail upon separate issues.

(g) "State" means the state or any of its agencies or any of its officials acting in his or her official capacity.

## § 8603. Interest.

If the state appeals an award made pursuant to this section and the award is affirmed in whole or in part, interest shall be paid on the amount of the award. Such interest shall run from the date of the award through the day before the date of the affirmance.

## § 8604. Annual report.

The department of audit and control shall file with the governor, the speaker of the assembly and the majority leader of the senate an annual report describing the number, nature and amount of each award in the previous fiscal year including the agency involved in each action, and other relevant information which might aid the legislature and the governor in evaluating the scope and impact of such awards.

## § 8605. Applicability.

(a) Nothing contained in this article shall be construed to alter or modify the other provisions of this chapter where applicable to actions other than actions against the state.

(b) Nothing contained in this article shall be deemed to authorize the institution of a civil action for the sole purpose of obtaining fees incurred by a party to an administrative proceeding.

CPLR

(c) Nothing contained in this article shall affect or preclude the right of any party to recover fees or other expenses authorized by common law or by any other statute, law or rule.

## 1992 AMENDMENTS

L. 1992, ch. 36, § 1, amended L. 1989, ch. 770, by omitting "except that the provisions of article 86 of the civil practice law and rules, as added by section one of this act, shall expire and be deemed repealed on March 31, 1992."

## 1989 AMENDMENTS

L. 1989, ch. 770, eff. April 1, 1990, created this new Article 86; Section 2 of that chapter provided that the new Article 86 "shall apply to all actions commenced on or after such date, except that the provisions of article 86 of the civil practice law and rules, as added by section one of this act, shall expire and be deemed repealed on March 31, 1992."

# ARTICLE 87

# PUNITIVE DAMAGE AWARDS; PUBLIC SHARE

[**Editor's note:** *L. 1992, ch. 55, eff. April 10, 1992 and deemed repealed on April 1, 1994, pursuant to L. 1992, ch. 55, § 427(dd).*]

CPLR

# ARTICLE 90

## FAILURE OR ADJOURNMENT OF TERM OF COURT

### SUMMARY OF ARTICLE

R 9001. No abatement by failure, adjournment, or change of time or place of term of court.

R 9002. Death, disability or incapacity of judge following verdict, report, decision, or determination of motion or special proceeding.

R 9003. Running of time when county judge disqualified from acting in a case.

### R 9001. No abatement by failure, adjournment, or change of time or place of term of court.

When a term of a court fails or is adjourned or the time or place of holding it is changed, all persons are bound to appear and all proceedings shall continue at the time and place to which the term is adjourned or changed, or, if it has failed, at the next term, with like effect as if the term had been held as originally appointed.

### R 9002. Death, disability or incapacity of judge following verdict, report, decision, or determination of motion or special proceeding.

The death, sickness, resignation, removal from or expiration of office or other disability or legal incapacity of a judge following his verdict, report, decision or determination of a motion or special proceeding in any matter in a civil judicial proceeding shall not affect its validity. Unless otherwise provided by rule of the chief administrator of the courts, any other judge of the same court may, on the application of a party, give effect to such verdict, report, decision or determination and make and sign an appropriate order or judgment based thereon, which shall have the same effect as if it had been made by the judge upon whose verdict, report, decision or determination it is based.

### CROSS REFERENCES

See **Judiciary Law** § 7-c in Appendix, *infra*, as to continuance of special proceeding before another officer.

### 1986 AMENDMENTS

L. 1986, ch. 355, eff. July 17, 1986, amended CPLR 9002 by adding "Unless otherwise provided by rule of the chief administrator of the courts" at the beginning of the second sentence.

### 1974 AMENDMENTS

Amended by proposal No. 4 of the Judicial Conference Report to the 1974 Legislature by adding the reference to a "determination of a motion or special proceeding." As stated by the 1974 Judicial Conference Report: "[A]t present there is no statute or rule providing that in case of death, sickness, resignation, removal from or expiration of office or other disability or legal incapacity of a judge after determining a motion or special proceeding, any judge of the same court may sign an order determining such motion or special proceeding. Thus, the proposed amendment would remove the present necessity in such case for duplicative proceedings."

### 1969 AMENDMENTS

Amendment promulgated by Judicial Conference Feb. 1, 1969 Report to the Legislature, effective Sept. 1, 1969, so as to permit any judge of the same court to sign the concluding order or judgment where the judge who rendered the verdict, report or decision cannot sign the concluding order or judgment because of "sickness, resignation, removal from or expiration of office or other disability or legal incapacity."

# R 9003. Running of time when county judge disqualified from acting in a case.

If a county judge is disqualified from acting in any case pending in his court and files a certificate pursuant to judiciary law section one hundred ninety-two, the time within which any proceeding may be taken, as fixed by statute or rule, does not begin to run until the certificate is filed.

### CROSS REFERENCES

Judiciary Law § 192 was repealed by L. 1964, ch. 53, eff. Sept. 1, 1964.

# ARTICLE 94

# ADMISSION TO PRACTICE

## SUMMARY OF ARTICLE

R 9401.   Committee.
R 9402.   Application for admission.
R 9403.   Referral to another judicial district.
R 9404.   Certificate of character and fitness.
R 9405.   Prior application.
R 9406.   Proof.
R 9407.   Filing.

## R 9401.   Committee.

The appellate division in each judicial department shall appoint a committee of not less than three practicing lawyers for each judicial district within the department, for the purpose of investigating the character and fitness of every applicant for admission to practice as an attorney and counselor at law in the courts of this state. Each member of such committee shall serve until his death, resignation or the appointment of his successor. A lawyer who has been or who shall be appointed a member of the committee for one district may be appointed a member of the committee for another district within the same department.

## R 9402.   Application for admission.

Every application for admission to practice pursuant to the provisions of paragraph a of subdivision one of section ninety of the judiciary law by a person who has been certified by the state board of law examiners, in accordance with the provisions of section four hundred sixty-four of said law, shall be referred by the appellate division to the committee for a district in its judicial department. Every application for admission to practice which is made on motion without the taking of the bar examination, pursuant to rules of the court of appeals and the provisions of paragraph b of subdivision one of section ninety of the judiciary law, by a person already admitted to practice in another jurisdiction, shall be referred by the appellate division to the committee for a district in its judicial department.

**1985 AMENDMENTS**

L. 1985, ch. 226, eff. June 15, 1985, amended CPLR 9402 to provide that the appellate division shall refer applications for admission to the committee in a district in its judicial department.

## R 9403.   Referral to another judicial district.

Notwithstanding rule 9402, any application for admission to practice pending before a committee, may be referred to the committee for another judicial district in the same or another department by order or direction of the presiding justice of the appellate division of the department embracing the district in which the application is pending. Such order or direction may be made only upon the written request of the chairman or acting chairman of the committee before which the application is pending and only upon his written certification either:

1. that the applicant, since he applied to take the bar examination or to dispense with such examination or since he applied on motion to be admitted to practice, has changed his actual residence to such other judicial district in the same or other department, or, if not a resident of the state, has acquired full-time employment in or changed his place of full-time employment to such other judicial district in the same or other department; or

2. that the majority of the members of such committee are not qualified to vote on the application or have disqualified themselves from voting or have refrained from voting thereon; or

3. that the members of such committee are equally divided in their opinion as* the application; or

4. that strict compliance with rule 9402 will cause undue hardship to the applicant.

* [**Editor's note:** So in original. Probably should read "as to."]

**1985 AMENDMENTS**

L. 1985, ch. 226, eff. June 18, 1985, amended CPLR 9403 to provide for transfer of an application for admission in the case of a non-resident acquiring full-time employment in a judicial district or where strict compliance with CPLR 9402 will cause undue hardship.

**1973 AMENDMENTS**

CPLR 9403 was amended by proposal No. 6 of the Judicial Conference Report to the 1973 Legislature, effective Sept. 1, 1973, to provide for the transfer of an application for admission to the bar from one judicial department to another.

## R 9404.   Certificate of character and fitness.

Unless otherwise ordered by the appellate division, no person shall be admitted to practice without a certificate from the proper committee that it has carefully investigated the character and fitness of the applicant and that, in such respects, he is entitled to admission. To enable the committee to make such investigation, the justices of the appellate division are authorized to prescribe and from time to time to amend a form of statement or questionnaire to be submitted by the applicant, including specifically his present and such past places of actual residence as may be required therein, listing the street and number, if any, and the period of time he resided at each place.

### 1973 AMENDMENTS

CPLR 9404 was amended by proposal No. 7 of the Judicial Conference Report to the 1973 Legislature, effective Sept. 1, 1973.

### 1965 AMENDMENTS

L. 1965, ch. 675, eff. Sept. 1, 1965.

## R 9405. Prior application.

In the event that any applicant has made a prior application for admission to practice in this state or in any other jurisdiction, then upon said statement or questionnaire or in an accompanying signed statement, he shall set forth in detail all the facts with respect to such prior application and its disposition. If such prior application had been filed in any appellate division of this state and if the applicant failed to obtain a certificate of good character and fitness from the appropriate character committee or if for any reason such prior application was disapproved or rejected either by said committee or said appellate division, he shall obtain and submit the written consent of said appellate division to the renewal of his application in that appellate division or in any other appellate division.

## R 9406. Proof.

No person shall receive said certificate from any committee and no person shall be admitted to practice as an attorney and counselor at law in the courts of this state, unless he shall furnish satisfactory proof to the effect:

1. that he supports the constitutions of the United States and of the state of New York; and

2. that he has complied with all the requirements of the applicable statutes of this state, the applicable rules of the court of appeals and the applicable rules of the appellate division in which his application is pending, relating to the admission to practice as an attorney and counselor at law.

### CROSS REFERENCES

See **Judiciary Law § 464** as to certification of non-residents employed within the state.

### 1985 AMENDMENTS

L. 1985, ch. 226, eff. June 18, 1985, amended CPLR 9406 by deleting subd. (2), mandating a six-month residency requirement for admission to practice, and amending

CPLR

subd. (1) to require applicants to prove they support the United States and New York constitutions.

### 1978 AMENDMENTS

L. 1978, ch. 294, eff. June 19, 1978, and applicable to applications for admission to practice made after June 1, 1975, eliminated from subd. (2) the former requirement that an applicant furnish proof that his residence in New York State has continued until the final disposition of his application.

### 1974 AMENDMENTS

Amended by proposal No. 5 of the Judicial Conference Report to the 1974 Legislature by deleting the second subdivision which provided that no person may be admitted to the bar in New York State unless he is a citizen of the United States. The remaining subdivisions were renumbered accordingly.

### 1965 AMENDMENTS

L. 1965, ch. 675, eff. Sept. 1, 1965, amended Subd. 3, now Subd. 2.

## R 9407. Filing.

Every application for admission to practice, together with all the papers submitted thereon, upon its final disposition by the appellate division shall be filed in the office of the clerk of such appellate division.

# ARTICLE 97

# RECORDS OF CLERKS OF THE COURTS

## SUMMARY OF ARTICLE

R 9701.    **Records to be kept by the clerk of appellate division.**
R 9702.    **Books to be kept by the clerks of other courts.**
R 9703.    **Form of records.**

## R 9701.   Records to be kept by the clerk of appellate division.

The clerk of the appellate division in each department shall keep:

1. a book, properly indexed, or an index, in which shall be entered the title of all proceedings in that court, with entries under each, showing the proceedings taken therein and the final disposition thereof; and

2. a book in which shall be indexed all undertakings filed in the clerk's office, with a statement of the proceedings in which they are given, and a statement of any disposition or order made of or concerning them; and

3. a book, properly indexed, or an index, which shall contain (a) the name of each attorney admitted to practice, in the department, with the date of the attorney's admission, and (b) the name of each person who has been refused admission or who has been disbarred, disciplined or censured by the court. The clerk of each department shall transmit to the clerk of the court of appeals and to the clerks of the other departments the names of all applicants who have been refused admission, and the names of all attorneys who have resigned or who have been disbarred, disciplined, censured or reinstated by the court.

### 1990 AMENDMENTS

L. 1990, ch. 623, eff. July 18, 1990, redesignated former subdivisions (3) and (4) as (2) and (3), respectively, and deleted subdivision (2); L. 1990, ch. 184, eff. May 24, 1990, deleted the reference in subdivision (3), clause (b), prior to its redesignation as subdivision (3) by L. 1990, ch. 623, eff. May 24, 1990, to "the names of all attorneys who have been admitted to practice."

### 1975 AMENDMENTS

CPLR 9701 was amended by Proposal No. 3 of the Judicial Conference Report to the 1975 Legislature, effective Sept. 1, 1975, to conform the language to the recordkeeping practices actually employed by the clerks of the Appellate Divisions.

## R 9702.  Books to be kept by the clerks of other courts.

The clerks of the other courts shall keep:

1. a "judgment-book," in which shall be recorded all judgments entered in their offices;

2. a book, properly indexed, in which shall be entered the title of all civil judicial proceedings, with proper entries under each denoting the papers filed and the orders made and the steps taken therein, with the dates of the filing of the several papers in the proceeding;

3. a book, properly indexed, in which shall be entered the name and address of each conservator, committee or guardian who is appointed pursuant to the provisions of the mental hygiene law, the title of the proceeding, the name and address of any surety, the papers filed, and any orders made or steps taken therein;

4. a book in which shall be recorded at length each undertaking of a public officer or any officer appointed by the court, filed in their offices, except the undertakings of receivers appointed under section 5228, with a statement showing when the undertaking was filed and a notation on the margin of the record showing any disposition, or order, made of or concerning it;

5. such other books, properly indexed, as may be necessary, or convenient, to contain the docket of judgments, the entry of orders, and all other necessary matters and proceedings; and

6. such other books as the chief administrator of the courts may direct to be kept.

### 1990 AMENDMENTS

L. 1990, ch. 184, eff. May 24, 1990, amended CPLR 9702 by deleting the phrase "the minutes of the court" in subdivision (5); L. 1990, Ch. 623, eff. July 18, 1990, amended CPLR 9702 by substituting the reference to the appellate divisions in subdivision (6) with "chief administrator of the courts."

### 1977 AMENDMENTS

L. 1977, ch. 28, eff. Sept. 1, 1977, amended CPLR 9702 by adding a new subdivision (3), and by renumbering the remaining subdivisions accordingly.

## R 9703.  Form of records.

A clerk shall keep books and records in such form and style as may be prescribed by the chief administrator of the courts.

### 1990 AMENDMENTS

L. 1990, ch. 623, eff. July 18, 1990, amended CPLR 9703 by designating that the form of books and records will now be as prescribed by the chief administrator of the courts.

# ARTICLE 98

# ACTIONS AGAINST VILLAGES

### SUMMARY OF ARTICLE

§ 9801.  **Actions against the village.**
§ 9802.  **Liability of villages in certain actions.**
§ 9803.  **Place of trial of actions and proceedings against villages.**
§ 9804.  **Notice of defects in certain actions.**

## § 9801.  Actions against the village.

1. No action shall be maintained against the village for a personal injury or injury to property alleged to have been sustained by reason of the negligence or wrongful act of the village or of any officer, agent or employee thereof, unless a notice of claim shall have been made and served in compliance with section fifty-e of the general municipal law.

2. Every such action shall be commenced pursuant to the provisions of section fifty-i of the general municipal law.

### CROSS REFERENCES

General Municipal Law § 50-e, referred to in paragraph (1), *supra*, appears in Appendix, *infra* . General Municipal Law § 50-i, referred to in paragraph (2), *supra*, appears in Appendix, *infra*.

### 1972 AMENDMENTS

L. 1972, ch. 890, § 3, eff. Sept. 1, 1973, added new CPLR Article 98 (CPLR 9801-9803) concerning actions against villages.

## § 9802.  Liability of villages in certain actions.

Except as provided otherwise in this chapter no action shall be maintained against the village upon or arising out of a contract of the village unless the same shall be commenced within eighteen months after the cause of action therefor shall have accrued, nor unless a written verified claim shall have been filed with the village clerk within one year after the cause of action shall have accrued, and no other action shall be maintained against the village unless the same shall be commenced within one year after the cause of action therefor shall have accrued, nor unless a notice of claim shall have been made and served in compliance with section fifty-e of the general municipal law. The omission to present a claim or to commence an action thereon within the respective periods of time above stated applicable to such claim, shall be a bar to any claim or action therefor against said village; but no action shall be brought upon any such claim until forty days have elapsed after the filing of the claim in the office of the village clerk.

### CROSS REFERENCES

See **General Municipal Law** §§ **50-e, 50-h and 50-i** in Appendix, *infra.*

## § 9803. Place of trial of actions and proceedings against villages.

The place of trial of all actions and proceedings against a village or any of its officers or boards shall be the county in which the village is situated.

## § 9804. Notice of defects in certain actions.

No civil action shall be maintained against the village for damages or injuries to person or property sustained in consequence of any street, highway, bridge, culvert, sidewalk or crosswalk being defective, out of repair, unsafe, dangerous or obstructed or for damages or injuries to persons or property sustained solely in consequence of the existence of snow or ice upon any sidewalk, crosswalk, street, highway, bridge or culvert unless written notice of the defective, unsafe, dangerous or obstructive condition, or of the existence of the snow or ice, relating to the particular place, was actually given to the village clerk and there was a failure or neglect within a reasonable time after the receipt of such notice to repair or remove the defect, danger or obstruction complained of or to cause the snow or ice to be removed, or the place otherwise made reasonably safe.

### CROSS REFERENCES

The provisions of this section are also found in **Village Law** § **6-628.** See also **Town Law §65-a,** as to liability of towns and town superintendents of highways, and notice requirements applicable thereto.

### 1973 AMENDMENTS

L. 1973, ch. 739, eff. Sept. 1, 1973, added new CPLR 9804.

# ARTICLE 100

# REPEAL; SAVING CLAUSES; EFFECTIVE DATE

### SUMMARY OF ARTICLE

§ 10001.  Repeal of the civil practice act.
§ 10002.  Abrogation of rules of civil practice.
§ 10003.  Pending and subsequent proceedings.
§ 10004.  Effect of unconstitutionality in part.
§ 10005.  Effective date.

## § 10001.  Repeal of the civil practice act.

Chapter nine hundred twenty-five of the laws of nineteen hundred twenty, entitled "An act in relation to the civil practice in the courts of the state of New York," and all acts amendatory thereof and supplemental thereto, constituting the civil practice act, as heretofore in effect, are hereby repealed.

## § 10002.  Abrogation of rules of civil practice.

The rules of practice adopted by the convention provided for by chapter nine hundred two of the laws of nineteen hundred twenty, as amended or supplemented by appropriate action of the justices of the appellate division in the several departments pursuant to section eighty-three of the judiciary law, comprising the rules of civil practice, as heretofore in effect, are hereby abrogated and shall no longer be in effect.

## § 10003.  Pending and subsequent proceedings.

This act shall apply to all actions hereafter commenced. This act shall also apply to all further proceedings in pending actions, except to the extent that the court determines that application in a particular pending action would not be feasible or would work injustice, in which event the former procedure applies. Proceedings pursuant to law in an action taken prior to the time this act takes effect shall not be rendered ineffectual or impaired by this act.

## § 10004.  Effect of unconstitutionality in part.

If any clause, sentence, paragraph, subdivision, section, rule or part of this chapter shall be adjudged by any court of competent jurisdiction to be invalid, such judgment shall not affect, impair or invalidate the remainder thereof, but shall be confined in its operation to the clause, sentence, paragraph, subdivision, section, rule or part thereof directly involved in the controversy in which such judgment shall have been rendered.

## § 10005.  Effective date.

This act shall take effect September first, nineteen hundred sixty-three.

# APPENDIX
## SELECTED PRACTICE PROVISIONS

## CONTENTS

| Titles included | Page |
|---|---|
| CONSTITUTION OF THE STATE OF NEW YORK | CONST-1 |
| BUSINESS CORPORATION LAW (BCL) | BCL-1 |
| COURT OF CLAIMS ACT | CCA-1 |
| CRIMINAL PROCEDURE LAW (CPL) | CPL-1 |
| DEBTOR AND CREDITOR LAW | DCL-1 |
| DOMESTIC RELATIONS LAW (DRL) | DRL-1 |
| EDUCATION LAW | ED-1 |
| ESTATES, POWERS AND TRUSTS LAW (EPTL) | EPTL-1 |
| GENERAL ASSOCIATIONS LAW | GAL-1 |
| GENERAL CONSTRUCTION LAW | GCL-1 |
| GENERAL MUNICIPAL LAW | GML-1 |
| GENERAL OBLIGATIONS LAW | GOL-1 |
| INSURANCE LAW | INS-1 |
| JUDICIARY LAW | JUD-1 |
| LIEN LAW | LIEN-1 |
| NEW YORK CITY CIVIL COURT ACT | NYCCCA-1 |
| PROFESSIONAL DISCIPLINARY RULES | PDR-1 |
| PUBLIC HEALTH LAW | PHL-1 |
| PUBLIC OFFICERS LAW | POL-1 |
| REAL PROPERTY LAW | RPL-1 |
| SURROGATE'S COURT PROCEDURE ACT (SCPA) | SCPA-1 |
| UNIFORM COMMERCIAL CODE (UCC) | UCC-1 |
| VEHICLE AND TRAFFIC LAW | VTL-1 |
| SPECIAL FEATURE: An Analysis of Practice Under New York's Commencement by Filing Law | CH.216-1 |
| COURT DIRECTORY | CD-1 |

App Pract Provs

# CONSTITUTION OF THE STATE OF NEW YORK

---

## SYNOPSIS OF SELECTED PROVISIONS

**Article III.**   **Legislature.**

§ 19.      [Private claims not to be audited by legislature; claims barred by lapse of time.]

**Article VI.**   **Judiciary.**

§ 1.      [Unified court system; courts of record; statewide service and execution.]

§ 3.      [Court of appeals; subject matter jurisdiction.]

§ 5.      [Appellate courts; power to determine appeal; transfer of appeal by court not authorized to review.]

§ 7.      [Supreme court; subject matter jurisdiction; new classes of actions.]

§ 8.      [Appellate terms authorized; composition; jurisdiction.]

§ 9.      [Court of claims continued; composition; jurisdiction.]

§ 11.     [County court; subject matter jurisdiction; appellate jurisdiction.]

§ 12.     [Surrogate's court continued; composition; subject matter jurisdiction.]

§ 13.     [Family court established; composition; subject matter jurisdiction.]

§ 15.     [New York City civil and criminal courts; merger authorized; subject matter jurisdiction.]

§ 16.     [District courts authorized; subject matter jurisdiction.]

§ 17.     [Town, village and city courts continued; subject matter jurisdiction.]

§ 18.     [Trial by jury.]

§ 19.     [Transfer of actions and proceedings.]

§ 28.     [Administrative supervision of the courts.]

§ 35.     [Abolition of certain courts; abolition of referee's office.] [Selections]

---

# ARTICLE III

# LEGISLATURE

## § 19. [Private claims not to be audited by legislature; claims barred by lapse of time]

The legislature shall neither audit nor allow any private claim or account against the state, but may appropriate money to pay such claims as shall have been audited and allowed according to law.

No claim against the state shall be audited, allowed or paid which, as between citizens of the state, would be barred by lapse of time. But if the claimant shall be under legal disability the claim may be presented within two years after such disability is removed.

# ARTICLE VI

# JUDICIARY

## § 1. [Unified court system; courts of record; statewide service and execution.]

a. There shall be a unified court system for the state. The state-wide courts shall consist of the court of appeals, the supreme court including the appellate divisions thereof, the court of claims, the county court, the surrogate's court and the family court, as hereinafter provided. The legislature shall establish in and for the city of New York, as part of the unified court system for the state, a single, city-wide court of civil jurisdiction and a single, city-wide court of criminal jurisdiction, as hereinafter provided, and may upon the request of the mayor and the local legislative body of the city of New York, merge the two courts into one city-wide court of both civil and criminal jurisdiction. The unified court system for the state shall also include the district, town, city and village courts outside the city of New York, as hereinafter provided.

b. The court of appeals, the supreme court including the appellate divisions thereof, the court of claims, the county court, the surrogate's court, the family court, the courts or court of civil and criminal jurisdiction of the city of New York, and such other courts as the legislature may determine shall be courts of record.

c. All processes, warrants and other mandates of the court of appeals, the supreme court including the appellate divisions thereof, the court of claims, the county court, the surrogate's court and the family court may be served and executed in any part of the state. All processes, warrants and other mandates of the courts or court of civil and criminal jurisdiction of the city of New York may, subject to such limitation as may be prescribed by the legislature, be served and executed in any part of the state. The legislature may provide that processes, warrants and other mandates of the district court may be served and executed in any part of the state and that processes, warrants and other mandates of town, village and city courts outside the city of New York may be served and executed in any part of the county in which such courts are located or in any part of any adjoining county.

*See also* Judiciary Law §§ 2, 2-b, *infra,* as to courts of record.

## § 3. [Court of appeals; subject matter jurisdiction.]

a. The jurisdiction of the court of appeals shall be limited to the review of questions of law except where the judgment is of death, or where the appellate division, on reversing or modifying a final or interlocutory judgment in an action or a final or interlocutory order in a special proceeding, finds new facts and a final judgment 'or a final order pursuant thereto is entered; but the right to appeal shall not depend upon the amount involved.

b. Appeals to the court of appeals may be taken in the classes of cases hereafter enumerated in this section;

In criminal cases, directly from a court of original jurisdiction where the judgment is of death, and in other criminal cases from an appellate division or otherwise as the legislature may from time to time provide.

In civil cases and proceedings as follows:

(1) As of right, from a judgment or order entered upon the decision of an appellate division of the supreme court which finally determines an action or special proceeding wherein is directly involved the construction of the constitution of the state or of the United States, or where one or more of the justices of the appellate division dissents from the decision of the court, or where the judgment or order is one of reversal or modification.

(2) As of right, from a judgment or order of a court of record of original jurisdiction which finally determines an action or special proceeding where the only question involved on the appeal is the validity of a statutory provision of the state or of the United States under the constitution of the state or of the United States; and on any such appeal only the constitutional question shall be considered and determined by the court.

(3) As of right, from an order of the appellate division granting a new trial in an action or a new hearing in a special proceeding where the appellant stipulates that, upon affirmance, judgment absolute or final order shall be rendered against him.

(4) From a determination of the appellate division of the supreme court in any department, other than a judgment or order which finally determines an action or special proceeding, where the appellate division allows the same and certifies that one or more questions of law have arisen which, in its opinion, ought to be reviewed by the court of appeals, but in such case the appeal shall bring up for review only the question or questions so certified; and the court of appeals shall certify to the appellate division its determination upon such question or questions.

(5) From an order of the appellate division of the supreme court in any department, in a proceeding instituted by or against one or more public officers or a board, commission or other body of public officers or a court or tribunal, other than an order which finally determines such proceeding, where the court

of appeals shall allow the same upon the ground that, in its opinion, a question of law is involved which ought to be reviewed by it, and without regard to the availability of appeal by stipulation for final order absolute.

(6) From a judgment or order entered upon the decision of an appellate division of the supreme court which finally determines an action or special proceeding but which is not appealable under paragraph (1) of this subdivision where the appellate division or the court of appeals shall certify that in its opinion a question of law is involved which ought to be reviewed by the court of appeals. Such an appeal may be allowed upon application (a) to the appellate division, and in case of refusal, to the court of appeals, or (b) directly to the court of appeals. Such an appeal shall be allowed when required in the interest of substantial justice.

(7) No appeal shall be taken to the court of appeals from a judgment or order entered upon the decision of an appellate division of the supreme court in any civil case or proceeding where the appeal to the appellate division was from a judgment or order entered in an appeal from another court, including an appellate or special term of the supreme court, unless the construction of the constitution of the state or of the United States is directly involved therein, or unless the appellate division of the supreme court shall certify that in its opinion a question of law is involved which ought to be reviewed by the court of appeals.

(8) The legislature may abolish an appeal to the court of appeals as of right in any or all of the cases or classes of cases specified in paragraph (1) of this subdivision wherein no question involving the construction of the constitution of the state or of the United States is directly involved, provided, however, that appeals in any such case or class of cases shall thereupon be governed by paragraph (6) of this subdivision.

### § 5.   [Appellate courts; power to determine appeal; transfer of appeal by court not authorized to review.]

a. Upon an appeal from a judgment or an order, any appellate court to which the appeal is taken which is authorized to review such judgment or order may reverse or affirm, wholly or in part, or may modify the judgment or order appealed from, and each interlocutory judgment or intermediate or other order which it is authorized to review, and as to any or all of the parties. It shall thereupon render judgment of affirmance, judgment of reversal and final judgment upon the right of any or all of the parties, or judgment of modification thereon according to law, except where it may be necessary or proper to grant a new trial or hearing, when it may grant a new trial or hearing.

b. If any appeal is taken to an appellate court which is not authorized to review such judgment or order, the court shall transfer the appeal to an appellate court which is authorized to review such judgment or order.

## § 7. [Supreme court; subject matter jurisdiction; new classes of actions.]

a. The supreme court shall have general original jurisdiction in law and equity and the appellate jurisdiction herein provided. In the city of New York, it shall have exclusive jurisdiction over crimes prosecuted by indictment, provided, however, that the legislature may grant to the city-wide court of criminal jurisdiction of the city of New York jurisdiction over misdemeanors prosecuted by indictment and to the family court in the city of New York jurisdiction over crimes and offenses by or against minors or between spouses or between parent and child or between members of the same family or household.

b. If the legislature shall create new classes of actions and proceedings, the supreme court shall have jurisdiction over such classes of actions and proceedings, but the legislature may provide that another court or other courts shall also have jurisdiction and that actions and proceedings of such classes may be originated in such other court or courts.

## § 8. [Appellate terms authorized; composition; jurisdiction.]

a. The appellate division of the supreme court in each judicial department may establish an appellate term in and for such department or in and for a judicial district or districts or in and for a county or counties within such department. Such an appellate term shall be composed of not less than three nor more than five justices of the supreme court who shall be designated from time to time by the chief administrator of the courts with the approval of the presiding justice of the appropriate appellate division, and who shall be residents of the department or of the judicial district or districts as the case may be and the chief administrator of the courts shall designate the place or places where such appellate terms shall be held.

b. Any such appellate term may be discontinued and re-established as the appellate division of the supreme court in each department shall determine from time to time and any designation to service therein may be revoked by the chief administrator of the courts with the approval of the presiding justice of the appropriate appellate division.

c. In each appellate term no more than three justices assigned thereto shall sit in any action or proceeding. Two of such justices shall constitute a quorum and the concurrence of two shall be necessary to decision.

d. If so directed by the appellate division of the supreme court establishing an appellate term, an appellate term shall have jurisdiction to hear and determine appeals now or hereafter authorized by law to be taken to the supreme court or to the appellate division other than appeals from the supreme court, a surrogate's court, the family court or appeals in criminal cases prosecuted by indictment or by information as provided in section six of article one.

App Pract Provs

e. As may be provided by law, an appellate term shall have jurisdiction to hear and determine appeals from the district court or a town, village or city court outside the city of New York.

## § 9. [Court of claims continued; composition; jurisdiction.]

The court of claims is continued. It shall consist of the eight judges now authorized by law, but the legislature may increase such number and may reduce such number to six or seven. The judges shall be appointed by the governor by and with the advice and consent of the senate and their terms of office shall be nine years. The court shall have jurisdiction to hear and determine claims against the state or by the state against the claimant or between conflicting claimants as the legislature may provide.

## § 11. [County court; subject matter jurisdiction; appellate jurisdiction.]

a. The county court shall have jurisdiction over the following classes of actions and proceedings which shall be originated in such county court in the manner provided by law, except that actions and proceedings within the jurisdiction of the district court or a town, village or city court outside the city of New York may, as provided by law, be originated therein: actions and proceedings for the recovery of money, actions and proceedings for the recovery of chattels and actions and proceedings for the foreclosure of mechanics liens and liens on personal property where the amount sought to be recovered or the value of the property does not exceed twenty-five thousand dollars exclusive of interest and costs; over all crimes and other violations of law; over summary proceedings to recover possession of real property and to remove tenants therefrom; and over such other actions and proceedings, not within the exclusive jurisdiction of the supreme court, as may be provided by law.

b. The county court shall exercise such equity jurisdiction as may be provided by law and its jurisdiction to enter judgment upon a counterclaim for the recovery of money only shall be unlimited.

c. The county court shall have jurisdiction to hear and determine all appeals arising in the county in the following actions and proceedings: as of right, from a judgment or order of the district court or a town, village or city court which finally determines an action or proceeding and, as may be provided by law, from a judgment or order of any such court which does not finally determine an action or proceeding. The legislature may provide, in accordance with the provisions of section eight of this article, that any or all of such appeals be taken to an appellate term of the supreme court instead of the county court.

d. The provisions of this section shall in no way limit or impair the jurisdiction of the supreme court as set forth in section seven of this article.

*See also* Judiciary Law § 190, *infra.*

## § 12. [Surrogate's court continued; composition; subject matter jurisdiction.]

a. The surrogate's court is continued in each county in the state. There shall be at least one judge of the surrogate's court in each county and such number of additional judges of the surrogate's court as may be provided by law.

b. The judges of the surrogate's court shall be residents of the county and shall be chosen by the electors of the county.

c. The terms of the judges of the surrogate's court in the city of New York shall be fourteen years, and in other counties ten years, from and including the first day of January next after their election.

d. The surrogate's court shall have jurisdiction over all actions and proceedings relating to the affairs of decedents, probate of wills, administration of estates and actions and proceedings arising thereunder or pertaining thereto, guardianship of the property of minors, and such other actions and proceedings, not within the exclusive jurisdiction of the supreme court, as may be provided by law.

e. The surrogate's court shall exercise such equity jurisdiction as may be provided by law.

f. The provisions of this section shall in no way limit or impair the jurisdiction of the supreme court as set forth in section seven of this article.

## § 13. [Family court established; composition; subject matter jurisdiction.]

a. The family court of the state of New York is hereby established. It shall consist of at least one judge in each county outside the city of New York and such number of additional judges for such counties as may be provided by law. Within the city of New York it shall consist of such number of judges as may be provided by law. The judges of the family court within the city of New York shall be residents of such city and shall be appointed by the mayor of the city of New York for terms of ten years. The judges of the family court outside the city of New York, shall be chosen by the electors of the counties wherein they reside for terms of ten years.

b. The family court shall have jurisdiction over the following classes of actions and proceedings which shall be originated in such family court in the manner provided by law: (1) the protection, treatment, correction and commitment of those minors who are in need of the exercise of the authority of the court because of circumstances of neglect, delinquency or dependency, as the legislature may determine; (2) the custody of minors except for custody incidental to actions and proceedings for marital separation, divorce, annulment of marriage and dissolution of marriage; (3) the adoption of persons; (4) the support of dependents except for support incidental to actions and proceedings in this state for marital separation, divorce, annulment of marriage or dissolution of marriage;

(5) the establishment of paternity; (6) proceedings for conciliation of spouses; and (7) as may be provided by law: the guardianship of the person of minors and, in conformity with the provisions of section seven of this article, crimes and offenses by or against minors or between spouses or between parent and child or between members of the same family or household. Nothing in this section shall be construed to abridge the authority or jurisdiction of courts to appoint guardians in cases originating in those courts.

c. The family court shall also have jurisdiction to determine, with the same powers possessed by the supreme court, the following matters when referred to the family court from the supreme court: habeas corpus proceedings for the determination of the custody of minors; and in actions and proceedings for marital separation, divorce, annulment of marriage and dissolution of marriage, applications to fix temporary or permanent support and custody, or applications to enforce judgments and orders of support and of custody, or applications to modify judgments and orders of support and of custody which may be granted only upon the showing to the family court that there has been a subsequent change of circumstances and that modification is required.

d. The provisions of this section shall in no way limit or impair the jurisdiction of the supreme court as set forth in section seven of this article.

## § 15.    [New York City civil and criminal courts; merger authorized; subject matter jurisdiction.]

a. The legislature shall by law establish a single court of city-wide civil jurisdiction and a single court of city-wide criminal jurisdiction in and for the city of New York and the legislature may, upon the request of the mayor and the local legislative body of the city of New York, merge the two courts into one city-wide court of both civil and criminal jurisdiction. The said city-wide courts shall consist of such number of judges as may be provided by law. The judges of the court of city-wide civil jurisdiction shall be residents of such city and shall be chosen for terms of ten years by the electors of the counties included within the city of New York from districts within such counties established by law. The judges of the court of city-wide criminal jurisdiction shall be residents of such city and shall be appointed for terms of ten years by the mayor of the city of New York.

b. The court of city-wide civil jurisdiction of the city of New York shall have jurisdiction over the following classes of actions and proceedings which shall be originated in such court in the manner provided by law: actions and proceedings for the recovery of money, actions and proceedings for the recovery of chattels and actions and proceedings for the foreclosure of mechanics liens and liens on personal property where the amount sought to be recovered or the value of the property does not exceed twenty-five thousand dollars exclusive of interest and costs, or such smaller amount as may be fixed by law; over summary proceedings to recover possession of real property and to remove tenants therefrom and over such other actions and proceedings, not within the exclusive jurisdiction of the supreme court, as may be provided by law. The court of city-wide civil jurisdiction shall further exercise such equity jurisdiction as may be provided by law and its jurisdiction to enter judgment upon a counterclaim for the recovery of money only shall be unlimited.

c. The court of city-wide criminal jurisdiction of the city of New York shall have jurisdiction over crimes and other violations of law, other than those prosecuted by indictment, provided, however, that the legislature may grant to said court jurisdiction over misdemeanors prosecuted by indictment; and over such other actions and proceedings, not within the exclusive jurisdiction of the supreme court, as may be provided by law.

d. The provisions of this section shall in no way limit or impair the jurisdiction of the supreme court as set forth in section seven of this article.

## § 16.  [District courts authorized; subject matter jurisdiction.]

a. The district court of Nassau county may be continued under existing law and the legislature may, at the request of the board of supervisors or other elective governing body of any county outside the city of New York, establish the district court for the entire area of such county or for a portion of such county consisting of one or more cities, or one or more towns which are contiguous, or of a combination of such cities and such towns provided at least one of such cities is contiguous to one of such towns.

b. No law establishing the district court for an entire county shall become effective unless approved at a general election on the question of the approval of such law by a majority of the votes cast thereon by the electors within the area of any cities in the county considered as one unit and by a majority of the votes cast thereon by the electors within the area outside of cities in the county considered as one unit.

c. No law establishing the district court for a portion of a county shall become effective unless approved at a general election on the question of the approval of such law by a majority of the votes cast thereon by the electors within the area of any cities included in such portion of the county considered as one unit and by a majority of the votes cast thereon by the electors within the area outside of cities included in such portion of the county considered as one unit.

d. The district court shall have such jurisdiction as may be provided by law, but not in any respect greater than the jurisdiction of the courts for the city of New York as provided in section fifteen of this article, provided, however, that in actions and proceedings for the recovery of money, actions and proceedings for the recovery of chattels and actions and proceedings for the foreclosure of mechanics liens and liens on personal property, the amount sought to be recovered or the value of the property shall not exceed fifteen thousand dollars exclusive of interest and costs.

App Pract Provs

e. The legislature may create districts of the district court which shall consist of an entire county or of an area less than a county.

f. There shall be at least one judge of the district court for each district and such number of additional judges in each district as may be provided by law.

g. The judges of the district court shall be apportioned among the districts as may be provided by law, and to the extent practicable, in accordance with the population and the volume of judicial business.

h. The judges shall be residents of the district and shall be chosen by the electors of the district. Their terms shall be six years from and including the first day of January next after their election.

i. The legislature may regulate and discontinue the district court in any county or portion thereof.

### § 17. [Town, village and city courts continued; subject matter jurisdiction.]

a. Courts for towns, villages and cities outside the city of New York are continued and shall have the jurisdiction prescribed by the legislature but not in any respect greater than the jurisdiction of the district court as provided in section sixteen of this article.

b. The legislature may regulate such courts, establish uniform jurisdiction, practice and procedure for city courts outside the city of New York and may discontinue any village or city court outside the city of New York existing on the effective date of this article. The legislature may discontinue any town court existing on the effective date of this article only with the approval of a majority of the total votes cast at a general election on the question of a proposed discontinuance of the court in each such town affected thereby.

c. The legislature may abolish the legislative functions on town boards of justices of the peace and provide that town councilmen be elected in their stead.

d. The number of the judges of each of such town, village and city courts and the classification and duties of the judges shall be prescribed by the legislature. The terms, method of selection and method of filling vacancies for the judges of such courts shall be prescribed by the legislature, provided, however, that the justices of town courts shall be chosen by the electors of the town for terms of four years from and including the first day of January next after their election.

### § 18. [Trial by jury.]

a. Trial by jury is guaranteed as provided in article one of this constitution. The legislature may provide that in any court of original jurisdiction a jury shall be composed of six or of twelve persons and may authorize any court which shall have jurisdiction over crimes and other violations of law, other than crimes prosecuted by indictment, to try such matters without a jury, provided, however, that crimes prosecuted by indictment shall be tried by a jury composed of twelve persons, unless a jury trial has been waived as provided in section two of article one of this constitution.

b. The legislature may provide for the manner of trial of actions and proceedings involving claims against the state.

## § 19. [Transfer of actions and proceedings.]

a. The supreme court may transfer any action or proceeding, except one over which it shall have exclusive jurisdiction which does not depend upon the monetary amount sought, to any other court having jurisdiction of the subject matter within the judicial department provided that such other court has jurisdiction over the classes of persons named as parties. As may be provided by law, the supreme court may transfer to itself any action or proceeding originated or pending in another court within the judicial department other than the court of claims upon a finding that such a transfer will promote the administration of justice.

b. The county court shall transfer to the supreme court or surrogate's court or family court any action or proceeding which has not been transferred to it from the supreme court or surrogate's court or family court and over which the county court has no jurisdiction. The county court may transfer any action or proceeding, except a criminal action or proceeding involving a felony prosecuted by indictment or an action or proceeding required by this article to be dealt with in the surrogate's court or family court, to any court, other than the supreme court, having jurisdiction of the subject matter within the county provided that such other court has jurisdiction over the classes of persons named as parties.

c. As may be provided by law, the supreme court or the county court may transfer to the county court any action or proceeding originated or pending in the district court or a town, village or city court outside the city of New York upon a finding that such a transfer will promote the administration of justice.

d. The surrogate's court shall transfer to the supreme court or the county court or the family court or the courts for the city of New York established pursuant to section fifteen of this article any action or proceeding which has not been transferred to it from any of said courts and over which the surrogate's court has no jurisdiction.

e. The family court shall transfer to the supreme court or the surrogate's court or the county court or the courts for the city of New York established pursuant to section fifteen of this article any action or proceeding which has not been transferred to it from any of said courts and over which the family court has no jurisdiction.

f. The courts for the city of New York established pursuant to section fifteen of this article shall transfer to the supreme court or the surrogate's court or the family court any action or proceeding which has not been transferred to them from any of said courts and over which the said courts for the city of New York have no jurisdiction.

g. As may be provided by law, the supreme court shall transfer any action or proceeding to any other court having jurisdiction of the subject matter in any other judicial district or county provided that such other court has jurisdiction over the classes of persons named as parties.

h. As may be provided by law, the county court, the surrogate's court, the family court and the courts for the city of New York established pursuant to section fifteen of this article may transfer any action or proceeding, other than one which has previously been transferred to it, to any other court, except the supreme court, having jurisdiction of the subject matter in any other judicial district or county provided that such other court has jurisdiction over the classes of persons named as parties.

i. As may be provided by law, the district court or a town, village or city court outside the city of New York may transfer any action or proceeding, other than one which has previously been transferred to it, to any court, other than the county court or the surrogate's court or the family court or the supreme court, having jurisdiction of the subject matter in the same or an adjoining county provided that such other court has jurisdiction over the classes of persons named as parties.

j. Each court shall exercise jurisdiction over any action or proceeding transferred to it pursuant to this section.

k. The legislature may provide that the verdict or judgment in actions and proceedings so transferred shall not be subject to the limitation or monetary jurisdiction of the court to which the actions and proceedings are transferred if that limitation be lower than that of the court in which the actions and proceedings were originated.

## § 28. [Administrative supervision of the courts.]

a. The chief judge of the court of appeals shall be the chief judge of the state of New York and shall be the chief judicial officer of the unified court system. There shall be an administrative board of the courts which shall consist of the chief judge of the court of appeals as chairman and the presiding justice of the appellate division of the supreme court of each judicial department. The chief judge shall, with the advice and consent of the administrative board of the courts, appoint a chief administrator of the courts who shall serve at his pleasure.

b. The chief administrator, on behalf of the chief judge, shall supervise the administration and operation of the unified court system. In the exercise of such responsibility, the chief administrator of the courts shall have such powers and duties as may be delegated to him by the chief judge and such additional powers and duties as may be provided by law.

c. The chief judge, after consultation with the administrative board, shall establish standards and administrative policies for general application throughout the state, which shall be submitted by the chief judge to the court of appeals, together with the recommendations, if any, of the administrative board. Such standards and administrative policies shall be promulgated after approval by the court of appeals.

## § 35. [Abolition of certain courts; abolition of referee's office.] [Selections]

a. The children's courts, the court of general sessions of the county of New York, the county courts of the counties of Bronx, Kings, Queens and Richmond, the city court of the city of New York, the domestic relations court of the city of New York, the municipal court of the city of New York, the court of special sessions of the city of New York and the city magistrates' courts of the city of New York are abolished from and after the effective date of this article and thereupon the seals, records, papers and documents of or belonging to such courts shall, unless otherwise provided by law, be deposited in the offices of the clerks of the several counties in which these courts now exist.

\*        \*        \*

k. The office of official referee is abolished, provided, however, that official referees in office on the effective date of this article shall, for the remainder of the terms for which they were appointed or certified, be official referees of the court in which appointed or certified or the successor court, as the case may be. At the expiration of the term of any official referee, his office shall be abolished and thereupon such former official referee shall be subject to the relevant provisions of section twenty-five of this article.

App Pract Provs

# BUSINESS CORPORATION LAW

### SYNOPSIS OF SELECTED PROVISIONS

**Article 3. Corporate name and service of process.**

§ 304.       Statutory designation of secretary of state as agent for service of process.

§ 306.       Service of process.

§ 307.       Service of process on unauthorized foreign corporation.

## Article 3. Corporate name and service of process.

### § 304. Statutory designation of secretary of state as agent for service of process.

(a) The secretary of state shall be the agent of every domestic corporation and every authorized foreign corporation upon whom process against the corporation may be served.

(b) No domestic or foreign corporation may be formed or authorized to do business in this state under this chapter unless in its certificate of incorporation or application for authority it designates the secretary of state as such agent.

(c) Any designation by a domestic or a foreign corporation of the secretary of state as such agent, which designation is in effect on the effective date of this chapter, shall continue. Every domestic or foreign corporation, existing or authorized on the effective date of this chapter, which has not designated the secretary of state as such agent, shall be deemed to have done so. Any designation prior to the effective date of this chapter by a foreign corporation of any agent other than the secretary of state shall terminate on the effective date of this chapter.

(d) Any designated post office address to which the secretary of state shall mail a copy of process served upon him as agent of a domestic corporation or a foreign corporation, shall continue until the filing of a certificate under this chapter directing the mailing to a different post office address.

### § 306. Service of process.

(a) Service of process on a registered agent may be made in the manner provided by law for service of a summons, as if the registered agent was a defendant.

(b)(1) Service of process on the secretary of state as agent of a domestic or authorized foreign corporation shall be made by personally delivering to and leaving with the secretary of state or a deputy, or with any person authorized by the secretary of state to receive such service, at the office of the department of state in the city of Albany, duplicate copies of such process together with the statutory fee, which fee shall be a taxable disbursement. Service of process on such corporation shall be complete when the secretary of state is so served. The secretary of state shall promptly send one of such copies by certified mail, return receipt requested, to such corporation, at the post office address, on file in the department of state, specified for the purpose. If a domestic or authorized foreign corporation has no such address on file in the department of state, the secretary of state shall so mail such copy, in the case of a domestic corporation, in care of any director named in its certificate of incorporation at the director's address stated therein or, in the case of an authorized foreign corporation, to such corporation at the address of its office within this state on file in the department.

(c) If an action or special proceeding is instituted in a court of limited jurisdiction, service of process may be made in the manner provided in this section if the office of the domestic or foreign corporation is within the territorial jurisdiction of the court.

(d) Nothing in this section shall affect the right to serve process in any other manner permitted by law.

## § 307. Service of process on unauthorized foreign corporation.

(a) In any case in which a non-domiciliary would be subject to the personal or other jurisdiction of the courts of this state under article three of the civil practice law and rules, a foreign corporation not authorized to do business in this state is subject to a like jurisdiction. In any such case, process against such foreign corporation may be served upon the secretary of state as its agent. Such process may issue in any court in this state having jurisdiction of the subject matter.

(b) Service of such process upon the secretary of state shall be made by personally delivering to and leaving with him or his deputy, or with any person authorized by the secretary of state to receive such service, at the office of the department of state in the city of Albany, a copy of such process together with the statutory fee, which fee shall be a taxable disbursement. Such service shall be sufficient if notice thereof and a copy of the process are:

(1) Delivered personally without this state to such foreign corporation by a person and in the manner authorized to serve process by law of the jurisdiction in which service is made, or

(2) Sent by or on behalf of the plaintiff to such foreign corporation by registered mail with return receipt requested, at the post office address specified

for the purpose of mailing process, on file in the department of state, or with any official or body performing the equivalent function, in the jurisdiction of its incorporation, or if no such address is there specified, to its registered or other office there specified, or if no such office is there specified, to the last address of such foreign corporation known to the plaintiff.

(c) (1) Where service of a copy of process was effected by personal service, proof of service shall be by affidavit of compliance with this section filed, together with the process, within thirty days after such service, with the clerk of the court in which the action or special proceeding is pending. Service of process shall be complete ten days after such papers are filed with the clerk of the court.

(2) Where service of a copy of process was effected by mailing in accordance with this section, proof of service shall be by affidavit of compliance with this section filed, together with the process, within thirty days after receipt of the return receipt signed by the foreign corporation, or other official proof of delivery or of the original envelope mailed. If a copy of the process is mailed in accordance with this section, there shall be filed with the affidavit of compliance either the return receipt signed by such foreign corporation or other official proof of delivery or, if acceptance was refused by it, the original envelope with a notation by the postal authorities that acceptance was refused. If acceptance was refused, a copy of the notice and process together with notice of the mailing by registered mail and refusal to accept shall be promptly sent to such foreign corporation at the same address by ordinary mail and the affidavit of compliance shall so state. Service of process shall be complete ten days after such papers are filed with the clerk of the court. The refusal to accept delivery of the registered mail or to sign the return receipt shall not affect the validity of the service and such foreign corporation refusing to accept such registered mail shall be charged with knowledge of the contents thereof.

(d) Service made as provided in this section shall have the same force as personal service made within this state.

(e) Nothing in this section shall affect the right to serve process in any other manner permitted by law.

App Pract Provs

# COURT OF CLAIMS ACT

―――――

## SYNOPSIS OF SELECTED PROVISIONS

**Article II.  Jurisdiction.**

**§ 10.  Time of filing claims and notice of intention to file claims. [Selection]**

―――――

## Article II.  Jurisdiction.

## § 10.  Time of filing claims and notice of intention to file claims. [Selection]

No judgment shall be granted in favor of any claimant unless such claimant shall have complied with the provisions of this section applicable to his claim.

*       *       *

5. If the claimant shall be under legal disability, the claim may be presented within two years after such disability is removed.

*       *       *

# CRIMINAL PROCEDURE LAW

---

## SYNOPSIS OF SELECTED PROVISIONS

**Article 50.** Compulsion of evidence by offer of immunity.

**§ 50.10.** Compulsion of evidence by offer of immunity; definitions of terms.
**§ 50.20.** Compulsion of evidence by offer of immunity.

---

**Article 50. Compulsion of evidence by offer of immunity.**

## § 50.10. Compulsion of evidence by offer of immunity; definitions of terms.

The following definitions are applicable to this article:

1. "Immunity." A person who has been a witness in a legal proceeding, and who cannot, except as otherwise provided in this subdivision, be convicted of any offense or subjected to any penalty or forfeiture for or on account of any transaction, matter or thing concerning which he gave evidence therein, possesses "immunity" from any such conviction, penalty or forfeiture. A person who possesses such immunity may nevertheless be convicted of perjury as a result of having given false testimony in such legal proceeding, and may be convicted of or adjudged in contempt as a result of having contumaciously refused to give evidence therein.

2. "Legal proceeding" means a proceeding in or before any court or grand jury, or before any body, agency or person authorized by law to conduct the same and to administer the oath or to cause it to be administered.

3. "Give evidence" means to testify or produce physical evidence.

## § 50.20. Compulsion of evidence by offer of immunity.

1. Any witness in a legal proceeding, other than a grand jury proceeding, may refuse to give evidence requested of him on the ground that it may tend to incriminate him and he may not, except as provided in subdivision two, be compelled to give such evidence.

2. Such a witness may be compelled to give evidence in such a proceeding notwithstanding an assertion of his privilege against self-incrimination if:

(a) The proceeding is one in which, by express provision of statute, a person conducting or connected therewith is declared a competent authority to confer immunity upon witnesses therein; and

(b) Such competent authority

(i) orders such witness to give the requested evidence notwithstanding his assertion of his privilege against self-incrimination, and

(ii) advises him that upon so doing he will receive immunity.

3. A witness who is ordered to give evidence pursuant to subdivision two and who complies with such order receives immunity. Such witness is not deprived of such immunity because such competent authority did not comply with statutory provisions requiring notice to a specified public servant of intention to confer immunity.

4. A witness who, without asserting his privilege against self-incrimination, gives evidence in a legal proceeding other than a grand jury proceeding does not receive immunity.

5. The rules governing the circumstances in which witnesses may be compelled to give evidence and in which they receive immunity therefor in a grand jury proceeding are prescribed in section 190.40.

# DEBTOR AND CREDITOR LAW

## SYNOPSIS OF SELECTED PROVISIONS

**Article 10.   Fraudulent Conveyances.**

§ 272.      **Fair consideration.**

**Article 10-A.   Personal Bankruptcy Exemptions.**

§ 282.      **Permissible exemptions in bankruptcy.**

§ 283.      **Aggregate individual bankruptcy exemption for certain annuities and personal property.**

§ 284.      **Exclusivity of exemptions.**

## Article 10.   Fraudulent Conveyances.

## § 272.   Fair consideration.

Fair consideration is given for property, or obligation,

a. When in exchange for such property, or obligation, as a fair equivalent therefor, and in good faith, property is conveyed or an antecedent debt is satisfied, or

b. When such property, or obligation is received in good faith to secure a present advance or antecedent debt in amount not disproportionately small as compared with the value of the property, or obligation obtained.

## Article 10-A.   Personal Bankruptcy Exemptions.

## § 282.   Permissible exemptions in bankruptcy.

Under section five hundred twenty-two of title eleven of the United States Code, entitled "Bankruptcy", an individual debtor domiciled in this state may exempt from the property of the estate, to the extent permitted by subsection (b) thereof, only (i) personal and real property exempt from application to the satisfaction of money judgments under sections fifty-two hundred five and fifty-two hundred six of the civil practice law and rules, (ii) insurance policies and annuity contracts and the proceeds and avails thereof as provided in section three thousand two hundred twelve of the insurance law and (iii) the following property:

1. Bankruptcy exemption of a motor vehicle. One motor vehicle not exceeding twenty-four hundred dollars in value above liens and encumbrances of the debtor.

2. Bankruptcy exemption for right to receive benefits. The debtor's right to receive or the debtor's interest in: (a) a social security benefit, unemployment compensation or a local public assistance benefit; (b) a veterans' benefit; (c) a disability, illness, or unemployment benefit; (d) alimony, support, or separate maintenance, to the extent reasonably necessary for the support of the debtor and any dependent of the debtor; and (e) all payments under a stock bonus, pension, profit sharing, or similar plan or contract on account of illness, disability, death, age, or length of service unless (i) such plan or contract, except those qualified under section 401 or 408 of the United States Internal Revenue Code of 1986, as amended, was established by the debtor or under the auspices of an insider that employed the debtor at the time the debtor's rights under such plan or contract arose, (ii) such plan is on account of age or length of service, and (iii) such plan or contract does not qualify under section four hundred one a, four hundred three a, four hundred three b, four hundred eight, four hundred nine or four hundred fifty-seven of the Internal Revenue Code of nineteen hundred eighty-six, as amended.

3. Bankruptcy exemption for right to receive certain property. The debtor's right to receive, or property that is traceable to: (i) an award under a crime victim's reparation law; (ii) a payment on account of the wrongful death of an individual of whom the debtor was a dependent to the extent reasonably necessary for the support of the debtor and any dependent of the debtor; (iii) a payment, not to exceed seventy-five hundred dollars on account of personal bodily injury, not including pain and suffering or compensation for actual pecuniary loss, of the debtor or an individual of whom the debtor is a dependent; and (iv) a payment in compensation of loss of future earnings of the debtor or an individual of whom the debtor is or was a dependent, to the extent reasonably necessary for the support of the debtor and any dependent of the debtor.

## § 283. Aggregate individual bankruptcy exemption for certain annuities and personal property.

1. General application. The aggregate amount the debtor may exempt from the property of the estate for personal property exempt from application to the satisfaction of a money judgment under subdivision (a) of section fifty-two hundred five of the civil practice law and rules and for benefits, rights, privileges, and options of annuity contracts described in the following sentence shall not exceed five thousand dollars. Annuity contracts subject to the foregoing limitation are those that are: (a) initially purchased by the debtor within six months of the debtor's filing a petition in bankruptcy, (b) not described in any paragraph of section eight hundred five (d) of the Internal Revenue Code of nineteen hundred fifty-four, and (c) not purchased by application of proceeds under settlement options of annuity contracts purchased more than six months

before the debtor's filing a petition in bankruptcy or under settlement options of life insurance policies.

2. Contingent alternative bankruptcy exemption. Notwithstanding section two hundred eighty-two of this article, a debtor, who (a) does not elect, claim, or otherwise avail himself of an exemption described in section fifty-two hundred six of the civil practice law and rules; (b) utilizes to the fullest extent permitted by law as applied to said debtor's property, the exemptions referred to in subdivision one of this section which are subject to the five thousand dollar aggregate limit; and (c) does not reach such aggregate limit, may exempt cash in the amount by which five thousand dollars exceeds the aggregate of his exemptions referred to in subdivision one of this section or in the amount of two thousand five hundred dollars, whichever amount is less. For purposes of this subdivision, cash means currency of the United States at face value, savings bonds of the United States at face value, the right to receive a refund of federal, state and local income taxes, and deposit accounts in any state or federally chartered depository institution.

## § 284. Exclusivity of exemptions.

In accordance with the provisions of section five hundred twenty-two (b) of title eleven of the United States Code, debtors domiciled in this state are not authorized to exempt from the estate property that is specified under subsection (d) of such section.

# DOMESTIC RELATIONS LAW

## SYNOPSIS OF SELECTED PROVISIONS

Article 11-A.   Special provisions relating to Divorce and Separation

§ 211.      Pleadings, proof and motions.

Article 13.   Provisions applicable to more than one type of matrimonial action.

§ 232.      Notice of nature of matrimonial action; proof of service.

§ 236.      Part B(4). Compulsory financial disclosure.

## Article 11-A.   Special provisions relating to Divorce and Separation.

### § 211.   Pleadings, proof and motions.

A matrimonial action shall be commenced by the filing of a summons with the notice designated in section two hundred thirty-two of this chapter, or a summons and verified complaint as provided in section three hundred four of the civil practice law and rules. A final judgment shall be entered by default for want of appearance or pleading, or by consent, only upon competent oral proof or upon written proof that may be considered on a motion for summary judgment. Where a complaint or counterclaim in an action for divorce or separation charges adultery, the answer or reply thereto may be made without verifying it, except that an answer containing a counterclaim must be verified as to that counterclaim. All other pleadings in a matrimonial action shall be verified.

## Article 13.   Provisions applicable to more than one type of matrimonial action.

### § 232.   Notice of nature of matrimonial action; proof of service.

a. In an action to annul a marriage or for divorce or separation, if the complaint is not personally served with the summons, the summons shall have legibly written or printed upon the face thereof: "Action to annul a marriage", "Action to declare the nullity of a void marriage", "Action for a divorce", or "Action for a separation", as the case may be, and shall specify the nature of any ancillary relief demanded. A judgment shall not be rendered in favor of the plaintiff upon the defendant's default in appearing or pleading, unless either (1) the summons and a copy of the complaint were personally delivered to the defendant; or (2) the copy of the summons (a) personally delivered to the defendant, or (b) served on the defendant pursuant to an order directing the method of service of the summons in accordance with the provisions of section three hundred eight or three hundred fifteen of the civil practice law and rules, shall contain such notice.

b. An affidavit or certificate proving service shall state affirmatively in the body thereof that the required notice was written or printed on the face of the copy of the summons delivered to the defendant and what knowledge the affiant or officer who executed the certificate had that he was the defendant named and how he acquired such knowledge. The court may require the affiant or officer who executed the affidavit or certificate to appear in court and be examined in respect thereto.

## § 236 Part B(4).　Compulsory financial disclosure.*

(a) In all matrimonial actions and proceedings in which alimony, maintenance or support is in issue, there shall be compulsory disclosure by both parties of their respective financial states. No showing of special circumstances shall be required before such disclosure is ordered. A sworn statement of net worth shall be provided upon receipt of a notice in writing demanding the same, within twenty days after the receipt thereof. In the event said statement is not demanded, it shall be filed with the clerk of the court by each party, within ten days after joinder of issue, in the court in which the proceeding is pending. As used in this part, the term "net worth" shall mean the amount by which total assets including income exceed total liabilities including fixed financial obligations. It shall include all income and assets of whatsoever kind and nature and wherever situated and shall include a list of all assets transferred in any manner during the preceding three years, or the length of the marriage, whichever is shorter; provided, however that transfers in the routine course of business which resulted in an exchange of assets of substantially equivalent value need not be specifically disclosed where such assets are otherwise identified in the statement of net worth. All such sworn statements of net worth shall be accompanied by a current and representative paycheck stub and the most recently filed state and federal income tax returns. Noncompliance shall be punishable by any or all of the penalties-prescribed in section thirty-one hundred twenty-six of the civil practice law and rules, in examination before or during trial.

b. As soon as practicable after a matrimonial action has been commenced, the court shall set the date or dates the parties shall use for the valuation of each asset. The valuation date or dates may be anytime from the date of commencement of the action to the date of trial.

> * [Editor's note: DRL Part B(4) applies to actions commenced on or after July 19, 1980. Identical provisions, contained in DRL 236 Part A(2), apply to actions commenced on or after September 1, 1975, but before July 19, 1980.]

# EDUCATION LAW

---

## SYNOPSIS OF SELECTED PROVISIONS

**Article 1.**    **Short title and definitions.**

**§ 2.**         **Definitions.**
**(13).**        **School officer.**

---

## Article 1.   Short title and definitions.

## § 2.   Definitions.

Whenever used in this chapter, the following terms shall have the respective meanings hereinafter set forth or indicated:

\*      \*      \*

13. School officer. The term "school officer" means a clerk, collector, or treasurer of any school district; a trustee; a member of a board of education or other body in control of the schools by whatever name known in a union free school district, central school district, central high school district, or in a city school district; a superintendent of schools; a district superintendent; a supervisor of attendance or attendance officer; or other elective or appointive officer in a school district whose duties generally relate to the administration of affairs connected with the public school system.

# ESTATES, POWERS AND TRUSTS LAW

---

## SYNOPSIS OF SELECTED PROVISIONS

**Article 7. Trusts.**

**Part 2. Rules governing trustees.**

**§ 7-2.3.**      Trust estate not to descend on death of trustee; appointment, duties and rights of successor trustee.

---

**Article 7. Trusts.**

**Part 2. Rules governing trustees.**

**§ 7-2.3. Trust estate not to descend on death of trustee; appointment, duties and rights of successor trustee.**

(a) On the death of the sole surviving trustee of an express trust, the trust estate does not vest in his personal representative or pass to his distributees or devisees, but, in the absence of a contrary direction by the creator, if the trust has not been executed, the trust estate vests in the supreme court or the surrogate's court, as the case may be, and the trust shall be executed by a person appointed by the court.

(b) Upon such notice to the beneficiaries of the trust as the court may direct of an application for the appointment of a successor trustee, unless the creator has directed otherwise, the court may appoint a successor trustee, even though the trust has terminated, whenever in the opinion of the court such appointment is necessary for the effective administration and distribution of the trust estate, subject to the following:

(1) A successor trustee shall give security in such amount as the court may direct.

(2) A successor trustee shall be subject to the same duties, as to accounting and trust administration, as are imposed by law on trustees and, in addition to the reasonable expenses incurred in the course of trust administration, shall be entitled to such commissions as may be fixed by any court having jurisdiction to pass upon such trustee's final account, which shall in no case exceed the commissions allowable by law to trustees.

# GENERAL ASSOCIATIONS LAW

---

## SYNOPSIS OF SELECTED PROVISIONS

Article 3.　Action or proceeding by or against unincorporated associations.

§ 12.　　　Action or proceeding by unincorporated association.
§ 13.　　　Action or proceeding against unincorporated association.

---

## Article 3.　Action or proceeding by or against unincorporated associations.

### § 12.　Action or proceeding by unincorporated association.

An action or special proceeding may be maintained, by the president or treasurer of an unincorporated association to recover any property, or upon any cause of action, for or upon which all the associates may maintain such an action or special proceeding, by reason of their interest or ownership therein, either jointly or in common. An action may likewise be maintained by such president or treasurer to recover from one or more members of such association his or their proportionate share of any moneys lawfully expended by such association for the benefit of such associates, or to enforce any lawful claim of such association against such member or members.

### § 13.　Action or proceeding against unincorporated association.

An action or special proceeding may be maintained, against the president or treasurer of such an association, to recover any property, or upon any cause of action, for or upon which the plaintiff may maintain such an action or special proceeding, against all the associates, by reason of their interest or ownership, or claim of ownership therein, either jointly or in common, or their liability therefor, either jointly or severally. Any partnership, or other company of persons, which has a president or treasurer, is deemed an association within the meaning of this section.

The service of summons, subpoena or other legal process of any court upon the president, vice president, treasurer, assistant treasurer, secretary, assistant secretary, or business agent, in his capacity as such, shall constitute service upon a labor organization. Such service shall be made on such individuals in the manner provided by law for the service of a summons on a natural person.

App Pract Provs

# GENERAL CONSTRUCTION LAW

## SYNOPSIS OF SELECTED PROVISIONS

**Article 2.    Meaning of terms.**

§ 20.        Day, computation.

§ 25.        Public holiday, Saturday or Sunday in contractual obligations; extension of time where performance of act authorized or required by contract is due on Saturday, Sunday or public holiday.

§ 25-a.      Public holiday, Saturday or Sunday in statutes; extension of time where performance of act is due on Saturday, Sunday or public holiday.

§ 25-b.      Injury to property.

§ 30.        Month, computation.

§ 31.        Month in statute, contract and public or private instrument.

§ 37-a.      Personal injury.

§ 58.        Year in statute, contract and public or private instrument.

§ 60.        Newspapers.

---

**Article 2.   Meaning of terms.**

**§ 20.   Day, computation.**

A number of days specified as a period from a certain day within which or after or before which an act is authorized or required to be done means such number of calendar days exclusive of the calendar day from which the reckoning is made. If such period is a period of two days, Saturday, Sunday or a public holiday must be excluded from the reckoning if it is an intervening day between the day from which the reckoning is made and the last day of the period. In computing any specified period of time from a specified event, the day upon which the event happens is deemed the day from which the reckoning is made. The day from which any specified period of time is reckoned shall be excluded in making the reckoning.

**§ 25.   Public holiday, Saturday or Sunday in contractual obligations; extension of time where performance of act authorized or required by contract is due on Saturday, Sunday or public holiday.**

1. Where a contract by its terms authorizes or requires the payment of money or the performance of a condition on a Saturday, Sunday or a public holiday,

or authorizes or requires the payment of money or the performance of a condition within or before or after a period of time computed from a certain day, and such period of time ends on a Saturday, Sunday or a public holiday, unless the contract expressly or impliedly indicates a different intent, such payment may be made or condition performed on the next succeeding business day, and if the period ends at a specified hour, such payment may be made or condition performed, at or before the same hour of such next succeeding business day, with the same force and effect as if made or performed in accordance with the terms of the contract.

2. Where time is extended by virtue of the provisions of this section, such extended time shall not be included in the computation of interest unless the contract so provides, except that when the period is specified as a number of months, such extended time shall be included in the computation of interest unless the contract otherwise provides.

3. Notwithstanding any other provision of law, all time deposits and certificates of deposit of banking organizations that mature on a Saturday, Sunday or bank holiday shall continue to accrue interest at the same rate fixed for the term of the deposit or certificate until the first banking day next succeeding the date of maturity, at which the principal and all accrued interest may be withdrawn, unless sooner withdrawn by the depositor.

### § 25-a. Public holiday, Saturday or Sunday in statutes; extension of time where performance of act is due on Saturday, Sunday or public holiday.

1. When any period of time, computed from a certain day, within which or after which or before which an act is authorized or required to be done, ends on a Saturday, Sunday or a public holiday, such act may be done on the next succeeding business day and if the period ends at a specified hour, such act may be done at or before the same hour of such next succeeding business day, except that where a period of time specified by contract ends on a Saturday, Sunday or a public holiday, the extension of such period is governed by section twenty-five of this chapter.

2. Where time is extended by virtue of the provisions of this section, such extended time shall not be included in the computation of interest, except that when the period is specified as a number of months, such extended time shall be included in the computation of interest.

### § 25-b. Injury to property.

"Injury to property" is an actionable act, whereby the estate of another is lessened, other than a personal injury, or the breach of a contract.

### § 30. Month, computation.

A number of months after or before a certain day shall be computed by counting such number of calendar months from such day, exclusive of the calendar month in which such day occurs, and shall include the day of the month in the last month so counted having the same numerical order in days of the month as the day from which the computation is made, unless there be not so many days in the last month so counted, in which case the period computed shall expire with the last day of the month so counted.

### § 31. Month in statute, contract and public or private instrument.

In a statute, contract or public or private instrument, unless otherwise provided in such contract or instrument or by law, the term month means a calendar month and not a lunar month.

### § 37-a. Personal injury.

"Personal injury" includes libel, slander and malicious prosecution; also an assault, battery, false imprisonment, or other actionable injury to the person either of the plaintiff, or of another.

### § 58. Year in statute, contract and public or private instrument.

The term year in a statute, contract, or any public or private instrument, means three hundred and sixty-five days, but the added day of a leap year and the day immediately preceding shall for the purpose of such computation be counted as one day. In a statute, contract or public or private instrument, the term year means twelve months, the term half year, six months, and the term a quarter of a year, three months.

App Pract Provs

### § 60. Newspapers.

a. In any case in which notice of any fact is required by law to be published or advertised in a newspaper, the term "newspaper" shall mean a paper of general circulation which is printed and distributed ordinarily not less frequently than once a week, and has been so for at least one year immediately preceding such publication or advertisement, and which contains news, articles of opinion (as editorials), features, advertising, or other matter regarded as of current interest, has a paid circulation and (except for such a paper which has been printed and distributed not less frequently than once a week for a period of ten years prior to January one, nineteen hundred seventy-five) has been entered at United States post-office as second-class matter. A publication which is distributed or made available primarily for advertising purposes to the public generally without consideration being paid therefor shall not be deemed to be a "newspaper" for the purpose of publication or advertisement of such notice required by law. Notwithstanding any provision of this subdivision to the contrary, a publication which was designated and publishing notice as an official newspaper prior to the year nineteen hundred forty and continued to be so designated and publishing for at least thirty years after such year shall be deemed to be a newspaper within the meaning of this subdivision.

b. The terms "daily newspaper" and "newspaper published each business day" in a statute, contract, or any public or private instrument, mean respectively, a newspaper customarily published on each business day of the year, whether or not such newspaper is published on any other day. The term "business day" when used herein does not include Saturdays, Sundays or legal holidays.

# GENERAL MUNICIPAL LAW

### SYNOPSIS OF SELECTED PROVISIONS

**Article 4.  Negligence and malfeasance of public officers; taxpayers' remedies.**

§ 50-e.     **Notice of claim.**
§ 50-h.     **Examination of claims.**
§ 50-i.     **Presentation of tort claims; commencement of actions.**

---

**Article 4.  Negligence and malfeasance of public officers; taxpayers' remedies.**

## § 50-e.  Notice of claim.

1. When service required; time for service; upon whom service required.

(a) In any case founded upon tort where a notice of claim is required by law as a condition precedent to the commencement of an action or special proceeding against a public corporation, as defined in the general construction law, or any officer, appointee or employee thereof, the notice of claim shall comply with and be served in accordance with the provisions of this section within ninety days after the claim arises except that in wrongful death actions, the ninety days shall run from the appointment of a representative of the decedent's estate.

(b) Service of the notice of claim upon an officer, appointee or employee of a public corporation shall not be a condition precedent to the commencement of an action or special proceeding against such person. If an action or special proceeding is commenced against such person, but not against the public corporation, service of the notice of claim upon the public corporation shall be required only if the corporation has a statutory obligation to indemnify such person under this chapter or any other provision of law.

2. Form of notice; contents. The notice shall be in writing, sworn to by or on behalf of the claimant, and shall set forth: (1) the name and post-office address of each claimant, and of his attorney, if any; (2) the nature of the claim; (3) the time when, the place where and the manner in which the claim arose; and (4) the items of damage or injuries claimed to have been sustained so far as then practicable but a notice with respect to a claim against a municipal corporation other than a city with a population of one million or more persons shall not state the amount of damages to which the claimant deems himself

entitled, provided, however, that the municipal corporation, other than a city with a population of one million or more persons, may at any time request a supplemental claim setting forth the total damages to which the claimant deems himself entitled. A supplemental claim shall be provided by the claimant within fifteen days of the request. In the event the supplemental demand is not served within fifteen days, the court, on motion, may order that it be provided by the claimant.

3. How served; when service by mail complete; defect in manner of service; return of notice improperly served.

(a) The notice shall be served on the public corporation against which the claim is made by delivering a copy thereof personally, or by registered or certified mail, to the person designated by law as one to whom a summons in an action in the supreme court issued against such corporation may be delivered or to an attorney regularly engaged in representing such public corporation.

(b) Service by registered or certified mail shall be complete upon deposit of the notice of claim, enclosed in a postpaid properly addressed wrapper, in a post office or official depository under the exclusive care and custody of the United States post office department within the state.

(c) If the notice is served within the period specified by this section, but in a manner not in compliance with the provisions of this subdivision, the service shall be valid if the public corporation against which the claim is made demands that the claimant or any other person interested in the claim be examined in regard to it, or if the notice is actually received by a proper person within the time specified by this section, and the public corporation fail to return the notice, specifying the defect in the manner of service, within thirty days after the notice is received.

(d) If the notice is served within the period specified by this section and is returned for the reason and within the time provided in this subdivision, the claimant may serve a new notice in a manner complying with the provisions of this subdivision within ten days after the returned notice is received. If a new notice is so served within that period, it shall be deemed timely served.

4. Requirements of section exclusive except as to conditions precedent to liability for certain defects or snow or ice. No other or further notice, no other or further service, filing or delivery of the notice of claim, and no notice of intention to commence an action or special proceeding, shall be required as a condition to the commencement of an action or special proceeding for the enforcement of the claim; provided, however, that nothing herein contained shall be deemed to dispense with the requirement of notice of the defective, unsafe, dangerous or obstructed condition of any street, highway, bridge, culvert, sidewalk or crosswalk, or of the existence of snow or ice thereon, where such notice now is, or hereafter may be, required by law, as a condition precedent to liability for damages or injuries to person or property alleged to have been

caused by such condition, and the failure or negligence to repair or remove the same after the receipt of such notice.

5. Application for leave to serve a late notice.

Upon application, the court, in its discretion, may extend the time to serve a notice of claim specified in paragraph (a) of subdivision one. The extension shall not exceed the time limited for the commencement of an action by the claimant against the public corporation. In determining whether to grant the extension, the court shall consider, in particular, whether the public corporation or its attorney or its insurance carrier acquired actual knowledge of the essential facts constituting the claim within the time specified in subdivision one or within a reasonable time thereafter. The court shall also consider all other relevant facts and circumstances, including: whether the claimant was an infant, or mentally or physically incapacitated, or died before the time limited for service of the notice of claim; whether the claimant failed to serve a timely notice of claim by reason of his justifiable reliance upon settlement representations made by an authorized representative of the public corporation or its insurance carrier; whether the claimant in serving a notice of claim made an excusable error concerning the identity of the public corporation against which the claim should be asserted; and whether the delay in serving the notice of claim substantially prejudiced the public corporation in maintaining its defense on the merits.

An application for leave to serve a late notice shall not be denied on the ground that it was made after commencement of an action against the public corporation.

6. Mistake, omission, irregularity or defect. At any time after the service of a notice of claim and at any stage of an action or special proceeding to which the provisions of this section are applicable, a mistake, omission, irregularity or defect made in good faith in the notice of claim required to be served by this section, not pertaining to the manner or time of service thereof, may be corrected, supplied or disregarded, as the case may be, in the discretion of the court, provided it shall appear that the other party was not prejudiced thereby.

7. Applications under this section. All applications under this section shall be made to the supreme court or to the county court: (a)in a county where the action may properly be brought for trial, (b)if an action to enforce the claim has been commenced, where the action is pending, or (c) in the event that there is no motion term available in any of the counties specified in clause (a) or (b) hereof, in any adjoining county.Where the application is for leave to serve a late notice of claim, it shall be accompanied by a copy of the proposed notice of claim.

8. Inapplicability of section. This section shall not apply to claims arising under the provisions of the workers' compensation law, the volunteer fire-fighters' benefit law, or the volunteer ambulance workers' benefit law or to claims against public corporations by their own infant wards.

App Pract Provs

## § 50-h. Examination of claims.

1. Wherever a notice of claim is filed against a city, county, town, village, fire district, ambulance district or school district the city, county, town, village, fire district, ambulance district or school district shall have the right to demand an examination of the claimant relative to the occurrence and extent of the injuries or damages for which claim is made, which examination shall be upon oral questions unless the parties otherwise stipulate and may include a physical examination of the claimant by a duly qualified physician. If the party to be examined desires, he or she is entitled to have such examination in the presence of his or her own personal physician and such relative or other person as he or she may elect. Exercise of the right to demand a physical examination of the claimant as provided in this section shall in no way affect the right of a city, county, town, village, fire district, ambulance district or school district in a subsequent action brought upon the claim to demand a physical examination of the plaintiff pursuant to statute or court rule.

2. The demand for examination as provided in subdivision one of this section shall be made by the chief executive officer or, where there is no such officer, by the chairman of the governing body of the city, county, town, village, fire district or school district or by such officer, agent or employee as may be designated by him for that purpose. The demand shall be in writing and shall be served personally or by registered or certified mail upon the claimant unless the claimant is represented by an attorney, when it shall be served personally or by mail upon his attorney. The demand shall give reasonable notice of the examination. It shall state the person before whom the examination is to be held, the time, place and subject matter thereof and, if a physical examination is to be required, it shall so state. If the place of examination is located outside the municipality against which the claim is made, the claimant may demand, within ten days of such service, that the examination be held at a location within such municipality. Such location shall be determined by the municipality. If a physical examination is to be required and there is no appropriate place for such an examination within the municipality, such examination shall be given at a location as close to such municipality as practicable. No demand for examination shall be effective against the claimant for any purpose unless it shall be served as provided in this subdivision within ninety days from the date of filing of the notice of claim.

3. In any examination required pursuant to the provisions of this section the claimant shall have the right to be represented by counsel. The examination shall be conducted upon oath or affirmation. The officer or person before whom the examination is had shall take down or cause to be taken down every question and answer unless the parties consent that only the substance of the testimony be inserted. The testimony so taken, together with the report of the examining physician where a physical examination is required, shall constitute the record of the examination. The transcript of the record of an examination shall not be

subject to or available for public inspection, except upon court order upon good cause shown, but shall be furnished to the claimant or his attorney upon request.

4. A transcript of the testimony taken at an examination pursuant to the provisions of this section may be read in evidence by either party, in an action founded upon the claim in connection with which it was taken, at the trial thereof or upon assessment of damages or upon motion. In an action by an executor or administrator to recover damages for a wrongful act, neglect or default by which a decedent's death was caused, the testimony of such decedent taken pursuant to the provisions of this section in respect of such wrongful act, neglect or default may be read in evidence.

5. Where a demand for examination has been served as provided in subdivision two of this section no action shall be commenced against the city, county, town, village, fire district or school district against which the claim is made unless the claimant has duly complied with such demand for examination, which compliance shall be in addition to the requirements of section fifty-e of this chapter. If such examination is not conducted within ninety days of service of the demand, the claimant may commence the action. The action, however, may not be commenced until compliance with the demand for examination if the claimant fails to appear at the hearing or requests an adjournment or postpone-ment beyond the ninety day period. If the claimant requests an adjournment or postponement beyond the ninety day period, the city, county, town, village, fire district or school district shall reschedule the hearing for the earliest possible date available.

### § 50-i.   Presentation of tort claims; commencement of actions.

1. No action or special proceeding shall be prosecuted or maintained against a city, county, town, village, fire district or school district for personal injury, wrongful death or damage to real or personal property alleged to have been sustained by reason of the negligence or wrongful act of such city, county, town, village, fire district or school district or of any officer, agent or employee thereof, including volunteer firemen of any such city, county, town, village, fire district or school district or any volunteer fireman whose services have been accepted pursuant to the provisions of section two hundred nine-i of this chapter, unless, (a) a notice of claim shall have been made and served upon the city, county, town, village, fire district or school district in compliance with section fifty-e of this chapter, (b) it shall appear by and as an allegation in the complaint or moving papers that at least thirty days have elapsed since the service of such notice and that adjustment or payment thereof has been neglected or refused, and (c) the action or special proceeding shall be commenced within one year and ninety days after the happening of the event upon which the claim is based; except that wrongful death actions shall be commenced within two years after the happening of the death.

2. This section shall be applicable notwithstanding any inconsistent provisions of law, general, special or local, or any limitation contained in the provisions of any city charter.

3. Nothing contained herein or in section fifty-h of this chapter shall operate to extend the period limited by subdivision one of this section for the commencement of an action or special proceeding.

# GENERAL OBLIGATIONS LAW

---

## SYNOPSIS OF SELECTED PROVISIONS

**Article 5.   Creation, definition and enforcement of contractual obligations.**

**Title 14.   Enforceability of clauses respecting choice of law and choice of forum in certain transactions.**

§ 5-1401.   Choice of law.
§ 5-1402.   Choice of forum.

**Article 7.   Obligations relating to property received as security.**

**Title 3.   Bonds and undertakings.**

§ 7-301.   Liability of surety on an undertaking.

**Article 15.   Modification and discharge of obligations.**

**Title 1.   Discharge of joint obligors.**

§ 15-102.   Co-obligor not a party.
§ 15-108.   Release or covenant not to sue.

**Article 17.   Revival or extension; waiver of defense or bar.**

**Title 1.   Obligations barred by statutes of limitation.**

§ 17-101.   Acknowledgment or new promise must be in writing.
§ 17-103.   Agreements waiving the statute of limitation.

---

**Article 5.   Creation, definition and enforcement of contractual obligations.**

**Title 14.   Enforceability of clauses respecting choice of law and choice of forum in certain transactions.**

### § 5-1401.   Choice of law

1. The parties to any contract, agreement or undertaking, contingent or otherwise, in consideration of, or relating to any obligation arising out of a transaction covering in the aggregate not less than two hundred fifty thousand dollars, including a transaction otherwise covered by subsection one of section 1-105 of the uniform commercial code, may agree that the law of this state shall govern their rights and duties in whole or in part, whether or not such contract,

App Pract Provs

agreement or undertaking bears a reasonable relation to this state. This section shall not apply to any contract, agreement or undertaking (a) for labor or personal services, (b) relating to any transaction for personal, family or household services, or (c) to the extent provided to the contrary in subsection two of section 1-105 of the uniform commercial code.

2. Nothing contained in this section shall be construed to limit or deny the enforcement of any provision respecting choice of law in any other contract, agreement or undertaking.

### § 5-1402.　Choice of forum.

1. Notwithstanding any act which limits or affects the right of a person to maintain an action or proceeding, including, but not limited to, paragraph (b) of section thirteen hundred fourteen of the business corporation law and subdivision two of section two hundred-b of the banking law, any person may maintain an action or proceeding against a foreign corporation, non-resident, or foreign state where the action or proceeding arises out of or relates to any contract, agreement or undertaking for which a choice of New York law has been made in whole or in part pursuant to section 5-1401 and which (a) is a contract, agreement or undertaking, contingent or otherwise, in consideration of, or relating to any obligation arising out of a transaction covering in the aggregate, not less than one million dollars, and (b) which contains a provision or provisions whereby such foreign corporation or non-resident agrees to submit to the jurisdiction of the courts of this state.

2. Nothing contained in this section shall be construed to affect the enforcement of any provision respecting choice of forum in any other contract, agreement or undertaking.

### Article 7.　Obligations relating to property received as security.

### Title 3.　Bonds and undertakings.

### § 7-301.　Liability of surety on an undertaking.

When any undertaking executed within or without the state specifies that it is to be void upon payment of an amount or performance of an act, the undertaking shall be deemed to contain a covenant either to pay the amount or to perform the act specified. In the event of payment, the amount recoverable from a surety shall not exceed the amount specified in the undertaking except that interest in addition to this amount shall be awarded from the time of default by the surety.

**Article 15.　Modification and discharge of obligations.**

**Title 1.　Discharge of joint obligors.**

**§ 15-102.　Co-obligor not a party.**

A judgment against one or more of several obligors, or against one or more of joint, or of joint and several obligors shall not discharge a co-obligor who was not a party to the proceeding wherein the judgment was rendered.

**§ 15-108.　Release or covenant not to sue.**

(a) Effect of release of or covenant not to sue tortfeasors. When a release or a covenant not to sue or not to enforce a judgment is given to one of two or more persons liable or claimed to be liable in tort for the same injury, or for the same wrongful death, it does not discharge any of the other tortfeasors from liability for the injury or wrongful death unless its terms expressly so provide, but it reduces the claim of the releasor against the other tortfeasors to the extent of any amount stipulated by the release or the covenant, or in the amount of the consideration paid for it or in the amount of the released tortfeasor's equitable share of the damages under article fourteen of the civil practice law and rules, whichever is the greatest.

(b) Release of tortfeasor. A release given in good faith by the injured person to one tortfeasor as provided in subdivision (a) relieves him from liability to any other person for contribution as provided in article fourteen of the civil practice law and rules.

(c) Waiver of contribution. A tortfeasor who has obtained his own release from liability shall not be entitled to contribution from any other person.

**Article 17.　Revival or extension; waiver of defense or bar.**

**Title 1.　Obligations barred by statutes of limitation.**

**§ 17-101.　Acknowledgment or new promise must be in writing.**

An acknowledgment or promise contained in a writing signed by the party to be charged thereby is the only competent evidence of a new or continuing contract whereby to take an action out of the operation of the provisions of limitations of time for commencing actions under the civil practice law and rules other than an action for the recovery of real property. This section does not alter the effect of a payment of principal or interest.

**§ 17-103.　Agreements waiving the statute of limitation.**

1. A promise to waive, to extend, or not to plead the statute of limitation applicable to an action arising out of a contract express or implied in fact or

in law, if made after the accrual of the cause of action and made, either with or without consideration, in a writing signed by the promisor or his agent is effective, according to its terms, to prevent interposition of the defense of the statute of limitation in an action or proceeding commenced within the time that would be applicable if the cause of action had arisen at the date of the promise, or within such shorter time as may be provided in the promise.

2. A promise to waive, to extend, or not to plead the statute of limitation may be enforced as provided in this section by the person to whom the promise is made or for whose benefit it is expressed to be made or by any person who, after the making of the promise, succeeds or is subrogated to the interest of either of them.

3. A promise to waive, to extend, or not to plead the statute of limitation has no effect to extend the time limited by statute for commencement of an action or proceeding for any greater time or in any other manner than that provided in this section, or unless made as provided in this section.

4. This section

a. does not change the requirements of the effect with respect to the statute of limitation, of an acknowledgment or promise to pay, or a payment or part payment of principal or interest, or a stipulation made in an action or proceeding;

b. does not affect the power of the court to find that by reason of conduct of the party to be charged it is inequitable to permit him to interpose the defense of the statute of limitation; and

c. does not apply in any respect to a cause of action to foreclose a mortgage of real property or a mortgage of a lease of real property, or to a cause of action to recover a judgment affecting the title to or the possession, use or enjoyment of real property, or a promise or waiver with respect to any statute of limitation applicable thereto.

# INSURANCE LAW

## SYNOPSIS OF SELECTED PROVISIONS

**Article 34.  Insurance contracts—property/casualty.**

§ 3420.      Liability insurance; standard provisions; right of injured person [Selections].

**Article 51.  Comprehensive motor vehicle insurance reparations [No-fault] [Selections].**

§ 5102.      Definitions.

§ 5103.      Entitlement to first party benefits; additional financial security required.

§ 5104.      Causes of action for personal injury.

§ 5108.      Limit on charges by providers of health services.

## Article 34.  Insurance contracts—property/casualty.

## § 3420.  Liability insurance; standard provisions; right of injured person [Selections].

\* \* \*

(g) No policy or contract shall be deemed to insure against any liability of an insured because of death of or injuries to his or her spouse or because of injury to, or destruction of property of his or her spouse unless express provision relating specifically thereto is included in the policy. This exclusion shall apply only where the injured spouse, to be entitled to recover, must prove the culpable conduct of the insured spouse.

## Article 51.  Comprehensive motor vehicle insurance reparations [No-fault] [Selections].

## § 5102.  Definitions.

In this chapter:

(a) "Basic economic loss" means, up to fifty thousand dollars per person of the following combined items, subject to the limitations of section five thousand one hundred eight of this article:

(1) All necessary expenses incurred for: (i) medical, hospital (including services rendered in compliance with article forty-one of the public health law, whether or not such services are rendered directly by a hospital), surgical, nursing, dental, ambulance, x-ray, prescription drug and prosthetic services; (ii) psychiatric, physical and occupational therapy and rehabilitation; (iii) any non-medical remedial care and treatment rendered in accordance with a religious method of healing recognized by the laws of this state; and (iv) any other professional health services; all without limitation as to time, provided that within one year after the date of the accident causing the injury it is ascertainable that further expenses may be incurred as a result of the injury. For the purpose of determining basic economic loss, the expenses incurred under this paragraph shall be in accordance with the limitations of section five thousand one hundred eight of this article.

(2) Loss of earnings from work which the person would have performed had he not been injured, and reasonable and necessary expenses incurred by such person in obtaining services in lieu of those that he would have performed for income, up to two thousand dollars per month for not more than three years from the date of the accident causing the injury. An employee who is entitled to receive monetary payments, pursuant to statute or contract with the employer, or who receives voluntary monetary benefits paid for by the employer, by reason of the employee's inability to work because of personal injury arising out of the use or operation of a motor vehicle, is not entitled to receive first party benefits for "loss of earnings from work" to the extent that such monetary payments or benefits from the employer do not result in the employee suffering a reduction in income or a reduction in the employee's level of future benefits arising from a subsequent illness or injury.

(3) All other reasonable and necessary expenses incurred, up to twenty-five dollars per day for not more than one year from the date of the accident causing the injury.

(4) "Basic economic loss" shall not include any loss incurred on account of death; subject, however, to the provisions of paragraph four of subsection (a) of section five thousand one hundred three of this article.

(5) "Basic economic loss" shall also include an additional option to purchase, for an additional premium, an additional twenty-five thousand dollars of coverage which the insured or his legal representative may specify will be applied to loss of earnings from work and/or psychiatric, physical or occupational therapy and rehabilitation after the initial fifty thousand dollars of basic economic loss has been exhausted. This optional additional coverage shall be made available and notice with explanation of such coverage shall be provided by an insurer at the first policy renewal after the effective date of this paragraph, or at the time of application.

(b) "First party benefits" means payments to reimburse a person for basic economic loss on account of personal injury arising out of the use or operation of a motor vehicle, less:

(1) Twenty percent of lost earnings computed pursuant to paragraph two of subsection (a) of this section.

(2) Amounts recovered or recoverable on account of such injury under state or federal laws providing social security disability benefits, or workers' compensation benefits, or disability benefits under article nine of the workers' compensation law, or medicare benefits, other than lifetime reserve days and provided further that the medicare benefits utilized herein do not result in a reduction of such person's medicare benefits for a subsequent illness or injury.

(3) Amounts deductible under the applicable insurance policy.

(c) "Non-economic loss" means pain and suffering and similar nonmonetary detriment.

(d) "Serious injury" means a personal injury which results in death; dismemberment; significant disfigurement; a fracture; loss of a fetus; permanent loss of use of a body organ, member, function or system; permanent consequential limitation of use of a body organ or member; significant limitation of use of a body function or system; or a medically determined injury or impairment of a non-permanent nature which prevents the injured person from performing substantially all of the material acts which constitute such person's usual and customary daily activities for not less than ninety days during the one hundred eighty days immediately following the occurrence of the injury or impairment.

(e) "Owner" means an owner as defined in section one hundred twenty-eight of the vehicle and traffic law.

(f) "Motor vehicle" means a motor vehicle as defined in section three hundred eleven of the vehicle and traffic law and also includes fire and police vehicles. It shall not include any motor vehicle not required to carry financial security pursuant to article six, eight or forty-eight-A of the vehicle and traffic law or a motorcycle, as defined in subsection (m) hereof.

(g) "Insurer" means the insurance company or self-insurer, as the case may be, which provides the financial security required by article six or eight of the vehicle and traffic law.

(h) "Member of his household" means a spouse, child or relative of the named insured who regularly resides in his household.

(i) "Uninsured motor vehicle" means a motor vehicle, the owner of which is (i) a financially irresponsible motorist as defined in subsection (j) of section five thousand two hundred two of this chapter or (ii) unknown and whose identity is unascertainable.

(j) "Covered person" means any pedestrian injured through the use or operation of, or any owner, operator or occupant of, a motor vehicle which has in effect the financial security required by article six or eight of the vehicle and traffic law or which is referred to in subdivision two of section three hundred twenty-one of such law; or any other person entitled to first party benefits.

App Pract Provs

(k) "Bus" means both a bus and a school bus as defined in sections one hundred four and one hundred forty-two of the vehicle and traffic law.

(l) "Compensation provider" means the state insurance fund, or the person, association, corporation or insurance carrier or statutory fund liable under state or federal laws for the payment of workers' compensation benefits or disability benefits under article nine of the workers' compensation law.

(m) "Motorcycle" means any motorcycle, as defined in section one hundred twenty-three of the vehicle and traffic law, and which is required to carry financial security pursuant to article six, eight or forty-eight-A of the vehicle and traffic law.

\*        \*        \*

### § 5103. Entitlement to first party benefits; additional financial security required.

(a) Every owner's policy of liability insurance issued on a motor vehicle in satisfaction of the requirements of article six or eight of the vehicle and traffic law shall also provide for; every owner who maintains another form of financial security on a motor vehicle in satisfaction of the requirements of such articles shall be liable for; and every owner of a motor vehicle required to be subject to the provisions of this article by subdivision two of section three hundred twenty-one of the vehicle and traffic law shall be liable for; the payment of first party benefits to:

(1) Persons, other than occupants of another motor vehicle or a motorcycle, for loss arising out of the use or operation in this state of such motor vehicle. In the case of occupants of a bus other than operators, owners, and employees of the owner or operator of the bus, the coverage for first party benefits shall be afforded under the policy or policies, if any, providing first party benefits to the injured person and members of his household for loss arising out of the use or operation of any motor vehicle of such household. In the event there is no such policy, first party benefits shall be provided by the insurer of such bus.

(2) The named insured and members of his household, other than occupants of a motorcycle, for loss arising out of the use or operation of (i) an uninsured motor vehicle or motorcycle, within the United States, its territories or possessions, or Canada; and (ii) an insured motor vehicle or motorcycle outside of this state and within the United States, its territories or possessions, or Canada.

(3) Any New York resident who is neither the owner of a motor vehicle with respect to which coverage for first party benefits is required by this article nor, as a member of a household, is entitled to first party benefits under paragraph two of this subsection, for loss arising out of the use or operation of the insured or self-insured motor vehicle outside of this state and within the United States, its territories or possessions, or Canada.

(4) The estate of any covered person, other than an occupant of another motor vehicle or a motorcycle, a death benefit in the amount of two thousand dollars for the death of such person arising out of the use or operation of such motor vehicle which is in addition to any first party benefits for basic economic loss.

(b) An insurer may exclude from coverage required by subsection (a) hereof a person who:

(1) Intentionally causes his own injury.

(2) Is injured as a result of operating a motor vehicle while in an intoxicated condition or while his ability to operate such vehicle is impaired by the use of a drug within the meaning of section eleven hundred ninety-two of the vehicle and traffic law.

(3) Is injured while he is: (i) committing an act which would constitute a felony, or seeking to avoid lawful apprehension or arrest by a law enforcement officer, or (ii) operating a motor vehicle in a race or speed test, or (iii) operating or occupying a motor vehicle known to him to be stolen, or (iv) operating or occupying any motor vehicle owned by such injured person with respect to which the coverage required by subsection (a) hereof is not in effect, or (v) a pedestrian, through being struck by any motor vehicle owned by such injured pedestrian with respect to which the coverage required by subsection (a) hereof is not in effect, or (vi) repairing, servicing or otherwise maintaining a motor vehicle if such conduct is within the course of a business of repairing, servicing or otherwise maintaining a motor vehicle and the injury occurs on the business premises.

(c) Insurance offered by any insurer to satisfy the requirements of subsection (a) of this section shall be offered: (1) without a deductible; and (2) with a family deductible of up to two hundred dollars (which deductible shall apply only to the loss of the named insured and members of that household). The superintendent may approve a higher deductible in the case of insurance policies providing additional benefits or pursuant to a plan designed and implemented to coordinate first party benefits with other benefits. The superintendent may approve appropriate deductible or co-insurance provisions for medical and other health care services provided through approved managed care programs.

(d) Insurance policy forms for insurance to satisfy the requirements of subsection (a) hereof shall be subject to approval pursuant to article twenty-three of this chapter. Minimum benefit standards for such policies and for self-insurers, and rights of subrogation, examination and other such matters, shall be established by regulation pursuant to section three hundred one of this chapter.

(e) Every owner's policy of liability insurance issued in satisfaction of article six or eight of the vehicle and traffic law shall also provide, when a motor vehicle covered by such policy is used or operated in any other state or in any Canadian province, insurance coverage for such motor vehicle at least in the minimum amount required by the laws of that state or province.

App Pract Provs

(f) Every owner's policy of liability insurance issued on a motorcycle or an all terrain vehicle in satisfaction of the requirements of article six or eight of the vehicle and traffic law or section twenty-four hundred seven of such law shall also provide for; every owner who maintains another form of financial security on a motorcycle or an all terrain vehicle in satisfaction of the requirements of such articles or section shall be liable for; and every owner of a motorcycle or an all terrain vehicle required to be subject to the provisions of this article by subdivision two of section three hundred twenty-one of such law shall be liable for; the payment of first party benefits to persons, other than the occupants of such motorcycle or all terrain vehicle, another motorcycle or all terrain vehicle, or any motor vehicle, for loss arising out of the use or operation of the motorcycle or all terrain vehicle within this state. Every insurer and self-insurer may exclude from the coverage required by this subsection a person who intentionally causes his own injury or is injured while committing an act which would constitute a felony or while seeking to avoid lawful apprehension or arrest by a law enforcement officer.

(g) A company authorized to provide the insurance specified in paragraph three of subsection (a) of section one thousand one hundred thirteen of this chapter or a corporation organized pursuant to article forty-three of this chapter may, individually or jointly, with the approval of the superintendent upon a showing that the company or corporation is qualified to provide for all of the items of basic economic loss specified in paragraph one of subsection (a) of section five thousand one hundred two of this article, provide coverage for such items of basic economic loss to the extent that an insurer would be required to provide under this article. Where a policyholder elects to be covered under such an arrangement the insurer providing coverage for the automobile shall be furnished with the names of all persons covered by the company or corporation under the arrangement and such persons shall not be entitled to benefits for any of the items of basic economic loss specified in such paragraph. The premium for the automobile insurance policy shall be appropriately reduced to reflect the elimination of coverage for such items of basic economic loss. Coverage by the automobile insurer of such eliminated items shall be effected or restored upon request by the insured and payment of the premium for such coverage. All companies and corporations providing coverage for items of basic economic loss pursuant to the authorization of this subsection shall have only those rights and obligations which are applicable to an insurer subject to this article.

(h) Any policy of insurance obtained to satisfy the financial security requirements of article six or eight of the vehicle and traffic law which does not contain provisions complying with the requirements of this article, shall be construed as if such provisions were embodied therein.

\*         \*         \*

## § 5104. Causes of action for personal injury.

(a) Notwithstanding any other law, in any action by or on behalf of a covered person against another covered person for personal injuries arising out of negligence in the use or operation of a motor vehicle in this state, there shall be no right of recovery for non-economic loss, except in the case of a serious injury, or for basic economic loss. The owner, operator or occupant of a motorcycle which has in effect the financial security required by article six or eight of the vehicle and traffic law, or which is referred to in subdivision two of section three hundred twenty-one of such law, shall not be subject to an action by or on behalf of a covered person for recovery for non-economic loss, except in the case of a serious injury, or for basic economic loss.

(b) In any action by or on behalf of a covered person, against a non-covered person, where damages for personal injuries arising out of the use or operation of a motor vehicle or a motorcycle may be recovered, an insurer which paid or is liable for first party benefits on account of such injuries has a lien against any recovery to the extent of benefits paid or payable by it to the covered person. No such action may be compromised by the covered person except with the written consent of the insurer, or with the approval of the court, or where the amount of such settlement exceeds fifty thousand dollars. The failure of such person to commence such action within two years after accrual gives the insurer a cause of action for the amount of first party benefits paid or payable against any person who may be liable to the covered person for his personal injuries. The insurer's cause of action shall be in addition to the cause of action of the covered person except that in any action subsequently commenced by the covered person for such injuries, the amount of his basic economic loss shall not be recoverable.

(c) Where there is no right of recovery for basic economic loss, such loss may nevertheless be pleaded and proved to the extent that it is relevant to the proof of non-economic loss.

## § 5108. Limit on charges by providers of health services.

(a) The charges for services specified in paragraph one of subsection (a) of section five thousand one hundred two of this article and any further health service charges which are incurred as a result of the injury and which are in excess of basic economic loss, shall not exceed the charges permissible under the schedules prepared and established by the chairman of the workers' compensation board for industrial accidents, except where the insurer or arbitrator determines that unusual procedures or unique circumstances justify the excess charge.

(b) The superintendent, after consulting with the chairman of the workers' compensation board and the commissioner of health, shall promulgate rules and regulations implementing and coordinating the provisions of this article and the workers' compensation law with respect to charges for the professional health services specified in paragraph one of subsection (a) of section five thousand one hundred two of this article, including the establishment of schedules for all such services for which schedules have not been prepared and established by the chairman of the workers' compensation board. Payments for medical and other health care services provided by managed care organizations pursuant to managed care programs approved pursuant to paragraph one of subsection (i) of section five thousand one hundred three of this article shall not exceed amounts otherwise payable by application of the fee schedules established by the superintendent or the chair of the workers' compensation board.

(c) No provider of health services specified in paragraph one of subsection (a) of section five thousand one hundred two of this article may demand or request any payment in addition to the charges authorized pursuant to this section. Every insurer shall report to the commissioner of health any patterns of overcharging, excessive treatment or other improper actions by a health provider within thirty days after such insurer has knowledge of such pattern.

# JUDICIARY LAW

---

## SYNOPSIS OF SELECTED PROVISIONS

**Article 2.**    **General provisions relating to courts and judges.**

| | |
|---|---|
| § 2. | Courts of record. |
| § 2-b. | General powers of courts of record. |
| § 7-c. | Continuance of special proceeding before another officer. |
| § 35-a. | Statements to be filed by judges or justices fixing or approving fees, commissions or other compensation for persons appointed by courts to perform services in actions and proceedings. |

**Article 5.**    **Supreme court.**

| | |
|---|---|
| § 140-b. | General jurisdiction of supreme court. |
| § 148-a. | [Repealed]. |

**Article 7.**    **County court.**

| | |
|---|---|
| § 190. | Jurisdiction of county court. |
| § 190-a. | When domestic or foreign corporation or joint-stock association deemed resident. |
| § 190-b. | Power of county court and county judge co-extensive with that of supreme court and supreme court justice. |

**Article 19.**    **Contempts (selections).**

| | |
|---|---|
| § 756. | Application to punish for contempt; procedure. |
| § 757. | Application to punish for contempt committed before referee. |
| § 760. | When application may be made. |
| § 761. | Notice to accused; service. |
| § 767. | When habeas corpus may issue. |
| § 770. | Final order directing punishment; exception. |
| § 772. | Punishment upon return of application. |
| § 773. | Amount of fine. |
| § 774. | Length of imprisonment and periodic review of proceedings. |
| § 775. | When court may release offender. |
| § 777. | Proceedings when accused does not appear. |

---

## Article 2. General provisions relating to courts and judges.

### § 2. Courts of record.

Each of the following courts of the state is a court of record:

1. The court for the trial of impeachments.

2. A court of the judiciary.

3. The court of appeals.

4. The appellate division of the supreme court in each department.

5. The supreme court.

6. The court of claims.

7. A county court in each county, except the counties of New York, Bronx, Kings, Queens, and Richmond.

8. The family court.

9. A surrogate's court in each county.

10. Each city court outside the city of New York.

11. The district court in each county or portion thereof in which such court shall be established.

12. The civil court of the city of New York and the criminal court of the city of New York.

All courts other than those specified in this section are courts not of record.

## § 2-b. General powers of courts of record.

A court of record has power

1. to issue a subpoena requiring the attendance of a person found in the state to testify in a cause pending in that court, subject, however, to the limitations prescribed by law with respect to the portion of the state in which the process of the local court of record may be served;

2. to administer an oath to a witness in the exercise of the powers and duties of the court and;

3. to devise and make new process and forms of proceedings, necessary to carry into effect the powers and jurisdiction possessed by it.

## § 7-c. Continuance of special proceeding before another officer.

In case of the death, sickness, resignation, removal from office, absence from the county, or other disabililty of an officer before whom or in whose court a special proceeding has been instituted, where no express provision is made by law for the continuance thereof, it may be continued before or in the court of

1. the officer's successor, or

2. if there is no successor capable of acting, any other officer residing in the same county before whom it might have been originally instituted, or

3. if there is neither a successor nor an officer specified in paragraph two capable of acting, an officer in an adjoining county who would originally have had jurisdiction of the subject matter had it occurred or existed in the latter county. An officer substituted, as prescribed by law, to continue a special proceeding instituted before another, may exercise all powers in the special proceeding, as if it had been originally instituted before him.

### § 35-a.  Statements to be filed by judges or justices fixing or approving fees, commissions or other compensation for persons appointed by courts to perform services in actions and proceedings.

1. (a) On the first business day of each week any judge or justice who has during the preceding week fixed or approved one or more fees or allowances of more than two hundred dollars for services performed by any person appointed by the court in any capacity, including but not limited to appraiser, special guardian, guardian ad litem, general guardian, referee, counsel, special referee, auctioneer, special examiner, conservator, committee of incompetent or receiver, shall file a statement with the office of court administration on a form to be prescribed by the state administrator. The statement shall show the name and address of the appointee, the county and the title of the court in which the services of the appointee were performed, the court docket index or file number assigned to the action or proceeding, if any, the title of the action or proceeding, the nature of the action or proceeding, the name of the judge or justice who appointed the person, the person or interest which the appointee represented, whether or not the proceeding was contested, the fee fixed or approved by the judge or justice, the gross value of the subject matter of the proceeding, the number of hours spent by the appointee in performing the service, the nature of the services performed and such other information relating to the appointment as the state administrator shall require. The judge or justice shall certify that the fee, commission, allowance or other compensation fixed or approved is a reasonable award for the services rendered by the appointee, or is fixed by statute. If the fee, commission, allowance or other compensation for services performed pursuant to an appointment described in this section is either specified as to amount by statute or fixed by statute as a percentage of the value of the subject matter of the action or proceeding, the judge or justice shall specify the statutory fee, commission or allowance and shall specify the section of the statute authorizing the payment of the fee, commission, allowance or other compensation.

(b) Paragraph (a) shall not apply to any compensation awarded to appointees assigned to represent indigent persons pursuant to Article 18-B of the county law, counsel assigned pursuant to section thirty-five of the judiciary law, law guardians or counsel appointed pursuant to the family court act, or referees appointed pursuant to section 78.25 of the mental hygiene law.

App Pract Provs

(c) Any judge or justice who fixes or approves compensation for services performed by persons appointed as referees to examine accounts of incompetents pursuant to section 78.25 of the mental hygiene law shall file, annually, with the office of court administration a statement containing such information regarding such appointments as the state administrator shall require.

2. The office of court administration shall annually submit to the appellate division of the supreme court in each of the judicial departments of the state a report containing a summary of the information contained in the statements filed with it pursuant to this section by the judges and justices sitting in courts in that department during the preceding year. Each appellate division of the supreme court shall keep and file such reports and shall have power to make such rules respecting the supervision of all such court appointees within its judicial department as it may deem necessary.

3. The statements and reports required by this section shall be matters of public record and available for public inspection. Each court may permit the information contained therein to be made available for publication at such times and in such manner as it may deem proper.

### Article 5. Supreme court.

### § 140-b. General jurisdiction of supreme court.

The general jurisdiction in law and equity which the supreme court possesses under the provisions of the constitution includes all the jurisdiction which was possessed and exercised by the supreme court of the colony of New York at any time, and by the court of chancery in England on the fourth day of July, seventeen hundred seventy-six, with the exceptions, additions and limitations created and imposed by the constitution and laws of the state. Subject to those exceptions and limitations the supreme court of the state has all the powers and authority of each of those courts and may exercise them in like manner.

### § 148-a. [Repealed].

### Article 7. County court.

### § 190. Jurisdiction of county court.

The jurisdiction of each county court, except the county courts of counties within the city of New York, extends to the following actions and special proceedings, in addition to the jurisdiction, power and authority conferred upon a county court in a particular case by special statutory provision:

1. An action for the partition of real property, for dower, for the foreclosure, redemption or satisfaction of a mortgage upon real property, for the foreclosure of a lien arising out of a contract for the sale of real property, for specific performance of a contract relating to real property, for the enforcement or

foreclosure of a mechanic's lien on real property, for reformation or rescission of a deed, contract or mortgage affecting real property, or to compel the determination of a claim to real property under article fifteen of the real property actions and proceedings law, where the real property to which the action relates is situated within the county; or to foreclose a lien upon a chattel in a case specified in section two hundred six of the lien law where the lien does not exceed twenty-five thousand dollars in amount and the chattel is found within the county.

2. An action in favor of the executor, administrator or assignee of a judgment creditor, or in a proper case in favor of the judgment creditor, to recover a judgment for money remaining due upon a judgment rendered in the same court.

3. An action for any other cause, where the defendant, or if there are two or more defendants, where all of them, at the time of the commencement of the action, reside in the county, or where a defendant has an office for the transaction of business within the county and the cause of action arose therein, or where the defendant is a foreign corporation that is doing business within the county and the cause of action arose therein and where the complaint in such action demands judgment for a sum of money only not exceeding twenty-five thousand dollars; or to recover one or more chattels the aggregate value of which does not exceed twenty-five thousand dollars with or without damages for the taking or detention thereof.

4. The custody of the person and the care of the property, concurrently with the supreme court, of a resident of the county who is adjudicated incompetent to manage his affairs by reason of age, drunkenness, mental illness or other cause or for whom a conservator has been appointed; and any special proceeding which the supreme court has jurisdiction to entertain for the appointment of a committee of the person or of the property of such an incompetent person or conservatee or for the sale or other disposition of the real property situated within the county of a person wherever resident who is incompetent, who is a conservatee, or who is an infant, or for the sale or other disposition of the real property, situated within the county, of a domestic religious corporation.

5. Notwithstanding any other provision of law to the contrary, any proceeding which the supreme court has jurisdiction to entertain to review the actions or determinations of the state board of parole.

6. An action for any claim against a restitution fund established by such court resulting from its criminal jurisdiction.

### § 190-a. When domestic or foreign corporation or joint-stock association deemed resident.

For the purpose of determining jurisdiction under section one hundred ninety, a domestic corporation or joint-stock association is deemed a resident of a county in which its principal place of business is established by or pursuant to a statute or by its articles of association, or in which its principal place of business or any part of its plant, shops, factories or offices is actually located, or in the case of a railroad corporation, in which any portion of the road operated by it is located, and a foreign corporation is to be deemed a resident of a county if it maintains any plant, store, office, warehouse or other facility for doing business within such county; and personal service of a paper by which an action or special proceeding is commenced, made within the county, as prescribed in the civil practice law and rules, is sufficient service thereof upon a domestic corporation wherever it is located.

### § 190-b.  Power of county court and county judge co-extensive with that of supreme court and supreme court justice.

1. Where a county court has jurisdiction of an action or a special proceeding, it possesses the same jurisdiction, power and authority in and over the same, and in the course of the proceedings therein, that the supreme court possesses in a like case; and it may render any judgment or grant either party any relief that the supreme court may render or grant in a like case, and may send its process and other mandates into any county of the state for service or execution and enforce obedience thereto in the same manner as the supreme court.

2. The county judge possesses the same power and authority in such action or special proceeding that a justice of the supreme court possesses in a like action or special proceeding brought in the supreme court.

3. The county judge possesses the same power and authority in a special proceeding which can be lawfully instituted before him out of court that a justice of the supreme court possesses in a like special proceeding instituted before him out of court.

### Article 19.   Contempts (selections).

### § 756.  Application to punish for contempt; procedure.

An application to punish for a contempt punishable civilly may be commenced by notice of motion returnable before the court or judge authorized to punish for the offense, or by an order of such court or judge requiring the accused to show cause before it, or him, at a time and place therein specified, why the accused should not be punished for the alleged offense. The application shall be noticed, heard and determined in accordance with the procedure for a motion on notice in an action in such court, provided, however, that, except as provided in section fifty-two hundred fifty of the civil practice law and rules or unless otherwise ordered by the court, the moving papers shall be served no less than ten and no more than thirty days before the time at which the application is noticed to be heard. The application shall contain on its face a notice that the purpose of the hearing is to punish the accused for a contempt of court, and that such punishment may consist of fine or imprisonment, or both, according to law together with the following legend printed or type written in a size equal to at least eight point bold type:

**WARNING:**

**YOUR FAILURE TO APPEAR IN COURT MAY RESULT IN YOUR IMMEDIATE ARREST AND IMPRISONMENT FOR CONTEMPT OF COURT.**

### § 757.  Application to punish for contempt committed before referee.

Where the offense is committed upon the trial of an issue referred to a referee appointed by the court, or consists of a witness's non-attendance, or refusal to be sworn or testify, before him, the application prescribed in this section may be made returnable before him or before the court. The application shall contain on its face a notice that the purpose of the hearing is to punish the accused for a contempt of court, and that such punishment may consist of fine or imprisonment, or both, according to law.

### § 760.  When application may be made.

An application may be made, either before or after the final judgment in the action, or the final order in the special proceeding.

### § 761.  Notice to accused; service.

An application to punish for contempt in a civil contempt proceeding shall be served upon the accused, unless service upon the attorney for the accused be ordered by the court or judge.

### § 767.  When habeas corpus may issue.

If the accused is in the custody of a sheriff, or other officer, by virtue of an execution against his person, or by virtue of a mandate for any other contempt or misconduct, or a commitment on a criminal charge, the court, upon proof of the facts, may issue a writ of habeas corpus, directed to the officer, requiring him to bring the accused before it, to answer for the offense charged. The officer to whom the writ is directed, or upon whom it is served, must bring him before the court, and detain him at the place where the court is sitting, until the further order of the court.

### § 770.  Final order directing punishment; exception.

Upon the return of an application to punish for contempt, or upon a hearing held upon a warrant of commitment issued pursuant to section seven hundred seventy-two or seven hundred seventy-three of this article, the court shall inform the offender that he has the right to the assistance of counsel, and when it appears that the offender is financially unable to obtain counsel, the court may in its discretion assign counsel to represent him. If it is determined that the accused has committed the offense charged; and that it was calculated to, or actually did, defeat, impair, impede, or prejudice the rights or remedies of a party to an action or special proceeding, brought in the court, or before the judge or referee; the court, judge, or referee must make a final order directing that he be punished by fine or imprisonment, or both, as the nature of the case requires. A warrant of commitment must issue accordingly, except as hereinafter provided. Where an application is made under this article and in pursuance of section two hundred forty-five of the domestic relations law or any other section of law for a final order directing punishment for failure to pay alimony and/or counsel fees pursuant to an order of the court or judge in an action for divorce or separation and the husband appear and satisfy the court or a judge before whom the application may be pending that he has no means or property or income to comply with the terms of the order at the time, the court or judge may, in its or his discretion, deny the application to punish the husband, without prejudice to the wife's rights and without prejudice to a renewal of the application by the wife upon notice and after proof that the financial condition of the husband is changed.

Where an application is made to punish an offender for an offense committed with respect to an enforcement procedure under the civil practice law and rules, if the offender appear and comply and satisfy the court or a judge before whom the application shall be pending that he has at the time no means or property or income which could be levied upon pursuant to an execution issued in such an enforcement procedure, the court or judge shall deny the application to punish the offender without prejudice to the applicant's rights and without prejudice to a renewal of the application upon notice and after proof that the financial condition of the offender has changed.

## § 772. Punishment upon return of application.

Upon the return of an application to punish for contempt, the questions which arise must be determined, as upon any other motion; and, if the determination is to the effect specified in section seven hundred and seventy, the order thereupon must be to the same effect as the final order therein prescribed.

Except as hereinafter provided, the offender may be committed upon a certified copy of the order so made, without further process. Where the commitment is ordered to punish an offense committed with respect to an enforcement procedure under the civil practice law and rules or pursuant to section two hundred forty-five of the domestic relations law, and the defendant has not appeared upon the return of the application, the final order directing punishment and commitment of the offender shall include a provision granting him leave to purge himself of the contempt within ten days after personal service of the order by performance of the act or duty the omission of which constitutes the misconduct for which he is to be punished, and the act or duty to be performed shall be specified in the order. Upon a certified copy of the order, together with proof by affidavit that more than ten days have elapsed since personal service thereof upon the offender, and that the act or duty specified has not been performed, the court may issue without notice a warrant directed to the sheriff or other enforcement officer of any jurisdiction in which the offender may be found. The warrant shall command such officer to arrest the offender forthwith and bring him before the court, or a judge thereof, to be committed or for such further disposition as the court in its discretion shall direct.

### § 773. Amount of fine.

If an actual loss or injury has been caused to a party to an action or special proceeding, by reason of the misconduct proved against the offender, and the case is not one where it is specially prescribed by law, that an action may be maintained to recover damages for the loss or injury, a fine, sufficient to indemnify the aggrieved party, must be imposed upon the offender, and collected, and paid over to the aggrieved party, under the direction of the court. The payment and acceptance of such a fine constitute a bar to an action by the aggrieved party, to recover damages for the loss or injury.

Where it is not shown that such an actual loss or injury has been caused, a fine may be imposed, not exceeding the amount of the complainant's costs and expenses, and two hundred and fifty dollars in addition thereto, and must be collected and paid, in like manner. A corporation may be fined as prescribed in this section.

If a fine is imposed to punish an offense committed with respect to an enforcement procedure under the civil practice law and rules or pursuant to section two hundred forty-five of the domestic relations law, and it has not been shown that such an actual loss or injury has been caused and the defendant has not appeared upon the return of the application, the order imposing fine, if any, shall include a provision granting the offender leave to purge himself of the contempt within ten days after personal service of the order by appearing and satisfying the court that he is unable to pay the fine or, in the discretion of the court, by giving an undertaking in a sum to be fixed by the court conditioned upon payment of the fine plus costs and expenses and his appearance and performance of the act or duty, the omission of which constitutes the misconduct for which he is to be punished. The order may also include a provision committing the offender to prison until the fine plus costs and expenses are paid, or until he is discharged according to law. Upon a certified copy of the order imposing fine, together with proof by affidavit that more than ten days have elapsed since personal service thereof upon the offender, and that the fine plus costs and expenses has not been paid, the court may issue without notice a warrant directed to the sheriff or other enforcement officer of any jurisdiction in which the offender may be found. The warrant shall command such officer to arrest the offender forthwith and bring him before the court, or a judge thereof,

App Pract Provs

to be committed or for such other disposition as the court in its discretion shall direct.

## § 774. Length of imprisonment and periodic review of proceedings.

1. Where the misconduct proved consists of an omission to perform an act or duty, which is yet in the power of the offender to perform, he shall be imprisoned only until he has performed it, and paid the fine imposed, but if he shall perform the act or duty required to be performed, he shall not be imprisoned for the fine imposed more than three months if the fine is less than five hundred dollars, or more than six months if the fine is five hundred dollars or more. In such case, the order, and the warrant of commitment, if one is issued, must specify the act or duty to be performed, and the sum to be paid. In every other case, where special provision is not otherwise made by law, the offender may be imprisoned for a reasonable time, not exceeding six months, and until the fine, if any, is paid; and the order, and the warrant of commitment, if any, must specify the amount of the fine, and the duration of the imprisonment. If the term of imprisonment is not specified in the order, the offender shall be imprisoned for the fine imposed three months if the fine is less than five hundred dollars, and six months if the fine imposed is five hundred dollars or more. If the offender is required to serve a specified term of imprisonment, and in addition to pay a fine, he shall not be imprisoned for the nonpayment of such fine for more than three months if such fine is less than five hundred dollars or more than six months if the fine imposed is five hundred dollars or more in addition to the specified time of imprisonment.

2. In all instances where any offender shall have been imprisoned pursuant to article nineteen of the judiciary law and where the term of such imprisonment is specified to be an indeterminate period of time or for a term of more than three months, such offender, if not then discharged by law from imprisonment, shall within ninety days after the commencement of such imprisonment be brought, by the sheriff, or other officer, as a matter of course personally before the court imposing such imprisonment and a review of the proceedings shall then be held to determine whether such offender shall be discharged from imprisonment. At periodic intervals of not more than ninety days following such review, the offender, if not then discharged by law from imprisonment, shall be brought, by the sheriff, or other officer, as a matter of course personally before the court imposing such imprisonment and further reviews of the proceedings shall then be held to determine whether such offender shall be discharged from imprisonment. Where such imprisonment shall have arisen out of or during the course of any action or proceeding, the clerk of the court before which such review of the proceedings shall be held, or the judge or justice of such court in case there be no clerk, shall give reasonable notice in writing of the date, time and place of each such review to each party or his attorney who shall have appeared of record in such action or proceeding, at their last known address.

### § 775.  When court may release offender.

Where an offender, imprisoned as prescribed in this article, is unable to endure the imprisonment, or to pay the sum, or perform the act or duty, required to be paid or performed, in order to entitle him to be released, the court, judge, or referee may, in its or his discretion, and upon such terms as justice requires, make an order, directing him to be discharged from the imprisonment.

Where the commitment was made to punish a contempt of court committed with respect to an enforcement procedure under the civil practice law and rules, and the offender has purged himself of contempt as provided in section seven hundred seventy-two or seven hundred seventy-three of this article, the court out of which the execution was issued shall make an order directing him to be discharged from the imprisonment.

### § 777.  Proceedings when accused does not appear.

Where a person has given an undertaking for his appearance, as prescribed in this article and fails to appear, on the return day of the application, the court may either issue a warrant of commitment, or make an order, directing the undertaking to be prosecuted; or both.

App Pract Provs

# LIEN LAW

## SYNOPSIS OF SELECTED PROVISIONS

**Article 10-A.** **Liens for taxes payable to the United States of America and other federal liens.**

**§ 243.**       **Fees.**

## Article 10-A.   Liens for taxes payable to the United States of America and other federal liens.

### § 243.   Fees.

The fee to be paid to the secretary of state or a clerk or register for filing and indexing each notice of lien or certificate or notice affecting any such lien shall be determined in accordance with the provisions of section ninety-six-a of the executive law. Such officers shall bill the district directors of internal revenue or other appropriate federal officers on a monthly basis for fees for documents filed by them.

App Pract Provs

# NEW YORK CITY CIVIL COURT ACT

———

## SYNOPSIS OF SELECTED PROVISIONS

Article 18.    **Small Claims.**

§ 1809.      Procedures relating to corporations, associations, insurers and assignees.

§ 1812.      Enforcement of small claims judgments.

———

## Article 18.   Small Claims.

### § 1809.   Procedures relating to corporations, associations, insurers and assignees.

1. No corporation, except a municipal corporation, public benefit corporation, school district or school district public library wholly or partially within the municipal corporate limit, no partnership or association, and no assignees of any small claim shall institute an action or proceeding under this article, nor shall this article apply to any claim or cause of action brought by an insurer in its own name or in the name of its insured whether before or after payment to the insured on the policy.

2. A corporation may appear in the defense of any small claim action brought pursuant to this article by an attorney as well as by any authorized officer, director or employee of the corporation provided that the appearance by a non-lawyer on behalf of a corporation shall be deemed to constitute the requisite authority to bind the corporation in a settlement or trial. The court or arbitrator may make reasonable inquiry to determine the authority of any person who appears for the corporation in defense of a small claims court case.

### § 1812.   Enforcement of small claims judgments.

(a) The special procedures set forth in subdivision (b) hereof shall be available only where:

1. there is a recorded judgment of a small claims court; and

2. (i) the aforesaid judgment resulted from a transaction in the course of the trade or business of the judgment debtor, or arose out of a repeated course of dealing or conduct of the judgment debtor, and (ii) there are at least two other

unsatisfied recorded judgments of a small claims court arising out of such trade or business or repeated course of dealing or conduct, against the judgment debtor; and

3. the judgment debtor failed to satisfy such judgment within a period of thirty days after receipt of notice of such judgment. Such notice shall be given in the same manner as provided for the service of a summons or by certified mail, return receipt requested, and shall contain a statement that such judgment exists, that at least two other unsatisfied recorded judgments exist, and that failure to pay such judgment may be the basis for an action, for treble the amount of such unsatisfied judgment, pursuant to this section.

(b) Where each of the elements of subdivision (a) of this section are present the judgment creditor shall be entitled to commence an action against said judgment debtor for treble the amount of such unsatisfied judgment, together with reasonable counsel fees, and the costs and disbursements of such action, provided, however, that in any such action it shall be a defense that the judgment debtor did not have resources to satisfy such judgment within a period of thirty days after receipt of notice of such judgment. The failure to pay a judgment obtained in an action pursuant to this section shall not be the basis for another such action pursuant to this section.

(c) Where the judgment is obtained in an action pursuant to subdivision (b), and arises from a business of the defendant, the court shall, in addition to its responsibilities under this article, advise the attorney general in relation to his authority under subdivision twelve of section sixty-three of the executive law, and if such judgment arises from a certified or licensed business of the defendant, advise the state or local licensing or certifying authority.

(d) Where a judgment has been entered in a small claims court and remains unsatisfied, the small claims clerk shall, upon request, issue information subpoenas, at nominal cost, for the judgment creditor and provide the creditor with assistance on their preparation and use. The court shall have the same power as the supreme court to punish a contempt of court committed with respect to an information subpoena.

[*Editor's Note: Article 18 of the Uniform District Court Act, the Uniform City Court Act and the Uniform Justice Court Act each contain provisions identical to NYCCCA §§ 1809 and 1812. See §§ 1809 and 1812 of UDCA, UCCA and UJCA.]

# PROFESSIONAL DISCIPLINARY RULES

### Part 1200. Disciplinary Rules of the Code of Professional Responsibility

§ 1200.1    Definitions.
§ 1200.2    Maintaining Integrity and Competence of the Legal Profession.
§ 1200.3    Misconduct.
§ 1200.4    Disclosure of Information to Authorities.
§ 1200.5    Responsibilities of a Supervisory Lawyer.
§ 1200.6    Publicity and Advertising.
§ 1200.7    Professional Notices, Letterheads and Signs.
§ 1200.8    Solicitation and Recommendation of Professional Employment.
§ 1200.9    Suggestion of Need of Legal Services.
§ 1200.10    Identification of Practice and Specialty.
§ 1200.10-a Client's Statement of Rights and Responsibilities in Domestic Relations Matters.
§ 1200.11    Fee for Legal Services.
§ 1200.12    Division of Fees Among Lawyers.
§ 1200.13    Agreements Restricting the Practice of a Lawyer.
§ 1200.14    Acceptance of Employment.
§ 1200.15    Withdrawal from Employment.
§ 1200.16    Aiding Unauthorized Practice of Law.
§ 1200.17    Dividing Legal Fees With a Nonlawyer.
§ 1200.18    Forming a Partnership with a Nonlawyer.
§ 1200.19    Preservation of Confidences and Secrets of a Client.
§ 1200.20    Refusing Employment When the Interests of the Lawyer May Impair Independent Professional Judgment.
§ 1200.21    Withdrawal as Counsel When the Lawyer Becomes a Witness.
§ 1200.22    Avoiding Acquisition of Interest in Litigation.
§ 1200.23    Limiting Business Relations with a Client.
§ 1200.24    Refusing to Accept or Continue Employment if the Interests of Another Client May Impair the Independent Professional Judgment of the Lawyer.
§ 1200.25    Settling Similar Claims of Clients.
§ 1200.26    Avoiding Influence by Others than the Client.
§ 1200.27    Conflict of Interest—Former Client.
§ 1200.28    Conflict of Interest—Organization as Client.
§ 1200.29    Membership in Legal Services Organization.
§ 1200.30    Failing to Act Competently.
§ 1200.31    Limiting Liability to Client.
§ 1200.32    Representing a Client Zealously.
§ 1200.33    Representing a Client Within the Bounds of the Law.
§ 1200.34    Performing the Duty of Public Prosecutor or Other Government Lawyer.

App Pract Provs

§ 1200.35   Communicating With One Of Adverse Interest.
§ 1200.36   Threatening Criminal Prosecution.
§ 1200.37   Trial Conduct.
§ 1200.38   Trial Publicity.
§ 1200.39   Communication with or Investigation of Jurors.
§ 1200.40   Contact with Witnesses.
§ 1200.41   Contact with Officials.
§ 1200.42   Action as a Public Official.
§ 1200.43   Statements Concerning Judges and Other Adjudicatory Officers.
§ 1200.44   Lawyer Candidate for Judicial Office.
§ 1200.45   Avoiding Even the Appearance of Impropriety.
§ 1200.46   Preserving Identity of Funds and Property of Others; Fiduciary
            Responsibility; Maintenance of Bank Accounts; Recordkeeping;
            Examination of Records.

Part 1300. Dishonored Check Reporting Rules for
Attorney Special, Trust and Escrow Accounts

§ 1300.1    Dishonored Check Reports.

Part 1400. Procedure for Attorneys in
Domestic Relations Matters

§ 1400.1    Application.
§ 1400.2    Statement of Client's Rights and Responsibilities.
§ 1400.3    Written Retainer Agreement.
§ 1400.4    Nonrefundable Retainer Fee.
§ 1400.5    Security Interests.
§ 1400.6    Closing Statement.
§ 1400.7    Fee Arbitration.

---

# Part 1200. Disciplinary Rules of the Code of Professional Responsibility

## § 1200.1   Definitions.*

As used in the disciplinary rules of the code of professional responsibility:

(a) *Differing interests* include every interest that will adversely affect either the judgment or the loyalty of a lawyer to a client, whether it be a conflicting, inconsistent, diverse, or other interest.

(b) *Law firm* includes, but is not limited to, a professional legal corporation, the legal department of a corporation or other organization and a legal services organization.

(c) *Person* includes a corporation, an association, a trust, a partnership, and any other organization or legal entity.

(d) *Professional legal corporation* means a corporation, or an association treated as a corporation, authorized by law to practice law for profit.

(e) *State* includes the District of Columbia, Puerto Rico, and other Federal territories and possessions.

(f) *Tribunal* includes all courts and all other adjudicatory bodies. A tribunal shall be deemed "available" when it would have jurisdiction to hear a complaint, if timely brought.

(g) *Bar association* includes a bar association of specialists as referred to in section 1200.10(b) of this Part.

(h) *Qualified legal assistance organization* means an office or organization of one of the four types listed in section 1200.8(d)(1) through (4), inclusive, that meets all the requirements thereof.

(i) Fraud does not include conduct, although characterized as fraudulent by statute or administrative rule, which lacks an element of scienter, deceit, intent to mislead, or knowing failure to correct misrepresentations which can be reasonably expected to induce detrimental reliance by another.

* [Editor's note: "Confidence" and "secret" are defined in section 1200.19(a) of this Part.]

### § 1200.2.  Maintaining Integrity and Competence of the Legal Profession.

(a) A lawyer is subject to discipline if the lawyer has made a materially false statement in, or has deliberately failed to disclose a material fact requested in connection with, the lawyer's application for admission to the bar.

(b) A lawyer shall not further the application for admission to the bar of another person that the lawyer knows to be unqualified in respect to character, education, or other relevant attributes.

### § 1200.3.  Misconduct.

(a) A lawyer shall not:

(1) Violate a disciplinary rule.

(2) Circumvent a disciplinary rule through actions of another.

(3) Engage in illegal conduct involving moral turpitude.

(4) Engage in conduct involving dishonesty, fraud, deceit, or misrepresentation.

(5) Engage in conduct that is prejudicial to the administration of justice.

(6) Unlawfully discriminate in the practice of law, including in hiring, promoting or otherwise determining conditions of employment, on the basis of

age, race, creed, color, national origin, sex, disability, marital status, or sexual orientation. Where there is available a tribunal of competent jurisdiction, other than a Departmental Disciplinary Committee, a complaint of professional misconduct based on unlawful discrimination shall be brought before such tribunal in the first instance. A certified copy of a determination by such tribunal, which has become final and enforceable, and as to which the right to judicial or appellate review has been exhausted, finding that the lawyer has engaged in an unlawful discriminatory practice shall constitute *prima facie* evidence of professional misconduct in a disciplinary proceeding.

(7) In domestic relations matters, begin a sexual relationship with a client during the course of the lawyer's representation of the client.

(8) Engage in any other conduct that adversely reflects on the lawyer's fitness to practice law.

## § 1200.4.   Disclosure of Information to Authorities.

(a) A lawyer possessing knowledge, not protected as a confidence or secret, of a violation of section 1200.3 of this Part that raises a substantial question as to another lawyer's honesty, trustworthiness or fitness in other respects as a lawyer shall report such knowledge to a tribunal or other authority empowered to investigate or act upon such violation.

(b) A lawyer possessing knowledge or evidence, not protected as a confidence or secret, concerning another lawyer or a judge shall reveal fully such knowledge or evidence upon proper request of a tribunal or other authority empowered to investigate or act upon the conduct of lawyers or judges.

## § 1200.5.   Responsibilities of a Supervisory Lawyer.

(a) A lawyer shall be responsible for a violation of the disciplinary rules by another lawyer or for conduct of a nonlawyer employed or retained by or associated with the lawyer that would be a violation of the disciplinary rules if engaged in by a lawyer if:

(1) the lawyer orders the conduct; or

(2) the lawyer has supervisory authority over the other lawyer or the nonlawyer, and knows or should have known of the conduct at a time when its consequences can be avoided or mitigated but fails to take reasonable remedial action.

## § 1200.6.   Publicity and Advertising.

(a) A lawyer on behalf of himself or herself or partners or associates, shall not use or disseminate or participate in the preparation or dissemination of any public communication containing statements or claims that are false, deceptive, misleading or cast reflection on the legal profession as a whole.

(b) Advertising or other publicity by lawyers, including participation in public functions, shall not contain puffery, self-laudation, claims regarding the quality of the lawyers' legal services, or claims that cannot be measured or verified.

(c) It is proper to include information, provided its dissemination does not violate the provisions of subdivisions (a) and (b) of this section, as to:

(1) education, degrees and other scholastic distinctions, dates of admission to any bar; areas of the law in which the lawyer or law firm practices, as authorized by the code of professional responsibility; public offices and teaching positions held; memberships in bar associations or other professional societies or organizations, including offices and committee assignments therein; foreign language fluency;

(2) names of clients regularly represented, provided that the client has given prior written consent;

(3) bank references; credit arrangements accepted; prepaid or group legal services programs in which the attorney or firm participates; and

(4) legal fees for initial consultation; contingent fee rates in civil matters when accompanied by a statement disclosing whether percentages are computed before or after deduction of costs and disbursements; range of fees for services, provided that there be available to the public free of charge a written statement clearly describing the scope of each advertised service; hourly rates; and fixed fees for specified legal services.

(d) Advertising and publicity shall be designed to educate the public to an awareness of legal needs and to provide information relevant to the selection of the most appropriate counsel. Information other than that specifically authorized in subdivision (c) of this section that is consistent with these purposes may be disseminated providing that it does not violate any other provisions of this rule.

(e) A lawyer or law firm advertising any fixed fee for specified legal services shall, at the time of fee publication, have available to the public a written statement clearly describing the scope of each advertised service, which statement shall be delivered to the client at the time of retainer for any such service. Such legal services shall include all those services which are recognized as reasonable and necessary under local custom in the area of practice in the community where the services are performed.

(f) If the advertisement is broadcast, it shall be prerecorded or taped and approved for broadcast by the lawyer, and a recording or videotape of the actual transmission shall be retained by the lawyer for a period of not less than one year following such transmission. All advertisements of legal services that are mailed, or are distributed other than by radio, television, directory, newspaper, magazine or other periodical, by a lawyer or law firm with an office for the practice of law in this state, shall also be subject to the following provisions:

(1) A copy of each advertisement shall at the time of its initial mailing or distribution be filed with the Departmental Disciplinary Committee of the appropriate judicial department.

(2) Such advertisement shall contain no reference to the fact of filing.

(3) If such advertisement is directed to a predetermined addressee, a list, containing the names and addresses of all persons to whom the advertisement is being or will thereafter be mailed or distributed, shall be retained by the lawyer or law firm for a period of not less than one year following the last date of mailing or distribution.

(4) The advertisements filed pursuant to this subdivision shall be open to public inspection.

(5) The requirements of this subdivision shall not apply to such professional cards or other announcements the distribution of which is authorized by section 1200.7 of this Part.

(g) If a lawyer or law firm advertises a range of fees or an hourly rate for services, the lawyer or law firm may not charge more than the fee advertised for such services. If a lawyer or law firm advertises a fixed fee for specified legal services, or performs services described in a fee schedule, the lawyer or law firm may not charge more than the fixed fee for such stated legal service as set forth in the advertisement or fee schedule, unless the client agrees in writing that the services performed or to be performed were not legal services referred to or implied in the advertisement or in the fee schedule and, further, that a different fee arrangement shall apply to the transaction.

(h) Unless otherwise specified in the advertisement, if a lawyer publishes any fee information authorized under this disciplinary rule in a publication which is published more frequently than once per month, the lawyer shall be bound by any representation made therein for a period of not less than 30 days after such publication. If a lawyer publishes any fee information authorized under this rule in a publication which is published once per month or less frequently, the lawyer shall be bound by any representation made therein until the publication of the succeeding issue. If a lawyer publishes any fee information authorized under this rule in a publication which has no fixed date for publication of a succeeding issue, the lawyer shall be bound by any representation made therein for a reasonable period of time after publication, but in no event less than 90 days.

(i) Unless otherwise specified, if a lawyer broadcasts any fee information authorized under this rule, the lawyer shall be bound by any representation made therein for a period of not less than 30 days after such broadcast.

(j) A lawyer shall not compensate or give any thing of value to representatives of the press, radio, television or other communication medium in anticipation of or in return for professional publicity in a news item.

(k) All advertisements of legal services shall include the name, office address and telephone number of the attorney or law firm whose services are being offered.

## § 1200.7.  Professional Notices, Letterheads and Signs.

(a) A lawyer or law firm may use professional cards, professional announcement cards, office signs, letterheads or similar professional notices or devices, provided the same do not violate any statute or court rule, and are in accordance with section 1200.6 of this Part, including the following:

(1) A professional card of a lawyer identifying the lawyer by name and as a lawyer, and giving addresses, telephone numbers, the name of the law firm, and any information permitted under section 1200.6 of this Part. A professional card of a law firm may also give the names of members and associates.

(2) A professional announcement card stating new or changed associations or addresses, change of firm name, or similar matters pertaining to the professional offices of a lawyer or law firm. It may state biographical data, the names of members of the firm and associates and the names and dates of predecessor firms in a continuing line of succession. It shall not state the nature of the practice except as permitted under section 1200.10 of this Part.

(3) A sign in or near the office and in the building directory identifying the law office. The sign shall not state the nature of the practice, except as permitted under section 1200.10 of this Part.

(4) A letterhead identifying the lawyer by name and as a lawyer, and giving addresses, telephone numbers, the name of the law firm, associates and any information permitted under section 1200.10 of this Part. A letterhead of a law firm may also give the names of members and associates, and names and dates relating to deceased and retired members. A lawyer may be designated "Of Counsel" on a letterhead if there is a continuing relationship with a lawyer or law firm, other than as a partner or associate. A lawyer or law firm may be designated as "General Counsel" or by similar professional reference on stationery of a client if the lawyer or the firm devotes a substantial amount of professional time in the representation of that client. The letterhead of a law firm may give the names and dates of predecessor firms in a continuing line of succession.

(b) A lawyer in private practice shall not practice under a trade name, a name that is misleading as to the identity of the lawyer or lawyers practicing under such name, or a firm name containing names other than those of one or more of the lawyers in the firm, except that the name of a professional corporation may contain "P.C." or such symbols permitted by law, and, if otherwise lawful, a firm may use as, or continue to include in its name the name or names of one or more deceased or retired members of the firm or of a predecessor firm in a continuing line of succession. Such terms as "legal clinic," "legal aid," "legal service office," "legal assistance office," "defender office" and the like, may be used only by qualified legal assistance organizations described in section 1200.8(d) of this Part, except that the term "legal clinic" may be used by any lawyer or law firm provided the name of a participating lawyer or firm is incorporated therein. A lawyer who assumes a judicial, legislative or public executive or administrative post or office shall not permit his or her name to remain in the name of a law firm or be used in professional notices of the firm during any significant period in which the lawyer is not actively and regularly practicing law as a member of the firm and, during such period, other members of the firm shall not use the lawyer's name in the firm name or in professional notices of the firm.

(c) A lawyer shall not hold himself or herself out as having a partnership with one or more other lawyers unless they are in fact partners.

(d) A partnership shall not be formed or continued between or among lawyers licensed in different jurisdictions unless all enumerations of the members and associates of the firm on its letterhead and in other permissible listings make clear the jurisdictional limitations on those members and associates of the firm not licensed to practice in all listed jurisdictions; however, the same firm name may be used in each jurisdiction.

## § 1200.8.  Solicitation and Recommendation of Professional Employment.

(a) A lawyer shall not, directly or indirectly, seek professional employment for the lawyer or a partner or associate of the lawyer from a person who has not sought advice regarding employment of the lawyer in violation of any statute or existing court rule in the judicial department in which the lawyer practices.

(b) A lawyer shall not compensate or give anything of value to a person or organization to recommend or obtain employment by a client, or as a reward for having made a recommendation resulting in employment by a client, except by any of the organizations listed in section 1200.8(d) of this Part.

(c) A lawyer shall not request a person or organization to recommend or promote the use of the lawyer's services or those of the lawyer's partner or associate, or any other affiliated lawyer as a private practitioner, other than by advertising or publicity not proscribed by section 1200.6 of this Part, except that:

(1) The lawyer may request referrals from a lawyer referral service operated, sponsored or approved by a bar association and may pay its fees incident thereto.

(2) The lawyer may cooperate with the legal service activities of any of the offices or organizations enumerated in section 1200.8(d)(1) through (4) of this Part and may perform legal services for those to whom the lawyer was recommended by such an office or organization to do such work if:

(i) The person to whom the recommendation is made is a member or beneficiary of such office or organization; and

(ii) The lawyer remains free to exercise independent professional judgment on behalf of the client.

(3) The lawyer may request such a recommendation from another lawyer or an organization performing legal services.

(d) A lawyer or the lawyer's partner or associate or any other affiliated lawyer may be recommended, employed or paid by, or may cooperate with one of the following offices or organizations which promote the use of the lawyer's services or those of a partner or associate or any other affiliated lawyer if there is no interference with the exercise of independent professional judgment on behalf of the client:

(1) a legal aid office or public defender office:

(i) operated or sponsored by a duly accredited law school;

(ii) operated or sponsored by a bona fide, non-profit community organization;

(iii) operated or sponsored by a governmental agency; or

(iv) operated, sponsored, or approved by a bar association;

(2) A military legal assistance office;

(3) A lawyer referral service operated, sponsored or approved by a bar association;

(4) Any bona fide organization which recommends, furnishes or pays for legal services to its members or beneficiaries provided the following conditions are satisfied:

(i) Neither the lawyer, nor the lawyer's partner, nor associate, nor any other affiliated lawyer nor any non-lawyer, shall have initiated or promoted such organization for the primary purpose of providing financial or other benefit to such lawyer, partner, associate or affiliated lawyer.

(ii) Such organization is not operated for the purpose of procuring legal work or financial benefit for any lawyer as a private practitioner outside of the legal services program of the organization.

(iii) The member or beneficiary to whom the legal services are furnished, and not such organization, is recognized as the client of the lawyer in the matter.

(iv) Any member or beneficiary who is entitled to have legal services furnished or paid for by the organization may, if such member or beneficiary so desires, select counsel other than that furnished, selected or approved by the organization for the particular matter involved; and the legal service plan of such organization provides appropriate relief for any member or beneficiary who asserts a claim that representation by counsel furnished, selected or approved would be unethical, improper or inadequate under the circumstances of the matter involved; and the plan provides an appropriate procedure for seeking such relief.

App Pract Provs

(v) The lawyer does not know or have cause to know that such organization is in violation of applicable laws, rules of court or other legal requirements that govern its legal service operations.

(vi) Such organization has filed with the appropriate disciplinary authority, to the extent required by such authority, at least annually a report with respect to its legal service plan, if any, showing its terms, its schedule of benefits, its subscription charges, agreements with counsel and financial results of its legal service activities or, if it has failed to do so, the lawyer does not know or have cause to know of such failure.

(e) A lawyer shall not accept employment when the lawyer knows or it is obvious that the person who seeks services does so as a result of conduct prohibited under this disciplinary rule.

(f) Advertising not proscribed under section 1200.6 of this Part shall not be deemed in violation of any provision of this disciplinary rule.

## § 1200.9.  Suggestion of Need of Legal Services.

(a) A lawyer who has given unsolicited advice to an individual to obtain counsel or take legal action shall not accept employment resulting from that advice, in violation of any statute or court rule.

(b) A lawyer may accept employment by a close friend, relative, former client (if the advice is germane to the former employment) or one whom the lawyer reasonably believes to be a client.

(c) A lawyer may accept employment which results from participation in activities designed to educate the public to recognize legal problems, to make intelligent selection of counsel or to utilize available legal services.

(d) A lawyer who is recommended, furnished or paid by a qualified legal assistance organization enumerated in section 1200.8(d)(1) through (4) of this Part, may represent a member or beneficiary thereof, to the extent and under the conditions prescribed therein.

(e) Without affecting the right to accept employment, a lawyer may speak publicly or write for publication on legal topics so long as the lawyer does not undertake to give individual advice.

(f) Subject to compliance with the provisions of section 1200.8(a) of this Part, if success in asserting rights or defenses of a client in litigation in the nature of a class action is dependent upon the joinder of others, a lawyer may accept employment from those contacted for the purpose of obtaining their joinder.

## § 1200.10.  Identification of Practice and Specialty.

(a) A lawyer or law firm may publicly identify one or more areas of law in which the lawyer or the law firm practices, or may state that the practice of the lawyer or law firm is limited to one or more areas of law.

(b) A lawyer who is certified as a specialist in a particular area of law or law practice by the authority having jurisdiction under the laws of this state over the subject of specialization by lawyers may hold himself or herself out as a specialist, but only in accordance with the rules prescribed by that authority.

### § 1200.10-a   Client's Statement of Rights and Responsibilities in Domestic Relations Matters.

In domestic relations matters to which Part 1400 of the joint rules of the Appellate Divisions is applicable, a lawyer shall provide a prospective client with a statement of client's rights and responsibilities at the initial conference and prior to the signing of a written retainer statement.

### § 1200.11.   Fee for Legal Services.

(a) A lawyer shall not enter into an agreement for, charge or collect an illegal or excessive fee.

(b) A fee is excessive when, after a review of the facts, a lawyer of ordinary prudence would be left with a definite and firm conviction that the fee is in excess of a reasonable fee. Factors to be considered as guides in determining the reasonableness of a fee include the following:

(1) The time and labor required, the novelty and difficulty of the questions involved and the skill requisite to perform the legal service properly.

(2) The likelihood, if apparent or made known to the client, that the acceptance of the particular employment will preclude other employment by the lawyer.

(3) The fee customarily charged in the locality for similar legal services.

(4) The amount involved and the results obtained.

(5) The time limitations imposed by the client or by circumstances.

(6) The nature and length of the professional relationship with the client.

(7) The experience, reputation and ability of the lawyer or lawyers performing the services.

(8) Whether the fee is fixed or contingent.

(c)A lawyer shall not enter into an arrangement for, charge, or collect:

(1) A contingent fee for representing a defendant in a criminal case; or

(2) Any fee in a domestic relations matter to which Part 1400 of the joint rules of the Appellate Divisions is applicable,

(A) The payment or amount of which is contingent upon the securing of a divorce or upon the amount of maintenance, support, equitable distribution, or property settlement; or

(B) Unless a written retainer agreement is signed by the lawyer and client setting forth in plain language the nature of the relationship and the details of the fee arrangement. A lawyer shall not include in the written retainer agreement a nonrefundable fee clause; or

(C) Based upon a security interest, confession of judgment or other lien, without prior notice to the client in a signed retainer agreement and approval from the Court after notice to the adversary. A lawyer shall not foreclose on a mortgage placed on the marital residence while the spouse who consents to the mortgage remains the titleholder and the residence remains the spouse's primary residence.

(3) A fee proscribed by law or rule of court.

(d) Promptly after a lawyer has been employed in a contingent fee matter, the lawyer shall provide the client with a writing stating the method by which the fee is to be determined, including the percentage or percentages that shall accrue to the lawyer in the event of settlement, trial or appeal, litigation and other expenses to be deducted from the recovery and whether such expenses are to be deducted before or after the contingent fee is calculated. Upon conclusion of a contingent fee matter, the lawyer shall provide the client with a written statement stating the outcome of the matter, and if there is a recovery, showing the remittance to the client and the method of its determination.

(e) In domestic relations matters to which Part 1400 of the joint rules of the Appellate Divisions is applicable, a lawyer shall resolve fee disputes by arbitration at the election of the client.

## § 1200.12.  Division of Fees Among Lawyers.

(a) A lawyer shall not divide a fee for legal services with another lawyer who is not a partner in or associate of the lawyer's law firm or law office, unless:

(1) The client consents to employment of the other lawyer after a full disclosure that a division of fees will be made.

(2) The division is in proportion to the services performed by each lawyer or, by a writing given to the client, each lawyer assumes joint responsibility for the representation.

(3) The total fee of the lawyers does not exceed reasonable compensation for all legal services they rendered the client.

(b) This disciplinary rule does not prohibit payment to a former partner or associate pursuant to a separation or retirement agreement.

## § 1200.13.  Agreements Restricting the Practice of a Lawyer.

(a) A lawyer shall not be a party to or participate in a partnership or employment agreement with another lawyer that restricts the right of a lawyer to practice law after the termination of a relationship created by the agreement, except as a condition to payment of retirement benefits.

(b) In connection with the settlement of a controversy or suit, a lawyer shall not enter into an agreement that restricts the right of a lawyer to practice law.

## § 1200.14.  Acceptance of Employment.

(a) A lawyer shall not accept employment on behalf of a person if the lawyer knows or it is obvious that such person wishes to:

(1) Bring a legal action, conduct a defense, or assert a position in litigation, or otherwise have steps taken for such person merely for the purpose of harassing or maliciously injuring any person.

(2) Present a claim or defense in litigation that is not warranted under existing law, unless it can be supported by good faith argument for an extension, modification, or reversal of existing law.

## § 1200.15.  Withdrawal from Employment.

(a) In general.

(1) If permission for withdrawal from employment is required by the rules of a tribunal, a lawyer shall not withdraw from employment in a proceeding before that tribunal without its permission.

(2) Even when withdrawal is otherwise permitted or required under section 1200.15(a)(1), (b) or (c), a lawyer shall not withdraw from employment until the lawyer has taken steps to the extent reasonably practicable to avoid foreseeable prejudice to the rights of the client, including giving due notice to the client, allowing time for employment of other counsel, delivering to the client all papers and property to which the client is entitled and complying with applicable laws and rules.

(3) A lawyer who withdraws from employment shall refund promptly any part of a fee paid in advance that has not been earned.

(b) Mandatory withdrawal.

A lawyer representing a client before a tribunal, with its permission if required by its rules, shall withdraw from employment, and a lawyer representing a client in other matters shall withdraw from employment, if:

(1) The lawyer knows or it is obvious that the client is bringing the legal action, conducting the defense, or asserting a position in the litigation, or is otherwise having steps taken, merely for the purpose of harassing or maliciously injuring any person.

(2) The lawyer knows or it is obvious that continued employment will result in violation of a disciplinary rule.

(3) The lawyer's mental or physical condition renders it unreasonably difficult to carry out the employment effectively.

App Pract Provs

(4) The lawyer is discharged by his or her client.

(c) Permissive withdrawal.

Except as stated in section 1200.15(a) of this Part, a lawyer may withdraw from representing a client if withdrawal can be accomplished without material adverse effect on the interests of the client, or if:

(1) The client:

(i) Insists upon presenting a claim or defense that is not warranted under existing law and cannot be supported by good faith argument for an extension, modification, or reversal of existing law.

(ii) Persists in a course of action involving the lawyer's services that the lawyer reasonably believes is criminal or fraudulent.

(iii) Insists that the lawyer pursue a course of conduct which is illegal or prohibited under the disciplinary rules.

(iv) By other conduct renders it unreasonably difficult for the lawyer to carry out employment effectively.

(v) Insists, in a matter not pending before a tribunal, that the lawyer engage in conduct which is contrary to the judgment and advice of the lawyer but not prohibited under the disciplinary rules.

(vi) Deliberately disregards an agreement or obligation to the lawyer as to expenses or fees.

(vii) Has used the lawyer's services to perpetrate a crime or fraud.

(2) The lawyer's continued employment is likely to result in a violation of a disciplinary rule.

(3) The lawyer's inability to work with co-counsel indicates that the best interests of the client likely will be served by withdrawal.

(4) The lawyer's mental or physical condition renders it difficult for the lawyer to carry out the employment effectively.

(5) The lawyer's client knowingly and freely assents to termination of the employment.

(6) The lawyer believes in good faith, in a proceeding pending before a tribunal, that the tribunal will find the existence of other good cause for withdrawal.

## § 1200.16.   Aiding Unauthorized Practice of Law.

(a) A lawyer shall not aid a non-lawyer in the unauthorized practice of law.

(b) A lawyer shall not practice law in a jurisdiction where to do so would be in violation of regulations of the profession in that jurisdiction.

## § 1200.17.  Dividing Legal Fees With a Nonlawyer.

(a) A lawyer or law firm shall not share legal fees with a nonlawyer, except that:

(1) An agreement by a lawyer with his or her firm, partner, or associate may provide for the payment of money, over a reasonable period of time after the lawyer's death, to the lawyer's estate or to one or more specified persons.

(2) A lawyer who undertakes to complete unfinished legal business of a deceased lawyer may pay to the estate of the deceased lawyer that proportion of the total compensation which fairly represents the services rendered by the deceased lawyer.

(3) A lawyer or law firm may include non-lawyer employees in a retirement plan, even though the plan is based in whole or in part on a profit-sharing arrangement.

## § 1200.18.  Forming a Partnership with a Nonlawyer.

(a) A lawyer shall not form a partnership with a nonlawyer if any of the activities of the partnership consist of the practice of law.

## § 1200.19.  Preservation of Confidences and Secrets of a Client.

(a) *Confidence* refers to information protected by the attorney-client privilege under applicable law, and *secret* refers to other information gained in the professional relationship that the client has requested be held inviolate or the disclosure of which would be embarrassing or would be likely to be detrimental to the client.

(b) Except when permitted under section 1200.19(c) of this Part, a lawyer shall not knowingly:

(1) Reveal a confidence or secret of a client;

(2) Use a confidence or secret of a client to the disadvantage of the client; and

(3) Use a confidence or secret of a client for the advantage of the lawyer or of a third person, unless the client consents after full disclosure.

(c) A lawyer may reveal:

(1) Confidences or secrets with the consent of the client or clients affected, but only after a full disclosure to them.

(2) Confidences or secrets when permitted under disciplinary rules or required by law or court order.

(3) The intention of a client to commit a crime and the information necessary to prevent the crime.

(4) Confidences or secrets necessary to establish or collect the lawyer's fee or to defend the lawyer or his or her employees or associates against an accusation of wrongful conduct.

(5) Confidences or secrets to the extent implicit in withdrawing a written or oral opinion or representation previously given by the lawyer and believed by the lawyer still to be relied upon by a third person where the lawyer has discovered that the opinion or representation was based on materially inaccurate information or is being used to further a crime or fraud.

(d) A lawyer shall exercise reasonable care to prevent his or her employees, associates, and others whose services are utilized by the lawyer from disclosing or using confidences or secrets of a client, except that a lawyer may reveal the information allowed by subdivision(c) of this section through an employee.

## § 1200.20.  Refusing Employment When the Interests of the Lawyer May Impair Independent Professional Judgment.

(a) Except with the consent of the client after full disclosure, a lawyer shall not accept employment if the exercise of professional judgment on behalf of the client will be or reasonably may be affected by the lawyer's own financial, business, property, or personal interests.

(b) A lawyer shall not act, or accept employment that contemplates the lawyer's acting, as an advocate before any tribunal if the lawyer knows or it is obvious that the lawyer ought to be called as a witness on behalf of the client, except that the lawyer may act as an advocate and also testify:

(1) If the testimony will relate solely to an uncontested issue.

(2) If the testimony will relate solely to a matter of formality and there is no reason to believe that substantial evidence will be offered in opposition to the testimony.

(3) If the testimony will relate solely to the nature and value of legal services rendered in the case by the lawyer or the lawyer's firm to the client.

(4) As to any matter, if disqualification as an advocate would work a substantial hardship on the client because of the distinctive value of the lawyer as counsel in the particular case.

(c) Neither a lawyer nor the lawyer's firm shall accept employment in contemplated or pending litigation if the lawyer knows or it is obvious that the lawyer or another lawyer in the lawyer's firm may be called as a witness other than on behalf of the client, and it is apparent that the testimony would or might be prejudicial to the client.

### § 1200.21. Withdrawal as Counsel When the Lawyer Becomes a Witness.

(a) If, after undertaking employment in contemplated or pending litigation, a lawyer learns or it is obvious that the lawyer ought to be called as a witness on behalf of the client, the lawyer shall withdraw as an advocate before the tribunal, except that the lawyer may continue as an advocate and may testify in the circumstances enumerated in section 1200.20(b)(1) through (4) of this Part.

(b) If, after undertaking employment in contemplated or pending litigation, a lawyer learns or it is obvious that the lawyer or a lawyer in his or her firm may be called as a witness other than on behalf of the client, the lawyer may continue the representation until it is apparent that the testimony is or may be prejudicial to the client at which point the lawyer and the firm must withdraw from acting as an advocate before the tribunal.

### § 1200.22. Avoiding Acquisition of Interest in Litigation.

(a) A lawyer shall not acquire a proprietary interest in the cause of action or subject matter of litigation he or she is conducting for a client, except that the lawyer may:

(1) Acquire a lien granted by law to secure the lawyer's fee or expenses.

(2) Except as provided in section 1200.11(c)(2) or (3) of this Part, contract with a client for a reasonable contingent fee in a civil case.

(b) While representing a client in connection with contemplated or pending litigation, a lawyer shall not advance or guarantee financial assistance to the client, except that:

(1) A lawyer may advance or guarantee the expenses of litigation, including court costs, expenses of investigation, expenses of medical examination, and costs of obtaining and presenting evidence, provided the client remains ultimately liable for such expenses.

(2) Unless prohibited by law or rule of court, a lawyer representing an indigent client on a pro bono basis may pay court costs and reasonable expenses of litigation on behalf of the client.

### § 1200.23. Limiting Business Relations with a Client.

(a) A lawyer shall not enter into a business transaction with a client if they have differing interests therein and if the client expects the lawyer to exercise professional judgment therein for the protection of the client, unless the client has consented after full disclosure.

(b) Prior to conclusion of all aspects of the matter giving rise to employment, a lawyer shall not enter into any arrangement or understanding with a client

App Pract Provs

or a prospective client by which the lawyer acquires an interest in literary or media rights with respect to the subject matter of the employment or proposed employment.

## § 1200.24.  Refusing to Accept or Continue Employment if the Interests of Another Client May Impair the Independent Professional Judgment of the Lawyer.

(a) A lawyer shall decline proffered employment if the exercise of independent professional judgment in behalf of a client will be or is likely to be adversely affected by the acceptance of the proffered employment, or if it would be likely to involve the lawyer in representing differing interests, except to the extent permitted under subdivision (c) of this section.

(b) A lawyer shall not continue multiple employment if the exercise of independent professional judgment in behalf of a client will be or is likely to be adversely affected by the lawyer's representation of another client, or if it would be likely to involve the lawyer in representing differing interests, except to the extent permitted under subdivision (c) of this section.

(c) In the situations covered by subdivisions (a) and (b) of this section, a lawyer may represent multiple clients if it is obvious that the lawyer can adequately represent the interest of each and if each consents to the representation after full disclosure of the possible effect of such representation on the exercise of the lawyer's independent professional judgment on behalf of each.

(d) While lawyers are associated in a law firm, none of them shall knowingly accept or continue employment when any one of them practicing alone would be prohibited from doing so under section 1200.20(a), 1200.24(a), (b) or (c), 1200.27 or 1200.45(b) of this Part except as otherwise provided therein.

## § 1200.25.  Settling Similar Claims of Clients.

(a) A lawyer who represents two or more clients shall not make or participate in the making of an aggregate settlement of the claims of or against the clients, unless each client has consented to the settlement after being advised of the existence and nature of all the claims involved in the proposed settlement, of the total amount of the settlement, and of the participation of each person in the settlement.

## § 1200.26.  Avoiding Influence by Others than the Client.

(a) Except with the consent of the client after full disclosure a lawyer shall not:

(1) Accept compensation for legal services from one other than the client.

(2) Accept from one other than the client any thing of value related to his or her representation of or employment by the client.

(b) A lawyer shall not permit a person who recommends, employs, or pays the lawyer to render legal service for another to direct or regulate his or her professional judgment in rendering such legal services.

(c) A lawyer shall not practice with or in the form of a professional corporation or association authorized to practice law for a profit, if:

(1) A nonlawyer owns any interest therein, except that a fiduciary representative of the estate of a lawyer may hold the stock or interest of the lawyer for a reasonable time during administration;

(2) A nonlawyer is a corporate director or officer thereof; or

(3) A nonlawyer has the right to direct or control the professional judgment of a lawyer.

### § 1200.27.   Conflict of Interest—Former Client.

(a) Except with the consent of a former client after full disclosure a lawyer who has represented the former client in a matter shall not:

(1) Thereafter represent another person in the same or a substantially related matter in which that person's interests are materially adverse to the interests of the former client.

(2) Use any confidences or secrets of the former client except as permitted by 1200.19(c) or when the confidence or secret has become generally known.

### § 1200.28.   Conflict of Interest—Organization as Client.

(a) When a lawyer employed or retained by an organization is dealing with the organization's directors, officers, employees, members, shareholders or other constituents, and it appears that the organization's interests may differ from those of the constituents with whom the lawyer is dealing, the lawyer shall explain that the lawyer is the lawyer for the organization and not for any of the constituents.

### § 1200.29.   Membership in Legal Services Organization.

(a) A lawyer may serve as a director, officer or member of a not-for-profit legal services organization, apart from the law firm in which the lawyer practices, notwithstanding that the organization serves persons having interests that differ from those of a client of the lawyer or the lawyer's firm, provided that the lawyer shall not knowingly participate in a decision or action of the organization:

(1) If participating in the decision or action would be incompatible with the lawyer's duty of loyalty to a client under Canon 5; or

(2) Where the decision or action could have a material adverse effect on the representation of a client of the organization whose interests differ from those of a client of the lawyer or the lawyer's firm.

App Pract Provs

## § 1200.30.  Failing to Act Competently.

(a) A lawyer shall not:

(1) Handle a legal matter which the lawyer knows or should know that he or she is not competent to handle, without associating with a lawyer who is competent to handle it.

(2) Handle a legal matter without preparation adequate in the circumstances.

(3) Neglect a legal matter entrusted to the lawyer.

## § 1200.31.  Limiting Liability to Client.

(a) A lawyer shall not seek, by contract or other means, to limit prospectively the lawyer's individual liability to a client for malpractice, or, without first advising that person that independent representation is appropriate in connection therewith, to settle a claim for such liability with an unrepresented client or former client.

## § 1200.32.  Representing a Client Zealously.

(a) A lawyer shall not intentionally:

(1) Fail to seek the lawful objectives of the client through reasonably available means permitted by law and the disciplinary rules, except as provided by subdivision (b) of this section. A lawyer does not violate this disciplinary rule, however, by acceding to reasonable requests of opposing counsel which do not prejudice the rights of the client, by being punctual in fulfilling all professional commitments, by avoiding offensive tactics, or by treating with courtesy and consideration all persons involved in the legal process.

(2) Fail to carry out a contract of employment entered into with a client for professional services, but the lawyer may withdraw as permitted under sections 1200.15, 1200.21 and 1200.24 of this Part.

(3) Prejudice or damage the client during the course of the professional relationship, except as required under section 1200.33 of this Part.

(b) In the representation of a client, a lawyer may:

(1) Where permissible, exercise professional judgment to waive or fail to assert a right or position of the client.

(2) Refuse to aid or participate in conduct that the lawyer believes to be unlawful, even though there is some support for an argument that the conduct is legal.

## § 1200.33.  Representing a Client Within the Bounds of the Law.

(a) In the representation of a client, a lawyer shall not:

(1) File a suit, assert a position, conduct a defense, delay a trial, or take other action on behalf of the client when the lawyer knows or when it is obvious that such action would serve merely to harass or maliciously injury another.

(2) Knowingly advance a claim or defense that is unwarranted under existing law, except that the lawyer may advance such claim or defense if it can be supported by good faith argument for an extension, modification, or reversal of existing law.

(3) Conceal or knowingly fail to disclose that which the lawyer is required by law to reveal.

(4) Knowingly use perjured testimony or false evidence.

(5) Knowingly make a false statement of law or fact.

(6) Participate in the creation or preservation of evidence when the lawyer knows or it is obvious that the evidence is false.

(7) Counsel or assist the client in conduct that the lawyer knows to be illegal or fraudulent.

(8) Knowingly engage in other illegal conduct or conduct contrary to a disciplinary rule.

(b) A lawyer who receives information clearly establishing that:

(1) The client has, in the course of the representation, perpetrated a fraud upon a person or tribunal shall promptly call upon the client to rectify the same, and if the client refuses or is unable to do so, the lawyer shall reveal the fraud to the affected person or tribunal, except when the information is protected as a confidence or secret.

(2) A person other than the client has perpetrated a fraud upon a tribunal shall promptly reveal the fraud to the tribunal.

## § 1200.34.  Performing the Duty of Public Prosecutor or Other Government Lawyer.

(a) A public prosecutor or other government lawyer shall not institute or cause to be instituted criminal charges when he or she knows or it is obvious that the charges are not supported by probable cause.

(b) A public prosecutor or other government lawyer in criminal litigation shall make timely disclosure to counsel for the defendant, or to a defendant who has no counsel, of the existence of evidence, known to the prosecutor or other government lawyer, that tends to negate the guilt of the accused, mitigate the degree of the offense or reduce the punishment.

## § 1200.35.  Communicating With One Of Adverse Interest.

(a) During the course of the representation of a client a lawyer shall not:

(1) Communicate or cause another to communicate on the subject of the representation with a party the lawyer knows to be represented by a lawyer in that matter unless the lawyer has the prior consent of the lawyer representing such other party or is authorized by law to do so.

(2) Give advice to a person who is not represented by a lawyer, other than the advice to secure counsel, if the interests of such person are or have a reasonable possibility of being in conflict with the interests of the lawyer's client.

## § 1200.36.   Threatening Criminal Prosecution.

(a) A lawyer shall not present, participate in presenting, or threaten to present criminal charges solely to obtain an advantage in a civil matter.

## § 1200.37.   Trial Conduct.

(a) A lawyer shall not disregard or advise the client to disregard a standing rule of a tribunal or a ruling of a tribunal made in the course of a proceeding, but the lawyer may take appropriate steps in good faith to test the validity of such rule or ruling.

(b) In presenting a matter to a tribunal, a lawyer shall disclose:

(1) Controlling legal authority known to the lawyer to be directly adverse to the position of the client and which is not disclosed by opposing counsel.

(2) Unless privileged or irrelevant, the identities of the clients the lawyer represents and of the persons who employed the lawyer.

(c) In appearing as a lawyer before a tribunal, a lawyer shall not:

(1) State or allude to any matter that he or she has no reasonable basis to believe is relevant to the case or that will not be supported by admissible evidence.

(2) Ask any question that he or she has no reasonable basis to believe is relevant to the case and that is intended to degrade a witness or other person.

(3) Assert personal knowledge of the facts in issue, except when testifying as a witness.

(4) Assert a personal opinion as to the justness of a cause, as to the credibility of a witness, as to the culpability of a civil litigant, or as to the guilt or innocence of an accused; but the lawyer may argue, upon analysis of the evidence, for any position or conclusion with respect to the matters stated herein.

(5) Fail to comply with known local customs of courtesy or practice of the bar or a particular tribunal without giving to opposing counsel timely notice of the intent not to comply.

(6) Engage in undignified or discourteous conduct which is degrading to a tribunal.

(7) Intentionally or habitually violate any established rule of procedure or of evidence.

## § 1200.38.   Trial Publicity.

(a) A lawyer participating in or associated with a criminal or civil matter shall not make an extrajudicial statement that a reasonable person would expect to be disseminated by means of public communication if the lawyer knows or reasonably should know that it will have a substantial likelihood of materially prejudicing an adjudicative proceeding.

(b) A statement ordinarily is likely to prejudice materially an adjudicative proceeding when it refers to a civil matter triable to a jury, a criminal matter, or any other proceeding that could result in incarceration, and the statement relates to:

(1) The character, credibility, reputation or criminal record of a party, suspect in a criminal investigation or witness, or the identity of a witness, or the expected testimony of a party or witness.

(2) In a criminal case or proceeding that could result in incarceration, the possibility of a plea of guilty to the offense or the existence or contents of any confession, admission, or statement given by a defendant or suspect or that person's refusal or failure to make a statement.

(3) The performance or results of any examination or test or the refusal or failure of a person to submit to an examination or test, or the identity or nature of physical evidence expected to be presented.

(4) Any opinion as to the guilt or innocence of a defendant or suspect in a criminal case or proceeding that could result in incarceration.

(5) Information the lawyer knows or reasonably should know is likely to be inadmissible as evidence in a trial and would if disclosed create a substantial risk of prejudicing an impartial trial.

(6) The fact that a defendant has been charged with a crime, unless there is included therein a statement explaining that the charge is merely an accusation and that the defendant is presumed innocent until and unless proven guilty.

(c) Provided that the statement complies with subdivision (a) of this section, a lawyer involved with the investigation or litigation of a matter may state the following without elaboration:

(1) The general nature of the claim or defense.

(2) The information contained in a public record.

(3) That an investigation of the matter is in progress.

(4) The scheduling or result of any step in litigation.

(5) A request for assistance in obtaining evidence and information necessary thereto.

App Pract Provs

(6) A warning of a danger concerning the behavior of a person involved, when there is reason to believe that there exists the likelihood of substantial harm to an individual or to the public interest.

(7) In a criminal case:

(i) The identity, age, residence, occupation and family status of the accused.

(ii) If the accused has not been apprehended, information necessary to aid in apprehension of that person.

(iii) The fact, time and place of arrest, resistance, pursuit, use of weapons, and a description of physical evidence seized, other than as contained only in a confession, admission, or statement.

(iv) The identity of investigating and arresting officers or agencies and the length of the investigation.

## § 1200.39.  Communication with or Investigation of Jurors.

(a) Before the trial of a case a lawyer connected therewith shall not communicate with or cause another to communicate with anyone the lawyer knows to be a member of the venire from which the jury will be selected for the trial of the case.

(b) During the trial of a case:

(1) A lawyer connected therewith shall not communicate with or cause another to communicate with any member of the jury.

(2) A lawyer who is not connected therewith shall not communicate with or cause another to communicate with a juror concerning the case.

(c) Subdivisions (a) and (b) of this section do not prohibit a lawyer from communicating with members of the venire or jurors in the course of official proceedings.

(d) After discharge of the jury from further consideration of a case with which the lawyer was connected, the lawyer shall not ask questions of or make comments to a member of that jury that are calculated merely to harass or embarrass the juror or to influence the juror's actions in future jury service.

(e) A lawyer shall not conduct or cause, by financial support or otherwise, another to conduct a vexatious or harassing investigation of either a member of the venire or a juror.

(f) All restrictions imposed by this section upon a lawyer also apply to communications with or investigations of members of a family of a member of the venire or a juror.

(g) A lawyer shall reveal promptly to the court improper conduct by a member of the venire or a juror, or by another toward a member of the venire or a juror or a member of his or her family of which the lawyer has knowledge.

### § 1200.40.   Contact with Witnesses.

(a) A lawyer shall not suppress any evidence that the lawyer or the client has a legal obligation to reveal or produce.

(b) A lawyer shall not advise or cause a person to hide or to leave the jurisdiction of a tribunal for the purpose of making the person unavailable as a witness therein.

(c) A lawyer shall not pay, offer to pay, or acquiesce in the payment of compensation to a witness contingent upon the content of his or her testimony or the outcome of the case. But a lawyer may advance, guarantee, or acquiesce in the payment of:

(1) Expenses reasonably incurred by a witness in attending or testifying.

(2) Reasonable compensation to a witness for the loss of time in attending or testifying.

(3) A reasonable fee for the professional services of an expert witness.

### § 1200.41.   Contact with Officials.

(a) A lawyer shall not give or lend anything of value to a judge, official, or employee of a tribunal except as permitted by section C(4) of Canon 5 of the Code of Judicial Conduct, but a lawyer may make a contribution to the campaign fund of a candidate for judicial office in conformity with section B(2) under Canon 7 of the Code of Judicial Conduct.

(b) In an adversary proceeding, a lawyer shall not communicate, or cause another to communicate, as to the merits of the cause with a judge or an official before whom the proceeding is pending, except:

(1) in the course of official proceedings in the cause.

(2) in writing if the lawyer promptly delivers a copy of the writing to opposing counsel or to an adverse party who is not represented by a lawyer.

(3) orally upon adequate notice to opposing counsel or to an adverse party who is not represented by a lawyer.

(4) as otherwise authorized by law, or by section A(4) under Canon 3 of the Code of Judicial Conduct.

### § 1200.42.   Action as a Public Official.

(a) A lawyer who holds public office shall not:

(1) Use the public position to obtain, or attempt to obtain, a special advantage in legislative matters for the lawyer or for a client under circumstances where the lawyer knows or it is obvious that such action is not in the public interest.

(2) Use the public position to influence, or attempt to influence, a tribunal to act in favor of the lawyer or of a client.

(3) Accept any thing of value from any person when the lawyer knows or it is obvious that the offer is for the purpose of influencing the lawyer's action as a public official.

## § 1200.43.  Statements Concerning Judges and Other Adjudicatory Officers.

(a) A lawyer shall not knowingly make false statements of fact concerning the qualifications of a candidate for election or appointment to a judicial office.

(b) A lawyer shall not knowingly make false accusations against a judge or other adjudicatory officer.

## § 1200.44.  Lawyer Candidate for Judicial Office.

(a) A lawyer who is a candidate for judicial office shall comply with the applicable provisions of Canon 7 of the Code of Judicial Conduct.

## § 1200.45.  Avoiding Even the Appearance of Impropriety.

(a) A lawyer shall not accept private employment in a matter upon the merits of which the lawyer has acted in a judicial capacity.

(b) Except as law may otherwise expressly permit:

(1) A lawyer shall not represent a private client in connection with a matter in which the lawyer participated personally and substantially as a public officer or employee, and no lawyer in a firm with which that lawyer is associated may knowingly undertake or continue representation in such a matter unless:

(i) The disqualified lawyer is effectively screened from any participation, direct or indirect, including discussion, in the matter and is apportioned no part of the fee therefrom; and

(ii) There are no other circumstances in the particular representation that create an appearance of impropriety.

(2) A lawyer having information that the lawyer knows is confidential government information about a person, acquired when the lawyer was a public officer or employee, may not represent a private client whose interests are adverse to that person in a matter in which the information could be used to the material disadvantage of that person. A firm with which that lawyer is associated may knowingly undertake or continue representation in the matter only if the disqualified lawyer is effectively screened from any participation, direct or indirect, including discussion, in the matter and is apportioned no part of the fee therefrom.

(3) A lawyer serving as a public officer or employee shall not:

(i) Participate in a matter in which the lawyer participated personally and substantially while in private practice or non-governmental employment, unless under applicable law no one is, or by lawful delegation may be, authorized to act in the lawyer's stead in the matter; or

(ii) Negotiate for private employment with any person who is involved as a party or as attorney for a party in a matter in which the lawyer is participating personally and substantially.

(c) A lawyer shall not state or imply that the lawyer is able to influence improperly or upon irrelevant grounds any tribunal, legislative body, or public official.

(d) A lawyer related to another lawyer as parent, child, sibling or spouse shall not represent in any matter a client whose interests differ from those of another party to the matter who the lawyer knows is represented by the other lawyer unless the client consents to the representation after full disclosure and the lawyer concludes that the lawyer can adequately represent the interests of the client.

### § 1200.46.  Preserving Identity of Funds and Property of Others; Fiduciary Responsibility; Maintenance of Bank Accounts; Recordkeeping; Examination of Records.

(a) *Prohibition against commingling.*

A lawyer in possession of any funds or other property belonging to another person, where such possession is incident to his or her practice of law, is a fiduciary, and must not commingle such property with his or her own.

(b) *Separate accounts.*

(1) A lawyer who is in possession of funds belonging to another person incident to the lawyer's practice of law, shall maintain such funds in a banking institution within the State of New York which agrees to provide dishonored check reports in accordance with the provisions of Part 1300 of these rules (22 NYCRR Part 1300). "Banking institution" means a state or national bank, trust company, savings bank, savings and loan association or credit union. Such funds shall be maintained, in the lawyer's own name, or in the name of a firm of lawyers of which he or she is a member, or in the name of the lawyer or firm of lawyers by whom he or she is employed, in a special account or accounts, separate from any business or personal accounts of the lawyer or lawyer's firm, and separate from any accounts which the lawyer may maintain as executor, guardian, trustee or receiver, or in any other fiduciary capacity, into which special account or accounts all funds held in escrow or otherwise entrusted to the lawyer or firm shall be deposited; provided, however, that such funds may be maintained in a banking institution located outside the State of New York if such banking institution complies with such Part 1300, and the lawyer has obtained the prior written approval of the person to whom such funds belong which specifies the name and address of the office or branch of the banking institution where such funds are to be maintained.

App Pract Provs

(2) A lawyer or the lawyer's firm shall identify the special bank account or accounts required by subdivision (b)(1) of this section as an "Attorney Special Account," or "Attorney Trust Account," or "Attorney Escrow Account," and shall obtain checks and deposit slips that bear such title. Such title may be accompanied by such other descriptive language as the lawyer may deem appropriate, provided that such additional language distinguishes such special account or accounts from other bank accounts that are maintained by the lawyer or the lawyer's firm.

(3) Funds reasonably sufficient to maintain the account or to pay account charges may be deposited therein.

(4) Funds belonging in part to a client or third person and in part presently or potentially to the lawyer or law firm shall be kept in such special account or accounts, but the portion belonging to the lawyer or law firm may be withdrawn when due unless the right of the lawyer or law firm to receive it is disputed by the client or third person, in which event the disputed portion shall not be withdrawn until the dispute is finally resolved.

(c) *Notification of receipt of property; safekeeping; rendering accounts; payment or delivery of property.*

A lawyer shall:

(1) promptly notify a client or third person of the receipt of funds, securities, or other properties in which the client or third person has an interest.

(2) identify and label securities and properties of a client or third person promptly upon receipt and place them in a safe deposit box or other place of safekeeping as soon as practicable.

(3) maintain complete records of all funds, securities, and other properties of a client or third person coming into the possession of the lawyer and render appropriate accounts to the client or third person regarding them.

(4) promptly pay or deliver to the client or third person as requested by the client or third person the funds, securities, or other properties in the possession of the lawyer which the client or third person is entitled to receive.

(d) *Required bookkeeping records.*

A lawyer shall maintain for seven years after the events which they record:

(1) the records of all deposits in and withdrawals from the special accounts specified in DR 9–102(B) and of any other bank account which records the operations of the lawyer's practice of law. These records shall specifically identify the date, source and description of each item deposited, as well as the date, payee and purpose of each withdrawal or disbursement.

(2) a record for special accounts, showing the source of all funds deposited in such accounts, the names of all persons for whom the funds are or were held, the amount of such funds, the description and amounts, and the names of all persons to whom such funds were disbursed.

(3) copies of all retainer and compensation agreements with clients.

(4) copies of all statements to clients or other persons showing the disbursement of funds to them or on their behalf.

(5) copies of all bills rendered to clients.

(6) copies of all records showing payment to lawyers, investigators or other persons, not in the lawyer's regular employ, for services rendered or performed.

(7) copies of all retainer and closing statements filed with the Office of Court Administration.

(8) all checkbooks and checkstubs, bank statements, prenumbered cancelled checks and duplicate deposit slips with respect to the special account specified in DR 9–102(B) and any other bank account which records the operations of the lawyer's practice of law.

Lawyers shall make accurate entries of all financial transactions in their records of receipts and disbursements, in their special accounts, in their ledger books or similar records, and in any other books of account kept by them in the regular course of their practice, which entries shall be made at or near the time of the act, condition or event recorded.

(e) *Authorized signatories.*

All special account withdrawals shall be made only to a named payee and not to cash. Such withdrawals shall be made by check or, with the prior written approval of the party entitled to the proceeds, by bank transfer.

Only an attorney admitted to practice law in New York State shall be an authorized signatory of a special account.

(f)(1) *Missing clients.*

Whenever any sum of money is payable to a client and the lawyer is unable to locate the client, the lawyer shall apply to the court in which the action was brought if in the unified court system, or, if no action was commenced in the unified court system, to the Supreme Court in the county in which the lawyer maintains an office for the practice of law, for an order directing payment to the lawyer of any fees and disbursements that are owed by the client and the balance, if any, to the Lawyers' Fund for Client Protection for safeguarding and disbursement to persons who are entitled thereto.

(2) *Designation of successor signatories.*

(i) Upon the death of a lawyer who was the sole signatory on an attorney trust, escrow or special account, an application may be made to the Supreme Court for an order designating a successor signatory for such trust, escrow or special account who shall be a member of the bar in good standing and admitted to the practice of law in New York State.

(ii) An application to designate a successor signatory shall be made to the Supreme Court in the judicial district in which the deceased lawyer maintained

App Pract Provs

an office for the practice of law. The application may be made by the legal representative of the deceased lawyer's estate; a lawyer who was affiliated with the deceased lawyer in the practice of law; any person who has a beneficial interest in such trust, escrow or special account; an officer of a city or county bar association; or counsel for an attorney disciplinary committee. No lawyer may charge a legal fee for assisting with an application to designate a successor signatory pursuant to this rule.

(iii) The Supreme Court may designate a successor signatory and may direct the safeguarding of funds from such trust, escrow or special account, and the disbursement of such funds to persons who are entitled thereto, and may order that funds in such account be deposited with the Lawyers' Fund for Client Protection for safeguarding and disbursement to persons who are entitled thereto.

(g) *Dissolution of a firm.*

Upon the dissolution of any firm of lawyers, the former partners or members shall make appropriate arrangements for the maintenance by one of them or by a successor firm of the records specified in DR 9–102(D). In the absence of agreement on such arrangements, any partner or former partner or member of a firm in dissolution may apply to the Appellate Division in which the principal office of the law firm is located or its designee for direction and such direction shall be binding upon all partners, former partners or members.

(h) *Availability of bookkeeping records; records subject to production in disciplinary investigations and proceedings.*

The financial records required by this Disciplinary Rule shall be located, or made available, at the principal New York State office of the lawyers subject hereto and any such records shall be produced in response to a notice or subpoena *duces tecum* issued in connection with a complaint before or any investigation by the appropriate grievance or departmental disciplinary committee, or shall be produced at the direction of the appropriate Appellate Division before any person designated by it. All books and records produced pursuant to this subdivision shall be kept confidential, except for the purpose of the particular proceeding, and their contents shall not be disclosed by anyone in violation of the lawyer-client privilege.

(i) *Disciplinary action.*

A lawyer who does not maintain and keep the accounts and records as specified and required by this Part, or who does not produce any such records pursuant to this Part, shall be deemed in violation of these rules and shall be subject to disciplinary proceedings.

## Part 1300. Dishonored Check Reporting Rules for Attorney Special, Trust and Escrow Accounts

### § 1300.1 Dishonored Check Reports.

(a) Special bank accounts required by Disciplinary Rule 9–102 (22 NYCRR 1200.46) shall be maintained only in banking institutions which have agreed to provide dishonored check reports in accordance with the provisions of this section.

(b) An agreement to provide dishonored check reports shall be filed with the Lawyers' Fund for Client Protection, which shall maintain a central registry of all banking institutions which have been approved in accordance with this section, and the current status of each such agreement. The agreement shall apply to all branches of each banking institution that provides special bank accounts for attorneys engaged in the practice of law in this state, and shall not be cancelled by a banking institution except on thirty days prior written notice to the Lawyers' Fund for Client Protection.

(c) A dishonored check report by a banking institution shall be required whenever a properly payable instrument is presented against an attorney special, trust or escrow account which contains insufficient available funds, and the banking institution dishonors the instrument for that reason. A "properly payable instrument" means an instrument which, if presented in the normal course of business, is in a form requiring payment under the laws of the State of New York.

(d) A dishonored check report shall be substantially in the form of the notice of dishonor which the banking institution customarily forwards to its customer, and may include a photocopy or a computer-generated duplicate of such notice.

(e) Dishonored check reports shall be mailed to the Lawyers' Fund for Client Protection, 55 Elk Street, Albany, New York 12210, within five banking days after the date of presentment against insufficient available funds.

(f) The Lawyers' Fund for Client Protection shall hold each dishonored check report for ten business days to enable the banking institution to withdraw a report provided by inadvertence or mistake; except that the curing of an insufficiency of available funds by a lawyer or law firm by the deposit of additional funds shall not constitute reason for withdrawing a dishonored check report.

(g) After holding the dishonored check report for ten business days, the Lawyers' Fund for Client Protection shall forward it to the attorney disciplinary committee for the judicial department or district having jurisdiction over the account holder, as indicated by the law office or other address on the report, for such inquiry and action that attorney disciplinary committee deems appropriate.

(h) Every lawyer admitted to the Bar of the State of New York shall be deemed to have consented to the dishonored check reporting requirements of this section.

App Pract Provs

Lawyers and law firms shall promptly notify their banking institutions of existing or new attorney special, trust, or escrow accounts for the purpose of facilitating the implementation and administration of the provisions of this section.

## Part 1400. Procedure for Attorneys in Domestic Relations Matters

### § 1400.1.  Application.

This Part shall apply to all attorneys who, on or after November 30, 1993, undertake to represent a client in a claim, action or proceeding, or preliminary to the filing of a claim, action or proceeding, in either Supreme Court or Family Court, or in any court of appellate jurisdiction, for divorce, separation, annulment, custody, visitation, maintenance, child support, or alimony, or to enforce or modify a judgment or order in connection with any such claims, actions or proceedings. This Part shall not apply to attorneys representing clients without compensation paid by the client, except that where the client is other than a minor, the provisions of section 1400.2 shall apply to the extent they are not applicable to compensation.

### § 1400.2.  Statement of Client's Rights and Responsibilities

An attorney shall provide a prospective client with a statement of client's rights and responsibilities, in a form prescribed by the Appellate Divisions, at the initial conference and prior to the signing of a written retainer agreement. If the attorney is not being paid a fee from the client for the work to be performed on the particular case, the attorney may delete from the statement those provisions dealing with fees. The attorney shall obtain a signed acknowledgement of receipt from the client. The statement shall contain the following:

### STATEMENT OF CLIENT'S RIGHTS AND RESPONSIBILITIES

Your attorney is providing you with this document to inform you of what you, as a client, are entitled to by law or by custom. To help prevent any misunderstanding between you and your attorney please read this document carefully.

If you ever have any questions about these rights, or about the way your case is being handled, do not hesitate to ask your attorney. He or she should be readily available to represent your best interests and keep you informed about your case.

An attorney may not refuse to represent you on the basis of race, creed, color, sex, sexual orientation, age, national origin or disability.

You are entitled to an attorney who will be capable of handling your case; show you courtesy and consideration at all times; represent you zealously; and preserve your confidences and secrets that are revealed in the course of the relationship.

You are entitled to a written retainer agreement which must set forth, in plain language, the nature of the relationship and the details of the fee arrangement. At your request, and before you sign the agreement, you are entitled to have your attorney clarify in writing any of its terms, or include additional provisions.

You are entitled to fully understand the proposed rates and retainer fee before you sign a retainer agreement, as in any other contract.

You may refuse to enter into any fee arrangement that you find unsatisfactory.

Your attorney may not request a fee that is contingent on the securing of a divorce or on the amount of money or property that may be obtained.

Your attorney may not request a retainer fee that is nonrefundable. That is, should you discharge your attorney, or should your attorney withdraw from the case, before the retainer is used up, he or she is entitled to be paid commensurate with the work performed on your case and any expenses, but must return the balance of the retainer to you. However, your attorney may enter into a minimum fee arrangement with you that provides for the payment of a specific amount below which the fee will not fall based upon the handling of the case to its conclusion.

You are entitled to know the approximate number of attorneys and other legal staff members who will be working on your case at any given time and what you will be charged for the services of each.

You are entitled to know in advance how you will be asked to pay legal fees and expenses, and how the retainer, if any, will be spent.

At your request, and after your attorney has had a reasonable opportunity to investigate your case, you are entitled to be given an estimate of approximate future costs of your case, which estimate shall be made in good faith but may be subject to change due to facts and circumstances affecting the case.

You are entitled to receive a written, itemized bill on a regular basis, at least every 60 days.

You are expected to review the itemized bills sent by counsel, and to raise any objections or errors in a timely manner. Time spent in discussion or explanation of bills will not be charged to you.

You are expected to be truthful in all discussions with your attorney, and to provide all relevant information and documentation to enable him or her to competently prepare your case.

You are entitled to be kept informed of the status of your case, and to be provided with copies of correspondence and documents prepared on your behalf or received from the court or your adversary.

You have the right to be present in court at the time that conferences are held.

You are entitled to make the ultimate decision on the objectives to be pursued in your case, and to make the final decision regarding the settlement of your case.

App Pract Provs

Your attorney's written retainer agreement must specify under what circumstances he or she might seek to withdraw as your attorney for nonpayment of legal fees. If an action or proceeding is pending, the court may give your attorney a "charging lien," which entitles your attorney to payment for services already rendered at the end of the case out of the proceeds of the final order or judgment.

You are under no legal obligation to sign a confession of judgment or promissory note, or to agree to a lien or mortgage on your home to cover legal fees. Your attorney's written retainer agreement must specify whether, and under what circumstances, such security may be requested. In no event may such security interest be obtained by your attorney without prior court approval and notice to your adversary. An attorney's security interest in the marital residence cannot be foreclosed against you.

You are entitled to have your attorney's best efforts exerted on your behalf, but no particular results can be guaranteed.

If you entrust money with an attorney for an escrow deposit in your case, the attorney must safeguard the escrow in a special bank account. You are entitled to a written escrow agreement, and may request that one or more interest-bearing bank accounts be used. You also are entitled to a written receipt, and a complete record concerning the escrow. When the terms of the escrow agreement have beenperformed, the attorney must promptly make payment of the escrow to all persons who are entitled to it.

In the event of a fee dispute, you may have the right to seek arbitration. Your attorney will provide you with the necessary information regarding arbitration in the event of a fee dispute, or upon your request.

Receipt Acknowledged:

. . . . . . . . . . . . . . . . . . . . . . . . . .
Attorney's signature

. . . . . . . . . . . . . . . . . . . . . . . . . .
Client's signature

. . . . . . . . . . . . . . . . . . . . . . . . . .
Date

## § 1400.3.  Written Retainer Agreement.

An attorney who undertakes to represent a party and enters into an arrangement for, charges or collects any fee from a client shall execute a written agreement with the client setting forth in plain language the terms of compensation and the nature of services to be rendered. The agreement, and any amendment thereto, shall be signed by both client and attorney, and, in actions in Supreme Court, a copy of the signed agreement shall be filed with the statement of net worth. Where substitution of counsel occurs after the filing of the net worth statement, a signed copy of the attorney's retainer agreement shall be filed with the court within 10 days of its execution. A copy of a signed amendment shall be filed within 15 days of signing. A duplicate copy of the filed agreement and any amendment shall be provided to the client. The agreement shall be subject to the provisions governing confidentiality contained in Domestic Relations Law § 235(1). The agreement shall contain the following information:

### RETAINER AGREEMENT

1. Names and addresses of the parties entering into the agreement;

2. Nature of the services to be rendered;

3. Amount of the advance retainer, if any, and what it is intended to cover;

4. Circumstances under which any portion of the advance retainer may be refunded. Should the attorney withdraw from the case or be discharged prior to the depletion of the advance retainer, the written retainer agreement shall provide how the attorney's fees and expenses are to be determined, and the remainder of the advance retainer shall be refunded to the client;

5. Client's right to cancel the agreement at any time; how the attorney's fee will be determined and paid should the client discharge the attorney at any time during the course of the representation;

6. How the attorney will be paid through the conclusion of the case after the retainer is depleted; whether the client may be asked to pay another lump sum;

7. Hourly rate of each person whose time may be charged to the client; any out-of-pocket disbursements for which the client will be required to reimburse the attorney. Any changes in such rates or fees shall be incorporated into a written agreement constituting an amendment to the original agreement, which must be signed by the client before it may take effect;

8. Any clause providing for a fee in addition to the agreed-upon rate, such as a reasonable minimum fee clause, must be defined in plain language and set forth the circumstances under which such fee may be incurred and how it will be calculated.

9. Frequency of itemized billing, which shall be at least every 60 days; the client may not be charged for time spent in discussion of the bills received;

10. Client's right to be provided with copies of correspondence and documents relating to the case, and to be kept apprised of the status of the case;

11. Whether and under what circumstances the attorney might seek a security interest from the client, which can be obtained only upon court approval and on notice to the adversary;

12. Under what circumstances the attorney might seek to withdraw from the case for nonpayment of fees, and the attorney's right to seek a charging lien from the court.

13. Should a dispute arise concerning the attorney's fee, the client may seek arbitration, which is binding upon both attorney and client; the attorney shall provide information concerning fee arbitration in the event of such dispute or upon the client's request.

## § 1400.4.    Nonrefundable Retainer Fee.

An attorney shall not enter into an arrangement for, charge or collect a nonrefundable retainer fee from a client. An attorney may enter into a "minimum fee" arrangement with a client that provides for the payment of a specific amount below which the fee will not fall based upon the handling of the case to its conclusion.

## § 1400.5.    Security Interests.

(a) An attorney may obtain a confession of judgment or promissory note, take a lien on real property, or otherwise obtain a security interest to secure his or her fee only where:

(1) the retainer agreement provides that a security interest may be sought;

(2) notice of an application for a security interest has been given to the other spouse; and,

(3) the court grants approval for the security interest after submission of an application for counsel fees.

(b) Notwithstanding the provisions of subdivision (a) of this section, an attorney shall not foreclose on a mortgage placed on the marital residence while the spouse who consents to the mortgage remains the titleholder and the residence remains the spouse's primary residence.

## § 1400.6.    Closing Statement.

A closing statement shall be filed with the clerk of the court in connection with every claim, action or proceeding in which a written retainer agreement is filed. The statement shall be subject to the provisions governing confidentiality contained in Domestic Relations Law § 235(1). The statement shall be filed within 15 days of entry of the judgment or other act concluding the case or terminating the retainer agreement and shall include the following information:

1. Caption of claim, action or proceeding.

2. Name and present address of client.

3. Date claim, action or proceeding was commenced and date settled, default entered or order or judgment entered.

4. Terms of settlement, order or judgment.

5. Amount of fees paid and dates of payment.

6. Whether security interest was obtained, amount thereof, date of court approval, and address, if any, of the secured property.

7. Amount of fee outstanding, terms of or payment schedule, if appropriate.

8. Date on which a copy of this closing statement has been forwarded to the client.

9. Date, attorney's name, address, telephone number and signature.

## § 1400.7.   Fee Arbitration.

In the event of a fee dispute between attorney and client, the client may seek to resolve the dispute by arbitration, which shall be binding upon both attorney and client and subject to review under CPLR Article 75, pursuant to a fee arbitration program established and operated by the Chief Administrator of the Courts and subject to the approval of the justices of the Appellate Divisions.

App Pract Provs

# PUBLIC HEALTH LAW

---

## SYNOPSIS OF SELECTED PROVISIONS

**Article 28.  Hospitals.**

**§ 2805-d.   Limitation of medical, dental or podiatric malpractice action based upon lack of informed consent.**

---

## Article 28.   Hospitals.

### § 2805-d.   Limitation of medical, dental or podiatric malpractice action based upon lack of informed consent.

1. Lack of informed consent means the failure of the person providing the professional treatment or diagnosis to disclose to the patient such alternatives thereto and the reasonably foreseeable risks and benefits involved as a reasonable medical, dental or podiatric practitioner under similar circumstances would have disclosed, in a manner permitting the patient to make a knowledgeable evaluation.

2. The right of action to recover for medical, dental or podiatric malpractice based on a lack of informed consent is limited to those cases involving either (a) non  emergency treatment, procedure or surgery, or (b) a diagnostic procedure which involved invasion or disruption of the integrity of the body.

3. For a cause of action therefore it must also be established that a reasonably prudent person in the patient's position would not have undergone the treatment or diagnosis if he had been fully informed and that the lack of informed consent is a proximate cause of the injury or condition for which recovery is sought.

4. It shall be a defense to any action for medical, dental or podiatric malpractice based upon an alleged failure to obtain such an informed consent that:

(a) the risk not disclosed is too commonly known to warrant disclosure; or

(b) the patient assured the medical, dental or podiatric practitioner he would undergo the treatment, procedure or diagnosis regardless of the risk involved, or the patient assured the medical, dental or podiatric practitioner that he did not want to be informed of the matters to which he would be entitled to be informed; or

(c) consent by or on behalf of the patient was not reasonably possible; or

(d) the medical, dental or podiatric practitioner, after considering all of the attendant facts and circumstances, used reasonable discretion as to the manner and extent to which such alternatives or risks were disclosed to the patient because he reasonably believed that the manner and extent of such disclosure could reasonably be expected to adversely and substantially affect the patient's condition.

# PUBLIC OFFICERS LAW

---

## SYNOPSIS OF SELECTED PROVISIONS

**Article 4. Powers and duties of public officers.**

§ 68.     Allowance of additional fees and expenses.

**Article 6. Freedom of information law.**

§ 84.     Legislative declaration.
§ 85.     Short title.
§ 86.     Definitions.
§ 87.     Access to agency records.
§ 88.     Access to state legislative records.
§ 89.     General provisions relating to access to records; certain cases.
§ 90.     Severability.

---

## Article 4.   Powers and duties of public officers.

## § 68.   Allowance of additional fees and expenses.

Where an officer or other person is required, in the course of a duty imposed upon him by law, to take an oath, to acknowledge an instrument, to cause an instrument to be filed or recorded, or to transmit a paper to another officer, he is entitled, in addition to the fees, or other compensation for the service, prescribed by law, to the fees necessarily paid by him, to the officer who administered the oath, or took the acknowledgment, or filed or recorded the instrument; and to the expense of transmitting the paper, including postage, where the transmission is lawfully made through the post-office.

## Article 6.   Freedom of information law.

## § 84.   Legislative declaration.

The legislature hereby finds that a free society is maintained when government is responsive and responsible to the public, and when the public is aware of governmental actions. The more open a government is with its citizenry, the greater the understanding and participation of the public in government.

As state and local government services increase and public problems become more sophisticated and complex and therefore harder to solve, and with the

App Pract Provs

resultant increase in revenues and expenditures, it is incumbent upon the state and its localities to extend public accountability wherever and whenever feasible.

The people's right to know the process of governmental decision-making and to review the documents and statistics leading to determinations is basic to our society. Access to such information should not be thwarted by shrouding it with the cloak of secrecy or confidentiality.

The legislature therefore declares that government is the public's business and that the public, individually and collectively and represented by a free press, should have access to the records of government in accordance with the provisions of this article.

## § 85.  Short title.

This article shall be known and may be cited as the "Freedom of Information Law."

## § 86.  Definitions.

As used in this article, unless the context requires otherwise:

1. "Judiciary" means the courts of the state, including any municipal or district court, whether or not of record.

2. "State Legislature" means the legislature of the state of New York, including any committee, subcommittee, joint committee, select committee, or commission thereof.

3. "Agency" means any state or municipal department, board, bureau, division, commission, committee, public authority, public corporation, council, office or other governmental entity performing a governmental or proprietary function for the state or any one or more municipalities thereof, except the judiciary or the state legislature.

4. "Record" means any information kept, held, filed, produced or reproduced by, with or for an agency or the state legislature, in any physical form whatsoever including, but not limited to, reports, statements, examinations, memoranda, opinions, folders, files, books, manuals, pamphlets, forms, papers, designs, drawings, maps, photos, letters, microfilms, computer tapes or discs, rules, regulations or codes.

## § 87.  Access to agency records.

1. (a) Within sixty days after the effective date of this article, the governing body of each public corporation shall promulgate uniform rules and regulations for all agencies in such public corporation pursuant to such general rules and regulations as may be promulgated by the committee on open government in conformity with the provisions of this article, pertaining to the administration of this article.

(b) Each agency shall promulgate rules and regulations, in conformity with this article and applicable rules and regulations promulgated pursuant to the provisions of paragraph (a) of this subdivision, and pursuant to such general rules and regulations as may be promulgated by the committee on open government in conformity with the provisions of this article, pertaining to the availability of records and procedures to be followed, including, but not limited to:

i. the times and places such records are available;

ii. the persons from whom such records may be obtained, and

iii. the fees for copies of records which shall not exceed twenty-five cents per photocopy not in excess of nine inches by fourteen inches, or the actual cost of reproducing any other record, except when a different fee is otherwise prescribed by statute.

2. Each agency shall, in accordance with its published rules, make available for public inspection and copying all records, except that such agency may deny access to records or portions thereof that:

(a) are specifically exempted from disclosure by state or federal statute;

(b) if disclosed would constitute an unwarranted invasion of personal privacy under the provisions of subdivision two of section eighty-nine of this article;

(c) if disclosed would impair present or imminent contract awards or collective bargaining negotiations;

(d) are trade secrets or submitted to an agency by a commercial enterprise or derived from information obtained from a commercial enterprise and which if disclosed would cause substantial injury to the competitive position of the subject enterprise;

(e) are compiled for law enforcement purposes and which, if disclosed, would:

i. interfere with law enforcement investigations or judicial proceedings;

ii. deprive a person of a right to a fair trial or impartial adjudication;

iii. identify a confidential source or disclose confidential information relating to a criminal investigation; or

iv. reveal criminal investigative techniques or procedures, except routine techniques and procedures.

(f) if disclosed would endanger the life or safety of any person;

(g) are inter-agency or intra-agency materials which are not:

i. statistical or factual tabulations or data;

ii. instructions to staff that affect the public;

iii. final agency policy or determinations; or

iv. external audits, including but not limited to audits performed by the comptroller and the federal government; or

(h) are examination questions or answers which are requested prior to the final administration of such questions.

(i) are computer access codes.

3. Each agency shall maintain:

(a) a record of the final vote of each member in every agency proceeding in which the member votes;

(b) a record setting forth the name, public office address, title and salary of every officer or employee of the agency; and

(c) a reasonably detailed current list by subject matter, of all records in the possession of the agency, whether or not available under this article.

4. (a) Each state agency which maintains records containing trade secrets, to which access may be denied pursuant to paragraph (d) of subdivision two of this section, shall promulgate regulations in conformity with the provisions of subdivision five of section eighty-nine of this article pertaining to such records, including, but not limited to the following:

(1) the manner of identifying the records or parts;

(2) the manner of identifying persons within the agency to whose custody the records or parts will be charged and for whose inspection and study the records will be made available;

(3) the manner of safeguarding against any unauthorized access to the records.

(b) As used in this subdivision the term "agency" or "state agency" means only a state department, board, bureau, division, council or office and any public corporation the majority of whose members are appointed by the governor.

## § 88. Access to state legislative records.

1. The temporary president of the senate and the speaker of the assembly shall promulgate rules and regulations for their respective houses in conformity with the provisions of this article, pertaining to the availability, location and nature of records, including, not limited to:

(a) the times and places such records are available;

(b) the persons from whom such records may be obtained;

(c) the fees for copies of such records, which shall not exceed twenty-five cents per photocopy not in excess of nine inches by fourteen inches, or the actual cost of reproducing any other record, except when a different fee is otherwise prescribed by law.

2. The state legislature shall, in accordance with its published rules, make available for public inspection and copying:

(a) bills and amendments thereto, fiscal notes, introducers' bill memoranda, resolutions and amendments thereto, and index records;

(b) messages received from the governor or the other house of the legislature, and home rule messages;

(c) legislative notification of the proposed adoption of rules by an agency;

(d) transcripts or minutes, if prepared, and journal records of public sessions including meetings of committees and subcommittees and public hearings, with the records of attendance of members thereat and records of any votes taken;

(e) internal or external audits and statistical or factual tabulations of, or with respect to, material otherwise available for public inspection and copying pursuant to this section or any other applicable provision of law;

(f) administrative staff manuals and instructions to staff that affect members of the public;

(g) final reports and formal opinions submitted to the legislature;

(h) final reports or recommendations and minority or dissenting reports and opinions of members of committees, subcommittees, or commissions of the legislature;

(i) any other files, records, papers or documents required by law to be made available for public inspection and copying.

(j) external audits conducted pursuant to section ninety-two of the legislative law and schedules issued pursuant to subdivision two of section ninety of the legislative law;

(k) any other files, records, papers or documents required by law to be made available for public inspection and copying.

3. Each house shall maintain and make available for public inspection and copying:

(a) a record of votes of each member in every session and every committee and subcommittee meeting in which the member votes;

(b) a record setting forth the name, public office address, title, and salary of every officer or employee; and

(c) a current list, reasonably detailed, by subject matter of any records required to be made available for public inspection and copying pursuant to this section.

> [**Editor's note:** Ch. 814 of L. 1987 relettered existing paragraph (j) as paragraph (k), and added the current paragraph (j). Paragraph (j) is effective until January 1, 1994, at which time it will be deemed repealed and paragraph (k) will be relettered as paragraph (j).]

## § 89. General provisions relating to access to records; certain cases.

The provisions of this section apply to access to all records, except as hereinafter specified:

1. (a) The committee on open government is continued and shall consist of the lieutenant governor or the delegate of such officer, the secretary of state

or the delegate of such officer, whose office shall act as secretariat for the committee, the commissioner of the office of general services or the delegate of such officer, the director of the budget or the delegate of such officer, and seven other persons, none of whom shall hold any other state or local public office except the representative of local governments as set forth herein, to be appointed as follows: five by the governor, at least two of whom are or have been representatives of the news media, one of whom shall be a representative of local government who, at the time of appointment, is serving as a duly elected officer of a local government, one by the temporary president of the senate, and one by the speaker of the assembly. The persons appointed by the temporary president of the senate and the speaker of the assembly shall be appointed to serve, respectively, until the expiration of the terms of office of the temporary president and the speaker to which the temporary president and speaker were elected. The four persons presently serving by appointment of the governor for fixed terms shall continue to serve until the expiration of their respective terms. Thereafter, their respective successors shall be appointed for terms of four years. The member representing local government shall be appointed for a term of four years, so long as such member shall remain a duly elected officer of a local government. The committee shall hold no less than two meetings annually, but may meet at any time. The members of the committee shall be entitled to reimbursement for actual expenses incurred in the discharge of their duties.

(b) The committee shall:

i. furnish to any agency advisory guidelines, opinions or other appropriate information regarding this article;

ii. furnish to any person advisory opinions or other appropriate information regarding this article;

iii. promulgate rules and regulations with respect to the implementation of subdivision one and paragraph (c) of subdivision three of section eighty-seven of this article;

iv. request from any agency such assistance, services and information as will enable the committee to effectively carry out its powers and duties; and

v. report on its activities and findings regarding articles six and seven of this chapter, including recommendations for changes in the law, to the governor and the legislature annually, on or before December fifteenth.

2. (a) The committee on public access to records may promulgate guidelines regarding deletion of identifying details or withholding of records otherwise available under this article to prevent unwarranted invasions of personal privacy. In the absence of such guidelines, an agency may delete identifying details when it makes records available.

(b) An unwarranted invasion of personal privacy includes, but shall not be limited to:

i. disclosure of employment, medical or credit histories or personal references of applicants for employment;

ii. disclosure of items involving the medical or personal records of a client or patient in a medical facility;

iii. sale or release of lists of names and addresses if such lists would be used for commercial or fund-raising purposes;

iv. disclosure of information of a personal nature when disclosure would result in economic or personal hardship to the subject party and such information is not relevant to the work of the agency requesting or maintaining it; or

v. disclosure of information of a personal nature reported in confidence to an agency and not relevant to the ordinary work of such agency.

(c) Unless otherwise provided by this article, disclosure shall not be construed to constitute an unwarranted invasion of personal privacy pursuant to paragraphs (a) and (b) of this subdivision:

i. when identifying details are deleted;

ii. when the person to whom a record pertains consents in writing to disclosure;

iii. when upon presenting reasonable proof of identity, a person seeks access to records pertaining to him.

2-a. Nothing in this article shall permit disclosure which constitutes an unwarranted invasion of personal privacy as defined in subdivision two of this section if such disclosure is prohibited under section ninety-six of this chapter.*

3. Each entity subject to the provisions of this article, within five business days of the receipt of a written request for a record reasonably described, shall make such record available to the person requesting it, deny such request in writing or furnish a written acknowledgment of the receipt of such request and a statement of the approximate date when such request will be granted or denied, including, where appropriate, a statement that access to the record will be determined in accordance with subdivision five of this section. Upon payment of, or offer to pay, the fee prescribed therefor, the entity shall provide a copy of such record and certify to the correctness of such copy if so requested, or as the case may be, shall certify that it does not have possession of such record or that such record cannot be found after diligent search. Nothing in this article shall be construed to require any entity to prepare any record not possessed or maintained by such entity except the records specified in subdivision three of section eighty-seven and subdivision three of section eighty-eight.

4. (a) Except as provided in subdivision five of this section, any person denied access to a record may within thirty days appeal in writing such denial to the head, chief executive or governing body of the entity, or the person therefor designated by such head, chief executive, or governing body, who shall within ten business days of the receipt of such appeal fully explain in writing to the person requesting the record the reasons for further denial, or provide access

to the record sought. In addition, each agency shall immediately forward to the committee on open government a copy of such appeal when received by the agency and the ensuing determination thereon.

(b) Except as provided in subdivision five of this section, a person denied access to a record in an appeal determination under the provisions of paragraph (a) of this subdivision may bring a proceeding for review of such denial pursuant to article seventy-eight of the civil practice law and rules. In the event that access to any record is denied pursuant to the provisions of subdivision two of section eighty-seven of this article, the agency involved shall have the burden of proving that such record falls within the provisions of such subdivision two.

(c) The court in such a proceeding may assess, against such agency involved, reasonable attorney's fees and other litigation costs reasonably incurred by such person in any case under the provisions of this section in which such person has substantially prevailed, provided, that such attorney's fees and litigation costs may be recovered only where the court finds that:

(i) the record involved was, in fact, of clearly significant interest to the general public; and

(ii) the agency lacked a reasonable basis in law for withholding the record.

5. (a)(1) A person acting pursuant to law or regulation who, subsequent to the effective date of this subdivision, submits any information to any state agency may, at the time of submission, request that the agency except such information from disclosure under paragraph (d) of subdivision two of section eighty-seven of this article. Where the request itself contains information which if disclosed would defeat the purpose for which the exception is sought, such information shall also be excepted from disclosure.

(2) The request for an exception shall be in writing and state the reasons why the information should be excepted from disclosure.

(3) Information submitted as provided in subparagraph one of this paragraph shall be excepted from disclosure and be maintained apart by the agency from all other records until fifteen days after the entitlement to such exception has been finally determined or such further time as ordered by a court of competent jurisdiction.

(b) On the initiative of the agency at any time, or upon the request of any person for a record excepted from disclosure pursuant to this subdivision, the agency shall:

(1) inform the person who requested the exception of the agency's intention to determine whether such exception should be granted or continued;

(2) permit the person who requested the exception, within ten business days of receipt of notification from the agency, to submit a written statement of the necessity for the granting or continuation of such exception;

(3) within seven business days of receipt of such written statement, or within seven business days of the expiration of the period prescribed for submission of such statement, issue a written determination granting, continuing or terminating such exception and stating the reasons therefor; copies of such determination shall be served upon the person, if any, requesting the record, the person who requested the exception, and the committee on public access to records.

(c) A denial of an exception from disclosure under paragraph (b) of this subdivision may be appealed by the person submitting the information and a denial of access to the record may be appealed by the person requesting the record in accordance with this subdivision:

(1) Within seven business days of receipt of written notice denying the request, the person may file a written appeal from the determination of the agency with the head of the agency, the chief executive officer or governing body or their designated representatives.

(2) The appeal shall be determined within ten business days of the receipt of the appeal. Written notice of the determination shall be served upon the person, if any, requesting the record, the person who requested the exception and the committee on public access to records. The notice shall contain a statement of the reasons for the determination.

(d) A proceeding to review an adverse determination pursuant to paragraph (c) of this subdivision may be commenced pursuant to article seventy-eight of the civil practice law and rules. Such proceeding must be commenced within fifteen days of the service of the written notice containing the adverse determination provided for in subparagraph two of paragraph (c) of this subdivision.

(e) The person requesting an exception from disclosure pursuant to this subdivision shall in all proceedings have the burden of proving entitlement to the exception.

(f) Where the agency denies access to a record pursuant to paragraph (d) of subdivision two of section eighty-seven of this article, the agency shall have the burden of proving that the record falls within the provisions of such exception.

(g) Nothing in this subdivision shall be construed to deny any person access, pursuant to the remaining provisions of this article, to any record or part excepted from disclosure upon the express written consent of the person who had requested the exception.

(h) As used in this subdivision the term "agency" or "state agency" means only a state department, board, bureau, division, council or office and any public corporation the majority of whose members are appointed by the governor.*

6. Nothing in this article shall be construed to limit or abridge any otherwise available right of access at law or in equity of any party to records.

7. Nothing in this article shall require the disclosure of the home address of an officer or employee, former officer or employee, or of a retiree of a public

App Pract Provs

employees' retirement system; nor shall anything in this article require the disclosure of the name or home address of a beneficiary of a public employees' retirement system or of an applicant for appointment to public employment; provided however, that nothing in this subdivision shall limit or abridge the right of an employee organization, certified or recognized for any collective negotiating unit of an employer pursuant to article fourteen of the civil service law, to obtain the name or home address of any officer, employee or retiree of such employer, if such name or home address is otherwise available under this article.*

**\*Editor's Note:**

Subdivision two-a of section eighty-nine takes effect Sept. 1, 1984, provided that agency actions necessary to the functioning of new Article Six-A of the Public Officers Law on such date shall be taken prior thereto.

Subdivision five of section eighty-nine applies only to records submitted on or after January 1, 1982.

Subdivision seven of section eighty-nine applies to any request pursuant to the Public Officers Law for which there is no final determination, including judicial review.

## § 90.  Severability.

If any provision of this article or the application thereof to any person or circumstances is adjudged invalid by a court of competent jurisdiction, such judgment shall not affect or impair the validity of the other provisions of the article or the application thereof to other persons and circumstances.

# REAL PROPERTY LAW

## SYNOPSIS OF SELECTED PROVISIONS

**Article 9.   Recording instruments affecting real property.**

§ 298.      Acknowledgments and proofs within the state.

§ 299.      Acknowledgments and proofs without the state, but within the United States or any territory, possession, or dependency thereof.

§ 299-a.   Acknowledgment to conform to law of New York or of place where taken; certificate of conformity.

§ 300.      Acknowledgments and proofs by persons in or with the armed forces of the United States.

§ 301.      Acknowledgments and proofs in foreign countries.

§ 301-a.   Acknowledgment to conform to law of New York or of foreign country; certificate of conformity.

## Article 9.   Recording instruments affecting real property.

### § 298.   Acknowledgments and proofs within the state.

The acknowledgment or proof, within this state, of a conveyance of real property situate in this state may be made: 1. At any place within the state, before (a) a justice of the supreme court; (b) an official examiner of title; (c) an official referee; or (d) a notary public.

2. Within the district wherein such officer is authorized to perform official duties, before (a) a judge or clerk of any court of record; (b) a commissioner of deeds outside of the city of New York, or a commissioner of deeds of the city of New York within the five counties comprising the city of New York; (c) the mayor or recorder of a city; (d) a surrogate, special surrogate, or special county judge; or (e) the county clerk or other recording officer of a county.

3. Before a justice of the peace, town councilman, village police justice or a judge of any court of inferior local jurisdiction, anywhere within the county containing the town, village or city in which he is authorized to perform official duties.

App Pract Provs

## § 299. Acknowledgments and proofs without the state, but within the United States or any territory, possession, or dependency thereof.

The acknowledgment or proof of a conveyance of real property situate in this state, if made (a) without the state but within the United States, (b) within any territory, possession, or dependency of the United States, or (c) within any place over which the United States, at the time when such acknowledgment or proof is taken, has or exercises jurisdiction, sovereignty, control, or a protectorate, may be made before any of the following officers acting within his territorial jurisdiction or within that of the court of which he is an officer: 1. A judge or other presiding officer of any court having a seal, or the clerk or other certifying officer thereof.

2. A mayor or other chief civil officer of any city or other political subdivision.

3. A notary public.

4. A commissioner of deeds appointed pursuant to the laws of this state to take acknowledgments or proofs without this state.

5. Any person authorized, by the laws of the state, District of Columbia, territory, possession, dependency, or other place where the acknowledgment or proof is made, to take the acknowledgment or proof of deeds to be recorded therein.

## § 299-a. Acknowledgment to conform to law of New York or of place where taken; certificate of conformity.

1. An acknowledgment or proof made pursuant to the provisions of section two hundred ninety-nine of this chapter may be taken in the manner prescribed either by the laws of the state of New York or by the laws of the state, District of Columbia, territory, possession, dependency, or other place where the acknowledgment or proof is taken. The acknowledgment or proof, if taken in the manner prescribed by such state, District of Columbia, territory, possession, dependency, or other place, must be accompanied by a certificate to the effect that it conforms with such laws. Such certificate may be made by

(a) An attorney-at-law admitted to practice in the state of New York, resident in the place where the acknowledgment or proof is taken, or by

(b) An attorney-at-law admitted to practice in the state, District of Columbia, territory, possession, dependency, or other place where the acknowledgment or proof is taken, or by

(c) Any other person deemed qualified by any court of the state of New York, if, in any action, proceeding, or other matter pending before such court, it be necessary to determine that such acknowledgment or proof conforms with the laws of such state, District of Columbia, territory, possession, dependency, or other place; or by the supreme court of the state of New York, on application for such determination. The justice, judge, surrogate, or other presiding judicial officer shall append to the instrument so acknowledged or proved his signed statement that he deemed such person qualified to make such certificate.

2. (a) The signature to such a certificate of conformity shall be presumptively genuine, and the qualification of the person whose name is so signed as a person authorized to make such certificate shall be presumptively established by the recital thereof in the certificate.

(b) The statement of a judicial officer appended to the instrument that he deemed the person making such certificate qualified shall establish the qualification of the person designated therein to make such certificate; and the recording, filing, registering or use as evidence of the instrument shall not depend on the power of the court to make the statement and proof shall not be required of any action, proceeding, matter or application in which or in connection with which the statement is made.

(c) When an instrument so acknowledged or proved is accompanied by the certificate of conformity and the statement of a judicial officer, if any be required, the acknowledgment or proof of the instrument, for the purpose of recording, filing or registering in any recording or filing office in this state or for use as evidence, shall be equivalent to one taken or made in the form prescribed by law for use in this state; and if the acknowledgment or proof is properly authenticated, where authentication is required by law, and if the instrument be otherwise entitled to record, filing or registering, such instrument, together with the acknowledgment or proof, the certificate of conformity and any certificate of authentication or statement of a judicial officer, may be recorded, filed or registered in any recording or filing office in this state, and shall be so recorded, filed or registered upon payment or tender of lawful fees therefor. In fixing the fees of a recording, filing or registering officer, the certificate of conformity and the statement of a judicial officer appended, if any, shall be treated as certificates of authentication required by other provisions of this chapter.

### § 300. Acknowledgments and proofs by persons in or with the armed forces of the United States.

The acknowledgment or proof of a conveyance of real property situate in this state, if made by a person enlisted or commissioned in or serving in or with the armed forces of the United States or by a dependent of any such person, wherever located, or by a person attached to or accompanying the armed forces of the United States, whether made within or without the United States, may be made before any commissioned officer in active service of the armed forces of the United States with the rank of second lieutenant or higher in the Army, Air Force or Marine Corps, or ensign or higher in the Navy or Coast Guard, or with equivalent rank in any other component part of the armed forces of the United States.

App Pract Provs

In addition to the requirements of sections three hundred and three, three hundred and four, and three hundred and six of this chapter, the certificate of an acknowledgment or proof taken under this section shall state (a) the rank and serial number of the officer taking the same, and the command to which he is attached, (b) that the person making such acknowledgment or proof was, at the time of making the same, enlisted or commissioned in or serving in or with the armed forces of the United States or the dependent of such a person, or a person attached to or accompanying the armed forces of the United States, and (c) the serial number of the person who makes, or whose dependent makes the acknowledgment or proof if such person is enlisted or commissioned in the armed forces of the Unites States. The place where such acknowledgment or proof is taken need not be disclosed.

No authentication of the officer's certificate of acknowledgment or proof shall be required.

Notwithstanding any of the provisions of this section, the acknowledgment or proof of a conveyance of real property situate in this state may also be made as provided in sections two hundred ninety-eight, two hundred ninety-nine, two hundred ninety-nine-a, three hundred one, and three hundred one-a, of this chapter.

## § 301. Acknowledgments and proofs in foreign countries.

The acknowledgment or proof of a conveyance of real property situate in this state may be made in foreign countries before any of the following officers acting within his territorial jurisdiction or within that of the court of which he is an officer: 1. An ambassador, envoy, minister, charge d'affaires, secretary of legation, consul-general, consul, vice-consul, consular agent, vice-consular agent, or any other diplomatic or consular agent or representative of the United States, appointed or accredited to, and residing within, the country where the acknowledgment or proof is taken.

2. A judge or other presiding officer of any court having a seal, or the clerk or other certifying officer thereof.

3. A mayor or other chief civil officer of any city or other political subdivision.

4. A notary public.

5. A commissioner of deeds appointed pursuant to the laws of this state to take acknowledgments or proofs without this state.

6. A person residing in, or going to, the country where the acknowledgment or proof is to be taken, and specially authorized for that purpose by a commission issued to him under the seal of the supreme court of the state of New York.

7. Any person authorized, by the laws of the country where the acknowledgment or proof is made, to take acknowledgments of conveyances of real estate or to administer oaths in proof of the execution thereof.

## § 301-a. Acknowledgment to conform to law of New York or of foreign country; certificate of conformity.

1. An acknowledgment or proof made pursuant to the provisions of section three hundred one of this chapter may be taken in the manner prescribed either by the laws of the state of New York or by the laws of the country where the acknowledgment or proof is taken. The acknowledgment or proof, if taken in the manner prescribed by the laws of such foreign country, must be accompanied by a certificate to the effect that it conforms with such laws. Such certificate may be made by

(a) An attorney-at-law admitted to practice in the state of New York, resident in such foreign country, or by

(b) A consular officer of the United States, resident in such foreign country, under the seal of his office, or by

(c) A consular officer of such foreign country, resident in the state of New York, under the seal of his office, or by

(d) Any other person deemed qualified by any court of the state of New York, if, in any action, proceeding, or other matter pending before such court, it be necessary to determine that such acknowledgment or proof conforms with the laws of such foreign country; or by the supreme court of the state of New York, on application for such determination.

The justice, judge, surrogate, or other presiding judicial officer shall append to the instrument so acknowledged or proved his signed statement that he deemed such person qualified to make such certificate.

2. (a) The signature to such a certificate of conformity shall be presumptively genuine, and the qualification of the person whose name is so signed as a person authorized to make such certificate shall be presumptively established by the recital thereof in the certificate.

(b) The statement of a judicial officer appended to the instrument that he deemed the person making such certificate qualified shall establish the qualification of the person designated therein to make such certificate; and the recording, filing, registering or use as evidence of the instrument shall not depend on the power of the court to make the statement and proof shall not be required of any action, proceeding, matter or application in which or in connection with which the statement is made.

(c) When an instrument so acknowledged or proved is accompanied by the certificate of conformity and the statement of a judicial officer, if any be required, the acknowledgment or proof of the instrument, for the purpose of recording, filing or registering in any recording or filing office in this state or for use as evidence, shall be equivalent to one taken or made in the form prescribed by law for use in this state; and if the acknowledgment or proof is properly authenticated, where authentication is required by law, and if the instrument be otherwise entitled to record, filing or registering, such instrument, together with the acknowledgment of proof, the certificate of conformity and any certificate of authentication or statement of a judicial officer, may be recorded, filed or registered in any recording or filing office in this state, or shall be so recorded, filed or registered upon payment or tender of lawful fees therefor. In fixing the fees of a recording, filing or registering officer, the certificate of conformity and the statement of a judicial officer appended, if any, shall be treated as certificates of authentication required by other provisions of this chapter.

# SURROGATE'S COURT PROCEDURE ACT

## SYNOPSIS OF SELECTED PROVISIONS

Article 3.    **Proceedings, pleadings and process.**

§ 315.      **Joinder and representation of persons interested in estates.**

Article 8.    **General provisions relating to bonds.**

§ 801.      **Amount; condition; number of sureties; obligees.**

Article 17.   **Guardians and custodians.**

§ 1708.     **Joint control subject to order.**

Article 18.   **Claims; debts and expenses.**

§ 1812.     **Leave to issue execution against decedent's real property.**

Article 22.   **Accounting.**

§ 2209.     **Affidavit to account.**

## Article 3.    Proceedings, pleadings and process.

### § 315.    Joinder and representation of persons interested in estates.

1. The provisions of this section shall apply in any proceeding in which all persons interested in the estate are required to be served with process. For the purposes of this section, the term "an interest in the estate" includes both interests in income and interests in principal.

2. Representation of class interests.

(a) Where an interest in the estate has been limited as follows, it shall not be necessary to serve process on any other person than as herein provided:

(i) In any contingency to the persons who shall compose a certain class upon the happening of a future event, the persons in being who would constitute the class if such event had happened immediately before the commencement of the proceeding.

(ii) To a person who is a party to the proceeding and the same interest has been further limited upon the happening of a future event to a class of persons described in terms of their relationship to such party, the party to the proceeding.

(iii) to unborn or unascertained persons, none of such persons, but if it appears that there is no person in being or ascertained, having the same interest, the court shall appoint a guardian ad litem to represent or protect the persons who eventually may become entitled to the interest.

(b) Where a party to the proceeding has a power of appointment it shall not be necessary to serve the potential appointees and if it is a general power of appointment it shall not be necessary to serve the takers in default of the exercise thereof.

3. Representation of contingent interests.

Where an interest in the estate has been limited to a person who is a party to the proceeding and the same interest has been further limited upon the happening of a future event to any other person it shall not be necessary to serve such other person.

4. Representation in probate proceeding. In a proceeding for probate of a testamentary instrument, the interests of the respective persons specified in subdivisions 2(a)(ii) and 3 of this section shall be deemed to be the same interest, whether or not their respective interests are in income or in principal or in both, provided that they are beneficiaries of the same trust or fund, that they have a common interest in proving or disproving the instrument offered for probate and that the person who is a party under subdivision 2(a)(ii) or the person to whom the interest has been limited under subdivision 3 would not receive greater financial benefit if such instrument were denied probate (in the case where such beneficiaries have a common interest in proving such instrument) or admitted to probate, (in the case where such beneficiaries have a common interest in disproving such instrument).

5. Representation of persons under a disability. If the instrument expressly so provides, where a party to the proceeding has the same interest as a person under a disability, it shall not be necessary to serve the person under a disability.

6. The decree or order entered in any such proceeding shall be binding and conclusive on all persons upon whom service of process is not required.

7. In any proceeding in which service of process upon persons interested in the estate may be dispensed with pursuant to the provisions of this section or section twenty-two hundred ten, in addition to such other requirements as may be applicable to the petition in the particular proceeding, the petition shall (i) set forth in a form satisfactory to the court the information required by subdivision three of section three hundred four with respect to the persons interested in the estate upon whom service of process may be dispensed with, the nature of the interests of such persons and the basis upon which service of process may be dispensed with, and (ii) state whether the fiduciary or any other person has discretion to affect the present or future beneficial enjoyment of the estate and, if so, set forth the discretion possessed and, if exercised, the manner in which it has been exercised. Notwithstanding the foregoing provisions of this

section and any provisions of the instrument to the contrary, if the court finds that the representation of a person's interest is or may be inadequate it may require that he be served. The basis for such finding shall be set forth specifically in the order.

8. Nonjudicial settlements of accounts of fiduciaries. Unless the instrument expressly provides otherwise, an instrument settling an account, executed by all the persons upon whom service of process would be required in a proceeding for the judicial settlement of the account, shall be binding and conclusive on all persons upon whom service of process would not be required to the same extent as that instrument binds the persons who executed it.

### Article 8. General provisions relating to bonds.

### § 801.  Amount; condition; number of sureties; obligees.

1. Amount. Whenever a fiduciary or legal life tenant shall be required to file a bond, the amount thereof, except where the court has reduced it or dispensed therewith, shall be fixed as follows:

*　　　　　*　　　　　*

(a) Guardian of the property of an infant

(a) Not less than:

i. Value of all personal property receivable by the guardian.

ii. Estimated gross rents of real property receivable by the guardian for three years.

iii. Estimated gross income for three years from sources other than moneys or other assets committed to the guardian for administration.

(c). i. Testamentary trustee, or executor required to hold, manage or invest property for the benefit of another,

ii. ancillary fiduciaries,

iii. guardian of the person of an infant,

iv. legal life tenant, or

v. any case not provided for in this article where the filing of a bond is required.

(c) In such amount as the court directs.

(d) In granting limited and restrictive letters pursuant to the provisions of 702 the court may dispense with a bond altogether or fix the amount at such sum as it may deem sufficient.

(e) In addition to such powers as are conferred by CPLR 2508, the court may at any time increase or decrease the bond of a fiduciary or legal life tenant when good reason therefore appears.

(f) In fixing the amount of a bond, the court may require evidence as to the character and value of the assets to be committed to the fiduciary and may examine the applicant or any other person under oath or take such other steps as it deems necessary.

2. Condition. Unless the court directs otherwise the condition of the bond shall be that the fiduciary will faithfully discharge his trust, obey all lawful decrees and orders touching the administration of the assets committed to him including but not limited to decrees or orders directing repayment of amounts allowed as advances on commissions and render a verified account of his administration whenever required to do so by the court. In the case of a legal life tenant the condition shall be that the principal account for and deliver to his successors in interest the property held as life tenant.

3. Sureties. The court may authorize or direct the execution and filing of a bond with a sole surety or with two or more sureties or it may dispense with sureties altogether when good reason therefor appears.

4. Obligees of bond. The bond of a fiduciary shall run to the people of the state for the security and benefit of the persons then or thereafter interested in the estate.

## Article 17.    Guardians and custodians.

## § 1708.    Joint control subject to order.

1. (a) The court may dispense with a bond wholly or partly and direct that the guardian jointly with a person or depositary designated collect and receive the moneys and other property of the infant as directed by order and that such moneys and property as it directs be deposited in the name of the guardian, subject to the order of the court, with a bank, savings bank, trust company, safe deposit company, or state or federal credit union designated in the order or invested in the name of the guardian, subject to the order of the court, in the shares of a savings and loan association or the savings account of a federal savings and loan association designated in the order, provided that no deposit or investment of the funds of any one infant in any single bank, savings bank, trust company, savings and loan association, federal savings and loan association, or state or federal credit union shall exceed the maximum amount insured by the federal deposit insurance corporation or the national credit union share insurance fund.

(b) The court may also dispense with a bond wholly or partly when it authorizes the guardian to purchase and invest in United States savings bonds, treasury bills, treasury notes, treasury bonds, or bonds of the state of New York or bonds or other obligations of any county, city, town, village or school district of the state of New York for the benefit of the infant and directs the guardian to deposit such bonds, bills, notes or other municipal obligations in joint custody with a bank, savings bank, trust company safe deposit company, or state or federal credit union invested in the name of the guardian, subject to the order of the court. The guardian shall collect and receive all interest and income from such United States savings bonds, treasury notes, treasury bonds or bonds of the state of New York or bonds or other obligations of any county, city, town, village or school district of the state of New York and deposit such interest and income in an account in the name of the guardian, subject to the order of the court, as authorized pursuant to this section with the bank, savings bank, trust company safe deposit company, or state or federal credit union having joint custody with the guardian of such United States savings bonds, treasury bills, treasury notes, treasury bonds, or bonds of the state of New York or bonds or other obligations of any county, city, town, village or school district of the state of New York.

(c) Such deposit or investment shall be withdrawn or removed only on the order of the court, except that no court order shall be required to pay over to the infant who has attained the age of eighteen years all the moneys so held unless the depository is in receipt of an order from a court of competent jurisdiction directing it to withhold such payment beyond the infant's eighteenth birthday.

2. All property of the infant not under joint control shall be secured by bond as provided in this act.

3. Where an infant is a beneficiary of a contract of life insurance under which moneys are payable to the infant or under which rights may accrue to the infant pursuant to election made by his guardian under the terms of the contract, the court may by order dispense wholly or partly with a bond and direct that the insurance company and the guardian shall make no withdrawal of the funds due to the infant under the contract except by joint check to the order of the guardian and a person designated by the court to receive such moneys.

4. The letters issued shall contain the substance of the order.

### Article 18.   Claims; debts and expenses.

### § 1812.   Leave to issue execution against decedent's real property.

For the purpose of procuring a decree granting leave to issue execution against a decedent's real property a judgment creditor shall present to the court a verified petition showing the facts and praying for such decree and that the person whose interest in the property will be affected by a sale by virtue of the execution and the fiduciary of the judgment debtor may be required to show cause why it should not be granted. Upon the presentation of the petition the court must issue process accordingly. The process must be served either personally or in such manner as directed by the court and upon the return thereof the court may make such decree as justice shall require.

**Article 22.    Accounting.**

**§ 2209.    Affidavit to account.**

To each account filed in the court, as prescribed in this article, must be appended the affidavit of the accounting party to the effect that the account contains according to the best of his knowledge and belief a true statement of all his receipts and disbursements on account of the estate and of all money or other property belonging to the estate which have come into his hands or been received by any other person by his order or authority for his use and that he does not know of any error or omission in the account to the prejudice of any creditor of, or person interested in, the estate.

# UNIFORM COMMERCIAL CODE

---

## SYNOPSIS OF SELECTED PROVISIONS

**Article 2. Sales.**

**§ 2-725.**     Statute of limitations in contracts for sale.

**Article 3. Commercial paper.**

**§ 3-122.**     Accrual of cause of action.

---

## Article 2. Sales.

### § 2-725. Statute of limitations in contracts for sale.

(1) An action for breach of any contract for sale must be commenced within four years after the cause of action has accrued. By the original agreement the parties may reduce the period of limitation to not less than one year but may not extend it.

(2) A cause of action accrues when the breach occurs, regardless of the aggrieved party's lack of knowledge of the breach. A breach of warranty occurs when tender of delivery is made, except that where a warranty explicitly extends to future performance of the goods and discovery of the breach must await the time of such performance the cause of action accrues when the breach is or should have been discovered.

(3) Where an action commenced within the time limited by subsection (1) is so terminated as to leave available a remedy by another action for the same breach such other action may be commenced after the expiration of the time limited and within six months after the termination of the first action unless the termination resulted from voluntary discontinuance or from dismissal for failure or neglect to prosecute.

(4) This section does not alter the law on tolling of the statute of limitations nor does it apply to causes of action which have accrued before this Act becomes effective.

App Pract Provs

**Article 3.　Commercial paper.**

**§ 3-122.　Accrual of cause of action.**

\*　　　\*　　　\*

(3) A cause of action against a drawer of a draft or an indorser of any instrument accrues upon demand following dishonor of the instrument. Notice of dishonor is a demand.

# VEHICLE AND TRAFFIC LAW

---

### SYNOPSIS OF SELECTED PROVISIONS

**Article 3. Exemption of non-resident owners and operators.**

§ 253.     Service of summons on non-residents.

§ 254.     Service of summons on residents who depart from state and on residents' executors or administrators who are non-residents or who depart from state.

---

### Article 3. Exemption of non-resident owners and operators.

### § 253. Service of summons on non-residents.

1. The use or operation by a non-resident of a vehicle in this state, or the use or operation in this state of a vehicle in the business of a non-resident, or the use or operation in this state of a vehicle owned by a non-resident if so used or operated with his permission, express or implied, shall be deemed equivalent to an appointment by such nonresident of the secretary of state to be his true and lawful attorney upon whom may be served the summons in any action against him, growing out of any accident or collision in which such non-resident may be involved while using or operating such vehicle in this state or in which such vehicle may be involved while being used or operated in this state in the business of such non-resident or with the permission, express or implied, of such non-resident owner; and such use or operation shall be deemed a signification of his agreement that any such summons against him which is so served shall be of the same legal force and validity as if served on him personally within the state and within the territorial jurisdiction of the court from which the summons issues, and that such appointment of the secretary of state shall be irrevocable and binding upon his executor or administrator. Where such non-resident has died prior to the commencement of an action brought pursuant to this section, service of process shall be made on the executor or administrator of such non-resident in the same manner and on the same notice as is provided in the case of the non-resident himself. Where an action has been duly commenced under the provisions of this section against a non-resident who dies thereafter, the court must allow the action to be continued against his executor or administrator upon motion with such notice as the court deems proper.

2. A summons in an action described in this section may issue in any court in the state having jurisdiction of the subject matter and be served as hereinafter provided. Service of such summons shall be made by mailing a copy thereof to the secretary of state at his office in the city of Albany, or by personally delivering a copy thereof to one of his regularly established offices, with a fee of ten dollars, and such service shall be sufficient service upon such non-resident provided that notice of such service and a copy of the summons and complaint are forthwith sent by or on behalf of the plaintiff to the defendant by certified mail or registered mail with return receipt requested. The plaintiff shall file with the clerk of the court in which the action is pending, or with the judge or justice of such court in case there be no clerk, an affidavit of compliance herewith, a copy of the summons and complaint, and either a return receipt purporting to be signed by the defendant or a person qualified to receive his certified mail or registered mail, in accordance with the rules and customs of the post-office department; or, if acceptance was refused by the defendant or his agent, the original envelope bearing a notation by the postal authorities that receipt was refused, and an affidavit by or on behalf of the plaintiff that notice of such mailing and refusal was forthwith sent to the defendant by ordinary mail; or, if the registered or certified letter was returned to the post office unclaimed, the original envelope bearing a notation by the postal authorities of such mailing and return, an affidavit by or on behalf of the plaintiff that the summons was posted again by ordinary mail and proof of mailing certificate of ordinary mail. Where the summons is mailed to a foreign country, other official proof of the delivery of the mail may be filed in case the post-office department is unable to obtain such a return receipt. The foregoing papers shall be filed within thirty days after the return receipt or other official proof of delivery or the original envelope bearing a notation of refusal, as the case may be, is received by the plaintiff. Service of process shall be complete when such papers are filed. The return receipt or other official proof of delivery shall constitute presumptive evidence that the summons mailed was received by the defendant or a person qualified to receive his certified mail or registered mail; and the notation of refusal shall constitute presumptive evidence that the refusal was by the defendant or his agent. Service of such summons also may be made by mailing a copy thereof to the secretary of state at his office in the city of Albany, or by personally delivering a copy thereof to one of his regularly established offices, with a fee of ten dollars, and by delivering a duplicate copy thereof with the complaint annexed thereto, to the defendant personally without the state by a resident or citizen of the state of New York or a sheriff, under-sheriff, deputy-sheriff or constable of the county or other political sub-division in which the personal service is made, or an officer authorized by the laws of this state, to take acknowledgments of deeds to be recorded in this state, or an attorney and/or counselor at law, solicitor, advocate or barrister duly qualified to practice in the state or country where such service is made, or by a United States marshall or deputy United States marshall. Proof of personal service without the state

shall be filed with the clerk of the court in which the action is pending within thirty days after such service. Personal service without the state is complete when proof thereof is filed. The court in which the action is pending may order such extensions as may be necessary to afford the defendant reasonable opportunity to defend the action.

3. As used in this section, the term "vehicle" means a "motor vehicle," "motorcycle," "semitrailer," and "trailer" as defined in sections one hundred twenty-five, one hundred twenty-three, one hundred forty-three and one hundred fifty-six, respectively, of this chapter, whether or not such vehicles are used or operated upon a public highway.

§ 254.　Service of summons on residents who depart from state and on residents' executors or administrators who are non-residents or who depart from state.

The provisions of section two hundred fifty-three of this chapter shall also apply (a) to a resident who departs from the state subsequent to the accident or collision and remains absent therefrom for thirty days continuously, whether such absence is intended to be temporary or permanent, and to any executor or administrator of such resident, and (b) to an executor or administrator of a resident if such executor or administrator is a non-resident or if, being a resident, he departs from the state and remains absent therefrom for thirty days continuously, whether such absence is intended to be temporary or permanent.

App Pract Provs

# SPECIAL FEATURE:
# NEW YORK'S COMMENCEMENT BY FILING LAW

by

## MARC ARKIN *

## 1995 REVISION

by

## PAUL H. ALOE **

# NEW YORK'S COMMENCEMENT BY FILING LAW

———

### SYNOPSIS

§ 1        Introduction
§ 2        Overview of Chapter 216
           [1]  General Provisions
           [2]  Statute of Limitations
           [3]  Personal Jurisdiction over the Defendant
           [4]  Transition Period
§ 3        Prior Law and the Legislative History of Chapter 216
§ 4        Courts in Which an Action Is Now Commenced by Filing
§ 5        Types of Actions in Which Commencement-By-Filing Applies
§ 6        Filing the Summons and Complaint
§ 7        If the Plaintiff Fails to Pay for the Index Number
§ 8        The Time in Which to Serve the Summons and Complaint After Filing
               with the Court
           [1]  When Service Must Be Effected

———

* Associate Professor, Fordham University School of Law

** Partner in the law firm of Rubin Baum Levin Constant & Friedman and member of the task force which participated in drafting the Commencement by Filing Act and chair, Committee on Civil Practice Law and Rules of the New York State Bar Association

[2]  Extensions of Time in General
[3]  Multi-Defendant Actions
[4]  Comparison with Federal Practice
[5]  If Filing with the Clerk Is Impeded
§ 9        Statute of Limitations
[1]  New Savings Provisions
[2]  Superseded Savings Provisions
§ 10       Special Proceedings
[1]  In General
[2]  Actions on Instruments for Payment of Money or Money Judgments
§ 11       Third-Party Proceedings
§ 12       Surrogate's Court
§ 13       Application to Diversity Actions in Federal Court
§ 14       Persons Excused from Paying Fees
§ 15       Transitional Provisions
App. A     New and Amended Statutory Provisions
App. B     Form Affidavit for Litigants Appearing as Poor Persons

## § 1    Introduction

On June 23, 1992, Governor Mario Cuomo signed legislation that fundamentally changed the procedure for commencement of lawsuits in the state of New York.[1]

The 1992 law which has no formal title other than Chapter 216 (but which is colloquially referred to as "commencement-by-filing")[2] operates primarily through amendments to CPLR 203, 304, 306-a, and through the creation of a new 306-b. Chapter 216, which took effect on July 1, 1992, also amends provisions of a number of other laws, including the Surrogate's Court Procedure Act, the Domestic Relations Law, the General Municipal Law, the Navigation Law, the Parks, Recreation and Historic Preservation Law, and the Vehicle and Traffic Law in order to conform with the new rules regarding the commencement of actions.[3]

Chapter 216 primarily concerns actions in Supreme Court and County Court. It changes the event that marks the commencement of a lawsuit and the tolling of the statute of limitations, from service of a summons on the defendant, to the filing of the summons and complaint (or the summons with notice) with the clerk of the court.[4]

---

[1]  Laws of 1992, Ch. 216, effective July 1, 1992.

[2]  *See* Blair & Aloe, *New Commencement by Filing Law: A Practitioner's Survival Guide*, N.Y.L.J., 6/26/92, p.1.

[3]  The text of each statute affected or added by Chapter 216 follows in Appendix A *infra*.

[4]  CPLR 304. A special proceeding is now commenced by filing a notice of petition (or an order to show cause) with the clerk of the court of the county in which the proceeding is brought. *Id.*

## § 2   Overview of Chapter 216

### [1]  General Provisions

The legislature has amended the CPLR so that, in the Supreme and County Courts, an action is now commenced when a summons and complaint, or a summons and CPLR 305(b) notice, is filed with the clerk of the court in the county in which the action is brought.[5] After filing of the initial process, the plaintiff has 120 days to file proof of service on the defendant with the court clerk.[6] Current methods of service are largely unaffected by the changes in the law.[7] If plaintiff fails to file proof of service and the defendant has not appeared within this 120-day period, the action is automatically "deemed dismissed" without prejudice.[8] Special proceedings are now commenced by filing a notice of petition (or an order to show cause) and a petition, which must be served on the defendant within 15 days of the expiration of the applicable statute of limitations.[9]

Prior to the enactment of Chapter 216, service of a summons had two functions it commenced the lawsuit, and it secured personal jurisdiction over the defendant. Now, commencement of the suit and obtaining personal jurisdiction are achieved by separate acts. The plaintiff must file to commence the action, and serve process to obtain personal jurisdiction over the defendant. Under the commencement-by-filing system, an action exists even though personal service has not yet been made on a named defendant.[10] These changes, important in themselves, have significant consequences in a number of practice areas.

### [2]   Statute of Limitations

Chapter 216 provides that a claim is interposed, and the statute of limitations tolled, when the plaintiff files a summons and complaint with the court clerk.[11] This means that a plaintiff now has complete control over the act that begins an action, a marked break with prior practice, in which the statute of limitations was tolled only when the plaintiff was able to effect service on the opposing party.

This increased control is not the only benefit for the plaintiff nearing the end of a limitations period. If a summons and complaint are filed with the court

---

[5] CPLR 304. During the remainder of this discussion, references to the filing of a summons and complaint should be read as including the alternative filing method (filing a CPLR 305(b) notice and summons).

[6] *See* § 10 *infra* for a discussion of the special requirements imposed on third-party plaintiffs.

[7] Moskowitz v. Lieberman, 158 Misc. 2d 1031, 602 N.Y.S.2d 752 (Sup. Ct. N.Y. Co. 1993).

[8] CPLR 306-b(a).

[9] CPLR 306-b(a). For a comprehensive discussion of the requirements for special proceedings, *see* § 9 *infra*.

[10] Evans v. Evans, 208 A.D.2d 223, 623 N.Y.S.2d 685 (1st Dept. 1995).

[11] CPLR 203(c).

before the expiration of the statute of limitations, the plaintiff has 120 days in which to serve the defendant and to file proof of service with the court.[12] If a plaintiff fails to meet that deadline, all is not lost, even if the statute of limitations has expired during the 120-day service period. Although the action is automatically "deemed dismissed," Chapter 216 contains a savings provision. The plaintiff may bring a new action complete with the purchase of a new index number against the defendant based on the same claim, with the requirement that the plaintiff effect service within 120 days of the date of the dismissal.[13]

Furthermore, if the statute of limitations would not have otherwise expired, the plaintiff may commence a new action without the aid of CPLR 306-b(b). Within the applicable statute of limitations period, there is no limit to the number of times that an action which has been "deemed dismissed" for failure to make service may be recommenced.[14]

### [3] Personal Jurisdiction over the Defendant

One of the chief practical consequences of the changes initiated by Chapter 216 is to discourage motions to dismiss for lack of personal jurisdiction based on ineffective service of process. Under prior practice, a defendant was able to assert the defense of lack of personal jurisdiction based on improper service at any time, even after the statute of limitations had expired with potentially disastrous consequences to the plaintiff.[15] This particular danger to plaintiffs arose because the Court of Appeals had held that the CPLR 205 six-month grace period in which to commence an action anew after its termination did not apply to actions dismissed for failure to obtain personal jurisdiction over the defendant.[16]

Even though Chapter 216 amends CPLR 205(a) specifically to exclude dismissals for improper service from the six-month grace period,[17] motions to dismiss based on improper service will have little value for a defendant under the new scheme. If the court dismisses an action for failure to effect proper service, the plaintiff will be able to commence a new action within 120 days

---

[12] This is a more generous arrangement than accorded under CPLR 203(b)(5), which grants the plaintiff 60 days in which to serve the summons on the defendant if the claim is first interposed by service on the sheriff. That provision is now only applicable in actions which are commenced by service in the lower courts.

[13] CPLR 306-b(b).

[14] See Blair & Aloe, New Commencement by Filing Law: A Practitioner's Survival Guide, N.Y.L.J., 6/26/92, p.1.

[15] See, e.g., Markoff v. South Nassau Community Hosp., 61 N.Y.2d 283, 473 N.Y.S.2d 766, 461 N.E.2d 1253 (1984) (holding, under prior practice, that if the complaint was dismissed for lack of proper service, the plaintiff's claim was lost because it was never commenced in the first place).

[16] Parker v. Mack, 61 N.Y.2d 114, 472 N.Y.S.2d 882, 460 N.E.2d 1316 (1984).

[17] This is because CPLR 306-b(b) permits recommencement where the dismissal is based on improper service. If the statute had not been so amended, then CPLR 306-b(b) and 205 could have been read to permit a plaintiff whose action is dismissed for improper service after the expiration of the limitations period to recommence the action more than once.

of the dismissal even if the statute of limitations expired after the original timely filing.[18] An Article 78 proceeding dismissed for failure to effect service may be started anew within 15 days.[19]

Under prior law, a plaintiff facing a motion to dismiss for lack of personal jurisdiction could sometimes render the motion moot by causing the defendant to be re-served with process before the action was dismissed.[20] Chapter 216 does not change this law. If there has been an appropriate filing within the limitations period, the action is timely commenced. If proof of service is filed within the 120 days, the automatic dismissal will not occur, even if the actual proof of service is subsequently deemed to have been defective.[21] If the defendant challenges service, the plaintiff may still subject the defendant to the personal jurisdiction of the court as long as the action has not been dismissed either because of an automatic dismissal under CPLR 306-b(a) for not filing proof of service, or because of a motion to dismiss under CPLR 3211(a).[22]

### [4] Transition Period

The CPLR changes enacted by Chapter 216 took effect on July 1, 1992, and apply to all actions commenced on or after that date. In order to ease the transition to the new filing system, and afford practitioners time to adjust and learn the statute, Chapter 216 provided a "window" period. Until December 31, 1992, an action could have been commenced, and the statute of limitations tolled, either by filing pursuant to the new act, or by traditional service of process, provided that the index number fee was paid by December 31, 1992. If the action was commenced within this window period, but the index number fee was not paid by December 31, 1992, then the action was automatically dismissed.[23] If within this window period, an action was dismissed for failure to purchase the index number and file before December 31, 1992, CPLR 205(a) does not apply

---

[18] CPLR 306-b(b).

[19] *Id.*

[20] *See, e.g.,* IBJ Schroder Bank & Trust Co. v. Zaitz, 170 A.D.2d 579, 566 N.Y.S.2d 871 (2d Dept. 1991); Kellner v. DeBushey Coach, Ltd., 138 A.D.2d 460, 526 N.Y.S.2d 115, 117 (2d Dept. 1988); Dashew v. Cantor, 85 A.D.2d 619, 445 N.Y.S.2d 24, 25 (2d Dept. 1981); Heusinger v. Russo, 96 A.D.2d 883, 466 N.Y.S.2d 36, 37 (2d Dept. 1983); Department of Hous. Preservation and Dev. v. Koenigsberg, 133 Misc. 2d 893, 509 N.Y.S.2d 270, 272 (Civ. Ct. N.Y. Co. 1986).

[21] *See* State St. Bank and Trust Co. v. Broadway/St. Nicholas Assocs., 214 A.D.2d 474, 625 N.Y.S.2d 217 (1st Dept. 1995).

[22] North Side Sav. Bank v. Arieh, 161 Misc. 2d 518, 614 N.Y.S.2d 706 (Sup. Ct. N.Y. Co. 1994) (court's holding that service of process was invalid did not result in dismissal where defendant was re-served since defendant was re-served with process in person and affidavit of service was filed within 120 days).

[23] Campbell v. Command Sec., Inc., — A.D.2d —, 628 N.Y.S.2d 775, 651 N.E.2d 1275 (2d Dept. 1995). *But see* Bloodgood v. Paradis, 160 Misc. 2d 290, 608 N.Y.S.2d 390 (Sup. Ct. Chenango Co. 1994) (the court held that the action was properly commenced where plaintiff mailed the fee prior to December 31, 1992 but it was not received until January 6, 1993).

to permit a second action if the statute of limitations has expired.[24] If the action was commenced before the window period (*i.e.*, before July 1, 1992), then the automatic dismissal did not occur.[25] On and after January 1, 1993, any attempt to commence an action in Supreme or County Court by service of a summons, is completely ineffective, and the service of unfiled process is a nullity.[26]

## § 3    Prior Law and the Legislative History of Chapter 216

Prior to Chapter 216, an action in New York was "commenced and jurisdiction acquired by service of a summons."[27] This one act tolled the running of the statute of limitations[28] and obtained personal jurisdiction over the defendant. As of July 1, 1992, all this has changed. An action is now commenced by filing the summons and complaint with the clerk of the court. Moreover, service of the summons and complaint is completely ineffective unless the summons bears an index number and the date of filing. Service of process is now necessary only to obtain personal jurisdiction over the defendant.

The history of Chapter 216 begins with New York's 1991 budgetary difficulties and the addition of CPLR 306-a to the statute books. Effective September 1, 1991, CPLR 306-a required the purchase of an index number for each lawsuit by mandating that a plaintiff file proof of service within 30 days of the commencement of an action.[29] CPLR 306-a(b) also required, for the first time, the purchase of a separate index number for a third-party action.

The legislature had designed the original CPLR 306-a as a revenue measure, hoping to force plaintiffs, including third-party plaintiffs, to file a summons in court within 30 days after service and to pay the $170 filing fee. Unfortunately, CPLR 306-a ran counter to the long-standing New York practice of conducting litigation without the benefit of an index number or the payment of any fee until court intervention or the filing of some paper became necessary.[30] Worse still from the standpoint of the legislature's goal, CPLR 306-a contained no real penalty for failure to comply with its requirements.[31] Not surprisingly, it was honored more in the breach than in the observance.

---

[24] Campbell v. Command Sec., Inc., — A.D.2d —, 628 N.Y.S.2d 775 (2d Dept. 1995).

[25] *See* Laws of 1992, Ch. 216, § 27; Siegel, *Imminent New Filing System Threatens Viability of Civil Lawsuits*, N.Y.L.J. 12/28/92, p. 1, col. 1; Siegel, N.Y. St. L. Dig., No. 391, July 1992.

[26] *See* Blair & Aloe, *New Commencement by Filing Law: A Practitioner's Survival Guide*, N.Y.L.J., 6/26/92, p.1.

[27] Former CPLR 304. The provision continued, a "special proceeding is commenced and jurisdiction acquired by service of a notice of petition or order to show cause."

[28] Former CPLR 203.

[29] Laws of 1991, Ch. 166, § 381.

[30] *See, e.g.*, CPLR 308(2) and 308(4) regarding the filing of an affidavit of service when certain methods of service are employed.

[31] CPLR 306-a(c) provided that if the summons had not been filed as required, the "court upon application shall order the filing thereof nunc pro tunc."

On March 31, 1992, the legislature responded by enacting Chapter 55 of the Laws of 1992. A broad-based revenue measure, the new act contained revisions to the CPLR designed to reinforce the demands of CPLR 306-a. Chapter 55 provided that an index number had to be purchased before service of the summons in an action and, more importantly, that service of the summons without an index number would have no effect.

Chapter 55, however, presented a number of problems, the most salient of which was that it required that a plaintiff file the summons before serving it, while retaining the existing rule that service on the defendant commenced the lawsuit. Chapter 55 also contained no time limit for service after filing a summons with the court.[32] These difficulties, among others, were addressed by a number of groups, which together with the Senate and Assembly Code Committees, drafted a bill containing a more comprehensive approach to the issue of commencement by filing.[33] The legislature adopted that bill as Chapter 216, which entirely superseded Chapter 55's civil procedure changes. As a result, Chapter 55 never became effective.[34]

## § 4. Courts in Which an Action Is Now Commenced by Filing

The revisions in practice brought about by Chapter 216 apply only in New York's Supreme and County Courts.[35] They do not apply in the New York City Civil Courts,[36] District Courts,[37] City Courts,[38] or Justice Courts.[39] The legislature has chosen to retain these lower courts as traditional "service courts" under the new act. The new commencement-by-filing system and its related procedural changes apply to all actions brought in County Court and Supreme Court on or after July 1, 1992. This includes proceedings commenced in the Appellate Division.[40]

---

[32] Other concerns were that a typographical error in the index number or insecure attachment of the proof of index number purchase (which was required to be attached to the summons) might result in the summons being treated as a nullity.

[33] The CPLR Committee of the Commercial and Federal Litigation Section of the New York State Bar Association had written a report in early 1992 proposing that the state shift to a commencement by filing system. The House of Delegates of the New York State Bar Association endorsed that report at its quarterly meeting in early April 1992. In scrambling to draft superseding legislation before Chapter 55 became effective, the legislature assembled a task force consisting of counsel from the Senate and Assembly Codes Committees and Judiciary Committees, representatives of the organized bar, court administrators and clerks, and other groups.

[34] Slutzky v. Aron Estates Corp., 157 Misc. 2d 749, 754, 597 N.Y.S.2d 997, 1001 (Sup. Ct. Rockland Co. 1993).

[35] Surrogate's Court already had a commencement by filing system in effect at the time the legislature adopted Chapter 216.

[36] N.Y.C. Civ. Ct. Act § 400, Laws of 1992, Ch. 216, § 15.

[37] U.D.C.A. § 400, Laws of 1992, Ch. 216, § 14.

[38] U.C.C.A. § 400, Laws of 1992, Ch. 216, § 16.

[39] U.J.C.A. § 400, Laws of 1992, Ch. 216, § 19.

[40] Spodek v. New York State Comm'r of Taxation & Fin., 85 N.Y.2d 760, 628 N.Y.S.2d 256 (1995).

The recommencement provisions of CPLR 306-b have also been held to apply to New York actions removed to federal court but subsequently dismissed for failure to effect proper service.[41]

## § 5   Types of Actions in Which Commencement-By-Filing Applies

One controversy that has arisen is whether certain kinds of actions are outside the commencement-by-filing statute because of the failure of the legislature to specifically include them in Chapter 216. The difficulty is that many statutes governing specific kinds of actions or proceedings refer to such actions or proceedings as being commenced by service. While Chapter 216 enumerated and changed many such statutes, it did not change them all, leaving some courts to conclude that specific kinds of proceedings were outside the scope of commencement-by-filing. This occurred principally in the area of real property tax assessment proceedings,[42] although the logic behind those cases could be applied to a broader class of statutes. In 1994, the legislature amended the statute to clarify that "filing" rather than "service" governs a host of proceedings, including Real Property Tax Actions.[43]

However, the legislature did not amend the statute in one particular area— election law proceedings. It was thought that this area was especially controversial and had divided the courts.[44] The cases excluding such proceedings from commencement-by-filing appear to run contrary to the legislative intent because CPLR 203(b)(2) and CPLR 304 (which permits commencement of actions without filing in certain limited exigent circumstances) were enacted specifically to deal with the problems encountered in election law proceedings.[45] On the other hand, the recommencement provision of CPLR 306-b(b) was thought by many to be inappropriate in election law proceedings because such proceedings must be decided quickly in light of impending elections, and thus the delay encountered by recommencement is inappropriate. Legislation was introduced in the 1995 legislative session to clarify that commencement-by-filing does apply to election law proceedings and to prevent recommencement under CPLR 306-b(b) in such proceedings.[46]

---

[41] Wilder v. Budget Rent a Car, 1995 U.S. Dist. LEXIS 7232 (S.D.N.Y. May 22, 1995).

[42] See In re Baker, N.Y.L.J., 4/21/93, p. 26, col. 1; McDonald's Corp. v. Assessor for Town of Hancock, 159 Misc. 2d 335, 604 N.Y.S.2d 485 (Sup. Ct. N.Y. Co. 1993).

[43] Laws of 1994, Ch. 563.

[44] See, e.g., Isabella v. Hotaling, 207 A.D.2d 648, 615 N.Y.S.2d 945, 947 (3d Dept. 1994), appeal denied, 84 N.Y.2d 801, 617 N.Y.S.2d 135 (1994) (filing requirements set forth in CPLR 304, as opposed to the various time periods contained in the new commencement-by-filing statutes enacted by the Laws of 1992, Ch. 216, do apply to election law proceedings); Ehle v. Wallace, 602 N.Y.S.2d 563, appeal denied, 82 N.Y.2d 653, 602 N.Y.S.2d 802 (1993) (respondent must be served before expiration of time to institute proceeding); Farmer v. King, Index No. 1761B/92 (Sup. Ct. Westchester Co., Oct. 19, 1992) (holding CPLR 306-b(b) inapplicable to election law proceedings).

[45] See Blair & Aloe, New Commencement by Filing Law: A Practitioner's Survival Guide, N.Y.L.J., 6/26/92, p.1.

[46] Assembly Bill A3953 (1995).

The recent case of *Spodek v. New York State Commissioner of Taxation and Finance*,[47] probably changes the landscape significantly. There, the Court of Appeals stated that the "legislature's intent that *all* actions and proceedings not specifically excluded should come under the operation of the 1992 commencement-by-filing act."[48] *Spodek* should thus foreclose the issue in favor of application of commencement-by-filing in actions in all non-excluded courts.

## § 6   Filing the Summons and Complaint

In order to commence an action under the new system, the plaintiff must file a summons and complaint, or a summons and CPLR 305(b) notice, with the clerk of the court of the county in which the action is brought. In the case of a special proceeding, a notice of petition or an order to show cause must be filed with the clerk. Filing is not considered complete unless the plaintiff delivers the index number fee to the clerk, along with the other required documents.[49] Where papers are mailed to the clerk, they are not deemed filed until they are actually received.[50] Purchasing an index number, without filing the summons and complaint, is jurisdictionally insufficient.[51]

Upon receipt of the required documents and fee, the clerk will now assign an index number to the action. The index number and the date of filing must appear on the summons.[52] The purpose of this requirement is to permit the defendant to determine that the action has been commenced and the date of the commencement for purposes of determining if the action is timely under the statute of limitations. Failure to include this information, however, is not intended to be a jurisdictional defect and should mandate dismissal only if it prejudices the defendant.[53]

---

[47] 85 N.Y.2d 760, 628 N.Y.S.2d 256 (1995).

[48] *Id.* at 765, 628 N.Y.S.2d at 259 (1995).

[49] CPLR 304.

[50] Enos v. City of Rochester, 206 A.D.2d 159, 619 N.Y.S.2d 459 (4th Dept. 1994).

[51] De Maria v. Smith, 197 A.D.2d 114, 610 N.Y.S.2d 689 (3d Dept. 1994) (statute of limitations not tolled where plaintiff purchased index number but did not file summons and complaint).

[52] CPLR 305(a). This section also specifies that any third-party summons must bear the index number of the *main* action (despite the requirement of CPLR 1007 that a *separate* fee be paid), the date of filing of the main action, and the date of filing of the third-party summons.

[53] The version of CPLR 306-a contained in the Laws of 1992, Ch. 55, explicitly announced that service of a summons without an index number was ineffective. That provision was omitted from Chapter 216 so that the statute would not provide that the omission of the index number or the date that the index number was purchased is necessarily fatal. If the omission does not result in prejudice to the defendants, then dismissal of the action is not warranted. *See* Cellular Tel. Co. v. Village of Tarrytown, 209 A.D.2d 57, 624 N.Y.S.2d 170 (2d Dept. 1995) (omission of the filing date did not result in prejudice where plaintiff served a duplicate copy of the summons with filing date shortly after service of the original summons); *see also* Yeger v. Yeger, N.Y.L.J., 4/2/93, p. 33, col. 1 (Sup. Ct. Kings Co. 1993); V. Alexander, 1993 Supp. Practice Commentary, McKinney's Consol. Laws of N.Y., Vol. 7B, CPLR C305:1, 1995 Pocket Part, p. 49 (West 1995).

Commence Filing

Similarly, a third-party plaintiff must file a third-party complaint with the court and pay the index number fee. The clerk will not, however, assign the action a separate number. Instead, the summons must bear the index number of the main action, and the filing dates of both the main and third-party actions.[54]

## § 7   If the Plaintiff Fails to Pay for the Index Number

CPLR 306-a(b) provides for the situation in which a person other than the plaintiff pays the filing fee—a situation that probably will be rare after the transition period is past.

CPLR 306–a(b) provides that if someone other than the plaintiff purchases the index number, that person is entitled to an order from the clerk of the court, requiring reimbursement by the plaintiff (or the third-party plaintiff) within 30 days of service of the order with notice of entry. If the plaintiff fails to comply, the paying individual may apply to the clerk for an order dismissing the action, but without prejudice.

## § 8   The Time in Which to Serve the Summons and Complaint After Filing with the Court

### [1] When Service Must Be Effected

Once a plaintiff has filed a summons and complaint with the clerk of the court, the plaintiff must file proof of service within 120 days.[55] The amended tolling provisions of CPLR 207 apply to CPLR 306-b(a), excluding from the calculation of the 120-day period any periods during which the defendant is absent from the state.[56] This time is also tolled if the defendant files for bankruptcy in the interim.[57] The filing of proof of service requirement is in addition to those found in other sections, such as CPLR 308(2) and (4). In other words, the plaintiff may have to file proof of service sooner because the method of service requires filing of service within a certain time-frame in order to complete service.

If the plaintiff fails to effect service and to file proof within the required time under CPLR 306-b(a), and the defendant does not appear, the action will be "deemed dismissed" without prejudice.[58] This dismissal is automatic. The clerk will not enter a formal order, but any attempted action after the automatic dismissal will be ineffective.[59] The purpose of the automatic dismissal provision,

---

[54] *See* § 11 *infra* for a more detailed discussion of third-party actions.

[55] In the case of a special proceeding, the period is 15 days from the expiration of the statute of limitations. *See* § 9 *infra*.

[56] Laws of 1992, Ch. 216, § 3.

[57] Beila Assocs. v. 27-29 W. 181 St. Assocs., Inc., 205 A.D.2d 320, 613 N.Y.S.2d 16 (1st Dept. 1994), *appeal dismissed without opinion,* 84 N.Y.2d 978, 622 N.Y.S.2d 916 (1994).

[58] CPLR 306-b(a).

[59] Counsel who engage in post-dismissal activity will risk sanctions under Part 130-1 of the Rules of the Chief Administrator of the Courts. *See* Williams v. Williams, 215 A.D.2d 980, 627 N.Y.S.2d

rather than requiring an order, as is the situation in federal court under Fed. R. Civ. P. 4(m), is because of the sheer volume of cases in New York state courts.

It is important to bear in mind that the automatic dismissal only occurs if, within the 120 days, the plaintiff fails to file proof of service and the defendant fails to appear. If the defendant appears within the 120-day period, there is no dismissal even if proof of service is not filed.

It is also important to bear in mind that the requirement of CPLR 306-b(a) is the filing of proof of service, not effective service. If proof of service is filed, but that service is subsequently contested, the action was still commenced.[60] Proof of service needs to be filed so that should a party discover an action in which the party has been named a defendant but not served, the party can ascertain from the public record if plaintiff is claiming to have made service. If the action is more than 120 days old, and there has been no proof of service filed, the named defendant has assurance that the action is dead, at least as to him. If service has been purportedly made, but in fact is improper, the defendant's remedy is to move to dismiss the action, if so inclined, and such motion should be granted if proper service has never been made.[61] An added protection for the defendant is that the plaintiff ordinarily must move for a default judgment within a year of the default or have the complaint dismissed as abandoned.[62]

It is also important to understand the purpose of the requirement under CPLR 306-b(a) that proof of service be filed. Under the former service system, the defendant would get actual notice of the lawsuit within the limitations period. Chapter 216 changed that. Under Chapter 216, all that is required is that the action be filed. Of course the defendant could, if so inclined, go to the public record to determine if an action has been filed against him, and in fact, certain electronic systems now list index number purchases along with defendants in the action. If the plaintiff commences an action against the defendant, and the defendant does not receive service, the defendant is entitled to determine from the public file if the plaintiff contends that the defendant has been served. If the public file reveals that the defendant has not been served after 120 days, the defendant is entitled to the assurance that the action is not against him and that there is nothing further the defendant need do or worry about with respect to that particular action. The plaintiff might commence a new action, of course, but this would require new service on the defendant.

Commence Filing

---

131 (3d Dept. 1995) (attorney sanctioned for submitting ex-parte order after automatic dismissal of action).

**60** State St. Bank and Trust Co. v. Broadway/St. Nicholas Assocs., 214 A.D.2d 474, 625 N.Y.S.2d 217 (1st Dept. 1995).

**61** *Id.*

**62** *See* CPLR 3215(c).

In some courts, the clerk will not accept an affidavit of service that a plaintiff attempts to file more than 120 days after the action is commenced. Nothing in Chapter 216 provides the clerk with such authority. Chapter 216 was designed to operate without the clerk needing to make a determination if the action has been dismissed or not. Thus, a clerk should accept an affidavit, even if it is filed more than 120 days after the action was commenced, although such filing, if it occurs after the action has been "deemed dismissed" under CPLR 306-b(a), will be a nullity. Of course there may be situations where the mere failure to file an affidavit within 120 days will not work an automatic dismissal, such as where the defendant has entered an appearance (which could occur if the defendant has answered the complaint)[63] within the 120-day period.

In the ordinary situation, a plaintiff who has experienced an automatic dismissal either for failure to serve the defendant or for failure to file proof of service within the 120-day period may simply begin all over again, filing a new action and purchasing a new index number. Matters are only slightly more complicated if the statute of limitations has run out sometime between the date the plaintiff timely commenced the original action and the date the 120-day service period expired. A plaintiff caught in that situation may take advantage of the new CPLR 306-b(b) to obtain an additional 120 days, measured from the date of dismissal, in which to commence a new action (limited, of course, to the same transaction or occurrence, or series of transactions or occurrences) and serve the defendant.

Since this second filing is a new action, the plaintiff must purchase a new index number and effect service of process all over again. Hopefully, with a full 240 days in which to serve the defendant (not counting periods excluded under tolling provisions such as CPLR 207), the plaintiff will be able to make the lawsuit stick.

The savings provision of CPLR 306-b(b), however, provides a little room for maneuvering by the dilatory. Once the dismissal occurs, either an automatic "deemed" dismissal for failure to file proof of service under CPLR 306-b(a), or for lack of personal jurisdiction, the 120-day clock starts to run. Within those 120 days, the plaintiff must not only commence a new action, but must also effect proper service on the defendant. If the plaintiff fails to serve the defendant within the second 120-day period, the action is time-barred. This provision means that the plaintiff whose action is dismissed after the expiration of the statute of limitations can only use CPLR 306-b once.

CPLR 306-b(b), unlike CPLR 306-b(a), does not state that an action will be "deemed dismissed" if plaintiff fails to file proof of service within 120 days of the original dismissal. However, since CPLR 306-b(b), unlike CPLR 306-b(a),

---

[63] CPLR 306-b(a) provides for automatic dismissal only if there has been no appearance and no affidavit filed within 120 days. Under CPLR 320, a defendant appears by serving an answer or a notice of appearance, or by making a motion which has the effect of extending the time to answer. CPLR 320 does not require the answer or notice of appearance to be filed to be effective.

requires actual service of process within the 120 days in order to invoke the savings provision, the "deemed dismissed" provision was thought to be unnecessary. If a plaintiff whose statute has expired fails to timely file pursuant to the provisions of CPLR 306-b(b), including making service within the second 120-day period, then that plaintiff's claim is time-barred.

### [2] Extensions of Time in General

CPLR 2004 provides that "[e]xcept where otherwise expressly prescribed by law, the court may extend any time fixed by any statute, rule or order for doing any act, upon such terms as may be just and upon good cause shown, whether the application for extension is made before or after the expiration of the time fixed." Chapter 216 makes no reference to CPLR 2004. During the drafting process, members of the task force observed that CPLR 2004 could not be used to extend an otherwise applicable statute of limitations.[64]

The courts have been divided on the availability of such extensions ranging from courts holding that CPLR 2004 extensions can be granted even after the 120-day period and others saying that it can never be granted.[65] Some courts have held that CPLR 2004 extensions should be granted where the application is made before the 120-day period expires and if it will not have the effect of extending the statute of limitations.[66] A number of authorities take the position that once automatic dismissal occurs, there is no longer any action in which the court can exercise its discretion under CPLR 2004.[67] That logic would appear to leave open the possibility that in a multi-party action, if any one party has been served, the court could still exercise discretion as to the unserved defendant since the action continues to exists.

While it is unclear how the courts will ultimately resolve this issue, the touchstone should be the statute of limitations. The purpose of CPLR 306-b is to ensure that the defendant receives notice of the suit within a set period after the statute of limitations would have otherwise expired. If the effect of the extension is to extend that time, than the application should be denied.

---

[64] *See* CPLR 201.

[65] Ressler Vineyards v. Kuhns, N.Y.L.J., 2/28/94, p. 28, col. 6 (Sup. Ct. N.Y. Co.) (CPLR 2004 permits court discretion to extent 120-day period even after the 120-day period has expired); Choice Card Products Citibank v. Federico, N.Y.L.J., 6/16/93, p. 30, col. 4 (Sup. Ct. Suffolk Co.) (court is without discretion to grant extension to file proof of service even if 120-day period has not expired because CPLR 306-b(a) constitutes clear law that cannot be circumvented by CPLR 2004).

[66] Norstar Bank of Upstate New York v. Wittbrodt, 154 Misc. 2d 260, 594 N.Y.S.2d 115 (Sup. Ct. Albany Co. 1993); *see also* Beaver Universal Corp. v. 1111 Jamaica Ave. Queens Leasing Corp., N.Y.L.J., 1/26/95, p. 32, col. 6 (Sup. Ct. Queens Co.).

[67] Green v. Kaladjian, 1994 WL 706337 (Sup. Ct. N.Y. Co. June 10, 1994); V. Alexander, Practice Commentaries, McKinney's Consol. Laws of N.Y., Vol. 7B, CPLR 306-b, C306-b:1, 1994 Pocket Part, p. 58 (West 1994); 1 Weinstein, Korn & Miller, New York Civil Practice—CPLR ¶ 306–b.02 (Matthew Bender); Blair & Aloe, *New Commencement by Filing Law: A Practitioner's Survival Guide*, N.Y.L.J., 6/26/92, p.1.

One thing, however, seems clear. A plaintiff who has already suffered an automatic dismissal under CPLR 306-b(a) should be unable to obtain an extension under CPLR 2004 for two reasons. First, the dismissed action no longer exists.[68] Second, the defendant has the right to rely on the public filing showing no purported service within 120 days as assurance that the defendant has been dismissed. At the very least, if the court grants the application, it should require service of its order on the defendant.

If the plaintiff makes the CPLR 2004 application before the action is dismissed, the request will not extend the outside date by which a defendant could properly be served; therefore, absent some prejudice to a defendant, the application should be granted.

Even if the court does deny the CPLR 2004 application, the result is unlikely to be tragic, merely expensive. As long as the statute of limitations has not expired, the plaintiff can simply for a fee commence a new action. If the statute of limitations has expired between commencement of the original action and the end of the 120-day period, CPLR 306-b(b) allows the plaintiff to obtain an additional 120 days for a fee in which to commence a new action on the same claim and serve the defendant.

Obviously, the issue is different if the statute of limitations expired during the original 120-day period, and the plaintiff is having difficulty effecting service during the second 120-day period, i.e., the one provided by CPLR 306-b(b). In other words, is a plaintiff likely to be successful in an application for an extension of the second 120-day period? Once again, it stands to reason that a plaintiff will be unsuccessful in seeking an extension of service time because to permit such an extension would violate the CPLR 201 prohibition against judicially extending the statute of limitations. While this result may seem harsh, it should be recalled that under the commencement-by-service system, the defendant had to be served within the limitations period or the action would be time-barred. If the plaintiff could not find the defendant within the limitations period, the plaintiff would have to apply for an order permitting service by publication. If, under Chapter 216, the plaintiff cannot find the defendant within the time permitted under CPLR 306-b for service, then the plaintiff is well advised to seek an order permitting service by publication.

### [3] Multi-Defendant Actions

Chapter 216 does not explicitly address the dilemma of a plaintiff who timely files a summons and complaint in an action against several defendants, but fails to serve one of the defendants within the necessary 120-day period while timely serving and filing proof of service on the other defendants. Nevertheless, it appears that the drafters intended that, if the unserved defendant fails to appear,

---

[68] This might not be the case in a multi-party action where there has been a timely filed proof of service or appearance by at least one of the defendants.

the action be deemed dismissed as to the unserved defendant but only as to the unserved defendant. This would certainly seem to be an appropriate occasion for the plaintiff to consider the various mechanisms for extending the time to serve or file pursuant to CPLR 2004. (*See* the discussion in § 8[2] *supra*). If efforts to secure an extension of time are unavailing, however, the plaintiff must then bring a new action against the unserved defendant, and pay a new index number fee.

The act also fails to state whether the clerk should or will issue a new index number in the new action brought against the unserved defendant. The simplest approach would be to follow the procedure used in third-party actions: use the same index number as the first action and indicate both that number and the date of filing of the second summons and complaint on the summons in the new action. Since this will be a new action, a fine sense of detail indicates that the plaintiff may also have to make a motion to consolidate it with the first action in order to get everyone back in the same lawsuit.

Another issue not addressed by Chapter 216 is the situation where the court grants the plaintiff leave to add additional parties after the action has been commenced. In that situation, when does the statute of limitations stop running against the newly added party? When must proof of service be filed with respect to the newly added party? Unfortunately, neither Chapter 216 nor anything else in the CPLR provides an explicit answer to these questions, even though plaintiff's claim may rise or fall on the answer.

In 1993, soon after the statute was enacted, the omission was recognized by certain of the drafters of Chapter 216. Senator Volker and Assemblyman Lentol introduced legislation that would have corrected the ambiguity.[69] Unfortunately, the bill was not acted upon by the legislature.

Under the former law, a claim was interposed against a newly added party upon service. On the other hand, a strong argument could be made that claims are no longer interposed by service but by filing, and it would be the filing of the pleading, not the service, that would interpose the claim. If the words

---

[69] Senate Bill 4301/Assembly Bill 6891 (1993). The bill would have added CPLR 203(h), which would have provided:

*Claim against new party where action commenced by filing.* Where a new party is added in a court where an action or proceeding is commenced by filing, any claim with respect to the new party, if not otherwise interposed because the party is united in interest with an original defendant, is interposed by the filing of a motion to add the new party together with the proposed pleading and summons to be served on the new party or, where such party may be added without motion, the filing of the summons and pleading to be served on such new party. Section 306-b of this chapter shall apply to newly added party in any such court, and proof of service with respect to such newly added defendant shall be filed within one hundred twenty days after entry of the order granting leave to add the party or, where no such order is required, the filing of the summons and the pleading to be served on such new party, provided that in an action or proceeding where the applicable statute of limitations is four months or less, such proof of service must be filed not later than fifteen days after the applicable statute of limitations expires.

"summons and complaint" referred to in CPLR 203(c) and 306-b(a) are read broadly to include the supplemental summons and complaint for the new party, then the filing of that instrument would seem to be the operative date that the claim is interposed.

The issue was presented in *Alvarez v. Thrifty Rent-A-Car Systems, Inc.*[70] There, the plaintiff moved for leave to join additional parties to the action and for an extension of time under CPLR 2004 for additional time to file proof of service on the new parties. The court noted that since the action was still viable (plaintiff had complied with CPLR 306-b(a) with respect to the original defendants), there was no reason not to grant the extension under CPLR 2004. In light of this decision, a plaintiff seeking to add new parties would be well advised to seek time within which to file proof of service under *Alvarez*. However, since CPLR 201 forbids the court from extending the statute of limitations, this might help the plaintiff if the statute of limitations expires after the supplemental summons and complaint have been filed but before service has been made on the defendant.

### [4] Comparison with Federal Practice

Under the Federal Rules of Civil Procedure, an action is commenced by filing a complaint with the clerk of the court. The clerk then issues the summons. Fed. R. Civ. P. 4(j) provides that a plaintiff must serve the summons and complaint within 120 days after filing the complaint. The federal rules require only that the plaintiff serve the defendant within the 120-day period; proof of service need only be filed within the defendant's answering time.[71] Moreover, failure to make proof of service does not affect the validity of service and, hence, has no jurisdictional consequences.[72] Should service within the 120-day period prove difficult, the plaintiff may turn to Fed. R. Civ. P. 6(b), which permits the court to enlarge the time for service. In fact, the plaintiff may make a motion to enlarge the service period even after the 120 days has expired, as long as the failure to serve the defendant resulted from "excusable neglect."

The revised CPLR may not be quite so flexible, although it still appears to be rather forgiving as long as the plaintiff pays the price of a new index number. After filing, the plaintiff must serve the defendant and file proof of service within 120 days of the date the summons and complaint were filed.[73] If the plaintiff fails to file proof of service, and the defendant does not make an appearance, the action is automatically "deemed dismissed" without prejudice.[74] If the statute

---

[70] 1995 WL 495114 (Sup. Ct. N.Y. Co., July 28, 1995).

[71] Fed. R. Civ. P. 4(g).

[72] *Id.*

[73] In the case of a special proceeding, the period is 15 days from the running of the statute of limitations. *See* § 9 *infra.*

[74] CPLR 306-b(a).

of limitations has not yet expired, the plaintiff who has experienced such an automatic dismissal can simply commence a new action by paying the fees and serving the defendant again. If the plaintiff wishes to avoid these expenses, it may prove possible to obtain an extension of time under CPLR 2004, although the law on that point is not altogether settled.[75] Thus, as long as a plaintiff is not facing statute of limitations problems, the CPLR operates quite similarly to federal law, particularly if the New York courts take an expansive view of the applicability of CPLR 2004 to the CPLR 306-b(a) deadlines.

Greater divergence from the federal system appears if the statute of limitations expires after the plaintiff commences an action, but before the 120-day period to serve the defendant and file proof of service has run out. CPLR 306-b(b) gives the plaintiff an additional 120 days, measured from the date of dismissal, in which to commence a new action, pay new index number fees and effect new service of process. Even if the plaintiff demonstrates diligent, although unsuccessful, efforts to serve the defendant a course available to the plaintiff under the federal rules failure to effect service within 120 days of filing will result in a dismissal. Presumably, courts cannot grant an extension of this deadline in order to serve the defendant because the result would be a judicial expansion of the statute of limitations, in violation of CPLR 201. The rule may not be quite so draconian if the plaintiff served the defendant during the required 120-day period and the sole defect was the plaintiff's failure to file proof of service with the court in a timely fashion. Since this could be construed as not operating to extend the statute of limitations, it is possible that a court might grant an extension pursuant to CPLR 2004.[76]

### [5] If Filing with the Clerk Is Impeded

CPLR 304 deals with the situation in which a plaintiff is running up against the expiration of the statute of limitations, needs to file a summons and complaint immediately, and discovers that the clerk's office is, for some reason, closed. If a judge finds that "circumstances prevent the immediate filing with the clerk of the court," the court may issue an order "requiring the subsequent filing at a specific time and date not later than five days thereafter." The court's signing of the order commences the action and tolls the statute of limitations.[77] Of course, the value of this provision is limited to times when, despite the unavailability of the clerk's office, it is possible for the plaintiff to secure the presence of a judge.

Moreover, CPLR 304 does not seem to address the situation in which a plaintiff is running up against the 120-day limit for filing proof of service with the clerk. In that circumstance, the plaintiff is apparently either left without a remedy or surrenders to the vagaries of CPLR 2004.[78]

---

[75] See § 8[2] supra.

[76] See § 8[2] supra.

[77] CPLR 304; CPLR 203(c)(2).

[78] See § 8[2] supra.

## § 9   Statute of Limitations

The revised CPLR 203(c) applies to all actions in Supreme and County Court, and provides that a claim is "interposed" against a defendant when the plaintiff files a summons and complaint with the clerk of the court.[79] A plaintiff may also apply to the court for an order permitting a delayed filing if circumstances prevent the immediate filing of the summons and complaint with the clerk.[80] In that case, the order must specify the date that the plaintiff must file the summons and complaint with the clerk no later than five days after the order and the claim is interposed against the defendant at the time the judge signs the order. Under New York law, every action must be interposed within the applicable limitations period. In other words, the statute of limitations stops running when the plaintiff files a summons and complaint with the clerk, or the court signs a five day (maximum) filing-extension order.

### [1] New Savings Provisions

A major concern of the practicing bar is the situation that arises when a plaintiff is unable to serve the defendant within the CPLR 306-b(a) 120-day period, the statute of limitations expires in the interim, and the action is deemed dismissed. CPLR 306-b(b) provides a new savings provision to deal with this concern. The plaintiff may now take advantage of an additional 120 days, measured from the date of dismissal, in which to commence a new action. Because this is a new action, however, the plaintiff must purchase a new index number and effect service of process within the second 120 period.[81]

### [2] Superseded Savings Provisions

CPLR 203(b), and in particular CPLR 203(b)(5), does not apply to actions commenced by filing.[82] This is hardly a dire turn of events, however, since CPLR 203(b)(5) no longer serves a valuable function. CPLR 203(b)(5) provides for service on the sheriff, or county clerk, in order to interpose a claim for statute of limitations purposes. Under prior practice, counsel running up against a limitations problem could deliver the summons to the sheriff of the county in which the defendant could be found and obtain another 60 days in which to effect service.[83] Now, in an ordinary action, simply by filing with the clerk,

---

[79] CPLR 203(c)(1). The CPLR employs the term "interposed" to indicate when the statute of limitations is tolled by bringing the claim against a defendant. An action is time-barred unless the claim is "interposed" within the applicable limitations period.

[80] CPLR 304.

[81] See § 7[1] and 7[2] supra for a complete discussion of CPLR 306-b(b).

[82] This continues to apply in actions commenced in "service" courts. See § 4 supra.

[83] CPLR 203(b)(5) states that a summons may be delivered to the sheriff of the county in which the defendant resides, is employed or is doing business, or, if none of these is known to the plaintiff after reasonable inquiry, of the county in which the defendant is known to have last done these things.

the plaintiff faced with statute of limitations problems obtains 120 days in which to serve the defendant not to mention the additional 120 days available if service is defective and the action is dismissed.[84]

CPLR 205 does not apply to dismissals under the provisions of Chapter 216.[85] An action dismissed for failure to comply with CPLR 306-b(a) may be recommenced under CPLR 306-b(b). In order to achieve the saving provision of CPLR 306-b(b), the plaintiff must not only commence an action within the second 120-day period, but must also effect actual service on the defendant within that same period. If this second step is not accomplished, then plaintiff will not have satisfied the conditions of CPLR 306-b(b). These provisions were designed to prevent the plaintiff from being able to indefinitely extend the statute of limitations by repeatedly filing the summons and complaint but never serving them on the defendant.

Likewise, CPLR 205(a) has been amended by Chapter 216 to provide that to satisfy the conditions of that statute, the plaintiff must not only commence the new action within six months of the dismissal, but must also make actual service on the defendant. Collectively, these provisions mean that the plaintiff will not be able to use CPLR 205 and 306-b(b) seriatim.

## § 10   Special Proceedings

### [1] In General

CPLR 304 provides that a special proceeding is commenced by filing a notice of petition or an order to show cause and a petition. Thus, the procedure is similar to an action, where the summons with notice or the summons and complaint must be filed.

Chapter 216 also makes some allowance for the short limitations period usually involved in special proceedings a mere four months in the case of Article 78 proceedings.[86] CPLR 306-b provides that, in an action or proceeding in which the statute of limitations is four months or less, proof of service must be filed with the court clerk no later than 15 days from the date on which the statute of limitations expires. The time for filing proof of service runs not from the filing of the summons and complaint, as in an ordinary action, but from the date the statute of limitations expires. Nevertheless, if proof of service is not filed within the required time, and the defendant has not appeared, the action will be deemed dismissed.

---

[84] CPLR 306-b(b).

[85] In Campbell v. Command Sec., Inc., — A.D.2d —, 628 N.Y.S.2d 775 (2d Dept. 1995), it was held that CPLR 205(a) could not be used where an action was commenced by service within the July 1, 1992 to December 31, 1992 "window" but was automatically dismissed because plaintiff failed to file the affidavit of service before December 31, 1992.

[86] CPLR 217.

If a special proceeding was timely commenced, but the statute of limitations expired during the period allotted for filing proof of service, the petitioner may take advantage of the time extension offered by CPLR 306-b(b). The petitioner will gain an additional 15 days, measured from the date of dismissal, in which to start a new proceeding, complete with new fees, and to serve the respondent.

### [2] Actions on Instruments for Payment of Money or Money Judgments

It is probably worth noting, as an aside, that Chapter 216 does not expressly treat actions under CPLR 3213, namely actions on instruments for payment of money or money judgments. A CPLR 3213 proceeding is, in essence, a motion for summary judgment complete with return date and an expedited schedule. The plaintiff need only serve a summons and notice of motion, along with any supporting papers. In a CPLR 3213 proceeding, there is no complaint to be filed. Nevertheless, since CPLR 3213 calls for the motion for summary judgment to be in lieu of the complaint, the motion should be filed along with the summons.

An interesting problem was revealed in *Federal Deposit Insurance Corp. v. Goodman.*[87] Plaintiff's legal assistant attempted to commence the CPLR 3213 action by going to the clerk's office, purchasing an index number, and then filing the papers. The clerk advised the legal assistant to file the papers in the motion support office, which she did. Plaintiff then commenced subsequent actions using this procedure. When the plaintiff prevailed on the motion, however, the clerk refused to enter the judgment because the summons had been filed with the motion support office, not with the "clerk." At the suggestion of the clerk, the plaintiff brought an Article 78 proceeding against the clerk, and sought an order from the court directing the clerk to accept the papers "nunc pro tunc."

The court refused to treat the motion support office as the clerk for purposes of the initial filing under CPLR 304, even though the clerk directed the legal assistant there, and perhaps, most significantly, the motion support office was performing one of the functions of the clerk of the court under the clerk's direction. The court granted "nunc pro tunc" orders in the instant case, but suggested that plaintiffs should have to file duplicate sets of papers in both offices and that the clerk's office should post a sign explaining this. As to filing of proof of service in such actions, however, the court held that the motion support clerk is an agent of the county clerk and that filing with the motion support clerk satisfies CPLR 306-b.

The decision in *Goodman* triggered corrective legislation in the 1995 legislative session. Assembly Bill 3807, introduced by Assemblyman Webrin, would have provided that the filing occurs when the papers are delivered to "or any other person designated by the clerk of the court for that purpose." That bill has not yet been acted on. Until such time, courts might consider whether

---

[87] N.Y.L.J., 7/13/95, p. 25, col. 5 (Sup. Ct. N.Y. Co. 1995).

papers filed in the motion support office, because of procedures established by the clerk, are nevertheless filed with the "clerk."

## § 11   Third-Party Proceedings

Chapter 216 introduces some changes in the area of third-party practice, the chief of which is that the third-party plaintiff must file the summons and complaint with the clerk of the court and must pay a separate index number fee.[88] However, the clerk will not assign the matter a separate index number.[89] The served copy of the third-party summons and complaint must bear the index number of the main action, and the dates of both the main filing and the third-party filing.[90]

Otherwise, the procedures governing a third-party action are similar to those that apply to the main action. For example, if someone other than the third-party plaintiff pays the index number fee, that person may recover the fee using the procedures outlined in CPLR 306-a(b).[91] Likewise, proof of service of the third-party summons and complaint must be filed within 120 days after filing. While third-party actions rarely involve statute of limitations problems,[92] the 120-day rule nonetheless applies to them and failure to comply with its dictates will cause the action to be deemed dismissed.[93] Of course, the third-party plaintiff may commence the third-party action for a second time, but it will cost a second filing fee.[94]

## § 12   Surrogate's Court

Chapter 216 made only one change to the Surrogate's Court Procedure Act, repealing SCPA 301, which implemented commencement by filing in the Surrogate's Court. Because SCPA 102 provides that the CPLR governs proceedings in the Surrogate's Court unless the SCPA specifically provides otherwise, SCPA 301 became unnecessary once Chapter 216 was in place. The result is a single change in Surrogate's Court practice, replacing the former 60-day period for filing proof of service with the 120-day period provided in CPLR 306-b.

Under Chapter 379 of the Laws of 1995, SCPA 301 was re-enacted. The new SCPA 301 becomes effective on October 1, 1995 and applies to all actions in the Surrogate's Court commenced on or after that date. The new statute is a

Commence Filing

---

[88] CPLR 305, CPLR 306-a, CPLR 1007.

[89] CPLR 306-a.

[90] CPLR 305.

[91] *See* § 6 *supra* for a complete discussion of this process.

[92] *See, e.g.*, Bay Ridge Air Rights v. State of New York, 44 N.Y.2d 49, 404 N.Y.S.2d 73, 375 N.E.2d 29 (1978). Third-party actions normally involve claims for indemnity and contribution; accordingly, they are covered by the six-year contract statute of limitations (CPLR 213(2)) and the period does not begin to run until the underlying claim is paid.

[93] CPLR 306-b(a).

[94] CPLR 306-b(b).

compromise for those who wanted to re-enact the previous version of SCPA 301, which provided only 60 days to make service after commencement-by-filing, but did not contain any re-commencement provision similar to CPLR 306-b(b).

The new SCPA 301 provides a parallel procedure to the CPLR but with important differences that could work mischief. It provides that a Surrogate's Court proceeding is commenced for purposes of the statute of limitations upon filing of the petition, provided that process is served within 120 days. However, when process is served by publication, the first publication must be made within one hundred twenty days of the filing of the petition. An important distinction, however, is that the requirement of the statute is not the filing of proof of service, as it is under CPLR 306-b(a), it is the *effecting* of service on any respondent. Thus, if proof of service is not validly made, the statute is presumably not satisfied. Another significant distinction is the "any respondent" language. Under CPLR 306-b(a), proof of service must be filed against each defendant, since each defendant is entitled to notice of the suit within a reasonable time of its filing. Under SCPA 301, there appears to be no such requirement.

SCPA 301(b) provides that if a proceeding is dismissed for failure to effect proper service, then the petitioner may commence a new proceeding despite the expiration of the statute of limitations within 120 days after the commencement of a proceeding upon the same instrument, transaction or occurrence, or transactions or occurrences, provided that service is also effected within such 120-day period. This provision appears similar to CPLR 306-b(b)'s requirement of commencement and service within the second 120-day period. It is unclear whether such service must be effected on any respondent or on all of them.

## § 13    Application to Diversity Actions in Federal Court

Chapter 216 will have significant effects on the statutes of limitations in diversity actions brought in New York federal courts. Rule 3 of the Federal Rules of Civil Procedure provides that a federal action is commenced by filing a complaint with the court; however, state law generally controls the time when an action is interposed for statute of limitations purposes.[95] Thus, under prior practice, the plaintiff in a federal diversity action in New York both had to file the complaint with the court in order to commence the action, and had to interpose the claim by one of the methods provided in CPLR 203 usually by service of process in order to toll the statute of limitations. The opportunities for confusion and litigation were legion[96] and dismissals were not unknown.[97]

---

[95] Walker v. Armco Steel, 446 U.S. 740, 64 L. Ed.2d 695, 100 S.Ct. 1978 (1980).

[96] *See, e.g.,* Datskow v. Teledyne, Inc., 899 F.2d 1298 (2d Cir. 1990), *cert. denied,* 111 S. Ct. 149, 112 L. Ed. 116, 498 U.S. 854 (1990) (resolving differences between state and federal practice by holding that, for purposes of CPLR 203(b)(5), filing with the clerk of the federal court is equivalent to delivery to the sheriff); Morse v. Elmira Country Club, 752 F.2d 35 (2d Cir. 1984) (holding mail service sufficient under Fed. R. Civ. P. 4(c)(2)(C)(ii) to interpose a claim for purposes of CPLR

Chapter 216 should eliminate most of this confusion. In a diversity action, filing the complaint will now presumably both commence the action and interpose the claim.[98] Once a plaintiff files a complaint, Fed. R. Civ. P. 4 governs the time in which the plaintiff must make service, the methods for service,[99] and the filing of proof of service. However, it seems that CPLR 306-b(b) will apply to diversity actions since it extends the limitations period in which an otherwise time-barred action may be brought. (*See* § 8[2] *supra* for a complete discussion of this issue.)

## § 14   Persons Excused from Paying Fees

CPLR 1101(d) and 1101(e) provide that the index number fee may be waived in actions commenced by poor persons, or in actions brought by organizations whose primary purpose is the provision of legal services to poor persons. In cases brought by poor persons, the poor person must file along with the summons and complaint an affidavit attesting to inability to pay the costs of the action.[100] If a judge approves the application, the plaintiff will receive written notice of the waiver. If the court denies the application, the plaintiff will receive notice that the fee must be paid within 120 days of the date of the order or the action will be dismissed.[101]

The court will also waive the index number fee in actions commenced by organizations devoted to the provision of legal services to poor persons. In order to obtain this waiver, an organization must file, along with the summons and complaint, an attorney's certification that it has determined the client is unable to pay the costs of the action.[102]

## § 15   Transitional Provisions

The changes in the CPLR enacted by Chapter 216 took effect on July 1, 1992, and apply to all actions commenced on or after that date. However, the legislature provided a six-month transition period in order for all parties concerned to become accustomed to its workings. Until December 31, 1992, an action could

---

203(b) (pre-Chapter 216), despite the defendant's failure to return acknowledgment form, requiring the plaintiff to make use of Fed. R. Civ. P. 4(c)(2)(C)(ii) alternative means of service after expiration of the limitations period).

[97] *See, e.g.,* Levy v. Pyramid Co. of Ithaca, 871 F.2d 9 (2d Cir. 1989) (action commenced by filing complaint in Maryland federal court, but transferred to New York federal court; action dismissed because the plaintiff failed to effect service within the New York statute of limitations period after the transfer).

[98] In the federal courts a summons cannot, strictly speaking, be filed with the clerk. Instead, the clerk issues the summons upon the filing of the complaint and delivers it to the plaintiff, who is then responsible for service on the defendant. Fed. R. Civ. P. 4(a) and 4(b).

[99] Fed. R. Civ. P. 4(c)(2)(C)(i) also incorporates by reference the state service rules.

[100] The official form is reproduced in Appendix B *infra*.

[101] CPLR 1101(d).

[102] CPLR 1101(e).

have been commenced, and the statute of limitations tolled, either by filing pursuant to the new act or by service of the summons, provided that the index number fee was paid by December 31, 1992. Failure to have paid the fee by that date with respect to an action commenced in the window period would result in the action being deemed dismissed without prejudice. If the statute of limitations did not expire by December 31, 1992, the dismissal would be of little moment. If it did expire, then CPLR 205(a) could not be used to recommence it.[103] Nor does CPLR 306-b(b), by its terms, apply to such a situation.[104]

---

[103] In Campbell v. Command Sec., Inc., — A.D.2d —, 628 N.Y.S.2d 775 (2d Dept. 1995).

[104] CPLR 306-b(b) applies only to dismissals for "failure to file proof of service pursuant to *this section* or for failure to effect proper service." (emphasis added). Thus, it would not be applicable to the transitional dismissal, which is not provided for in CPLR 306-b.

# APPENDIX A*
## New and Amended Statutory Provisions

———

### Civil Practice Law and Rules

§ 203. **Method of computing periods of limitation generally.**

(a) Accrual of cause of action and interposition of claim. The time within which an action must be commenced, except as otherwise expressly prescribed, shall be computed from the time the cause of action accrued to the time the claim is interposed.

(b) Claim in complaint where action commenced by service. In an action which is commenced by service, a claim asserted in the complaint is interposed against the defendant or a co-defendant united in interest with such defendant when:

1. the summons is served upon the defendant; or

2. first publication of the summons against the defendant is made pursuant to an order, and publication is subsequently completed; or

3. an order for a provisional remedy other than attachment is granted, if, within thirty days thereafter, the summons is served upon the defendant or first publication of the summons against the defendant is made pursuant to an order and publication is subsequently completed, or, where the defendant dies within thirty days after the order is granted and before the summons is served upon the defendant or publication is completed, if the summons is served upon the defendant's executor or administrator within sixty days after letters are issued; for this purpose seizure of a chattel in an action to recover a chattel is a provisional remedy; or

4. an order of attachment is granted, if the summons is served in accordance with the provisions of section 6213; or

5. the summons is delivered to the sheriff of that county outside the city of New York or is filed with the clerk of that county within the city of New York in which the defendant resides, is employed or is doing business, or if none of the foregoing is known to the plaintiff after reasonable inquiry, then of the county in which the defendant is known to have last resided, been employed or been engaged in business, or in which the cause of action arose; or if the defendant is a corporation, of a county in which it may be served or in which the cause of action arose; provided that:

———

* The sequence of the statutes in this Appendix follows the order in which the amendments appear in Chapter 216.

(i) the summons is served upon the defendant within sixty days after the period of limitation would have expired but for this provision; or

(ii) first publication of the summons against the defendant is made pursuant to an order within sixty days after the period of limitation would have expired but for this provision and publication is subsequently completed; or

(iii) the summons is served upon the defendant's executor or administrator within sixty days after letters are issued, where the defendant dies within sixty days after the period of limitation would have expired but for this provision and before the summons is served upon the defendant or publication is completed.

6. in an action to be commenced in a court not of record, the summons is delivered for service upon the defendant to any officer authorized to serve it in a county, city or town in which the defendant resides, is employed or is doing business, or if none of the foregoing be known to the plaintiff after reasonable inquiry, then in a county, city or town in which defendant is known to have last resided, been employed or been engaged in business, or, where the defendant is a corporation, in a county, city or town in which it may be served, if the summons is served upon the defendant within sixty days after the period of limitation would have expired but for this provision; or, where the defendant dies within sixty days after the period of limitation would have expired but for this provision and before the summons is served upon the defendant, if the summons is served upon his executor or administrator within sixty days after letters are issued.

(c) Claim in complaint where action commenced by filing. In an action which is commenced by filing, a claim asserted in the complaint is interposed against the defendant or a co-defendant united in interest with such defendant when:

1. the summons and complaint or summons with notice is filed with the clerk of the court; or

2. a court signs an order after finding that circumstances prevent the immediate filing of the summons and complaint or summons with notice with the clerk of the court. The court shall specify in the order the time and date, no later than five days after the signing of the order, by which such filing is to occur.

(d) Defense or counterclaim. A defense or counterclaim is interposed when a pleading containing it is served. A defense or counterclaim is not barred if it was not barred at the time the claims asserted in the complaint were interposed, except that if the defense or counterclaim arose from the transactions, occurrences, or series of transactions or occurrences, upon which a claim asserted in the complaint depends, it is not barred to the extent of the demand in the complaint notwithstanding that it was barred at the time the claims asserted in the complaint were interposed.

(e) Effect upon defense or counterclaim of termination of action because of death or by dismissal or voluntary discontinuance. Where a defendant has served an answer containing a defense or counterclaim and the action is terminated because of the plaintiff's death or by dismissal or voluntary discontinuance, the time which elapsed between the commencement and termination of the action is not a part of the time within which an action must be commenced to recover upon the claim in the defense or counterclaim or the time within which the defense or counterclaim may be interposed in another action brought by the plaintiff or his successor in interest.

(f) Claim in amended pleading. A claim asserted in an amended pleading is deemed to have been interposed at the time the claims in the original pleading were interposed, unless the original pleading does not give notice of the transactions, occurrences, or series of transactions or occurrences, to be proved pursuant to the amended pleading.

(g) Time computed from actual or imputed discovery of facts. Except as provided in article two of the uniform commercial code or in section two hundred fourteen-a of this chapter, where the time within which an action must be commenced is computed from the time when facts were discovered or from the time when facts could with reasonable diligence have been discovered, or from either of such times, the action must be commenced within two years after such actual or imputed discovery or within the period otherwise provided, computed from the time the cause of action accrued, whichever is longer.

## § 205.  Termination of action.

(a) New action by plaintiff. If an action is timely commenced and is terminated in any other manner than by a voluntary discontinuance, a failure to obtain personal jurisdiction over the defendant, a dismissal of the complaint for neglect to prosecute the action, or a final judgment upon the merits, the plaintiff, or, if the plaintiff dies, and the cause of action survives, his or her executor or administrator, may commence a new action upon the same transaction or occurrence or series of transactions or occurrences within six months after the termination provided that the new action would have been timely commenced at the time of commencement of the prior action and that service upon defendant is effected within such six-month period.

(b) Defense or counterclaim. Where the defendant has served an answer and the action is terminated in any manner, and a new action upon the same transaction or occurrence or series of transactions or occurrences is commenced by the plaintiff or his successor in interest, the assertion of any cause of action or defense by the defendant in the new action shall be timely if it was timely asserted in the prior action.

(c) Application. This section also applies to a proceeding brought under the workers' compensation law.

## § 207.   Defendant's absence from state or residence under false name.

If, when a cause of action accrues against a person, he is without the state, the time within which the action must be commenced shall be computed from the time he comes into or returns to the state. If, after a cause of action has accrued against a person, that person departs from the state and remains continuously absent therefrom for four months or more, or that person resides within the state under a false name which is unknown to the person entitled to commence the action, the time of his absence or residence within the state under such a false name is not a part of the time within which the action must be commenced. If an action is commenced against a person described above, the time within which service must be made on such person in accordance with subdivisions (a) and (b) of section three hundred six-b of this chapter shall be computed in accordance with this section. This section does not apply:

1. while there is in force a designation, voluntary or involuntary, made pursuant to law, of a person to whom a summons may be delivered within the state with the same effect as if served personally within the state; or

2. while a foreign corporation has one or more officers or other persons in the state on whom a summons against such corporation may be served; or

3. while jurisdiction over the person of the defendant can be obtained without personal delivery of the summons to the defendant within the state.

## § 304.   Method of commencing action or special proceeding.

An action is commenced by filing a summons and complaint or summons with notice with the clerk of the court in the county in which the action is brought. A special proceeding is commenced by filing a notice of petition or order to show cause and a petition with the clerk of the court in the county in which the special proceeding is brought. Where a court finds that circumstances prevent immediate filing with the clerk of the court, the signing of an order requiring the subsequent filing at a specific time and date not later than five days thereafter shall commence the action. For purposes of this section, and for purposes of section two hundred three of this chapter, filing shall mean the delivery of the summons with notice or summons and complaint to the clerk together with any fee required as specified in rule twenty-one hundred two of this chapter for filing.

## R 305.   Summons; supplemental summons; amendment.

[Editor's note: only (a) amended]

(a) Summons; supplemental summons. A summons shall specify the basis of the venue designated and if based upon the residence of the plaintiff it shall specify the plaintiff's address, and also shall bear the index number assigned and the date of filing with the clerk of the court. A third-party summons shall also specify the date of filing of the third-party summons with the clerk of the court. The summons in an action arising out of a consumer credit transaction shall prominently display at the top of the summons the words "consumer credit transaction" and, where a purchaser, borrower or debtor is a defendant, shall specify the county of residence of a defendant, if one resides within the state, and the county where the consumer credit transaction took place, if it is within the state. Where, upon order of the court or by stipulation of all parties or as of right pursuant to section 1003, a new party is joined in the action and the joinder is not made upon the new party's motion, a supplemental summons specifying the pleading which the new party must answer shall be filed with the clerk of the court and served upon such party.

### § 306-a.   Index number in an action commenced in supreme or county court.

(a) Upon filing the summons and complaint or summons with notice with the clerk of the court in an action commenced in supreme or county court, an index number shall be assigned and the fee required by subdivision (a) of section eight thousand eighteen of this chapter shall be paid. Upon the filing of a summons and complaint against a person not already a party, as permitted under section one thousand seven or rule one thousand eleven of this chapter, the fee required by subdivision (a) of section eight thousand eighteen of this chapter shall be paid, but a separate index number shall not be assigned.

(b) If a person other than the plaintiff or third-party plaintiff who served the summons or third-party summons obtains the index number and pays the fee therefor, the clerk shall issue an order directing the plaintiff or the third-party plaintiff to pay such person the amount of the fee paid. If such fee is not paid within thirty days of service of the order with notice of entry, the person who paid the fee, in addition to any other remedies available at law, may apply to the clerk for an order dismissing the action without prejudice.

### § 306-b.   Filing proof of service in an action commenced in supreme or county court.

(a) Proof of service of the summons and complaint, summons with notice, or of the third-party summons and complaint shall be filed with the clerk of the court within one hundred twenty days after the date of filing of the summons and complaint, summons with notice or third-party summons and complaint, provided that in an action or proceeding where the applicable statute of limitations is four months or less, such proof of service must be filed not later than fifteen days after the date on which the applicable statute of limitations expires. If proof of service is not filed and there has been no appearance by the defendant within the time provided in this section for filing proof of service, the action or third-party action shall be deemed dismissed as to the non-appearing party with respect to whom no proof of service has been filed, without prejudice and without costs.

Commence Filing

(b) If an action dismissed for failure to file proof of service pursuant to this section or for failure to effect proper service was timely commenced, the plaintiff may commence a new action, despite the expiration of the statute of limitations after the commencement of the original action, upon the same transaction or occurrence or series of transactions or occurrences within one hundred twenty days of such dismissal provided that service upon the defendant is effected within such one hundred twenty day period. Where the claim asserted is in a proceeding against a body or officer which must be commenced within four months or less, the plaintiff must commence the new action and serve the defendant with* fifteen days of such dismissal.

## § 312-a.   Personal service by mail.

[Editor's note: only (b)(1) amended]

(b) Completion of service and time to answer. 1. The defendant, defendant's attorney or an employee of the attorney must complete the acknowledgement of receipt and mail or deliver a copy of it within thirty days from the date of receipt. Service is complete on the date the signed acknowledgement of receipt is mailed or delivered to the sender. The signed acknowledgement of receipt shall constitute proof of service.

## § 1007.   When third-party practice allowed.

After the service of his answer, a defendant may proceed against a person not a party who is or may be liable to that defendant for all or part of the plaintiff's claim against that defendant, by filing pursuant to section three hundred four of this chapter a third-party summons and complaint with the clerk of the court in the county in which the main action is pending, for which a separate index number shall not be issued but a separate index number fee shall be collected. The third-party summons and complaint and all prior pleadings served in the action shall be served upon such person within one hundred twenty days of the filing. A defendant serving a third-party complaint shall be styled a third-party plaintiff and the person so served shall be styled a third-party defendant. The defendant shall also serve a copy of such third-party complaint upon the plaintiff's attorney simultaneously upon issuance for service of the third-party complaint on the third-party defendant.

## § 1101.   Motion for permission to proceed as a poor person; affidavit; certificate; notice; waiver of fee; when motion not required.

(a) Motion; affidavit. Upon motion of any person, the court in which an action is triable, or to which an appeal has been or will be taken, may grant permission to proceed as a poor person. Where a motion for leave to appeal as a poor person is brought to the court in which an appeal has been or will be taken, such court

---

* [Editor's note: So in original. Should probably read "within."]

shall hear such motion on the merits and shall not remand such motion to the trial court for consideration. The moving party shall file an affidavit setting forth the amount and sources of his or her income and listing his or her property with its value; that he or she is unable to pay the costs, fees and expenses necessary to prosecute or defend the action or to maintain or respond to the appeal; the nature of the action; sufficient facts so that the merit of the contentions can be ascertained; and whether any other person is beneficially interested in any recovery sought and, if so, whether every such person is unable to pay such costs, fees and expenses. An executor, administrator or other representative may move for permission on behalf of a deceased, infant or incompetent poor person.

(b) Certificate. The court may require the moving party to file with the affidavit a certificate of an attorney stating that the attorney has examined the action and believes there is merit to the moving party's contentions.

(c) Notice. If an action has already been commenced, notice of the motion shall be served on all parties, and notice shall also be given to the county attorney in the county in which the action is triable or the corporation counsel if the action is triable in the city of New York.

(d) Waiver of fee in certain cases. A plaintiff may seek to commence his or her action without payment of the fee required by filing the form affidavit, attesting that such plaintiff is unable to pay the costs, fees and expenses necessary to prosecute or defend the action, which shall be available in the clerk's office along with the summons and complaint or summons with notice or third-party summons and complaint. The case will be given an index number, or, in courts other than the supreme or county courts, any necessary filing number and the application will be submitted to a judge of the court. If the court approves the application, the plaintiff will by written order be given notice that all fees and costs relating to the filing and service shall be waived. If the court denies the application the plaintiff will by written order be given notice that the case will be dismissed if the fee is not paid within one hundred twenty days of the date of the order.

(e) When motion not required. Where a party is represented in a civil action by a legal aid society or a legal services or other nonprofit organization, which has as its primary purpose the furnishing of legal services to indigent persons, or by private counsel working on behalf of or under the auspices of such society or organization, all fees and costs relating to the filing and service shall be waived without the necessity of a motion and the case shall be given an index number, or, in a court other than the supreme or county court, an appropriate filing number, provided that a determination has been made by such society, organization or attorney that such party is unable to pay the costs, fees and expenses necessary to prosecute or defend the action, and that an attorney's certification that such determination has been made is filed with the clerk of the court along with the summons and complaint or summons with notice or third-party summons and complaint or otherwise provided to the clerk of the court.

Commence Filing

## § 1319.  Service of summons.

An order of attachment granted before service is made on the defendant against whom the attachment is granted is valid only if, within sixty days after the order is granted, a summons is served upon the defendant or first publication of the summons against the defendant is made pursuant to an order and publication is subsequently completed, except that a person upon whom the order of attachment is served shall not be liable for acting upon it as if it were valid without knowledge of the invalidity. If the defendant dies within sixty days after the order is granted and before the summons is served upon him or her or publication is completed, the order is valid only if the summons is served upon his or her executor or administrator within sixty days after letters are issued. Upon such terms as may be just and upon good cause shown the court may extend the time, not exceeding sixty days, within which the summons must be served or publication commenced pursuant to this section, provided that the application for extension is made before the expiration of the time fixed.

## § 6213.  Service of summons.

An order of attachment granted before service is made on the defendant against whom the attachment is granted is valid only if, within sixty days after the order is granted, a summons is served upon the defendant or first publication of the summons against the defendant is made pursuant to an order and publication is subsequently completed, except that a person upon whom the order of attachment is served shall not be liable for acting upon it as if it were valid without knowledge of the invalidity. If the defendant dies within sixty days after the order is granted and before the summons is served upon him or publication is completed, the order is valid only if the summons is served upon his executor or administrator within sixty days after letters are issued. Upon such terms as may be just and upon good cause shown the court may extend the time, not exceeding sixty days, within which the summons must be served or publication commenced pursuant to this section, provided that the application for extension is made before the expiration of the time fixed.

## § 7102.  Seizure of chattel on behalf of plaintiff.

[Editor's note: only (a) amended]

(a) Seizure of chattel. When the plaintiff delivers to a sheriff an order of seizure, the papers on which the order was granted, and the undertaking and, if an action to recover a chattel has not been commenced, a summons and complaint bearing the index number and the date of filing with the clerk of the court, he shall seize the chattel in accordance with the provisions of the order and without delay.

## Uniform District Court Act

### § 400.   Method of commencing action or special proceeding.

Section three hundred four of the civil practice law and rules shall not apply in this court. An action is commenced in this court and jurisdiction acquired by service of a summons. A special proceeding is commenced and jurisdiction acquired by service of a notice of petition or order to show cause.

———

## New York City Civil Court Act

### § 400.   Method of commencing action or special proceeding.

Section three hundred four of the civil practice law and rules shall not apply in this court. An action is commenced in this court and jurisdiction acquired by service of a summons. A special proceeding is commenced and jurisdiction acquired by service of a notice of petition or order to show cause.

Commence Filing

# Uniform City Court Act

## § 400.   Method of commencing action or special proceeding.

Section three hundred four of the civil practice law and rules shall not apply in this court. An action is commenced in this court and jurisdiction acquired by service of a summons. A special proceeding is commenced and jurisdiction acquired by service of a notice of petition or order to show cause.

## § 409.   Summons; filing; proof of service.

[Editor's note: UCCA Subdivision (a) of section 409 of the uniform city court act is repealed and subdivisions (b) and (c) are relettered subdivisions (a) and (b).]

## § 411.   Summons or notice of petition; filing nunc pro tunc.

Where a summons in an action, or a petition or notice of petition in a special proceeding, has not been filed within the time prescribed by law, or by the rules of the court if such rules shall require filing pursuant to section 409 (a) of this act, the court may order the filing thereof nunc pro tunc. In such instance the court may in its discretion extend the responding time of the other party.

## Uniform Justice Court Act

### § 400.  Method of commencing action or special proceeding.

Section three hundred four of the civil practice law and rules shall not apply in this court. An action is commenced in this court and jurisdiction acquired by service of a summons. A special proceeding is commenced and jurisdiction acquired by service of a notice of petition or order to show cause.

---

Commence Filing

## Domestic Relations Law

### § 211.   Pleadings, proof and motions.

A matrimonial action shall be commenced by the filing of a summons with the notice designated in section two hundred thirty-two of this chapter, or a summons and verified complaint as provided in section three hundred four of the civil practice law and rules. A final judgment shall be entered by default for want of appearance or pleading, or by consent, only upon competent oral proof or upon written proof that may be considered on a motion for summary judgment. Where a complaint or counterclaim in an action for divorce or separation charges adultery, the answer or reply thereto may be made without verifying it, except that an answer containing a counterclaim must be verified as to that counterclaim. All other pleadings in a matrimonial action shall be verified.

## General Municipal Law

### § 504-a.   Abandoned dwellings and mortgage foreclosures in Nassau, Suffolk or Westchester county.

1. Following site designation, pursuant to section five hundred four of this article, a municipality or an urban renewal or community development agency in Nassau, Suffolk or Westchester county may certify a one, two or three family dwelling as abandoned. Upon such certification, an action to foreclose any mortgage on such dwelling may be commenced by*. Process in such action shall be served pursuant to subdivision four upon natural persons who are record owners.

2. Said certification of abandonment may be made if such municipality or agency finds that: (a) all or a part of the subject property lies within an area that has been designated by the governing body as in need of urban renewal, pursuant to such section five hundred four; (b) the subject property has been vacant for sixty consecutive days; and, (c) in the opinion of the certifying municipality or agency the subject property has become a danger to life, public health or public safety and/or has, because of its physical condition and appearance, caused a blighting influence to surrounding properties and is adversely affecting neighborhood property values.

3. Said premises shall be deemed vacant within the meaning of paragraph (b) of subdivision two of this section if three or more of the following conditions exist: (a) termination of service by the lighting company, which termination has lasted for fifteen days; or (b) termination of telephone service by the telephone company, which termination has lasted for fifteen days; or (c) failure to maintain the premises in reasonably good repair; or (d) information from the neighbors that the premises have been vacant for sixty days or more; or (e) accumulation of mail at the premises; or (f) blatant evidence of vandalism; or (g) lack of furnishings inside the premises.

4. Upon said certification of abandonment, the certifying municipality or agency may file or record in the office of the clerk of each county in which all or a part of the subject property is situated, without fee, a certification containing such findings and the facts upon which it is based, describing the property and providing that an action to foreclose any mortgage on said property, may be commenced by filing of the summons and verified complaint with personal service to be made either as provided in subdivisions one through four of section three hundred eight of the civil practice law and rules, or, with respect to natural persons who are record owners, by publishing, without the necessity for a court order, of a copy of the summons together with notice to the defendant, a brief statement of the nature of the action and the relief sought, the sum of

---

*[Editor's note: So in original.]

money for which judgment may be taken in case of default, and a brief description of the property, at least once in each of three successive weeks in a newspaper in the English language of general circulation in the municipality wherein all or a part of the property lies and by mailing a copy of the summons and verified complaint to the last known address of the record owner or owners of the premises, certified mail, return receipt requested and by tacking a copy of the summons and verified complaint, to the front door of the premises. Service shall be deemed complete twenty days after the last date of publication, date of mailing or date of posting, whichever occurs last.

5. All other parties to the lawsuit, other than record owners, shall be served with the summons and verified complaint as presently provided in the CPLR.

# Navigation Law

## § 48. Negligence in use or operation of vessel attributable to owner

**[Editor's note:** only (1) amended]

1. Every owner of a vessel used or operated upon the navigable waters of the state or any tidewaters bordering on or lying within the boundaries of Nassau and Suffolk counties, shall be liable and responsible for death or injuries to person or property resulting from negligence in the use or operation of such vessel, in the business of such owner, or otherwise, by any person using or operating the same with the permission, express or implied, of such owner.

The use or operation by a non-resident or non-residents of a vessel in this state, or the use or operation in this state of a vessel in the business of a non-resident, or the use or operation in this state of a vessel owned by a non-resident if so used or operated with his permission, express or implied, shall be deemed equivalent to an appointment by such non-resident of the secretary of state to be his true and lawful attorney upon whom may be served the summons in any action against him, growing out of any accident or collision in which such non-resident may be involved while using or operating such vessel in this state or in which such vessel may be involved while being used or operated in this state in the business of such non-resident or with the permission, express or implied, of such non-resident owner; and such use or operation shall be a signification of his agreement that any such summons against him which is so served shall be of the same legal force and validity as if served on him personally within the state and within the territorial jurisdiction of the court from which the summons issues, and that such appointment of the secretary of state shall be irrevocable and binding upon his executor or administrator. Where such non-resident has died prior to the commencement of an action brought pursuant to this section, service of process shall be made on the executor or administrator of such non-resident in the same manner and on the same notice as is provided in the case of the non-resident himself. Where an action has been duly commenced under the provisions of this section against a non-resident who dies thereafter, the court must allow the action to be continued against his executor or administrator upon motion with such notice as the court may deem proper.

## § 74. Service of summons & complaint on non-residents.

**[Editor's note:** only (1) amended]

1. The use, operation, navigation or maintenance by a non-resident, or in his business, of a vessel in waters of this state; or owned by a non-resident and used, operated, navigated or maintained with his permission in waters of this state, shall be deemed equivalent to an appointment by such non-resident of the secretary of state to be his true and lawful attorney upon whom may be served

the summons and complaint in any action against him, growing out of any accident or collision in which such non-resident may be involved while using, operating, navigating or maintaining such vessel in waters of this state, or in which such vessel may be involved while being used, operated, navigated or maintained in such waters in the business of the non-resident, or with the permission, expressed or implied, of such non-resident, and such use, operation, navigation or maintenance shall be deemed a signification of his agreement that any such summons and complaint against him which is so served shall be of the same legal force and validity as if served upon him personally within the state and the territorial jurisdiction of the court from which the summons issues, and that such appointment of the secretary of state shall be irrevocable and binding upon his executor or administrator. Where such non-resident has died prior to the commencement of an action brought pursuant to this section, service of summons and complaint shall be made on the executor or administrator of such non-resident in the same manner and on the same notice as is provided in the case of the non-resident himself. Where an action has been duly commenced under the provisions of this section against a non-resident who dies thereafter, the court must allow the action to be continued against his executor or administrator upon motion with such notice as the court deems proper.

# Parks, Recreation and Historic Preservation Law

## § 25.27.   Service on nonresidents and certain residents, administrators or executors.

[Editor's note: only (1) amended]

1. The use or operation by a nonresident of a snowmobile in this state, or the use or operation in this state of a snowmobile in the business of a nonresident or the use or operation in this state of a snowmobile owned by a nonresident if so used or operated with his permission, express or implied, shall be deemed equivalent to an appointment by such nonresident of the secretary of state to be his true and lawful attorney upon whom may be served the summons in any action against him, growing out of any accident or collision in which such nonresident may be involved while using or operating such snowmobile in this state or in which such snowmobile may be involved while being used or operated in this state in the business of such nonresident or with the permission, express or implied, of such nonresident or with the permission, express of * implied, of such nonresident owner. Such use or operation shall be deemed a signification of his agreement that any such summons against him which is so served shall be of the same legal force and validity as if served on him personally within the state and within the territorial jurisdiction of the court from which the summons issues, and that such appointment of the secretary of state shall be irrevocable and binding upon his executor or administrator. Where such nonresident has died prior to the commencement of an action brought pursuant to this section, service of process shall be made on the executor or administrator of such nonresident in the same manner and on the same notice as is provided in the case of the nonresident himself. Where an action has been duly commenced under the provisions of this section against a nonresident who dies thereafter, the court shall allow the action to be continued against his executor or administrator upon motion with such notice as the court deems proper.

---

* [Editor's note: So in original. Should probably read "or."]

# Vehicle and Traffic Law

### § 253.  Service of summons on non-residents.

[Editor's note: only (1) amended]

1. The use or operation by a non-resident of a vehicle in this state, or the use or operation in this state of a vehicle in the business of a non-resident, or the use or operation in this state of a vehicle owned by a non-resident if so used or operated with his permission, express or implied, shall be deemed equivalent to an appointment by such non-resident of the secretary of state to be his true and lawful attorney upon whom may be served the summons in any action against him, growing out of any accident or collision in which such non-resident may be involved while using or operating such vehicle in this state or in which such vehicle may be involved while being used or operated in this state in the business of such non-resident or with the permission, express or implied, of such non-resident owner; and such use or operation shall be deemed a signification of his agreement that any such summons against him which is so served shall be of the same legal force and validity as if served on him personally within the state and within the territorial jurisdiction of the court from which the summons issues, and that such appointment of the secretary of state shall be irrevocable and binding upon his executor or administrator. Where such non-resident has died prior to the commencement of an action brought pursuant to this section, service of process shall be made on the executor or administrator of such non-resident in the same manner and on the same notice as is provided in the case of the non-resident himself. Where an action has been duly commenced under the provisions of this section against a non-resident who dies thereafter, the court must allow the action to be continued against his executor or administrator upon motion with such notice as the court deems proper.

## APPENDIX B

# FORM AFFIDAVIT FOR LITIGANTS PROCEEDING AS POOR PERSONS

_____ COURT OF _____

COUNTY OF _____

_____ , Plaintiff
(Petitioner)

v.

_____ , Defendant
(Respondent)

AFFIDAVIT IN SUPPORT OF APPLICATION FOR WAIVER OF FILING AND SERVICE FEES AND COSTS AND TO PROCEED AS A POOR PERSON

The undersigned, being duly sworn, says:

1. I am the plaintiff or petitioner in this case. This statement is made in support of my request (a) for waiver of the index number fee and/or any other filing and service fees and costs, and (b) to proceed in this case as a poor person.

2. I support myself and _____ others in my household.

3. My only source of income is (check one):
   [  ]  Public assistance
   [  ]  Social security/SSI
   [  ]  Other _____

4. The amount of income I receive each month is $_____.

5. Check one of the items below:
   [  ]  I do not have a bank account.
   [  ]  I have a bank account with approximately $_____ in the account.

6. I own the following property which has an estimated value as indicated: [IF NONE, WRITE "NONE"]

<u>LIST PROPERTY</u>                    <u>VALUE</u>

_____        _____
_____        _____
_____        _____

Commence Filing

7. I have no other savings, property or assets.

8. I am unable to pay the costs, fees and expenses necessary to assert my rights in this case.

9. No one else who is able to pay any required costs and fees has a beneficial interest in the results of this case.

10. The facts of my case are described in my court papers, which are attached.

11. I have made no prior request for this relief in this case.

WHEREFORE, I request (a) that all fees relating to the filing and service of this action or proceeding be waived, and (b) that I be permitted to proceed in this case in all respects as a poor person.

_____

(Signature)

Sworn to before me
this _____ day of _____, 19_____.

# COURT DIRECTORY

---

## STATE-WIDE COURT ADMINISTRATIVE OFFICES

**Office of Court Administration**

270 Broadway
New York, New York 10007
Honorable Jonathan Lippman, Chief Administrative Judge
(518) 473-6087
(212) 417-2000 (New York City Office)

**Commission on Judicial Conduct**

801 Second Avenue, 13th Floor
New York, New York 10017
(212) 949-8860

Agency Building I
38-40 State Street, 1st Floor
Albany, New York 12207
(518) 474-5617

227 Alexander Street, Room 710
Rochester, New York 14607
(716) 232-5756

**Lawyers' Fund for Client Protection**

55 Elk Street
Albany, New York 12210-2305
(518) 474-8438
(800) 422-3863 (within New York State)

**Department of State, Division of Corporations and State Records**

162 Washington Avenue
Albany, New York 12231
(518) 473-2492
Corporate Search: 1-900-835-2677

Secretary of State Executive Offices
270 Broadway
New York, New York 10007
(212) 417-5800

## NEW YORK STATE COURTS
### Court of Appeals

Court of Appeals Hall
20 Eagle Street
Albany, New York 12207-1095
(518) 455-7700

### Appellate Division
### First Department

27 Madison Avenue
New York, New York 10010
(212) 340-0400

### Second Department

45 Monroe Place
Brooklyn, New York 11201
(718) 875-1300

### Third Department

Justice Building
South Mall
Albany, New York 12223
(518) 474-3609

mailing address:
P.O. Box 7288
Capitol Station
Albany, New York 12224

### Fourth Department

501 Hall of Justice
Civic Center Plaza
Rochester, New York 14614
(716) 428-1000

### Court of Claims

Justice Building, Empire State Plaza
P.O. Box 7344
Capitol Station
Albany, New York 12224
(518) 465-8881

5 World Trade Center, 8th Floor
New York, New York 10048
(212) 775-0100

## COUNTY DIRECTORY
### Albany County

(Third Department, Third Judicial District)

Supreme Court

Albany County Court House
Albany, New York 12207
Chief Clerk: (518) 487-5019

Surrogate's Court

Albany County Court House, Rm 125
Albany, New York 12207
(518) 487-5393
Chief Clerk: (518) 487-5390

County Court

Albany County Court House
Albany, New York 12207
(518) 487-5013

Family Court
1 Van Tromp Street
Albany, New York 12207
(518) 427-3500

City Court

Civil Court
City Hall, Room 209
Eagle & Corning Pl.
Albany, New York 12207
(518) 434-5113

P.O. Box 678
Cohoes, New York 12047-0678
(518) 237-7646

City Hall
15th Street & Broadway
Watervliet, New York 12189
(518) 270-3803

Sheriff

Albany County Court House
Albany, New York 12207
(518) 487-5400

## Allegany County

(Fourth Department, Eighth Judicial District)

Supreme Court

Court House
Belmont, New York 14813
(716) 268-5813

Surrogate's Court

Court House
Belmont, New York 14813
(716) 268-5815

County Court

Court House
Belmont, New York 14813
(716) 268-5813

Family Court

Court House
Belmont, New York 14813
(716) 268-5816

Sheriff

7 Court Street
Belmont, New York 14813
(716) 268-9211

## Bronx County

(First Department, Twelfth Judicial District)

Supreme Court

851 Grand Concourse
Bronx, New York 10451
Civil Division: (718) 590-3722, 3
First Deputy Chief Clerk, Civil Branch: (718) 590-3714

Surrogate's Court

851 Grand Concourse, Rm. 406
Bronx, New York 10451
(718) 590-3611

Family Court

900 Sheridan Avenue
Bronx, New York 10451
(718) 590-3318, 9

Civil Court

851 Grand Concourse
Bronx, New York 10451
(718) 590-3000

## Broome County

(Third Department, Sixth Judicial District)

Supreme Court

Court House
Binghamton, New York 13902-1766
(607) 778-2448

Surrogate's Court

Court House
Binghamton, New York 13902-1766
(607) 778-2111

County Court

Justice Building, 4th Floor
Hawley Street
Binghamton, New York 13901
(607) 778-2431, 2418

Family Court

Justice Building
Hawley Street
Binghamton, New York 13901
(607) 778-2156

City Court

Governmental Plaza
38 Hawley Street
Binghamton, New York 13901
(607) 772-7006

Sheriff

897 Upper Front Street
Binghamton, New York 13905
(607) 778-2492

## Cattaraugus County

(Fourth Department, Eighth Judicial District)

Supreme Court

County Center
303 Court Street
Little Valley, New York 14755
(716) 938-9111

Surrogate's Court

Court House
Little Valley, New York 14755-1096
(716) 938-9111, Ext. 327

County Court

Court House
Little Valley, New York 14755
(716) 938-9111, Ext. 387, 8

Family Court

1701 Lincoln Avenue, Suite 1140
Olean, New York 14760-1152
(716) 373-8035

City Court

Municipal Building
P.O. Box 631
Olean, New York 14760-0631
(716) 376-5620

Municipal Center
225 Wild Wood Ave.
Salamanca, New York 14779
(716) 945-4153

Sheriff

County Office Building
Little Valley, New York 14755
(716) 938-9111

## Cayuga County

(Fourth Department, Seventh Judicial District)

Supreme Court

Court House
154 Genessee Street
Auburn, New York 13021-3474
(315) 255-4320

Surrogate's Court

Court House
154 Genessee Street
Auburn, New York 13021-3471
(315) 255-4316

County Court

Court House
Auburn, New York 13021-3474
(315) 255-4320

Family Court

Court House, Third Floor
Auburn, New York 13021-3476
(315) 255-4306

City Court

153 Genesee Street
Auburn, New York 13021-3434
(315) 253-1570

Sheriff

P.O. Box 518
Auburn, New York 13021
(315) 253-1222

## Chautauqua County

(Fourth Department, Eighth Judicial District)

Supreme Court

Court House
1 North Erie Street
P.O. Box 292
Mayville, New York 14757-0292
(716) 753-4266

Surrogate's Court

Gerace Office Building
P.O. Box C
Mayville, New York 14757-0299
(716) 753-4339

County Court

Court House
1 North Erie Street
P.O. Box 292
Mayville, New York 14757-0292
(716) 753-4266

Family Court

Gerace Office Building
P.O. Box 149
Mayville, New York 14757
(716) 753-4351

City Court

Dunkirk City Court—City Hall
342 Central Ave.
Dunkirk, New York 14048-2122
(716) 366-2055

City Hall
Municipal Building
200 East 3rd Street
Jamestown, New York 14701
(716) 483-7561, 2

Sheriff

Sheriff's Office
P.O. Box 128
Mayville, New York 14757
(716) 753-2131

### Chemung County

(Third Department, Sixth Judicial District)

Supreme Court

203 Lake Street, 6th Floor
Elmira, New York 14902-0588
(607) 737-2847
Chief Clerk: (607) 737-2084

Surrogate's Court

P.O. Box 588
224 Lake St.
Elmira, New York 14902-0588
(607) 737-2946, 2819

County Court

Court House
203 Lake Street
P.O. Box 588
Elmira, New York 14902-0588
(607) 737-2084

Family Court

203 William Street
P.O. Box 588
Elmira, New York 14902-0588
(607) 737-2902, 2903

City Court

City Hall
317 East Church Street
Elmira, New York 14901
(607) 737-5681

Sheriff

211 William Street
Elmira, New York 14902-0588
(607) 737-2930

## Chenango County

(Third Department, Sixth Judicial District)

Supreme Court

Court House
5 Court Street
Norwich, New York 13815
(607) 337-1740
Court Clerk: (607) 337-1457

Surrogate's Court

County Office Building
5 Court Street
Norwich, New York 13815
(607) 337-1827, 1822

County Court

County Office Building
5 Court Street
Norwich, New York 13815
(607) 337-1825

Family Court

County Office Building
5 Court Street
Norwich, New York 13815
(607) 337-1820

City Court

45 South Broad Street
Norwich, New York 13815
(607) 334-1224

Sheriff

14 West Park Place
Norwich, New York 13815
(607) 334-2000

## Clinton County

(Third Department, Fourth Judicial District)

Supreme Court

County Government Center
137 Margaret Street
Plattsburgh, New York 12901-2933
(518) 565-4715

Surrogate's Court

County Government Center
137 Margaret Street
Plattsburgh, New York 12901-2933
(518) 565-4630

County Court

County Government Center
137 Margaret Street
Plattsburgh, New York 12901-2933
(518) 565-4657

Family Court

County Government Center
137 Margaret Street
Plattsburgh, New York 12901-2933
(518) 565-4658

City Court

City Hall
41 City Hall Place
Plattsburgh, New York 12901
(518) 563-7870

Court Directory

Sheriff

25 McCarthy Drive
Plattsburgh, New York 12901
(518) 561-1810

## Columbia County

(Third Department, Third Judicial District)

Supreme Court

Court House
401 Union Street
Hudson, New York 12534
(518) 828-7858

Surrogate's Court

Court House
401 Union Street
Hudson, New York 12534
(518) 828-0414

County Court

Court House
401 Union Street
Hudson, New York 12534
(518) 828-7909

Family Court

Court House 401 Union Street
Hudson, New York 12534
(518) 828-0315

City Court

429 Warren Street
Hudson, New York 12534
(518) 828-3100

Sheriff

85 Industrial Tract
Hudson, New York 12534
(518) 828-3344

## Cortland County

(Third Department, Sixth Judicial District)

Supreme Court

Court House
46 Greenbush Street, Suite 301
Cortland, New York 13045-2725
(607) 753-5010
Chief Clerk: (607) 753-5013

Surrogate's Court

Court House
46 Greenbush Street, Suite 301
Cortland, New York 13045-2725
(607) 753-5355

County Court

Court House
46 Greenbush Street, Suite 301
Cortland, New York 13045-2725
(607) 753-5010

Family Court

Court House
46 Greenbush Street, Suite 301
Cortland, New York 13045-2725
(607) 753-5353

City Court

25 Court Street
Cortland, New York 13045
(607) 753-1811

Sheriff

Court House
54 Greenbush Street
Cortland, New York 13045
(607) 753-3311

## Delaware County

(Third Department, Sixth Judicial District)

Supreme Court

Court House
3 Court Street
P.O. Box 231
Delhi, New York 13753
(607) 746-2131

Surrogate's Court

Court House
3 Court Street
Delhi, New York 13753
(607) 746-2126

County Court

Court House
3 Court Street
Delhi, New York 13753
Clerk: (607) 746-2131

Family Court

Court House
3 Court Street
Delhi, New York 13753
(607) 746-2298

Sheriff

Court House Square
P.O. Box 326
Delhi, New York 13753
(607) 746-2336

## Dutchess County

(Second Department, Ninth Judicial District)

Supreme Court

Court House
Poughkeepsie, New York 12601-3203
(914) 486-2260

Surrogate's Court

Court House
10 Market Street
Poughkeepsie, New York 12601-3203
(914) 486-2235

County Court

Court House
10 Market Street
Poughkeepsie, New York 12601-3203
(914) 486-2260

Family Court

28 Market Street
Poughkeepsie, New York 12601-3204
(914) 486-2500

City Court

463 Main Street
Beacon, New York 12508
(914) 831-7480

Civic Center Plaza
P.O. Box 300
Poughkeepsie, New York 12601
(914) 451-4091

Sheriff

150 North Hamilton Street
Poughkeepsie, New York 12602
(914) 452-0400

## Erie County

(Fourth Department, Eighth Judicial District)

Supreme Court

Erie County Hall
92 Franklin Street
Buffalo, New York 14202
(716) 851-3291

Surrogate's Court

Erie County Hall
92 Franklin Street
Buffalo, New York 14202
(716) 854-7867

County Court

Erie County Hall
92 Franklin Street
Buffalo, New York 14202
Chief Clerk: (716) 858-8452

Family Court

25 Delaware Avenue
Buffalo, New York 14202
(716) 858-8100

City Court

50 Delaware Avenue
Buffalo, New York 14202
(716) 847-8200

City Hall
714 Ridge Road
Lackawanna, New York 14218-1588
(716) 827-6486

City Hall
200 Niagara Street
Tonawanda, New York 14150
(716) 693-3484, 5, 6

Sheriff

10 Delaware Avenue
Buffalo, New York 14202
(716) 858-7608

## Essex County

(Third Department, Fourth Judicial District)

Supreme Court

Essex County Government Center
P.O. Box 217
Elizabethtown, New York 12932
(518) 873-3370, 1

Surrogate's Court

County Court Building
P.O. Box 505
Elizabethtown, New York 12932
(518) 873-3384, 5

County Court

Essex County Government Center
P.O. Box 217
Elizabethtown, New York 12932
(518) 873-3370, 1

Family Court

Court House
Elizabethtown, New York 12932
(518) 873-3320

Sheriff

Court House
P.O. Box 278
Elizabethtown, New York 12932
(518) 873-3346

## Franklin County

(Third Department, Fourth Judicial District)

Supreme Court

Court House
63 West Main Street
Malone, New York 12953-1817
(518) 481-1749

Surrogate's Court

Court House
63 West Main Street
Malone, New York 12953-1893
(518) 481-1737

County Court

Court House
63 West Main Street
Malone, New York 12953-1893
(518) 481-1749

Family Court

Court House
63 West Main Street
Malone, New York 12953-1893
(518) 481-1742

Commissioner of Jurors

63 West Main Street
Malone, New York 12953

Sheriff

Box 196T
R.R. #2 Bear Hill Road
Malone, New York 12953
(518) 483-6795, 6

## Fulton County

(Third Department, Fourth Judicial District)

Supreme Court

223 West Main Street
Johnstown, New York 12095
(518) 762-0539

Surrogate's Court

County Building
223 West Main Street
Johnstown, New York 12095
(518) 762-0685

County Court
223 West Main Street

County Building
P.O. Box 485
223 West Main Street
Johnstown, New York 12095
(518) 762-0539

Family Court

County Building
223 West Main Street
Johnstown, New York 12095
(518) 762-3840

City Court

City Hall
Frontage Road
Gloversville, New York 12078
(518) 773-4527

City Hall
33-41 East Main Street
Johnstown, New York 12095
(518) 762-0007

Sheriff
2712 State Highway 29
P.O. Box 20
Johnstown, New York 12095
(518) 762-3151

## Genesee County

(Fourth Department, Eighth Judicial District)

Supreme Court

Genesee County Building 1
P.O. Box 462
Batavia, New York 14021-0462
(716) 344-2550, Ext. 239

Surrogate's Court

Genesee County Building 1
P.O. Box 462
Batavia, New York 14021-0462
(716) 344-2550, Ext. 237

County Court

Genesee County Building 1
P.O. Box 462
Batavia, New York 14021-0462
(716) 344-2550, Ext. 239

Family Court

Genesee County Building 1
P.O. Box 462
Batavia, New York 14021-0462
(716) 344-2550, Ext. 228

City Court

City Hall
10 West Main Street
P.O. Box 385
Batavia, New York 14021-0385
(716) 343-8180, Exts. 232, 233, 234

Sheriff

14 West Main Street
P.O. Box 151
Batavia, New York 14021-0151
(716) 343-0911

## Greene County

(Third Department, Third Judicial District)

Supreme Court

Greene County Court House
320 Main Street
Catskill, New York 12414
(518) 943-2230
Chief Clerk: (518) 943-2230

Surrogate's Court

Greene County Court House
320 Main Street
Catskill, New York 12414
(518) 943-2484

County Court

Greene County Court House
320 Main Street
Catskill, New York 12414
(518) 943-2050
Chief Clerk: (518) 943-2050

Family Court

Greene County Court House
320 Main Street
Catskill, New York 12414
(518) 943-5711

Sheriff

80 Bridge Street
Catskill, New York 12414
(518) 943-3300

## Hamilton County

(Third Department, Fourth Judicial District)

Supreme Court

No sessions held (*See Fulton County for information*)

Surrogate's Court

Chambers
P.O. Box 780
Indian Lake, New York 12842-0780
(518) 648-5411

County Court

*mailing address*:
P.O. Box 780
Indian Lake, New York 12842-0780

*Court sessions held at*:
Court House
Lake Pleasant, New York 12108
(518) 548-3211

Chambers
P.O. Box 780
Indian Lake, New York 12842-0780
(518) 648-5411

Sheriff
P.O. Box 210
South Shore Road
Lake Pleasant, New York 12108
(518) 548-3113

## Herkimer County

(Fourth Department, Fifth Judicial District)

Supreme Court

Court House
P.O. Box 907
Herkimer County Court House
320 N. Main Street
Herkimer, New York 13350-0749
(315) 867-1186
Chief Clerk: (315) 867-1209

Surrogate's Court

Court House
P.O. Box 907
Herkimer County Court House
320 N. Main Street
Herkimer, New York 13350-0749
(315) 867-1170

County Court

Court House
P.O. Box 907
Herkimer County Court House
320 N. Main Street
Herkimer, New York 13350-0749
(315) 867-1171
Chief Clerk: (315) 867-1209

Family Court

Herkimer County Office Building
P.O. Box 749
119 Mary Street
Herkimer, New York 13350-0749
(315) 867-1139

City Court

City Hall
659 East Main Street
Little Falls, New York 13365
(315) 823-1690

Sheriff

109-111 Mary Street
P.O. Box 709
Herkimer, New York 13350-0709
(315) 867-1167

## Jefferson County

(Fourth Department, Fifth Judicial District)

Supreme Court

Dulles State Office Building, 10th Floor
317 Washington Street
Watertown, New York 13601
(315) 782-9290
Chief Clerk: (315) 782-9290

Surrogate's Court

County Office Building, 7th Floor
175 Arsenal Street
Watertown, New York 13601-2562
(315) 785-3019

County Court

Jefferson Couny Court House
195 Arsenal Street
Watertown, New York 13601-2577
(315) 785-3044

Family Court

County Office Building
County Office Building
175 Arsenal Street, 5th Floor
Watertown, New York 13601-2560
(315) 785-3001

City Court

Municipal Building
245 Washington Street
Watertown, New York 13601
(315) 785-7785

Sheriff

753 City Center Drive West
Watertown, New York 13601
(315) 786-2600

## Kings County

(Second Department, Second Judicial District)

Supreme Court
Civic Center
Montague Street
Brooklyn, New York 11201
(718) 643-8076, 8077

Surrogate's Court
2 Johnson Place
Brooklyn, New York 11201
(718) 643-5262

Family Court
283 Adams Street
Brooklyn, New York 11201
(718) 643-4546

Civil Court
141 Livingston Street
Brooklyn, New York 11201
(718) 643-5069

Under Sheriff
Municipal Building
210 Joralemon Street
Brooklyn, New York 11201
(718) 802-3543

## Lewis County

(Fourth Department, Fifth Judicial District)

Supreme Court

Court House
P.O. Box 232
7660 State Street
Lowville, New York 13367-1396
(315) 376-5333
Court Clerk: (315) 376-5380

Surrogate's Court

County Court House
7660 State Street
Lowville, New York 13367-1396
(315) 376-5344

County Court

County Court House
7660 State Street
Lowville, New York 13367-1396
(315) 376-5366

Family Court

County Court House
7660 State Street
Lowville, New York 13367-1396
(315) 376-5345

Sheriff

Public Safety Building
P.O. Box 233
Lowville, New York 13367
(315) 376-3511

## Livingston County

(Fourth Department, Seventh Judicial District)

Supreme Court

Livingston County Court House
2 Court Street
Geneseo, New York 14454-1030
(716) 243-7060

Surrogate's Court

Livingston County Court House
2 Court Street
Geneseo, New York 14454-1030
(716) 243-7095

County Court

Livingston County Court House
2 Court Street
Geneseo, New York 14454-1030
(716) 243-7060

Family Court

Livingston County Court House
2 Court Street
Geneseo, New York 14454-1030
(716) 243-7070

Sheriff

4 Court Street
Geneseo, New York 14454
(716) 243-7120

## Madison County

(Third Department, Sixth Judicial District)

Supreme Court

North Court Street
P.O. Box 545
Wampsville, New York 13163-0545
(315) 366-2267

Surrogate's Court

Court House
North Court Street
P.O. Box 607
Wampsville, New York 13163
(315) 366-2392

County Court

Court House
North Court Street
P.O. Box 545
Wampsville, New York 13163
(315) 366-2266

Family Court

Court House
North Court Street
P.O. Box 607
Wampsville, New York 13163
(315) 366-2291

City Court

109 North Main Street
Oneida, New York 13421
(315) 363-1310

Sheriff
P.O. Box 16
Wampsville, New York 13163
(315) 366-2289

## Monroe County

(Fourth Department, Seventh Judicial District)

Supreme Court
400 Hall of Justice
Rochester, New York 14614-2185
(716) 428-2020
Chief Clerk: (716) 428-5001

Surrogate's Court
304 Hall of Justice
Rochester, New York 14614-2186
(716) 428-5200

County Court
400 Hall of Justice
99 Exchange Street
Rochester, New York 14614-2184
(716) 428-2331

Family Court
300 Hall of Justice
99 Exchange Street
Rochester, New York 14614-2187
(716) 428-5429

City Court
1 Hall of Justice
99 Exchange Blvd.
Rochester, New York 14614
Civil: (716) 428-2444

Sheriff
130 South Plymouth Avenue
Rochester, New York 14614
(716) 428-5780, 1

## Montgomery County

(Third Department, Fourth Judicial District)

Supreme Court

Court House
P.O. Box 1500
Fonda, New York 12068
(518) 853-4516

Surrogate's Court

Court House
Broadway
P.O. Box 1500
Fonda, New York 12068-1500
(518) 853-8108

County Court

Court House
Broadway
P.O. Box 1500
Fonda, New York 12068
(518) 853-3431, 3834

Family Court

Court House
Broadway
P.O. Box 1500
Fonda, New York 12068
(518) 853-8133

City Court
Public Safety Building, Room 208
Amsterdam, New York 12010
(518) 842-9510

Sheriff
Sheriff's Office
5 Park Street
Fonda, New York 12068
Civil: (518) 853-5500

## Nassau County

(Second Department, Tenth Judicial District)

Supreme Court

Supreme Court Building
100 Supreme Court Dr.
Mineola, New York 11501
(516) 571-2966
Chief Clerk: (516) 571-2903

Surrogate's Court

262 Old Country Road
Mineola, New York 11501
(516) 571-2082
Chief Clerk - Referee: (516) 571-2082

County Court

County Court House
262 Old Country Road
Mineola, New York 11501
(516) 571-2800, 2801
Chief Clerk: (516) 571-2720

Family Court

1200 Old Country Road
Westbury, New York 11590
(516) 571-9033
Chief Clerk: (516) 571-9030

District Court

First District Court

99 Main Street
Hempstead, New York 11550
Civil Court: (516) 572-2264

Second District Court

Town Hall
99 Main Street
Hempstead, New York 11550
(516) 572-2264

Third District Court
435 Middleneck Road
Great Neck, New York 11023
(516) 482-0702

Fourth District Court
87 Bethpage Road
Hicksville, New York 11801
(516) 931-0231

City Court
13 Glen Street
Glen Cove, New York 11542-2776
(516) 676-0109

1 West Chester Street
Long Beach, New York 11561
(516) 431-1000

Sheriff

County Office Building
240 Old Country Road
Mineola, New York 11501
(516) 571-2113

## New York County

(First Department, First Judicial District)

Supreme Court

60 Centre Street
New York, New York 10007-1474
(212) 374-8357
Chief Clerk and Executive Officer, Civil Branch: (212) 374-4422

Surrogate's Court

31 Chambers Street
New York, New York 10007
(212) 374-8233

Family Court

60 Lafayette Street
New York, New York 10013
(212) 374-8791

Civil Court

111 Centre Street
New York, New York 10013
(212) 374-8174
Civil Court Information Line (*all 5 boroughs*): (212) 791-7000

Sheriff
31 Chambers Street
New York, New York 10007
(212) 788-8730, 1

## Niagara County

(Fourth Department, Eighth Judicial District)

Supreme Court

775 3rd Street
Niagara Falls, New York 14302-1710
(716) 278-1800

Surrogate's Court

Court House
175 Hawley Street
Lockport, New York 14094-2758
(716) 439-7130

Niagara County Civil Building
3rd and Cedar Street
Niagara Falls, New York 14302-1710
(716) 278-1821

County Court

Court House
175 Hawley Street
Lockport, New York 14094-2758
Clerk: (716) 434-3272

Family Court

Court House
175 Hawley Street
Lockport, New York 14094-2758
(716) 434-1992

County Building
775 3rd Street
Niagara Falls, New York 14302-0366
(716) 284-3158

City Court
Lockport Municipal Building
One Locks Plaza
Lockport, New York 14094
Civil: (716) 439-6660

Public Safety Building
520 Hyde Park Boulevard
Niagara Falls, New York 14302-2725
Civil: (716) 286-4505

City Hall
216 Payne Ave.
North Tonawanda, New York 14120-5446
(716) 693-1010

Sheriff
P.O. Box 496
5526 Niagara Street
Lockport, New York 14095
(716) 439-9370

## Oneida County

(Fourth Department, Fifth Judicial District)

Supreme Court

Court House
800 Park Ave.
Utica, New York 13501
(315) 798-5889, 90
Deputy Chief Clerk III: (315) 798-5556

Surrogate's Court

Elizabeth Street Court House
800 Park Ave.
Utica, New York 13501
(315) 798-5866

County Court

Court House
800 Park Ave.
Utica, New York 13501
(315) 798-5716

Family Court

Court House
800 Park Ave.
Utica, New York 13501-2294
(315) 798-5925

Court House
302 North James Street
Rome, New York 13440-5196
(315) 337-7492

City Court

Justice Building
301 North James Street
Rome, New York 13440
(315) 337-6440

601 Sherrill Road
Sherrill, New York 13461
(315) 363-0996

413 W. Oriskany Street
Utica, New York 13502
(315) 724-8157

Sheriff

Law Enforcement Building
6065 Judd Road
Oriskany, New York 13424
(315) 765-2225

## Onondaga County

(Fourth Department, Fifth Judicial District)

Supreme Court

Court House
401 Montgomery St.
Syracuse, New York 13202
(315) 435-2030
Chief Clerk: (315) 435-2030

Surrogate's Court

Court House
401 Montgomery Street
Syracuse, New York 13202-2173
(315) 435-2101

County Court

Court House
401 Montgomery Street
Syracuse, New York 13202
(315) 435-2040

Family Court

Onondaga County Court House
401 Montgomery Street
Syracuse, New York 13202
(315) 435-2090

City Court

Public Safety Building
511 South State Street
Syracuse, New York 13202-2179
(315) 477-2785

Sheriff

407 South State Street
Syracuse, New York 13202
(315) 435-3044

## Ontario County

(Fourth Department, Seventh Judicial District)

Supreme Court

Court House
27 North Main Street
Canandaigua, New York 14424-1447
(716) 396-4239

Surrogate's Court

Court House
27 North Main Street
Canandaigua, New York 14424-1447
(716) 396-4055

County Court

Court House
27 North Main Street
Canandaigua, New York 14424-1447
(716) 396-4239

Family Court

Court House
27 North Main Street
Canandaigua, New York 14424-1447
(716) 396-4272

City Court

City Hall
2 North Main Street
Canandaigua, New York 14424-1448
(716) 396-5011

City Hall
47 Castle Street
Geneva, New York 14456
(315) 789-6560

Sheriff

Sheriff's Office
74 Ontario Street
Canandaigua, New York 14424
(716) 394-4560

## Orange County

(Second Department, Ninth Judicial District)

Supreme Court

Orange County Government Center
255 Main Street
Goshen, New York 10924
(914) 294-5151, Ext. 6065

Surrogate's Court

Surrogate's Court House
30 Park Place
Goshen, New York 10924
(914) 291-2193

County Court

Orange County Government Center
255-275 Main Street
Goshen, New York 10924
(914) 294-5151, Ext. 6020

Family Court

Orange County Government Center
255-275 Main Street
Goshen, New York 10924
(914) 294-5151, Ext. 6094

City Court

2 James Street
Middletown, New York 10940
(914) 346-4050

Public Safety Building
57 Broadway
Newburgh, New York 12550
(914) 565-3208

14-18 Hammond Street
Port Jervis, New York 12771-2495
(914) 858-4034

Sheriff

40 Erie Street
Goshen, New York 10924
(914) 294-3303

## Orleans County

(Fourth Department, Eighth Judicial District)

Supreme Court

Court House
Court House Square
Albion, New York 14411-1497
(716) 589-5458

Surrogate's Court

Surrogate's Office
Court House Square
Albion, New York 14411-1497
(716) 589-4457

County Court

Court House
Court House Square
Albion, New York 14411-1497
(716) 589-5458
Court Clerk: (716) 589-5458

Family Court

Court House
Court House Square
Albion, New York 14411-1497
(716) 589-4457

Sheriff

26 Platt Street
Albion, New York 14411-9998
(716) 589-5528

## Oswego County

(Fourth Department, Fifth Judicial District)

Supreme Court

Court House
25 East Oneida Street
Oswego, New York 13126-2693
(315) 349-3277

Surrogate's Court

Court House
25 East Oneida Street
Oswego, New York 13126-2693
(315) 349-3295

County Court

Court House
46 East Bridge
Oswego, New York 13126
(315) 349-8391
Court Clerk: (315) 349-3280

Family Court

Public Safety Center
39 Churchill Road
Oswego, New York 13126
(315) 349-3350

City Court

Municipal Building
141 South First Street
Fulton, New York 13069
(315) 593-8400

Conway Municipal Center
20 West Oneida Street
Oswego, New York 13126
(315) 343-0415

Sheriff

Route 57
Oswego, New York 13126
(315) 349-3302 *or* (800) 582-7583

## Otsego County

(Third Department, Sixth Judicial District)

Supreme Court

County Office Building
197 Main Street
P.O. Box 710
Cooperstown, New York 13326
(607) 547-4364

Surrogate's Court

Surrogate's Office
County Office Building
Cooperstown, New York 13326
(607) 547-4213

County Court

Court Chambers
197 Main Street
Cooperstown, New York 13326
(607) 547-4364
Chief Clerk: (607) 547-4364

Family Court

197 Main Street
Cooperstown, New York 13326
(607) 547-4264

City Court

Public Safety Building
81 Main Street
Oneonta, New York 13820
(607) 432-4480

Sheriff

Sheriff's Office

197 Main Street
Cooperstown, New York 13326
(607) 547-4271

## Putnam County

(Second Department, Ninth Judicial District)

Supreme Court

County Office Building
40 Gleneida Ave.
Carmel, New York 10512
(914) 225-3641, Ext. 337

Surrogate's Court

Court House
40 Gleneida Ave.
Carmel, New York 10512
(914) 225-3641, Ext. 293

County Court

Court House
40 Gleneida Ave.
Carmel, New York 10512
(914) 225-3641, Ext. 336

Family Court

County Office Building
40 Gleneida Ave.
Carmel, New York 10512
(914) 225-3641, Ext. 287

Sheriff

3 County Center
Carmel, New York 10512
(914) 225-4300

## Queens County

(Second Department, Eleventh Judicial District)

Supreme Court

Civil Term:

120-55 Queens Boulevard
Kew Gardens, New York 11424
(718) 520-3037

88-11 Sutphin Boulevard
Jamaica, New York 11435
(718) 520-3713
Court Clerk: (718) 520-3136

Surrogate's Court

88-11 Sutphin Boulevard
Jamaica, New York 11435
(718) 520-3132

Family Court

89-14 Parsons Boulevard
Jamaica, New York 11432
(718) 520-3991

Civil Court

120-55 Queens Boulevard
Kew Gardens, New York 11424
(718) 520-3610

Under Sheriff

42-71 65th Place
Woodside, New York 11377
(718) 803-0918

## Rensselaer County

(Third Department, Third Judicial District)

Supreme Court

Court House
Congress and 2nd Street
Troy, New York 12180
(518) 270-3711, 2

Surrogate's Court

Court House
Congress and 2nd Street
Troy, New York 12180
(518) 270-3724

County Court

Court House
Congress and 2nd Street
Troy, New York 12180
(518) 270-3738
Chief Clerk: (518) 270-3711

Family Court

Court House Annex
105 3rd Street
Troy, New York 12180
(518) 270-3761

City Court

City Hall
505 Broadway
Rensselaer, New York 12144
(518) 462-6751

City Hall
Monument Square
Troy, New York 12180
(518) 273-2434

Sheriff

P.O. Box 1076
1504 Fifth Avenue
Troy, New York 12180
(518) 270-5448

## Richmond County

(Second Department, Second Judicial District)

Supreme Court

County Court House
18 Richmond Terrace
Staten Island, New York 10301
(718) 390-5396
Court Clerk: (718) 390-5396

Surrogate's Court

County Court House
18 Richmond Terrace
Staten Island, New York 10301
(718) 390-5400

Family Court

100 Richmond Terrace
Staten Island, New York 10301
(718) 390-5462

Civil Court

927 Castleton Avenue
Staten Island, New York 10310
(718) 390-5416

Under Sheriff

350 Saint Marks Place
Staten Island, New York 10301
(718) 876-5308

## Rockland County

(Second Department, Ninth Judicial District)

Supreme Court

Court House
1 South Main Street
New City, New York 10956
Civil: (914) 638-5388
Chief Clerk: (914) 638-5393

Surrogate's Court

Court House
1 South Main Street
New City, New York 10956
(914) 638-5393

County Court

Court House
1 South Main Street
New City, New York 10956
Civil: (914) 638-5393
Chief Clerk: (914) 638-5393

Family Court

Rockland County Office Building
11 New Hempstead Rd.
New City, New York 10956
(914) 638-5300

Sheriff

55 New Hempstead Road
New City, New York 10956
(914) 638-5456

## St. Lawrence County

(Third Department, Fourth Judicial District)

Supreme Court

Court House
48 Court Street
Canton, New York 13617-1194
(315) 379-2219

Surrogate's Court

48 Court Street
Canton, New York 13617-1199
(315) 379-2217, 9427

County Court

Court House
48 Court Street
Canton, New York 13617-1199
(315) 379-2219
Chief Clerk: (315) 379-2219, 2200

Family Court

Court House
48 Court Street
Canton, New York 13617-1199
(315) 379-2410

City Court

330 Ford Street
Ogdensburg, New York 13669
(315) 393-3941

Sheriff

Court House
48 Court Street
Canton, New York 13617
(315) 379-2222

## Saratoga County

(Third Department, Fourth Judicial District)

Supreme Court

30 McMaster Street
Ballston Spa, New York 12020-0600
(518) 885-2224

Surrogate's Court

30 McMaster Street
Ballston Spa, New York 12020-0600
(518) 884-4722

County Court

30 McMaster Street, Building 2
Ballston Spa, New York 12020-0600
(518) 885-5381

Family Court

Saratoga County Municipal Center
35 West High Street
Ballston Spa, 12020-0600
(518) 885-2226

City Court

City Hall
36 North Main Street
Mechanicville, New York 12118
(518) 664-9876

City Hall
474 Broadway
Saratoga Springs, New York 12866
(518) 587-3550

Sheriff

Saratoga County Municipal Center
6010 County Farm Road
Ballston Spa, New York 12020-0600
(518) 885-6761
Civil Division: (518) 885-2269

## Schenectady County

(Third Department, Fourth Judicial District)

Supreme Court

612 State Street
Schenectady, New York 12305-2114
(518) 388-4323

Surrogate's Court

Court House
612 State Street
Schenectady, New York 12305-2113
(518) 388-4293

County Court

Court House
612 State Street
Schenectady, New York 12305
(518) 388-4215

Family Court

620 State Street
Schenectady, New York 12305-2114
(518) 388-4305

**City Court**

Civil:
City Hall
Jay Street, Room 215
Schenectady, New York 12305
(518) 382-5077, 8

**Sheriff**

Schenectady County Jail
Veeder Avenue
Schenectady, New York 12305
Civil: (518) 388-4304

## Schoharie County

(Third Department, Third Judicial District)

**Supreme Court**

Court House
300 Main Street
P.O. Box 669
Schoharie, New York 12157-0669
(518) 295-8342

**Surrogate's Court**

Court House
300 Main Street
Schoharie, New York 12157-0669
(518) 295-8383, 7

**County Court**

Court House
300 Main Street
Schoharie, New York 12157-0669
(518) 295-8342

**Family Court**

Court House
300 Main Street
Schoharie, New York 12157-0669
(518) 295-8383, 7

**Sheriff**

Box 6891
Schoharie, New York 12157-0089
(518) 295-8114, 8888

## Schuyler County

(Third Department, Sixth Judicial District)

Supreme Court

Court House
105 9th Street
Watkins Glen, New York 14891
(607) 535-7760

Surrogate's Court

Court House
105 9th Street
Watkins Glen, New York 14891
(607) 535-7144

County Court

Court House
105 9th Street
Watkins Glen, New York 14891
(607) 535-7015
Chief Clerk: (607) 535-7760

Family Court

Court House
105 9th Street
Watkins Glen, New York 14891
(607) 535-7143

Sheriff

106 10th Street
Watkins Glen, New York 14891
(607) 535-8222

## Seneca County

(Fourth Department, Seventh Judicial District)

Supreme Court

Court House
48 W. Williams Street
Waterloo, New York 13165
(315) 539-7021

Surrogate's Court

Court House
48 W. Williams Street
Waterloo, New York 13165
(315) 539-7531

County Court

Court House
48 W. Williams Street
Waterloo, New York 13165
(315) 539-7021

Family Court

Court House
48 W. Williams Street
Waterloo, New York 13165-1338
(315) 539-6291

Sheriff
48 W. Williams Street
Waterloo, New York 13165
(315) 539-9241

## Steuben County

(Fourth Department, Seventh Judicial District)

Supreme Court

3 East Pulteney Square
Bath, New York 14810-1575
(607) 776-7879

Surrogate's Court

13 Pulteney Square
Bath, New York 14810-1598
(607) 776-7126

County Court

Court House
3 East Pulteney Square
Bath, New York 14810-1575
(607) 776-7879
Court Clerk: (607) 776-7879

Family Court

Court House
3 East Pulteney Square
Bath, New York 14810-1621
(607) 776-9631, Ext. 3450

City Court

City Hall
12 Civic Center Plaza
Corning, New York 14830-2884
(607) 936-4111

108 Broadway
Hornell, New York 14843-0627
(607) 324-7535

Sheriff
Steuben County Jail
P.O. Box 271
Bath, New York 14810
(607) 776-7671

## Suffolk County

(Second Department, Tenth Judicial District)

Supreme Court

235 Griffing Avenue
Riverhead, New York 11901
(516) 852-2333

Surrogate's Court

320 Center Drive
Riverhead, New York 11901
(516) 852-1745

County Court

210 Center Drive
P.O. Box 9007
Riverhead, New York 11901-9007
(516) 852-1462
Chief Clerk: (516) 852-2121

District Court

First District Court

Civil:
400 Carleton Avenue
P.O. Box 9072
Central Islip, New York 11722
(516) 853-5404

Second District Court

375 Commack Road
Deer Park, New York 11729
(516) 854-1950

Third District Court

1850 New York Avenue
Huntington Station, New York 11746
(516) 854-4545

**Fourth District Court**

North County Complex Building C158
Veterans' Memorial Highway
Hauppauge, New York 11787
(516) 853-5406

**Fifth District Court**

P.O. Box 9081
400 Carleton Ave.
Central Islip, New York 11722
(516) 853-7615

**Sixth District Court**

150 West Main Street
Patchogue, New York 11772
(516) 854-1440

**Family Court**

400 Carleton Avenue
P.O. Box 9076
Central Islip, New York 11722-9076
(516) 853-4647, 8

**Sheriff**

100 Center Drive
Riverhead, New York 11901-3389
(516) 852-2200

## Sullivan County

(Third Department, Third Judicial District)

**Supreme Court**

Court House
Monticello, New York 12701
(914) 794-4066

**Surrogate's Court**

Government Center
100 North Street
Box 5012
Monticello, New York 12701
(914) 794-3513, Ext. 157

**County Court**

Court House
Monticello, New York 12701
(914) 794-1248
Chief Clerk: (914) 794-4066

Family Court

Government Center
100 North Street
Monticello, New York 12701
(914) 794-3000, Ext. 5026

Sheriff

County Jail
Monticello, New York 12701
(914) 794-7100

## Tioga County

(Third Department, Sixth Judicial District)

Supreme Court
16 Court Street
P.O. Box 307
Owego, New York 13827
(607) 687-0544

Surrogate's Court
Court Annex Building
20 Court Street
P.O. Box 10
Owego, New York 13827
(607) 687-1303

County Court
Court Annex
16 Court Street
Owego, New York 13827
(607) 687-0338

Family Court
Court Annex Building
20 Court Street
P.O. Box 10
Owego, New York 13827
(607) 687-1730

Sheriff

103 Corporate Drive
Owego, New York 13827
(607) 687-1010

## Tompkins County

(Third Department, Sixth Judicial District)

Supreme Court

Court House
320 N. Tioga Street
P.O. Box 70
Ithaca, New York 14851-0070
(607) 272-0466

Surrogate's Court

Court House
320 N. Tioga Street
P.O. Box 70
Ithaca, New York 14851-0070
(607) 277-0622

County Court

Court House
320 N. Tioga Street
P.O. Box 70
Ithaca, New York 14851-0070
(607) 272-0466

Family Court

Court House
320 N. Tioga Street
P.O. Box 70
Ithaca, New York 14851-0070
(607) 277-1517

City Court

118 E. Clinton St.
Ithaca, New York 14850
(607) 273-2263

Sheriff

779 Warren Road
Ithaca, New York 14850
(607) 257-1345

## Ulster County

(Third Department, Third Judicial District)

Supreme Court

Court House
285 Wall Street
Kingston, New York 12401-0906
Clerks: (914) 339-5680
Filings: (914) 331-9300, Ext. 252

Surrogate's Court
240 Fair Street
P.O. Box 1800
Kingston, New York 12401-0800
(914) 340-3348

County Court

Court House
285 Wall Street
Kingston, New York 12401-0906
(914) 339-5680

Family Court
P.O. Box 3658
16 Lucas Avenue
Kingston, New York 12402
(914) 340-3600

City Court

1 Garraghan Drive
Kingston, New York 12401
(914) 338-2974

Sheriff

Golden Hill Drive
Kingston, New York 12401-0906
(914) 338-0939

## Warren County

(Third Department, Fourth Judicial District)

Supreme Court

Warren County Municipal Center
Route U.S. 9
Lake George, New York 12845
(518) 761-6429, 31

Surrogate's Court

Warren County Municipal Center
Route U.S. 9
Lake George, New York 12845
(518) 761-6514

County Court

Warren County Municipal Center
Route U.S. 9
Lake George, New York 12845
(518) 761-6547

Family Court

Warren County Municipal Center
Route U.S. 9
Lake George, New York 12845
(518) 761-6500

City Court

42 Ridge Street
Glens Falls, New York 12801
(518) 798-4714

Sheriff

Warren County Municipal Center
Route U.S. 9
Lake George, New York 12845
(518) 761-6477

## Washington County

(Third Department, Fourth Judicial District)

Supreme Court

Court House
383 Broadway
Fort Edward, New York 12828
(518) 746-2521

Surrogate's Court

Court House
383 Broadway
Fort Edward, New York 12828
(518) 746-2545

County Court

Court House
383 Broadway
Fort Edward, New York 12828
(518) 746-2521
Clerk: (518) 746-2521

Family Court

Court Directory

Court House
383 Broadway
Fort Edward, New York 12828
(518) 746-2501

Sheriff

East Broadway
Box 2003
Salem, New York 12865
(518) 854-9245

## Wayne County

(Fourth Department, Seventh Judicial District)

Supreme Court

54 Broad Street
Lyons, New York 14489-1178
(315) 946-5457

Surrogate's Court

54 Broad Street
Lyons, New York 14489-1173
(315) 946-5430

County Court

54 Broad Street
Lyons, New York 14489-1134
(315) 946-5459

Family Court

54 Broad Street
Lyons, New York 14489-1180
(315) 946-5420

Sheriff

County Jail
7368 Route 31
Lyons, New York 14489-9107
(315) 946-9711

## Westchester County

(Second Department, Ninth Judicial District)

Supreme Court
111 Grove Street
White Plains, New York 10601
(914) 285-3800

Surrogate's Court

140 Grand Street
White Plains, New York 10601
(914) 285-3712
Chief Clerk: (914) 285-3725

County Court
111 Grove Street
White Plains, New York 10601
(914) 285-3800
Chief Clerk: (914) 285-4336

Family Court

111 Grove Street
White Plains, New York 10601
(914) 285-3600

420 North Avenue
New Rochelle, New York 10801
(914) 633-1290

53 South Broadway
Yonkers, New York 10701
(914) 966-6400

City Court

City Court Building
Roosevelt Square
Mount Vernon, New York 10550-2019
(914) 665-2400

90 Beaufort Place
New Rochelle, New York 10801
(914) 654-2291

2 Nelson Avenue
Peekskill, New York 10566
(914) 737-3405

21 Third Street
Rye, New York 10580
(914) 967-1599

77 South Lexington Avenue
White Plains, New York 10601
(914) 422-6050

Robert W. Cacace Justice Center
100 South Broadway
Yonkers, New York 10701
(914) 377-6377

Sheriff
Saw Mill River Parkway
Hawthorne, New York 10532
(914) 741-4400

## Wyoming County

(Fourth Department, Eighth Judicial District)

Supreme Court

Court House
143 North Main Street
Warsaw, New York 14569-1193
(716) 786-3148

Surrogate's Court

Court House
143 North Main Street
Warsaw, New York 14569-1193
(716) 786-3148

County Court

Court House
143 North Main Street
Warsaw, New York 14569-1193
(716) 786-3148

Family Court

Court House
143 North Main Street
Warsaw, New York 14569-1193
(716) 786-3148

Sheriff

151 North Main Street
Warsaw, New York 14569
(716) 786-8989

## Yates County

(Fourth Department, Seventh Judicial District)

Supreme Court

Court House
226 Main Street
Penn Yan, New York 14527-1191
(315) 536-5129

Surrogate's Court
108 Court Street
Penn Yan, New York 14527-1176
(315) 536-5130

County Court

Court House
226 Main Street
Penn Yan, New York 14527-1191
(315) 536-5126

Family Court

Court House
108 Court Street
Penn Yan, New York 14527-1182
(315) 536-5127

Sheriff
Public Safety Building
227 Main Street
Penn Yan, New York 14527
(315) 536-5182

# INDEX

[References are to CPLR Sections, Rules and Appendices.]

## A

### ABANDONED CASES
Dismissal of
- Appropriate entry by clerk, authorization without need for order . . . 3404
- Supreme or county court, cases deemed abandoned . . . 3404

### ABSENCE FROM STATE
Statutes of limitations, tolling of
- Designated person for receipt of summons, voluntary or involuntary designation; existence of . . : 207
- Jurisdiction over defendant, ability to obtain without personal service within state . . . 207

### ACCELERATED JUDGMENTS
Affidavit prior to default as verification of pleading . . . 3201
Default judgment (See DEFAULT AND DEFAULT JUDGMENTS)
Judgment by confession (See CONFESSION OF JUDGMENT)
Motion to dismiss (See DISMISSAL MOTIONS)
Offer to compromise (See COMPROMISE OF CLAIM)
Offer to liquidate damages conditionally . . . . 3220
Submitted facts, action on . . . 3222
Summary judgment, motion for (See SUMMARY JUDGMENT)
Tender of payment . . . 3219
Voluntary discontinuance (See VOLUNTARY DISCONTINUANCE OF ACTION)
Want of prosecution, removal from calendar for neglect to prosecute . . . 3216; 3404

### ACCIDENT AND ACCIDENT REPORTS
Airplane accidents, testimony as to . . . 4519
Class actions (See CLASS ACTIONS)
Disclosure required, scope of . . . 3101(g)
Motor vehicle, personal injuries arising out of negligent use of
- Statement of serious injury or economic loss greater than basic economic loss
  - Bill of particulars . . . 3043
  - Requirement . . . 3016(g)
- Testimony as to . . . 4519
Personal injuries arising out of negligent use of motor vehicle (See subhead: Motor vehicle, personal injuries arising out of negligent use of)

### ACCIDENT AND ACCIDENT REPORTS—Cont.
Vessel, testimony as to accidents involving . . . 4519

### ACCOUNTINGS
Corporation, action by or on behalf of; specified party defendants . . . 213
Express trust proceedings (See EXPRESS TRUST PROCEEDINGS)
Temporary receiver, maintenance and inspection of accounts . . . 6404
Time for commencement; last transaction by either party, computation from . . . 206(d)

### ACKNOWLEDGMENTS
Certification of . . . 4538
Undertakings . . . 2502(d)

### ACTIONS BY OR AGAINST STATE (See STATE, ACTIONS BY OR AGAINST)

### ADDITIONAL ALLOWANCES (See DISBURSEMENTS AND ADDITIONAL ALLOWANCES)

### ADJOURNMENT
Health care arbitration . . . 7558(c)
Term of court . . . 9001

### AD LITEM GUARDIAN (See GUARDIAN AD LITEM)

### ADMINISTRATORS (See EXECUTORS AND ADMINISTRATORS)

### ADMISSIONS
Blood genetic marker tests . . . 4518(d),(e)
Disclosure (See DISCLOSURE)
DNA tests . . . 4518(d),(e)
Documents (See PAPERS, subhead: Admissions)
Effect of . . . 3123(b)
Notice to admit . . . 3123(a)
Papers (See PAPERS, subhead: Admissions)
Photographs (See PHOTOGRAPHS, subhead: Admissions)

### ADMISSION TO PRACTICE
Appellate division
- Committee, appointment of . . . 9401
- Questionnaires or statements, preparation of to aid investigation of character . . . . . 9404
Application for admission
- Filing upon final disposition, requirement . . . 9407

I–1

[References are to CPLR Sections, Rules and Appendices.]

**ADMISSION TO PRACTICE**—Cont.

Application for admission—Cont.

    Generally . . . 9402

    Prior application, existence of . . . 9405

    Referral to other judicial district, when authorized . . . 9403

Certificate of character and fitness . . . 9404

Character and fitness, certificate of . . . 9404

Committee

    Appointment by appellate division in each judicial department . . . 9401

    Certificate of character and fitness, issuance by committee . . . 9404

    Questionnaires or statements, preparation of to aid investigation into character . . . . 9404

Compliance with all applicable rules and statutes relating to admission to practice, requirement for proof of . . . 9406(2)

Loyalty, proof of . . . 9406(1)

Motion, admission on . . . 9402

Proof

    Compliance with all applicable rules and statutes relating to admission to practice . . . 9406(2)

    Generally . . . 9406

    Loyalty . . . 9406(1)

    Residence . . . 9406(2)

Records of, maintenance by court clerks . . . . 9701(3),(4)

Referral of application to another jurisdiction . . . 9403

Refusal of admission, court clerk's records of . . . 9701(3),(4)

Residence

    Generally . . . 9403

    Proof of . . . 9406(2)

**ADULTERY**

Incompetency of spouse to testify . . . 4502(a)

**ADVERSE POSSESSION**

Statute of limitations . . . 212

**AFFIDAVITS**

(See also specific subject headings)

Opposing affidavits (See DISMISSAL MOTIONS)

Public officers, affidavits of . . . 4520

Statements subscribed and affirmed by expert treated as . . . 2106

Undertakings (See UNDERTAKINGS)

Verification of pleading

    Affidavit of, form . . . 3021

    Utilization of verified pleading . . 105(u)

**AFFIRMATIONS** (See OATHS AND AFFIRMATIONS)

**AFFIRMATIVE DEFENSES**

Foreign country money judgments, enforcement of . . . 5303

Pleading of

    Requirement . . . 3018(b)

    Surprise of adverse party, matters if not pleaded likely to cause . . . 3018(b)

**AGENT AND PRINCIPAL** (See PRINCIPAL AND AGENT)

**AGENT ORANGE**

Personal injuries of military personnel with service in Indochina, statute of limitations . . . 214-b

**AGRICULTURE**

Inspection certificates issued by Department of Agriculture . . . 4529

**ALIEN NONRESIDENT**

Warring country, citizen, resident or sojourner in; tolling of statutes of limitations . . . 209(b)

**ALIMONY**

Long-arm jurisdiction in action for . . . 302(b)

Statute of limitations . . . 211

**ALLOWANCES** (See DISBURSEMENTS AND ADDITIONAL ALLOWANCES)

**ALTERNATE JURORS**

Generally . . . 4106

**ALTERNATIVE PLEADINGS**

Allowance . . . 3014

**AMENDED AND SUPPLEMENTAL PLEADINGS**

Additional or subsequent transactions or occurrences, inclusion of . . . 3025(b)

Claims included in, statute of limitations; time claim deemed interposed . . . 203(f)

Evidence, conformity to; ground of amendment . . . 3025(c)

Leave of court or stipulation of parties; additional or subsequent transactions . . . 3025(b)

Responses to, time limits . . . 3025(d)

Without leave of court, when authorized . . . . 3025(a)

**AMENDMENTS** (See specific subject headings)

**ANNULMENT OR DISSOLUTION OF MARRIAGE**

Fraud as ground for, statute of limitations on . . . 214

"Matrimonial action," term including . . 105(p)

**ANNULMENT OR DISSOLUTION OF MAR-RIAGE**—Cont.

Statute of limitations on fraud as grounds for . . . 214

**ANSWER**

Additional time to serve, situations allowing . . . 3012(c)

Appearance of defendant
    Authority . . . 320(a)
    Motion by defendant, extension of time to answer effected by . . . 320(a)

Article 78 proceedings (See ARTICLE 78 PROCEEDINGS)

Authorization for . . . 3011

Counterclaim against defendant, inclusion in answer, allowance . . . 3011

Cross-claim against defendant, inclusion in answer, allowance . . . 3011

Goods sold and delivered, answer to itemized verified complaint; specificity required . . . . 3016(f)

Interrogatory, to (See INTERROGATORIES)

Reply to counterclaim, defined . . . 3011

Service of answer or reply, time for . . 3012(a)

Special proceedings
    Service of, time limits . . . 403(b)
    When utilized . . . 402

Third-party defendant . . . 1008

Verification of, when required . . . 3020(b)

**APPEALS**

Affirmation of judgment or order, grounds of decision; required statement where no opinion given . . . 5522

Appealable paper . . . 5512(a)

Appeal as of right, time for taking . . . 5513(a)

Appellate division, appeal to (See COURT OF APPEALS)

Appellate term (See APPELLATE TERM)

Briefs and appendices
    Appellant's brief and appendix, content . . . 5528(a)
    Citations with, method . . . 5529(e)
    Filing copies of brief, requirements . . . . 5530
    Form . . . 5529
    Headings on pages . . . 5529(c)
    Joint appendix . . . 5528(d)
    Margin, bound . . . 5529(a)(3)
    Noncompliance . . . 5528(e)
    Numbering of pages . . . 5529(b)
    Omissions . . . 5529(d)
    Paper requirements . . . 5529(a)
    Points, division by . . . 5528(a)(4)

**APPEALS**—Cont.

Briefs and appendices—Cont.
    Questions and answers, paragraphing of . . . 5529(f)
    Reply brief and appendix . . . 5528(c)
    Reproduction methods . . . 5529(a)
    Respondent's . . . 5528(b)
    Service of copies of brief upon opponent, requirements . . . 5530
    Type size . . . 5529(a)(2)
    Typewritten, permissibility . . . 1102(c)

Clerk of court fee for filing notice of . . . . . . 8022(b)

Costs (See COSTS, subhead: Appeal, costs upon)

County clerks' fees for filing notice of . . . . . 8022(a)

Court of appeals (See COURT OF APPEALS)

Cross-appeals
    Filing of records . . . 5530(b)
    Timeliness . . . 5513(c)

Defects in form . . . 5520(c)

Description of actions filed . . . 5531

Disbursement on . . . 8301(a)

Disposition of . . . 5522

Enforcement of judgment pending appeal, stay of (See subhead: Stay of enforcement of judgment or order pending appeal)

Entry of order . . . 5524(a)

Ex parte orders, review of . . . 5704

Extension of time
    Alternate method of appeal . . . 5514(a)
    Attorney, disability of . . . 5514(b)
    Generally . . . 5514(c)

Fee for filing, notice of
    Clerk of court . . . 8022(b)
    County clerks . . . 8022(a)

Filing
    Notice of fee for
        Clerk of court . . . 8022(b)
        County clerks . . . 8022(a)
    Record on appeal (See subhead: Record on appeal)

Final judgment, appeal from; scope of review . . . 5501(a)

Foreign country money judgment, stay in case of appeal . . . 5306

Habeas corpus (See HABEAS CORPUS)

In camera interviews . . . 4019(b)

Money judgments, enforcement of (See MONEY JUDGMENT—ENFORCEMENT PROCEDURES)

Notice of
    Fee for filing
        Clerk of court . . . 8022(b)
        County clerks . . . 8022(a)

**APPEALS**—Cont.

Notice of—Cont.
    Generally . . . 5515
    Permission, motion for . . . 5516
Object, consequences for failure to . . . . . . 5501(a)(3)
Omitted acts . . . 5520(a)
Out-of-court orders, entry of . . . 5512(b)
Parties authorized to appeal . . . 5511
Permission to appeal, motion for
    Appellate division, grant by (See COURT OF APPEALS)
    Copy to clerk of court of appeals, requirement for . . . 5513(3); 5515(2)
    Court of appeals (See COURT OF APPEALS)
    Notice of motion . . . 5516
    Order granting, entry, appeal taken from time of . . . 5515(1)
    Right, instead of as of . . . 5520(b)
    Time for motioning . . . 5513(b)
Poor persons, appeals by
    Briefs and appendices, typewritten; permissibility . . . 1102(c)
    Stenographer's transcript, no fee for . . . . 1102(b)
Preferences . . . 5521
Record on appeal
    Certification of, stipulation by parties in lieu of . . . 5532
    Contents . . . 5526
    Description of action, inclusion . . . 5531
    Filing requirements
        Cross-appeal, upon . . . 5530(b)
        Generally . . . 5530(a)
        Special rules as to . . . 5530(c)
    Form of . . . 5526
    Page headings . . . 5526
    Statement in lieu of . . . 5527
    Statement prefixed, description of action . . . 5531
    Testimony, page headings for . . . 5526
Referees
    Appeal from judgment entered on referee's report . . . 5525(b)
    Review of findings on appeal . . . 4511(c)
Remittitur of order and record on appeal, procedure . . . 5524(b)
Restitution of property or rights, power of court to order . . . 5523
Simplified Procedure for Court Determination of Disputes, limitations . . . 3037
Stay of enforcement of judgment or order pending appeal
    Action defended by insurer . . . 5519(b)

**APPEALS**—Cont.

Stay of enforcement of judgment or order pending appeal—Cont.
    Affirmation or modification of appealed judgment or order, effect . . . 5519(e)
    Continuation of stay on affirmed or modified judgment . . . 5519(e)
    Court order for stay . . . 5519(c)
    Denial of motion to appeal, effect . . . . . 5519(e)
    Foreign country money judgments . . . . . 5306
    Insurer as defendant . . . 5519(b)
    Limitation of stay . . . 5519(c)
    Medical malpractice . . . 5519(g)
    Proceedings after stay . . . 5519(f)
    Sale of perishable goods by court of origin, stay not applicable to . . . 5519(f)
    Undertaking required . . . 5519(d)
    Without court order; conditions permitting . . . 5519(a)
Subsequent orders
    No effect on appeal, specification of orders having . . . 5517(a)
    Review upon motion . . . 5517(b)
Substitution of parties
    Extension of time for procedural steps . . 1022
    Time for substitution . . . 1021
Time limitations
    Appeal as of right . . . 5513(a)
    Cross-appeal . . . 5513(c)
    Permission to appeal, motion for . . . . . . 5513(b)
Transcript of proceedings (See TRANSCRIPT OF ACTION OR PROCEEDING)
Undertakings
    Appeal by state or municipality . . . . . . 2512(2)
    Stay of enforcement pending appeal . . . . 5519(d)
Venue, order changing . . . 511(d)

**APPEARANCE BY DEFENDANT**

Answer, service of; appearance made by
    Authority . . . 320(a)
    Motion by defendant, extension of time to answer effected by . . . 320(a)
Attorney appearance for defense or prosecution of civil action (See ATTORNEYS)
Class actions
    Court's discretion as to . . . 907
    Notice as to . . . 907
Demand for complaint, appearance not per se constituted by . . . 3012(b)

[References are to CPLR Sections, Rules and Appendices.]

**APPEARANCE BY DEFENDANT**—Cont.

Jurisdiction over defendant (See subhead: Personal jurisdiction conferred by)

Limited appearance, when allowed

Authority . . . 314

No personal jurisdiction conferred by . . . 320(c)

Quasi in rem jurisdiction, applicability to . . . 320(c)

Notice of appearance, service of, method for making appearance . . . 320(a)

Personal jurisdiction conferred by

Authority . . . 320(b)

Non-resident in matrimonial actions or family court proceedings . . . . 302(b)

No personal jurisdiction conferred

Defending on merits after objection asserted, objection subsequently failing, effect . . . 320(c)

Limited appearance . . . . . . 320(c); 320(c)(1)

Motions to dismiss based on . . . . . 320(c)

Motion to dismiss for lack of personal jurisdiction, motion or answer asserting . . . 320(b); 3211(a)

Publication of summons, defendant's appearance during, completion of publication established by . . . 320(d)

Special appearance, objection to personal jurisdiction; motion to dismiss . . . 3211(a)(8)

Time to make appearance

Extension . . . 3012(d)

Summons served to defendant affecting, manner of . . . 320(a)

**APPELLATE DIVISION**

Admission to practice

Certificate of character and fitness . . . . . 9404

Committee, appointment of . . . 9401

Affirmance, statement as to disposition of facts on . . . 5712(b)

Appeals from (See COURT OF APPEALS)

Appellate terms, appeals from . . . 5703(a)

Article 78 proceedings . . . 7804(g), (h)

Calendar practice, control by chief administrator of courts . . . 3401

Costs on appeal, award of; amount authorized . . . 8203(a)

County courts, from

Appeals as of right . . . 5701(a)

Appeals by permission . . . 5701(c)

Orders not appealable as of right . . . . . 5701(b)

**APPELLATE DIVISION**—Cont.

Dissent by one or more justices, statement of . . . 5712(a)

Ex parte orders, review of . . . 5704(a)

Modification, order of . . . 5712(c)

Money judgments contested as excessive or inadequate, determination . . . 5501(c)

Original instance, appeals to appellate division from courts of . . . 5702

Permission to appeal

Court of appeals, to (See COURT OF APPEALS)

Generally . . . 5701(c)

Place for appeal . . . 5711

Preliminary injunction by . . . 5518

Records of clerk of court . . . 9701

Reversal, order of . . . 5712(c)

Right, appeal as of . . . 5701

Scope of review on appeal . . . 5501(c)

Supreme Court, from

Appeals as of right . . . 5701(a)

Appeals by permission . . . 5701(c)

Orders not appealable as of right . . . . . 5701(b)

Temporary restraining order by . . . 5518

**APPELLATE TERM**

Appeals to appellate division . . . 5703(a)

Costs on appeal, award of . . . 8203(b)

Ex parte orders, review of . . . 5704(b)

Questions of law and fact, review of . . . . . . 5501(d)

**APPENDICES** (See APPEALS, subhead: Briefs and appendices)

**APPRAISERS AND APPRAISALS**

Disclosure of appraisal report in condemnation proceedings . . . 3140

Sheriff reimbursed for payment of compensation to appraisers . . . 8013(b)

**ARBITRATION PROCEEDINGS**

Agency making award by confession . . . . . . 7508(c)

Agreement to arbitrate, enforceability . . . 7501

Amount of recovery, limitation as to . . . 3405

Application to court

Limitations of time . . . 7502(b)

Provisional remedies . . . 7502(c)

Special proceeding for purpose of, when authorized . . . 7502(a)

Subsequent applications, motions for . . . 7502(a)

Venue . . . 7502(a)

Arbitrator

Appointment by court, when authorized . . . 7504

[References are to CPLR Sections, Rules and Appendices.]

**ARBITRATION PROCEEDINGS**—Cont.

Arbitrator—Cont.

Confession, award by . . . 7508(c)

Failure to act; court appointment of successor, application by party for . . . 7504

Judicial hearing officer as . . . 3405

Majority decision of . . . 7506(e)

Modification of award . . . 7509

Oath prior to hearing testimony . . . . . . 7506(a)

Oaths, administer . . . 7505

Powers . . . 7505

Subpoenas, issue . . . 7505

Attorneys, representation by . . . 7506(d)

Award

Action based upon, statute of limitations . . . 215

Appeal as of right . . . 5601(d)

Appeal by permission . . . 5602(a)(1)

Confession, award by (See subhead: Confession, award by)

Confirmation of award

Generally . . . 7510

Judgment entered upon confirmation . . . 7514(a)

Delivery of copy to each party in manner agreed upon . . . 7507

Form . . . 7507

Modification of (See subhead: Modification of award)

Time limits, extension agreements . . . . . 7507

Vacation of (See subhead: Vacation of award)

Claim for, commencement of action on, limitations period, computation . . . 204(b)

Compel arbitration effect on stay of action, application to . . . 7503(a)

Confession, award by

Agency making award . . . 7508(c)

Arbitrator making award . . . 7508(c)

Availability . . . 7508(a)

Person making award . . . 7508(c)

Time of award . . . 7508(b)

Confirmation of award

Generally . . . 7510

Judgment entered upon confirmation . . . 7514(a)

Conservatee, controversy concerning . . . 1209

Corruption as grounds for vacation of award . . . 7511(b)(1)

Court of appeals (See COURT OF APPEALS)

Death of party to agreement, effect . . . 7512

Delivery of award . . . 7507

Demand for arbitration . . . 7503(c)

**ARBITRATION PROCEEDINGS**—Cont.

Determination of issue, agreement as to method, enforcement as arbitration agreement . . 7601

Dismiss on ground of arbitration and award, motion to . . . 3211(a)(5)

Evidence . . . 7506(c)

Extension of time

Award . . . 7507

Modification of award by arbitrator . . . . 7509

Fees and expenses involved

Generally . . . 7513

Payment, provisions for . . . 3405

Reduction or disallowance, court's discretion as to . . . 7513

Fraud as grounds for vacation of award . . . . . 7511(b)(1)

Health care (See HEALTH CARE ARBITRATION)

Hearing

Adjournment or postponement, arbitrator's discretion as to . . . 7506(b)

Evidence, determination by arbitrator on . . . 7506(c)

Majority determination and rendering of award . . . 7506(e)

Rehearing on vacation of award . . . . . . 7511(d)

Representation by attorney, right to . . . . 7506(d)

Time and place, appointment by arbitrator . . . 7506(b)

Waiver of requirements as to, written consent of parties required . . . 7506(f)

Incompetent party

Continuance of proceedings . . . 7512

Controversy involving, submission to arbitration, necessity of court order . . 1209

Infant, controversy involving, necessity for court order . . . 1209

Judgment on award

Confirmation, judgment upon . . . 7514(a)

Entry . . . 7514(a)

Judgment-roll . . . 7514(b)

Jury trial de novo following arbitrators determination . . . 3405

Limitation as to maximum amount of recovery . . . 3405

Malpractice actions . . . 3045

Modification of award

Application, time limits . . . 7511(a)

Arbitrator's modification . . . 7509

Confirmation of award on motion to modify . . . 7511(e)

Extension of time . . . 7509

**ARBITRATION PROCEEDINGS**—Cont.
Modification of award—Cont.
  Grounds for modifying . . . 7511(c)
  Miscalculation of figures as grounds for
    . . . 7511(c)(1)
  Time of application . . . 7511(a)
Notice of intention to arbitrate . . . 7503(c)
Oaths
  Arbitrator's oath . . . 7506(a)
  Power of arbitrator to administer . . 7505
Prejudice . . . 7511(b)(2)
Provisional remedies . . . 7502(c)
Rehearing on vacation of award . . . 7511(d)
Special proceedings for purpose of application to
  court, when authorized . . . 7502(a)
Statutes of limitations
  Application at discretion of arbitrators . . .
    7502(b)
  Claim, commencement of action on . . . .
    204(b)
  One-year period . . . 215
  Stay of action, application for . . 7503(c)
Stay of action, application for
  Application to compel arbitration effect on
    . . . 7503(a)
  Generally . . . 7503(b)
  Time limitation . . . 7503(c)
  Waiver of right to declare null and void
    . . . 7503(c)
Subpoenas, power of arbitrator to issue . . 7505
Time
  Application to court . . . 7502(b)
  Award, time for making . . . 7507
  Confession, award by . . . 7508(b)
  Hearing . . . 7506(b)
  Stay of action, application for . . 7503(c)
  Vacation of award, time for application
    . . . 7511(a)
Vacation of award
  Confirmation of award on denial of motion
    to modify or vacate . . . 7511(e)
  Corruption as grounds for . . . 7511(b)(1)
  Excessive or improper exercise of powers of
    arbitrator . . . 7511(b)(1)
  Fraud as grounds for . . . 7511(b)(1)
  Grounds for . . . 7511(b)
  Prejudice . . . 7511(b)(2)
  Procedural irregularities as ground . . . . .
    7511(b)(1)
  Rehearing . . . 7511(d)
  Time of application . . . 7511(a)
Venue . . . 7502(a)
Waiver
  Consent of parties at hearing, written . . .
    7506(f)

**ARBITRATION PROCEEDINGS**—Cont.
Written agreement to submit to arbitration, effect
  . . . 7501

**ARMED FORCES**
Satisfaction of money judgment against members,
  exempt personal property . . . 5205(e)

**ARREST**
Sheriff's fees for serving or executing order of
  arrest . . . 8011(h)

**ARTICLE 78 PROCEEDINGS**
Abuse of discretion, review of . . . 7803(3)
Affidavits
  Answering . . . 7804(e)
  Generally . . . 7804(d)
  Service, time for . . . 7804(c)
Answer
  Certified transcripts of records, filing of
    . . . 7804(e)
  Service, time for . . . 7804(c)
  Verification . . . 7804(d)
Appearance by judicial officer . . . 7804(i)
Appellate division, transfer to . . . 7804(g), (h)
Attorney General
  Service of papers in proceeding against bo-
    dies or officers after expiration in office
    . . . 7804(c),(i)
Body, definition of term . . . 7802(a)
Certiorari to review, writ of, relief previously
  obtained by; applicability of Article 78 proceed-
  ing to . . . 7801
Contempt proceedings, review of . . . 7801(2)
Counterclaim, reply to . . . 7804(d)
Criminal proceedings . . . 7804(i)
Custody proceedings . . . 7804(i)
Default judgments . . . 7804(e)
Discipline imposed, review of . . . 7803(3)
Dismissal . . . 7804(f); 7806
Duty specifically enjoined by law, review of
  . . . 7803(1)
Evidence, review of . . . 7803(4)
Expiration of term of office, proceeding after
  . . . 7802(b)
Filing of answer and certified transcript of records
  . . . 7804(e)
Hearing and determination . . . 7804(g)
Joinder of parties
  Prohibition . . . 7802(c)
  Successors in office . . . 7802(b)
Judgment, relief granted by . . . 7806
Judicial officer, appearance by . . . 7804(i)
Jurisdiction, review of excess of . . . 7803(2)
Law questions . . . 7803(3)
Limitations on applicability of Article . . 7801

[References are to CPLR Sections, Rules and Appendices.]

**ARTICLE 78 PROCEEDINGS**—Cont.

Mandamus, writ of, relief previously obtained by; applicability of Article 78 proceeding to . . . 7801

Notice of petition
    Generally . . . 7802(d)
    Service, time for . . . 7804(c)

Objections in point of law . . . 7804(f)

Officer, definition of term . . . 7802(a)

Parties to proceeding . . . 7802

Penalty, review of . . . 7803(3)

Petition, notice of
    Generally . . . 7804(d)
    Service of, time for . . . 7804(c)

Pleadings . . . 7804(d)

Prohibition, writ of, relief previously obtained by; applicability of Article 78 proceeding to . . . 7801

Questions raised . . . 7803

Referees . . . 7804(h),(i)

Remedies, adequacy of other . . . 7801(1)

Reply
    Counterclaim, reply to . . . 7804(d)
    Service, time for . . . 7804(c)

Service of papers . . . 7804(c),(i)

Show cause order . . . 7804(c)

Special proceeding . . . 7804(a)

Statute of limitations . . . 217

Stay of proceedings, power of court to order, authorization . . . 7805

Successors, joinder of . . . 7802(b)

Time
    Affidavits, service of . . . 7804(c)
    Answer, service of . . . 7804(c)
    Notice of petition, service of . . . 7804(c)
    Reply, service of . . . 7804(c)

Transcript of records, filing of . . . 7804(e)

Transfer to appellate division . . . 7804(g), (h)

Trial of issues of fact . . . 7804(h)

Venue . . . 506; 7804(b)

**ASSAULT AND BATTERY**

Statute of limitations . . . 215

**ASSIGNMENTS**

Venue provisions . . . 503(e)

**ASSOCIATION, UNINCORPORATED** (See UNINCORPORATED ASSOCIATION)

**ASSUMPTION OF RISK**

Establishment of . . . 1411

**ATTACHMENT**

Abatement or discontinuance of action, effect . . . 6224

**ATTACHMENT**—Cont.

Adverse claims, procedure for determination of
    Fraudulent adverse claim determined, payment of plaintiff's reasonable expenses by claimant . . . 6221
    Questions of facts disputed, separate trial by court order . . . 6221

Affidavit of plaintiff on motion, necessary showings . . . 6212(a)

Annulment of attachment . . . 6224

Burden of proof in motion for vacation or modification of attachment . . . 6223(b)

Common carrier as garnishee, additional undertaking required as to . . . 6217

Confirmation . . . 6211(b)

County clerk's fees for filing or recording notice of . . . 8021(a)(10)

Crime, actions for forfeiture of proceeds of (See FORFEITURE OF PROCEEDS OF CRIME)

Crime victim, order of attachment for damages brought by . . . 6201(4)

Damages for wrongful attachment . . . 6212(e)

Debts against which money judgment may be enforced, attachability of . . . 6202

Demand by defendant for paper on which order granted, service on plaintiff after levy of property . . . 6212(d)

Discharge of attachment . . . 6222

Disclosure procedure, availability after order of attachment . . . 6220

Disposition of attached property . . . 6226

Docketing, attachment at time of lien upon real property; priority of lien . . . 5203(a)

Failure to proceed . . . 6214(e)

Filing of attachment order . . . 6212(c)

Forfeiture proceeding for proceeds of crime (See FORFEITURE OF PROCEEDS OF CRIME)

Garnishee
    Discharge of obligation of, how effected . . . 6204
    Proper garnishee, determination of . . . . . 6202

Grounds for obtaining order . . . 6201

Habeas corpus (See HABEAS CORPUS, subhead: Attachment warrant pursuant to writ)

Levy
    Personal property (See subhead: Personal property)
    Real property . . . 6216

Matrimonial action, unavailability in . . . 6201

Modification or vacation
    Burden of proof in motion for vacation or modification of attachment . . . 6223(b)
    Motion . . . 6223(a)

[References are to CPLR Sections, Rules and Appendices.]

**ATTACHMENT—Cont.**

Motion papers

    Affidavit . . . 6212(a)

    Damages . . . 6212(e)

    Demand for papers by defendant . . . . . 6212(d)

    Filing . . . 6212(c)

    Undertaking . . . 6212(b)

Notice of . . . 6210

Order of attachment without notice

    Contents . . . 6211

    Ex parte order, authorization . . . 6211

    Necessary specification and directions . . . 6211

Personal property

    Levy upon

        Delivery, proceeding to compel . . . 6214(d)

        Effect . . . 6214(b)

        Failure to proceed after 90 days . . . 6214(e)

        Method . . . 6214(a)

        Seizure of property levied on by service . . . 6214(c)

    Rights of attaching creditor . . . 6203

    Transferee's rights . . . 6203(1),(2)

Priority of attachment orders . . . 6226

Proceeding to compel payment, delivery or transfer, commencement against garnishee

    Authorization . . . 6214(d)

    Failure to proceed within 90 days after levy by service, voidance of levy to extent not fulfilled as result . . . 6214(e)

Property against which money judgment may be enforced, attachability . . . 6202

Real property, levy upon . . . 6216

Return of attached property or proceeds therefrom, power of court to direct . . . 6225

Seizure

    Generally . . . 6215

    Service, seizure of property levied on by . . . 6214(c)

Service of (See SERVICE OF SUMMONS AND PAPERS)

Sheriff's duties (See SHERIFF, CONSTABLE AND OTHER OFFICERS)

Statute of limitation, computation of . . 203(b); 6213

Undertaking

    Discharge of attachment . . . 6222

    Procedure . . . 6212(b)

Vacation or modification

    Burden of proof in motion for vacation or modification of attachment . . . 6223(b)

    Motion . . . 6223(a)

**ATTACHMENT—Cont.**

Wrongful attachment, damages for . . . 6212(e)

**ATTORNEY GENERAL**

Article 78 proceedings, service of papers in, responsibilities as to . . . 7804(c),(i)

Intervention as of right, notice to attorney general where constitutionality in issue . . . 1012(b)

State bodies or officers, papers served upon

    Notice of petition, where action commenced by . . . 7804(c)

    Preliminary injunction, notice of motion for . . . 6311

    Show cause order . . . 2214(d); 7804(c)

**ATTORNEYS**

Admission to practice (See ADMISSION TO PRACTICE)

Affirmation in lieu of affidavit . . . 2106

Appearance

    Corporation, requirement . . . 321(a)

    Natural person on own behalf, defense or prosecution by

        Authorization . . . 321(a)

        Infant or incompetent, disallowance . . . 321(a)

    Party's ability to act in own behalf where attorney appeared, consent of court . . . 321(a)

    Real property actions, authority for appearance in

        Agency or wholly-owned corporation of United States . . . 322(c)

        Non-resident defendant's attorney . . . 322(b)

        Plaintiff's attorney . . . 322(a)

    Voluntary association, requirement . . . . 321(a)

Arbitration, representation during . . . 7506(d)

Attorney-client privilege . . . 4503(a)

Certification of copies of papers in litigation by, authorization . . . 2105

Change of attorneys . . . 321(b)

Civil actions, prosecution or defense by attorney in . . . 321(a)

Confidential communications to, privilege against disclosure . . . 4503(a)

Corporation, defense or prosecution of civil action by attorney . . . 321(a)

Death, removal or disability

    Appeal, time for taking . . . 5514(b)

    Prior to judgment, further proceedings against party; conditions to . . . 321(c)

Defined for purposes of CPLR . . . 105(c)

Disability (See subhead: Death, removal or disability)

Index

[References are to CPLR Sections, Rules and Appendices.]

**ATTORNEYS—Cont.**

District attorney defined, forfeiture-proceeds of crime . . . 1310(14)

Endorsement by attorney of papers served of filed . . . 2101(d)

Fees (See ATTORNEYS' FEES)

Forfeiture of proceeds of crime; fees and expenses, exemption of property acquired as payment for . . . 1311(12)

Incompetent persons (See INCOMPETENT PERSONS)

Index or listing of attorneys and present standing, court clerk's maintenance of . . . 9701(3),(4)

Infants (See INFANTS AND MINORS)

Poor person, assignment of attorney for . . . . . 1102(a)

Real property actions, appearance in (See subhead: Appearance)

Referee in action, designation of attorney in good standing . . . 4312(1)

Removal (See subhead: Death, removal or disability)

Service of papers upon . . . 2103(b)

Statements subscribed and affirmed by; treatment as affidavits . . . 2106

Third-party action, service of complaint on plaintiff's attorney in . . . 1007

Trustee of an express trust, advance payment fees to . . . 8005

Verification of pleadings by, when authorized . . . 3020(d)(3)

Withdrawal of . . . 321(b)

**ATTORNEYS' FEES**

Class actions . . . 909

Forfeiture of proceeds of crime, exemption from . . . 1311(12)

Health care arbitration

    Award of fees . . . 7564(b)

        Contingency fee agreements . . . 7552(c)

Malpractice actions . . . 5031(c)

State, actions against (See STATE, ACTIONS BY OR AGAINST, subhead: Counsel fees and expenses, award of)

**AUCTIONS**

Money judgments, enforcement of

    Auction to satisfy, notice of; personal property . . . 5233(b)

**AUDIO-VISUAL MATERIALS**

Disclosure, scope of . . . 3101(i)

**AUTOMOBILE ACCIDENTS** (See ACCIDENT AND ACCIDENT REPORTS)

# B

**BAIL**

Habeas corpus (See HABEAS CORPUS)

**BANK ACCOUNTS**

Infant or incompetent's funds, court's rights to deposit . . . 1206(c)

**BANKRUPTCY**

Debtor and Creditor Law . . . App

Dismiss action, discharge in bankruptcy as ground . . . 3211(a)(5)

**BILL OF PARTICULARS**

Amendment of . . . 3042(b)

Authorization . . . 3041

Demand for

    Failure to comply with . . . 3042(c)

    Penalties for refusal to comply with . . . . 3042(d)

    Procedure for making . . . 3042(a)

Failure to comply with demand for . . 3042(c)

Generally . . . 3041

Improper or burdensome demands, service of . . . 3042(e)

Interrogatories, service in addition to demand for bill; leave of court as condition to allowance . . . 3130

Negligence actions

    Verification . . . 3044

Penalties for refusal to comply with . . 3042(d)

Personal injury actions

    Discretion of court to grant bill . . . . . . 3043(c)

    Specified particulars . . . 3043(a)

    Supplemental bill without leave . . . . . . 3043(b)

Service of improper or burdensome demands . . . 3042(e)

Supplemental bill without leave . . . 3043(b)

Verification

    Generally . . . 3044

    Negligence actions . . . 3044

**BLOOD GENETIC MARKER TEST**

Admissibility as evidence . . . 4518(d),(e)

Certification of . . . 4518(e)

Paternity actions . . . 4518(d)

**BLOOD TEST**

Blood genetic marker test, admissibility of . . . 4518(d),(e)

Business records, results admissible as . . . . . 4518(c)

**BLOOD TEST**—Cont.

Disclosure

Blood relationship, controversy involving; notice by adverse party to submit to blood examination . . . 3121(a)

DNA test, admissibility of . . . 4518(d),(e)

Paternity test . . . 4518(d)

**BONDS AND NOTES**

Mortgage on real property securing, actions on, statute of limitations; six-year period . . 213

Performance (See UNDERTAKINGS)

Principal or interest of, action to recover

State bond, 20-year statute of limitations . . . 211

Statutes of limitations

20-year statute of limitations . . . 211

Six-year period . . . 213

**BRIDGES**

Villages, actions against . . . 9804

**BRIEFS**

Appeals (See APPEALS, subhead: Briefs and appendices)

Health care arbitration . . . 7563(a)

**BUILDING CONTRACTORS**

Fees for filing of loan contracts . . 8021(b)(10)

**BURDEN OF PROOF**

Damages recoverable . . . 1412

Forfeiture of proceeds of crime

Attachment, vacating or modifying . . . . 1329(2)

"Real property instrumentality of crime" . . . 1311(3)(b)(v)

Limited liability of persons jointly liable . . . . 1603

**BUSINESS CORPORATION LAW (BCL)**

Selected practice provisions . . . App

**BUSINESS RECORDS**

Evidence, as (See EVIDENCE)

# C

**CALENDAR PRACTICE**

Abandoned cases, dismissal of

Appropriate entry by clerk, authorization without need for order . . . 3404

Supreme or county court, cases deemed abandoned . . . 3404

Chief administrator of the courts, control by . . 3401

Malpractice actions, pre-trial conferences in . . 3406(b)

**CALENDAR PRACTICE**—Cont.

Note of issue (See NOTE OF ISSUE)

Placement of case on calendar, procedure . . . . 3402(a)

Preferences for trial (See PREFERENCES FOR TRIAL)

Pre-trial conferences in malpractice actions . . . 3406(b)

**CENSUS** (See POPULATION)

**CERTIFICATES AND CERTIFICATION**

Acknowledgment, certification of . . . 4538

Agriculture, inspection certificates issued by United States . . . 4529

Blood genetic marker tests . . . 4518(e)

Business records . . . 4518(c)

Copy of order delivered to county treasurer, requirements for certification of . . . 2607

Depositions, certification by presiding officer . . . 3116(b)

Deposits into court . . . 2607

DNA tests . . . 4518(e)

Fees

County clerks . . 8020(f); 8021(a),(c),(e),(f)

Oaths . . . 8009(1)

Foreign law, final certification; who may make . . . 4542(b)

Marriage certificate as evidence of marriage . . 4526

Oaths

Fees . . . 8009(1)

Officers administering oath to persons in armed forces . . . 2309(d)

Other states, oaths administered in . . . . . 2309(c)

Official record of court or government office, authentication of certificates of

Officer of another jurisdiction . . 4540(c)

Officer of state . . . 4540(b)

Public officers, certificates of . . . 4520

Satisfaction of judgment, entry of . . . 5021(c)

Sealer's certificate as to standard of measurement . . . 4534

**CERTIORARI TO REVIEW** (See ARTICLE 78 PROCEEDING)

**CHARACTER COMMITTEE** (See ADMISSION TO PRACTICE)

**CHATTEL ACTIONS**

Additional parties, requirement for service on . . . 7103(d)

Affidavit for recovery of chattel . . . 7102(c)

Availability . . . 7101

[References are to CPLR Sections, Rules and Appendices.]

**CHATTEL ACTIONS**—Cont.

Damages

    Defendant having special property within of less value than chattel . . . 7108(b)(2)

    Taking or detaining chattel, action for; three-year limitations period . . . 214

    Value greater than damages sustained by defendant . . . 7108(b)(1)

    Wrongful taking . . . 7108(a)

Depositions; location of chattel, testimony by deposition to ascertain . . . 7112

Disposition of chattel by sheriff . . . 7102(f)

Enforcement of judgment and order (See ENFORCEMENT OF JUDGMENT AND ORDER, subhead: Real property or chattel)

Impounding chattel

    Generally . . . 7103(b)

    Undertaking required, amount . . 7103(b)

Injunction or restraining order to prevent removal of unique chattel from state or other disposition, court grant of . . . 7109(a)

Judgments

    Award not made . . . 7108(b)

    Contempt, enforceable by . . . 7109(b)

    Execution on . . . 7108(a)

    Failure to make . . . 7108(c)

    Generally . . . 7108(a)

Location of chattel, testimony by deposition to ascertain . . . 7112

Out-of-state service subsequent to seizure, no personal jurisdiction resulting . . . 314

Papers on which order granted

    Affidavit, requirement for . . . 7102(c)

    Seizure upon delivery to sheriff . . . . . . 7102(a)

    Service of copy on persons from whose possession seizure is being made . . . . 7102(b)

Parties, additional . . . 7103(d)

Perishable property, sale of . . . 7105

Provisional remedy, seizure as

    Limitations period, running of . . . 203(b)

    Recovery . . . 6001

Reclaiming chattel

    Generally . . . 7103(a)

    Less than all chattels . . . 7104

Recovery of chattel, three-year limitations period on actions for . . . 214

Restraining order

    Removal of chattel from state or other disposition . . . 7102(d)(2)

    Return of chattel to defendant . . . . . . 7103(c)(2)

Returning chattel to defendant

    Less than all chattels returned, effect . . . 7104

**CHATTEL ACTIONS**—Cont.

Returning chattel to defendant—Cont.

    Notice to sheriff and all parties required prior to order for return . . . 7103(c)(1)

    Personal property, exempt; court order for return . . . 7103(c)(1)

    Restraining order . . . 7103(c)(2)

    Security and conditions of return, court's discretion as to . . . 7103(c)(1)

    Value greater to defendant than to plaintiff, court order for return . . . 7103(c)(1)

Return of sheriff . . . 7107

Seizure of chattel on behalf of plaintiff

    Affidavit, contents of . . . 7102(c)

    Disposition of chattel by sheriff . . . . . . 7102(f)

    Interposition of claim, seizure as provisional remedy for purpose of determining . . . 203(b)

    Order of seizure . . . 7102(d)

    Perishable property, sale by sheriff . . . . 7105

    Prerequisites . . . 7102(a)

    Prior to commencement of action, procedure for seizure . . . 7102

    Provisional remedy, seizure as

        Limitations period, running of . . . . . 203(b)

        Recovery . . . 6001

    Restraining order preventing removal of chattel from state or other disposition . . . 7102(d)(2)

    Search for chattel

        Affidavit provision for . . . 7102(c)

        Order of seizure, inclusion . . . . . . 7102(d)(1)

        Powers as to . . . 7110

    Service on

        Out-of-state service subsequent to seizure, no personal jurisdiction resulting . . . 314

        Person in control of chattel . . . . . . 7102(b)

    Two or more chattels, seizure of . . 7104

    Undertaking (See subhead: Undertakings pursuant to)

Service of papers . . . 7102(b)

Sheriff's recovery of chattel

    Authority for . . . 7102(a)

    Breaking open and entering building on seizure or execution . . . 7102(c); 7110

    Disposition of chattel, generally . . . . . . 7102(f)

    Fees and expenses

        Generally . . . 8011(e)

**CHATTEL ACTIONS**—Cont.

Sheriff's recovery of chattel—Cont.

Fees and expenses—Cont.

Payment to sheriff on request . . . . 7106(a)

Filing of return within 20 days after delivery of chattel, requirement for . . . 7107

Liability of sheriff for damages incurred in wrongful delivery of chattel, limitation as to . . . 7106(b)

Powers of sheriff . . . 7110

Return of sheriff . . . 7107

Statutes of limitations (See STATUTES OF LIMITATIONS)

Undertakings pursuant to

Action on undertaking after final judgment, return of execution required prior to . . . 7111

Failure of surety to justify, delivery of chattel to plaintiff . . . 7103(a)

Impounding of chattel . . . 7103(b)

Reclaiming of chattel, requirement for . . . 7103(a)

Seizure of chattel by sheriff on behalf of plaintiff

Amount . . . 7102(e)

Exception to plaintiffs' surety by person claiming lien or security interest . . . 7102(e)

Execution . . . 7102(e)

Failure of surety to justify, return of chattel to person from whom seized . . . 7102(f)

Prerequisite for . . . 7102(a)

Unique chattel

Judgment enforceable by contempt . . . . 7109(b)

Preliminary injunction . . . 7109(a)

Temporary restraining order . . . 7109(a)

Value of property, award of

Exceptions . . . 7108(b)

Failure of jury to fix sum . . . 7108(c)

Venue for actions to recover chattel . . . 508

Wrongful taking, damages for . . . 7108(a)

**CHILDREN** (See INFANTS AND MINORS)

**CHIROPRACTORS**

Confidential communications with patient, privileged status of . . . 4504

**CITY** (See GOVERNMENTAL SUBDIVISIONS)

**CIVIL FORFEITURE**

Proceeds of crime (See FORFEITURE OF PROCEEDS OF CRIME)

**CIVIL FORFEITURE**—Cont.

Recovery of penalty or forfeiture (See PENALTIES)

**CIVIL PRACTICE ACT**

Repeal of . . . 10001

Substitution and succession by CPLR . . . 101

**CIVIL PRACTICE LAW AND RULES (GENERALLY)**

Abrogation of rules of civil practice . . . 10002

Amendment of rules . . . 102

Citation, manner of . . . 101

Civil Practice Act as predecessor . . . 101

Construction, liberal . . . 104

Effective date . . . 10005

Invalidity of part

No impairment of remainder . . . 10004

Saving clause . . . 10004

New rules, adoption . . . 102

Pending and subsequent proceedings, effect on . . . 10003

Rescission of rules . . . 102

Saving clause . . . 10004

Type size requirement . . . 105(t)

**CLASS ACTIONS**

Appearance of parties

Court's discretion as to . . . 907

Notice as to . . . 907

Attorney's fees, recovery from class opponent, court's discretion as to . . . 909

Compromise of action, court approval of, requirement . . . 908

Conduct of proceeding, court's discretion as to, considerations . . . 907

Description of class . . . 903

Dismissal or discontinuance of action, approval of court, requirement for . . . 908

Judgment

Embracing entire class; unfavorable decision no effect on . . . 905

Favorable to class; recovery of legal fees, court's discretion as to . . . 909

Payment, terms of, court's discretion as to . . . 907

Maintenance as class action, court consideration as to

Plaintiff's motion for order to determine, time for filing . . . 902

Random sampling of members to determine opinion as to litigation . . . 904

Member of class, court's discretion as to . . . . 903

Notice of

Burden of costs, court's discretion as to . . . 904

[References are to CPLR Sections, Rules and Appendices.]

**CLASS ACTIONS**—Cont.

Notice of—Cont.

Content, approval by court, requirement . . . 904

Determination of action, notice to members required . . . 908

During conduct of proceeding; court order for . . . 907

Expense involved, preliminary determination . . . 904

Method, court's discretion as to . . . 904

Relief, action for; court's discretion as to necessity . . . 904

Order allowing

Description of class, requirement . . . 903

Plaintiff's motion to maintain as class action, time for filing . . . 902

Partial class actions, authority for . . . 906

Prerequisites to action by representative parties on behalf of all . . . 901

Privity concept formerly under § 1005, elimination; Judicial Committee opinion . . . 901

Recovery of penalty, bar to maintenance as class action . . . 901

Subclasses, treatment as classes . . . 906

**CLERGY**

Confidential communications . . . 4505

**CLERK OF COURT**

Agent for service of summons, designation as . . . 303

Appeal, filing notice of . . . 8022(b)

Default judgments, entry by clerk . . . 3215(a)

Defined . . . 105(e)

Docketing of judgments . . . 2222; 5018(a)

Entry of judgment

Generally . . . 5016(a)

Real property, affecting . . . 2222; 5018(a)

Fees for services performed by

Advance, payable in . . . 8016(a)

Appeal, filing notice of . . . 8022(b)

Exemption of state and county agencies and officers from . . . 8017

Judgment-roll on appeal, certifying . . . . 8016(b)

Records and books of

Appellate division, clerk of . . . 9701

Attorney admissions, disbarments, censure, discipline and refusals of admission . . . 9701(3),(4)

Conservators, committees or guardians appointed by court . . . 9702(3)

Form and style of maintenance . . . 9703

Itemization . . . 9702

Judgments entered, book of . . . 9702(1)

**CLERK OF COURT**—Cont.

Records and books of—Cont.

Minute books . . . 9702(5)

Proceedings of all types, book or card index of . . . 9701(1); 9702(2)

Undertakings, records of . . . . . 9701(2); 9702(4)

Section and block index maintained by . . . . . 2222; 5018(a)

Taxation of costs, computation by clerk . . . . . 8401

**COLLATERAL ESTOPPEL**

Affirmative defense, pleading as . . . 3018(b)

Dismiss action, motion to; collateral estoppel as basis . . . 3211(a)(5)

**COMMENCEMENT OF ACTION OR PRO-CEEDING**

Index number, assignment and payment of fee of . . . 306-a

Methods of . . . 304

New York's Commencement by Filing Law . . App

Petition or order to show cause, service of . . . 304

Special proceedings, methods of commencement . . . 304

Statute of limitations (See STATUTES OF LIMITATIONS)

Summons, effect of statute of limitations on service of . . . 203(b)

**COMMISSIONER OF FINANCE OF NEW YORK CITY**

Fees for services performed . . . 8010

**COMMISSIONS**

Depositions outside state . . . 3108

Receivers

Allowance when funds deposited . . . . . 8004(b)

Generally . . . 8004(a)

Service upon, personal . . . 312

Trustees . . . 8005

Verification by . . . 3020(d)(2)

**COMMODITY MARKET REPORTS**

Evidence, admissibility of . . . 4533

**COMMON CARRIER**

Attachment, additional undertaking to carrier garnishee . . . 1323; 6217

Venue, fixing of; residence as basis

Place where cause of action arose, additional place of residence for venue . . 503(c)

Principal office of corporation, county of as residence for venue purpose . . . 503(c)

[References are to CPLR Sections, Rules and Appendices.]

**COMPARATIVE NEGLIGENCE**
Affirmative defense, pleading as . . . 3018(b)
Defined . . . 1411
Retroactivity . . . 1413

**COMPETENCY OF WITNESSES** (See WIT-
NESSES)

**COMPLAINT**
Authorization for . . . 3011
Counterclaim deemed asserted in, cause of action
in . . . 3019(d)
Default judgments
    Amount demanded in, judgment for . . . .
    3215(a)
    Summons served without complaint; re-
    quired notice provision . . . 305(b)
Defined . . . 105(b)
Demand for complaint . . . 3012(b)
Interpleader complaint, defined . . . 3011
Particularity, requirement for . . . 3016
Relief, inclusion of demand for . . . 3017
Summary judgment in lieu of complaint (See
SUMMARY JUDGMENT, subhead: Service in
lieu of complaint)
Summons, service with . . . 3012
Third-party (See THIRD-PARTY PRACTICE)
Verification, requirement for . . . 3016

**COMPROMISE OF CLAIM**
Offer to compromise . . . 3221

**COMPTROLLER, STATE OF NEW YORK**
Public retirement system established for public
employees at issue, notice to state comptroller
. . . 1012(c)
Special proceeding against, venue for . . 506(b)
Venue for special proceeding against . . 506(b)

**COMPUTED AXIAL TOMOGRAPHS**
Evidence, admissibility as . . . 4532-a
Personal injury actions, admissibility in . . . . .
4532-a

**CONDEMNATION PROCEEDING**
Appraisal reports intended for use at trial, rules
regarding exchanges; adoption by appellate
division of each judicial department . . 3140

**CONFESSION OF JUDGMENT**
Affidavit of defendant . . . 3218(a)
Entry of judgment . . . 3218(b)
Execution of judgment, sums not due . . . . . .
3218(c)
Installment buyers, purchases under $1500; disal-
lowance of confessed judgment . . . 3201
Joint debtors, confession of judgment . . . . . .
3218(d)

**CONFESSIONS** (See ARBITRATION PRO-
CEEDINGS, subhead: Confession, award by)

**CONFIDENTIAL COMMUNICATIONS** (See
EVIDENCE)

**CONSERVATEE**
Controversy concerning, permissibility of arbitra-
tion . . . 1209
Costs in action, liability for . . . 1205
Distributee, as
    Generally . . . 1206
    Value of property . . . 1206(b)
Personal service upon, requirements as to . . . .
309(c)
Security for costs . . . 8501(b)
Settlement of action or claim . . . 1207
Voluntary discontinuance of action via stipulation,
prohibition against . . . 3217(a)(2)

**CONSERVATOR**
Book kept by clerk of court of . . . 9702(3)
Guardian ad litem
    Motion by conservator to appoint, permissi-
    bility . . . 1202
    Notice of motion for, service of . . . 1202
Personal service on a conservatee and . . 309(c)
Residence for purpose of venue; county of ap-
pointment and of actual residence, conservator
deemed resident of both . . . 502(b)
Security for costs, requirement as to court's discre-
tion . . . 8501(b)
Substitution for conservatee, designation as; title
and text as to . . . 1016
Suits by or against; no requirement of joinder
. . . 1004
Undertaking, cost of . . . 8006
Venue determination . . . 503(b)

**CONSOLIDATION OF ACTIONS**
Actions pending before same court, power of court
to join; conditions to order . . . 602(a)
Common questions of law and fact, actions involv-
ing . . . 602(a)
Costs, award of . . . 8104
Different courts, actions pending in; removal and
consolidation of, court's power to order . . .
602(b)
Generally . . . 602
Health care arbitration . . . 7556(c)

**CONSTABLES** (See SHERIFF, CONSTABLE
AND OTHER OFFICERS)

**CONSTITUTIONALITY**
Intervention as of right, notice to attorney general
where constitutionality in issue . . . 1012

**CONSUMER CREDIT TRANSACTIONS**
Defined . . . 105(f)
Joinder of claims involving . . . 601(b)
Summons (See SUMMONS)
Venue
    Misplacement of
        Completion of service . . . 513(c)
        Rejection . . . 513(a); 513(b)
        Summons, statement included in . . 305(a)

**CONTEMPT OF COURT**
Enforcement of money judgment, power of court
    to punish for contempt . . . 5210
Subpoena, noncompliance . . . 2308(a), (b)

**CONTRACT ACTION**
Default action, notice required for . . . . . . . .
    3215(g)(3)
Election of remedies (See ELECTION OF REME-
    DIES)
General Obligations Law . . . App
Interest, recovery of, action for breach of perfor-
    mance of contract . . . 5001(a)
Printed contracts in small print . . . 4544
Simplified procedure, contract to submit existing
    or future controversy
        Enforcement of . . . 3033(1)
        Jury trial, waiver of, contract constituting
        . . . 3033(1)
Statutes of limitations (See STATUTES OF LIMI-
    TATIONS)
Venue, contract fixing; execution prior to com-
    mencement of action . . . 501

**CONTRIBUTION**
Amount of . . . 1402
Cause of action for, asserting . . . 1403
Claim for . . . 1401
Indemnity, rights of . . . 1404
Persons entitled to damages not affected, right of
    . . . 1404
Subrogation, rights of . . . 1404

**CONTRIBUTORY NEGLIGENCE**
Damages, no bar to recovery of (See NEGLI-
    GENCE ACTIONS)

**CONVERSION ACTION**
Election of remedies . . . 3002(c)

**CONVEYANCES**
Certification of acknowledgment . . . 4538
Real property situated outside state . . . 4524

**CORONER**
Official acts done or omitted, liability arising from
    . . . 215

**CORPORATIONS (GENERALLY)**
Actions by or on behalf of . . . 213
Attorney, defense or prosecution of civil action by;
    requirement . . . 321(a)
Business Corporation Law (BCL) . . . App
Default judgment . . . 3215(g)(4)
Director of corporation, actions against, statute of
    limitations on . . . 213
Dissolution, substitution of proper party upon
    . . . 1017
Domestic corporation (See DOMESTIC CORPO-
    RATIONS)
Foreign corporation (See FOREIGN CORPORA-
    TIONS)
Garnishee for enforcement of money judgment;
    president or treasurer as proper garnishees
    . . . 5201(c)(1)
Gross negligence of directors, officers or trustees;
    particularity in complaint as to specific cause of
    action . . . 3016(h)
Intentional infliction of harm by directors, officers
    or trustees; particularity in complaint as to
    specific cause of action . . . 3016(h)
Interrogatory sent to, manner of answering . . .
    3133(b)
Not-for-profit corporation law
    Motion to dismiss on grounds of § 720(a)
        immunity . . . 3211(a)(11)
    Verified complaint, requirement, actions
        based on § 720(a) . . . 3016
Officer of corporation, actions against; statute of
    limitations . . . 213
Personal service upon, method of effecting . . .
    311(a); 311(b)
Place of incorporation, particularity regarding;
    statement in complaint . . . 3015(b)
Pleadings
    Corporate directors, officers or trustees, neg-
        ligence of; particularity in complaint as to
        cause of action . . . 3016(h)
    Corporate status of party, statement in com-
        plaint, requirements . . . 3015(b)
Referee for determination of issue involving . .
    4317(a)
Shareholder, actions against; statute of limitations
    on . . . 213
Small claims action against, defense by share-
    holder or corporate officer . . . 321(a)
Status as corporation, statement in complaint;
    requirement . . . 3015(b)
Statute of limitations
    Employee or stockholder, against; six-year
        period . . . 213
    Six-year period . . . 213

**CORPORATIONS (GENERALLY)**—Cont.

Substitution of party upon dissolution, court order . . . 1017

Summons served pursuant to business corporation law § 306(b), service of summons by mail in addition to . . . 3215(g)(4)

Venue, corporation for purpose of fixing . . . . 503(c)

## COSTS

Additional allowances (See DISBURSEMENTS AND ADDITIONAL ALLOWANCES)

Amount of costs
    Action, costs involved in . . . 8201
    Appellate division, appeal to . . . 8203
    Court of Appeals, appeal to . . . 8204
    Motion, costs awarded on, amount authorized . . . 8202

Appeal, costs upon
    Appellate division . . . 8203(a)
    Appellate term . . . 8203(b)
    Entitlement to . . . 8107

Appellate division, amount of costs on appeal to . . . 8203(a)

Appellate term, amount of costs on appeal to . . . 8203(b)

Award of costs, specification of . . . 8108

Conservatee, liability of . . . 1205

Consolidated actions, costs awarded in . . 8104

Counterclaims to recover damages
    Injury to property actions . . . 8303-a
    Malpractice actions . . . 8303-a
    Personal injury actions . . . 8303-a
    Wrongful death actions . . . 8303-a

Court of Appeals, amount of costs on appeal . . . 8204

Damages
    Counterclaims to recover (See subhead: Counterclaims to recover damages)
    Frivolous claims to recover (See subhead: Frivolous claims to recover damages)

Default judgments (See DEFAULT AND DEFAULT JUDGMENTS, subhead: Costs, default judgment for)

Denial of costs, specification of . . . 8108

Disbursements (See DISBURSEMENTS AND ADDITIONAL ALLOWANCES)

Fiduciary, costs awarded against . . . 8110

Frivolous claims to recover damages
    Injury to property actions . . . 8303-a
    Malpractice actions . . . 8303-a
    Personal injury actions . . . 8303-a
    Wrongful death actions . . . 8303-a

Health care arbitration . . . 7553

Higher courts, limitation of costs for actions brought in . . . 8102

**COSTS**—Cont.

Incompetent persons, liability of . . . 1205

Infants' liability for . . . 1205

Injury to property actions
    Counterclaims in action to recover damages for, costs upon . . . 8303-a
    Frivolous claims in action to recover damages for, costs upon . . . 8303-a

Malpractice actions
    Counterclaims in action to recover damages for, costs upon . . . 8303-a
    Frivolous claims in action to recover damages for, costs upon . . . 8303-a

Motion, costs awarded upon court's discretion as to . . . 8106

Multiple plaintiffs or defendants, method for awarding costs . . . 8105

Notice of pendency, cancellation of . . 6514(d)

Personal injury actions
    Counterclaims to recover damages for . . . 8303-a
    Frivolous claims to recover damages for . . . 8303-a

Poor persons, responsibility for costs and fees by . . . 1102(d)

Prevailing party, costs awarded to
    Discretion of court regarding . . . 8101
    Separate issues, parties prevailing upon . . . 8103

Property paid into court, cost of administrating; party responsible . . . 2603

Public officers, recovery of costs by . . 8109(b)

Removed action, costs awarded in . . . 8104

Security for costs (See SECURITY FOR COSTS)

Separate issues, parties prevailing on . . . 8103

Severed actions, costs awarded in . . . 8104

Simplified procedure . . . 3036(9)

Specification of denial or award of costs . . . . 8108

State, actions by or against (See STATE, ACTIONS BY OR AGAINST)

Wrongful death actions
    Counterclaims to recover damages for . . . 8303-a
    Frivolous claims to recover damages for . . . 8303-a

## COUNTERCLAIMS

Article 78 proceedings; reply to counterclaim . . . 7804(d)

Complaint, cause of action in counterclaim deemed asserted in . . . 3019(d)

Costs upon counterclaims to recover damages (See COSTS, subhead: Counterclaims to recover damages)

[References are to CPLR Sections, Rules and Appendices.]

## COUNTERCLAIMS—Cont.

Death of plaintiff

Generally . . . 203(d)

New action . . . 205(b)

Default judgment . . . 3215(h)

Defined . . . 3019(a)

Dismiss, impropriety of interposition, basis of motion . . . 3211(a)(6)

Foreign country money judgments, enforcement of . . . 5303

Health care arbitration . . . 7564(b)

Injury to property actions, costs upon counterclaims in action to recover damages for . . . 8303-a

Interposition of counterclaim for less than amount in complaint . . . 3215(h)

Jury trial of facts arising under, assertion in . . 4102(c)

Malpractice actions, costs upon frivolous claims in actions to recover damages for . . . 8303-a

Nominal plaintiff, counterclaim against; assertion of claim against person beneficially interested . . . 3019(c)

Personal injury actions, costs upon counterclaims in action to recover damages for . . . 8303-a

Provisional remedies available . . . 6001

Reply to . . . 3011

Statutes of limitations (See STATUTES OF LIMITATIONS)

Third-party defendant, counterclaim by; right available to . . . 1008

Trustee, counterclaims against . . . 3019(c)

Verification where complaint not verified, allowance . . . 3020(a)

Wrongful death actions, costs upon counterclaims in action to recover damages for . . . 8303-a

## COUNTIES

Clerks (See COUNTY CLERKS)

Judge disqualified from acting in case, running of time from date certificate filed . . . 9003

Personal service on . . . 311(a)

Venue for trial

Actions against county, county as proper place . . . 504

Designated . . . 509

## COUNTY CLERKS

Copies of illegible papers . . . 8019(b)

Express trusts, filing of instruments settling accounts of . . . 7705

Fees paid to (See FEES, subhead: County clerks)

General duties . . . 8021

Jury trial, filing demand for . . . 8020(c)

Notice to clerk prior to entry, requirement of court . . . 8019(c)

## COUNTY CLERKS—Cont.

Page and type size acceptable to . . . 8019(e)

Taxation of costs . . . 8401

## COUNTY COURTS

Appeals to appellate division from (See APPELLATE DIVISION)

Motions (See MOTIONS)

## COUNTY TREASURERS

Fees of . . . 8010

Property paid into court (See DEPOSITS INTO COURT)

## COURT OF APPEALS

Appeal as right, grounds for . . . 5601

Appellate division

Nonfinal determination by, appeal as of right based on . . . 5601(d)

Orders from (See APPELLATE DIVISION)

Permission to appeal, grant by appellate division (See subhead: Permission to appeal)

Reversal or substantial modification of judgment by appellate division (See subhead: Reversal or substantial modification of judgment by appellate division)

Arbitration proceedings

Final award

Appeal as of right . . . 5601(d)

Appeal by permission . . 5602(a)(1)

Promulgation of rules for by chief judge . . . 3405

Certified question, appeal on

Disposition upon determination . . . 5614

Fact questions to which no findings made, prior determination of; presumption as to . . . 5612(b)

Constitutional grounds, appeal as of right based on . . . 5601(b)

Costs on appeal to, award of, amount authorized . . . 8204

Disposition of appeal

Certified questions . . . 5614

New trial or hearing, disposition on appeal from order granting . . . 5615

Reversal or modification of judgment by appellate division . . . 5613

Dissent on stated question of law, ground for appeal as of right . . . 5601(a)

Finality of, method of determining . . . 5611

Law questions, review of . . . 5501(b)

Lower courts, appeals as of right from . . . . . 5601(a)

New trial or hearing, appeal from order granting

Appeal as of right . . . 5601(c)

[References are to CPLR Sections, Rules and Appendices.]

**COURT OF APPEALS**—Cont.

New trial or hearing, appeal from order granting—Cont.

Disposition of . . . 5615

Nonfinal determination by appellate division, appeal as of right based upon . . . 5601(d)

Permission to appeal

Appellate division, grant by

Content of granting order . . . 5713

Copy of order . . . 5515(3)

When authorized . . . 5602

Generally . . . 5602

Questions of fact, presumptions of

Certified questions, presumptions in appeal of . . . 5612(b)

Prior determinations, presumptions as to . . . 5612

Remittance for determination of facts not considered by and raised in appellate division . . . 5613

Review of, when authorized . . . 5501(b)

Reversal or substantial modification of judgment by appellate division

Disposition upon . . . 5613

Remittance for determination of facts not considered by and raised in appellate division . . . 5613

Treatment by appellate division, presumption as to . . . 5612(a)

**COURT OF CLAIMS**

Court of Claims Act . . . App

**COURTS (GENERALLY)**

Appeals, court of (See COURT OF APPEALS)

Appellate Division (See APPELLATE DIVISION)

Claims Act, Court of . . . App

County courts (See COUNTY COURTS)

Court not of record, commencement of action in; statute of limitations . . . 203(b)

Decisions of court

Form of decisions . . . 4213(b)

Requests for findings of fact, submittal . . . 4213(a)

Time for decision . . . 4213(c)

Default judgments, entry by court (See DEFAULT AND DEFAULT JUDGMENTS, subhead: Entry of judgment)

Defined for purposes of CPLR . . . 105(g)

Directory . . . App

Forum non conveniens (See FORUM NON CONVENIENS)

Issues to be decided by courts . . . 4211

Judiciary Law . . . App

Personal service upon . . . 312

**COURTS (GENERALLY)**—Cont.

Stenographer's fees . . . 8002

**CPLR** (See CIVIL PRACTICE LAW AND RULES (GENERALLY))

**CREDITORS** (See DEBTOR AND CREDITOR)

**CRIME, PROCEEDS OF**

Forfeiture actions (See FORFEITURE OF PROCEEDS OF CRIME)

**CRIME VICTIM**

Attachment order for damages brought by . . . 6201(4)

Civil action by; one-year statute of limitations . . . 215

Patient as, identification by dentist of . . . . . . 4504(b)

Statutes of limitations

Action by crime victim . . . 213-b

Civil action following criminal action . . . 215

**CRIMINAL PROCEDURE LAW (CPL)**

Selected practice provisions . . . App

**CRIMINAL PROSECUTIONS**

Article 78 proceedings . . . 7804(i)

Civil and criminal prosecution, violation of right admitting of both; prohibition against merger . . . 106

Criminal Procedure Law (CPL) . . . App

**CROSS-CLAIMS**

Answer to . . . 3011

Complaint, cause of action in cross-claim deemed asserted in . . . 3019(d)

Defined . . . 3019(b)

Foreign country money judgments, enforcement of . . . 5303

Health care arbitration . . . 7564(b)

Jury trial of facts arising under, assertion in . . . 4102(c)

Provisional remedies available . . . 6001

Third-party defendant, availability to . . . 1008

Verification of where complaint not verified, allowance . . . 3020(a)

**CUSTODIANS**

Property paid into court, liability of custodian for . . . 2608

**CUSTODY OF CHILD**

Article 78 proceedings . . . 7804(i)

[References are to CPLR Sections, Rules and Appendices.]

# D

## DAMAGES

Attachment, wrongful . . . 6212(e)

Chattel actions (See CHATTEL ACTIONS)

Costs

    Counterclaims to recover (See COSTS, subhead: Counterclaims to recover damages)

    Frivolous claims to recover (See COSTS, subhead: Frivolous claims to recover damages)

Counterclaims to recover (See COSTS, subhead: Counterclaims to recover damages)

Evidence; prima facie proof of damages, documents qualifying as . . . 4533-a

Frivolous claims to recover (See COSTS, subhead: Frivolous claims to recover damages)

Health care arbitration (See HEALTH CARE ARBITRATION)

Increased damages granted by statute; single damages specified in verdict or report, increased amount in judgment . . . 4018

Joint tortfeasor, proof of payment by . . 4533-b

Liquidation of . . . 3220

Medical malpractice action (See MALPRACTICE ACTIONS)

Negligence (See NEGLIGENCE ACTIONS)

Personal injury actions (See PERSONAL INJURY ACTIONS)

Preliminary injunction, damages sustained by reason of; ascertaining . . . 6315

Subpoena, noncompliance of . . . 2308(b)

Summary judgment, triable issue of fact limited to amount or extent of damage . . . 3212(c)

Temporary restraining order, damages sustained by reason of; ascertaining . . . 6315

Undertaking by state or municipality, damages fixed in lieu of . . . 2512(2)

## DEATH

Attorneys

    Appeal, time for taking . . . 5514(b)

    Prior to judgment, further proceedings against; conditions to . . . 321(c)

Counterclaim, death of plaintiff effect on

    Generally . . . 203(d)

    New action . . . 205(b)

Creditor, death of

    Malpractice actions, judgments in . . 5035

    Personal injury, injury to property and wrongful death actions . . . 5045

Entry of judgment after death of party . . . . . 5016(d)

Judge following verdict, death of . . . 9002

Statutes of limitations (See STATUTES OF LIMITATIONS)

## DEATH—Cont.

Substitution of parties (See SUBSTITUTION OF PARTIES)

## DEBT

Enforcement of money judgment against

    Attachment, subject to . . . 6202

    Generally . . . 5201(a)

## DEBTOR AND CREDITOR

Attachment, creditor's rights in personal property . . . 1314

Creditor, death of

    Malpractice actions, judgments in . . 5035

    Personal injury, injury to property and wrongful death actions . . . 5045

Debtor and Creditor Law . . . App

Forfeiture of proceeds of crime . . . 1314

Garnishment (See GARNISHMENT)

Money judgments, enforcement of (See MONEY JUDGMENT—ENFORCEMENT PROCEDURES)

## DEBTOR AND CREDITOR LAW

Selected practice provisions . . . App

## DECLARATORY JUDGMENT

Declination by court to render, grounds for . . . 3001

Demand for relief . . . 3017(b)

Further relief, availability of; immateriality . . . 3001

Judicial controversy, involving . . . 3001

Supreme court, judgment rendered by . . 3001

## DEFAMATION (See LIBEL ACTION; SLANDER ACTION)

## DEFAULT AND DEFAULT JUDGMENTS

Adult incapable of prosecuting or defending rights, default judgment entered against, conditions to allowance . . . 1203

Article 78 proceedings . . . 7804(e)

Claim, default judgment limited to amount of . . . 3215(a)

Complaint

    Amount demanded in, judgment for . . . . . 3215(a)

    Dismissal of complaint for failure to enter judgment within one year . . . 3215(c)

    Summons served without complaint; required notice provision . . . 305(b)

Contractual obligation, notice for . . 3215(g)(3)

Corporation served pursuant to business corporation law § 306(b), additional service of summons by mail to . . . 3215(g)(4)

Costs, default judgment for

    Application to clerk, right of defendant . . . 3215(a)

[References are to CPLR Sections, Rules and Appendices.]

**DEFAULT AND DEFAULT JUDGMENTS—** Cont.

Costs, default judgment for—Cont.
  Grounds for entry . . . 3215(a)
  Time for making application . . . 3215(a)
Counterclaim for less than amount in complaint, interposition without . . . 3215(h)
Disclosure proceedings, notice requirements in . . . 3105
Dismissal of complaint for failure to enter judgment within one year . . . 3215(c)
Entry of judgment
  Clerk, entry by . . . 3215(a)
  Complaint, amount demanded in; judgment for . . . 3215(a)
  Court, entry by
    Cases where clerk cannot enter judgment, application to court authorized . . . 3215(a)
    Notices (See subhead: Notices)
    Place for making motion . . 3215(e)
    Procedure . . . 3215(b)
  Failure to enter default within one year, disposition of complaint by court . . . . 3215(c)
  Less than all defendants, judgment entered against, severance of action by clerk . . . 3215(a)
  Summons with notice, amount stated in, judgment for . . . 305(b); 3215(a)
Failure to enter default within one year, disposition of complaint by court . . . 3215(c)
Infants, default judgment entered against, conditions to allowance . . . 1203
Issuance, grounds for . . . 3215(a)
Judicially declared incompetent, default judgment entered against, conditions to allowance . . . 1203
Law office failure, excusable default due to . . . 2005
Less than all defendants, judgment entered against, severance of action by clerk . . . 3215(a)
Matrimonial action, written finding of fact; condition to entry of judgment . . . 3215(b)
Multiple defendants . . . 3215(d)
Notices
  Appearance of defendant, effect of . . . . 3215(g)(2)
  Contractual obligation, notice for . . . . . 3215(g)(3)
  Corporation, service of summons on . . . . 3215(g)(4)
  Nonappearance . . . 3215(g)(3)
  Requirements . . . 3215(g)(1)
Place for making motion . . . 3215(e)

**DEFAULT AND DEFAULT JUDGMENTS—** Cont.

Proof on application, required showings . . . . . 3215(f)
Settlement stipulation for entry of default judgment . . . 3215(i)
Severance, entry against less than all defendants . . . 3215(a)
Simplified procedure . . . 3036(4)
Sum certain or ascertainable, actions for . . . . 3215(a)
Summons, service of
  Complaint, default judgment based on summons served without; required notice provision . . . 305(b)
  Corporation served pursuant to business corporation law § 306(b), additional service of summons by mail to . . . 3215(g)(4)
  Entry of judgment, summons without notice; amount stated in . . . 305(b); 3215(a)
  Sum certain or ascertainable, actions for . . . 305(b)
Time for application to clerk . . . 3215(a)
Verified complaint, use as affidavit of facts constituting claim . . . 3215(f)

**DEFECT IN PROCEDURE** (See IRREGULARITY, MISTAKE OR DEFECT IN PROCEDURE)

**DEFENSE** (See specific subject headings)

**DEMAND FOR RELIEF**
Declaratory judgments . . . 3017(b)
Generally . . . 3017(a)
Malpractice actions . . . 3017(c)
Municipal corporations, actions against . . . . . 3017(c)

**DENTISTS**
Affirmation in lieu of affidavit . . . 2106
Confidential communications with patient, privileged status of . . . 4504(a)
Identification of patient as crime victim . . . . . 4504(b)
Malpractice (See MALPRACTICE ACTIONS)

**DEPOSITIONS**
Address of party possessing assigned cause of action, demand for . . . 3118
Certification by presiding officer . . . 3116(b)
Changes in form or substance by witness . . . . 3116(a)
Commission for depositions outside state, issuance of . . . 3108
Conduct during . . . 3113
Cross-questions, time for service of . . 3109(a)

[References are to CPLR Sections, Rules and Appendices.]

**DEPOSITIONS—Cont.**

Designation of deponent . . . 3106(d)

Documentary evidence or exhibit as part of deposition, handling of . . . 3116(c)

English language, conduct of examination in language other than . . . 3114

Errors and irregularities in transcription
>  Motion to suppress deposition on basis of, due diligence requirement . . . 3116(e)
>  Notice requirements . . . 3112
>  Waiver of, how effected . . . 3116(e)

Examination and cross-examination of deponent, extent permitted . . . 3113(c)

Exhibits, attachment and return with deposition . . . 3116(c)

Expenses related to taking of, party responsible for . . . 3116(d)

Fees . . , 8301(a)(2)

Filing requirement . . . 3116(b)

Health care arbitration (See HEALTH CARE ARBITRATION)

Impeachment of witnesses, use for purpose of . . . 3117(a)

Letters rogatory, issuance of; when permitted . . . 3108

Medical witnesses . . 3101(d)(1)(ii); 3117(a)(4)

Notice requirements
>  Errors in notice, waiver of, how effected . . . 3112
>  Oral questions, depositions upon . . . . . . 3102(a); 3107
>  Written questions . . . 3102(a); 3109(a)

Oath of witness, administration of . . . 3113(b)

Officers taking, objections to
>  Competency of witness . . . 3115(d)
>  Disqualification . . . 3115(c)
>  Effect on deposition . . . 3115(a)
>  Errors . . . 3115(b)
>  Form of written questions . . . 3115(e)
>  Recording by officer . . . 3113(b)

Oral questions; notice requirements . . . . . . . 3102(a)(4); 3107

Person not a witness . . . 3106(b)

Persons before whom taken, authorized persons; specification . . . 3113(a)

Place for taking . . . 3108; 3110

Priority of . . . 3106(a)

Prisoners, of; leave of court as condition . . . . 3106(c)

Production of books, papers and other things . . . 3111

Recross-questions, time for service of . . . . . . 3109(a)

Redirect questions, time for service of . . . . . 3109(a)

**DEPOSITIONS—Cont.**

Signing by witness, effect of . . . 3116(a)

Subpoenas
>  Generally . . . 3106(b)
>  Money judgment (See SUBPOENAS, subhead: Money judgment, proceeding for enforcement)

Subsequent actions between same parties or representatives concerning same subject matter, use of former depositions; allowance . . 3117(d)

Substitution of parties, effect on use of depositions . . . 3117(d)

Transcription of testimony
>  Errors and irregularities in transcription (See subhead: Errors and irregularities in transcription)
>  Requirement . . . 3113(b)

Translation fees, payment by examining party; witnesses ignorant of English language . . . . 3114

Use at trial, hearing of motion or interlocutory proceeding
>  Any person's deposition made before party or party's representative, use by adverse party for any purpose, conditions . . . . 3117(a)(3)
>  Effect . . . 3117(d)
>  Impeachment of witness, use for purpose of, availability to any party . . . 3117(a)
>  Partial use, availability of remainder part for use by adverse party . . . 3117(b)
>  Party's or representative's deposition; use for any purpose by adversely interested party . . . 3117(a)(2)
>  Subsequent actions concerning same subject and parties or representatives, use of former depositions at . . . 3117(d)
>  Substitution of parties, effect on right to use . . . 3117(c)

Videotaping of pretrial examinations . . 3113(b)

Within state, notice of taking deposition as . . . 3110

Witnesses
>  Impeachment of, deposition used for . . . 3117(a)
>  Medical . . . 3101(d)(1)(ii); 3117(a)(4)
>  Oath . . . 3113(b)
>  Prisoners . . . 3106(c)
>  Signing by . . . 3116(a)

Written questions, depositions taken on
>  Cross- or recross-questions, service of, time limitations . . . 3109(a)
>  Notice requirements, contents . . 3102(a); 3109(a)

[References are to CPLR Sections, Rules and Appendices.]

**DEPOSITIONS**—Cont.
Written questions, depositions taken on—Cont.
  Officer before whom deposition to be taken
    Delivery of notice and copies of written questions served to . . . 3109(b)
    Designation in notice . . . 3109(a)
    Objection to form of written questions . . . 3115(e)
  Requirements to permit . . . 3108
  Responding questions, service of, time limitations for . . . 3109(a)

**DEPOSITS INTO COURT**
Certification of copy of order delivered to county treasurer, requirement . . . 2607
Commissioner of Finance, New York City
  Delivery of money and securities . . . . . 2601(b)
Contents of order, requirements . . . 2607
Control of money or securities deposited
  Court's power over . . . 2601(a)
  Subsequent control . . . 2601(d)
Costs of administrating, party responsible . . . . 2603
County treasurer
  Certification of copy of order delivered to county treasurer, requirement . . . 2607
  Delivery of money or securities to
    Authorization . . . 2601(b)
    Commissioner of Finance of New York City, treatment as county treasurer . . . 2601(b)
Custodian, payment by pursuant to court order; liability for; good faith requirement . . 2608
Delivery of money and securities, parties involved . . . 2601(b)
Depository's duties
  Book entries, required inclusions . . 2605
  Statements to appellate division of appropriate supreme court, transmittal of . . . . 2605
Discharge of party; money deposited, discharge to extent of sum deposited . . . 2601(a)
Disposition of property by
  Conditions prerequisite to order . . . 2701
  Disobedience of direction to sell as contempt; disposal of property by sheriff . . . 2703
  Enforcement of court order . . . 2703
  Purchase by party to action, claim not prejudiced by . . . 2702
  Sale of property . . . 2702
  Value of property, likelihood to decrease during pendency, motion for sale precipitated by . . . 2702

**DEPOSITS INTO COURT**—Cont.
Expenses of administrating, party responsible for . . . 2603
Fifty dollars, property or income thereof not exceeding, no necessity for court order . . 2607
Gross sum, payment in lieu of income derived from deposited money
  Calculation of gross sum, method . . 2604
  Real Property Actions and Proceedings Law, calculation of gross sum pursuant to, authorization . . . 2604
Money, deposit of; discharge of party to extent deposited . . . 2601(a)
Other than money or securities, payment of; disposition . . . 2602
Payment out of court, order for
  Documents accompanying motion on notice; requirements . . . 2606(2)
  Motion on notice . . . 2606(1)
  Special proceeding as method; documents accompanying petition, requirement . . . 2606(2)
Referee for sale of property, deposit of property by, required procedure . . . 2609
Securities, payment into court . . . 2601(b)
Special proceedings for order for payment out of court . . . 2606(2)
Title to deposited funds . . . 2601(c)
Warehouse or safe deposit company, storage of other than money or security deposits in; power of court to direct . . . 2602

**DISABILITIES**
Attorneys
  Appeal, time for taking . . . 5514(b)
  Prior to judgment, further proceedings against; conditions to . . . 321(c)
Moving party, disability of
  Dismiss, motion to . . . 3211(a)(5)

**DISBURSEMENTS AND ADDITIONAL ALLOWANCES**
Admissibility of . . . 4518(f)
Appeal, disbursements on . . . 8301(a)
Certification of . . . 4518(f)
Discretionary additional allowances
  Enforcement motion . . . 8303(b)
  Generally . . . 8303(a)
Real property actions, additional allowances in
  Action settled . . . 8302(c)
  Amount of allowance . . . 8302(b)
  Determination of claim . . . 8302(a)(3)
  Foreclosure . . . 8302(d)
  Partition . . . 8302(a)(2)
Taxable disbursements, authorization
  Action or appeal, disbursements involved in, specification . . . 8301(a)

**DISBURSEMENTS AND ADDITIONAL AL-LOWANCES**—Cont.

Taxable disbursements, authorization—Cont.

Motion, disbursements on, specification . . . 8301(b)

Party not awarded costs . . . 8301(c)

Publication expenses . . . 8301(a)(3)

Reasonable fee of private persons as basis . . . 8301(d)

Referee's fees . . . 8301(a)(1)

Sheriff's fees . . . 8301(a)(8)

Title searches, fees for . . . 8301(a)(10)

Undertakings for stay of enforcement of judgment . . . 8301(a)(11)

Witness' fees . . . 8301(a)(1)

**DISCLOSURE**

Accident reports, scope of disclosure as to . . . 3101(g)

Addresses, demands for; service of written notice of . . . 3118

Admissions of papers, documents and photographs

Denial, penalty for unreasonable . . . . . . 3123(c)

Effect of . . . 3123(b)

Notice to admit . . . 3123(a)

Penalty for unreasonable denial . . . . . . 3123(c)

After commencement of trial; order of trial court on notice

Condition to obtaining disclosure . . . . . 3102(d)

Order of trial court on notice, condition to obtaining disclosure . . . 3102(d)

Appraisal reports at appropriation proceeding, exchanges of . . . 3140

Appropriation proceeding, appraisal reports intended for use at trial . . . 3140

Attachment order, availability of disclosure after grant of . . . 6220

Audio-visual materials, scope of disclosure as to . . . 3101(i)

Before commencement of action

Court order as condition . . . 3102(c)

Real property action involving title . . . . 3102(c)

Referee to take testimony, appointment by court . . . 3102(c)

When authorized . . . 3102(c)

Blood relationship, controversy involving; notice by adverse party to submit to blood examination . . . 3121(a)

Books, papers and things in possession of person to be examined, permissibility . . . 3111

Compelling disclosure

Application to court, when available . . . . 3124

**DISCLOSURE**—Cont.

Compelling disclosure—Cont.

Place for making motion to compel . . . . 3125

Condemnation proceedings, appraisal reports intended for use at trial, exchanges of . . 3140

Defaulting party, notice requirements of disclosure article to . . . 3105

Depositions, taking of (See DEPOSITIONS)

Devices for obtaining information . . . 3102(a)

Documents, admission as to (See subhead: Admissions of papers, documents and photographs)

Expert witnesses

Generally . . . 3101(a)(3)

Trial preparation . . . 3101(d)(1)

Express trusts, examination of trustees of . . . . 408; 7701

Extent authorized . . . 3101

Failure to comply with disclosure provisions, proponent's remedies . . . 3124

Forfeiture of proceeds of crime

Information, order for . . . 1326

Health care arbitration; disclosure of communications to arbitration panel . . . 7557

Hospital records, authorization to obtain . . . . 3121(a)

Insurance agreements, discovery of existence and contents, authorization . . . 3101(f)

Interrogatories (See INTERROGATORIES)

Judgment creditor, availability to . . . 5223

Jurisdiction outside state, action pending in; testimony of witness within state required . . . . 3102(e)

Material prepared for litigation . . . 3101(d)(2)

Mental examination (See subhead: Physical or mental examination)

Notice as method for obtaining . . . 3102(b)

Notice to admit

Admissions of papers, documents and photographs . . . 3123(a)

Objections to

Notices of withholding due to . . 3122(b)

Time limitations for . . . 3122(a)

Papers, admissions of (See subhead: Admissions of papers, documents and photographs)

Penalties

Demands or refusals, unreasonable . . . . 3124

Denial, unreasonable . . . 3123(c)

Willful noncompliance . . . 3126

Persons required to disclose . . . 3101(a)

Photographs, admissions of (See subhead: Admissions of papers, documents and photographs)

Physical or mental examination

Blood relationship, controversy involving; notice by adverse party to submit to blood examination . . . 3121(a)

[References are to CPLR Sections, Rules and Appendices.]

**DISCLOSURE—Cont.**

Physical or mental examination—Cont.

Notice of examination, time to be specified on . . . 3121(a)

Objection to, motion specifying; time for service of notice of motion . . . 3122

Physicians' reports, exchange of copies by parties . . . 3121(b)

Submission to . . . 3121(a)

Privileged matter, unavailability upon objection . . . 3101(b)

Protective orders

Abuse, prevention of . . . 3103(a)

Suppression of information improperly obtained . . . 3103(c)

Suspension of disclosure pending application for protective order . . . 3103(b)

Referees (See subhead: Supervision of disclosure)

Responses, amendment or supplementation of . . . 3101(h)

Scope, generally . . . 3101

Special proceedings, disclosure during, requirements . . . 408

State as party to action, availability of disclosure . . . 3102(f)

Statement of party to action, availability to same party . . . 3101(e)

Stay of disclosure . . . 3214(b)

Stipulation as method . . . 3102(b)

Supervision of disclosure

Authority for . . . 3104(a)

Expenses of referee, payment by court . . . 3104(e)

Motion for supervision, permissibility by any party . . . 3104(a)

Powers of supervisor . . . 3104(c)

Referee as supervisor, selection by stipulation . . . 3104(b)

Referral to supervising judge, all motions preliminary to trial . . . 3214(a)

Review of referee's order, right to . . . . . 3104(d)

Testimony, take; prior to commencement of action . . . 3102(c)

Work product . . . 3101(c)

**DISCONTINUANCE** (See VOLUNTARY DISCONTINUANCE OF ACTION)

**DISCOVERY**

(See also DISCLOSURE)

Health care arbitration (See HEALTH CARE ARBITRATION)

Inspection

Grounds for . . . 3120

Non-party, discovery against . . . 3120(b)

**DISCOVERY—Cont.**

Inspection—Cont.

Objection to, motion specifying; time for service of notice of motion . . 3122(a)

Party to action, discovery against . . . . . 3120(a)

Property, inspection of . . . 3120

Time to be specified on notice of inspection . . . 3120(a)(2)

Statutes of limitations (See STATUTES OF LIMITATIONS)

**DISCRIMINATION**

Income execution, discrimination against employees based upon . . . 5252

Wage assignment, discrimination against employees based upon . . . 5252

**DISMISSAL MOTIONS**

(See also SUMMARY JUDGMENT)

Abandoned cases

Appropriate entry by clerk, authorization without need for order . . . 3404

Supreme or county court, cases deemed abandoned . . . 3404

Arbitration and award as ground . . 3211(a)(5)

Architects and engineers, standards for motions to dismiss in actions against licensed . . . . . . 3211(h)

Authorization . . . 3211

Bankruptcy, discharge in; basis of motion . . . . 3211(a)(5)

Collateral estoppel, action not maintainable due to; basis of motion . . . 3211(a)(5)

Counterclaim improperly interposed, basis of motion . . . 3211(a)(6)

Defense neither stated nor meritorious

Basis for motion to dismiss . . . 3211(b)

Pleading again in event motion granted, permission requested in opposing papers; requirements for allowance . . . 3211(e)

Disability of moving party as ground . . . . . 3211(a)(5)

Documentary evidence, defense founded upon; basis of motion . . . 3211(a)(1)

Engineers and architects, standards for motions to dismiss in actions against licensed . . . . . . 3211(h)

Evidence permitted during hearing of motion . . . 3211(c)

Extension of time to plead, service of motion resulting in . . . 3211(f)

Failure to prosecute (See FAILURE TO PROSECUTE)

Failure to state cause of action in pleading

Basis for motion to dismiss . . . 3211(a)(7)

**DISMISSAL MOTIONS**—Cont.

Failure to state cause of action in pleading—Cont.
Pleading again in event motion granted, permission requested in opposing papers, necessary showings . . . 3211(e)

Forum non conveniens
Court's discretion to stay or dismiss action on motion of party
Contracts to which GOL § 51402 applies, mandatory enforcement of choice of forum clauses in . . 327(b)
Domicile or residence of any party within state as no bar to court's action . . . 327(a)

Grounds
Enumeration . . . 3211(a)
Nonwaivable grounds, specification . . . . 3211(e)
Number of grounds in single motion . . . 3211(e)

Hearing of motion
Evidence permitted during . . . 3211(c)
Immediate trial of issues raised by motion, power of court to order . . . 3211(c)
Summary judgment, motion for; authorization for court to treat motion to dismiss as . . . 3211(c)

Infancy as ground . . . 3211(a)(5)

Judgment dismissing claim, effect of . . . 5013

Jurisdictional defect as ground
Personal jurisdiction over defendant, lack of, basis of motion . . . 3211(a)(8)
Quasi-in-rem jurisdiction, lack of . . . . . 3211(a)(9)
Subject matter jurisdiction, court lacking, basis of motion . . . 3211(a)(2)

Legal incapacity of plaintiff, basis of motion . . . 3211(a)(3)

Necessary party, nonjoinder of; basis of motion . . . 3211(a)(10)

Nonjoinder of party . . . 3211(a)(10)

Not-for-profit corporation law, § 720(a) immunity as ground . . . 3211(a)(11)

Number of grounds assertible in one motion . . . 3211(e)

Opposing affidavit
Facts justifying opposition, possible existence but unavailability of, shown by affidavit
Continuance to permit further affidavits, court order, authorization . . . 3211(d)
Remedies . . . 3211(d)

Payment as ground . . . 3211(a)(5)

**DISMISSAL MOTIONS**—Cont.

Pending action on same cause of action between same parties, discretion of court regarding pretrial disposition . . . 3211(a)(4)

Public petition and participation, standards for motions to dismiss in cases involving . . . . . 3211(g)

Release of moving party, motion based upon . . . 3211(a)(5)

Res judicata, motion based upon . . 3211(a)(5)

Single motion to dismiss, extent allowed, requirement . . . 3211(e)

Statute of frauds, motion based upon . . . . . . 3211(a)(5)

Statute of limitations
Affirmative action to recover on claim in defense . . . 203(e)
Motion based upon . . . 3211(a)(5)

Subject matter jurisdiction, court lacking; basis of motion . . . 3211(a)(2)

Substitution motion not made within reasonable time as grounds, court's discretion as to dismissal on merits . . . 1021

Summary judgment, dismissal motion treated as . . . 3211(c)

Third-party complaint, dismissal without prejudice of . . . 1010

Time for making motions; service of responsive pleading, any time prior to . . . 3211(e)

Waiver of grounds for dismissal
Nonwaivable grounds, specification . . . . 3211(e)

**DISPOSITIONS**

Appeals . . . 5522

Court of appeals (See COURT OF APPEALS)

Forfeiture of proceeds of crime; disposition of attached property after execution . . . 1332

Incompetent persons (See INCOMPETENT PERSONS, subhead: Disposition of proceeds of incompetent's claim, methods)

Infants and minors; disposition of proceeds of claim, methods . . . 1206

Property (See DEPOSITS INTO COURT)

**DISSOLUTION OF MARRIAGE** (See ANNULMENT OR DISSOLUTION OF MARRIAGE)

**DISTRICT ATTORNEY**

Defined under forfeiture-proceeds of crime . . . 1310(14)

**DIVORCE ACTION**

Matrimonial actions
Divorce action as term included in . . . . 105(p)

[References are to CPLR Sections, Rules and Appendices.]

**DIVORCE ACTION**—Cont.
Matrimonial actions—Cont.
Generally (See MATRIMONIAL ACTIONS)
Misconduct of party, specification of . . 316(c)
Pleadings, particularity of statements required for
. . . 3016(c)
Summons not personally delivered, defense by
person to whom . . . 317

**DNA TEST**
Admissibility as evidence . . . 4518(d),(e)
Certification of . . . 4518(e)
Paternity actions . . . 4518(d)

**DOCKETING OF JUDGMENT**
Change of docket, certificate issued by proper
clerk, entry . . . 5019(d)
Clerk of court . . . 5018(a)
Electronic method of . . . 5018(d)
Form, necessary inclusions in docket book . . .
5018(c)
Joint liability of two or more persons, judgment
upon; indication of defendants "not summoned"
. . . 5018(a)
Judgment creditor, change in; entry on docket of
judgment . . . 5019(c)
Maintaining, method of . . . 5018(d)
Money judgment, judgment-roll filing of; docket-
ing subsequent to . . . 5018(a)
Order docketed as judgment . . . 2222
Real property
Lien upon, attachment at time of docking;
priority of lien . . . 5203(a)
Satisfaction or partial satisfaction, entry on docket
of judgment
Docketing in other counties, transcripts of
docket judgment . . . 5020(d)
Small claims actions; satisfied, partially satisfied,
and unsatisfied, entry on docket . . . 5021(b)
Subsequent judgment or order affecting docketed
judgment, entry upon docket of judgment . .
5019(b)
Time for . . . 5018(a)
Transcript of judgment, filing of; docketing based
upon . . . 5018(a)
United States' court judgment of . . . 5018(b)

**DOING BUSINESS** (See FOREIGN CORPORA-
TIONS; NONRESIDENT)

**DOMESTIC CORPORATIONS**
Corporations generally (See CORPORATIONS
(GENERALLY))
Defined for purposes of CPLR . . . 105(h)
Security for costs, exemption from . . . 8501(a)

**DOMESTIC CORPORATIONS**—Cont.
Venue for trial, residence of corporation for purpose of fixing
Principal office, corporation deemed resident
of county where
Authority . . . 503(c)
Railroad or other common carrier,
place cause of action arose; additional place of residence . . 503(c)
Verification of pleading, execution by officer of
domestic corporation . . . 3020(d)(1)

**DOMESTIC RELATIONS LAW (DRL)**
Selected practice provisions . . . App

**DOWER ACTION**
Jury trial of fact issues, authorization for . . . .
4101(2)

**DRL** (See DOMESTIC RELATIONS LAW
(DRL))

# E

**EAVESDROPPING**
Admissibility as evidence . . . 4506
Suppress, motion to . . . 4506

**EDUCATION**
Education Law . . . App
Infant (See INFANTS AND MINORS, subhead:
Support, maintenance or education, property of
infant applied for purpose of; petition to court)

**EDUCATION LAW**
Selected practice provisions . . . App

**EJECTMENT ACTION**
Jury trial of fact issues, authorization for . . . .
4101(2)

**ELECTION OF REMEDIES**
Agent and undisclosed principal, causes of action
existing against . . . 3002(b)
Arbitration of damages
Malpractice actions . . . 3045
Authorization . . . 3002
Contracts
Action generally . . . 3002(c)
Reformation of contract, action on . . . . .
3002(d)
Rescission of fraudulently induced contract,
claim for damages joined with . . . . .
3002(e)
Conversion action . . . 3002(c)
Fraud or misrepresentation, rescission of contract
and damages; claims for . . . 3002(e)

**ELECTION OF REMEDIES**—Cont.

Malpractice actions . . . 3045

Reformation of agreement . . . 3002(d)

Rescission of fraudulently induced contract, claim for damages joined with . . . 3002(e)

Several persons, causes of action existing against . . . 3002(a)

Vendee's lien on real property, no denial resulting from form of action chosen . . . 3002(f)

**ELECTROMYOGRAMS**

Evidence, admissibility as . . . 4532-a

Personal injury actions, admissibility in . . . . . 4532-a

**ELECTRONIC TECHNOLOGY**

Reproduction of original document, admissibility of electronically stored . . . 4539(b)

Service of papers by electronic means

    Definition . . . 2103(f)

    Generally . . . 2103(b)(5)

**EMPLOYEE-EMPLOYER RELATIONSHIP**

Discrimination against employees based upon wage assignments . . . 5252

Employee organization's breach of duty of fair representation; statute of limitations . . . 217

**ENFORCEMENT OF JUDGMENT AND ORDER**

Allowance at discretion of court, additional award to judgment creditor . . . 8303(b)

Alternative method of enforcement, judgments to which applicable, specification . . . 5105

Contempt, enforcement by . . . 5104

Execution, enforcement by (See subhead: Real property or chattel)

Exempt property (See MONEY JUDGMENT— ENFORCEMENT PROCEDURES)

Money judgments (See MONEY JUDGMENT— ENFORCEMENT PROCEDURES)

Real property or chattel

    CPLR 5230, compliance with . . . 5102

    Possession of, judgment or order awarding Authorization . . . 5102

        Death of party against whom enforcement sought, effect . . . 5102

    Sale of real property for (See REAL PROPERTY ACTIONS, subhead: Sale for enforcement of money judgment)

Stay of enforcement pending appeal (See APPEALS)

Trustee of fiduciary, dereliction of duty, judgment directing payment of sum of money . . . . . 5105(2)

**ENTERPRISE CORRUPTION**

Civil actions notice . . . 1355

Civil remedies . . . 1353

Joinder of parties . . . 1354

**EPTL** (See ESTATES, POWERS AND TRUSTS LAW (EPTL))

**EQUITY SUIT**

Action at law and, distinctions between . . . . . 103(a)

**ERRORS** (See IRREGULARITY, MISTAKE OR DEFECT IN PROCEDURE)

**ESTATES**

Estates, Powers and Trusts Law (EPTL) . . . . App

Infant, guardian of

    Management of estate, direction by court order; discretion of court . . . 1210(d)

**ESTATES, POWERS AND TRUSTS LAW (EPTL)**

Selected practice provisions . . . App

**EVIDENCE**

Abstract companies, searches by . . . 4523

Admission to practice (See ADMISSION TO PRACTICE, subhead: Proof)

Age of child, proof of . . . 4516

Agriculture inspection certificates issued by Department of Agriculture . . . 4529

Airplane accidents, testimony as to . . . 4519

Ancient maps, surveys and real property records . . . 4522

Arbitration hearing; determination by arbitrator on . . . 7506(c)

Attorney-client privilege . . . 4503(a)

Authentication

    Certified acknowledgment or proof of writing, prima facie evidence of authenticity . . . 4538

    Handwriting of person claimed to be author, writing containing, comparison with disputed writing . . . 4536

    Official record of court or governmental office, authentication of (See subhead: Official record of court or governmental office, authentication of)

    Self-authentication of newspapers and periodicals . . . 4532

    Subscribing witness, writings not requiring; proof of . . . 4537

Automobile accidents, testimony as to . . 4519

Axial tomographs, admissibility of . . . 4532-a

Blood genetic marker test, admissibility of . . . 4518(d),(e)

[References are to CPLR Sections, Rules and Appendices.]

**EVIDENCE**—Cont.
Business records
    Generally . . . 4518(a)
    Hospital bills . . . 4518(b)
    Hospital records in custody of warehouse
       . . . 4518(c)
    Reproduction or copy of original, basis for
       admissibility of . . . 4539(a)
Certificate or affidavit of public officer . . 4520
Child, proof of age of . . . 4516
Chiropractor-patient privilege . . . 4504
Clergy-communicant, communications between,
    privilege against disclosure . . . 4505
Collateral sources of payment, admissibility of
    Medical malpractice actions . . . 4545(a)
    Personal injury, injury to property or wrong-
       ful death
           Public employer, certain actions against
              . . . 4545(b)
           Recovery of costs, loss of earnings or
              economic loss . . . 4545(c)
    Public employer, certain actions against;
     personal injury, injury to property or
       wrongful death . . . 4545(b)
Commodity market reports, admissibility of . . .
    4533
Common law, rules of evidence at, availability
    . . . 4543
Competency of witnesses (See WITNESSES)
Computed axial tomographs, admissibility of
    . . . 4532-a
Confidential communications
    Attorney-client, communications between
       . . . 4503(a)
    Chiropractor-patient privilege . . . 4504
    Clergy-communicant, communications be-
       tween . . . 4505
    Dentist-patient, communications between
       . . . 4504
    Nurse-patient, communications between
       . . . 4504
    Physician-patient, communications between
       . . . 4504
    Podiatrist-patient, communications between
       . . . 4504
    Psychologist-client, communications be-
       tween . . . 4507
    Rape crisis counselor-client, communica-
       tions between
           Generally . . . 4510(b)
           Limitations on waiver . . . 4510(d)
           Waiver of confidentiality, privilege of
              . . . 4510(c)
    Social worker-client, communications be-
       tween . . . 4508

**EVIDENCE**—Cont.
Confidential communications—Cont.
    Spouses, communications between . . . . .
       4502(b)
Contributory negligence . . . 4519
Conveyances
    Certification of acknowledgment . . 4538
    Real property outside state . . . 4524
Damages, prima facie proof of . . . 4533-a
Death, presumption of . . . 4527(a)
Decedent
    Mental and physical condition, disclosure of
       . . . 4504(c)
    Personal transaction or communication with
       witness, admissibility into evidence . . .
       4519
Dentist-patient, communications between, privi-
    lege against disclosure . . . 4504(b)
Depositions of witnesses (See DEPOSITIONS)
Disclosure (See DISCLOSURE)
Dismissal motions
    Documentary evidence, defense founded
       upon; basis of motion . . . 3211(a)(1)
    Evidence permitted during hearing of motion
       . . . 3211(c)
DNA test, admissibility of . . . 4518(d),(e)
Eavesdropping
    Admissibility . . . 4506
    Suppress, motion to . . . 4506
Electromyograms, admissibility of . . . 4532-a
Electronically stored reproduction of original,
    admissibility of . . . 4539(b)
Expert opinion . . . 4515
Facts, proof of . . . 4543
Fetal heart rate monitor strips, admissibility of
    . . . 4532-a
Foreign records and documents, authentication
    and proof of . . . 4542
Handwriting of alleged author, comparison with
    disputed writing for authentication purposes
    . . . 4537
Hospital bill, admissibility as business record
    . . . 4518(b)
Hospital records in custody of warehouse . . . .
    4518(c)
Human leucocyte antigen test, records of . . . .
    4518(c)
Impeachment of witnesses
    Depositions . . . 3117(a)
    Prior inconsistent statements . . . 4514
Injury to property
    Collateral sources of payment, admissibility
       of
           Public employer, certain actions against
            . . . 4545(b)

EVIDENCE—Cont.

Injury to property—Cont.

Collateral sources of payment, admissibility of—Cont.

Recovery of costs, loss of earnings or economic loss . . . 4545(c)

Insurance payments as collateral source of payment, admissibility of

Malpractice actions . . . 4545(a)

Interrogatories, use of (See INTERROGATORIES)

Joint tortfeasors, proof of payments by . . . . . 4533-b

Judicial notice of law

Copies of statutes and cases . . . 4511(d)

Determination by court . . . 4511(c)

Foreign law . . . 4511(b)

Mandatory notice . . . 4511(a)

Matter to be judicially noticed . . 4511(d)

Permissive notice . . . 4511(b)

Justice of the peace, proceedings before; proof of . . . 4541

Lack of official record, statement signed by public officer in charge of specified records, effect . . . 4521

Library records . . . 4509

Magnetic resonance images, admissibility of . . 4532-a

Malpractice actions

Insurance payments as collateral sources of payment, admissibility of . . . 4545(a)

Loss of earnings and impairment of earning ability as . . . 4546

Maps, surveys and real property records of ancient age . . . 4522

Marriage certificate, prima facie evidence of marriage established by . . . 4526

Missing persons

Death, presumption of . . . 4527(a)

Present status of, report by authorized party pursuant to law of United States; prima facie evidence of status . . . 4527(b)

Negligence cases . . . 4519

Newspapers and periodicals, self-authenticity of . . . 4532

New York simplified procedure for court determination of disputes, rules of evidence during (See SIMPLIFIED PROCEDURE)

Nurse-patient privilege . . . 4504

Official record of court or government office, authentication of

Certificates

Officer of another jurisdiction . . . . 4540(c)

Officer of state . . . 4540(b)

EVIDENCE—Cont.

Official record of court or government office, authentication of—Cont.

Copies permitted . . . 4540(a)

Printed tariff or classification subject to public service commission . . . 4540(d)

Paternity test, records of . . . 4518(d)

Personal injury actions

Collateral sources of payment, admissibility of

Public employer, certain actions against . . . 4545(b)

Recovery of costs, loss of earnings or economic loss . . . 4545(c)

Computed axial tomographs, admissibility of . . . 4532-a

Electromyograms, admissibility of . . . . . 4532-a

Fetal heart rate monitor strips, admissibility of . . . 4532-a

Magnetic resonance images, admissibility of . . . 4532-a

Position emission tomographs, admissibility of . . . 4532-a

Sonograms, admissibility of . . . 4532-a

X-rays, admissibility of . . . 4532-a

Personal injury cases . . . 4519

Physician-patient privilege . . . 4504

Pleadings, conforming to evidence; motion to amend pleadings for purpose of . . . 3025(c)

Podiatrist-patient privilege . . . 4504

Population, certificate of

Conclusive evidence . . . 4530(b)

Prima facie evidence . . . 4530(a)

Positron emission tomographs, admissibility of . . . 4532-a

Printed contracts in small print . . . 4544

Prior testimony, admissibility . . . 4517

Privileges

Confidential communications (See subhead: Confidential communications)

Psychologist-client privilege . . . 4507

Public officer's affidavit or certificate . . . 4520

Real property, evidence pertaining to

Abstract companies, searches by . . 4523

Conveyance

Certification of acknowledgment . . . 4538

Outside state . . . 4524

Title insurance companies, searches by . . . 4523

Receipt of evidence

Authorized person as qualified to administer related oath or affirmation . . . 2309(a)

[References are to CPLR Sections, Rules and Appendices.]

**EVIDENCE**—Cont.

Referees reviewing of findings on appeal . . . . 4511(c)

Reproduction or copy of original business records, admissibility of . . . 4539(a)

Self-incrimination, privilege against . . . 4501

Service of notice, affidavit as prima facie evidence of . . . 4531

Simplified procedure (See SIMPLIFIED PROCE-DURE)

Social worker-client, communications between, privilege against disclosure . . . 4508

Sonograms, admissibility of . . . 4532-a

Spousal privilege
 Confidential communications . . . 4502(b)
 Incompetency where adultery is issue . . . 4502(a)

Stock market report, admissibility of report . . . 4533

Summary judgment, motion for . . . 3212(b)

Surveys
 Maps and other real property records . . . 4522
 Standard of measurement used by surveyor . . . 4534

Tender of payment pursuant to CPLR, fact of tender known to jury; prohibition against . . . 3219

Uniform Commercial Code, Article 9; copy of statements filed pursuant to . . . 4525

Vessel, testimony as to accidents involving . . . 4519

Videotaping testimony at pretrial examination . . . 3113(b)

Waiver limitations . . . 4508(b)

Weather conditions, prima facie evidence of; what constitutes . . . 4528

Wills; probate, validity or construction of, actions involving, attorney-client privilege applied to . . . 4503(b)

Writings, proof of (See subhead: Authentication)

Wrongful death actions
 Collateral sources of payment, admissibility of
  Public employer, certain actions against . . . 4545(b)
  Recovery of costs, loss of earnings or economic loss . . . 4545(c)

X-rays, admissibility of . . . 4532-a

**EXAMINATION BEFORE TRIAL** (See DE-POSITIONS)

**EXECUTION ON JUDGMENTS**

Form of execution, necessary inclusions . . . . . 5230(a)

**EXECUTION ON JUDGMENTS**—Cont.

Income execution (See INCOME EXECUTION)

Issuance
 Place for issuance . . . 5230(b)
 Satisfaction or vacation of judgment, issu-ance any time prior to . . . 5230(b)

Orders
 Defined . . . 5230(e)

Return of execution, time limitations and exten-sions . . . 5230(c)

Sheriff
 Fees (See SHERIFF, CONSTABLE AND OTHER OFFICERS, subhead: Fees)
 Records, requirements for . . . 5230(d)

**EXECUTORS AND ADMINISTRATORS**

Security for costs . . . 8501(b)

Summons served upon, interposition of claim against decedent; statute of limitations
 Provisional remedy order, death of defendant within 30 days thereafter; delivery within 60 days of issuance of letters . . 203(b)
 Sheriff, summons delivered to . . . 203(b)

Venue
 County of appointment and actual residence, residence in both for venue purposes . . . 503(b)
 Specification of representatives . . 503(b)

**EX PARTE PROCEEDINGS**

Appellate division, review of orders by . . . . . 5704(a)

Appellate term, review of orders by . . 5704(b)

Motions (See MOTIONS)

**EXPENSES** (See COSTS; FEES)

**EXPERT WITNESSES** (See WITNESSES, sub-head: Expert witnesses)

**EXPRESS TRUST PROCEEDINGS**

Attorney-trustee, advance payment of fees to . . . 8005

Availability . . . 7701

Commissions of trustees . . . 8005

County clerk, filing of instruments settling ac-counts . . . 7705

Disclosure of
 Trustees, examination of . . . 408; 7701

Filing instrument settling trust, allowance . . . . 7705

Joinder and representation of persons interested in estates; SCPA provisions governing . . 7703

Judicial settlement of trustee's accounts, petition of trustee . . . 7702

Order on filing instrument settling account . . . 7706

**EXPRESS TRUST PROCEEDINGS**—Cont.

Recording of instruments settling accounts . . . 7705

Referee to examine and audit trustee's account, appointment of . . . 7704

Trustees, examination of . . . 7701

Verified account accompanying petition by trustee for settlement . . . 7702

**EXTENSION OF TIME**

Appeals (See APPEALS, subhead: Extension of time)

Arbitration

    Award . . . 7507

    Modification of award by arbitrator . . . . 7509

Delay, excusable . . . 2005

Dismissal, extension of time to plead for . . . . 3211(f)

Execution on judgment, return of . . . 5230(c)

Generally . . . 2004

Incompetent persons . . . 208

Infants . . . 208

Law office failure; excusable delay . . . 2005

Mentally ill persons, action accruing in favor of; extension of statute of limitations period . . . 208

Periods fixed by law, extension by court; prohibition against . . . 201

Substitution of parties . . . 1022

Termination of action, new action by plaintiff or personal representative; six-month extension to bring action . . . 205(a)

Time to appear or plead . . . 3012(d)

# F

**FAILURE TO PROSECUTE**

Dismissal of action

    Conditions precedent to, specification . . . 3216(b)

    Note of issue (See subhead: Note of issue)

Note of issue

    Demand by party seeking dismissal for service and filing of note

        Calendar, note of issue placed on . . . 3216(d)

        Compliance with received demand within specified period, effect . . . 3216(c)

        Failure to comply with demand, discretion of court regarding . . 3216(e)

        Requirement . . . 3216(b)(3)

Scope of provision . . . 3216(a)

**FAMILY COURT PROCEEDINGS**

Jurisdiction over non-resident

    Support or alimony, demand for . . 302(b)

Support or alimony, demand for

    Jurisdiction over non-resident . . . 302(b)

**FEES**

Appeal, filing notice of

    Clerk of court . . . 8022(b)

    County clerks . . . 8022(a)

Arbitration proceedings (See ARBITRATION PROCEEDINGS)

Attorneys' fees (See ATTORNEYS' FEES)

Clerks of court (See CLERK OF COURT)

Commissioner of Finance of New York City . . . 8010

County clerks

    Appeal, filing notice of . . . 8022(a)

    Building loan contracts, filing of . . . . . . 8021(b)(10)

    Calendar fees . . . 8020(a); 8020(b)

    Certificates and certification . . . 8020(f); 8021(b),(c),(e),(f)

    Chattel mortgages . . . 8021(b)(5)

    Clerk of court, fees for services rendered in capacity as . . . 8020

    Copies of records . . . 8019(f)

    Exemplification . . . 8020(f)

    Exemptions . . . 8019(d)

    Federal tax liens . . . 8021(g)

    Filing fees . . . 8021(b)

    Foreclosure notices . . . 8021(a)(3)

    Generally . . . 8019

    Hospital liens, filing notices of . . . . . . . 8021(b)(6)

    Index number fees

        Additional services where index number assigned . . . 8018(d)

        Amount . . . 8018(a)

        Endorsement . . . 8018(c)

        Exemptions from payment . . . . . . 8018(b)

    Instruments, recording of . . . 8021(b)(11)

    Legible copies requirement by county clerk, fee prescribed for . . . 8019(b)

    Maps . . . 8021(a)(3),(e)

    Mechanics' liens, filing notices of . . . . . 8021(b)(4)

    New York City . . . 8021(a),(b),(c)

    Notice of attachment filing or recording . . . 8021(a)(10)

    Notice of pendency, filing or recording . . . 8021(a)(10)

    Other than as clerk of court, fees for service rendered in capacity as . . . 8021

[References are to CPLR Sections, Rules and Appendices.]

**FEES**—Cont.
County clerks—Cont.
    Production of records . . . 8020(h)
    Searches . . . 8020(g); 8021(d)
    Services where sheriff is party or otherwise disqualified, fees for performance . . . . 8015
    Transcripts, filing of . . . 8021(b)(7)
    Transferred cases, calendar fees . . . . . . 8020(b)
    Uniform Commercial Code . . . 8021(f)
    Wages, filing assignment of order for payment of . . . 8020(c), (e); 8021(b)(3)
County treasurer, fees for . . . 8010
Disbursements (See DISBURSEMENTS AND ADDITIONAL ALLOWANCES)
Oaths and affirmations
    Administration and certification . . . . . . 8009(1)
    Witnesses to execution of instruments, swearing of . . . 8009(2)
Papers, transmission of . . . 8008
Poor persons, responsibility for costs and fees by . . . 1102(d)
Printer's fees . . . 8007
Publication fees . . . 8301(a)(3)
Receivers, commissions of
    Allowance when funds depleted . . . . . . 8004(b)
    Generally . . . 8004(a)
Referees (See REFEREES)
Removal of case, previous payments; crediting provisions . . . 326(c)
Sheriff's fees (See SHERIFF, CONSTABLE AND OTHER OFFICERS)
State, actions against (See STATE, ACTIONS BY OR AGAINST, subhead: Counsel fees and expenses, award of)
Stenographers . . . 8002
Subpoenas (See SUBPOENAS)
Transcripts (See TRANSCRIPT OF ACTION OR PROCEEDING)
Trustees' commissions . . . 8005

**FELONY**
Forfeiture of proceeds or instrumentality of crime; "specified felony offense"
    Adduction of evidence to contradict establishment of elements of . . . 1331(3-a)
    Defined . . . 1310(4-b)

**FETAL HEART RATE MONITOR STRIPS**
Evidence, admissibility as . . . 4532-a
Personal injury actions, admissibility in . . . . . 4532-a

**FIDUCIARY**
Bonds required of (See UNDERTAKINGS, subhead: Fiduciary bonds)
Costs awarded against . . . 8110
Trustee of fiduciary, dereliction of duty; judgment directing payment of sum of money . . . . . 5105(2)

**FORECLOSURE**
Additional allowances in . . . 8302(d)
Fees of county clerks . . . 8021(a)(3)
Referee on, commissions to . . . 8003(b)

**FOREIGN CORPORATIONS**
Authorized foreign corporation
    Venue for trial, residence of corporation for purpose of fixing, section establishing . . . 503(c)
Corporations generally (See CORPORATIONS (GENERALLY))
Defined for purposes of CPLR . . . 105(h)
Jurisdiction over
    Real property located in state, ownership, use or possession; personal jurisdiction based upon . . . 302(a)
    Tortious acts committed by unauthorized foreign corporation, jurisdiction based on (See subhead: Tortious acts of unauthorized foreign corporation, personal jurisdiction based on)
    Transacting business within state by unauthorized corporation, act arising from, basis for personal jurisdiction . . 302(a)
    Unauthorized foreign corporation, personal jurisdiction over . . . 302
Long-arm statute (See subhead: Jurisdiction over)
Outside state, place of tortious act; injury to person or property within state caused by
    Conditions . . . 302(a)
    Doing business regularly within state, condition to applicability of subdivision . . . 302(a)
    Persistent course of conduct in state, engagement of corporation in, condition to applicability of subdivision . . . 302(a)
    Soliciting business regularly in state, condition to applicability of subdivision . . . 302(a)
    Substantial income derived from goods used, consumed or services rendered in state, condition to applicability of subdivision . . . 302(a)
Service of summons on, officer within state for purpose of; inapplicability of tolling section of statute of limitations . . . 207

[References are to CPLR Sections, Rules and Appendices.]

FOREIGN CORPORATIONS—Cont.

Tortious acts of unauthorized foreign corporation, personal jurisdiction based on
    Defamation of character, specific exception from applicability of subdivision . . . . 302(a)
    Within state, place of commission . . . . . 302(a)
Unauthorized foreign corporation, personal jurisdiction over . . . 302
Venue, residence of corporation for purpose of fixing . . . 503(c)
Verification of pleadings by, attorney or agent effecting; authorization . . . 3020(d)(3)

FOREIGN COUNTRY MONEY JUDGMENTS

Action on judgment, enforcement by . . . 5303
Affirmative defense, judgment as . . . 5303
Appeal, stay in case of . . . 5306
Citation of article . . . 5309
Conflict with other final judgment, ground for non-recognition . . . 5304(b)(5)
Contrary agreement for settlement, existence of; ground for non-recognition . . . 5304(b)(6)
Counterclaim, assertion in . . . 5303
Cross-claim, assertion in . . . 5303
Defined . . . 5301(b)
Due process of law, no provision for in foreign system; ground for non-recognition . . . . . . 5304(a)(1)
Final judgment where rendered, applicability of article to . . . 5302
"Foreign state" defined . . . 5301(a)
Forum for foreign trial, inconvenience where action solely based upon personal service; ground for non-recognition . . . 5304(b)(7)
Fraud, judgment obtained by . . . 5304(b)(3)
Full faith and credit, entitlement to (See FULL FAITH AND CREDIT, FOREIGN JUDGMENT ENTITLED TO)
Income deduction order based on . . . 5242(c)
Interpretation of article, uniformity of . . 5308
Non-recognition, grounds for
    Conflict with other final judgment . . . . . 5304(b)(5)
    Contrary agreement for settlement, existence of . . . 5304(b)(6)
    Forum for foreign trial, inconvenience where action solely based upon personal service . . . 5304(b)(7)
    Fraud, judgment obtained by . . . . . . . . 5304(b)(3)
    Notice of proceedings, insufficiency of . . 5304(b)(2)
    Personal jurisdiction over defendant by foreign court, lack of . . . 5304(a)(2)

FOREIGN COUNTRY MONEY JUDGMENTS—Cont.

Non-recognition, grounds for—Cont.
    Public policy of state, cause of action repugnant to . . . 5304(b)(4)
    Subject matter jurisdiction, lack of . . . . 5304(b)(1)
Notice of proceedings in foreign court, insufficiency of; ground for non-recognition . . . . 5304(b)(2)
Order, support enforcement . . . 5242(c)
Personal jurisdiction over defendant by foreign court
    Basis of jurisdiction sufficient to give, enumeration of . . . 5305
    Lack of, ground for non-recognition . . . . 5304(a)(2)
Public policy of state, cause of action repugnant to; ground for non-recognition . . 5304(b)(4)
Recognition of . . . 5303
Situations not covered by article, recognition of, allowance . . . 5307
Stay in case of appeal . . . 5306
Subject matter jurisdiction, lack of in foreign court; ground for non-recognition . . . . . . . 5304(b)(1)
Summary judgment in lieu of complaint, enforcement by . . . 5303

FOREIGN LAW

Complaint or defense based upon, substance of foreign law; inclusion in pleading . . 3016(e)
Final certification, who may make . . . 4542(b)
Judicial notice of . . . 4511(b)
Pleadings, complaint or defense based on . . . . 3016(e)
Records or documents, proof of . . . 4542

FORFEITURE

Crime, proceeds of (See FORFEITURE OF PROCEEDS OF CRIME)
State's action to recover penalty or (See PENALTIES)

FORFEITURE OF PROCEEDS OF CRIME

Actions generally . . . 1311
Adverse claims, proceedings to determine . . . . 1327
Affidavits to support filing of judgment or settlement, requirements for . . . 1311(11)
Amount recoverable . . . 1311(8)
Attachment
    Adverse claimants, determination of rights of . . . 1327
    Annulment of order . . . 1330

[References are to CPLR Sections, Rules and Appendices.]

**FORFEITURE OF PROCEEDS OF CRIME—**
Cont.

Attachment—Cont.

Common carrier, additional undertaking to . . . 1323

Creditor's rights in personal property . . . 1314

Discharge of . . . 1328

Disclosure of information, order . . . 1326

Disposition of attachment property after execution . . . 1332

Duties of claiming agent after levy . . . . 1324

Garnishee of debt or property, proper . . . 1313

Inventory of property . . . 1324(2)

Levy on personal property by seizure . . . 1321

Levy on personal property by service of order

    Effect of levy . . . 1320(2)

    Failure to proceed, effect . . 1320(5)

    Method of levy . . . 1320(1)

    Payment or delivery, proceeding to compel . . . 1320(4)

    Prohibition of transfer . . . 1320(2)

    Seizure by claiming agent . . . . . . 1320(3)

Levy on real property . . . 1322

Liability for damages by claiming authority . . . 1318(4)

Motion papers

    Affidavits and other written evidence . . . 1318(1)

    Damages, liability of claiming authority for . . . 1318(4)

    Demand for papers by defendant . . 1318(3)

    Filing . . . 1318(2)

Obligation to defendant, discharge of garnishee's . . . 1315

Order of attachment

    Confirmation of order granted without notice . . . 1317(2)

    Notice, on . . . 1316

    Notice, without . . . 1317

    Service of summons . . . 1319

Priority among orders of attachment . . . . 1332

Return of property . . . 1331

Service of summons . . . 1319

Statement of garnishee . . . 1325

Transferee of debt owed defendant, enforcement against . . . 1314

**FORFEITURE OF PROCEEDS OF CRIME—**
Cont.

Attachment—Cont.

Vacating or modifying

    Burden of proof . . . 1329(2)

    Motion . . . 1329(1)

Attorney's fees and expenses, exemption of property acquired as payment for . . . 1311(12)

Burden of proof

    Attachment, vacating or modifying . . . . 1329(2)

    "Real property instrumentality of crime" . . . 1311(3)(b)(v)

Claiming agent

    Defined . . . 1310(12)

    Directions to . . . 1331

    Duties after levy . . . 1324

    Levy on personal property by service of order

        Duties after levy . . . 1324

        Seizure by claiming agent . . . . . . 1320(3)

    Seizure by, levy on personal property by service of order . . . 1320(3)

Claiming authority

    Commencement by . . . 1311(1)

    Defined . . . 1310(11)

    Notice of pendency cancellation by . . . 1347(5)

Constitutionality of Article 13-A

    Separability of invalid provisions . . 1351

Criminal liability of defendant concealing or disposing of specified property . . . 1311(9)

Definitions . . . 1310

Dismissal of action . . . 1311(4)

Disposal of property

    Generally . . . 1349(1)

    Priority, order of . . . 1349(2)

District attorney defined . . . 1310(14)

Fair consideration defined . . . 1310(13)

Filing of stipulations or settlement agreements . . . 1311(11)

Generally . . . 1311

"Instrumentality of crime" defined . . . 1310(4)

Jury trial on issue of fact, right of defendant to . . . 1311(2)

Motion papers

    Attachment (See subhead: Attachment)

    Preliminary junction . . . 1334

Notice of pendency

    Cancellation of

        Claiming authority, by . . . 1347(5)

        Costs and expenses . . . 1347(3)

        Discretionary . . . 1347(2)

        Mandatory . . . 1347(1)

[References are to CPLR Sections, Rules and Appendices.]

**FORFEITURE OF PROCEEDS OF CRIME—**
Cont.
Notice of pendency—Cont.
  Cancellation of—Cont.
    Motion for . . . 1347
    Stipulation, by . . . 1347(4); 6514(d)
    Undertaking for . . . 1348
  Constructive notice, as . . . 1343
  Content . . . 1344(2)
  Designation of index . . . 1344(2)
  Duration . . . 1346
  Filing . . . 1343,1344(1)
  Generally . . . 1343
  Indexing . . . 1344(2),(3)
  Service of summons . . . 1345
Personal property, levy on (See subhead: Attachment)
Post-conviction forfeiture crime
  Defined . . . 1310(5)
  Generally . . . 1311(1)(a)
Pre-conviction forfeiture crime
  Defined . . . 1310(6)
  Generally . . . 1311(1)(b)
Preliminary injunction
  Affidavit on motion for . . . 1334
  Damages sustained by reason of, ascertaining . . . 1337
  Grounds for . . . 1333
  Motion papers . . . 1334
  Vacating or modifying . . . 1336
Preservation of other rights and remedies . . . . 1352
Procedures governing, generally . . . 1350
"Proceeds of crime" defined . . . 1310(2)
Property subject to forfeiture defined . . . . . . 1310(1)
Provisional remedies (See subhead: Remedies, provisional)
"Real property instrumentality of crime"
  Burden of proof . . . 1311(3)(b)(v)
  Defined . . . 1310(4-a)
  "Dwelling" defined . . . 1311(4-a)(b)
  Generally . . . 1311(1)
  "Owner" defined . . . 1311(4-a)(b)
  Protection of lawful interests, court orders for . . . 1311(4-a)(a)
Rebuttable presumptions
  Criminal defendant, action against . . . . . 1311(3)(d)
  Evidence in rebuttal, admissibility of . . . 1311(3)(e)
  Noncriminal defendant, action against . . . 1311(3)(c)

**FORFEITURE OF PROCEEDS OF CRIME—**
Cont.
Receiver, temporary
  Accounts . . . 1341
  Appointment . . . 1338(1)
  Duration of receivership . . . 1338(3)
  Joinder of moving party . . . 1338(1)
  Oath . . . 1339
  Powers of . . . 1338(2)
  Removal . . . 1342
  Undertaking by . . . 1340
Remedies, provisional
  (See also specific subheads, e.g., Attachment)
  Election of . . . 1312(2)
  Generally . . . 1312(1)
  Grounds for granting . . . 1312(3)
  Modification of remedy by court . . . . . . 1312(4)
Remission . . . 1311(7)
Sealing of papers, motion for . . . 1311(6)
Service of summons
  Attachment, order of . . . 1319
  Notice of pendency . . . 1345
  Notice or summons and verified complaint . . . 1311(5)
"Specified felony offense"
  Adduction of evidence to contradict establishment of elements of . . . 1311(3-a)
  Defined . . . 1310(4-b)
Subpoena duces tecum (See SUBPOENAS)
"Substituted proceeds of crime" defined . . . . . 1310(3)
Temporary receiver (See subhead: Receiver, temporary)
Temporary restraining order
  Damages sustained by reason of, ascertaining . . . 1337
  Generally . . . 1333; 1335(1)
  Grounds for . . . 1333
  Service . . . 1335(2)
  Transfer of assets prevented by . . . 1316
  Vacating or modifying . . . 1336
Undertakings
  Notice of pendency cancellation, undertaking for . . . 1348
  Temporary receiver . . . 1340
Venue . . . 1311(10)

**FORMS, OFFICIAL**
Appendix of; adoption, amendment and rescission of . . . 107

[References are to CPLR Sections, Rules and Appendices.]

**FORUM NON CONVENIENS**
Court's discretion to stay or dismiss action on motion of party
  Contracts to which GOL § 51402 applies, mandatory enforcement of choice of forum clauses in . . . 327(b)
  Domicile or residence of any party within state as no bar to court's action . . . . . 327(a)
  General Obligations Law . . . App

**FRAUD**
Annulment of marriage, statute of limitations . . . 214
Arbitration award; fraud as grounds for vacation of award . . . 7511(b)(1)
Benefits received by party asserting fraud, restoration of prior to judgment . . . 3004
Commencement of action; statute of limitations . . . 213
Damages resulting from fraudulently induced contract, claim joined with demand for rescission; no bar for inconsistency . . . 3002(e)
Foreign country money judgment obtained by . . . 5304(b)(3)
Pleading cause of action or defense of . . . . . 3016(b)
Rescission of contract induced by fraud as remedy . . . 3002(e)
Statutes of limitations (See STATUTES OF LIMITATIONS)

**FREEDOM OF INFORMATION LAW** (See PUBLIC OFFICERS LAW)

**FRIVOLOUS CLAIMS**
Costs upon frivolous claims to recover damages (See COSTS, subhead: Frivolous claims to recover damages)
Health care arbitration . . . 7564(b)
Injury to property actions, costs upon frivolous claims in action to recover damages for . . . 8303-a
Malpractice actions, costs upon frivolous claims in action to recover damages for . . . 8303-a
Personal injury actions, costs upon frivolous claims in action to recover damages for . . . 8303-a
Wrongful death actions, costs upon frivolous claims in action to recover damages for . . . 8303-a

**FULL FAITH AND CREDIT, FOREIGN JUDGMENT ENTITLED TO**
Action on judgment, right of judgment creditor to proceed by way of, unimpairment of . . 5406

**FULL FAITH AND CREDIT, FOREIGN JUDGMENT ENTITLED TO**—Cont.
Citation of article . . . 5408
Filing requirements . . . 5402(a)
"Foreign judgment," defined for purpose of article . . . 5401
Notice of filing sent judgment debtor . . . 5403
Status of foreign judgment . . . 5402(b)
Stay of enforcement, grounds for order of . . . 5404
Summary judgment in lieu of complaint, motion for . . . 5406
Uniformity of interpretation . . . 5407

# G

**GARNISHMENT**
Attachment and garnishee
  Discharge of obligation of, how effected . . . 6204
  Proper garnishee, determination of . . . . . 6202
Enforcement procedures for money judgments (See MONEY JUDGMENT—ENFORCEMENT PROCEDURES)
Forfeiture of proceeds of crime; proper garnishee of debt or property . . . 1313
Garnishee defined . . . 105(i)
Income execution (See INCOME EXECUTION)
Partnership, interest in
  Enforcement of money judgment; proper garnishee specified . . . 5201(c)(3)

**GENERAL ASSOCIATIONS LAW**
Selected practice provisions . . . App

**GENERAL CONSTRUCTION LAW**
Selected practice provisions . . . App

**GENERAL MUNICIPAL LAW**
Selected practice provisions . . . App

**GENERAL OBLIGATIONS LAW**
Selected practice provisions . . . App

**GOVERNMENTAL SUBDIVISIONS**
Cities
  Personal service on . . . 311(a)
  Venue for actions against . . . 504
County
  Actions against, proper place of trial, designation . . . 504
  Personal service on; persons who may be served, specification of . . . 311(a)
District corporation, venue for actions against . . . 504
New York City (See NEW YORK CITY)

**GOVERNMENTAL SUBDIVISIONS**—Cont.

Park district, personal service on; persons who may be served, specification of . . . 311(a)

School district

Personal service on; persons who may be served, specification of . . . 311(a)

Venue for actions against . . . 504

Service on, personal

Cities . . . 311(a)

Counties . . . 311(a)

Park district . . . 311(a)

School district . . . 311(a)

Sewage district . . . 311(a)

Town . . . 311(a)

Village . . . 311(a)

Sewage district, personal service on; persons who may be served, specification of . . . 311(a)

Town

Personal service on; persons who may be served, specification of . . . 311(a)

Venue for actions against . . . 504

Venue . . . 504

Verification by . . . 3020(d)(2)

Village (See VILLAGES)

**GUARDIAN AD LITEM**

Adult incapable of prosecuting or defending rights, representation of . . . 1201

Appointment of . . . 1202

Compensation . . . 1204

Conservator

Motion by conservator to appoint, permissibility . . . 1202

Notice of motion, service on conservator . . . 1202

Property of infant or incompetent, disposition of . . . 1206

Representation by . . . 1201

Security for costs . . . 8501(b)

Surrogate's Court Procedure Act . . . App

**GUARDIANS**

Incompetents (See GUARDIAN AD LITEM)

Infant (See INFANTS AND MINORS, subhead: Guardian of infant)

# H

**HABEAS CORPUS**

Affixing and mailing copy of petition, when authorized . . . 7005

Appeals

Bail, release not stayed by appeal taken by state . . . 7011

Judgment refusing to grant habeas corpus, appeal from . . . 7011

**HABEAS CORPUS**—Cont.

Appeals—Cont.

Notice for purpose of, recipient of . . . . . 7011

Return of writ . . . 7011

Attachment warrant pursuant to writ

Accompanying or preceding writ . . 7007

Compelling obedience to disregarded writ, directed to sheriff of county in which served person may be found . . 7006(b)

Detention as criminal offense, apprehension of responsible person ordered . . . 7007

Discharge of detained person as final judgment, enforcement, order issued for . . . 7010(a)

Immediate appearance of detained person before court, issuance of warrant of attachment with writ to ensure . . . 7007

Precept to immediately bring up detained person, issuance by court . . . 7006(c)

Bail, questions concerning; determination at hearing

Appeal taken by state, release not stayed by . . . 7011

Denial of bail where matter of right or abuse of discretion, forthwith admittance as final judgment; amount and time and place of release to be specified . . . 7010(b)

Excessive amount, final judgment reducing . . . 7010(b)

Child-abuse proceeding, petition by party in ; subsequent to order of family court . . . . . . 7002(a)

Common law writ of habeas corpus, applicability of article to . . . 7001

Content of writ . . . 7004

Criminal offense, detention constituting

Apprehension of person responsible for detention, warrant preceding or accompanying writ . . . 7007

Defects in writ, disobedience based upon; disallowance . . . 7006(a)

Determination of proceeding

Appeal . . . 7011

Denial of bail as constituting abuse of discretion, final judgment as to . . . 7010(b)

Discharge of person detained, final judgment as . . . 7010(a)

Excessive amount of bail as constituting abuse of discretion, final judgment as to . . . 7010(b)

Remand to detention, final judgment as . . . 7010(c)

Discharge of detained person, judgment directing

Defect in form of commitment not valid reason for discharge . . . 7010(a)

[References are to CPLR Sections, Rules and Appendices.]

**HABEAS CORPUS**—Cont.

Discharge of detained person, judgment directing—Cont.

    Detainment by person not entitled where other so entitled not valid reason for discharge . . . 7010(a)

    Enforcement of discharge by order of attachment . . . 7010(a)

    Re-detention on same charge after discharge, prohibition . . . 7012

Expenses in transporting person under detention, payment by petitioner; court's discretion as to . . . 7004(e)

Hearing

    Custody during proceeding, court's discretion as to . . . 7009(e)

    Notice of hearing required

        Detainment by order of family court during pendency of proceeding, service of notice of hearing upon judge . . . 7009(a)(2)

        District attorneys, service upon . . . 7009(a)(3)

        Eight-day or other notice at discretion of court . . . 7009(a)

        Recipient of notice as party for appeal purposes . . . 7011

        Service of notice in civil case . . . . 7009(a)(1)

    Reply to return, oral or written denial or allegation of facts showing person as entitled to discharge . . . 7009(b)

    Sickness or infirmity of detained person, effect . . . 7009(d)

    Summary nature of hearing prescribed . . . 7009(c)

Immediate appearance of detained person before court, issuance of warrant of attachment with writ to ensure . . . 7007

Issuance of writ

    Denial, grounds for . . . 7003(a), (b)

    Violation by judge or court, penalty for . . . 7003(c)

    When required . . . 7003(a)

Notices (See subhead: Hearing)

Obedience to writ

    Attachment warrant to compel full obedience, issuance against person served . . . 7006(b)

    Compelling obedience . . . 7006(b)

    Precept to bring up detained person . . . . 7006(c)

    Sheriff disobedient to writ, warrant of attachment to designate specific substitute for execution . . . 7006(b)

**HABEAS CORPUS**—Cont.

Obedience to writ—Cont.

    Sickness or infirmity of detained person, disobedience of writ . . . 7006(a)

Petitioning for

    Content of petition, necessary recitals . . . 7002(c)

    Eligible parties, specification . . . 7002(a)

    Infants in child abuse proceeding, subsequent to order of family court . . . . . . 7002(a)

    Legality of detention determined in prior proceeding, no requirement for court issuance on successive petitions . . 7003(b)

    Person illegally imprisoned . . . 7002(a)

    Successive petitions for writ . . . 7003(b)

    To whom made . . . 7002(b)

Remand of person to detention, final judgment as . . . 7010(c)

Retention after discharge for same cause, when authorized . . . 7012

Return of writ

    Affidavit, return consisting of

        Content . . . 7008(b)

        Service and filing requirement . . . . 7008

    Appeal from judgment on return . . 7011

    Before whom returnable, specification in issuance of writ . . . 7004(c)

    Forthwith returnable

        Authority to specify . . . 7004(d)

        Within 24 hours of service, definition as . . . 7008(a)

    Person upon whom writ or copy is served as making return regardless of direction of writ . . . 7006(a)

    When returnable . . . 7004(d)

Security for costs . . . 8501(a)

Service of writ, methods . . . 7005

Show cause as to continued detention

    Appeal from judgment on refusal . . 7011

    Generally . . . 7003(a)

Sickness or infirmity of detained person, effect

    Hearing, disposition of . . . 7009(d)

Special proceeding, defined as . . . 7001

Undertaking by petitioner, court's discretion as to amount . . . 7004(e)

Warrant (See subhead: Attachment warrant pursuant to writ)

Writ of certiorari to inquire into detention, applicability of article to . . . 7001

**HANDWRITING**

Proof of writing by comparison . . . . 4536

[References are to CPLR Sections, Rules and Appendices.]

## HEALTH CARE ARBITRATION
Adjournment . . . 7558(c)
Applicability of article . . . 7551
Arbitration administrator
    Defined . . . 7550(a)
    Rules of . . . 7558(b)
    Selection of arbitrators . . . 7554
Arbitrators
    Associate arbitrators
        Appointment of . . . 7554(b)
        Communication with candidates . . .
        7555(b)
        Screening of proposed candidates
        . . . 7555(a)
    Chairperson
        Appointment of . . . 7554(a)
        Subpoenas, power to issue . . . 7560
    Communication with candidates . . . . . .
    7555(b)
    Decision of panel . . . 7563(b)
    Fees and expenses . . . 7562(b)
    Mutual agreement on . . . 7554(d)
    Salary . . . 7562(b)
    Screening of proposed candidates . . . . .
    7555(a)
    Selection of . . . 7554
Associate arbitrators
    Appointment of . . . 7554(b)
    Communication with candidates . . . . . .
    7555(b)
    Screening of proposed candidates . . . . .
    7555(a)
Attorney's fees
    Award of . . . 7564(b)
    Contingency fee agreements . . . 7552(c)
Briefs . . . 7563(a)
Chairperson
    Appointment of . . . 7554(a)
    Subpoenas, power to issue . . . 7560
Communications to arbitration panel, disclosure of
    . . . 7557
Consent of parties . . . 7556(d)
Consolidation of proceedings . . . 7556(c)
Costs of proceedings . . . 7553
Counterclaims . . . 7564(b)
Cross-claims . . . 7564(b)
Damages, determination of . . . 7552(c)
Decision of panel
    Form of . . . 7564(a)
    Judicial review of decision . . . 7565
    Majority vote . . . 7563(b)
    Modification of decision . . . 7565
Demand for arbitration
    Generally . . . 7556(a)

## HEALTH CARE ARBITRATION—Cont.
Demand for arbitration—Cont.
    Service within time limits, stay of action
        effect on . . . 7556(d)
Depositions
    Evidence, as . . . 7561(a)
    Generally . . . 7558(a)
    Taking requirements . . . 7561(b)
Disclosure of communications to arbitration panel
    . . . 7557
Discovery
    Enforcement of procedures . . . 7561(c)
    Generally . . . 7558(a)
    Requirements . . . 7558(b)
Expert witness, neutral . . . 7559(c)
Frivolous claims . . . 7564(b)
Health care provider defined . . . 7550(d)
Health maintenance organization
    Defined . . . 7550(c)
Hearing
    Briefs . . . 7563(a)
    Generally . . . 7559(a)
    Testimony, recording of . . . 7559(b)
Hospital defined . . . 7550(b)
Incompetent persons . . . 7556(b)
Judicial review of decision . . . 7565
Minors . . . 7556(b)
Modification of decision . . . 7565
Proceedings
    Consolidation of proceedings . . . 7556(c)
    Costs of . . . 7553
    Generally . . . 7552(a)
Standards of duty, practice or care . . . 7552(b)
Stay of action; demand of arbitration served within
    time limits, effect on . . . 7556(d)
Stenographers, use of at hearing . . . 7559(b)
Subpoenas . . . 7560
Witnesses
    Expert witness, neutral . . . 7559(c)
    Fees . . . 7562(a)

## HEALTH INSURANCE BENEFITS
Defined . . . 5241(a)(11)
Income execution (See INCOME EXECUTION)
Support enforcement (See INCOME EXECU-
TION)

## HERBICIDES
Personal injury actions involving military personnel with service in Indochina . . . 214-b

## HOMESTEAD EXEMPTION (See MONEY
JUDGMENT—ENFORCEMENT PROCE-
DURES)

## HOSPITAL OR MEDICAL RECORDS
Authority to obtain . . . 3121(a)

[References are to CPLR Sections, Rules and Appendices.]

**HOSPITAL OR MEDICAL RECORDS**—Cont.
Business records
> Hospital bill as; admissibility into evidence
> . . . 4518(b)
> Hospital records in custody of warehouse
> . . . 4518(c)

Disclosure of records for examination . . . . . .
3121(a)
Fees for filing notices of lien . . . 8021(b)(6)
Incompetent persons, settlement of action by
. . . 1208(c)
Infants, settlement of action by . . . 1208(c)
Subpoena duces tecum, production of records
pursuant to (See SUBPOENAS, subhead: Hos-
pital or medical records, production of)
Warehouse, records in custody of . . . 4518(c)

**HUMAN LEUCOCYTE ANTIGEN TEST**
Business records, results admissible as . . . . .
4518(c)

**HUSBAND AND WIFE** (See MATRIMONIAL
ACTIONS; SPOUSES)

# I

**IMPEACHMENT OF WITNESSES**
Depositions . . . 3117
Prior inconsistent statements . . . 4514

**IMPLEADER** (See THIRD-PARTY PRAC-
TICE)

**IN CAMERA INTERVIEWS**
Appeals . . . 4019(b)
Infants, recording . . . 4019(a)

**INCOME DEDUCTION**
Order, support enforcement
> Contents of payment . . . 5242(g)
> Employers failure to deduct . . . 5242(e)
> Errors, order to correct . . . 5242(a)
> Foreign judgment or order, income deduc-
> tion based on . . . 5242(c)
> Payment, court's criteria for determining
> likelihood of . . . 5242(b)
> Priority of order . . . 5242(d)
> Process, issuance of . . . 5242(f)

**INCOME EXECUTION**
Default in payment by judgment debtor, execution
against garnishee (See subhead: Garnishee,
execution against)
Discrimination against employee . . . 5252
Earnings
> Defined . . . 5231(c)
> Disposable earnings defined . . . 5231(c)

**INCOME EXECUTION**—Cont.
Failure to serve judgment debtor as condition
. . . 5231(d)
Form of execution . . . 5231(c)
Garnishee, execution against
> Default in installment payment by judgment
> creditor as condition . . . 5231(d)
> Duties of . . . 5231(e)
> Failure to serve judgment debtor as condition
> . . . 5231(d)
> Proceeding against for accrued installments,
> judgment creditor commencing, when au-
> thorized . . . 5231(e)
> Service of execution upon; notice to debtor,
> inclusion in execution . . . 5231(a)
Health insurance benefits
> Defined . . . 5241(a)(11)
> Income deduction for . . . 5241(g)(2)
> Issuance for . . . 5241(b)(2),(g)(2),(3)
Installments, withholding of . . . 5231(f)
Issuance . . . 5231(b); 5241(b)
Levy upon money payable by municipal corpora-
tion or state . . . 5231(h)
Medical support enforcement . . . . . . . . . .
5241(b)(2),(g)(2)
Modification, motions for, authorization . . . . .
5231(i)
Priority, delivery to another sheriff . . . 5231(j)
Service of execution
> Certified-mail-return-receipt-requested, ser-
> vice by; copies by regular mail . . . . .
> 5231(d)
> Failure to serve . . . 5231(e)
> Manner of service . . . 5231(d)
> Time limitation . . . 5231(d)
Sheriff, fixed fees of
> Judgment debtor
>> Levy upon default or failure to serve
>> . . . 8011(d)
>> Service upon . . . 8011(c)
Statement on . . . 5231(g)
Support enforcement
> Creditor defined . . . 5241(a)(3)
> Date of withholding defined . . . . . . . .
> 5241(a)(10)
> Debtor defined . . . 5241(a)(2)
> Deduction from income . . . 5241(g)(1)
> Default defined . . . 5241(a)(7)
> Employer defined . . . 5241(a)(4)
> Form of execution for support enforcement
> . . . 5241(c)(1)
> Health insurance benefits (See subhead:
> Health insurance benefits)
> Income deduction order for (See INCOME
> DEDUCTION, subhead: Order, support
> enforcement)

[References are to CPLR Sections, Rules and Appendices.]

**INCOME EXECUTION—Cont.**

Support enforcement—Cont.
    Income defined . . . 5241(a)(6)
    Income payor defined . . . 5241(a)(5)
    Issuance . . . 5241(b)(1)
    Levy . . . 5241(f)
    Medical support enforcement . . . . . . .
        5241(b)(2),(g)(2)
    Mistake of fact defined . . . 5241(a)(8)
    Mistake of fact, procedure for assertion of
        . . . 5241(e)
    Money payable by state, levy upon . . . .
        5241(i)
    Notice to debtor . . . 5241(d)
    Order of support defined . . . 5241(a)(1)
    Priority . . . 5241(h)
    Support collection unit defined . . . . . . .
        5241(a)(9)

**INCOMPETENT PERSONS**

Appearance by . . . 1208(d)
Arbitration involving
    Continuance of proceedings . . . 7512
    Controversy involving incompetent persons,
        submission to arbitration; necessity of
        court order . . . 1209
Attorneys, settlement of action by
    Affidavit . . . 1208(b)
    Papers by attorney for adverse party, prepa-
        ration of . . . 1208(f)
    Representation requirement . . . 1208(e)
Benefits received by party asserting incompetency,
    restoration prior to judgment . . . 3004
Committee for judicially declared incompetent
    Residence for purpose of venue; county of
        appointment and of actual residence, com-
        mittee deemed resident of both . . . . .
        503(b)
    Substitution of committee in action against
        incompetent . . . 1016
Conservatee
    Distributee, as . . . 1206
    Value of property . . . 1206(b)
Costs, liability for . . . 1205
Default judgment against judicially declared in-
    competent, conditions to allowance . . . 1203
Disposition of proceeds of incompetent's claim,
    methods
    Exceptions . . . 1206
    Payment to infant at 18 years of age, no court
        order required . . . 1206(c)
    Prior references to age 21 deemed to desig-
        nate age 18 . . . 1206(c)
Guardian ad litem (See GUARDIAN AD LITEM)
Health care arbitration . . . 7556(b)

**INCOMPETENT PERSONS—Cont.**

Judicially declared incompetent
    Default judgment entered against, conditions
        to allowance . . . 1203
    Guardian ad litem, representation by; situa-
        tions necessitating . . . 1201
    Representation by committee, authorization
        . . . 1201
Mentally ill persons, action accruing in favor of;
    extension of statute of limitations period . . .
    208
Personal service on judicially declared incompe-
    tent, manner of effecting . . . 309(b)
Poor person, motion to proceed as; representative
    making . . . 1101(a)
Representation of
    Attorney . . . 1208(e)
    Authorized persons . . . 1201
Security for costs . . . 8501(b)
Settlement of action by
    Affidavit of incompetent's representative,
        necessary inclusions . . . 1208(a)
    Appearance of person before court, require-
        ment for . . . 1208(d)
    Attorney's affidavit . . . 1208(b)
    Medical or hospital report . . . 1208(c)
    Motion for settlement . . . 1207
    Papers required, preparation by attorney for
        adverse party . . . 1208(f)
    Procedure . . . 1208
    Representation . . . 1208(e)
    Special proceeding for purpose of . . 1207
Sheriff's fees for receiving precept to inquire as to
    . . . 8011(h)
Simplified procedure, CPLR provisions applicable
    . . . 3036(8)
Statute of limitation on action commenced by
    . . . 208
Substitution of committee in action against . . .
    1016
Voluntary discontinuance of action via stipulation,
    prohibition against; incompetent as party . . .
    3217(a)(2)

**INCONSISTENT ACTIONS OR RELIEF** (See
ELECTION OF REMEDIES)

**INCONVENIENT FORUM** (See FORUM NON
CONVENIENS)

**INDEMNIFICATION**

Collateral sources of payment, awards reduced to
    extent of indemnification by
    Medical malpractice actions . . . 4545(a)
    Public employer, certain actions against;
        personal injury and wrongful death . . .
        4545(b)

**INDEMNIFICATION**—Cont.

Contribution, effect of . . . 1404

Indemnitor for executing or attaching officer, substitution of . . . 1020

Substitution of parties

   Indemnitor for executing or attaching officer, substitution of . . . 1020

**INDEXING REQUIREMENTS**

Notice of pendency

   Electronic indexing . . . 6511(d)

   Requirements . . . 6511(c)

**INDIVIDUAL RETIREMENT ACCOUNTS (IRAS)**

Exemption from money judgments, trusts qualifying as . . . 5205(c)(2)

**INFANTS AND MINORS**

Accrual of action, infant plaintiff at time of, extension of limitations period . . . 208

Adult spouse, infant residing with

   Proceeds of infant's claim distributed to, discretion of court to order . . . 1206(a)

   Representation of infant, when allowed . . . 1201

Age of child, proof of . . . 4516

Appearance by . . . 1208(d)

Arbitration of controversy involving, court order authorizing . . . 1209

Attorneys, settlement of action by

   Affidavit . . . 1208(b)

   Papers by attorney for adverse party, preparation of . . . 1208(f)

   Representation requirement . . . 1208(e)

Benefits received by party asserting infancy, restoration of prior to judgment . . . 3004

Child-abuse proceeding

   Habeas corpus writ, petition by party in child-abuse proceeding; subsequent to order of family court . . . 7002(a)

Costs, liability for . . . 1205

Default judgment and entered against, conditions to allowance . . . 1203

Defined . . . 105(j)

Dismiss, infancy of moving party as ground . . . 3211(a)(5)

Disposition of proceeds of infant's claim, methods . . . 1206

Education of, allowance for; petition (See petition to court; subhead: Support, maintenance or education, property of infant applied for purpose of)

Estate management by guardian, direction by court order; discretion of court . . . 1210(d)

Guardian ad litem (See GUARDIAN AD LITEM)

**INFANTS AND MINORS**—Cont.

Guardian of infant

   Appointment, petition for

      Contents . . . 1210(a)

      Order of appointment, filing certified copy, requirement . . . 1210(e)

      Persons authorized to petition . . . . 1210(a)

   Estate management, direction by court order; discretion of court . . . 1210(d)

   Hearing for purpose of selecting, inquiries during . . . 1210(b)

   Notice of petition for application of infant's property for support, maintenance or education, when required . . . 1211(b)

   Surrogate's Court Procedure Act . . . App

   Undertaking, order of court regarding . . . 1210(c)

Habeas corpus writ, petition by party in child-abuse proceeding; subsequent to order of family court . . . 7002(a)

Health care arbitration . . . 7556(b)

In camera interviews, recording . . . 4019

Infancy defined . . . 105(j)

Maintenance of, allowance for; petition concerning (See petition to court; subhead: Support, maintenance or education, property of infant applied for purpose of)

Personal service of summons upon, manner of effecting . . . 309(a)

Poor person, motion to proceed in action as, representative making . . . 1101(a)

Representation of infant

   Attorney . . . 1208(e)

   Generally . . . 1201

Settlement of action by

   Affidavit of infant's representative, necessary inclusions . . . 1208(a)

   Appearance of infant before court, requirement for . . . 1208(d)

   Attorney's affidavit . . . 1208(b)

   Medical or hospital report . . . 1208(c)

   Motion for settlement . . . 1207

   Papers required, preparation by attorney for adverse party . . . 1208(f)

   Procedure . . . 1208

   Representation . . . 1208(e)

   Special procedure for purpose of . . 1207

Statute of limitations, extension . . . 208

Support, maintenance or education, property of infant applied for purpose of; petition to court

   Contents, necessary inclusions . . 1211(a)

   Notice of petition, parties entitled to . . . 1211(b)

   Place of petitioning . . . 1211(a)

Index

[References are to CPLR Sections, Rules and Appendices.]

**INFANTS AND MINORS**—Cont.
Undertaking, order of court regarding
Guardian . . . 1210(c)
Voluntary discontinuance of action via stipulation,
prohibition against; infant as party to action
. . . 3217(a)(2)

**INJUNCTIONS**
Obscene prints and articles . . . 6330
Preliminary injunctions (See PRELIMINARY IN-
JUNCTION)

**IN REM JURISDICTION** (See QUASI-IN-
REM JURISDICTION)

**INSANE PERSONS** (See INCOMPETENT PER-
SONS)

**INSPECTION**
Certificates issued by United States Department of
Agriculture as evidence, inspection . . . 4529
Discovery (See DISCOVERY)

**INSURANCE**
Admissibility of insurance payments in medical
malpractice actions . . . 4545(a)
Appeal in action defended by insurer, stay of
enforcement under policy pending appeal . .
5519(b)
Disclosure of . . . 3101(f)
Insurance Law . . . App
Medical malpractice actions; admissibility of in-
surance payments as collateral source of pay-
ment . . . 4545(a)
Stay of enforcement pending appeal, insurer as
defendant . . . 5519(b)
Superintendent duties . . . 5039; 5049
Surety in judicial undertaking, authorization of
insurance company as . . . 2502(a)(1)

**INSURANCE LAW**
Selected practice provisions . . . App

**INTENTIONAL TORTS**
Corporate directors, officers or trustees, intentional
infliction of harm by; particularity in complaint
as to specific cause of action . . . 3016(h)

**INTEREST RECOVERY**
Counsel fees and expenses, award of; state, actions
against . . . 8603
Judgment, computation of interest from . . . . .
5003
Order directing payment of money, docketing as
judgment, computation of interest from date of
docketing . . . 5003
Overcharge of interest, action for; statutes of
limitations . . . 215

**INTEREST RECOVERY**—Cont.
Rate of interest authorized . . . 5004
State, actions against; counsel fees and expenses,
award of . . . 8603
Statutes of limitations; overcharge of interest,
action for . . . 215
Verdict, report or decision; recovery of interest to
Authorization . . . 5001
Civil penalty, imposition of . . . 5001(a)
Date from which interest computed
Civil penalty, imposition of . . . . .
5001(b)
Determination . . . 5001(b)
Specification in verdict, report, or deci-
sion . . . 5001(c)
Final judgment, date of entry, interest com-
puted to; authorization . . . 5002
Total sum awarded including interest to
verdict, basis of interest . . . 5002

**INTERLOCUTORY PROCEEDINGS**
Depositions (See DEPOSITIONS, subhead: Use at
trial, hearing of motion or interlocutory proceeding)
Entry of judgment . . . 5016(e)

**INTERPLEADER**
Claimant defined . . . 1006(a)
Complaint defined . . . 3011
Defensive interpleader . . . 1006(b)
Jurisdictional basis; deposit of money into court or
retention to credit of action as
Authorization . . . 1006(g)
Service without state, basis for . . . . 314;
1006(g)
"Specific property within state" under CPLR
314(2), deposited or retained sum as
. . . 1006(g)
Objection to, former grounds for; abolition . . .
1006(d)
Pending action on same claim between stakeholder
and claimant in state court, effect on stakehold-
er's attempted interpleader . . . 1006(c)
Special proceeding, after commencement, interpleader disallowed without court's leave . . .
401
Stakeholder
Defined . . . 1006(a)
Discharge of, partial or complete . . . . .
1006(f)
Independent liability to claimant, issue
raised; court's discretion over . . . . . .
1006(e)

[References are to CPLR Sections, Rules and Appendices.]

**INTERROGATORIES**

Answers to

Forms of . . . 3133(b)

General verdict of jury accompanied by answers to interrogatories . . . 4111(c)

Service of, time requirements for . . . . . 3133(a)

Bill of particulars, demand for in addition to service of written interrogatory; leave of court as condition to allowance . . . 3130

Copies of papers and other items relevant to answers, requirement for . . . 3131

Corporation, answer to interrogatory by; manner of making answer . . . 3133(b)

Deposition in addition to service of written interrogatory, leave of court as condition to allowance . . . 3130

Examination of relevant papers and items in possession, custody, or control of answering party; opportunity to examine or copies required . . . 3131

Matrimonial action . . . 3130

Negligence actions, use of interrogatory in . . . 3130

Objections to

Answers, amendments to . . . 3133(c)

Forms of . . . 3133(b)

Service of, time requirements for . . . . . 3133(a)

Parties to action, use of interrogatories limited to . . . 3132

Partnership, answer to interrogatory by, manner of making answer . . . 3133(b)

Scope of use . . . 3131

Service of, requirements . . . 3132

Use, generally . . . 3130

Verdict of jury

General verdict accompanied by answers to interrogatories . . . 4111(c)

Wrongful death action, use of interrogatory in, disallowance . . . 3130

**INTERVENTION**

Attorney general of state, intervention as of right; constitutionality of state statute in issue . . . 1012(b)

Comptroller of state, intervention as of right; public retirement benefits in issue . . 1012(c)

Notices

Attorney general, notice to . . . 1012(b)

Comptroller of state, notice to . . 1012(c)

Permission, intervention by . . . 1013

Pleadings proposed by intervenor, motion to intervene accompanied by . . . 1014

**INTERVENTION—Cont.**

Public retirement benefits as issue, intervention by state comptroller upon notification by court . . . 1012(c)

Right, as matter of, situations

Constitutionality of state statute, action involving, attorney general's right to defend statute . . . 1012(b)

Property action, possible adverse effect on intervenor . . . 1012(a)

Representation of intervenor's interest, actual or possible inadequacy . . 1012(a)

Special proceedings, allowance in, permission of court as condition . . . 401

Statutory authorization, right to intervene conferred by . . . 1012(a)

Substituted parties (See SUBSTITUTION OF PARTIES)

**INTER VIVOS TRUSTS** (See EXPRESS TRUST PROCEEDINGS)

**IRAS** (See INDIVIDUAL RETIREMENT ACCOUNTS (IRAs))

**IRREGULARITY, MISTAKE OR DEFECT IN PROCEDURE**

Correction

During action, allowance by court . . . . . 2001

Judgment, effect on . . . 5019(a)

Depositions (See DEPOSITIONS, subhead: Errors and irregularities in transcription)

Disregard of, when allowed . . . 2001

Erroneous court ruling, disregard of where no substantial right thereby prejudiced . . . 2002

Judicial sale, irregularity in; sale set aside by court as result . . . 2003

Relief against mistake of law, no bar to . . . . . 3005

Six-year statute of limitations . . . 213

# J

**JAIL**

Prisoners (See PRISONERS)

Subpoenas (See SUBPOENAS)

**JOINDER OF CLAIMS**

Generally . . . 601

Consumer credit transactions, involving . . . . . 601(b)

Venue conflicts, resolution by court . . . 502

**JOINDER OF PARTIES**

Adding or dropping misjoined parties; court's discretion . . . 1003

[References are to CPLR Sections, Rules and Appendices.]

**JOINDER OF PARTIES—Cont.**

Article 78 proceedings
    Prohibition . . . 7802(c)
    Successors in office . . . 7802(b)

Class action (See CLASS ACTIONS)

Contribution among tortfeasors (See JOINT TORTFEASORS)

Dismiss action, nonjoinder of necessary party as ground for motion to . . . 3211(a)(10)

Enterprise corruption, civil actions . . . 1354

Express trusts, SCPA provisions governing . . . 7703

Impleader (See THIRD-PARTY PRACTICE)

Interpleader (See INTERPLEADER)

Misjoinder of party . . . 1003

Necessary parties . . . 1001

No necessity for, representative parties, actions by and against; specified parties . . . 1004

Nonjoinder of
    Dismissal of action without prejudice as result . . . 1003

Permissive joinder of plaintiff or defendant . . . 1002

Special proceedings, joinder by leave of court . . . 401

Temporary receiver
    Joinder of moving party . . . 6401(a)

Third-party practice (See THIRD-PARTY PRACTICE)

Venue conflicts, resolution by court . . . 502

**JOINT LIABILITY**

Actions based on, service of summons on less than all named defendants, effect . . . 1501

Defendants not summoned, indication upon judgment . . . 5018(a)

Limited liability of persons jointly liable
    Application . . . 1602
    Burden of proof . . . 1603
    Generally . . . 1601
    Non-economic loss, definition of . . 1600

Property of co-obligor not served in original action, judgment against for unpaid sum of original judgment; subsequent action . . 1502

Provisional remedies in subsequent action against co-obligor . . . 1502

**JOINT TORTFEASORS**

Mitigation of damages, proof of payment or settlement with another joint tort-feasor . . 4533-b

Payments by joint tort-feasor, proof offered in mitigation of damages; hearing as method . . . 4533-b

**JOINT TRIAL**

(See also CONSOLIDATION OF ACTIONS)

**JOINT TRIAL—Cont.**

Actions pending before same court, power of court to join, conditions to order by court . . . . . 602(a)

Authorization . . . 602

Common questions of law and fact, actions involving . . . 602(a)

Different courts, actions pending in, removal and joinder of action; court's power to order . . . 602(b)

Motion for joint trial, requirement . . . 602

Power of court to order, conditions to exercise . . . 602

**JUDGES**

Administrative judges, relief from judgment or order on application of . . . 5015(c)

County judge disqualified from acting, running of time . . . 9003

Death, disability or incapacity of following verdict . . . 9002

Defined for purposes of CPLR . . . 105(g)

Voir dire, judge's presence during; right of any party to require . . . 4107

**JUDGMENT CREDITOR**

Change in, filing requirements . . . 5019(c)

Death of, effect of
    Malpractice actions . . . 5035
    Personal injury actions . . . 5045

Definition . . . 105(l)

Disclosure, compel . . . 5223

Money judgments, enforcement of (See MONEY JUDGMENT—ENFORCEMENT PROCEDURES)

**JUDGMENT DEBTOR**

Definition . . . 105(m)

Foreign judgment, notice of filing . . . 5403

Income execution
    Failure to serve judgment debtor as condition . . . 5231(d)
    Sheriff, fixed fees of
        Levy upon default or failure to serve judgment debtor . . . 8011(d)
        Service upon judgment debtor . . . . 8011(c)

Money judgments, enforcement of (See MONEY JUDGMENT—ENFORCEMENT PROCEDURES)

Satisfaction-piece, copy mailed to by person entitled to force judgment . . . 5020(a)

**JUDGMENTS**

Action upon judgment
    Complaint, necessary inclusions in . . . . 3016(d)

[References are to CPLR Sections, Rules and Appendices.]

**JUDGMENTS**—Cont.

Action upon judgment—Cont.

    Money judgments (See subhead: Money judgments)

Arbitration (See ARBITRATION PROCEEDINGS)

Article 78 proceedings . . . 7806

Assignment of periodic installments . . . 5038

Chattel actions (See CHATTEL ACTIONS)

Class actions (See CLASS ACTIONS)

Confession of judgment (See CONFESSION OF JUDGMENT)

Contents . . . 5011

Decision of court, entry of judgment upon . . . 5016(c)

Declaratory judgment (See DECLARATORY JUDGMENT)

Default judgment (See DEFAULT AND DEFAULT JUDGMENTS)

Defined . . . 105(k); 5011

Determination basis . . . 5031

Dismissal of claim by, effect . . . 5013

Docketing of judgment (See DOCKETING OF JUDGMENT)

Enforcement (See ENFORCEMENT OF JUDGMENT AND ORDER)

Entry of judgment

    Clerk of court . . . 5016(a)

    Death of party, effect upon entry after . . 5016(d)

    Final judgment after interlocutory judgment . . . 5016(e)

    Signing and filing by clerk, entry effectuated by . . . 5016(a)

    Verdict, judgment upon . . . 5016(b)

Foreign judgment (See FOREIGN COUNTRY MONEY JUDGMENTS)

Full faith and credit, foreign judgment entitled to (See FULL FAITH AND CREDIT, FOREIGN JUDGMENT ENTITLED TO)

Interest, recovery and computation of (See INTEREST RECOVERY)

Interlocutory judgment, motion for final judgment after direction of . . . 5016(e)

Irregularities in papers or procedures, no substantial right of party affected; effect upon judgment . . . 5019(a)

Judgment creditor (See JUDGMENT CREDITOR)

Judgment lien or levy, release of on appeal

    Undertaking for purpose of . . . 5204

Judgment-roll

    Appeal, fee for certification on . . 8016(b)

    Arbitration proceedings . . . 7514(b)

    Content . . . 5017(b)

**JUDGMENTS**—Cont.

Judgment-roll—Cont.

    Filing requirement . . . 5017(a)

    Preparation, persons responsible . . . . . . 5017(a)

    Real property judgment lien, duration; measurement from filing of judgment roll . . . 5019(b)

    Simplified procedure, contents of judgment-roll . . . 3036(7)

Liquidation of damages . . . 3220

Malpractice actions

    Adjustment of payments . . . 5036

    Death of creditor, effect of . . . 5035

    Determination, basis for . . . 5031

    Failure to make payment . . . 5034

    Periodic installments . . . 5038

    Security

        Form of . . . 5032

        Insurers . . . 5039

        Posting and maintaining . . . 5033

    Settlements . . . 5037

Money judgments

    Appellate Division, determination, money judgments contested as excessive or inadequate . . . 5501(c)

    Enforcement of (See MONEY JUDGMENT—ENFORCEMENT PROCEDURES)

    General Obligations Law, actions authorized under, inapplicability of section to . . . 5014

    Maintenance, conditions to . . . 5014

    Periodic payment of (See subhead: Periodic payment of)

Payments

    Appellate Division, determination; money judgments contested as excessive or inadequate . . . 5501(c)

    Enforcement of (See MONEY JUDGMENT—ENFORCEMENT PROCEDURES)

    Periodic payment of (See subhead: Periodic payment of)

    Prompt payment following settlement (See subhead: Prompt payment following settlement)

Periodic payment of

    Medical, dental, or podiatric malpractice actions (See subhead: Malpractice actions)

    Personal injury, injury to property and wrongful death actions (See subhead: Personal injury, injury to property and wrongful death actions)

[References are to CPLR Sections, Rules and Appendices.]

**JUDGMENTS**—Cont.
Personal injury, injury to property and wrongful
   death actions
      Adjustment of payments . . . 5046
      Death of creditor, effect of . . . 5045
      Determination, basis for . . . 5041
      Failure to make payment . . . 5044
      Periodic installments, assignment of . . . .
        5048
      Security
          Form of . . . 5042
          Insurers . . . 5049
          Posting and maintaining . . . 5043
      Settlements . . . 5047
Pleadings
      Extent satisfied, disclosure in pleading . .
        3016(d)
      Jurisdiction of body rendering judgment or
        decision, no necessity to specifically plead
        . . . 3015(c)
Prompt payment following settlement
      Failure to pay . . . 5003-a(e)
      Future installment payments, applicability to
        . . . 5003-a(f)
      Judicial approval of settlement . . . . . .
        5003-a(d)
      Municipality or subdivision not indemnified
        by state, payment by . . . 5003-a(b)
      Public benefit corporation indemnified by
        state, payment by . . . 5003-a(c)
      Tender defined . . . 5003-a(g)
      Time limitation . . . 5003-a(a)
Referee to determine, decision of; entry of judg-
   ment upon . . . 5016(c)
Relief from
      Administrative judge, on application of
        . . . 5015(c)
      Generally . . . 2005
      Motion, on . . . 5015(a)
      Restitution . . . 5015(d)
      Stipulation, on . . . 5015(b)
Satisfaction of judgment (See DEPOSITS INTO
   COURT; SATISFACTION OF JUDGMENT)
Severance ordered, judgment upon part of cause
   of action where . . . 5012
Simplified procedure
      Entry and enforcement provisions of CPLR
        . . . 3036(8)
      Judgment-roll, contents . . . 3036(7)
Submitted controversy
      Commencement . . . 3222(a)
      Subsequent proceedings . . . 3222(b)
Subsequent judgment or order affecting, entry
   upon docket of judgment . . . 5019(b)

**JUDGMENTS**—Cont.
Summary judgment (See SUMMARY JUDG-
   MENT)
Taxation of amount inserted in judgment . . . .
   8401
Tender of payment pursuant to CPLR . . 3219
Unsatisfied judgment against one of several parties
   against whom causes of action exist, no bar to
   action against others . . . 3002(a)

**JUDICIAL HEARING OFFICER**
Appearance at Article 78 proceeding . . 7804(i)
Arbitrator, officer as . . . 3405
Article 78 proceedings, appearance at . . . . . .
   7804(i)
Defined . . . 105(n)
Powers of . . . 4301
Referee
      Designation as . . . 3104(b)
      Fees . . . 8003(c)
      Powers of . . . 4301

**JUDICIAL NOTICE** (See EVIDENCE, subhead:
   Judicial notice of law)

**JUDICIAL PROCEEDINGS, CIVIL**
Action at law and equity suit, distinction abolished
   . . . 103(a)
Defined . . . 105(d)
Form of proceedings . . . 103(a)

**JUDICIAL SALES**
Irregularity in, sale set aside by court as result
   . . . 2003

**JUDICIARY LAW**
Selected practice provisions . . . App

**JURISDICTION**
Alimony, long-arm jurisdiction in action for . .
   302(b)
Appearance of defendant, jurisdiction conferred
   by (See APPEARANCE BY DEFENDANT)
Chattel actions
      Out-of-state service subsequent to seizure,
        no personal jurisdiction resulting . . 314
Disclosure
      Action pending in jurisdiction outside state,
        testimony of witness within state required
        . . . 3102(e)
Dismissal motions (See DISMISSAL MOTIONS)
Extrajurisdictional proceedings, service in connec-
   tion with
      Court order
          Pursuant to . . . 328(a)
          Without . . . 328(b)
      Recognition or enforcement of decree . . .
        328(c)

[References are to CPLR Sections, Rules and Appendices.]

**JURISDICTION**—Cont.

Foreign corporations, unauthorized (See FOR-EIGN CORPORATIONS)

Foreign court, personal jurisdiction over defendant by

Basis of jurisdiction sufficient to give, enumeration of . . . 5305

Lack of, ground for non-recognition . . . . 5304(a)(2)

Forum, inconvenient (See FORUM NON CONVENIENS)

Grounds for jurisdiction previous to CPLR, retention of, authorization . . . 301

In rem jurisdiction, service without state, judgment sought affecting title or interest in property within state . . . 314

Long-arm statute

Alimony . . . 302(b)

Non-domestics . . . 302

Matrimonial actions (See MATRIMONIAL ACTIONS)

Non-domiciliary, jurisdiction over (See NONRESIDENT)

Personal jurisdiction

Appearance of defendant, jurisdiction conferred by (See APPEARANCE BY DEFENDANT)

Non-domestics (See NONRESIDENT)

Service without state, personal jurisdiction resulting from

Authority . . . 313

Persons subject to . . . 313

Unauthorized foreign corporations, personal jurisdiction over (See FOREIGN CORPORATIONS)

Property within state, service made outside state, no personal jurisdiction resulting

Attachment order, levy on property pursuant to . . . 314

Chattel, seizure of, in actions to recover . . . 314

Interest in or title to specified property, judgment affecting, authority . . . 314

Persons authorized to make service . . . . 314

Quasi-in-rem jurisdiction

Attachment order, property within state levied upon pursuant to, service of summons made without state . . . 314

Removal jurisdiction (See REMOVAL OF ACTION)

Subject matter jurisdiction, lack of, motion to dismiss action based upon . . . 3211

**JURISDICTION**—Cont.

Tortious acts, commission in person or through agent

Within state . . . 302(a)

Without state . . . 302(a)

Without state (See subhead: Extrajurisdictional proceedings, service in connection with)

**JURORS**

Alternate jurors . . . 4106

Challenges

Cause, for . . . 4110

Disqualification of juror for relationship . . . 4110(b)

Favor, to . . . 4110(a)

Generally . . . 4108

Disagreement among . . . 4113

Disqualification of juror for relationship . . . . . 4110(b)

Examination of (See VOIR DIRE)

Excuse by stipulation of parties, allowance . . . 4108

Inhabitants as jurors, competency of . . 4110-a

Instruction of, requests for . . . 4110-b

Number of jurors, six as authorized . . . 4104

Oath to, administration of . . . 2309(a)

Peremptory challenges . . . 4109

Persons constituting jury, six as authorized number . . . 4105

Qualification of, objection to, challenge as Method . . . 4108

Relationship to party, disqualification due to . . . 4110(b)

Sheriff's fee for notifying jurors to attend . . . . 8011(k)

Swearing in of, requirement . . . 4105

Verdicts by (See JURY TRIAL)

**JURY TRIAL**

Advisory jury

Submission of issues of fact to . . . 4212

Verdict, confirmation or rejection of . . . . 4403

Arbitration, jury trial de novo following . . . . 3405

Chattel, action to recover, jury trial of fact issues authorized . . . 4101(2)

Constitution granting . . . 4101(3)

Counterclaim, issues of facts arising upon . . . 4102(c)

County clerk filing demand for . . . 8020(c)

Cross-claim, issues of facts arising upon . . . . 4102(c)

Demand for jury trial, issues triable of right

County clerk filing demand . . . 8020(c)

[References are to CPLR Sections, Rules and Appendices.]

**JURY TRIAL**—Cont.

Demand for jury trial, issues triable of right—Cont.

  Issues to be tried by jury, specification in demand . . . 4102(b)

  Local rules . . . 4102(d)

  Methods of making demand . . . 4102(a)

  Noncompliance with procedure, power of court to remedy . . . 4102(e)

  Revelation of issues triable by jury during trial, demand by adverse party for jury trial . . . 4103

  Waiver of jury trial (See subhead: Waiver of jury trial)

Direction of new trial, disagreement by jury resulting in . . . 4113(b)

Disagreement by jury . . . 4113

Dower, action for, jury trial of fact issues; authorization . . . 4101(2)

Ejectment, action for, fact issues tried by jury; authorization . . . 4101(2)

Enumerated actions . . . 4101

Examination of jurors (See VOIR DIRE)

Forfeiture of proceeds of crime, fact issues in actions for . . . 1311(2)

Instruction of the jury, request for . . . 4110-b

Issues triable by jury . . . 4101; 4103

Jurors (See JURORS)

Local rules on trial by . . . 4102(d)

Notice of issue, demand for jury trial contained in . . . 4102(a)

Nuisance, action for abatement of and damages for . . . 4101(2)

Post-trial motions . . . 4404(a)

Premises, jury's inspection of . . . 4110-c

Real property claim, determination of . . . . . . 4101(2)

Removal of action

  Waiver of jury trial

    Proper jurisdiction, inoperativeness of prior waiver . . . 322(b)

    Supreme court to surrogate's court, right to jury trial preserved in later proceeding . . . 325(e)

Revelation of issues triable by jury

  During trial, opportunity given adverse party to demand jury trial . . . 4103

  Prior to trial, specified issues . . . 4101

Simplified Procedure for Court Determination of Disputes, submission of controversy under, waiver of jury trial constituted by . . . 3031

Special proceedings, fact issues triable of right by jury

  Demand for jury trial, opportunity given parties, requirement . . . 410

**JURY TRIAL**—Cont.

Special proceedings, fact issues triable of right by jury—Cont.

  Waiver, how effected . . . 410

Specification of issues . . . 4102(b)

Statute granting . . . 4101(3)

Sum of money only, action for, fact issues tried by jury; authorization . . . 4101(1)

Tender of payment pursuant to CPLR known to jury, prohibition against . . . 3219

Third-party claim, issues of fact arising upon . . . 4102(c)

Verdicts of jury

  Disagreement among jurors, procedure . . . 4113(a)

  Entry of verdict . . . 4112

  Five-sixths of jurors rendering, allowance . . . 4113(a)

  General verdict

    Answers to interrogatories, accompanied by . . . 4111(c)

    Defined . . . 4111(a)

  Itemized verdicts

    Malpractice actions . . . 4111(d)

    Personal injury, public employer for . . . 4111(e)

    Special and general damages . . . . . 4111(f)

    Wrongful death, public employer for . . . 4111(e)

  Special verdict

    Defined . . . 4111(a)

    Procedure . . . 4111(b)

Village, action against

  Person acting as justice or juror . . 4110-a

Voir dire (See VOIR DIRE)

Waiver of jury trial

  Appear, failure to . . . 4102(c)

  Removal of action

    Court with proper jurisdiction, inoperativeness of prior waiver . . 325(b)

    Supreme court to surrogate's court, right to jury trial preserved in later proceeding . . . 325(e)

  Revelation of issues triable by jury during trial, opportunity to demand jury trial given adverse party; failure as waiver . . . 4103

  Withdrawal of demand, effect on . . . . . 4102(c)

Waste, action for, jury trial of fact issues; authorization . . . 4101(2)

# K

**KEOGH PLANS**
Exemption from money judgments, trusts qualifying as . . . 5025(c)(2)

# L

**LABOR DISPUTE**
Employee organization's breach of duty of fair representation; statute of limitations . . . 217
Temporary restraining order, issuance in action arising from, prohibition against . . . 6313(a)

**LANDLORD AND TENANT**
Tenants' action based on landlord's retaliatory behavior . . . 215

**LAW OFFICE FAILURE**
Delay or default resulting from, court excusal of . . . 2005

**LEASES**
Printed leases, admissible in evidence . . 4544

**LETTERS**
Patent, letters
    Annulment for specified grounds, actions to recover property by state or subsequent patentee; statute of limitations . . . 212
Rogatory, letters
    Issuance of, when permitted . . . 3108

**LIBEL ACTION**
Damages, action for, statute of limitations . . . 215
Pleadings, particularization of words complained of . . . 3016(a)

**LIBRARIES**
Circulation records as evidence . . . 4509
Subpoenas (See SUBPOENAS)

**LICENSES AND PERMITS**
Consumer affairs, department of
    License to do business under; pleading requirements . . . 3015(e)

**LIEN LAW**
Selected practice provisions . . . App

**LIENS**
Attachment at time of docketing, priority of lien . . . 5203(a)
Election of remedies
    Vendee's lien on real property, no denial resulting from form of action chosen . . . 3002(f)

**LIENS—Cont.**
Federal tax liens, fees for services rendered in relation to . . . 8021(g)
Lien Law . . . App
Mechanics' liens, fees for filing notices of . . . 8021(b)(4)
Money judgments, enforcement of (See Judgment debtor; MONEY JUDGMENT—ENFORCEMENT PROCEDURES, subheads: Judgment creditor, rights of)
Real property surety lien (See UNDERTAKINGS)
Undertaking for purpose of release of judgment lien or levy on appeal . . . 5204
Vendee's lien on real property, no denial resulting from form of action chosen . . . 3002(f)

**LIMITATIONS OF TIME** (See STATUTES OF LIMITATIONS)

**LIMITED APPEARANCE** (See APPEARANCE BY DEFENDANT)

**LIS PENDENS** (See NOTICE OF PENDENCY)

**LONG-ARM STATUTE**
Alimony . . . 302
Non-domestics . . . 302
Unauthorized foreign corporation, personal jurisdiction over, acts giving rise to (See FOREIGN CORPORATIONS, subhead: Jurisdiction over)

# M

**MAGNETIC RESONANCE IMAGES (MRI)**
Evidence, admissibility as . . . 4523-a
Personal injury actions, admissibility in . . . . . 4532-a

**MAGNETIC TAPE**
Restraining notice on . . . 5222(g)

**MAIL**
Service of summons and papers (See SERVICE OF SUMMONS AND PAPERS)

**MALICIOUS PROSECUTION ACTION**
Statute of limitations, one-year period . . . 215

**MALPRACTICE ACTIONS**
Appeals, stay of enforcement . . . 5519(g)
Arbitration of damages . . . 3045
Attorney's fees, payment of . . . 5031(c)
Certificate of merit to accompany complaint . . 3012-a
Collateral source of payment . . . 4545(a)
Commencement of action, statute of limitations (See subhead: Statute of limitations)

**MALPRACTICE ACTIONS**—Cont.

Complaint not served with summons, notice required, exception as to requirement for sum for which default judgment may be taken . . . . 305(b)

Costs upon counterclaims in actions to recover damages for . . . 8303-a

Costs upon frivolous claims in actions to recover damages for . . . 8303-a

Counterclaims in actions to recover damages for, costs upon . . . 8303-a

Damages
>  Arbitration . . . 3045
>  Evidence, loss of earnings and impairment of earning ability as . . . 4546
>  Verdict . . . 4111(d)

Demand for relief . . . 3017(c)

Deposition of expert witnesses . . 3101(d)(1)(ii)

Disclosure, scope of, requirement . . 3101(d)(1)

Election of remedies . . . 3045

Evidence
>  Insurance payments as collateral source of payment, admissibility of . . . 4545(a)
>  Loss of earnings and impairment of earning ability as . . . 4546

Frivolous claims in actions to recover damages for, costs upon . . . 8303-a

Insurance payments as collateral source of payment, admissibility of . . . 4545(a)

Judgments (See JUDGMENTS, subhead: Malpractice actions)

Lack of informed consent as ground
>  Expert medical testimony not offered by plaintiff, mandatory granting of judgment . . . 4401-a

Mandatory filing . . . 3406(a)

Pre-calendar conference . . . 3406(b)

Preferences for trial . . . 3403(a)(5)

Publication, service of summons by
>  Default judgment sum, bar to publication of . . . 316(a)

Public Health Law . . . App

Settlements . . . 5037

Statute of limitations
>  Commencement of action within 2-1/2 years . . . 214-a
>  Foreign object in patient's body, commencement of action based on discovery of . . . 214-a
>  Stay of enforcement pending appeal . . . . 5519(g)
>  Three year period . . . 214

Supplemental demand . . . 3017(c)

Trial preference . . . 3403(a)(5)

**MALPRACTICE ACTIONS**—Cont.

Verdict
>  Itemization, requirement for . . . 4111(d)

**MANDAMUS, WRIT OF** (See ARTICLE 78 PROCEEDINGS)

**MANDATES (GENERALLY)**

Execution of . . . 2223

Officers receiving mandate, duties of . . . 2223

Return of . . . 2223

**MAPS**

Evidence
>  Ancient maps, surveys and records affecting real property . . . 4522

Fees of county clerks . . . 8021(a)(3),(e)

**MARRIAGE CERTIFICATE**

Prima facie evidence of marriage . . . 4526

**MATRIMONIAL ACTIONS**

Annulment of marriage (See ANNULMENT OR DISSOLUTION OF MARRIAGE)

Attachment order, prohibition . . . 6201

Default judgment, entry of; written finding of fact as condition . . . 3215(b)

Defined; specific actions included . . . 105(p)

Distributive awards, personal jurisdiction over . . . 302(b)

Domestic Relations Law (DRL) . . . App

Interrogatories . . . 3130(2)

Jurisdiction
>  Distributive awards . . . 302(b)
>  Maintenance actions for . . . 302(b)
>  Nonresident of defendant . . . 302(b)
>  Support and alimony, demand for . . . . . 302(b)
>  Without state not giving personal jurisdiction, service . . . 314

Maintenance, actions for, personal jurisdiction over nonresident defendants . . . 302(b)

Misconduct of party, specification of . . 316(c)

Nonresident defendant, personal jurisdiction over . . . 302(b)

Partial summary judgment, availability of . . . . 3212(e)

Personal service (See SERVICE OF SUMMONS AND PAPERS)

Referees (See REFEREES)

Service of summons (See SERVICE OF SUMMONS AND PAPERS)

Special relief in, personal jurisdiction over nonresident defendant . . . 302(b)

Summary judgment, motion for; limitations on availability
>  Partial summary judgment . . . 3212(e)

[References are to CPLR Sections, Rules and Appendices.]

**MATRIMONIAL ACTIONS—Cont.**

Support or alimony, demand for, exercise of personal jurisdiction over nonresident respondent or defendant by court . . . 302(b)

Uncontested actions, referee in . . . 4312(5)

**MECHANICS' LIENS**

Fees for filing notices of . . . 8021(b)(4)

**MEDICAL MALPRACTICE** (See MALPRACTICE ACTIONS)

**MEDICAL RECORDS** (See HOSPITAL OR MEDICAL RECORDS)

**MENTALLY ILL PERSONS** (See INCOMPETENT PERSONS)

**MILITARY PERSONNEL**

Agent Orange (phenoxy herbicides), personal injury actions involving . . . 214-b

Oaths taken before officers in armed forces . . . 2309(d)

Personal injury actions involving

    Statutes of limitations and

        Agent Orange (phenoxy herbicides); service in Indochina . . . 214-b

**MINORS** (See INFANTS AND MINORS)

**MISCONDUCT**

Divorce action

    Specification of misconduct of party . . . . 316(c)

**MISSING PERSONS**

Death, presumption of; prima facie evidence establishing . . . 4527(a)

Present status of, report by authorized party pursuant to law of United States; prima facie evidence of status . . . 4527(b)

**MISTAKE IN PROCEDURE** (See IRREGULARITY, MISTAKE OR DEFECT IN PROCEDURE)

**MOBILE HOMES**

Homestead exemption, applicability . . 5206(a)

**MONEY JUDGMENT—ENFORCEMENT PROCEDURES**

Adverse claims to property held for satisfaction of judgment, determination of . . . 5239

Appeal

    Release of levy or lien

        Motion upon notice by judgment debtor, effect . . . 5204

        Undertaking on appeal given by judgment debtor, requirement . . 5204

**MONEY JUDGMENT—ENFORCEMENT PROCEDURES—Cont.**

Appeal—Cont.

    Stay, conditions precedent for . . . . . . . 5519(a)(2); 5519(a)(3)

Armed forces' member, exempt personal property . . . 5205(e)

Arrest of judgment debtor, warrant for

    Grounds for issuance . . . 5250

Auction to satisfy, notice of; personal property . . . 5233(b)

Contempt of court, power of court to punish for . . . 5210

Corporate interest, subject of enforcement as; president or treasurer as proper garnishee . . 5201(c)(1)

Debt against money judgment

    Attachment, subject to . . . 6202

    Generally . . . 5201(a)

Decedent estate, right or interest in as subject of enforcement; proper garnishee specified . . . 5201(c)(2)

Defined . . . 105(q)

Discharge of garnishee's obligation . . . 5209

Disclosure, availability of to judgment creditor . . . 5223

Disobedience of specified procedures, punishment as contempt . . . 5251

Execution against property (See EXECUTION ON JUDGMENTS)

Exemptions

    Armed forces' member . . . 5205(e)

    Homestead (See subhead: Homestead exemption)

    Personal property (See subhead: Personal property, enforcement against)

    Security deposits

        Rental of real property for residence . . . 5205(g)

        Utilities, deposits with . . . 5205(g)

    Trust (See subhead: Trust exemption)

Foreign country money judgments (See FOREIGN COUNTRY MONEY JUDGMENTS)

Garnishee, proper

    Corporate interest, president or treasurer as proper garnishee . . . 5201(c)(1)

    Decedent estate, right or interest in . . . . 5201(c)(2)

    Discharge of garnishee's obligation . . . . 5209

    Negotiable instrument . . . 5201(c)(4)

    Partnership interest . . . 5201(c)(3)

    Proper party as . . . 5201(a)

Homestead exemption

    Owner's death, after . . . 5206(b)

[References are to CPLR Sections, Rules and Appendices.]

**MONEY JUDGMENT—ENFORCEMENT PROCEDURES**—Cont.

Homestead exemption—Cont.

Sale of homestead exceeding ten thousand dollars . . . 5206(e)

Suspension of occupation as affecting . . . 5206(c)

Ten thousand dollars, exceeding . . . . . . 5206(d)

Types of property . . . 5206(a)

Income execution (See INCOME EXECUTION)

Income exemptions

Judgment debtor's personal services . . . . 5205(d)(2)

Limitations . . . 5205(d)

Matrimonial awards . . . 5205(d)(3)

Trust income . . . 5205(d)(1)

Individual Retirement Accounts as trust exemption from . . . 5205(c)(2)

Installment payment order . . . 5226

Judgment creditor, rights of

Disclosure, compelling . . . 5223

Personal property, rights in

Execution creditor and transferee of debt or property, superiority of rights . . . 5202(a)

Exempt personal property (See subhead: Personal property, enforcement against)

Judgment creditor and transferee of debt or property, priority of rights . . . 5202(b)

Real property, liens upon; priority of

Docketing of money judgment, attachment of lien from time of . . . . . 5203(a)

Duration of lien . . . 5203(a)

Extension of lien . . . 5203(b)

Notice of levy pursuant to execution, filing of, attachment of lien from time of . . . 5203(a)

State or state agency as judgment debtor, effect . . . 5203(a)(5)

Transfers having superior rights, enumeration . . . 5203(a)

Judgment debtor

Arrest of . . . 5250

Death, enforcement after . . . 5208

Income exemptions, personal services of judgment debtor . . . 5205(d)(2)

Payment or delivery of property of debtor (See subhead: Payment or delivery of property of debtor)

Payments of debts owed to . . . 5227

**MONEY JUDGMENT—ENFORCEMENT PROCEDURES**—Cont.

Judgment debtor—Cont.

Real property, liens upon; priority of

Decedent's estate, award to judgment debtor as representative of : . . . . 5203(a)(6)

Judgment entered after death of judgment debtor . . . 5203(a)(4)

Municipal corporation as judgment debtor . . . 5203(a)(5)

Restraining notice along with notice to Exemptions . . . 5222(e)

Procedure . . . 5222(d)

State as . . . 5207

Keogh plans as trust exemption from . . . . . . 5202(c)(2)

Modification of procedure, power of court over . . . 5240

Negotiable instrument, property or debt evidenced by, garnishment of . . . 5201(c)(4)

Obligor

Defined . . . 5232(d)

Notice to . . . 5232(c)

Orders

Defined . . . 5222(f); 5230(e)

Partnership interest, subject of enforcement, proper garnishee specified . . . 5201(c)(3)

Payment or delivery of property of debtor

Documents to effect . . . 5225(c)

Notice . . . 5225(a)

Property not in possession . . . 5225(b)

Service . . . 5225(a)

Personal property, enforcement against

Execution creditors, priority among . . . . 5234(b)

Exemptions

Animals trained to assist disabled persons . . . 5205(h)

Armed forces' member . . . 5205(e)

Cause of action for damages for injury to, exemption from satisfaction; duration of exemption . . . 5205(b)

Income (See subhead: Income exemptions)

Life insurance policies, for . . . . . . 5205(i)

Life sustaining or maintaining systems . . . 5205(h)

Medical/dental accessions to body . . . 5205(h)

Milk proceeds where produced on judgment debtor's farm; Agriculture and Markets Law . . . 5205(f)

**MONEY JUDGMENT—ENFORCEMENT PROCEDURES**—Cont.
Personal property, enforcement against—Cont.
  Exemptions—Cont.
      Permanently disabled persons, aid to . . . 5205(h)
      Trust (See subhead: Trust exemption)
  Judgment creditors, priority among . . . . 5234(c)
  Notice to judgment debtor . . . 5232(c)
  Obligor
      Defined . . . 5232(d)
      Notice to . . . 5232(c)
  Sale of
      Notice of sale, posting requirements . . . 5233(b)
      Order for immediate sale, discretion of court over . . . 5233(c)
      Proceeds of sale, distribution rights . . . 5234(a)
      Public auction, method of sale . . . . 5233(a)
      Unsalable material . . . 5233(d)
  Seizure, levy by . . . 5232(b)
  Service of execution, levy by . . . 5232(a)
  Sheriff, directions to . . . 5238
  Surplus after payment to judgment creditor, payment to judgment debtor . . 5234(a)
Prior to entry of judgment, extent of enforcement authorized . . . 5229
Privilege on examination; immunity
  Criminal Procedure Law, grant of immunity in accordance with . . . 5211
  False swearing . . . 5251
  Power of court to grant . . . 5211
Proceedings for enforcement
  Contempt, power of court to punish for . . . 5210
  Court for commencing . . . 5221(a)
  Place for commencing . . . 5221(a)
  Restraining notice, issuance, authorization (See subhead: Restraining notice)
Property, execution against (See EXECUTION ON JUDGMENTS)
Protective orders, issuance by court . . . 5240
Real property
  Exemptions
      Burying ground; conditions to exemption . . . 5206(g)
      Homestead exemption (See subhead: Homestead exemption)
  Levy upon . . . 5235
  Liens upon, priority of (See Judgment debtor; subheads: Judgment creditor, rights of)

**MONEY JUDGMENT—ENFORCEMENT PROCEDURES**—Cont.
Real property—Cont.
  Sale (See REAL PROPERTY ACTIONS, subhead: Sale for enforcement of money judgment)
  Sheriff, directions to . . . 5238
Receivership
  Extension of . . . 5228(b)
  Receiver, appointment of . . . 5228(a)
Restraining notice
  Disobedience of . . . 5251
  Effect and duration of restraint . . 5222(b)
  Magnetic tape, in form of . . . 5222(g)
  Notice to judgment debtor and
      Exemptions . . . 5222(e)
      Procedure . . . 5222(d)
  Obligor, notice to . . . 5222(d)
  Service of . . . 5222(a)
  Signature of clerk or attorney who issued notice . . . 5222(a)
  Subsequent notice . . . 5222(c)
  Willful disobedience of, punishment for . . . 5251
Sale of property (See subheads for specific types of property)
Security deposits, exemption
  Rental of real property for residence . . . 5205(g)
  Utilities, deposits with . . . 5205(g)
State as judgment debtor, inapplicability of procedures to . . . 5207
Statutes of limitations (See STATUTES OF LIMITATIONS)
Subpoena, availability of (See SUBPOENAS)
Trust exemption
  Additions to asset . . . 5205(c)(5)
  Retirement plans/benefits . . . 5205(c)(2)
  Spendthrift trusts . . . 5205(c)(3)

**MORTGAGES**
Bonds or notes, mortgage on real property securing; six-year statute of limitations . . . 213
Chattel mortgages, county clerks' fees . . . . . 8021(b)(5)
County clerks' fees
  Chattel mortgages, county clerks' fees . . 8021(b)(5)
  Foreclosure . . . 8021(a)(3)
Foreclosure
  Additional allowances in . . . 8302(d)
  Fees of county clerks . . . 8021(a)(3)
Statute of limitations
  Bonds or notes, mortgage on real property securing; six-year statute of limitations . . . 213

[References are to CPLR Sections, Rules and Appendices.]

**MORTGAGES—Cont.**
Statute of limitations—Cont.
   Ten-year period . . . 212

**MOTIONS**
Attachment (See ATTACHMENT)
Class action, motion by plaintiff for maintenance as . . . 902
Correction of pleadings . . . 3024
Costs awarded upon court's discretion as to . . 8106
County court actions
   Exclusion of action by rule of chief administrator of courts . . . 2213(c)
   Ex parte motions, place for making motion . . . 2213(a)
   Supreme court or justice thereof, motion made before
      CPLR 1207, motion under; inapplicability of section to . . . 2213(b)
Cross motions, service of notice demanding relief on moving party, time for serving . . . 2215
Defined . . . 2211
Depositions of witnesses, use at hearing of motion (See DEPOSITIONS, subhead: Use at trial, hearing of motion or interlocutory proceeding)
Dismissal motions (See DISMISSAL MOTIONS)
Ex parte motions
   Chief administrator of courts, exclusion by rule of . . . 2212(d)
   County court action . . . . 2213(c)
   Prior motion for similar relief, disclosure of result and new facts concerning, affidavit accompanying motion including; requirement . . . 2217(b)
   Supreme court actions . . . 2212(b)
Fact issue raised on motion . . . 2218
Motion term, motion noticed to be heard before . . . 2212(a)
Notice, motion on
   Answering affidavit, time for serving . . . 2214(b)
   Papers to be furnished court . . . 2214(c)
   Service of, notice effected by . . . 2211
   Show cause order
      Grant by court in lieu of notice motion . . . 2214(d)
      Notice motion, in lieu of; grant of show cause order . . . 2214(d)
   Specificity, requirements . . . 2214(a)
   Time for serving . . . 2214(b)
Pleading, motion to correct . . . 3024
Post-trial motions (See TRIAL)
Prior motions, motion affecting . . . 2221(a)
   Chief administrator of courts, exclusion by rule of . . . 2217(d),2221(b)

**MOTIONS—Cont.**
Prior motions, motion affecting—Cont.
   Ex parte motion, result of prior motion for similar relief and new facts, disclosure in accompanying affidavit; requirement . . . 2217(b)
Relief demanded by other than moving party, time for service of notice . . . 2215
Show cause orders (See SHOW CAUSE ORDERS)
Special proceedings (See SPECIAL PROCEEDINGS)
Summary judgment (See SUMMARY JUDGMENT)
Supreme court actions
   Chief administrator of courts, exclusion by rule of . . . 2212(d)
   County court or judge, supreme court motions heard by, chief administrator of courts' rules providing for, authorization . . . 2212(c)
   Ex parte motions, place motion may be heard . . . 2212(b)
   Motion on notice, place motion noticed to be heard
      County adjoining county in which action triable . . . 2212(a)
      Judicial district in which action triable . . . 2212(a)
   Supreme court or justice thereof, motion made before, CPLR 1207 motions under; inapplicability of section to . . 2213(b)
Transfer of, allowance . . . 2217(c)
Trial motions (See TRIAL)

**MOTOR VEHICLES**
Accidents (See ACCIDENT AND ACCIDENT REPORTS)
Vehicle and Traffic Law . . . App

**MRI** (See MAGNETIC RESONANCE IMAGES)

**MUNICIPAL CORPORATIONS**
Demand for relief . . . 3017(c)
Income execution payable by, levy of . . . . . . 5231(h)
Subpoenas (See SUBPOENAS)
Undertakings
   Exceptions . . . 2512(2)
   Name of, undertaking in . . . 2513

# N

**NEGLIGENCE ACTIONS**
Assumption of risk (See subhead: Contributory negligence)

[References are to CPLR Sections, Rules and Appendices.]

**NEGLIGENCE ACTIONS**—Cont.
Bill of particulars
    Verification . . . 3044
Comparative negligence (See COMPARATIVE NEGLIGENCE)
Contributory negligence
    Affirmative defenses . . . 3018(b)
    Burden of pleading and proof . . . 1412
    Culpability as determining amount of diminution . . . 1411; 1412
    Effectivity, date of . . . 1413
Corporate directors, officers or trustees, gross negligence of; particularity in complaint as to specific cause of action . . . 3016(h)
Culpable conduct, considerations; Judicial Conference opinion as to . . . 1411
Damages recoverable
    Contributory negligence or assumption of risk (See subhead: Contributory negligence)
    Culpability as factor . . . 1411
Interrogatory in, use of . . . 3130
Pleadings (See PLEADINGS (GENERALLY))
Verification
    Bill of particulars . . . 3044

**NEGOTIABLE INSTRUMENTS**
Signature, admission of absent specific denial . . . 3015(d)

**NEWSPAPERS AND PERIODICALS**
Authenticity . . . 4532

**NEW TRIAL** (See TRIAL)

**NEW YORK CITY**
Commencement by Filing Law, New York's . . . App
Commissioner of finance
    Deposits into court . . . 2601(b)
    Fees for services performed . . . 8010
New York Civil Court Act . . . App
Personal service upon, manner of effecting; corporation counsel or party designated in writing by, personal service upon . . . 311(a)
Statute of limitations, tolling of . . . 203(b)
Venue
    Actions . . . 504
    Transit authority, action against . . 505(b)

**NEW YORK CITY CIVIL COURT ACT**
Selected practice provisions . . . App

**NEW YORK CITY TRANSIT AUTHORITY**
Venue in action against . . . 505(b)

**NEW YORK STATE**
Commencement by Filing Law . . . App

**NEW YORK STATE**—Cont.
Constitution of . . . App

**NON-DOMICILIARIES** (See NONRESIDENT)

**NONRESIDENT**
Alien-nonresident
    Warring country, citizen, resident or sojourner in; tolling of statutes of limitations . . . 209(b)
Attachment orders, authorization . . . 6201
Family Court proceedings, demand for support or alimony . . . 302(b)
Jurisdiction
    Appearance, effect of . . . 302(c)
    Generally . . . 302
    Matrimonial actions . . . 302(b)
    Tortious acts, commission in person or through agent
        Within state . . . 302(a)
        Without state . . . 302(a)
Long-arm statute . . . 302
Matrimonial actions, personal jurisdiction over . . . 302(b)
Plaintiff in court of state, designation of agent for service of process by use of court . . . 303
Real property located in state, ownership, use or possession, personal jurisdiction based upon . . . 302(a)
Tortious acts, commission in person or through agent; basis of jurisdiction
    Within state . . . 302(a)
    Without state . . . 302(a)
Transacting business within state, acts arising from, basis of personal jurisdiction . . 302(a)

**NOTE OF ISSUE**
Additional parties, effect upon calendar position . . . 3402(b)
Bill of particulars, amendment of . . . 3042(b)
Dismissal motion, noncompliance with written demand for service of note as basis . . . . . . 3216(a)
Failure to prosecute (See FAILURE TO PROSECUTE)
Function . . . 3402
Order of trials, determination, filing of note as basis . . . 3403
Placement of case on calendar, filing as method . . . 3402
Rules regulating hearing of causes . . . 3401
Written demand for service of note, claimant's failure to comply with, basis for dismissal motion . . . 3216(a)

**NOT-FOR-PROFIT CORPORATION LAW**
Motion to dismiss on grounds of § 720(a) immunity . . . 3211(a)(11)

[References are to CPLR Sections, Rules and Appendices.]

**NOT-FOR-PROFIT CORPORATION LAW—**
Cont.
Verified complaint, requirement, actions based on
§ 720(a) . . . 3016

**NOTICE OF PENDENCY**
Cancellation of
    Costs and expenses . . . 6514(c)
    Discretionary cancellation . . . 6514(b)
    Forfeiture of proceeds of crime (See FOR-
      FEITURE OF PROCEEDS OF CRIME)
    Mandatory cancellation . . . 6514(a)
    Plaintiff, cancellation by . . . 6514(e)
    Security for plaintiff . . . 6515
    Stipulation, cancellation by . . . 6514(d)
    Undertaking for . . . 6515
Complaint, filing with notice of pendency . . . .
  6511(a)
Constructive notice to specified parties . . 6501
Content, necessary inclusions . . . 6511(b)
County clerk's fees for filing or recording . . .
  8021(a)(10)
Death of defendant prior to completed service,
  effectivity of notice . . . 6512
Duration . . . 6513
Extension of time
    Duration of notice . . . 6513
Filing requirements . . . 6511(a)
Forfeiture of proceeds of crime (See FORFEI-
  TURE OF PROCEEDS OF CRIME)
Indexing
    Electronic indexing . . . 6511(d)
    Requirements . . . 6511(c)
Provisional remedy, notice of pendency as . . . .
  6001
Real property, action in which judgment would
  affect; utilization of notice of pendency in
  . . . 6501
Service of summons
    Death of defendant prior to . . . 6512
    Generally . . . 6512
Undertaking for cancellation . . . 6515

**NOTICE OF PETITION**
Article 78 proceedings
    Generally . . . 7802(d)
    Service, time for . . . 7804(c)
Infant's support, property applied to
    Parties entitled to notice of petition . . . .
    1211(b)
Special proceedings (See SPECIAL PROCEED-
  INGS)
Summons (See SUMMONS)

**NOTICES** (See Specific subject headings)

**NUISANCE**
Jury trial of fact issues, action for abatement of and
  damages for nuisance . . . 4101(2)

**NURSES**
Confidential communications . . . 4504

# O

**OATHS AND AFFIRMATIONS**
Administration, qualified persons . . . 2309(a)
Arbitrator
    Arbitrator's oath . . . 7506(a)
    Power of arbitrator to administer . . 7505
Armed forces of United States, officer's certificate
  of oath or affirmation, necessary inclusions
  . . . 2309(d)
Attorney, affirmation of in lieu of affidavit . . .
  2106
Certificates
    Officers administering oath to persons in
      armed forces . . . 2309(d)
    Other states, oaths administered in . . . . .
      2309(c)
Dentist, affirmation of in lieu of affidavit . . . .
  2106
Depositions, oath administered during . . . . . .
  3113(b)
Evidence, receipt of, authorized person as quali-
  fied to administer related oath or affirmation
  . . . 2309(a)
Fees
    Administration and certification . . . . . .
      8009(1)
    Witnesses to execution of instruments,
      swearing of . . . 8009(2)
Form of oath or affirmation . . . 2309(b)
Juror or jurors, administration of oath to; autho-
  rized person . . . 2309(a)
Oath of office, inapplicability of section to . . .
  2309(a)
Osteopath, affirmation of in lieu of affidavit . . .
  2106
Outside state, administration, treatment; accompa-
  nying certificates . . . 2309(c)
Physician, affirmation of in lieu of affidavit . . .
  2106
Referee, oath of . . . 4315
Temporary receiver, oath of
    Forfeiture of proceeds of crime, action for
      . . . 1339
    Generally . . . 6402

**OBJECTIONS**
Charge made or refused to be made to jury,
  objection to; time for interposing . . . 4017

[References are to CPLR Sections, Rules and Appendices.]

**OBJECTIONS**—Cont.

Exceptions to rulings, no necessity for . . 4017

Failure to object, consequences . . 4017; 4110-b; 5501(a)(3)

Instructions to the jury, failure to give; request for . . . 4110-b

Ruling or order of court, objection to

    Formal exception, no necessity for . . . . 4017

    Time for interposing objection . . . 4017

**OBSCENE PRINTS, MOTION PICTURES AND ARTICLES**

Injunction for . . . 6330

Seizure, generally . . . 5233(d)

**OPENING AND CLOSING STATEMENTS**

Generally . . . 4016

**ORDERS (GENERALLY)**

Appellate court order, signature requirements . . . 2219(b)

Defined . . . 5222(f); 5230(e)

Docketing order as judgment by clerk, request of party . . . 2222

Entry of . . . 2220(a)

Filing requirements . . . 2220(a)

Form . . . 2219(a)

Provisional remedy, order pertaining to . . . . . 2219(a)

Relief from

    Administrative judge, on application of . . . 5015(c)

    Motion, on . . . 5015(a)

    Restitution . . . 5015(d)

    Stipulation, on . . . 5015(b)

Service of order, method . . . 2220(b)

Time for granting . . . 2219(a)

Writing requirement . . . 2219(a)

# P

**PAPERS**

Admissions

    Effect of . . . 3123(b)

    Notice to admit . . . 3123(a)

    Penalty for unreasonable denial . . . . . . 3123(c)

Attorney's endorsement . . . 2101(d)

Caption on papers, required content . . 2101(c)

Contract print size smaller than 8 point or illegible, bar to submission as evidence involving consumer transaction or residential lease . . 4544

Copies

    Certification by attorney admitted to practice in courts of state, authorization . . 2105

**PAPERS**—Cont.

Copies—Cont.

    Interrogatories, papers relevant to answers; requirement for copies . . . 3131

    Service or filing of, when authorized . . . 2101(e)

Defect in form, no substantial right prejudiced thereby

    Disregard of defect and leave to correct, allowance . . . 2101(f)

    Waiver of defect, how effected . . 2101(f)

English language requirement . . . 2101(b)

Filing requirements . . . 2102

Form of papers, requirements for

    Contract print size 8 point or greater, requirement for consumer transaction or residential lease . . . 4544

    Exceptions . . . 2101(a)

Interrogatories, copies of papers . . . 3131

Legibility . . . 2101(a)

Motion papers, rules pertaining to . . . 2214

Service of (See SERVICE OF SUMMONS AND PAPERS)

Size . . . 2101(a)

Statements by attorney, physician, osteopath, or dentist admitted to practice in the state; treatment as affidavit; qualifications . . . 2106

Stipulations outside court, binding effect of; requirements . . . 2104

Transmission of, fees and expenses for . . 8008

Type size requirements . . . 105(t)

**PARK DISTRICT**

Service of summons . . . 311(a)

**PARTIES, JOINDER OF** (See JOINDER OF PARTIES)

**PARTITION**

Additional allowances in . . . 8302(a)(2)

Summons not personally delivered, defense by person to whom . . . 317

**PARTNERSHIP**

Garnishment of interest in, enforcement of money judgment; proper garnishee specified . . . . . 5201(c)(3)

Interrogatory sent to, manner of answering . . . 3133(b)

Name of partnership, suits by or against brought in . . . 1025

Personal service upon (See SERVICE OF SUMMONS AND PAPERS)

Venue for trial, residence of partnership as basis, section establishing . . . 503(d)

[References are to CPLR Sections, Rules and Appendices.]

**PATERNITY TEST**
Blood genetic marker test . . . 4518(d)
DNA test . . . 4518(d)
Evidence, records of test as . . . 4518(d)

**PENALTIES**
Aggrieved person, action by . . . 7202
Common informer
    Collusive or fraudulent recovery, action not
      barred by . . . 7203(c)
    Maintainable . . . 7203(a)
    Service of summons, authorization . . . .
    7203(b)
Crime, proceeds of (See FORFEITURE OF PRO-
    CEEDS OF CRIME)
Disclosure (See DISCLOSURE)
Forfeiture
    Action by state . . . 7201
    Aggrieved person, action by . . . 7202
    Common informer (See subhead: Common
      informer)
    Good faith reliance on judicial decision,
      defense of . . . 7205
    Partial recovery . . . 7204
    Recognizance . . . 7201(c)
    Statutory penalty or forfeiture . . 7201(a)
    Treason, conviction of . . . 7201(b)
Good faith reliance on judicial decision, defense
    of . . . 7205
Partial recovery . . . 7204
Statutes of limitations, three-year period . . 214
Treason, conviction of . . . 7201(b)

**PENSION PLANS**
Periodic payments under, action for sums due; no
    bar to action to recover future payments when
    due . . . 3003

**PEREMPTORY CHALLENGE** (See VOIR
DIRE)

**PERFORMANCE BONDS** (See UNDERTAK-
INGS)

**PERISHABLE PROPERTY**
Chattel action, seizure of
    Sale of perishable property . . . 7105
Sale of
    Seizure of chattel action . . . 7105
    Stay of enforcement pending appeal . . . .
    5519(f)

**PERMISSIVE JOINDER** (See JOINDER OF
PARTIES)

**PERSONAL INJURY ACTIONS**
Agent Orange, military personnel with service in
    Indochina . . . 214-b

**PERSONAL INJURY ACTIONS**—Cont.
Assumption of risk established, recovery of dam-
    ages (See subhead: Damages recoverable)
Bill of particulars (See BILL OF PARTICU-
    LARS)
Collateral sources of payment, admissibility of
    Public employer, certain actions against
      . . . 4545(b)
      Recovery of costs, loss of earnings or eco-
        nomic loss . . . 4545(c)
Contributory negligence established, recovery of
    damages (See subhead: Damages recoverable)
Costs upon counterclaims in action to recover
    damages for . . . 8303-a
Costs upon frivolous claims in action to recover
    damages for . . . 8303-a
Counterclaims in action to recover damages for
    personal injury action, costs upon . . 8303-a
Damages recoverable
    Assumption of risk no bar to recovery
      Burden of proof . . . 1412
      Culpability, effect . . . 1411; 1412
      Effectivity, date of . . . 1413
    Contributory negligence no bar to recovery
      Burden of proof . . . 1412
      Culpability as determining amount of
        diminution . . . 1411; 1412
      Effectivity, date of . . . 1413
    Culpable conduct as factor . . . 1411
Evidence (See EVIDENCE)
Frivolous claims in action to recover damages for,
    costs upon . . . 8303-a
Judgments, periodic payment of (See JUDG-
    MENTS, subhead: Personal injury, injury to
    property and wrongful death actions)
Motor vehicle accidents (See ACCIDENT AND
    ACCIDENT REPORTS)
Public employer; certain actions against
    Admissibility of collateral source of payment
      . . . 4545(b)
    Itemized verdict . . . 4111(e)
Statutes of limitations
    Agent Orange; actions involving; military
      personnel with service in
      Indochina . . . 214-b
    Recovery of damages, three-year period
      . . . 214
    Three-year period . . . 215
    Toxic substances, latent effects of exposure
      to, discovery of injury . . . 214-c
Terminally ill plaintiffs, trial preferences for (See
    PREFERENCES FOR TRIAL)
X-rays as evidence, admissibility of . . 4532-a

**PERSONAL PROPERTY (GENERALLY)**
Attachment of (See ATTACHMENT)

## PERSONAL PROPERTY (GENERALLY)—Cont.

Deposit of (See DEPOSITS INTO COURT, subhead: Disposition of property by)

Enforcement against (See MONEY JUDGMENT—ENFORCEMENT PROCEDURE)

Exempt property (See MONEY JUDGMENT—ENFORCEMENT PROCEDURES)

Levy upon (See FORFEITURE OF PROCEEDS OF CRIME, subhead: Attachment)

Property within state, service made outside state, judgment sought affecting interest or title to specified property . . . 314

Sheriff's fees for sale of . . . 8011(g)

## PERSONAM JURISDICTION (See JURISDICTION)

## PETITION

(See also COMPLAINT; specific subject headings)

Notice of petition (See NOTICE OF PETITION)

## PHENOXY HERBICIDES (AGENT ORANGE)

Personal injury actions involving military personnel with service in Indochina . . . 214-b

## PHOTOGRAPHS

Admissions

    Effect of . . . 3123(b)

    Notice to admit . . . 3123(a)

    Penalty for unreasonable denial . . . . . . 3123(c)

## PHYSICAL OR MENTAL EXAMINATIONS, PRETRIAL (See DISCLOSURE, subhead: Physical or mental examination)

## PHYSICIANS

Affirmation of in lieu of affidavit . . . 2106

Confidential information, physician-patient privilege . . . 4504

Malpractice actions (See MALPRACTICE ACTIONS)

Statements subscribed and affirmed by; treatment as affidavits . . . 2106

## PLAINTIFF (GENERALLY)

Defined . . . 105(b)

Petitioner in special proceeding as . . . 105(b)

Terminally ill plaintiff, trial preference for . . . 3403(a)(6)

## PLEADINGS (GENERALLY)

Affirmative defenses

    Requirement . . . 3018(b)

    Surprise of adverse party, matters if not pleaded likely to cause . . . 3018(b)

## PLEADINGS (GENERALLY)—Cont.

Alternative pleading, allowance . . . 3014

Amended and supplemental pleadings (See AMENDED AND SUPPLEMENTAL PLEADINGS)

Answer (See ANSWER)

Article 78 proceedings . . . 7804(d)

Bill of particulars (See BILL OF PARTICULARS)

Complaint (See COMPLAINT)

Condition precedent in contract action, performance or occurrence of . . . 3015(a)

Corporate directors, officers or trustees, negligence of; particularity in complaint as to cause of action . . . 3016(h)

Corporate status of party, statement in complaint, requirements . . . 3015(b)

Correction of pleadings

    Scandalous or prejudicial matter . . . . . . 3024(b)

    Time limits . . . 3024(c)

    Vague or ambiguous pleadings . . 3024(a)

Counterclaims (See COUNTERCLAIMS)

Cross-claims (See CROSS-CLAIMS)

Demand for relief (See DEMAND FOR RELIEF)

Dismissal motions (See DISMISSAL MOTIONS)

Divorce actions, particularity of statement required for . . . 3016(c)

Extension of time . . . 3012(d)

Foreign law, cause of action or defense based upon, statement of substance of foreign law . . . 3016(e)

Form and content

    Consecutively numbered paragraphs . . . . 3014

    Incorporation by reference, prior allegations, allowance . . . 3014

    Separate causes of action or defenses, statement of

        Inconsistent actions or defenses stated, immateriality . . . 3014

        Separately numbered and state, authorization . . . 3014

    Single allegation where practicable, each paragraph containing . . . 3014

    Statements included, particularity of

        Requirement . . . 3013; 3015

        Specified matters, particularity required as to . . . 3015

Fraud, pleading cause of action or defense . . . 3016(b)

Hypothetical pleading, allowance . . . 3014

Inconsistent causes of action or defenses, inclusion in pleadings, allowance . . . 3014

Interpleader complaint (See INTERPLEADER)

[References are to CPLR Sections, Rules and Appendices.]

**PLEADINGS (GENERALLY)**—Cont.

Judgment, action on; information regarding
    Extent satisfied, disclosure in pleading . .
      3016(d)
    Jurisdiction of body rendering judgment or
      decision, no necessity to specifically plead
      . . . 3015(c)
Labor or service performed, itemization of claims
    by plaintiff . . . 3016(f)
Libel or slander action, particularity of pleading
    regarding . . . 3016(a)
Liberal construction of, authorization . . . 3026
Marked pleadings, copies furnished by trial judge
    . . . 4012
Motions to correct, time limits . . . 3024(c)
Negligence
    Corporate directors, officers or trustees, par-
      ticularity in complaint as to cause of action
      . . . 3016(h)
    Personal injuries arising out of negligence in
      use or operation of motor vehicle
      Bill of particulars . . . 3043
      Statement of serious injury or eco-
        nomic loss greater than basic eco-
        nomic loss; requirement . . . . . .
        3016(g)
Negotiable instrument, signature on, admission of
    absent specific denial . . . 3015(d)
Particularity . . . 3013
Personal injuries arising out of negligence in use
    or operation of motor vehicle
    Bill of particulars . . . 3043
    Statement of serious injury or economic loss
      greater than basic economic loss; require-
      ment . . . 3016(g)
Responsive pleadings
    Affirmative defenses . . . 3018(b)
    Denials . . . 3018(a)
Sale and delivery of goods, pleadings involving
    . . . 3016(f)
Scandalous or prejudicial matter contained in,
    motion to strike, authorization . . . 3024(b)
Separation action, particularity required in com-
    plaint . . . 3016(c)
Service
    Additional time to answer . . . 3012(c)
    Authorization . . . 3012(a)
    Demand for complaint where summons
      served without complaint . . . 3012(b)
    Extension of time for . . . 3012(d)
Special proceedings (See SPECIAL PROCEED-
    INGS)
Specific actions, particularity of pleadings regard-
    ing . . . 3016

**PLEADINGS (GENERALLY)**—Cont.

Striking of pleadings (See STRIKING OF
    PLEADINGS)
Subsequent pleadings, new or additional claims
    included in, service on non-appearing party
    . . . 3012(a)
Third-party complaint (See THIRD-PARTY
    PRACTICE)
Types, specification . . . 3011
Undue influence, circumstances involved; detailed
    statement setting forth . . . 3016(b)
Vague or ambiguous pleading, motion for more
    definite statement, authorization . . . 3024(a)
Verification (See VERIFICATION)

**PODIATRISTS**
Confidential communications with patient, privi-
    leged status of . . . 4504
Malpractice (See MALPRACTICE ACTIONS)

**POOR PERSON, ACTIONS BY OR AGAINST**
Affidavit establishing status . . . 1101(a), (b)
Appeals by
    Briefs and appendices, typewritten; permissi-
      bility . . . 1102(c)
    Stenographer's transcript, no fee for . . . .
      1102(b)
Attorney, assignment of . . . 1102(a)
Beneficially interested persons in recovery, disclo-
    sure in affidavit establishing status as poor
    person . . . 1101(a)
Costs and fees
    Responsibility for . . . 1102(d)
    Waiver of . . . 1101(d)
County attorney in which action triable, notice of
    motion to proceed as poor person given to
    . . . 1101(c)
Deceased person, representative of; motion on
    decedent's behalf to proceed as poor person
    . . . 1101(a)
Distribution of recovery in favor of . . . 1103
Finance administrator, notice of motion for per-
    mission to proceed as poor person given to,
    requirement; actions triable in New York . . .
    1101(c)
Incompetent, representative of; motion on incom-
    petent's behalf to proceed as poor person . .
    1101(a)
Infant, representative of; motion on infant's behalf
    to proceed as poor person . . . 1101(a)
Legal services furnished for poor person, waiver
    of costs and fees without motion when . . . .
    1101(e)
Permission to proceed as poor person . . . 1101
Privileges . . . 1102

[References are to CPLR Sections, Rules and Appendices.]

**POOR PERSON, ACTIONS BY OR AGAINST**—Cont.

Recovery or favorable settlement, distribution of . . . 1103

Stenographer's transcript on appeal, no charge for . . . 1102(b)

**POPULATION**

Certificate of population as evidence
    Conclusive evidence . . . 4530(b)
    Prima facie evidence . . . 4530(a)

Evidence, certificate of population as
    Conclusive evidence . . . 4530(b)
    Prima facie evidence . . . 4530(a)

**POSITRON EMISSION TOMOGRAPHS**

Evidence, admissibility as . . . 4532-a

Personal injury actions, admissibility in . . . . . 4532-a

**PRECLUSION ORDERS** (See BILL OF PARTICULARS)

**PREFERENCES FOR TRIAL**

Appeals . . . 5521

Interests of justice as basis for grant . . . . . . . 3403(a)(3)

Malpractice action . . . 3403(a)(5)

Preliminary conference in personal injury actions involving terminally ill plaintiffs
    Discovery proceedings, schedule for completion of . . . 3407(b)(1)
    Procedures . . . 3407(b)
    Request for conference . . . 3407(a)

Procedure for obtaining . . . 3403(b)

Seventy-five years of age, applicant being, basis for grant of preference . . . 3403(a)(4)

Specific preferences, enumeration of . . . 3403

State, actions by or against, preference authorized . . . 3403(a)(1)

Statutory provision, specific authorization under . . . 3403(a)(2)

Terminally ill plaintiff
    Generally . . . 3403(a)(6)
    Preliminary conference in personal injury actions involving terminally ill plaintiffs (See subhead: Preliminary conference in personal injury actions involving terminally ill plaintiffs)

**PREJUDICE**

Arbitration award, as grounds for vacation of . . . 7511(b)(2)

Permissive joinder of parties, prejudices and expenses resulting from . . . 1002(c)

Pleadings, correction of . . . 3024(b)

**PRELIMINARY INJUNCTION**

Affidavit of plaintiff, necessary showings . . . . 6312(a)

Appellate division, by . . . 5518

Attorney general, service upon . . . 6311

Damages resulting from, ascertainment of . . . . 6315

Forfeiture of proceeds of crime (See FORFEITURE OF PROCEEDS OF CRIME)

Grounds for obtaining . . . 6301

Issue of fact raised by defendant, effect of . . . 6312(c)

Modification of pending appeal or determination of motion for permission to appeal, power of appellate division . . . 6314

Modification or vacatur, undertaking required . . . 6314

Notice of motion for . . . 6311

Notice to defendant, grant conditioned upon . . 6311

Provisional remedy, injunction as . . . 6001

Service upon attorney general . . . 6311

State bodies or officers, service upon . . . 6311

Temporary restraining order prior to . . . 6301

Undertaking
    Another action, stay of proceedings in; amount required . . . 6312(b)(1)
    Modification or vacatur, undertaking required . . . 6314
    Money judgment, stay of proceedings for; amount required . . . 6312(b)(3)
    Recovery of real property, stay of proceedings for; amount required . . 6312(b)(2)

Unique chattel . . . 7109(a)

**PRESUMPTIONS**

Agriculture, inspection certificates issued by United States . . . 4529

Certified acknowledgment or proof of writing, authenticity of . . . 4538

Court of appeals (See COURT OF APPEALS, Questions of fact, presumptions of)

Death of missing person . . . 4527

Marriage certificate as evidence of marriage . . 4526

Missing person, presumption of death of . . . . 4527

Population, certificate of . . . 4530(a)

Questions of fact, presumptions of (See COURT OF APPEALS)

Rebuttable presumptions (See FORFEITURE OF PROCEEDS OF CRIME)

Sealer's certificate as to standard of measurement . . . 4534

Service of papers or posting notice, affidavit of . . . 4531

Index

[References are to CPLR Sections, Rules and Appendices.]

**PRESUMPTIONS—Cont.**

Weather conditions issued by United States Weather Bureau . . . 4528

**PRIMA FACIE EVIDENCE** (See PRESUMPTIONS)

**PRINCIPAL AND AGENT**

Misconduct of agent; statutes of limitations . . . 206(b)

Non-domiciliary, agent of, acts done by; personal jurisdiction over non-domiciliary predicated upon . . . 302

Service of summons, agent for (See SERVICE OF SUMMONS AND PAPERS, subhead: Agents for service)

Statutes of limitations; misconduct of agent . . . 206(b)

Undisclosed principal and agent, causes of action existing against; disclosure of principal, effect . . . 3002(b)

**PRINTERS**

Fees . . . 8007

**PRISONERS**

Depositions of, leave of court as condition . . . 3106(c)

Fees for sheriffs . . . 8011(j)

Forfeiture of proceeds of crime (See FORFEITURE OF PROCEEDS OF CRIME)

Habeas corpus, petition for, person illegally imprisoned making . . . 7002(a)

Sheriff's fees . . . 8011(j)

Statute of limitations . . . 215

Subpoena (See SUBPOENAS)

**PRIVACY, RIGHT OF**

Violation of right, action for damages, statute of limitations . . . 215

**PROCEEDINGS**

Special proceedings (See SPECIAL PROCEEDINGS)

**PROCEEDS OF CRIME, CIVIL FORFEITURE OF** (See FORFEITURE OF PROCEEDS OF CRIME)

**PROFESSIONAL DISCIPLINARY RULES**

Selected practice provisions . . . App

**PROHIBITION, WRIT OF** (See ARTICLE 78 PROCEEDINGS)

**PROOF** (See EVIDENCE)

**PROOF OF SERVICE** (See SERVICE OF SUMMONS AND PAPERS)

**PROPERTY**

Chattel real, classification as real property for purposes of CPLR . . . 105(s)

Costs upon counterclaims in action to recover damages for injury to . . . 8303-a

Costs upon frivolous claims in action to recover damages for injury to . . . 8303-a

Counterclaims in action to recover damages for injury to property, costs upon . . . 8303-a

Disposition of property (See DEPOSITS INTO COURT)

Frivolous claims in action to recover damages for injury to property, costs upon . . . 8303-a

Injury to property

    Collateral sources of payment, admissibility of

        Public employer, certain actions against . . . 4545(b)

        Recovery of costs, loss of earnings or economic loss . . . 4545(c)

    Counterclaims in action to recover damages for, costs upon . . . 8303-a

    Frivolous claims in action to recover damages for, costs upon . . . 8303-a

Property paid into court (See DEPOSITS INTO COURT)

Public property, misappropriation or spoliation of; statute of limitations . . . 213

Statute of limitations; public property, action based on spoliation or other misappropriation of . . . 213

**PROPERTY PAID INTO COURT** (See DEPOSITS INTO COURT)

**PROTECTIVE ORDERS**

Disclosure (See DISCLOSURE)

Enforcement of money judgments . . . 5240

**PROVISIONAL REMEDIES**

Arbitration, application to court for . . 7502(c)

Availability . . . 6001

Counterclaim, cause of action contained in . . . 6001

Cross-claim, cause of action contained in . . . . 6001

Forfeiture of proceeds of crime (See FORFEITURE OF PROCEEDS OF CRIME, subhead: Remedies, provisional)

Injunction (See PRELIMINARY INJUNCTION)

Motion for, contents . . . 6001

Receivership as . . . 6001

Seizure of chattel as provisional remedy

    Limitations period, running of . . . 203(b)

    Recovery . . . 6001

[References are to CPLR Sections, Rules and Appendices.]

**PROVISIONAL REMEDIES**—Cont.
Temporary restraining order (See TEMPORARY RESTRAINING ORDER)
Types, specification . . . 6001

**PSYCHOLOGIST**
Confidential communications . . . 4507

**PUBLICATION**
Fees . . . 8301(a)(3)
Required publication not possible as specified, court remedy as to . . . 2401(1)
Service, by (See SERVICE OF SUMMONS AND PAPERS, subhead: Publication, service by)
Suspended or terminated prior to completion of required publication, completion in other newspaper without court order . . . 2401(2)
Time period of publication, computation . . . . 2402

**PUBLIC EMPLOYEES**
General Municipal Law . . . App
Personal injury and wrongful death, certain actions against public employer for
  Admissibility of collateral source of payment . . . 4545(b)
  Itemized verdict . . . 4111(e)

**PUBLIC EMPLOYERS**
Personal injury, certain actions against public employer for
  Admissibility of collateral source of payment . . . 4545(b)
  Itemized verdict . . . 4111(e)

**PUBLIC HEALTH LAW**
Selected practice provisions . . . App

**PUBLIC OFFICERS**
Affidavits of . . . 4520
Costs, recovery of . . . 8109(b)
Public Officers Law . . . App
Substitution of public officers
  Designation by official title . . . 1023
  Generally . . . 1019
Undertakings
  Exceptions . . . 2512(2)
  Name of, undertaking in . . . 2513
Venue (See VENUE)

**PUBLIC OFFICERS LAW**
Selected practice provisions . . . App

**PUBLIC RETIREMENT BENEFITS**
Retirement benefits system established for at issue, notice to state comptroller, requirement for . . . 1012(c)

**PUBLIC SERVICE COMMISSION**
Special proceeding against, venue for . . 506(b)
Tariffs or classification, authentication of . . . . 4540(d)
Venue for special proceeding against . . 506(b)

# Q

**QUASI-IN-REM JURISDICTION**
Attachment order, levy on defendant's property in state pursuant to, service of summons without state . . . 314
Dismissal, jurisdictional defect as grounds for . . . 3211(a)(9)
Limited appearance based on, no personal jurisdiction conferred by . . . 320(c)

# R

**RAILROADS** (See COMMON CARRIER)

**RAPE CRISIS COUNSELOR**
Confidential communications between client and (See EVIDENCE)
Definition . . . 4510(a)(2)

**REAL PROPERTY ACTIONS**
Additional allowances (See DISBURSEMENTS AND ADDITIONAL ALLOWANCES)
Attachment of (See ATTACHMENT)
Attorney's authority to appear in action (See ATTORNEYS, subhead: Appearance)
Chattel actions (See CHATTEL ACTIONS)
Conveyances
  Certification of acknowledgment . . 4538
  Outside state . . . 4524
Damages for property injury
  Contributory negligence or assumption of risk established, recovery not barred . . 1411
  Culpable conduct as factor . . . 1411
Definition for purposes of CPLR . . . 105(r)
Disclosure proceeding prior to commencement of action . . . 3102(c)
Evidence (See EVIDENCE)
Forfeiture actions by state (See FORFEITURE OF PROCEEDS OF CRIME)
Homestead exemption (See MONEY JUDGMENT—ENFORCEMENT PROCEDURES, subhead: Homestead exemption)
Jury trial . . . 4101(2)
Liens on real property (See LIENS)
Money judgment (See MONEY JUDGMENT—ENFORCEMENT PROCEDURES)
Mortgage on real property . . . 212

[References are to CPLR Sections, Rules and Appendices.]

**REAL PROPERTY ACTIONS**—Cont.

Notice of pendency, filing of (See NOTICE OF PENDENCY)

Proper party defendants, specification of . . 212

Property within state, made outside state, judgment sought affecting interest or title to specified property; no personal jurisdiction resulting
    Authority . . . 314
    Persons authorized to make service . . . . 314

Real Property Law . . . App

Receiver, appointment of . . . 5106

Redemption from mortgage, action by mortgagor . . . 212

Referee, appointment of . . . 5103(b)

Sale for enforcement of money judgment
    Conveyance to sheriff . . . 5107; 5236(f)
    Disposition of proceeds, priority . . . . . . 5236(g)
    Entry of judgment, effect . . . 5103(a)
    Execution, sale pursuant to . . . 5236
    Failure of title of property sold, recovery of purchase price from paid judgment creditors . . . 5237
    Generally . . . 5106
    Irregularity in sale, effect . . . 5237
    Judgment creditors, failure to respond to notice, effect . . . 5236(e)
    Mortgaged property . . . 5236(b)
    Notice of sale . . . 5236(c)
    Place of sale
        County where property is situated . . . 5103(a)
        Generally . . . 5236(a)
        Other than county in which judgment is entered . . . 5103(a)
    Postponement of sale, request for notice of . . . 5236(d)
    Procedure . . . 5236
    Proceeds from sale, distribution among judgment creditors, priority of . . . 5236(g)
    Proof of, filing . . . 5236(f)
    Public auction . . . 5236(a)
    Receiver, appointment of . . . 5106
    Referee appointed for . . . 5103(b)
    Reversal or setting aside of judgment, effect . . . 5237
    Time of sale . . . 5236(a)

Sheriff's fees for sale of . . . 8011(g)

Statutes of limitations (See STATUTES OF LIMITATIONS)

Venue for trial . . . 507

Voluntary discontinuance of action, without order; exclusion of parcels of land . . . 3217(a)(3)

**REAL PROPERTY LAW**

Selected practice provisions . . . App

**RECEIVERS AND RECEIVERSHIP**

Accounts, maintenance and inspection of . . . . 6404

Commissions of receivers
    Allowance when funds depleted . . . . . . 8004(b)
    Generally . . . 8004(a)

Crime, for property subject to action for forfeiture of proceeds of (See FORFEITURE OF PROCEEDS OF CRIME)

Forfeiture of proceeds of crime (See FORFEITURE OF PROCEEDS OF CRIME, subhead: Receiver, temporary)

Money judgment, enforcement of
    Appointment of receiver for purpose of, procedure . . . 5228(a)
    Extension of receivership . . . 5228(b)

Oath of temporary receiver . . . 6402

Provisional remedy, receivership as . . . 6001

Removal upon motion or own initiative, power of court making appointment . . . 6405

Substitution of parties, order of . . . 1017

Temporary receiver
    Appointment of, authorization . . 6401(a)
    Duration of receivership . . . 6401(c)
    Forfeiture of proceeds of crime (See FORFEITURE OF PROCEEDS OF CRIME, subhead: Receiver, temporary)
    Joinder of moving party . . . 6401(a)
    Powers of . . . 6401(b)
    Removal of . . . 6405
    Undertaking by, amount set by court . . . 6403

Undertaking by temporary receiver, amount set by court . . . 1340; 6403

**RECORDS AND RECORDING**

Appeals (See APPEALS)

Clerk of court (See CLERK OF COURT, subhead: Records and books of)

Express trusts, recording of instruments settling accounts of . . . 7705

Foreign records, proof of . . . 4542

Paternity test, record of . . . 4518(d)

Sheriff's records of executions . . . 5230(d)

Undertaking, maintenance by county clerk . . . 9701(2); 9702(4)

**RECOVERY ACTIONS**

Chattel, action to try right of possession (See CHATTEL ACTIONS)

State's action to recover forfeiture or penalty (See PENALTIES)

[References are to CPLR Sections, Rules and Appendices.]

**REFEREES**

Appeal
Judgment entered on referee's report . . . 5525(b)
Review of findings on appeal . . . 4511(c)

Appointment and delegation of power by court, authorization . . . 4001

Article 78 proceedings . . . 7804(h),(i)

Attorney, designation in good standing . . . . . 4312(1)

Conduct of trial
Referee to determine, trial by; applicability of court trial provisions . . . 4318
Referee to report, trial by . . . 4320(a)

Corporation, referee for determination of issue involving . . . 4317(a)

Decision of
Court's decision, requirements pertaining to; compliance of referee's decision with . . . 4319
Filing requirement . . . 4319

Deposit by referee appointed to sell property . . . 2609

Designation of
Number authorized . . . 4312(1)
Objections to designation by all parties . . . 4312(2)

Determination of issue, referee for purpose of
Any party's motion or on court's own initiative, reference based on . . . 4317(b)
Conduct of trial by . . . 4318
Consent of parties . . . 4317(a)
Decision of referee . . . 4319
Delegation of powers, order of reference containing . . . 4311
Entry of judgment upon . . . 5016(c)
Powers authorized . . . 4301
Stipulation by parties, filing of, order of reference entered upon . . . 4317(a)

Disclosure (See DISCLOSURE, subhead: Supervision of disclosure)

Evidence, review of findings on appeal . . . . . 4511(c)

Express trusts, appointment of referee to examine and audit trustee's accounts . . . 7704

Fees and expenses
Commissions upon sale of real property . . . 8003(b)
Computation of . . . 4321
Consent to fee . . . 8003(a)
Disbursement taxable . . . 8301(a)(1)
Judicial hearing officer as referee . . . . . 8003(c)

Foreclosure, commission to act as referee on . . . 8003(b)

**REFEREES**—Cont.

Judicial hearing officer
Designation as referee . . . 3104(b)
Fees . . . 8003(c)
Powers of . . . 4301

Matrimonial action
Designation of referee for, requirements . . . 4312(2)
Uncontested action . . . 4312(5)

More than one, designation of
Action authorized by majority . . . 4316
Procedure during hearing . . . 4316

Motion for trial by referee, time limitation . . . 4015

Notice of order of reference . . . 4313

Number designated . . . 4312(2)

Oath of referee . . . 4315

Order of reference . . . 4311

Performance of act, referee for purpose of
Delegation of powers, order of reference containing . . . 4311
Powers authorized . . . 4301

Powers of
Administration of oaths by referee to inquire and report . . . 4201
All powers of court in performing like function, referee-to-determine . . . 4301
Court delegation of . . . 4001
Determine, powers to . . . 4301
Order of reference as specifying . . 4311
Report, powers to . . . 4201

Qualifications . . . 4312

Report, referee for purpose of
Conduct of trial by . . . 4320(a)
Confirmation or rejection by judge, motion directed at . . . 4403
Filing requirements . . . 4320(b)
Oaths, administration of . . . 4201
Powers . . . 4201
Submission of issues of fact to . . . 4212
Subpoenas, issuance of . . . 4201
Transcript and exhibits, filing with report . . . 4320(b)

Review of findings on appeal . . . 4511(c)

Sale of real property
Commissions upon . . . 8003(b)
Judgment or order directing, appointment of referee for purpose of . . . 5103(b)

Special referee . . . 4312(2)

Subpoenas, issuance of . . . 4201

Successor referee . . . 4314

Supervision of disclosure (See DISCLOSURE, subhead: Supervision of disclosure)

Trial by referee
(See also subhead: Conduct of trial)

[References are to CPLR Sections, Rules and Appendices.]

**REFEREES**—Cont.
Trial by referee—Cont.
    Motion for, time for . . . 4015
    Order of reference . . . 4311
Trustee's account, examination and auditing, referee's appointment for . . . 7704

**REFORMATION OF INSTRUMENTS**
Election of remedies . . . 3002(d)

**RELEASE**
Dismiss, release of moving party as ground for motion to . . . 3211(a)(5)

**REMEDIES**
Election of (See ELECTION OF REMEDIES)
Provisional remedies (See PROVISIONAL REMEDIES)

**REMITTITUR**
Appeal . . . 5524(b)

**REMOVAL OF ACTION**
Calendar conditions as factor . . . 325(d)
Costs awarded in . . . 8104
Forum non conveniens
    Court's discretion to stay or dismiss action on motion of party
        Contracts to which GOL § 51402 applies, mandatory enforcement of choice of forum clauses in . . 327(b)
        Domicile or residence of any party within state as no bar to court's action . . . 327(a)
Grounds for removal . . . 325
Jury trial, waiver of
    Supreme court to surrogate's court, right to jury trial preserved in later proceeding . . . 325(e)
    Waiver of, removal to proper jurisdiction; inoperativeness of prior waiver . . . . . 322(b)
Limited jurisdiction, court of
    On consent of . . . 325(c)
    Removal to or from . . . 325(b)
    Without consent of . . . 325(d)
Lower court, removal to
    Damages sustained apparently less than amount demanded, reduction to sum within jurisdictional limits of lower court . . . 325(c); 325(d)
    From one lower court to another . . . . . . 325(g)
Mistaken choice of court, commencement of action in; removal upon motion in supreme court . . . 325(a)

**REMOVAL OF ACTION**—Cont.
Previous payments, crediting provisions . . . . . 326(c)
Procedures on removal
    Fees and disbursements, previous payments; crediting provisions . . . 326(c)
    Order of removal, filing certified copy with clerk of court where action pending . . 326(b)
    Papers and records in action, delivery to clerk of court to which action removed . . . 326(b)
    Stay of proceedings during, order directing . . . 326(a)
Stay of proceedings during, order directing . . . 326(a)
Supreme court, motion to remove; ground for granting
    County court judge, incapacitation of . . . 325(f)
    Mistaken choice of court, commencement of action in . . . 325(a)
Surrogate's court, removal to; action affecting decedent's estate
    Jury trial, right preserved in later proceeding . . . 325(e)
    Prior order by surrogate's court for removal . . . 325(e)
Undertaking of party, effect of removal on . . . 2504(b)

**REPLEVIN** (See CHATTEL ACTIONS)

**REPLY**
Article 78 proceedings
    Counterclaim, reply to . . . 7804(d)
    Service, time for . . . 7804(c)
Special proceedings
    Service of, time limits . . . 403(b)
    When utilized . . . 402

**RESCISSION**
Fraud or misrepresentation as basis . . 3002(e)

**RESIDENCE**
Admission to practice
    Generally . . . 9403
    Proof of . . . 9406(2)
False name, statutes of limitations on use of (See STATUTES OF LIMITATIONS, subhead: False name, residence in state under)
Nonresident (See NONRESIDENT)
Statutes of limitations (See STATUTES OF LIMITATIONS, subhead: False name, residence in state under)
Venue (See VENUE)

[References are to CPLR Sections, Rules and Appendices.]

**RES JUDICATA**
Dismiss based upon, motion to . . . 3211(a)(5)

**RESPONSIVE PLEADINGS**
Affirmative defenses . . . 3018(b)
Denials . . . 3018(a)

**RESTITUTION**
Appeals; restitution of property or rights, power of court to order . . . 5523
Relief from judgment or order . . . 5015(d)

**RESTORATION OF BENEFITS**
Judgment unnecessary, before . . . 3004

**RESTRAINING NOTICES**
Money judgments, enforcement of (See MONEY JUDGMENT—ENFORCEMENT PROCEDURES)

**RETIREMENT BENEFITS**
Money judgment, exemption from application to satisfaction of . . . 5205(c)
Periodic payments under retirement or pension contract, action for sum due; no bar to action to recover future payments when due . . . 3003

# S

**SALE OF GOODS**
Pleading of . . . 3016(f)

**SATISFACTION OF JUDGMENT**
Entry of satisfaction
Certificate by issuing county clerk as authority for entry in any county where docketed . . . 5021(c)
Debtor and Creditor Law, instrument of discharge filed pursuant to, entry conditioned upon . . . 5021(a)(4)
Deposit of sum of money, condition to entry . . . 5021(a)(3)
Order of court, entry pursuant to . . . . . 5021(a)(2)
Return of execution by sheriff, entry upon . . . 5021(b)
Satisfaction- or partial satisfaction-piece, filing of; condition to entry . . . . . . . 5021(a)(1)
Execution on judgment, issuance prior to . . . . 5230(b)
Exemption (See MONEY JUDGMENT—ENFORCEMENT PROCEDURES, subhead: Personal property, enforcement against)
Satisfaction-piece or partial satisfaction-piece
Attorney's execution of . . . 5020(b)

**SATISFACTION OF JUDGMENT**—Cont.
Satisfaction-piece or partial satisfaction-piece—Cont.
Demand by judgment debtor, failure to respond, penalty for . . . 5020
Docketing in other counties, transcripts of docket judgment . . . 5020(d)
Execution and delivery of . . . 5020(a), (b)
Filing requirement . . . 5020
Full satisfaction of judgment, filing requirements following; failure to execute or refusal to satisfy . . . 5020(c)
Judgment debtor, copy mailed to by person entitled to enforce judgment . . 5020(a)
Statutory penalty on failure to file . . . . . 5020(c)
Who may execute . . . 5020
Unclaimed or undeliverable payment requiring deposit of certified check with clerk of court . . . 5020-a

**SAVING CLAUSE** (See CIVIL PRACTICE LAWS AND RULES (GENERALLY))

**SCHOOL DISTRICT**
Personal service on; persons who may be served, specification of . . . 311(a)
Specification . . . 311(a)
Venue for actions against . . . 504

**SEALED INSTRUMENT, ACTION ON**
Six-year statute of limitations . . . 213

**SECURITY DEPOSITS**
Personal property exemption from application to satisfy money judgment
Rental of real property for residence . . . 5205(g)
Utilities, deposits with . . . 5205(g)

**SECURITY FOR COSTS**
Assignee for benefit of creditors . . . 8501(b)
Committee of incompetent required to give security . . . 8501(b)
Conservatee's estate, protection of . . . 8501(b)
Conservator, requirement as to court's discretion . . . 8501(b)
Dismissal on failure to give security . . . 8502
Domestic corporation, exemption for . . 8501(a)
Executors and administrators required to give security . . . 8501(b)
Failure to give security . . . 8502
Foreign corporation's license to do business in state, exemption for . . . 8501(a)
Guardian ad litem . . . 8501(b)
Habeas corpus petitioner . . . 8501(a)

[References are to CPLR Sections, Rules and Appendices.]

**SECURITY FOR COSTS**—Cont.

Incompetent persons, protection of estate of . . 8501(b)

Motion, discretionary . . . 8501(b)

Stay of proceedings . . . 8502

Time for payment of security . . . 8502

Trustee for benefit of creditors . . . 8501(b)

Undertaking . . . 8503

**SEIZURE OF CHATTEL** (See CHATTEL ACTIONS)

**SELF INCRIMINATION**

Privilege against . . . 4501

**SEPARATE TRIAL**

Authority . . . 603

Permissive joinder of parties, prejudices and expenses resulting from . . . 1002(c)

Third-party complaint, order of separate trial; court's discretion over . . . 1010

**SEPARATION ACTION**

Matrimonial actions

Generally (See MATRIMONIAL ACTIONS)

Separation action as term including . . . . 105(p)

Pleading involving, particularity required in complaint . . . 3016(c)

Summary judgment, availability of motion, limitations . . . 312(b)

**SERVICE OF SUMMONS AND PAPERS**

Affidavit . . . 4531

Agents for service

Attorney, designation as agent . . . 303

Clerk of court, designation as agent . . . . 303

Courts of state, use by person not subject to personal jurisdiction; designation of agent in separate action . . . 303

Designation of agent, generally . . . 318

Matrimonial actions, inapplicability of section to . . . 308

Personal service on natural person, delivery to agent designated under CPLR 318 . . . 308

Amendments; proof of service . . . 305(c)

Article 78 proceedings . . . 7804(c),(i)

Attachment order

Death of defendant prior to service, effect . . . 6213

Extension of time limitation . . . 6213

Service outside of state, authorization . . . 314; 314(3)

Sixty-day limitation for service . . . 6213

**SERVICE OF SUMMONS AND PAPERS**—Cont.

Attorney general (See ATTORNEY GENERAL, subhead: State bodies or officers, papers served upon)

Attorney, service upon . . . 2103(b)

Boards and commissions, personal service on, persons who may be served . . . 312

Chattel actions . . . 314

Commencement of action

Generally . . . 304

Statute of limitations, effect . . . 203(b)

Common informer, action to recover statutory penalty or forfeiture by, service of summons . . . 7203(b)

Complaint, service with . . . 3012

Conservatee, personal service upon . . . 309(c)

Corporation, personal service upon . . . 311(a); 311(b)

Costs and disbursements, taxation of

Bill of costs . . . 8403

Re-taxation, notice of . . . 8403

County, personal service on

Method . . . 311(a)

Persons may be served, specification . . . 311(a)

Court order, manner of making personal service directed by . . . 308

Courts, three or more judges, personal service on . . . 312

Default judgment (See DEFAULT AND DEFAULT JUDGMENTS, subhead: Summons, service of)

Defense by person to whom not personally, delivered

Annulment, action for, inapplicability of section to . . . 317

Conditions to allowance, necessary findings by court

Actual notice not received . . . 317

Appearance, party's failure to make . . . 317

Meritorious defense, existence of . . 317

CPLR 318 agent, inapplicability of section to . . . 317

Divorce action, inapplicability of section to . . . 317

Effect of successful defense, court's order of restitution . . . 317

Partition, action for, inapplicability of section to . . . 317

Time for asserting defense

Entry of judgment, knowledge of, computation from . . . 317

[References are to CPLR Sections, Rules and Appendices.]

**SERVICE OF SUMMONS AND PAPERS—**
Cont.

Defense by person to whom not personally, delivered—Cont.

Time for asserting defense—Cont.

Limitation; more than five years after entry of judgment . . . 317

Divorce action . . . 317

Electronic means, service by

Definition . . . 2103(f)

Generally . . . 2103(b)(5)

Extrajurisdictional proceedings, service in connection with

Court order

Pursuant to . . . 328(a)

Without . . . 328(b)

Recognition or enforcement of decree, effect on . . . 328(c)

Filing

Generally . . . 2103(d)

Papers . . . 2102

Forfeiture, action to recover . . . 7203(b)

Forfeiture of proceeds of crime (See FORFEITURE OF PROCEEDS OF CRIME)

Governmental subdivisions, personal service on (See GOVERNMENTAL SUBDIVISIONS)

Income execution (See INCOME EXECUTION)

Incompetent person, personal service upon committee and incompetent within state . . . . . . 309(b)

Infant, personal service upon, methods . . . . . 309(a)

Interposition of claim, service of summons upon defendant

Method . . . 203(b)

Provisional remedy order, death of defendant within 30 days thereafter; delivery within 60 days of issuance of letters . . 203(b)

Sheriff, summons delivered to . . . 203(b)

Joint liabilities, action based on; service on less than all named defendants . . . 1501

Mail, personal service by

Acknowledgment of receipt; form . . . . . 312-a(d)

Affirmation . . . 312-a(c)

Certified mail to specified officer of state agency . . . 307

Completion of service . . . 312-a(b)

Definition of mailing . . . 2103(f)

Disbursements . . . 312-a(f)

Form . . . 312-a(d)

Natural person, upon . . . 308

Overnight mail service of attorneys . . . . 2103(b)(6)

Procedure of service . . . 312-a(a)

**SERVICE OF SUMMONS AND PAPERS—**
Cont.

Mail, personal service by—Cont.

Publication in matrimonial actions . . . . . 316(b)

Statement of service; form . . . 312-a(d)

Subsequent service . . . 312-a(e)

Substituted service . . . 308

Time to answer . . . 312-a(b)(2)

Matrimonial actions

Personal service on natural person . . 308

Publication, service by

Mailing to accompany . . . 316(b)

Order necessary to direct . . . 316(b)

Time of completion . . . 316(c)

Service without state, no personal jurisdiction resulting . . . 314

Medical malpractice actions, default judgment sum as bar to publication . . . 316(a)

Methods . . . 2103

Natural person, personal service (See subhead: Personal service, methods)

Notice contained in summons without complaint

Object of action . . . 305(b)

Relief sought . . . 305(b)

Sum to be taken in case of default, actions for sums certain or ascertainable by computation . . . 305(b)

Notice of pendency

Death of defendant prior to service . . . . 6512

Generally . . . 6512

Order, service of; method . . . 2220

Overnight mail, service of attorneys by . . . . . 2103(b)(6)

Parties . . . 2103(e)

Partnerships

Affixing copy of summons to actual place of business . . . 310(c)

Agent or employee authorized by appointment to receive service . . . 310(d)

Court motion of service . . . 310(e)

Generally . . . 310(a)

Managing or general agent, personal service upon . . . 310(b)

Personal service, methods

Conservatee, personal service upon . . . . 309(c)

Corporation, personal service upon . . . . 311(a); 311(b)

County, personal service on

Method . . . 311(a)

Persons may be served, specification . . . 311(a)

[References are to CPLR Sections, Rules and Appendices.]

**SERVICE OF SUMMONS AND PAPERS—**
Cont.
Personal service, methods—Cont.
    Governmental subdivisions (See GOVERN-
      MENTAL SUBDIVISIONS)
    Incompetent persons . . . 309(b)
    Infant, service on . . . 309(a)
    Mailing (See subhead: Mail, personal service
      by)
    Natural person, service on
      Agent for service designated under
        CPLR 318, delivery upon, personal
        service on principal affected by
        . . . 308
      Delivery to person within state . . . .
        308
      Impracticability of specified methods
        for service, court-ordered method
        authorized . . . 308
      Mailing, by . . . 308
      Matrimonial actions, exception . . . .
        308
      Substituted service (See subhead: Sub-
        stituted service)
    Partnership (See subhead: Partnerships)
    Proof of service . . . 306(b)
    State, service upon . . . 307
    Without state (See subhead: Without state,
      place of service)
Persons serving . . . 2103(a)
Preliminary injunction . . . 6311
Proof of service
    Acknowledgment . . . 306(d)
    Admission of service . . . 306(e)
    Amendment, allowance; power of court over
      . . . 305(c)
    Elements of . . . 306
    Filing
      Failure to file proof of service, dis-
        missal of action for . . . 306-b
      Time limitations for . . . 306-b
    Requirements of
      Form . . . 306(d)
      Other service . . . 306(c)
      Personal service . . . 306(b)
    Subpoenas . . . 2303
    Substituted service, time and place for filing
      proof . . . 308
Publication, service by
    Appearance by defendant during publication
      period; completion of publication estab-
      lished as result . . . 320(d)
    Authority . . . 315
    Duration of publication; four successive
      weeks, at least once in each week of,
      requirement . . . 316(a)

**SERVICE OF SUMMONS AND PAPERS—**
Cont.
Publication, service by—Cont.
    Matrimonial actions
      Mailing to accompany . . . 316(b)
      Order necessary to direct . . . 316(b)
      Time of completion . . . 316(c)
    Order directing service by publication
      Contents, requirements . . 316(a), (b)
      Default judgment, sum . . . 316(a)
      Divorce action, necessity for order to
        direct . . . 316(b)
      Matrimonial action, necessity for order
        to direct . . . 316(b)
      Medical malpractice actions, default
        judgment sum as bar to publication
        . . . 316(a)
      Separation action, necessity for order
        to direct . . . 316(b)
    Outside state, place of service
      Authority for service by publication
        . . . 315
      Court order on motion directing publi-
        cation, contents . . . 316
      Inability to effect service by other pre-
        scribed method, due diligence re-
        quirement, necessary showing . . .
        315
    Time for publication, 20 days after order
      granted, first publication required to be
      made within . . . 316(c)
    Two newspapers, publication in, requirement
      . . . 316(a)
Recovery of statutory penalty or forfeiture, action
    by common informer . . . 7203(b)
Sheriff or authorized officer
    Service of summons . . . 8011(h)
    Time limitation on delivery (See STAT-
      UTES OF LIMITATIONS)
State bodies or officers, proceedings against com-
    menced by service; requirement for service
    upon attorney general . . . 7804(c)
State, personal service upon, manner of effecting
    . . . 307
Statute of limitations (See STATUTES OF LIMI-
    TATIONS)
Subpoena (See SUBPOENAS)
Substituted service
    Completion of service, time requirement
      . . . 308
    Court order, manner of service directed by;
      impracticability of specified methods, nec-
      essary showing . . . 308
    Mailing and affixing summons . . . 308

**SERVICE OF SUMMONS AND PAPERS—** Cont.

Substituted service—Cont.
Place for service on substituted party, specification . . . 308
Time for filing . . . 308
Temporary restraining order . . . 6313(b)
Undertakings . . . 2505
Venue (See VENUE)
Without state, place of service
In rem jurisdiction resulting . . . 314
Matrimonial action, service without state
No personal jurisdiction resulting . . 314
Persons authorized to make service . . . 314
No personal jurisdiction resulting
Authority . . . 314
Property within state, service outside state; judgment sought affecting interest to title to specified property . . . 314
Publication, service by, court order directing; authority and conditions to . . . 315
Specified actions . . . 314
Personal jurisdiction resulting, generally . . . 313
Property within state, service outside state; no personal jurisdiction resulting
Attachment order, action commenced and property levied pursuant to . . . 314
Title to or interest in specified property, judgment sought affecting . . 314

**SETTLEMENT OF ACTION**

Default judgment, entry upon failure to comply with stipulation of settlement . . . 3215(i)
Incompetent, settlement of claim or action by, methods (See INCOMPETENT PERSONS)
Infant, settlement of claim or action by, methods (See INFANTS AND MINORS)
Prompt payment following (See JUDGMENTS)
Proof, mitigation of damages and . . . 4533–b

**SEVERANCE**

Authority . . . 603
Costs awarded in . . . 8104
Default judgment, entry against less than all defendants . . . 3215(a)
Permissive joinder of parties, prejudices and expenses resulting from, court's power to order separate relief and trials as remedy . . . . . . 1002(c)

**SEVERANCE—**Cont.

Special proceedings, court's power regarding, authorization . . . 407
Summary judgment, cause of action of . . . . . 3212(e)(1)

**SEWAGE DISTRICTS**

Service of summons . . . 311(a)

**SHERIFF, CONSTABLE AND OTHER OFFICERS**

Advance payment as reimbursement for expenses . . . 8013(d)
Arrest, fees for serving or executing order of . . . 8011(h)
Attachment orders, duties pursuant to
After, levy, sheriff's duties
Inventory . . . 6218(b)
Retention of property . . . 6218(a)
Directions to levy property in which defendant has interest, order of attachment specifying . . . 6211
Execution issued on judgment against defendant, priority of duties as to . . . 6226
Fees . . . 8011(a)
Personal property, levy by service of order . . . 6214(a), (b)
Poundage fees . . . 8012(b)(3)
Priority among two or more orders against same defendant . . . 6226
Real property, levy upon . . . 6216
Return of property on direction of court . . . 6225
Seizure of personal property as alternate means of levy . . . 6215
Seizure of property capable of delivery . . . 6214(c); 6215
Chattel, seizure of (See CHATTEL ACTIONS)
Civil process, service of (See subhead: Fees)
Claiming agent defined, forfeiture of proceeds of crime, New York City . . . 1310(12)
Constables' services, fees for . . . 8011(k)
Executions against property
Fees
Collection of fees . . . 8014
Generally . . . 8011(b)
Records, requirement of . . . 5230(d)
Expenses, reimbursement for
Advance payment, sheriff's discretion as to necessity . . . 8013(d)
Appraisal of attached property . . 8013(b)
Collection on execution against property, where authorized . . . 8014
Fees (See subhead: Fees)
Generally . . . 8013(c), 8013(d)
Publication of notice of sale . . . 8013(a)

[References are to CPLR Sections, Rules and Appendices.]

**SHERIFF, CONSTABLE AND OTHER OFFI-CERS**—Cont.

Fees

Additional compensation at court's discretion . . . 8012(c)

Arrest, serving or executing order of . . . 8011(h)

Attachment . . . 8011(a)

Chattel, recovery of
Generally . . . 8011(e)
Payment to sheriff on request . . . . 7106(a)

Collection on execution, nonstatutory designation of payment . . . 8014

Constables' services . . . 8011(k)

Copies . . . 8011(i)

Disbursement of, taxable . . . 8301(a)(8)

Execution against property
Collection of fees . . . 8014
Generally . . . 8011(b)

Income execution; judgment debtor, service upon . . . 8011(c)

Incompetency precept . . . 8011(h)

Judgment debtor, income execution served upon . . . 8011(c)

Jurors, notification and attendance of . . . 8011(k)

Prisoners, handling . . . 8011(j)

Returns . . . 8011(i)

Sales of real or personal property . . . . . 8011(g)

Subpoenas, service of . . . 8011(h)

Summary proceeding . . . 8011(f)

Summons, service of . . . 8011(h)

Undertakings . . . 8011(i)

View, attending . . . 8011(k); 8012(a)(3)

Forfeiture of proceeds of crime, claiming agent defined, New York City . . . 1310(12)

Income execution, fees for
Judgment debtor
Levy upon default or failure to serve . . . 8011(d)
Service upon . . . 8011(c)

Incompetency precept, fees for . . . 8011(h)

Inventory of seized property pursuant to attachment order . . . 6218(b)

Jurors, fees for notification and attendance of . . . 8011(k)

Mailed payment to creditor returned as undeliverable or unclaimed, procedure for satisfaction; notification to sheriff . . . 5020-a

Mileage fees for specified services
Generally . . . 8012(a)
New York City . . . 8012(d)

**SHERIFF, CONSTABLE AND OTHER OFFI-CERS**—Cont.

Poundage fees
Attachment order, levy by . . . 8012(b)(3)
Collection of money . . . 8012(b)(1)
Levy by virtue of execution . . 8012(b)(2)

Prisoners, fees for handling . . . 8011(j)

Property in which judgment debtor has interest held by, directions by court regarding . . . . 5238

Sales of real or personal property, fees for . . . 8011(g)

Statutes of limitations (See STATUTES OF LIMITATIONS)

Subpoenas, fees for service of . . . 8011(h)

Summary proceeding, fees for . . . 8011(f)

Summons
Delivery to sheriff, time limitation (See STATUTES OF LIMITATIONS)
Sheriff's fees for service of summons . . . 8011(h)

Undertakings
Fees for . . . 8011(i)
Public officer, damages fixed in lieu of undertaking by . . . 2512(2)

View, attending; fees . . . 8011(k); 8012(a)(3)

**SHOW CAUSE ORDERS**

Article 78 proceedings . . . 7804(c)

Death of party and substitution of parties; dismissal of action by court . . . 1021; 5016(d)

Habeas corpus
Appeal from judgment on refusal . . 7011
Generally . . . 7003(a)

Notice motion, in lieu of; grant of show cause order . . . 2214(d)

Service in lieu of notice of petition, order granted by court; authorization . . . 403(d)

Service of . . . 2211

State bodies or officers, order upon
Generally . . . 2214(d)
Procedure . . . 7804(c)

**SIDEWALKS**

Villages, actions against . . . 9804

**SIMPLIFIED PROCEDURE**

Appeal from, limitations on right . . . 3037

Authorization . . . 3035

Commencement by service of summons, no necessity for, authorization . . . 3031

Contract to submit existing or future controversy
Enforcement of . . . 3033(1)
Jury trial, waiver of, contract constituting . . . 3033(1)

[References are to CPLR Sections, Rules and Appendices.]

## SIMPLIFIED PROCEDURE—Cont.

Costs and disbursements, discretion of court to award . . . 3036(9)

Court determination . . . 3036

Death of parties, CPLR provisions regarding, applicability to simplified procedure . . . . . 3036(8)

Default judgment, when authorized . . 3036(4)

Evidence during

    Admissibility, rules related to, dispensing of . . . 3036(1)

    Expert witness, evidence obtained by . . . 3036(2)

    Technicality of, compliance with; limitation on . . . 3035(b); 3036(1)

Implementation . . . 3035(a)

Incompetency of parties, CPLR provisions related to, applicability to simplified procedure . . . . 3036(8)

Judgments

    Entry and enforcement provisions of CPLR . . . 3036(8)

    Judgment-roll, contents . . . 3036(7)

Jury trial, waiver of submission of controversy under simplified procedure constituting . . . . 3031

Note of issue, filing of . . . 3036(6)

Pleadings, no necessity for . . . 3031

Practice under . . . 3035(c)

Pretrial conference

    Questions of law, disposition of . . . . . . 3035(a)

    Scope . . . 3036(5)

Purpose . . . 3035(a)

Settlement by court on motion, dispute over terms

    Authorization . . . 3033(2)

    Execution or noncompliance with contract, substantial question regarding . . . . . . 3034(3)

    Motion procedure . . . 3034

Statement of parties

    Contents . . . 3032

    Filing requirement . . . 3031

    Necessary recitals . . . 3031

    Signing and acknowledgment of . . 3031

Stay of other action or proceeding, when authorized . . . 3036(3)

Venue . . . 3036(8)

## SLANDER ACTION

Damages, action for; statute of limitations . . . 215

Pleading, particularization of words complained of . . . 3016(a)

## SMALL CLAIMS ACTIONS

Corporation as defendant, appearance by shareholder or corporate officer . . . 321(a)

Unsatisfied judgments, entry on judgment docket . . . 5021(b)

## SOCIAL WORKERS

Confidential communications . . . 4508

## SOLE PROPRIETORSHIP

Interrogatory sent to, manner of answering . . . 3134(a)

## SONOGRAMS

Evidence, admissibility as . . . 4532-a

Personal injury actions, admissibility in . . . . . 4532-a

## SPECIAL PROCEEDINGS

Answer and reply

    Service of, time limits . . . 403(b)

    When utilized . . . 402

Arbitration, application to court for . . 7502(a)

Article 78 proceedings (See ARTICLE 78 PROCEEDINGS)

Commencement, methods of . . . 304

Defects in papers, motion to correct

    Petitioner, objection by . . . 405(c)

    Specified defects . . . 405(a)

    Time limits . . . 405(b)

Defined . . . 105(b)

Disclosure during, permission of court required for . . . 408

Enforcement of agreement that issue or controversy be determined by person named or to be selected . . . 7601

Express trust (See EXPRESS TRUST PROCEEDINGS)

Habeas corpus as . . . 7001

Hearing, procedure upon, papers furnished court by parties . . . 409(a)

Incompetent persons, settlement of action by . . . 1207

Infants, settlement of action by . . . 1207

Interpleader, allowance, condition to . . . 401

Intervention, when allowed . . . 401

Joinder, allowance, condition to . . . 401

Judgment, court's determination entered as . . . 411

Jury trial, fact issues triable of right by jury

    Demand for jury trial, opportunity given parties, requirement . . . 410

    Waiver, how effected . . . 410

Money judgment, enforcement, proceedings for purpose of (See MONEY JUDGMENT—ENFORCEMENT PROCEDURES)

[References are to CPLR Sections, Rules and Appendices.]

**SPECIAL PROCEEDINGS**—Cont.

Motions
    Defects in papers, motions to correct (See
        subhead: Defects in papers, motions to
        correct)
    Time for . . . 406
Notice of petition
    Affidavits in support, accompaniment . . .
        403(a)
    Service with petition and affidavits
        Manner of service . . . 403(c)
        Specification thereon, requirements
            . . . 403(a)
        Time for . . . 403(b)
Objections in point of law, manner of and time for
    raising
    Petitioner, objections by . . . 404(b)
    Respondent, objections by . . . 404(a)
Papers furnished court upon hearing . . . 409(a)
Parties, how denominated . . . 401
Petition
    Adverse party, absence of, necessary recitals
        . . . 402
    Complaint in action, compliance with re-
        quirements for . . . 402
    Notice of (See subhead: Notice of petition)
Pleadings and procedure
    Action
        Pleadings authorized in, discretion of
            court regarding use of . . . 402
        Procedure for . . . 103(b)
    Answer and reply
        Service of, time limits . . . 403(b)
        When utilized . . . 402
    Defects in papers, motion to correct
        Petitioner, objection by . . . 405(c)
        Specified defects . . . 405(a)
        Time limits . . . 405(b)
    Denomination . . . 402
    Time for noticing motion; motions made
        prior to time petition notice to be heard
        . . . 406
Procedure for action . . . 103(b)
Property paid into court, disbursement of . . . .
    2606(2)
Reply and answer
    Service of, time limits . . . 403(b)
    When utilized . . . 402
Severance of claims or party, power of court to
    order, authorization . . . 407
Show cause order; service in lieu of notice of
    petition, order granted by court; authorization
    . . . 403(d)
Striking of pleadings
    Correction of defects in papers . . 405(a)

**SPECIAL PROCEEDINGS**—Cont.

Striking of pleadings—Cont.
    New matter contained in answer . . . . . .
        404(b)
Summary determinations by court, extent allowed
    . . . 409(b)
Third-party practice, when allowed . . . 401
Trials of issues of fact
    Jury trial, issues triable of right by
        Demand for jury trial, opportunity
            given parties, requirement . . 410
        Waiver, how effected . . . 410
    When allowed . . . 410
Trusts, special proceedings relating to (See EX-
    PRESS TRUST PROCEEDINGS)
Venue (See VENUE)

**SPOUSES**

Adultery, incompetency of spouse to testify . .
    4502(a)
Confidential communications between . . . . . .
    4502(b)
Marriage certificate, prima facie evidence of mar-
    riage established by . . . 4526
Matrimonial actions (See MATRIMONIAL AC-
    TIONS)
Witness where spouse is party to action, compe-
    tency as . . . 4512

**STAKEHOLDERS** (See INTERPLEADER)

**STATE, ACTIONS BY OR AGAINST**

Costs, recovery of
    Counsel fees and expenses, award of (See
        subhead: Counsel fees and expenses,
        award of)
    Municipal corporation, action by state in
        behalf of . . . 8109(a)
    Public officers, actions by . . . 8109(b)
Counsel fees and expenses, award of
    Annual report . . . 8604
    Applicability . . . 8605
    Application for fees . . . 8601(b)
    Definitions . . . 8602
    Interest . . . 8603
    New York State Equal Access to Justice Act,
        intent of . . . 8600
    When awarded . . . 8601(a)
Disclosure rules, availability when state party to
    action . . . 3102(f)
Expenses, award of (See subhead: Counsel fees
    and expenses, award of)
Forfeiture of proceeds of crime (See FORFEI-
    TURE OF PROCEEDS OF CRIME)
Name of state, action brought in
    No necessity for; situation . . . 1301

[References are to CPLR Sections, Rules and Appendices.]

## STATE, ACTIONS BY OR AGAINST—Cont.

Name of state, action brought in—Cont.

When required; actions brought in people's behalf . . . 1301

Personal service upon state, method; attorney-general or assistant, delivery to within state . . . 307

Preliminary injunction to restrain public officer from performing statutory duties, notice of motion for . . . 6311

Procedure, action by state . . . 1303

Relation or information of person, action by attorney general based on; conditions . . . 1302

Statute of limitations

Cause of action, commencement of action on . . . 202

Twenty-year period, action to sue for or with respect to real property . . . 211

Trial preference, allowance of . . . 3403

Undertaking by, damages fixed in lieu of . . . . 2512(2)

## STATUTES OF LIMITATIONS

Abbreviation after notice; action to recover money . . . 216

Absence of defendant from state

Designated person for receipt of summons, voluntary or involuntary designation, existence of . . . 207

Foreign corporation, officer within state . . . 207

Jurisdiction over defendant, ability to obtain without personal service within state . . . 207

Account, mutual, open and current, time for commencement of action; last transaction, computation from . . . 206(d)

Accrual of cause of action . . . 203(a)

Accrued actions at time of effective date, status under CPLR

Accrued but not barred actions, longer of applicable limitations periods, action to be governed by . . . 218

Barred action at time of effective date . . . 218

Action accruing without state . . . 202

Agent, misconduct of . . . 206(b)

Alimony . . . 211

Amended pleading, claim asserted in; original pleading, claim deemed interposed at time of; condition . . . 203(f)

Annulment or dissolution of marriage, fraud as grounds for . . . 214

Appeal (See APPEALS, subhead: Time limitations)

## STATUTES OF LIMITATIONS—Cont.

Arbitration (See ARBITRATION PROCEEDINGS, subhead: Statutes of limitations)

Architects and engineers, notice of claim requirement in action involving licensed; effect on tolling of statute of limitations . . . 214-d

Article 78 proceedings . . . 217

Assault and battery . . . 215

Body or officer, proceeding against; 4-month limitations period . . . 217

Bond or note

Six-year period . . . 213

Twenty-year period . . . 211

Chattel actions

Damages for taking or detaining . . . 214

Interposition of claim, seizure as provisional remedy for purposes of determining . . . 203(b)

Recovery of . . . 214

Three-year period . . . 214

Common informer, actions to recover statutory penalties . . . 215

Computation methods . . . 203

Contract action, express or implied contracts

Interpleader situation, reduction of period to one year after notice given to adverse claimant; conditions . . . 216

Six-year limitations period . . . 213

Uniform Commercial Code, limitations period contained in; exception from subdivision . . . 213

Coroners, actions based on liability for acts or omissions of . . . 215

Corporations

Employee or stockholder, against; six-year period . . . 213

Six-year period . . . 213

Counterclaim

Death of party, action terminated due to . . . 203(e)

Dismissal or voluntary discontinuance of action . . . 203(e)

Interposition of, time for; computation

Same transaction, counterclaim arising from . . . 203(d)

Service of claim, counterclaim not barred at time of . . . 203(d)

New action by plaintiff or successor in interest, timeliness of . . . 205(b)

Termination of action for any reason . . . 205(b)

County judge disqualified from case . . . 9003

Court not of record, commencement of action in; statute of limitations

Authorized officer, delivery of summons for service to; time for interposing claim . . . 203(b)

[References are to CPLR Sections, Rules and Appendices.]

**STATUTES OF LIMITATIONS**—Cont.

Crime victim, action by . . . 213-b

Death of potential party

Claimant's death, commencement of action by representative, extension of one year from date of death; conditions to . . . . 210

Letters, accrual prior to grant of . . . 210

Party against whom a cause of action exists, death of

Eighteen months after date of death, extension of time for action against representative . . . 210

Defense

Bar to service of claim . . . 203(d)

Death terminating action, effect . . 203(e)

Dismissal or voluntary discontinuance terminating effect . . . 203(d)

Interposition . . . 203(d)

New action, effect . . . 205(b)

Same transaction, defense arising from, permissibility to extent of demand notwithstanding time bar . . . 203(d)

Termination of action for any reason; new action by plaintiff or successor in interest, timeliness of defense, determination . . 205(b)

Demand as condition to commencement of action, right to make demand . . . 206(a)

Discovery of facts, actual or imputed discovery; cases where limitations period computed from

Annulment of marriage on ground of fraud . . . 214

Commencement of action . . . 203(g)

Fraud, action based on . . . 213

Medical, dental, or podiatric malpractice; foreign object in patient's body . . . . . 214-a

Mistake, action based on . . . 213

Phenoxy herbicides, personal injury caused by . . . 214-b

Public property, spoliation or other misappropriation; state action . . . 213

Toxic substances, personal injury caused by . . . 214-c

Dismissal or voluntary discontinuance of action, affirmative action to recover on claim in defense . . . 203(e)

Dismiss based upon, motion to . . . 3211(a)(5)

Employee organization's breach of duty of fair representation . . . 217

Engineers and architects, notice of claim requirement in action involving licensed; effect on tolling of statute of limitations . . . 214-d

Execution on judgment, return of . . . 5230(c)

**STATUTES OF LIMITATIONS**—Cont.

Extension of limitations period (See EXTENSION OF TIME)

False imprisonment . . . 215

False name, residence in state under

Designated person for receipt of summons, existence of; inapplicability of tolling section . . . 207

Foreign corporation, officer within state . . . 207

Jurisdiction over defendant, ability to obtain without personal service within state; inapplicability of tolling section . . . 207

False words causing special damages . . . 215

Fraud action

Annulment or dissolution of marriage . . . 214

Six-year period . . . 213(8)

Incompetent person, statute of limitation on commenced by . . . 208

Infancy, extension due to . . . 208

Insanity, extension due to . . . 208

Intentional torts . . . 215

Interest overcharge or penalty for; one-year limitations period . . . 215

Interposition of claim, commencement of applicable period; computation factor

Amended pleading, claim in; deemed related back to original pleading . . . 203(f)

Co-defendant united in interest, claim asserted against . . . 203(b)

Court not of record, officer authorized to serve summons, delivery of summons to; time for interposing claim . . . 203(b)

First publication of summons pursuant to order, subsequent completion of publication; method of interposing claim . . . . 203(b)

Methods, generally . . . 203(b)

Order for time and date of filing . . . . . . 203(c)

Sheriff, delivery of summons (See subhead: Sheriff, constable and other officers)

Summons, filing of . . . 203(c)

Summons, service of (See subhead: Summons, service of)

Landlord's retaliatory behavior against tenant . . . 215

Legal notice, publication of, method of computing publication period . . . 2402

Liability, penalty or forfeiture, statute imposing; action to recover upon . . . 214

Libel and slander . . . 215

Limitations period, measurement of

Commencement of applicable period . . . 203(a)

**STATUTES OF LIMITATIONS**—Cont.

Limitations period, measurement of—Cont.
 Methods . . . 203
Malicious prosecution, one-year period . . 215
Malpractice actions (See MALPRACTICE ACTIONS)
Mistake, action based on; 6-year limitations period . . . 213
Money judgment, action on; expiration of 20-year statute of limitations giving rise to presumption of payment
 Conclusive presumption . . . 211
 Enforcement order, property acquired by, payment deemed established by . . 211
 Exceptions . . . 211
 Levy upon execution, property acquired by, payment deemed established by . . 211
 Part payment, exception to presumption by virtue of . . . 211
 Signed acknowledgment of indebtedness within 20-year period, exception to presumption . . . 211
Mortgages
 Bonds or notes, mortgage on real property securing; six-year statute of limitations . . . 213
 Redemption, commencement in ten years . . . 212
New York City . . . 203(b)
Notice of claim requirement in actions against licensed engineers and architects . . . 214-d
Officer or body, proceeding against; 4-month limitations period . . . 217
One-year period
 Arbitration award . . . 215
 Common informer, actions to recover statutory penalties . . . 215
 Coroners, actions based upon liability for acts or omissions of . . . 215
 Criminal action, civil action commenced after termination of . . . 215
 Interest overcharge, action for . . . 215
 Landlord's retaliatory behavior against tenant . . . 215
 Malicious prosecution action . . . 215
 Prisoners . . . 215
 Sheriff, actions based upon liability for acts or omissions of . . . 215
Personal injury actions (See PERSONAL INJURY ACTIONS)
Prisoners . . . 215
Privacy, right of . . . 215
Real property actions
 Grantee's or patentee's actions for real property . . . 211

**STATUTES OF LIMITATIONS**—Cont.

Real property actions—Cont.
 Incumbrances, covenant against; breach . . . 206(c)
 Possession to recover, commencement in ten years . . . 212
 Residential rent overcharge, commencement in four-years . . . 213-a
 Seizing covenant of; breach . . . 206(c)
 State, actions brought by . . . 211
Rent overcharge . . . 213-a
Sealed instrument, action upon; six-year period . . . 213
Sheriff, constable or other officers
 Acts or omissions of officer, action upon liability for . . . 215
 Delivery of summons to . . . 203(b)
 Three-year period, nonpayment of money collected . . . 214
Six-year period
 Bond or note . . . 213
 Contracts . . . 213
 Corporation against employee or stockholder, action on behalf of . . . 213
 Fraud . . . 213
 Mistake, action based upon . . . 213
 Public property, action based on spoliation or other misappropriation . . . 213
 Sealed instrument, action upon . . . 213
Specific law prescribing, time limit different from CPLR provision, specific law controlling . . . 201
Stay of action, court or statute authorizing; time for commencement excluding duration of stay . . . 204(a)
Stockholders' derivative actions
 Employee or stockholder, against; six-year period . . . 213
Summons, filing of; method of interposing claim . . . 203(c)
Summons, service of
 Appearance of defendant during publication period, publication deemed completed due to . . . 320(d)
 First publication, claim interposed by . . . 203(b)
 Foreign corporation, computation of time . . . 207
 Method of interposing claim . . . 203(b)
 New York City . . . 203(b)
 Provisional remedy order, death of defendant within 30 days thereafter; delivery within 60 days of issuance of letters . . 203(b)
 Sheriffs (See subhead: Sheriff, constable or other officers)

[References are to CPLR Sections, Rules and Appendices.]

**STATUTES OF LIMITATIONS**—Cont.

Support payments . . . 211

Ten-year period

Adverse possession for specified period prior to commencing action . . . 212

Letters patent, time for commencing of action of ejectment after annulment of . . 212

Mortgage, action to redeem from . . . 212

Three-year period

Annulment of marriage . . . 214

Chattel actions (See subhead: Chattel actions)

Malpractice actions . . . 214

Penalty or forfeiture . . . 214

Personal injury action . . . 215

Sheriff, constable or other officer for non-payment of money collected . . . 214

Tolling of statute

New York City . . . 203(b)

War tolling provisions

Alien subject or citizen of hostile country . . . 209(b)

Citizen or subject of enemy country, necessary party to action, inability of person to commence action without . . . 209(b)

Enemy or enemy occupied territory, action accruing in . . . 209(a)

Resident or sojourner of country at war with United States or allies, necessary party to action, inability of person to commence action without . . . 209(c)

Twenty-year period

Bond or note . . . 211

Grantee's action for or with respect to real property . . . 211

Money judgment, presumption of payment of (See 20-year statute of limitations; subhead: Money judgment, action)

State's action to sue for or with respect to real property . . . 211

Villages, actions against . . . 9802

Voluntary discontinuance of action; counterclaim, affirmative action to recover in . . . 203(e)

War tolling provisions (See subhead: Tolling of statute)

Workmen's compensation proceedings, termination and commencement of new action, time limitation for; applicability of CPLR section . . . 205(c)

Written agreement fixing, shorter time prescribed by, allowance . . . 201

**STATUTORY CONSTRUCTION**

General Construction Law . . . App

**STAY OF PROCEEDINGS**

Appeals (See APPEALS)

Arbitration (See ARBITRATION PROCEEDINGS)

Article 78 proceedings . . . 7805

Authority of court to order, limitation on . . . . 2201

Commencement of action, court or statute authorizing; time for commencement excluding duration of stay . . . 204(a)

Disclosure . . . 3214(b)

Foreign country money judgments, appeal of . . . 5306

Foreign judgment, grounds for stay of enforcement . . . 5404

Forum non conveniens

Contracts to which GOL § 51402 applies, mandatory enforcement of choice of forum clauses in . . . 327(b)

Domicile or residence of any party within state as no bar to court's action . . . . . 327(a)

Health care arbitration; demand of arbitration served within time limits, stay of action effect on . . . 7556(d)

Pending actions stay in, court's authority to grant . . . 2201

Undertaking for stay of enforcement of judgment as disbursement taxable, expenses securing . . . 8301(a)(11)

Venue change, stay of proceedings order for purpose of; when allowed . . . 511(c)

**STENOGRAPHERS**

Fees . . . 8002

Health care arbitration hearing . . . 7559(b)

**STIPULATIONS**

Disclosure, method of . . . 3102(b)

Notice of pendency, cancellation of . . 1347(4); 6514(d)

Outside court, binding effect; requirements . . . 2104

Relief from judgment or order on . . . 5015(b)

Voluntary discontinuance of action via stipulation, prohibition against; incompetent as party . . . 3217(a)(2)

**STOCKHOLDERS' DERIVATIVE ACTION**

Statute of limitations; 6-year limitations period . . . 213

**STOCK MARKET REPORTS**

Evidence, admissibility of . . . 4533

[References are to CPLR Sections, Rules and Appendices.]

**STREETS AND HIGHWAYS**

Notice of dangers of defects prior to accident required for maintenance of action against village . . . 9804

**STRIKING OF PLEADINGS**

Scandalous or prejudicial matter . . . 3024(b)

Special proceeding

    Correction of defects in papers . . 405(a)

    New matter contained in answer . . . . . . 404(b)

Subpoena, disobedience of . . . 2308(a)

**SUBMITTED CONTROVERSY**

Commencement . . . 3222(a)

Subsequent proceedings . . . 3222(b)

**SUBPOENAS**

Arbitrator's power to issue . . . 7505

Attendance pursuant to, time provisions on subpoena . . . 2305(a)

Books, papers and things, production of

    Deposition, at . . . 3111

    Duces tecum subpoena, use of . . 2305(c)

    Inspection and audit of records . . 2305(c)

    Subpoena duces tecum, service of

        Issuance by court of subpoena . . . . 2307

        Money judgments, enforcement of . . . 5224(a)(2)

        Reproduction of items required . . . 2307

        Time limits on production . . . 2307

Contempt of court, noncompliance with subpoena punishable as . . . 2308(a),(b)

Costs for noncompliance with non-judicial subpoena, imposition of, authorization . . . . . . 2308(b)

Damages sustained by noncompliance, liability for . . . 2308(a), (b)

Depositions

    Money judgments, enforcement of (See subhead: Money judgment, proceeding for enforcement)

    Production of books, papers and things . . . 3111

Disobedience of, liability for

    Contempt of court, punishable as . . . . . 2308(a),(b); 5251

    Judicial subpoena, noncompliance with . . . 2308(a)

    Money judgment, proceeding for enforcement of . . . 5251

    Non-judicial subpoena, noncompliance with . . . 2308(b)

**SUBPOENAS—Cont.**

Disobedience of, liability for—Cont.

    Pleadings of disobedient party, striking of, authorization where judicial subpoena disobeyed . . . 2308(a)

Duces tecum subpoena

    Attendance in compliance with, substitution by suitable party, allowance . . 2305(b)

    Books, papers and things, production of (See subhead: Books, papers and things, production of)

    Forfeiture action (See subhead: Forfeiture–proceeds of crime)

    Hospital or medical records of municipal corporation, production of (See subhead: Hospital or medical records, production of)

    Money judgment, proceeding for enforcement

        Production of books and papers required by . . . 2301

        Use of, authorization . . . 5224(a)(2)

    Municipal corporation or state, department of (See subhead: Municipal corporation or state, department of)

    Original record or document where certified copy admissible, subpoena to compel production of issued by court; requirement . . . 2302(b)

    Service of (See subhead: Books, papers and things, production of)

    Time of possession . . . 2305(c)

Fees

    Attendance fees . . . 8001(a)

    Compliance with subpoena . . . 5224(b)

    Examination before trial, person subpoenaed upon . . . 8001(b)

    Mileage fees . . . 8001(a)

    Sheriff's fees for service of . . . 8011(h)

    Subpoenaed person, payments in advance for fees and traveling expenses incurred by . . . 2303

    Transcript of record to comply with subpoena . . . 8001(c)

Forfeiture of proceeds of crime

    Application for . . . 1311-a(1),(2)

    Granting of application, terms for . . . . . 1311-a(3)

    Issuance of . . . 1311-a(4)

    Notice requirements . . . 1311-a(4),(5)

Function . . . 2301

Health care arbitration . . . 7560

Hospital or medical records, production of

    Certified transcript or production, authorization . . . 2306(a)

**SUBPOENAS**—Cont.

Hospital or medical records, production of—Cont.

Delivery to clerk, manner of . . . 2306(b)

Time for service of subpoena . . . 2306(a)

Issuance

Court order, issuance by, when necessary . . . 2302(b)

Without court order, persons authorized . . . 2302(a)

Jail, commitment of disobedient person to

Grounds . . . 2308(a), (b)

Review of proceedings, requirements . . . 2308(c)

Warrant of commitment, particularity of, requirement . . . 2308(a),(b)

Libraries, service of subpoena duces tecum to . . . 2307

Modification of, motion for . . . 2304

Money judgment, proceeding for enforcement

Authorization . . . 5221(b)

Depositions, subpoena requiring attendance for taking of

Authorization . . . 5224(a)(1)

Conduct of examination . . 5224(d)

Submission of deposition to witness for perusal; signing by witness . . . . 5224(e)

Subsequent examination . . . 5224(f)

Time and place of examination . . . 5224(c)

Disobedience of subpoena . . . 5251

Fees for compliance with subpoena . . . . 5224(b)

Information subpoena . . . 5224(a)(3)

Subpoena duces tecum

Production of books and papers required by . . . 2301

Use of, authorization . . . 5224(a)(2)

Types authorized . . . 5224(a)

Motion to quash . . . 2304

Municipal corporation or state, service of subpoena duces tecum to department of . . 2307

New York State Labor Relations Board, issued before . . . 2310

Noncompliance with (See subhead: Disobedience of, liability for)

Non-judicial subpoena, noncompliance with . . 2308(b)

Original record or document where certified copy admissible, production of

Court clerk issuance without court order . . . 2302(a)

Court-issued, requirement . . . 2302(b)

Notice requirement . . . 2302(b)

**SUBPOENAS**—Cont.

Original record or document where certified copy admissible, production of—Cont.

Psychiatric clinical records under Mental Hygiene Law, court order . . . 2302(a)

Penalty not to exceed $50, noncomplying person subject to . . . 2308(a),(b)

Prisoner's attendance, subpoena compelling . . . 2302(b)

Psychiatric clinical records, court order . . . . . 2302(a)

Referee's power to issue . . . 4201

Service of

Authorization for service in same manner as summons . . . 2303

Books, papers and things, production of (See subhead: Books, papers and things, production of)

Libraries (See subhead: Libraries)

Municipal corporation or state, department of (See subhead: Municipal corporation or state, department of)

Proof of . . . 2303

Sheriff's fees for . . . 8011(h)

Sheriff's fees for service of . . . 8011(h)

Traveling expenses and fees advance payment to subpoenaed person, authorization . . . 2303; 2305

Without court order, issuance . . . 2302(a)

**SUBROGATION**

Contribution, effect of . . . 1404

**SUBSTITUTED SERVICE** (See SERVICE OF SUMMONS AND PAPERS)

**SUBSTITUTION OF PARTIES**

Appeals

Extension of time for procedural steps . . 1022

Time for substitution . . . 1021

Conservator, substitution of . . . 1016

Corporate dissolution, proper party substituted by court . . . 1017

Death of party

Claim by or against not extinguished, substitution of proper party, court order . . . 1015(a)

Joint parties, rights and liabilities surviving, no abatement of action resulting . . . . 1015(b)

No timely substitution; dismissal of action by court, show cause order . . . . . 1021; 5016(d)

Depositions, effect on use of . . . 3117(d)

Dismissal for failure to substitute . . . 1021

[References are to CPLR Sections, Rules and Appendices.]

**SUBSTITUTION OF PARTIES—Cont.**

Dissolution of corporate party, proper party substituted by court . . . 1017

Extension of time for effecting . . . 1022

Final judgment, event requiring substitution occurring after . . . 1021

Incompetency of party, adjudication, substitution of committee, requirement . . . 1016

Indemnitors for executing or attaching officer . . . 1020

Procedure, motion to substitute, persons entitled to make motion . . . 1021

Public officers

Designation by official title . . . 1023

Generally . . . 1019

Receiver, order of substitution of proper party . . . 1017

Transfer of interest, substitution or joinder of transferee, discretion of court to order . . . . 1018

Unknown party, designation of; subsequent knowledge of identity or name . . . 1024

**SUMMARY JUDGMENT**

Architects and engineers, standards for summary judgment in actions against licensed . . . . . 3212(i)

Complaints (See subhead: Service in lieu of complaint)

Damages, amount or extent, triable issue of fact limited to . . . 3212(c)

Dismissal motion treated as . . . 3211(c)

Engineers and architects, standards for summary judgment in actions against licensed . . . . . 3212(i)

Entry of summary judgment, abeyance pending determination of remaining cause of action; direction by court . . . 3212(e)(2)

Foreign country money judgment, enforcement by summary judgment in lieu of complaint authorization . . . 5303

Immediate trial . . . 3212(c)

Limitation of issues of fact for trial . . 3212(g)

Matrimonial action, availability of partial summary judgment . . . 3212(e)

Opposing affidavits, facts probable but unavailable to justify opposition contained in; court's power to remedy . . . 3212(f)

Partial summary judgment, grants of

Abeyance of entry of summary judgment, pending determination of remaining cause of action . . . 3212(e)(2)

Authorization . . . 3212(e)

Incontrovertible facts, ascertainment of; specification in court's order . . 3212(g)

**SUMMARY JUDGMENT—Cont.**

Partial summary judgment, grants of—Cont.

Matrimonial action, availability in . . . . . 3212(e)

Severance of summarily judged cause of action, power of court to grant . . . . . 3212(e)(1)

Proof in support of motion, evidence permitted . . . 3212(b)

Public petition and participation, standards for summary judgment in cases involving . . . . 3212(h)

Service in lieu of complaint

Article 54 procedure, allowance in . . . . 5406

Authorization . . . 3213

Foreign judgment . . . 5406

Instrument for payment of money only, actions based upon . . . 3213

Judgment, action based upon . . . 3213

Procedure . . . 3213

Severance of summarily determined cause of action, power of court to grant . . . 3212(e)(1)

Time for making motion . . . 3212(a)

Unavailability of facts to opposing party . . . . 3112(f)

**SUMMARY PROCEEDINGS**

Sheriff, fixed fees of . . . 8011(f)

**SUMMONS**

Agent for service of (See SERVICE OF SUMMONS AND PAPERS)

Consumer credit transaction, action on

Generally . . . 305(a)

Misplacement of venue

Completion of service . . . 513(c)

Rejection . . . 513(a),(b)

Defined . . . 105(b)

Index number

Assignment and fee payment

Generally . . . 306-a

Person other than plaintiff . . 306-a

Generally . . . 305(a)

Joinder of new party; supplemental summons required to be served . . . 305(a)

Misplacement of venue (See statement included in summons; subhead: Venue, basis for)

Personal service, methods (See SERVICE OF SUMMONS AND PAPERS)

Proof of service (See SERVICE OF SUMMONS AND PAPERS)

Publication of summons pursuant to order (See SERVICE OF SUMMONS AND PAPERS)

Service of summons (See SERVICE OF SUMMONS AND PAPERS)

[References are to CPLR Sections, Rules and Appendices.]

**SUMMONS**—Cont.

State, personal service upon, manner of effecting (See SERVICE OF SUMMONS AND PAPERS)

Supplemental summons, requirement of service of; joinder of new party . . . 305(a)

Third-party summons

Generally . . . 305(a)

Index number, assignment and fee payment by person other than plaintiff . . 306-a

Venue, basis for; statement included in summons

Defendant's residence as basis . . . 305(a)

Misplacement

Completion of service . . . 513(c)

Rejection . . . 513(a),(b)

Requirement . . . 305(a)

Residence of plaintiff as basis, address, specification, requirement . . . 305(a)

**SUPPLEMENTAL PLEADINGS** (See AMENDED AND SUPPLEMENTAL PLEADINGS)

**SUPPORT ENFORCEMENT**

Income deduction, order for (See INCOME DEDUCTION)

Income execution (See INCOME EXECUTION)

**SUPPORT PAYMENTS**

Admissibility of . . . 4518(f)

Certification of . . . 4518(f)

Demand for, exercise of personal jurisdiction over respondent or defendant by court . . . 302(b)

Jurisdiction over non-resident . . . 302(b)

Statute of limitations . . . 211

**SUPREME COURTS**

Appeals to appellate division from (See APPELLATE DIVISION)

Declaratory judgment . . . 3001

Motions (See MOTIONS)

Place of trial of action pending in another court, change of . . . 604

Removal of case; grounds for granting

County court judge, incapacitation of . . . 325(f)

Mistaken choice of court, commencement of action in . . . 325(a)

Venue for special proceedings against . . . . . . 506(b)

**SURETY ARRANGEMENT IN JUDICIAL PROCEEDINGS** (See UNDERTAKINGS)

**SURROGATE'S COURT**

Removal to, action affecting decedent's estate

Jury trial, right preserved in later proceeding . . . 325(e)

**SURROGATE'S COURT**—Cont.

Removal to, action affecting decedent's estate—Cont.

Prior order by surrogate's court for removal . . . 325(e)

**SURROGATE'S COURT PROCEDURE ACT (SCPA)**

Joinder and representation of persons interested in estates; SCPA provisions governing . . 7703

Selected practice provisions . . . App

**SURVEYS**

Evidence

Maps and other real property records . . . 4522

Standard of measurement used by surveyor . . . 4534

# T

**TARIFFS OR CLASSIFICATIONS**

Authentication for evidence . . . 4540(d)

**TAXATION AND FINANCE DEPARTMENT**

Special proceeding against state tax commission, commencement; venue of . . . 506(b)

Venue of special proceeding against state tax commission . . . 506(b)

**TAXATION OF COSTS AND DISBURSEMENTS**

Bill of costs, service of . . . 8403

Clerk's duty . . . 8401

Computation by clerk . . . 8401

County clerk . . . 8401

Disbursements taxable (See DISBURSEMENTS AND ADDITIONAL ALLOWANCES, subhead: Taxable disbursements, authorization)

Judgment, insertion of amount taxed in . . 8401

Judicial review of taxation or re-taxation . . . . 8404

Notice of taxation

Generally . . . 8402

Re-taxation, notice of . . . 8403

Re-taxation

Judicial review of . . . 8404

Notice of . . . 8403

Service of papers

Bill of costs . . . 8403

Re-taxation, notice of . . . 8403

Valuation of property . . . 8401

**TEMPORARY RESTRAINING ORDER**

Appellate division, by . . . 5518

Chattel, return of . . . 7103(c)(2)

[References are to CPLR Sections, Rules and Appendices.]

**TEMPORARY RESTRAINING ORDER—**
Cont.

Damages resulting from, ascertainment of . . . . 6315

Forfeiture of proceeds of crime (See FORFEITURE OF PROCEEDS OF CRIME)

Immediate and irreparable harm, necessary showing of . . . 6301; 6313(a)

Labor dispute, prohibition of issuance in action arising from . . . 6313(a)

Modification or vacatur of
    Power of court over . . . 6314
    Undertaking required . . . 6314

Notice not necessary . . . 6313(a)

Preliminary injunction hearing, issuance prior to . . . 6301

Service of, manner . . . 6313(b)

Statutory duties performed by public officer or municipal corporation, prohibition of restraining order as to . . . 6313(a)

Undertaking
    Modification or vacatur, undertaking required . . . 6314
    Prior to granting temporary restraining order, court's discretion as to undertaking . . . 6313(c)

Unique chattel . . . 7109(a)

**TENDER**
Procedure . . . 3219
Safekeeping . . . 3219
Withdrawal . . . 3219

**TERMINATION OF ACTION**
Death of plaintiff causing . . . 203(e)
New action by plaintiff
    Six-month extension to bring action . . . . 205(a)
    Timeliness of defense . . . 205(b)
    Workmen's Compensation Law, application to proceedings under . . . 205(c)

**TERM OF COURT**
Continuance of proceedings at adjoined time and place during or new term, authorization . . . 9001

Death, disability or incapacity of judge following verdict . . . 9002

Disqualification of county judge, effect upon statute of limitations . . . 9003

**THIRD-PARTY PRACTICE**
Amendment of complaint by plaintiff, time for . . . 1009

Answer asserted by third-party defendant, service of . . . 1008

**THIRD-PARTY PRACTICE—Cont.**

Appeal, right of, availability to third-party defendant . . . 1008

Attorney, service of complaint in third-party action on plaintiff's . . . 1007

Complaint in third-party action
    Defined . . . 3011
    Dismissal without prejudice . . . 1010
    Filing . . . 1007
    Plaintiff's attorney, service on . . . 1007
    Separate trial . . . 1010
    Service . . . 1007

Counterclaim, right to, availability to third-party defendant . . . 1008

Cross-claim, right to, availability to third-party defendant . . . 1008

Defenses of defendant against plaintiff, availability to third-party defendant . . . 1008

Dismissal without prejudice of third-party complaint, determination by court, factors . . . . 1010

Interpleader (See INTERPLEADER)

Intervention (See INTERVENTION)

Jury trial of facts arising under, assertion in action where no right to jury trial exists . . 4102(c)

Plaintiff in third-party complaint
    Amendment of complaint within 20 days after service of answer to complaint on plaintiff's attorney . . . 1009
    Defendant serving complaint as . . . 1007
    Service of third-party defendant . . . 1007

Pleadings required to be served . . . 1007

Separate trial of third-party complaint, court's order, determinative factors . . . 1010

Special proceeding, allowance during, condition to . . . 401

Successive proceedings, authorization . . . 1011

Third-party defendant, impleaded party denominated as . . . 1007

Third-party plaintiff, defendant denominated as . . . 1007

Verification of third-party claim where complaint not verified, allowance, effect . . . 3020(a)

When authorized . . . 1007

**TIME EXTENSIONS** (See EXTENSION OF TIME)

**TITLE INSURANCE COMPANIES**
Disbursement, fees for title searches as . . . . . 8301(a)(10)

Evidence, searches as . . . 4523

**TOLLING PROVISIONS** (See STATUTES OF LIMITATIONS)

**TORTS**
Jurisdiction; acts commissioned in person or through agency
    Within state . . . 302(a)
    Without state . . . 302(a)

**TOWNS**
Actions against, proper place of trial, designation . . . 504
Personal service on; persons who may be served, specification . . . 311(a)

**TOXIC SUBSTANCES**
Personal injury actions involving, statute of limitations . . . 214-c
Statutes of limitations; personal injury actions . . . 214-c

**TRAFFIC VIOLATIONS**
Vehicle and Traffic Law . . . App

**TRANSCRIPT OF ACTION OR PROCEEDING**
Appeal of proceeding, preparation of transcript upon
    Failure of respondent to timely amend or object
        Affirmation of compliance by appellant, requirement for inclusion . . . 5525(c)(2)
        Notice of settlement to respondent, requirement for . . . 5525(c)(3)
        Transcript deemed correct without stipulation or settlement . . 5525(c)(2)
    Number of copies to be provided, appellate division's discretion as to . . . 5525(a)
    Omission of part, stipulation by parties to appeal . . . 5525(b)
    Poor person, party permitted to appeal as; no charge for transcripts . . . 1102(b)
    Portion of record provided . . . 5525(b)
    Referee's report, judgment entered upon . . . 5525(b)
    Reporter, request to . . . 5525(a)
    Respondent's proposed amendments or objections . . . 5525(c)(1)
    Service of transcript and amendments on respondent, time for . . . 5525(c)(1)
    Statement in lieu of transcript, submittal to judge or referee . . . 5525(d)
    Stenographic report, service of; request to . . . 5525(a)
    Submittal to judge or referee, procedure . . . 5525(c)(1)
    Time for settlement, special limitations by appellate division . . . 5525(e)

**TRANSCRIPT OF ACTION OR PROCEEDING**—Cont.
Appeal of proceeding, preparation of transcript upon—Cont.
    Trial without jury, no transcript necessary . . . 5525(b)
Article 78 proceedings; transcript of records, filing of . . . 7804(e)
Depositions (See DEPOSITIONS)
Docketing of judgment based upon filing of transcript . . . 5018(a)
Fees
    Clerks of court . . . 8016(a)(5)
    County clerks . . . 8021(b)(7)
    Index number fees . . . 8018(a)
Subpoena, comply with; fees . . . 8001(c)

**TRANSIT AUTHORITY** (See NEW YORK CITY TRANSIT AUTHORITY)

**TRANSPORTATION DEPARTMENT**
Special proceeding against, venue of . . 506(b)

**TRIAL**
Advisory jury, use of . . . 4212
Calendar practice
    Generally (See CALENDAR PRACTICE)
    Trial preferences (See PREFERENCES FOR TRIAL)
Conduct of trial, regulation by court . . . 4011
Consolidation of actions (See CONSOLIDATION OF ACTIONS)
Duration of trial . . . 4014
Evidence (See EVIDENCE)
Examination before trial (See DEPOSITIONS)
Form of decision, oral or written . . . 4213(b)
Increased damages, statute granting, judgment entered for increased amount . . . 4018
Issues to be decided by court . . . 4211
Joint trial (See JOINT TRIAL)
Jury trial (See JURY TRIAL)
Marked pleadings, copies furnished trial judge . . . 4012
Materials for obtaining . . . 3101(2)
Motions during trial
    Continuance, motion for . . . 4402
    Judgment
        Generally . . . 4401
        Post-trial judgment . . . 4401-a
    New trial, motion for . . . 4402
    Report of referee to report, confirmation or rejection of, motion . . . 4403
    Verdict of advisory jury, confirmation or rejection of, motion . . . 4403

[References are to CPLR Sections, Rules and Appendices.]

**TRIAL**—Cont.

New trial
    Appeal from order granting, court of appeals
        Appeal as of right . . . 5601(c)
        Disposition of . . . 5615
    Motion for during trial . . . 4402
    Post-trial motion for . . . 4404
    Verdict, confirmation or rejection by judge
       . . . 4403
Objections, formalities regarding (See OBJEC-
    TIONS)
Opening and closing statements . . . 4016
Place of trial
    Generally (See VENUE)
    Other than courthouse, when allowed . . .
      4013
    Where action triable, defined . . . 105(q)
Post-trial motions
    Judgment, motion for
        Jury cases . . . 4404(a)
        Nonjury cases . . . 4404(b)
    Place for making motion . . . 4405
    Single motion regarding, requirement . . .
      4406
    Time for making motion . . . 4405
Preferences (See PREFERENCES FOR TRIAL)
Referee, trial by (See REFEREES)
Requests for findings of fact, submittal . . . . .
    4213(a)
Separate trial (See SEPARATE TRIAL)
Sequence in which issues tried, determination by
    court, authorization . . . 4011
Severance (See SEVERANCE)
Time for decision; agreement of parties to extend
    . . . 4213(c)

**TRUSTS AND TRUSTEES**

Counterclaims against trustees . . . 3019(c)
Estates, Powers and Trusts Law (EPTL) . . . .
    App
Express trusts (See EXPRESS TRUST PRO-
    CEEDINGS)
Security for costs . . . 8501(b)

**TYPE SIZE REQUIREMENT**

Calculation of . . . 105(t)

# U

**UNAUTHORIZED FOREIGN CORPORA-
TION**

Jurisdiction over, personal . . . 302

**UNDERTAKINGS**

Acknowledgment, form of . . . 2502(d)

**UNDERTAKINGS**—Cont.

Additional or new undertaking, motion upon no-
    tice for, court's power over . . . 2508
Affidavits
    Form of . . . 2502(a)
    Real property surety lien, undertaking by
      natural person
        Filing of duplicate original, require-
          ment . . . 2503(c)
        Necessary inclusions . . . 2503(b)
Appeal
    State or municipality . . . 2512(2)
    Stay of enforcement . . . 5519(d)
Attachment
    Discharge of attachment . . . 6222
    Procedure . . . 6212(b)
Certificate of qualification, exception following
    . . . 2506(a)
Change of parties, effect . . . 2504(b)
Chattel actions (See CHATTEL ACTIONS, sub-
    head: Undertakings pursuant to)
Conditions to . . . 2502(c)
Control of assets, agreement between principal and
    surety, conditions to allowance . . . 2509
Covenant of surety to pay upon nonperformance
    of condition, obligation including undertaking
    defined as . . . 2501(1)
Damages assessed in lieu of . . . 2512(2)
Defined . . . 2501
Deposit of legal tender or unregistered United
    States bonds, undertaking consisting of . . . .
    2501(2)
Disbursement taxable, expenses in securing under-
    taking to stay enforcement of judgment as
    . . . 8301(a)(11)
Exception to surety, written notice of exception;
    service of
      Certificate of qualification, exception follow-
        ing . . . 2506(a)
      Justification of surety, motion to justify made
        within 10 days of service of notice of
        exception (See subhead: Justification of
        surety)
      No exception taken, effect . . . 2506(b)
      Sheriff, notice of exception served upon,
        when authorized . . . 2506(a)
      Time limitations . . . 2506(a)
Fees payable to sheriff . . . 8011(i)
Fiduciary bonds
    Accounting . . . 2510(a)
    Discharge of surety . . . 2510(a)
    Premium on undertaking, reimbursement on
      . . . 8006
    Settlement of account . . . 2510(b)

[References are to CPLR Sections, Rules and Appendices.]

**UNDERTAKINGS—Cont.**

Filing of undertaking and service of copy upon adverse party

    Clerk with whom filed, specification . . . . 2505

    Effect . . . 2505

Forfeiture of proceeds of crime

    Notice of pendency cancellation, undertaking for . . . 1348

    Temporary receiver . . . 1340

General Obligations Law . . . App

Guardian of infant . . . 1210(c)

Habeas corpus writ, undertaking by petitioner in amount fixed by court . . . 7004(e)

Insurance company as surety, authorization of . . . 2502(a)(1)

Judgment lien or levy, release of on appeal, undertaking for purpose of . . . 5204

Justification of surety

    Certificate of qualification, issued pursuant to Insurance Law, acceptance in lieu of justification . . . 2507(a)

    Failure to justify after notice of exception served, effect . . . 2507(b)

    Motion to justify; notice of exception to surety, time to motion to justify measured from service of . . . 2507(a)

Municipal corporation, undertaking by

    Damages fixed . . . 2512(2)

    Name of, undertaking in . . . 2513

Notice of pendency, cancellation of

    Forfeiture of proceeds of crime . . . 1348

    Undertaking on motion of aggrieved person for . . . 6515

Preliminary injunction (See PRELIMINARY INJUNCTION)

Principal as party to obligation, joinder of, no necessity for . . . 2501(1)

Public officers

    Exceptions . . . 2512(2)

    Name of, undertaking in . . . 2513

Real property surety lien, undertaking by natural person greater than $1000

    Affidavits

        Filing of duplicate original, requirement . . . 2503(c)

        Necessary inclusions . . . 2503(b)

    Creation of lien . . . 2503(a)

    Release of lien by clerk or register of appropriate county, conditions

        Consent to release, acknowledgment by benefited party . . . 2503(d)(1)

        Court order, discharge of surety by; release effected by . . 2503(d)(2)

**UNDERTAKINGS—Cont.**

Real property surety lien, undertaking by natural person greater than $1000—Cont.

    Surety bond liens docket of county clerk's or register's office, recording of undertaking in . . . 2503(a),(c)

Receiver, temporary

    Forfeiture of proceeds of crime . . . 1340

    Undertaking in amount set by court . . . . 6403

Record of, maintenance by court clerks . . . . . 9701(2); 9702(4)

Removal of action, effect on liability . . . . . . 2504(b)

Security for costs . . . 8503

Service upon adverse party . . . 2505

Sheriff's fees for . . . 8011(i)

State, undertaking by, no requirement for . . . . 2512

Stay of enforcement of judgment as disbursement taxable, expenses securing undertaking for . . . 8301(a)(11)

Surety

    Affidavit of (See subhead: Affidavits)

    Certificate of qualification, exception following . . . 2506(a)

    Control of assets by agreement with surety . . . 2509

    Exception to (See service of; subhead: Exception to surety, written notice of exception)

    Insurance company as, qualifications . . . 2502(a)(1)

    Justification of (See subhead: Justification of surety)

    Liability of . . . 2511

    Natural person as

        Affidavit accompanying undertaking, necessary inclusions . . 2502(a)(2)

        Attorney as, disallowance . . . . . . 2502(a)(2)

        Real property lien (See subhead: Real property surety lien, undertaking by natural person greater than $1000)

Temporary restraining order

    Modification or vacatur, undertaking required . . . 6314

    Prior to granting of, court's discretion as to . . . 6313(c)

Two or more undertakings, same instrument containing, allowance . . . 2502(b)

Waiver of, method . . . 2504(a)

**UNDUE INFLUENCE**

Pleading, circumstances constituting the wrong; detailed statement setting forth . . . 3016(b)

[References are to CPLR Sections, Rules and Appendices.]

**UNIFIED COURT SYSTEM**
Administrative officers of, review of determinations by . . . 1026

**UNIFORM COMMERCIAL CODE**
County clerks' fees . . . 8021(f)
Evidence of filing under Article 9 . . . 4525
Selected practice provisions . . . App

**UNIFORM ENFORCEMENT OF FOREIGN JUDGMENTS ACT** (See FULL FAITH AND CREDIT, FOREIGN JUDGMENT ENTITLED TO)

**UNINCORPORATED ASSOCIATION**
Actions by or against, General Associations Law governing . . . 1025
General Associations Law . . . App
Venue for trial, residence of association for purpose of fixing, establishment . . . 503(d)

**UNJUST ENRICHMENT**
Benefits received by party seeking avoidance of transaction, restoration of as condition to judgment, court's power to order . . . 3004

**UNKNOWN PARTY**
Designation of, subsequent knowledge of identity or name . . . 1024

# V

**VEHICLE AND TRAFFIC LAW**
Selected practice provisions . . . App

**VENDOR-VENDEE**
Vendee's lien on real property, no denial resulting from form of action chosen . . . 3002(f)

**VENUE**
Appeal; order changing venue . . . 511(d)
Arbitration proceedings; applications to court . . . 7502(a)
Article 78 proceedings . . . 506; 7804(b)
Assignments . . . 503(e)
Business, individually owned, residence of owner as proper place of trial . . . 503(d)
Change of venue
    Appeal from order changing venue . . . . 511(d)
    Ends of justice promoted, ground for change . . . 510
    Impartial trial, inability to have, reasonable belief in; ground for change . . . 510
    Improper county, designation, ground for change (See subhead: Improper county designated, basis for change of venue)

**VENUE**—Cont.
Change of venue—Cont.
    Jury, actions or issues triable without, transfer in court's discretion . . . 512
    Motion to change, necessity for . . . 510
    Stay of proceedings order for purpose of, grant by court, when allowed . . 511(c)
    Subsequent proceedings; delivery of records to clerk of new county . . . 511(d)
    Witness' convenience, ground for change . . . 510
Chattel, action to recover . . . 508
Common carrier, residence as basis
    Place where cause of action arose, additional place of residence for venue . . 503(c)
    Principal office of corporation, county of as residence for venue purpose . . . 503(c)
Comptroller, special proceeding against . . . . . 506(b)
Conflicting provisions . . . 502
Conservator . . . 503(b)
Consumer credit transactions (See CONSUMER CREDIT TRANSACTIONS, subhead: Venue)
Contract fixing venue, execution prior to commencement of action, enforceability . . . 501
County
    Actions against, county as proper place of trial . . . 504
    Designated . . . 509
Defendant's residence as basis . . . 503(f)
Demand for change of venue, service of, improper county designated as ground (See subhead: Improper county designated, basis for change of venue)
District corporation, actions against . . . 504
Executors, administrators and other personal representatives
    County of appointment and actual residence, residence in both for venue purposes . . . 503(b)
    Specification of representatives . . 503(b)
Forfeiture of proceeds of crime, actions for . . . 1311(10)
Governmental entities, actions against; proper place for trial . . . 504
Improper county designated, basis for change of venue
    Authorization . . . 510
    Demand for change
        Motion for change by defendant, within 15 days after service of demand where no consent given . . . 511(b)
        Time for serving, with or prior to answer . . . 511(a)

VENUE—Cont.

Improper county designated, basis for change of venue—Cont.

    Motion for change by defendant, place motion to be made . . . 511(b)

Joinder of claims or parties, conflicts of venue arising from, court's power . . . 502

New York City

    Actions . . . 504

    Exception granted to . . . 504

    Transit authority, action against . . 505(b)

Officer or body, special proceeding against (See subhead: Special proceedings)

Partnership, residence as basis of venue, section establishing . . . 503(d)

Plaintiff designating, authorization . . . 509

Principal office, corporation deemed resident of county where

    Authority . . . 503(c)

    Railroad or other common carrier, place cause of action arose; additional place of residence . . . 503(c)

Public authorities, actions involving

    Facilities involved in action, county containing, proper place of trial . . . 505(a)

    Principal office, county of, proper place of trial . . . 505(a)

    State laws, authorities constituted under, applicability of section to . . . 505(a)

    Transit Authority, New York City; actions involving . . . 505(b)

Public service commission, special proceeding against . . . 506(b)

Railroad or other common carrier, place cause of action arose, additional place of residence . . . 503(c)

Real property action . . . 507

Residence as basis

    Assignee in action for sum of money only . . . 503(e)

    Commencement of action, either party's county of residence at time of, proper place for trial . . . 503(a)

    Consumer credit transaction, action on . . 503(f)

    Defendant's residence . . . 503(f)

    Domestic or authorized foreign corporation, principal office, county in which located as residence . . . 503(c)

    Executors, administrators and other personal representatives . . . 503(b)

    More than one county, residence of party in . . . 503(a)

    Partnership . . . 503(d)

    Unincorporated association . . . 503(d)

VENUE—Cont.

School district, actions against . . . 504

Simplified procedure . . . 3036(8)

Special proceedings

    Article 78 proceedings . . . 506

    Comptroller . . . 506(b)

    Judicial district wherein proceeding triable, any county within

        Exception; Education Law § 4404 . . . 506(b)

        Exception; officer or body, special proceedings against . . . 506(b)

        General rule . . . 506(a)

    Officer of body, proceedings against

        Commissioner of education . . . . . 506(b)

        County court judge . . . 506(b)

        Court of general sessions judge . . . 506(b)

        Supreme court justice . . . 506(b)

    Public service commission . . . 506(b)

    State tax commission . . . 506(b)

    Transportation department . . . 506(b)

    Water resources board . . . 506(b)

State Tax Commission, special proceeding against . . . 506(b)

Stay of proceedings pending change of . . . . . 511(c)

Summons (See SUMMONS)

Town, actions against . . . 504

Transportation department, special proceeding against . . . 506(b)

Unincorporated association, residence as basis of venue . . . 503(d)

Village, action against . . . 504

Water resources board, special proceeding against . . . 506(b)

VERDICTS

General verdict; entry of judgment upon where jury trial of right . . . 5016(b)

Instructions by court to facilitate, sufficiency of . . . 4111(b),(c)

Interest recoveries (See INTEREST RECOVERY)

Itemized verdict

    Appellate Division, determination, money judgments contested as excessive or inadequate . . . 5501(c)

    Malpractice actions . . . 4111(d)

Jury trial (See JURY TRIAL)

Special verdict; entry of judgment upon, appropriateness of judgment directed by court . . . . 5016(b)

[References are to CPLR Sections, Rules and Appendices.]

**VERIFICATION**

Affidavit of

Form of . . . 3021

Utilization as verified pleading, permissibility . . . 105(u)

Answer, verification of, when required . . . . . 3020(b)

Article 78 proceedings . . . 7804(d)

Bill of particulars . . . 3044

Board or commission, execution by officer of . . . 3020(d)(2)

Complaint, requirement . . . 3016

Construction of verified pleadings . . . 3023

Counterclaim where complaint not verified, allowance . . . 3020(a)

Cross-claim where complaint not verified, allowance . . . 3020(a)

Default judgment, use of verified complaint as affidavit of facts constituting claim . . . . . . 3215(f)

Defective verification, treatment by adverse party . . . 3022

Defense unrelated to merits, verification of, requirement . . . 3020(c)

Defined . . . 3020(a)

Domestic corporations, execution by officer of . . . 3020(d)(1)

Execution of, necessary parties; specification . . . 3020(d)

Foreign corporation, execution by . . 3020(d)(3)

Governmental subdivisions, execution by officer of . . . 3020(d)(2)

State, verification by . . . 3020(d)(2)

Subsequent pleadings, effect of verified pleading upon . . . 3020(a)

Third-party claim where complaint not verified, allowance . . . 3020(a)

**VIDEOTAPES**

Deposition, use at . . . 3113(b)

Pretrial examination, testimony during . . . . . 3113(b)

**VILLAGES**

Bridges, defective condition of . . . 9804

Contracts, actions involving; requirements for notice of claim . . . 9801(1); 9802

Defects, notice of . . . 9804

Notice of defects or dangers on public ways, requirements for prior written notice . . 9804

Personal service on; persons who may be served, specifications . . . 311(a)

Proper place of trial, designation . . . 504; 9803

Residents of village as justices or jurors . . . . 4110-a

**VILLAGES**—Cont.

Sidewalk or crosswalk as unsafe or dangerous . . . 9804

Streets and highways, condition of . . . 9804

Time limitations . . . 9802

Venue for actions against . . . 504

**VOIR DIRE**

Judge's presence during, right of any party to require . . . 4107

**VOLUNTARY DISCONTINUANCE OF ACTION**

Conservatee, unilateral discontinuance via stipulation . . . 3217(a)(2)

Effect . . . 3217(c)

Incompetent for whom committee appointed, party to action being, disallowance of discontinuance via stipulation . . . 3217(a)(2)

Infant as party, unilateral discontinuance prohibited . . . 3217(a)(2)

Interested nonparties, existence of, unilateral discontinuance via stipulation prohibited . . . . . 3217(a)(2)

Notice of discontinuance, service upon all parties . . . 3217(a)(1)

Parcels of land, exclusion without order . . . . . 3217(a)(3)

Statutes of limitations; counterclaim, affirmative action to recover in . . . 203(e)

Stipulation, by . . . 3217(a)(2)

# W

**WAGE ASSIGNMENTS**

County clerks' fees for filing . . . . 8020(c), (e); 8021(b)(3)

Discrimination against employees based upon . . . 5252

**WAIVER**

Arbitration proceedings; consent of parties at hearing, written . . . 7506(f)

Dismissal, specification of nonwaivable grounds for . . . 3211(e)

Jury trial (See JURY TRIAL, subhead: Waiver of jury trial)

Limitations on . . . 4508(b)

Undertaking, waiver of . . . 2504(a)

**WANT OF PROSECUTION** (See FAILURE TO PROSECUTE)

**WAR**

Statutes of limitations, tolling of (See STATUTES OF LIMITATIONS)

[References are to CPLR Sections, Rules and Appendices.]

**WASTE, ACTION FOR**
Jury trial of fact issues, authorization . . . . . .
   4101(2)

**WATER RESOURCES BOARD**
Special proceeding against, venue for . . 506(b)
Venue for special proceedings against . . . . . .
   506(b)

**WILLS**
Attorney-client privilege, applicability to actions
   involving; limitations on privilege . . 4503(b)
Defined . . . 7703
Statute of limitations in action to establish will,
   Judicial Conference opinion as to . . . 213

**WITNESSES**
Competency of witnesses
   Adultery, action founded upon; competency
      of spouses to testify against each other
      . . . 4502(a)
   Conviction of crime, competency not af-
      fected by . . . 4513
   Interest in event, incompetency not estab-
      lished by reason of . . . 4512
   Party to action, witness being; incompetency
      not established by reason of . . . 4512
   Spouse of party, witness being; incompe-
      tency not established by reason of . . .
      4512
Conviction of crime, history of witness including
   . . . 4513
Depositions (See DEPOSITIONS)
Disclosure of expert witnesses
   Generally . . . 3101(a)(3)
   Trial preparation . . . 3101(d)(1)
Expert witnesses
   Disclosure
      Generally . . . 3101(a)(3)
      Trial preparation . . . 3101(d)(1)
   Health care arbitration . . . 7559(c)
   Questions eliciting opinion of; form of ques-
      tion . . . 4515
   Simplified procedure, evidence obtained
      . . . 3036(2)
Fees as taxable disbursement . . . 8301(a)(1)
Health care arbitration
   Expert witness, neutral . . . 7559(c)
   Fees . . . 7562(a)
Impeachment of witnesses
   Depositions . . . 3117(a)
   Prior inconsistent statements . . . 4514
Party to action, witness being, incompetency to
   testify not established as result . . . 4512

**WITNESSES**—Cont.
Privileges against testifying (See EVIDENCE,
   subhead: Confidential communications)
Spouse of party, witness as, incompetency as
   witness not established as result . . . 4512
Subscribing witness, proof of writings not requir-
   ing; authentication . . . 4537
Swearing of witness to execution of instruments
   . . . 8009(2)
Unavailable witness, prior testimony by . . . . .
   4517
Venue change for convenience of . . . 510

**WORKMEN'S COMPENSATION PROCEED-
ING**
Termination of action, new action on same cause,
   commencement of, time limitations for; applicability of CPLR section . . . 205(c)

**WORK PRODUCT RULE**
Disclosure . . . 3101(c)

**WRONGFUL DEATH ACTIONS**
Collateral sources of payment, admissibility of
   Public employer, certain actions against
      . . . 4545(b)
      Recovery of costs, loss of earnings or eco-
         nomic loss . . . 4545(c)
Contributory negligence or assumption of risk no
   bar to recovery . . . 1411
Costs upon counterclaims in action to recover
   damages for . . . 8303-a
Costs upon frivolous claims in action to recover
   damages for . . . 8303-a
Counterclaims in action to recover damages for
   wrongful death action, costs upon . . 8303-a
Frivolous claims in action to recover damages for
   wrongful death action, costs upon . . 8303-a
Interrogatory in, use of . . . 3130
Joint tort-feasor, proof of payment by . . . . . .
   4533-b
Judgments, periodic payment of (See JUDG-
   MENTS, subhead: Personal injury, injury to
   property and wrongful death actions)
Public employer, certain actions against
   Admissibility of collateral source of payment
      . . . 4545(b)
   Itemized verdict . . . 4111(e)

# X

**X-RAYS**
Evidence, admissibility as . . . 4532-a
Personal injury actions, admissibility in . . . . .
   4532-a